Encyclopedia of the

War of 1812

Encyclopedia of the
War of 1812

David S. Heidler
and Jeanne T. Heidler, editors

ABC-CLIO

Santa Barbara, California
Denver, Colorado
Oxford, England

Library of Congress Cataloging-in-Publication Data

Heidler, David Stephen, 1955–
    Encyclopedia of the War of 1812 / David S. Heidler and Jeanne T. Heidler.
        p.   cm.
    Includes bibliographical references and index.
    1. United States—History—War of 1812—Encyclopedias.
I. Heidler, Jeanne T.   II. Title.
E354.H46   1997
973.5'2'03—dc21   97-34085
                                                          CIP

ISBN 0-87436-968-1

04 03 02 01 00 99 98 97   10 9 8 7 6 5 4 3 2 1

ABC-CLIO, Inc.
130 Cremona Drive, P.O. Box 1911
Santa Barbara, California 93116-1911

This book is printed on acid-free paper ∞.
Manufactured in the United States of America

———❦———

To the memory of

Clare D. Heidler, Jr. (1913–1996)
Jane Autry Heidler (1914–1996)
Robert D. Twiggs (1957–1995)

"As much beauty as could die."
—Ben Jonson

———❦———

Contents

*Encyclopedia of
the War of 1812, 1*

Acknowledgments

Dr. Richard N. Blanco first envisioned this project, and without his encouragement and support in its early stages, we would possibly yet be forlorn and wandering. Dick's untimely death in 1994 not only deprived us of an adviser and a friend but left the scholarly world bereft. He is still missed, still mourned.

The contributors who have made this encyclopedia possible were simply delightful colleagues. Their work was diligently thorough and its arrival always timely, and the suggestions that frequently accompanied their efforts have marked an improvement in every instance. A few of our contributors have, in fact, made such vital contributions to the project that they have earned our special gratitude and thus warrant a special mention. Dr. John C. Fredriksen, a celebrated scholar known for his fine bibliography on the War of 1812, thoughtfully provided us with names and addresses of potential contributors and kindly sent a large box of material he had compiled over the many years he has spent investigating the war. Dr. Spencer C. Tucker helped us construct style sheets, provided sage advice about word allocations and deadlines, and made available to us his considerable knowledge about naval matters during the Early Republic. Likewise, Comdr. Tyrone G. Martin has helped to untangle the mysteries of naval lore and lexicon. Dr. Frederick Drake not only made a physically voluminous contribution to the encyclopedia, he also supplied us with invaluable perspectives from the British and Canadian side of the conflict. Dr. Harold D. Langley, Dr. Rory Cornish, and Dr. William A. Paquette furnished leads on illustrations and maps and offered graphic items from their own extensive collections.

Dr. Ronald Aichele and Dr. Beatrice Spade of the University of Southern Colorado and Col. Carl Reddel and Col. Mark Wells of the U.S. Air Force Academy offered support and encouragement at every turn. Bea's loan of a scanner saved hours of labor. Chuck Howard spent more time behind a photocopy machine than he probably cares to remember, and Carlos Salinas, Jack Swope, and Gary Perkins of the University of Southern Colorado's computer center made sure the computer behaved.

Dr. Junius P. Rodriguez introduced us to ABC-CLIO in an act of such signal kindness that we are simply unable to find words sufficient to convey our appreciation. Indeed, we are comforted only by the realization that Junius so routinely commits acts of signal kindness that he must be accustomed to friends whose "thank yous" really mean much more. Todd Hallman at ABC-CLIO was the perfect blend of enthusiasm and encouragement, and Rolf Janke raised a glass to our good health and the project's conclusion with such sober surety that we were inclined to believe both were likely events. Connie Oehring has made production chores appear effortless, which in itself was not easy at all, as copy editors Libby Barstow and Beth Partin might be willing to testify. For all the patience shown us, we are thankful.

Family and friends were supportive, and our parents Joseph and Sarah Twiggs have made dark days light with just the right words at the right times. Our other parents and our brother, to whom we have dedicated this book, had eagerly awaited its appearance. Now they await us. We are grateful for their memory.

Jeanne T. Heidler
and David S. Heidler
Colorado Springs, Colorado

The War of 1812: An Overview

In the summer of 1812, the titanic clash of the great European powers was entering its final act. Napoleon Bonaparte, emperor of the French, led a half million men into Russia even as French armies continued their four-year fight with the British on the Iberian Peninsula—the Spanish ulcer, Bonaparte had called it. The wars marked by this final, violent chapter had been going on for almost two decades, spending Europe's resources and disrupting the peaceful commerce of the world. In June 1812, when the United States of America declared war on Great Britain, it was a gesture that seemingly had nothing to do with alliances of old Europe or the colliding egos of bemedaled marshals and proud princes. And yet it had everything to do with those things—and more.

The crisis between the United States and Great Britain that erupted into the War of 1812 stemmed from the European wars of the French Revolution and their successors, the Napoleonic Wars. Americans viewed consequent violations of their neutral rights by both France and Great Britain as a serious blow to national honor. On occasion they were willing to fight for that honor, as the brief undeclared Quasi-War with France from 1798 to 1800 demonstrated. The peace convention with France ending the Quasi-War and the 1803 purchase of Louisiana by Thomas Jefferson's administration that eliminated contiguous territorial contact between the United States and France helped to ease tensions between those two nations. The renewal of the death struggle between Great Britain and France in 1803, however, not only revived tensions between the United States and France but increased the strain with Great Britain as well.

Each of the two warring powers tried to prevent the United States from supplying the needs of the other. Both countries seized American ships. The Orders in Council issued by the British and the Berlin, Milan, and other assorted decrees issued by Napoleon restricted American trade, but many Americans came to see British violations as more obnoxious, especially when those violations included the practice of impressment.

The tensions between the United States and Great Britain nearly led to war in 1807 with the *Chesapeake-Leopard* Affair. Rather than resorting to war, as many Americans urged, Pres. Thomas Jefferson retaliated for the seizure of four sailors from the USS *Chesapeake* by experimenting with economic coercion. At his urging, Congress in December 1807 passed the Embargo Act, ending most international trade for the United States.

The experiment failed. Not only was the act widely evaded, but it did more harm to American commerce than to either the British or the French economies. Domestically it damaged the standing and popularity of the Jeffersonian Democratic Republicans and threatened the chances of James Madison, Jefferson's handpicked successor, in the election of 1808. Madison fought off the challenge of disaffected Jeffersonian James Monroe for the party's nomination and carried the election in the fall, but he inherited myriad problems that would prove politically and emotionally overwhelming.

Immediately before Madison assumed office, Congress admitted the failure of the embargo and replaced it with the Non-Intercourse Act, eliminating trade only with Great Britain and France. When this measure was also ineffective, Congress passed Macon's Bill No. 2. Drafted in the spring of 1810 with little direction from President Madison, this act reopened trade with the world with a provision to maintain trade with either belligerent if it dropped its commercial restrictions and to resume nonintercourse with the other. Napoleon leaped at the chance to cripple his British enemy. In the late summer of 1810, he indicated his willingness to revoke the Berlin and Milan Decrees as they applied to the United States. Though Napoleon had no intention of stopping his assault on American trade and demonstrated as much with his actions, President Madison took him at his word and resumed nonintercourse with the British.

Throughout 1811, the United States and Great Britain thus moved closer to war. The British government refused to make any concessions to American demands regarding neutral rights, and many Americans became convinced that the British goal was to restore the colonial relationship of the seventeenth and eighteenth centuries in all but name. Furthermore, western Americans suspected a British role in the growing nativist movement among American Indians, particularly those gathered around the popular Tecumseh and his brother Tenskwatawa (the Prophet). The origins of this movement had nothing to do with British intrigue, but westerners nonetheless became convinced of British involvement. With the aim of securing the frontier, the governor of the Indiana Territory, William Henry Harrison, received authorization in the fall of 1811 to march against Tecumseh and Tenskwatawa's settlement at Prophet's Town to chastise the natives. His expedition culminated in the Battle of Tippecanoe and the destruction of Prophet's Town. Ironically, it also fulfilled the prophecy of earlier rumors when it caused the northwestern Indians to form an alliance with the British.

Increasing pressure compelled President Madison to summon the 12th Congress into session on 4 November 1811. Congress was sharply divided between the Federalist minority and a factionalized Democratic Republican majority, but a group of young Republicans known as War Hawks assumed a conspicuous—and some would say dominant—role. The War Hawks urged immediate redress of American grievances against Great Britain through war. With one of their leaders, young Henry Clay of Kentucky, elected Speaker of the House, they controlled key committees and pushed their agenda on the president.

The intractable attitude of the British government moved the United States closer to war during the winter and spring of 1812. Congress was reluctant to pay for military increases, and considerable debate abounded as to how a war should be fought, but President Madison finally succumbed to the pressure with a war message on 1 June 1812. After a short debate the House agreed, and after a longer one the Senate did as well. On 18 June 1812, the United States declared war on Great Britain. Nobody in America knew that plans were well in progress in London to repeal the Orders in Council, and when those plans reached fruition four days after the U.S. declaration of war, trans-Atlantic communication would delay the news for another month.

By then war had not only officially commenced with a documented declaration; fighting had as well. Lacking a better way to prosecute a conflict against an enemy several thousand miles away, the Madison administration planned to fight the British forces at their closest location, which was Canada. Federalists wryly noted the inconsistency of fighting on land to protect maritime rights, but Madison justifiably felt the country had to do something. In any event, westerners such as Henry Clay saw the acquisition of Canada as a legitimate and achievable war aim.

William Hull, governor of the Michigan Territory and new commander of all American forces in the northwest,

was ordered to invade Canada from Detroit and to seize as much of Upper Canada as practical. The resulting campaign was a disaster. Hull's invasion failed, and he surrendered Detroit to the British. The remaining campaigns of 1812 saw little improvement in American fortunes. Hull's successor, William Henry Harrison, found mobilization of militia and volunteer forces so difficult that he was unable to launch a concentrated move into Michigan. In the northeast, Brig. Gen. Henry Dearborn, discovering that New England militias were not only difficult to organize but were frequently unwilling to serve, ended any hopes for a campaign against Montreal in 1812. Two attempts to invade Canada along the Niagara Frontier failed miserably.

The only salvation for American morale in the early months of the War of 1812 was the small American navy. With confident British counterparts unprepared for the skill of American seamen, U.S. naval officers such as Isaac Hull, Stephen Decatur, and William Bainbridge scored impressive naval victories in the summer and fall of 1812. By 1813, however, the British began to adjust policies to fit circumstances: The Admiralty ordered captains to avoid individual combat with American warships and tightened a blockade around important American ports. Many intrepid American captains of 1812 were soon bottled up in harbors while British naval forces raided American coastlines with impunity. By 1814, American coastal towns from Maine into Chesapeake Bay and down to Georgia were being roughly visited by British raiding parties.

In the spring of 1813, Americans renewed their efforts to invade Canada. Dearborn mounted a halfhearted offensive across the Niagara River at Fort George, and the result was virtually no territorial gain. Indeed, U.S. forces suffered several significant losses as they tried to extend their hold deeper into Upper Canada. To the west, however, young Oliver Hazard Perry built an American fleet on Lake Erie that succeeded in defeating an entire British squadron in September 1813. Perry's victory opened the way for William Henry Harrison to reoccupy Detroit and from there to pursue and defeat British forces under Brig. Gen. Henry Procter at the Battle of the Thames. This battle did not end the war in the northwest, but Tecumseh's death at the Thames broke the back of his Indian confederation.

In the northeast, Henry Dearborn resigned in the wake of his failures. His successors were Maj. Gen. James Wilkinson and Maj. Gen. Wade Hampton, and the War Department planned for them to coordinate an invasion along two different routes to converge on Montreal. It would have been a dubious plan even for congenial commanders, but Wilkinson and Hampton feuded with one another. Finally, the indecision of both commanders prevented either offensive from coming close to Montreal.

By 1814, younger, more vigorous officers were emerging in the American ranks to replace elderly Revolutionary War veterans. Jacob Brown, Andrew Jackson, George Izard, Winfield Scott, and Edmund Pendleton Gaines prosecuted the war with energy and imagination. In March 1814, Andrew Jackson crushed the fighting spirit of the Red Stick Creeks in the Mississippi Territory, effectively ending the Creek War there. By late spring of 1814, Jacob Brown prepared to launch an invasion across the Niagara River into Canada. After taking Fort Erie, Brown moved north toward Lake Ontario in hopes of coordinating his movements with Commodore Isaac Chauncey there to secure Upper Canada.

As the Americans enjoyed these successes, the British hatched plans of their own. The defeat and abdication of Napoleon in the spring of 1814 freed British forces in Europe for campaigning in America. By summer, British veterans were arriving in North America to take part in offensives against several points in the United States. One offensive was planned for the Lake Champlain route into New York; a raid-in-force was launched in Chesapeake Bay; and another campaign was planned for the Gulf of Mexico, its ultimate objective New Orleans. By midsummer 1814, the first two of these plans were under way, and a promising campaign season for the United States had taken an ominous turn. Jacob Brown, failing to join Chauncey, pulled back to Fort Erie. In August, the British raid into the Chesapeake put the U.S. government to flight and resulted in the burning of Washington's public buildings. Yet in September, when the British assailed Baltimore, American forces there repulsed attacks at Northpoint and on Fort McHenry. To the north, the U.S. army and naval forces on Lake Champlain also proved to be up to the task on both land and lake, compelling the British to retreat to Canada after the Battles of Plattsburg and Plattsburg Bay.

American victories at Baltimore and Plattsburg lifted sagging American morale, but some parts of the country persisted in dissent. New England still chafed under the war's effect on commerce and suffered the afflictions of British raiding parties. In the fall of 1814, as the section's anger grew, perceptions of neglect by the national government resulted in Massachusetts calling for a convention of New England delegates to discuss grievances. Though moderate in tone, the Hartford Convention (December 1814 to January 1815) would cause many in other parts of the country to question New England's loyalty for years to come.

American and British negotiators had worked in Ghent, Belgium, since August 1814 to reach an agreement ending the Anglo-American conflict. Finally, on 24 December 1814, peace commissioners signed a treaty. Negotiations had been difficult, but there had always been the overarching American advantage that the British had not wanted to fight the United States while fighting Napoleon, and that after Napoleon was defeated, the colossal and protracted effort of battling him had made the British tired of war. The Treaty of Ghent settled nothing that the War of 1812 was supposed to be about, but by Christmas Eve 1814, it was enough for it merely to stop the war.

Andrew Jackson had not yet fought the British at New Orleans when the American and British commissioners signed the treaty in Ghent. But when Jackson did fight the British on 8 January 1815, the crushing American victory at New Orleans would join in the American mind with the news of peace. The two events were thus popularly linked even as the treaty arrived in the capital almost simultaneously with the emissaries from the Hartford Convention. Jackson had destroyed the British at New Orleans, and the news of that victory followed by news of peace destroyed the Federalist party.

With the immediate and unanimous ratification by the Senate of the Treaty of Ghent, the war ended. It would leave a mixed legacy. The celebrations that greeted the end of the war masked the fact that the United States had achieved none of Madison's stated goals in the War of 1812. Serious divisions within the government had hampered the war effort, and threats of secession had almost divided the nation. Yet the conflict had also spawned determination in many Americans to strengthen the nation and to eliminate the weaknesses made apparent by the war.

The War of 1812 was a watershed. It marked the end of the Jeffersonian insistence that a militia was the only way to defend republican liberty. It marked the end of the first American party system with the demise of the hapless Federalists amid charges of disloyalty and secession. It marked the end of whatever American introversion and insecurity lingered from the faltering days of the Confederation, and it ushered in an age of expansion and limitless optimism. It provided the country with proof of American resilience. Hobbled by the military ineptitude of bad generals or beset by the unshakable indifference of the occasional patriot, the country had not only survived; in some memorable cases it had triumphed. Many people charged with patriotic enthusiasm would describe the War of 1812 as a second war of independence and would call the period after it the "Era of Good Feelings." It says much about the complicated nature of this conflict and its aftermath that neither label was really correct.

Organization of This Book

Alphabetical entries account for the bulk of the information in this encyclopedia. Every effort has been made to adhere to consistent and standard methods that will make finding information easy, but invariably some arbitrary (and to some minds perhaps eccentric) decisions regarding organization have been necessary.

We have elected to list naval battles alphabetically using the name of the U.S. vessel first, regardless of the outcome of the contest. Items whose identifying name is preceded by a descriptor or other qualifier have been listed under the name (as in Ghent, Treaty of), and forts and battles are listed alphabetically under their individual names (as in Amanda, Fort, or Lundy's Lane, Battle of). To avoid unintended anachronisms, main titles and headwords for biographical entries do not include military rank or title. The exceptions are those whose names require a title for identification (as in Castlereagh, Viscount, Robert Stewart).

Spellings of certain names and places varies widely in primary sources, and those variations have been continued by the secondary authorities. In all events, we have attempted to use the most common or what seems the most accurate spelling, but we do so knowing that some will take exception to Sacket's rather than Sackett's Harbor or Chippewa rather than Chippawa. The participants in this early-nineteenth-century event did not have copy editors, much to the chagrin of those who now labor in the vineyard of consistency.

Finally, should your search through the alphabetical entries prove fruitless, please consult the index. Listings there will include all proper names and where they occur throughout the encyclopedia.

Maps

USS Chesapeake vs.
HMS Shannon

USS Enterprise vs.
HMS Boxer

USS Argus vs.
HMS Pelican

Liverpool
London
Bristol

Halifax

Boston

USS Constitution vs.
HMS Guerrière

USS Essex vs.
HMS Alert

Azores

New York

Prince-de-
Neufchatel vs.
HMS Endymion

General Armstrong vs.
British squadron

USS Constitution vs.
HMS Cyane and Levant

Chesapeake
Bay

Maderia

USS President vs.
HMS Endymion,
Pomone, and Tenedos

USS Wasp vs.
HMS Frolic

USS United States vs.
HMS Macedonian

Chasseur vs.
HMS St. Lawrence

Cuba

North

Atlantic

USS Hornet vs.
HMS Peacock

Ocean

Cape Verde
Is.

Equator

USS Constitution vs.
HMS Java

South

Atlantic

Ocean

USS Essex vs.
HMS Phoebe
and Cherub

Valparaiso

Map 1 The war at sea

Map 2 The southern theater

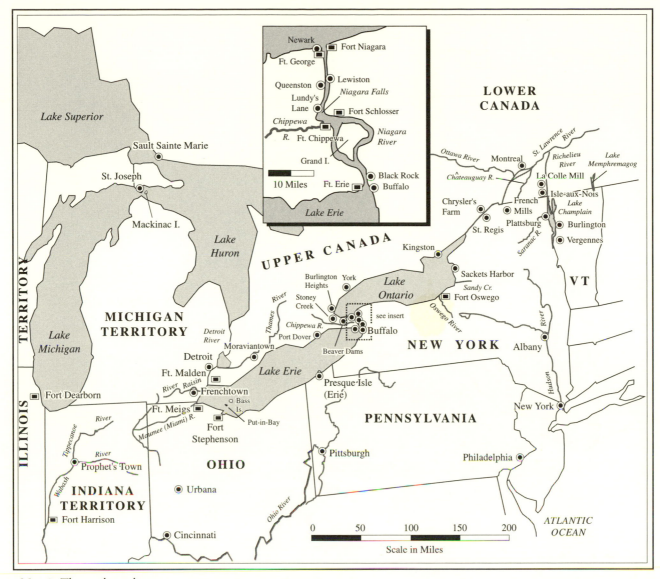

Map 3 The northern theater

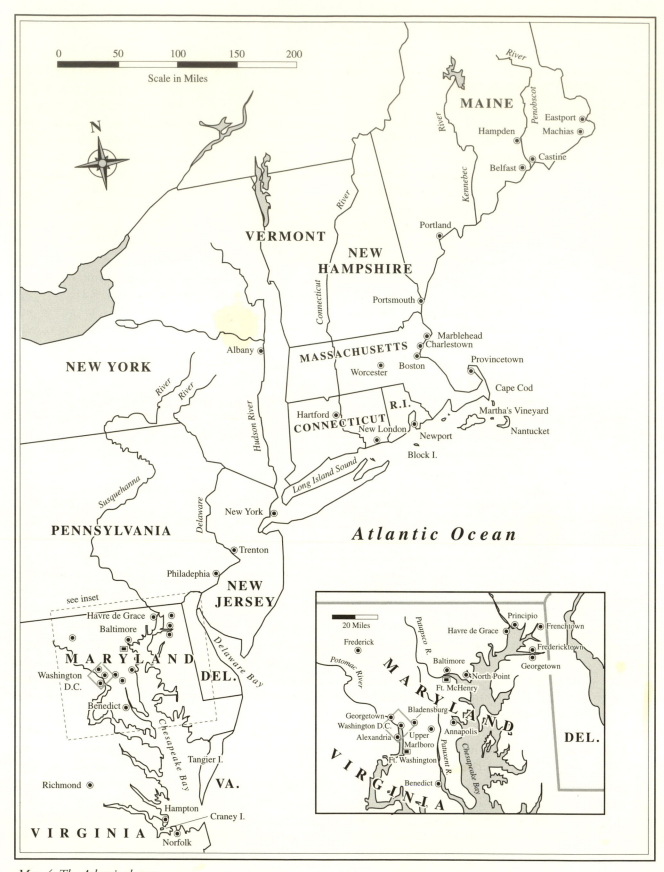

Map 4 The Atlantic theater

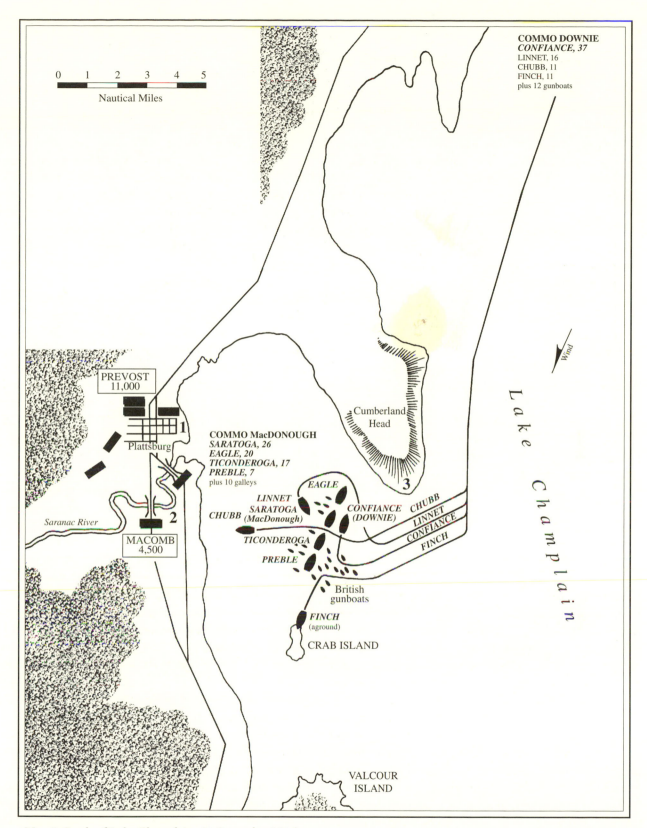

COMMO DOWNIE
CONFIANCE, 37
LINNET, 16
CHUBB, 11
FINCH, 11
plus 12 gunboats

0 1 2 3 4 5
Nautical Miles

Wind

PREVOST
11,000

1

Plattsburg

COMMO MacDONOUGH
SARATOGA, 26
EAGLE, 20
TICONDEROGA, 17
PREBLE, 7
plus 10 galleys

Cumberland
Head

3

Saranac River

2

MACOMB
4,500

EAGLE

LINNET
SARATOGA
CHUBB *(MacDonough)*

CHUBB
LINNET
CONFIANCE
(DOWNIE)
CONFIANCE
FINCH

TICONDEROGA

PREBLE

British
gunboats

FINCH
(aground)

CRAB ISLAND

L a k e   C h a m p l a i n

VALCOUR
ISLAND

Map 5 Battle of Lake Champlain, 11 September 1814

xxi

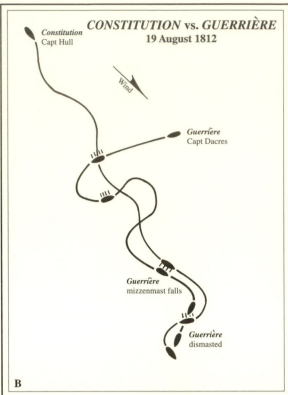

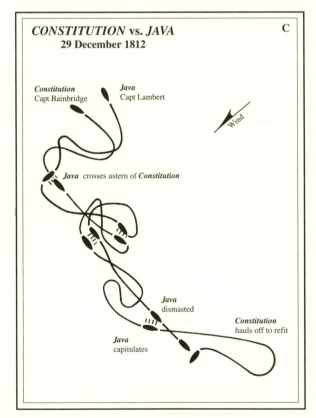

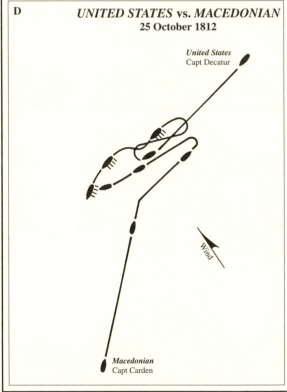

Map 6 (A) The Constitution *captures several merchant ships near Cape Race; (B)* Constitution *vs.* Guerrière; *(C)* Constitution *vs.* Java; *(D)* United States *vs.* Macedonian

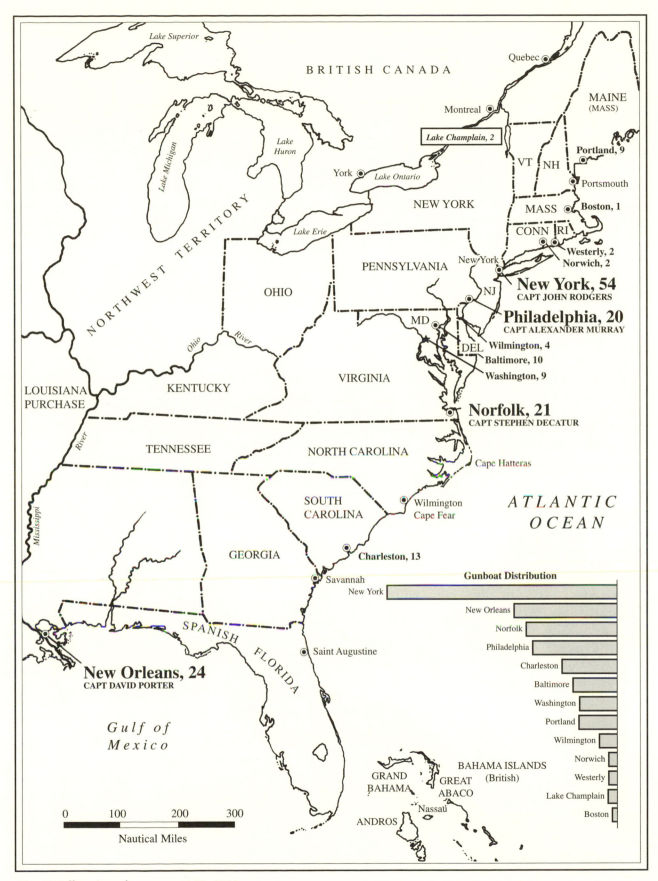

Map 7 *Jefferson's gunboat navy, 1807–1809*

Labels visible on the map:

- BRITISH CANADA
- Quebec
- Montreal
- *Lake Superior*
- *Lake Michigan*
- *Lake Huron*
- York
- *Lake Ontario*
- *Lake Erie*
- NORTHWEST TERRITORY
- MAINE (MASS)
- *Lake Champlain, 2*
- **Portland, 9**
- VT NH
- Portsmouth
- MASS **Boston, 1**
- CONN RI
- **Westerly, 2**
- **Norwich, 2**
- NEW YORK
- PENNSYLVANIA
- New York
- **New York, 54**
  CAPT JOHN RODGERS
- NJ
- **Philadelphia, 20**
  CAPT ALEXANDER MURRAY
- MD
- **Wilmington, 4**
- DEL
- **Baltimore, 10**
- **Washington, 9**
- OHIO
- *Ohio* River
- KENTUCKY
- VIRGINIA
- LOUISIANA PURCHASE
- *Mississippi* River
- **Norfolk, 21**
  CAPT STEPHEN DECATUR
- TENNESSEE
- NORTH CAROLINA
- Cape Hatteras
- SOUTH CAROLINA
- Wilmington Cape Fear
- *ATLANTIC OCEAN*
- GEORGIA
- **Charleston, 13**
- Savannah
- SPANISH FLORIDA
- Saint Augustine
- **New Orleans, 24**
  CAPT DAVID PORTER
- *Gulf of Mexico*
- GRAND BAHAMA
- GREAT ABACO
- BAHAMA ISLANDS (British)
- Nassau
- ANDROS

Scale: 0 100 200 300 Nautical Miles

Gunboat Distribution
- New York
- New Orleans
- Norfolk
- Philadelphia
- Charleston
- Baltimore
- Washington
- Portland
- Wilmington
- Norwich
- Westerly
- Lake Champlain
- Boston

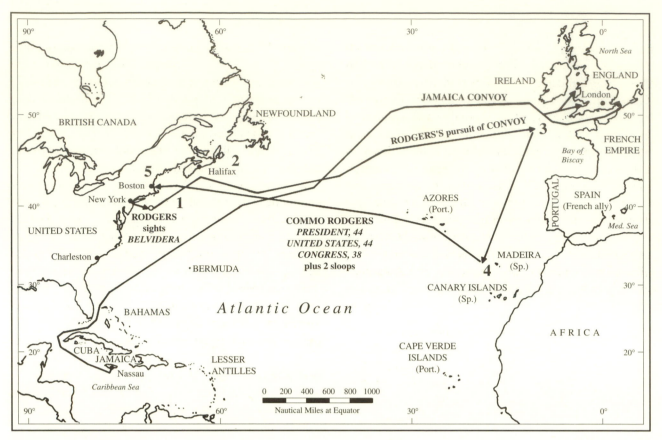

Map 8 Cruise of the U.S. fleet, June–August 1812

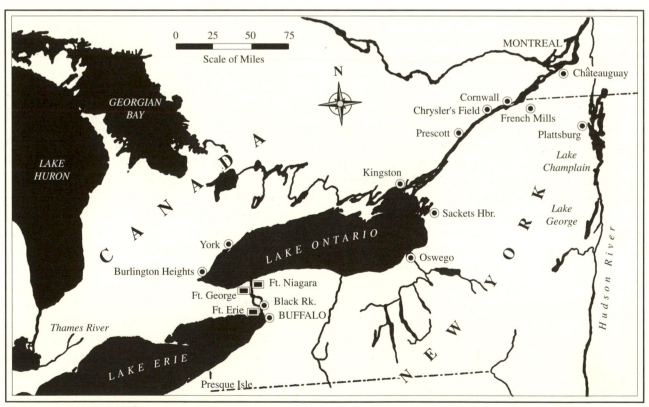

Map 9 The northern front

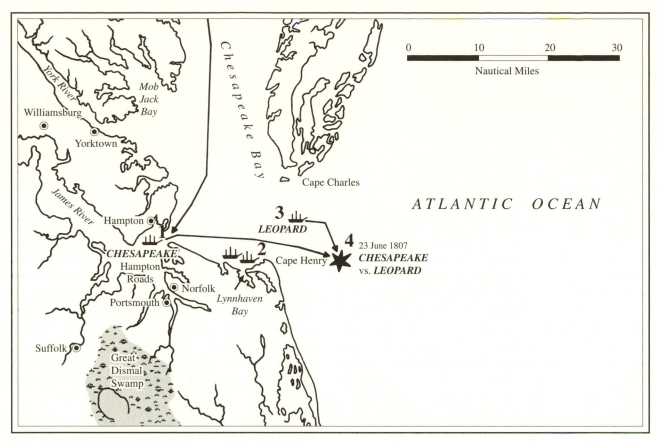

Map 10 Chesapeake *vs.* Leopard

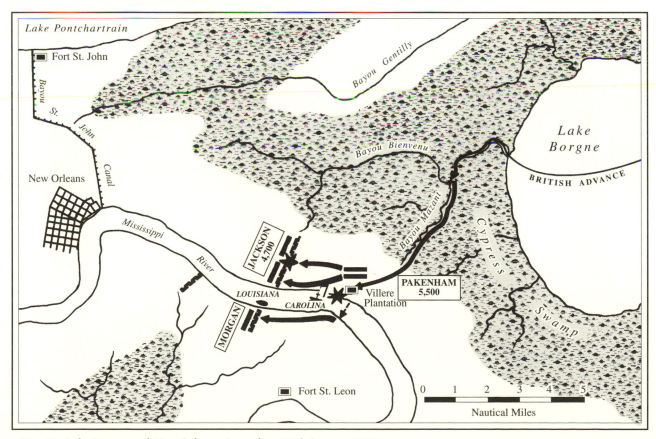

Map 11 Lake Borgne and New Orleans, December 1814–January 1815

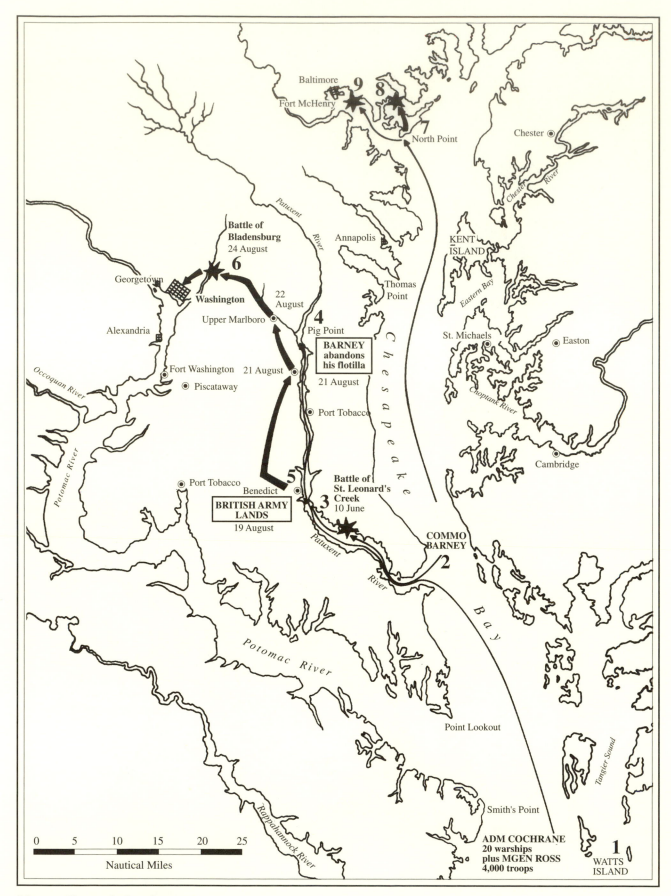

Baltimore
Fort McHenry
9
8
7
North Point
Chester

Patuxent

**Battle of
Bladensburg**
24 August
6

Annapolis
Thomas
Point

River

KENT
ISLAND

Eastern Bay

Georgetown

22
August

Washington

Upper Marlboro

4
Pig Point

St. Michaels

Easton

Alexandria

21 August

**BARNEY
abandons
his flotilla**
21 August

Choptank River

Occoquan River

Fort Washington

Piscataway

Port Tobacco

Chesapeake

Potomac River

Port Tobacco
Benedict

5

**BRITISH ARMY
LANDS**
19 August

**Battle of
St. Leonard's
Creek**
10 June

3

Cambridge

Patuxent

**COMMO
BARNEY**

2

River

Bay

Potomac River

Point Lookout

Tangier Sound

Rappahannock River

| 0 | 5 | 10 | 15 | 20 | 25 |

Nautical Miles

Smith's Point

**ADM COCHRANE
20 warships
plus MGEN ROSS
4,000 troops**

1
WATTS
ISLAND

Map 12 Chesapeake Bay theater

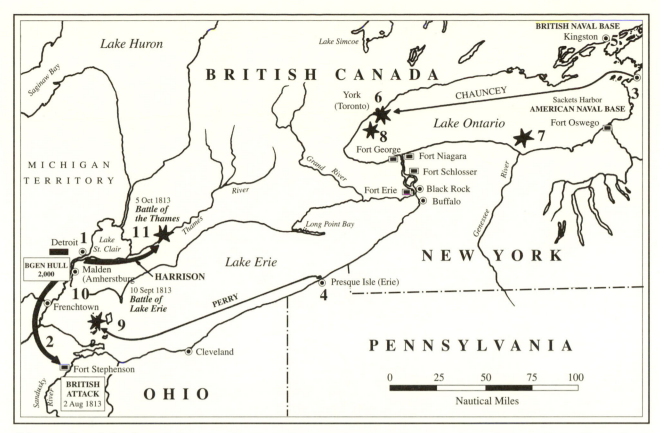

Map 13 Great Lakes theater

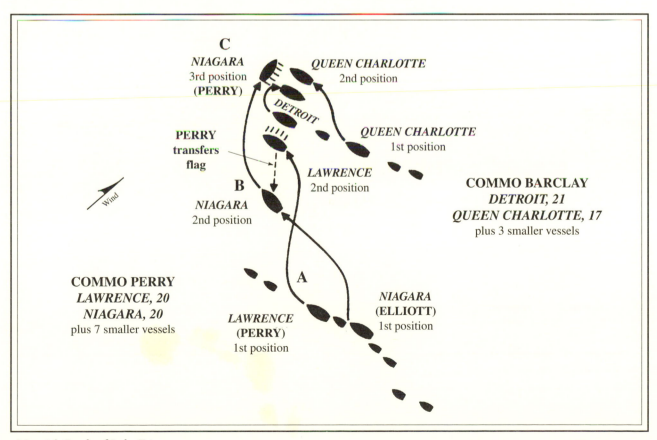

Map 14 Battle of Lake Erie

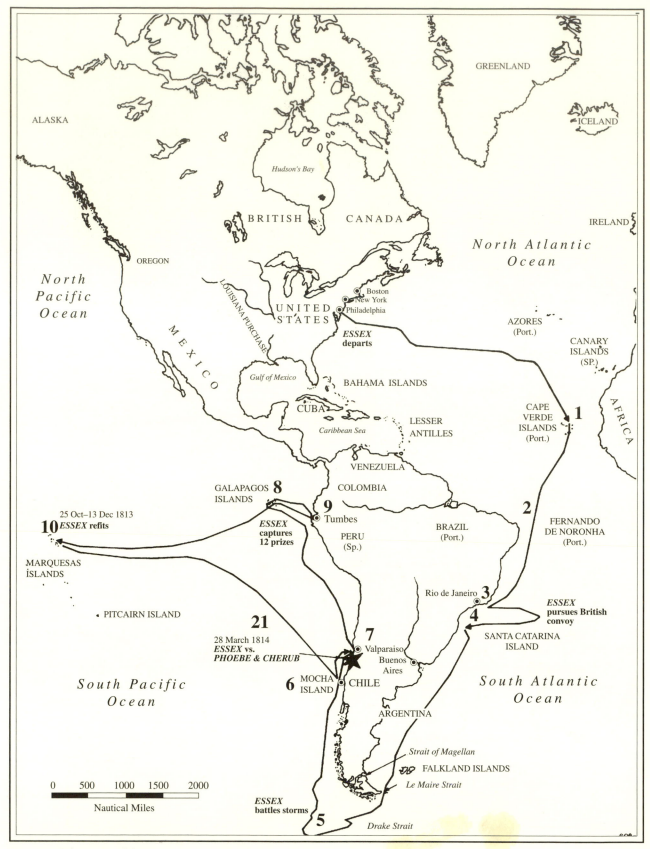

GREENLAND

ICELAND

ALASKA

North Pacific Ocean

OREGON

BRITISH   CANADA

Hudson's Bay

IRELAND

North Atlantic Ocean

UNITED STATES

Boston
New York
Philadelphia

***ESSEX* departs**

AZORES
(Port.)

CANARY ISLANDS
(SP.)

AFRICA

Gulf of Mexico

BAHAMA ISLANDS

CUBA

Caribbean Sea

LESSER ANTILLES

VENEZUELA

COLOMBIA

CAPE VERDE ISLANDS
(Port.)

1

2

FERNANDO DE NORONHA
(Port.)

GALAPAGOS ISLANDS **8**

9
Tumbes

***ESSEX* captures 12 prizes**

PERU
(Sp.)

BRAZIL
(Port.)

25 Oct–13 Dec 1813
10 ***ESSEX* refits**

MARQUESAS ISLANDS

PITCAIRN ISLAND

21

28 March 1814
ESSEX* vs. *PHOEBE & CHERUB

Rio de Janeiro **3**

4

***ESSEX* pursues British convoy**

SANTA CATARINA ISLAND

7 Valparaiso

6 MOCHA ISLAND   CHILE

Buenos Aires

South Pacific Ocean

South Atlantic Ocean

ARGENTINA

0   500   1000   1500   2000

Nautical Miles

***ESSEX* battles storms**

5

Strait of Magellan
FALKLAND ISLANDS

Le Maire Strait

Drake Strait

MEXICO

LOUISIANA PURCHASE

Map 15 The cruise of the Essex

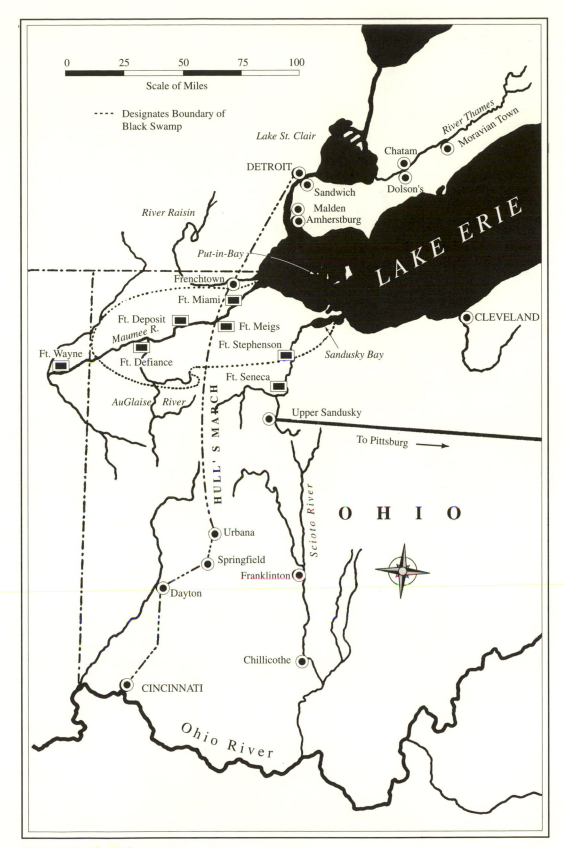

Map 16 Northwest front

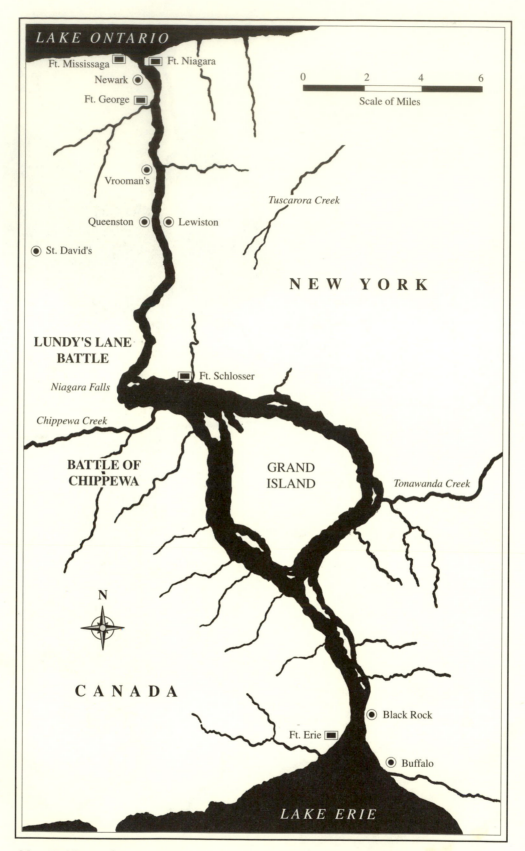

Map 17 Niagara front

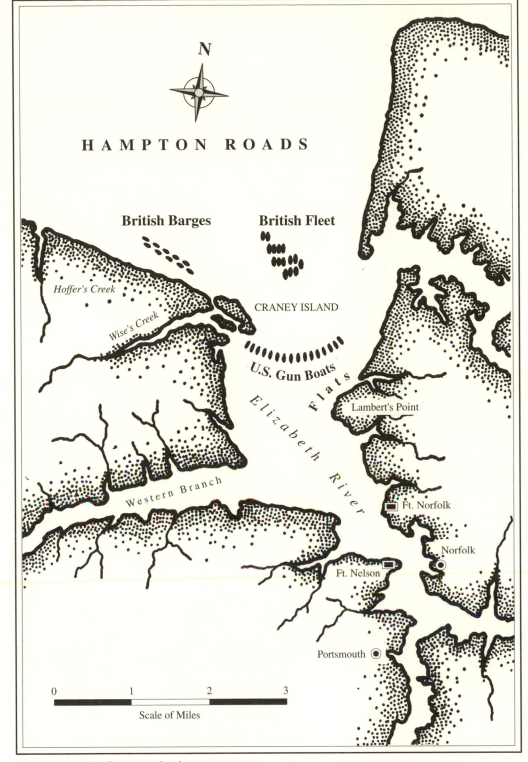

N

HAMPTON ROADS

British Barges   **British Fleet**

Hoffer's Creek

CRANEY ISLAND

Wise's Creek

U.S. Gun Boats

Flats

Elizabeth River

Lambert's Point

Western Branch

Ft. Norfolk

Norfolk

Ft. Nelson

Portsmouth

| 0 | 1 | 2 | 3 |

Scale of Miles

Map 18 Battle of Craney Island

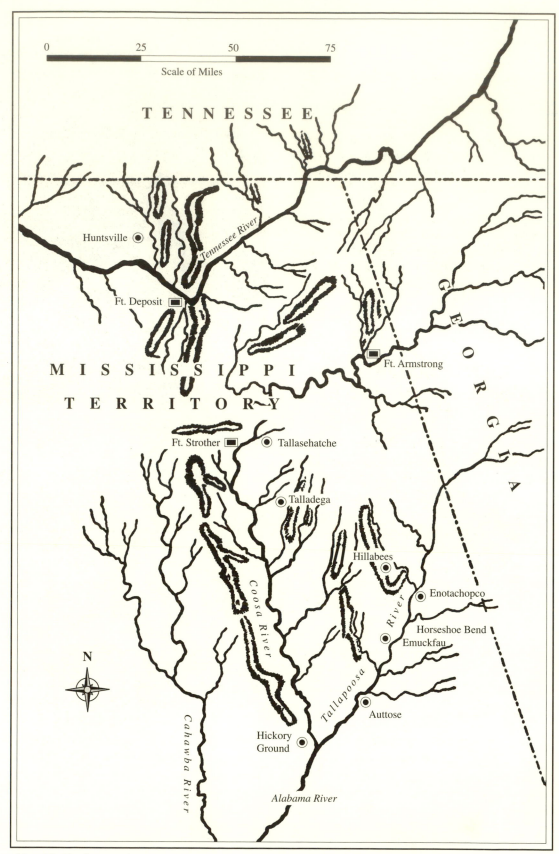

Map 19 Creek campaign

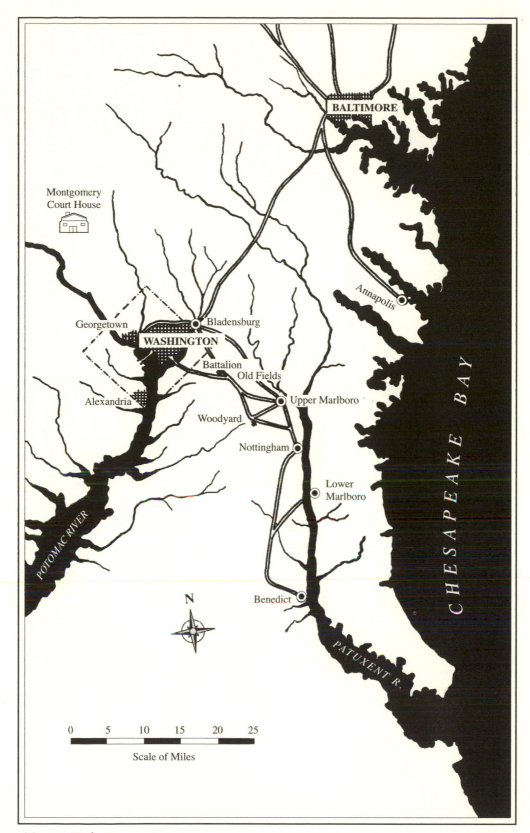

Map 20 Washington campaign

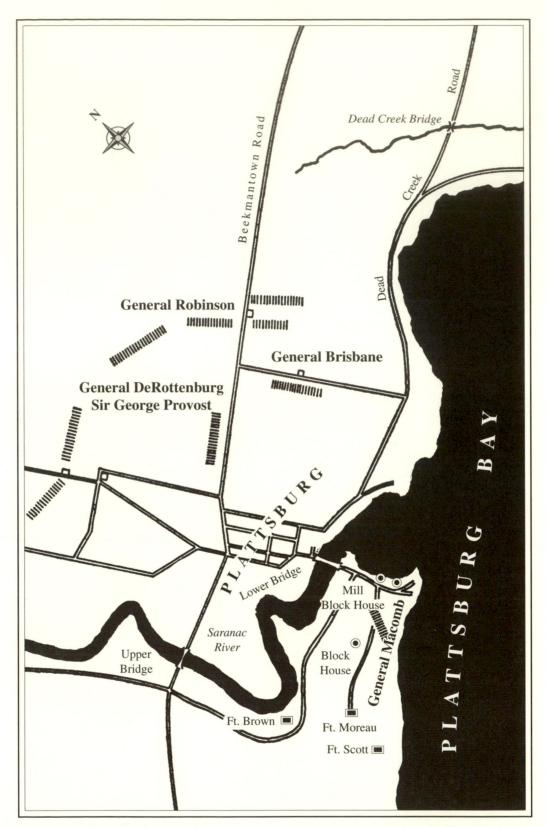

Map 21 *Battle of Plattsburg (land)*

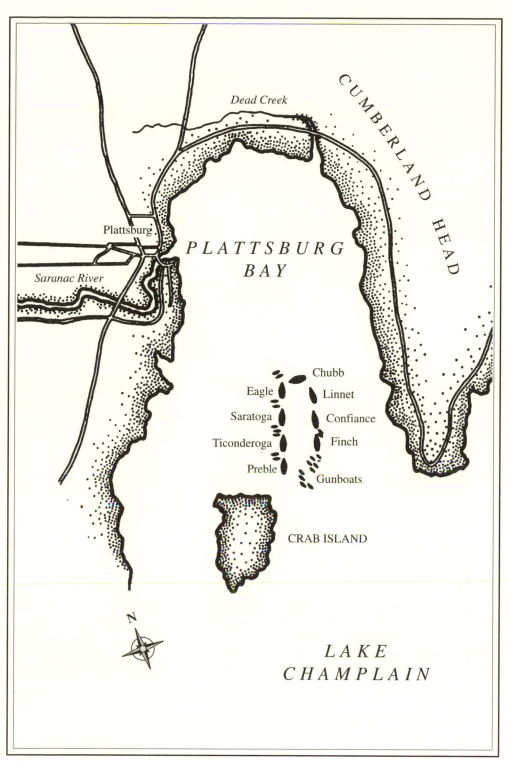

Dead Creek

CUMBERLAND HEAD

Plattsburg

Saranac River

PLATTSBURG BAY

Chubb
Eagle   Linnet
Saratoga   Confiance
Ticonderoga   Finch
Preble   Gunboats

CRAB ISLAND

N

LAKE CHAMPLAIN

Map 22 Battle of Plattsburg (sea)

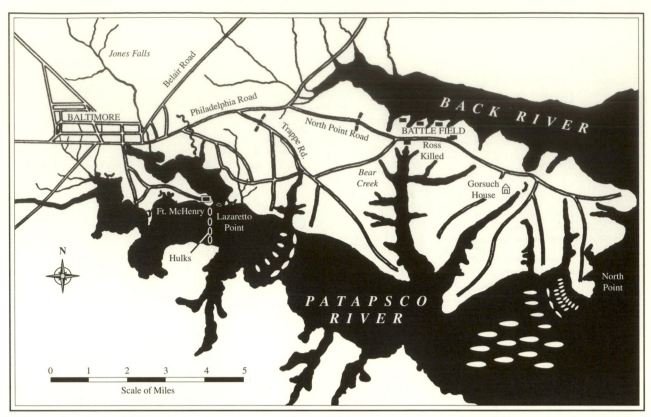

Map 23 Battle of Baltimore

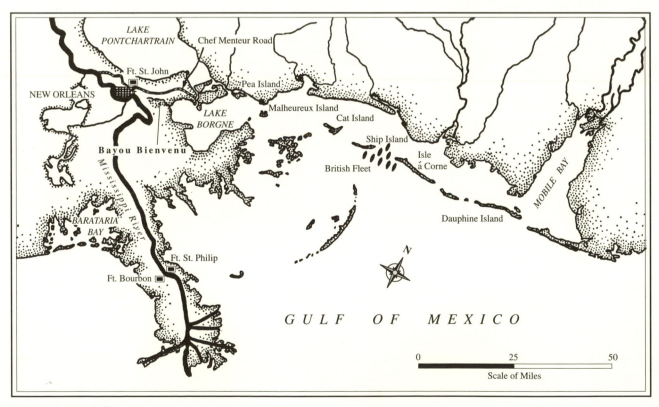

Map 24 New Orleans campaign

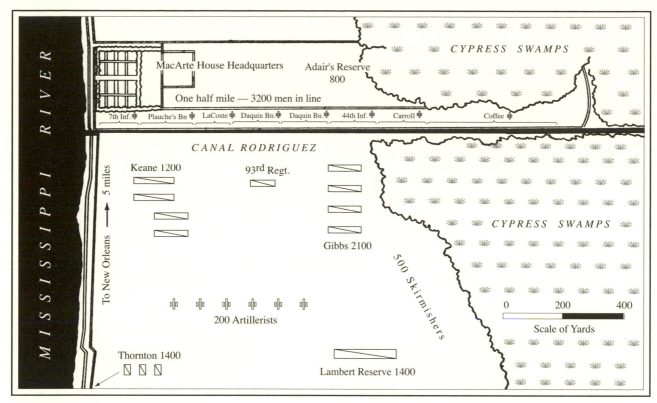

Map 25 New Orleans, January 8

A

ADAIR, JOHN
1757–1840
U.S. militia officer

Born in South Carolina, John Adair moved to Kentucky in 1786. He participated in the Indian wars of the 1790s and became prominent in Kentucky politics. From 1805 to 1807, he represented Kentucky in the U.S. Senate, but his involvement with Aaron Burr's schemes temporarily damaged Adair's popularity.

Though of advanced years during the War of 1812, he was eager to participate and volunteered to serve as Gov. Isaac Shelby's aide when William Henry Harrison invited the governor to join the invasion of Canada after Oliver Hazard Perry's victory on Lake Erie. Consequently, Adair was present at the Battle of the Thames. As a result of his activities in that campaign, he received a brevet rank of brigadier general in the Kentucky militia and the post of adjutant general.

When Andrew Jackson called for militia reinforcements for his defense of the Gulf of Mexico in the fall of 1814, Adair raised a force and marched to New Orleans, arriving on 2 January 1815. He left Kentucky so quickly that he did not adequately arm his men. Approximately half of his 700 men arrived at New Orleans without weapons. General Jackson scrounged up what he could for the remainder. At the final British offensive of the campaign on 8 January, Adair's men—perhaps because of their poor arms—were placed as a reserve behind men commanded by Gen. William Carroll in the area that would receive the brunt of the British assault. The men who had brought their own guns, however, had brought rifles, partly giving rise to the now-disputed story that the British were defeated because the U.S. forces were mainly armed with rifles.

Following the war, Adair returned to Kentucky, his political reputation restored. In 1820, he was elected governor and served for four years in that position. At the age of 74,

in 1831, he was elected to the U.S. House of Representatives. After one term, he retired from public life and died in Harrodsburg, Kentucky, in 1840.

—Jeanne T. Heidler and David S. Heidler

See also: Carroll, William; Harrison, William Henry; New Orleans, Battle of; Shelby, Isaac; Thames, Battle of the
Further Reading
Leger, William G. "The Public Life of John Adair." Ph.D. diss., University of Kentucky, 1960.

ADAMS, JOHN QUINCY
1767–1848
U.S. diplomat

Born in Braintree (Quincy), Massachusetts, to John Adams and Abigail Smith Adams, John Quincy Adams spent much of his youth abroad accompanying his father on his many diplomatic missions during the American Revolution. Much of the younger man's early education occurred in France, Spain, and the Netherlands. In 1781, Adams traveled to Russia as secretary for Francis Dana, U.S. minister to the czar. When John Adams received an appointment as one of the U.S. peace commissioners to Paris, young Adams went to Paris as one of his father's secretaries.

After his return to the United States, Adams entered Harvard as a junior and graduated after attending for one year. He read law and began his practice in Boston, but soon politics proved irresistible. He first wrote anonymous essays that were published in northeastern newspapers and that dealt mainly with diplomatic topics. The identity of the author was soon an open secret, and John Quincy Adams thereby gained a reputation as something of an expert in foreign affairs. This purported expertise and the fact

John Quincy Adams

that his father was George Washington's vice president prompted Washington to appoint the younger Adams minister to the Dutch Republic in 1794 and minister to Portugal in 1796. When John Adams won the presidency, he made his son minister to Prussia in 1797.

Following his father's defeat in a bid for reelection in 1800, John Quincy Adams returned to the United States in 1801 and became involved in Massachusetts politics. In 1803, the Massachusetts legislature elected him to the U.S. Senate, although once seated in that body, he rapidly gained a reputation for diverging from fellow Federalists in many of his views. He publicly broke with the party in 1807, a step prompted by his disagreement with Federalists concerning the *Chesapeake-Leopard* incident and by his subsequent support for the Embargo Act. Eventually, Adams would privately muse that the embargo had been a mistake, especially after he knew how easily his native New England had evaded it. But at the time, his break from the Federalists cost him reelection to the Senate in 1808.

Republicans soon rewarded him in 1809, when newly inaugurated Pres. James Madison appointed Adams minister to Russia. While in Russia, he continued to follow U.S. domestic developments as closely as possible. He also per-

sisted in his belief that economic coercion was preferable to war in securing neutral rights for the United States from the British and French. By 1812, though, Adams had come to see British trade restrictions as an attempt to revive colonialism. If the United States did not protect its rights, even by war, the country would become hopelessly dependent on the British. As Adams posted these thoughts home to his parents, Napoleon Bonaparte began his invasion of Russia.

Strangely, it was Russia's war with France that produced the first serious attempt to resolve the Anglo-American conflict. Only a year after the beginning of the War of 1812, Czar Alexander I mounted an effort to end Great Britain's war with the United States so that Great Britain, Russia's ally, could devote its full energies to defeating Napoleon. Alexander instructed Foreign Minister Count Romanzoff to approach Minister Adams and the British about the possibility of the czar's mediating a peace settlement. Adams passed the offer on to President Madison, who eagerly accepted it.

Shortly after Congress opened its session in May 1813, Madison asked it to confirm the appointments of John Quincy Adams, James A. Bayard, and Albert Gallatin as the U.S. peace commissioners to Russia. Although Adams and Bayard were confirmed, the Senate refused to confirm Gallatin, who had already departed for Europe. When Bayard and Gallatin arrived in St. Petersburg carrying the U.S. acceptance of the czar's offer, the commissioners did not know that Gallatin lacked congressional confirmation. In any event, it made little difference, because neither an official acceptance nor any commissioners had arrived from London. Throughout the summer and into the fall rumors circulated that the British would resist an outside power's dictating their trade policies and hence had refused the czar's offer. Meanwhile, the three Americans waited.

British foreign secretary Lord Castlereagh did not want to appear unreasonable about ending the war, so he conveyed to President Madison the British government's offer of direct negotiations with the United States. Madison accepted and immediately submitted the names of John Quincy Adams (as head of the commission), James A. Bayard, Henry Clay, and Jonathan Russell. Several weeks later, after learning that Gallatin was still in Europe, Madison included him in the peace commission. This time Congress confirmed all five men.

Bayard and Gallatin had impatiently left Russia to engage in some unofficial diplomacy with the British before word reached St. Petersburg of this new development. Once Adams heard about his role in the direct talks, he also made his way to western Europe to join his fellow commissioners in the summer of 1814. Lord Castlereagh had suggested that it might be convenient to conduct negotiations in London, but Adams and Clay adamantly insisted that negotiations take place on neutral ground. This was possibly the last point of complete agreement between Adams and Clay during all of the negotiations, but it was responsible for removing discussions from the British capital. After the British agreed to meet at Ghent in Belgium, the U.S. commissioners traveled there to await their counterparts.

The British commissioners were Dr. William Adams, Lord Gambier, and Henry Goulburn. Only Goulburn held a high post in the current ministry: undersecretary to Lord Bathurst in the Colonial Office and to Castlereagh in the Foreign Office. The group in sum proved inferior in political rank to the delegates from the United States. Lord Castlereagh reserved his best diplomats for the upcoming Congress of Vienna and sent to Ghent three mediocrities whose most imaginative gesture throughout the negotiations was to be late for them. The British commissioners thought that reinforcements freed from the European war and bound for North America would turn the military tide there to their negotiating advantage. When they did arrive they exceeded their instructions and demonstrated no diplomatic flexibility. They made plain their preconceived notion that the United States should be grateful that Britain was willing to talk at all.

Thus, negotiations officially began on 8 August 1814. The list of nonnegotiable British terms included an Indian buffer state carved from U.S. territory, adjustments of the Canadian border at various points to the advantage of Canada, the elimination of U.S. fishing rights in Canadian waters, and the demilitarization of the Great Lakes. Adams, who tended toward pessimism, was convinced by the British demeanor at Ghent and this list of incredible demands that the talks were a waste of time. He grew glum and testy. The desultory work habits of his fellow commissioners annoyed and discouraged him. To his mind his compatriots drank too much, smoked too much, and stayed up too late. Henry Clay was the worst offender on all counts, Adams sourly noted, and he no doubt blamed Clay for leading the others away from work to indulgent degradation. So nobody pleased him, and he brooded over the arrogant tone of written messages sent by the British commissioners. Britain would remain adamantly tied to its original terms, he thought, and his fellow Americans would continue personal amusements rather than steeling themselves for equally adamant responses.

Yet several surprises awaited this disconsolate diplomat. As it happened, the British commissioners' arrogance angered their superiors in London almost as much as it infuriated the Americans. Adams suddenly noticed such a change in British behavior that it was obvious that the commissioners had been reined in. In fact, the lengthy interval between U.S. proposals and British responses led him to believe that the British negotiators were now required to submit their responses to London for approval. Even so, his British counterparts continued to press their original terms, albeit more pleasantly.

To make matters worse, Henry Clay irritated Adams's frayed nerves by suggesting that New England's fishing rights could be offered as a concession to the British. To a New Englander, such a suggestion was simple blasphemy. Perhaps to get back some of his own, Adams suggested conceding free British navigation of the Mississippi River as a bargaining ploy. Clay exploded, saying that westerners would never agree to such a move. When Albert Gallatin stepped in to smooth ruffled feathers, Adams took notice. Privately, he gave Gallatin much credit for the success of the United States at Ghent.

Adams almost lost to the other commissioners on the issue of territorial concessions. They believed that the British would not make a treaty unless some guarantees were made for Canadian security and that part of those guarantees would have to include a chunk of Massachusetts, specifically a large part of the future state of Maine. Adams stubbornly protected his native state's interests, and in the end the British did not insist upon such a concession. In fact, Henry Clay had been right in insisting that the British delegation originally had been merely bluffing. Ultimately, the British did not insist on much of anything. Regarding the Indian buffer state, Adams informed British commissioner Henry Goulburn that the American people would never leave such a large amount of territory in Indian hands. The British government then decided to accept instead the assurance that all lands in the hands of Indians at the start of the conflict would be returned to them at its conclusion. Adams and his fellow commissioners also gained some flexibility when Madison and Secretary of State James Monroe dropped the elimination of impressment as a U.S. condition for peace. The removal of that restriction on their actions left Adams and the others free to negotiate any treaty within reason if the British would cooperate.

By December, British negotiators at Vienna were in an increasingly weak position because a coalition between the czar and the king of Prussia threatened the European settlement. Lord Castlereagh thus was ready for the war in North America to come to an end. Attempting to stop a land grab by the Russians and Prussians, Castlereagh could not have the negotiations at Ghent held up on the basis of British attempts to grab U.S. territory. In many ways the British difficulties at Vienna gave Adams and the others the breach they needed. The Treaty of Ghent, which thus returned both nations to status quo antebellum, was signed on 24 December 1814. The following day was Christmas, and John Quincy Adams broke his solemnity to make merry. He joined his colleagues for dinner as the guests of the British commissioners.

Adams left Ghent for London shortly after the signing of the treaty. Gallatin and Clay joined him there to negotiate trade matters with Britain. With surprising quickness they reached an agreement satisfactory to both nations. Shortly after the war, President Madison appointed Adams U.S. minister to Great Britain. He began negotiations on what became known as the Rush-Bagot Agreement, demilitarizing the Great Lakes. Appointed Pres. James Monroe's secretary of state, Adams returned to the United States in 1817. As secretary of state, he was responsible for numerous diplomatic triumphs, including the Adams-Onís Treaty (the Transcontinental Treaty) and state papers including the Monroe Doctrine.

In 1824, Adams ran for president and was elected by the House of Representatives after none of the candidates received a majority of the electoral college votes. Ironically, his selection by the House resulted from support he received from his old nemesis at Ghent, Henry Clay. Adams then appointed Clay his secretary of state, an action that led to charges by the supporters of Andrew Jackson that Adams and Clay had made a "corrupt bargain."

Following Adams's defeat by Jackson in the election of 1828, Adams returned briefly to private life before accepting election in 1830 to the House of Representatives from his Massachusetts congressional district. He served in the House for the remainder of his life, often serving as the spokesman for antislavery forces, especially in his long fight to secure the repeal of the Gag Rule, a legislative sanction forbidding the reading of abolitionists petitions on the floor of Congress. Worn out by his labors, John Quincy Adams collapsed in Congress on 21 February 1848 and died two days later.

—Jeanne T. Heidler and David S. Heidler

See also: Alexander I; Bathurst, Henry, Third Earl Bathurst; Bayard, James Asheton; Castlereagh, Viscount, Robert Stewart; Clay, Henry; Embargo Act; Gallatin, Albert; Ghent, Treaty of; Goulburn, Henry; Impressment; Madison, James; Monroe, James; Russell, Jonathan

Further Reading

Adams, John Quincy. *Memoirs of John Quincy Adams: Comprising Portions of His Diary from 1795 to 1848.* Ed. Chauncey Worthington Ford. 7 vols. Philadelphia: J. B. Lippincott, 1874–1877.

Bemis, Samuel Flagg. *John Quincy Adams and the Foundations of American Foreign Policy.* New York: Alfred A. Knopf, 1969.

Nagel, Paul C. *John Quincy Adams: A Public Life, A Private Life.* New York: Alfred A. Knopf, 1997.

Perkins, Bradford. *Castlereagh and Adams: England and the United States, 1812–1823.* Berkeley: University of California Press, 1964.

Russell, Greg. *John Quincy Adams and the Public Virtues of Diplomacy.* Columbia: University of Missouri Press, 1995.

Willwerth, Mary Elizabeth. "John Quincy Adams as Minister to Russia, 1809–1814: The Ideals and Realities Confronting His Mission." Master's thesis, Eastern Illinois University, 1992.

AFRICAN AMERICANS

Wars are often crucibles of social change because military necessity can force policies that modify prevailing patterns of discrimination and oppression. The War of 1812 opened doors of opportunity for some slaves and freedmen. It also required the adoption of enlistment policies that questioned fundamental assumptions about slavery. African Americans served with distinction during the war, despite restrictions placed on their participation.

Andrew Jackson's skillful recruitment and adroit use of the Battalion of Free Men of Color at New Orleans is the most celebrated African American chapter in the War of 1812. Yet it was as sailors, not soldiers, that most enslaved or free African Americans served. In 1812, even severe troop shortages did not soften whites' prejudices against blacks in service. A congressional act of 3 March 1813, however, authorized the enlistment of free blacks in the U.S. Navy. Eventually they constituted 10 to 20 percent of U.S. crews on the Upper Lakes. Tales of such gallant African American sailors as the heroic John Johnson and the "Black Hercules," Richard Seavers, flourished in African American communities after the war. Some black seamen escaped British impressment to fight for the United States. Official accounts describe their contributions in many naval battles, including the decisive engagement on Lake Erie.

African Americans contributed to the war effort outside the navy as well. Black soldiers performed mostly menial tasks when scattered throughout white troop regiments, including regiments from southern states. Free black women and men worked to build defensive fortifications in many cities and towns, most notably at Grays Ferry in Philadelphia. After the fall of Washington, D.C., more than 2,500 free blacks labored continuously for two days to erect defenses protecting Philadelphia. Many African Americans used the war as an opportunity to prove themselves capable and loyal to the United States, hoping that the nation would reward their military and civil service after the war. In spite of widespread African American support for the United States, persistent fears of slave insurrections and defections to the British heightened racial tension during the war.

Of course, not all enslaved or free African Americans considered a U.S. victory to be in their best interests. John Hope Franklin points out that the perception that victorious Americans would extend slavery limited African American military participation. Also, areas such as New England and the Mid-Atlantic states, from which free black enlistees were most likely to come, dissented against the war.

Some African Americans fought for the British, who frequently promised freedom at the end of the conflict. A 200-man unit of black marines was part of the British forces in the major Chesapeake campaigns, including Bladensburg, Washington, and Baltimore. Unfortunately for these British enlistees, the British government did not keep its word. After the war, many of these men were resold into slavery in the West Indies. Recognizing the profitability of these transactions for the British, the United States sought and in 1828 secured indemnities for the sale of fugitive slaves.

Louisiana's Battalion of Free Men of Color deserves special mention, both for its notoriety and for its significance. Gen. Andrew Jackson delivered a stirring speech to the free black men of New Orleans after Gov. William C.C. Claiborne had authorized their enrollment in the militia. A bitter struggle had preceded Claiborne's edict, and he restricted enlistment to free black landholders and to slaves who had their owners' consent. These men were organized into four companies of 64 men each, designated the Battalion of Free Men of Color, and commanded by white captains. The first African Americans commissioned as second lieutenants in a state militia formed part of the command structure.

Jackson's plea to Louisiana's free African Americans was spurred by military necessity. He needed soldiers in 1814. Furthermore, he considered black inclusion in U.S. forces a way to counter British recruitment of blacks as spies, guides, messengers, and laborers. During the Battle of New Orleans, the Free Men of Color held a key position near Jackson's main forces on the banks of the Mississippi. They earned praise for their hard work in building extensive fortifications —sometimes called the "cotton-bag" defenses— that shielded U.S. troops. In spite of their notable achievements in defending the city, the black soldiers nevertheless were banned from participation in the victory celebration. Worse, they were denied many of the bonuses Jackson had promised, such as federal pensions and pay equal to that of white enlistees, 160-acre land grants to each man, and freedom for the enslaved.

In his address to "the Free Colored Inhabitants of Louisiana" on 21 September 1814, Jackson called his audience "Sons of Freedom" and called on them to defend the liberty of all Americans in the war against the British. For the many African Americans who answered his call, the aftermath of the war was especially disheartening. Jackson's words rang hollow as black soldiers found themselves reenslaved by the country they had fought to defend. Although the Treaty of Ghent did include a clause requiring both the United States and Great Britain to discourage the slave trade, the U.S. victory in the war was a bitter event for most African Americans. Black men and women would have to wait nearly fifty years before their war for freedom would begin.

—*Elizabeth Lutes Hillman*

See also: Baltimore, Battle of; Bladensburg, Battle of; Claiborne, William Charles Coles; Ghent, Treaty of; Jackson, Andrew; Lake Erie Campaign; New Orleans, Battle of

Further Reading

Crane, Jay David, and Elaine Crane, eds. *The Black Soldier: From the American Revolution to Vietnam.* New York: William Morrow, 1971.

Foner, Jack D. *Blacks and the Military in American History: A New Perspective.* New York: Praeger, 1974.

Franklin, John Hope. *From Slavery to Freedom: A History of Negro Americans.* 4th ed. New York: Alfred A. Knopf, 1974.

George, Christopher T. "Mirage of Freedom: African Americans in the War of 1812." *Maryland Historical Magazine* 91 (Winter 1996).

Wilson, Joseph T. *The Black Phalanx: A History of the Negro Soldiers of the United States in the Wars of 1775–1812, 1861–1865.* Hartford: American, 1888.

ALEXANDER I
1777–1825?
Russian czar, 1801–1825

Alexander I ascended to the throne in 1801 after his father, Paul I, was assassinated. During the early years of his reign, Alexander's position was not entirely secure. Moody, deeply religious, and mystical, the new czar was emotionally unstable and prone to change policies if given the proper inspiration. Furthermore, although Alexander considered reforms for Russia, he had to contend with profound challenges to his empire's existence.

French threats to Russia multiplied during the first half of Alexander's 25-year reign. Russian armies suffered defeats, as did their potential European allies, as the French subjugated Europe. In 1807, Napoleon and Alexander concluded a treaty at Tilsit, but over time this peace became precarious. When Russia began to flout the restrictions of Napoleon's Continental System, Alexander slowly realized that a French invasion of Russia was likely. Accordingly, he sought alliances that might deter Napoleon's punishment. Because Britain was the only major power not under Napoleon's control, positive Anglo-Russian relations became imperative.

Russian relations with the United States were also important. U.S.-Russian trade prospered through Baltic Sea routes. Encouraging this trade was a major pursuit of John Quincy Adams, who became U.S. minister in St. Petersburg in 1809. Adams sought commercial agreements with the Russian government and dealt extensively with Count Nicholas Romanzoff, the Russian foreign minister since 1807. As Alexander's representative, Romanzoff sought to unite all potential anti-Napoleonic powers. Thus he became alarmed as Anglo-American relations deteriorated during 1811 and 1812. In April 1812, Russian diplomats held discussions with their British counterparts in Sweden in the hope of staving off an Anglo-American war. The resultant Swedish-Russian-British treaty, signed on 18 July 1812, marked a significant boost to the anti-French effort. Furthermore, the Russians urged the British to repeal their Orders in Council. In the end, however, the Russian efforts could not prevent the War of 1812.

Napoleon invaded Russia on 22 June 1812 and advanced rapidly on Moscow. News of Anglo-American hostilities reached St. Petersburg in September, at the same time as the disastrous Battle of Borodino and the French occupation of Moscow. Alexander faced the greatest crisis of his reign and was determined to remove any obstacle to expelling Napoleon. Consequently, he proposed to mediate between the British and Americans.

On 18 September, Romanzoff instructed Baron Nicolay to offer mediation when he arrived in London. At about the same time, Romanzoff contacted Lord Cathcart, British minister to Russia. On 21 September, Romanzoff met with Adams and revealed Alexander's mediation offer. Adams proved receptive and immediately notified his State Department. On 24 February 1813, news of Alexander's proposed mediation reached Washington. On 8 March 1813, Count Andrei Daschkov, Russian minister to the United States, formally conveyed the offer to Secretary of State James Monroe. Three days later, Monroe formally accepted the Russian initiative.

James Madison's administration embraced the Russian offer without consulting Congress or assessing Britain's inclinations. On 25 May, however, Madison called the Senate into special session to discuss the Russian proposal. He also appointed Secretary of the Treasury Albert Gallatin and Sen. James Bayard to join Adams as peace commissioners. The Senate confirmed Adams and Bayard, but Gallatin and Bayard departed on 9 May 1813 prior to the Senate rejection of the treasury secretary in a fit of political pique. Later in 1813, the Senate did confirm Gallatin's commission, but he had already been in Europe for months without legitimate credentials.

Some Britons saw the War of 1812 as a semidomestic quarrel and therefore opposed any outside intervention. The British remembered the Russian sponsorship of the League of Armed Neutrality of 1780 that had so chagrined them during the American Revolution, and they had no intention of encouraging a sequel. Also, they were wary of postwar Russian intentions in central and eastern Europe. London told Lord Cathcart to decline the offer.

Bayard and Gallatin reached St. Petersburg on 21 July 1813 and soon deduced that their mission was futile. Alexander was in Germany fighting Napoleon, removing the czar as a persuasive force in the capital. Romanzoff's rapidly waning power diminished his worth to the Americans. Bayard and Gallatin left Russia empty-handed in January 1814.

Napoleon's defeat in Russia profoundly changed the balance of power in Europe. Forced on the defensive, he soon faced a growing number of determined and vengeful enemies. Alexander, for one, was resolved to destroy Napoleon, but the 1812 campaign had exhausted the Russian army. As Russia became more dependent on British financial subsidies, the czar's preoccupation with myriad domestic and diplomatic issues pushed U.S.-Russian relations into the background.

In the fall of 1813, Romanzoff nevertheless repeated his mediation offer to the British, who rebuffed him again. In October 1813, the new British minister in St. Petersburg immediately began undermining Romanzoff's reputation and authority. Meanwhile, Viscount Castlereagh, the British foreign minister, wrote to Monroe on 4 November 1813 proposing direct negotiations. When Monroe accepted the British proposal on 5 January 1814, Russian mediation efforts became moot. Romanzoff resigned shortly afterward, and Alexander directed his attention to the Congress of Vienna. With significant European issues under discussion, relations with the United States rapidly dwindled in importance.

U.S. diplomats tried to secure Alexander's support for their efforts at the peace negotiations in Ghent. On 17 June 1814, the czar, then in Britain, received Gallatin and Levett Harris, secretary to the U.S. peace delegation. Even though Alexander charmed the Americans, he did little to help them challenge British demands.

Alexander hoped his Anglo-American diplomacy would enhance Russia's power in Europe. When his efforts with the United States became less likely to produce these results, he abandoned them. For the Madison administration, Alexander's mediation offer seemed a way to end an unpopular war. Although Russia remained an absolute monarchy with political institutions repellent to the United States, some Americans retained a friendly regard for Russians because of their attempts at mediation.

—*James Biedzynski*

See also: Adams, John Quincy; Bayard, James Asheton; Castlereagh, Viscount, Robert Stewart; Gallatin, Albert; Madison, James; Monroe, James; Orders in Council

Further Reading

Bolkhovitinov, Nikolai N. *The Beginnings of Russian-American Relations, 1775–1815.* Cambridge: Harvard University Press, 1975.

Ford, Chauncey Worthington, ed. *The Writings of John Quincy Adams.* 7 vols. New York: Macmillan, 1913–1917.

Golder, F. A. "The Russian Offer of Mediation in the War of 1812." *Political Science Quarterly* 31 (September 1916): 360–391.

Shulim, Joseph I. "The United States Views Russia in the Napoleonic Age." *Proceedings of the American Philosophical Society* 102 (30 April 1958): 148–159.

Troyat, Henri. *Alexander of Russia: Napoleon's Conqueror.* New York: E. P. Dutton, 1982.

ALLEN, WILLIAM HENRY
1784–1813
Captain, U.S. Navy

William Henry Allen was born in Providence, Rhode Island, on 21 October 1784, into a distinguished family. He entered the navy in the spring of 1800 and served on the frigate *George Washington* under Capt. William Bainbridge. After several years of duty in the Mediterranean, Allen joined the *Chesapeake* as a third lieutenant in command of a gun division. In the *Chesapeake's* ill-fated encounter with the *Leopard* on 22 June 1807, Allen fired the only shot against the British ship. According to legend, Allen grabbed a coal from the galley with his bare hand and used it to discharge the cannon, but as the official records contain no mention of an injured hand, most likely he used tongs to handle the coal. Allen and the other officers of the *Chesapeake* were so outraged at Commodore James Barron's cowardice that they successfully petitioned the secretary of the navy for Barron's trial and punishment.

After earning promotion to first lieutenant, Allen joined Commodore Stephen Decatur on the frigate *United States* in 1809. He distinguished himself in the 25 October 1812 encounter with the British frigate *Macedonian* (49 guns) that resulted in her capture. Decatur credited the victory to Allen's exceptionally fine gun crew and rewarded him with the honor of bringing the *Macedonian* to port.

As a result of these actions, Allen took command of the *Argus* (20 guns). On 18 June 1813, with William Harris Crawford, the new U.S. minister to France on board, Allen successfully eluded the British blockades of New York and the Biscay coast and landed Crawford in L'Orient in Brittany. Then Allen turned his attention to British shipping in the English Channel and the Irish Sea. For 31 days the *Argus* preyed upon unconvoyed British shipping, seizing and burning 19 vessels with cargoes worth an estimated $2,000,000, a record unmatched by any other U.S. vessel in the war. Allen earned the respect of his British adversaries by permitting the crews of his prizes to keep their personal belongings and later releasing them on parole. Even so, British shippers, panicked by mounting property losses and rising insurance rates, pressured the Admiralty to order several men-of-war to pursue and destroy the bold interloper from the United States.

On August 13, within sight of the Welsh coast, the *Argus* captured her last prize, a merchantman sailing from Oporto with a cargo of wine. Allen failed to prevent his crew from consuming a portion of the wine before burning the prize. Thus when the British brig *Pelican* (21 guns), commanded by Capt. John Forcyce Maples, came up on the U.S. ship just off St. David's Head in the early morning of 14 August, many of the sailors on the *Argus* were in no condition to fight effectively. Nevertheless, the courageous, or perhaps reckless, Allen refused to flee. The *Pelican* closed in, and the battle ensued.

Allen fell in the first few moments of the fight, his left thigh smashed by a round shot. Only after excessive bleeding caused him to faint was he taken below. The *Argus* continued to fight under the command of 2d Lt. William Howard Allen, but on this day the British gunners were far more effective than their U.S. counterparts, whose poor performance has been attributed to bad powder or overfatigue. When the two ships came together and the British prepared to board, the *Argus* made no attempt to resist and surrendered, one-quarter of her crew already dead or wounded and the remainder demoralized.

After Allen was transferred to the *Pelican,* the surgeon

from the *Argus* amputated Allen's leg immediately, but gangrene set in. When the *Pelican* and its prize landed in Plymouth, the British moved Allen to a hospital. There he died on 18 August 1813. The British buried him with military honors.

—*Charles H. McArver, Jr.*

See also: Allen, William Howard; Bainbridge, William; Barron, James; *Chesapeake-Leopard* Affair; Crawford, William H.; Decatur, Stephen, Jr.; *United States* versus *Macedonian*

Further Reading

Adams, Henry. *History of the United States of America during the Administrations of Thomas Jefferson and James Madison.* 4 vols. New York: Albert & Charles Boni, 1930.

Beirne, Francis F. *The War of 1812.* New York: E. P. Dutton, 1949.

Forester, C. S. *The Age of Fighting Sail: The Story of the Naval War of 1812.* Garden City, NY: Doubleday, 1956.

ALLEN, WILLIAM HOWARD
1790–1822
Lieutenant, U.S. Navy

Born in Hudson, New York, on 8 July 1790, Allen joined the U.S. Navy in 1801 and became a lieutenant in 1811. During the contest between USS *Argus* and HMS *Pelican* on 14 August 1813, command eventually devolved to Lt. William Howard Allen after the severely wounded captain of the *Argus,* William Henry Allen, lost so much blood that he fainted. Lieutenant Allen was no relation to the captain. Lieutenant Allen gallantly continued the fight until the severely crippled *Argus* was forced to haul down her colors.

After the war, Allen commanded the USS *Alligator.* On 9 November 1822, he died aboard that ship while fighting pirates off the Cuban coast.

—*William A. Paquette*

AMANDA, FORT
1812–1815
U.S. garrison and supply depot

Ohio troops under the command of Col. Thomas Pogue built this post on the west bank of the Auglaize River, a short distance from present-day Criders-ville, Ohio. It was one of several small fortifications constructed by the Ohio militia in northwestern Ohio during the autumn of 1812. The post, with Fort Barbee and Fort Jennings, guarded the supply route from Piqua to Fort Winchester (Defiance, Ohio). The fortification contained four blockhouses connected by a log palisade 11 feet high and 170 feet long. Two of the blockhouses were used to store flour, corn, and oats; a third was used to store salted meats. Several small cabins also stood within the stockade to house the garrison.

During the spring of 1813, Capt. Daniel Hosbroock commanded the garrison and enlarged the facilities, although the exact nature of his changes is unknown. The post was abandoned after the war, in 1815. Today, the Ohio Historical Society administers the site. It contains the graves of 75 men who died at the fort during the War of 1812.

Colonel Pogue named Fort Amanda in honor of his youngest daughter, Hannah Amanda Pogue

—*Larry L. Nelson*

Further Reading

Gilpin, Alec R. *The War of 1812 in the Old Northwest.* East Lansing: The Michigan State University Press, 1958.

Johnson, David R. "Fort Amanda—A Historical Redress." *Northwest Ohio Quarterly* 48 (1976): 102–106.

Knopf, Richard C., ed. *Document Transcriptions of the War of 1812 in the Old Northwest.* 10 vols. Columbus: Ohio Historical Society, 1956–1962.

ANTIWAR SENTIMENT
1812–1815

According to Samuel Eliot Morison, domestic opposition to the War of 1812 was as widespread as to any war in U.S. history, including the Vietnam War. Most opponents based their opposition to Madison's policies on economic and political grounds. Northeastern merchants worried about the destruction of commercial prosperity in the United States, whereas Federalist politicians insisted that the anti-British policies of the Republicans represented subservience to Napoleonic France and a threat to U.S. independence.

Jeffersonian Republicans' reaction to the declaration of war on 18 June 1812 was lukewarm. The vote in the House of Representatives was 79 to 49, with 14 absent, and in the Senate it was 19 to 13. Thirty-four congressmen accused the Madison administration of pressuring them to vote for the war. Many said the war was one of conquest, with Canada the main object. They predicted that the enterprise would lead to heavy costs and more taxes.

Politics played a major role in opposition to the war. New England Federalists feared that western expansion would weaken the political influence of the eastern seaboard. They believed the war would invite the British navy to destroy their maritime commerce and invade their coastal towns. Federalists also exhibited some alarms traditionally associated with Republicans. Three days after the declaration of war, former Pres. John Adams proclaimed: "The danger of our government is, that the General will be a man of more popularity than the President, and the army possess more power than the Congress."

Federalist opposition also appeared in other parts of the Union. In Baltimore, violent riots broke out in June and July 1812, after the newspaper *The Federalist-Republican* printed editorials criticizing the war. Congressman Harmanus Bleecker of New York told the House that the war "might expose our happy form of Government—our excellent political institutions—to a dangerous trial." Congressman Daniel Sheffey from Staunton, Virginia, reinforced Bleecker's sentiments, noting that "uniformity of action is only desirable where there is a uniformity of sentiment; and that, on most subjects, will only exist where the mind is enchained by the fear which despotic power inspires."

The clearest examples of tepid support occurred when the federal government tried to institute universal conscription. Congressmen from the South and the West, regions that strongly supported the war, expressed grave doubts about the draft. When it became clear, however, that few were willing to serve voluntarily, Madison instructed Secretary of War James Monroe to devise a plan that would increase the ranks of the nation's army. After much deliberation, in November 1814 Monroe presented a plan to Congress that called for organizing the militia into groups of 100 men between the ages of 18 and 25. Each group would furnish four men for actual service, replacing them as necessary. If it had to, the federal government could draft the four men, although substitutes would be permitted.

Debate in Congress over this plan was acrimonious. Sen. David Daggett of Connecticut argued that no country could "compel any man to become a soldier for life, during a war, or for any fixed time." Sen. Christopher Gore of Massachusetts insisted that such a draft was "the first step on the odious ground of conscription . . . in a manner presumed to be the least disgusting." Sen. Jeremiah Mason of New Hampshire pointed out: "Nor is it believed that with this construction, the Constitution would have been adopted by a single state of the Union."

Despite such opposition, the bill passed in the Senate. It failed in the House, however, where Federalists exerted considerable pressure. Leading Federalist Daniel Webster of New Hampshire delivered one of the main speeches against the plan. His colleague from Massachusetts, Morris S. Miller, also played a major role in defeating it. In late 1814, the Hartford Convention approved a resolution stating that except in cases of actual invasion or insurrection, the states of Massachusetts, Connecticut, and Rhode Island would retain control of their militia. The convention placed on record the following statement: "An iron despotism can impose no harder servitude upon the citizen, than to force him from his home and occupation, to wage offensive wars, undertaken to gratify the pride or passions of his master."

The strongest opposition to the war occurred in New England. Church leaders condemned the war as "immoral" and "useless." Federalist clergymen, such as the Reverend Brown Emerson, observed that "war is a dreadful calamity, the scourge of Almighty Jehovah, in recompense for the crying sins of the people."

Political leaders also joined in the chorus of dissent. Josiah Quincy of Massachusetts complained that a successful conquest of Canada would lead to a permanent military establishment. Laban Wheaton, also of the Bay State, feared that liberty would fall victim to a war for foreign conquest. Massachusetts governor Caleb Strong declared a public fast as a way to atone for a war "against the notion from which we are descended, and which for many generations has been the bulwark of the religion we profess."

New England governors refused to call out the state militia. Maine sent a strong antiwar bloc to Congress. Samuel Fessenden of New Gloucester declared it "time to take our rights into our own hands. . . . We ought to establish a customs house by law, and the sooner we come at issue with the general government the better." In November 1814, the results of congressional elections in six of seven districts in Maine put antiwar Federalists into office.

Massachusetts was by far the most virulent in antiwar sentiment. The legislature called for establishing a peace party. In July 1812, delegates from 53 towns attended a convention in Northampton. They signed a petition declaring the war to be "neither just, necessary, nor expedient" and urged Madison to reach a quick peace settlement. Governor Strong even sponsored a secret mission to make peace with the British. In November 1814, he dispatched Thomas Adams, Federalist member of the General Court from occupied Castine, to Gen. Sir John Sherbrooke at Halifax. Adams was to ascertain the British government's position should a conflict ensue between Governor Strong and President Madison

Talk of secession dominated Federalist politics in Massachusetts. The most serious threat was the Reunion of the Original Thirteen States movement promoted by John Lowell and the Essex Junto. The Junto consisted of upper-class families from Essex County whose habit of intermarriage worked to preserve their privileged status. These celebrated families included the Cabots, Lowells, Lees, Jacksons, and Higginsons. The Essex Junto could boast of such political leaders as John Lowell, Harrison Gray Otis, Judge Isaac Parker, and Sen. Timothy Pickering.

Lowell's proposal called for the original thirteen states to draft a new federal Constitution to protect New England's maritime and commercial interests. Lowell actually was sponsoring a secessionist plan aimed at kicking the West out of the Union. As preposterous as the idea was, it gained support from Senator Pickering, Gouverneur Morris of New York, and Charles Carroll of Maryland. The most respected of Boston's Federalist newspapers endorsed the idea and called for New England states to meet in Hartford, Connecticut, to discuss it.

From 15 December 1814 to 5 January 1815, delegates from Massachusetts, Connecticut, and Rhode Island gathered in Hartford. The convention heard proposals for seizing customs houses, impounding federal revenues, declaring neutrality, nullifying conscription, prohibiting new western states from outvoting charter members of the Union, and stopping Jeffersonian embargoes. Nonetheless, the three state legislatures had selected some cautious delegates. The convention did issue a states' rights manifesto designed to revive New England's national power, but moderates such as George Cabot, Joseph Lyman, Harrison Gray Otis, and Benjamin Hazard used their influence to thwart Lowell's radical proposals.

Throughout the war New York Federalists, like their New England counterparts, tried to pressure the Madison administration into a peace settlement with England. As early as the spring of 1812, town meetings organized by the Federalists throughout the state petitioned Congress to end the embargo. When war was declared, an antiwar Federalist majority took control of the Assembly. Federalists arranged drives to send antiwar petitions to Congress. Some 300 residents of Washington County, for instance, signed a petition opposing the war. In August 1812, a huge antiwar rally was held in New York City. Federalists established a Committee of Correspondence seeking to coordinate antiwar activists in New York and other states, and in September 1812 the Federalist state convention issued a proclamation rejecting the "doctrine . . . that when war is once declared all inquiry into its justice . . . ought to cease. . . ." Even Lt. Gov. DeWitt Clinton flirted with antiwar Federalists. His prowar Republican colleagues were so angry that they refused to renominate him for office at their February 1813 Republican state caucus.

Military musters and federal demands on the militia excited special enmity in New York. Federal militia in the upper Hudson Valley refused to report for duty. In the summer of 1812, militia refused to participate in raids into Canada and would not cross the Niagara River in October 1812 during the Battle of Queenston. In the winter of 1812–1813, large numbers of militiamen deserted their units and returned to their farms. When Gov. Daniel D. Tompkins called out 5,000 men for the 1813 campaign, only 1,500 reported. Rensselaer County so resisted the draft that several companies were without any men.

It is clear that antiwar sentiment was prevalent, particularly among Federalists in the Northeast. The restrictive trade policy spawned it and the declaration of war solidified it. During the war, Federalists reaped some local political benefits from their resistance. Andrew Jackson's victory at New Orleans and the news from Ghent of the peace treaty, however, shattered the efficacy of Federalist dissent.

One lasting result of the antiwar agitation was the creation of peace societies at war's end. In 1815, Presbyterian merchant David Low Dodge formed the New York Peace Society. Under his leadership, the society distributed antiwar tracts and argued that war violated the basic principles of Christianity. The Massachusetts Peace Society was also created in 1815. By the mid-1820s there were 50 city, county, and state peace societies in the United States. In 1828, Harvard graduate William Ladd founded the national peace organization, American Peace Society. It has been argued, then, that the first organized peace movement in the United States and in recorded history resulted from the War of 1812.

—*Charles F. Howlett*

Further Reading

Curti, Merle. *Peace or War: The American Struggle, 1636–1936.* New York: W. W. Norton, 1936.

DeBenedetti, Charles. *The Peace Reform in American History.* Bloomington: Indiana University Press, 1980.

Ekirch, Arthur A., Jr. *The Civilian and the Military.* New York: Oxford University Press, 1956.

Morison, Samuel Eliot. "Dissent in the War of 1812." In *Dissent in Three American Wars,* ed. Samuel Eliot Morison, Frederick Merk, and Frank Freidel. Cambridge: Harvard University Press, 1970.

Strum, Harvey. "The Politics of the New York Antiwar Campaign, 1812–1815." *Peace and Change* 8 (September 1982): 7–18.

APPLING, DANIEL
1787–1817
Brevet colonel of the First Rifle Regiment

Georgia-born Daniel Appling entered the army as a second lieutenant in the newly organized Regiment of Riflemen. As war with Britain loomed, Appling was promoted first to captain and then in April 1812 to major. The regiment never operated as one unit; its companies were scattered among the several U.S. armies, the riflemen always at the front. Appling's battalion was stationed at Sacket's Harbor, the largest U.S. naval base on the Great Lakes.

After the British raid on Oswego in early May 1814, the Americans faced a problem. So far the British had not discovered 36 heavy naval guns and 10 large rope cables at Oswego Falls, 8 miles upriver from Oswego. The guns and cable were necessary to fit the ships nearing completion at the Sacket's Harbor shipyard. Because of their weight and the poor condition of the roads, the guns and cable had to be moved by water the 60 miles to Sacket's Harbor. However, the Royal Navy squadron on Lake Ontario was blockading the U.S. base, and when the British commander, Sir James Yeo, learned of the guns, he was anxious to prevent them from reaching the shipyard.

At dusk on 28 May, 19 bateaux under the command of Master Commandant Melancthon Woolsey left Oswego laden with guns and cable. Daniel Appling and 150 of his riflemen defended the valuable cargo. About as many Oneida warriors moved by land adjacent to the small flotilla to assist if needed. One of the U.S. boats fell behind and was captured. Learning of the valuable cargo up ahead, the British launched a squadron of gunboats in fast pursuit.

The following day, Woolsey pulled into Big Sandy Creek, several miles short of his destination, to send out scouts before proceeding. The next morning, the British squadron entered the Big Sandy and carefully searched for the bateaux. Sighting the masts of the U.S. ships in the distance, the British disembarked nearly 200 marines and sailors and moved upstream to seize the guns so vital to the U.S. fleet.

Aware of the British advance, Appling concealed his riflemen and Oneida warriors in the woods about a half mile in front of the bateaux. When the British came into view, Appling opened fire. The initial fusillade cut down dozens of British, and the survivors tried to withdraw. Appling, however, sent a force around their flank that effectively cut off retreat. Appling reported killing 14 sailors and marines

and taking 161 prisoners. One American was killed and two wounded in this one-sided affair. The prisoners were marched off to Sacket's Harbor while local militia turned out to manhandle the guns and cable the few remaining miles to the shipyard.

Hurt by the loss of his sailors to Appling's ambush and alarmed by the arrival of the guns at Sacket's Harbor, Sir James Yeo called off the blockade. The army recognized Appling's important contribution, and for an engagement that lasted less than 15 minutes, he was brevetted to lieutenant colonel.

Appling later served at Plattsburg, where he commanded a covering force that disputed the advance of thousands of British regulars on the weak U.S. defenses. Performing with distinction, Appling's riflemen helped stall the formidable British attack.

After the postwar demobilization, Daniel Appling was chosen to remain in active service. He resigned his commission in the summer of 1816. The following spring, Appling died in Montgomery, Alabama.

—*Richard V. Barbuto*

See also: Woolsey, Melancthon Taylor; Yeo, James Lucas
Further Reading
Frame, Nat. "The Battle of Sandy Creek and Carrying the Cables for the 'Superior.'" *Jefferson County Historical Society Transactions* 3 (1895): 32–40.

ARGUS VERSUS *PELICAN*
14 August 1813

After receiving orders to transport William H. Crawford, the new U.S. minister to France, the commander of the U.S. brig *Argus*, Master Commandant William H. Allen, set sail from New York to France on 18 June 1813. When the minister was safely in France, Allen cruised north on 20 July, and from 23 July to 13 August the *Argus* took 19 prizes. That proved to be the largest number for any U.S. naval vessel in the war.

On 14 August at 4:00 A.M., Allen had just set his nineteenth prize on fire when Commander John F. Maples, commanding the powerful British brig *Pelican*, saw the *Argus* moving away from the burning ship and gave chase. Shortly after 5:30 A.M., the *Pelican* closed with *Argus*, and the battle began. The weariness of Allen's crew after their successful patrol, combined with the somewhat larger size and more heavily armed state of the *Pelican*, created a favorable situation for Maples. Within 45 minutes, the *Argus* surrendered to the *Pelican* after the British ship had pounded the *Argus* with accurate broadsides that inflicted damage to her hull, masts, sails, and rigging. The casualties on board the *Argus* were 6 dead or mortally wounded, including Allen, and 18 wounded. The *Pelican* only had 2 dead and 5 wounded.

—*R. Blake Dunnavent*

Further Reading
Dye, Ira. *The Fatal Cruise of the* Argus: *Two Captains in the War of 1812*. Annapolis, MD: United States Naval Institute, 1994.

ARMISTEAD, GEORGE
1780–1818
U.S. officer

George Armistead, the commander of Fort McHenry during the British bombardment, emerged from the War of 1812 as one of its great popular heroes. He was born in New Market, Virginia, on 10 April 1780 to a prominent family of English and German origin that first settled in America in 1635. His particular branch of the family showed a strong inclination for military service, and four of George Armistead's brothers were also army or militia officers. One of his brothers was killed in action at Fort Erie in 1814, and his youngest brother, Walker, was the third graduate of West Point. One of George Armistead's nephews, Lewis, also became an army officer and later, as a Confederate general, was killed in action at Gettysburg.

George Armistead was appointed a second lieutenant in the Seventh U.S. Infantry in January 1799. He made first lieutenant the following year and transferred to the Corps of Artillerists and Engineers in February 1801. He made captain in 1806, and the following year he assumed command of the artillery company that is currently the U.S. Army's Third Battalion, Second Air Defense Artillery. In March 1813, Armistead became the major of the Third Regiment of Artillery, which had been raised the previous year. During the early part of the war, he served in Canada and distinguished himself during the capture of Fort George on 18 May 1813. Secretary of War John Armstrong apparently had a great deal of faith in Armistead's abilities. In September 1813, Armstrong ordered General Wilkinson to remove Capt. Nathaniel Leonard from the command of Fort Niagara and replace him with Armistead. Wilkinson left Leonard in command, however, and Armstrong later maintained that had Armstrong's order been followed, Fort Niagara would not have been lost.

Armistead assumed command of Fort McHenry in early 1814. His command included the fort itself, the Lazaretto Battery directly across the channel, and a small flotilla of gunboats. In the days just prior to the British attack on 13 September, Armistead had little time for sleep as he organized his defenses. The entire garrison consisted of roughly 1,000 men. One regular company of U.S. artillery and a company of Baltimore militia manned the 21 cannon inside the fort itself. Two companies of sea fencibles and two companies of volunteer artillery manned the 36 guns in a series of outer earthworks just above the high tide water level. In between the outworks and the fort, about 600 infantry occupied a series of trenches. Fifteen of the guns in the outer positions were huge 42-pounders, on loan from France.

The British opened their bombardment of Fort McHenry just before 7:00 A.M. on 13 September 1814. The main attacking force consisted of five of the Royal Navy's eight-bomb ketches and the rocket ship *Erebus*. The typical "bomb" carried two mortars, a 10-inch and a 13-inch, that could hurl a 200-pound shell 4,200 yards. The best range the defenders could achieve with their biggest guns was only 2,000 yards. While the British ships sat out of range of the U.S. cannon and poured fire into the fort, Armistead did everything he could to increase the range of his guns. He tried the dangerous practices of overloading the powder charges and elevating the tubes beyond normal limits. Fortunately none of the tubes burst, but three of his guns tore their own carriages apart. By about 10:00 A.M., Armistead concluded there was nothing he could do but ride out the firestorm.

During the ensuing bombardment, the British managed to take out one of the Americans' 24-pounders. Another shell crashed through the roof of the fort's powder magazine, but to the garrison's good fortune, the shell was a dud. Armistead hastily had the powder moved outside the fort and dispersed, so that any more hits could only set off single barrels rather than sending up the entire fort. Armistead had supposedly known all along that the magazine was not "bomb proof" but kept it to himself to avoid panic among his troops. Armistead had other things to worry about, too. His wife at that moment was in Gettysburg giving birth to their first child.

After about eight solid hours of pounding, the British assumed the lack of fire from the fort meant the Americans were out of action. About 3:00 P.M., Adm. Alexander Cochrane ordered three of the bombs and the rocket ship in for the kill. Armistead had been waiting for just this moment. He held his fire until the British ships came well within range and then opened up with everything in the fort. The surprised British quickly disengaged, pulled back out of range, and resumed their shelling. The Americans resumed their grim wait.

The firing continued throughout the night. The British made one attempt to launch a landing party against the fort under cover of darkness in order to take it from the rear, but the U.S. gunners spotted the British and drove them off before they could land. Meanwhile, British colonel Arthur Brooke on the land had assumed command after the death of Gen. Robert Ross and was requesting naval gunfire support so he could attack Baltimore. In order to cover Brooke, the fleet would have to come back within range of the guns at Fort McHenry, and Cochrane was loath to do that. Finally, about 7:00 A.M. on 14 September, Cochrane halted the entire operation and recalled Brooke and the infantry. In 24 hours the British fired some 1,500 shells. About 400 landed inside the fort, and most of the rest burst directly overhead. The only U.S. casualties were 4 dead and 24 wounded. Armistead, however, fell delirious with fever and exhaustion after five days of super-human effort holding his beleaguered command together.

After the British withdrew, President Madison immediately sent Armistead a brevet promotion to lieutenant colonel, and the citizens of Baltimore presented the Hero of Fort McHenry with a silver punch bowl that was an exact scale replica of a 13-inch British bombshell. To his immense relief Armistead also learned that his wife had delivered a healthy baby girl. Armistead wrote to her, "So you see, my dear wife, all is well, at least your husband has got a name and standing that nothing but divine providence could have given him, and I pray to my Heavenly Father that we may long live to enjoy." He did not, though. George Armistead died in Baltimore on 25 April 1818 at the age of 38. The cause of death was heart disease, apparently aggravated by the strain of the siege at Fort McHenry.

—David T. Zabecki

See also: Baltimore, Battle of; McHenry, Fort; Star-Spangled Banner, The

Further Reading

Armstrong, John. *Notices of the War of 1812.* New York: Whiley & Putman, 1840.

Birkhimer, William E. *Historical Sketch of the Organization, Administration, Materiel and Tactics of the Artillery, United States Army.* Washington, DC: Chapman, 1884.

Downey, Fairfax. *The Sound of the Guns.* New York: David McKay, 1955.

McKenney, Janice. *Air Defense Artillery: Army Lineage Series.* Washington, DC: Center of Military History, 1985.

Powell, William. *List of Officers of the Army of the United States, 1777–1900.* New York: L. R. Hammersly, 1900.

Trussell, J.B.B., Jr., "Cannon Hold the Breach." *Field Artillery Journal* 39 (Nov.-Dec. 1949): 258–269.

ARMSTRONG, JOHN
1758–1843
U.S. secretary of war

Born to John Armstrong and Rebecca Lyon Armstrong in Pennsylvania, the younger Armstrong attended but did not graduate from the College of New Jersey (Princeton). Before he could complete his studies, he volunteered to fight in the American Revolution. Because his father, a veteran of the French and Indian War, had met many notable people, including George Washington and Hugh Mercer, during that conflict, Armstrong obtained a commission before he turned 20.

During the Revolution, Armstrong had a varied career, fighting at Trenton and Princeton before attaching himself to Gen. Horatio Gates and moving to the New York theater. As Gates's aide, Armstrong carried the message from Gates to Benedict Arnold at Bemis Heights on 7 October 1777 that ordered Arnold back to headquarters. Armstrong did not reach Arnold until the future traitor had already been shot in the thigh, thus placing Armstrong in the lamentable position of adding Gates's insult to Arnold's injury. Otherwise, Armstrong enjoyed relatively unbroken luck. For example, illness prevented him from accompanying his mentor Gates on the disastrous Camden campaign of 1780.

Perhaps Armstrong's most notable activity during the Revolution did not come until the war was almost over. As part of the large body of officers headquartered at Newburgh, New York, in the last months of the war, Armstrong was again in the company of his friend Gates. He also shared the concerns of many officers that Congress did not intend to provide them with sufficient rewards for their sacrifices during the war. Congress, at one point desperate for experienced officers, had promised to remunerate those who remained in service for the war's duration with a pension of half-pay for life. With the war drawing to a close at the end of 1782, Congress gave every sign of intending to break that promise.

Armstrong began discussing recourse with several disaffected officers. They agreed that putting their views in writing would most effectively apprise other officers and Congress of their seriousness. Armstrong's offer to draft this statement meant that he would write the first of the so-called Newburgh Addresses. At the time of their appearance, these addresses had only an anonymous author. When in later years it became known that Armstrong wrote them, the news hurt his public career. The real intentions of the officers involved is still in question, but scholars then and since have interpreted the addresses as threatening a military coup if the discontented officers' demands were not met.

After the Revolution, Armstrong returned to Pennsylvania and became involved in state politics. After serving briefly in the Confederation's Congress, he was appointed a judge in the new Northwest Territory. He remained in the position only briefly before returning to Pennsylvania. Yet his marriage into the powerful Livingston family of New York prompted him to leave his native state, become a resident of New York, and manage his wife's property.

In the 1790s Armstrong leaned toward the Federalist Party, but the passage of the Alien and Sedition Acts in 1798 caused him to become a Democratic Republican. In 1800, New York Republicans sent him to the U.S. Senate. He did not remain long, resigning his seat at the end of 1801 owing to his wife's and his own illnesses. His return to the Senate in 1803 was interrupted when Pres. Thomas Jefferson appointed him to become the U.S. minister to France.

Armstrong's tenure in France produced mixed results, but he did face overwhelming tasks. The six years he served at Napoleon's court presented him with a continuous series of frustrations. He tried to persuade the French to recognize the Floridas as included in the Louisiana Purchase, tried to induce Napoleon to return confiscated U.S. ships and cargoes, and attempted to ameliorate the effects of the Berlin Decree (1806) and the Milan Decree (1807). His own government could prove exasperating as well. In his dispatches to Jefferson, Armstrong told the president that the embargo was not having the desired effect on France and that U.S. shipping actually suffered more. Armstrong had come to believe that the United States should either use war to force concessions or do nothing.

Even these potentially divisive issues with the French did not damage Armstrong's good relations with his hosts, but by 1810 his patience had ebbed. He was obviously nonplussed when the French government asked him how the United States and France could improve their relationship. The French apparently were serious in their attempt at settlement, but years of Napoleon's manipulations had seasoned Armstrong to suspicion, and he met their gesture accordingly. He insisted on complete restoration of U.S. ships and cargoes as a basis for talks. In short, Armstrong's response seemed so obstinately arbitrary that it angered Napoleon. The emperor first announced the sale of all U.S.

property currently under dispute. He then issued the Rambouillet Decree, which authorized the seizure of all U.S. property that had entered the country since 20 May 1809. Napoleon patronizingly justified his action by explaining that he was merely helping the United States enforce the Non-Intercourse Act of 1809.

This behavior irreparably alienated Armstrong. When he received unofficial word of Macon's Bill No. 2, he did not relate the possible implications for France. Napoleon, however, saw an opportunity for trickery. The act opened trade to both Great Britain and France, but if one dropped its restrictions on U.S. trade, the United States would resume nonintercourse with the other. Napoleon saw this situation as a way to hurt the British with a U.S. cat's-paw. When the Duc de Cadore sent Armstrong a vaguely worded letter implying that the Berlin and Milan Decrees would no longer be enforced after November 1810, Armstrong sent the letter to Pres. James Madison. He left it to the president to decide if the letter fulfilled the terms of Macon's Bill No. 2. Armstrong was tired of the whole business; he left France in October 1810.

Back in the United States, Armstrong retired to his estates. As war loomed with Great Britain in early 1812, he supported the war measures taken by Congress, and when war was declared, he found himself in demand. Men such as Armstrong with military experience were much sought after, and he received a commission as a brigadier general with command of the defenses of New York City. When the Madison administration forced William Eustis to resign as secretary of war at the end of 1812, Armstrong was mentioned to replace him.

Yet Armstrong had developed a reputation for being difficult. Correspondingly, he had few political friends and many enemies. To complicate the situation for President Madison, the two most important members of his cabinet, Secretary of State James Monroe and Secretary of the Treasury Albert Gallatin, strongly opposed Armstrong's appointment to the War Department. The military failures of 1812, however, daunted suitable candidates for the job, and Madison reluctantly but finally offered it to Armstrong. The new secretary assumed his chores with many people hoping he would fail.

His personal difficulties aside, Armstrong inherited an inefficient, understaffed bureaucracy in the War Department. The supply system was antiquated and in shambles. The natural proliferation of officers in wartime led to innumerable confusions about rank, seniority, and jurisdiction. One of the first things Secretary Armstrong did was to supervise the composition of "Rules and Regulations of the Army of the United States." This much-needed and long-overdue document served as the model of all future editions of army regulations. Next, Armstrong secured an increase in the number of general officers. He divided the country into nine military districts, with his office as the clearinghouse for operations in each. Eustis had taken a disastrously nonchalant approach to military affairs. Armstrong, who fancied himself a military expert, planned to correct that practice.

Still, Armstrong's interest in improving military performance was tempered by the need for economy. He believed that fortifications, particularly in coastal areas, constituted an expense yielding little value. His critics accused him of neglecting the defense of important areas, including Washington, D.C. Armstrong planned to provide vulnerable areas with more regular soldiers, believing that regulars in the duration and flexibility of their service would result in additional economies. He thus encouraged officers to avoid using militia as much as possible. Armstrong quickly discovered, however, that the regular forces could not recruit enough men to eliminate the need for militia. He therefore reluctantly proposed to the cabinet and eventually to Congress that conscription be implemented. James Monroe led the opposition in the cabinet and worked behind the scenes to have the measure defeated in Congress. Recruiting continued to be a problem, though. When Monroe later replaced Armstrong as secretary, he made virtually the same conscription proposal to Congress. Reaping what he had sowed, Monroe was also rebuffed.

Armstrong's abrasive personality certainly did not help his work with either Congress or his subordinates. The position of secretary of war had never been tested by a real conflict, and Armstrong perceived his duty more widely than his predecessors ever had. He believed that during war the secretary should direct officers in the field to insure implementing the government's policies. Few people, in or out of the military, would likely have disagreed with him about the principle. Problems arose over how he chose to implement it.

Armstrong's poor relations with most of his generals sprang from his habit of sending orders directly to their subordinates. This practice meant that general officers in every theater never could be sure how many men they actually commanded or where these men were. Armstrong's cavalier disregard for chain of command would eventually bring about the resignation of Maj. Gen. William Henry Harrison.

Armstrong also differed with many of his generals about how to win the war. Early in his tenure he became so focused on taking the Canadian port of Kingston that other operations were either discounted or ignored altogether. In spite of such mental concentration, however, his orders to officers in the field could be confusing and sometimes contradictory. His instructions also tended to grant so much discretion that one could wonder why he had bothered to draft them, especially to officers inclined toward caution. So although many resources were aimed toward Kingston, activities on that front were uncoordinated. Meanwhile, Harrison's and Oliver Hazard Perry's campaigns against the British in the Western Theater and on Lake Erie received scant attention from Armstrong. The upcoming campaign against the Creek Indians in Alabama was virtually ignored.

The problems that this lack of coordination brewed in the proposed invasions of Canada quickly became evident. Though Armstrong traveled to New York, ostensibly to insure cooperation between Gens. James Wilkinson and Wade Hampton, he for once refused to interfere with their separate invasions, and consequently they remained separate invasions to the very dismal end of the failed campaign. Both Wilkinson and Hampton would go into winter quarters posting no gains for the United States.

By the spring of 1814, criticism directed at Armstrong and his department had become shrill. Harrison resigned in a huff, and Armstrong filled the vacant major general's position with militia general Andrew Jackson without first clearing the appointment with Madison. The president in fact grew steadily angrier with what he viewed as Armstrong's aloof attitude and became much more active in the day-to-day administration of the war. Naturally, Armstrong resented Madison's increased oversight, interpreting it as an unsubtle commentary on his competence.

By the summer of 1814, the secretary had become testy and sullen. Perhaps seeking to assert his independence, Armstrong continued to fill vacancies in the officer ranks without consulting Madison. Finally on 13 August 1814, the president's patience ran out. Madison formally reprimanded his secretary and outlined specific guidelines about how appointments would be handled in the future. The action was long overdue, but the timing for this reprimand could not have been worse. Armstrong sank into an even deeper pout, his emboldened critics pressed for his removal, and the British entered Chesapeake Bay.

Armstrong had always been accused of neglecting defenses for Washington, D.C. He had countered that the capital was in no danger, and he would not waste money erecting defenses for an area so obviously safe from enemy assault. In the summer of 1814, as alarm about the capital's vulnerability grew strident, Madison intervened. Over Armstrong's protests, William Winder was given command of Washington's defense. Madison had made the appointment partly to appease Winder's Federalist uncle, the governor of Maryland, but that made no difference to the secretary of war. Armstrong now did little else but brood.

On those occasions when he stirred from his sulk, Armstrong disagreed with or directly disapproved of Winder's plans for defending the city. Their most material difference concerned the timing of when to call out the surrounding state militias. Winder wanted them called out immediately so that he could position and train them at the likely approaches to the city. Yet Armstrong had a theory about militia. He believed that they fought best on the spur of the moment and that giving them time to fret about impending battles only assured their flight from them. Armstrong won this argument.

By the morning of 24 August 1814, the British force that had moved up the Patuxent River clearly intended to march on Washington. At last proved wrong about the capital's being a target, Armstrong would now see his theory on militia readiness tested. As Winder prepared his defenses with a hastily assembled militia, he sent a letter to Armstrong in Washington asking the secretary's advice about troop placement. The courier assumed that the emergency would have Armstrong conferring with the president at the executive mansion, so he delivered Winder's note there. Armstrong was not with Madison, but the president naturally thought the letter significant, so he read it before sending it on to Armstrong. The secretary was furious that Madison would open a message intended for Armstrong. Later, when Madison tried to wrest an opinion from Armstrong about the rapidly unfolding military situation, he sourly conveyed that the U.S. militia did not stand a chance.

When Madison finally convinced Armstrong to go to the U.S. defenses at Bladensburg, the secretary apparently misunderstood the president to mean that he could take command there. Madison and much of his cabinet arrived later and disabused Armstrong of the faulty impression. The secretary then washed his hands of the whole affair.

The rout at Bladensburg was not John Armstrong's fault (indeed, Secretary of State James Monroe had badly placed the crucial body of troops), but Armstrong's failures preceded the engagement. He failed to foresee the need for better defensive works in the vicinity of the capital, and his attitude toward Winder eliminated even a fighting chance for the U.S. forces. As the Americans retreated through Washington, criticisms about the secretary's neglect of the capital took on new life. When Winder decided not to make a stand on Capitol Hill and pulled the army beyond Georgetown, Washington's citizens blamed Armstrong. After the British evacuated a smoldering Washington, cries for Armstrong's head grew louder.

Madison and Monroe returned to Washington on 27 August. Armstrong was still absent, so the president made Monroe interim secretary of war. When Armstrong reap-peared on 29 August, wide hostility from both citizens and militia greeted him. Several militia units declared for the record that they would not continue to serve if Armstrong remained in office. He offered his resignation to President Madison; instead of accepting it, Madison agreed that an extended trip home for Armstrong would possibly allow tempers to cool. The gesture only postponed the inevitable, hastened by Armstrong himself. While on his way home, he wrote a letter to the *Baltimore Patriot* newspaper defending his conduct. After the publication of the letter, Armstrong sent his resignation to Madison and retired to his estates in New York.

The failure to defend Washington ended John Armstrong's participation in the War of 1812 and for the most part concluded his public career. He did not attempt to justify himself again in print until 1816. Then, in an unsuccessful attempt to block the election of his old nemesis, James Monroe, to the presidency, he accused Monroe of a conspiracy to ruin his career by undermining his activities as secretary of war. Armstrong published attacks on Monroe and other enemies for the rest of his life, but he devoted his real energies to managing his considerable properties. Through it all, his family remained loyal and devoted, and when Armstrong died in 1843, his children were around him.

—Jeanne T. Heidler and David S. Heidler

See also: Bladensburg, Battle of; Cadore Letter; Eustis, William; Macon's Bill No. 2; Monroe, James; Rambouillet Decree; Winder, William H.

Further Reading

Skeen, C. Edward. *John Armstrong, Jr., 1758–1843: A Biography.* Syracuse, NY: Syracuse University Press, 1981.

ARMSTRONG, ROBERT
1792–1854
General; U.S. consul

Robert Armstrong was born in Abingdon, Virginia, on 28 September 1792. His father, Trooper Armstrong, had been a Revolutionary War soldier. The family moved to Tennessee during Robert Armstrong's youth, but he returned to Abingdon to attend school. When the war broke out, he left school and enlisted in a Tennessee volunteer artillery company as a sergeant and later joined Andrew Jackson's command as a lieutenant. He served in Jackson's campaign against the Creeks and distinguished himself at

Enitachopco on 24 January 1814. There he was wounded. According to Jackson, Armstrong's courageous action saved the U.S. army from a disastrous and "shameful" defeat. Subsequently, he served as Jackson's aide-de-camp at New Orleans.

After the war Armstrong played a prominent role in Tennessee politics. He had eloped to the Hermitage in June 1814 with Margaret Nicol, daughter of a prominent Nashville merchant, and after Jackson had interceded on Armstrong's behalf with the girl's father, Armstrong entered the family business. In 1829, Jackson appointed him postmaster of Nashville. When the Second Seminole War broke out in 1835, Jackson designated Armstrong as a brigadier general in command of two volunteer regiments from middle Tennessee. After a short campaign that ended in the decisive battle of Wahoo Swamp, he returned to Tennessee to run for governor in 1837. However, he did little campaigning, and his Whig opponent, Newton Cannon, convinced the voters that Democratic policies were responsible for the economic depression. The result was a decisive defeat for Armstrong. He continued to be active in politics, managing the Democratic campaign in Tennessee in 1839 and championing James K. Polk's nomination for the presidency in 1844. Jackson demonstrated his regard for his old friend when he willed Armstrong his military sword. Armstrong served as U.S. consul to Liverpool between 1845 and 1849. He became proprietor of the Washington *Union* in 1851 and printer for the House of Representatives. He died in Washington on 23 February 1854.

—*Charles H. McArver, Jr.*

Further Reading

Ewing, Robert. "Portrait of General Robert Armstrong." *Tennessee Historical Magazine* 5 (July 1919): 75–80.

Moore, John Trotwood, and Austin P. Foster, eds. *Tennessee the Volunteer State, 1769–1923*. 4 vols. Chicago: S. J. Clarke Publishing, 1923.

Parton, James. *Life of Andrew Jackson*. 3 vols. New York: Mason Brothers, 1860.

Tennessee Historical Magazine 5 (July 1919): 75–80.

ARTILLERY

Artillery at the start of the nineteenth century was little different from the black-powder, smooth-bore, muzzle-loading big guns that had been in general use for the previous several hundred years. In the post-Napoleonic period, artillery began a series of rapid technological advances that continue to the present day. During the War of 1812, however, artillery pieces still had limited accuracy, slow rates of fire, and maximum ranges that seldom reached beyond 2,000 yards. Most field guns had maximum effective ranges closer to 900 yards.

Artillery was also among the least mobile of a military commander's war fighting assets. Most field artillery was drawn by horses, with the crews walking alongside. The guns were converted from two- to four-wheel loads by hitching them to a limber that also served as an ammunition chest. The complete gun section included a second vehicle, called a caisson, to haul ammunition. During the early nineteenth century, most caissons had four wheels. They later evolved into two-wheeled vehicles hooked to a second limber. By the early 1800s most countries were starting to experiment with horse artillery, units in which all the cannoneers were mounted. But such units played an insignificant part in the War of 1812.

Then, as now, the various types of cannon fell into three general categories, based on their construction and ballistic characteristics: guns, mortars, and howitzers. The gun was the most widely used artillery piece of the day. Long in relationship to the size of its bore, it fired a solid projectile at a high velocity and flat trajectory. Guns were used primarily for their impact and battering effect. The mortar was a short, stubby weapon that fired exploding projectiles at high angles. Although the mortar had a shorter range than a gun of the same size, it could engage targets in defilade by shooting over intermediate obstructions. The howitzer, which also fired exploding projectiles, fell in between the gun and the mortar. Howitzers generally had shorter barrels and larger calibers than guns and could fire at higher angles, but not as high as mortars. The main advantage of the howitzer was that it was mounted on a field carriage. That made it more mobile than the mortar, which was usually mounted on a solid wood block. Howitzers could also fire solid shot, but they rarely did so because they did not have the hitting power of guns.

The artillery of the day was also classified by function and size. On the one hand, garrison pieces were heavy and relatively immobile; they were employed to defend fixed fortifications—mostly seacoast forts. Garrison guns were mounted on heavy solid carriages, similar to those used on ships. Field pieces, on the other hand, had to be lighter and more mobile because they moved with the army. Size classification depended on the type of weapon. Guns were classified by the weight of the iron ball they fired, whereas howitzers and mortars were size classified by the diameters of their bores. During the War of 1812, the more widely used field pieces on both sides included 3-, 6-, and 12-pounder guns and the 5.5-inch howitzer.

Artillery ammunition fell into two broad categories: exploding and nonexploding. Solid shot, a cast-iron sphere, was the basic nonexploding round for the gun. Sometimes solid shot was heated to red-hot temperatures before firing, to produce an incendiary effect against flammable targets, such as ships or ammunition. The Americans used red hot shot against Fort George in 1813. Scatterable shot was another type of nonexploding ammunition. Used almost exclusively against human targets, it produced an effect like a huge shotgun. One form was canister, or case shot, consisting of small iron balls packed into a tin cylinder and fired (usually point-blank) into advancing troops. The other form was grapeshot, a group of iron balls (larger than canister) tied around a central wooden spindle and base. Grape was particularly effective in breaking up cavalry charges. It had a greater effective range than canister but less than half that of ball shot.

Exploding projectiles, called shells (or bombs), were hollow iron spheres filled with a charge and triggered by a tapered wooden fuse packed with a quick-burning substance. The shell was the primary round for the mortar and the howitzer. Prior to the nineteenth century, guns fired only nonexploding ammunition. In 1784, Lt. Henry Shrapnel of the Royal Artillery invented the spherical case round (later called shrapnel) for the gun. This round consisted of a thin-walled iron sphere filled with smaller shot and a bursting charge, which could be set to explode in the air at a given distance from the gun. The new round produced the effects of canister but at greatly extended ranges. The main disadvantage of spherical case was the difficulty of estimating the proper fuse setting to achieve good effect on the target. The British used spherical case for the first time in the War of 1812 at Queenston Heights.

Black powder, a mechanical mixture of saltpeter (potassium nitrate), sulfur, and charcoal, was the basic propellant for all firearms. By the early 1800s the standard recipe for war powder was a 75-15-10 mix. For hundreds of years, a ladle on a long pole had been the standard method of feeding powder into the cannon tube. By the middle of the nineteenth century, prepackaged powder cartridges had been developed. A projectile and powder cartridge packaged as a single unit were called fixed-ammunition. Cartridges were made of either cotton cloth or flannel; but all artillerymen preferred the more expensive flannel because it burned more evenly and rarely left a smoldering residue in the tube. In any event, the gun crew had to swab out the tube with a wet sponge after each shot to make sure any hot residue did not prematurely set off the next round.

Artillery gunnery in those days was more of an art than the exact science it has since become. Aiming was accomplished by visually aligning a notch on the muzzle of the tube with one on the breech. The crude carriages of the day did not absorb the recoil from firing, and the gun had to be reaimed after each round. Indirect fire techniques lay almost a hundred years in the future, and the gunner could only aim at what he could see. High-angle fire at hidden targets with a mortar or howitzer was not really aimed fire and appropriately was called "firing at random." Experience and "feel" were the major factors in a gunner's accuracy. Rough elevation and range tables did exist, but the gunner seldom had time to use them in combat.

A 6-pounder field gun typically had a crew of nine men, commanded by a sergeant, with an officer commanding two guns. Firing the piece required a series of nine distinct steps:

1. Advance sponge
2. Tend vent
3. Sponge piece
4. Handle cartridge
5. Charge piece
6. Ram down cartridge
7. Prime
8. Take aim
9. Fire

A well-trained crew could fire as many as 12 unaimed rounds in a minute. Unaimed rounds were seldom effective, however, and no crew could keep that rate up for very long. Sustained rates of fire in combat were closer to one or two rounds every minute.

Slow rates of fire and relative inaccuracy meant that the guns had to be massed to achieve any worthwhile effect. Because of their flat trajectory as well as the gunners' requirement to see the target, field guns could not fire over the heads of the supported troops. That meant that during offensive operations, artillery had to be positioned in front of or to the flanks of the infantry. A round of solid shot hitting a closely packed formation of infantry produced between two and four casualties. At 500 yards, a 6- or 12-pounder with an average gunner had slightly better than an 80 percent probability of a hit against a line of troops. Artillery seldom was used in a counterfire role because the field guns were too inaccurate, and another gun was just too small a target. For example, during the artillery duel on 1 January 1815 at New Orleans, the Royal Artillery failed to knock out their U.S. counterparts. The British guns only fell silent themselves when they ran out of ammunition.

Field guns in forward positions were always in danger of being captured, so the practice of spiking came into being. Spiking a gun involved jamming some metal obstruction into the vent. Gun crews usually carried special tools for just such a contingency. These spikes were long enough to hit the bottom of the inside of the bore and would bend over or flair out when driven into the vent. As a field expedient, a bayonet could be jammed into the vent and snapped off. Artillery artificers of the period were generally well trained in the techniques of drilling out vents, and spiking rarely put a gun out of action for more than just a few hours.

A gun crew about to be overrun would spike its piece before abandoning it, hoping to make it inoperable to the enemy after capture. An attacking force, on the other hand, might themselves spike a gun they had just captured if they knew they could not keep it. When Col. William Thornton's column overran Capt. Daniel Patterson's battery at New Orleans, the Americans started to spike their guns so the British could not turn them on Jackson's positions across the river. When Thornton's troops pulled back, they finished spiking the guns so the Americans could not move back in and use them on the withdrawing British.

U.S. Artillery

In the beginning of the U.S. Army there was only the artillery. When the Revolutionary War ended, Congress disbanded the entire Continental Army on 20 June 1784. The one exception was a single company of artillerymen left to guard the military supplies at West Point. Today's U.S. Army grew from that one company, originally raised by Alexander Hamilton in 1776. That same unit manned the guns at Fort St. Philip during the War of 1812. Today it is the First Battalion, Fifth Field Artillery, the only U.S. military unit to have served continuously on active duty since the Revolution.

By October 1786, the fledgling U.S. Army had rebounded to the point at which its artillery consisted of a whole battalion. Prior to the nineteenth century, artillery and engineers were closely related in most armies, and in 1794 they were combined in the U.S. Army as the Corps of Artillerists and Engineers. In 1802, the engineers and artillery split, and a 20-company Regiment of Artillerists was formed. In 1808, Congress authorized a ten-company Regiment of Light Artillery, which was supposed to be the same type of horse artillery unit that many European armies were then starting to field. Only one company was ever mounted prior to the war, and that lasted only a few months. A colonel for the new regiment was not even appointed until 1812.

Throughout most of the period between the Revolution and the War of 1812, U.S. artillerymen often served as infantry on the frontier. Some cannoneers never even saw a cannon. The defenses along the Atlantic and Gulf coasts had some 927 heavy guns, but many of these were obsolete relics from the Revolution. In all except a few key locations, they were manned by local militia.

With the coming of the war, Congress hastily authorized two additional 20-company artillery regiments on 11 January 1812. The Second and Third Regiments were designated as part of the "additional military force," and appointments in them were considered to be somehow inferior to an appointment in the First Artillery, a part of the "permanent peace establishment." On 12 May 1814, the three artillery regiments on foot were consolidated to form the Corps of Artillery, consisting of 12 battalions of four companies each. The main flaw in this new organization was the lack of an overall commander. The new corps, in fact, had no colonel's positions. Half of the battalions had lieutenant colonels as commanders, and the other half had majors. The Regiment of Light Artillery remained separate until 1 June 1821, when all U.S. artillery units were again consolidated and reformed as four new numbered regiments.

Various militia and volunteer artillery units participated in the War of 1812. In July 1813, Congress authorized a Corps of Sea Fencibles "for defense of ports and harbors of the United States." Two companies of sea fencibles, along with two companies of the First Maryland Artillery Regiment, manned the guns at Fort McHenry. Seven other companies of the First Maryland defended Baltimore from firing positions on Hampstead Hill during Ross's attack. Maj. George Peter's Georgetown Artillery was one of the few militia units to fight well at Bladensburg. Perhaps the most significant U.S. volunteer artillerymen of the war were the odd assortment of freebooters and "hellish banditti" that served Jackson's guns at New Orleans.

From the earliest colonial times, artillery practice in the United States closely followed that of the Royal Artillery. During the Revolution, Henry Knox carefully built his Continental Artillery along the lines of his British counterparts. Following the Revolution, however, U.S. artillery slowly shifted to the French model. By the start of the War of 1812, most U.S. artillery carriages were based on the French Gribeauval System. Cannon tubes continued to follow British designs for a few more years, but Secretary of War Dearborn ordered a shift from brass to iron tubes as a cost-saving measure.

Since artillery units almost never served or trained as artillery in the years following the Revolution, the United States entered the War of 1812 with virtually no artillery tactical doctrine. Some artillery manuals had been written in the United States after the Revolution, but they were never adopted by the War Department. The first official U.S. manual of artillery tactics, *The Maneuvers Horse Ar-*

tillery, was not adopted until 1 August 1812. The book was originally written in Paris in 1800 by Gen. Tadeusz Kosciuszko, a hero of both the American and Polish Revolutions. Kosciuszko based his tactical system on then current French practice and modified it according to his own knowledge of field conditions in the United States.

In general, the U.S. Army handled its artillery poorly in the Canadian theater, although the artillery had some of the best officers in the army at the start of the war. Seven of the 12 brevets conferred in 1813 went to artillery officers. Yet because officers like George Izard, Winfield Scott, and Alexander Macomb were so competent and efficient, they were assigned to other critical areas. Macomb's command of the Third Artillery was really just an adjunct to his duties as an infantry commander. The Third, in fact, served almost entirely as infantry. By March 1814, there was not a single colonel serving with any of the four artillery regiments. Only once did a senior artillery officer actually have command of all the U.S. guns in a major field force. When James Wilkinson was at Sacket's Harbor preparing for his push on Montreal, he issued an order in October 1813 assigning Gen. Moses Porter as commander of all artillery troops. Shortly after, however, Porter had to withdraw from field duty because of illness.

U.S. artillery was either neglected or misused while senior U.S. commanders continually lamented their lack of it. In August 1812, Gen. Henry Dearborn wrote from Greenbush, N.Y., "I am in want of experienced artillerists. We have none here of any kind." When Izard assumed command at Plattsburg in May 1814, he reported to the secretary of war that his three companies of light artillery had only one officer each and 40 horses total.

Yet the U.S. Army did manage to produce a few outstanding lower-echelon artillery commanders in the northern theater. Capt. Nathan Towson was unquestionably the best U.S. artillery company commander of the war. Like his British counterpart, Maj. William Holcroft, Towson seems to have fought almost everywhere in the Canadian theater. Maj. Jacob Hindman was one of the few effective artillery battalion commanders. Hindman's battalion supported Jacob Brown's force during the 1814 Niagara Campaign.

With two exceptions U.S. artillery performed no better in the Atlantic coast fighting than it did in the north. During the bombardment of Fort McHenry, U.S. artillerymen under Maj. George Armistead achieved no startling feats of gunnery. They were able to engage the enemy for a period of only about 30 minutes because the British bomb vessels fired mostly from beyond the range of the fort's guns. That Armistead's inexperienced troops withstood the 24 hours of pounding and still managed to return effective fire was really their greatest accomplishment.

The best U.S. field artillery fight occurred at Bladensburg. Ironically, it was a Navy show. When almost all of the U.S. army broke and ran, Commodore Joshua Barney's five big 18-pounder naval guns planted in the middle of the Washington Road killed 200 and wounded 50 of Ross's troops. Before the British finally flanked them, Barney's sailors suffered more than 20 percent casualties, including the commodore himself.

New Orleans was the most decisive U.S. artillery battle since Yorktown. Despite facing British guns that were more numerous, heavier, and manned by superior crews, the U.S. gunners rode out the artillery duel on 1 January 1815 and generally returned effective fire. Assuming the defensive and operating on interior lines, they had the advantage of more time and more readily available resources to prepare and deeply entrench their firing positions.

Andrew Jackson assembled one of the strangest collections of American field artillerymen ever. On the east side of the river, his 15 guns were grouped into seven battery positions along his line. He only had five heavy guns: one 32-pounder, three 24-pounders, and one 18-pounder. Jackson's nominal artillery commander was Capt. Enoch Humphreys, a regular army officer. During the battle, however, each of the batteries fought independently. One of the batteries was commanded by a regular army corporal; another was commanded by Gen. Garrijues Flaugeac, an exile from Napoleon's army; yet another was commanded by Dominique You, the brother of buccaneer Jean Lafitte. Over on the west side of the river, Navy captain Daniel Patterson planted two 12-pounder naval guns, positioning them to shoot into the British left flank. By the time the British attacked again on 8 January, Patterson had emplaced a total of 16 guns on the west bank. Most were positioned to shoot across the river, but some pointed down river to protect the position's front.

To the credit of the U.S. gunners, they ignored the Royal Artillery's counterbattery fire during the attack on 8 January and concentrated their own fire on the British infantry with canister and grape. Despite the long-cherished belief in the performance of the Americans' rifles that day, many historians now agree it was primarily artillery fire that mauled the attacking troops. An analysis of British casualties does much to support the claim. Some regiments, such as the Fourth Foot, were out of rifle range, yet suffered disproportionately higher casualties than regiments such as the 44th, which led Gen. Samuel Gibbs's column. The Rifle Brigade, which covered Gibbs's front with a skirmish line, suffered only 11 killed. This was because a widely spread skirmish line was among the most difficult of targets for artillery to engage. Finally, George Gleig and other British eyewitnesses have described the mangled condition of the troops who died in the assault. That only could have been the work of artillery.

British Artillery

Britain's Royal Regiment of Artillery was (and still is) not a single regiment but rather a corps consisting of that entire arm. At the start of the War of 1812, the Royal Artillery included 12 troops of the Royal Horse Artillery (RHA), ten battalions of ten companies each of foot artillery, a 12 company invalid battalion, and the Corps of Royal Artillery Drivers.

The standard artillery company had 5 officers, 95 men, and 6 guns. Although the horse companies had their own horses, the foot companies did not, and all necessary transportation was supposed to come from the Corps of Drivers. In 1822, the drivers were disbanded and consolidated into the foot companies. A Royal Horse Artillery troop had 5 officers, 144 men, and 187 horses. In 1813, the RHA formed a number of rocket detachments armed with the new Congreve Rocket. The following year these rocket detachments were grouped into the First and Second Rocket Troops. The invalid companies were manned by partially disabled troops performing garrison duties in England only. The British allocated artillery on the basis of three tubes for every 1,000 men—a formula they used from Cromwell through World War II.

At the higher levels, British artillery had a complicated and cumbersome command and control structure. Until 1855, both the Royal Artillery and the Royal Engineers came under the Board of Ordnance, rather than under the War Office like the rest of the British army. During military operations, the senior artillery commander in the field reported directly to the master general of ordnance in London rather than to the force commander. By the early 1800s, however, strong British field commanders, such as Wellington, usually managed to exercise direct control over their supporting artillery.

Unlike some of the more fashionable regiments in the British army, the Royal Artillery was a thoroughly middle-class establishment. It was one of the only regiments never to use the system of purchasing commissions. Rather than taking their training with the rest of the army at the Royal Military College at Sandhurst, gunner and sapper officers received their training at the Royal Military Academy at Woolwich—known as the Shop because of the technical nature of its curriculum. The Royal Artillery's history contains many stories similar to that of William Johnstone, who enlisted in the Royal Artillery in 1752 and died a lieutenant general in 1802.

At the start of the War of 1812, the Royal Artillery had nine companies in Canada under the command of Maj.

Gen. George Glasgow. Two of those companies had served continuously in Canada since their evacuation from New York City at the end of the American Revolution. In 1813, some of the newly formed RHA rocket detachments went to Canada. When the Peninsular War ended in 1814, the British increased the Royal Artillery's strength in Canada to 14 companies. The Canadian Militia Artillery also fielded several companies that usually operated under the close direction of the senior Royal Artillery officer present.

None of the campaigns in the Canadian theater involved large masses of British guns operating under the direction of a senior artillery commander. They were rather a series of soldiers' battles with small batteries or even single guns engaged. In most of these northern battles, the British had fewer guns than their opponents. At the start of the war, Capt. William Holcroft's company was the Royal Artillery's only field unit in Upper Canada. The other eight Royal Artillery companies manned the garrison guns at Quebec, Montreal, and Halifax. Holcroft's company, heavily augmented by militia artillery, provided virtually all the support to British field operations through the middle of 1814. During the 1814 Niagara Campaign, Holcroft's gunners were joined by the company of Capt. J. Maclachlan, newly arrived from England.

Lundy's Lane was one of the few northern battles in which both sides were almost evenly matched for guns. Facing the Americans' three 18-pounders and six 12-pounders were two 24-pounders and seven 6-pounders of the British. The British guns were also supported by a Royal Marine Artillery rocket detachment. The British started the battle with their guns in a superior position on high ground. The British battery tore into the U.S. lines and played havoc with the U.S. guns, which could not elevate high enough to return fire effectively. The 21st U.S. Infantry finally took the British battery from the flank in a surprise night attack. U.S. artillery quickly occupied the hill, and the British unsuccessfully counterattacked the position three times in the dark. The Americans beat back the counterattacks but were later ordered to withdraw from the hill after Gen. Jacob Brown was wounded by a British rocket. The Americans did not have enough horses to draw off both the captured British guns and their own, so they extracted their own first and then tried to return for the captured guns. By that time, however, the British gunners had reoccupied the position and had taken possession of their guns.

When the British opened the Chesapeake Bay campaign of 1814, Maj. Gen. Robert Ross's force had three Royal Artillery companies plus a rocket half-company from the Royal Marine Artillery. Two of the Royal Artillery companies had seen many months of hard service in the Peninsula, and the third had served in Italy. They lacked horses to draw their guns. As a result, Ross marched on Washington supported only by one 6-pounder and two 3-pounders, and even these were dragged overland by seamen. At Bladensburg, British rockets terrified the raw U.S. militiamen, and their first and second defensive lines quickly folded. When the British reached the position held by Commodore Joshua Barney, their one 6-pounder under Capt. Adam Crawford traded shots with Barney's five 18-pounders until the British infantry finally managed to flank the U.S. position.

After suffering repulse at Baltimore and losing Ross to a U.S. sharpshooter's bullet, the British moved south. In November 1814, a fourth artillery company joined the force at New Orleans. When Gen. Edward Pakenham arrived to assume command the following month, he was accompanied by Col. Alexander Dickson, who assumed overall command of the British guns. New Orleans was the only battle of the War of 1812 where a higher-level commander controlled all the British artillery on the field. It was also one of the few battles in which the British had a superior number of guns. Transportation, though, remained the Royal Artillery's biggest problem, and in this battle it proved their undoing.

The British did manage to drag enough guns over the 80-mile line of communications that stretched from the fleet to their field positions. They could not, however, bring up enough ammunition. During the artillery duel on 1 January 1815, the British had 22 cannon throwing a salvo of 276 pounds, to the Americans' 15 guns throwing 225 pounds. Dickson's gunners actually registered more direct hits, knocking out three American guns and losing only one in the process. But the flimsy British firing emplacements resulted in fairly high casualties among the gun crews. After three hours of firing, Dickson simply ran out of ammunition. Even with enough ammunition, Dickson doubted his hastily constructed battery platforms could have withstood much more firing. Almost all of his bigger guns were actually naval pieces. Since they were not mounted on field carriages, they were much more difficult to transport over land and could only fire from specially constructed platforms.

During the week following the artillery duel, the British moved up more heavy guns and painstakingly built up their ammunition reserves. When the Seventh Fusiliers and the 43rd Foot marched up from the fleet, each man carried an artillery round in his knapsack. The Royal Artillery supported the British attack on 8 January with 26 guns that threw a salvo weight of 360 pounds. They concentrated their fire on the U.S. batteries. But the U.S. guns ignored the counterbattery fire and poured grape and canister into the advancing ranks of redcoats. When the British infantry finally fell back, the artillery had to abandon their exposed guns because they had no means of extracting them from the forward positions.

The greatest irony of the campaign came a few days later when Dickson learned that an ordnance ship had just arrived at the fleet anchorage. The ship carried 26 cannon on field carriages, including two heavy howitzers. If Dickson had possessed those guns on New Year's Day, the Battle of New Orleans might have turned out quite differently. Now it was too late. The British army retreated down the Mississippi on 19 January. Having no means to transport his heavy guns on their bulky naval carriages, Dickson had no choice but to spike and abandon his pieces.

Canadian Militia Artillery

British major general Isaac Brock did not trust the Canadian militia, and the events of the War of 1812 largely vindicated his opinion. Canada's militia artillery, in contrast, did perform well in the war. Of the 5,455 Canadian militiamen who served in Upper Canada between 1812 and 1815, 350 were artillerymen. Although this was only 6.4 percent, that was a substantially higher ratio than the 500 Royal Artillerymen out of the force of some 13,000 British regulars who served in Canada during the War of 1812.

Several militia artillery units existed prior to the outbreak of hostilities. The Loyal Company of Artillery, formed at St. John in 1793, claims to be the third-oldest artillery unit in the British Commonwealth today. Both the First and Second Regiments of Lincoln Militia had artillery companies—that of the First commanded by Capt. John Powell and that of the Second commanded by Capt. James Kerby. After the war started, at least three other militia field artillery companies were raised. The Incorporated Artillery Company of Capt. Alexander Cameron also saw action in Upper Canada; the Royal Militia Artillery was formed in Lower Canada; and the Mississippi Volunteer Artillery served in the Far West. Two companies of drivers were also formed: Capt. Isaac Swayze's Troop of Provincial Royal Artillery Drivers supported both militia and Royal Artillery field batteries in Upper Canada; and the Corps of Provincial Royal Artillery Drivers served in Lower Canada.

At the start of the war, William Holcroft's company was the only Royal Artillery unit in Upper Canada. Until the end of 1813, almost all the fighting in the Niagara Peninsula involved Holcroft's unit, augmented by the militia companies of Powell and Kerby and later by Cameron's and supported by Swayze's drivers. At Queenston Heights, most of the men behind the guns on the Canadian side of the river were militia gunners. At Fort George in 1813,

Holcroft's regulars manned the field guns in front of the fort, and Powell's militia gunners (assisted by one of Holcroft's sergeants) served the garrison guns of the fort itself.

After Gen. John Vincent evacuated Fort George on 27 May, he disbanded the bulk of his militia. That marked the end of the service of the two Lincoln artillery companies. With one exception, no militia artillery participated in any of the fighting in 1814. In July of that year a force of volunteers under Capt. William McKay, called the Michigan Fencibles, attacked Fort Shelby, the U.S. outpost at Prairie du Chien. McKay's only heavy firepower was an ancient 3-pounder manned by the Fencibles and commanded by Royal Artillery Sgt. James "One Gun" Keating, a veteran of the Napoleonic wars. Fort Shelby had six guns and was also protected by the 14-gun *Governor Clark*, a U.S. gunboat on the Mississippi River.

When the Canadians reached the fort on 17 July, Keating engaged the formidably armed gunboat. After three hours of trading shots, the *Clark*'s crew cut her cable and drifted downstream to safety. Keating then turned his attention on the fort, but he had expended most of his ammunition against the boat. He was down to three rounds, plus another three rounds of usable U.S. shot that had been fired at him. In full view of the fort, he began heating up his rounds for hot shot. That apparently was too much for the U.S. garrison, which surrendered before Keating could get his first round loaded. Keating's feat earned him a militia commission and command of the Mississippi Volunteer Artillery.

Royal Marine Artillery

The Royal Marine Artillery fought in every major theater of the War of 1812, with the exception of the Northwest. Each of the three Royal Marine battalions deployed to North America was composed of six infantry companies and an artillery company. Each battalion also had a Royal Marine Artillery rocket half-company as a special attachment. A typical Royal Marine Artillery company was made up of 1 captain, 4 lieutenants, 4 sergeants, 4 corporals, 6 bombardiers, 2 drummers, and 60 gunners. A rocket half-company had 1 lieutenant, 4 noncommissioned officers, and 20 gunners. The Royal Navy's rocket ship *Erebus* also carried a Royal Marine Artillery half-company to work the rockets, and Royal Marine artillerymen manned the large 10-inch and 13-inch mortars on the Royal Navy's five bomb vessels that served in U.S. waters.

Two Royal Marine battalions arrived off Chesapeake Bay with Adm. Sir George Cockburn's squadron in June 1813. The Royal Marine Artillery company of the First Battalion was commanded by Capt. Thomas A. Parke, with Lt. G. E. Balchild in charge of the rocket half-company. Capt. Richard Parry commanded the Second Royal Marine Artillery company, and Lt. J. H. Stevens the rockets. Their first action came on 22 June when both Royal Marine Artillery companies participated in the attack on Craney Island, Virginia, while both rocket half-companies engaged U.S. shore positions from armed launches. Two days later, Royal Marine Artillery units took part in the attack on Hampton.

The four Royal Marine Artillery units continued to participate in operations off Chesapeake Bay until early September, when Adm. John Borelase Warren took the fleet to Halifax. On 22 September, the Royal Marine battalions were ordered ashore in response to a request for help from Gen. Sir George Prevost. The First battalion with its artillery marched up the St. Lawrence to Lower Canada while the Second moved farther upriver into Upper Canada. Parke's First Royal Marine Artillery Company fought at La Colle Mill on 30 March 1814. Parry's Second Royal Marine Artillery Company participated in the attack on Oswego on 5 May 1814, with Stevens's rocket half-company supporting the landing parties from armed launches.

Shortly after the attack on Oswego, the Admiralty disbanded the two Royal Marines battalions in Canada and ordered the troops distributed in small parties to the various ships of the lake flotillas. The Royal Marine Artillery companies were supposed to be split into sections and assigned to the various St. Lawrence forts until more Royal Artillery units could arrive from England. Despite these orders, Royal Marine artillerymen continued to see field service for several more months. Parke's First Royal Marine Artillery Company fought as a complete unit at Plattsburg on 11 September 1814, serving with the Royal Artillery on shore while Balchild's rocket half-company manned a mortar battery and later made up part of Prevost's rear guard. Parry's Second Royal Marine Artillery Company was split into a number of small detachments that served with the Royal Artillery at the Battle of Chippewa and at Lundy's Lane. A rocket section under Royal Marine Artillery sergeant Austin also fought at Lundy's Lane, firing from a position in the church graveyard just behind the British guns. During Gen. Gordon Drummond's unsuccessful attack on Fort Erie on 15 August, a Royal Marine Artillery detachment accompanied the center assault column. In the protracted siege that followed, the Royal Marine Artillery manned two of Drummond's batteries.

A third Royal Marine battalion, meanwhile, arrived off Chesapeake Bay in July 1814. The Royal Marine Artillery company was commanded by Capt. John Harrison, with Lt. John Lawrence in charge of the rocket half-company.

Both Royal Marine Artillery units participated in the various raids along the Potomac in July and August, including the 22 August raid on Pig Point that resulted in the destruction of Commodore Joshua Barney's flotilla. At the battle of Bladensburg and the subsequent march on Washington, Harrison's Royal Marine Artillery Company accompanied Gen. Robert Ross's "Right Brigade," and Lawrence's rocket half-company went with the "Light Brigade." It was Lawrence's rockets that so frightened the inexperienced U.S. militia at Bladensburg. Both Royal Marine Artillery units also participated in the attack on North Point just below Baltimore.

While Harrison's and Lawrence's units were fighting on land, Royal Marine Artillerymen served on the rocket and bomb vessels that accompanied Capt. James A. Gordon's raid up the Potomac River. Lt. T. S. Beauchant commanded the Royal Marine Artillery half-company on the rocket ship *Erebus*. The Royal Marine Artillery detachments on the bomb ships were commanded by Lt. A. J. Moore on the *Devastation*, Lt. Robert Wright on the *Aetna*, and Lt. H. A. Napier on the *Meteor*. After capturing and destroying Fort Washington on 27 August, Gordon's force had to fight its way back down the river, finally rejoining the fleet on 9 September. The *Erebus* and the three bomb ships were then joined by the bomb ships *Terror* and *Volcano*. These six vessels made up the attack force against Fort McHenry on 13–14 September. The Royal Marine Artillery detachment on the *Terror* was commanded by Lt. J. Walker, and the detachment on the *Volcano* was commanded by Lt. J. P. Furzer.

After Ft. McHenry and Baltimore, all Royal Marines units in the Chesapeake area were sent south for operations along the Georgia coast. The only exception was Lieutenant Lawrence's 26-man unit that accompanied the force moving on New Orleans. In November 1814, the First Royal Marine Battalion, including Parke's Royal Marine Artillery Company, was reconstituted in Quebec and sent south in support of Georgia coastal operations.

For the New Orleans expedition Lawrence's men shed their rockets and were armed with three 5.5-inch mortars on field carriages. The detachment landed at New Orleans as part of the advance guard and participated in the sinking of the *Louisiana*. During the artillery duel of 1 January 1815, the Royal Marine Artillery detachment manned a battery position on the right flank of the Royal Marine Artillery rocket detachment. Like the rest of the British artillery, the Royal Marine Artillery gunners worked under a severe ammunition shortage, having only 30 rounds for each of their mortars. During the British attack on 8 January, Lawrence's detachment accompanied Col. William Thornton's column on the west bank of the river.

The day after the final British defeat on land, the bomb ships *Aetna*, *Meteor*, and *Volcano* started their ten-day firefight with Fort St. Philip, 70 miles downriver from New Orleans. The Royal Marine Artillery detachment in the *Volcano* was now under the command of Lt. Robert Henry. (Lt. Furzer had been killed in a fight with the U.S. privateer *Saucy Jack* off Jamaica on 31 October.)

After the British withdrew from New Orleans, Lawrence's Royal Marine Artillery detachment took part in the siege and occupation of Fort Bowyer in February 1815. Parke's Royal Marine Artillery Company, meanwhile, was sent back to Canada in January, leaving only Harrison's Royal Marine Artillery Company to support operations off the Georgia coast. The Royal Marine's last action of the war came in February 1815 when Harrison's Royal Marine Artillery Company and Royal Marine Artillery detachments in the *Terror*, *Devastation*, and *Erebus* participated in the expeditions up the Savannah River and the St. Mary's River in south Georgia.

—*David T. Zabecki*

See also: Armistead, George; Dickson, Alexander; Holcroft, William; Porter, Moses; Thornton, William; Towson, Nathan

Further Reading

Birkhimer, William E. *Historical Sketch of the Organization, Administration, Materiel and Tactics of the Artillery, United States Army.* Washington, DC: Chapman, 1884.

Browne, James Alex. *England's Artillerymen.* London: Hall, Smart, and Allen, 1865.

Downey, Fairfax. *The Sound of the Guns.* New York: McKay, 1955.

Duncan, Francis. *History of the Royal Regiment of Artillery.* Vol. 2. London: John Murray, 1872.

Fraser, Edward, and L. G. Carr-Laughton. *The Royal Marine Artillery: 1804–1923.* London: The Royal United Services Institution,1930.

Heitman, F. B. *Historical Register of the United States Army.* Washington, DC: The National Tribune, 1890.

Hughes, B. P. *Honor Titles of the Royal Artillery.* Woolwich: Royal Artillery Institution, 1974.

———. *Open Fire: Artillery Tactics from Marlborough to Wellington.* Strettington, Sussex, England: Antony Bird Publications, 1983.

Kosciuszko, Tadeusz. *The Manoeuvres of Horse Artillery.* New York: U.S. Military Philosophical Society, 1808.

Laws, M.E.S. *Battery Records of the Royal Artillery: 1716–1859.* Woolwich: Royal Artillery Institution, 1952.

Mauncy, Albert. *Artillery through the Ages.* Washington, DC: U.S. Government Printing Office, 1949.

Nicolson, G.W.L. *The Gunners of Canada.* Toronto: McClelland and Stewart, 1967.

Peterson, Harold L. *Round Shot and Rammers*. South Bend, IN: South Bend Replicas, 1969.
Reilly, Robin. *The British at the Gates*. New York: G. P. Putnam's Sons, 1974.
U.S. Department of War. *A System of Exercise and Instruction of Field Artillery Including Manoeuvres for Light or Horse Artillery*. Boston: Hilliard, Gray, 1829.

ASPINWALL, THOMAS
1786–1876
U.S. officer

Born in Boston, the grandson of Revolutionary War hero William Aspinwall, who was killed at Concord, Thomas Aspinwall graduated from Harvard and had begun the practice of law when war started with Great Britain in 1812. Granted a major's commission in the Ninth Infantry Regiment, Aspinwall fought in several of the major campaigns and battles of the northern theater.

By the spring of 1813, he had been breveted a lieutenant colonel. In May of that year, he and reinforcements for Sacket's Harbor were transported via gunboats on Lake Erie just as Adm. Sir James Lucas Yeo's major British invasion force was descending on Sacket's Harbor from Kingston. As Aspinwall's little expedition neared the harbor, British Indian allies in canoes and British landing boats nearly overtook it. Most of Aspinwall's force made it ashore and reached U.S. defenses by the night of 28 May 1813. Lieutenant Colonel Aspinwall was thus present at the successful defense of Sacket's Harbor.

A few months later Aspinwall joined the preparations for Gen. James Wilkinson's invasion of Canada. In this disastrous campaign, Aspinwall drew special mention for his courage in the otherwise dismal U.S. showing at Chrysler's Farm in November 1813.

In 1814, Aspinwall returned to the Niagara Frontier and fought in the major engagements during this last summer of the war. He assumed command of the first brigade at Lundy's Lane when Brig. Gen. Winfield Scott was wounded. As the commander of the Ninth Infantry Regiment, Aspinwall held the U.S. left in the defense of Fort Erie on 15 August. The failure of the British on that occasion led to a prolonged siege that was broken on 17 September when Maj. Gen. Jacob Brown ordered a sortie from Fort Erie against the British artillery positions. Aspinwall and his Ninth Regiment formed part of the second U.S. division, with the goal of securing the two batteries in the British center. The assault was successful, though Aspinwall

received such a severe injury that he lost an arm. He was breveted a colonel for his actions on 17 September.

Following the war, Aspinwall resigned his commission. Pres. James Madison appointed him to serve as U.S. consul in London, a post he held for 37 years. He then returned to Boston, where he died in 1876.

—*Jeanne T. Heidler and David S. Heidler*

See also: Chrysler's Farm, Battle of; Lundy's Lane, Battle of; Sacket's Harbor, Battle of
Further Reading
Smith, C. Charles. "Memoirs of Colonel Thomas Aspinwall." *Massachusetts Historical Society Proceedings* 3 (1891): 30–81.

ASTOR, JOHN JACOB
1763–1848
U.S. businessman

The War of 1812 marked both extremes of success and failure for John Jacob Astor. Although he succeeded in winning legal and actual dominance of the Great Lakes fur trade, his dream of establishing the fur trade with China out of Astoria foundered in the confusions caused by the war.

Astor arrived in New York from Waldorf, Germany, in 1783 and opened a musical instrument store. By 1785, he was building a fur trade in upstate New York. He offered the Indians there a better price and demanded low prices and high quality from his suppliers. He competed fiercely with the Montreal traders, ignoring a variety of regulations and laws that impeded his goal of controlling the Great Lakes trade.

During the War of 1812, Astor successfully lobbied Congress to pass a law in 1814 that reserved the fur trade on U.S. soil to U.S. citizens. Since the British had constituted his only competition, Astor now had his monopoly. His available labor force, however, was mostly French Canadian. Astor was forced to go back to Congress to gain exemptions for certain classifications: voyageurs, habitants, and small traders. With his labor supply secure, he forced the Montreal trading houses to sell him their assets. For the next several decades, Astor's company made a fortune in the Great Lakes.

Still, Astor believed that the Rocky Mountains held far more furs than the Great Lakes region and that far more lucrative markets awaited him in China. After studying the

John Jacob Astor

Further Reading

Brannon, Gary. *The Last Voyage of the* Tonquin: *An Ill-fated Expedition to the Pacific Northwest.* Waterloo, Ont.: Escart Press, 1992.

Flandrau, Grace. *Astor and the Oregon Country.* St. Paul, MN: Great Northern Railway, 1926.

Haeger, John D. *John Jacob Astor: Business and Finance in the Early Republic.* Detroit: Wayne State University Press, 1991.

Keeling, Mildred Roberta. "John Jacob Astor and the Settlement of Astoria." Master's thesis, Southwest Texas State University, 1940.

Parton, James. *Life of John Jacob Astor, To Which Is Appended a Copy of His Last Will.* New York: American News, 1865.

Scott, Anne Simpson. "John Jacob Astor and the Settlement of the Northwest." Master's thesis, Arkansas State College, 1961.

record of the Lewis and Clark expedition, he began establishing a series of posts to the Pacific. Russian claims to the Northwest complicated his plans, but after making a deal with Alexander Baranov's Russian America Company, Astor established Astoria on the Columbia River in 1811. The outbreak of the War of 1812 disrupted his plans, however, when his own employees sold the post to the British North West Company. Astor tried to persuade the U.S. Navy to help retake the post, but he was unable to do so.

Even with the failure of Astoria, Astor's business activities continued throughout the war. In fact, one of his letters to a contact in Canada alerted British forces there to the declaration of war before Gen. William Hull knew about it. Nor did the war prevent Astor from maintaining a lucrative trade with Canada. He was also one of the biggest subscribers to war bonds, though he usually insisted that he be allowed to purchase the bonds at a discount.

By the time of his death in 1848, Astor had defined and dominated the fur trade in the Great Lakes region and provided a basis for the U.S. claim to the Oregon territory. Astor demonstrated in his quest for monopoly a finely honed entrepreneurial spirit and competitive edge worthy of late-nineteenth-century businessmen.

—*Kurt E. Leichtle*

See also: Astoria, Fort

ASTORIA, FORT
U.S. fur-trading post, Columbia River

Astoria was a fur-trading post built and operated by John Jacob Astor's Pacific Fur Company. News of the United States' declaration of war reached Astoria 15 January 1813, brought by Donald McKenzie, one of Astor's employees. In November 1810, Simon McGillvray of the North West Company had asked the British government to send a British expedition to gain possession of the mouth of the Columbia River. The British therefore had already dispatched a warship and had built a military fort and settlement at the mouth of the Columbia.

The war now furnished the opportunity to capture Astor's post. The *Isaac Todd*, a North West Company storeship, sailed from London in March 1813, escorted by the frigate HMS *Phoebe* and sloops HMS *Cherub* and HMS *Racoon*. The *Racoon*, commanded by Capt. William Black, was dispatched to capture Astoria. In September, when North West Company traders John George McTavish, Duncan McKenzie, and Angus Bethune arrived with several canoes filled with furs, they proposed that Astoria be sold to the North West Company, and Duncan McDougall, Astor's agent, agreed. The Canadians took possession and supplied the Pacific Fur Company employees with wages and provisions. Most of Astor's employees joined the North West Company, and the British replaced the American flag with their own.

When the *Racoon* arrived on 13 December 1813, Black took possession in the name of King George, after whom the fort was renamed. The *Isaac Todd* arrived 28 April

1814. The terms of the Treaty of Ghent restored the fort to U.S. control in 1818.

—*Frederick C. Drake*

See also: Astor, John Jacob

Further Reading

Campbell, Marjorie W. *The North West Company.* Vancouver: Douglas & McIntyre, 1957. Reprint, 1983.

Davidson, Charles Gordon. *The North West Company.* Publications in History, vol. 7. Berkeley: University of California, 1918.

Elliot, T. C. "Sale of Astoria, 1813." *Oregon Historical Quarterly* 33 (March 1932): 43–50.

Franchere, Gabriel. *Adventures at Astoria, 1810–1814.* Norman: University of Oklahoma Press, 1967.

———. *Journal of a Voyage to the North West Coast of North America during the Years, 1811, 1812, 1813 and 1814.* Vol. 45. Ed. W. Kaye Lamb. Toronto: Champlain Society, 1969.

Gough, Barry M. *The Royal Navy and the North West Coast of North America, A Study of British Maritime Ascendancy, 1810–1914.* Vancouver: University of British Columbia Press, 1971.

Irving, Washington. *Astoria.* Vol. 3. London: R. Bentley, 1836.

Judson, Katherine B. "The British Side to the Restoration of Fort Astoria." *Oregon Historical Society Quarterly* 20 (1919): 305–330.

Merk, Frederick. "The Genesis of the Oregon Question." *Mississippi Valley Historical Review* 36 (1949–1950): 583–612.

Porter, Kenneth W. *John Jacob Astor, Businessman.* 2 vols. Cambridge: Harvard University Press, 1931.

Ronda, James. *Astoria and Empire.* Lincoln: University of Nebraska Press, 1990.

Ross, Alexander. *Adventures of the First Settlers on the Oregon or Columbia River.* Chicago: R. R. Donnelly, 1913.

Sands, Harold, "Canada's Conquest of Astoria: How Montrealers Peacefully Secured the American Fort on the Pacific Coast." *Canadian Magazine* 42 (1914): 464–468.

Tate, Vernon D., ed. "Spanish Documents Relating to the Voyage of the *Racoon* to Astoria and San Francisco." *Hispanic American Historical Review* 18 (May 1938): 183–191.

planned a hit-and-run attack against the village of Autosse. The town was on the southern bank of the Tallapoosa River about 20 miles above its juncture with the Coosa in Mississippi Territory. After a 60-mile march, Floyd's small army reached Autosse on the morning of 29 November 1813.

Floyd separated his army into three columns, placing his artillery in front of the right column. He planned to surround the enemy town by extending his flanks toward Calabee Creek. He would employ the friendly Indians to prevent any escape across the creek. As Floyd approached Autosse, however, he discovered another small town about a quarter-mile downstream. This forced him to extend his left flank so he could destroy both towns.

Autosse put up a good fight, but U.S. artillery and small arms fire proved too much for them. By 9 A.M., the battle was over, with at least 200 Indians dead and 400 dwellings destroyed. General Floyd suffered 11 killed and 54 wounded. With that successful result, Floyd returned to his base on the Chattahoochee River.

—*John M. Keefe*

See also: Calabee, Battle of; Creek War; Georgia

Further Reading

Halbert, H. S., and T. H. Ball. *The Creek War of 1813 and 1814.* Chicago: Donohue and Henneberry, 1895.

Martin, Joel W. *Sacred Revolt: The Muskogees' Struggle for a New World.* Boston: Beacon Press, 1991.

Owsley, Frank Lawrence, Jr. *Struggle for the Gulf Borderlands: The Creek War and the Battle of New Orleans, 1812–1815.* Gainesville: University Presses of Florida, 1981.

Rowland, Dunbar. *Andrew Jackson's Campaign against the British, or the Mississippi Territory in the War of 1812.* New York: Macmillan, 1926.

AUTOSSE, BATTLE OF
29 November 1813

In mid-November 1813, Gen. John Floyd left Georgia accompanied by 950 Georgia militia and 400 friendly Creek warriors under William McIntosh and the son of Mad Dog. With only limited supplies available, Floyd knew that he could not sustain a long campaign, so he

B

BACON, EZEKIEL
1776–1870
U.S. congressman

Born in Boston, Massachusetts, the son of John Bacon, Ezekiel Bacon graduated from Yale in 1794, studied law, and opened a private practice by 1800. Shortly thereafter he entered state politics as a Democratic Republican and served two terms in the state legislature. He entered the Tenth Congress in 1807 as a replacement for a congressman who resigned, but he was elected in his own right to the 11th and 12th Congresses. In the 12th Congress, he served as the chair of the House Committee on Ways and Means.

Bacon was considered a strong supporter of the Madison administration, and it fell to him in Ways and Means to bring secretary of the treasury Albert Gallatin's controversial plan to finance the war before the House. He did so four months before war was declared. Even Democratic Republicans found this move irregular, and Bacon had a difficult time persuading his fellow members that the government should embark upon the unpopular plan of securing a $10 million loan, increasing customs duties, and implementing internal taxes. After all, as some congressmen pointed out, the United States had fought its last war with Great Britain over the issue of internal taxes. The best Bacon could do was secure approval of the loan and agreement to a resolution stating that in the event of war the other measures would be enacted.

Because the war was already underway when the second session of the 12th Congress convened in November 1812, Bacon had less to do regarding taxation issues. He further alienated himself from his state's mainly Federalist delegation, however, by favoring an administration-sponsored bill that made it illegal to arrest a soldier for debt. After faint-hearted soldiers experienced combat, they would entreat friends and relatives to charge them with debt so they could be arrested and hence removed from the war. The ruse also had the consequence of depleting military units. The bill passed but only over vehement Federalist objections that some men had enlisted to avoid their creditors and this bill would only encourage that practice.

The growing unpopularity of the war in New England ruined any hopes Bacon had of returning to the 13th Congress, but the administration rewarded his loyalty with an appointment in 1814 as the first comptroller of the U.S. Treasury. After the war, he resigned that position and moved to New York, where he practiced law and engaged in local politics. Before Bacon died in Utica, New York, in 1870, he was the last living congressman who had served during the Madison administration.

—*Jeanne T. Heidler and David S. Heidler*

See also: U.S. Congress
Further Reading
Barlow, William, and David O. Powell. "Congressman Ezekiel Bacon of Massachusetts and the Coming of the War of 1812." *Historical Journal of Western Massachusetts* 6 (Spring 1978): 28–41.

BAINBRIDGE, WILLIAM
1774–1833
Captain, U.S. Navy

Born to Tory parents living in New Jersey during the Revolution, William Bainbridge's early years were a period of flights from his parents' vengeful foes and fights with taunting peers. Bainbridge first went to sea in 1789, but little is known of his merchant service until he became a ship's master in 1793 at the age of 18. In March 1797, at St. Eustatius, he married Susan Heyliger, the granddaughter of a former governor-general.

William Bainbridge

Bainbridge was in Philadelphia during the spring and summer of 1798 when the U.S. Navy was being formed. He accepted a commission as a lieutenant in August and immediately took command of the schooner USS *Retaliation*. In November, while impetuously investigating two ships off Antigua, he found himself under the guns of a superior French force and had to surrender his ship, the first officer of the U.S. Navy to do so.

Bainbridge, promoted to master commandant in 1799 and to captain in 1800, continued to exhibit an impetuous nature. While commanding the light frigate USS *George Washington* in 1800, he found himself under the guns of the bey of Algiers and was forced to make a trip to Constantinople flying the bey's flag and bearing gifts to his Ottoman master. In October 1803, when in command of the frigate USS *Philadelphia*, Bainbridge was on blockade duty off Tripoli when he rashly pursued a smaller craft into reef-strewn inshore waters. Too late, he realized his error, and the frigate ran aground while attempting to clear offshore. Bainbridge had to surrender his ship to the Tripolitans and spent the next 19 months as a prisoner of war. On each occasion, he emerged blameless, and thanks to his political acumen and powerful friends in the govern-

ment, he actually was promoted ahead of those previously senior to him.

The outbreak of the War of 1812 found Bainbridge taking command of the Boston Navy Yard. The USS *Constitution* returned there from her victory over HMS *Guerrière*, and her captain, Isaac Hull, wished relief. Bainbridge gained the command. On 29 December 1812, off Brazil, he defeated HMS *Java* in a hard-fought battle and returned to resume command of the Boston Yard for the remainder of the war.

Following a brief voyage to the Mediterranean at war's end, Bainbridge devoted himself to regaining command of the Boston Yard and to vendettas against contemporaries who had achieved fame in the Barbary War while he was a prisoner. His attempts to have Capts. Charles Stewart and Isaac Hull punished failed, but his involvement in the Barron-Decatur controversy helped to push that argument to the duel that caused Decatur's death.

After one more cruise to the Mediterranean, Bainbridge spent the rest of his career commanding one of the Navy yards or as a member of the Board of Naval Commissioners, serving for a time as its president. He died in Philadelphia on 27 July 1833. The Bainbridges had no children.

The U.S. Navy has named four ships for Commodore Bainbridge.

—*Tyrone G. Martin*

See also: *Constitution* versus *Java*

Further Reading

Dearborn, Henry A.S. *The Life of William Bainbridge Esq., of the United States Navy.* Ed. James Barnes. Princeton: Princeton University Press, 1931.

Harris, Thomas. *The Life and Services of Commodore William Bainbridge, United States Navy.* Philadelphia: Carey Lea and Blanchard, 1837.

Long, David F. *Ready To Hazard.* Hanover, NH: University Press of New England, 1981.

Martin, Tyrone G. *A Most Fortunate Ship.* Annapolis, MD: Naval Institute Press, 1997.

BALTIMORE, BATTLE OF
12–14 September 1814

Baltimore was a prime target for British military strategists. Its population of some 45,000 made it the third-largest city in the United States, and it boasted one of the best harbors on the east coast. In 1812, Baltimore had been a hotbed of prowar activity. During the war, privateers

The American confidence that was gained when Baltimoreans unexpectedly repelled a British attack is clearly demonstrated in this political cartoon by William Sculp.

launched from its docks accounted for more than 500 prizes taken from the British merchant marine. As a result of this wartime success, Baltimore's warehouses bulged with loot and plunder. Maj. Gen. Robert Ross, Vice Adm. Sir Alexander Cochrane, and Rear Adm. George Cockburn, buoyed by their successes against Washington and Alexandria in August 1814, decided to turn their attention to this Republican stronghold on the Chesapeake.

The Americans had sensed that Baltimore would someday become a battleground. Accordingly, Samuel Smith, U.S. senator and major general of the Maryland Militia, ordered the town fortified in mid-1813. Eventually more than 10,000 troops, mostly militia, congregated around the city, building trenches and constructing breastworks. Star-shaped Fort McHenry, a brick fortification garrisoned by U.S. regulars under the command of Maj. George Armistead, dominated the water approaches. Other batteries also emerged, some mounting large cannon borrowed from the French sloop-of-war *L'Eole*, stranded in port by the British blockade.

When news of the disaster at Bladensburg and the subsequent burning of Washington's public buildings began filtering into Baltimore, Smith and his command knew that their city would be next. Defeatism and pessimism were compounded by arguments over command authority. The Committee of Vigilance and Safety, Baltimore's de facto government, and Gov. Levin Winder of Maryland agreed to place General Smith in charge of the city's defense, superseding Brig. Gen. William Henry Winder, the federal officer in charge of the district. General Winder, while correctly the senior officer and nephew of the governor, enjoyed no confidence among the troops at Baltimore owing to his defeats at Bladensburg and Washington. Replacing a regular officer with one from the militia was regarded as highly irregular, but most of the garrison's soldiers sustained the action.

Before long, Smith had instilled confidence in the Americans and had shaped his forces into a creditable army. Brigades formed, including the 500 sailors under Commodore John Rodgers, a few dozen marines, a pair of U.S. regular regiments, the militias of Pennsylvania and Virginia, and the remnants of the Maryland militia. Seven generals—William H. Winder, Thomas Forman, Walter Smith, John Stricker, Douglass, Singleton, and Tobias

Stansbury—led these units as they continued building defenses along the brow of Hampstead Hill.

Admiral Cochrane, his ships sailing northward toward Baltimore, was unaware of the preparations by the Americans. In any event, he was unconcerned, given the U.S. militia's performance in defense of the nation's capital. He planned a two-pronged assault on the city, with General Ross landing on the North Point Peninsula and moving against the land defenses while the ships of the Royal Navy reduced Fort McHenry.

In the early afternoon of Sunday, 11 September, signal guns in Baltimore announced the arrival of the British flotilla. Smith ordered Brigadier General Stricker to take his 3,200-man brigade—composed of the 5th, 27th, 39th, and 51st Maryland militia regiments, a few companies of Pennsylvanians, and Maj. William Pinkney's battalion of riflemen—to North Point to determine British intentions. By nightfall, Stricker had placed his men into a line of battle at a narrow spot halfway down the North Point peninsula between Bread and Cheese Creek to the north and Bear Creek to the south. Capt. John Montgomery's battery of six 4-pounders covered Long Log Lane, the main road leading to Baltimore. That night, the British put ashore their infantry strike force under General Ross and Admiral Cockburn. Shuttled by barges and whaleboats from the fleet in the Patapsco River, the soldiers began landing around 4:00 A.M. By sunrise, all 4,700 were on shore and formed up for the march to Baltimore. Four units, the 4th, 21st, 44th, and 85th regiments of foot, composed the bulk of the command, supplemented by 600 sailors and marines and a few companies of light infantry.

By late morning, 12 September, Stricker's scouts and skirmishers discovered the British just a few miles away at the farm of Robert Gorsuch. Stricker braced his command for the attack, but it never came. As the day passed, he feared a night attack and determined to provoke a fight during the daylight. Accordingly, he dispatched a few cavalrymen, two companies of militia, and a company of riflemen to attract the enemy's attention. At around 1:30 P.M., the Americans traded volleys with a 60-man British vanguard.

General Ross, ordering up his regiments to support the developing battle, chose to lead the fight himself until the bulk of his troops arrived. A U.S. rifleman felled the unescorted Ross, putting a fatal bullet in his chest. Unaware of this development, the Maryland militiamen retreated to Stricker's main line. The British column, now under the command of Col. Arthur Brooke, began its assault on the U.S. position an hour later. As the battle evolved, the 44th and 85th regiments of foot charged the U.S. center. In a savage 20-minute melee, these two units routed Stricker's brigade and captured two guns. More than 163 Americans

lay dead or wounded, and another 50 were taken prisoner. The British had lost half as many.

Meanwhile, 16 frigates, rocket ships, and bomb brigs moved into position less than 3 miles away from Fort McHenry to complete the campaign. Early the next morning, 13 September, the bombardment of Fort McHenry began while the army moved into position to take Baltimore. For the next 20 hours, Cochrane's warships pounded Fort McHenry but without significant effect. The following evening, the British also failed in an amphibious night attack against Baltimore's defenses. Unable to reduce the stubborn forts and facing a well-fortified enemy in superior numbers, the British prudently decided to abandon the campaign and withdrew their forces back into the Chesapeake.

—*Donald Frazier*

See also: Armistead, George; McHenry, Fort; Smith, Samuel; Star-Spangled Banner, The; Stricker, John; Winder, William H.

Further Reading

Hoyt, William D. "Civilian Defense in Baltimore, 1814–1815." *Maryland Historical Magazine* 39 (1944): 7–23.

Lord, Walter. *The Dawn's Early Light.* New York: W. W. Norton, 1972.

Robinson, Ralph. "Controversy over the Command at Baltimore in the War of 1812." *Maryland Historical Magazine* 39 (1944): 117–224.

BALTIMORE RIOTS
June–July 1812

The civil disruptions known as the Baltimore Riots culminated in a mob attack on a Federalist newspaper critical of the War of 1812. The event resulted in at least one death and considerable destruction.

At the time of the War of 1812, the city of Baltimore was a flourishing commercial center. The *Federal Republican* was the newspaper that served mercantile interests. Baltimore merchants, like their New England brethren, had suffered from the restrictive commercial measures of the Jeffersonian embargoes. The war with Great Britain heightened differences between supporters of Madison and his Federalist opponents, and the *Federal Republican* added its voice to support the latter. Alexander Hanson, the newspaper's 26-year-old editor and co-owner, immediately denounced the declaration of war and declared his publication's intention of continuing its criticisms.

On Saturday, 20 June 1812, two days after Congress had declared war, the *Federal Republican* published an editorial stating: "We mean to represent, in as strong colors as we are capable, that the war is unnecessary, inexpedient, and entered into from partial, personal, and, as we believe, motives bearing upon their front marks of undisguised foreign influence which cannot be mistaken."

On Monday evening, 22 June, a mob led by a French apothecary demolished the newspaper's offices. The mob then marched to the wharves, where it torched some ships and damaged adjacent property owned by Federalist merchants. Not to be silenced, the *Federal Republican* continued publication for five weeks from the lower portion of Hanson's house in Georgetown, near Washington, D.C. Finally it was announced that the paper would resume publication from new offices in Baltimore. When supporters of the war gave every sign of planning another attack on the paper, city officials showed little interest in protecting it.

Federalists, however, rose to the newspaper's defense. Gen. Henry "Lighthorse Harry" Lee mounted plans to defend its new Baltimore office on Charles Street, and 20 other well-armed Federalists joined him, Revolutionary War general James Lingan prominent among them. On 27 June, the newspaper was published from the Baltimore office. That evening, the anti-Federalist mob marched to it and began throwing stones. When the mob forced open the front door, Lee and his men immediately opened fire, wounding several mob leaders and killing another.

City magistrates called out two companies of militia under Brig. Gen. John Stricker to restore order. A cavalry troop under Maj. William Barney was also dispatched to the scene, but nobody in authority evinced any determined resolve to challenge the mob. Indeed, Stricker's response was so nonchalant as to suggest his sympathies were with the assailants. At daylight, Mayor Edward Johnson and General Stricker reached a truce with the defenders, some of whom were seriously injured. The authorities guaranteed the Federalists safe conduct to the county jail, where all would answer to charges of murder. They were also promised military protection while in custody.

The defenders marched the mile to the jail surrounded by Stricker's militia. The mob pelted this makeshift parade with cobblestones before turning to its destructive business of ransacking Hanson's offices while militiamen passively stood by. That night the mob gathered outside the county jail and intimidated the guard at the gate. When he allowed them to enter, the frightened prisoners elected to try their luck with flight. As they rushed out of the jail, some escaped by mingling with the mob, but others were waylaid

to face an ugly, extended beating marked by hideous torture. Lee was crippled for the rest of a life shortened by injuries sustained that night—he would die in 1818. Lingan, 70 years old, died at the hands of the people deaf to his pleas for mercy and indifferent to his reminders of his service in the Revolution. Alexander Hanson's injuries were so dire that he would die in 1819 at only 33 years of age.

The Maryland legislature later conducted an investigation into the affair and issued a stinging report criticizing the negligence of city officials. Prominent Maryland Republicans, however, blamed the publishers of the *Federal Republican*. The paper was condemned as treasonable, and its fate was mourned only by its political supporters. The city of Baltimore produced its own report that whitewashed the affair with scores of euphemisms and ended by exculpating authorities of any neglect or wrongdoing. Mob atrocities were thus overlooked in Baltimore and elsewhere. In some circles, in fact, such behavior was applauded as nothing more than a patriotic gesture of support for Pres. James Madison's call to arms. The Baltimore Riots had an icy effect on Federalist dissent, not only in Maryland but throughout the nation.

—*Charles F. Howlett*

See also: Hanson, Alexander Contee; Lee, Henry; Stricker, John
Further Reading

Cassell, Frank A. "The Great Baltimore Riot of 1812." *Maryland Historical Magazine* 70 (1975): 241–259.

Fischer, David Hackett. *The Revolution of American Conservatism: The Federalist Party in the Era of Jeffersonian Democracy.* New York: Harper & Row, 1965.

Hickey, Donald R. "The Darker Side of Democracy: The Baltimore Riots of 1812." *Maryland Historian* 7 (1976): 1–14.

White, Patrick C.T. *A Nation on Trial: The War of 1812.* New York: John Wiley & Sons, 1965.

BANGOR, MAINE
See Castine, Maine

BARATARIAN PIRATES

U.S. officials often described a lawless maritime organization operating from the Gulf Coast of Louisiana as being composed of pirates. The men actually were privateers operating under letters-of-marque from France, republican

Cartagena, and other Latin American revolutionary governments. They used the so-called Island of Barataria and other isolated Louisiana coastal areas as their base. Barataria is land that extends west from the mouth of the Mississippi River to the Bayou Lafourche and south from New Orleans to the Gulf of Mexico. From that location the Baratarians operated a prosperous smuggling ring supplying contraband goods, including slaves, to the settlers of the region.

First meeting as a smugglers' association in 1805, this band was composed of men of various nationalities and ultimately led by the brothers Pierre and Jean Lafitte; other influential members included Dominique Youx (also known as Dominique You, Alexander Frederic, Frederic You), Vincent Gambie, Louis Chighizola, and Renato Beluche. Their base on the island of Grand Terre by 1810 included 40 warehouses, slave pens, a hospital, residences, and a fort with cannon. Conservative estimates put the Baratarian force at 3,000, but it probably numbered more than 5,000 men. The Baratarians coordinated an elaborate network of ships, warehouses, and depots. They boldly maintained warehouses in the Crescent City.

In the years before the War of 1812, the Baratarians plundered U.S., English, Spanish, and neutral merchantmen. They disregarded international neutrality laws by seizing any vessel that could yield a profit, especially Spanish slave ships bound for Cuba. The U.S. Navy in the Gulf found it impossible to prevent the illegal importation and consumption of contraband goods supplied by the Baratarians. After the beginning of the war, their piratical activities subsided as British naval forces constantly patrolled the Gulf Coast and U.S. gunboats scoured its many estuaries.

The U.S. Navy and revenue service fought a minor conflict with the Baratarians beginning in the fall of 1812. In November, U.S. dragoons commanded by Capt. Andrew Hunter Holmes ambushed several pirogues loaded with contraband, taking the Lafitte brothers prisoner in the struggle. The following year, in October 1813, revenue officials unsuccessfully attacked a Baratarian cargo. A federal agent was killed in that encounter. In January 1814, the pirates captured a group of revenue agents and killed customs agent John B. Stout during the attack. So while the United States had been fighting a war with Britain for two and a half years, the most significant action along the Gulf Coast had taken place against these pirates.

On 16 September 1814, Master-Commandant Daniel Patterson and Col. Robert Ross, wanting to break the pirates' power, led a joint army-navy expedition against Barataria Bay. The U.S. force met little resistance and seized several privateers and prizes as well as 80 prisoners, including Renato Beluche and Dominique Youx. During the melee, Lt. Thomas ap Catesby Jones boarded one of the

schooners to extinguish a fire that had already done considerable damage. Apparently, the Baratarians left a quantity of powder in the schooner's open cabin, hoping the explosion would destroy all vessels.

Two weeks before the U.S. assault on Barataria, Royal Navy captain Nicholas Lockyer, commanding the sloop *Sophie*, delivered dispatches to Jean Lafitte proposing an alliance between the pirates and British forces. Lafitte secretly advised Louisiana governor William Claiborne about the British offer, however, and proposed instead that Baratarians help the Americans. Claiborne sent copies to Maj. Gen. Andrew Jackson. Thus, U.S. officials learned of British plans against New Orleans, and Lafitte declined the British offer.

Jackson initially refused the offer of help from the "hellish banditti," but after learning of the defeat of U.S. gunboats on Lake Borgne on 14 December, he realized New Orleans needed more defensive assistance. As British forces prepared their assault, the Louisiana legislature passed a resolution providing amnesty for any Baratarian who aided in the defense of New Orleans. The pirates in jail were released, Jean Lafitte offered his services to Jackson, and Baratarian powder and shot were delivered to U.S. troops. Some 300 to 400 Baratarians served at Forts Bayou St. John, Petites Coquilles, and St. Philip; others formed an artillery company that saw considerable action at Chalmette on 8 January 1815. In fact, Baratarian men and resources significantly helped Jackson in his defense of the city. The supplies they provided helped ensure a U.S. victory.

In February 1815, Pres. James Madison pardoned the Lafitte brothers and the Baratarians in recognition for their services at the Battle of New Orleans. Afterward, although many of the privateers/pirates returned to peaceful pursuits, others resumed their lawless activities in the Gulf. Some began filibustering against Spanish colonies, using Galveston, Texas, as a base of operations. After the War of 1812, increased British and U.S. naval patrols worked for a decade to end the Baratarian threat in the Gulf. By 1825 the age of piracy in that region had ended.

—*Gene A. Smith*

See also: Lafitte, Jean; Louisiana; New Orleans, Battle of
Further Reading
Arthur, Stanley Clisby. *Jean Lafitte, Gentleman Rover.* New Orleans: Harmanson, 1952.
De Grummond, Jane Lucas. *The Baratarians and the Battle of New Orleans.* Baton Rouge, LA: Legacy Publishing, 1961.
———. *Renato Beluche: Smuggler, Privateer and Patriot, 1780–1860.* Baton Rouge: Louisiana State University Press, 1983.

Faye, Stanley. "The Great Stroke of Pierre Laffite." *Louisiana Historical Quarterly* 23 (1940): 733–826

Gayarre, Charles. "Historical Sketch of Pierre and Jean Lafitte; The Famous Smugglers of Louisiana." *Magazine of American History* 10 (1883).

Latour, A. Lacarriere. *Historical Memoir of the War in West Florida and Louisiana in 1814–15*. N.p., 1816. Reprint, 1864.

Vogel, Robert C. "Jean Lafitte, the Baratarians, and the Historical Geography of Piracy in the Gulf of Mexico." *Gulf Coast Historical Review* 5 (1990): 63–77.

BARCLAY, ROBERT HERIOT
1786–1837
British naval officer

Born on 18 September 1786, the son of the Reverend Peter Barclay, minister at Kettle Manse, Fifeshire, Scotland, Robert Barclay entered the Royal Navy as an 11-year-old midshipman posted to HMS *Anson* (44 guns) and, in February 1805, to Lord Nelson's HMS *Victory*. As acting lieutenant in HMS *Swiftsure* (74 guns), Barclay fought at Trafalgar on 21 October 1805 and helped to rescue 170 men of the crippled French *Redoubtable* in the ensuing gale. He served on board HMS *Diana* (38 guns) during 1808 in the English channel, and in November 1809 he lost his left arm during an attack on a French convoy. Between July 1810 and October 1812 he remained a lieutenant on the North American station in the schooner *Bream*, the small frigate *Æolus*, the sloop *Tartarus*, and the frigate *Iphigenia*.

In April 1813, Barclay was one of three naval lieutenants appointed by Adm. Sir John Borlase Warren to the Great Lakes station, but Sir James Lucas Yeo arrived to supersede him. After declining command of the St. Lawrence River gunboats, Barclay was appointed to command the Canadian Provincial Marine squadron on Lake Erie.

With Barclay at Amherstburg, Essex County, in July were 7 British seamen; Captain Robert Finnis, who arrived in late July; 108 members of the Canadian Provincial Marine; 54 of the Royal Newfoundland Fencibles; and 106 soldiers of the 41st Foot. Thirty-six sailors joined Barclay later. Commander in Chief Sir George Prevost informed Barclay and Fort Malden's army commander, Brig. Gen. Henry Procter, that "the ordnance and the naval stores you require must be taken from the Enemy whose resources on Lake Erie must become yours." Indeed, British guns, ammunition, and seamen were in short supply, and provisions were virtually exhausted. Desperate for supplies, Barclay sailed 10 September 1813 to engage his opposite number, Master Commandant Oliver Hazard Perry.

Barclay's six-vessel squadron, headed by the newly built ship HMS *Detroit* and the smaller HMS *Queen Charlotte*, was much inferior to Perry's nine vessels, spearheaded by the powerful 22-gun brigs USS *Lawrence* and USS *Niagara*. Perry's total firepower outgunned Barclay's vessels by 1,536 pounds to 887 pounds (57.7 percent) and in broadside weight by 936 to 496 pounds (52.9 percent). That calculated to a U.S. advantage of 304 to 208 pounds in long guns and 632 to 288 pounds in carronades. Barclay's force nonetheless compelled Perry's flagship USS *Lawrence* to surrender, and when Barclay retired, badly injured, he believed the battle won. Perry brought up his second fresh brig, USS *Niagara*, however, and commanding from her deck quickly compelled the damaged and entangled British vessels to surrender. Every British officer was either killed or wounded.

The battle confirmed Perry's command of the lake gained in August, opened the way for Gen. William Henry Harrison's invasion of Upper Canada in October, and redeemed the loss of Michilimackinac and Detroit in July and August 1812. Barclay returned to England, where a court-martial exonerated him, but not until 1824 was he posted to another vessel. He married Agnes Cossar of Westminster on 11 August 1814 and fathered several children. Barclay died on 8 May 1837.

—*Frederick C. Drake*

See also: Lake Erie Campaign; Perry, Oliver Hazard

Further Reading

Barclay, R. H. "Commander Barclay's Account of the Battle of Lake Erie." *Journal of American History* 8 (1914): 123–128.

Buckie, Robert. "'His Majesty's Flag Has Not Been Tarnished': The Role of Robert Heriot Barclay." *Journal of Erie Studies* 17, no. 2 (Fall 1988): 85–102.

Burt, Blanche A. "Sketch of Robert Heriot Barclay, R. N." *Ontario Historical Society Papers and Records* 14 (1916): 169–178.

"The Court Martial of Commander Robert Barclay: Important Documentary Evidence Concerning the Battle of Lake Erie Never Before Published." *Journal of American History* 8 (1914): 129–146.

Drake, Frederick C. "A Loss of Mastery: The British Squadron on Lake Erie, May–September, 1813." *Journal of Erie Studies* 17 (Fall 1988): 47–75.

Marshall, John. *Royal Naval Biography*. Vol. 3, pt. 1, pp. 186–195. London: Rees, Orme, Brown and Green, 1831.

Peckham, Howard. "Commodore Perry's Captive." *Ohio History* 72 (1963): 220–227.

Stacey, Charles P. "Another Look at the Battle of Lake Erie." *Canadian Historical Review* 39 (1958): 41–51.

Welsh, William J., and David C. Skaggs, eds. *War on the Great Lakes: Essays Commemorating the 175th Anniversary of the Battle of Lake Erie.* Kent, OH: Kent State University Press, 1991.

BARCLAY, THOMAS
1753–1830
British consul general; British commissioner on prisoner exchanges, 1812–1814

Thomas Barclay, son of Henry Barclay, rector of Trinity Church, New York, was a Columbia College graduate who studied the law under John Jay. Thomas Barclay served in the American Revolution under British generals William Howe and Henry Clinton and rose to the rank of major. British defeat forced Barclay to flee with his family to Nova Scotia. There he continued to serve the Crown as Speaker of the Nova Scotia assembly and adjutant general of the militia.

Between 1796 and 1828, Thomas Barclay ably served the British government in the United States as a commissioner under the Jay Treaty, as a commissioner for the care and exchange of prisoners, and as a commissioner under articles four and five of the Treaty of Ghent (1814–1828). From 1801 to 1812, Barclay was also the British consul general in New York, a post that was next in importance to the British minister in Washington. As consul general, Barclay wrote strong letters to London protesting British impressment of U.S. sailors and successfully interceded to win the release of U.S. natives held on British men-of-war. Thomas Barclay's letters affirmed his sincere conviction that the Royal Navy should stop impressing U.S. seamen. He cited specific instances of those who were undoubtedly U.S. citizens being forced to serve on British ships. Nevertheless, in 1807, an angry New York mob attacked Barclay's residence to protest British interference with U.S. trade.

The declaration of war by the United States in 1812 ceased Barclay's duties as consul general. His U.S. birth and extensive contacts with political leaders of the United States, however, led the British Crown to appoint Barclay as His Majesty's commissioner on prisoner exchanges, a post he held until the end of the war (1812 to 1814). Barclay's new duties brought him to Washington, D.C., but fears that Barclay could be a British spy forced his confinement in nearby Bladensburg, Maryland. When the British advanced on Washington in 1814, Barclay reluctantly left Bladensburg for Baltimore only two hours before the fighting began there.

A sincere and devout Christian, Barclay showed such compassion for the poor and provided such honorable service for the Crown that he won praise both from George III and George IV. The crown also awarded him a substantial Crown pension. Barclay chose to remain in New York as a Treaty of Ghent commissioner. He died there in 1830.

—*William A. Paquette*

Further Reading

Dunn, Mary A. "The Career of Thomas Barclay." Ph.D. diss., Fordham University, 1974.

Lord, Walter. *The Dawn's Early Light.* New York: W. W. Norton, 1972.

BARKER, JACOB
1779–1871
New York merchant and banker

Jacob Barker was born to Robert Barker and Sarah Folger Barker on Swan Island, Massachusetts (Maine). When only an infant, Jacob Barker lost his father and was raised by his Quaker mother on Nantucket. At the age of 16, Barker enlisted as a seaman on a merchant vessel headed for New York City. Once there, he left his brief seafaring career to become a clerk. By judicious saving and investing, he established his own firm when only 22. After weathering some financial difficulties, he emerged as a power in New York financial circles.

Unlike many of the merchants of New York, Barker staunchly supported Thomas Jefferson and the Democratic Republican Party. He opposed war with Great Britain because of the financial disruption it promised, but once war was declared he became one of James Madison's staunchest supporters. Barker practiced costly patriotism, for the war did in fact destroy his shipping business. Nevertheless, he devoted himself to raising money for the government. Those labors required him to spend much time in Washington, D.C., and he became close with high officers of the government, including President Madison.

As the British approached the capital in August 1814, Barker reportedly made Madison a strange offer: He would personally blow up the capitol rather than allow it to fall into British hands. As President Madison rode with the military defenders of the city on 24 August, Barker was one of several people who stopped at the executive mansion to urge Dolley Madison to leave Washington. With several other friends, he tried to remove Gilbert Stuart's large portrait of George Washington from its frame so it could be taken to safety.

After Mrs. Madison left, Barker stayed at the mansion to save what valuables he could from looters and the British. A half hour after Mrs. Madison's departure, the president arrived. In a surreal scene, Barker, Madison, and several aides sat for a while, numbly relating stories about the day's events. Finally, the president also left the city. Barker remained, though, packing away items and finding a cart for the cumbersome Washington portrait. At last, he left the city to take the painting to a farmhouse outside Georgetown.

The next day, Barker rode to Montgomery Court House, the headquarters of what was left of the retreating U.S. army. When he learned that the men there had no rations, Barker immediately rode with Robert De Peyser to Baltimore. With his own money he purchased several wagon loads of food and paid for their transport to the U.S. camp.

After the British evacuation of Washington, Barker returned the Washington portrait to the executive mansion. He was proud of the part he had played in saving it. His efforts to help finance the war had produced mixed results, but Barker was a quiet patriot. He sacrificed his business and gave tirelessly of his time for his country in its greatest hour of need. His business fortunes recovered after the war. He died in Philadelphia at the age of 92.

—*Jeanne T. Heidler and David S. Heidler*

See also: Madison, Dolley Payne; Washington, British Capture of
Further Reading
Barker, Jacob. *Incidents in the Life of Jacob Barker*. Washington, DC: N.p., 1855.

BARLOW, JOEL
1754–1812
Poet; minister to France, 1811–1812

Born in Redding, Connecticut, Barlow was a leading poet of the Early National period and served the United States as a diplomat. A Yale graduate, he spent three years as chaplain for the Third Massachusetts Brigade during the American Revolution. As a member of the conservative "Hartford Wits," Barlow contributed to *The Anarchiad* (1786–1787). His other works included *The Vision of Columbus* (1787), *The Hasty Pudding* (1796), and *The Columbiad* (1807).

Barlow spent much of his life overseas. By the 1790s, he had become a dedicated republican. While in London, Barlow joined the Society for Constitutional Information. He fervently defended the revolution in France and became an honorary French citizen. Additionally, Barlow served as U.S. consul to Algiers, ransoming some U.S. sailors held captive by the Barbary pirates.

In 1811, Barlow became U.S. minister to France, succeeding John Armstrong. The previous year, Napoleon had craftily suggested that France would cease enforcing the Berlin and Milan Decrees if the United States stopped trading with Britain. Yet French depredations against U.S. shipping had continued. So the poet-diplomat had two major goals: first, to receive payment for the illegal seizure of U.S. ships; second, to secure normal commercial relations with the French.

For a year, Barlow could not bring a change in Bonaparte's policy. Then in the spring of 1812, the British appeared inclined to repeal the Orders in Council if the French officially withdrew the Berlin and Milan Decrees. Barlow tried to extract a formal pronouncement from Napoleon's government that France had not placed the United States under the stipulations of the Berlin and Milan Decrees since November 1810. After some effort, he managed to obtain an equivocal though formal note from the French government to that effect. The USS *Wasp* carried this document from Barlow to Jonathan Russell, the U.S. chargé d'affaires in London. The dispatch helped to bring about the British revocation of the Orders in Council that summer, although the action was too late to avert the declaration of war by the United States.

When Napoleon undertook his Russian invasion, Barlow accepted the emperor's invitation for a meeting and traveled from Paris to Wilna, Lithuania, Bonaparte's winter headquarters. Napoleon's purpose for the meeting remains unknown because it never occurred. Barlow, taken ill by the rigors of his journey, completed his final poem, a condemnation of the horrible devastation caused by Napoleon's campaigns that was entitled "Advice to a Raven in Russia." He concluded with the wish that the world would "hurl from his blood-built throne this king of woes." Barlow rapidly succumbed to pneumonia and died on 26 December 1812. He was buried in Poland.

—*S. Kirk Bane*

Further Reading
Brant, Irving. "Joel Barlow, Madison's Stubborn Minister." *William and Mary Quarterly* 25 (October 1958): 438–451.
Ford, Arthur L. *Joel Barlow*. New York: Twayne, 1971.

Woodress, James. *A Yankee's Odyssey: The Life of Joel Barlow.* Philadelphia: Lippincott, 1958.

BARNEY, JOSHUA
1759–1818
U.S. naval officer

Joshua Barney

Joshua Barney was an energetic, capable naval commander in the War of 1812. Born in Baltimore County, Maryland, on 6 July 1759, Barney went to sea at an early age, commanding his first vessel while still in his teens. He served with distinction in the Revolutionary War as a captain of privateers and in the Continental Navy. He was an officer in the French Navy from 1796 to 1802 and left that service a commodore. Returning to Baltimore, in May 1812 he sold his home and retired to a farm at Elkridge.

When the War of 1812 began, Barney despaired of a navy command because of the loss of his seniority while he was in French service, so he turned to privateering. Late in 1812, in one of the most successful privateering ventures of the war, his 12-gun *Rossie* took 18 British vessels, two of them in hard-fought engagements. Unfortunately for Barney, financial return from the cruise was slight, and he again retired.

In the summer of 1813, Barney drafted a comprehensive defense scheme for the Chesapeake Bay area and sent it to Secretary of the Navy William Jones. Much of the bay and its tributaries were navigable only to shallow-draft vessels, and the British often had to rely on barges. Barney's plan was to build a flotilla of shallow-draft oared vessels capable of seeking out the British barges when they were away from the cover of Royal Navy warships. In August 1813 Jones responded by offering Barney command of an upper Chesapeake flotilla at Baltimore. To avoid offending high-ranking naval officers, Jones gave Barney no regular or permanent rank in the navy; his commission was that of sailing master commandant—"captain in the Flotilla Services of the United States."

Initially, Barney's flotilla consisted of eight barges and galleys built for the navy at Baltimore, some city barges, and other vessels to be supplied by the navy. He added to this by purchase and construction. The British, meanwhile, increased their presence in the bay and also built barges. When informed of the British activities, Barney's reaction was, "I am anxious to be at them."

Beginning in April, Barney made several attempts to engage the British. Unfortunately for the Americans, the end result was that Barney's flotilla was bottled up in the Patuxent River. In June the flotilla fought several battles with the British but could not escape the Patuxent, and a British advance by water and land forced Barney to destroy his boats on August 22. He and his men then marched to Washington.

Barney's flotillamen and marines were defending one of two bridges over the eastern branch of the Potomac that guarded access to the navy yard when news came of the British advance. In a conference with Pres. James Madison, Barney insisted on marching to Bladensburg. In the Battle of Bladensburg, fought on 24 August, Barney and his flotillamen and marines were virtually the only Americans to gain credit. Barney directed the fire of a battery of five guns. He was wounded in the thigh by a musket ball and taken prisoner. Later the city of Washington presented him with a sword of honor in recognition of his achievement.

Barney died at Pittsburgh on 1 December 1818.

—Spencer C. Tucker

See also: Bladensburg, Battle of; Chesapeake Bay Campaign, 1813–1814; Patuxent River, Battles of

Further Reading
Footner, Hulbert. *Sailor of Fortune: The Life and Adventures of Commodore Barney, U.S.N.* New York: Harper, 1940.
Paine, Ralph D. *Joshua Barney: A Forgotten Hero of Blue Water.* New York: Century, 1924.
Shomette, Donald G. *Flotilla: Battle for the Patuxent.* Solomons, MD: The Calvert Marine Museum Press, 1981.

BARRIE, ROBERT
1774–1841
British naval officer

Born on 5 May 1774 at St. Augustine, Florida, Robert Barrie was the son of Dr. Robert Barrie of Sanquhar, Scotland, and Dorothea Gardner. The younger Barrie entered the Royal Navy on 5 June 1788 as a midshipman and served from 1790 to 1795 on board HMS *Discovery,* Capt. George Vancouver's surveying expedition of the North American Pacific coast. Barrie was promoted to lieutenant in 1795, served in the West Indies in 1800, and earned promotion to commander on 23 October 1801 and to captain on May 1802. He enjoyed great success on HMS *Pomone* in the Mediterranean and captured Napoleon's brother, Lucien Bonaparte, in October 1811.

Barrie sailed "the old tub" HMS *Grampus* (50 guns) to Barbados in January 1813, then transferred to HMS *Dragon* (74 guns), which he happily described as "as desirable a ship as any in the Navy." He noted that "if Nathan [the United States] does not make peace we shall have some fun with his sea ports this summer." In April, he was off the Delaware and Sandy Hook seeking USS *Constitution* and USS *Congress.* He rejoined Sir John Borlase Warren's fleet in the Chesapeake and predicted that "Nathan will have very little trade." Remembering the exploits of his old command, he brashly stated that HMS *Pomone* "would have done Nathan's business."

In Chesapeake Bay during 1814, as part of Rear Adm. George Cockburn's advanced squadron, Barrie took over 85 prizes and worried about "a dirty peace." Later, he led the attack on Castine, Maine, and supervised the considerable destruction of Bangor.

On 24 October 1816, he married Julia Wharton Ingilby and went to live in France. From 1819 to 1825 and from 1827 to 1834 he was senior commander, naval forces, Great Lakes, then returned to a knighthood in England. Barrie died on 7 June 1841.

—*Frederick C. Drake*

See also: Castine, Maine; Chesapeake Bay Campaign, 1813–1814
Further Reading
Brock, T. L. "Commissioner Robert Barrie and His Family in Kingston, 1819–1834." *Historic Kingston* 23 (1975): 1–18.
———. "H. M. Dock Yard, Kingston under Commissioner Robert Barrie, 1819–1834." *Historic Kingston* 16 (1968): 3–22.
———. "Sir Robert Barrie." *Dictionary of Canadian Biography.* Vol. 7, *1836–1850,* pp. 50–51. Toronto: University of Toronto Press, 1979.
MacLaren, D. H. "British Naval Officers of a Century Ago. Barrie and Its Streets—A History of Their Names." *Ontario Historical Society Papers and Records* 17 (1919): 106–112.
Marshall, John. *Royal Naval Biography.* Vol. 2, pt. 2, pp. 729–735. London: Hurst, Rees, Orme, Brown and Green, 1824.
Spurr, John W. "The Royal Navy's Presence in Kingston. Part 1: 1813–1836." *Historic Kingston* 25 (1977): 63–77.

BARRON, JAMES
1789–1851
U.S. naval officer

James Barron was born in Virginia in 1789 to a family rich in naval heritage. His father, James Barron, was the captain of a merchant ship and had commanded a portion of the naval forces of Virginia during the Revolution. His elder brother, Samuel Barron, also distinguished himself in the navy and eventually attained the rank of commodore. James followed these examples, and after serving as an apprentice aboard his father's ship for several years, he entered the U.S. Navy as a lieutenant. He was commissioned on 9 March 1798 and was so successful on his first tour aboard the frigate *United States,* commanded by Commodore John Barry, that he was promoted to captain in 1799. It is noteworthy that while serving on the *United States,* Barron commanded a young sailor named Stephen Decatur, who noticed his courage in action and would have many future opportunities to comment on it.

After his promotion, Captain Barron was given command of the frigate *Essex* in the squadron under the command of his brother. This squadron was a part of the fleet under Commodore Edward Preble bound for the Mediterranean Sea to deal with the Barbary pirates. When his brother took over for Commodore Preble as commander in chief of the naval forces in the European region, Barron was given command of the larger vessel USS *President.* He remained in the Mediterranean for the

James Barron

next five years, serving bravely and revealing a natural seamanship.

In 1806, Barron was promoted to the rank of commodore, and the following year he was assigned to command the USS *Chesapeake*, a posting that would haunt him for the rest of his life. At Norfolk, the *Chesapeake* was hurriedly outfitted with an inexperienced crew and poorly prepared equipment. Nevertheless, the ship set sail on 22 June 1807, with Master Commandant Charles Gordon directing its navigation. Once it had cleared to open water, the *Chesapeake* was waylaid by the British frigate *Leopard*. In addition to her disadvantage in men and equipment, the *Chesapeake*'s 36 guns could hardly have matched the *Leopard*'s 50.

The commander of the British vessel demanded the return of four British deserters he alleged were aboard the ship. When Barron refused to comply with this demand, the British frigate opened fire on the *Chesapeake*, killing three and wounding 18, one of these being Commodore Barron himself. Efforts to get the ship ready for battle were belated and ineffectual, so Barron ordered the flag lowered. The *Chesapeake* had fired only one gun. The British boarded the U.S. ship and took away four crewmen. The British government later disavowed the actions of the British commander of the *Leopard*, but the U.S. govern-

ment and, more specifically, the navy were not so forgiving of Commodore Barron.

In January 1808, Barron was court-martialed on charges of disgraceful and premature surrender of his ship. He contended, however, that the negligence of the navy had rendered him powerless to resist the overwhelming strength of the British vessel. The court-martial, which was presided over by Capt. John Rodgers, acquitted Commodore Barron of cowardice and some other minor charges, but it found him guilty for "neglecting, on the probability of an engagement, to clear his ship for action." This verdict caused Barron's suspension for five years without pay. He would never again hold a significant command in the U.S. Navy. He spent the next ten years abroad.

Barron returned to the United States after the War of 1812 with the intention of reentering the navy. Fellow officers, however, were vehement in their criticism of his conduct, especially his absence from the country during the war. Barron considered Commodore Stephen Decatur to be the ringleader of those opposing him and challenged him to a duel. The duel took place on 22 March 1820 in Bladensburg, Maryland. Commodore Barron was severely wounded in the thigh, but Decatur was fatally wounded and died several hours later. Decatur's death only resulted in opinion turning further against Barron. He died in Norfolk, Virginia, on 21 April 1851.

—*John Barron*

See also: Chesapeake-Leopard Affair; Decatur, Stephen, Jr.
Further Reading
Stevens, William O. *An Affair of Honor: The Biography of Commodore James Barron, U.S.N.* Norfolk: Norfolk County Historical Society of Chesapeake, Virginia, in cooperation with the Earl Gregg Swem Library of the College of William and Mary, 1969.

BATHURST, HENRY, THIRD EARL BATHURST
1762–1834
British statesman

Lord Bathurst was an accomplished and high-ranking minister throughout the reign of George III. In Lord Liverpool's ministry, he functioned as secretary for war and the colonies. The post made him directly responsible for the war with the United States. In 1812 and 1813, the Peninsular War was Bathurst's primary concern; Britain could spare reinforcements for Canada only in driblets. He also ordered minor punitive expeditions in Chesapeake Bay that culminated in the sack of Hampton and Havre de Grace. Following the fall of Napoleon and the release of British military and naval assets for war in North America, Bathurst's policies for the conflict with the United States became more serious.

In the spring of 1814, Bathurst authorized military occupation of islands in Passamaquoddy Bay on the Maine–New Brunswick border. He expected that the United States eventually would concede to these as British holdings. By June, the influx of Peninsula veterans to Canada was sufficient, Bathurst believed, to have Gov. Gen. George Prevost begin offensive operations before summer's end. Prevost was to reduce Sacket's Harbor, New York, and destroy the U.S. naval establishments on both Lake Erie and Lake Champlain. Furthermore, British forces were to regain Detroit and restore the Michigan Territory to the Indians as a buffer state. Only in this manner, Bathurst felt, could Britain assure the "ultimate security" of His Majesty's North American possessions. Considering the relative weakness of the United States in 1814, his goals seemed attainable.

Unfortunately for the British, their defeats at Plattsburg and Baltimore in September 1814 dashed Bathurst's plans. He nonetheless wanted *uti possidetis* (state of possession) to be the basis for peace negotiations at Ghent. This stance insured British control of Fort Niagara, Mackinac, and northern Maine as territorial concessions. The U.S. commissioners flatly rejected these conditions, and on 3 November 1814, Bathurst sought advice from the duke of Wellington. The duke signaled his willingness to go to Canada if ordered but cautioned Bathurst that without control of the lakes little could be accomplished. Furthermore, Wellington said that considering recent defeats, Britain was not justified in demanding territorial concessions; these were simply not worth the price of prolonging the war. Considering the explosive situation at the Congress of Vienna, both Wellington and Lord Liverpool wanted the U.S. affair concluded quickly. Bathurst relented and authorized the British commissioners at Ghent to adopt status quo antebellum as their negotiating position. One month later the treaty was signed.

Bathurst, despite his wartime bellicosity toward the United States, was cordial and moderate toward John Quincy Adams while negotiating over the fisheries and boundary matters in 1817. He remained a visible presence in British politics for many years and from 1828 to 1830 served as lord president of the Council under the duke of Wellington's ministry.

—*John C. Fredriksen*

See also: Castlereagh, Viscount, Robert Stewart
Further Reading
Bickley, Francis, ed. *Report on the Manuscripts of Earl Bathurst.* London: T. B. Hart, 1923.
Grenville, Richard. *Memoirs of the Court and Cabinets of George the III.* 4 vols. London: Hurst and Blackett, 1853–1855.
Perkins, Bradford. *Castlereagh and Adams: England and the United States, 1812–1823.* Berkeley: University of California Press, 1964.
Wellesley, Arthur, ed. *Supplementary Dispatches, Correspondence and Memoranda of Field Marshal Arthur Duke of Wellington K.G.* 15 vols. London: N.p., 1858–1872.

BAYARD, JAMES ASHETON
1767–1815
Federalist congressman and senator; diplomat

Born as the second son of the surgeon James Bayard and his wife, Agnes, on 28 July 1767, young James Bayard was reared on the family estate at Bohemia Manor, Maryland. After the death of his father in 1770 and of his mother in 1774, James went to live with his uncle, John Bayard, and in 1784 graduated from the College of New Jersey (Princeton), demonstrating great interest in history, philosophy, and jurisprudence. That same year Bayard embarked upon a career in law, first studying under Joseph Reed and then under Reed's partner, the eminent Philadelphia attorney Jared Ingersoll; in 1787 Bayard was admitted to the bar in both Philadelphia and New Castle, Delaware. In 1795, he married Ann Bassett, the daughter of Delaware's chief justice Richard Bassett, a prominent Federalist. Between 1797 and 1801, Bayard served as Delaware's congressman. He denounced France in 1798 for its intimidating conduct during the XYZ Affair, supported that year the Alien and Sedition Acts, and, as leader of the minority party, spoke against Republican efforts to repeal the 1801 Judiciary Act.

Bayard served as a senator from Delaware between 1805 and 1813 and became involved with major issues concerning the War of 1812. In 1807 the Delawarean denounced the British attack on the USS *Chesapeake*, maintaining that the "honor, rights, and independence" of the United States must be preserved. Between 1809 and 1812, Bayard revealed a moderate stance about Republican measures di-

James Asheton Bayard

rected against England. He nonetheless believed that the 1809 Non-Intercourse Act was ruining the U.S. economy. A year later, he stated that the Madison administration should enter into negotiations with the British over the issue of impressment. Yet even as Bayard labeled Republican expansionists as "warmongers," he denounced the British for violating the neutral rights of the United States and called for measures to strengthen the U.S. Navy.

Two years later, on 16 June 1812, Bayard delivered a speech to the Senate in which he maintained that the United States was not prepared for war, that an embargo should be imposed against England for 90 days, and that efforts should be made to reconcile U.S. and British differences over the issues of neutral rights and impressment. Yet the pleas of this moderate Federalist were ignored, and war against Great Britain was proclaimed two days later.

Bayard participated in diplomatic activities of the War of 1812. After Czar Alexander I offered to mediate the Anglo-American conflict, President Madison, who respected the moderate views of the Delaware Federalist, appointed Bayard in April 1813 to serve as a commissioner in St. Petersburg with Albert Gallatin and John Quincy Adams. Bayard and Gallatin received instructions from Secretary of State James Monroe that an Anglo-American pact must contain a clause about impressment. They sailed on the ship *Neptune* for Russia on 9 May 1813 and reached St. Petersburg on 21 July. After several meetings with Russian foreign minister Count Romanzoff, Bayard on 21 September observed that "the object of our mission was quite distant." After Britain in January 1814 made clear its rejection of Russian mediation efforts and soon thereafter agreed to direct negotiations with the United States, Bayard went to Ghent to serve as a representative during the Anglo-American peace conference. At Ghent, Bayard especially favored the abolition of impressment, U.S. rights to North Atlantic fisheries, and the navigation of U.S. ships on the Mississippi River. The Delawarean signed the Treaty of Ghent, which was based on the principle of status quo antebellum and contained nothing about impressment and the rights of neutrals. He insisted, however, that the 1814 Peace of Christmas Eve was the most "favorable as could be expected under existing circumstances."

The entire episode took its toll on Bayard. He was quite ill when he arrived from England at Wilmington, Delaware, on 31 July 1815. He died six days later.

—*William Weisberger*

See also: Ghent, Treaty of
Further Reading
Borden, Morton. *The Federalism of James A. Bayard.* New York: Columbia University Press, 1955.
Donnan, Elizabeth, ed. *The Papers of James A. Bayard. Annual Report of the American Historical Association for the Year 1913.* Vol. 2. N.p., 1915.
Engelman, Fred L. *The Peace of Christmas Eve.* London: Hart-Davis, 1960.
Perkins, Bradford. *Castlereagh and Adams: England and the United States, 1812–1823.* Berkeley: University of California Press, 1964.
Stagg, J.C.A. *Mr. Madison's War: Politics, Diplomacy, and Warfare in the Early American Republic, 1783–1830.* Princeton: Princeton University Press, 1983.

BAYNES, EDWARD
d. 1829
British officer

Col. Edward Baynes served as one of Gen. Sir George Prevost's subordinate officers on the northeastern end of Lake Ontario in 1813 and continued to serve under Prevost for the remainder of the war as the general's adjutant general. Perhaps Baynes's most dubious distinction throughout the war was to serve as commander of the force that Prevost ordered to take Sacket's Harbor in May 1813. Though Prevost accompanied the expedition, Baynes had direct command of the 750-man contingent.

Transported by Adm. Sir James Yeo's squadron from Kingston on 27 May, the ships were close enough to the harbor on 28 May to disembark the men into smaller boats for the trip to the mainland. Coming ashore on Horse Island on the morning of 29 May, Baynes and his men had to traverse a narrow causeway before striking at the harbor. U.S. artillery had made the British landing uncomfortable, and their trip across the causeway would have been even more difficult had militia Brig. Gen. Jacob Brown put a more experienced force in front to challenge the British passage. Almost at the first shot from the British regulars, Brown's New York militia ran, allowing Baynes to move his men across the causeway with relative ease.

As Baynes moved toward town, however, Brown's regulars put up a much stiffer resistance, aided by their artillery. Baynes had no artillery, and Yeo's ships could not get close enough to help with the naval guns. After Baynes threw his men against the U.S. defenses for two hours, they were exhausted. Through a ruse, Brown coaxed some of the militia to move back toward the British lines, which convinced Prevost that the entire British force was in danger of envelopment. He ordered a retreat. Brown tried to cut off the withdrawal, but Baynes successfully guided his men back to their boats.

Following the failure at Sacket's Harbor, Baynes remained part of Prevost's staff for the remainder of the war. He achieved the rank of major general by the end of the conflict. As Prevost's adjutant general during the Plattsburg campaign, it fell to Baynes to order the withdrawal of British land forces after the British naval force had suffered defeat there.

—*Jeanne T. Heidler and David S. Heidler*

See also: Brown, Jacob J.; Prevost, George; Sacket's Harbor, Battle of
Further Reading
"The Battle of Sackett's Harbor." *Military and Naval Magazine of the United States* 1 (1833): 7–25.

BEANES, WILLIAM
1749–1828

The son of William and Mary (Bradley) Beanes, William Beanes was born near Croome, in Prince George's County, Maryland, on 24 January 1749. Nothing is known of his early years except that as a child of parents who had emigrated from Scotland and who became large landowners, he grew up in a comfortable rural environment. Throughout his life he spoke with a Scottish accent. Presumably he graduated from a public school, or he may have been educated by a private tutor. It is known that he began the study of medicine under one of the medical men in his neighborhood. As soon as he felt qualified, he began practicing medicine on his own. On 25 November 1773, he married Sarah Hawkins Hanson, the niece of John Hanson, who later became the president of the First Continental Congress.

Beanes was one of the leaders in Prince George's County who supported Boston's resistance to the Coercive Acts. After the battle of Lexington, he offered his services at a general hospital established in Philadelphia by the Continental Congress. In 1779 he bought property outside of the town of Upper Marlboro in Prince George's County, Maryland, built a home there and began practicing medicine in the area. He also engaged in farming and eventually became a major landowner and the proprietor of the local gristmill. By the end of the eighteenth century, he was regarded as an experienced practitioner of medicine, and in 1799 he was one of the founders of the Medical and Chirurgical Faculty of Maryland, a predecessor of the state Medical Board. His interest in religious matters showed in his work to establish the Trinity Protestant Episcopal Church in Upper Marlboro. When the church was organized in 1810, he was elected as its first senior warden.

In the War of 1812, Beanes would achieve some celebrity as a result of events during the British invasion of Maryland in the summer of 1814. When the British landed near Benedict, Maryland, and marched to Upper Marlboro, about 16 miles from Washington, they found the town mostly deserted except for its most prominent citizen, Dr. Beanes. The doctor offered Maj. Gen. Robert Ross the use of his home as a headquarters, and the general accepted it. This act of courtesy and the doctor's friendly manner—perhaps all springing from his Federalist political sentiments—apparently led Ross to conclude that the doctor was in sympathy with the British. The lack of any U.S. resistance in the town helped to confirm the idea that this was a safe area for the invaders.

After the British marched to Washington and burned some of the public buildings in the city, they again stopped briefly in Upper Marlboro before returning to their ships. When some British deserters began plundering small farms, Robert Bowie, a former governor of Maryland who owned property in the area, decided to do something about it. He enlisted Beanes's help, and the doctor persuaded several local people to join a makeshift constabulary. These citizens seized six or seven of the deserters and confined them in the local jail. One escaped and informed Ross about what had happened. Furious to think that he had been misled by the doctor's earlier hospitality and apparently believing that some sort of pledge of neutrality had been given or implied, Ross ordered the arrest of Beanes, Bowie, and four other men.

British soldiers seized Beanes and two of his guests at his home after midnight, scarcely giving him time to dress. General Ross subsequently released Bowie and the other citizens he had in custody, but he insisted on taking Beanes back to the British ships. Protests from U.S. Brig. Gen. William H. Winder proved fruitless. Some of the doctor's friends appealed to Francis Scott Key, a lawyer in Georgetown, D.C., to secure the release of Dr. Beanes. Key obtained the consent of Pres. James Madison, and in the company of John S. Skinner, the U.S. agent in charge of prisoner exchanges, the two boarded a flag of truce ship and proceeded down Chesapeake Bay in search of the British force.

They were received on board the flagship of Vice Adm. Sir Alexander Cochrane and met with General Ross. Ross refused to release Beanes and spoke harshly about the doctor. Skinner then gave Ross some letters from wounded British soldiers left behind after the Battle of Bladensburg that related the kind treatment they had received at the hands of the Americans. The letters touched Ross and softened his anger toward Beanes, who was now promised release, but not until after a planned attack on Baltimore. Key visited Beanes, finding him confined in the forward part of the flagship among British soldiers and sailors, who were subjecting him to rough treatment. No officer would speak to him, and he had not had a change of clothing since his arrest.

Released now from confinement, Beanes accompanied Key and Skinner to the truce ship where they awaited the outcome of the attack on Fort McHenry at the entrance of Baltimore's harbor. Throughout the night of 13 September 1814, the three men listened to Cochrane's booming cannon and swooshing Congreve Rockets and wondered about the fate of the fort. When daylight revealed that the fort was still in U.S. hands and that the British had broken off the attack and were withdrawing, Key had the inspiration for his famous "Star Spangled Banner." Beanes, Key, and Skinner were released and reached Baltimore on the evening of 16 September. Dr. Beanes's friends saw to it that he returned home safely.

Beanes spent the rest of his life at his home on Academy Hill in Upper Marlboro. His wife died in July 1822, and he died on 12 October 1828. The couple had no children.

In preparation for the centennial of the attack on Fort McHenry, a society was formed in 1913 to restore Beanes's tomb. Subsequently, historical markers were placed to identify his tomb and the site of his home.

—*Harold D. Langley*

See also: Baltimore, Battle of; Key, Francis Scott; Ross, Robert; Star-Spangled Banner, The; Upper Marlboro, Maryland; Washington, British Capture of

Further Reading

Magruder, Caleb Clark, Jr. "Dr. William Beanes, The Incidental Cause of the Authorship of the Star-Spangled Banner." *Records of the Columbia Historical Society* 22 (1919): 207–225.

BEAUMONT, WILLIAM
1785–1853
Army surgeon; renowned physiologist

William Beaumont was born in Lebanon, Connecticut, on 21 November 1785. As a young man, he moved to Champlain in northern New York, where he worked as a schoolteacher and in his brother's store. Immediately prior to the War of 1812, he studied medicine as an apprentice in St. Albans, Vermont, and in June 1812 was licensed to practice medicine and surgery by the Third Medical Society of Vermont.

In September 1812, Beaumont went to Plattsburg, New York, to volunteer as a surgeon's mate in the U.S. Army. He was assigned to the Sixth Regiment of U.S. Infantry. When Beaumont had started his medical training, he had also begun to keep medical and general journals. These were often rough and cursory, but they provide very useful information on medical conditions during the first year of the War of 1812.

Beaumont accompanied Gen. Henry Dearborn's forces north to the Canadian border in November 1812 and after their retreat remained with the Sixth Regiment in Plattsburg. He was shocked by the inadequate preparations for the care of the sick and wounded and was disappointed that there had been no effective U.S. military action on the Lake Champlain front. For a time in January 1813, he planned to return to private life and start a civilian practice in Plattsburg, but he remained in the army, and in March went with his regiment to Sacket's Harbor.

Beaumont was in the U.S. attack on York (Toronto), Upper Canada, in April 1813 and in his journal gives a dramatic description of the severe injuries inflicted on the U.S. troops by the British magazine explosion that killed the U.S. commander, Brig. Gen. Zebulon Pike. After the York attack, Beaumont sailed with the U.S. troops to the Niagara River and in May was with the vanguard that captured Fort George. After that engagement, he served in the U.S. military hospitals at Newark, Upper Canada, and Lewiston, New York.

Because none of Beaumont's journals for the last year and a half of the war exists, he is not a source for details on medical conditions in that period, although his letters give some information. He apparently accompanied Gen. James Wilkinson's expedition down the St. Lawrence late in 1813 and endured the rigors of the winter quarters at French Mills on the Salmon River. Beaumont's last major service in the War of 1812 was during the British attack on Plattsburg in September 1814. In that attack, he was attached to a U.S. artillery company and received favorable mention for his bravery.

In June 1815, Beaumont resigned from the army and entered private practice in Plattsburg. He re-enlisted in 1820, and at Mackinac in 1822 he was given the chance to achieve permanent fame when he was summoned to treat the French Canadian voyageur, Alexis St. Martin, who had suffered a severe wound in his stomach. Beaumont's ensuing research on human digestion earned him a lasting reputation as the first renowned physiologist in the United States. After leaving the army, Beaumont spent the last part of his life in St. Louis with his wife, Deborah Green Platt, and his three children. He died there on 25 April 1853.

—*Reginald Horsman*

See also: Medicine, Army; Pike, Zebulon Montgomery; York, Battle of

Further Reading

Myer, Jesse S. *Life and Letters of Dr. William Beaumont.* St. Louis: C. V. Mosby, 1912.

Nelson, Rodney B. *Beaumont: America's First Physiologist.* Geneva, IL: Grant House, 1990.

Pitcock, Cynthia DeHaven. "The Career of William Beaumont, 1785–1853: Science and the Self-Made Man in America." Ph.D. diss., Memphis State University, 1985.

BEAVER DAMS, BATTLE OF

24 June 1813

U.S. forces under Gen. Henry Dearborn took Fort George in late May 1813 and made a brief attempt to extend U.S. positions deeper into Canada but then pulled back to concentrate around Fort George. General Dearborn was ill much of the time, and Maj. Gen. Morgan Lewis was transferred to Sacket's Harbor, so day-to-day command of the troops around Fort George fell to Brig. Gen. John Boyd.

After consulting with the bedridden Dearborn, Boyd decided in late June 1813 to extend U.S. positions out from Fort George by driving the small British force from Beaver Dams. This British garrison consisted of barely a company of regulars under Lt. James Fitzgibbon and approximately 450 Indians nominally under the command of a Frenchman, Capt. Dominique Ducharme.

To command the expedition, Dearborn and Boyd chose Lt. Col. Charles G. Boerstler, who had at his disposal the 14th Infantry Regiment; parts of the 4th, 6th, and 23rd Regiments; an artillery company; and 20 light dragoons. Before departing Fort George, Boerstler failed to have the route adequately scouted but did make an effort to keep the expedition a secret from Canadian civilians in nearby Newark.

Boerstler led his men out of Fort George at nightfall on 23 June and marched until reaching Queenston around midnight. Unfortunately for the success of his mission, Boerstler did not take as great care with the civilians around Queenston as he had at Newark. Laura Secord, the wife of a Canadian militiaman, overheard the route the Americans planned to take, tricked one of the sentries into letting her beyond the pickets, and made it to Lieutenant Fitzgibbon in time to warn him. The young lieutenant now had time to arrange his Indian allies in a wooded area just outside of Beaver Dams.

Leaving Queenston on the morning of 24 June, Boerstler again did not take care to scout his front or flanks. The Indians struck after Boerstler's men were well into the wooded area, catching them completely by surprise. In spite of Boerstler's receiving a wound early in the attack that forced him to take refuge in a wagon, his men fought so bravely and tenaciously that most of Fitzgibbon's Indian allies disappeared. As Boerstler's men clawed their way to an open area with a clear avenue of escape, Boerstler, who still had command, was about to order the retreat when Lieutenant Fitzgibbon approached carrying a truce flag.

Fitzgibbon demanded that the Americans surrender. He informed the U.S. commander that approximately 1,500 regulars and 700 Indians were within minutes of surrounding Boerstler's men. Fitzgibbon claimed that he would be unable to restrain the Indians from butchering the U.S. soldiers. Boerstler hesitated and asked for terms: specifically, that the wounded be protected from the Indians, that his officers be allowed to retain their sidearms, and that the handful of U.S. militiamen who had accompanied the expedition be paroled at once. Fitzgibbon cheerfully agreed, and Boerstler surrendered 484 officers and men to less than half that number. He discovered the ruse shortly after his men had surrendered their weapons. By that time, many Indians had returned and set about murdering wounded Americans.

The disaster at Beaver Dams had tremendous repercussions along the Niagara Frontier and in Washington. On the front, British Gen. John Vincent responded to the victory at Beaver Dams by tightening his positions nearer Fort George and instituting raids across the Niagara River into the United States. In Washington, the growing criticism of General Dearborn's handling of the war in the north reached a crescendo in Congress. Secretary of War John Armstrong consequently had to remove the old warrior.

—Jeanne T. Heidler and David S. Heidler

See also: Boerstler, Charles G.; Boyd, John Parker; Fitzgibbon, James; Secord, Laura Ingersoll
Further Reading
Cruikshank, Ernest A. *The Battle of Fort George.* Niagara Falls, Ont.: Niagara Historical Society, 1904.
Keefer, Frank H. *Beaver Dams.* Thorold, Ont.: Thorold Post Printers, 1914.

Thomas Hart Benton

BENTON, THOMAS HART
1782–1858
Lawyer; soldier; statesman

Thomas Hart Benton, one of the most prominent U.S. statesmen of the antebellum period, gained fame as an advocate of sound currency, a promoter of westward expansion, and a leading supporter of Andrew Jackson. Early in Benton's long career, he experienced a frustrating interlude as an officer during the War of 1812.

As a youth, Benton emigrated from North Carolina to Tennessee, where he was admitted to the bar in 1806. He established a lucrative practice in Nashville, served in the state senate, and earned the friendship of Gen. Andrew Jackson, one of Tennessee's most prominent citizens.

At the outbreak of the War of 1812, young Benton dreamed of military glory. He helped recruit a regiment of Tennessee volunteers for service under Jackson. Originally commissioned as a captain, Benton was soon promoted to lieutenant colonel and became Jackson's aide-de-camp. Jackson's men were pressed into federal service and or-

dered to march south to combat Britain's Creek Indian allies. However, owing to the intrigues of James Wilkinson, the highest-ranking general in the U.S. Army, Jackson's forces were abruptly disbanded after several weeks of marching. A disgruntled Benton rightly suspected Wilkinson of jealousy toward Jackson and possible disloyalty to the U.S. cause.

Returning to Tennessee, Benton joined his brother, Jesse, in an unseemly quarrel with Maj. William Carroll, a quartermaster in Jackson's army. Carroll turned Jackson against the Benton brothers, and the feud culminated in a brawl in a Nashville hotel in which Jackson received a pistol ball he carried for the rest of his life. Now persona non grata in Tennessee, Benton emigrated to Missouri. There he established a law practice and published the *St. Louis Enquirer.*

Despite killing a man in a duel, in 1821 Benton was elected one of Missouri's first U.S. senators. During his thirty-year Senate career, the Missourian promoted hard money so enthusiastically he was dubbed "Old Bullion." Reconciled with Jackson, he became Old Hickory's leading spokesman in Congress. Benton also ardently promoted cheap land for settlers, a transcontinental railroad, and other measures that benefited western development.

Though a slaveholder himself, Benton came to oppose the proslavery policies of John C. Calhoun and other southern statesmen as dangerous to the Union. His opposition to the Compromise of 1850 for conceding too much to the South caused his defeat when he ran for reelection in 1851. Undaunted, Benton won election to the House of Representatives in 1852, only to lose two years later for voting against the Kansas-Nebraska Act that he correctly feared would renew slavery agitation with bloody results. An unsuccessful bid for governor of Missouri as an independent in 1856 proved the old statesman's last hurrah in politics. He spent the remaining two years of his life writing his valuable memoir, *Thirty Years' View*, and compiling a 16-volume abridgment of the debates of Congress that he completed the day before he died.

—*Ricky Earl Newport*

Further Reading
Benton, Thomas Hart. *Thirty Years' View*. 2 vols. New York: D. Appleton, 1854–1856.
Chambers, William Nisbet. *Old Bullion Benton: Senator from the New West. Thomas Hart Benton, 1782–1858*. Boston: Little, Brown, 1956.
Rogers, Joseph M. *Thomas H. Benton*. Philadelphia: George W. Jacobs, 1905.
Smith, Elbert B. *Magnificent Missourian: The Life of Thomas Hart Benton*. Philadelphia: J. B. Lippincott, 1958.

BERKELEY, GEORGE CRANFIELD
1753–1818
British admiral; member of Parliament, 1783–1810

The officer responsible for the *Chesapeake-Leopard* incident of 1807, George Berkeley was a son of the Fourth Earl of Berkeley. The family was politically powerful and had been prominent in the development of Virginia during the colonial period. His family connection was responsible for George Berkeley's naval advancement and his own election to Parliament for Gloucestershire in 1783.

Berkeley entered the Royal Navy in 1766 under the command of his cousin, Rear Adm. Augustus Keppel. He served under some of the most famous officers of the period, including Capts. James Cook and John Jervis, Earl St. Vincent. Present at the victory at Ushant in 1778, Berkeley was in U.S. waters during the Revolution and became a captain in 1780. Following the Peace of Paris in 1783, he

supported the administration of William Pitt the Younger, and although his active service was often criticized, his political connections helped his advancement to rear admiral in 1805 and gained him the command of the Halifax Station in 1806. Specifically, he owed his appointment to Lord Howick, who had served during the American Revolution and had remained a stalwart anti-American. William Grenville, the prime minister at the time of Berkeley's promotion, had misgivings about Berkeley's appointment to Canadian waters. Those misgivings were reinforced by Berkeley's constant stream of complaints about Jefferson and the United States.

Berkeley seriously tested Anglo-American relationships regarding neutral rights and impressment. Aware that deserters from the Royal Navy were receiving protection from local authorities in the United States, Berkeley also believed Jefferson would back down when confronted by British power. He instructed his subordinates to stop and search U.S. vessels for deserters. On 22 June 1807, Capt. Salusbury P. Humphreys, aboard Berkeley's flagship HMS *Leopard*, stopped the U.S. frigate USS *Chesapeake* to remove a notorious deserter, a London tailor, Jenkin Radford. After a fruitless discussion, Humphreys, who actually doubted the wisdom of Berkeley's orders, finally fired a shot across the bow of the *Chesapeake*. After a ten-minute action, the U.S. commander, Commodore James Barron, struck his colors, and the *Chesapeake* was boarded. Four mariners, including Radford, who was later hanged at Halifax, were removed. Although the other three—two of whom were African Americans—were clearly Americans, they were perceived as deserters from the Royal Navy. Nonetheless, Humphreys had violated U.S. sovereignty, and there was an outcry for war against Britain. Jefferson employed restraint and attempted to use the incident to persuade London to abandon its policy of impressment.

Both Barron and Humphreys personally suffered because of this unfortunate incident. The former was court-martialed for failing to prepare his ship for action; Humphreys was placed on half-pay in 1808 and never received another command. Admiral Berkeley, true to form, escaped punishment. Recalled from the Halifax Station in 1810, he was placed in command off the coast of Portugal, retired from the service in 1812, and was knighted in 1813. He died in February 1818.

—*Rory T. Cornish*

See also: Barron, James; *Chesapeake-Leopard* Affair
Further Reading
Gaines, Edward E. "George Cranfield Berkeley and the *Chesapeake-Leopard* Affair of 1807." In *America in the Middle Period: Essays in Honor of Bernard Mayo*, ed. John Bales. Charlottesville: University of Virginia Press, 1973.

BERLIN DECREE
21 November 1806

The Berlin Decree issued by Napoleon Bonaparte proclaimed the British Isles to be in a state of blockade by land and sea. The decree prohibited all commerce with British ports, and all goods from either British or British colonial ports were liable to seizure. The Berlin Decree marked the inauguration of Napoleon's formal use of economic warfare against his enemies, particularly Great Britain. It also saw the official beginning of the Continental Blockade, a boycott of imported goods, by means of which Napoleon tried to destroy Great Britain by economic pressures. The French defeat at Trafalgar, 21 October 1805, had proved Napoleon could not defeat Britain on the seas. Therefore, he turned to the type of economic strategy that French revolutionaries had employed when they had banned British products in 1793. In 1803 Napoleon expanded this exclusion to a "coast system" extending as far as Hanover.

Napoleon's pretext for the Berlin Decree was the British naval blockade, beginning in May 1806, of the European coastline from Brest to Elbe. Before the Berlin Decree, French measures against British trade were not entirely successful, as British and colonial goods entered Europe through Dutch and north German ports. The French at first did not seriously enforce the Berlin Decree against Americans. Then in the summer of 1807, Napoleon began seizing U.S. ships. However, unlike the British, the French never impressed U.S. seamen, a practice that made the British highly unpopular in the United States.

Initially, Great Britain mocked Napoleon's Berlin Decree. The London *Times* reflected this attitude when it trumpeted, "His decree will have as little effect on British commerce as his navy has." Nevertheless, the British did retaliate. In January and November 1807, they issued Orders in Council prohibiting maritime trade between ports controlled by France and its allies. All neutral ships had to call at British ports or submit to search by British authorities. In addition, the British ordered neutral vessels to pay duties and seek licenses for trade with enemy ports. This meant all ships bound for continental Europe initially had to pass through British ports.

Napoleon responded with the Milan Decrees of 23 November and 17 December 1807. They ordered the capture of any neutral ships that either stopped at British ports or submitted to British search. By this time, French maritime trade had suffered severe disruption. There were now no neutrals.

In theory, the Milan Decrees closed the door to U.S. commerce. If U.S. ships ignored British regulations, they could be seized by the French. In practice, trade continued by way of special licenses and wholesale evasion. The U.S. reaction to the economic war between France and Great Britain was part of the reason for passage of the Embargo Act of 23 December 1807, which prohibited U.S. ships from trading with Europe and banned some English manufactured goods from entering the continent. Jefferson's intention in issuing the act was to force the belligerents to abandon their controls. In practice, it hurt the Americans more than either the British or the French.

Napoleon responded to the U.S. embargo with the Decree of Bayonne, 17 April 1808, stating that U.S. vessels entering European ports should be sequestered. Congress repealed the Embargo Act in March 1809 and replaced it with the Non-Intercourse Act, which reopened trade with all countries except Britain and France. This act was equally ineffective in gaining concessions. These measures hurt U.S. commerce, and so in May 1810, Americans resumed trading with the belligerents.

In August 1810, Napoleon offered to lift the blockade of the United States if the British revoked their Orders in Council. The proposal proved popular in the United States. The U.S. government declared that nonintercourse with Britain would recommence if the British did not revoke their Orders in Council by February 1811.

The Berlin Decree and its progeny seriously impinged upon the British economy. Napoleon's enforcement of the policy varied but was vigorous on those occasions when he applied it. The year 1811 was disastrous for British exports, and the outlook continued to be grim until Napoleon's retreat from Moscow.

By the end of 1811, the Continental Blockade had collapsed, yet Great Britain's Tory government had insisted on maintaining the Orders in Council. This policy helped to provoke the U.S. declaration of war in June 1812. In the same month, the Tories revoked the Orders under pressure from Whigs and industrialists, but it was too late for the news to reach the United States. The War of 1812, therefore, was a direct outgrowth of the commercial war between France and Great Britain.

—*Leigh Whaley*

See also: Milan Decree; Orders in Council; Rambouillet Decree
Further Reading
Crouzet, François. *L'Economie Britannique et le Blocus Continental 1806–1813.* 2 vols. Paris: Economica, 1988.

Perkins, Bradford. *Prologue to War: England and the United States 1805–1812.* Berkeley and Los Angeles: University of California Press, 1963.

Further Reading

Northern, William J. *Men of Mark in Georgia.* 6 vols. Atlanta: Caldwell Publishers, 1910. Reprint, Spartanburg, SC: Reprint Company, 1974.

BIBB, WILLIAM WYATT
1781–1820
U.S. congressman and senator

Born in Georgia to William Bibb, a Revolutionary War veteran, and Sally Wyatt Bibb, the younger Bibb received his medical degree from the University of Pennsylvania in 1801. While practicing medicine in Georgia, he also entered politics, serving terms in the lower and upper houses of the Georgia legislature. In 1805, Bibb's district sent him to the U.S. House of Representatives, where he remained until assuming William Crawford's Senate seat in 1813 when Pres. James Madison appointed Crawford minister to France.

In 1811, Bibb, a Democratic Republican, ran for Speaker of the House as a representative of the party's peace faction, thus challenging the leader of the War Hawks, Henry Clay. Bibb was defeated 75 to 38. Once the war started, however, Bibb was a loyal supporter of the administration, often working as a compromiser both in the struggles that threatened to divide his own party and in the disagreements with Federalists.

Perhaps his most significant contribution during the war came in the fall of 1814 when the army desperately needed more men. To raise the 30,000 additional regulars, Secretary of War James Monroe asked Congress for a conscription law. Senator Bibb proposed a compromise bill to draft 80,000 militia for two-years service. These men would serve under state officers and would be eligible for service only in their home states or adjoining states. The bill passed the Senate, but the House would not consent to it. Though stymied in that initiative, Bibb at the same time proposed another bill to increase the amount of land granted to enlistees from 160 acres to 320 acres and to allow minors between the ages of 18 and 21 to enlist without the approval of parents or guardians. This bill passed both houses.

Following the war, Pres. James Monroe appointed Bibb the first (and only) territorial governor of Alabama. When Alabama became a state, Bibb was chosen its first state governor. He died at the age of 38 from injuries sustained in a riding accident.

—*Jeanne T. Heidler and David S. Heidler*

BIDDLE, JAMES
1783–1848
U.S. naval officer

As one of America's first "sailor-statesmen," James Biddle can be listed as one of the fathers of the U.S. Navy. Although he is best known for his later naval and diplomatic successes during cruises with the Caribbean, Mediterranean, Asiatic, and South American Squadrons, his contribution to the efforts of the United States during the War of 1812 was significant. His superb seamanship and courage played a tremendous role in two successful frigate actions against the British: *Wasp* versus *Frolic* and *Hornet* versus *Penguin*.

A prominent Philadelphia family, the Biddles produced a host of soldiers, sailors, politicians, and businessmen in the young United States. James's uncle, Nicholas Biddle, rose to the rank of commodore of a five-ship squadron during the American Revolution but was tragically killed in action in 1778. After serving as a merchant marine captain, Charles Biddle, James's father, pursued a successful mercantile and political career in Pennsylvania. James started his own naval career in 1800 when he was commissioned a midshipman on board the frigate *President*. In 1802, he joined the *Constellation* for an uneventful cruise in the Mediterranean. The following year, he was taken prisoner after the unfortunate grounding of the *Philadelphia* in Tripoli Harbor.

After his release, the Navy Department gave him command of a coastal gunboat. During this assignment, he spent a great deal of time surveying South Carolina harbors as possible naval bases. In early 1807, he was promoted to lieutenant but took an extended leave from the navy to sail with the merchant marine. Upon his return to active duty, Biddle served in a variety of roles, including commands in gunboats and a sloop and lieutenancies aboard the *Constitution* and *President*.

Within weeks of the outbreak of the War of 1812, the Navy Department assigned Biddle as first lieutenant to Master Commandant Jacob Jones of the 18-gun sloop *Wasp*. While patrolling off the Virginia coast on 17 October 1812, Jones and Biddle closed with a British convoy, escorted by HMS *Frolic* (18 guns). A day earlier, both vessels

James Biddle

and New London for more than a year, but in January 1815 he finally slipped out to sea. His orders were to interdict British shipping in the South Atlantic and eventually to join a U.S. squadron at Tristan da Cunha. After an unproductive two-month cruise, Biddle spotted HMS *Penguin* approaching Tristan on 23 March 1815. The *Penguin*, commanded by Capt. James Dickinson, Royal Navy, was trying to intercept a U.S. privateer in the South Atlantic.

The vessels rapidly closed and began a 15-minute exchange of close-range broadsides. Although the two ships threw about the same weight of metal, Captain Dickinson had the disadvantage of an inexperienced crew. Soon that crew had no captain, for Dickinson himself was mortally wounded during this initial exchange. After a brief collision that tore away much of the sails and rigging of both ships, Biddle wore and presented a fresh broadside. Unable to respond, *Penguin* struck her colors. Only 22 minutes had passed since the opening rounds were fired. The British vessel lost one-third of her crew, most of her guns were disabled, and her masts were either gone or tottering. *Hornet* had only suffered 11 casualties, most of them from light wounds. Biddle had taken a musket ball through his chin and neck, but he remained in command and recovered rapidly. As for his ship, the *Hornet* had not received a single hull hit from *Penguin*'s guns. The *Penguin*, on the other hand, was so severely damaged that she had to be scuttled the next day.

Hornet joined USS *Peacock*, another U.S. sloop, for a cruise around South Africa and into the Indian Ocean. In late April, *Hornet* barely escaped HMS *Cornwallis* (74 guns). During the harrowing chase, Biddle had lightened ship by jettisoning most of his ammunition and necessities. Heading to a port to replace equipment, he arrived on 9 June at San Salvador, Brazil, and there learned that the war had ended five months earlier. He also discovered his promotion to post-captain, the highest attainable rank in the U.S. Navy at the time.

After the war, Biddle commanded squadrons in the Mediterranean, Caribbean, and Far East and won fame for promoting U.S. interests abroad. While on his Mediterranean cruise, he represented the U.S. government by signing a commercial treaty with Turkey. Later, he set up the U.S. Legation at Canton. During the Mexican War, his squadron cooperated with U.S. Army units off the coast of California.

Biddle's 48 years of naval service finally ended after a three-year cruise on the USS *Columbus*. Seven months after his return to the United States, he died on 1 October 1848.

had ridden out a gale that had damaged *Frolic*'s topsails and main yard. Jones and his opponent, Capt. Thomas Whinyates, Royal Navy, opened the engagement at less than 60 yards in heavy seas. While Jones's gunners fired at *Frolic*'s hull, the British aimed at *Wasp*'s sails and rigging. Although both vessels suffered extensive damage to their sails, masts, and rigging, the Americans gradually gained the upper hand. *Frolic* was unable to maneuver effectively, and her bow crashed into *Wasp*'s waist, giving Jones the opportunity to rake his adversary prior to boarding. Lieutenant Biddle led the boarding party, which accepted the surrender of the British survivors. *Frolic* had suffered 90 casualties out of a crew of 110 sailors, whereas Jones lost only ten of his command.

This contest between equals clearly demonstrated that the Americans were more than a match for their Royal Navy adversaries. Unfortunately, Jones was unable to bring his prize into port because HMS *Poictiers* (74 guns) arrived on the scene four hours after *Frolic*'s surrender. Unable to escape or resist, Jones surrendered, and the ships were taken to Bermuda. Jones, Biddle, and the crew were soon exchanged, and upon their return to the United States, the Navy Department promoted both officers. In early 1813, Biddle took command of the USS *Hornet* (20 guns), sister ship of the *Wasp*.

Stronger British warships blockaded Biddle in New York

—*John J. Abbatiello*

See also: *Hornet* versus *Penguin*; *Wasp* versus *Frolic*

Further Reading

Long, David F. *Sailor-Diplomat: A Biography of Commodore James Biddle, 1783–1848.* Boston: Northeastern University Press, 1983.

Nicholas Biddle

BIDDLE, NICHOLAS
1786–1844
Lawyer; financial expert

Born on 8 January 1786, Nicholas Biddle attained considerable success in several careers: banking and finance, diplomacy, politics, literature, academic scholarship, architecture, and government service. He came from a wealthy Philadelphia merchant family. Nicholas Biddle was a gifted student who enrolled at the University of Pennsylvania when he was ten years of age and was graduated from the College of New Jersey (Princeton). He later was awarded a master's degree from Princeton, the youngest graduate of that university in its history. After college, he studied law and was admitted to the bar when he was 18. While a student, he mastered French, Italian, modern and classical Greek, and Latin.

Upon completing his legal studies in 1804, Biddle became secretary to Gen. John Armstrong, the U.S. minister to France. Biddle was described as a handsome young man, slightly above average in height, with a fair complexion, chestnut hair, and an oval face. A gifted conversationalist, he served the U.S. diplomatic establishment in Europe until July 1807. Biddle worked first in France and later for James Monroe when he was minister to Great Britain. In helping to address great diplomatic problems with these countries, Nicholas Biddle became a talented international lawyer well acquainted with commercial issues. Biddle also became an ardent U.S. nationalist.

While in Europe in 1806, Nicholas Biddle took a leave of absence to take an unusual grand tour to see places of historic interest. He is thought to be the first American to have visited Greece. He became a great devotee of Greek history and architecture, an enthusiasm evident in the style of his estate, called Andalusia, and in some of the public buildings he influenced, such as the Second Bank of the United States in Philadelphia. Some of his friends called him Nick the Greek.

When Biddle returned to Philadelphia, he practiced law and contributed articles to literary and scientific journals. He became the editor of the prestigious *Portfolio* and

established such a reputation that Col. William Clark asked him to edit the journals of the Lewis and Clark expedition. Biddle had nearly completed the project when he was elected to the Pennsylvania legislature as a Federalist; he turned the manuscript over to Paul Allen to complete it. While in the legislature, Biddle acquired national standing as an expert on banking and government finance after delivering an important speech opposing the dissolution of the First Bank of the United States. He predicted the economic problems of inadequate credit and inflation that would occur during the War of 1812. In 1811, Biddle married a wealthy Philadelphia heiress and thus became independently wealthy for the rest of his life.

When war was declared in 1812, Biddle, who held a reserve military commission, was unable to serve because of a serious leg injury. Although a Federalist, he supported the war effort in his journal's editorials. He criticized those radical New England Federalists who flirted with secession. By 1814, Biddle had become a Republican. He advised Secretary of State Monroe during the war and was an active member of the Philadelphia Defense Committee. Elected to the Pennsylvania State Senate in 1814, he delivered an important speech opposing the Hartford Convention's recommendations.

After the war, Biddle combined occasional service in the state capital with the life of a gentleman farmer, editor, and part-time attorney in Philadelphia. He hoped for a national position and finally was selected by Pres. James Monroe as one of the directors of the Second Bank of the United States. He served as one of the bank's directors for 19 of the next 20 years and was its president for much of that period. Pres. Andrew Jackson clashed with Biddle in what became known as the Bank War. After Jackson had destroyed the Second Bank of the United States, Biddle ran the Bank of the United State of Philadelphia, a state bank, for several years and continued his literary work. He died in Philadelphia on 27 February 1844.

—*George E. Frakes*

Further Reading

Cappon, Lesser J. "Who Is the Author of 'History of the Expedition under the Command of Captains Lewis and Clark' (1814)?" *William and Mary Quarterly* 19, no. 2 (1962): 257–268.

Govern, Thomas Pain. *Nicholas Biddle, Nationalist and Public Banker, 1786–1844.* Chicago: University of Chicago Press, 1959.

BIDDLE, THOMAS
1790–1831
Major, U.S. Army

Thomas Biddle was born in Philadelphia on 21 November 1790. He entered the U.S. Army on 9 April 1812 as a captain in the Ninth U.S. Infantry. That July he transferred to the Second U.S. Artillery. He distinguished himself at the capture of Fort George in May 1813; and the following month at Stoney Creek he commanded a company of artillery fighting as infantry. During the 1814 Niagara Campaign, Biddle commanded one of the four artillery companies in Maj. Jacob Hindman's battalion. At Lundy's Lane on 25 July 1814, Biddle was wounded early in the battle. Later, however, he accompanied the force of U.S. artillerymen that moved up to take control of the British guns after their firing position on high ground was overrun by the 21st U.S. Infantry in a flank attack. Biddle helped defend the position from three successive British counterattacks. When the Americans were ordered to pull back and regroup, Biddle brought off a British gun, which turned out to be the only one retained by the Americans in that battle.

Although still suffering from the effects of the shoulder wound he received at Lundy's Lane, Biddle commanded a small two-gun battery at Fort Erie during the British siege that August. In the early morning hours of 15 August, a force of about 100 Royal Artillerymen seized control of the fort's main northeast bastion. They held the position against determined opposition for about two hours, when the bastion exploded for still-mysterious reasons. As the British tried to pull out of the shattered position, Biddle moved a fieldpiece up and enfiladed their withdrawal, inflicting heavy casualties on the survivors. Biddle received a brevet promotion to major for "gallant conduct in the defense of Fort Erie."

In December 1814, Biddle became aide-de-camp to General Izard. Biddle remained in the army after the war, and on 17 May 1815 he took command of the artillery company that today is the U.S. Army's Fifth Battalion, First Field Artillery. In January 1820, Biddle transferred back into the infantry. That August he received a substantive promotion to major in the Paymaster's Department, which was then headed by Nathan Towson, one of his former fellow company commanders from Hindman's battalion. Biddle held that position for the remainder of his life. He was killed in a duel with Spencer Pettis on 29 August 1831 in St. Louis. Because of Biddle's poor eyesight, the firing distance was reduced to 5 feet. Both men were killed on the first volley.

—*David T. Zabecki*

See also: Artillery; Hindman, Jacob; Lundy's Lane, Battle of; Towson, Nathan

Further Reading

Armstrong, John. *Notices of the War of 1812.* New York: Whiley & Putnam, 1840.

Birkhimer, William E. *Historical Sketch of the Organization, Administration, Materiel and Tactics of the Artillery, United States Army.* Washington, DC: Chapman, 1884.

Downey, Fairfax. *The Sound of the Guns.* New York: David McKay, 1955.

Heitman, F. B. *Historical Register of the United States Army.* Washington, DC: The National Tribune, 1890.

McKenney, Janice E. *Field Artillery, Regular Army and Reserve: Army Lineage Series.* Washington, DC: Center for Military History, 1985.

BIG WARRIOR

d. 1825
Headman, Upper Creek Indian
town of Tuckabatchee

Big Warrior (Tustennuggee Thlucco), the physically imposing and wealthy chief of Tuckabatchee, led the faction of the Creek National Council that sought peaceful accommodation with the United States during the early nineteenth century. His decision to execute members of the Red Stick nativist movement caused the Creek War of 1813–1814 and drew the Creeks into the War of 1812.

Big Warrior's son, Tuskeneah, introduced Tecumseh to the Creeks in 1811. The Shawnee chief brought to the Creeks the message of his brother, Tenskwatawa, who advocated a militant pan-Indian alliance, a nativist religious revival, and the repudiation of Anglo-American influence. Many Creeks—known as Red Sticks—were receptive to Tecumseh's message because it reinforced a nativist religious revival already underway in the Creek Nation. Big Warrior, however, refused to affiliate with the prophetic movement and urged conciliation with the United States.

After Red Sticks killed some white settlers in 1812 and 1813, the Creek National Council ordered the execution of several of their leaders, including Little Warrior. This order ignited the Creek War of 1813–1814 as the Red Sticks, in retaliation, attacked and laid siege to Tuckabatchee. Big Warrior, however, escaped to Coweta, the home of his ally Little Prince. There, the accommodationist leaders appealed for and received assistance from the United States and from southern natives. After several battles, Andrew Jackson's combined U.S. and Indian troops administered a devastating defeat to the Red Sticks at Horseshoe Bend.

After the U.S. victory, Jackson demanded that the Creeks sign the Treaty of Fort Jackson. The agreement, which required the Creek Nation to cede large tracts of land to the federal government, made no distinction between the Red Sticks and the Creeks who fought with Jackson. Only one Red Stick was present at the treaty signing. Big Warrior, Little Prince, and other Creek leaders who had allied with the United States were forced to sign the humiliating treaty for the entire Creek Nation.

After this slight, Big Warrior quietly repudiated his accommodationist leanings, secretly adopted the Red Stick position, and requested British assistance to continue the war against the United States. The Treaty of Ghent and the victory at New Orleans dashed Big Warrior's plans for vengeance.

In 1825, Big Warrior died while in Washington protesting the infamous Treaty of Indian Springs.

—*Tim Alan Garrison*

See also: Creek War; Horseshoe Bend, Battle of; Little Prince; Red Sticks; Tuckabatchee

Further Reading

Dowd, Gregory Evans. *A Spirited Resistance: The North American Indian Struggle for Unity, 1745–1815*. Baltimore: Johns Hopkins University Press, 1992.
Green, Michael D. *The Politics of Indian Removal: Creek Government and Society in Crisis*. Lincoln: University of Nebraska Press, 1982.
Griffith, Benjamin W., Jr. *McIntosh and Weatherford, Creek Indian Leaders*. Tuscaloosa: University of Alabama Press, 1988.
Heidler, David S., and Heidler, Jeanne T. *Old Hickory's War: Andrew Jackson and the Quest for Empire*. Mechanicsburg, PA: Stackpole Books, 1996.
Wright, J. Leitch, Jr. *Creeks and Seminoles: The Destruction and Regeneration of the Muscogulge People*. Lincoln: University of Nebraska Press, 1986.

BIGELOW, ABIJAH

1775–1860
U.S. congressman

Born in Westminster, Massachusetts, Abijah Bigelow graduated from Dartmouth College in 1795. A few years later he began practicing law and became involved in local politics. From 1807 to 1809, he served in the state legislature, and in 1810 he entered the 11th Congress as a Federalist. He remained in Congress until the end of the War of 1812.

Like most Federalists, Bigelow strongly opposed the U.S. declaration of war against Great Britain. In Congress he was especially critical of what he viewed as the discriminatory methods of financing the war. He thought that Secretary of the Treasury Albert Gallatin's proposal to secure large loans would lead to widespread inflation and that the taxes should be more equitably collected across the entire country. The administration's use of customs duties as the primary means of taxation, Bigelow argued, unduly burdened the already weak New England economy so dependent on the import trade.

Bigelow persistently criticized the Madison administration's handling of war finances and the conduct of the war until its end. He left national politics in disgust in 1815. Returning to Massachusetts, Bigelow returned to private practice and remained active in local politics. He died in Worcester, Massachusetts, in 1860.

—*Jeanne T. Heidler and David S. Heidler*

See also: U.S. Congress
Further Reading
Brigham, Clarence, ed. "Letters of Abijah Bigelow, Member of Congress to His Wife, 1810–1815." *American Antiquarian Society Proceedings* 40 (1930): 305–406.

BISSHOPP, CECIL
1783–1813
British army officer

Born on 25 June 1783, the eldest son of Sir Cecil Bisshopp of West Sussex, Bisshopp joined the Foot Guards as an ensign on 20 September 1799. He served as private secretary to Rear Adm. Sir John Borlase Warren at the coronation of Czar Alexander I in 1801. Otherwise, his service took him to Corunna, Spain, in January 1809 and saw him participating in the ill-fated Walcheren expedition in the Netherlands in July 1809. In 1811 and 1812, he sat briefly in Parliament for Newport. By August 1812, he was a lieutenant colonel and sailing for Canada as inspecting field officer of militia.

Bisshopp's troops at Chippewa and Fort Erie repulsed Alexander Smyth's probe at Frenchmen's Creek in November 1812. After the loss of Fort George on 27 May 1813, Bisshopp withdrew from Chippewa and joined Brig. Gen. John Vincent at Burlington Heights near Hamilton. During the night action at Stoney Creek on 6 June, Bisshopp commanded the reserves. On 11 July, he led a force of regulars and militia across the river to Black Rock near Buffalo, destroyed the batteries, and burned several schooners, the barracks, blockhouses, naval yard, and storehouses. The raid also captured eight guns.

A U.S. prisoner described Bisshopp as "a mild humane-looking man and about 36 years of age, rather tall and well made and a man of exceeding few words." During a counterattack organized by Brig. Gen. Peter B. Porter, Bisshopp was wounded in the left thigh, wrist, and upper right arm. He lingered painfully for five days and died on 16 July 1813, presumably of shock or blood poisoning. He is buried in Lundy's Lane cemetery.

—*Frederick C. Drake*

Further Reading
Allen, Robert S. "Cecil Bisshopp." *Dictionary of Canadian Biography*. Vol. 5, *1801–1820,* pp. 82–83. Toronto: University of Toronto Press, 1979.
Cruikshank, Ernest A. *The Documentary History of the Campaign upon the Niagara Frontier.* 9 vols. Vol. 3, pp. 319–322; Vol. 4, pp. 20, 225–233; Vol. 6, pp. 223–224, 230; Vol. 9, p. 359. Welland, Ont.: Lundy's Lane Historical Society, 1896–1908.
Green, Ernest. "Some Graves on Lundy's Lane." *Publications of the Niagara Historical Society* 22 (1911): 4–6.
Wood, William H. *Select British Documents of the Canadian War of 1812.* 3 vols. Vol. 1, pp. 650–651, 654–658; Vol. 2, pp. 163–164. Toronto: Chaplain Society, 1920–1928.

BLACK ROCK, NEW YORK

Situated on the front lines during the war, the village of Black Rock suffered the fate of many border towns. Black Rock was on the eastern shore of the Niagara River 2 miles below Buffalo and 1.5 miles across the water from Fort Erie in Upper Canada. Named for a rock ledge protruding over the river that could shelter small vessels, Black Rock had been the site of ferry service into Upper Canada. Immediately below Black Rock, the Niagara bifurcates around Squaw Island. The eastern channel was the site of the Black Rock navy yard. Throughout the war, many of Black Rock's houses and public buildings served as quarters for U.S. soldiers and sailors.

Alexander Smyth embarked his army twice from the navy yard (28 November and 1 December 1812) only to disembark without crossing the Niagara. Smyth's abortive invasion attempts brought ridicule upon him but also reflected the general unpreparedness of the Army of the Center, as the force along the Niagara was known. The military situation remained quiet until the early hours of 11 July 1813, when British Lt. Col. Cecil Bisshopp landed a party of about 250 regulars and militia just below Squaw Island. Moving quickly, the raiders burned a schooner and the barracks and blockhouse at Black Rock and captured several guns and boats and considerable foodstuffs. War Hawk and militia brigadier general Peter B. Porter gathered a force of regulars, militia, and Seneca Indian volunteers and attacked the British sharply, forcing their withdrawal across the river. Bisshopp was mortally wounded in this otherwise successful raid.

Although Bisshopp had respected private property in Black Rock, the Americans did not do so when abandoning Fort George in December. The burning of Newark prompted swift retaliation, and Black Rock was not spared. On the evening of 29 December 1813, Maj. Gen. Phineas Riall led a mixed force of regulars, militia, and native warriors across the Niagara River below Black Rock. At daybreak, Riall's command moved on Black Rock and easily brushed aside a larger force of New York militia, many of whom ran at the first sound of gunfire. The British continued their raid and seized Buffalo easily. Over the next two days the twin villages were torched. Only one house in Black Rock survived, because it sheltered women and children.

The Niagara Frontier remained unprotected by regulars until mid-April, when Winfield Scott arrived at Buffalo to train his brigade. Embarking from Black Rock on 3 July, Scott defeated the British two days later at Chippewa. Following the Battle of Lundy's Lane, the U.S. army withdrew to Fort Erie, and Black Rock saw its last action of the war. Lt. Gen. Gordon Drummond, whose army followed the Americans south to Fort Erie, hoped to coax them back across the river by threatening Black Rock and Buffalo. On the night of 2 August 1814, Lt. Col. John Tucker led nine companies of British regulars across the Niagara. They were stopped cold about a mile north of Black Rock by Maj. Ludowick Morgan and a small battalion of riflemen. Failing in this flanking maneuver, Drummond opened the seven-week-long unsuccessful siege of Fort Erie. By October, the war was all but over along the Niagara River. Buffalo's rapid growth after the opening of the Erie Canal eventually swallowed up the village of Black Rock.

—Richard V. Barbuto

See also: Niagara Campaigns
Further Reading
Babcock, Louis L. *The War of 1812 on the Niagara Frontier.* Buffalo: Buffalo Historical Society, 1927.

BLADENSBURG, BATTLE OF
24 August 1814

In 1814, the British took the offensive in North America on several fronts. One was a mid-Atlantic campaign. Substantial land reinforcements came through Bermuda, including 2,500 battle-hardened regulars detached from the duke of Wellington's forces in France and commanded by Maj. Gen. Robert Ross. Preceded by naval units under Vice Adm. Alexander Cochrane, this force arrived in Chesapeake Bay on 15 August and headed for Tangier Island. Counting the forces of Rear Adm. Sir George Cock-

burn already on hand, Cochrane had at his disposal 20 warships—four were ships of the line—and many transports and store ships. With a battalion of 700 marines detached to operate with the soldiers, total British ground strength was more than 4,500 men.

To confuse the Americans about the real intent of his operations, Cochrane detached two squadrons of frigates. He sent one up the Potomac River and the other up Chesapeake Bay to a point above Baltimore. At noon on 19 August, the main British force started up the Patuxent. Cochrane masked his designs on Washington, D.C., by making it appear that his target was Capt. Joshua Barney's flotilla in the Patuxent. Cochrane explained in his report to the Admiralty that this strategy "afforded a pretext for ascending that river to attack him near its source, above Pig Point, while the ultimate destination of the combined force was Washington, should it be found that the attempt might be made with any prospect of success."

British troops landed at Benedict, 25 miles up the Patuxent. On 20 August, they began the march along the river's west bank while flanked by light British vessels that followed their progress. Their immediate objective was Barney's flotilla. On 22 August, the land forces reached Upper Marlboro, 40 miles upriver. Thus just abreast of Upper Marlboro at Pig Point, the U.S. flotilla at Pig Point found itself cornered. Barney had foreseen the inevitable result. To save his men, he abandoned his boats on 21 August, leaving a few men to destroy them at the last minute. The skeleton crews accomplished this on 22 August as the British approached.

Cockburn argued strongly for an attack on Washington, and finally Ross agreed. One approach to the capital was along the eastern branch of the Potomac to a point where two bridges spanned the river. This was the most direct route, and Barney's flotillamen were soon defending the bridge that led to the Washington Navy Yard. The second route, 8 miles longer, would require the British to continue northwest to Bladensburg. Ross and Cockburn opted for the latter as less risky and more likely to afford surprise. During the night of 23 August, British troops reached Bladensburg. The marines remained at Upper Marlboro in case the expedition met with failure and needed to retire.

The defense of the national capital, commanded by Brig. Gen. William Winder, resulted in an unmitigated military disaster. Although Winder labored under the severe handicap of having to rely on what was essentially a militia force, virtually no preparations anticipated a British attack on Washington. The end of fighting in Europe indicated the need to strengthen the defenses of both Washington and Baltimore, and the wooded terrain in the area would have made that a relatively easy task. Even a last-minute felling

This plan of the Battle of Bladensburg shows how the outnumbered British were easily able to beat back General Winder's troops on August 24 and march on to Washington in another blow to American morale.

of trees and destruction of roads and bridges might have prevented the descent on Washington.

As early as 1 July, Pres. James Madison had warned his cabinet that he expected an attack on Washington. Madison himself selected Winder to command a newly created Tenth Military District covering Maryland, northern Virginia, and the District of Columbia. Madison chose Winder in part because his uncle, Levin Winder, was the governor of Maryland and a critic of the war. General Winder had only about 500 regulars available for his defense, and many of them were shut up in forts. As a result, on 4 July the government informed nearby states of a massive call for 93,500 militia. Winder could not, however, order any of them into active service until there was imminent danger.

The danger became more than imminent as the British approached Bladensburg. The clash there occurred on 24 August. Winder had approximately 6,000 men to oppose 4,000 British soldiers. The U.S. forces, however, were badly placed at Bladensburg because Secretary of State James Monroe had arrived on the field and changed Brig. Gen. Tobias Stansbury's deployments. Many of the militiamen broke and ran after a few volleys. Militia performance was

almost universally deplorable throughout the war, and Bladensburg was among the worst. The British use of Congreve Rockets especially terrified the green troops.

Belatedly, on 24 August, Joshua Barney had received permission to march his 400 seamen and marines to Bladensburg. They reached the field after the battle had begun and were virtually the only Americans to gain credit that day. Some served a battery of five guns; the remainder of the men supported the battery, acting as infantry. Barney's men fired their navy 12- and 18-pounders to prevent the enemy advance on the Washington Pike. They fought virtually alone. Winder himself contributed to the defeat by ordering the militiamen to retire before they had really been tested. Insufficiently trained to retire in good order, the militia was soon in full flight. Only the sailors and marines held firm, but the British worked around them. Barney himself was wounded and taken prisoner.

By 4:00 P.M. the Battle of Bladensburg was over. It had lasted three hours. British casualties in the battle were 64 killed and 185 wounded; U.S. casualties were 10 or 12 killed, 40 wounded. About 100 Americans were captured.

The rout at Bladensburg allowed the British to take Washington that night and burn its public buildings. They left the next day and reembarked at Benedict on 30 August.

—*Spencer C. Tucker*

See also: Barney, Joshua; Chesapeake Bay Campaign, 1813–1814; Cochrane, Alexander; Cockburn, George; Congreve Rockets; Militia in the War of 1812; Monroe, James; Ross, Robert; Stansbury, Tobias; Winder, William H.

Further Reading

Lloyd, Alan. *The Scorching of Washington. The War of 1812.* New York: David McKay, 1975.

Lord, Walter. *The Dawn's Early Light.* New York: W. W. Norton, 1972.

Muller, Charles G. *The Darkest Day: 1814, the Washington-Baltimore Campaign.* Philadelphia: Lippincott, 1963.

BLAKELY, JOHNSTON
1781–1814
U.S. naval officer

Born in Seaford, Ireland, Johnston Blakely immigrated to the United States with his family when he was an infant and grew up in North Carolina. He entered the U.S. Navy at the age of 19 as a midshipman and rose quickly in this service to the command of the USS *Enterprise* in 1811.

Considered one of the most promising of the rising crop of young officers in the navy, Blakely commanded the *Enterprise* until 1813. The following year he received command of the new sloop USS *Wasp* (22 guns) at Portsmouth, New Hampshire.

On 1 May 1814, Blakely miraculously eluded the British blockade outside Portsmouth and immediately sailed for the British Isles. Within days of his arrival, the *Wasp* captured five British merchant vessels. On 28 June, he had his first encounter with a British war vessel, HMS *Reindeer* (18 guns). After only about half an hour of combat, the *Reindeer* surrendered. The British ship had received such heavy damage in the engagement, however, that Blakely was forced to burn her the following day. Blakely's *Wasp* had also received damage and was low on supplies, so he immediately set out for L'Orient, France.

Blakely stayed in France for almost two months, repairing and resupplying the *Wasp*. On 27 August, he set sail again. On the night of 1 September, he encountered HMS *Avon*. After a short engagement, the *Avon* signaled surrender, but before Blakely could take possession of the ship, he spotted sails that eventually forced his flight. On 21 September he had another chance, however, when HMS *Atlanta* (8 guns) was spotted and easily taken. Blakely dispatched the *Atlanta* with a prize crew to Savannah, Georgia, and continued his sail. The *Wasp* was last spotted by a Swedish ship east of the island of Madeira on 9 October. It was never seen again and was presumed lost at sea. During Blakely's five-month cruise, he captured 14 ships.

—*Jeanne T. Heidler and David S. Heidler*

See also: Wasp versus Avon; Wasp versus Reindeer
Further Reading
Pratt, Fletcher. "Johnston Blakely, the Carolina Sea Raider." *United States Naval Institute Proceedings* 76 (1950): 996–1007.

BLOOMFIELD, JOSEPH
1753–1823
U.S. brigadier general

Born to Dr. Moses Bloomfield and Sarah Ogden Bloomfield in Woodbridge, New Jersey, Joseph Bloomfield studied law as a young man. Before he could begin his practice, he became a captain in the Third New Jersey Regiment at the beginning of the Revolutionary War. He fought until 1778, when an injury forced his res-

ignation. Following the Revolution, he served as an officer in the New Jersey militia and in a number of political posts, including governor of New Jersey.

At the beginning of the War of 1812, James Madison gave Bloomfield command of the Third Military District, centered in New York, with the rank of brigadier general. By the fall of 1812, Bloomfield had recruited approximately 8,000 men around Plattsburg, where he trained and prepared them for a campaign against Canada along the Lake Champlain route. Before the campaign could commence, however, Gen. Henry Dearborn arrived to take command of the campaign. Later in the war, Bloomfield prepared Philadelphia defenses for a possible British attack.

Following the war, Bloomfield served two terms in Congress and died in 1823 as a result of a carriage accident that year.

—*Jeanne T. Heidler and David S. Heidler*

See also: Dearborn, Henry
Further Reading
Nelson, William. *Some Notices of Governor Joseph Bloomfield.* Newark, NJ: Daily Advertiser Printing House, 1886.

BLOUNT, WILLIE
1768–1835
Governor of Tennessee, 1809–1815

Willie (pronounced Wiley) Blount was born on 18 April 1768, the son of Jacob and Hannah Baker Blount of North Carolina. He was the half-brother of William Blount, governor of the Southwest Territory. Willie Blount studied at what are now Princeton and Columbia Universities and became a member of the bar in North Carolina. He came to Tennessee while William was territorial governor and served him as a private secretary from 1790 to 1796. Blount married while thus employed, but the date is uncertain. He fathered two daughters. In 1802, he settled in Clarksville, Montgomery County, Tennessee, where he practiced law and farmed.

Because of the political organization William Blount had created in Tennessee, Willie was well placed to achieve political advancement. In 1807, Willie Blount was elected to the state legislature and in 1809 was elected governor, a post he held until 1815.

One of the first problems Governor Blount faced was frontier defense. Andrew Jackson, one of two militia commanders in the state, had proposed a reorganization of the militia with Blount's encouragement. With Jackson's endorsement, Blount also proposed removing Indians to areas west of the Mississippi River.

In November 1812, the War Department told Blount about troop requirements to defend New Orleans. Of these, some 1,500 Tennessee militiamen would serve under Gen. James Wilkinson, a man Jackson had denounced as a "publick villain." The Madison administration, however, had suggested that Blount not place Jackson in command. Blount disregarded the administration's wishes. Part of his reason stemmed from military need. Jackson's units were better prepared for rapid muster. But it was political motives that chiefly guided Blount's decision to select Jackson. The governor did not want to alienate a popular ally who lived in a part of the state important for Blount's election. For his part, Jackson owed a considerable debt to Blount. The man who became the Hero of New Orleans had the chance to achieve that fame because Willie Blount ignored the wishes of the War Department.

The first military effort by Jackson's volunteers ended at Natchez when the War Department dismissed them in February 1813. Already displeased with the federal government's seeming indifference, Blount reacted sharply to news of the Fort Mims Massacre. On his own authority, he mobilized Jackson's militia. The governor also raised more money than authorized by Washington to sustain the state's volunteers, even securing personal loans to do so. When federal authorization did come, Blount asked Washington to pay him a commission on the $300,000 he had raised. Not until 1830, however, when his friend Jackson was president, did Blount receive the compensation.

Willie Blount made significant contributions to the war effort in the South. He selected Jackson to command volunteers and took prompt action to provide a well-equipped force with sustaining financial support. The result was military success. As Blount said, the War of 1812 helped to prove "that a republican government is not only best calculated to promote the happiness of man, in time of tranquility, but capable also of withstanding the rude shocks of war. . ."

Blount died on 10 September 1835.

—*Thomas H. Winn*

See also: Jackson, Andrew; Mims, Attack on Fort; Wilkinson, James

Further Reading

Clark, Mary. "Willie Blount: Governor of Tennessee, 1809–1815." In *Governors of Tennessee I, 1790–1835*, ed. Charles W. Crawford. Memphis: Memphis State University Press, 1979.

Moser, Harold, ed. *The Papers of Andrew Jackson.* Vol. 2, 1804–1813. Knoxville: University of Tennessee Press, 1984.

Peeler, Elizabeth H. "The Policies of Willie Blount as Governor of Tennessee, 1809–15." *Tennessee Historical Quarterly* 1 (December 1942): 309–327.

White, Robert H., ed. *Messages of the Governors of Tennessee.* Vol. 1, *1796–1821.* Nashville: Tennessee Historical Commission, 1952.

BLUE-LIGHT FEDERALISTS
See Connecticut

BOB SMITH

The new U.S. Navy adopted many Royal Navy customs, one of which was the issuance of grog, a mix of rum and water, twice daily. The word grog came from the nickname of Rear Adm. Edward Vernon, inventor of the concoction, who favored a boat cloak made of grogram and so was known as Old Grog. When Robert Smith became secretary of the navy in the Jefferson administration, he noted that not only was U.S. rye whiskey cheaper than rum but also the sailors preferred it. In 1806, he ordered that rye replace grog. U.S. tars followed British practice and began calling their drink Bob Smith.

—*Tyrone G. Martin*

BOERSTLER, CHARLES G.
1778–?
Colonel, 14th U.S. Infantry

Charles G. Boerstler, a native of Maryland, was commissioned a lieutenant colonel in the newly raised 14th U.S. Infantry on 12 March 1812. After mustering 300 men, Boerstler marched them north to the Niagara Frontier. Once there, the regimental colonel, William H. Winder, took command. Winder and Boerstler had their hands full with the new officers and raw recruits of the 14th Infantry, and training proceeded slowly. Pay was late, food inadequate, weapons unserviceable, and in October the men were still in their linen summer jackets. Despite these problems, Brig. Gen. Alexander Smyth chose Boerstler and the 14th Infantry to spearhead the invasion of Canada.

In the early hours of 28 November, Boerstler and 200 of his men embarked from Black Rock in 11 boats. Seven boats managed to land, but alert British pickets drove off the others. Boerstler's mission was to destroy the bridge over Frenchman's Creek so British reinforcements could not interfere with the main landing. Boerstler fought his way to the bridge only to discover that his men had left the axes in the boats. Doing what damage they could, Boerstler and his men returned to the U.S. shore. Smyth aborted the main attack, and the 14th wintered over in Buffalo.

When Winder became a brigadier general in March 1813, Boerstler succeeded him to command of the regiment. Boerstler and the 14th moved to Fort George following its capture in May. Although the British had been driven from Fort George, they had not been destroyed. In fact, at Stoney Creek on 6 June, they mauled a U.S. column. Emboldened by their success, the British drew in closer to Fort George. The U.S. commander, Brig. Gen. John P. Boyd, needed to regain the initiative, so he planned a raid to destroy a British outpost near Beaver Dams. Boerstler, eager for a chance to fight, was to lead the attack.

Boerstler's force of 700 included cavalry and artillery built around the 14th Infantry. Setting out from Fort George on 23 June, Boerstler's column marched on muddy roads as his men caught glimpses of Indians in the distance. On 24 June, as they approached Beaver Dams, the Americans entered a forest. As they pushed farther into the woods, Indians to their rear cut the Americans off. Soon firing broke out everywhere. Although wounded in the thigh, Boerstler led a charge that failed to drive off the native warriors. The thick woods made his cannon and cavalry useless, so Boerstler contemplated a fighting withdrawal. He could not, however, leave his many wounded to the mercy of the Indians. The fighting continued for several hours until a regular British officer, Lt. James Fitzgibbon, appeared with a white flag. Fitzgibbon told Boerstler that only surrender would save the Americans from massacre. Tricked into believing that his force was outnumbered and despairing of any alternative, Boerstler surrendered. Fitzgibbon paroled the militia and marched the regulars into captivity. Boerstler himself managed to evade capture and return to U.S. territory.

Unknown to him at the time, Boerstler had received a promotion to full colonel on 20 June. When the army demobilized in 1815, it dropped Charles Boerstler from its rolls. That same year a court of inquiry concluded that his surrender at Beaver Dams had been justified.

—*Richard V. Barbuto*

See also: Beaver Dams, Battle of; Black Rock, New York; Boyd, John Parker; Fitzgibbon, James; George, Fort; Smyth, Alexander; Stoney Creek, Battle of; Winder, William H.

Further Reading

Berton, Pierre. *Flames across the Border: The Canadian-American Tragedy, 1813–1814*. Boston: Little, Brown, 1981.

Stanley, George F.G. *The War of 1812: Land Operations*. Canadian War Museum Historical Publication 18. Toronto: Macmillan, 1983.

BONAPARTE, NAPOLEON

See Napoleon I

BOWYER, FORT
Mobile, Mississippi Territory

Situated on Mobile Point, a 4-mile-wide sandy peninsula that commanded the narrow entrance to Mobile Bay, Fort Bowyer served as an important U.S. post on the Gulf of Mexico. Its location surveyed the mouth of the Alabama and Tombigbee river systems and the coast of Spanish West Florida.

Spanish forces under Capt. Cayetano Perez evacuated Mobile in April 1813. Capt. Reuben Chamberlain, U.S. Army, began building the bastion shortly afterward. Gen. Thomas Flournoy ordered Col. John Bowyer to Mobile Point in June 1813 to complete construction of the fort. The stronghold was a semicircular seaside redoubt of 400 feet. Bluffs skirting both sides of the peninsula surrounded the fortification. When completed, the fort consisted of a sand exterior 15 feet thick at the summit with pine lining the interior. The fort had no casemates, but it boasted nine cannon.

In early July 1814, the fort's vulnerability to a landward attack from the east worried Flournoy. He evacuated the position, moving troops, cannon, and stores to nearby Fort Charlotte at Mobile, 30 miles southeast across the bay. Bowyer was transferred to Plattsburg, New York, never to have the opportunity to defend the fort that bore his name.

By early August 1814, Gen. Andrew Jackson, learning that British forces in Spanish Florida intended to attack Mobile, sent Maj. William Lawrence with 160 men to reconstruct the fort. Lawrence and his men worked diligently over the next month, adding wooden batteries and mounting at least 14 guns. A British force of marines and Indians arrived on 12 September 1814, but the fort repulsed their attack two days later. In February 1815, less than two months after the British defeat at New Orleans, British forces overwhelmed Lawrence's garrison, capturing the bastion. The Treaty of Ghent returned Fort Bowyer to the United States. Years after the war, its name was changed to Fort Morgan.

—Gene A. Smith

See also: Flournoy, [John] Thomas; Ghent, Treaty of; Jackson, Andrew; Lawrence, William; Mobile, Battles of

Further Reading

Brown, Wilburt S. *The Amphibious Campaign for West Florida and Louisiana, 1814–1815: A Critical Review of Strategy and Tactics at New Orleans.* University: University of Alabama Press, 1969.

Coker, William S. "The Last Battle of the War of 1812: New Orleans. No, Fort Bowyer!" *Alabama Historical Quarterly* 43, no. 1 (1981): 43–63.

De Grummond, Jane Lucas *The Baratarians and the Battle of New Orleans.* Baton Rouge, LA: Legacy Publishing, 1961.

Latour, A. Lacarriere. *Historical Memoir of the War in West Florida and Louisiana in 1814–15.* Gainesville: University of Florida Press, 1964.

Owsley, Frank L., Jr., *Struggle for the Gulf Borderlands: The Creek War and the Battle of New Orleans, 1812–1815.* Gainesville: University Presses of Florida, 1981.

BOYD, JOHN PARKER
1764–1830
U.S. officer

John Boyd was born in Newburyport, Massachusetts, to James Boyd and Susanna Boyd. Though too young to serve in the American Revolution, Boyd entered the army as an ensign in 1784. Finding advancement difficult in the small regular establishment following the Revolution, Boyd traveled to India in 1789, where he hired out his services to various Indian princes.

In 1808, Boyd returned to the United States. He obtained a colonel's commission and command of the Fourth Infantry. In 1811, he commanded that regiment when sent to join William Henry Harrison's militia forces in Indiana. Boyd and his men marched with Harrison to Prophet's Town in November of that year and participated in the Battle of Tippecanoe.

When war began with Great Britain in 1812, Boyd was promoted to brigadier general. He served throughout the war on the Canadian border under Henry Dearborn and then James Wilkinson. Under the former, he led his brigade during the second assault on the British positions at Fort George in May 1813. By the middle of June 1813, however, Dearborn had given up most of the territory gained in this campaign.

After the British captured John Chandler and William Winder, two of Dearborn's other brigade commanders, Boyd urged Dearborn to allow him to expand U.S. control from Fort George. Boyd decided to attack the British outpost at Beaver Dams. His field commander for the expedition, Lt. Col. Charles G. Boerstler, led his men out on the night of 25 June. They had tried to keep their target a secret, but the wife of a Canadian militiaman, Laura Secord, overheard the plan and took it to the British. The British commander thus had time to prepare an Indian ambush for Boerstler. Though Boerstler fought his way through the ambush, the attack so unnerved him that he surrendered to the inferior British force.

This disaster possibly revealed Boyd's strategic shortcomings. Contemporaries described him as courageous but limited, something Boyd would have another opportunity to prove when James Wilkinson replaced Dearborn in the fall of 1813. The aged Wilkinson took a long time to prepare his part of another northern invasion. Finally setting out in October, he halted his army on 8 November to confer with his officers. Boyd and several other general officers urged Wilkinson to continue the invasion toward Montreal. Wilkinson reluctantly agreed.

As the expedition made its way down the St. Lawrence, British gunboats following behind and British forces along the shore made the passage miserable. On 10 November, the expedition neared the rapids at Longue Saute. Fearing what awaited them along this dangerous stretch, Wilkinson sent Brig. Gen. Jacob Brown on land to clear the area. Wilkinson then waited until the morning of 11 November to send the rest of the army down the rapids. By then, however, the British gunboats and shore force had caught up to him from behind. To avoid harassment on the trip down the rapids, Wilkinson sent Boyd to dislodge the British land force.

The British force, commanded by Col. Joseph Morrison, drew up for battle on Chrysler's Farm. Though Boyd had almost double Morrison's strength, he attacked before properly organizing his force. He also placed his artillery badly. Boyd consequently lost control of the battle at its outset, as his units entered the fray piecemeal with no apparent coordination. In spite of U.S. strength, the outnumbered British held the field, and Wilkinson had to run the rapids the next day with the British still very close on his heels.

It was all for nothing. Wilkinson learned shortly afterward that Wade Hampton's force would not join the march on Montreal. So Wilkinson, always reluctant about the invasion, now resolved to abandon it. He went into winter quarters at French Mills, having only Boyd's defeat at Chrysler's Farm to show for his trouble.

John Boyd served the last years of the war as he had the first, without distinction. When the war ended, he was one of the officers chosen for dismissal in the reduction of the regular force. He died in Boston in 1830.

—*Jeanne T. Heidler and David S. Heidler*

See also: Beaver Dams, Battle of; Boerstler, Charles G.; Brown, Jacob J.; Chandler, John; Chrysler's Farm, Battle of; Dearborn, Henry; George, Fort; Harrison, William Henry; Montreal; Morrison, Joseph Wanton; Prophet's Town; Secord, Laura Ingersoll; Tippecanoe, Battle of; Wilkinson, James; Winder, William H.
Further Reading
Boyd, John P. *Documents and Facts Relative to Military Operations during the Late War.* N.p., 1816.

BOYLE, THOMAS
1776?–1825
U.S. privateer captain

According to tradition, Thomas Boyle was born in Marblehead, Massachusetts, although his background was obscure. As a young man he moved to Baltimore, Maryland, and used it as his base of operations before and during the War of 1812. Before the war, he commanded various merchant vessels, and once war began, he became the captain of the schooner *Comet* (14 guns). From July to October 1812, he captured prizes worth more than a half million dollars. He set out again from Baltimore in December, eluding British warships guarding the entrance to Chesapeake Bay. During the next year, he added significantly to his prize total.

Beginning in 1814, he assumed command of the *Chasseur* (16 guns), a ship Baltimoreans affectionately referred to as the "Pride of Baltimore." Aboard this swift vessel, Boyle would make his reputation as one of the war's most daring and ingenious U.S. privateers. He spent much of 1814 around the British Isles, wreaking havoc on British merchant shipping there. Ridiculing British paper blockades of the North American coast, Boyle sent word to London that he alone was establishing a blockade of Great Britain. The boastful declaration tweaked British pride, but

his actions seriously injured them. Insurance rates soared for merchant vessels leaving British ports, and insurance became unobtainable for ships traveling between England and Ireland. As he captured almost a score of prizes, Boyle continued to evade numerous British warships.

Leaving British waters at the end of 1814, Boyle sailed for the West Indies. On 26 February 1815, he spotted the sails of what he thought was a rich British merchantman. As he closed, however, he realized his quarry was actually the HMS *Lawrence* (13 guns). Boyle later explained that he would never have sought an engagement with a Royal Navy ship because it would have brought him under the superior gunnery training of hardened crews. Yet he outgunned the *Lawrence*, so he decided to engage her. Within fifteen minutes, the *Lawrence* had surrendered.

Following the war, Boyle returned to the merchant trade. He died at sea in 1825.

—*Jeanne T. Heidler and David S. Heidler*

See also: Privateering
Further Reading
Hopkins, Fred W. *Tom Boyle, Master Privateer.* Cambridge, MD: Tidewater Press, 1976.

BRADY, HUGH
1768–1851
U.S. officer

Born in Pennsylvania, Hugh Brady entered the army as an ensign in the 1790s and served under Maj. Gen. Anthony Wayne in the Fallen Timbers campaign. By 1799, Brady had risen to the rank of captain in the Fourth Infantry Regiment. He left the army in 1800, but he returned at the commencement of war with Great Britain in 1812. Given command as the colonel of the 22nd Regiment of Infantry, Brady saw action on the northern frontier.

The 22nd's most important contributions came in the summer of 1814 in the Battles of Chippewa and Lundy's Lane. In the latter battle, Brady's regiment was a part of Brig. Gen. Winfield Scott's First Brigade. As the British artillery tore into the brigade, Brady's 22nd became tangled with the 11th Regiment when its ammunition ran out and it began to fall back. In the confusion, Brady was badly wounded, though he and his regiment held their own until Maj. Gen. Jacob Brown's reinforcements arrived. Brady and a number of other officers were angry with Brown after the battle because they felt that he did not praise their conduct enough in the battle report.

Following the war, Brady remained in the army and served in the Mexican-American War while in his late seventies. Before he died in Detroit in 1851, Brady reached the brevet rank of major general.

—*Jeanne T. Heidler and David S. Heidler*

See also: Brown, Jacob J.; Chippewa, Battle of; Lundy's Lane, Battle of; Scott, Winfield
Further Reading
Bales, George C. "General Hugh Brady." *Michigan Pioneer* 7 (1877–1878): 573–579.

BROCK, ISAAC
1769–1812
British general

Born in St. Peter Port, Guernsey, 6 October 1769, Isaac Brock was the eighth son of John Brock and Elizabeth De Lisle. He was educated in Guernsey, England, and Rotterdam. He never married. He died at Queenston Heights, Upper Canada (now Ontario), on 13 October 1812.

In 1785, Brock joined the Eighth (King's) Regiment of Foot as an ensign. He became a lieutenant in 1790 and then exchanged into the 49th Foot, where he became a captain. With his regiment, he served in Barbados and Jamaica. He purchased a majority in 1795 and a lieutenant colonelcy in 1797 and by the end of that year was in command of the 49th as its senior lieutenant colonel.

He first saw action in 1799 as part of Sir Ralph Abercromby's expedition to Holland. He suffered a slight wound there while leading a charge across the sand dunes. In 1801, he and his regiment were on Lord Nelson's ships when they attacked Copenhagen. The following year, he took his regiment to Canada. He became a colonel in 1805 and a major general in 1811.

During the decade after his arrival in Canada, at different times he commanded the garrison at Quebec, all the forces in Canada, and finally, beginning in September 1811, the troops in Upper Canada. He also became the administrator of that colony, replacing absent Lt. Gov. Francis Gore. Because Brock was eager for military distinction, he frequently requested to return to Europe. When at last he received approval, however, he decided to remain in Upper Canada because conflict with the United States appeared imminent. Barely four months later, the U.S. government declared war.

Brock called for reinforcements of regulars and energetically pursued other measures to prepare Upper Canada's defenses. In February 1812, he sought support, through the prominent fur trader Robert Dickson, of the western Indians. In March, he obtained from the Upper Canadian assembly an amended militia act that allowed for the formation of voluntary flank companies in each militia battalion. By the end of May, these companies were forming and their training was well underway. They would prove to be the most effective militia forces in Upper Canada.

Unlike the commander of the forces, Sir George Prevost, Brock believed that Upper Canada was defensible. In fact, he thought the most efficacious strategy would be an offensive. By attacking the Americans, particularly in the west, one could win Indian support. Disregarding Prevost's desire for restraint, Brock authorized Capt. Charles Roberts, the officer commanding Fort St. Joseph, to attack Michilimackinac. He caught the U.S. garrison by surprise, and his bloodless victory brought the Indians of the Upper Lakes over to the British. Their presence at Detroit in August would contribute significantly to its capture.

Brock had to meet the legislature in York (now Toronto) before he was free to leave (on 5 August) for Amherstburg to challenge Brig. Gen. William Hull's invasion. He sent ahead York militia volunteers and followed in open boats with men of the 41st Foot and of the Oxford, Norfolk, and Lincoln militias. After a brief conference at the Mohawk village on the Grand River, Brock arrived at Amherstburg's Fort Malden on 13 August. There he met Tecumseh. The next day he conferred with his officers and Indian leaders and decided to attack Detroit. Never one to waste time, on 15 August Brock demanded Hull's surrender. Brock ominously warned that once battle began, he would be unable to control the Indians. This was exploiting Hull's fears, for Brock was well informed about that general's demoralized state and the insubordination among his troops. Early on 16 August, Brock's and Tecumseh's forces crossed the Detroit River, and to their surprise Hull surrendered the fort without firing a shot.

For several reasons, the victory proved crucial to the successful defense of Upper Canada. It eliminated the main U.S. force in the Michigan Territory and put the area under British control for more than a year. The victory also won the British widespread Indian support and a large supply of weapons that Upper Canada badly needed. Most important, Brock saw the frustrating defeatism of Upper Canadians evaporate. Instead, the colony exhibited an increased determination to resist invasion by the United States. As for Brock, his fame rested upon this startling victory. For it he later became not only a knight but "the hero of Upper Canada."

Brock hurried back to the Niagara Frontier. Maj. Gen. Roger Sheaffe had arrived and reinforcements for the 49th were on their way. Recognizing the potential U.S. naval threat on the lakes, Brock intended to attack both Sacket's Harbor and U.S. vessels near Buffalo. Yet Prevost's orders blocked the initiative. The governor had arranged an armistice with the U.S. commander in chief, Maj. Gen. Henry Dearborn.

Brock strengthened the defenses along the Niagara River—for example, building artillery positions—but he knew that U.S. forces greatly outnumbered his own. He guessed that the invasion would target Fort Erie or Fort George rather than Queenston. When the attack came there on 13 October, he at first thought it was a diversion. Nevertheless, he rushed to Queenston from Fort George, ordering militia units along the road to follow him.

Halfway up a steep escarpment from Queenston village, an 18-pounder in a redan covered the landing. As Brock arrived at this position, U.S. soldiers suddenly appeared on the crest above the battery. The surprised British fled down to the village. Brock rallied his forces (a weak company of the 49th and a few York militia) and led a charge against the enemy, firing from behind trees and logs. Over 6 feet tall and in his scarlet uniform tunic, Brock stood out as an obvious target. Within minutes, he was shot in the chest and died almost immediately. There are several versions of his alleged last words, yet no solid proof exists that he said anything, much less what it might have been.

His aide-de-camp, Lt. Col. John Macdonell, hurriedly led a second charge, during which he also fell to a fatal wound. Sheaffe succeeded to Brock's command and successfully ended the battle that afternoon, but Brock's death overshadowed the victory.

Brock's loss was a blow to the defense of Canada, yet it also motivated both militia and regulars. Although Brock commanded only briefly in the war, no other British or Canadian commander would inspire such affection and respect. With aggressive strategy and bold leadership, he proved that Upper Canada could be defended against great odds. Many saw his charge up Queenston Heights as heroic rather than imprudent, and Upper Canadians thirsted for heroes during and after the war. They strongly supported a movement to erect an impressive monument to Brock on the Heights. After the first monument was destroyed, a second was raised, and the "hero of Upper Canada" as well as Macdonell are buried in its base.

—*Wesley B. Turner*

See also: Dearborn, Henry; Detroit, Surrender of; Erie, Fort; George, Fort; Hull, William; Malden, Fort; Michigan Territory; Michilimackinac, Fort; Prevost, George; Queenston, Battle of; Sacket's Harbor, Battle of; Sheaffe, Roger Hale; Tecumseh

Further Reading

Stacey, C. P. "Sir Isaac Brock." *Dictionary of Canadian Biography*, F. G. Halpenny, gen. ed. Vol. 5, pp. 109–115. Toronto: University of Toronto Press, 1983.

Stanley, G.F.G. *The War of 1812. Land Operations.* Ottawa: National Museums of Canada, 1983.

Tupper, Ferdinand Brock. *The Life and Correspondence of Major-General Sir Isaac Brock, K.B.* 2d ed. London: Simpkin, Marshall, 1847.

Zaslow, Morris, ed. *The Defended Border. Upper Canada and the War of 1812.* Toronto: Macmillan, 1964.

BROKE, PHILIP BOWES VERE
1776–1841
British naval officer

Eldest son of Philip Bowes Broke and Elizabeth Beaumont, Philip was born in Broke Hall, Nacton, Suffolk, on 9 September 1776. He entered the Royal Academy, Portsmouth Dockyard, in 1788 and was posted midshipman to the sloop HMS *Bull Dog* on 25 June 1792 under Capt. George Hope. He then went to HMS *L'Eclair* and was present at the siege of Toulon and Bastia. He saw action aboard HMS *Romulous* (36 guns) at Toulon on 11 June 1794 and Genoa on 13–14 March 1795. He was again at Toulon on 13 July 1795, this time aboard the flagship HMS *Britannia* (100 guns). As third lieutenant of the HMS *Southampton* (32 guns), he was in action at Cape St. Vincent on 14 February 1797. He participated in Sir John Borlase Warren's destruction of a French invasion squadron off Ireland on 12 October 1798. Promoted to commander in January 1799, Broke achieved post-captain on 14 February 1801. He went on half-pay and married Sarah Louisa, daughter of Sir William Middleton, on 25 November 1802.

Broke commanded HMS *Druid* in the English Channel during April 1805 and then off the Irish coast. On 31 August 1806, Broke was appointed to HMS *Shannon* (38 guns), an 18-pounder frigate. In short order, he molded a taut, disciplined crew with daily artillery training. The *Shannon* protected whalers off Spitzbergen, participated in the reduction of Madeira in December 1807, and for the next four years cruised off Brest and Plymouth. Broke then joined Vice Adm. Herbert Sawyer's Halifax squadron in September 1811. After war was declared, Broke was part of a small frigate squadron that pursued USS *Constitution* in an epic chase of two days beginning on 17 July 1812.

On 1 June 1813, HMS *Shannon* was blockading Boston alone when USS *Chesapeake* (38 guns) under Capt. James Lawrence sailed, accompanied by numerous pleasure craft. The *Chesapeake* mounted 28 long 18-pounders, main deck, and 18, 32-pound carronades, quarter deck and forecastle. She could throw 1,134 pounds of metal total; her broadside delivered 570 pounds. *Shannon's* starboard broadside—the one to engage this action—fired 538 pounds. This was thus the first wartime encounter of equal 18-pounder frigates.

The *Chesapeake* came on too quickly and, in rounding toward the *Shannon*, exchanged broadsides with her. The *Shannon's* first broadside wounded Lawrence and a hundred of his crew. The *Chesapeake* meanwhile overshot the British frigate on her weather quarter, luffed into the wind, then slowly drifted back into the *Shannon's* starboard bow. In the artillery duel that followed, the *Chesapeake* received a devastating 362 shots while only throwing 158 into the *Shannon*. The vessels were lashed together, and Broke's boarders overpowered the opposition in less than 11 minutes. The *Chesapeake* lost 67 dead and 97 wounded, the *Shannon* 33 dead and 50 wounded.

Lawrence died en route to Halifax on 4 June. Broke had taken a blow to his head from the butt end of a musket. The wound bared his brain, and he never fully recovered. After convalescence, he returned to England, was elevated to a baronetcy on 25 September 1813, and received a KCB on 3 January 1815 and a gold medal. In July 1830, he was promoted to rear admiral of the Red.

Although Broke fathered eleven children, the wound he sustained that day in action against the *Chesapeake* plagued him for the rest of his life. He died 2 January 1841 in London, where he was seeking medical relief for his injury. He is buried in St. Martin's parish church, Nacton.

—*Frederick C. Drake*

See also: *Chesapeake* versus *Shannon;* Lawrence, James
Further Reading
"Biographical Memoir of Sir Philip Bowes Vere Broke." *Naval Chronicle* 33 (1815): 1–22.
Brighton, John G. *Admiral Sir Philip B. V Broke, bart., K. C. B.: A Memoir.* London: Low, Marston, 1866.
Kenneth, Allen. "Broke and the *Shannon.*" In *Sea Captains and Their Ships.* London: Oldham Press, 1965.
Laughton, John Knox. "Broke, Sir Philip Bowes Vere." *Dictionary of National Biography.* Vol. 2, pp. 1294–1295. London: Oxford University Press, 1937–1938.
Marshall, John. *Royal Naval Biography.* Vol. 2, pt. 1, pp. 367–381. London: Hurst, Rees, Orme, Brown and Green, 1824.

BROOKE, ARTHUR
1772–1843
British officer

Born in Ireland, the son of Francis Brooke, Arthur Brooke joined the British army as an ensign in 1792 with the 44th Regiment. He remained with that regiment until 1815. He fought in Flanders in 1794 and 1795 and thereafter rose in the ranks. He earned promotion to captain while serving in the West Indies in 1798, to major while fighting in the Egyptian campaign in 1801 and 1802, and to lieutenant colonel and commander of the regiment while stationed on Malta from 1804 to 1812. Brooke attained the rank of colonel while serving in the Peninsular Campaign in 1813.

Following Napoleon's abdication in the spring of 1814, Brooke and his regiment joined Maj. Gen. Robert Ross in his expedition to Chesapeake Bay. Leading the 44th in the march on Washington, Brooke commanded the right flank at Bladensburg that routed the U.S. left and opened the way to the U.S. capital. Following the burning of Washington, Brooke returned to the Patuxent River with the bulk of the army.

In the subsequent Baltimore campaign, Brooke served as Major General Ross's second in command in the landing at North Point on 11 September. He therefore assumed command of the expedition when Ross was killed by a U.S. rifleman. After repelling the small U.S. force that had killed Ross, Brooke decided to delay an attack on U.S. positions in his front. These Americans, commanded by Baltimore militia brigadier general John Stricker, were considered the cream of the local militia. Because they sported uniforms with a cut that was unusual for militia, Brooke and his officers temporarily mistook them for regulars.

Brooke took the time to plan his assault carefully. He placed his artillery to take out U.S. guns, aimed Congreve Rockets to disorient Stricker's infantry, and then attacked with the view of surrounding Stricker's force. The plan very nearly worked. At the least, it caused a general retreat of the U.S. militiamen. Yet Bread and Cheese Creek gave the Americans a point behind which to rally and prevented the isolation and capture of pockets of Stricker's army. By the time Americans had concentrated behind the creek, it was nearly dark, and Brooke called off the attack for the night. It was a move that allowed Stricker's withdrawal during the night to the main defenses outside of Baltimore.

Brooke moved cautiously toward Baltimore the following morning (13 September). He had to march his army through dense Godly Wood, picking his way around the obstacles Stricker's men had left in his path. When he emerged from the forest at about 10:00 a.m., he faced formidable entrenchments and batteries the Americans had erected to protect Baltimore's eastern approach. A brief reconnaissance revealed to Brooke that defenses northeast of the city were the weakest, and he decided to attack there. As the British moved north, however, they collided with a strong, mobile U.S. force blocking their path. Brooke ordered his men back and contemplated a direct assault from due east. He abandoned this idea after determining the maneuver would leave both of his flanks exposed.

Having wasted the day, Brooke then decided on a surprise night attack. He ordered campfires stoked to convince Americans that the British planned no more fighting that day. It promised to be a rainy night, so Brooke could also count on poor visibility to cloak his design. For Brooke's plan to work, however, a number of events had to occur almost simultaneously. A diversionary attack at the southern end of the U.S. defenses had to take place immediately before the main attack on the northern part. Before the diversion could occur, though, Adm. Alexander Cochrane's naval guns in the Patapsco River would have to silence "Rogers's Bastion," an emplacement of 20 heavy U.S. guns just south of the diversion's objective. Yet Cochrane's failure to reduce Fort McHenry meant that he could not get close enough to use his guns against the U.S. battery. An attempt to land a force from his ships in the U.S. rear also failed.

When it became clear that Cochrane could not fulfill his part of the plan, Brooke and Adm. George Cockburn, who had accompanied the land assault, decided to withdraw. At about 2:00 A.M. on 14 September, Brooke began leading his army back to North Point. The Americans first thought the withdrawal a trick, but soon enough a small force was in harrying pursuit. Before Brooke could turn his army to fight, his rear guard sharply repelled the Americans, who quickly returned to their lines. After camping for the night near North Point, Brooke and his men were back aboard ship by the morning of 15 September.

Though he remained in the army, Colonel Brooke never saw combat again following the War of 1812. He was nevertheless promoted to major general in 1819 and achieved the rank of lieutenant general before his death in London in 1843.

—*Jeanne T. Heidler and David S. Heidler*

See also: Bladensburg, Battle of; Chesapeake Bay Campaign, 1813–1814; Cochrane, Alexander; Cockburn, George; Congreve Rockets; McHenry, Fort; Ross, Robert; Stricker, John

Further Reading
Jenkins, B. Wheeler. "The Shots that Saved Baltimore." *Maryland Historical Magazine* 77 (1982): 362–364.

BROWN, JACOB J.
1775–1828
U.S. officer

Born in Bucks County, Pennsylvania, to Samuel Brown and Abi White Brown, members of old Quaker families, young Brown received a good education as a child. He was thus able to make a living for a time as a schoolteacher when his father suffered financial reverses. After briefly working as a surveyor in the Northwest, he moved to New York, first to New York City and then to the frontier area around Lake Ontario, where he established an estate and founded Brownville.

As a prominent citizen of the state, Brown was offered a state militia commission. He abandoned his Quaker upbringing of pacifism to accept command of the local regiment. He worked so diligently to organize and train the men under his command that he rose in the state officers' estimation to the rank of brigadier general by 1811, the rank he held at the outbreak of the War of 1812.

Situated in an area certain to see hostilities, Brown's frontier militia command put him into action very soon. After participating in a skirmish at Ogdensburg, New York, his next major action gained him a wider reputation. In May 1813, Gen. Sir George Prevost heard that Sacket's Harbor was defended by only 160 men and determined to deprive Commodore Isaac Chauncey's fleet of a safe haven. Hearing that Prevost had left Kingston accompanied by Adm. Sir James Yeo's fleet, Brown immediately summoned all militia and regulars in the area to Sacket's Harbor. The last of his reinforcements arrived just as Yeo's ships approached the harbor.

Brown commanded approximately 400 regulars and 500 militia against a British regular force under the immediate command of Col. Edward Baynes and the overall

Jacob J. Brown

command of Prevost. When the British landed on 29 May and approached Brown's defenses, he placed his militia in front, perhaps in the hopes that the regulars behind them would give them courage. It was a false hope. Confronted by the martial assurance of the crack British regulars, the U.S. militiamen broke and ran. Brown's regulars stood, however, and using the wooded terrain and obstacles that had been prepared for them were able to inflict enormous casualties on the still-advancing British. Nevertheless, Brown needed more men to hold the harbor. He knew that the fleeing militiamen were still too frightened to rejoin the fight, so sending word to them that the British were on the run, he invited them to join the chase. Thinking they could take part in the final victory, about 300 militiamen returned. When Prevost saw their approach, he believed that Brown was receiving reinforcements on the British flank, so he withdrew.

Brown's defense of Sacket's Harbor gained him a national reputation when the country was in great need of good military news. Secretary of War John Armstrong awarded Brown a regular commission as a brigadier general in July 1813. In the fall, as a new regular officer, he was assigned to the impending campaign against Montreal commanded by Maj. Gen. James Wilkinson. Though this expedition ended disastrously, Brown's role in it further enhanced his reputation.

Most of the army moved down the St. Lawrence River aboard boats as Brown's brigade took turns with others trying to clear the banks of British pursuers. When the army approached the Longue Saute, an 8-mile stretch of rapids, the British in the rear closed in. To complicate the U.S. position further, scouts reported that the British occupied a fortified position at the other end of the rapids. While part of the army fought the Battle of Chrysler's Farm on 11 November, Brown took his brigade by land down the rapids to clear the British from the area.

An unimpressive U.S. performance at Chrysler's Farm was mitigated by word from Brown that he had successfully cleared away the British at the end of the rapids. The army proceeded down the watercourse, but at the other end Wilkinson learned that he would not be joined against Montreal by the army under Maj. Gen. Wade Hampton. Wilkinson abandoned the campaign and put the army into winter quarters at French Mills. Wilkinson had been ill for most of the campaign, and he now took to his bed and turned the army over to Brown. The Americans endured miserable conditions for two months until Brown received orders in February 1814 to take the army to Sacket's Harbor. After a dreary march back, Brown replaced General Wilkinson as commander of the Army of the North.

Throughout the spring and early summer of 1814, Brown planned how he would use his new command, especially as reinforcements made their way to Lake Ontario. Confusing orders from Secretary of War John Armstrong led Brown to think he had authorization to invade Canada across the Niagara River. On 3 July 1814, he crossed the river with about 3,500 men in three columns, two brigades of regulars under Brig. Gens. Winfield Scott and Eleazar Ripley and militia under Brig. Gen. Peter B. Porter. After Americans fired a few rounds at Fort Erie, the British garrison there surrendered. Leaving a small force to occupy the fort, Brown sent Scott's brigade up the Canadian bank of the Niagara River toward Lake Ontario. Brown meanwhile sent word to Commodore Isaac Chauncey at Sacket's Harbor to rendezvous with the army so they could cooperate in a joint campaign against the British along the lake.

Learning that Brown had crossed the Niagara, British brigadier general Phineas Riall marched his army toward Fort Erie. Scott ran into Riall on 5 July when he noticed the presence of British soldiers and Indians in the woods to his left. Thinking that it was only a small party of the enemy, he sent Porter and his militia into the trees to clear them. Porter's men soon scampered back to report that the main British army waited just ahead. In fact, Riall was not only just ahead, he had brought his army across the Chippewa River and was quickly advancing on Scott as the Americans hastily formed for battle. Scott's well-trained men—he drilled them incessantly—executed a series of difficult maneuvers as Riall recklessly advanced under the mistaken impression that Brown's invasion force was mainly militia. As the two armies clashed, Riall soon discovered his error. After intense fighting, the British withdrew across the river, and Brown continued his advance to Lake Ontario.

When the U.S. army arrived at the lake on 10 July, Brown was surprised not to find Chauncey's squadron waiting on him. Three days later, Brown had become so concerned about increasing British forces in the area that he sent a pleading letter to Sacket's Harbor. Brown did not know that Chauncey lay dangerously ill, but even if Chauncey had been healthy, the petulant commodore had no intention of making his fleet the servant of the army. Brown, deprived of Chauncey's cooperation, had to retreat toward Fort Erie to reestablish lines of supply and communication. Riall had been reinforced by the overall British commander, Lt. Gen. Gordon Drummond, and these forces threatened to isolate Brown from his base.

Moving across the Chippewa River, Brown hoped to delay the oncoming British by sending Scott back to engage their advance units. Scott found the British army well placed along Lundy's Lane, the sound of Niagara Falls thundering nearby. Significantly outnumbered, the Americans were soon in trouble. The battle turned into a savage affair, continuing even after dark as Brown brought the rest of the army up about 9:00 P.M. to assume command of the field. Brown sent Col. James Miller to take a British hilltop battery, but by the time Miller succeeded, both Scott and Brown had been seriously wounded and forced to leave the field. Brown's wounds, a musket shot in the thigh and severe bruises from a spent artillery ball, temporarily knocked him out of the war. Scott's wounds were more serious, ending his participation in the War of 1812.

The battle finally spent itself, and the U.S. army withdrew to Fort Erie. There Brig. Gen. Edmund Pendleton Gaines took command in Brown's absence. While Brown recovered, the British began a formal siege of Fort Erie and staged an attack on the fort on 15 August. The Americans successfully repulsed the attack, but the British brought in heavy guns for daily artillery bombardments. On 29 August, one of the British shells crashed through Gaines's room in the fort, so severely wounding him that he had to relinquish command. Brown, though not completely recovered from his own wounds, returned.

The British artillery barrages became intolerable. Many of Brown's officers urged him to evacuate the fort and retreat to the U.S. side of the river, but he refused. Instead, he planned a surprise sortie to take the British artillery. On the night of 17 September, in the midst of a rainstorm, the foray commenced in two columns. After intense fighting around the batteries, the Americans spiked the guns of two of three British batteries and returned to the fort. Drummond lifted the siege on 21 September.

Although of little strategic value, Brown's Niagara Campaign and the successful defense of Fort Erie lifted the country's spirits at an important time. Much of the nation was hearing about British advances in eastern New York and the destruction of Washington, D.C., so the plucky persistence along the Niagara became important psychologically. As a result, Brown emerged from the War of 1812 a national hero.

When the army was reduced following the war, Brown remained in service as the senior ranking officer. When Congress cut the number of major generals from two to one in the army reduction of 1821, Brown received the distinction of becoming the first commanding general of the army. He held that position until his death in 1828.

—Jeanne T. Heidler and David S. Heidler

See also: Armstrong, John; Baynes, Edward; Chauncey, Isaac; Chippewa, Battle of; Chrysler's Farm, Battle of; Drummond, Gordon; Erie, Fort; Gaines, Edmund Pendleton; Hampton, Wade; Kingston, Upper Canada; Lundy's Lane, Battle of; Miller, James; Ogdensburg, Battle of; Porter, Peter Buell; Prevost, George; Riall, Phineas; Ripley, Eleazar Wheelock; Sacket's Harbor, New York; Scott, Winfield; Wilkinson, James; Yeo, James Lucas

Further Reading

Babcock, Louis L. *The War of 1812 on the Niagara Frontier.* Buffalo: Buffalo Historical Society, 1927.

Cruikshank, E. A., ed. *The Documentary History of the Campaign upon the Niagara Frontier 1812–1814.* 9 vols. Welland, Ont.: Lundy's Lane Historical Society, 1896–1908.

Hoard, Gerard C. *Major General Jacob Jennings Brown.* Watertown, NY: Hungerford, Holbrook, 1979.

BROWN, NOAH
1770–?
Shipbuilder; merchant

Noah Brown was born at "Salem" county, northern New York, and raised in Stamford, Delaware County. He and three brothers survived captivity by Indians, who killed his father in 1780. Trained as a house carpenter from 1785 to 1792, Brown then worked in New York until 1804. After he and his brother Adam built a North West Company schooner, the *Work,* at Newark, Upper Canada, in 1804, Noah was employed at the Forman Cheesman Yard in New York. Next spring, the brothers built a whale ship at Sag Harbor, Long Island, and in 1807 worked at George Peek's shipyard. The two cut live oak in North Carolina for the frigate *New York* from 1807 to 1808, built five navy gunboats in 1809, repaired the *Brooklyn*, and built the privateers *General Armstrong, Paul Jones, Prince de Neufchatel, Warrior, Yorktown,* and *Zebra* at New York from 1812 to 1814.

In January 1813, when Commodore Isaac Chauncey hired Henry Eckford to build lake vessels, he appointed Noah to work with Daniel Dobbins at Erie, Pennsylvania. From late February to June 1813, Brown finished three gunboats, a despatch schooner, and Perry's brigs *Lawrence* and *Niagara.*

Noah and Adam built the U.S. sloop *Peacock* at Corlears Hook, New York, from July through September 1813. By March 1814, they were working for Master Commandant Thomas Macdonough on Lake Champlain, building the ship *Saratoga* (26 guns) and nine gunboats and converting the steamer *Vincennes* into *Ticonderoga* (17 guns). In June, they commenced the brig *Eagle* (18 guns), launched August 11. They returned to New York to build Robert Fulton's *Demologus* and his torpedo-boat *Mute.* They next worked with Eckford on two 120-gun ships at Sacket's and Henderson's Harbors.

After the war, Noah was elected assistant alderman of New York's Tenth Ward in 1815 and 1816 as a Republican. He ceased shipbuilding in 1833 after completing the ferryboat *Sussex.*

—*Frederick C. Drake*

See also: Chauncey, Isaac; *Demologus;* Macdonough, Thomas
Further Reading

Brown, Noah. "The Remarkable Statement of Noah Brown." *Journal of American History* 8 (1914): 103–108.

"Career of Daniel Dobbins now for the first time compiled from original documents," including "The Dobbins Papers, Early Days on the Lakes, and Episodes of the War of 1812, written by Captain William W. Dobbins from the Papers and Reminiscences of His Father," ed. Frank H. Severance. *Publications of the Buffalo Historical Society* 8 (1905): 257–379.

Chapelle, Howard. *The History of the American Sailing Navy: The Ships and Their Development.* New York: W. W. Norton, 1949.

———. *The Search for Speed under Sail 1700–1855.* New York: W. W. Norton, 1967.

Crisman, Kevin J. *The* Eagle: *An American Brig on Lake Champlain during the War of 1812.* Shelburne, VT: New England Press; Annapolis, MD: Naval Institute Press, 1987.

Rosenburg, Max. *The Building of Perry's Fleet on Lake Erie.* Harrisburg, PA: Historical and Museum Commission, 1950.

Thorpe, Francis N. "The Building of the Fleet." *Pennsylvania Magazine of History and Biography* 37 (1913): 257–297.

BROWNSTOWN, BATTLE OF
5 August 1812

As William Hull became increasingly nervous about his supply and communication lines during his invasion of Canada, on 4 August 1812 he dispatched Maj. Thomas Van Horne back to Detroit to lead an expedition of about 200 men south from there to reopen those lines. Rather than taking back paths out of Detroit as suggested by Hull, Van Horne left the town by the main road, carrying with him communications from Hull outlining what he viewed as his increasingly precarious position.

As Van Horne neared Brownstown, he stopped his small force at a French settler's house to obtain water. The Frenchman warned Van Horne that a party of Indians was preparing an ambush closer to town. Van Horne apparently did not believe him, because he took no special precautions as he set out again toward Brownstown. Before reaching the town, Van Horne's men were fired on by a party consisting primarily of Indians led by Tecumseh. Van Horne, fearing that his attackers were planning to surround his army, ordered a retreat, which threw the already frightened men into a panic. Some reports claim that Tecumseh accomplished this task with as few as 25 warriors. One of the things left behind in the flight was Hull's mail, which was delivered to the British at Fort Malden. Van Horne and most of his men eventually made it back to Detroit, losing 17 killed and several wounded. His failure to open the lines out of Detroit further agitated an already anxious Hull.

—*Jeanne T. Heidler and David S. Heidler*

See also: Detroit, Surrender of; Hull, William; Malden, Fort; Tecumseh
Further Reading

Quaife, Milo M. "The Story of Brownstown." *Burton Historical Collection Leaflet* 4 (1926): 65–80.

BUFFALO, NEW YORK

No other town in the United States saw more of the war than Buffalo. Its 400 residents made Buffalo the largest village on the U.S. shore of the Niagara River. Hundreds and sometimes thousands of soldiers camped nearby throughout the conflict. Named after nearby Buffalo Creek, the frontier village guarded the eastern end of Lake Erie where it rapidly narrowed into the Niagara River. Fort Erie, a British post, was directly west across the Niagara's southern mouth, and nearby was a large Seneca reservation. Buffalo's commercial rival, Black Rock, sat 2 miles downriver.

The first major action near Buffalo occurred on 9 October 1812 when U.S. Navy lieutenant Jesse D. Elliott led a daring night raid across the river. The raiders captured two brigs anchored under Fort Erie's guns and brought them to the U.S. shore. This small victory heartened Americans demoralized by Hull's surrender of Detroit in August.

After the defeat at Queenston Heights, Brig. Gen. Alexander Smyth assumed command of U.S. forces on the Niagara Frontier. Smyth marshaled his troops at Buffalo, but his two attempts to invade Upper Canada were dismal failures. Buffalo daily faced the British at Fort Erie during 1813. After the Battle of Fort George, the British had pulled back from their line on the river, but the Americans abandoned Fort George in December, burning the Upper Canada village of Newark in the process. British retaliation brought the war into the streets and homes of Buffalo.

After seizing Fort Niagara on 19 December, Lt. Gen. Gordon Drummond ordered his subordinate, Maj. Gen. Phineas Riall, to exploit this success. On the evening of 29 December, Riall crossed the Niagara below Black Rock and in the early morning hours attacked that village. More than 2,000 U.S. militia and a handful of Iroquois warriors rallied to defend Black Rock and Buffalo. This untrained and largely inexperienced force was no match for Riall's regulars and Indians. After a feeble defense, the defenders broke and fled. The village trustees of Buffalo implored Dr. Cyrenius Chapin, an occasional leader of irregular raiders, to negotiate a surrender of the village. Chapin received Riall's assurance that private property was safe, but over the next two days the British burned Buffalo and nearly every structure along the U.S. side of the Niagara. Only Fort Niagara remained. Some of Riall's Indian allies killed and scalped about a dozen civilians. Nearly the entire population fled eastward into the snowy forests, refugees from what had become a cruel war.

Buffalo rebounded. When Winfield Scott marched his brigade into the ruins of the village in April, confidence returned. Buffalo became the base for Jacob Brown's invasion of Canada in July, and reinforcements and supplies from Buffalo sustained Fort Erie during its six-week siege. After the war, Buffalo became the western terminus of the Erie Canal and a starting point for an epic westward expansion.

—*Richard V. Barbuto*

See also: Black Rock, New York; Brown, Jacob J.; Detroit, Surrender of; Drummond, Gordon; Elliott, Jesse Duncan; Erie, Fort; George, Fort; Hull, William; Newark, Upper Canada; Niagara Campaigns; Queenston, Battle of; Riall, Phineas; Scott, Winfield; Smyth, Alexander

Further Reading
Babcock, Louis L. *The War of 1812 on the Niagara Frontier.* Buffalo: Buffalo Historical Society, 1927.

BURBECK, HENRY
1754–1848
U.S. Army officer

At the start of the War of 1812, Henry Burbeck was the Grand Old Man of U.S. artillery. He was born in Boston on 8 June 1754, the son of William Burbeck, a provincial British officer at Castle William in Boston Harbor. At the start of the Revolutionary War, William Burbeck was the lieutenant colonel of Gridley's Massachusetts Artillery Regiment, and his son, Henry, became a first lieutenant in that same unit. Henry Burbeck fought at Bunker Hill and was one of the few officers retained when Gridley's Regiment was converted to Henry Knox's Continental Artillery Regiment.

Henry Burbeck served as an artillery officer throughout the entire Revolution. He fought at Brandywine, Germantown, and Monmouth and was present during the long winter at Valley Forge. On 12 September 1777, he was promoted to captain and given command of a company in the Third Continental Artillery after its commanding officer was killed at Brandywine. One of Burbeck's lieutenants in that company was Moses Porter. At the end of the war, Burbeck received a brevet promotion to major in September 1783 and left the continental service that following November.

Burbeck returned to military service on 20 October 1786 as a captain in the newly formed battalion of U.S. Artillery. He was given command of a newly raised company that today is the U.S. Army's First Battalion, Fourth Air Defense Artillery. From August 1787 to April 1790, Burbeck was the post commander at West Point. He then spent several years on the western frontier serving under Gen. Anthony Wayne in the war against the western Indians. Burbeck became the major-commandant of the Battalion of U.S. Artillery in 1791, the lieutenant colonel commandant of the Corps of Artillerists and Engineers in 1798, and the colonel of the Regiment of Artillerists in 1802. In the spring of 1810, Burbeck served as the president of a board of officers convened by Secretary of War William Eustis to review Winfield Scott's claim to a major's vacancy in the Regiment of Light Artillery. Scott was the senior captain in that regiment, but at the time he was under suspension by sentence of court-martial. The board ruled against Scott, and the majority went to Abraham Eustis, who, incidentally, was the secretary's nephew.

Burbeck served as the commander of the Regiment of Artillerists until May 1814, when the three U.S. foot artillery regiments were consolidated to form the Corps of Artillery. Although he was the senior U.S. artillery officer at the start of the war, he saw little actual field service. At first, he commanded the defenses of New York Harbor. In 1813, he was the senior ranking colonel in the U.S. Army. That year he was brevetted brigadier general and assigned command of the Second Military District, headquartered at New London. There he encountered problems with the Rhode Island militia, which refused to recognize the authority of the federal government over that of the state. Burbeck handled the problem by dismissing the militia organization from federal service, thus placing the expense of defending Rhode Island on the state. Rhode Island quickly fell back into line.

Burbeck retired from the U.S. Army in June 1815. He died at the age of 94 in New London, Connecticut, on 2 October 1848.

—*David T. Zabecki*

See also: Eustis, William; Porter, Moses; Rhode Island; Scott, Winfield

Further Reading

Birkhimer, William E. *Historical Sketch of the Organization, Administration, Materiel and Tactics of the Artillery, United States Army.* Washington, DC: Chapman, 1884.

Downey, Fairfax. *The Sound of the Guns.* New York: David McKay, 1955.

Heitman, F. B. *Historical Register of the United States Army.* Washington, DC: The National Tribune, 1890.

McKenney, Janice. *Air Defense Artillery: Army Lineage Series.* Washington, DC: Center of Military History, 1985.

BURLINGTON, VERMONT

Burlington, Vermont, became a shipbuilding town and army supply depot in spring 1813 when U.S. Army lieutenant Thomas Macdonough commenced building new vessels and renamed his small 1812 flotilla (*Hunter* became *Growler* and *Bull Dog* became *Eagle*), which had win-

tered in Shelburne Bay on Lake Champlain. Virginian Gen. Thomas Parker, transferred from the Niagara Frontier and commanding the first brigade—the 4th, 30th, and 31st regiments—thus found himself guarding a huge depot of military stores at Burlington. He assumed these stores would attract the British. At the end of July, Parker's fears were realized when Lt. Col. John Murray and Capt. Thomas Everard attacked Plattsburg, Swanton, and Champlain with 946 officers and men. They burned public property, the barracks, and the hospital and destroyed lake bateaux and naval stores. Gen. Wade Hampton, who arrived to take command at Burlington early in July, made preparations to defend the town.

Macdonough's *President* and the two gunboats were moored directly under the high bank of the encampment. Two partially completed sloops filled with men from the garrison swung on spring cables and sported six guns each. E. S. Churchill's company of artillery manned a 12-gun battery in the encampment. Hampton evacuated women and children, and the town labored to hide private property before the British arrived.

It all amounted to a hollow alarm. On 1 August, British vessels did begin bombarding the town, and the next day, U.S. observers in the college belfry battled the heat and humidity as much as the British salvos. The British flotilla began firing shortly after 2 P.M., but after discharging 200 shot at long range, the ships left, having done little injury to Burlington.

—*Frederick C. Drake*

See also: Hampton, Wade; Macdonough, Thomas

Further Reading

Bellico, Russell P. *Sails and Steam in the Mountains: A Maritime and Military History of Lake George and Lake Champlain.* New York: Purple Mountain Press, 1992.

Coit, Daniel. "The British Attack on Burlington." *Vermont History* 29 (1961): 82–86.

Hill, Henry W. "Otter Creek in History." *Vermont Historical Society Proceedings* 8 (1913–1914): 138.

BURN, JAMES
d. 1823
U.S. officer

Though originally from South Carolina, James Burn made his home in Virginia and then Pennsylvania. As part of the military buildup occasioned by the Quasi-War,

Burn entered the U.S. Army as a captain of cavalry in March 1799, only to see his regiment disbanded in June 1800 with the end of hostilities with France.

As war loomed with Great Britain in 1812, Burn's regular army experience and his service as a cavalryman with the Virginia militia made him a potential asset to the U.S. Army. When the War Department created the Second Light Dragoon Regiment, Burn was made its colonel and commander. From the beginning, however, dragoon units were neglected by the War Department. For example, Burn's commission was not delivered until 6 July 1812, four months after the creation of the regiment. Even with commission finally in hand, Burn was not allowed to recruit the entire regiment at once. Once he began assembling men in upstate New York, most were without full uniforms well into the winter, and only half of them had horses by the fall, an unfortunate situation for new dragoons in need of training. These difficulties were surmounted, but the War Department then scattered Burn's companies from the Niagara Frontier to the Northwest. Burn probably never had his entire regiment, fully horsed and equipped, in one place throughout the entire war.

While his horsemen were being scattered to the winds, Burn kept two companies along the Niagara, where he remained for much of the war. As part of Maj. Gen. Henry Dearborn's campaign against Fort George on 25 May 1813, Burn and his two companies had the job of crossing the Niagara River south of Fort George to prevent the British retreating from the fort from reaching Queenston. As he prepared to cross the river, however, withering fire from the British batteries on the other side pinned down his force. After the British had evacuated Fort George and their retreat became general, the British artillerymen left with their guns, and Burn crossed the river.

As he brought his first company ashore, Burn met Col. Winfield Scott, and together they decided to pursue the beleaguered British garrison. As the two officers waited for Burn's second company to come across the river, an order from Dearborn's headquarters called off the attack. Allowing the entire British force to escape then necessitated a series of expeditions over the next few weeks to give the Americans at Fort George some breathing room. One of those expeditions resulted in the Battle of Stoney Creek on 5 June 1813, in which Burn and his dragoons took part.

Inexplicably, the dragoons were placed at the rear of the army under Brig. Gens. William Winder and John Chandler. The British surprised the U.S. camp on 5 June and captured both Winder and Chandler, leaving Burn as the senior ranking officer and hence in command of the confused and frightened U.S. force. After consulting the other officers, Burn decided to withdraw.

The following year the First and Second Dragoons were consolidated into one, and Burn assumed command of the new regiment. When the war ended, however, Congress deemed horse units too expensive to maintain, and the dragoons were disbanded. Burn consequently left the army for the last time and died in Frankfort, Pennsylvania, in 1823.

—*Jeanne T. Heidler and David S. Heidler*

See also: Chandler, John; George, Fort; Scott, Winfield; Stoney Creek, Battle of; Winder, William H.

Further Reading

Coleman, Margaret. *The American Capture of Fort George, Ontario.* Ottawa: Department of Northern and Indian Affairs, 1977.

BURNT CORN, BATTLE OF
27 July 1813

Burnt Corn, the opening battle of the Creek War of 1813 and 1814, transformed a civil war within the Creek Nation into a larger conflict with the United States. That conflict, in turn, introduced a new era of total warfare to the Mississippi Territory. U.S. soldiers and militiamen not only battled their opponents with guns but also destroyed their crops and homes.

Up to 1813, Agent Benjamin Hawkins successfully shielded the 30,000-member Creek Nation from white settlers while at the same time introducing the Indians to ways of white men. There were, however, conservative tribesmen who believed their nation was under siege. White settlements already peppered the Alabama and Georgia countrysides. What could the Creek Nation do? The Red Sticks, a faction of Creek leaders dazzled by Anglo-Indian victories in the Northwest and by promises of aid from Spanish colonists in Florida, decided to take matters into their own hands. They inspired several massacres that triggered a civil war within the Creek Nation. The conflict was between the war faction, represented by the youthful Red Sticks and their 4,000 supporters, and the accommodationists, represented by tribal elders and their followers. The Battle of Burnt Corn tipped the balance of power in favor of the Red Sticks, who were reassured by the British that if the Red Sticks faced defeat at the hands of the Americans, British ships would evacuate the Indians to Cuba. As a result, what began as a tribal dispute became a war against the United States.

In July 1813, Peter McQueen, a leader of the war faction, took 350 men to Pensacola, Florida, to obtain arms. News of McQueen's activities quickly reached Col. James Caller of Washington County, Mississippi Territory, the senior military officer in the area. To prevent a major Creek uprising, Caller believed he had to seize McQueen's munitions. The colonel mustered 180 militiamen and began his search.

On 27 July 1813, he found McQueen's pack train 80 miles north of Pensacola at Burnt Corn Creek. When Caller and his men overwhelmed the dozen Indians guarding the train, they thought they had won a bloodless victory. The Americans did not notice the nearly 100 tribesmen in the woods and swamp nearby. When the undisciplined militiamen became preoccupied with their captured goods, the Red Sticks counterattacked. The Americans fled in panic for several miles before they finally organized a rational retreat.

The number of dead and injured in the Battle of Burnt Corn remains unknown, but it was an obvious (and uncommon) victory. The Red Sticks were eager to fight on, but they had no plans for a long-term war, nor did they have good leadership, sufficient arms, or the promised support of the British. Nevertheless, the Creek War lasted over one year, primarily because of U.S. supply shortages, the constant turnover of militia, and jurisdictional disputes between the Sixth and Seventh U.S. Military Districts.

—*Peter R. Faber*

See also: Creek War; Hawkins, Benjamin; McQueen, Peter; Red Sticks

Further Reading

Millett, Allan R., and Peter Maslowski. *For the Common Defense.* New York: The Free Press, 1984.
Owsley, Frank L., Jr. *Struggle for the Gulf Borderlands: The Creek War and the Battle of New Orleans, 1812–1815.* Gainesville: University Presses of Florida, 1981.
Tucker, Glenn. *Poltroons and Patriots.* Indianapolis: Bobbs-Merrill, 1954.

BURROWS, WILLIAM
1785–1813
U.S. naval officer

William Burrows, son of Lt. Col. W. W. Burrows, first commandant of the U.S. Marine Corps, entered the U.S. Navy as a midshipman in November 1799. His first assignment started in January 1800 aboard the gunship *Portsmouth.* Sailing to France under the command of

Daniel McNeill, Burrows saw naval action that captured two French privateers. After further study in French and navigation, Burrows was promoted to lieutenant aboard the *Constitution* and saw action in the Tripolitan war.

Between 1808 and 1813, Burrows moved from enforcing the embargo with naval patrols along the Delaware River to distinguishing himself aboard the *President* and *Hornet.* Neither his intrepidity nor seamanship earned him recognition, however. Disappointed that he was not promoted, Burrows resigned. The navy refused the resignation. Instead, the government gave Burrows a year's furlough that he spent on a merchant ship in India and China. As Burrows returned home aboard the *Thomas Penrose,* the British captured the ship. After a temporary incarceration in Barbados, Burrows was paroled and returned to the United States, where the navy gave him command of the sloop *Enterprise* (16 guns).

Sailing from Portsmouth, New Hampshire, on 5 September 1813, Burrows saw action the next day against HMS *Boxer.* After an intense hour of exchange, the *Boxer,* raked and without her main-topmast, surrendered. Severely wounded during battle, Burrows continued to command his ship and lived long enough to accept the surrender of the *Boxer.* Burrows and HMS *Boxer*'s Captain Blythe, who also died in the battle (he had been cut in two by chain shot), were buried in adjacent graves in Portland, Maine. Congress posthumously awarded William Burrows a gold medal. The *Enterprise*'s victory was the first since the loss of the *Chesapeake* in June 1813 and restored national morale.

—*William A. Paquette*

See also: *Enterprise* versus *Boxer*

Further Reading

Dudley, William S., ed. *The Naval War of 1812; A Documentary History.* 2 vols. Washington, DC: Department of the Navy, 1985–1992.

BUTLER, WILLIAM O.
1791–1880
U.S. Army officer

William O. Butler was born in Kentucky to Percival Butler and Mildred Hawkins Butler. Butler graduated from Transylvania University shortly before the United States declared war against Great Britain in 1812. Leaving his law studies, Butler enlisted in the army. Because of his excellent performance, he quickly rose to the officer ranks.

William O. Butler

As part of the Kentucky forces under William Henry Harrison and Maj. Richard M. Johnson in September 1812, Butler was sent to Fort Wayne in that month. Serving under Brig. Gen. James Winchester and operating out of Fort Wayne, Butler was wounded and captured by the British on 22 January 1813 at the Battle of Frenchtown.

He was fortunate to escape the fate of many at the River Raisin, when Col. Henry Procter's Indian allies systematically murdered the wounded.

After Butler's exchange, he was commissioned a captain in the Kentucky Volunteers; after raising his company, he traveled to Alabama in time to serve under Maj. Gen. Andrew Jackson in the latter's campaign against Pensacola and in the defense of New Orleans.

At New Orleans, on the night of 23 December 1814, Butler led one of the attacks on Maj. Gen. John Keane's British advanced landing force. Though this attack did not succeed in repulsing the British, it did cause the British to halt their advance in anticipation of the arrival of their overall commander, Lt. Gen. Sir Edward Pakenham. Butler's actions on 23 December 1814 and in the final defeat of the British on 8 January 1815 earned him the praise of Major General Jackson and eventual elevation to the general's staff.

Following the War of 1812, Butler resumed the study of law, though he returned to military service briefly as a volunteer general in the Mexican-American War. Entering politics, Butler served in the Kentucky state legislature and in the U.S. Congress.

—*Jeanne T. Heidler and David S. Heidler*

See also: Frenchtown, Battles of; Harrison, William Henry; Jackson, Andrew; Johnson, Richard Mentor; Keane, John; New Orleans, Battle of; Pakenham, Edward; Pensacola, Battle of; Procter, Henry; Wayne, Fort; Winchester, James

Further Reading

Roberts, Gerald F. "William O. Butler, Kentucky Cavalier." Master's thesis, University of Kentucky, 1971.

C

CABOT, GEORGE
1752–1823
Massachusetts merchant; U.S. senator

Born in Salem, Massachusetts, to John Cabot and Elizabeth Higginson Cabot, George Cabot attended Harvard College but left before graduation. He then entered a maritime career, first as a cabin boy, then as captain of a schooner in his older brothers' merchant fleet. He proved so successful at the business side of trading that his brothers accepted him as a partner in 1777. During the American Revolution, the firm reaped steady profits in privateering. After the Revolution, Cabot became involved in banking and other investments and was so successful that he retired from business before he turned 45.

Retirement allowed Cabot to engage another interest that he had been pursuing intermittently since the Revolution—politics. In 1791, he began serving his first term as a U.S. senator from Massachusetts. In the Senate, he quickly joined the faction associated with Secretary of the Treasury Alexander Hamilton, the core of what would become the Federalist Party. Nothing apparently held Cabot's interest for long, however, and he resigned from the Senate in 1796.

Over the next few years, Cabot and members of other old Massachusetts families began relocating to Boston, where they became the nucleus of business and political power in the state. Though officially retired from public life, Cabot became something of an elder statesmen for this tight-knit, aristocratic group. Because of his measured approach to what most New England Federalists considered the great crises of the age—Thomas Jefferson's election, the embargo, and the War of 1812—he generally diverted them from drastic action.

Still, no one mistook his deliberate demeanor for indifference about these issues. Before the War of 1812 began, Cabot was one of those hard-line Federalists who defended British violations of neutral shipping and the British use of impressment. Even as tensions with Great Britain increased, he continued to believe an Anglo-American alliance would benefit the United States. Once the war began, he urged Massachusetts to protect its rights from federal encroachment but stopped short of advocating secession.

When the call went out for delegates to assemble at the Hartford Convention, Cabot led the Massachusetts delegation. The convention chose him for its president. When John Adams heard this news, the former president remarked that Cabot's true ambition was to be elected president of New England. Yet, Adams misjudged Cabot's diffidence—some would have called it laziness. His presence at the convention at least assured that secessionist firebrands would not prevail. The constitutional amendments proposed by the convention might have seemed radical to those outside New England, but Cabot and the more moderate members of the convention prevented any serious discussion of disunion.

Following the War of 1812, Cabot resumed his role as the sage of Boston society. He died at his home in 1823.

—*Jeanne T. Heidler and David S. Heidler*

See also: Embargo Act; Federalist Party; Hartford Convention; Impressment
Further Reading
Lodge, Henry Cabot. *Life and Letters of George Cabot.* Boston: Little, Brown, 1878.

CADORE LETTER
5 August 1810

The United States tried to protect its neutral rights in the midst of Napoleonic Wars by employing economic coercion against England and France. The restrictive trade system, however, had shown itself to be a dismal failure by the advent of James Madison's administration.

The Embargo of 1807 had been replaced by the less obnoxious but equally ineffective Non-Intercourse Act, and when that latter measure was about to expire, Congress strained for a way to escape the economic tribulations of economic coercion without seeming to abandon the policy. The result was Macon's Bill No. 2. Under its stipulations, the United States would resume trade with both Britain and France but would cease trading with one nation upon the other's abandonment of its objectionable practices against neutral U.S. commerce.

The obvious cynicism and cunning of Macon's Bill No. 2 fairly begged for a duplicitous response from the master of duplicity himself, Napoleon. On 5 August 1810, Napoleon's foreign secretary, the Duc de Cadore, dispatched a letter to U.S. minister John Armstrong. Its language was deliberately vague, but the Cadore letter seemed to indicate the revocation of Napoleon's commercial restrictions aimed at U.S. commerce. The revocation, however, was contingent upon the United States' either compelling Britain's repeal of the Orders in Council or instituting unrestricted U.S. economic warfare against the British that would include both nonimportation and nonexportation.

As such, the Cadore letter announced a policy that in fact promised nothing, but Madison leapt at the opportunity with a proclamation on 2 November 1810 in which he announced the reinstitution of nonimportation against Britain should that nation not repeal the Orders in Council. Under the terms of Macon's Bill, there was a three-month grace period, but Madison's rashness had already done the damage. Critics then and since have criticized the president's quick and apparently unquestioning acceptance of the Cadore letter's inexplicit and groundless pledge, pointing out that it made the United States an unwitting participant in Napoleon's Continental System. In any event, the president's action contributed to the worsening of Anglo-American relations that would eventually provoke the U.S. declaration of war.

—Jeanne T. Heidler and David S. Heidler

See also: Armstrong, John; Berlin Decree; Embargo Act; Macon's Bill No. 2; Milan Decree; Napoleon I; Orders in Council

Further Reading

Egan, Clifford L. *Neither Peace nor War: Franco-American Relations, 1803–1812.* Baton Rouge: Louisiana State University Press, 1983.

CALABEE, BATTLE OF
27 January 1814
Mississippi Territory (Alabama)

In the summer of 1811, Tecumseh enlisted the support of the Creek Indians to fight the United States. After acquiring arms at Spanish Pensacola, a Creek faction called Red Sticks fended off a U.S. attack at Burnt Corn. Then in August 1813, Red Sticks massacred a U.S. settlement at Fort Mims, Mississippi Territory (now Alabama). The state of Georgia authorized Gen. John Floyd to raise a volunteer militia, and on 29 November 1813, Floyd defeated a substantial Creek force in the Battle of Autosse.

After a six-week lull, Floyd opened a new campaign with 1,300 Georgia and Carolina volunteers, including a cavalry company and 400 Allied Creeks. He advanced along the Old Federal Road and established a supply base in what is now Macon County, Alabama. Floyd heard about large numbers of hostiles building fortifications at Hoithlewallee, a nearby village. He immediately advanced and reached the Calabee Swamp (near modern Tuskegee) on 26 January 1814. Finding high ground bordering the swamp, he camped his men in a pine forest there.

A larger Red Stick force had gathered across the swamp at McGirth's Still House Stream to hold council. The Creek numbers had increased to 1,800, possibly the largest Red Stick force assembled during the war. Although the Creek numbers were impressive, many lacked guns and carried only bows and arrows or war clubs. William Weatherford, known as Red Eagle, was present and addressed the council. This great war chief proposed that the Creeks wait until Floyd's army crossed Calabee Creek before launching their attack. After a prolonged discussion, Weatherford's plan was rejected. Disappointed in the decision, he left the council and returned to his smaller force at Polecat Springs.

About an hour and a half before sunrise on 27 January, Creek warriors stealthily approached Floyd's camp, attacked the sentries, and fiercely poured into the encampment. Although completely surprised, Floyd's troops quickly regrouped. The volunteer force then made the melee a general engagement. Using his cannon, Floyd repulsed the Red Sticks after fierce hand-to-hand fighting. The hostile Creeks made several desperate but unsuccessful attempts to capture the cannon. As a result, the artillerymen suffered the heaviest casualties. During the violent fighting, most of the Allied Creeks deserted Floyd's forces and fled from the combat. Uchee warriors, led by their famous chief, Captain Timpoochee Barnard, fought bravely with Floyd's militia. Shortly after sunrise, Floyd reorganized his troops and led a charge against the Red Sticks. Although the Indians fought bravely, militia bayonets routed them. The cavalry regiment, rifle company, and loyal Indians pursued them through the Calabee Swamp. The Battle of Calabee was over.

As in most battles with Indians, exact Creek losses were uncertain. Floyd's militia counted 70 Red Sticks dead and 132 wounded. Floyd's army suffered 17 dead and 132 wounded. The Allied Creek force had 5 killed and 15 wounded.

Concerned about his wounded, Floyd returned to Fort Mitchell. Following his withdrawal, the Creeks repossessed the battlefield.

—*Brigitte F. Cole*

See also: Autosse, Battle of; Burnt Corn, Battle of; Creek War; Georgia; Mims, Attack on Fort; Red Sticks; Weatherford, William

Further Reading

Brewer, Willis. *Alabama: Her History, Resources, War Record, and Public Men.* Montgomery, AL: Barrett and Brown, 1872.

Owen, Thomas McAdory. *History of Alabama and Dictionary of Alabama Biography.* Vol. 1. Chicago: S. J. Clarke Company, 1921.

Owsley, Frank Lawrence, Jr. *Struggle for the Gulf Borderlands: The Creek War and the Battle of New Orleans, 1812–1815.* Gainesville: University Presses of Florida, 1981.

Pickett, Albert J. *History of Alabama, and Incidentally of Georgia and Mississippi, from the Earliest Period.* N.p., 1851. Reprint, Tuscaloosa, AL: Willo Publishing, 1962.

White, George. *Historic Collection of Georgia.* New York: Pudney and Russell, 1855.

Woodward, Thomas S. *Woodward's Reminiscences of the Creek, or Muscogee Indians.* N.p., 1859. Reprint, Mobile, AL: Southern University Press for Graphics, 1965.

CALHOUN, JOHN C.
1782–1850
South Carolina congressman; statesman

Those who know John C. Calhoun only as the advocate of states' rights and the defender of the Old South may have some difficulty in recognizing "the young Hercules who carried the war [of 1812] on his shoulders."

Born into a moderately prosperous Scottish-Irish family near Abbeville, South Carolina, on 18 March 1782, Calhoun received little education until he enrolled in Moses Waddel's famous academy. Blessed with exceptional intelligence, Calhoun did well there and at Yale College, from which he graduated in 1804. After studying law at Tapping Reeves's Connecticut school and with Henry W. DeSaussure in Charleston, Calhoun gained admission to the bar in December 1807. Although a successful lawyer, he did not enjoy the work. A speech in which he denounced British aggression after the *Chesapeake-Leopard* incident led to his 1808 election to the lower house of the South Carolina legislature. Two years later Calhoun won election to the U.S. House of Representatives as a Jeffersonian Republican. In 1811, he married a cousin, Floride Calhoun, who brought to the marriage considerable property.

The South Carolinian came to the 12th Congress as one of the new, talented members of the House who demanded an aggressive policy toward Great Britain. Federalist Josiah Quincy said the War Hawks were "young politicians, half-hatched, the shell still on their heads, and the pin feathers not yet shed." The tall, wiry young man with piercing eyes attracted notice from the start with his ardor, intelligence, and speaking ability. Although Calhoun knew and used the usual oratorical techniques, he preferred to rely on the compelling power of carefully reasoned argument. When messmate Henry Clay of Kentucky was elected Speaker, he appointed Calhoun to the important Committee on Foreign Relations. Calhoun was soon its head. The South Carolinian was appalled by the weakness of the national administration. "Our executive officers are most incompetent men," Calhoun wrote a friend, "and will let the best of causes I fear perish in their hands." Secretary of State James Monroe was the exception; he worked well with the War Hawks. Unfortunately, as the nation moved toward war, Secretary of War William Eustis and Secretary of the Navy Paul Hamilton were, in Calhoun's opinion, incompetent.

In the debate over the Army Bill, the redoubtable John Randolph argued that the United States should support Great Britain's fight for civilization against Napoleon Bonaparte. The United States must fight Britain, Calhoun replied, or give up its right to trade freely. To defend its rights, the nation had to be strong militarily. When Pres. James Madison finally succumbed to such pressure for war, Calhoun wrote the committee's report and introduced the war measure.

Calhoun urged an active prosecution of the conflict. "We have had a peace like a war," he told the House in June 1812. "In the name of Heaven let us not have the only thing that is worse, a war like a peace." Overly optimistic, he predicted that within four weeks the United States would have all of Upper Canada and part of Lower Canada. Reelected to the House without opposition in 1812, Calhoun redoubled his efforts for victory as a series

John C. Calhoun

of defeats alarmed the nation. He and the other War Hawks forced the resignation of Secretary Eustis.

Opposition to the war existed largely in New England. Calhoun understood the concerns of that section better than most of the War Hawks, and he argued for commercial concessions that would restore national unity. Only then, he thought, could the country successfully prosecute the war with vigor. He wanted to repeal the embargo and nonintercourse acts, but when that effort failed in December 1813, he voted with the majority for the sake of party unity. In fact, the demands of party unity sometimes required that he defend policies he found disagreeable. Nevertheless, he was one of the few members who could successfully challenge John Randolph, and he clashed frequently with Daniel Webster, an able young spokesman for the New England interests. As New England opposition to the war increased, Calhoun asked a fundamental question: How far can opposition be safely carried before it ceases to be a right and becomes an abuse?

In early 1814, Calhoun finally secured congressional authorization to secure substantial loans for the conduct of the war. A boycott by eastern bankers made the act ineffective, however. In April, Calhoun guided the repeal of the embargo and nonimportation acts. Their economic pressure had failed to prevent war, he told the House, and they should have been repealed when the war started. Calhoun was at his home ill with fever when the British burned many of Washington's public buildings in August 1814. Reporting to Congress a month late, he found it meeting in Blodgett's Hotel, which housed the Patent Office.

He increasingly occupied himself with the future of the young republic. Calhoun reshaped Secretary of the Treasury Alexander J. Dallas's recommendation for a new national bank, but his proposal was rejected in January 1815. Calhoun and Webster collaborated on an alternate scheme that passed Congress but fell to President Madison's veto on constitutional grounds. Meanwhile, Calhoun pushed for a bill to draft 80,000 militia into the army, but opponents stripped the bill of its essential features. In any event, the end of the war made it moot.

When word of the peace treaty reached Washington in February 1815, Calhoun declared, "To all practical purposes, we have attained complete success." When he examined the treaty in detail, however, he was disappointed. Convinced that the Treaty of Ghent was nothing more than a truce, he urged the establishment of a strong postwar military that could ensure the nation's rights.

Strongly nationalistic, Calhoun deplored "refined arguments on the constitution" that would limit federal powers needed to strengthen and unify the nation. An excellent secretary of war in the Monroe administration, Calhoun was elected vice president in 1824 and 1828. He resigned from that position to defend South Carolina's nullification effort in 1832 and 1833. In and out of the Senate until 1850, he served as secretary of state during part of Tyler's administration, and he continued to be an unsuccessful presidential aspirant. He became known for his advocacy of states' rights, the "positive good" defense of slavery, and his intriguing theory of the concurrent majority, a means of safeguarding minority rights. Shortly before his death on 31 March 1850, Calhoun predicted the dissolution of the Union within 12 years, probably following a presidential election. By then, few Americans remembered the ardent young nationalist of the War of 1812.

—*Lowell H. Harrison*

See also: Clay, Henry; U.S. Congress; War Hawks
Further Reading

Bartlett, Irving H. *John C. Calhoun: A Biography.* New York: W. W. Norton, 1993.

Coit, Margaret L. *John C. Calhoun: American Portrait.* New York: Houghton Mifflin, 1950.

Meriwether, Robert L., ed. *The Papers of John C. Calhoun, 1801–1817.* Columbia: University of South Carolina Press, 1959.

Nevin, John. *John C. Calhoun and the Price of Union*. Baton Rouge: Louisiana State University Press, 1988.

Wiltse, Charles M. *John C. Calhoun: Nationalist, 1782–1828*. Indianapolis: Bobbs-Merrill, 1944.

CAMPBELL, GEORGE W.
1769–1848
U.S. senator; secretary of the treasury

George W. Campbell

A native of Scotland and son of Archibald Campbell and Elizabeth Mackay Campbell, George W. Campbell moved to North Carolina as a child with his family. After graduating from Princeton College and studying law, he began practicing law in Knoxville, Tennessee. He entered politics in 1803 with a successful bid for a seat from Tennessee in the U.S. House of Representatives, where he served three terms. After leaving the House he sat on the Tennessee Supreme Court but returned to Congress as a U.S. Senator in 1811.

As part of the War Hawk faction in congress, Campbell spoke in favor of war with Great Britain and became a staunch ally of the Madison administration. In fact, during the war some viewed Campbell as one of the administration's strongest supporters in the Senate. Pres. James Madison turned to Campbell when Secretary of the Treasury Albert Gallatin became a peace commissioner to the British government in 1814. During Gallatin's absence in Europe, Secretary of the Navy William Jones performed Gallatin's duties. Because no one knew how long the peace negotiations would last, Madison appointed Campbell as a permanent replacement for Gallatin.

Campbell's selection was not a popular one. He had no experience with financial affairs, and he inherited a disorganized Treasury Department. Further, as Campbell had been one of the few unquestioning supporters of Madison in the Senate, in Campbell's appointment to the Treasury the president lost one of his best spokesmen in Congress.

As secretary of the treasury, Campbell learned that his predecessor had been right to recommend the imposition of internal taxes to an unreceptive Congress. As the country slipped deeper into debt, Campbell met increasing difficulty finding funds to finance the war. During the summer of 1814, with the British threatening to advance on all fronts, finding money occupied almost all of Campbell's time. His health began to fail, and after preparing a cursory financial report to Congress recommending internal taxes, he asked Madison to let him quit the treasury. With cabinet burdens removed, Campbell's health improved almost immediately. Soon the Tennessee legislature returned him to the Senate.

Following the War of 1812, Campbell sat in the Senate until serving briefly in 1818 as U.S. minister to Russia. Following his return from Russia, he devoted most of his remaining years to business activities. He always strongly supported Andrew Jackson in political affairs. He died in 1848 a wealthy man.

—*Jeanne T. Heidler and David S. Heidler*

See also: Gallatin, Albert; Jones, William; Madison, James; War Hawks

Further Reading

Jordon, Weymouth T. *George Washington Campbell of Tennessee: Western Statesman*. Tallahassee: Florida State University, 1955.

CAMPBELL, JOHN B.
d. 1814
U.S. officer

Born in Virginia, John B. Campbell entered the army in March 1812 as lieutenant colonel of the 19th Infantry Regiment. Serving in the Army of the Northwest at the beginning of the war, Campbell was dispatched by William Henry Harrison on 25 November 1812 to destroy the Miami villages along the Mississiniwa River. En route, Campbell stopped at Dayton, Ohio, to procure horses. By mid-December, he had started for his target. Several days out, he fought a short engagement and destroyed one village, moving to destroy several deserted villages as well. He returned to the first village to camp and reconnoiter, and on the morning of 18 December Miamis fell upon Campbell and his men. Though Campbell repelled the attack, intelligence reported that a larger body of Indians was nearby and that they were commanded by Tecumseh. With his men suffering terribly from the cold, Campbell did not want to risk another engagement against larger numbers. So he retreated to Greenville, Ohio. Harrison commended Campbell's actions on the Mississiniwa, and soon he obtained a brevet promotion to colonel.

By 1814, Campbell had been promoted to colonel of the 11th Infantry Regiment. In May 1814 he loaded his regiment on small craft in Lake Erie and made for Port Dover on the Canadian side. In retaliation for the British destruction of Buffalo the previous winter, Campbell ordered Port Dover destroyed. Even some of his own men questioned the destruction of private property. The United States attempted to prevent British retaliation for the act by reprimanding Campbell, but the British used his actions at Port Dover as an excuse for their destructive raids in the Chesapeake Bay region that summer.

Back in command of the 11th Infantry in July 1814, Campbell was badly wounded at the Battle of Chippewa on 5 July 1814. His wounds kept him from his regiment, and he never recovered, dying on 28 August 1814.

—*Jeanne T. Heidler and David S. Heidler*

See also: Chippewa, Battle of; Harrison, William Henry; Tecumseh
Further Reading
Bannister, J. A. "The Burning of Dover." *Western Ontario Historical Notes* 21 (1965): 1–25.

CANNING, GEORGE
11 April 1770–8 August 1827
British statesman; British secretary of
state for foreign affairs

George Canning was born in London of an Anglo-Irish background. His father, George Canning, of Garvagh, Londonderry, came to London in disgrace in 1757, dabbled in supporting John Wilkes, and married Mary Anne Costello, an actress and the penniless daughter of John Costello, a Connaught squire. The younger Canning enjoyed support from his uncles, Stratford Canning of Garvagh and the Reverend William Leigh and his wife, Elizabeth. Canning's brilliance at Hyde Abbey School, Winchester, Eton, and Christ Church, Oxford, also gained him notice. At Oxford, he befriended Robert Banks Jenkinson, Lord Liverpool, who became the prime minister during the last stages of the Napoleonic wars.

Witty with his friends and sarcastic toward his enemies, Canning was an extraordinarily effective orator in an age that distrusted oratory. Possessed of exceptional talent, he also displayed a restless ambition, a quality his enemies labeled as arrogance. Many expected him to join the Whigs, but he entered the House of Commons as a disciple of Pitt. Eventually he led a small faction—a dozen "Canningites"— in the House of Commons before the War of 1812. His bitter rivalry with Viscount Castlereagh, a member of Lord Liverpool's Tory government from 1812 to 1822, resulted in a duel on 21 September 1809. Canning suffered a slight wound in his left thigh, but it kept him out of office for considerable periods. Before the chill reality of wandering in the political wilderness hit home in 1815 and 1816, he preferred it to serving in a cabinet with Castlereagh.

From 1807 to 1809, Canning was secretary of state for foreign affairs in the Portland administration. He was thus the author of the 8 September 1807 preemptive strike on the Danish fleet to prevent its falling into Napoleon's hands. He also gained the agreement of the prince regent of Portugal to turn over the Portuguese fleet hours before Marshal Junot's troops entered Lisbon to seize it. He negotiated with William Pinkney, U.S. minister in London in 1808, seeking a mutual removal of trade restrictions and Orders in Council. The effort proved unsuccessful. Toward Europe, Canning operated a hard-line policy designed to keep nations out of Napoleon's orbit, and after Tilsit, he argued for and planned attacks on Denmark and Holland to further that end.

In 1809, Canning instructed David Montagu Erskine,

George Canning

his minister in Washington, to ask the U.S. government to reopen trade with Great Britain, deny a resumption of trade with France, accept the Rule of 1756 (trade not permitted in peace was not permitted in war), and allow the Royal Navy to police these provisions. Erskine's agreement with Pres. James Madison called for a resumption of British trade, cessation of French trade, and the repeal of the Orders in Council. Canning curtly disavowed this arrangement, stating that Erskine had exceeded his instructions. Thus was wrecked a promising attempt to deal with angry differences over impressment, trade regulations, Orders in Council, and Napoleonic decrees. Canning recalled Erskine, and the agreement miscarried. The United States reinstituted the Non-Intercourse Act.

In 1809, when Lord Bathurst replaced Canning as foreign secretary, Canning left government office. In 1812, he declared himself in favor of Catholic emancipation and headed the polls in the Liverpool election, then the second city in the kingdom. He had little contact with the United States through the War of 1812. From September 1814 until he resigned in July 1815 he was the head of a special embassy to Lisbon, Portugal, on the expectation that the prince regent and the House of Braganza would return. He later acknowledged it as the greatest political mistake of his life, and it was the nadir of his political fortunes. He approved Castlereagh's peace settlements in 1815 and re-

joined the government the following year as a supporter of his old adversary's foreign policy.

After a two-year absence, Canning returned to government as foreign secretary from 1822 to 1827. During those five years, prior to becoming prime minister, he developed a system that was grounded in the advancement of English commercial interests and that utilized a balance of power against the pretensions of Austrian foreign minister Clemens von Metternich. He also negotiated a convention with the United States for the suppression of the slave trade in 1824, but the U.S. Senate refused to ratify it.

—*Frederick C. Drake*

See also: Bathurst, Henry, Third Earl Bathurst; Castlereagh, Viscount, Robert Stewart; Liverpool, Robert Banks Jenkinson, Second Earl of; Madison, James; Napoleon I; Non-Intercourse Act; Orders in Council; Pinkney, William

Further Reading

Aspinall, A. "The Canningite Party." *Transactions of the Royal Historical Society,* 4th ser., 17 (1934): 177–226.

Hinde, Wendy. *George Canning.* London: Collins, 1973.

Marriott, John A.R. *George Canning and His Times: A Political Study.* London: John Murray, 1907.

Perkins, Bradford. "George Canning, Great Britain, and the United States, 1807–1809." *American Historical Review* 63 (October 1957): 1–22.

———. *Prologue to War: England and the United States, 1805–1812.* Berkeley and Los Angeles: University of California Press, 1963.

Petrie, Charles. *George Canning.* London: Eyre & Spottiswoode, 1930, 1946.

Rolo, Paul Jacques Victor. *George Canning: Three Biographical Studies.* London: Macmillan, 1965.

Stapleton, Augustus G. *George Canning and His Times.* London: J. W. Parker, 1859.

Temperley, Harold W.V. *The Foreign Policy of Canning, 1822–1827: England, the Neo-Holy Alliance, and the New World.* London: Frank Cass, 1966.

CANNON, NAVAL

The warships of the U.S. and British navies had as their main armaments long guns and carronades. Both types were muzzle-loaders and were identified by the weight of the solid shot they fired—for instance, a 24-pounder long gun.

The long guns were just that: cast-iron cannon ranging in length from about 8 to more than 10 feet and weighing upward of 4 tons each. Each was mounted on a wooden carriage with four fixed trucks (wheels) and was manned by a crew of 9 (British) to 14 (U.S.) men. Training (directing) the gun was done by levering it from side to side; elevation was accomplished with a quoin (wedge)inserted under the rear end of the gun. The normal powder charge weighed one-quarter what the shot did, and a trained crew could be expected to sustain fire at the rate of a shot about every three minutes. Long guns in use in the two navies ranged from 9- to 32-pounders in the rated units. Effective ranges of 1,000 yards and more were the norm, and random shot could travel more than 3,000 yards.

The carronade, named for Carron, Scotland, the site of its creation, was a short, lightweight, large-bore weapon. Generally weighing under 2 tons and measuring less than 4 feet long, it could be carried in greater numbers higher in a ship than could long guns and still not affect the vessel's stability. A carronade's crew numbered six (British) to nine (U.S.) men, and could sustain a somewhat higher rate of fire than a long gun's crew. Mounted on a slide, it was easier to train, and instead of requiring the use of the quoin, most had a built-in elevating screw. The shorter barrel meant a greatly reduced range, and a normal powder charge was only about one-sixteenth of the shot weight. Maximum effective range was on the order of 400 yards, and within that range, because of its large bore, the gun was popularly known as the "smasher." The two navies employed carronades from 12- to 68-pounders.

In addition to these two main types, during the war there appeared at least two efforts to combine the range of the long gun with the lightness of the carronade. In Britain, it was called a gunade; in the United States, a Columbiad. Neither was employed in great numbers, nor were the guns particularly successful.

—*Tyrone G. Martin*

See also: Artillery; Columbiad; Naval Ordnance; Rates
Further Reading
Hogg, Ian, and John Batchelor. *Naval Gun.* Poole: Blandford Press, 1978.
Lavery, Brian. *Nelson's Navy.* Annapolis, MD: Naval Institute Press, 1989.
Tucker, Spencer C. *Arming the Fleet.* Annapolis, MD: Naval Institute Press, 1989.

CARDEN, JOHN SURMAN
1771–1858
British Navy officer, HMS *Macedonian*

Born 15 August 1771, Carden became a midshipman in 1788. He saw action on board HMS *Marlborough* in 1794 and earned promotion to lieutenant, then to commander (25 October 1798) and to post-captain (22 January 1806). He commanded HMS *Sheerness* at Helder (1800) and the Red Sea and fought in the Mediterranean, India (1803), and Egypt, where his performance earned him high commendation from Rear Adm. John Sprat Ranier. He also served aboard *Queen Charlotte* (100 guns), *Ville de Paris* (100 guns), *Ocean* (98 guns), and *Mars* (74 guns), and during the War of 1812 he commanded HMS *Macedonian* (38 guns).

On 25 October 1812, the *Macedonian*, a frigate carrying 18-pounders, encountered USS *United States* (44 guns), a 24-pounder frigate commanded by Capt. Stephen Decatur. In an engagement of two hours and ten minutes, the *United States* pulverized the *Macedonian* into what Carden later described in his report as "a perfect wreck and unmanageable log." *Macedonian* sustained 36 dead, 36 severely wounded, and 32 slightly wounded. The *United States* lost 5 dead and 7 wounded. *Macedonian*'s broadside compared at 63.2 percent to that of the *United States*, and *Macedonian*'s crew was 62.9 percent of that of the *United States* (301 to 478).

Several writers—Theodore Roosevelt, C. S. Forester, and William James—criticized Carden for not closing quickly on the *United States*, but such criticism does not take into account the intense fire of a superior opponent and the heavy sea. In fact, Carden's court-martial exonerated him and his disciplined crew, and Secretary to the Admiralty John Wilson Croker defended Carden before the House of Commons. The cities of Worcester and Gloucester and the Borough of Tewkesbury unanimously voted him the Freedom of the Cities and Borough. Carden was later promoted to admiral. He died at Ramoan rectory, Ballycastle, County Antrim, on 22 April 1858.

—*Frederick C. Drake*

See also: Croker, John Wilson; Decatur, Stephen, Jr.; *United States* versus *Macedonian*
Further Reading
Forester, Cecil S. *The Age of Fighting Sail: The Story of the Naval War of 1812.* Garden City, NY: Doubleday, 1956.

James, William. *Naval History of Great Britain from 1793–1820.* Vol. 6, p. 114. London: R. Bently, 1837.

Mahan, Alfred Thayer. *Sea Power in Its Relations to the War of 1812.* London: Sampson, Low, Marston & Company, 1905.

Marshall, John. *Royal Naval Biography.* Vol. 2, pt. 2, pp. 1007–1019. London: Hurst, Rees, Orme, Brown and Green, 1824.

Roosevelt, Theodore. *The Naval War of 1812.* New York: G. P. Putnam's Sons, 1882.

CARROLL, WILLIAM

3 March 1788–22 March 1844
Tennessee militia officer

Born to Thomas and Mary Carroll near Pittsburgh, William Carroll's father was an employee of and later a partner with Albert Gallatin in the hardware business. The younger Carroll migrated to Tennessee in 1810 and married Cecelia Bradford in about 1813. The couple had three sons. In Nashville, Carroll established a nail factory that expanded into a successful enterprise. It would eventually include a steamboat, the *General Jackson,* constructed for him at Pittsburgh. He would thus become a major promoter of the transportation revolution after the War of 1812.

Carroll became involved in Tennessee militia affairs by helping to organize a company that chose him as its captain. In November 1812, Maj. Gen. Andrew Jackson appointed Carroll brigade inspector. Jackson effusively praised Carroll's conduct, referring to him as the "indefatigable" Carroll who was "the best Brigade Major in the armies of the U.S.—he ought and must be at the head of a regiment."

Jackson's preference for Carroll led to jealousy, perhaps even to a duel. Carroll's excellent performance, however, increasingly won him Jackson's growing favor. Carroll displayed initiative, leadership, and courage during the Creek War of 1813–1814 at the battles of Talladega, Emuckfau, Enitachopco, and especially at Tohopeka (Horseshoe Bend), where Carroll was wounded. Moreover, he proved especially successful in mollifying his men, who resented changes in their terms of enlistment. When Tennessee units, mustered under state control, moved to federal command, Carroll's men proved reliable, whereas Jackson had to threaten others to remain for the campaign's duration.

In 1814, the Madison administration made Jackson a major general in the regular army. William Carroll succeeded him as major general of the Tennessee militia's Second Division. Jackson applauded the appointment because he thought Carroll would "give energy and proper tone to the militia."

Expecting a British invasion of Louisiana, Jackson ordered Carroll to move by land to Natchez as quickly as possible. Carroll moved his forces by boat down the Mississippi River, reaching Natchez 18 days later, on 13 December 1814. Aware of the lengthy time in transport, he apologized for "disobeying orders."

Carroll arrived at New Orleans on 20 December with more than 3,000 troops. They formed the center of Jackson's line behind the Rodriguez Canal and delivered the accurate, withering volleys that helped devastate Pakenham's British forces.

Throughout the southern campaigns of the war, William Carroll played a pivotal role. He proved that Jackson's confidence in him was well founded. Carroll at New Orleans provided Jackson with disciplined and well-armed troops, showing that militia forces properly led and supplied could perform well against regulars.

—*Thomas H. Winn*

See also: Creek War; Emuckfau Creek, Battle of; Enitachopco Creek, Battle of; Gallatin, Albert; Horseshoe Bend, Battle of; Jackson, Andrew; New Orleans, Battle of; Pakenham, Edward; Talladega, Battle of; Tennessee

Further Reading
Owsley, Frank Lawrence, Jr., *Struggle for the Gulf Borderlands: The Creek War and the Battle of New Orleans, 1812–15.* Gainesville: University Presses of Florida, 1981.

Walker, Margaret L. "The Life of William Carroll." Master's thesis, University of Tennessee, 1929.

CASS, LEWIS

1782–1866
U.S. officer

The oldest child of Mary Gilman Cass and her husband, Jonathan, who was a Revolutionary War veteran and a craftsman, Lewis Cass was born in Exeter, New Hampshire, on 9 October 1782. In 1792, he entered Phillips Exeter Academy. The young Cass, who was a classmate of Daniel Webster, learned much from the academy's demanding master, Benjamin Abbot. Cass showed special interest in the classics and in history, and in 1799 he completed his studies at Exeter. That year he accompanied his family to Delaware; he taught Latin at the Wilmington

Academy, and in 1800 he moved on to Ohio. He resided in Marietta for two years, preparing for a career in law, first under Return Jonathan Meigs and then under Matthew Backus. In 1802, Cass was admitted to the Ohio bar. He moved to Zanesville to begin his legal practice and tried cases in Ohio's Third Circuit. Two years later he was elected as the first prosecutor of Muskingum County.

The year 1806 proved eventful for the ambitious Cass. He married Elizabeth Spencer of Vienna, Virginia, and won election to the Ohio House of Representatives. He also drafted and introduced in the Ohio legislature a bill to grant the governor emergency powers to act against Aaron Burr's shadowy conspiracy to establish an empire in the Southwest. Pres. Thomas Jefferson rewarded Cass for his opposition to Burr's schemes by appointing him as U.S. marshal for Ohio. Cass in turn became a devoted member of the Republican Party.

Cass enhanced his political and legal reputation in 1808 by successfully defending Ohio Supreme Court justice George Tod when he was impeached by the Ohio legislature. Between 1808 and 1812, Cass was involved with the Masonic Grand Lodge of Ohio, serving as its deputy grand master between 1808 and 1809 and as its grand master between 1810 and 1812. The lodge, counting among its ranks Gov. Samuel Huntington, George Tod, Jacob Burnet, and Henry Brush, provided a haven for moderate Republican leaders in the Ohio country.

Believing that war against the British "was both just and necessary," Cass was active in the first phases of the northwestern campaign. He closed his Zanesville law office and went to Dayton in May 1812, where Gov. Return Jonathan Meigs appointed him colonel of the Third Ohio Regiment under the command of Gen. William Hull, territorial governor of Michigan and the commander of the Northwest Army. In June, Cass led his army to Detroit and on 12 July crossed into Canada, taking Sandwich without opposition from the British.

Four days later, Cass launched an attack against a bridge over the River Aux Canards. Soon to be dubbed the Hero of the Tarontee for such early successes, he seized this bridge about 4 miles from Fort Malden, taking two prisoners and losing none of his men. With no specific instructions from Hull, however, Cass retreated to Sandwich in disgust. Such neglect and indecision on Hull's part only worsened. Cass led an expedition to the River Raisin to help troops under Capt. Henry Brush, and upon returning, he heard about Hull's surrender of Fort Detroit to Gen. Isaac Brock. The dejected Cass returned to Detroit, reportedly broke his sword rather than surrender it, and vehemently spoke against Hull during his court-martial two years later.

In 1813, Cass was promoted to brigadier general and with Gen. Duncan McArthur was placed in the Eighth Military District under the command of Gen. William Henry Harrison. Commander Oliver Hazard Perry, after his naval victory at Put-In-Bay on 10 September 1813, controlled Lake Erie for the United States and two weeks later began transporting Harrison's troops to the vicinity of Detroit. British general Henry Procter began a retreat, and Harrison's troops passed the ruins of Fort Malden. Cass occupied Sandwich with his 27th Infantry. Six days later, on 5 October, Cass was with Harrison's army at the Battle of the Thames. After this major victory, he returned to Detroit and on 14 October was appointed military administrator of Michigan and Upper Canada.

Like other officers in the War of 1812, Cass became a national leader. As Michigan's territorial governor, he negotiated with the Indians at Fort Meigs in 1817, forcing them to cede lands in portions of Michigan and Ohio. He helped to establish the University of Michigan and the Michigan Agricultural Society. During the 1820s and 1830s, he encouraged the development of Detroit to attract settlers. He served in the Senate in 1845 and again in 1851 as a Democrat, staunchly supporting the U.S. stance against Britain in the Oregon dispute and defending the Compromise of 1850. Cass ran as the Democratic presidential nominee in 1848, advocating popular sovereignty, but lost to the Whig Zachary Taylor. Cass served as secretary of state in the James Buchanan administration between 1857 and 1860. He died on 17 June 1866.

—*William Weisberger*

See also: Brock, Isaac; Harrison, William Henry; Hull, William; Lake Erie Campaign; Malden, Fort; McArthur, Duncan; Meigs, Return Jonathan; Michigan Territory; Ohio; Perry, Oliver Hazard; Procter, Henry; Thames, Battle of the; Webster, Daniel

Further Reading

Gilpin, Alec R. *The Territory of Michigan, 1805–1837.* East Lansing: Michigan State University Press, 1970.

Woodward, Frank B. *Lewis Cass: The Last Jeffersonian.* New Brunswick, NJ: Rutgers University Press, 1950.

CASTINE, MAINE

On 6 June 1814, Earl Bathurst, British secretary of state for war and the colonies, ordered Sir John Coape Sherbrooke, lieutenant governor of Nova Scotia, to attack settlements and seize territory "which at present intercepts the communication between Halifax and Quebec." After two years of licensed trade and smuggling between Nova Scotia, New Brunswick, and the Maine district of Massachusetts, New Brunswickers hoped to reattach the Madawaska territory and secure communications with Canada. Seizing substantial portions of the Maine District at the least could extract U.S. concessions at the peace negotiations, permanently readjusting the boundary.

Pursuant to this new policy, in the summer of 1814 New England coastal settlements were increasingly subjected to British depredations. On 21 June, an expedition under Sir Robert Barrie attacked Thomaston and St. George west of Penobscot Bay and captured four vessels in the river. Next, on 11 July, Sir Thomas Masterman Hardy in *Ramillies* (74 guns) and Lt. Col. Andrew Pilkington mounted a raid against Eastport and the Passamaquoddy Islands "to occupy and maintain possession of the islands." Moose Island and Fort Sullivan surrendered (the British renamed it Fort Sherbrooke), and U.S. Army major Purley Putnam, the 40th regiment, and 87 defenders were captured. Hardy bombarded Stonington on 11 and 12 August, but he had no intention of taking the town.

Sherbrooke planned the Penobscot expedition led by Rear Adm. Edward Griffith and Maj. Gen. Gerard Gosselin, with ten war vessels and ten troop transports conveying the 29th, 62nd, and 98th regiments, totaling about 2,500 troops. On 1 September, Castine fell when Lt. Col. William Douglas landed infantry on the isthmus. The defenders, 40 regulars and 100 militiamen, fled after spiking four 4-pounder guns. Gosselin and the 600-strong 29th, escorted by the frigate HMS *Bacchante*, took Belfast on the west side of the bay. Escorted by HMS *Dragon's* tenders and barges, the *Dragon's* Captain Robert Barrie and Lt. Col. Henry John headed upriver with 700 men from the Royal Artillery detachment and companies of the 29th, 60th, 62nd, and 98th regiments. The force reached Bucksport before dark, camped overnight in thick fog, and reached Frankfort at 2:00 P.M. on 2 September.

They then moved against U.S. forces at Hampden. There, British marines and troops attacked militia and seamen defending the USS *Adams*, a frigate in Hampden for hull repairs. Taking 81 prisoners, the British lost 10 killed and wounded to the defenders' 94. U.S. captain Charles Morris destroyed his ship, the *Adams*, by setting her on fire just before escaping the British assault. The British next captured Bangor, and the following day militia general Blake surrendered his forces. Several vessels were captured. The expedition returned via Hampden and captured all merchant vessels.

Meanwhile, a second force under Pilkington and Capt. Hyde Parker headed for Machias, situated 77 miles to the east. It landed at Buck's Harbor, made a tedious night march, and captured Fort O'Brien and Machias. Troops occupied the captured territory, and on 18 September the expedition returned to Halifax.

Castine and several other Maine settlements were occupied for eight months. Customs fees collected there were used to commence the building of what later became Dalhousie University. Yet peace negotiations did not secure the conquest. Instead, the terms of the Treaty of Ghent restored the captured section of Maine territory to the United States.

—*Frederick C. Drake*

See also: Barrie, Robert; Bathurst, Henry, Third Earl Bathurst; Ghent, Treaty of; Griffith, Edward; Hampden, Maine; Hardy, Thomas Masterman; Maine, District of; Morris, Charles; Sherbrooke, John Coape; Stonington, Connecticut, Bombardment of

Further Reading

Ballard, William. "Castine, October 1, 1814." *Bangor Historical Magazine* 2 (1996): 45–51.

Burroughs, Peter. "Sir John Coape Sherbrooke." *Dictionary of Canadian Biography*. Vol. 6, *1812–1830*, pp. 712–716. Toronto: University of Toronto Press, 1979.

Clark, George. "Military Operations at Castine, Maine." *Worcester Society of Antiquity* 18 (1899): 18–38.

Copp, Walter Ronald. "Military Activities in Nova Scotia during the War of 1812." *Collections of the Nova Scotia Historical Society* 24 (1938): 57–58, 74.

Harvey, D. C. "The Halifax-Castine Expedition." *Dalhousie Review* 18 (Spring 1938-1939): 207–213.

Stanley, George. "British Operations on the Penobscot in 1814." *Journal of the Society for Army Historical Research* 19 (autumn 1940).

———. "The Castine Expedition." In *The War of 1812: Land Operations*. Ottawa: National Museums of Canada; Ottawa: Macmillan of Canada, 1983.

Sutherland, David. "Halifax Merchants and the Pursuit of Development, 1783–1850." *Canadian Historical Review* 59 (1978): 1–17.

Wheeler, George A. "British Occupation in 1815." In *Castine Past and Present*. Boston: Rockwell, Churchill Press, 1896.

———. *History of Castine, Penobscot and Brooksville*. Bangor, ME: Burt, Robinson, 1875.

CASTLEREAGH, VISCOUNT, ROBERT STEWART

1769–1822
Marquis of Londonderry;
British foreign minister, 1812–1822

Born to Robert Stewart, Marquis of Londonderry, and Sarah Frances Conway Stewart in Ireland, Lord Castlereagh (as he was generally known as an adult) was educated in Ireland and at Cambridge University, traveled throughout Europe, and returned to Ireland, where he was elected to the Irish House of Commons. When war erupted between France and Great Britain, he became a lieutenant colonel in the Londonderry militia while continuing his political career.

During the French Revolution, Castlereagh formed many of his political opinions that reflected a growing conservatism with age. He gained both credit and condemnation for his efficient handling of the Irish uprising of 1798, but the British government was predictably pleased. Castlereagh thus began his rise in political circles. In 1802, he accepted a position in Lord Addington's cabinet and became the cabinet's leading expert on foreign affairs. Serving in a variety of ministries before the outbreak of the War of 1812, Castlereagh also became increasingly interested in military affairs as the war with Napoleon proceeded.

During much of Spencer Perceval's ministry, Castlereagh was out of the cabinet but not out of voice, as his volubly expressed opinions in the House of Commons showed. In February 1812, he returned to the cabinet as foreign secretary. Following the assassination of Spencer Perceval in May 1812, the cabinet began debating the repeal of the Orders in Council. The Non-Intercourse Act of the United States was causing considerable distress, particularly in the textile industry, and Castlereagh as foreign secretary bore much of the criticism for the British policy that had inspired U.S. commercial retaliation. It fell to Castlereagh to make the announcement to Parliament that the Orders would be lifted effective 23 June, five days after the United States declared war on Great Britain.

When word reached Great Britain that the United States had declared war, Castlereagh met toward the end of August 1812 with U.S. chargé d'affaires Jonathan Russell. Russell's instructions from Washington were to seek peace on the basis of Britain's revoking the Orders in Council and renouncing the right of impressment as well. Castlereagh impatiently explained to Russell that the repeal of the Orders should be sufficient for the United States. The right of impressment, he insisted, was a British domestic concern and none of the United States' business. Castlereagh smugly found it strange that so soon after declaring war, the United States seemed so eager for peace.

Throughout the first two years of the War of 1812, Castlereagh directed his primary interests and efforts to defeating Napoleon. He encouraged Russian resistance, monitored insurgents throughout Europe, organized a coalition against Napoleon, and worked with the British cabinet on grand strategy. Under the weight of these labors, the foreign secretary regarded the war with the United States as an annoying distraction. When Czar Alexander I offered to mediate the Anglo-American conflict, however, Castlereagh took notice.

Though Pres. James Madison quickly accepted the czar's offer and sent Albert Gallatin and Sen. James Bayard to St. Petersburg to begin the negotiations, Castlereagh immediately refused to participate. Not only was the foreign secretary suspicious of the czar's motives, he also rejected anything that made Britain seem dependent on another power to solve its problems. Yet Castlereagh did not want to seem unreceptive to peace. As an alternative, he sent word to Madison offering direct Anglo-American negotiations.

President Madison did not receive Castlereagh's offer until November 1813. He immediately accepted it. This opportunity seemed more likely to result in a treaty than the czar's offer, so Madison expanded the U.S. delegation to reflect a cross section of political views in the United States. The commission included Speaker of the House Henry Clay, U.S. chargé to London Jonathan Russell, James Bayard and Albert Gallatin (both still in Europe), and U.S. minister to Russia John Quincy Adams.

Lord Castlereagh suggested London as the location for the meetings, and before the other commissioners arrived, Albert Gallatin traveled there to begin informal talks with the foreign secretary. The other U.S. delegates, however, preferred a more neutral location, finally selecting Ghent across the channel in Belgium. Castlereagh was preoccupied with the abdication of Napoleon and arrangements for the Congress of Vienna, so Gallatin abandoned his private negotiations and traveled to Ghent in July 1814.

The men chosen by Castlereagh to meet the U.S. commissioners were singularly untalented. The British foreign secretary needed his more skillful diplomats in Vienna. The legation of Lord Gambier (a man inexperienced in diplomatic negotiations), Henry Goulburn (a young, stubborn undersecretary), and Dr. William Adams (a nonentity) revealed that Lord Castlereagh and the British cabinet regarded negotiations with the United States as secondary in importance.

Because the end of the European war meant that large numbers of British soldiers could now go to the United States, the British legation arrived in Ghent expecting to dictate terms. Castlereagh's instructions were to end New England fishing rights in Canadian waters, establish an Indian buffer state in the Northwest, and secure recognition of Britain's right of impressment. If possible, the British also wanted Louisiana ceded to Spain and an extension of the Canadian border into northern New York. When Castlereagh's envoys placed these demands before the Americans, they responded that the British position fell so far beyond their powers that they could not even discuss it. When the British negotiators insisted that theirs were the only acceptable terms, almost the entire U.S. delegation deduced that Lord Castlereagh was not serious about concluding a treaty. The exception was Henry Clay. He believed the foreign secretary was bluffing. Under his urging, the U.S. commissioners tried a bluff of their own. After declaring further talks on British terms as useless, the U.S. delegation prepared to go home.

When Castlereagh heard that the Americans were packing, he instructed his commissioners to be more conciliatory. If the negotiations broke down over these points, it would appear that the British were only continuing the war to acquire territory, and Castlereagh wanted to avoid any impression that might compromise British influence at the Congress of Vienna. Therefore, as Castlereagh prepared to depart for Vienna, negotiations at Ghent resumed.

At that, Castlereagh's active part in the talks at Ghent ended. He left the supervision of his commissioners to Lord Bathurst. Yet the final outcome at Ghent would significantly impinge on Castlereagh's deliberations in Vienna. When Czar Alexander I and the king of Prussia contrived to acquire massive land cessions in central Europe, Castlereagh arranged an alliance between Great Britain, France, and Austria to prevent it. With the war still raging in North America and his two allies fatigued from defeating Napoleon, it was less likely that Castlereagh could back any threats leveled at Russo-Prussian greed. Castlereagh's makeshift alliance troubled Alexander, however, and when word reached Vienna of the peace signed at Ghent, the prospect of the British soldiers returning from North America persuaded the czar to abandon his scheme.

Lord Castlereagh's accomplishments during the Napoleonic wars and at the Congress of Vienna sealed his reputation as Europe's premier diplomat. Following the Congress he continued as foreign secretary until his death, working constantly to maintain the balance of power created in Vienna. In his relations with the United States, particularly with U.S. minister to Great Britain John Quincy Adams, Castlereagh forged a grudging friendship of conve-nience, eventually resolving many problems left over from the War of 1812.

In 1822, worn out by almost ceaseless toil, and perhaps suffering from some undiagnosed physical or mental malady, Lord Castlereagh committed suicide.

—*Jeanne T. Heidler and David S. Heidler*

See also: Adams, John Quincy; Alexander I; Bathurst, Henry, Third Earl Bathurst; Bayard, James Asheton; Canning, George; Clay, Henry; Diplomacy; Gallatin, Albert; Ghent, Treaty of; Goulburn, Henry; Impressment; Madison, James; Napoleon I; Non-Intercourse Act; Orders in Council; Perceval, Spencer; Russell, Jonathan

Further Reading
Bartlett, C. J. *Castlereagh.* New York: Scribner, 1966.
Derry, John W. *Castlereagh.* London: Lane, 1976.
Perkins, Bradford. *Castlereagh and Adams: England and the United States, 1812–1823.* Berkeley: University of California Press, 1964.
Webster, Sir Charles. *The Foreign Policy of Castlereagh.* 2 vols. London: Barnes and Noble, 1925–1931, 1934.

CAULK'S FIELD, BATTLE OF
30 August 1814

While the main British squadron was engaged in the raid on Washington, D.C., in August 1814, Sir Peter Parker was sent with his ship HMS *Menelaus* across Chesapeake Bay to raid the interior and presumably keep militia forces there pinned down. On the night of 30 August, while anchored off the upper Eastern Shore of Maryland, Parker received word of an encampment of about 200 militiamen near Chestertown. Determined to disperse them, he ordered the *Menelaus* to put into one of the deep water creeks nearby.

At about 11:00 P.M., Parker led a party of about 260 sailors and marines ashore and made for the position of the Maryland militiamen. The militia commander, Col. Philip Reed, had been alerted to the British approach, so he stationed a skirmish line across a road running through Caulk's Field and placed the remainder of his men behind a slight rise to the side of the road. When the British approached the first line of militiamen, the Americans fired and then withdrew, leading the British to think that would be their only opposition. As they continued along the road, however, the remainder of the Americans opened fire, leading to a general engagement. In the early going, Parker was shot in the thigh and bled to death before his men could return him to the ship.

Having received far more resistance than they were used to in their raids and with their commander mortally wounded, the British decided to withdraw. Unbeknownst to them, however, the Americans were almost out of ammunition and on the verge of retreat themselves.

Of relatively little strategic importance, the Battle of Caulk's Field cost the Royal Navy one of its most promising young officers.

—Jeanne T. Heidler and David S. Heidler

See also: Parker, Peter
Further Reading
Tucker, Lillian H. *Battle of Caulk's Field, 150th Anniversary Commemoration.* Chestertown, MD: Kent County News, 1964.
———. "Sir Peter Parker: Commander of the H.M.S. *Menelaus* in the Year 1814." *Bermuda Historical Quarterly* 1 (1944): 189–245.

CHANDLER, JOHN
1762–1841
U.S. officer

Born in Epping, New Hampshire, to Joseph Chandler and Lydia Eastman Chandler, John Chandler served in the army and navy during the American Revolution. Following the Revolution he moved with a group of his neighbors to what would become the state of Maine. There he became involved in local and Massachusetts state politics and even served two terms in the U.S. House of Representatives. In the midst of all of these obligations, Chandler served as an officer in the Massachusetts militia. When war with Great Britain erupted in June 1812, he was the major general of the 17th Division.

In November 1812, Chandler received a commission as a brigadier general in the U.S. Army and resigned from the Massachusetts Militia. Chandler served the first part of the war as the commander of one of the three brigades that made up the Army of the North under General Henry Dearborn. Chandler's brigade served as part of the reserve in the battle to take Fort George. He and his men saw almost no action in that engagement, and there was some speculation that using them would have prevented the British escape.

Ordered to pursue the British along with the brigade of Brig. Gen. William Winder, Chandler and the two brigades caught up to the British near Stoney Creek. Pulling back to camp for the night, the Americans were surprised before dawn on 6 June by the British commanded by Brig. Gen. John Vincent. In the confusion of the dark, both Chandler and Winder stumbled into the British lines and were captured. Though the results of the battle were not decisive, the British suffered more casualties than the Americans.

Chandler was exchanged the following spring, and in the summer of 1814, he assumed command of regular forces along the New England coast at Portland, Massachusetts (Maine). While there he participated in drawing up a plan of defense for the town and coast with citizens' groups and the local militia. He was transferred to Portsmouth, New Hampshire, before the plan could be implemented.

When word of peace reached the United States, Chandler resigned from the army and returned to northern Massachusetts, where he reentered politics and business. In politics, Chandler actively worked for the separation of Maine from Massachusetts and served in the convention that drafted Maine's state constitution. The legislature then elected Chandler one of its first two senators, and for the remainder of his life, he was an active participant in Democratic politics in the state and the nation.

—Jeanne T. Heidler and David S. Heidler

See also: Stoney Creek, Battle of; Vincent, John; Winder, William H.
Further Reading
Talbot, George F. "General John Chandler of Monmouth, Maine, with Extracts from His Autobiography." *Collections of the Maine Historical Society* 9 (1887): 167–205.

CHÂTEAUGUAY, BATTLE OF
26 October 1813

The Battle of Châteauguay resulted in the defeat of the eastern wing of a two-pronged U.S. advance on Montreal in the fall of 1813. Maj. Gen. Henry Dearborn's victories at York and Fort George had not yielded strategic gains, so Secretary of War John Armstrong revised his strategy. Armstrong correctly concluded that cutting the British supply line east of Kingston would be decisive to the war effort.

When the administration bowed to pressure to replace Dearborn, it chose Maj. Gen. James Wilkinson. Armstrong, Wilkinson, and Commodore Isaac Chauncey met at Sacket's Harbor to plan an attack before the campaign season ended. After prolonged debate, they decided to advance on Montreal along two routes. Wilkinson would move his force by water from Sacket's Harbor down the St. Lawrence River. The second column, starting from Plattsburg, would march along the Châteauguay River to the St. Lawrence and there rendezvous with Wilkinson's army.

Maj. Gen. Wade Hampton commanded the army stationed around Lake Champlain. Like Wilkinson, Hampton was a veteran of the Revolution. Wilkinson and Hampton hated each other, a fact well known throughout the army. Nonetheless, Armstrong persuaded Hampton to cooperate with Wilkinson, at least during this campaign.

On 21 October, Hampton started his troops down the Châteauguay. When they approached the border, nearly all of the 1,400 New York militiamen refused to cross. Hampton pressed on with 4,000 partially trained and largely inexperienced regulars.

On 25 October, Hampton's column came upon log barricades and abatis blocking the road along the river. Swampy woods, impassable to Hampton's wagons and guns, flanked both sides of the river. Hampton knew he would need the road to support his advance on Montreal. About 1,700 Canadian fencibles and militia and a few Indians, all under Napoleonic war veteran Lt. Col. Charles de Salaberry, defended the log barriers. Hampton sent a strong force to the opposite side of the river so it could move through the forest and gain the Canadians' rear. The sound of the flank attack the next morning would signal Hampton to begin his frontal assault. That evening, however, Hampton heard that Armstrong had ordered winter quarters built for Hampton's army, not near Montreal but south of the Canadian border! It became obvious to Hampton that the secretary himself was pessimistic as to U.S. prospects.

Even worse, Hampton's tactics for the Battle of Châteauguay did not mesh. The flanking column got lost in the marshy woods. A smaller, but determined Canadian force fought these Americans to a standstill the next morning. Discovering that his plan had miscarried, Hampton launched an attack that became little more than a two-hour firefight before the first barricade. After losing about 50 men, Hampton called off the offensive. Citing widespread sickness among his men and a lack of supplies, Hampton ignored Wilkinson's orders to continue to Montreal. So one prong of the last U.S. offensive of 1813 fell to its commander's confusion and suspicion, induced more by mistrust of his superiors than by enemy action. Hampton resigned in disgust in March 1814.

—*Richard V. Barbuto*

See also: Armstrong, John; Chauncey, Isaac; Dearborn, Henry; George, Fort; Hampton, Wade; Kingston, Upper Canada; Montreal; Sacket's Harbor, New York; Salaberry, Charles-Michel d'Irumberry de; Wilkinson, James; York, Battle of

Further Reading
Guitard, Michelle. *The Militia of the Battle of the Châteauguay.* Ottawa: Parks Canada, 1983.
Mahon, John K. *The War of 1812.* Gainesville: University Presses of Florida, 1972.
Stanley, George F.G. *The War of 1812: Land Operations.* Canadian War Museum Historical Publication 18. Toronto: Macmillan, 1983.
Suthern, Victor. *Defend and Hold: The Battle of Châteauguay.* Ottawa: Balmuir Book Publishing, n.d.

CHATHAM, UPPER CANADA
4 October 1813

When Brig. Gen. Henry Procter began his retreat into Upper Canada in September 1813, the withdrawal dispirited Procter's Indian allies, especially Tecumseh. For months, Tecumseh had perceived Procter as a coward, and this latest retreat from U.S. soil prompted the Shawnee to threaten abandoning the British.

To placate Tecumseh and his Indian allies, Procter described the retreat as intended only to find stronger ground on which they would finally defeat the Americans. He promised Tecumseh that when the entire British and Indian force reached the point where the Thames River forked at Chatham, they would make a stand. As the retreat progressed, however, Procter sent an engineering officer ahead to examine the ground around Chatham. The report was anything but encouraging. The area did not provide defensible ground, said the engineer, who suggested it would be better to move farther up the Thames.

Procter did not tell Tecumseh, who was following at some distance, of the change in plans. Instead, Procter continued his retreat past Chatham toward Moraviantown. When Tecumseh arrived at Chatham and saw no defensive preparations there, he was furious at yet another sign of Procter's cowardice. Many Indians with Tecumseh abandoned the expedition at this point, but Tecumseh knew that the American William Henry Harrison was at his heels. The Shawnee determined to at least delay the Americans.

Taking up position on the other side of a partially destroyed bridge at McGregor's Creek on 4 October 1813, the remaining Indians stood in the way of Harrison's advancing army. Harrison thought he had encountered the entire British force, so he arranged his men for battle and had two 6-pounder fieldpieces brought up. Tecumseh's Indians had never grown used to artillery fire, and the first shots from the guns scattered them.

Following the skirmish at Chatham, Tecumseh reluctantly joined Procter at Moraviantown, where the British general at last had determined to make his stand against Harrison.

—*Jeanne T. Heidler and David S. Heidler*

See also: Harrison, William Henry; Procter, Henry; Tecumseh; Thames, Battle of the
Further Reading
Ermatinger, C. O. "The Retreat of Procter and Tecumseh." *Ontario Historical Society Papers and Records* 17 (1919): 11–21.

CHAUNCEY, ISAAC
1772–1840
U.S. naval officer

Isaac Chauncey was born on 20 February 1772 at Black Rock, Fairfield County, Connecticut, to Wolcott and Ann Brown Chauncey, a lineal descendant of Charles Chauncey, second president of Harvard. When only 19 years old, Isaac Chauncey was commanding the ship *Jenny*, owned by the Schermerhorns, New York shipowners. After joining the navy he was appointed first lieutenant of the frigate USS *President* on 11 June 1799, rank dating from 17 September 1798. On that ship he served with Commodore Thomas Truxtun in the West Indies during the last year of the Quasi-War with France.

In 1801, Chauncey was placed sixth on the permanent list of lieutenants. He participated in the Tripolitan war from 1802 to 1805 as acting commander of the flagship *Chesapeake* and later as the commander of the frigates *New York* and *John Adams*. In Commodore Preble's attack on Tripoli, 28–29 August 1804, Chauncey served on the flagship USS *Constitution* and was commended by Preble. After that Chauncey's promotions were virtually guaranteed. He became master-commandant on 18 May 1804 and captain on 24 April 1806. On furlough after this last promotion, he voyaged to the West Indies on a vessel belonging to John Jacob Astor. From 1807 to 1812, Chauncey had command of the New York Navy Yard. This duty brought security and a house for his family as well as

a network of rich acquaintances from Chauncey's work procuring supplies.

Following William Hull's disaster at Detroit in August 1812, Chauncey was appointed to command at Lakes Ontario and Erie in September 1812 (Champlain was left outside his authority) and worked to recruit men; hire shipwrights, riggers, and blacksmiths; and develop supply contracts. He persuaded the crew of the *John Adams* to volunteer en masse and eventually arrived at Sacket's Harbor with 700 sailors and shipwrights. He worked effectively with Lt. Melancthon T. Woolsey to procure a small squadron of converted merchant schooners. Led by the brig *Oneida* (18 guns), the construction of which Woolsey had supervised in 1808, this squadron had seized command of Lake Ontario from the ineffective Canadian Provincial Marine by November 1812. Chauncey had already contracted with New York shipwright Henry Eckford to build the ship *Madison* (26 guns). Finished in 45 days and launched in November, she commanded Lake Ontario by the end of 1812.

With the opening of the campaign in April 1813, Chauncey effectively supported Henry Dearborn's invasion of York on 27 April with the *Madison*, *Oneida*, and 14 schooners, some heavily armed with nine and ten guns. Chauncey then landed Dearborn's army to capture Fort George on 27 May. After helping reduce Fort George, Chauncey returned to Sacket's Harbor to find his base had been attacked. On 28–29 May, a newly arrived party of Royal Navy "Lakers" under Sir James Lucas Yeo had joined the Kingston garrison led by Sir George Prevost for the assault. In essence, Yeo seized the initiative and effectively neutralized Chauncey's support of the U.S. army in the Upper Niagara peninsula by attacking its rear at Forty Mile Creek and capturing its supply boats. The U.S. army, defeated at Stoney Creek on 6 June 1813, was driven back to Fort George and penned there for the rest of the year.

In the ensuing naval contest, Yeo and Chauncey each sought to engage on terms most suitable to his own squadron. Yeo's was smaller, heavily armed with carronades, and sailed together well as a war squadron. Chauncey's had many more ships and was led by the large new frigate *General Pike*, a ship as big as the ocean-going *Essex* and commanded by the seasoned Arthur Sinclair. Chauncey also had many more long guns. Yet he had to tow his rather ineffective schooners or risk a divided squadron vulnerable to defeat in detail.

Under these circumstances, the two commodores played an intricate cat-and-mouse game, but there is no evidence to support Charles Oscar Paullin's pejorative comment that "both commanders were wary and excessively cautious" or James L. Mooney's view that "both commanders suffered from a common naval malady, fearing defeat more than they desired victory." Both commodores knew that the stakes included the whole of Upper Canada. Yeo kept attacking Chauncey's supply bases on the southern shore of Lake Ontario, but Yeo's orders described his main task as defensive: to maintain possession of the Canadian provinces. That meant supplying the British army in the Niagara peninsula.

Chauncey's role was to attack the British squadron, defeat it, and reduce British lake bases to open the way for the U.S. army. Running actions in August 1813 saw Yeo best Chauncey twice. Yet the critical turning point came on 28 September when Chauncey finally trapped Yeo at the west end of Lake Ontario on a lee shore with an east wind and forced the British squadron to flee to Burlington Bay. Only Chauncey's apprehension about water depth caused him to haul off, and as he failed to pursue into the bay the British squadron escaped. This incident occurred just three weeks after Perry's decisive victory on Lake Erie, meaning that Yeo's thorough destruction at Burlington Bay could have been the decisive moment in the war, but Chauncey let it slip by.

Toward the end of the 1813 season, Chauncey initially was ordered to support the intended invasion of Kingston by Gen. James Wilkinson's army. When plans changed the target to Montreal, Chauncey successfully escorted Wilkinson down the St. Lawrence. After internal feuding and administration vacillation ended this invasion with both armies in winter camp, Chauncey was informed that Sacket's Harbor and his squadron there would have no protection unless he brought William Henry Harrison's army down the lake from Fort George. Braving terrific gales and blinding snowstorms, Chauncey's squadron executed a masterful removal of Harrison's army. The entire episode embittered Chauncey, however, and from it grew his contempt for army commanders who wished to use his vessels merely as transports.

At Sacket's Harbor, Chauncey organized a large-scale shipbuilding program, established a hospital, built a rope walk, and erected barracks for his seamen. By 1814, his large ships included the USS *Superior* (64 guns), the largest ship then in the U.S. Navy, and the smaller but enormously powerful frigate *Mohawk* (44 guns). Yet the work wore Chauncey down. Careworn, ill, and with his ship construction program lagging, he failed to appear in support of Gen. Jacob Brown's attack on the Niagara peninsula forts in July 1814. When this campaign ended with Brown's retreat from Lundy's Lane to Fort Erie and eventually to Buffalo, the two began an acrimonious correspondence as they attempted to lay blame for the campaign's failure. All of it was published in newspapers,

prompting President Madison to consider replacing Chauncey with Stephen Decatur. Decatur's suggestions, however, to blockade Kingston with sunken vessels was rightly ridiculed by Chauncey as born of Decatur's ignorance about Kingston's lake depth and channel width. Madison relented, and Chauncey remained in command.

Over the winter of 1814–1815, he visited New York and Washington to finalize plans for mammoth line-of-battle ships and hired the New York shipbuilders Henry Eckford and Noah and Adam Brown to build them. One, named *New Orleans* after Andrew Jackson's victory of 8 January 1815, was planked and ready for launching when the Senate ratified the Peace of Ghent in February 1815.

Chauncey was a skilled organizer, but he could not delegate responsibility effectively. He never appointed an officer, as Yeo did at Kingston, to superintend the administrative affairs at Sacket's Harbor. Thus myriad administrative details distracted him from his most important objective of destroying Yeo and dominating Lake Ontario. He lost sight of the strategy that to win the Upper Province his forces would have to smash British naval strength, and he was outdueled or outsmarted by Yeo on critical occasions.

His subordinate, Oliver Hazard Perry, had destroyed the British squadron on Lake Erie on 10 September 1813, but Chauncey never managed the same feat on Lake Ontario. Yet Paullin's judgment that "it is obvious that among the naval commanders of the War of 1812 he is not of the first rank" is too harsh. It ignores the difficulties imposed by army interference and financial stringency. It does not take into account the overly ambitious strategy formulated by the Madison administration, attempting to rebound from a year of military disasters by pursuing an aggressive war in the north. In spite of this, Sacket's Harbor under Chauncey became the largest naval station in the United States and built more ships during the war than any other naval yard.

After the war, Chauncey took command in 1815 of the *Washington* (74 guns) at Portsmouth, New Hampshire. Starting in 1816, he commanded for two years in the Mediterranean, where he negotiated a treaty with Algiers. From 1822 to 1824, he was one of three post-captains who made up the Board of Navy Commissioners in Washington. From 1825 to 1832, he again commanded the New York Navy Yard but in 1832 returned to Washington as a navy commissioner and president of the Board. He was married to Catherine Sickels, and two of his sons, Charles W. and John S. Chauncey, became naval officers. He died on 27 January 1840 and was buried in the Congressional Cemetery.

—*Frederick C. Drake*

See also: Brown, Jacob J.; Dearborn, Henry; Decatur, Stephen, Jr.; Detroit, Surrender of; George, Fort; Harrison, William Henry; Hull, William; Kingston, Upper Canada; Lake Ontario; Perry, Oliver Hazard; Sacket's Harbor, New York; Stoney Creek, Battle of; Wilkinson, James; Woolsey, Melancthon Taylor; Yeo, James Lucas

Further Reading

Fowler, William C. "Isaac Chauncey." *Memorials of the Chauncey Family.* Vol. 1. Boston: W. H. Dutton, 1894.

Haller, Willis C., Gerard Hoard, and Robert Marshall. *The Building of Chauncey's Fleet.* N.p., 1983.

Mooney, James L. "Isaac Chauncey." In *James Madison and the American Nation 1751–1836,* ed. Robert Rutland. New York: Simon & Schuster, 1994.

Paullin, Charles Oscar. "Isaac Chauncey." *Dictionary of American Biography.* Vol. 3, pp. 40–41. New York: Charles Scribner's Sons, 1936.

Pratt, Fletcher. "An Anomaly: Isaac Chauncey." In *Preble's Boys.* New York: Sloane, 1950.

CHEROKEE INDIANS

In the early nineteenth century, the Cherokee occupied a region around the Smoky Mountains in North Carolina, South Carolina, Tennessee, north Georgia, and north Alabama. Their support for the United States arose partly from favorable trade relations and partly from hatred of the British-allied Iroquois, who had sold Cherokee northern land claims a generation earlier. The Lower Cherokee lived in the piedmont of South Carolina and Georgia and had become few in number. The Middle Towns were in North Carolina. To their west, higher in the Appalachians, stood the Valley Towns. Beyond the Smoky Mountains in Tennessee lived the so-called Overhill Cherokee. The tribe probably numbered about 13,000, including some adopted blacks and whites. Each group varied somewhat in its alliances and connections with non-Cherokee neighbors. At the end of the Revolution, all had lost some territory to the Americans.

For years before the War of 1812, the Cherokee nation suffered a crisis of identity and culture. Having made peace with the Americans, they expected to continue as a nation on their own territory. How they would accommodate a partly subservient relationship with the United States became a great controversy. As the traditional towns splintered, Christian missionaries arrived, and the population began expanding after a long decline. A nativist cult, now usually called the Cherokee Ghost Dance, flourished among the poorer element. The earthquakes that shook the southeast between December 1811 and April 1812 were seen by some as mystical events that only exacerbated tensions between nativists and accommodationists. Thus at the outbreak of war the Cherokee, though inclined to support the United States, were highly unsettled.

This religious awakening resembled that of the Shawnee, and some Cherokee warriors met with Tecumseh when he visited the Creek town of Tuckabatchee in 1811. Yet Tecumseh's plans for an Indian confederation attracted only a few Cherokee. Economic, cultural, and even blood ties with white Americans were too strong, and the chiefs who led the nation discredited the traditionalists. Col. Return Jonathan Meigs, the federal Cherokee agent, correctly reported to Washington that a British alliance would not tempt the Cherokee nation. Nevertheless, the Cherokee could not avoid involvement in the Creek Civil War that blended into the southeastern frontier phase of the War of 1812. Many enlisted in the fight against the Red Stick Creeks, and some enrolled as U.S. soldiers. For example, Pathkiller, the elderly principal chief, became an honorary colonel. In the campaigns of October 1813 to January 1814 and of March 1814, Cherokee warriors took part in five engagements. Thirty-six were killed, and 51 were wounded.

In a skirmish at Turkeytown in October, the Cherokee aided in the rout of a Red Stick band. Several hundred Creeks (including women and children) were killed, but no Cherokees. On 9 November, Andrew Jackson's raid on Talladega employed some Cherokee soldiers. Ten days later, when Gen. James White attacked the Hillabee towns, 400 Cherokees accompanied his troops. In January 1814, Jackson's army was in dire straits at Emuckfau Creek when the arrival of Cherokee and Allied Creek warriors turned the tide of battle. During Jackson's retreat, Red Sticks again attacked him at Enitachopco Creek, and many of the Indian soldiers were killed.

In March 1814, Jackson set out from Fort Strother for another campaign against the Red Sticks. Most of his Cherokee soldiers were new recruits, but they contributed vitally to the decisive battle at Horseshoe Bend (Tohopeka). Cherokee warriors crept behind Red Stick lines and stole canoes to cut off Creek leader Menewa's retreat. Eighteen Cherokees were killed and 36 wounded in this battle.

Horseshoe Bend concluded the Cherokee part in the war. They held several hundred Red Sticks prisoner for awhile but eventually released most of them. They did, however, keep a few black slaves captured in the campaigns. Yet for all that, the Cherokee suffered acute losses in this conflict. In the closing months of the war, U.S. militiamen passing through Cherokee country destroyed extensive amounts of Cherokee property. The federal government forgot its promise of pensions and wages on the same level as white militia. And finally, 2.2 million acres of land claimed by the tribe were lost in the Treaty of Fort Jackson, even though the treaty's ostensible purpose was to punish the Red Sticks. In spite of commendable efforts by Colonel Meigs, these wrongs were never redressed. In 1816, after meetings between Cherokee leaders and Pres. James Madison, the government agreed to compensation, but a storm of outrage from western settlers and Andrew Jackson blocked the agreement.

—*Thomas S. Martin*

See also: Creek War; Meigs, Return Johnathan
Further Reading

Calloway, Colin G. *Crown and Calumet: British-Indian Relations, 1783–1815.* Norman: University of Oklahoma Press, 1987.

Cotterill, R. S. *The Southern Indians: The Story of the Civilized Tribes before Removal.* Norman: University of Oklahoma Press, 1954.

McLoughlin, William G. *Cherokee Renascence in the New Republic.* Princeton: Princeton University Press, 1986.

CHESAPEAKE BAY CAMPAIGN
1813–1814

The principal British blockade, backed by combined operations, was in Chesapeake Bay, heartland of the Virginian and Maryland tobacco trade and a major trading area for U.S. foreign and coastal trade. Chesapeake Bay provided water access to Washington, the national capital; Annapolis, the Maryland state capital; and the thriving ports of Baltimore and Alexandria. Two navy yards, Washington and Norfolk, and two frigates, *Constellation* at Norfolk and *Adams* in the Potomac, lay within the waters of the bay. Baltimore was also a wartime privateer base. The shores of Virginia and Maryland provided tempting prize-money bait for British naval officers intent on punishing the Virginian Republican aristocracy, who, they surmised, brought on the war. By early 1813, Virginia governor James Barbour was acutely aware of the need to defend his state's sea borders.

On 21 November 1812, Adm. Sir John Borlase Warren, commanding the combined squadrons of the Halifax, Leeward Islands, and Jamaica stations, had suggested to the Admiralty plans for a limited blockade of Delaware and Chesapeake Bays; a "flying army and squadron" to destroy naval resources, vessels, forts, dockyards and arsenals; and a blockade to seize ships and magazines from Charlestown to New York. By 6 February 1813, when Warren finally received Admiralty notification to implement the plan, he had 3 sail of the line, 15 18-pounder frigates, 6 smaller frigates, 29 sloops of war, and 15 smaller vessels for the entire coast and the West Indies. A reinforcement in spring 1813 of 3 sail of the line, 1 50-gun ship, 8 smaller frigates, and 4 sloops, sent to deal with the possibility of any escaping French squadron, allowed Warren to commence a limited occupation of Chesapeake Bay, using Lynnhaven Bay as a fleet anchorage.

Two ships of the line and five or six frigates took station to intercept all intercourse by water. Warren also employed about 700 marines, accompanied by artillery, and 600 men of the 102nd regiment "to harass and alarm the Enemy," capture and destroy trade and shipping, "and carry all hostile effect into his harbours." Attacks by ships' boats began in February and lasted until August 1813. The waters of the Chesapeake ceased to serve as a highway for U.S. commerce. Capt. Alfred Thayer Mahan commented accurately that "these blockades were supported . . . by an accumulation of naval force entirely beyond the competition of the American navy. . . . The movements of the British had passed wholly beyond control."

As Warren's force sealed the capes, the local population of Norfolk feared an attack. Mail traffic was reduced to a canoe passing from Hampton or Newport News. Philip Barraud, surgeon at the Norfolk naval hospital, noted "we are now shut up from every possible communication with them. The tenders and boats from their Ships pop up the River without interruption & I have no doubt will alarm & endanger the shores of our Rivers full or much worse then they have done our Town." British forces took possession of Sharps, Tilghman, Poplar, and Tangier Islands, and the latter remained a British base throughout the war.

When Rear Adm. Sir George Cockburn aboard HMS *Marlborough* (74 guns) joined Warren as second-in-command, he engaged in punitive warfare and raided Urbanna, at Carter's Creek, Lancaster County, and Westmoreland County. The Severn River, 100 miles above Hampton, was blocked. By 16 April, a division of three 74s, 12 frigates, and smaller vessels were stationed at the mouth of the Patapsco River, a dozen miles from Baltimore. Cockburn's frigates attacked towns and villages of the Upper Chesapeake; invaded Frenchtown on the River Elk with its stores of flour, army clothing, saddles, bridles and cavalry equipment on 29 April; destroyed the Cecil or Principi foundry 3 or 4 miles to the northward; attacked the Havre de Grace battery; and smashed numerous cannon waiting to be shipped. Georgetown and Fredericktown were attacked next, and cutting-out expeditions went up the Sassafras.

In this long romp through the upper Chesapeake, Cockburn's force suffered seven wounded: five in the attack on Georgetown and Fredericktown, one at Havre de Grace, and one at Frenchtown. Baltimore editor Hezekiah Niles wrathfully denounced Cockburn's diversionary raids as being conducted by "a band of robbers," characterized as "the water winnebagoes" who caused "wanton violence—such horrid deviations from the rules and practices of civilized war—such purely savage proceedings." Cockburn himself was castigated as "one of the veriest wretches in existence." Such condemnation denoted effectiveness.

Cockburn also raided the southern Chesapeake as his squadron moved down the bay to rejoin Warren's fleet. Mahan preached the obvious conclusions: "There could be no doubt as to which party was getting the worst, undergoing besides almost all the suffering and quite all the harassment. This is the necessary penalty of the defensive, when inadequate."

Defenders had some successes against the occupying force. On 19 June, Warren brought 2,650 reinforcements, mainly marines and marine artillery from Bermuda under Sir Sidney Beckwith, 300 of the 102nd regiment commanded by Lt. Col. Charles James Napier, and 250 of two independent French companies, the Canadian Chasseurs. These forces attacked Craney Island on 22 June 1813 in 50 ships' boats from 13 sail anchored near Norfolk, carrying roughly 1,300 men. Craney Island was reinforced by local militia, the USS *Constellation,* and fourteen gunboats forming a crescent line of battle across the channel, backed by two forts, one on each river bank. The British attack was repulsed on an ebbing tide as the leading boats grounded 300 yards from the island. A flanking movement by Beckwith with a detachment of nearly 800 around Pig's Point, Nansemond River, recoiled when it ran into militia artillery. The attack was bungled, and Beckwith's and Napier's party lost 71 men. Total British casualties in the Norfolk attack were 88 killed and wounded, 62 missing, including 9 seamen killed, 8 wounded, and 10 missing. Warren blamed the failure on the extreme shoalness of the water on the sea side and the difficulty of getting across from the land side, but it was an inept attack on an ebb tide. Napier reflected, "Our attack on Craney Island was silly" and added, "it was the wrong place to attack, we should not have lost more men in striking at the town. . . .Our good Admirals are such bad generals . . . Cockburn thinks himself a Wellington! And Beckwith is sure the navy never produced such an Admiral as himself." Despite this combined operational failure, a British frigate lay off Newport News, three ships of the line were in the

Roads, and the *Constellation* and gunboats still lay under the fort.

When Hampton was attacked, the Canadian Chasseurs behaved with great brutality to avenge the massacre of comrades in a stranded boat at Craney Island. Hampton was occupied for three days and then evacuated at night. Outrages were committed that evoked a storm of protest from Americans, who reproached Beckwith for the conduct of the troops and threatened retaliation in kind. Philip Barraud complained that "vast enormities were practised in so much that we are sending off our wives & children. . . . The accursed Enemy by his Characters at Hampton is prepared to let loose a miserable Warfare. We must meet it Severely—God will protect us." Beckwith expressed regret and notified U.S. Gen. Robert B. Taylor that Warren had determined before the attack to send away the foreign troops, who had been trained under Bonaparte, "as men too lawless to be trusted" but indicated "they had been excited by the murder of their comrades in the stranded boat."

After Hampton, Warren sent some of the larger fleet units and transports out of the bay. By 5 July only one ship of the line was seen. Warren never had more than 2,600 troops, and the militia in the surrounding districts considerably outnumbered them, but Warren and Cockburn could always gain a local superiority for a period long enough to create havoc in the larger towns in the Chesapeake. The Hampton business, however, led Warren to rein in the troops. His naval forces remained, and the Chesapeake was, as Mahan termed it, "not so much blockaded as occupied."

In the bay, the U.S. government maintained a flotilla of gunboats, schooners, and great rowing barges for defense purposes. They aided the militia against small foraging parties but were not particularly effective in attacking frigates such as the *Junon* on 29 July, after she had grounded temporarily on Crow's Shoal on an ebb tide.

On 6 August, Warren used Napier's 102nd and the marine artillery to take possession of Kent Island, a central point between Annapolis, Baltimore, Washington, and the eastern shore. Kent was to serve as a refreshment area for ships' crews and troops. The island also became a gathering point for escaping slaves, who acted as guides, messengers, and pilots on board the troop transports. The loss of the escaped slaves meant severe economic losses for Virginian and Maryland planters, who began to pressure the state legislatures and Govs. James Barbour of Virginia and Levin H. Winder of Maryland to provide military protection.

Warren ultimately justified his small-scale raiding and combined operations in the bay as a means to detain U.S. troops otherwise destined for Canada, "as well as creating great alarm & Distress among the people." When Warren's force left, it transported about 300 bay slaves, some of whom he placed in the army and navy, some as workmen in Nova Scotia, and a few in the Bermuda dockyard. Warren left Robert Barrie in HMS *Dragon* (74 guns) in possession of Kent Island and in control of the Chesapeake blockaders with one ship of the line, two frigates, ten brigs, and three schooners. Barrie continued Warren's policy of raiding such places as the Pleasure House Barracks (21 September) and estates along the Potomac River. Between 6 September and 25 December, Barrie's ships took 69 vessels, and the bay remained occupied during the winter months.

In April 1814, as the Napoleonic empire crumbled, Warren was replaced by Vice Adm. Sir Alexander Inglis Forester Cochrane, whose naval force was joined by the Second battalion of 1,080 Royal Marines from Canada. Gen. Robert Ross embarked 2,000 troops from the Gironde in five troopships escorted by two line of battle ships. Rear Adm. Pulteney Malcolm also brought out to Bermuda the *Royal Oak* together with four frigates, two or three sloops, and the *Devastation* and *Meteor* (bomb vessels). In late April, British barges again entered the lower Rappahannock to Carter's Creek, capturing schooners, stealing sheep, and freeing slaves. The Baltimore gunboat flotilla was blockaded in the Patuxent River. Capt. Charles Gordon, on the trapped USS *Constellation*, still tried to raise the blockade but could not obtain troops from the army to assist him.

Cochrane kept George Cockburn's and Robert Barrie's advanced squadrons into the Chesapeake while he waited in Bermuda for the troops. They divided the Chesapeake between them, Barrie taking the upper part, Cockburn the lower. Although the work of Cockburn's and Barrie's smaller raiding parties from their squadrons was reminiscent of the small 1813 activity, the persistent blockade of the commerce of individual citizens as well as warships continued, and more powerful attacks were threatened against major cities.

Opposing Cochrane's overwhelming bay force was a small flotilla of gunboats commanded by Joshua Barney, a Revolutionary War Marylander who had enjoyed success in 1812 as a privateersman. He suggested to Secretary of the Navy William Jones that a small squadron of barges or row-galleys with light oars, light sails, and one heavy gun could defend the Chesapeake waters. By spring 1814, Barney had 18 vessels. He attempted raids on British-held Tangier Island but ran into the British fleet coming north up the bay and retreated. By 31 May, Barney's flotilla began harassing ships' boats from Albion and St. Lawrence, but his force was blockaded behind Drum Point near the entrance of the Patuxent until 7 June. Barrie sent his boats up the river after Barney's flotilla had retreated to St. Leonard's

Creek, a wide but shallow arm of the eastern bank of the river. Despite various skirmishes, the two forces neutralized each other's efforts.

Barrie thereupon began a policy of annoying the countryside's inhabitants and small towns in an effort to entice Barney's flotilla out from its anchorage, using local indignation as a spur. From 5 to 16 June, Barrie's marines and seamen, including a newly trained black corps in the *Dragon's* boats, raided the shores of the Patuxent, burning tobacco stores and houses. Calverton, Huntingtown, Prince Frederick, Benedict, and Lower Marlboro were all attacked. The force pushed on to Marlboro, where Barrie expected much sterner opposition, as the town was only 18 miles from Washington, but here he was disappointed in his wishes to try his marines against regulars, for he met no opposition.

Barrie's policy was eventually successful. After his boats and marines destroyed a battery at Chissinisack on 24 June 1814, Barney's flotilla came out and skirmished with the British boats on 26 June near the mouth of St. Leonard's Creek. A five-gun battery also fired on the *Loire* (38 guns), but the guns of the battery rolled back down the bluff. After an hour's cannonading, Barney withdrew up the creek. The British frigate was hulled once and lost some rigging, but she was not badly damaged. Barney's flotilla retreated once more up the Patuxent, and he scuttled two gunboats (Nos. 137 and 138) to prevent their capture, before moving north to White's Landing and then to Nottingham. Barney fell ill as the British burned St. Leonard's.

While waiting for Cochrane's main force to arrive from Bermuda, George Cockburn placed his squadron in the lower Potomac and informed Cochrane of the weakness of the surrounding countryside and the lack of patriotic spirit among its people. He also indicated that the U.S. Treasury was without sufficient funds and voiced the thought that no country could be more unfit for war than the United States. "I doubt if the American Government knew decidedly every particular of the intended attack on them," he stated, "whether it would be possible for them to adopt with sufficient Promptitude any effective means to avert the Blow." Cockburn then tipped his head in the direction of Washington. "I shall strongly advocate their seizing in the first instance the Capital," he confided to Barrie, "as that is always a hard Blow to begin with and is in this instance so easy to be effected within 48 Hours after Landing such a Force at Benedict." He moved his anchorage to Drum Point and left two frigates and a brig to deceive any watchers into thinking his move related to the blockade of Barney's flotilla.

On 18 July, Cockburn attacked Leonard's Town, the

capital of Maryland County, where the U.S. 38th regiment was stationed. He burned the regiment's stores, arms, flour and provisions, together with a schooner. British marines attacked Nominy Ferry and returned to the ships bringing off "135 refugee Negroes, two captured Schooners a large quantity of tobacco, dry goods and cattle and four prisoners." They lost one killed and four wounded. On 6 August, Cockburn reported that Coon River inlet was "the only inlet on the Virginia side of the Potomac which I had not visited," so he ordered an attack there by the battalion of marines. Somewhat laconically he noted to Cochrane "that having finished with the Virginia side of the Potomac as detailed to you in my letter of the 8th I crossed over on the 11th with the squadron and anchored them close to George's Island at the entrance of St. Mary's Creek." The marines made a number of excursions but found no militia or anyone armed. Having completed his round of visits of the whole countryside bordering on the Potomac, Cockburn proceeded to join Cochrane on 14 August, preparatory to the attack on Washington, Alexandria, and Baltimore. By then Thomas Browne, later a governor of Florida but then a member of Virginian general John P. Hungerford's staff, overestimated the British Chesapeake fleet at "seventy-odd ships of the line, spread out from the mouth of Chesapeake Bay up the Potomac, above where we were stationed; we could often see the men on the decks of the ships."

Cockburn's and Barrie's Chesapeake raiding provided ample opportunity for Madison's government to prepare an organized defense of the region. A cabinet meeting of 1 July surveyed the available troops. A thousand regulars were on hand, with 150 marines and Joshua Barney's 500 flotilla-men. The neighboring states of Virginia, Maryland, North Carolina, and the District of Columbia could muster a potential 93,000 militia. A new military district, the Tenth, was created on 2 July and placed under the command of Gen. William H. Winder, a relative of the federalist governor of Maryland. Winder was assigned all of the regulars and 15,000 militia who had not yet been mobilized; he began to reconnoiter his territory and his command, preparing for an anticipated attack. His calls for reinforcements went unheeded, and recruits trickled in only slowly. The British fleet's work in the Chesapeake and the arrival of troops from Bermuda laid the basis for extended attacks on Washington (24 August), which was burned; Alexandria, which was ransomed; and Baltimore, which successfully resisted. Because the Madison administration did not anticipate a serious attack, the disastrous consequences that followed were the logical result of its indecisiveness. The occupation of the Chesapeake always gave the initiative to the British occupying forces, until most of the

heavy units were withdrawn in October to join the attack on New Orleans.

—*Frederick C. Drake*

See also: Barney, Joshua; Barrie, Robert; Cochrane, Alexander; Cockburn, George; Craney Island, Battle of; Hampton, Virginia; Napier, Charles (British army officer); Norfolk, Virginia; Ross, Robert; Warren, John Borlase; Washington, British Capture of; Winder, Levin; Winder, William H.

Further Reading
Barraud, E. M. *Barraud: The Story of a Family.* London: Research Publishing Company, 1967.
Calderhead, William L. "Naval Innovation in Crisis: War in the Chesapeake 1813." *American Neptune* 36 (July 1976): 206–221.
Cassell, Frank A. "Slaves of the Chesapeake Bay Area and the War of 1812." *Journal of Negro History* 57 (1972): 144–155.
Garitee, Jerome R. *The Republic's Private Navy: The American Privateering Business as Practiced by Baltimore during the War of 1812.* Middletown, CT: Wesleyan University Press, 1977.
Hanson, George A. *Old Kent: The Eastern Shore of Maryland.* Baltimore: John P. Des Forges, 1876.
Hoge, William A. "The British Are Coming. . . . Up the Potomac." *Northern Neck Historical Magazine* 14 (December 1964): 1269.
Mahan, Alfred Thayer. *Sea Power in its Relation to the War of 1812.* 2 vols. Boston: Little, 1919.
Mayhew, Dean R. "Jeffersonian Gunboats in the War of 1812." *American Neptune* 32 (April 1982): 108–113.
Napier, Lieutenant-General Sir W. *The Life and Opinions of General Sir Charles James Napier G. C. B.* London: N.p., 1857.
Niles' Weekly Register, Vol. 4 and 5.
Shomette, Donald G. "The Much Vaunted Flotilla." In *Ships on the Chesapeake: Maritime Disasters on Chesapeake Bay and Its Tributaries, 1608–1978.* Centreville, MD: Tidewater Publications, 1982.
Shomette, Donald G., and Fred W. Hopkins, Jr., "The Search for the Chesapeake Flotilla." *American Neptune* 43 (January 1983): 5–19.

CHESAPEAKE-LEOPARD AFFAIR
22 June 1807

The *Chesapeake-Leopard* incident was the most important naval confrontation between the United States and Britain before the War of 1812 and in itself a cause of the conflict. It was the culmination of a long history of mistrust between the United States and Britain following the American Revolution.

In 1807, several French warships sought refuge in Chesapeake Bay. While the Royal Navy maintained its vigil, several British seamen deserted to the U.S. shore. Some deserters found their way aboard U.S. Navy ships, including the frigate *Chesapeake* (38 guns), fitting out at Norfolk for the Mediterranean. British authorities demanded that Americans return the deserters. The United States government refused.

On the morning of 22 June 1807, the *Chesapeake* weighed anchor and sailed from Hampton Roads, Commodore James Barron nominally in command. Secretary of the Navy Robert Smith had ordered Barron to assume command of the U.S. Mediterranean squadron, but in regard to the *Chesapeake*, Barron had briefly visited the ship only twice. Master Commandant Charles Gordon was in actual command of the frigate and had prepared her for sea. As the *Chesapeake* tacked to get off shore, her movements were mirrored by HMS *Leopard* (50 guns), commanded by Capt. Salusbury Humphreys. The *Leopard* then approached the *Chesapeake* and hailed, her captain saying he had dispatches. The "dispatch," brought aboard by a British lieutenant, turned out to be a general circular from the Royal Navy commander in North America, Vice Adm. Sir George Berkeley, ordering his captains to search for deserters from specified British warships.

Humphreys did his best to moderate the order's tone, but he insisted on mustering the *Chesapeake*'s crew. Barron denied he had any deserters on board and said that, in any case, the British had no right to search a U.S. Navy vessel. After more than 40 minutes of fruitless discussion, Humphreys recalled the lieutenant and ordered his crew to open fire.

The *Chesapeake* was wholly unready, her gun deck littered with baggage, powder horns unfilled, and matches unlit. Worse, nothing had been done while the British lieutenant was aboard to prepare for the possibility of battle. The *Chesapeake*'s crew got off only one shot before Barron struck the ship's colors. In the uneven exchange the British fired several broadsides that killed three Americans. Eighteen others suffered wounds, including Barron, who exhibited outstanding personal bravery under fire. Humphreys refused Barron's surrender of the *Chesapeake* as a prize of war. Instead, he mustered the Americans and took off four men identified as deserters (one from the *Halifax* and three from the *Melampus*). The *Leopard* then sailed away, having created a diplomatic tumult of the first order.

The United States simply exploded in indignation, and many even clamored for war. Citizens in Norfolk destroyed British naval property. State governments called up militia, and the federal government ordered gunboats into service. The war of words that followed spread both anger and fear. The Hampton Roads area braced for a British attack.

Pres. Thomas Jefferson resolutely avoided war, but in July he did order British warships from U.S. waters. Time soon cooled belligerent passions among the public, but official rancor over the incident persisted, especially in discussions of impressment. The *Chesapeake-Leopard* affair also profoundly affected the U.S. Navy. A board of inquiry investigated the affair, and the courts-martial that followed bitterly divided the officer corps and even led to duels. Barron's court found him guilty of neglecting "on the probability of an engagement, to clear the ship for action." Suspended from the navy for five years, he never again had a command afloat. Gordon, responsible for preparing the frigate for sea, escaped any penalty, possibly owing to family connections.

London finally conceded the affair was a mistake, but the admission meant little to Jenkin Radford, the deserter from the *Halifax*. In August 1807, a Royal Navy court-martial found him guilty of mutiny, desertion, and contempt (insolence to a British naval officer). Condemned to death, Radford soon swung from the yardarm of the *Halifax*. The three deserters from the *Melampus* received sentences of 500 lashes each. This sentence was, however, remitted, and the three were simply subjected to "temporary" imprisonment. One died in captivity, but the other two eventually returned to Boston and rejoined the crew of the *Chesapeake*.

U.S. Navy officers yearning for revenge against the British got a taste of it in the *President–Little Belt* incident of 18 May 1811. Bitterness over the *Chesapeake-Leopard* affair lingered, however, even after the War of 1812. When Barron sought reinstatement in the navy, Stephen Decatur reproached him for staying out of the country during the war. The two fought a duel that left Decatur mortally wounded. For his part, Barron at least had the satisfaction of outliving the other principals in the affair. He died in 1851 at 83, the oldest living U.S. Navy officer.

—*Spencer C. Tucker*

See also: Barron, James; Berkeley, George Cranfield; Decatur, Stephen, Jr.; *President–Little Belt* Incident

Further Reading

Emmerson, John Cloyd. *The* Chesapeake *Affair of 1807: An Objective Account of the Attack by HMS* Leopard *upon the U.S. Frigate* Chesapeake *off Cape Henry, Va., June 22, 1807, and Its Repercussions.* Portsmouth, VA: privately printed, 1954.

Stevens, William O. *An Affair of Honor. The Biography of Commodore James Barron, U.S.N.* Norfolk: Norfolk County Historical Society of Chesapeake, Virginia, in cooperation with

A Robert Dodd painting of the demoralizing defeat of the U.S.S. Chesapeake *by the British* Shannon. *The 15-minute fight was a boost to British morale, as the* Chesapeake *was the first American frigate to be lost in the war.*

the Earl Gregg Swem Library of the College of William and Mary, 1969.

Tucker, Spencer C., and Frank T. Reuter. *Injured Honor: The Chesapeake-Leopard Affair, June 22, 1807.* Annapolis, MD: Naval Institute Press, 1996.

CHESAPEAKE VERSUS SHANNON
1 June 1813

On 1 June 1813, off Boston Harbor, the Royal Navy frigate *Shannon* (38 guns), commanded by Capt. Philip Bowes Vere Broke, defeated the U.S. Navy frigate *Chesapeake* (38 guns), commanded by Capt. James Lawrence. It was the first U.S. Navy frigate loss in the War of 1812 and a boost to British pride.

Lawrence had only taken command of the *Chesapeake* on 18 May. A capable, brave, and resourceful officer, he also was inclined to rashness. The *Chesapeake*, then fitting out at Boston, had a reputation as an unlucky ship, dating back to the *Chesapeake-Leopard* affair of 1807, and most of her crew had departed when their enlistments expired. Lawrence found it hard to recruit replacements; most seamen preferred to ship in privateers. A number of foreigners were in the crew, including Englishmen and Portuguese. A few men from the *Constitution* joined, and they and the remaining crew from the *Chesapeake* would have been an excellent nucleus, given time for training. Unfortunately, the Americans were not to have that opportunity. The officers were also largely new to the ship, although First Lt. Augustus Ludlow had been a third lieutenant on the frigate's latest cruise.

Captain Philip Broke of the *Shannon* was one of the best frigate captains in the Royal Navy and had been in command of the *Shannon* since September 1806. His crew was well trained and seasoned, and the frigate had been cruising the North American coast for 18 months. More than anyone else, Broke was responsible for the development of improved gunnery practices. Unlike most Royal Navy captains, who gave little attention to gunnery, Broke insisted on realistic training. He reinforced proficiency with daily drills and simulated firing. Not only did he train his gun crews to carry out concentrated fire (aligning all guns to fire on one area), but at his own expense he fitted the *Shannon's* guns with dispart sights and gunners' quadrants. He also developed a ballistics pendulum for regulating gun position in horizontal firing. As a consequence, the *Shannon* was greatly superior in gunnery to most British frigates.

On paper the two frigates compared equally as far as ordnance was concerned. The *Chesapeake* mounted 50 guns (26 in broadside): 28 long 18s on the gun deck; on the spar deck, 2 long 12s, 1 long 18, and 19 carronades (18 of them 32s and 1 a 12). Her broadside weight of metal was 542 pounds. Her crew complement was 379 men. The *Shannon* carried 52 guns: on the gun deck, 28 were 18s; on the spar deck, 4 were long 9s, 1 was a long 6, 16 were 32-pounders, and 3 were 12-pounder carronades. Her broadside weight of metal was thus 550 pounds, and she had a crew complement of 330 men.

Early on 1 June, Broke sent Lawrence a challenge to battle. Such figurative tossing of the gauntlet was common practice in the two navies, each trying to affect more bravado than the other. Lawrence, who needed no such invitation, had sailed before it arrived. His own earlier successes against Royal Navy vessels led Lawrence to believe he could defeat his opponent. On 1 June, then, the *Chesapeake* weighed anchor at noon and sailed out of Boston harbor.

The battle took place about 18 miles from Boston lighthouse and began about 5:50 P.M. Although the *Chesapeake's* fire did considerable damage to the *Shannon*, she herself suffered far more. About 6:00 the two frigates fell apart. The *Shannon's* anchor snagged the *Chesapeake's* quarter port, grappling her stern quarter against the *Shannon's* starboard side. Broke ordered the ships lashed together, main battery fire halted, and boarders forward.

British fire had claimed a disproportionate share of the U.S. officers. The fourth lieutenant was killed, and First Lieutenant Ludlow was mortally wounded. Lawrence himself, conspicuous in dress uniform on the quarterdeck, also fell. Mortally wounded, he was carried below.

At 6:02, Broke led a boarding party of about 20 men aboard the *Chesapeake*. Many of the *Chesapeake's* crew deserted their posts, and only the marines stood firm to a man. By 6:05, only 15 minutes after the battle had begun, it was all over. The Americans suffered 61 killed or mortally wounded and 85 severely or slightly wounded. The *Shan-*

non lost 33 men killed or mortally wounded and 50 wounded, including Broke. Surprisingly, in the short battle the *Chesapeake's* guns inflicted more damage to the *Shannon's* hull than the *Java*, *Guerrière*, or *Macedonian* had to their opponents, and in turn the U.S. frigate suffered less damage than was normal in such engagements. Superior British training and discipline had decided the battle.

The British took the *Chesapeake* into Halifax, where she was repaired and taken into the Royal Navy. Captain Lawrence and Lieutenant Ludlow were buried with full military honors. Broke was made a baronet and his lieutenants promoted. Lawrence achieved immortality with his final order, issued as he was being carried below: "Don't give up the ship."

—*Spencer C. Tucker*

See also: Broke, Philip Bowes Vere; *Chesapeake-Leopard* Affair; Halifax, Nova Scotia; Lawrence, James
Further Reading
Padfield, Peter. *Broke and the* Shannon. London: Hodder and Stoughton, 1968.
Poolman, Kenneth. *Guns off Cape Ann. The Story of the* Shannon *and the* Chesapeake. London: Evans Brothers, 1961.
Roosevelt, Theodore. *The Naval War of 1812.* New York: G. P. Putnam's Sons, 1882.
Tucker, Spencer C., and Frank T. Reuter. *Injured Honor: The* Chesapeake-Leopard *Affair, June 22, 1807.* Annapolis, MD: Naval Institute Press, 1996.

CHEVES, LANGDON
1776–1857
Republican congressman

Langdon Cheves was born in Abbeville District, South Carolina, on 17 September 1776 but spent most of his youth residing with genteel relatives in Charleston. Although he did not receive a classical education, he became one of the most successful attorneys in his native state. He read law in the offices of Judge William Marshall and in 1797 was admitted to the state bar. Within a decade his legal practice, based in Charleston, had a statewide clientele.

Many of his close legal colleagues, including Marshall, were Federalists, yet throughout Cheves's active political career he was a firm Jeffersonian Republican. He was so outspoken in his professed loyalties that a longtime rival, Joseph Alston, referred to Cheves as the "political Jesuit."

In 1802, he was elected to the South Carolina House of Representatives by the voters of the Parishes of St. Michael's and St. Philip's (Charleston District). Cheves held this seat until 1809, when the legislature appointed him state attorney general. The following year, he was elected to the U.S. House of Representatives, where he became part of a notable quartet of legislators from South Carolina. The other members of this group were John C. Calhoun, William Lowndes, and David R. Williams. All four were active War Hawks, a collection of vocal congressional Republicans who advocated war with Great Britain.

In 1812, Cheves actively backed the retention of Henry Clay of Kentucky as Speaker of the House. Clay accordingly awarded Cheves with the chairmanship of the Committee of Ways and Means. During his years in Congress, Cheves was also an influential member on the Committee of Naval Affairs. After the declaration of war against the British in June 1812, Cheves was a key framer of many subsequent military appropriation bills. He relished direct oratorical confrontations with antiwar opponents, such as Rep. Daniel Webster of New Hampshire.

When the 13th Congress convened in March 1814 the lower house was obliged to select a new presiding officer. Pres. James Madison had recently appointed Clay to the U.S. delegation that was attending the peace conference in Ghent, Belgium. The Republican majority elected Clay's personal choice for the office, Langdon Cheves. It was House Speaker Cheves who announced to his colleagues in January 1815 that the Treaty of Ghent had been finalized the previous month.

In May 1815 Cheves declined Madison's request that he join the administration as secretary of the treasury. Moreover, Cheves announced to constituents in Charleston that he would not stand for reelection in 1816. Instead, he returned home to accept a seat on the South Carolina Court of Appeals. Cheves also intended to rebuild his once-extensive private law practice.

On 6 March 1819, Pres. James Monroe appointed Cheves to succeed William Jones as president of the troubled Second National Bank of the United States. Cheves's retrenchment policy meant fewer loans, higher interest rates, and a sharp reduction of legal tender bank notes in circulation. Debtors and entrepreneurs were enraged by these moves, but the bank became quite solvent during Cheves's management, which ended with his resignation in May 1822. He was succeeded by Nicholas Biddle.

Cheves's long absence from South Carolina precluded any direct role in state politics, but he quietly became a political power broker. Never a fanatical defender of slavery, he also regarded the activities of the abolitionists as quite worrisome. In 1850, he agreed to represent South Carolina

at the Nashville Convention but remained optimistic that the respective sectional issues could be resolved within the existing constitutional framework.

Until his death Cheves remained an active attorney with a flourishing practice. He owned considerable property around the state, especially a valuable rice plantation in Beaufort District. On 26 June 1857, Cheves suddenly died in Columbia, South Carolina, while visiting one of his married daughters. He was buried in Magnolia Cemetery in Charleston.

—*Miles S. Richards*

See also: Biddle, Nicholas; Calhoun, John C.; Clay, Henry; Ghent, Treaty of; Jones, William; Lowndes, William; U.S. Congress; War Hawks; Williams, David Rogerson

Further Reading

Ford, Lacy K. *Origins of Southern Radicalism*. New York: Oxford University Press, 1988.

Hammond, Bray. *Banks and Politics in America from the Revolution to the Civil War*. New York: Oxford University Press, 1957.

Leiding, Harriet Kershaw. *Charleston: Historic and Romantic*. Philadelphia: Lippincott, 1931.

Wolfe, James Harold. *Jeffersonian Democracy in South Carolina*. Chapel Hill: The University of North Carolina Press, 1940.

CHICAGO MASSACRE
15 August 1812

The Chicago Massacre stemmed from Gen. William Hull's disastrous campaign in the Michigan area. With the fall of Fort Michilimackinac to the British, Hull ordered the evacuation of the now vulnerable Fort Dearborn, located near the mouth of the Chicago River. Hull wanted Capt. Nathan Heald, a regular army officer from Massachusetts, to relocate his garrison and local settlers to Fort Wayne. Before Heald left, however, Hull also ordered him to give his supplies—including surplus firearms and ammunition—to the unfriendly Potawatomi and Winnebago tribes in the area. After largely following Hull's wishes, Captain Heald on 12 August 1812 led 54 lightly armed soldiers and about 39 settlers toward Fort Wayne. The party soon confronted 500 Potawatomi, who commenced a ferocious attack, killing or wounding two-thirds of Heald's people. Those who survived became prisoners of war.

The Chicago Massacre's legacy was threefold: It temporarily destroyed any trace of U.S. authority over Lake

Michigan, it exposed the area west of the Ohio and Maumee Rivers to British attack, and it eliminated the westernmost staging area of a planned three-prong assault into Canada.

—Peter R. Faber

See also: Dearborn, Fort; Hull, William; Michilimackinac, Fort; Wayne, Fort

Further Reading

Coles, Harry L. *The War of 1812.* Chicago: University of Chicago Press, 1965.

Frazier, Arthur H. "The Military Frontier: Fort Dearborn." *Chicago History* 9 (1980): 80–85.

Horsman, Reginald. *The War of 1812.* New York: Knopf, 1969.

Tucker, Glenn. *Poltroons and Patriots.* Indianapolis: Bobbs-Merrill, 1954.

CHIPPEWA, BATTLE OF
5 July 1814

In the early morning hours of 3 July 1814, the United States renewed its offensive on the Niagara front. Acting upon the suggestion of Secretary of War John Armstrong, Gen. Jacob Brown ordered his army of 4,800 men across the Niagara River into Canada. After taking Fort Erie, a British outpost near the juncture of Lake Erie and the Niagara River, Brown moved his army north along the Niagara. He hoped to rendezvous with a small U.S. fleet on Lake Ontario, then to march west and conquer all of Upper Canada.

Brown's early capture of Fort Erie triggered an immediate British reaction. The area commander, Maj. Gen. Phineas Riall, gathered 2,000 troops to face the U.S. army. For most of that hot and clear 4 July, small numbers of British delayed Brown's lead element, the First Brigade commanded by Winfield Scott.

By nightfall, Scott stopped his advance at the Chippewa River. Riall had established a strong position on the north bank. The Americans doubled back 1 mile and encamped behind Street's Creek. The next morning the militia of both armies engaged in desultory skirmishing on the plain between the Chippewa and Street's Creek. By noon, however, Jacob Brown had grown impatient. Not only had there been no general battle, but intermittent sniper fire harassed his lines. Riall had successfully positioned a number of Canadian militia and allied

Mohawk Indians in a forest west of the plain. Brown responded by ordering his Third Brigade to clear the woods. It proved a most unpleasant task. Around 4:00 P.M. the Third Brigade entered the woods single-file, only to run into a reinforced column of enemy militia and Indians. Within moments, the weaker U.S. contingent scrambled wildly for the rear.

The attack upon the Third Brigade was part of a general British advance. Phineas Riall had also ordered his three regiments of regulars to fix bayonets and cross the Chippewa. The sudden British movement surprised the Americans. Winfield Scott, mildly contemptuous of the British, believed there would be no battle. By 5:00 P.M., he had even prepared to drill his brigade on the plain. Jacob Brown, however, was worried. He heard the rattle of musketry in the forest and saw the dust kicked up by the attacking British regulars. He promptly ordered a disbelieving Scott to cross the creek and ready for battle. It did not take long for Scott to realize British intentions. Cannonballs landed near his brigade. Scott then ordered the 25th Infantry into the woods to guard the flank left unsecured by the Third Brigade's inglorious retreat.

Yet Phineas Riall was only slightly less confused than Winfield Scott about what lay in front of him. From his position near the Chippewa, Riall saw Scott's brigade on the march. He quickly noticed that the enemy wore nonstandard gray coats and not the prescribed blue uniforms of U.S. regulars. For a few brief moments, Riall thus believed his opposition was inferior militia. As Scott's soldiers dressed their lines and marched steadily through the British cannonade, Riall changed his opinion, exclaiming: "Those are Regulars, by God!"

The battle unfolded quickly. The artillery of both sides inflicted heavy casualties. As the Americans pressed forward, Scott extended his lines to create a concave formation, a maneuver that apparently bewildered the British. They marched steadily forward. When no more than 70 yards apart, both sides stopped and delivered a volley of musketry. With that the tide of battle suddenly shifted. Scott's concave formation caught the British in a cross fire. U.S. artillery destroyed a British caisson, leaving the redcoats without any functioning artillery. Unable to stand his ground any longer, Riall signaled retreat. He used a reserve regiment to cover his troops as they scampered across the sole bridge over the Chippewa.

Dead and wounded soldiers littered the battlefield. The British suffered 515 casualties, whereas the Americans counted 318 total losses. Although a tactical victory for Jacob Brown, he had not inflicted the crippling defeat necessary for strategic success. Indeed, twenty days later Brown fought again at Lundy's Lane, where he suffered

The bloody struggle raged on as the tides were turned, and American troops gained the upper hand to eventually beat the British at the Battle of Chippewa.

such losses that he was forced all the way back to Fort Erie. His strategic objective of conquering Upper Canada had vanished.

The significance of Chippewa was, however, more intangible. For two years of the war, U.S. regulars had generally met disaster. This changed at Chippewa. From that point forward, the British would be more wary of U.S. regulars. More importantly, Chippewa served as a vital turning point in the institutional development of the U.S. military. The battle would provide future generations of U.S. regulars with a tradition of combat steadiness previously wanting.

—*Kyle S. Sinisi*

See also: Armstrong, John; Brown, Jacob J.; Erie, Fort; Lake Ontario; Riall, Phineas; Scott, Winfield

Further Reading

Berton, Pierre. *Flames across the Border: The Canadian-American Tragedy, 1813–1814.* Boston: Little, Brown, 1981.

Elliott, Charles W. *Winfield Scott: The Soldier and the Man.* New York: Macmillan, 1937.

Kimball, Jeffrey. "The Battle of Chippawa: Infantry Tactics in the War of 1812." *Military Affairs* 31 (Winter 1967-1968): 169–186.

CHITTENDEN, MARTIN
1763–1840
U.S. representative; governor of Vermont

Born in Connecticut, Martin Chittenden spent most of his life in Vermont. After graduating from Dartmouth College, Chittenden almost immediately entered politics. He sat in the Vermont General Assembly, and beginning in 1803, he served four terms in the U.S. House of Representatives. In 1811 and 1812, his brother-in-law, Jonas Galusha, defeated him in the election for governor, but the 1813 election was thrown into the Vermont General Assembly. Chittenden finally edged Galusha to become governor.

Before his defeat, Governor Galusha had answered Gen.

Wade Hampton's request for Vermont militia to help him invade Canada. This required the Vermont men to travel to New York. The Republican Galusha supported the war, and even new Federalist governor Chittenden was not a strong opponent of it. Yet Chittenden did not think he had the constitutional authority to send Vermont militia out of the state.

Chittenden did not want to undermine Hampton's campaign. After the invasion failed, he sent an officer to retrieve the Vermont militia. Some of Vermont's Republican officers refused to obey the governor's order, but most of the militia, discouraged by the failed invasion, returned home. By that time, Chittenden's position had gained national attention. Throughout the country, Republicans predictably condemned his lack of patriotism while Federalists lauded his principled constitutionalism. In April 1814, requests for Vermont militia to protect Lake Champlain's eastern shore revived the issue. The task did not require the men to leave the state, so Chittenden ordered 1,500 men to the lake. The men resented being reorganized by the regular officers, however, and most refused to muster.

A few months later, the British moved on Plattsburg, New York, and federal officers again requested that Chittenden supply Vermont militia for the town's protection. Chittenden's constitutional reservations persisted, but the country's high peril prompted him to ask the Vermont militia to volunteer for the duty. This gesture apparently satisfied both political camps, because in the same year he again defeated brother-in-law Galusha for the governorship.

Chittenden was required to forward Massachusetts's proposal for a convention at Hartford, Connecticut, to the Vermont General Assembly. The legislature declined to participate in the convention. When Galusha defeated Chittenden the following year for the governorship, Chittenden retired to his farm.

—*Jeanne T. Heidler and David S. Heidler*

See also: Federalist Party; Hampton, Wade; Hartford Convention; Plattsburg, Battle of; U.S. Congress; Vermont
Further Reading
Heaton, John L. *The Story of Vermont.* Boston: Lothrop, 1889.
Sharp, Solomon P. *Mr. Sharp's Motion, Relating to the Conduct of Martin Chittenden, Governor of Vermont, in ... Ordering the Militia of That State, Engaged in the Service of the United States, to Withdraw from Their Service.* Washington, DC: A. & G. Way, Printers, 1814.

CHOCTAW INDIANS

One of the so-called Five Civilized Tribes of the Old South, the Choctaw were an ethnically mixed people who occupied three river valleys in modern Mississippi: the Pearl, Chickasawhay, and Pascagoula. Their language became the basis of a trading pidgin used throughout the region until the nineteenth century. The population centered around the Six Towns, the chief of which was Koweh Chito. Their spiritual center was and is the mound called Nanih Waiya, in modern Winston County, Mississippi. Like most tribes, the Choctaw were matrilineal, and observers remarked on the apparent equality and labor sharing of the sexes. According to William Bartram in 1777, they were "most ingenious and industrious husbandmen, having large plantations, or country farms . . . their territories are more generally cultivated, and better inhabited than any other Indian republic that we know of."

By the time of the War of 1812, treaty and cession had fractured the Choctaw homeland, displacing many of its 20,000 or so people. They had surrendered most land along the Gulf Coast and the Alabama and Tombigbee Rivers to the United States, which wanted the land for a buffer against Spain. The few sources of information about the situation before the Revolution are contradictory and confusing, suggesting considerable disruption. Many roads cut through Choctaw country, and the liquor trade suffered few restrictions.

Tecumseh's visit to the Choctaws, though a key event in their history, is not well documented. Coming from Chickasaw country, his entourage passed through the Six Towns (the region between today's Meridian and Macon) and was treated with respect. In a council at Hoentubbee's Town, in the presence of the great Pushmataha, the Shawnee asked the Choctaws to join his grand alliance. Pushmataha liked the idea of Indian cooperation, but he would not countenance war against the Americans. Tecumseh stayed for two weeks in Moshulitubbee's Town, where he addressed an even larger council. Then the Choctaws politely asked him to leave their country. He continued on to the Creek Upper Towns, where he had better luck.

The Choctaws declared war on the Red Stick Creeks immediately after the attack on Fort Mims. During the Creek Civil War, the Choctaws prevented the Red Sticks from making much headway in the Mississippi Territory. Choctaw warriors scouted for Gen. John Coffee when he preceded Jackson's army into Alabama in September 1813, and they took part in Col. Gilbert Russell's offensive against the Creeks in February 1814.

The British courted southeastern Indians, including the Choctaws, during the War of 1812. As late as the summer of 1814, Royal Marine major Edward Nicholls sent emissaries to the Choctaws. The British hoped that their attacks on Mobile and Baton Rouge would be successful enough to win Choctaws to their colors. Yet these Indians remained friendly to the United States, fighting bravely under Andrew Jackson's command at Pensacola and New Orleans. At New Orleans, Choctaw sharpshooters played a major role in demoralizing British pickets. They also slowed Col. Robert Rennie's advance on Jackson's lines in the first stages of the battle. And on 8 January, a large contingent under Capt. Pierre Jugeat defended a key sector of Jackson's lines in the swampy area along the river.

Unlike recent historians, contemporaries acknowledged that the more famous victories of Creek, Cherokee, and white leaders alike might not have been possible without timely Choctaw assistance. Of course, this loyalty was not entirely altruistic: Throughout the war, federal agent Silas Dinsmoor kept U.S. supplies flowing into Choctaw country.

Ironically, in spite of such Choctaw aid to the United States, the tribe continued to lose its land rapidly after the war. In 1816, they ceded all their remaining territory east of the Tombigbee. The U.S. government removed them to the West after the Treaty of Dancing Rabbit Creek in 1830.

—*Thomas S. Martin*

See also: Coffee, John; Creek War; Jackson, Andrew; Mims, Attack on Fort; Mobile, Battles of; New Orleans, Battle of; Nicholls, Edward; Red Sticks; Tecumseh

Further Reading

Calloway, Colin G. *Crown and Calumet: British-Indian Relations, 1783–1815.* Norman: University of Oklahoma Press, 1987.

Cotterill, R. S. *The Southern Indians: The Story of the Civilized Tribes before Removal.* Norman: University of Oklahoma Press, 1954.

Owsley, Frank Lawrence, Jr. *Struggle for the Gulf Borderlands: The Creek War and the Battle of New Orleans, 1812–1815.* Gainesville: University Presses of Florida, 1981.

Reeves, Carolyn Keller. *The Choctaw before Removal.* Jackson: University Press of Mississippi, 1985.

CHRYSLER'S FARM, BATTLE OF

11 November 1813

The Battle of Chrysler's Farm marked the defeat of the 1813 campaign by the United States to seize Montreal. After seizing Fort George in May 1813, Maj. Gen. Henry Dearborn failed to drive the British from the Niagara Peninsula. Secretary of War John Armstrong then reconsidered the U.S. strategy.

The key to Upper Canada was the well-defended naval base at Kingston on Lake Ontario. Armstrong reasoned that Kingston would fall if the Americans could sever the St. Lawrence River, the British line of communication to Kingston. After Pres. James Madison replaced Dearborn with Maj. Gen. James Wilkinson, Armstrong met Wilkinson and Commodore Isaac Chauncey at Sacket's Harbor to plan the campaign. After much debate, they settled on a two-pronged attack aimed at Montreal. Wilkinson would command the left or western wing. Maj. Gen. Wade Hampton, who commanded the U.S. army stationed around Lake Champlain, would lead the right wing. Hampton and Wilkinson detested each other, and Armstrong struggled to keep the peace between the two.

On 17 October, Wilkinson's 8,000 inadequately trained regulars, most of whom had never seen combat, departed Sacket's Harbor en route for the St. Lawrence River. The Americans rowed or sailed in hundreds of open bateaux through wind and sleet. Dozens of boats and scores of men perished in the storm. Chauncey did not seal Kingston harbor, so a small flotilla of British gunboats followed Wilkinson. Traveling the banks of the St. Lawrence, about 800 regulars commanded by Lt. Col. Joseph Morrison also shadowed the Americans.

When Wilkinson's army came upon an 8-mile stretch of rapids, the general ordered the men onto the northern shore while the lightened boats navigated the rough water. A vanguard, under Brig. Gen. Jacob Brown, cleared the Canadian shoreline of British opposition all the way to the end of the rapids.

While the Americans were camped near John Chrysler's farm, Morrison's force, though slender, nevertheless drew closer. Too sick to take the field, Wilkinson ordered Brig. Gen. John P. Boyd, an officer of considerable combat experience, to drive off Morrison's men. Boyd attacked Morrison piecemeal with four brigades. The well-trained and disciplined British soldiers drove back each U.S. assault. Superior British firepower stopped a mounted attack before the dragoons could close with pistol and saber. The Americans charged with spirit, but they could neither fire nor maneuver as quickly as their enemy. Boyd broke off the attack after suffering over 400 casualties, more than twice as many as Morrison. The Americans might have tried again had not Wilkinson learned of Hampton's retreat to New York following his defeat at Châteauguay on 26 October. Wilkinson hastily convened a council of war that endorsed his proposal to end the campaign and go into winter quarters.

Wilkinson was quick to lay the blame for the failed campaign on Hampton's refusal to cooperate. Armstrong would have none of it, however. In March 1814, he relieved Wilkinson of his command and ordered him to stand for a court-martial. Wilkinson won acquittal, but the army dropped him from its rolls in 1815.

—*Richard V. Barbuto*

See also: Boyd, John Parker; Brown, Jacob J.; Châteauguay, Battle of; Chauncey, Isaac; Hampton, Wade; Kingston, Upper Canada; Montreal; Morrison, Joseph Wanton; Sacket's Harbor, New York; Wilkinson, James

Further Reading

Elliott, Charles W. "The Indispensable Conquest." *Infantry Journal* 45 (July-August 1938): 334–342.

Mahon, John K. *The War of 1812*. Gainesville: University Presses of Florida, 1972.

Stanley, George F.G. *The War of 1812: Land Operations*. Canadian War Museum Historical Publication 18. Toronto: Macmillan, 1983.

Way, Ronald L. "The Day of Crysler's Farm." *Canadian Geographical Journal* 62 (1961): 184–217.

CHRYSTIE, JOHN
d. 1813
U.S. officer

A resident of New York, John Chrystie entered the U.S. Army as a first lieutenant of the Sixth Infantry in May 1808. By the outbreak of the War of 1812, Chrystie had risen to the rank of lieutenant colonel in the 13th Infantry Regiment. Assigned to the Niagara Frontier, Chrystie participated in the disastrous campaign against Queenston in October 1812.

On the night of 10 October 1812, Chrystie arrived at Four-Mile Creek with 350 men of the 13th, along with about 30 boatloads of supplies. As one of the senior regular officers present, Chrystie believed he should command the attack rather than militia colonel Solomon Van Rensselaer, nephew of the overall commander of the expedition, Maj. Gen. Stephen Van Rensselaer. Chrystie and his fellow officers ignored the fact that the younger Van Rensselaer was a former regular officer who had served under Anthony Wayne at Fallen Timbers. Van Rensselaer, wounded at that engagement, had seen more combat experience than Chrystie or any of the others. In recognition of his rank and status, Chrystie led 300 regulars across the Niagara in the first wave of the attack on 13 October.

On the night of 12 October, he moved his men into position, taking care not to alert the British of the U.S. plans. He arrived at the point of embarkation in Lewiston about midnight. Early the next morning, he loaded his men into 13 boats and set out for the other shore. Three of the boats, however, lost maneuverability in the river's eddies. One of those boats happened to be carrying Chrystie. No one knew his whereabouts for hours.

Meanwhile, the fight on Queenston Heights fiercely unfolded. Colonel Van Rensselaer was severely wounded and carried from the field. Had Chrystie been present, he would have assumed command, but no one had yet heard from him, so command devolved to one of Chrystie's subordinates, Capt. John Wool. Chrystie finally reappeared in the late afternoon after the U.S. retreat had started. He was just in time to receive a minor wound during the withdrawal. No formal accusations resulted, but Solomon Van Rensselaer privately implied that Chrystie's behavior on 13 October was cowardly.

In any event, his conduct that day did not hurt his career. In March 1813, he achieved the rank of colonel and became the commander of the 23rd Infantry Regiment. After participating in Dearborn's campaign against Fort George in May 1813, he died of natural causes there on 22 July 1813.

—*Jeanne T. Heidler and David S. Heidler*

See also: Dearborn, Henry; Queenston, Battle of; Van Rensselaer, Solomon; Van Rensselaer, Stephen; Wool, John Ellis

Further Reading

Redway, Jacques W. "General Van Rensselaer and the Niagara Frontier." *New York State Historical Association Proceedings* 8 (1909): 14–22.

CLAGHORN, GEORGE
1748–1824
U.S. shipbuilder

George Claghorn was born in Chilmark, Massachusetts. He served as an officer in the Revolutionary War and was wounded at Bunker Hill. Following the war he became a shipbuilder in New Bedford, Massachusetts. His skills soon gained him the attention of the Washington administration and the contract to construct the USS *Constitution* in 1794.

When the United States' problems with Algerian pirates temporarily came to an end, construction on the ship was halted until the country edged toward war with France in 1797. Congress then authorized the ship's completion, and it was launched on 21 October 1797. After his completion of the *Constitution*, Claghorn becomes an obscure figure. He died in Rhode Island in 1824.

—*Jeanne T. Heidler and David S. Heidler*

Further Reading

Emery, William M. *Colonel George Claghorn, Builder of the* Constitution. New Bedford, MA: Old Dartmouth Historical Society, 1931.

CLAIBORNE, FERDINAND L.
1773–1815
U.S. militia and volunteer officer

Born in Virginia, Ferdinand Claiborne entered the U.S. Army as a young man. Starting with a commission as an ensign in 1793, Claiborne became a first lieutenant, First U.S. Infantry Regiment, in 1794. He fought under Gen. Anthony Wayne at Fallen Timbers; following the war with the northwestern Indians, he continued to serve in that part of the country. Before resigning his commission in 1802, Claiborne rose to the rank of captain. Perhaps because of his brother W.C.C. Claiborne's position as territorial governor of the Louisiana Territory, Ferdinand Claiborne moved to the southwest, where he settled in the Mississippi Territory. He quickly rose to prominence in the young territory, serving in the territorial legislature and in 1811 becoming brigadier general of the territorial militia.

When war broke out with Great Britain, Claiborne accepted the position of colonel of the Mississippi Volunteers, U.S. Army, and in March 1813 became that force's commander at the rank of brigadier general. When a group of Mississippi Territory militia attacked a group of Red Stick Creek Indians at Burnt Corn Creek on 27 July 1813, U.S. military involvement in what had been a Creek civil war began.

General Claiborne did not have enough men at his disposal to stage an offensive against the Red Sticks. He expected Red Sticks to seek revenge for the attack at Burnt Corn, however, so he used his limited forces to reinforce various frontier forts throughout the eastern part of the territory. As part of this effort, Claiborne dispatched Maj.

Ferdinand L. Claiborne

Daniel Beasley with 170 militiamen to the Tensaw River. Beasley scattered about 50 of his men at outposts along the river and took the remaining 120 to Fort Mims, where most of them, including Beasley, were killed when the Red Sticks attacked on 30 August 1813. The very morning before the attack, Beasley had sent word to Claiborne that he had received a false report of an impending assault.

When Claiborne heard about the massacre at Fort Mims, he was so short of men that he could not send even a burial party for three weeks, let alone any substantive relief. Maj. Gen. Thomas Flournoy, commander of the Seventh Military District headquartered in New Orleans, authorized Claiborne, however, to call more militia into the field, march to the confluence of the Tombigbee and Alabama Rivers, and destroy any Red Sticks in his path. Claiborne was to build a fort and await reinforcements from the Third and Seventh U.S. Infantry Regiments.

While Claiborne put this plan into motion, Flournoy received word from Secretary of War John Armstrong that because the Creek War was occurring in both the Sixth and Seventh Military Districts, Armstrong was giving command of the entire war to Maj. Gen. Thomas Pinckney, commander of the Sixth Military District. This decision so angered Flournoy that he sent his regulars back to New Orleans and dismissed Claiborne's Mississippi Dragoon regiment. When Claiborne wanted to continue the campaign and questioned Flournoy's decision regarding the dragoons, Flournoy reprimanded him. Claiborne persisted, however, and ultimately Flournoy relented. He even allowed the Third Infantry to join the campaign.

On 13 November, Claiborne began the campaign with about 1,200 militiamen and regulars. William Weatherford's town, the Holy Ground, was his objective. As Claiborne moved up the Alabama River, he established Fort Claiborne and other forts to prevent Red Sticks from gaining his rear. Garrisoning these posts meant that his army was smaller as it approached the Holy Ground on the morning of 23 December 1813.

The inhabitants of the town knew about Claiborne's movements and had already evacuated the women and children. Many of the warriors who remained, however, did not prepare an adequate defense because they had been told by one of their prophets, Josiah Francis (Hillis Hadjo), that he had created an invisible ring around the town that would kill any white men who crossed it. When Claiborne attacked in three succeeding columns about noon and his men did not die, many of the Red Sticks fled. Those who remained under William Weatherford put up a desperate fight, but in the end they too had to flee. Weatherford escaped only at the last minute by swimming his horse across the Alabama River.

After taking what food they could carry, Claiborne's men burned the town. The following day, 24 December, Claiborne marched the men upriver; there, after a brief battle, they burned another town. Since his militiamen's enlistments were to expire in January, Claiborne moved back to Fort Claiborne, where his men were mustered out of U.S. service. Claiborne also resigned his volunteer commission on 17 January 1814. The Third Infantry stayed to garrison the forts.

Claiborne's campaign against the Red Sticks had immense impact on the Creek War. By clearing the Alabama River of Red Sticks and fortifying the area to prevent their return, Claiborne forced the Red Sticks to concentrate their activities east of that area just as Andrew Jackson began the campaign that would result in their devastating defeat at Tohopeka (Horseshoe Bend).

Ferdinand Claiborne died in the Mississippi Territory in February 1815.

—*Jeanne T. Heidler and David S. Heidler*

See also: Burnt Corn, Battle of; Claiborne, William Charles Coles; Creek War; Flournoy, [John] Thomas; Horseshoe Bend, Battle of; Jackson, Andrew; Mims, Attack on Fort; Pinckney, Thomas; Red Sticks; Weatherford, William

Further Reading
Owsley, Frank Lawrence, Jr. *Struggle for the Gulf Borderlands: The Creek War and the Battle of New Orleans, 1812–1815.* Gainesville: University Presses of Florida, 1981.

CLAIBORNE, WILLIAM CHARLES COLES
1775–1817
Governor of Louisiana

W. C. C. Claiborne's distinguished political career as a Tennessee congressman, territorial governor of Mississippi, governor of the Territory of Orleans, and governor of Louisiana embodied the developing western perspective and spirit of Jeffersonian republicanism.

William Charles Coles Claiborne, son of Col. William and Mary (Leigh) Claiborne, was born in Sussex County, Virginia, in 1775. He attended Richmond Academy and studied briefly at the College of William and Mary until financial difficulties ended his formal instruction at age 15. John Beckley, a fellow Virginian who was clerk of the U.S. House of Representatives, hired Claiborne as an assistant in his office. In this capacity, Claiborne met the leading statesmen of the period, including his mentor and later benefactor, Thomas Jefferson.

Claiborne decided to study law when North Carolina congressman John Sevier recognized the young clerk's talent and offered encouragement. Claiborne returned to Virginia for studies, and upon passing the bar, moved to the frontier in 1794 to practice criminal law in Sullivan County, Tennessee. Representing his county in the 1796 statehood convention, Claiborne helped to draft the original Tennessee constitution. When Sevier became governor of Tennessee, he appointed Claiborne, then only 21 years old, to serve as a judge on the state supreme court. In August 1797, Tennessee voters chose Claiborne to complete Andrew Jackson's unexpired congressional term and reelected him in subsequent elections, though he remained under the legal constitutional age to hold the office.

Claiborne chaired the congressional committee that supervised the Mississippi Territory, and in that capacity he investigated allegations of political impropriety leveled against Gov. Winthrop Sargent. On 25 May 1801, President Jefferson replaced Sargent with Claiborne, and he arrived at Natchez on November 23. Despite intense rivalry between vying factions, Governor Claiborne maintained a moderate course resulting in substantive progress for the territory and its inhabitants. Creation of new counties, settlement of land claims, and reforms in public health, education, and internal security were provincial successes during Claiborne's tenure. Additionally, continuing negotiations with regional Indian tribes and with Spanish Louisiana educated the young governor in larger national policy issues.

Upon the purchase of Louisiana in 1803, Jefferson sent Claiborne and Gen. James Wilkinson to New Orleans as his commissioners to accept the orderly transfer from French to U.S. authority. Jefferson's appointment of Claiborne as governor of the Territory of Orleans was implicit in this arrangement, and Claiborne remained at New Orleans to begin the challenge of making the recently purchased territory truly American. Conversant in neither French nor Spanish, unfamiliar with local customs and practices, and Protestant in a Roman Catholic region, Claiborne faced many cultural obstacles in governing this new territory. Creoles remained suspicious of the governor and leery of Americanization.

Claiborne was an enigmatic leader. Contemporaries sometimes mistook his prudence for indecision when facing difficulties, but he shunned rashness. Instead, he frequently sought counsel and approval from peers and superiors. During crises, most notably the Burr conspiracy and the Battle of New Orleans, Claiborne seemed to demonstrate weakness by consigning extraordinary powers upon Generals Wilkinson and Jackson. His manner of leadership generated vociferous criticism, but Claiborne was an honorable man who was always ready to answer for his actions. He even fought a duel when Daniel Clark charged him with incompetence for abdicating responsibilities during the Burr affair.

Criticism notwithstanding, Claiborne enjoyed certain accomplishments as a territorial governor. In 1810, he secured the Baton Rouge district as the United States annexed the West Florida parishes, joining them to the Territory of Orleans. In January 1811, he directed the effective military suppression of the German Coast slave insurrection, an uprising that threatened New Orleans. And in 1812, he saw Louisiana become the eighteenth state with himself its first elected governor.

The War of 1812 imperiled Louisiana with threats from without and within. The British might invade and plantation districts might revolt, but Claiborne remained confident. Militia enlistment was meager, however, and few Creoles joined the 44th Infantry, newly created for coastal defense. Claiborne nevertheless overestimated Louisiana's troop strength in official communications with Gen. Andrew Jackson. When Jackson arrived in December 1814, he declared martial law and initiated aggressive procedures

for defending New Orleans. Jackson scornfully deprecated Louisiana loyalty. Yet Claiborne's faith in the Louisiana militia's valor and fervent civilian patriotism vindicated his earlier confidence about the fidelity of Louisiana's citizens.

In 1817, Louisiana residents elected Claiborne to the U.S. Senate, completing the cycle of his political journey, but he died before taking office. A competent emissary of Jeffersonian republicanism, Claiborne effectively administered demanding frontier regions and prepared diverse communities for statehood.

—*Junius P. Rodriguez*

See also: Jackson, Andrew; New Orleans, Battle of; Sevier, John; Wilkinson, James

Further Reading

Claiborne, Nathaniel Herbert. *Notes on the War in the South; with Biographical Sketches of the Lives of Montgomery, Jackson, Sevier, and Late Gov. Claiborne, and Others.* Richmond, VA: William Ramsay, 1819.

Claiborne, W.C.C. *The Official Letter Books of W.C.C. Claiborne.* 6 vols. Jackson, MS: State Department of Archives and History, 1917.

Hatfield, Joseph T. *William Claiborne: Jeffersonian Centurion in the American Southwest.* Lafayette: University of Southwestern Louisiana, 1976.

CLARK, WILLIAM
1770–1838
Explorer; Indian agent; governor of Missouri Territory

William Clark was born in Virginia and reared in Kentucky. He gained frontier experience as an officer in Gen. Anthony Wayne's Indian campaigns of the 1790s. In 1804, Clark's friend Meriwether Lewis tapped him as coleader for their celebrated expedition through the Louisiana Purchase. Clark's fortitude, skill in negotiating with Indians, and meticulous journal keeping helped insure the success of the Lewis and Clark expedition.

In 1807, Pres. Thomas Jefferson appointed Clark superintendent of Indian affairs for the Louisiana Territory. In 1813, Pres. James Madison gave him additional duties as governor of the newly organized Missouri Territory.

During the War of 1812, Governor Clark capably defended the western frontier from attack by Britain's Indian allies. He ordered gunboats built and staffed them with volunteer crews to patrol the Mississippi River. In May

1814, he accompanied an expedition consisting of Seventh Regiment detachments and some 200 militia from St. Louis to Prairie du Chien on the Wisconsin River. The meager British presence there fled before Clark's arrival in June, so the Americans secured the strategic site without resistance and erected Fort Shelby there. After the war, Clark helped negotiate a series of treaties that restored peace with the Indian nations in the West.

Clark continued to serve as territorial governor until Missouri achieved statehood in 1821. That year he was defeated in the state's first gubernatorial election. Though respected for his talents as an explorer and Indian negotiator, Clark's aristocratic demeanor and association with unpopular fur-trading interests proved fatal to his political career. The old frontiersman remained as federal Indian agent for the trans-Mississippi region until his death in St. Louis in 1838.

—*Ricky Earl Newport*

See also: Prairie du Chien
Further Reading

Foley, William E. *The Genesis of Missouri: From Wilderness Outpost to Statehood.* Columbia: University of Missouri Press, 1989.

Holt, Glen E. "After the Journey Was Over: The St. Louis Years of Lewis and Clark." *Gateway Heritage* 2 (fall 1981): 42–48.

Rogers, Ann. "William Clark: A Commemoration." *Gateway Heritage* 9 (summer 1988): 12–15.

Steffen, Jerome O. *William Clark: Jeffersonian Man on the Frontier.* Norman: University of Oklahoma Press, 1977.

Thwaites, Reuben Gold. "William Clark: Soldier, Statesman." *Washington Historical Quarterly* 1 (July 1907): 234–251.

CLAY, GREEN
1757–1826
U.S. militia officer

Born in Virginia, the son of Charles Clay, Green Clay moved to Kentucky as a young man, where he became a surveyor. As was customary, he accepted payment for his services in land, and within a short time he had accumulated enormous holdings. As one of the largest landowners in the area (still part of Virginia), Clay quickly rose to political prominence. When Kentucky became a state, he continued his political involvement with terms in both the lower house of the Kentucky legislature and in the state senate.

At the beginning of the War of 1812, Clay obtained a commission as a major general of the Kentucky militia. Clay did not see combat until 1813, when he marched 1,200 men to Fort Defiance to aid in Maj. Gen. William Henry Harrison's defense of Ohio.

When Harrison learned that Gen. Henry Procter and his Indian allies under Tecumseh intended to attack Fort Meigs on the south bank of the Maumee River, Harrison took 300 of his men to relieve the fort. He left Clay with instructions to bring his militiamen when summoned. On 1 May 1813, Procter began his siege, facing his artillery toward Fort Meigs from the north bank of the Maumee. The next day Harrison sent word to Clay to begin his movement down the river. Clay's people would travel on flatboats specially constructed to provide them protection from snipers along the shore.

As Clay made his way downriver, he received additional instructions from Harrison to divide his forces into two parts. One part, 800 strong, was to land near Procter's battery on the north bank to spike its guns and then retire to the fort. The remainder of Clay's men were to fight their way into the fort through the Indians encamped above it.

Clay placed Col. William Dudley in command of the 800 men assigned to disable the British battery. Dudley's attack on 5 May was so fierce that the British gunners and the Indians nearby immediately ran. Dudley's men, however, were so excited by their quick victory that they spent only a brief time disabling the guns before continuing their pursuit of the enemy. By then, other Indians in the vicinity were alerted by the attack and set a trap for the impulsive militiamen, who charged directly into the ambush. Approximately 80 percent of the Kentuckians were killed or captured, and with the full knowledge of Procter, the Indians tortured about 20 of these captives to death before Tecumseh stopped the slaughter. In the meantime, Clay had led the remainder of his men safely into Fort Meigs. There the garrison had watched helplessly the grisly fate of the other Kentuckians.

Even as Clay's force was arriving, Procter and Tecumseh had fallen to quarreling, and most of the Indians were drifting away. As a result, Procter lifted the siege on 9 May. With the fort free from any immediate threat, Harrison marched most of his army to Cleveland to cooperate with the navy under Oliver Hazard Perry. Harrison left Green Clay in command of Fort Meigs.

Harrison's departure from western Ohio with the main U.S. army, however, again inspired Procter and Tecumseh in July to drive the remaining Americans from their positions. As the problem with Fort Meigs was its strong position and excellent construction, Tecumseh proposed a plan to Procter to draw the Americans out of the fort. Out of sight but within hearing of the fort, Procter's troops and Tecumseh's warriors would stage a fake battle. The hope was that when Clay heard the commotion, he would believe a relief force was being attacked and would leave the fort to render help. On 20 July, Procter's army arrived in the vicinity of Fort Meigs and began the mock battle. In spite of pleas from several officers to help their fellow Americans, Clay was not expecting a relief force and refused to leave the fort.

Procter left the area on 28 July to try his luck at nearby Fort Stephenson. Following Procter's failure there and the subsequent British evacuation of Ohio, Clay marched his men to Detroit. Their enlistment terms were due to expire soon, however, so Clay was unable to participate in the fall invasion of Canada. He returned to Kentucky, ending his military career.

After the war, Clay returned to his business pursuits and became locally famous for innovative farming techniques on his estate, White Hall. He died in Kentucky at the age of 69.

—*Jeanne T. Heidler and David S. Heidler*

See also: Harrison, William Henry; Meigs, Fort; Procter, Henry; Tecumseh

Further Reading

Hammack, James W., Jr. *Kentucky and the Second American Revolution: The War of 1812.* Lexington: University of Kentucky Press, 1976.

Henry Clay

CLAY, HENRY
1777–1852
Speaker of the House of Representatives

Born in Hanover County, Virginia, on 12 April 1777, Henry Clay received limited education in local schools. When he was 15, the family moved to Kentucky, leaving the lad in Virginia. Henry clerked in a store, then worked for the clerk in the High Court of Chancery. Chancellor George Wythe employed Clay as a copyist and directed his studies, and in 1797 Clay secured his law license. Soon afterward he moved to Lexington, Kentucky, where he established a successful practice. In 1799, he married Lucretia Hart, daughter of Thomas Hart, a wealthy Lexington merchant. Seven of their 11 children died before Clay's death on 29 June 1852.

Noted as a defense attorney in criminal cases, Clay prospered and acquired Ashland, an estate near Lexington. His 1798 speech against the Sedition Act won public acclaim, though his advocacy of gradual emancipation in 1799 concerned some slaveholders. In 1803, he won election as a Jeffersonian Republican to the Kentucky House of Representatives for the first of several terms. His legislative abilities were recognized in 1808 by his election as Speaker. Clay's service in the House was interrupted by two appointments (1806 to 1807 and 1810 to 1811) to serve out unexpired terms in the U.S. Senate.

By 1810, Clay was convinced that repeated violations of U.S. rights justified war against both France and Great Britain. He told the Senate on 22 February 1810 that he preferred "the troubled ocean of war . . . to the tranquil, putrescent pool of ignominious peace." He preferred war against Great Britain. British violations had been more numerous, and they habitually stirred up Indians in the Northwest. Moreover, the British could be attacked in Canada. He assured his fellow senators that the Kentucky militia alone could seize Montreal and Upper Canada. Thus, the man John Randolph of Roanoke called the Cock of Kentucky became the major spokesman for the War Hawks in the Republican Party.

Clay preferred the House of Representatives to the more sedate Senate, and in 1810 he won election to the House.

When the 12th Congress met on 4 November 1811, Henry Clay brought with him a strong nationalism, extraordinary speaking abilities, and a charismatic personality. War fever was sweeping much of the country in 1811, and the defeat of Indians at Tippecanoe Creek on 7 November whetted western demands for a final solution to the Indian problem. Already noted as the ablest of the War Hawks, Clay won the contest for Speaker. It was a surprising victory for a freshman congressman, but Clay's persuasiveness had already become legendary. A political enemy refused to be introduced to Clay for fear that he would fall victim to the Kentuckian's charm.

Clay transformed the speakership and became more powerful than any of his predecessors. Fair and evenhanded in his presiding role, he did more than direct the House's business. He appointed other War Hawks to key committees and blocked the disruptive tactics of eccentric John Randolph and Federalist Josiah Quincy. Clay also refused to let his presiding duties restrict his oratorical talent. Often he temporarily left the Speaker's chair to participate in debates, proving especially effective in the committee of the whole. He became the tireless political leader of the House, working outside the chamber to forge compromises and build winning coalitions.

The War Hawks resolutely pushed for war, shoving their "Old Republican" colleagues in James Madison's administration and the nation along with them. They walked a fine line between supporting and manipulating Madison himself. They paid him homage as head of their party and admonished him for avoiding a war he clearly did not want. Although in 1811 Clay had voted against rechartering the Bank of the United States on strict constitutional scruples, he rejected strict construction to advocate legislation preparing the country for war. He failed to augment the navy, but he did secure the House's approval for increased taxes. For his part, Madison wanted a second term and realized his need for War Hawk support to attain it. The reluctant president moved down the road to war.

An embargo act in 1812 served as a prelude to war, and Madison sent his war message to Congress on 1 June. It passed the House on 4 June by a vote of 79 to 49 and the Senate on 17 June by 19 to 13. Both the sizable opposition and a delay in the Senate vote revealed strong opposition from New England. Josiah Quincy commented, "Henry Clay was the man whose influence and power more than that of any other produced the war of 1812."

Clay believed that "Mr. Madison is totally unfit for the storm of War" and that most of the administration leaders were even less qualified, so he worked tirelessly to secure the measures needed for victory. Clay helped to obtain William Henry Harrison's appointment to the northwestern command and to supply him with Kentucky troops. The Speaker also defended the administration against Federalist attacks. In a major speech on 8–9 January 1813, Clay denounced conspirators who sought dissolution of the Union and those who wanted peace at any price. "An honorable peace," he warned, "is attainable only by an efficient war." If the nation would only use its ample resources, peace would be won at Halifax or Quebec. Congress passed a bill to raise 20 infantry regiments for one year's service. They were to invade Canada.

His colleagues again elected him Speaker, for the 13th Congress in 1813, but by then Clay saw the need for an end to the war. It would have to end honorably, however. Great Britain rejected Russia's offer to mediate a peace with the United States, but strained by the long struggle with France, the British offered to enter direct negotiations. Clay accepted membership on the five-man commission that met their British counterparts in Ghent. He was to become a stubborn spokesman for U.S. claims.

Clay and fellow peace commissioner John Quincy Adams clashed frequently over matters of personality and policy. Regional concerns such as fishing rights and the use of the Mississippi River put them at odds. Luckily, these internal disagreements did not subvert the U.S. position. In fact, both U.S. and British positions gradually moved from impracticality to partial accommodation. The end of the Napoleonic wars, for example, meant that the irresolvable issue of neutral rights could be ignored.

Clay's skill at Brag, a card game that rewarded shrewd bluffing, proved useful in the negotiations. He foresaw a British willingness to withdraw from extreme positions, and though not pleased with all parts of the treaty, he accepted it as the best arrangement then possible. The provision for several joint commissions was promising, and as if to prove the new spirit of conciliation, Clay, Adams, and Albert Gallatin went to England and negotiated a trade agreement. While there, Clay became interested in Hereford cattle, which he later helped introduce into the United States.

After the war, Henry Clay returned to the House and continued his distinguished public career. He became a National Republican and then a Whig leader as new party alignments developed, but the presidency eluded him. Even so, during the first half of the nineteenth century Clay was one of the nation's most important statesmen. As representative, senator, and secretary of state, he formulated an integrated national program called the American System. He earned fame as the Great Compromiser who helped resolve several sectional crises, the last of which was in 1850. Clay's proposals became the Compromise of

1850, but by then his energy and talent flagged under the rigors of age. Henry Clay died two years later.

—*Lowell H. Harrison*

See also: Adams, John Quincy; Ghent, Treaty of; U.S. Congress; War Hawks

Further Reading

Hopkins, James F., ed. *The Papers of Henry Clay.* Vol. 1, *The Rising Statesman, 1797–1814;* Vol. 2, *The Rising Statesman, 1815–1820.* Lexington: University of Kentucky Press, 1959 and 1961.

Mayo, Bernard. *Henry Clay: Spokesman for the West.* Boston: Houghton Mifflin, 1937.

Peterson, Merrill D. *The Great Triumvirate: Webster, Clay and Calhoun.* New York: Oxford University Press, 1987.

Remini, Robert V. *Henry Clay: Statesman for the Union.* New York: W. W. Norton, 1992.

Van Deusen, Glyndon G. *The Life of Henry Clay.* Boston: Little, Brown, 1937.

CLINTON, DEWITT
1769–1828
New York politician;
mayor of New York City

Born on 2 March 1769 in Little Britain, New York, to a distinguished colonial family, DeWitt Clinton graduated from Columbia College, New York City, in 1786. He began practicing law in 1790. At age 28, he entered the state senate, serving from 1798 to 1802 and again from 1806 to 1811. In addition, he was mayor of New York City for ten years between 1803 and 1815.

In 1802, Clinton entered the U.S. Senate, but he resigned the next year to become mayor of New York and gradually turned against Pres. Thomas Jefferson during the next four years. Clinton had admired Jefferson, but disagreements over maritime issues, especially impressment, estranged them. As New York's mayor, Clinton asked Jefferson to help protect the city's harbor, because he felt New York's commercial interests were of national concern. The British had been blockading New York, and Jefferson sympathized with Clinton's difficulties, but the president did nothing. Clinton remained embittered over Jefferson's seeming indifference to a foreign policy beneficial to commerce.

Clinton and his uncle, George Clinton, led an antiadministration faction in Congress known as the Clintonians. These staunch Republicans, who represented northern commercial regions, clamored for more protection of trade. The Clintonians believed that English and French policies destructive to U.S. commerce had to be combated. They put little confidence in the administration's measures. Jefferson's commercial restrictions had brought economic depression to the northern states but had not forced Napoleon to repeal the Berlin and Milan Decrees nor the British Admiralty to revoke the Orders in Council. The Clintonians became a rallying point for those opposed to commercial restrictions, advocating instead negotiations supported by military preparations.

Clinton initially opposed the embargo of 1807, contending that merchants had the right to counter foreign attacks in any way they felt appropriate, even if that meant arming their ships. Although the threat of party discipline persuaded Clinton to moderate his opposition, the embargo worked severe hardship on New York's maritime trade and grain producers. The Clintonian newspaper, the *American Citizen*, denounced the embargo as "unconstitutional, unenforceable and destined to destroy America's commerce."

Between 1808 and 1810, Clinton bided his time, doing little to oppose James Madison. All that changed when the administration employed the stipulations of Macon's Bill No. 2. After Napoleon supposedly revoked the Berlin and Milan Decrees against Americans, the United States decreed nonintercourse against Britain. When it became evident that Napoleon had no plans to respect U.S. shipping rights, however, a new surge of antirestriction sentiment arose. In Clinton's mind, Madison had merely continued Jefferson's anticommercial and antimanufacturing policies.

Clinton stood for the presidency in 1812 and became the first major politician in the Republican Party to state that commerce was as important as agriculture to the U.S. economy. Jeffersonian trade policies continued by Madison had frustrated the Clinton faction's desire for a balanced and expanding economy. The attempt to overthrow the Virginia Dynasty and its preference for agricultural interests resulted in the Clinton bid for the presidency. In fact, the war was the major issue in the campaign. Madison described the war as necessary for the defense of U.S. rights. Clinton adopted a cautious course in this regard. In antiwar regions, he was portrayed as desirous of negotiation. In prowar areas, followers portrayed him as a guarantor of quick victory. As one critic acidly noted, "In the west he was a friend of war . . . in the east . . . a friend of peace."

When Congress declared war on 18 June 1812, Clinton clarified his position. He had opposed war, he said, because the country was ill prepared for it. And he questioned Madison's motives, stating that they were derived more from political necessity than from a desire to protect U.S. trade.

Defeated in the presidential election, Clinton continued to condemn the Madison administration's lack of military preparation. Meanwhile, Clinton worked vigorously to improve the defenses of New York City, serving on the city's Committee of Defense and involving himself in the construction of fortifications. Gov. Daniel D. Tompkins refused Clinton's request for a brigadier general's appointment, however. New York Madisonians did not want to give Clinton the chance to enhance his political prominence. Clinton's report describing New York's defense needs specified the construction of military camps at Brooklyn and Harlem Heights. He noted the continued presence of British warships and underscored the city's vulnerability to attack from sea. The British, wrote Clinton, would surely judge New York City a major target because of the city's immense wealth.

In July 1814, an exasperated Mayor Clinton headed a committee that reported on the city's unredressed exposure and dismissed the national government's preparations as only creating an "army on paper." As late as October 1814, Clinton was preparing the city for an expected British invasion. The attack never materialized, and four months later, news of peace arrived.

Until the end of the war, Clinton fought for the extension of free trade, a stronger navy, and better coastal defenses. He never relented in his criticism of the Madison administration for its lack of preparation in war. His persistence proved politically costly. Madisonians denied Clinton renomination as lieutenant governor in 1813, and two years later they ousted him as mayor. After the war, Clinton served New York as the prime mover in the Erie Canal project.

—*Leigh Whaley*

See also: Embargo Act; Madison, James; New York; Tompkins, Daniel D.
Further Reading
Bobbe, Dorothie. *DeWitt Clinton*. New York: Minton, Balch, 1933.
Brown, Roger Hamilton. *The Republic in Peril: 1812*. New York: Columbia University Press, 1964.
Campbell, William W., ed. *Life and Writings of DeWitt Clinton*. New York: Baker, 1849.
Sirey, Steven E. *DeWitt Clinton and the American Political Economy*. New York: Peter Lang, 1989.

COBBETT, WILLIAM
1762–1835
British journalist and reformer

Born on 9 March 1763, in Farnham, Surrey, William Cobbett was a self-educated essayist, journalist, politician, reformer, and agriculturist. A stint in the British army saw him in Nova Scotia for part of his tour. Discharged in 1791, he soon faced prosecution in England for a pamphlet condemning British army practices and calling for improved conditions. He sought refuge in the United States for an extended stay from October 1792 to January 1800.

Cobbett at best regarded the United States with ambivalence. In Philadelphia, he earned notoriety as a radical journalist and pamphleteer under the nom de plume Peter Porcupine. His style included savage and sarcastic attacks directed both at individual Americans and at U.S. society in general. British émigré Joseph Priestly and the American Dr. Benjamin Rush were favorite targets. When Rush successfully sued Cobbett for libel, the acid-penned pamphleteer returned to England.

Cobbett sometimes receives credit for revolutionizing journalism in the United States by encouraging political partisanship in the press. He could be an occasionally outspoken advocate for U.S. rights, but his only consistent feature was his vehemence. He defended the British right of search in the *Chesapeake-Leopard* affair of 1807 but took the part of the United States in the *President–Little Belt* incident of 1811. During the War of 1812, he praised the success of U.S. frigates with pamphlets such as "The Pride of Britannia Humbled," "The Queen of the Ocean Unqueened," and "The American Cock Boats." He returned to Philadelphia in May 1817 during a British crackdown on radicalism and remained until October 1819.

Cobbett's unabated agitation for a variety of causes, including the reform of the English political system, was to earn him a seat in the Reform Bill Parliament of 1832. He died on 18 June 1835 at Guilford, England.

—*Eugene L. Rasor*

See also: *Chesapeake-Leopard* Affair
Further Reading
Cobbett, William. *The Autobiography of William Cobbett*. Ed. William Reitzel. London: Faber, 1933, 1967.
———. *Peter Porcupine in America*. Ithaca: Cornell University Press, 1994.

William Cobbett

Cole, G.D.H. *The Life of William Cobbett*. London: Collins, 1924, 1947.

Gaines, Pierce W. *William Cobbett and the U.S., 1792–1835*. Worcester: American Antiquarian, 1971.

Spater, George. *William Cobbett: The Poor Man's Friend*. 2 vols. Cambridge: Cambridge University Press, 1982.

COCHRANE, ALEXANDER
1758–1832
Admiral, Royal Navy

Born 22 April 1758, the younger son of the eighth earl of Dundonald, Alexander Forester Inglis Cochrane pursued a career in the Royal Navy that saw him a postcaptain by the end of the American Revolution. Recalled to active duty in 1790, he commanded a frigate prior to the war with France, a ship of the line on the North American station, the Channel fleet, the Quiberon Bay and Ferrol expeditions, and the landings in Egypt. From 1800 to 1806, he combined naval command with service in Parliament. Peace in 1802 saw a brief lull in his active service, but he was recalled in 1803 when hostilities resumed. He became a rear admiral in 1804, commanding the squadron off Ferrol. In 1805, he was sent to the Caribbean in pursuit of a French squadron, then was made commander in chief at the Leeward Islands. For his performance as second in command at the battle of St. Domingo the following year, he was created a knight of the Order of the Bath. In 1810, he became governor of Guadeloupe.

When the Admiralty recalled Adm. Sir John Borlase Warren in 1814, Cochrane was appointed to command from Bermuda, a newly defined North American station of which the Caribbean islands were not part. Immediately, on 2 April, he issued a proclamation aimed largely at slaves, stipulating that Americans who so desired could join the British forces or be relocated to live freely in British North America or the Caribbean. About 300 former slaves subsequently served in the Chesapeake region as British marines. Americans charged Cochrane with fomenting a slave uprising; British critics, conversely, alleged that some blacks who answered the offer were subsequently sold as slaves in the West Indies. At the least, U.S. charges about fomenting domestic insurrections gained credence when Cochrane authorized arming Indians in Florida.

Early in June, Lt. Gen. Sir George Prevost, governor-general of Upper Canada, wrote to Cochrane to suggest British coastal raids in retaliation for U.S. depredations in Canada. Cochrane had already been overseeing coastal raids in the Chesapeake Bay region. Now he issued orders for the destruction of towns along the coast of the United States, greatly increasing pressure on the New England states. Two 74-gun ships with attendant vessels now patrolled from Long Island to Nantucket, and another such squadron cruised from Nantucket to New Brunswick. The new deployment's first victim was the island of Nantucket. By threatening to cut off food and fuel shipments to the community, Cochrane compelled its inhabitants to declare their neutrality and withhold their taxes from the United States.

After receiving about 5,000 marine and infantry reinforcements, by late summer of 1814 Cochrane was planning a concentrated attack somewhere on the coast of the United States to relieve pressure on Canada. In August, he sent 4,000 troops under the command of Maj. Gen. Robert Ross to destroy U.S. gunboats in the Patuxent River and attack Washington. After the burning of Washington, Cochrane turned to Baltimore, disembarking Ross and 4,500 men 15 miles from the city on 11 September while he sailed up the Patapsco River. Cochrane's bombardment of Fort McHenry on the night of 13 August failed to reduce the fort, and General Ross was killed in action against U.S. forces. Consequently, Baltimore was spared Washington's fate.

As early as June, Cochrane had pressed the Admiralty to seize New Orleans. With that object in mind, he had begun preparations by arming and training Indians on the southern coast. He intended to use Ross's troops, augmented by 2,000 more from Europe, to capture Mobile and advance on New Orleans via Lake Pontchartrain. Ross's death, the repulse of a British attack on Mobile on 12 September, and Andrew Jackson's seizure of Pensacola on 7 November ended that plan.

While awaiting a replacement for Ross, Cochrane developed a new plan. Since attacking from Lake Pontchartrain was unfeasible and the approach to New Orleans via the Mississippi River well guarded, Cochrane decided to attack via Lake Borgne. On 14 December, British forces captured the U.S. gunboats on the lake, making possible a British advance through Bayou Bienvenu. Two days before Christmas, the British were within 7 miles of New Orleans. As recently arrived Gen. Sir Edward Pakenham planned his attack on the city's defenses, Cochrane sought to lend support. He ordered the Villeré Canal extended from Lake Borgne to the Mississippi River and directed that 1,200 men be ferried across the river to flank Jackson's forces. Though the movement was successful, the general assault on Jackson's lines failed. Thwarted at New Orleans, Cochrane and Gen. John Lambert on 11 February captured Fort Bowyer outside Mobile, when they heard of the war's end.

Returning to England, Cochrane was promoted to admiral in 1819 but did not receive another command until he was made commander in chief at Plymouth in 1821. He died in Paris on 26 January 1832.

—*Joseph M. McCarthy*

See also: Baltimore, Battle of; Jackson, Andrew; Lambert, John; McHenry, Fort; New Orleans, Battle of; Pakenham, Edward; Prevost, George; Ross, Robert; Warren, John Borlase

Further Reading
Forester, Cecil Scott. *The Age of Fighting Sail: The Story of the Naval War of 1812.* Garden City, NY: Doubleday, 1956.
Humphries, B. "Sir Alexander Cochrane and the Conclusion of the American War, 1814–1815." Master's thesis, Liverpool University, 1960.
Owsley, Frank L., Jr. *Struggle for the Gulf Borderlands: The Creek War and the Battle of New Orleans, 1812–1815.* Gainesville: University Presses of Florida, 1981.

COCKBURN, GEORGE
1772–1853
Admiral of the fleet, Royal Navy

As the second son of Sir James Cockburn, George Cockburn was slated for a career at sea at the age of nine. After serving aboard a number of vessels in the British Isles, the Mediterranean, and other stations, he reached the rank of lieutenant at the age of 21. Serving in Lord Hoods's squadron during the French wars of the 1790s, Cockburn gained command of his own sloop, HMS *Speedy*. Moving up to the frigate HMS *Meleager* in 1794, Cockburn was involved in the battles off Toulon in 1795. Shortly thereafter, Cockburn served under and became a friend of Lord Nelson. As commander of the frigate HMS *Minerve*, Cockburn served the remainder of the war in the Mediterranean, preying primarily on privateers and capturing many prizes.

As war again loomed in 1803, Cockburn commanded HMS *Phaeton* in the East Indies. He moved to the West Indies in 1808 as commander of HMS *Pompee* and aided in the capture of Martinique. Until 1812, he served off the coast of Spain, aiding the forces of the deposed king of Spain and rising to the rank of rear admiral. In August, after word reached Europe of the U.S. declaration of war, he was sent to North American waters to serve under the command of Sir John Borlase Warren. Warren immediately directed Cockburn to Chesapeake Bay to destroy enemy supplies in that region.

Cockburn arrived in Chesapeake Bay in February 1813 aboard HMS *Marlborough* with numerous supporting craft. After sending part of his force to harass other areas, such as Delaware Bay, Cockburn moved up the Chesapeake; after threatening Baltimore, he moved to the Elk River. Though he always claimed that he would respect private property unless local citizens resisted his force, in the upper bay Cockburn took little pains to distinguish between private and public property. Reaching the area off the commercial port of Frenchtown, Maryland, in late April 1813, Cockburn ordered the mercantile establishments and warehouses along the shore looted and then had the warehouses burned.

Moving next to the small town of Havre de Grace, he woke the citizens on the night of 2 May 1813 with Congreve Rockets, setting several houses and businesses on fire. He said a shore battery on the town docks and the presence of militiamen justified his actions. The rockets chased everyone from town, leaving only an elderly Irishman named John O'Neil to man the battery. When a British shore party captured the lone artilleryman, Cockburn let him go as a reward for his pluck. O'Neil's quixotic resistance, however, gave Cockburn a reason, he thought, to destroy much of the town.

Cockburn then sent a raiding party inland to destroy a cannon foundry at Principio, Maryland. Moving across the bay to the Eastern Shore of Maryland, Cockburn then burned the towns of Georgetown and Fredericktown because a few local militiamen had fired on his men. After leaving the Eastern Shore, Cockburn moved down the bay to rendezvous with Admiral Warren. Cockburn's force alone had not been strong enough to attack Norfolk, but the addition of Warren's ships convinced both men that such an assault now was possible. The presence in Norfolk harbor of the USS *Constellation* made the port even more attractive. Yet the attack failed on 22 June 1813, and Cockburn turned his attention to the lightly defended town of Hampton.

Cockburn's attack on Hampton, Virginia, is one of the most controversial actions of the War of 1812. After landing outside the city on 25 June 1813, British landing parties quickly overwhelmed the approximately 450 militiamen protecting the outskirts. The British then quickly occupied the town. The following day, before leaving the area, occupying soldiers and sailors went on a rampage that shocked even the British officers. Not only did they steal or destroy private property, they also committed rape and murder. When investigations revealed the full extent of the barbarous behavior at Hampton, Cockburn and other officers blamed the Canadian Chasseurs—French deserters who elected to fight for the British rather than be imprisoned.

Cockburn's Chesapeake raids had gained him notoriety throughout the United States by the end of the summer of 1813. The U.S. press referred to him by a variety of names, all reflecting condemnation. When ashore conducting raids, Cockburn avidly read whatever newspapers he could find, so he was fully acquainted with U.S. sentiments toward him.

After the raid on Hampton, Cockburn spent the remainder of the summer raiding along the coast of the Carolinas. In 1814, he was back in the Chesapeake, however, in preparation for a major British expedition there. British naval and land forces were flush with reinforcements, thanks to the end of the European war, and Cockburn was champing at the bit to engage in something other than mere coastal raiding. His officers and men, now fully acquainted with the waters and currents of the Chesapeake, also were eager to commence the 1814 summer campaign.

Vice Adm. Sir Alexander Cochrane had replaced Admiral Warren. Maj. Gen. Robert Ross led a land force of the duke of Wellington's veterans to accompany Cochrane. The expedition's ostensible purpose was to stage large-scale raids as a diversion for the larger British effort out of Canada. Cochrane was also under instructions to retaliate for the May 1814 destruction of the Canadian town of Port Dover. Cochrane, Cockburn, and Ross also hoped to make a lasting impression on U.S. citizens in the vicinity of the U.S. capital.

On 15 August 1814, the three men held a council of war aboard ship at the mouth of the Potomac River. They decided that Ross would raid deep into the interior with Washington, D.C., as a possible target of opportunity. While this expedition progressed, Cockburn would take some of his smaller craft up the Patuxent River to eliminate the only U.S. naval force opposing him on the bay—Commodore Joshua Barney's flotilla of one sloop and 13 gunboats. Cornered by Cockburn, Barney destroyed most of his vessels and retreated inland, leaving Cockburn free to join Ross's march on Washington.

On 22 August, Cockburn joined Ross as he headed toward Bladensburg. Two days later, the two commanders received word from Cochrane to abandon the expedition and return to the ships. Although technically in supreme command, Cochrane could only offer what amounted to a strong suggestion at this point, however. During joint operations, British military practice placed the army commander in complete control once he took his men ashore. Cockburn was thus able to persuade Ross to ignore the instructions and continue the campaign. Although Cockburn was present at the Battle of Bladensburg, he left the direction of the fighting to Ross. Once in Washington, however, Cockburn came into his own.

Witnesses attested to the fun Cockburn had looting the public buildings of the U.S. capital. Riding a white mare that trailed her foal, he moved around the city having the time of his life. He spent most of his time telling soldiers and sailors what they could steal and burn. Under Cockburn's orders, anyone caught stealing private property was flogged. Cockburn's scrupulous protection of private property did not extend, however, to the offices of the *National Intelligencer,* published by Joseph Gales. Cockburn derisively referred to him as "Josey," because Gales had been one of Cockburn's severest critics in the U.S. press. Now the admiral took it as a personal quest to destroy Gales's offices. When ladies whose residences neighbored the *Intelligencer* implored Cockburn to shield their homes from risk by not burning the newspaper's offices, Cockburn satisfied himself with having the *Intelligencer's* house dismantled by brute force. According to some witnesses, Cockburn insisted that all of the *c*'s in Gales's type be destroyed so the *Intelligencer* could not publish any more stories about the admiral.

Aglow from their destructive triumph over Washington, the three British commanders pondered their next target, the rich port of Baltimore. After awaiting the return of various detachments sent out as diversions for the Washington raid, Cochrane set out in early September. Cockburn had developed a taste for land operations in Washington. In any event, he apparently did not want to play subordinate to Cochrane in the water approach to Baltimore, so he accompanied Ross's infantry when the army landed outside Baltimore. On the morning of 12 September, Ross and Cockburn stopped for breakfast at the farm of Robert Gorsuch. While the family served the officers food, Cockburn and Ross laughed as their men slaughtered and cooked the family's barn animals. For the British, it was a light amusement for an otherwise heavy day. Shortly after leaving the Gorsuch farm, Cockburn and Ross ran into a small U.S. force under Maj. Richard Heath. As Ross moved forward to direct his men, a U.S. sharpshooter shot him dead.

Cockburn continued on with Ross's successor, Col. Arthur Brooke. Failing to penetrate Baltimore's defenses from the east, Brooke decided to await the outcome of the naval bombardment of Fort McHenry. After listening to the attack from 13 September until dawn the following day, Brooke realized that Cochrane's force had not forced its way into the harbor. Cochrane sent another of his suggestions to abandon the effort, and this time Brooke and Cockburn agreed that retreat was necessary. They turned back to North Point.

Following the British failure to take Baltimore, Cockburn continued his raids in the Chesapeake. Colder weather rather than the Americans chased him south. On 1 January 1815, he landed on Cumberland Island and began raiding the Georgia coast. On 13 January, he moved up the St. Mary's River to attack the town of the same name. Performing what had become a familiar routine, he looted public storehouses there and moved briefly into the interior to recruit slaves for further raiding. When Cockburn heard in February that peace had been concluded, he was planning an assault on Savannah and talking of provoking a general slave uprising to bring the southern states under British control.

Cockburn returned to England during Wellington's final campaign to defeat Napoleon. Shortly after Waterloo, the Admiralty assigned Cockburn to command HMS *Northumberland*, the ship that would transport Bonaparte to St. Helena. Once there, Cockburn remained the governor of the island until 1816. Continuing his naval service, Cockburn became admiral of the fleet in 1851.

—*Jeanne T. Heidler and David S. Heidler*

See also: Barney, Joshua; Brooke, Arthur; Campbell, John B.; Chesapeake Bay Campaign, 1813–1814; Cochrane, Alexander; Craney Island, Battle of; Gales, Joseph; Hampton, Virginia; Havre de Grace, Maryland, Attack on; Ross, Robert; Warren, John Borlase

Further Reading

Evans, Sir George De Lacy. *Facts Relating to the Capture of Washington, In Reply to Some Statements Contained in the Memoirs of Admiral Sir George Cockburn, G.C.B.* London: H. Colburn, 1829.

Pack, A. James. *The Man Who Burned the White House: Admiral Sir George Cockburn, 1772–1853.* Emsworth, U.K.: Mason, 1987.

COCKE, JOHN
1772–1854
U.S. militia officer

Born in Brunswick, Virginia, young John Cocke moved with his parents to Tennessee. There he studied law and began his own practice in Hawkins County in 1793. He also became increasingly involved in Tennessee politics as a frequent member of the Tennessee legislature.

When word reached Tennessee of the Red Stick Creek attack on Fort Mims in the Mississippi Territory (now Alabama), the state legislature called on Gov. Willie Blount to supplement the 1,500 Tennessee militia then in service with 3,500 additional men. Blount gave command of the East Tennessee Division to John Cocke, with the understanding that he was to march his men into the Creek nation and rendezvous with the West Tennessee Division under Maj. Gen. Andrew Jackson. Once the two forces were joined, Jackson was to have overall command.

Assembling his men at Knoxville, Cocke marched them into the Creek country ready to do battle. He quickly encountered the same difficulties, however, that were plaguing Jackson to the west—a thoroughly corrupt, inefficient supply system that left him with no rations to begin a campaign. To make matters worse, he received frequent messages from Jackson urging him to join the West Tennessee forces at Jackson's base in Fort Strother. Cocke knew that once he arrived at Fort Strother, any military glory and the political dividends it would yield back home would belong to Jackson. So instead of obeying the instructions of his nominal superior, Cocke built his own advanced base, 70 miles east of Jackson, which he named Fort Armstrong.

Still without rations, in November Cocke decided to make one strike at the enemy before his funds completely ran out. He chose as his target a group of Creek settlements known as the Hillabee towns. The Creeks of those towns had been among the most hostile to U.S. expansion. In the middle of November 1813, Cocke's men destroyed three Hillabee towns, killed several dozen warriors, and captured several hundred women and children. Cocke did not know that these towns had sued Jackson for peace and that he in turn had promised them their safety.

Jackson was already angry at Cocke for refusing to join him at Fort Strother, and he believed Cocke was also hoarding supplies. Moreover, if Cocke had followed orders, he would have known better than to attack peaceful Hillabees under Jackson's protection. Yet Jackson needed Cocke's men and supplies if he was to mount a major campaign against the Red Sticks. So Old Hickory held his temper and again invited Cocke to join him.

When Cocke accepted the invitation and arrived at Fort Strother on 12 December, Jackson quickly discerned the reason for his rival's sudden cooperation. Enlistment terms for almost all of Cocke's division were due to expire within weeks, and he did not even have enough food to get them back to Tennessee. Jackson, similarly distressed, ordered Cocke to escort the militia back to Tennessee and inform Governor Blount that they needed another army.

Governor Blount called for a new enlistment of six-month militia from East Tennessee, and Cocke marched them back to Jackson. The new men found Fort Strother most uncomfortable and chronically short of rations. When grumbling turned to talk of mutiny, Cocke addressed the men in such a way as to imply sympathy with their complaints. He also encouraged anger against the governor for raising their entire force from East Tennessee rather than having the rest of the state share the burden. Cocke, of course, was sympathizing with past and future constituents, and perhaps he confused his role of militia commander with that of accommodating politician. Andrew Jackson would clear that up for him. When Jackson heard Cocke's speech to the men, he simply snapped. He ordered Cocke's arrest and confinement, but by then Cocke had left the fort to return to Tennessee. Jackson's reach was long, however, and Cocke was arrested there, but his trial occurred in East Tennessee among his friends and supporters. They cheerfully acquitted him.

Following the war, Cocke remained active in Tennessee politics and served four terms in the U.S. House of Representatives from 1819 to 1827.

—*Jeanne T. Heidler and David S. Heidler*

See also: Creek War; Hillabee Massacre, Creek Territory; Jackson, Andrew; Red Sticks; Tennessee

Further Reading
Akers, Frank H. "The Unexpected Challenge; The Creek War of 1813–1814." Ph.D. diss., Duke University, 1975.
Cocke, John A. *A Letter to the Honorable John H. Eaton, Dec. 16, 1818*. Knoxville: Heiskell, Brown, 1819.

CODRINGTON, EDWARD
1770–1851
British naval officer; rear admiral of the Red, 1814

Born on 27 April 1770, Edward Codrington entered the navy as a midshipman on 18 July 1783 at Channel station. Promoted to lieutenant on 17 June 1793, he served as Earl Howe's signal officer aboard HMS *Queen Charlotte* during the "glorious First of June." He was promoted to commander on 7 October 1794 and post-captain on 6 April 1795. He fought on HMS *Orion* at Trafalgar, 17 October 1805, and received a gold medal and the thanks of both houses of Parliament. He saw action at Schelde, 14–15 August 1808, and from April 1811 to April 1813 commanded a detached squadron on the Spanish coast.

In January 1814, Codrington took the frigate HMS *Forth* to the North American station. Promoted to rear admiral on 4 June, he replaced Sir Henry Hotham as captain of the fleet under Sir Alexander Inglis Forester Cochrane. Codrington directed fleet movements during the attacks on Washington, Alexandria, Baltimore, and New Orleans. An able fleet administrator, he was critical of the favoritism that had guided the appointments of Cochrane's predecessor, Sir John Borlase Warren.

Codrington's postwar honors included the KCB, 2 January 1815, and the GCMG, 1832. As vice admiral (1825) and commander in chief, Mediterranean station (1826), he commanded the English, Russian, and French fleet that destroyed the Turkish fleet at Navarino Bay, 20 October 1827. He was elected to Parliament for Davenport (1832–1839), promoted to admiral of the Blue (10 January 1837), and appointed commander in chief, Portsmouth (29 November 1839). Codrington died on 28 April 1851.

—*Frederick C. Drake*

See also: Cochrane, Alexander
Further Reading
Bourchier, Lady, ed. *Codrington's Memoir of Admiral Sir Edward Codrington*. Vol. 1; Vol. 2, pp. 309–343. London: Longmans, Green, 1873.

Laughton, John Knox. "Sir Edward Codrington." *Dictionary of National Biography.* London: Oxford University Press, 1937–1938.

Marshall, John. *Royal Naval Biography.* Vol. 1, pt. 2, pp. 635–638, 872–873. London: Hurst, Rees, Orme, Brown and Green, 1823.

COFFEE, JOHN
1772–1833
Brigadier general of Tennessee volunteers

Born in Prince Edward County, Virginia, John Coffee moved with his pioneering family to frontier North Carolina. There he apparently received some education. Following his father's death in 1797, Coffee relocated his family to Davidson County, Tennessee. A successful merchant, land surveyor, and developer, he quickly became one of the region's most prominent citizens. His early business dealings netted a partnership with Andrew Jackson, with whom he developed a close and lasting friendship. In 1809, Coffee married Rachel Jackson's niece.

Coffee had no military training, yet when war broke out in 1812 he raised a mounted company for service with Jackson's volunteer army. Elevated to colonel and given command of a regiment, Coffee led his men to Mississippi Territory but was ordered back to Tennessee before seeing any action.

The following year Coffee played a significant role in Jackson's campaign against Creek Indians in Alabama. Promoted to brigadier general, he was conspicuous in Jackson's victories at Tallushatchee, Talladega, and Emuckfau. Despite a wound received at Emuckfau, Coffee was with Jackson at Horseshoe Bend two months later. In November 1814, Coffee and his well-traveled volunteers participated in the invasion of Spanish Florida and the capture of Pensacola. Only weeks later, responding to British landings near New Orleans, Coffee's brigade rushed to join Jackson's hastily arranged defense.

On 23 December 1814, Coffee commanded the left wing in the night attack at Villeré Plantation. During the climactic Battle of New Orleans on 8 January 1815, Coffee's riflemen anchored Jackson's left, a 1,000-yard stretch of forbidding, wooded swamp.

After the war, Coffee returned to land speculation and development. Eventually he became a leading planter in northern Alabama, an area he helped open for settlement as surveyor of the public lands. Coffee increasingly retreated from public life but nevertheless remained one of Jackson's most trusted friends and advisers. He died in 1833.

—David Coffey

See also: Creek War; Emuckfau Creek, Battle of; Horseshoe Bend, Battle of; Jackson, Andrew; New Orleans, Battle of; Pensacola, Battle of; Talladega, Battle of; Tallushatchee, Battle of

Further Reading

Boom, Aaron. "John Coffee—Citizen Soldier." *Tennessee Historical Quarterly* 22 (1963): 223–237.

Halbert, H. S., and T. H. Ball. *The Creek Indian War.* Tuscaloosa: University of Alabama Press, 1969.

Owsley, Frank Lawrence, Jr. *Struggle for the Gulf Borderlands: The Creek War and the Battle of New Orleans 1812–1815.* Gainesville: University Presses of Florida, 1981.

COLPOYS, EDWARD GRIFFITH
See Griffith, Edward

COLUMBIAD
Ordnance

The Columbiad was the first U.S. shell gun. It was a short, rather light piece of ordnance designed as an alternative to the carronade and was usually designated as an 18-pounder. It may have been a rebored cannon. Lt. George Bomford (1750–1848), later head of the Army Ordnance Department, is credited with inventing the Columbiad. The gun was named either for a popular song of the time written by a friend of Bomford or for the Columbia Foundry of Henry Foxall. The earliest known definition of a Columbiad appeared in 1811: "a gun of a new construction lately cast at Faxall's [Foxall's Columbia] foundry, on the Potomack. . . ."

The Columbiad was a chambered ordnance that combined certain features of the gun, howitzer, and mortar and fired either shot or shell. It was employed during the War of 1812 both in coast defense and aboard some U.S. Navy vessels, although its use on shipboard seems to have been limited largely to gunboats and a few larger vessels, all of them on the Great Lakes. Two sloops on Lake Champlain had Columbiads as a part of their original armament: The *President* had six 18-pounder Columbiads and four long

12-pounders, and the *Montgomery* had seven long 9-pounders and two 18-pounder Columbiads. A 50-pounder Columbiad of about 7.4-inch smooth bore remains in the U.S. Military Academy collection at West Point as Old Trophy No. 310.

The Columbiad is usually regarded as a transitional piece between the carronade and Paixhans gun: Some Americans later charged that Col. Henri Paixhans of France simply expropriated Bomford's invention.

—*Spencer C. Tucker*

See also: Cannon, Naval; Naval Ordnance; Rates
Further Reading
Lewis, Emanuel Raymond. "The Ambiguous Columbiads." *Military Affairs* 28, no. 3 (Fall 1964): 111–22.

COMBS, LESLIE
1793–1881
Soldier, 1812–1813;
politician, 1827–1857

Leslie Combs enlisted in the Kentucky militia soon after the outbreak of hostilities in 1812. He served as a scout and messenger under James Winchester during the River Raisin Campaign. Carrying messages between Winchester and William Henry Harrison, Combs avoided capture following the Battle of the River Raisin (22 January 1813).

Combs reenlisted and served under Gen. Green Clay during the spring 1813 relief expedition to Fort Meigs. As Clay's column approached Fort Meigs, Combs volunteered to lead a small party through enemy lines carrying word of the Kentuckians' advance to the post's commander, General Harrison. An Indian ambush turned Combs and his party back even as they moved within sight of the fort. On 5 May 1813, Clay's force arrived at the U.S. garrison, and he was detached with nearly 800 others to attack British artillery batteries on the north side of the Maumee River. The assault, commanded by Col. William Dudley, was at first successful. The British managed an effective countercharge, however, that left Dudley dead and the batteries again in British hands. The deadly engagement ended with nearly 600 Kentuckians either dead or captured. Combs, wounded and captured, later had to run the gauntlet at the British camp. Eventually paroled, he spent the remainder of the war in Kentucky practicing law.

Combs was elected to the Kentucky House of Repre-

sentatives in 1827. He served intermittently until 1857, acting as that body's speaker in 1846.

—*Larry L. Nelson*

See also: Clay, Green; Frenchtown, Battles of; Meigs, Fort; Winchester, James
Further Reading
Combs, Leslie. *Col. Wm. Dudley's Defeat Opposite Fort Meigs. May 5th, 1813. Official Report from Captain Leslie Combs to General Green Clay.* Cincinnati: Spiller & Gates, 1869.
Narrative of the Life of General Leslie Combs: Embracing Incidents in the History of the War of 1812. Washington, DC: American Whig Review Office, 1852.
Quisenberry, Anderson. *Kentucky in the War of 1812.* Baltimore: Genealogical Publishing Company, 1969.

CONGRESS, UNITED STATES
See U.S. Congress

CONGREVE ROCKETS

Rockets predate cannon. Rockets were probably first developed by the ancient Chinese, but there are few records of significant rocket use in war until the very close of the eighteenth century. In 1792 and again in 1799, Tippoo Sahib of Mysore used rockets to good effect against the troops of the Honorable East India Company at the sieges of Seringapatam. As a result, the Board of Ordnance asked the Royal Laboratory at Woolwich to provide the technical expertise to equip British troops with war rockets. The Royal Laboratory could not help, but Lt. William Congreve of the Hanoverian Army learned about the problem and started an independent study of war rockets.

Congreve most probably learned about the rocket question from his father, Gen. Sir William Congreve, Bart., who at the time was comptroller of the Royal Laboratory. Sir William was also a prominent artillery technician who had invented the block trail. In 1814, Col. William Congreve succeeded his father as comptroller of the Royal Laboratory and also inherited his title. The two Sir William Congreves are therefore often confused as the same person.

Working at his own expense, Congreve initially could get no more than 500 or 600 yards in range from his rockets. Through tedious trial and error he managed to reach

2,000 yards with a 6-pounder rocket. In 1804, he switched from a paper case to an iron case and decreased the length of the stabilizing stick. The resulting 32-pounder rocket was 3.5 feet long and 4 inches in diameter, with a 15-foot-long stick and a maximum range of 3,000 yards. Congreve's experiments included very heavy rockets, up to 300-pounders, multiple rockets, and even a compound rocket. The 1813 edition of R. W. Adye's *Pocket Gunner and Bombardier* listed the most commonly used size and warhead combinations:

Size	Warhead	Maximum Range
42-pounder	carcass and shell	3,500 yards
32-pounder	carcass	3,000 yards
32-pounder	shell	3,000 yards
32-pounder	case (large)	2,500 yards
32-pounder	case (small)	3,000 yards
32-pounder	explosion	3,000 yards
12-pounder	case (large)	2,000 yards
12-pounder	case (small)	2,500 yards

The 32-pounder was the one most widely used as a general-purpose weapon. The carcass warhead carried as much incendiary materiel as a 10-inch howitzer round. Rockets with exploding warheads were detonated by an external fuse set along the rocket body. Prior to launching, the firing crew cut the detonating fuse to the appropriate length. The fuse was then ignited by the propelling charge from the rocket's vent. The firing crew could vary range by altering the angle of launch. Congreve developed a transportable firing frame, but the rockets also could be fired simply by leaning them against a parapet at the appropriate angle.

Congreve Rockets were used for the first time in war during the British attack on Boulogne Harbor. On 18 October 1806, the Royal Navy fired 200 rockets into the town from 18 vessels. The British made a similar attack against Copenhagen in 1807, firing 2,500 rockets; most of the town burned. The Royal Artillery officially adopted the Congreve Rocket in January 1813, when 194 officers and men were added to the Royal Horse Artillery to form rocket detachments. In October that same year Congreve Rockets were used in the field for the first time at Leipzig. In 1814, the various Royal Horse Artillery rocket detachments were reorganized into the First and Second Rocket Troops. A Rocket Troop consisted of three divisions, each with two subdivisions. Each subdivision had five sections of three troopers and two ammunition drivers. A well-trained section could fire two to three rockets per minute.

By 1814 Congreve Rockets had become a standard part of the ammunition of most British warships. Under Congreve's personal direction, the Royal Navy also refitted two small sloops, the *Erebus* and the *Galguo*, as rocket vessels. Each rocket vessel carried a 25-man detachment of the Royal Marine Artillery. The Royal Marine Artillery also formed rocket half-companies to fight on land. Congreve referred to these units as "rocket infantry."

The first use of Congreve Rockets in the War of 1812 came during the naval attack on Lewes, Delaware, on 6 April 1813. Throughout the course of the war elements of three Royal Marine Artillery rocket half-companies and the Royal Marine Artillery detachment in the *Erebus* employed their weapons in several engagements along the Atlantic Coast and in Canada. Congreve Rockets were used in the field for the first time at Lundy's Lane, where a stick from one of the weapons wounded U.S. commander Gen. Jacob Brown. A Royal Marine Artillery rocket half-company also fought on land at Bladensburg. That same unit fought on shore again a few weeks later at North Point below Baltimore. At about the same time, their comrades on the *Erebus* attacked Fort McHenry. During the New Orleans operation, Congreve Rockets were fielded by the Royal Horse Artillery. Capt. Henry Lane commanded a 40-man detachment of the Second Rocket Troop, armed with 150 rockets. Lane's force made up part of the British rear guard during the later withdrawal.

Congreve was naturally very enthusiastic about his new weapon system. In his 1814 book, *Details of the Rocket System*, he called it "ammunition without ordnance, . . . the soul of artillery without the body." According to Congreve, the technical advantage of the rocket was "the facility of firing a great number of rounds in a short time, or even instantaneously, with small means." But Congreve's rockets had relatively poor accuracy, and they saw no significant use in war after the Battle of Waterloo in June 1815. In the battles around Washington and Baltimore they actually produced little significant effect on the ground. The "rockets' red glare" did, however, alarm green U.S. troops, causing many to flee the battlefield in terror.

—*David T. Zabecki*

See also: Baltimore, Battle of; Lundy's Lane, Battle of; McHenry, Fort; New Orleans, Battle of; Star-Spangled Banner, The

Further Reading
Congreve, Sir William. *The Details of the Rocket System*. London: J. Whiting, 1814. Reprint: Ottawa, Ont. Museum Restoration Service, 1970.
Downey, Fairfax. *Cannonade*. New York: Doubleday, 1966.
Duncan, Francis. *History of the Royal Regiment of Artillery*. London: John Murray, 1873.

Graves, Donald. *Sir William Congreve and the Rocket's Red Glare*. Bloomfield, Ont.: Museum Restoration Service, 1989.

Hogg, O.F.G. *Artillery: Its Origin, Heyday, and Decline*. London: Hurst and Company, 1970.

Rogers, H.C.B. *A History of Artillery*. Secaucus, NJ: The Citadel Press, 1975.

CONJOCTA CREEK, BATTLE OF
3 August 1814

After the battle of Lundy's Lane, the Left Division of Maj. Gen. Jacob Brown fell back to Fort Erie and entrenched itself. This positioned the U.S. army on the Canadian side of the Niagara River, opposite Buffalo, New York. At length, the British Right Division under Lt. Gen. Gordon Drummond advanced and began a formal investment of Fort Erie. Drummond was cognizant of the strength of Brown's position and resorted to a stratagem to spare himself a costly siege. Though strongly posted, Fort Erie was totally dependent upon Buffalo for supplies of every description, which arrived nightly by means of a fleet of small boats. Drummond anticipated that if Buffalo were captured, the U.S. garrison would either be forced to confront his superior numbers in the open or face starvation. On the night of 2 August 1814, he dispatched a select force of 600 light troops commanded by Col. John G.P. Tucker, 41st Foot, with instructions to cross the Niagara River and storm the town.

Fortunately for the Americans, General Brown recognized the precarious nature of his supply line and took active measures to protect it. On 2 August, he entrusted Buffalo's defense to a composite battalion of the First and Fourth U.S. Riflemen. Their commander, Maj. Ludowick Morgan, had observed British activity along the Niagara River and deduced that an attack was imminent. That evening, Morgan secretly erected breastworks along the south bank of Conjocta Creek, directly above the town. Morgan also took the added precaution of removing the ties from a bridge spanning the creek directly in his front. Early on the morning of 3 August, pickets alerted him that enemy forces had crossed the river above town as expected and were pushing south.

Tucker's force, which contained some of the best light companies in the Right Division, confidently advanced along the riverbank until reaching Conjocta Creek. There it paused and was in the process of replacing the bridge ties when Morgan blew his whistle and commenced a point-blank fire upon the milling soldiers. The deadly fusillade panicked the British, who fell back to the trees to exchange shots at long range. Morgan's men ceased firing and hid behind their breastworks to conserve ammunition. A second attempt to repair the bridge was also repulsed. Thwarted by this bridge, Tucker tried turning the U.S. right flank by sending troops along the creek, but they encountered militia and riflemen posted there for such a contingency and withdrew. Having lost the element of surprise and fearful of U.S. reinforcements, Tucker called off the attack after two hours, reembarked, and returned to Canada. British losses were 12 killed, 21 wounded, and 6 taken prisoner. Morgan's casualties were 2 killed and 8 wounded. General Drummond was so incensed by the conduct of his troops in this defeat that he publicly authorized officers to shoot any soldier cowering under fire.

Conjocta Creek was a small but brilliantly conducted affair with immense strategic implications. Had Tucker succeeded in capturing Buffalo, the Fort Erie garrison would have been eliminated as a military force. The aggressive Drummond would then have been free to ravage western New York, Erie, or Detroit at his leisure. Defeat, however, insured that the British would be forced to undertake a siege for which they were poorly prepared. For this reason alone Conjocta Creek must be ranked as one of the decisive engagements of the War of 1812 and a clear strategic triumph for the United States. Unfortunately, Major Morgan, the Hero of Conjocta, fell in a minor skirmish outside Fort Erie on 13 August.

—*John C. Fredriksen*

See also: Brown, Jacob J.; Buffalo, New York; Drummond, Gordon; Erie, Fort

Further Reading

Fredriksen, John C., ed. "The Memoirs of Jonathan Kearsley." *Indiana Military History Journal* 10 (1985): 4–16.

Graves, Donald, ed. *Merry Hearts Make Light Days: The War of 1812 Journal of Lieutenant John Le Couteur, 104th Foot*. Ottawa: Carleton University Press, 1993.

Whitehorne, Joseph. *While Washington Burned: The Battle of Fort Erie*. Baltimore, MD: Nautical & Aviation Publishing Company of America, 1992.

CONNECTICUT

A heavily Federalist state, Connecticut opposed the United States' declaration of war against Great Britain in June 1812. The Connecticut legislature declared that James Madison's administration and the U.S. Congress had acted foolishly in committing the country to a war it was so financially and militarily ill-equipped to fight. When shortly thereafter the national government asked for a requisition of militia to help man New England forts while the regular army undertook an invasion of Canada, Connecticut governor Roger Griswold joined fellow governors of Massachusetts and Rhode Island by refusing. All three governors claimed that the Constitution gave them command over their state militias. Federal law, they said, proscribed calling those militias into service unless the country was invaded or in immediate threat of invasion.

Of all the New England states, Connecticut most assiduously guarded the command of its militia. This spawned controversy in the spring of 1813 when Adm. Sir Thomas S. Hardy's British fleet arrived off New London. Militia forces were called out to patrol the coastal areas, and local citizens rushed to the shoreline to fire at British vessels as they chased New London trading ships back to port. In June 1813, the Madison administration dispatched Brig. Gen. Henry Burbeck to assume command of New London's defense. When the local militia forces refused to place themselves under his authority, Burbeck removed them from federal service. This action meant that the federal government would neither pay nor supply any Connecticut forces that remained in service.

Burbeck's actions temporarily put the citizens of New London in a dither. Since Capt. Stephen Decatur had taken refuge in New London's harbor with the USS *United States*, USS *Hornet*, and the British prize ship *Macedonian*, it seemed likely the British would strike the town to capture or destroy these ships. Under the press of this potential crisis, Gov. John Cotton Smith and Burbeck reached an accommodation. Smith sent Maj. Gen. William Williams of the militia to New London, where he technically outranked Burbeck. A new muster of militia nominally served under Williams, but Burbeck arranged the defense of the town. Meanwhile, Decatur moved his ships out of harm's way up the Thames River.

By fall, Decatur was impatient to escape the confines of New London and decided to make a run for it. He quietly moved his ships back to New London harbor to try his escape to open seas on the night of 12 December. As he prepared to leave the harbor, however, he heard that the British had been alerted to his movements by someone flashing blue lights at the mouth of the river. His chance of surprise gone, Decatur had to stay in the harbor and would not have another chance to leave. It was never precisely determined who was responsible for these blue-lanterned signals, but the episode gave rise to the term "blue-light Federalists" to signify those who so opposed the war that they actually aided the British.

The British remained off of New London into the spring of 1814. In April, they sent ashore a raiding party to destroy some of the coastal batteries in the vicinity of the port. British sailors managed to spike several guns and destroy some boats in the Connecticut River before the alarm was sounded. Sailors from Decatur's ships and local militia tried to prevent the British force from returning to its ships but were too late.

The arrangement between Burbeck and the Connecticut militia worked well during crisis, but by late spring of 1814, Burbeck chafed under the arrangement and began quarreling with local and state officials. Seeking to reestablish harmony, the administration replaced him with a Connecticut Federalist, Col. Jacob Kingsbury. The new regular commander did not question the state's authority over the Connecticut militia.

In July 1814, the situation for the Connecticut coastline again looked bleak, thus requiring a commander with more military acumen than political popularity. The more experienced Brig. Gen. Thomas Cushing replaced Kingsbury. Cushing was not without persuasive powers, though. He had served most recently in Massachusetts and had convinced militia there of the benefits of federal service. He hoped to do the same in Connecticut. At first things went smoothly when, responding to a greater British naval force off the coast, new militia units were summoned to New London. These new troops served directly under two militia brigadier generals, who immediately deferred to Cushing upon their arrival. It was only a mildly awkward arrangement that separated the militia and regulars into discrete entities under one commander. In short, the militia units were commanded by militia officers who were nonetheless commanded by the regular officer, Cushing.

The compromise satisfied the militia perfectly, but it irked Connecticut politicians who persisted in their doctrine of a state-controlled militia. When Governor Smith sent militia major general Augustine Taylor to New London, he insisted upon assuming absolute command of the Connecticut forces. Cushing could not hide his exasperation. He declared that if the Connecticut men were under state control, Connecticut could pay for them. As before, when the militia had been dismissed from federal service over the command controversy, federal pay and supplies were immediately cut off. The state treasury now had to bear Connecticut's defense.

When the legislature convened a month later in October, its members were livid. The unexpected burden of supplying and paying militia forces had put the state's finances in turmoil. Relations with the national government continued to deteriorate through the fall of 1814. When Congress passed a law that permitted minors between the ages of 18 and 21 to enlist in the army without parental permission, the Connecticut legislature made the practice illegal within the state. This worsening federal relationship also explains why the Connecticut legislature enthusiastically accepted the invitation from Massachusetts to send delegates to a New England convention. Connecticut lieutenant governor Chauncey Goodrich led the state's delegation to the meeting that was hosted by Connecticut and thus became known as the Hartford Convention. After the convention, the Connecticut legislature joined Massachusetts to endorse its resolutions and proposed constitutional amendments.

For all this turmoil, when the war ended it had left Connecticut virtually untouched. The state's coastline suffered little palpable damage, and no major military engagements took place within it. What did suffer damage, however, was Connecticut's reputation. Many throughout the nation viewed the home of the blue-light Federalists and the Hartford Convention as the most disloyal state during the war.

—*Jeanne T. Heidler and David S. Heidler*

See also: Burbeck, Henry; Decatur, Stephen, Jr.; Griswold, Roger; Hardy, Thomas Masterman; Hartford Convention; Kingsbury, Jacob; New London, Connecticut; Smith, John Cotton
Further Reading
Buckley, William E., ed. "Letters of Connecticut Federalists, 1814–1815." *New England Quarterly* 3 (1930): 316–331.
Hickey, Donald R. "New England's Defense Problem and the Genesis of the Hartford Convention." *New England Quarterly* 50 (December 1977): 587–604.

CONNER, DAVID
1792–1856
U.S. naval officer

Born in Harrisburg, Pennsylvania, to David Conner and Abigail Rhodes Conner, young Conner went to Philadelphia as a teenager to work for his brother. At the age of 17 he received an appointment as a midshipman and began a lifelong naval career. In 1811, Conner began service aboard the sloop USS *Hornet* (18 guns), where he would remain throughout the War of 1812.

The *Hornet* had returned from Great Britain just a month before the declaration of war. Within weeks, she saw her first action, capturing the British privateer *Dolphin*.

Appointed prize-master of the captured ship, Conner was captured when the British retook the ship. By the end of the year, he had been exchanged and was serving as third lieutenant aboard the *Hornet* under James Lawrence when she engaged the HMS *Peacock* on 24 February 1813. After 15 minutes, the *Peacock*, in danger of sinking, surrendered. Conner led a detail to the disabled vessel to supervise her crew's rescue while trying to save the ship itself. He lightened the *Peacock* by throwing her guns overboard and patched her hull below the waterline, but it was too late. Conner jumped into the launch just before the *Peacock* sank, but three of his own men and nine British crewmen perished with her.

His performance in this and future actions earned him promotion to first lieutenant by war's end, a rank he held under Capt. James Biddle in the *Hornet*'s final engagement of the conflict. In this contest against the HMS *Penguin* the Americans triumphed in 20 minutes, but Conner received a severe hip wound that would plague him for two years.

Following the War of 1812, Conner rose steadily in the navy and by the Mexican-American War commanded the naval forces that blockaded Mexico's Gulf coast and landed Gen. Winfield Scott's invading army in March 1847. Conner died in Philadelphia in 1856.

—*Jeanne T. Heidler and David S. Heidler*

See also: Biddle, James; *Hornet* versus *Peacock*; *Hornet* versus *Penguin*; Lawrence, James
Further Reading
Henkels, Stanislaus V. *The Correspondence of Commodore David Conner, U.S. Navy during the War of 1812 and Mexican War.* Philadelphia: Self-published, 1914.

CONSTITUTION VERSUS CYANE AND LEVANT
20 February 1815

USS *Constitution*, commanded by Capt. Charles Stewart, had been two months on cruise when, on the afternoon of 20 February 1815, she encountered the British light frigate *Cyane* and the corvette *Levant*. The British had departed Tangier three days earlier and, unbeknownst to the Americans, were the rear guard of a West Indies–bound convoy.

Stewart clapped on sail to close the *Cyane*, separated from *Levant* by several miles. The *Constitution*'s main royal mast cracked, however, and required replacement. By the time he again was closing, Stewart found the two Britons formed in column with 100 yards between them. The big U.S. frigate closed to a position abeam of them, to starboard about 600 yards, with the wind coming from astern, slightly on the larboard quarter. From this position, she opened the battle with a double-shotted broadside.

Smoke soon enveloped the combatants, but the British quickly realized they would have to shorten the range or their carronades would have little effect. Each sought to close. Stewart, completely blinded by the smoke, ceased fire to let it clear away ahead. When it did, he saw *Cyane* apparently trying to cut under his stern. Loosing a broadside at the assumed position of *Levant*, he backed his ship and struck *Cyane* with withering blasts. The smaller British ship reeled away with most of her rigging destroyed and a half-dozen guns out of action.

By this time, the sun had set, but Stewart saw *Levant* apparently trying to cut ahead of him. Charging ahead, he wore short and delivered two withering raking broadsides at the British ship's stern, sending her staggering off into the darkness. He then continued around to gain a position within 50 yards of *Cyane*'s larboard quarter. His foe surrendered before he could fire. The Americans spent the next hour removing the British officers and placing a prize crew aboard.

With one enemy secured, Stewart went hunting for the other. In just a quarter hour, he discovered *Levant* returning to the fray. The two ships exchanged broadsides as they passed at close range on opposite courses. Stewart wore short, however, and hit his foe with a raking broadside from astern. As his enemy decided to run before the wind, the U.S. captain went in chase. Two 24-pounder long guns shifted to fire out of her forwardmost ports allowed *Constitution* to keep up a damaging fire as she closed in, ultimately heading for a position on the enemy's larboard quarter. She was reaching that position shortly after 10 P.M., when *Levant* signaled her surrender.

Captain Stewart received a gold medal from Congress for his victory, but because the battle occurred at the war's end it never received the notoriety of the ship's earlier triumphs. Captain, crew, and ship had performed splendidly, and their triumph should have become a textbook classic.

—*Tyrone G. Martin*

See also: Stewart, Charles
Further Reading
Forester, C. S. *The Age of Fighting Sail.* Garden City, NY: Doubleday, 1956.
Fowler, William M., Jr. *Jack Tars & Commodores.* Boston: Houghton Mifflin, 1984.
Mahan, Alfred T. *Sea Power in Its Relations to the War of 1812.* Boston: Little, Brown, 1905.
Martin, Tyrone G. *A Most Fortunate Ship.* Annapolis, MD: Naval Institute Press, 1997.

CONSTITUTION VERSUS *GUERRIÈRE*
19 August 1812

Early on the afternoon of 19 August 1812, when some 600 miles due east of Boston on a southerly course, USS *Constitution,* under the command of Capt. Isaac Hull, made contact with a ship to the southeast, steering a westerly course. Soon each recognized the other as an enemy frigate. Capt. James R. Dacres of HMS *Guerrière* slowed to let his foe close. The wind was northerly.

Shortly after 4:00 P.M., the Briton opened fire at long range. Hull continued to close cautiously, yawing to either side to throw off his enemy's aim. At about 5:00, Dacres grew impatient and turned downwind, a maneuver of challenge. Hull set his main topgallant sail and closed to starboard. As he began to overlap the enemy, he opened fire with double-shotted guns at half-pistol-shot distance.

After 20 minutes of firing, *Guerrière*'s mizzenmast fell to starboard, causing the ship to veer in that direction. Before either side could prevent it, *Guerrière* crashed into *Constitution*'s larboard mizzen shrouds, wrecking a quarter boat. As the *Constitution*'s forward motion caused her to swing astern, *Guerrière* bumped into her several more times and smashed Hull's gig in the stern davits before breaking free.

Hull next maneuvered to take a position on *Guerrière*'s larboard bow and unleashed at least two broadsides, which staved in the Briton's two forwardmost gun ports, leaving a single gaping maw. Seeing the enemy ship largely immobilized by the tangle of her downed mast, Hull moved to get across her bow to deliver a devastating rake down her length. He cut it too close, however, and a second collision resulted, *Guerrière* this time snagging Hull's starboard mizzen shrouds. Both sides attempted to board through a hail of countering musket fire, but it was too heavy. *Constitution*'s continuing movement again caused the ships to pull apart. The resultant whipping of the *Guerrière*'s jibboom overstressed her wounded foremast, and it fell to starboard. Its weight took the impaired mainmast with it. At that point, *Guerrière* became unmanageable. Hull drew off eastward a short distance and made a few necessary rigging repairs. He then returned and was about to resume fire when the *Guerrière* surrendered. It was just about sunset.

Inexperienced in combat, Isaac Hull fought this contest as one would have expected: cautiously and without polish. He owed his victory as much to luck and Captain Dacres's contempt as to his own skill. When Hull returned to Boston about ten days later, however, he "revised" his action report to make it appear that he had finished his enemy in about 35 minutes with no collisions. It was the kind of tale of derring-do badly needed by the public in the United States—a fable of Brother Jonathan outwitting John Bull—and Hull was accordingly lionized. Congress promptly awarded him a gold medal. And USS *Constitution* henceforth was known as Old Ironsides.

—*Tyrone G. Martin*

See also: Dacres, James Richard; Hull, Isaac
Further Reading
Fowler, William M., Jr. *Jack Tars & Commodores*. Boston: Houghton Mifflin, 1984.

Grant, Bruce. *Captain of Old Ironsides*. Chicago: Pellegrini and Cudahy, 1947.

Martin, Tyrone G. "Isaac Hull's Victory Revisited." *The American Neptune* 47 (winter 1987): 14–21.

CONSTITUTION VERSUS JAVA
29 December 1812

The British frigate *Java* was en route to India when she met USS *Constitution,* under the command of Commodore William Bainbridge, off the coast of Brazil on 29 December 1812. Although the British ship was smaller and heavily laden with supplies and personnel for the Indian station, she was faster than her opponent. Both sides were eager to do battle.

The fray opened at long range shortly after 2:00 P.M. The *Java* was on *Constitution's* larboard quarter and the wind nearly on the beam as the two sailed to the southeast. British shooting was quite good, and Bainbridge was wounded in the thigh early on. When he saw his enemy moving ahead of him and threatening to turn across his bow, he fired a broadside and wore round to the southwest, placing *Java* once more astern, this time to starboard. Again, the British ship came charging up and ahead, and again Bainbridge wore—back to the southeast. Yet a third time, *Java* began closing from the larboard quarter but instead, on drawing abeam, suddenly wore to starboard and

delivered raking fire at the *Constitution's* stern. Bainbridge was hit a second time, and his ship's wheel was shot away. Since *Constitution* failed to maneuver, the British captain, Henry Lambert, assumed she was running and turned to pursue up her windward side.

But Bainbridge was not through. Supported by a pair of midshipmen, he arranged a temporary steering rig and prepared to close on his antagonist as she came abeam. As the *Java* did so, a lucky U.S. shot tore away her jibboom and caused her to turn up into the wind, out of control. Seeing this, Bainbridge wore his injured ship around and got in a rake of *Java's* larboard quarter before reversing his swing and resuming his original course. Now, it was Lambert's turn to try to regain the advantage. He brought his ship under control and attempted to grapple the U.S. ship amidships and board her. The plan misfired, however, as *Java* struck *Constitution* farther aft and had her foremast shot away before falling astern.

The balance now was in Bainbridge's favor. He wore his ship across *Java's* bow, raking her, and continued on around to cross her stern and do it again before reversing course for another stern rake. Then he took up a position off *Java's* starboard quarter from which he could pound her with impunity. When he had beaten her virtually mastless, he drew off ahead and spent some time making emergency rigging repairs. Shortly after 5:00, he was about to rake her again from ahead when *Java* surrendered, her captain mortally wounded.

When the British Admiralty learned of the defeat, it ordered that henceforth U.S. heavy frigates should be fought only by two or more Britons of similar force. Bainbridge earned himself a congressional gold medal and became another U.S. naval hero.

—*Tyrone G. Martin*

See also: Bainbridge, William
Further Reading
Dudley, William S., ed. *The Naval War of 1812: A Documentary History*. Vol. 1. Washington, DC: Naval Historical Center, 1985.

Forester, C. S. *The Age of Fighting Sail*. Garden City, NY: Doubleday, 1956.

Long, David F. *Ready To Hazard*. Hanover, NH: University Press of New England, 1981.

Martin, Tyrone G. *A Most Fortunate Ship*. Annapolis, MD: Naval Institute Press, 1997.

This aggressive clash and American victory between the now familiar Constitution *and the British frigate* Java *so surprised the British that an order was issued that no lone British ship should engage an American frigate.*

COOK'S MILLS, BATTLE OF
19 October 1814

On 12 October 1814, the Right Division under Maj. Gen. George Izard completed its arduous trek from Plattsburg, New York, and reached the Niagara Frontier. There it was united with the battle-hardened veterans of Maj. Gen. Jacob Brown's Left Division at Fort Erie. Their combined forces totaled nearly 7,000 well-trained and equipped soldiers, the largest aggregate of military power the United States possessed in this war. However, the two leaders were at cross purposes over how to best deploy it. The aggressive Brown wanted to immediately attack British forces under Lt. Gen. Gordon Drummond, which were strongly entrenched behind the Chippewa River. Izard, the senior officer, declined to sacrifice his men in frontal assaults and preferred luring Drummond out into the open. On 15 October, the Americans commenced a spirited bombardment of the British position, but Drummond refused to move. Demonstrations in front of Drummond's line followed, but Brown, angered by what he considered Izard's indecision, marched his division for Sacket's Harbor. Faced with the onset of winter, Izard resorted to one final ploy to evict Drummond from his works.

Intelligence had been received that quantities of grain were stored at Cook's Mills on Lyon's Creek, a tributary of the Chippewa. On 17 October, Izard dispatched Gen. Daniel Bissell's brigade, 900 strong, to attack the mill, turn Drummond's right, and force him into action. Poor roads precluded artillery support, but Bissell arrived at Cook's Mills on the evening of 18 October. A heavy skirmish between his riflemen and the Glengarry Fencibles convinced him that sizable enemy forces were in the vicinity. His suspicions were confirmed on 19 October when U.S. outposts across the creek were attacked by 750 British troops under Lt. Col. Christopher Myers, 100th Foot. As Bissell's riflemen and light troops disputed Myers's advance, Bissell deployed for an immediate counterattack.

The U.S. line surged across Lyon's Creek under heavy fire that included artillery and rockets. Holding the 15th and 16th Infantry in reserve, Bissell ordered Maj. Isaac D. Barnard's 14th Infantry to charge the enemy in front while the Fifth Infantry, under Maj. Ninian Pinkney, turned their left flank. Both movements were successful, and Myers, perceiving himself outnumbered, withdrew from Cook's Mills in orderly fashion. The victorious Americans sustained 12 killed and 55 wounded to a British loss of 1 killed and 35 wounded. The U.S. troops returned to Cook's Mills and burned 200 bushels of wheat intended for the enemy. When it became apparent that even this provocation would not budge Drummond, Bissell ordered his brigade back along Lyon's Creek. He rejoined General Izard at Fort Erie without incident.

On the surface, Cook's Mills appears to have been an insignificant skirmish. It is notable, however, in being the last encounter between regular forces in Canada during the War of 1812. Moreover, that the Americans clearly prevailed in this stiff little action was rendered even more significant because their opponents included the 82nd Foot, formerly of Wellington's army. The victory reflects credit upon General Izard, who had properly drilled and instructed his men at Plattsburg during the summer. Had Bissell's men lacked this preparation, a meeting with such seasoned British troops might have ended disastrously.

—*John C. Fredriksen*

See also: Brown, Jacob J.; Drummond, Gordon; Izard, George
Further Reading
Einstein, Lewis, ed. "Recollections of the War of 1812 by George Hay, Eighth Marquis of Tweedale." *American Historical Review* 32 (1926): 69–78.
Fredriksen, John C. "Niagara, 1814: The American Quest for Tactical Parity in the War of 1812 and Its Legacy." Ph.D. diss., Providence College, 1993.
Graves, Donald E., ed. *Merry Hearts Make Light Days: The War of 1812 Journal of Lieutenant John Le Couteur, 104th Foot.* Ottawa: Carleton University Press, 1993.

COPUS MASSACRE

15 September 1812

William Hull's surrender of Detroit in August 1812 caused consternation among the settlers of northern Ohio, who feared an increase in Indian attacks along the frontier. Several such incidents in that state culminated in September with what has come to be known as the Copus Massacre.

James Copus, a Pennsylvanian of German ancestry, in 1809 had moved with his family to Richland County, Ohio, eventually settling along the Black Fork River, near present-day Mifflin. Copus belonged to the Methodist Church, and he frequently preached to the large Indian population in the region. Several other white families settled in the vicinity of the Copus farm. Upon the outbreak of war, Copus reluctantly participated in negotiations to remove a peaceful Delaware village from nearby Greentown. Copus was against the removal of the Delaware, but to avoid bloodshed he persuaded their chief, Pamoxet, also known as Captain Armstrong, to remove to Piqua, Ohio. Despite assurances that the Delawares' remaining property would be protected, stragglers from the soldiers sent to escort them almost immediately burned the village. This deceit infuriated the Indians.

In September 1812, a fatal attack on the family of Frederick Zimmer drove Copus and other settlers to the blockhouse at nearby Beam's Mill. After remaining there for about five days, however, Copus returned to his farm on 14 September, accompanied by his family and nine soldiers. That evening Copus and his family stayed in their cabin while the soldiers slept in a nearby barn. Copus became alarmed by the continuous barking of his dogs, and he urged the soldiers to return to his cabin. They showed little concern over the possibility of an Indian attack, and the following morning seven of the men carelessly left their weapons leaning against Copus's cabin while they went to a nearby spring to bathe. At the spring a large party of Indians—according to some writers, it may have numbered as many as 45—attacked the soldiers. These Indians almost certainly included Greentown Indians angry at James Copus for his part in their forced removal.

Five of the soldiers were quickly killed and scalped. Another escaped into the woods but was shot in the bowels and found dead weeks later. The seventh soldier, George Dye, was wounded but managed to reach the Copus cabin, where he joined forces with the Copus family and with the two soldiers who had not gone to the spring. James Copus was wounded early in the fight while helping Dye into the cabin and died about an hour later. The three remaining soldiers defended the cabin against attacks that lasted for several more hours. Another soldier and James Copus's ten-year-old daughter, Nancy, were both wounded.

When it became apparent that the Indians had left, a soldier ran to the Beam's Mill Blockhouse for help. The commander, a Captain Martin, had promised to bring an additional detachment to Copus's farm the previous evening. Instead, after scouting the area and detecting no

Indian signs, Martin's force had encamped away from the Copus farm and did not reach the scene until after the battle. Unable to overtake the attackers, Martin's force buried the white dead and returned to the blockhouse.

The Copus Massacre was the last Indian attack in Richland County. The surviving members of the Copus family remained at the blockhouse for several months. They eventually traveled to Claysville, Ohio, for the duration of the war. Mrs. Copus remarried and survived until 1862. A monument was later erected at the battle site, and residents held a commemoration on the battle's centennial in September 1912.

—David Coles

See also: Ohio
Further Reading

Campbell, R. M. "The Copus Hill Tragedy." *Journal of American History* 16 (1922): 50–54.
Galbreath, Charles B. *History of Ohio.* 5 vols. Chicago: The American Historical Society, 1925.
Graham, A. A. *History of Richland County.* N.p., 1880.
Howe, Henry. *Historical Collections of Ohio.* 2 vols. Cincinnati: C. J. Krehbiel, 1904.
Williams, Eugene Ellis. "The Copus Battle Centennial." *Ohio Archaeological and Historical Publications* 21 (1912): 379–395.

COVINGTON, LEONARD
1768–1813
U.S. officer

Born in Maryland, Leonard Covington entered the army for the first time in 1792. He served under Gen. Anthony Wayne, who commended Covington for bravery in the Fallen Timbers campaign. He left the army as a captain in 1795 and returned to Maryland. From 1805 to 1807, he represented Maryland in the U.S. House of Representatives. He reentered the army in 1809 at the rank of lieutenant colonel.

Breveted to the rank of brigadier general in August 1813 for his early service in the war, Covington commanded the Third Brigade in Maj. Gen. James Wilkinson's invasion of Canada in the fall of 1813. Covington's brigade made up one of the two brigades (Brig. Gen. John Boyd's was the other) in Maj. Gen. Morgan Lewis's division.

On 11 November 1813, the army's boats neared the Longue Salte, 8 miles of continuous rapids. Boyd's brigade and much of Covington's brigade were landed to repel the British approach at Chrysler's Farm. As Covington prepared his men for the attack, he mistook the British in front of him for Canadian militia and attacked before his men were fully ready. This and subsequent attacks were repelled in a typical display of the disorganized U.S. assault. While trying to take some British artillery later in the battle, Covington was mortally wounded. He died two days later. His body was taken to the U.S. winter quarters at French Mills, where he was buried. French Mills was later renamed Fort Covington in his honor.

—*Jeanne T. Heidler and David S. Heidler*

See also: Boyd, John Parker; Chrysler's Farm, Battle of; Lewis, Morgan; Wilkinson, James
Further Reading

Wailes, Benjamin Leonard Covington. *Memoir of Leonard Covington.* Natchez, MS: Natchez Printing and Stationery Co., 1928.
Way, Ronald L. "The Day of Crysler's Farm." *Canadian Geographical Journal* 62 (1961): 184–217.

COX, WILLIAM STITGREAVES
1790–1874
Lieutenant, U.S. Navy

Command of the *Chesapeake* devolved upon naval lieutenant William Cox after HMS *Shannon's* three broadsides decimated the *Chesapeake's* crew and seriously wounded its captain, James Lawrence, on 1 June 1813. Though neither ship suffered serious damage, the *Chesapeake* was more vulnerable because it sustained damage to its foresail, leaving its stern and crew exposed to enemy fire. The continued fire from HMS *Shannon* caused additional U.S. casualties and also caused the *Chesapeake's* larboard quarter to tangle with the *Shannon's* forerigging. British captain Sir Philip Broke ordered the *Chesapeake* boarded. All U.S. officers on board the *Chesapeake* suffered wounds except acting Lieutenant Cox, who carried Captain Lawrence below deck and took no part in the melee above.

The capture of the *Chesapeake* was the first British capture of a U.S. vessel in the War of 1812. Some have argued that the humiliating defeat of the *Chesapeake* required a scapegoat. The *Chesapeake's* wounded Lt. George Budd filed charges against Lt. William Cox, asserting that Cox should have been on deck fighting the British rather than with Lawrence. Some *Chesapeake* crewmen testified that

Cox was following Lawrence's orders. William Cox was tried, found guilty on two counts, and dishonorably discharged from the navy in 1814.

Later naval historians doubted Cox's guilt because the *Chesapeake* was fresh from refitting and manned by a green crew. Court testimony revealed that Lieutenant Cox fought his guns bravely until the crew deserted. He rushed on deck to repel the boarders, probably unaware that as the only senior uninjured officer on the *Chesapeake*, he was in command.

His descendants vigorously fought William Cox's conviction. They forced Pres. Theodore Roosevelt to apologize for his published statements that William Cox "acted basely." William Cox's conviction stood until 1952, when his great-grandson, Electus D. Litchfield, persuaded Georgia congressman Eugene Cox (no relation) to introduce a motion for exoneration. A joint resolution of Congress accomplished that objective. The U.S. government restored William Cox to the rank of third lieutenant as of 1874, the year he died.

—*William A. Paquette*

See also: Broke, Philip Bowes Vere; *Chesapeake* versus *Shannon*; Lawrence, James
Further Reading
Lansen, Arthur. "Scapegoat of the *Chesapeake-Shannon* Battle." *United States Naval Institute Proceedings* 79 (1953): 528–531.

CRANEY ISLAND, BATTLE OF
22 June 1813

In mid-June 1813, Adm. Sir John Warren returned to Chesapeake Bay with troop reinforcements under Col. Sir John Beckwith. The British had the goal of taking the *Constellation*, blockaded at Norfolk and defended by a line of 19 small gunboats. Thus on 20 June 1813, 13 Royal Navy vessels, including three 74s, one 64, four frigates, and three transports, took position to attack Norfolk.

Craney Island, guarding the mouth of the Elizabeth River, was the key to Norfolk's defense. Charged with Norfolk's land defense, Brig. Gen. Robert B. Taylor had tried to bolster the island's weak fortification with a battery of seven guns (two 24-pounders, one 18, and four 6s) and had placed another across the river at Lamberts Point.

Luckily for the Americans, Warren could not get his ships of the line close enough to bombard Craney Island.

Instead, at dawn on 22 June, the British came ashore on the mainland northwest of the island. This contingent made its way to Wise's Creek opposite Craney, but the island's batteries forced the British inland. At the same time, however, the British were deploying a force of barges against the island proper.

U.S. captain Joseph Tarbell had ordered three lieutenants and 100 seamen to man a small battery on the island's northwest side. There were only about 150 Americans on Craney Island, including men from the *Constellation*. Nonetheless, their well-directed fire sank three large British boats, including the 50-foot-long *Centipede*. Capt. John Cassin later wrote that the men of the *Constellation* "fired their 18 pounders more like riflemen than Artillerists. I never saw such shooting and seriously believe they saved the Island." Some British troops got ashore, but they quickly fell back to launch Congreve Rockets. Soon they drew fire from the gunboats protecting the Elizabeth River, and Gunboat No. 67 placed such a withering bombardment that even these British stalwarts had to disperse. The Americans estimated the attackers at 2,500 to 3,000 men, exclusive of seamen, and their losses at 400 men.

On 23 June, the British landed troops at Newport News under cover of Congreve Rockets. Two days later, Hampton fell after stubborn resistance, its 500 defenders overwhelmed by sheer weight of numbers. After destroying Hampton's defenses and committing a number of outrages against civilians, the British raided up the James River beyond Smithfield.

Americans feared another British assault on Craney Island, and Cassin strengthened its garrison and mounted 36 cannon there. The British did not return to Norfolk, however. Instead, they moved into Chesapeake Bay and its tributaries to plunder. On 11 July, they returned to their Lynnhaven Bay anchorage.

—*Spencer C. Tucker*

See also: Warren, John Borlase
Further Reading
Emmerson, John C., Jr., comp. *War in the Lower Chesapeake & Hampton Roads Area, 1812–1815, as Reported in the* Norfolk Gazette & Publick Ledger *& the* Norfolk & Portsmouth Herald. Portsmouth, VA: N.p., 1946.
Hallahan, John M. *The Battle of Craney Island*. Portsmouth, VA: Saint Michael's Press, 1986.

CRAWFORD, WILLIAM H.
1772–1834
U.S. senator; minister to France

One of 11 children born to Joel Crawford and Fanny Harris Crawford in Virginia, William Harris Crawford moved with his family to South Carolina and then to Georgia when still a small child. After a good education at one of the finer rural academies in the South, Crawford tried teaching and the law before settling on a political career. After serving for a few years in the Georgia legislature, Crawford was sent to the U.S. Senate in 1807.

Arriving within days of the vote on the Embargo Bill, Crawford requested a delay in the voting while he studied the measure. When his motion for delay was defeated, Crawford voted against the measure. Though Crawford would later come to support the embargo as preferable to war, his refusal to agree to measures he did not fully understand set the pattern for his very reflective public career.

Though he considered himself a good Democratic Republican, Crawford defies easy categorization during the years before the War of 1812. He considered war preferable to submission, but he did not feel that the United States was or would be capable of challenging the British on the seas. He opposed the increase in naval construction supported by many War Hawks because he did not believe the country could create a match for the Royal Navy. Rather, he believed that any increase in U.S. military capabilities should focus on the army. Properly armed Americans could conceivably challenge the British in Canada.

Crawford also felt that the resources of the United States should be used to acquire the Floridas. He told the Madison administration the best way to achieve that objective and recommended former Georgia governor George Mathews as an appropriate person to carry out a covert annexation scheme. At first secretively supportive, the Madison administration ultimately disavowed Mathews's actions in east Florida in the spring of 1812 when war loomed with Britain. An angry Crawford continued to push for Florida's annexation even after war had commenced against Great Britain.

In spite of his reservations regarding U.S. preparedness, Crawford voted with the majority in the Senate for a declaration of war on 18 June 1812. As the conflict progressed, however, he viewed the Madison administration with increasing dismay. At one point, he communicated his misgivings directly to his friend, Secretary of State James Monroe, and thereafter the administration began taking

Crawford's counsel. When Secretary of War William Eustis resigned at the end of 1812, Crawford's advice had become so important to the administration that he was consulted on a replacement. After running through several candidates, Madison offered the job to Crawford, but he refused, pleading a lack of qualifications.

Yet Crawford continued as an informal intimate of the government's highest councils. When word arrived of Joel Barlow's untimely death, Madison turned to Crawford to replace Barlow as minister to France. Crawford reluctantly accepted, in the belief that he could positively guide negotiations with France regarding U.S. trade. Setting sail on 18 June 1813 from New York City aboard the USS *Argus*, Crawford began a frustrating two-year mission to France. He started his negotiations with France from a difficult position. Napoleon had maintained the right to seize U.S. shipping in French ports with the Rambouillet Decree, a proclamation that posed as retaliation for the United States' Nonimportation Act of 1809. After the effective date of the act, Bonaparte declared, all U.S. shipping entering French ports or on the high seas would be subject to seizure. Against these obnoxious assertions, Crawford had a hard task: to gain the removal of French restrictions on U.S. trade and indemnification for goods already confiscated while also maintaining friendly relations with France. The most talented and seasoned diplomat would have found this a nearly impossible chore.

Two shipping cases consumed most of Crawford's energies. They concerned the merchant vessels *Nancy* and *Decatur*. The *Nancy* case greeted Crawford on his arrival. The ship, en route from the United States to Lisbon, had been stopped by two French ships, who had removed the *Nancy*'s crew and burned the ship in the Atlantic Ocean. Crawford's tireless efforts failed to persuade Napoleon to disavow the action, and the case remained unresolved until the Bourbon restoration. The *Decatur* incident actually occurred during Napoleon's first exile, when the French detained the ship as a privateer. Since France was then at peace with the British, the monarchy held that privateers could not legally dispose of their goods in neutral French ports. Again, Crawford's arguments proved fruitless. The *Decatur* was not released until after the United States and Great Britain were at peace.

In addition to such time-consuming functions, Crawford supervised the activities of all U.S. consuls in western Europe and reported regularly to the administration on the military and political situations there. His information sometimes was especially valuable, as when he warned of the French retreat from Spain at the end of 1813. The Madison administration thus had several months warning about the likelihood of British veterans from Wellington's Spanish campaign being used against the United States.

When Napoleon's military disasters finally forced his abdication in the spring of 1814, Crawford hoped the new government under Louis XVIII would be more receptive to U.S. terms. Disappointed in this expectation, Crawford spent the summer of 1814 informing U.S. peace commissioners at Ghent about the European political scene. Following the peace, Crawford was so discouraged by his failure to obtain redress from the French that he asked to be relieved. Shortly after Crawford's return to the United States on 1 August 1815, President Madison appointed him secretary of war. Crawford held the post until October 1816, when he took the reins of the Treasury Department during Madison's last months in office. Crawford remained at Treasury under Madison's successor, James Monroe. At the War and Treasury Departments, Crawford earned a reputation as an extremely able administrator, but in both positions he also gained the lasting enmity of a rising star in U.S. politics—Maj. Gen. Andrew Jackson. This relationship would have a direct bearing on Crawford's political future.

During the presidency of James Monroe, Crawford achieved such prominence in national political circles that the Republican caucus nominated him for president in the election of 1824. By that time, however, most people perceived the caucus system as a vestige of elitism that had outlived its usefulness in a time of rising democracy. Crawford accordingly was challenged in the election by fellow Democratic Republicans John Quincy Adams, Andrew Jackson, and Henry Clay. Afflicted during the campaign season by what appeared to be a partially incapacitating stroke, Crawford scored only a distant third in the electoral college.

His health partially rebounded, but Crawford's defeat in the election meant an end to his national political career. He returned to Georgia, where he remained active in local affairs until his death in 1834.

—*Jeanne T. Heidler and David S. Heidler*

See also: Barlow, Joel; Embargo Act; Mathews, George; Napoleon I; Patriot War

Further Reading

Mooney, Chase C. *William H. Crawford, 1772–1834.* Lexington: The University Press of Kentucky, 1974.

Shepard, Helen Louise. "The National Political Career of William H. Crawford, 1807–1825." Master's thesis, Indiana University, 1940.

CREEK WAR
1813–1814

Spiritual, philosophical, ethnic, and political differences and the stress caused by land hunger of white Americans caused the Creek Nation to erupt in civil war in 1813. Because this war occurred during the War of 1812, white Americans jumped to the erroneous conclusion that the British had inspired internal strife within the Creek Nation. The civil war partly sprang from white pressure for land cessions that led some Creeks to target isolated white and mixed-blood settlements. These two factors led to U.S. intervention in the civil war. The conflict thus merged with the War of 1812.

The Creek Nation lay within western Georgia and the eastern part of the Mississippi Territory (now Alabama) and consisted of two sections. The Lower Creeks resided in the eastern part of the nation, along and near the Chattahoochee River. The Upper Creek towns were situated almost due west of the Lower Creeks. As a confederation of different ethnic groups, ethnic and language differences partly divided these two sections. The activity of U.S. Creek agent Benjamin Hawkins deepened these divisions. Living among the Creeks (primarily Lower Creeks) since 1796, Hawkins had instituted a policy that he believed would save the Creeks from extinction and make them more acceptable to their white neighbors. Hawkins encouraged the Creeks to accept what he called a "civilization" program that included white methods of farming, adoption of private property, and the establishment of government. Many Lower Creeks living near Hawkins and white Georgians appeared receptive to Hawkins's plan, especially those who reaped the economic benefits of trade and commerce with whites. Upper Creeks, living farther away from Hawkins and other whites, grew alarmed over white expansion and were irritated by disreputable whites moving through their lands on the new federal road completed in 1810.

These differences became critical in 1811 when a spiritual revival swept through the Upper Creek towns. Seeking total reversion to native ways as the best defense against growing white influence, the movement coincided with a visit of the great Shawnee leader, Tecumseh. Because his mother was Creek, to this matrilineal Creek society Tecumseh was Creek also. He came south in 1811 to persuade southern Indians to join northwestern Indians in a confederation against further white expansion. Upper Creeks especially listened attentively to Tecumseh's message, and a party of them traveled back to the Northwest with him.

In the spring of 1812, a series of murders of whites within the Creek Nation prompted Benjamin Hawkins to summon the Creek Council. This body dispatched a group of Creeks called law menders to execute the perpetrators. As Little Warrior's band returned from their trip north with Tecumseh, they attacked a settlement on the Duck River in Tennessee. Another expedition of law menders executed Little Warrior and his compatriots. Creeks killing Creeks, however, only steeled the determination of the group known as Red Sticks to resist acculturation. The term *Red Stick,* which designated those nativist Creeks who went to war against their fellow Creeks, derived from the Creek practice of sending bundles of sticks, the number of which indicated the days until an event. If the sticks were red, the event was a war.

The Creek National Council was dominated by Creeks who supported Hawkins's plans, so the acculturationists became the Red Sticks' obvious targets. As hostilities escalated between the Red Sticks, mostly from the Upper Towns, and other Creeks, Georgia, Tennessee, and the Mississippi Territory wanted to put down the Red Sticks with militia. Hawkins resisted such a plan because he feared that a white invasion of the Creek Nation would only conclude with a sizable Creek land cession.

The situation became more critical in the summer of 1813, however, when Red Sticks besieged the town of Tuckabatchee. The town was the home of Big Warrior, an important Creek headman. When Tuckabatchee sent out a call for reinforcements and weapons, Hawkins knew that he could no longer forestall white involvement. In the meantime, the Red Sticks, too, had internationalized the conflict by sending emissaries to Spanish Pensacola to seek weapons and ammunition.

One of these parties, led by Red Stick leader Peter McQueen, successfully procured powder and lead from Spanish authorities in July 1813. As he returned with his supplies on 27 July 1813, Mississippi territorial militia attacked his force at Burnt Corn Creek. Col. James Caller's militiamen caught these Red Sticks by surprise. To save themselves, they abandoned their pack animals, but they soon regrouped in a nearby swamp, counterattacked the militiamen, and scattered them. This Red Stick victory at Burnt Corn Creek helped their recruiting among fellow Creeks. One Creek who joined the Red Sticks following the battle was William Weatherford (Red Eagle), who would prove to be one of their most effective military leaders.

By August 1813, Red Sticks were led by a diverse group of men, ranging from religious prophets like Josiah Francis (Hillis Hadjo) to battle leaders like Peter McQueen and William Weatherford. The methods of the prophets and the militarists differed considerably. The prophets employed magic to protect warriors in battle, whereas militarists relied on complex strategy to harry and expel the enemy Creek and white presence in the nation.

Before Burnt Corn Creek, scattered white and mixed-blood farms made attacks easy. After that engagement, however, families began huddling together in makeshift forts. One such fort was Fort Mims near the Alabama River. Situated in the southwestern part of what is now Alabama, the stockade had been built by a mixed-blood farmer named Samuel Mims. By mid-August about 300 people, including 120 militiamen, had crowded into the fort. About noon on 30 August 1813, approximately 750 Red Sticks led by William Weatherford attacked the fort, easily gaining entry because the compound's gate was open. Several hours of heavy fighting ended in a Red Stick victory that was followed by the systematic murder of survivors. Only a few dozen inhabitants of the fort escaped.

The Red Stick attack on Fort Mims terrified the frontier from Canada to Mobile. It also insured a more active role for the United States in the Creek War. When surrounding state and territorial militias were called out, Secretary of War John Armstrong appointed Maj. Gen. Thomas Pinckney, commander of the Sixth Military District, to coordinate the war effort. This decision angered Maj. Gen. Thomas Flournoy, commander of the Seventh Military District, because the Creek War lay partly in his district. His resentment almost led him to withhold forces marching against the Creeks from the Mississippi Territory, but Mississippi Volunteer brigadier general Ferdinand L. Claiborne persuaded Flournoy to let the expedition proceed.

Claiborne planned to march his army to the confluence of the Coosa and Tallapoosa Rivers. There he hoped to join the East Tennessee Militia under Maj. Gen. John Cocke, the West Tennessee Militia under Maj. Gen. Andrew Jackson, and the Georgia Militia under Maj. Gen. John Floyd. Regular forces from both the Sixth and Seventh Districts were to coordinate efforts with these militia initiatives.

Mississippi forces began the campaign when Claiborne led part of his force out of St. Stephens in the second week of October. He made little progress, however, before General Flournoy, angry over the command controversy, withdrew a large part of the army. When Flournoy partly relented, Claiborne set out again in mid-November with about 1,200 men. Moving up the Alabama River with the Creek town of the Holy Ground as his objective, Claiborne erected posts along the way to secure control of the area and prevent a Red Stick retreat to the south.

Because Claiborne's march was slow, Red Sticks knew about his movements. Yet their prophets at the Holy Ground convinced most warriors that white men who crossed an invisible line set by the prophets would die. Because Red Sticks thought few defensive measures necessary, Claiborne's attack on 23 December 1813 only had to contend with a few dozen warriors led by William Weatherford. After putting up a stiff and costly resistance, Weatherford escaped by swimming his horse across the Alabama River. Claiborne moved north to destroy another nearby town and then moved back down the Alabama River to Fort Claiborne. Most of his men's terms of service had expired, and they were mustered out of service, so only regulars remained to garrison the forts and control the area.

Such a circumstance set the tone for much of the Creek War. Problems of communication and supply combined with short militia terms of service to plague every facet of the U.S. campaign against the Red Sticks. The delay of Claiborne's campaign had prevented him from rendezvousing with the Tennessee and Georgia expeditions, but it was not the last time that it would happen. Similar delays and problems prevented other campaigns from achieving any semblance of coordination as well.

Maj. Gen. John Floyd, commanding the Georgia militia, also had planned to meet the other armies at the Coosa and Tallapoosa Rivers. Major General Pinckney instructed Floyd to establish a supply post at the Chattahoochee River and then move toward his objective, establishing forts along the way. Floyd was ready to march his 2,000 men against the Red Sticks in September 1813, except that he could not accumulate enough food to supply a campaign. Not until mid-November did Floyd have enough rations to leave his camp at Fort Hawkins and stage a raid against the Red Sticks. By then, expiring militia terms had reduced his army to fewer than 1,000 men.

Nevertheless, Floyd constructed Fort Mitchell on the Chattahoochee and joined forces with about 400 Allied Creeks under William McIntosh. Floyd then set out for the Red Stick town of Autosse on the Tallapoosa River. His army attacked on the morning of 29 November, but because the settlement was really two towns spread out over a considerable area, Floyd's men were unable to cut off the Red Stick retreat. After destroying the town, Floyd had to retrace his steps to Fort Mitchell. He had run out of food. Much to the dismay of the returning Georgians, so had the fort. Expected supplies had not arrived and would not arrive until the end of December. Floyd's men scrounged off the land, but they could not accumulate enough rations to stage another march into Red Stick country. When food finally arrived, Floyd barely had time to plan another raid before the enlistments of his men expired on 22 February 1814. He left Fort Mitchell in mid-January, stopping briefly about 40 miles west to build a small fortification he dubbed Fort Hull. He then proceeded to Calabee Creek to

establish a strong base for operations in the surrounding area.

In the predawn hours of 27 January 1814, a Red Stick force fell upon Floyd's Calabee camp, catching the sleeping men and even the sentries completely by surprise. Had it not been for two artillery pieces, the entire U.S. army might have been destroyed. Even though Floyd fought off the attack, he suffered 169 casualties and was forced back to Fort Hull and then to Fort Mitchell. Most of his men were then mustered out of service. Regulars and a few hardy militiamen remained in the Creek Nation to garrison the forts erected by Claiborne and Floyd, but it was left to the two armies coming out of Tennessee to mount any further offensive actions against the Red Sticks.

After Gov. Willie Blount called out 3,500 Tennesseans in September 1813, Maj. Gen. Andrew Jackson, commander of the West Tennessee militia, set Huntsville as the rendezvous point for his army. Maj. Gen. John Cocke began preparing his force at Knoxville. Brig. Gen. John Coffee arrived in Huntsville ahead of Jackson to begin preparations for the campaign and encountered the same difficulties plaguing the Mississippi and Georgia militias—no rations and very little immediate prospect of receiving any. Jackson and Coffee also believed that it would be necessary to recruit Cherokees if they were to have a sufficient force to operate against the Red Sticks. Without food, this prospect seemed unlikely as well.

Hoping to solve both problems with one solution, Jackson ordered Coffee to take approximately 600 men to destroy the Red Stick settlements south of Huntsville on the Black Warrior River and bring back the food stored in those towns. While this expedition got underway in mid-October, Jackson marched the rest of the army south to the Tennessee River and built Fort Deposit as a supply base. After Coffee rejoined him, Jackson remained at Fort Deposit only a few days. He left for Ten Islands, where Red Sticks reportedly were congregating.

On 3 November 1813, Jackson sent Coffee ahead to attack the town of Tallushatchee. Coffee surrounded the town and killed every adult male in the town. He captured 84 women and children. Stopping his march near the site of the town, Jackson constructed Fort Strother. He expected General Cocke's army and the supplies brought by that force to join him there, but as he waited Jackson heard that the Allied Creek town of Talladega was under attack and needed assistance. The town was only a day's march, so Jackson left Fort Strother with only a small force and took his army to Talladega.

When Jackson attacked the Red Sticks besieging Talladega on 9 November, he tried to surround them, but the Creeks found an opening and most escaped. Although about one-third of the Red Sticks engaged were killed, Jackson could not seal his victory because of Fort Strother's weakness. He returned there to await General Cocke.

Governor Blount had made it clear that once both armies reached the area of hostilities Jackson would be in overall command. Cocke, however, was reluctant to give up his independent command by joining forces with the West Tennesseans. In fact, while Jackson marched in relief of Talladega, Cocke ordered part of his army to attack the Red Stick settlements at the Hillabee Towns. What Cocke did not know was that the Hillabees had secured from Jackson a grant of peace. Cocke's campaign undid that arrangement and convinced the Hillabees that they should continue the war.

Meanwhile, Jackson was in danger of having to abandon the campaign altogether because of the impending expiration of the terms of enlistment of about half his force. Then Jackson learned that Cocke had decided to join him after all, engendering a fugitive hope that the entire enterprise could be salvaged. When Cocke arrived at Fort Strother on 12 December, Jackson quickly learned otherwise. Virtually all of Cocke's men were due to return home within a few weeks. Jackson sent Cocke back to Tennessee to raise a new force. When everyone departed, Jackson was left at Fort Strother with fewer than 150 men.

By early January, Jackson had about 1,000 volunteers at Fort Strother, but most of them had enlisted for only 60 days. Jackson knew that he would not be able to wait until more men arrived to accomplish anything, so in mid-January he decided to stage a raid south out of Fort Strother. Jackson's foray took place about the same time as General Floyd's second invasion of the Creek Nation, and Jackson hoped that these simultaneous movements would so divide the Red Sticks that they could be defeated piecemeal. The coincidental action was the closest thing to a coordinated movement between the various militia forces during the Creek War.

On 21 January, Jackson camped near a Red Stick position on Emuckfau Creek. Near dawn the next morning Red Sticks attacked his camp. Jackson's men repeatedly drove off the attackers and they eventually withdrew, but Jackson suffered so many casualties that he too had to begin a withdrawal to Fort Strother. On 24 January, his army was crossing Enitachopco Creek when Red Sticks struck the U.S. rear guard. Jackson thought he had prepared the rear elements of his force to wheel and envelop the Indians, but only the center of Jackson's line held. Grapeshot from his 6-pounder prevented the Red Sticks from overrunning the entire army.

Jackson had not done tremendous damage to the Red Sticks with his raid, but his ability to mount any campaign at all convinced Major General Pinckney to place most of the resources for the war against the Creeks in Jackson's hands. At Fort Strother, as Jackson's new Tennessee army trickled in and Pinckney sent him the 39th Infantry Regiment, Jackson began preparations for mounting a decisive campaign against one of the primary Red Stick strongholds—a bend in the Tallapoosa River called Tohopeka (Horseshoe Bend).

Jackson's preparations included instilling rigid discipline in his new militia army. Regulars drilled the men relentlessly. Even officers were arrested if they dared complain or sided with those who did. One teen-aged private who disobeyed orders was tried and executed as an example. Thus shaped, the army began the campaign on 14 March. Moving down the Coosa River by land and boats, Jackson stopped the army only long enough to build a base called Fort Williams before moving out again for the Red Stick stronghold at Tohopeka. Accompanying Jackson's army from Fort Williams was a significant body of Cherokees and Allied Creeks under William McIntosh. These Indian contingents would prove invaluable in preventing the retreat of the Red Sticks from Tohopeka.

Leaving Fort Williams on 24 March, Jackson made directly for the fortified Red Stick position on the Tallapoosa. The Creeks in the bend of the river had built a strong series of breastworks across the entrance to their encampment. Jackson sent his Indian allies and mounted troops to the other side of the river to prevent escape across its shallow waters. He then launched his attack shortly after 10:00 A.M. on 27 March 1814. Some of his Indian allies and mounted troops had crossed the river and fired at the rear of the Red Stick position as Jackson's artillery opened up on the breastworks. After softening up the Red Stick position with artillery and rifle fire for about two hours, the 39th led the attack on the breastworks. After securing the fortifications, Jackson's forces isolated different groups of Red Sticks and killed them piecemeal.

The fighting continued throughout the day into the night. When it ended, approximately 800 Red Sticks lay dead on the field or floating in the river. Approximately 350 women and children were captured along with three warriors. A few women and children were accidentally killed during the battle. No reliable reports counted the number of warriors who managed to escape, but at least several dozen did so. The Red Sticks were not totally destroyed, but the blow delivered by Jackson on 27 March caused many of them to lose heart and flee southward to Florida.

Jackson moved to the confluence of the Coosa and Tallapoosa Rivers, where his men erected Fort Jackson. From there he operated against Red Stick remnants and met with commanders of Mississippi, Georgia, South Carolina, and North Carolina militias and regular forces. In April, Major General Pinckney arrived at Fort Jackson. As militia and regulars patrolled the countryside, they soon realized that any Red Sticks left in the vicinity were in no position to resist further. In fact, most were starving and willing to surrender simply to receive the military rations that were handed out to them. Even William Weatherford rode into Jackson's camp and surrendered. According to some reports, Jackson was so impressed by Weatherford's courage and candor that he allowed him to go home. Whatever Jackson's reasons, he did release Weatherford, who returned to his home and lived out his life as an Alabama planter.

With the Creek War seemingly at an end, Secretary of War John Armstrong instructed Pinckney to negotiate a treaty to compensate the United States for the expense of the war and forever separate Creeks from foreign influence. Not only had Spanish officials supplied Red Sticks, but in the last months of fighting rumors told about the British landing a force on the Gulf Coast of Florida to cooperate with the Red Sticks. Requiring a land cession from the Creeks that would cut them off from the coast would remedy this potential problem.

Armstrong initially appointed Pinckney and Creek agent Hawkins to conduct the Creek negotiations, but Tennesseans and Georgians viewed both men as too sympathetic to Indians and worked hard for their removal. Ultimately Secretary Armstrong agreed and appointed Jackson to conduct the negotiations. Jackson by then had also been rewarded with a regular commission as a brigadier general, and when William Henry Harrison resigned his commission, Armstrong gave the vacant major generalship to Jackson.

So it was as a major general in the U.S. Army that Andrew Jackson instructed Agent Hawkins to assemble all the Creek leaders he could find at Fort Jackson in early August to sign a treaty. Hawkins could find no Red Sticks—most had fled to Florida. In the early summer of 1814, the British had arrived there, too. And though the British under Maj. Edward Nicholls proved to be too little and too late, the presence of British and Red Sticks in Florida agitated an already nervous southern frontier. After Jackson completed his treaty arrangements at Fort Jackson, he intended to do something about it.

When Jackson met with Creeks in the first week of August, only one Red Stick leader was present. All other Creek leaders had been allied with the United States during the Creek War. Therefore it came as a tremendous surprise when the treaty terms ceded their lands as well as those of the Red Sticks. Jackson's terms, which he explained were nonnegotiable, called for the cession of approximately one-

half of the Creek Nation to the United States, 23 million acres in all. On 9 August, the Creeks ended the Creek War by reluctantly signing or making their marks on the Treaty of Fort Jackson.

Jackson promptly marched to Spanish Pensacola to roust out the British there and prevent its use as a possible base. He then marched to even greater glory at New Orleans. The Creek War was officially over, but it had left scars that would not heal easily. The Red Sticks who had fled to Florida joined forces with their Seminole kinsmen to resist U.S. expansion into the territory ceded by the Fort Jackson Treaty. Their hostility to the United States would fester over the next few years, eventually prompting another war with Andrew Jackson—the First Seminole War.

—*Jeanne T. Heidler and David S. Heidler*

See also: Autosse, Battle of; Big Warrior; Burnt Corn, Battle of; Calabee, Battle of; Claiborne, Ferdinand L.; Cocke, John; Emuckfau Creek, Battle of; Enitachopco Creek, Battle of; Flournoy, [John] Thomas; Floyd, John; Fort Jackson, Treaty of; Georgia; Hawkins, Benjamin; Hillabee Massacre, Creek Territory; Horseshoe Bend, Battle of; Jackson, Andrew; McIntosh, William; McQueen, Peter; Mims, Attack on Fort; Pinckney, Thomas; Red Sticks; Talladega, Battle of; Tallushatchee, Battle of; Tecumseh; Weatherford, William

Further Reading
Heidler, David S., and Jeanne T. Heidler. *Old Hickory's War: Andrew Jackson and the Quest for Empire.* Mechanicsburg, PA: Stackpole Books, 1996.
Owsley, Frank L., Jr. *Struggle for the Gulf Borderlands: The Creek War and the Battle of New Orleans, 1812–1815.* Gainesville: University Presses of Florida, 1981.

CRITTENDEN, JOHN JORDAN
1787–1863
U.S. statesman

The son of John and Judith (Harris) Crittenden, John J. Crittenden was born near Versailles, Kentucky, on 10 September 1786. He began the practice of law after completing a sound education at William and Mary College in 1807. He soon moved to Russellville in Logan County, where the legal field was less crowded. In 1810 he became an aide to Gov. Ninian Edwards and the attorney general for the Illinois Territory. Crittenden returned to Logan County in 1811 and in May married Sarah Lee. After her death he married Mrs. Maria K. Todd in 1826,

John Jordan Crittenden

and after her death, Mrs. Elizabeth Ashby in 1853. Crittenden was the father of nine children. Elected to the state House of Representatives in 1811 as a Jeffersonian Republican, he was reelected for six consecutive terms.

Like many westerners, Crittenden became convinced that only war could stop British encouragement of Indian agitation in the Northwest. In 1812, he not only supported the declaration of war, he accompanied Gen. Samuel Hopkins as an aide when Hopkins led 2,000 mounted volunteers against Indians in the Illinois Territory. The expedition accomplished little other than burning a few deserted villages, but it seemed a good start. When Crittenden returned to Congress, he labored to insure Kentucky's active participation in the war.

In 1813, Gov. Isaac Shelby mustered volunteers for another force that he would lead in person, and Crittenden joined another expedition as the commander's aide. This campaign culminated in the British defeat at the Battle of the Thames. For his part, Crittenden performed staff duties expeditiously, and both Shelby and Gen. William Henry Harrison praised his efforts. Of course, Crittenden's postwar political career benefited from this military service.

Indeed, Crittenden went on to hold a staggering number of state and national public offices. During his career, he was a state legislator, U.S. senator, U.S. district attorney, Kentucky secretary of state, U.S. attorney general, governor, and U.S. congressman. Through it all, he remained a devout nationalist. Crittenden's famous compromise plan failed to avert secession and the Civil War in 1861. His

family reflected the nation's division: One son became a Union major general, the other a Confederate. John J. Crittenden died in Frankfort on 26 July 1863.

—*Lowell H. Harrison*

See also: Edwards, Ninian; Hopkins, Samuel; Shelby, Isaac
Further Reading
Coleman, Ann Mary Crittenden. *The Life of John J. Crittenden.* 2 vols. Philadelphia: J. B. Lippincott, 1871.
Kirwan, Albert D. *John J. Crittenden: The Struggle for the Union.* Lexington: University of Kentucky Press, 1962.

CROCKETT, DAVID "DAVY"
1786–1836
Congressman; folk hero

Davy Crockett was born on 17 August 1786 in eastern Tennessee to pioneering parents of modest means. The family had settled on the Nolichucky River in the Cherokee country. While growing up, Crockett often left home on adventures; he thus received little formal education. He mostly worked as a cattle driver during his long absences from home. After his roamings, he returned to eastern Tennessee and married Polly Findley in 1806. He moved his wife and two sons to middle Tennessee in 1811.

His first home away from the mountains was near Fayetteville in Lincoln County, near the line with Mississippi Territory. Here, he proved a poor farmer but skilled hunter. His wife died in 1813, prompting Crockett to move 80 miles west to modern Giles County. Here he received appointment as a justice of the peace.

In 1813, at age 27, Crockett left his home to participate in Andrew Jackson's war against the Red Stick faction of the Creek Nation. As a scout in Gibson's Tennessee militia, Crockett was on hand for the rout of Creek warriors at the Battle of Tallushatchee on 2 November 1813 but took no active part in the battle. His term of enlistment expired shortly thereafter, and he returned home. Later, he claimed that he had helped lead the militia mutiny against General Jackson at Fort Strother. Crockett reenlisted for a second term in the late summer of 1814, joining Jackson's army at Pensacola before returning home for a final time that December. Overall, his military service in the War of 1812 was mostly composed of guarding horse herds or scouting and foraging expeditions.

After the war, Crockett turned his somewhat exaggerated claims of service against the Red Sticks to political advantage and won election to the Tennessee legislature in 1821. Crockett moved to modern Dyer County near the Mississippi River and represented this district in the statehouse starting in 1823. In 1827 and 1829, Crockett won seats in the U.S. Congress as a Democrat; there he became a champion of settlers' (or squatters') rights. Crockett was among the emerging anti-Jackson faction that would ultimately become the Whig Party but felt the political consequences in his defeat in 1831. With the help of his Whig allies, Crockett returned to Congress in 1833, but he suffered defeat again in 1835.

Increasingly disgusted by his political misfortunes, Crockett is reported to have said "You can all go to Hell and I'm going to Texas" at his campaign concession speech. In November 1835, the defeated politician left his native Tennessee to seek his fortune in Texas, then in the midst of a revolution against Mexico. Crockett, leading some 27 Tennessee volunteers, reinforced the garrison at the Alamo. On 6 March 1836, Crockett and a handful of other defenders were reported to have been taken alive by the assaulting Mexican soldiers who overran the fortress. Staff officers, on orders of Mexican general Antonio Lopez de Santa Anna, summarily executed Crockett and the other prisoners, who had managed to outlive the rest of the slain garrison by just a few minutes.

—*Donald S. Frazier*

See also: Creek War; Jackson, Andrew
Further Reading
Shackford, James A. *David Crockett: The Man and the Legend.* Chapel Hill: University of North Carolina Press, 1956.

CROGHAN, GEORGE
1791–1849
U.S. officer

Born to William Croghan and Lucy Clark Croghan (sister of George Rogers Clark and William Clark) in Louisville, Kentucky, George Croghan graduated from William and Mary College just in time to join William Henry Harrison as an aide in the campaign that resulted in the Battle of Tippecanoe. At the beginning of the War of 1812, Harrison's patronage secured the 21-year-old Croghan a commission as a captain in the regular army.

The first year of the war saw him serving at Fort Defiance and then at Fort Meigs in Ohio. Croghan distinguished himself sufficiently to earn a promotion to major

before he turned 22. In the summer of 1813, Harrison gave Croghan command of Fort Stephenson on the Lower Sandusky River in Ohio. With a garrison of approximately 160 regulars, Croghan assumed command at a perilous time in western Ohio. Gen. Henry Procter's British army, Canadian militia, and about 2,000 Indians under Tecumseh had been trying since the spring to gain a foothold on the southern side of Lake Erie.

In late July, after failing to reduce Fort Meigs, Procter and his Indian allies made their way to Fort Stephenson. Major General Harrison, in command of the U.S. army in the Northwest, had anticipated that Procter might turn to the small, undermanned Fort Stephenson. He sent word to Croghan that if Procter had artillery, Croghan was to evacuate the fort, burn it, and march to safety. Meanwhile, Harrison made his way with about 800 men to the makeshift Fort Seneca, some 10 miles removed from Fort Stephenson. He then sent more emphatic orders to Croghan to abandon the fort. By then Croghan's scouts had spotted Tecumseh's Indians closing around the fort, and the young commander feared that if he tried to march his men out, they would fall to ambush. He sent word to Harrison that he intended to hold the fort.

Harrison exploded over Croghan's disobedience. He sent word to Fort Stephenson relieving Croghan of command. According to some accounts, when Croghan received these orders, he made his way to Fort Seneca to plead his case before his old mentor, Harrison. Harrison reportedly was so impressed with Croghan's zeal that he restored the young man to his command and gave him permission to try to hold his position.

Procter arrived outside Fort Stephenson on 31 July. He planned to attack it with approximately 400 regulars and an equal number of Indians. Tecumseh was to use the remainder of his Indians to prevent U.S. reinforcements from reaching Croghan. For his part, Croghan also had a plan. Clearly outnumbered and outgunned, he examined his fortifications for their weakest point and made arrangements that anticipated Procter's attack there. Croghan placed his one artillery piece, a 6-pounder nicknamed "Old Betsy," at the weak point, but he covered the gun so the attackers would not see it until they were in range.

On the morning of 1 August, Procter demanded Croghan's surrender. In what had become a standard ploy, Procter mused that once the attack began, he would be unable to restrain his Indian allies from inflicting terrible atrocities on Croghan's men. Croghan stated brusquely that he had no intention of surrendering, so Procter opened up with his artillery. At 5:00 P.M., he launched his main attack on the fort.

Croghan had prepared for Procter's salient precisely.

George Croghan

When the British attack came within range, the Americans uncovered "Old Betsy" and let loose with grapeshot. The British line staggered, and the Indians recoiled. The British regulars then reformed and charged again. "Old Betsy" shattered their line again. By now, more than 100 British soldiers lay dead or wounded, and the rest withdrew. Procter suggested that the Indians, whose number was approximately 2,000, stage the next assault. Surveying the havoc occasioned by "Old Betsy," they declined. So far Croghan had only lost one man. He expected a night attack, though one never materialized. Instead, during the night Procter withdrew. He never invaded the United States again.

George Croghan immediately became a national hero for a country bereft of them. Harrison, in contrast, had heard the sounds of the attack on Fort Stephenson 10 miles away, and had never left Fort Seneca—a bit of caution that generated considerable criticism. Harrison would redeem himself, however, at the Battle of the Thames less than three months later.

Brevetted a lieutenant colonel for his actions at Fort Stephenson, Croghan would never live up to the potential displayed there. When in the following year he was given command of the U.S. attempt to take Fort Michilimackinac on Mackinac Island, he proved surprisingly inept at offensive warfare. In the expedition he commanded approximately 700 men, about half regulars and half militia. After leaving Detroit on 3 July aboard three brigs with two gunboat escorts, the Americans spent two weeks fruitlessly searching for British supply bases. Arriving at Mackinac on 26 July, the ships could not find a place to anchor without coming within range of the fort's artillery. To make matters worse, the ship's guns could not be sighted to reach the fort. Frustrated by the situation, Croghan loaded his men in boats on 4 August and landed on the north side of the island.

The time taken for this maneuver allowed Fort Michilimackinac's commander, Col. Robert McDouall, to arrange his defenses. Leaving only a small garrison in the fort, McDouall moved approximately 150 men to breastworks on its outer approaches. Anchored by dense forest on both sides and covered by two artillery pieces, McDouall's line was further protected by his 350 Indian allies in the trees on either side. Moving uphill from the north shore of the island, Croghan tried to avoid McDouall's strong position in the center by sending most of his men into the trees to attack its flanks.

The result was chaos. While Croghan's right flanking column was being ambushed by Indians, the left became lost in the forest. Meanwhile, McDouall had all but abandoned the center of his line because of a false report that more Americans were landing in his rear. Because of U.S. blunders, he returned before Croghan knew he was gone. Realizing the hopelessness of the attack, Croghan called it off and returned to his boats.

Following the war, Croghan's life and career continued their downward spiral. Never able to recapture the glory of his stand at Fort Stephenson, he nevertheless continued in the military, serving adequately as the army's inspector general. He accompanied Gen. Zachary Taylor's invasion of northern Mexico in the opening stages of the Mexican-American War. In 1849, Croghan died, a victim of the cholera outbreak within the army at New Orleans.

—*Jeanne T. Heidler and David S. Heidler*

See also: Harrison, William Henry; McDouall, Robert; Michilimackinac, Fort; Procter, Henry; Stephenson, Fort; Tecumseh; Tippecanoe, Battle of

Further Reading

Bowlus, Bruce. "A 'Signal Victory': The Battle for Fort Stephenson, August 1–2, 1813." *Northwest Ohio Quarterly* 63 (1991): 43–57.

Gilpin, Alec R. *The War of 1812 in the Old Northwest.* East Lansing: Michigan State University Press, 1958.

State Archeological and Historical Society of Ohio. *93rd Anniversary of the Battle of Fort Stephenson; Reinterment of Remains of Major Geo. Croghan, Beneath the Monument Erected in His Honor on Fort Stephenson, Fremont, Ohio. Thursday August 2, 1906.* Columbus: Ohio State Archeological and Historical Society, 1907.

CROKER, JOHN WILSON
1780–1857
British politician;
journalist and literary essayist

John Croker was born in Ireland, the son of a senior customs official. He was educated at Trinity College, Dublin, and trained in London for the law at Lincoln's Inn. After beginning a successful legal career, he entered Parliament in 1807 as a Tory. He quickly made close political connections with the leading figures in his party: George Canning, Lord Castlereagh, Robert Peel, and, among the Irish contingent of his circle, the rising star Sir Arthur Wellesley, later to be the duke of Wellington. Croker made himself useful as a clever speaker with a sharp tongue. With slashing partisanship he defended the government against discrediting scandal—the commander in chief's mistress was selling army officers commissions—and excused its poor military record against Napoleon. In October 1809, he was rewarded with a post in the newly formed Perceval government as secretary to the Admiralty, a position he held over the following 22 years.

In May 1812, when Perceval was assassinated, the new prime minister, Lord Liverpool, asked Croker to stay on in his rather shaky administration. Croker, although not a policy maker, became one of the leading politicians responsible for defending the navy and the government during the War of 1812. This he did with great vigor in the House of Commons and with his prolific journalism. His earlier pamphlet, "A Key to the Orders in Council," made use of his polemical talents to explain British trade regulations in the economic war against Napoleon. It also made the factual case for government policies that caused friction with the United States.

Croker incautiously stated at the outset of the fighting in 1812 that the Americans would be taught a lesson. With Britain's military efforts concentrated on the defeat of Napoleon rather than the war with the United States, unexpected British naval reverses embarrassed Croker's boast. In Parliament, fierce Whig attacks criticized the government for its record of defeat and for the success of U.S. privateering raids on British commerce. Radical member of Parliament Samuel Whitbread continuously raised questions about official corruption in the navy. Croker bore the brunt of this criticism. Writing under the pseudonym Nereus, he defended the government in his "Letter on the Subject of the Naval War with America" (1813). In Parliament, his well-practiced defense was politically effective. His harsh partisanship earned him condemnation at the time and subsequently from Whig and Tory alike. The historian Thomas Macaulay thought Croker "a bad man," and Benjamin Disraeli lampooned Croker in his novel *Coningsby*.

Disgusted by the movement toward democracy, Croker retired from Parliament after passage of the first Reform Bill (1831–1832). He remained active in partisan politics to the end of his long life, however, as a contributor to the *Quarterly Review*.

—*S. J. Stearns*

See also: Canning, George; Castlereagh, Viscount, Robert Stewart

Further Reading

Brightfield, M. F. *John Wilson Croker*. Berkeley and Los Angeles: University of California Press, 1940.

Jennings, Louis J., ed. *The Croker Papers: The Correspondence and Diaries of the Rt. Honorable John Wilson Croker, Secretary to the Admiralty from 1809 to 1831*. 3 vols. London: John Murray, 1884.

D

DACRES, JAMES RICHARD
1788–1853
British naval officer

Born to Vice Adm. James Richard Dacres, the younger Dacres entered the navy at the age of eight aboard his father's ship, HMS *Sceptre*. Showing a keen aptitude for the sea, Dacres gained command of his own sloop, HMS *Elk,* at the age of 17 and of the HMS *Bacchante* in 1806; he was given command of the frigate *Guerrière* in March 1811. The *Guerrière* was a French vessel captured in 1806.

Before the advent of hostilities between the United States and Great Britain, Dacres patrolled the Atlantic coastline of the United States and was reported to be especially vigilant about reclaiming British deserters from U.S. merchant vessels. His alleged seizure of a deserter off a merchantman out of New York City in April 1811 was reputed to be one of the causes for the confrontation between HMS *Little Belt* and USS *President*.

After the declaration of war, Dacres continued to operate off the U.S. coastline, and it was approximately 600 miles off Boston that he and his crew encountered Isaac Hull and USS *Constitution* on 19 August 1812. Dacres had reputedly issued a challenge to all U.S. frigates that he was ready to do battle, and according to some reports he was contemptuous of U.S. seamanship. He apparently changed his mind on the 19th.

After what amounted to a slugfest, with *Constitution* having the advantage in maneuverability and firepower, Dacres was forced to surrender his sinking ship. During the engagement Dacres suffered a wound from U.S. sharpshooters firing from the *Constitution*'s rigging, but he recovered before his exchange could be arranged. A court-martial in Halifax later cleared Dacres of any blame in losing the ship.

Though such a surrender often cut short promising careers, Dacres was given command of HMS *Tiber* in 1814, and before the end of his career he achieved the rank of vice admiral.

—*Jeanne T. Heidler and David S. Heidler*

See also: Constitution versus *Guerrière;* Hull, Isaac
Further Reading
Fowler, William M., Jr. *Jack Tars & Commodores.* Boston: Houghton Mifflin, 1984.
Martin, Tyrone G. "Isaac Hull's Victory Revisited." *American Neptune* 47 (Winter 1987): 14–21.

DALE, SAMUEL
1772–1841
Pioneer; soldier; statesman

Known as the "Daniel Boone of Alabama," Samuel Dale spent much of his life on the frontier. He was born in Rockbridge County, Virginia, but grew up in Glade Hollow along the Clinch River in Washington County. In 1783, his family moved to Greene County, Georgia. Both parents died in 1792, leaving him responsible for his seven younger siblings.

The following year he became a scout in a company raised by Capt. Jonas Fauche. After entering federal service, the company took up quarters on the Oconee River at Fort Mathews. In 1794, Dale distinguished himself in several engagements with the Muscogees along the Chattahoochee River. He commanded Fort Republic on the Apalachee River in Georgia until his unit was disbanded in 1796. Over the next ten years he traded among the Creeks and Cherokees, established a trading post in what became Jones County, Georgia, and served as a guide for immigrants going to the Mississippi Territory. Around 1810, he moved to Clarke County in what would become Alabama.

Dale played a prominent role in the Creek War. On one of his trading excursions in October 1811, he was present at Tuckabatchee when Tecumseh appealed to the Creek

Indians for support against the Americans. Dale advised Indian agent Col. Benjamin Hawkins of the danger, but Hawkins failed to heed the warning. When hostilities began in 1813, Captain Dale joined the militia under Col. James Caller. He achieved a measure of fame on 12 January 1813, at the so-called Canoe Fight, which took place at the mouth of Randon's Creek in Monroe County, Alabama. There he and two associates paddled a canoe out to engage another canoe filled with Indian warriors. In the bloody hand-to-hand combat that ensued, Dale and his friends overcame and killed their nine adversaries. He was not as successful at the Battle of Burnt Corn (1813), where he suffered a wound when Red Stick Creeks defeated the Americans. He also took part in Gen. Ferdinand L. Claiborne's Econochaca campaign and in Colonel Russell's Cahaba old towns expedition. In 1814 Dale became one of Andrew Jackson's couriers during the Battle of New Orleans and subsequently served again with Jackson during his Seminole campaign.

Dale was active in early Alabama and Mississippi politics. He was a delegate to the Alabama constitutional convention, served in the state assembly from 1817 to 1829, became a general in the Alabama militia, and had a county named after him. In the spring of 1818, during the administration of Gov. W. W. Bibb, Dale helped pacify the Indians who opposed the Fort Jackson Treaty. He erected Fort Dale at Poplar Spring and helped finish Fort Bibb. In 1831 he took charge of moving the Choctaw Indians to the trans-Mississippi west. However, an injury prevented him from completing this mission. He stayed in Lauderdale County, Mississippi, and became its first representative to the state legislature. He died in Daleville, Mississippi, on 23 May 1841.

—*Charles H. McArver, Jr.*

See also: Creek War; Hawkins, Benjamin
Further Reading
Brewer, Willis. *Alabama, Her History, Resources, War Record, and Public Men from 1540 to 1872.* N.p., 1872. Reprint, Spartanburg, SC: The Reprint Company, Publishers, 1975.

Pickett, Albert James. *History of Alabama ... Annals of Alabama, 1819–1900 by Thomas McAdory Owen.* Birmingham, AL: The Webb Book Company, Publishers, 1900.

Tucker, Glenn. *Poltroons and Patriots.* 2 vols. New York: Bobbs-Merrill, 1954.

DALLAS, ALEXANDER
1759–1817
U.S. secretary of the treasury

Alexander Dallas was born in Jamaica to Robert Dallas and Sarah Cormack Hewett Dallas. His parents returned to their home in Great Britain, where Alexander grew to manhood. After reading law, young Alexander moved first to Jamaica and then in 1783 to the United States, establishing residence in Philadelphia to practice law. By the early 1790s, Dallas had become involved in Pennsylvania politics. He supported Thomas Jefferson, and in 1801 the new president appointed Dallas U.S. district attorney for the Eastern District of Pennsylvania.

Albert Gallatin left the Treasury Department during the War of 1812, and James Madison wanted to appoint Dallas, his staunch supporter and Gallatin's friend, to the position of secretary. Dallas, however, had made political enemies in Pennsylvania, particularly among the more radical Democrats, and they refused to support his appointment. Secretary of War John Armstrong also counted himself among the Pennsylvanian's enemies, thus promising to make cabinet service disagreeable for Dallas. George W. Campbell became Gallatin's successor, but in September 1814 poor health forced his resignation. By then, Armstrong had also left the cabinet, so Madison appointed Dallas to the treasury post.

The new secretary of the treasury believed that dire times called for desperate action. His treasury empty, Dallas could not even cover the interest on the country's enormous debt. He immediately prepared comprehensive reports for Congress that detailed measures necessary to save the country from bankruptcy. One of his most important recommendations called for increasing internal taxes. He also urged the creation of a second national bank to stabilize the currency. Meanwhile, Dallas temporarily suspended interest payments on the current debt. Although the creation of a new national bank would have to wait two more years, Congress realized the immediate gravity of the situation and agreed to the large tax increase and currency inflation.

Because President Madison had refused to see the Hartford Convention's emissaries, it fell to Dallas and Secretary of State James Monroe to receive them. Dallas was noncommittal but courteous to his visitors. By then, the political crisis of the war had passed with news of the Treaty of Ghent. The financial consequences of the conflict, however, remained to be calculated. Dallas's tough approach to

Alexander Dallas

meeting those consequences helped avert economic calamity and put the nation on a good footing to establish a strong postwar economy.

Alexander Dallas died in 1817, less than two years after the war.

—*Jeanne T. Heidler and David S. Heidler*

See also: Armstrong, John; Gallatin, Albert; Hartford Convention
Further Reading
Dallas, Alexander James. *Life and Writings of Alexander James Dallas.* Philadelphia: J. B. Lippincott, 1871.
Walters, James Raymond, Jr. *Alexander James Dallas: Lawyer, Politician, Financier, 1759–1817.* New York: Da Capo Press, 1969.

DANE, NATHAN
1752–1835
Massachusetts Federalist

Son of Daniel Dane and Abigail Burnham Dane, Nathan Dane was born in Ipswich, Massachusetts. After graduating from Harvard College in 1778, he stud-

ied law and began practicing in 1782 in Beverly, Massachusetts. In the same year, he became involved in state politics as a representative to the state legislature. He gained a statewide reputation and began serving in Congress under the Articles of Confederation in 1785. In 1787, he was responsible for including the clause prohibiting slavery in the Northwest Ordinance.

In the Massachusetts ratification debate over the Constitution, Dane opposed the document. After it went into effect, he returned to his private legal practice. He remained active in state politics and legal matters, but he never returned to national politics except to serve as a presidential elector in 1812.

Though a staunch Federalist, and hence a strong opponent of the war with Great Britain, Dane was considered a moderate in a state known for its radical opposition to the war. When the Hartford Convention was called in the fall of 1814 to ventilate New England opposition, Dane agreed to be a member of the Massachusetts delegation, in spite of a growing deafness that had compelled his increasing withdrawal from public life. He later explained that he had attended the convention to prevent any radical action, and he was considered a voice of reason throughout the convention.

Following the war, Dane's deafness forced his complete retirement from public life. He thus had time to complete several legal texts he had been working on for years. He died in Beverly in 1835.

—*Jeanne T. Heidler and David S. Heidler*

See also: Federalist Party; Hartford Convention
Further Reading
Johnson, Andrew J. "The Life and Constitutional Thought of Nathan Dane." Ph.D. diss., Indiana University, 1964.

DARTMOOR PRISON

Thousands of U.S. prisoners of war wallowed in this dank, foreboding jail in southwest England. Dartmoor Prison's conditions were abysmal, but they were not a product of deliberate malice as much as they were the result of administrative shortcomings and inadequate resources. An ineffectual U.S. foreign service did little to ameliorate the situation.

Apparently Dartmoor officials exerted considerable pressure on U.S. prisoners to enlist in the British navy. Dartmoor held more than 5,000 men when the Treaty of

Ghent ended the war, but only some 75 Americans had enlisted in the British service to escape the dismal conditions. Meanwhile, U.S. agent Reuben G. Beasley had done little to protect the U.S. prisoners at Dartmoor. A prison culture of self-help and survival naturally developed.

When the first U.S. prisoners of war arrived in 1813, there were about 8,000 French captives from the Napoleonic wars behind Dartmoor's dank walls. The prison was by then four years old and had never been anything but cold, damp, dark, and unhealthy. Notorious as a "depot of living death," Dartmoor was as ugly to captor as it was to captive. British guards, for instance, were cycled through the prison every two to three months as a form of punishment duty.

The prison part of the complex consisted of seven barracks, each able to hold 1,500 men. About 1,000 "coloured people" were segregated as inmates. Some interracial association occurred, but it was always informal and usually secretive. For example, the black barracks, Number 4, was the "center of religious activity" in the prison. One chronicler found at least two whites attending the Methodist sermons in Number 4.

Upon entering Dartmoor Prison, an inmate would receive a hammock, a blanket, a horse rug, a bed, a yellow jacket, a pair of trousers, a waistcoat, a pair of wooden shoes, and a cap. Prisoners also had a small cash allowance for purchases from local market vendors allowed access to the prison. Oddly enough, the diet has been described by one historian as more nutritious than that of contemporary Americans.

On 31 December 1814, a week after the treaty signing at Ghent, agent Beasley visited his countrymen at Dartmoor for the first and last time. He brought them extra clothing but little else. Because Beasley did not have a plan for prisoner transportation, Americans at Dartmoor not only languished there after the peace, but the British continued adding to prisoner ranks well into March 1815. Not until that month did the British officially inform prisoners about the peace, now three months old. It is likely that rumors had preceded the formal announcement, but now enraged U.S. inmates burned Beasley in effigy, and tensions mounted toward a confrontation with guards.

The result was the Dartmoor Massacre of 6 April 1815. Prison commandant Capt. T. G. Shortland had unwisely reduced rations. On 4 April, prisoners' complaints grew vehement as they demanded bread rather than hard biscuits, but Shortland rebuffed them. Two days later, prisoners had become sullenly insubordinate, and when a few stepped outside the limits of their courtyard, jittery guards fired on them. Seven prisoners died, and 31 were wounded. One American described the incident as "butch-

ery, barbarity and inveteracy." Prisoner Charles Andrews said it was "murderous" and labeled its perpetrators "bloody butchers" who acted with "cool and deliberate malice." Lord Castlereagh, the British foreign secretary, called it an "unfortunate incident." A British investigation eventually exonerated the guards under a ruling of justifiable homicide, but Castlereagh offered his regrets and British compensation to the families of the dead prisoners.

—Stephen Piscitelli

Further Reading

Andrews, Charles. *The Prisoners' Memoirs or Dartmoor Prison.* New York: Self-published, 1815.

Horrid Massacre at Dartmoor Prison. Boston: Nathaniel Conerly, 1815.

Horsman, Reginald. "The Paradox of Dartmoor Prison." *American Heritage*, 26, no. 2 (February 1975): 13–17

Melish, John. *A Description of Dartmoor Prison, with an Account of the Massacre of the Prison.* Philadelphia: Self-published, 1815.

DE ROTTENBURG, BARON FRANCIS
1757–1832
British officer

Born in Poland and of partly Swiss extraction, Baron Francis de Rottenburg served in the French army during the French Revolution and then received a commission in the British army during the Napoleonic wars. He was sent to Canada in 1810 as a brigadier general and was promoted the following year to major general.

Before the outbreak of the War of 1812 and during the first year of that conflict, de Rottenburg commanded British forces in Lower Canada and was headquartered in Montreal. Immediately after the declaration of war, de Rottenburg began preparing Montreal's defenses, expecting that city to be one of the first U.S. targets. He continued his preparations into the fall of 1812 but found it increasingly difficult to persuade farmers in Lower Canada to sell their produce to the army. As a result, he issued a proclamation, stopping just short of declaring martial law in the province but making it mandatory for farmers to sell to the army. For this action, de Rottenburg was later censured by the legislature of Lower Canada.

Fortunately for de Rottenburg, during his tenure as commander in Lower Canada, he never had to defend against a major invasion by the United States. In June 1813, however, thanks to the attack on and destruction of York, Upper Canada, while it was under the command of Maj. Gen. Roger H. Sheaffe, de Rottenburg was transferred to a more active theater. De Rottenburg became the commander in Upper Canada and was replaced in Lower Canada by Lieut. Gen. Sir Gordon Drummond.

De Rottenburg took command in Upper Canada with the knowledge that the governor general of Canada, Sir George Prevost, viewed that theater as expendable as long as Montreal and Quebec remained safe. This knowledge almost immediately put de Rottenburg at odds with Brig. Gen. Henry Procter, operating in concert with Tecumseh's Indian confederacy in the Northwest. As Procter failed to dislodge the various positions occupied by Americans under William Henry Harrison in that theater, and Oliver Hazard Perry prepared to launch his squadron on Lake Erie, de Rottenburg was under constant pressure almost from the beginning of his command in Upper Canada to supply more troops to western Upper Canada. Although Prevost had authorized de Rottenburg to release some units to aid Procter, de Rottenburg felt constrained by Prevost's views and therefore did not supply Procter with the men he requested.

Following the U.S. victory on Lake Erie and Procter's subsequent retreat eastward, the misunderstandings between the two officers increased. Procter hoped that de Rottenburg would bring an army west to meet him so that they could together repulse Harrison's offensive. Not only did de Rottenburg have no intention of joining with Procter, he at first sent orders to Procter not to retreat east at all. He then changed his orders to instruct Procter that if he must retreat, to do so slowly and to do nothing to alienate his Indian allies. In the end, even though Procter escaped the debacle at the Battle of the Thames, he later blamed his superiors, including de Rottenburg, for his disastrous campaign.

In December 1813, de Rottenburg was again transferred to Lower Canada, where Gov. Gen. Prevost intended to take personal command of an invasion of the United States. In the upcoming campaign into Lake Champlain, de Rottenburg, who even though present throughout the war thus far had had very little combat experience in it, was appointed to serve as Prevost's second in command. Like his superior, however, he took very little part in the Battle of Plattsburg.

Following the war, de Rottenburg returned to England, where he continued in the army, rising to the rank of lieutenant general. He died in Portsmouth.

—*Jeanne T. Heidler and David S. Heidler*

See also: Drummond, Gordon; Montreal; Plattsburg, Battle of; Prevost, George; Procter, Henry; Sheaffe, Roger Hale; Tecumseh; Thames, Battle of the; York, Battle of

Further Reading

Everest, Allan S. *British Objectives at the Battle of Plattsburg*. Champlain, NY: Moorsfield Press, 1960.

Lauriston, Victor. "The Case for General Procter." *Kent Historical Society Papers* 7 (1951): 7–17.

DE SALABERRY, CHARLES-MICHEL D'IRUMBERRY

See Salaberry, Charles-Michel d'Irumberry de

DEARBORN, FORT

At the commencement of the War of 1812, Fort Dearborn on the bank of the Chicago River was garrisoned by a company of troops, 54 regulars and 12 militia, under Capt. Nathan Heald. Nine women and 18 children were also in the fort. It had two block houses and a stockade but was more a trading post than a military stronghold, supplied by merchant schooners from Buffalo through Lakes Huron and Michigan.

When Michilimackinac fell on 25 July 1812, Brig. Gen. William Hull, at Detroit to attack Amherstburg and Fort Malden, ordered Heald to evacuate Fort Dearborn. Heald emptied the fort's liquor into the river, destroyed the surplus arms and ammunition, and pulled out on 15 August 1812. Four hundred hostile Potawatomi and Winnebago Indians, aware of the British victory at Michilimackinac, attacked the column. Twenty-six regulars, all the militia, two women and 12 children were killed. The survivors fell under the protection of the Potawatomi chief, Blackbird. Some escaped and some were ransomed by British officers. Fort Dearborn was burned.

The massacre, the capitulations at Michilimackinac and Detroit (17 August—two days after the massacre), and Stephen Van Rensselaer's defeat at Queenston on 13 October persuaded the Upper Mississippi and Missouri Indians to join the Shawnee chieftains Tecumseh and the Prophet and consequently the British war effort. Fort Wayne, on the Maumee, remained as the sole U.S. military post in the old Northwest. The combined military disasters led Pres. James Madison to remove his secretary of war, William Eustis.

—*Frederick C. Drake*

See also: Chicago Massacre
Further Reading
Barnhart, John D. "A New Letter about the Massacre at Fort Dearborn." *Indiana Magazine of History* 41 (1945): 187–199.
Bateman, Newton. "The Story of Fort Dearborn." In *Historical Encyclopedia of Illinois.* 2 vols., vol. 2, pp. 630–636. Chicago: Munsell Publishing, 1905.
Burton, Charles M. "The Fort Dearborn Massacre." *Magazine of American History* 18 (1912): 74–85.
"Chicago Massacre." In *Free Trade and Sailors' Rights: A Bibliography of the War of 1812.* Comp. John C. Fredriksen. Westport, CT: Greenwood Press, 1985.
Frazier, Arthur H. "The Military Frontier: Fort Dearborn." *Chicago History* 9 (1980): 80–85.
Hamilton, Henry R. "Fort Dearborn Massacre." In *The Epic of Chicago.* Chicago: Willett, Clark, 1932.

Henry Dearborn

DEARBORN, HENRY
1751–1829
Secretary of war, 1801–1809; senior major general, 1812–1813

Born at Hampton, New Hampshire, on 23 February 1751 to Simon and Sarah Dearborn, Henry Dearborn was a fine junior officer and an able secretary of war, but in the War of 1812 he proved to be a poor theater commander. His military career began in 1775. After hearing of the fighting at Lexington, he left his medical practice, formed his own unit, fought at Breed's Hill, and was captured by the British during the assault on Quebec in 1776. Promoted to lieutenant colonel after he was exchanged by the British in 1777, Dearborn served in the Third New Hampshire Regiment and fought with distinction at Ticonderoga and Freeman's Farm. Passing the winter of 1777–1778 at Valley Forge, he then saw action at the Battle of Monmouth and in July 1781 was appointed to Gen. George Washington's staff as the deputy quartermaster general. After Cornwallis's surrender at Yorktown, Dearborn was discharged from the army on 1 March 1783.

Following his discharge, Dearborn helped to form the New Hampshire Society of Cincinnati and in 1785 moved to Maine, where he built a home on the Kennebec River (near the present town of Gardiner). A respected businessman and speculator, he was appointed to the rank of brigadier general and became a major general of militia. Between 1789 and 1798, Dearborn served as a U.S. marshal for the District of Maine, as a district representative to

the state congress, and finally, in 1798, as a member of the state House of Representatives. When Jefferson won the presidency, the president-elect offered Dearborn the post of secretary of war, and for a short period he served as the secretary of the navy.

At the War Department, Dearborn furthered Jefferson's desire to bring about a "chaste reformation" of the army. This entailed developing a program for national security while protecting republican government from autocratic Federalists. The Military Peace Establishment Act of 1802 became central to the task of "Republicanizing" the army. It provided for army staff reorganization, strength reduction, and restructuring. Dearborn purged outspoken Federalists from the regular army's officer corps and set up new military and civil positions for faithful Republicans. By 1806, Dearborn's actions and the death, discharge, or resignation of other Federalist army officers meant that more than half of the officer corps had been appointed by Jefferson. Moreover, the 1802 act created the U.S. Military Academy to educate future republican military leaders in republican principles as well as the fundamentals of reading, writing, geography, history, and mathematics. Even the dress standards of the army changed to reflect the "Republican" look—fashionable shoe-buckles were eliminated, and short hair and common trousers became the style.

As secretary of war, Dearborn also introduced new technology, adding to the army's inventory Whitney muskets, new gun cartridges, and a new light artillery formation. Dearborn also negotiated Indian treaties that ceded millions of acres to the government, separating these Indians from foreign influences and eventually providing starting points from which to explore the new Louisiana Purchase. After the *Chesapeake-Leopard* affair in 1807, Dearborn sought to build up the army, increase arms production, and construct fortifications. Ever the economizer, Dearborn eliminated the position of quartermaster general (as directed by the 1802 act) and divided those duties between himself and three civilian military agents. Under his careful scrutiny, this highly centralized system worked well. It was ironic that as the army's senior major general during the War of 1812, Dearborn saw the same logistical system severely hamper his battlefield effectiveness.

Near the end of his second term, Jefferson granted Dearborn's request for another position and appointed him post collector of customs at Boston. When the War of 1812 broke out, Pres. James Madison offered Dearborn the job of senior major general of the army. Reluctantly he accepted and received command of the northeast theater from the Niagara River to the New England coast. He set up headquarters at Albany and traveled to Boston to supervise recruiting. Dearborn also began organizing New England coastal defenses.

That few New England governors saw the need to call out their militia irritated Dearborn. The states would not supply the manpower necessary for coastal defense. New England indifference and the shortcomings of undermanned, poorly administered ordnance and quartermaster departments also delayed preparations for the invasion of Canada. Meanwhile, news from Halifax that the British had repealed the Orders in Council in June 1812 made a cessation of hostilities seem possible. On 9 August 1812, Dearborn agreed to an armistice with Canada's governor-general, Sir George Prevost.

Dearborn later drew considerable criticism not only for signing the armistice—which Madison immediately terminated, effective 8 September—but for failing to give Gen. William Hull at Detroit timely notice of its existence. The British obtained Hull's plans, countered them, and captured Detroit.

By the end of 1812, the U.S. Army had suffered defeat at Queenston on the Niagara River and had only marched to the Canadian border on a fruitless expedition. As the Americans went into winter quarters, Dearborn requested that Madison accept his resignation. He wanted to "retire to the shades of private life, and remain a mere interested spectator." His request was denied.

As Madison began his second term in 1813, he ap-

pointed John B. Armstrong as the new secretary of war, replacing William Eustis, who had resigned in the aftermath of the 1812 fiasco. Armstrong abandoned the idea of capturing Montreal and decided instead to attack Kingston, Ontario, hoping its fall would stop the flow of supplies on the St. Lawrence River. Then the army could head west to capture York (present-day Toronto), Fort George, and finally Montreal.

Kingston's supposedly heavy fortifications, however, made Dearborn reluctant to attack there. He convinced Armstrong that the army should attack York and Fort George first. Dearborn won both engagements, but he also allowed the British army to escape. In late May, he abandoned the campaign after the British almost captured the U.S. base at Sacket's Harbor. His health failing and with this last campaign marked by delay, indecision, and ineptitude, Dearborn was relieved of command on 6 July 1813. Despite Dearborn's repeated requests for a court of inquiry, Madison did not press the issue.

Upon returning to New York, Dearborn took command of the city's defenses. In a strange and ironical twist, he later presided over the court-martial that condemned Hull for surrendering Detroit, even though many believed Dearborn's actions had abetted the disaster. Following Dearborn's honorable discharge from the Army on 15 June 1815, Madison nominated him for secretary of war. Federalists so stridently questioned Dearborn's military record, however, that Madison withdrew the nomination. In 1822, Pres. James Monroe appointed Dearborn U.S. minister to Portugal. Dearborn retired from government service in 1824 and died on 6 June 1829 at his home in Roxbury, Massachusetts.

—Mark R. Grandstaff

See also: Armstrong, John; George, Fort; Hull, William; Queenston, Battle of

Further Reading

Crackel, Theodore J. *Mr. Jefferson's Army: Political and Social Reform of the Military Establishment, 1801–1809.* New York: New York University Press, 1987.

Goodwin, Daniel. *The Dearborns.* Chicago: Fergus Printing, 1884.

DECATUR, STEPHEN, JR.
1779–1820
U.S. naval officer

Contemporaries considered Stephen Decatur the foremost naval hero of his time, and subsequent generations of writers have widely endorsed this view. He certainly looked the part. Standing 5 feet 10 inches tall, he possessed an imposing physique along with a shock of curly brown hair that lent his features a roguish cast. Already renowned for his daring actions against Tripoli in 1804, Decatur cemented his reputation for boldness and valor with his capture of the British frigate *Macedonian* during the early months of the War of 1812. Historian Charles Lee Lewis titled his 1937 biography of Decatur *The Romantic Decatur*, extolling his subject as "the very embodiment of the chivalrous patriotic youth."

If Decatur exemplified this heroic ideal, he also exhibited some of the less noble traits all too characteristic in the early navy's officer corps. He had a hair-trigger temper when it came to matters of personal honor and prerogative. He could also be ruthless to anyone who failed to measure up to his rigid standards or who in some way obstructed his quest for glory. Combative by nature and driven to excel, Decatur never backed away from a challenge. This combustible mix of qualities helped him gain the fame he coveted while also serving to bring about the senseless tragedy that ended his life on a dueling field in Maryland.

Decatur came from maritime stock. He was born on 5 January 1779 in the Eastern Shore village of Sinepuxent, Maryland. His father, the senior Stephen, was a successful merchant captain who enjoyed a second career as a privateer during the American Revolution. Volunteering for service during the Quasi-War with France, the elder Decatur secured a permanent place for himself in U.S. naval history by taking the first prize of the war.

His father's career notwithstanding, Stephen had little direct contact with the sea during his formative years. His sole taste of seafaring as a youngster came from a voyage he took to Europe at the age of eight. Otherwise, he spent most of his childhood in Philadelphia with his feet firmly rooted on the ground. He attended the Protestant Episcopal Academy and afterward studied briefly at the University of Pennsylvania before securing a job as a clerk in a Philadelphia shipping firm. In 1798, however, the desire to seek service afloat proved too strong for him. He appealed to John Barry, a family friend and the captain of the frigate *United States*, who was happy to use his influence on Decatur's behalf. With his newly minted midshipman's warrant in hand, Decatur reported aboard the *United States* in May 1798.

Despite his lack of nautical experience, Decatur quickly showed an aptitude for his new calling. His maiden cruise with Barry during the summer of 1798 was enlivened by the capture of several French prizes, and Decatur handled himself well enough to gain a promotion to lieutenant. It was during this first voyage on the *United States* that De-

Stephen Decatur, Jr.

catur was befriended by one of the frigate's lieutenants, James Barron. Appointed head of Decatur's watch, Barron took the novice midshipman under his wing and helped ease his transition into the complex world of a sailing warship.

In June 1801, Decatur joined the frigate *Essex* as her first lieutenant and sailed to the Mediterranean in company with Commodore Richard Dale's squadron "of training and observation." The 22-year-old lieutenant had already developed a prickly sense of honor and had shown no qualms about resorting to violence to defend it. In 1799, he wounded the mate of a merchant ship in a duel. While in the Mediterranean, he became embroiled in two other affairs of honor. A Spanish officer did not respond to Decatur's challenge, but in a far more serious incident, Decatur acted as Midshipman Joseph Bainbridge's second when he shot and killed the secretary to the British governor-general of Malta. Bainbridge and Decatur narrowly avoided arrest on charges of murder, and the two young officers were ordered to return to the United States. Unhappy with this outcome, an angry Decatur twice threatened to resign his commission. On both occasions, James Barron's temperate advice caused him to reconsider.

Despite his ignominious departure, Decatur soon returned to the Mediterranean, this time with an independent command, the brig *Argus*. Arriving at Gibraltar in November 1803, the *Argus* came under the scrutiny of the squadron's stern commodore, Edward Preble, who noted approvingly, "The order she is in does great credit to her commander." Decatur would soon have opportunity to show that he could do more than run a taut ship.

On 31 October 1803, the frigate *Philadelphia* ran aground in Tripoli Harbor and was captured. By the end of January 1804, Preble resolved to strike back, and he gave Decatur the honor of delivering the blow. On the evening of 16 February, Decatur and a picked force of 75 volunteers steered a captured Tripolitan ketch into the enemy's harbor and tied up next to the *Philadelphia*. Within minutes, Decatur's force boarded the frigate, overpowered her guards, and set the vessel ablaze. Decatur then led his men back to the ketch and safety, his hazardous mission complete at the cost of only one minor wound.

The destruction of the *Philadelphia* drew plaudits from all quarters. Lord Horatio Nelson called it "the most bold and daring act of the age," and Secretary of the Navy Robert Smith showed his appreciation by authorizing Decatur's immediate promotion, making him at age 25 the youngest captain in U.S. naval history. But Preble and Decatur were not done yet. In early August 1804, Preble launched a direct attack on Tripoli's defenses. Once again Decatur was prominent, commanding a division of gunboats in the assault. In the action that followed, Decatur captured two enemy gunboats after fierce hand-to-hand struggles with their crews.

Decatur returned to the United States in 1805, where he was honored and feted for his stirring deeds. While making the rounds of the Norfolk social scene toward the end of the year, the newly anointed naval hero made the acquaintance of Susan Wheeler, the daughter of the town's mayor. They were married the following March, and a few months later Decatur settled happily into his new position as commander of the Norfolk Navy Yard. He was still there in June 1807 when Commodore James Barron brought the *Chesapeake* limping back to Hampton Roads after her humiliating encounter with the HMS *Leopard*. Decatur had already begun to distance himself from Barron after an earlier misunderstanding. The incident had occurred the previous year when Barron made public mention of Decatur's betrothal to a Philadelphia woman, unaware that Decatur had severed the engagement and was courting Miss Wheeler. Although the mistake was an innocent one, Decatur still took offense at Barron's embarrassing disclosure. The *Chesapeake* affair, however, poisoned their relationship forever. Decatur openly expressed his contempt

for Barron's actions. Serving as one of the judges at Barron's court-martial, Decatur joined the court in sentencing his former mentor to a five-year suspension from duty.

Decatur spent the next two years in command of the *Chesapeake*, performing the thankless task of enforcing Thomas Jefferson's trade embargo. In 1809, he transferred his pennant to the *United States*, but the dull work of patrolling the country's territorial waters continued.

Late May 1812 found him in charge of a small squadron operating out of Norfolk. Commodore John Rodgers commanded another squadron based in New York. With war clearly imminent, Secretary of the Navy Paul Hamilton consulted Decatur and Rodgers for their ideas on naval strategy. Decatur urged Hamilton to dispatch ships singly or in pairs on long-range commerce-raiding missions. Rodgers disagreed, insisting that the fastest frigates should concentrate in a single division, and the entire fleet should occasionally do the same for particular missions.

While Hamilton mulled this conflicting counsel, Rodgers unilaterally settled the matter. Immediately after war was declared, Rodgers met Decatur at Sandy Hook, asserted his seniority, and set off with both squadrons to intercept a large British convoy bound from Jamaica to England. To silence any objections from his junior subordinate, Rodgers shrewdly cut a deal with Decatur, agreeing to a fifty-fifty split of the prize money.

Rodgers need not have bothered: Their 70-day cruise netted just seven prizes. Worse for Rodgers and Decatur, when they returned to Boston, they saw the battle-scarred *Constitution*, fresh from her recent triumph over the HMS *Guerrière*. Decatur could at least take consolation in one fact: Isaac Hull's success against the *Guerrière* convinced Hamilton to divide the fleet into two-ship raiding squadrons. In October, Decatur sailed from Boston in the *United States*, accompanied by the *Argus*. The two ships parted company four days out, and Decatur proceeded to steer in a southeasterly direction, intending to attack British shipping in the vicinity of the Canary Islands.

On the morning of 25 October, however, instead of a merchantman, his lookouts spied the British frigate *Macedonian* (38 guns). British pride had widely dismissed the *Constitution*'s victory over the *Guerrière* as a fluke, but this second duel of the war demonstrated that a medium frigate like the *Macedonian* was no match for a U.S. 44. Decatur handled his ship smartly throughout the 90-minute battle, using the heavier armament and superior gunnery of the *United States* to pound his opponent into a wreck. Decatur had his victory, but he was now determined to go Hull one better. Dismissing any thoughts of continuing his cruise, he resolved to repair the *Macedonian* and escort his prize home. On 4 December, Decatur made his triumphant entry at New London. His capture of the *Macedonian* created a sensation, and once more a grateful nation showered him with honors. He also collected $30,000 in prize money from the government.

In the spring of 1813, Decatur prepared for another extended cruise, leading a squadron composed of the *United States*, the refurbished *Macedonian*, and the sloop *Hornet*. He set sail in late May through the eastern end of Long Island Sound, hoping to elude the British blockading force off Sandy Hook. The British were guarding this route, too, so Decatur put in at New London rather than engage an enemy squadron of uncertain size. New London, however, turned out to be more a prison than a sanctuary when several British warships immediately took up station outside the port. Decatur stayed busy through the end of 1813 organizing New London's harbor defenses. He also toyed with the idea of arranging a fight between his two frigates and two of the British blockaders. But neither the duel nor an opportunity to escape materialized. Finally in the spring of 1814, the Americans stripped the *United States* and the *Macedonian* and hauled them up the Thames River, where they remained until the end of the war.

In May 1814, Decatur took command of the *President*, then being outfitted at New York. New York's vulnerability, however, prompted the Navy Department to cancel his cruise, instead ordering him to take charge of the port's naval defenses. Not until 1815 was he free again to go to sea. On the night of 14 January, Decatur tried to run the *President* to open water. Everything went wrong. First, a piloting error ran the *President* aground on the bar at Sandy Hook. It took two hours to float her free, and she suffered extensive damage. Westerly winds made it impossible to turn back, so Decatur pressed on. Daybreak revealed three enemy warships only 2 miles ahead of him. Outnumbered and hurt even before trading fire, Decatur ran, but her damage made the *President* plodding prey for her pursuers. Although U.S. gunners scored some hits, the uneven contest ended with Decatur's hauling down his flag sometime around midnight.

The defeat was bitter even if meaningless—the *President's* surrender came three weeks after the Treaty of Ghent. Yet even before a court of inquiry had delivered a verdict on Decatur's loss of the *President*, the new navy secretary, Benjamin Crowninshield, offered him a choice of assignments. Decatur elected to take charge of one of the squadrons then preparing for service against Algiers in the Mediterranean. Once in the Mediterranean, Decatur's squadron of ten sail overawed the dey of Algiers with relative ease. From Algiers, the commodore and his fleet proceeded to show the flag at Tripoli and Tunis. He received a hero's welcome upon his arrival at New York on 12 November 1815. For the third time in ten years, Decatur was the toast of the nation.

Life took a quiet turn for Decatur after the war and his Mediterranean escapades. He accepted a seat on the three-man Board of Navy Commissioners and relocated to Washington, taking up residence with his wife in a mansion opposite the White House. There he tended to his new administrative duties with his usual zeal, advising the secretary of the navy on such matters as coastal defense and warship construction.

In 1818, however, James Barron returned to the United States after living abroad for a decade and applied to the Navy Department for reinstatement. The government denied his request. As Barron brooded over this rebuff, he heard that Decatur had publicly disparaged his character. Barron dashed off a note to Decatur demanding an explanation and thus triggered an exchange of letters. The two officers finally agreed to settle their differences with a duel at Bladensburg, Maryland, on the morning of 22 March 1820. Barron suffered a flesh wound in the thigh, but his shot struck Decatur in the groin. He died within the day.

—Jeff Seiken

See also: Barron, James; *Chesapeake-Leopard* Affair; Hamilton, Paul; New London, Connecticut; Rodgers, John; *United States* versus *Macedonian*

Further Reading

Dunne, W.M.P. "Pistols and Honor: The James Barron–Stephen Decatur Conflict, 1798–1807." *The American Neptune* 50, no. 4 (1990): 245–259.

Guttridge, Leonard F., and Jay D. Smith. *The Commodores*. New York: Harper & Row, 1969.

Lewis, Charles L. *The Romantic Decatur*. Philadelphia: University of Pennsylvania Press, 1937.

MacKenzie, Alexander S. *Life of Stephen Decatur, A Commodore in the Navy of the United States*. Boston: Charles C. Little and James Brown, 1846.

Schroeder, John H. "Stephen Decatur: Heroic Ideal of the Young Navy." In *Command under Sail: Makers of the American Naval Tradition*, ed. James C. Bradford. Annapolis, MD: Naval Institute Press, 1985.

DECLARATION OF WAR, U.S.
See U.S. Congress

DELAWARE INDIANS

The British gave the name Delaware to an Algonquin-speaking confederation whose members resided in and around the mid-Atlantic's Delaware River Valley. Calling themselves Lenni Lenape, meaning "men of our nation" or "genuine men," these mainly agrarian natives were also called "grandfather" by many eastern Woodland peoples in recognition of their long-established heritage, duly recorded in the epic Walum Olum (Red Tally). The tribe befriended William Penn, whose Great Treaty with Chief Tamenend of the Unami clan and other Delawares in 1683 led to the establishment of Pennsylvania.

By the mid-eighteenth century, European encroachment and conflict with the Iroquois had pushed the Delaware into the Ohio country. Siding with the French in the French and Indian War, they participated in the defeat of General Braddock in western Pennsylvania. Later, at Fort Pitt in 1778, the Delaware had the distinction of signing the first treaty between an Indian tribe and the United States, though part of the clan favored the British during the Revolution. Following the 1782 massacre of Christianized Delawares at the Moravian mission of Gnadenhutten (Ohio), some bands moved farther west or north, all the while remaining angry over continued U.S. transgression on the frontier. As anger turned to open hostility, the Delaware and their allies were defeated at the Battle of Fallen Timbers in 1794. They signed the Treaty of Greenville the following year.

When the 1809 Treaty of Fort Wayne annexed more Indian lands to the United States, many Delawares, especially those in the Indiana Territory, rallied to Tecumseh's call for defiance. Less antagonistic Delawares, however, participated in the Piqua Council of August 1812, then visited the prophet, seeking Indian nonalignment as the War of 1812 engulfed the Northwest Territory. Unsuccessful in their mission, the Delaware remained a divided people throughout the conflict. Signing of the July 1814 Treaty of Greenville was followed by acceptance of the 1818 Treaty of Saint Mary's, in which the Delawares ceded all Indiana land claims to the United States. In 1829, the final tribal holdings in Ohio were signed away, and the remaining Delawares moved to Kansas.

—*William E. Fischer, Jr.*

See also: Tecumseh
Further Reading
Ferguson, Roger J. "The White River Indiana Delawares: An Ethnohistoric Synthesis, 1795–1867." Ed.D. diss., Ball State University, 1972.
Sugden, John. *Tecumseh's Last Stand.* Norman, OK: University of Oklahoma Press, 1985.
Weslager, C. A. *The Delaware Indians: A History.* New Brunswick, NJ: Rutgers University Press, 1972.

DEMOLOGUS

In 1813, Robert Fulton submitted plans to Pres. James Madison for a steam warship. Secretary of the Navy William Jones and several influential captains supported the idea, so in March 1814 Congress authorized the vessel's construction. Fulton was placed in charge of the project. Named the *Demologus* (Voice of the People), the new vessel was launched at the end of October 1814. After Fulton's death in February 1815, she was renamed the *Fulton* and subsequently she was called the *Fulton I.*

At the time of her commissioning in June 1815, the *Fulton* was the first steam frigate in any navy in the world. Yet she was not a true frigate. Designed as a catamaran, her hulls protected the center paddle wheel, and her intended use was as a harbor defense vessel for New York City. In fact, Fulton envisioned her as a mobile battery exclusively under steam propulsion, but Capt. David Porter, who took command of the frigate while she was under construction, insisted on the addition of a two-master lateen sail rig. The change required bulwarks on the spar deck to protect men working the sails and added greatly to the *Fulton's* weight without enhancing her fighting qualities.

With a length of 153 feet 2 inches and beam of 56 feet, the *Fulton* was the largest steamer in the world. The steam engine could produce 120 horsepower and could push her 2,475 tons at 5.5 miles per hour. Her 58-inch wooden bulwarks made her presumably shot proof, and her 30 guns made her theoretically formidable. She carried long 32-pounders on her trial run, but the plan was to arm her with large Columbiads. War's end came before she was ready for service. She became a receiving ship at the Brooklyn Navy Yard until she blew up in 1829 in an accidental explosion of her magazine.

—*Spencer C. Tucker*

See also: Fulton, Robert; Torpedoes
Further Reading
Canney, Donald L. *The Old Steam Navy.* Vol. 1, *Frigates, Sloops, and Gunboats, 1815–1885.* Annapolis, MD: Naval Institute Press, 1990.

DEPOSIT, FORT(S)

During the Creek War in 1813–1814, U.S. forces moving against the Red Stick faction of the Creek Nation established a number of supply depots in Alabama. Andrew Jackson's forces erected three such posts, but only one was officially named Fort Deposit. It was situated in Marshall County at Thompson's Creek, then at the southernmost point of the Tennessee River.

Gen. Ferdinand L. Claiborne's Mississippi forces established two supply depots when they invaded Creek territory. One of these, named Fort Deposit, was established in Lowndes County. This Fort Deposit was the only supply depot to become a permanent settlement. It is located 25 miles south of Hayneville, the county seat of Lowndes County.

—*Henry S. Marks*

See also: Creek War
Further Reading

Holland, James W. "Andrew Jackson and the Creek War: Victory at the Horseshoe." *The Alabama Review* 21 (October 1968): 243–275.

Jenkins, William H. "Alabama Forts, 1700–1838." *The Alabama Review* 12 (July 1959): 163–180.

DESHA, JOSEPH
1768–1842
Congressman, 1807–1819;
militia general, 1813

Joseph Desha was born in Monroe County, Pennsylvania, but migrated westward with his family in 1781. The Deshas moved first to Kentucky; a year later they settled in the Cumberland District of Tennessee. Joseph spent his youth as an Indian fighter. In 1792, he returned to Kentucky, where he resided for the rest of his life. He participated in Gen. Anthony Wayne's 1794 expedition against the Northwest Indians. His distinguished service in this campaign assisted his entrance into Kentucky politics. In 1807, he was elected to the U.S. House of Representatives.

As a congressman, Desha stood out immediately as a fervent nationalist and advocate of tough measures against Great Britain and France. He strongly supported the Jefferson administration's Embargo Act and related enforcement legislation. In the 12th Congress, he served on the influential House Foreign Relations Committee, whose members Speaker Henry Clay carefully selected for their willingness to confront Britain over blockades and impressment. Desha did not disappoint Clay. Although Desha seldom spoke during the 1811–1812 session, he did vote for nine of 11 war measures the committee brought before the House. Desha supported a resolution to arm merchant vessels, a bill to increase the regular army to 25,000 men, and a bill authorizing the president to accept volunteer corps into U.S. service. Desha was among the 79 representatives who voted for the declaration of war against Britain on 4 June 1812. Historians usually classify him among the War Hawks.

During the war, Desha advocated larger professional armies and longer enlistment terms. In the summer of 1813, he left Washington in response to Kentucky governor Isaac Shelby's call for militia to join Maj. Gen. William Henry Harrison's campaign to drive the British out of Detroit and conquer Upper Canada. In September, Shelby gave General Desha command of the second division of the 3,500-man army assembled on the Ohio River at Newport. Desha's unit comprised the second and fifth brigades and the 11th regiment. The Kentucky militia later proved instrumental in forcing the British to evacuate Detroit and routing them at the Battle of the Thames River (5 October 1813) in present-day southern Ontario. At the latter engagement, Desha's command held the U.S. left wing against the British army's Indian allies.

Desha returned to congressional service for the remainder of the war. The abandonment of Canada as a territorial objective and the willingness to ignore impressment and maritime rights in the effort to secure peace displeased him. He was thus disappointed by the Treaty of Ghent. Desha retired from Congress in 1819 after serving six consecutive terms. His War of 1812 service made him popular in Kentucky, and he later served the state as governor (1824–1828). He died at Georgetown in Scott County.

—*Michael S. Fitzgerald*

See also: Thames, Battle of the; U.S. Congress
Further Reading

Clark, Thomas D. "Kentucky in the Northwest Campaign." In *After Tippecanoe: Some Aspects of the War of 1812,* ed. Philip P. Mason. East Lansing: Michigan State University Press, 1963.

Hammack, James W. *Kentucky and the Second American Revolution: The War of 1812.* Lexington: University Press of Kentucky, 1976.

Horsman, Reginald. "Who Were the War Hawks?" *Indiana Magazine of History* 60 (June 1964): 121–136.

Quaife, Milo M., ed. "Governor Shelby's Army in the River Thames Campaign." *The Filson Club Historical Quarterly* 10 (July 1936): 135–165.

DETROIT, SURRENDER OF
16 August 1812

During the summer of 1812, Fort Detroit and the nearby town of the same name became the base of operations for the U.S. Northwestern Army under Revolutionary War veteran Gen. William Hull. After recruiting a force of volunteers and militia, primarily from Ohio, Hull arrived at Detroit on 5 July. He expected to receive word of the declaration of war before beginning an invasion of Canada, but Secretary of War William Eustis had dispatched this crucial intelligence through the regular mail. Hull had thus sent his papers to Detroit aboard the schooner *Cuyahoga*. British general Isaac Brock, fully aware of the outbreak of hostilities, captured the schooner as it sailed past Fort Malden. Brock thus knew all of Hull's plans, including the strength and disposition of U.S. forces.

Hull paused at Detroit for a week amid the grumbling of his impatient militia. Finally, official word of the war arrived with orders to begin the invasion. Hull crossed the Detroit River and made for Fort Malden. He outnumbered the British at Malden by almost two to one, but as his army moved toward its target, Hull became increasingly agitated about the security of his supply lines. Two separate detachments checking the lines into Detroit were attacked by Indians under Tecumseh and were forced back to Detroit. When Hull heard that Mackinac Island had surrendered to the British, he feared that all northwestern Indians would soon descend upon his army. His alarm obscured his advantages, so he immediately retreated to Detroit. This move seriously damaged the army's morale and raised questions among his subordinates about Hull's competence.

In the meantime, Brock received not only reinforcements but additional intelligence about his opponent. When contents of a captured U.S. mailbag revealed how dispirited the U.S. army was, Brock planned to capture Detroit. To unnerve already edgy Americans, he dispatched a message, which exaggerated his number of Indian allies, in such a way as to assure its capture. Brock then moved on Detroit, reaching the Detroit River to prepare a siege by constructing a battery emplacement for his largest guns—two 18-pounders.

Watching this activity from Fort Detroit, Hull's artillerists asked the general's permission to fire at the British preparations. The Americans had 28 artillery pieces, including several 24-pounders, but Hull refused to allow them to fire. On 15 August, Brock sent Maj. J. B. Glegg to Fort Detroit under flag of truce. Brock demanded Hull's surrender. Brock implied that if he were forced to storm the fort, he would not be able to control his Indian allies. Hull revealed how unsettling this prospect was by waiting two hours before rejecting Brock's demand.

As the British prepared to cross the river, U.S. major Thomas Jesup made ready to stop them. Jesup correctly anticipated where most British troops would come ashore, but when he requested permission to place a battery to prevent the British landing, Hull refused. Hull's irrational behavior—he refused to come out of his quarters or to allow any defense preparations—prompted some of his subordinates to consider relieving him of command. They lost their nerve, however.

While Hull crouched in his quarters, the British began to move unmolested across the Detroit River. Regulars and militiamen in Fort Detroit were joined by the men, women, and children of the town, all to crowd together on the afternoon of 15 August as British artillery opened up on them. Hull's own daughter and grandchildren were in the fort. The bombardment continued into the night and picked up again the next morning as British soldiers and their Indian allies surrounded the town. The British moved their batteries closer, too, and some of the hits became deadly accurate. Civilians shrieked in terror when a British shell killed a group of officers.

Without consulting anyone, Hull soon summoned his son and aide to carry a note to the British under a flag of truce. The general also ordered a white flag raised over the fort. Any doubt about what this meant was dispelled when British officers entered the fort to negotiate terms. Hull had surrendered the fort, the town, and a detachment under Cols. Duncan McArthur and Lewis Cass that had been sent out of Detroit to meet reinforcements and supplies. The British paroled the volunteers and militia and made the regulars prisoners of war, to be transported to Canada.

The surrender of Detroit was a devastating blow to U.S. morale. What should have been the beginning of a successful invasion of Canada had turned into an ignominious defeat. Not only had a strategic position been surrendered to the British, but the entire Northwest would remain vulnerable to British designs for the next year. When Hull was later exchanged, he was court-martialed, convicted, and sentenced to death. Pres. James Madison commuted the sentence because of Hull's age and Revolutionary War service.

—*Jeanne T. Heidler and David S. Heidler*

See also: Brock, Isaac; Cass, Lewis; Hull, William; Jesup, Thomas Sidney; Malden, Fort; McArthur, Duncan
Further Reading
Cruikshank, E. A., ed. *Documents Relating to the Invasion of Canada and the Surrender of Detroit 1812.* Ottawa: Government Printing Bureau, 1913.

DICKSON, ALEXANDER
1777–1840
British army officer

Alexander Dickson was the leading British artilleryman of the early nineteenth century. A member of a military dynasty, he was the third son of Adm. William Dickson, the brother of Adm. Sir Collingwood Dickson, and the father of another famous British gunner, Gen. Sir Collingwood Dickson, VC.

Dickson entered the Royal Military Academy at Woolwich in 1793 and left the following year as a second lieutenant. He served as an artillery officer at the capture of Minorca, the siege of Malta, and the abortive siege of Buenos Aires. During the Peninsular War, Dickson obtained a commission in the Portuguese Artillery at a higher rank than he held in the British army. He became one of the few artillery officers Wellington ever trusted. Wellington eventually used Dickson's Portuguese rank to make him chief of all allied artillery in the peninsula, placing him over the heads of several more senior Royal Artillery officers. Dickson commanded the Portuguese Artillery at Salamanca, Badajoz, and Ciudad Rodrigo; and he commanded the allied artillery at Vittoria, San Sebastian, and Tolouse.

Command of the British Artillery at New Orleans in January 1815 was a dark spot in Dickson's otherwise brilliant career. Both technically and tactically, he faced several severe handicaps. His single biggest problem was that the army's forward positions were over 80 miles away from its supply base with the fleet. This long line of communications over bad roads was always stretched to the breaking point, making it impossible to get sufficient numbers of heavy guns and adequate amounts of ammunition to the front line. Compounding this problem, most of the available heavy guns were mounted on naval rather than field carriages. That made them even more difficult to move

over land, and it also meant that Dickson's troops had to construct stable firing platforms before the guns could be used effectively. The marshy ground south of New Orleans made that task almost impossible. Dickson did his best with what he had, but in the end it was not good enough.

Dickson arrived at the fleet's main anchorage with General Pakenham's party on 25 December 1814. That same day he moved up to the forward British positions and assumed command of the guns. At that point he had only 12 guns, the heaviest being two 9-pounders. He immediately ordered more guns and ammunition up from the fleet. On 26 December, Dickson wanted to fire on the *Carolina*, but Pakenham overruled his artillery commander because he did not believe the 9-pounders could range the target. Pakenham wanted to wait for the arrival of the 18-pounders that Dickson had ordered. When the 18-pounders did not arrive on 27 December, Pakenham relented. About eight o'clock that morning, Dickson's 9-pounders opened up on the *Carolina* with hot shot—Dickson was famous in the Royal Artillery for his fondness for using hot shot. Two and a half hours later the *Carolina* exploded and sank, but the British gunners had expended nearly a third of their ammunition.

Dickson was later criticized for not engaging the *Louisiana* as well, which was about a mile farther upstream. The *Louisiana*, however, was at the extreme range of Dickson's guns. Given his limited ammunition supply, he probably made the right decision in placing all of his efforts on the one sure target, rather than trying for both and running the risk of neutralizing neither. If there was any major blunder in this action, it was Pakenham's in not taking the advice of his artillery commander. The day's delay in attacking the *Carolina* gave Andrew Jackson that much more time to strengthen his defenses.

After the abortive reconnaissance-in-strength on 28 December, Pakenham decided to wait for the heavy guns to neutralize the well-entrenched and effective U.S. artillery. Between 28 and 30 December, the Royal Navy delivered eight 18-pounders and four 24-pounders—all on naval carriages. During the night of 31 December, Dickson's troops put forth a superhuman effort to construct a series of five battery positions 800 yards from the U.S. lines. But there was too little time and the ground was too weak to allow doing the job properly. Ammunition remained a problem. Each of the 18-pounders had 68 rounds, but the 24-pounders had only 40. Dickson knew he did not have enough for a major fight.

The British opened the artillery duel at nine o'clock on New Year's Day, 1815. The weak and unleveled battery platforms affected the accuracy of the guns, and the concussion from each round of the heavy guns made the platforms that much weaker. Three hours later, when the British stopped firing, many of the Americans believed it was because they had neutralized Dickson's guns. The British, in fact, had simply run out of ammunition. Dickson later noted in his journal, "[We] only ceased for want of Ammunition, for we had not one piece of heavy Ordnance disabled." He also noted that "even if there had been Sufficient Ammunition, the nature of our Batteries were such the men could not have gone on for many hours longer." Dickson, through no fault of his own, had failed to win the artillery battle. But Adm. Edward Codrington called the failure "a blot on the artillery escutcheon."

Dickson had one more key role to play in the battle, and that earned him even more criticism. On 8 January, after the main British assault on the east bank was beaten back and Pakenham was killed, Gen. John Lambert ordered Dickson to cross over to the west bank to evaluate Col. William Thornton's situation. Thornton had been sent across the river to secure a U.S. battery there and turn it on Jackson's right. Although Thornton had succeeded in carrying the Americans' first line and taking Daniel Patterson's battery, Dickson reported that the position would require an additional 2,000 troops to hold and exploit. Both Admiral Codrington and Col. John Burgoyne, the chief engineer, strongly disagreed, but Lambert took Dickson's advice and ordered the troops to withdraw. For that decision, Dr. Carson Ritchie would later blame Dickson for the entire debacle. "It was not Pakenham," said Ritchie, "but Sir Alexander Dickson who lost the third battle of New Orleans."

The remainder of Dickson's career dispelled any questions created by his performance at New Orleans. He returned to Europe in time to fight at Waterloo and later supported the Prussian army with artillery at the sieges of Philipeville and Marienburg. For those actions he was awarded the Prussian Order Pour le Merite (later known as the Blue Max). He became a knight commander of the Guelphic Order (KCH) and a knight grand cross of the Bath (GCB). At the time of his death in 1840, he held the two top positions in the Royal Artillery: director general of artillery and master gunner St. James' Park. For a month after his death all Royal Artillery officers were ordered to wear black crepe on their swords.

—David T. Zabecki

See also: New Orleans, Battle of; Pakenham, Edward; Thornton, William (British officer)
Further Reading
Browne, James Alex. England's Artillerymen. London: Hall, Smart, and Allen, 1865.

Duncan, Francis. History of the Royal Regiment of Artillery. Vol. 2. London: John Murray, 1873.
Kane, John. List of Officers of the Royal Regiment of Artillery. 4th ed. London: Royal Artillery Institute, 1890.
Reilly, Robin. The British at the Gates. New York: G.P. Putnam's Sons, 1974.

DICKSON, ROBERT
1765?–1823
Fur trader; British Indian Department agent

Robert Dickson was born in Dumfries, Scotland, and entered the fur trade as a merchant in the Niagara region following the Revolutionary War. In 1786, he began his own trading firm at Michilimackinac, and by 1797 he was living in Spanish territory west of the Mississippi River. Shortly afterward, he was one of the leading merchants among the semimigratory Sioux living in the Minnesota and Upper Great Lakes region.

His loyalty to the British government and mounting concern about U.S. encroachment in his trading area led him to support Crown efforts during the War of 1812. As early as June 1812, Dickson was rallying the region's Native Americans to the British cause. On 18 June, the first day of the war, he led nearly 300 warriors to the British post at St. Joseph Island, Ontario. On 17 July 1812, he assisted in the successful attack against Michilimackinac by commanding nearly 400 Indians. This victory secured the alliance between the British government and the Indians of the area. On 1 January 1813, he was appointed agent and superintendent for the Indians of the western nations. Later in 1813, he recruited nearly 1,400 native allies for the second siege of Fort Meigs (21–24 July) and personally took part in the unsuccessful 1 August attack upon Fort Stephenson.

The following year he participated in the defense of Michilimackinac and assisted in the capture of the U.S. schooners Tigress and Scorpion. By war's end Dickson had been promoted to the rank of lieutenant colonel. He retired from the Indian department in 1815.

—Larry L. Nelson

See also: Michilimackinac, Fort
Further Reading
Horsman, Reginald. "British Indian Policy in the Northwest, 1897–1812." Mississippi Valley Historical Review 45 (1958–1959): 51–66.

Thwaites, Reuben Gold et al., eds. *Collections of the State Historical Society of Wisconsin.* 31 vols., Vol. 11, pp. 271–315; Vol. 12, pp. 133–153. Madison, WI: Democratic Printing Company, State Printers, 1854–1931.

Tohill, L. A. "Robert Dickson, British Fur Trader on the Upper Mississippi." *North Dakota Historical Quarterly* 2 (1928): 5–29; 3 (1929): 83–128, 182–203.

DIPLOMACY
1807–1815

Various students of the War of 1812 have postulated a variety of reasons for the United States' reluctant entry into the war, its early desire to seek an amicable peace, and its later acceptance of the diplomatic results of status quo antebellum. Despite the variety of opinion, one fact seems indisputable: The overriding factor leading to Pres. James Madison's declaration of war was the demand for neutral rights. Neutral rights were the focus of Madison's war message and the salient reason for mounting public hostility toward the British. More important than ideology, internal rifts between the Federalists and the Republicans, and the desire to prove that the United States was indeed independent of its former caretaker was the desire to extend trade routes and keep money flowing into U.S. coffers from open trade with Europe.

The conflict with Great Britain began as early as 1803 with the renewal of war in Europe. With the British occupied in a protracted land and sea war with Napoleon, the neutral Americans stood to profit handsomely by taking over trade with the French and Spanish West Indies from the British. In 1805, however, a British prize court ruled in the case of the *Essex* that the practice of shipping French and Spanish goods through U.S. ports while en route to other countries did not neutralize enemy goods. Then, in 1806 and 1807, the British established a series of Orders in Council that in essence set up a naval blockade of Europe. Ships heading for Europe had to accept British inspection and obtain licenses or have their goods confiscated. By 1807, the British increasingly interfered with U.S. shipping, not only to keep goods from reaching Napoleon's forces but also to cripple competition with British merchant shipping. Americans responded with several reprisals, most notably Jefferson's Embargo Act of 1807. Nevertheless, the depredations against the maritime rights of the United States continued. As Anglo-American relations deteriorated, the few attempts at reconciliation came to nothing, and at least one ruined the career of earnest

young David Erskine, the British minister to Washington. When Erskine negotiated the revocation of the Orders in Council, he exceeded his instructions and suffered public repudiation and recall by his own government.

Yet if neutral rights had been the only issue, the United States could have gone to war with both France and Britain in 1812. Napoleon retaliated against Britain's blockade with his own Continental System, as enacted by the Berlin Decree of 1806 and the Milan Decree of 1807. These two acts resulted in a virtual blockade of the British Isles and specified that neutral ships that complied with British regulations could be seized when they reached European ports. Between 1807 and 1812, the two belligerents and their allies confiscated more than 900 U.S. ships. Little wonder that the repeal of such measures became the foremost objective of U.S. foreign policy in the years before 1812.

Despite French interference with the neutral rights of the United States, the British list of offenses was far longer than that of the French and included impressment, incitement of Native Americans, and instigation of trouble in Florida. Furthermore, some Americans supported the war in hopes of forcing the British to concede Canada. They hoped that the declaration of war itself would be enough to win such a concession from the enemy. To this end the U.S. declaration of war was a ruse contrived to coerce the British into taking U.S. demands seriously.

Such a ruse, however, could have serious consequences. One was starting a war that was neither desirable nor winnable—at least with the public support and the state of the U.S. military at the time. Perhaps that is why, on 18 June 1812, the day the war was declared, President Madison sent Secretary of State James Monroe to apprise the British minister, Augustus J. Foster, that the United States had declared war but desired a quick peace. Five days later, Madison invited Foster to the White House to outline the United States' terms. Madison, hoping to avoid "any serious collision," told the minister that peace could be restored if the British rescinded the Orders in Council and banned impressment.

Ironically, the Orders in Council had already been repealed before the declaration of war by the United States, but the news did not arrive early enough to influence the U.S. decision. After a decade of unsuccessfully checking Napoleon's advances, British policy makers had been rethinking their economic blockade for some time. A nation that heavily relied on trade could not long withstand the repercussions from its own Orders in Council that closed the entire coast of Napoleonic-controlled Europe. These orders not only caused U.S. resentment to grow because of seizure of U.S. shipping but also hurt British manufacturers and consumers. Pressure by these two groups eventually forced the British government to rescind the Orders in Council.

On 26 June 1812, the Madison administration, unaware of the repeal of the Orders, dispatched a note to Jonathan Russell, the U.S. chargé d'affaires in London, authorizing him to open negotiations for an armistice. Russell told the British that they would have to give up the Orders in Council and impressment; the United States in turn would guarantee that no British seamen would serve on U.S. ships.

The British rejected Russell's offer because the Orders in Council had already been rescinded. Thus, within two weeks of the declaration of war, only the issue of impressment stood in the way of peace. The British foreign minister, Lord Castlereagh, declared that the British could not renounce the right of impressment "without the certainty of an arrangement . . . to secure its object." Castlereagh knew that impressment had not been a major issue since the abortive Monroe-Pinkney Treaty and the attack on the *Chesapeake* in 1807. He reasoned that once the U.S. government heard of the cancellation of the Orders, the war would be over. In fact, by July the British government was so sure that the repeal of the Orders would end the war that it instructed its navy to ignore any attacks from privateers sent to sea prior to the time the Americans received news of the revocation of the Orders.

The Americans insisted that Britain renounce impressment and failed to comment on the cancellation of the Orders. Thus, having heard nothing from the U.S. government by October 13, some ten weeks after the declaration of war, the British authorized general reprisals against the United States. Britain, however, continued to seek peace. Its ministry had instructed Sir John Borlase Warren, the naval commander on the U.S. station, to seek an armistice. Moreover, Foster attempted to negotiate a cease-fire in Halifax. His encouragement led British administrators in Canada to sign an armistice with U.S. general Henry Dearborn. The Madison administration did not recognize the agreement because it did not end impressment. Hence, 1812 ended with two reluctant belligerents both interested in peace but now locked in a land and naval war.

In early March 1813, Andrei Daschkov, the Russian minister to Washington, suggested that his government would be willing to mediate a new round of negotiations between the two warring nations. Russia stood to gain from an amicable peace settlement because it relied both on trade with the United States and on British aid in the Napoleonic wars. The Anglo-American war kept the trade from Russian consumers and kept the British focused on the problems in North America rather than on the European continent.

The U.S. government was pleased to negotiate with the Russians. After all, the campaign in Canada had gone poorly; the treasury was almost depleted; and the Federalists remained defiant. Furthermore, the war in Europe had turned in Britain's favor. It would not be too long before the United States might have to face the entire might of the British empire. Secretary Monroe and other U.S. officials saw the value of ending the war before the European war came to a climax.

U.S. officials still had grandiose hopes for major British concessions. By July 1813, Madison had sent Albert Gallatin and James A. Bayard to join U.S. minister John Quincy Adams at St. Petersburg in an effort to gain maritime concessions, end impressment, and obtain the "whole of Canada" as well. Meanwhile, the British had rejected Russia's mediation offer, but poor communication kept the U.S. peace envoys in Russia until January 1814. On their way back to the United States, Gallatin and Bayard visited London and conducted informal negotiations with Alexander Baring, a respected British banker. It became apparent that the British would not budge on the impressment issue.

Hoping to convince the Americans of his desire to end the conflict, Lord Castlereagh in November 1813 sent word that Britain desired to open direct talks with the Americans "for the restoration of peace." Nevertheless, he warned in a letter to Monroe, he would continue to insist on the right of impressment. In spite of this warning, Madison accepted the offer to negotiate. He also appointed Henry Clay, Speaker of the House and preeminent War Hawk, to join the U.S. delegation. The U.S. commissioners then were John Quincy Adams, Jonathan Russell, James Bayard, Albert Gallatin, and Henry Clay. They met with British negotiators in August 1814 at the Belgian city of Ghent.

Negotiations lasted through December. Meanwhile, the war had ended in Europe, the attitude in England toward the United States turned vindictive, and the British government remained tight-lipped about the negotiations at Ghent. Few British officials, however, wanted to enter into a long, protracted war with the United States—it was a "millstone" to be avoided. They felt that the British people had already suffered much from the lack of trade, higher taxes, and death toll of the Napoleonic wars. Madison, conversely, had released information to the U.S. public by mid-October about the scope of British demands at Ghent. He then skillfully rallied Federalist support for the war. Aside from those who applauded the Hartford Convention planned for December 1814 to consider antiwar measures and anti-Republican tactics, many Federalists began to agree with Madison that the only alternative was resistance or disgrace.

As the negotiations dragged on, the U.S. envoys quarreled among themselves, expected little success, and at best hoped to blame all futility on their British counterparts. British commissioners could not match the talents of their U.S. counterparts. Ultimately, the Americans waged an ingenious diplomatic battle, creatively ignoring instructions from the Madison administration to demand the cession of Canada and to take up the issue of maritime rights. In fact, they never even mentioned impressment. They believed, as did Secretary of State James Monroe, that the United States had demonstrated its feelings about impressment by resisting it.

British concessions took more time. At first British diplomats demanded that their Native American allies be made parties to any peace process and that their boundaries be recognized. The British had previously suggested—and now at Ghent demanded—that an independent Indian state be created as a buffer between the United States and Canada. They changed their minds only when Americans threatened to withdraw from the negotiations. London quickly sent word to the U.S. delegation that the buffer state idea was only a suggestion, and it was never discussed again. All that remained of British assurances to their Indian allies was Article IX of the treaty, a weak pledge that the United States would restore Indian lands held in 1811. Americans were now free to expand westward, free from the threat of British intervention.

When negotiations began, the British were optimistic about extracting territorial concessions from the Americans. By the time the Indian question was settled, however, the United States had repelled the British invasion of New York and had defeated the British on Lake Champlain in September. Although the British ministry now only hoped to obtain minor territorial concessions, acquiring land hardly seemed justified in light of the new military situation. The duke of Wellington, fresh from the battlefields of Napoleonic Europe and now offered direction of the war with the United States, told his superiors that Britain's inability to control the Great Lakes gave it "no right from the state of the war to demand any concession of territory from America." In October, Britain withdrew the demand for territory.

By the end of November, discussions focused on Britain's desire to continue to use the Mississippi River as an outlet from Canada. Recognizing that the Americans would hesitate to continue such an agreement, the British planned to deny a U.S. request for continued fishing rights off the coast of British North America. In the end, both sides simply agreed not to discuss these questions.

On Christmas Eve 1814, the negotiators signed a peace treaty that either ignored or deferred all relevant issues. The agreement established peace on the basis of status quo antebellum. John Quincy Adams and the other U.S. delegates to Ghent believed that the treaty was more an armistice than a lasting peace. But by 1817, the United States and Great Britain were on the road to reconciliation—something that the U.S. envoys at Ghent would never have predicted in 1814. Trade relations with Britain were restored. The Rush-Bagot Agreement of 1817 and the Convention of 1818 settled several disputes left unresolved at Ghent. In effect, the two compacts removed the threat of naval competition on the Great Lakes, established an unfortified border between the United States and Canada, set the northern limit to the Louisiana Purchase at the 49th parallel, restored U.S. fishing rights off Newfoundland and Labrador, and opened Oregon to joint occupation.

In the years following the war, Britons and Americans formed their own interpretations of the war. Because the United States had neither won Canada nor forced Britain to renounce impressment, some Britons saw the war as a British victory. Many Americans viewed it differently. The United States had stood up to the British, defied their demands, and fought the conquerors of Napoleon to a draw.

Perhaps to a lesser extent, Americans did have something to celebrate. Militarily, they had been powerful enough to force the British ministry to concede that halfway measures were not enough. It became obvious that war with the United States would require a full commitment of English soldiers and money—a commitment that neither the ministry nor the British people was willing to make. Ultimately, the War of 1812 revived flagging U.S. nationalism, cleared the way for an expanded overseas trade, and reinforced the notion that the "Great Experiment" would undoubtedly continue—at least for the time being.

—*Mark R. Grandstaff*

See also: Adams, John Quincy; Bayard, James Asheton; Berlin Decree; Castlereagh, Viscount, Robert Stewart; Clay, Henry; Dearborn, Henry; Embargo Act; *Essex* Decision; Foster, Augustus John; Gallatin, Albert; Ghent, Treaty of; Impressment; Milan Decree; Monroe, James; Orders in Council; Russell, Jonathan

Further Reading

Bartlett, C. J. *Defense and Diplomacy: Britain and the Great Powers, 1815–1914.* Manchester, England: University of Manchester Press, 1993.

Perkins, Bradford. *Castlereagh and Adams.* Berkeley and Los Angeles: University of California Press, 1964.

Stagg, J.C.A. *Mr. Madison's War: Politics, Diplomacy, and Warfare in the Early American Republic, 1783–1830.* Princeton: Princeton University Press, 1983.

DOBBINS, DANIEL
1776–1856
U.S. naval officer

Daniel Dobbins was born near Lewistown, Mifflin County, Pennsylvania, on 5 July 1776. When Jay's Treaty (ratified in 1795) opened the Great Lakes to U.S. commerce, 19-year-old Dobbins shrewdly observed the need for increased lake transport. At Erie he learned the salt trade and the Buffalo-to-Erie coastline. After 1800, he commanded vessels such as *Good Intent, Ranger, General Wilkinson,* and the schooner *Salina* in the salt and provisions trade for Rufus Seth Reed and for Porter, Barton & Co. of Black Rock.

On 17 July 1812, Dobbins's *Salina* and the schooner *Mary* were captured when Michilimackinac fell. Both vessels were retaken at Detroit by Gen. William Hull's forces, then recaptured by Gen. Isaac Brock when Hull surrendered Detroit on 17 August. Dobbins escaped and rode to Washington to confirm news of the western disasters for Pres. James Madison and Secretary of War William Eustis. An emergency cabinet meeting questioned Dobbins about building vessels on the Upper Lakes.

In September, Secretary of the Navy Paul Hamilton appointed Dobbins a sailing master in the U.S. Navy and authorized $2,000 for him to commence construction at Erie. Dobbins engaged Ebenezer Crosby of Buffalo to build four gunboats. The designs of two of them were altered by Commodore Isaac Chauncey in December.

As an officer of Oliver H. Perry's growing squadron, Dobbins had a chance to share the glory of the U.S. triumph on Lake Erie. Ironically, however, he was commanding the *Ohio,* procuring supplies in Buffalo, during Perry's victorious action of 10 September 1813. After the war Dobbins continued in the navy, but in 1820, in a court-martial for fighting with another sailing master, he was sentenced to an 18-month suspension without pay and publicly reprimanded at the Erie Navy Yard. He served as sailing master until 1826, then entered the Revenue Marine. He alternated with Capt. Gilbert Knapp, being removed by Whig presidents and reinstated by Democratic presidents. Dobbins's son, Decatur, an army lieutenant, committed suicide after killing a man. Dobbins himself died on 29 February 1856.

—*Frederick C. Drake*

See also: Lake Erie Campaign; Perry, Oliver Hazard

Further Reading
Dobbins, William W. *History of the Battle of Lake Erie and Reminiscences of the Flagships* Lawrence *and* Niagara. Erie, PA: Ashby Printing, 1913.
Drugan, A. J. "Dan Dobbins—The Unsung Hero of the Battle of Lake Erie." *Columbus Dispatch Magazine* (September 1963): 6–21.
Ilisevich, Robert D. *Daniel Dobbins: Frontier Mariner.* Erie, PA: Crawford County Historical Society Publications, 1993.
Metcalf, Clarence S. "Daniel Dobbins, Sailing Master, U.S.N., Commodore Perry's Right Hand Man." *Inland Seas* 14 (1958): 88–96, 181–191.
Severance, Frank H., ed., and William Dobbins. "The Dobbins Papers: Early Days on the Lakes and Episodes of the War of 1812." *Publications of the Buffalo and Erie County Historical Society* 8 (1905): 257–379.

DOWNIE, GEORGE
d. September 1814
British naval officer

Downie was one of four captains sent to join Sir James Lucas Yeo. He superseded Capt. Peter Fisher, who had been in command of the British squadron on Lake Champlain since 1813. Downie arrived at Isle aux Noix on 1 September 1814 and took command two days later. Capt. Daniel Pring was ordered to HMS *Linnet*. Fisher, who had taken command initially from Pring, was sufficiently disturbed to request a court-martial to investigate his conduct while in command.

Downie's squadron consisted of one brig, *Linnet* (16 guns); two captured sloops, renamed the *Broke* and the *Shannon;* and about ten row galleys and gunboats of one or two guns each. He found a frigate being built, the *Confiance,* which was to mount 36 guns, but she was incomplete. On 7 and 8 September, accompanied by *Linnet,* the *Confiance* was moved from the wharf at Isle aux Noix, and by sweeping, towing, warping, and sailing she reached a position off Chazy. Carpenters still worked fashioning her decks. Downie exercised the crew at the great guns, but they had no gun locks. He asked Captain Upton of HMS *Junon* at Quebec for his frigate's locks, but they never arrived. *Confiance* went into action with carronade locks fitted and bound in place to the long guns with copper hoops.

Letters exchanged from 7 to 10 September between Downie and Sir George Prevost, commanding the army, pressed Downie into action, for the army was pushing south along the western shore of the lake. Prevost's letters revealed a startling ignorance about the amount of time it took to bring parts of a squadron together and train the crews. Downie insisted that he would not take his vessels into action until they were ready. He reminded Prevost on 8 September that "the Ship was not ready—She is not ready now—and until she is ready, it is my duty, not to hazard the Squadron before an Enemy who will be superior in force." He also told Prevost's aide-de-camp when he arrived bearing another letter, "I am responsible for the Squadron I command, and no man shall make me lead it into action before it is in fit condition." This experienced captain was nobody's dupe.

Downie observed American Thomas Macdonough's position from Cumberland head and ordered his squadron to follow the *Confiance* as she moved along Macdonough's line. The *Confiance* was to fire on each vessel until she reached the U.S. flagship USS *Saratoga* and the brig USS *Eagle*. Then she was to sail between them.

The wind, however, prevented this maneuver, and the British line straggled. The result was that the *Linnet* fought against the *Eagle* and the *Confiance* against the *Saratoga* and *Ticonderoga*. Fifteen minutes into the battle, a cannonball struck Downie, killing him instantly. Command of *Confiance* devolved on his first lieutenant, who commanded the ship for two and a quarter hours. When Macdonough warped *Saratoga* round and brought fresh broadsides to bear, the *Confiance* was forced to surrender.

A Royal Navy court-martial exonerated Downie, portraying him as the victim of undue pressure by Sir George Prevost.

—*Frederick C. Drake*

See also: Lake Champlain, Battle of; Macdonough, Thomas; Yeo, James Lucas
Further Reading
Everest, Allan S. *The War of 1812 in the Champlain Valley*. Syracuse, NY: Syracuse University Press, 1981.
Wood, William H. *Select British Documents of the Canadian War of 1812*. 3 vols., Vol. 3, pp. 380, 395, 414, 441–442, 459, 463, 470. Toronto: Chaplain Society, 1920–1928.

DRUMMOND, GORDON
1772–1854
British general

Born in Quebec City on 27 September 1772, the youngest son of Colin Drummond of Perthshire and Catherine Oliphant of Rossie, in Scotland, Gordon was

educated in Britain. In 1807 he married Margaret Russell of Brancepeth Castle, and they had three children, two of them born in Canada. He died in London on 10 October 1854.

In 1789, Drummond entered the British army as an ensign in the First (The Royal Scots) Regiment of Foot. His rise was rapid: lieutenant in the 41st Foot in March 1791, a captain in January 1792, a major in the Eighth (King's) Foot in February 1794, and "junior lieutenant colonel" in March. In that year, he first saw active service in the Netherlands campaign under the duke of York. He became colonel on 1 January 1798, a brigadier general in 1804, and a major general the following year.

Before Drummond arrived in Canada, he served in the West Indies and the Mediterranean. In July 1808, he arrived in Quebec City to serve under the governor, Sir James Craig. Drummond was promoted to the rank of lieutenant general in June 1811, at which time he was commander of the forces in Canada, but he left in October to take up an appointment in Ireland. He returned to Canada in 1813 in order to succeed Major General Francis, Baron de Rottenburg, as commander of the forces in and administrator of Upper Canada (now Ontario).

Drummond was to demonstrate an aggressiveness and determination in combat not seen in the two previous commanders of Upper Canada, Major Generals Sir Roger Sheaffe and Rottenburg. As soon as Drummond arrived in the colony, he issued orders to stop or reverse the movement of units toward Lower Canada, and he hurried to the Niagara Frontier. There he found that Col. John Murray had moved into Fort George immediately after the hasty U.S. departure. Drummond decided to follow up this advance at once by seizing Fort Niagara. Its capture—by a surprise night attack—on 19 December gave the British effective control over the mouth of the Niagara River. Along with their possession of Fort George and Fort Mississauga (constructed in 1814) this control enabled them to deny that strategic anchorage to U.S. warships. Drummond never lost sight of the importance of holding on to all these positions and reaped the benefits later when Commodore Isaac Chauncey's fleet was unable to deliver supplies to Gen. Jacob Brown's army.

Determined to defend Upper Canada, Drummond persistently demanded more reinforcements and supplies from Sir George Prevost, recommended strengthening existing fortifications as well as undertaking new ones (Forts Mississauga and Drummond, the latter on Queenston Heights), and supported plans to attack U.S. bases. This led to the raid against Oswego on 6 May. Although the British did not carry out all the destruction they had hoped, their action did delay Chauncey's shipbuilding program. This raid also demonstrated the ability of Drummond and Commander Sir James Yeo to cooperate effectively in planning and executing combined operations.

Drummond was in Kingston when General Brown invaded the Niagara Frontier, captured Fort Erie, defeated Maj. Gen. Phineas Riall at Chippewa, and advanced north of Queenston, thereby threatening Fort George. Drummond acted decisively by shifting westward what forces he could muster and hurrying in that direction as soon as he was able. He arrived at York (Toronto) on 22 July and reached Fort George on the 25th, after sending orders to Lt. Col. John Tucker to lead a sortie southward from Fort Niagara. To deal with this apparent threat to his flank, Brown sent Brig. Gen. Winfield Scott with his brigade northward to menace Fort George. Out of these complicated maneuvers came the clash at Lundy's Lane between advanced elements of the two opposing armies. A full-scale battle developed after Drummond, bringing the 89th Foot and detachments of the Royal Scots, the King's, and the 41st, countermanded Riall's order to retreat. Drummond's will to fight was matched by the determination of the U.S. generals. The outcome was the bloodiest battle on Canadian soil during the war, with almost 900 U.S. casualties and over 800 British. Despite being wounded in the neck, Drummond continued to command throughout. He recognized the strategic significance of holding the high ground where the British guns were sited, and for control of that ground the battle was fought. Drummond's reputation was greatly enhanced by what the British and Canadians regarded as a victory.

The Battle of Lundy's Lane ended late on 25 July, and the Americans fell back to Fort Erie. By 1 August, Drummond had moved his headquarters to within a few miles of the fort, and the very next day he sent a raiding party across the river against Black Rock. The siege of Fort Erie had begun, but Drummond's battlefield successes were not to be repeated. His 15 August assault on the fort ended disastrously for the British. Drummond put the principal blame on De Watteville's Regiment, but much of the fault in fact lay with his own generalship. His plan of a three-pronged night attack was too complicated, and the preliminary artillery barrage sacrificed the advantage of surprise while failing to inflict significant damage on the defenses or casualties among the defenders.

Afterward, Drummond simply held on until winter put an end to campaigning. He supported plans and efforts to establish a naval base on Lake Erie and to open a road to a good harbor on Lake Huron, but in his time little was achieved.

Drummond also served as civil administrator of Upper Canada, generally with success. He presided over one session of the Upper Canadian assembly, which passed additional laws to support the war effort, including strong measures against traitors. During his term, the largest treason trial of the war was held at Ancaster, where 15 men were found guilty and sentenced to death. After deliberating over the implications and consulting legal officials, Drummond decided to reprieve seven, leaving their fate to be decided by the home government. Another problem that Drummond inherited was food shortages and the refusal of some farmers to sell supplies to the army. Like his predecessor, Rottenburg, Drummond was forced to impose martial law to meet the army's needs, but he stressed that it was to be applied carefully and mildly. Such a measure was never popular, but indications are that Drummond was both a successful and well-liked civil governor.

In April 1815, he was sworn in as administrator of Lower Canada and commander of the troops, replacing Sir George Prevost, who had been recalled to England. Drummond supervised the transition to peace between Canada and the United States under the Treaty of Ghent. For example, he directed the return of Michilimackinac to U.S. control. He departed for Britain in May 1816. There he lived quietly as a peacetime soldier. Promoted to general in May 1825, he was at the time of his death the senior general in the British army.

—*Wesley B. Turner*

See also: Brown, Jacob J.; de Rottenburg, Baron Francis; Erie, Fort; Lundy's Lane, Battle of; Prevost, George; Scott, Winfield; Sheaffe, Roger Hale; Yeo, James Lucas

Further Reading

Graves, Donald E. *The Battle of Lundy's Lane on the Niagara in 1814*. Baltimore, MD: The Nautical & Aviation Publishing Company of America, 1993.

Stanley, G.F.G. *The War of 1812. Land Operations*. Ottawa: National Museums of Canada, 1983.

Stickney, Kenneth. "Sir Gordon Drummond." *Dictionary of Canadian Biography*, F. G. Halpenny, gen. ed. Vol. 8, pp. 236–239. Toronto: University of Toronto Press, 1979.

Zaslow, Morris, ed. *The Defended Border. Upper Canada and the War of 1812*. Toronto: Macmillan, 1964.

DRUMMOND, WILLIAM
d. 1814
British officer

William Drummond, the nephew of Lt. Gen. Sir Gordon Drummond, British commander on the Niagara Frontier in 1814, served under his uncle in the British attempt to recoup British losses on the Niagara in the summer of 1814. Contemporaries described Drummond as an accomplished and magnetic officer, but they also noted a cruel streak. His conduct at Fort Erie revealed it.

To take Fort Erie in August 1814, Lieutenant General Drummond planned a night attack for 14–15 August. He gave his nephew, William Drummond, command of the attack on the old part of the fort, the U.S. right. Before the attack, Drummond told fellow officers that he did not expect to survive it. The assault on the right began at about 2:00 A.M. on 15 August, when Drummond (sometimes referred to as Drummond of Kelty to distinguish him from his more famous relative) led his 250 men against the fort. He was supported on his right by Lt. Col. Hercules Scott.

The main attack on the U.S. left faltered, leaving Drummond and Scott to secure at least part of the U.S. works. Scott was killed early, and thus the entire offensive fell to Drummond. Scott's charge against Battery Douglass had failed, and in the early stages of Drummond's attempt to force entry into the fort it appeared he would suffer a similar fate. The smoke from the guns combined with the darkness, however, to let him probe north for weaknesses. Finding one, he erected his scaling ladders to gain entrance to an upper floor. As Drummond bounded over the wall into the fort, several Americans heard him shout to his men to give no quarter. As good as his word, when Drummond encountered a severely wounded U.S. artillery officer begging for mercy, he shot the man with his pistol. A bullet soon found Drummond's heart, and Americans repeatedly bayoneted him. No quarter had become their watchword as well.

Drummond's death early in the effort spared him from the explosion that likely would have killed him anyway. As British soldiers pressed their attack, Fort Erie's powder magazine on the floor below blew up, killing many of Drummond's men. Spectacularly, it also ended the British attempt to take the fort.

—*Jeanne T. Heidler and David S. Heidler*

See also: Drummond, Gordon; Erie, Fort
Further Reading
Whitehorne, Joseph. *While Washington Burned: The Battle for Fort Erie, 1814.* Baltimore, MD: The Nautical and Aviation Company Publishing Company of America, 1992

DUANE, WILLIAM
1760–1835
U.S. journalist

Born to Irish immigrants in New York near Lake Champlain, William Duane was taken to Ireland by his mother when he was five years old. He was forced to learn the trade of a printer when his mother disinherited him for marrying a Protestant. He moved to Calcutta, India, in 1787 to start a newspaper called the *Indian World*. After being ejected from India for criticizing the East India Company, Duane spent a brief time in England and then migrated to the United States. Benjamin Franklin Bache employed him on the Philadelphia *Aurora*. He became the editor of that newspaper when Bache died in 1798.

Under Duane the *Aurora* became the leading Jeffersonian newspaper, a role that caused Duane's arrest for violation of the Sedition Act. Jefferson became president before Duane came to trial, so he was never prosecuted.

During the administration of Thomas Jefferson, Duane made British impressment of U.S. seamen the *Aurora*'s primary point of protest. He insisted that the issue should command as much attention as British and French violations of neutral trading rights. While urging the administration to action, Duane also engaged in a personal feud with Jefferson's secretary of the treasury, Albert Gallatin, that stemmed from the awarding of government printing contracts. The quarrel carried into politics in Pennsylvania—also Gallatin's adoptive state—and was still underway when war with Great Britain commenced in 1812.

When the war began, Gallatin's cabinet rival, Secretary of War John Armstrong, used this disagreement with Duane to anger Gallatin. Armstrong appointed Duane an adjutant-general in the army. Duane had developed an interest in military strategy before the war, but he was nothing more than an armchair amateur. Accordingly, he never achieved military glory, though he did begin to picture himself as a military expert. During the conflict, he published two instruction manuals for soldiers—*Handbook for Riflemen* and *Handbook for Infantry*. He also continued to edit the *Aurora*, writing about military matters and criticizing Federalists for condemning as inhumane the use of Robert Fulton's torpedoes.

Following the war, Duane ran the *Aurora* until 1822. He divided the remaining years of his life between travel and involvement in Pennsylvania politics.

—*Jeanne T. Heidler and David S. Heidler*

See also: Armstrong, John; Gallatin, Albert; Impressment

E

ECONOCHACA, BATTLE OF
23 December 1813
Creek War

Gen. Ferdinand L. Claiborne was determined to march on the Creek town of Econochaca. William Weatherford had erected the town, commonly called the Holy Ground, after the massacre at Fort Mims. It was designed as a safe haven for Creek Indians. The Creek prophets claimed that the town was protected by an indiscernible barricade that would destroy white men attempting to broach it. On 13 December 1813, Claiborne departed Fort Claiborne with approximately 1,000 men, consisting of Mississippi volunteers, a detachment from the Third U.S. Infantry Regiment, a battalion of horse, and 150 Choctaws.

After marching 100 miles, they reached Econochaca, situated on a bluff overlooking the Alabama River. On 23 December 1813, Claiborne advanced forward in three columns; the right commanded by Maj. Joseph Carson, the center under Col. Gilbert Russel composed of the regulars, and the left under Maj. Henry Cassells. Carson's column was the first to reach the town and came under immediate fire. His Mississippi volunteers held their ground, forcing the Indians to flee. The fighting ended before Cassells or Russel could get their columns into the fight. Claiborne then laid Econochaca to ashes. Two hundred houses were destroyed, and 33 Indians were killed in the action. The Americans lost only one dead and 20 wounded. Although a small battle, the loss of the town destroyed the prophets' credibility and severely damaged Red Stick morale.

—*John M. Keefe*

See also: Claiborne, Ferdinand L.; Creek War; Weatherford, William
Further Reading

Halbert, H. S., and T. H. Ball. *The Creek War of 1813 and 1814.* Chicago: Donohue and Henneberry, 1895.
Martin, Joel W. *Sacred Revolt: The Muskogees' Struggle for A New World.* Boston: Beacon Press, 1991.
Owsley, Frank Lawrence, Jr. *Struggle for the Gulf Borderlands.* Gainesville: University Presses of Florida, 1981.

EDWARDS, NINIAN
1775–1833
Illinois territorial governor, 1809–1818

Ninian Edwards was born 17 March 1775 in Montgomery County, Maryland. After attending Dickinson College in Carlisle, Pennsylvania, he moved to Kentucky in 1795 and began practicing law. In addition to serving in the state legislature, he was commissioned a major in the militia. A series of judicial appointments culminated in Edwards's becoming chief justice of the commonwealth of Kentucky in 1808.

In 1809, Edwards was appointed governor of the newly created and sparsely populated Illinois Territory. A territorial governor's powers were much more extensive than those of a state governor. From the beginning, Edwards's main problem was the hostility of many of the territory's Indians and the absence of an effective force of regular army troops. The deterioration of relations between Indians and settlers accelerated during 1810 and 1811.

In June 1811, Edwards wrote Secretary of War William Eustis that there was a growing number of hostile Indians near the Mississippi River and that he had ordered a series of blockhouses built in advance of white settlements. In July, after several settlers were killed, Edwards called out three companies of militia. He also supported Indiana territorial governor William Henry Harrison's plan to move against Tecumseh and Tenskwatawa (the Prophet) at Prophet's Town on the Tippecanoe River near present-day Lafayette, Indiana. Harrison's victory at the Battle of Tippecanoe, however, only increased raiding in the Illinois Territory.

After learning of the 18 June 1812 declaration of war,

Edwards moved territorial militia units to the northern line of settlement. Col. William Russell's arrival with two companies of U.S. Rangers at least partially relieved Edwards's worry about a lack of regular army troops. In October, Edwards and Russell started north from near modern Edwardsville with fewer than 400 mounted Illinois troops and U.S. Rangers. After burning two Kickapoo villages on a fork of the Sangamon River, they conducted a forced march to a large Kickapoo and Potawatomi village at the head of Peoria Lake. After a surprise dawn attack on horseback, Edwards reported that 24 to 30 Indians were killed without the loss of a single soldier.

Although he was active in early 1813 in sending out patrols and completing a string of 17 forts along the frontier between the Mississippi and Kaskaskia Rivers, the Peoria campaign was the highlight of Edwards's military career. In June 1813, Missouri territorial governor Benjamin Howard was appointed brigadier general to command both the Missouri and Illinois Territories. Edwards's active participation in the war thus came to a conclusion.

Edwards subsequently served as a U.S. senator from Illinois and in 1826 was elected governor of the state. He died 20 July 1833, at Belleville, Illinois.

—Robert J. Holden

See also: Illinois Territory
Further Reading
Edmunds, R. David. *The Potawatomis, Keepers of the Fire.* Norman: University of Oklahoma Press, 1978.
Edwards, Ninian Wirt. *History of Illinois from 1778 to 1833 and Life and Times of Ninian Edwards.* Springfield, IL: Illinois Journal Company, 1870.
Gilpin, Alec R. *The War of 1812 in the Old Northwest.* East Lansing: Michigan State University Press, 1958.
Holden, Robert J. "Ninian Edwards and the War of 1812: The Military Role of a Territorial Governor." *Selected Papers in Illinois History, 1980.* Springfield, IL: Illinois State Historical Society, 1980.
Reynolds, John. *My Own Times: Embracing Also the History of My Life.* Chicago: Fergus Printing Company, 1879.

ELLICOTT, JOSEPH
1760–1826
Land agent; intelligence agent, western New York

Pennsylvania-born Joseph Ellicott displayed an early aptitude for science and mechanics. He worked in his family's flour mill business in Maryland before joining his brothers in western Pennsylvania as a surveyor. As a surveyor, Ellicott was responsible for placing the southwestern boundary of New York State in 1789. In 1791, he surveyed Washington City and drew the boundary between Georgia and Creek Indian lands.

In 1794, the Holland Land Company hired Joseph Ellicott first to explore and later to survey western New York and Pennsylvania (1797). The 3,000,000 acres in western New York were opened to settlement in 1800 after being divided into townships 6 miles square. Appointed land agent by the Holland Land Company, Ellicott established his office at Batavia, New York, and acted as the "patroon" of western New York for 21 years. He arranged for road openings, internal surveys, land sales, payment collections, and the granting of deeds and mortgages.

Ellicott founded the city of Buffalo after excluding the site from Indian lands. In 1803, Buffalo was surveyed and laid out in a pattern similar to that of Washington, D.C. Ellicott's position as both landowner and land agent allowed him to become the Democratic Party boss for western New York.

During the turbulence of the Jefferson and Madison administrations, commercial considerations usually guided Joseph Ellicott's political stance. He opposed Jefferson's Embargo Act of 1807 because land sales dropped, yet he accepted the Non-Importation Acts of 1809 and Macon's Bill No. 2 in 1810 because land sales increased. Western New York War Hawk Peter B. Porter won election to Congress and urged an increase in national military forces along the Niagara. Ellicott, who opposed Porter, urged strengthening only local defenses because he believed there would be no war with Britain. Although a strong Democratic Republican partisan, Ellicott supported New York native son DeWitt Clinton against James Madison in the 1812 presidential election.

During the War of 1812, Ellicott sent letters to the Holland Land Company's agent general in which he substantially detailed British movements in Ontario and western New York. Although he did not engage in active military duty, Ellicott disapproved of the appointments of Generals Stephen Van Rensselaer and Alexander Smyth. When the British burned Buffalo on 30 December 1813, the remnants of the U.S. army established headquarters at Batavia. Refugees also sought shelter there. Ellicott turned his land office into a hospital, received army officers into his home, persuaded citizens to take in soldiers and refugees, and reunited families separated by the war. He was appointed one of three commissioners to distribute relief money given by New York State to its counties. Both the Holland Land Company and Ellicott gave additional financial aid. Ellicott donated his own land near the Batavia arsenal for the construction of barracks and storage shelters.

After the war, Ellicott encouraged the Holland Land Company's involvement in the construction of the Erie Canal. He was appointed a canal commissioner in 1816, but deteriorating mental health plagued him. By 1821, he had succumbed to what appears to have been clinical depression. He resigned from the land company and became a virtual recluse. Ellicott never married, and his last years were tortured ones spent in a mental asylum. He died in 1826.

—*William A. Paquette*

See also: Buffalo, New York
Further Reading

Babcock, James Locke. *Joseph Ellicott, the Founder of Buffalo.* Batavia, NY: Batavia Times, 1934.

Chazanof, William. *Joseph Ellicott and the Holland Land Company: The Opening of Western New York.* Syracuse, NY: Syracuse University Press, 1970.

Wyckoff, William. "Joseph Ellicott and the Western New York Frontier: Environmental Assessment, Geographical Strategies, and Authored Landscapes, 1797–1811." Ph.D. diss., Syracuse University, 1982.

ELLIOTT, JESSE DUNCAN
1782–1845
U.S. naval officer

Maryland-born Jesse Duncan Elliott was the son of a Revolutionary War patriot killed by Indians. The orphaned Elliott had few advantages but at age 20 entered school, intent on a naval career. Elliott's early career at sea consisted of appointments as midshipman on the frigate *Essex* (1804), lieutenant aboard the *Chesapeake* (1807), and acting lieutenant on the schooner *Enterprise* (1809). In 1810, Elliott carried important documents to the U.S. minister in London and saw service on the *John Adams* and the *Argus*.

When war with Great Britain was declared in 1812, the newly married Elliott was stranded in Norfolk. Proceeding north to New York City, Elliott joined with Commodore Isaac Chauncey and was sent to Presque Isle on Lake Erie to build a fleet of ships. On 9 October 1812, Elliott captured two British vessels there, HMS *Detroit* (the former U.S. brig *Adams* that had been captured at Detroit) and HMS *Caledonia*. Heavy bombardment from British shore artillery forced Elliott to beach and then destroy the *Detroit*. The *Caledonia*, however, became the nucleus for the Lake Erie flotilla that included the *Lawrence* and *Niagara*.

Jesse Elliott was Oliver Hazard Perry's main contender for the command of the Lake Erie fleet. Perry's seniority won. Elliott was transferred to Lake Ontario as captain of the *Madison*, Commodore Chauncey's flagship. After Elliott was promoted to master commandant in 1813, he and Chauncey successfully took York (now Toronto) on 24 July 1813. In August 1813, Elliott joined Commodore Perry as second in command with 100 men aboard the *Niagara*, where he took part in the Battle of Lake Erie against the British. After Perry's 10 September 1813 victory on Lake Erie, Elliott assumed temporary command of the Lake Erie fleet before his transfer to the sloop *Ontario*.

Charges were later made that during the Battle of Lake Erie, Elliott allowed the *Lawrence* to take the brunt of British fire for two hours before coming to the *Lawrence*'s assistance. It was after the war that the controversy became so publicly visible that Elliott challenged Perry to a duel. Perry declined but lodged charges against Elliott, alleging, among other things, that Elliott had displayed conduct unbecoming an officer. Horrified by the political implications of this quarrel, Pres. James Monroe refused to act on Perry's charges. The debate over this feud continued even after the deaths of both men.

After the War of 1812, Jesse Elliott's naval service spawned additional controversy. Tried on charges of misconduct alleged during his command of the Mediterranean squadron (1835–1838), he suffered a four-year suspension without pay, though two years' pay was later remitted. He was the commandant of the navy yard in Philadelphia (1844), where he died in 1845.

—*William A. Paquette*
—*Frederick C. Drake, contributing*

See also: Chauncey, Isaac; Lake Erie Campaign; York, Battle of
Further Reading

Altoff, Gerard T. "The Perry-Elliott Controversy." *Northwest Ohio Quarterly* 60 (autumn 1988): 135–152.

Belovarac, Allan. "A Brief Overview of the Battle of Lake Erie and the Perry-Elliott Controversy." *Journal of Erie Studies* 17 (fall 1988): 3–6.

Elliott, Jesse. *Address . . . delivered, November 14, 1843, in Washington County, Maryland . . . to His Early Companions, with an Appendix of Historical Facts and Documents.* N.p., 1844.

———. *A Biographical Notice of Commodore Jesse D. Elliott . . . Containing a Review of the Controversy between Him and the Late Commodore Perry.* N.p., 1835.

Palmer, Michael A. "A Failure of Command, Control, and

Communication: Oliver Hazard Perry and the Battle of Lake Erie." *Journal of Erie Studies* 17 (fall 1899): 7–26.

Roske, Ralph, and Richard W. Donely. "The Perry-Elliott Controversy: A Bitter Footnote to the Battle of Lake Erie." *Northwest Ohio Quarterly* 34 (1962): 111–123.

Westcott, Allen. "Commodore Jesse Duncan Elliott: The Stormy Petrel of the Navy." *United States Naval Institute Proceedings* 54 (1928): 773–778.

ELLIOTT, MATTHEW
1739?–1814
British Indian agent

Elliott was born in County Donegal, Ireland, in about 1739 and came to the United States in 1761. He settled in western Pennsylvania and in the years before the American Revolution traded out of Pennsylvania among the Shawnee Indians in the Ohio country. During the Revolution, Elliott fled from Pittsburgh to join the British in Detroit and for the rest of the war served as a British Indian agent. After the Revolution, he settled in Amherstburg, Upper Canada, where he traded. In the 1790s he again served the British among the Indians. Acting as assistant to Alexander McKee, Elliott was extremely active in encouraging the Indians to resist U.S. expansion beyond the Ohio River. In 1796, he became superintendent of Indian affairs at Amherstburg. At the end of the following year he was dismissed after a quarrel with the military authorities about his use of supplies. He remained an exceedingly influential figure in the Amherstburg-Detroit frontier region, cultivating an extensive and prosperous farm and serving as a member of the Upper Canadian House of Assembly. For many years he lived with a Shawnee woman, and she bore him two sons. One son, Alexander, who was educated as a lawyer, was killed in the War of 1812. In 1810, Elliott married Sarah Donovan. She also bore him two sons.

In 1808, in an atmosphere of deteriorating Anglo-American relations, Elliott was reappointed as superintendent at Amherstburg. In the years immediately prior to the War of 1812, Elliott helped advise and supply Indians from U.S. territory south of the Great Lakes. They were encouraged to visit Fort Malden at Amherstburg, and Elliott urged them to be prepared to serve the British should war break out between Great Britain and the United States. He gave support to the Indian confederacy that was being organized by Tecumseh and his brother Tenskwatawa (the Shawnee Prophet).

Although over 70 years old, Elliott was active in the field during the War of 1812, working with the Indians while holding the rank of lieutenant colonel in the Essex County militia. He led 600 Indians when Maj. Gen. Isaac Brock captured Detroit in August 1812 and in the next month went on Maj. Adam C. Muir's unsuccessful expedition against Fort Wayne.

The British had difficulty in supplying their troops and their many Indian allies in the Detroit region. In the winter of 1812–1813, Elliott took many Indians to winter at the rapids of the Maumee River in northwestern Ohio. In January 1813, he led the Indians when Col. Henry Procter defeated the Americans at Frenchtown. The Frenchtown victory caused great bitterness among the Americans because after the victory, when Procter and Elliott had returned to Amherstburg, Britain's Indian allies killed some of the captured U.S. wounded. This behavior only heightened the hatred of U.S. frontiersmen toward members of the British Indian Department.

Relations between Elliott and Colonel Procter were extremely poor. Procter was highly critical of Elliott, but Elliott continued to bear the main responsibility for organizing Indian support for British forces along the Detroit frontier region. Elliott was again in the field in the spring of 1813, coordinating the Indian forces in the sieges of Fort Meigs and Fort Stephenson in Ohio. There was further controversy at Fort Meigs, because once again U.S. prisoners were killed by the British Indian allies. At Fort Stephenson, relations between Procter and Elliott continued to deteriorate as they blamed one another for the failure of the attack on the fort.

When in September 1813 the British fleet on Lake Erie was defeated at the battle of Put-in-Bay, Procter's supply line was cut, and he decided he would have to withdraw from the Detroit frontier region. Elliott and the Indians wanted Procter to engage the Americans before withdrawing from the region, but Procter insisted on a retreat before the U.S. land forces arrived at Amherstburg, demoralizing the Indians. Elliott accompanied Procter's force and the Indians on the retreat and was present at the battle of the Thames when William Henry Harrison's forces overtook Procter's army. Procter, who disregarded the advice of Elliott and Tecumseh regarding the best defensive position, suffered a crushing defeat. Tecumseh was killed.

Elliott accompanied the remnant of the British force to Burlington at the head of Lake Ontario. He died there on 7 May 1814.

—Reginald Horsman

See also: Detroit, Surrender of; Frenchtown, Battles of; Malden, Fort; Meigs, Fort; Procter, Henry; Stephenson, Fort; Tecumseh; Tenskwatawa; Thames, Battle of the

Further Reading

Calloway, Colin. *Crown and Calumet: British-Indian Relations, 1783–1815.* Norman: University of Oklahoma Press, 1987.

Horsman, Reginald. *Matthew Elliott: British Indian Agent.* Detroit: Wayne State University Press, 1964.

———. "The Role of the Indian in the War." In *After Tippecanoe: Some Aspects of the War of 1812,* ed. Philip P. Mason. East Lansing: Michigan State University Press, 1963, pp. 60–77.

EMBARGO ACT

Provocation from Great Britain and France, in the form of the Orders in Council, the *Chesapeake-Leopard* Affair, and the decision to strictly enforce the Continental System, led Pres. Thomas Jefferson in 1807 to request enactment of the Embargo Act. This controversial measure eliminated U.S. trade with the other nations of the world, by which means Jefferson hoped to force the two belligerent powers to respect the neutral trading rights of the United States. The resulting 15-month experiment in economic warfare caused minor inconveniences to England while severely disrupting the U.S. economy. Faced with growing opposition to the measure at home, Jefferson asked Congress to repeal the act in the waning days of his administration.

The attack on the *Chesapeake* dramatically increased anti-British sentiment in the United States and quite possibly could have resulted in war between the two nations in 1807. At that time, however, as diplomatic historian Thomas Bailey writes, Jefferson "was still firmly committed to peace at almost any price." Economic sanctions might provide an opportunity to force both Britain and France to respect the neutral rights of the United States short of a declaration of war. In April 1806, Congress had passed the Non-Importation Act to limit the importation of certain British manufactured goods until an agreement could be reached. Jefferson also dispatched James Monroe and William Pinkney on a mission to London to conduct negotiations.

The Non-Importation Act briefly went into effect in November 1806, resulting in several seizures, but Jefferson recommended its suspension after just five weeks, primarily to encourage British concessions in the negotiations. Congress subsequently suspended the act through the summer of 1807 and authorized Jefferson to continue its suspension through the next legislative session. On 14 December, the law again went into effect, although ships that had sailed before this date had six months to return with any goods.

On this same day, news reached the United States from John Armstrong in France that Napoleon's Berlin Decree would henceforth be applied to all nations, including the United States. As Jefferson biographer Dumas Malone notes, "It was to become increasingly clear that, in the eyes of the French no less than the English, there were no more neutrals." Jefferson also informed Congress of a British proclamation calling for a continuation of the policy of impressment. "The validity of papers of naturalization," Malone continued, "on which Americans had so long relied, was denied. By this proclamation the sanction of the highest British authority was given to policies and practices which were regarded by Jefferson and Madison . . . as infringements on American sovereignty and a denial of basic human rights."

Despite the reservations of Albert Gallatin, who stated that, in regard to both domestic and foreign policy, "I prefer war to a permanent embargo," Jefferson asked Congress to enact a formal embargo on 18 December 1807. The president stated that the objective of the measure was to "keep our seamen and property from capture, and to starve the offending nations." By a wide margin the legislature adopted the act on 22 December.

The original Embargo Act, which would be revised and strengthened over the next year, forbade U.S.-registered vessels from leaving the United States for any foreign ports. Coastwide trade was allowed under the measure, although a heavy bond equal to double the value of the ship and cargo was required for these purposes, and trade to U.S. ports adjacent to foreign territory was also prohibited. Revenue officials inspected all vessels upon their arrival, and naval and revenue ships were authorized to stop any suspicious vessel. Despite these enforcement provisions, smuggling activities became rampant, particularly between U.S. and Canadian ports. Several loopholes also limited the law's effectiveness. Some ships left U.S. ports before the act became official. U.S. ships could still travel to foreign ports to pick up U.S. property, and foreign ships could bring goods to the United States if they left only with ballast. All of these provisions could be used to circumvent the law's intention. Nevertheless, by 1808 U.S. exports had declined to barely one-fifth of their level the previous year. The act infuriated New England shipping interests as well as southern and western farmers who exported their crops. On a positive note, the reduction in European imports did spur domestic manufacturing. Still, widespread opposition to the embargo led to a resurgence of the Federalist Party, especially in New England.

Opponents of the Embargo, including many in Jefferson's own administration, hoped that the president might ask for repeal of the measure at the opening of the December 1808 legislative session. Instead, in his annual message to Congress, he made no indication of his desire to do so. Opposition continued to grow during late 1808 and early 1809, and it became even more vocal after the passage of the harsh measures of the Enforcement Act of 1809.

Most frustrating to Jefferson was the embargo's limited impact on England and France. Historian Reginald Horsman contends that although the Embargo Act "certainly caused some consternation in England, it had little effect on those who created policy." British merchants and manufacturers who relied on trade with the United States and were thus hurt most by the embargo supported the Whig Party, which already opposed the Orders in Council. In Parliament in early 1808, Whigs criticized the Orders as both illegal and a detriment to U.S.-British relations. Meetings in Liverpool and in other ports and manufacturing cities led to petitions to repeal the Orders. Whigs argued that "England was not only losing the trade of the only important neutral but also was driving her into the arms of France." The British government, however, refused to be swayed by these opposition protests, insisting that the Orders remain in force as an integral part of the struggle against Napoleon. Increased trade to Central and South America largely offset the decline in commerce with the United States, and in fact the Tory leadership was pleased with the embargo.

Growing domestic opposition and an intractable England and France forced Jefferson to reluctantly ask for the Embargo's repeal. On 1 March 1809, days before leaving office, the president signed legislation repealing the act and replacing it with the Non-Intercourse Act. This new law continued the restrictions on trade with the two belligerents while enabling U.S. ships to trade with neutral nations. If either England or France reversed or modified its maritime policies to the benefit of the United States, trade with that nation might resume.

In retrospect the Embargo Act had failed by almost every measure. Abroad the act failed to end either the Orders in Council or the Continental System, and at home it had revitalized the Federalist opposition and hurt Republican morale. Federalist strength in Congress doubled after the 1808 elections, and the party tripled its electoral vote in the presidential election. Widespread smuggling undermined the embargo, even among its proponents. In 1807, in the aftermath of the *Chesapeake-Leopard* incident, Jefferson might easily have brought the nation into war with Great Britain. Ironically, by early 1809 such enthusiasm had largely passed. Jefferson left office in March 1809, leaving James Madison to deal with the thorny issue of foreign trade. Further negotiations and legislation, in the form of Macon's Bill No. 2, failed to settle the issue with Great Britain and ultimately led to war in 1812.

—*David Coles*

See also: Macon's Bill No. 2; Non-Intercourse Act; Trade Restrictions
Further Reading
Horsman, Reginald. *The Causes of the War of 1812*. Philadelphia: University of Pennsylvania Press, 1962.
Jennings, Walter W. *The American Embargo, 1807–1809*. Iowa City: University of Iowa Press, 1921.
Malone, Dumas. *Jefferson the President: Second Term, 1805–1809*. Boston: Little, Brown, 1974.
Perkins, Bradford. *Prologue to War: England and the United States, 1805–1812*. Berkeley: University of California Press, 1961.
Rutland, Robert A. *Madison's Alternatives: The Jeffersonian Republicans and the Coming of War, 1805–1812*. Philadelphia: J. B. Lippincott, 1975.
Sears, Louis M. *Jefferson and the Embargo*. Durham, NC: Duke University Press, 1927.
Spivak, Burton. *Jefferson's English Crisis: Commerce, Embargo, and the Republican Revolution*. Charlottesville: University of Virginia Press, 1979.

EMUCKFAU CREEK, BATTLE OF
22 January 1814

Gen. Andrew Jackson decided to attack the large encampment of hostile Creeks at Emuckfau Creek in present-day Alabama as a diversion for Gen. John Floyd's advance from Georgia. On 15 January 1814, with 800 volunteers, 200 friendly Indians, and one 6-pounder, Jackson crossed the Coosa River. It was to be the only time in the Creek War that a U.S. force conducted an offensive against a superior Indian force.

Late in the night of 21 January, Jackson's forces came upon a well-beaten path leading to the Creek encampment. Jackson decided to halt and conduct a reconnaissance before venturing any farther. He then formed his forces in a large hollow square. At 6:00 A.M., about 900 hostile Indians fell upon Jackson's left flank. The Indians were checked until first light, when Gen. John Coffee led forward a party of men, pushing the Indians back. Coffee then pursued the Indians with about 400 men. Upon reaching the Indian encampment, Coffee realized that the

Indians were too numerous, so he returned to the main U.S. force. This retreat encouraged the Indians, who once again attacked Jackson's position. General Coffee again counterattacked and after some difficulty repelled them.

Jackson returned to Fort Strother, fighting while en route another brief, but fierce, action at Enitachopco Creek. Twenty men were killed and 75 wounded in the campaign. Even though Jackson had not scored a major victory, the Madison administration eagerly embraced any report that was not bad news. As a result, the battles, and Jackson's role in them, were celebrated.

—*John M. Keefe*

See also: Coffee, John; Creek War; Enitachopco Creek, Battle of; Jackson, Andrew
Further Reading
Martin, Joel W. *Sacred Revolt: The Muskogees' Struggle for A New World.* Boston: Beacon Press, 1991.
Owsley, Frank Lawrence, Jr. *Struggle for the Gulf Borderlands.* Gainesville: University Presses of Florida, 1981.
Rowland, Dunbar. *Andrew Jackson's Campaign against The British, Or The Mississippi Territory in the War of 1812.* New York: Macmillan, 1926.

ENITACHOPCO CREEK, BATTLE OF
24 January 1814

After two months delay awaiting reinforcements and supplies, Andrew Jackson, with about 1,000 men, felt comfortable enough to make a raid from his base at Fort Strother against Red Stick Creek positions. After one engagement on 22 January 1814 at Emuckfau, he decided to move back to Fort Strother to await more men and supplies before undertaking a major campaign.

His route back to Fort Strother carried him across Enitachopco Creek. Since he knew that Red Sticks in fairly large numbers were in the vicinity, he decided to camp for the night on 23 January before crossing the creek the next day. Realizing the possibility of an attack in his rear, Jackson warned his officers to have the men ready to turn and fight at a moment's notice. Just as he expected, after much of the army was across the creek, Red Sticks fell on the rear guard in a ferocious assault.

Jackson had intended his right and left columns to wheel around and recross the creek above and below the Indians to envelop their position. Faced with the Indians, however,

both columns panicked and ran, leaving only the men in the center to stand their ground against the Red Sticks. Jackson finally repelled the Creek assault by bringing up his one artillery piece, a 6-pounder, and firing grapeshot into the attackers. He then made his way back to Fort Strother.

Though neither the Battle of Emuckfau nor that of Enitachopco was a great victory for Jackson, both battles inflicted heavy casualties on the Red Sticks. Also, news of these battles reached the rest of the country just as it was learning of the disastrous invasions of Canada out of New York, thus providing some good military news at an otherwise dismal time.

—*Jeanne T. Heidler and David S. Heidler*

See also: Emuckfau Creek, Battle of; Jackson, Andrew
Further Reading
Owsley, Frank Lawrence, Jr. *Struggle for the Gulf Borderlands.* Gainesville: University Presses of Florida, 1981.

ENTERPRISE VERSUS BOXER
5 September 1813

The "lucky little *Enterprise*" was a 14-gun U.S. Navy schooner, altered to a brig, commanded by Lt. William Burrows. Her sister ships, the *Nautilus* and *Vixen,* had both been captured by the British and later wrecked. On 1 September 1813, *Enterprise* sailed from Portsmouth, New Hampshire, with 120 men. After chasing a schooner suspected of being a British privateer, the *Enterprise* set a course for Monhegan Island, Maine, an area in which British vessels had been reported. On 5 September, in a bay near Pemaquid Point, a British brig was discovered getting underway.

This was the Royal Navy's 14-gun brig *Boxer* (Capt. Samuel Blyth, 66 men). This ship, whose flag was ordered nailed to the mast by her glory-seeking captain, set a course directly for the *Enterprise,* with an engagement ensuing in mid-afternoon. During a 40-minute melee, the *Enterprise* gained a favorable position that allowed her to rake the bow of the British vessel. The battered *Boxer* surrendered and lowered her colors only after the U.S. warship, which had been lightly damaged in the fray, stopped firing. U.S. dead and wounded were listed at 12 and British at 21.

Both Lieutenant Burrows and Captain Blyth were mortally wounded early in this engagement and were buried side by side with full military honors in Portland, Maine. Command of the *Enterprise* in this action fell to Lt. Edward

Charles del et Sculp gloats over American victories in this 1813 etching. James Madison pounds King George III, while presumably similar things are taking place between the two ships in the background.

R. McCall, who, like Burrows, was awarded a gold medal by Congress for gallantry.

—*Robert J. Bunker*

See also: Burrows, William
Further Reading
Hill, F. Stanhope. *The "Lucky Little* Enterprise" *and Her Successors in the United States Navy, 1776–1900.* Boston: F. Stanhope Hill, 1900.
Picking, Sherwood. *Sea Fight off Monhegan:* Enterprise *and* Boxer. Portland, ME: Machigonne Press, 1941.

ERIE, FORT

Fort Erie was the southern anchor of the British defensive line along the Niagara River. Situated at the easternmost end of Lake Erie, its guns threatened vessels approaching the entrance of the Niagara. As early as 1750, the French had a trading post at this strategic point. The British built two fortifications there following the French and Indian War, but both were destroyed in violent lake storms. Reconstruction began in 1805 but was not completed by the start of the war. In 1812, Fort Erie consisted of two stone barracks enclosed by two earthen and two masonry bastions.

In October 1812, naval lieutenant Jesse Elliott and a daring band of U.S. raiders cut out two British brigs from under the guns of the fort, but combat was otherwise limited to intermittent salvos between the British and the U.S. shore batteries across the river. Following the capture of Fort George in May 1813, Brig. Gen. John Vincent ordered the evacuation of the Niagara River defensive line. The garrison at Fort Erie dutifully blew up or burned as much of the fortifications as they could and then proceeded to join Vincent at Burlington Heights. Americans occupied the ruins of Fort Erie but soon departed. The focus of the fighting by then was along the north shore of the Niagara Peninsula. In December, the British reoccupied Fort Erie following Lt. Gen. Gordon Drummond's winter offensive that had cleared U.S. forces from both shores of the Niagara River.

Fort Erie was the first objective of Maj. Gen. Jacob Brown's 1814 campaign. In the early hours of 3 July, Brig. Gen. Winfield Scott crossed the Niagara River with his brigade of regulars, landing just north of the fort. Brig. Gen. Eleazar Ripley landed his regular brigade a few hours later on the shore of Lake Erie, west of the fort. The two bodies of troops united, surrounding the British garrison of 137. As the Americans approached, a Royal Artillery gun fired. The round exploded over the heads of the color guard of the 25th U.S. Infantry, wounding four corporals. The British commander, considering that further resistance was futile in face of such a large force, surrendered. As the British crossed the Niagara River in captivity, the 25th U.S. Infantry planted its colors on the ramparts. As Brown marched his army, designated as the Left Division, northward to beat the British in open battle, a small U.S. garrison labored to improve the fort's defenses.

After an impressive victory at Chippewa, the Left Division failed to defeat Drummond's army at Lundy's Lane and withdrew to Fort Erie. Drummond followed slowly, discovering as he approached the fort that the Americans had enhanced it by extending a long earthen wall, fronted by a ditch and abatis, from the fort to Snake Hill on the shore of Lake Erie. The Americans, commanded by Brig. Gen. Edmund P. Gaines, were within a long, slender entrenched camp, their backs to the water.

Drummond brought up guns from Fort George and opened a bombardment on 13 August. In the early hours of 15 August, Drummond threw three assault columns against the Americans, who fended off the first two attacks. The last column, under the command of Col. William Drummond, forced its way into a bastion. For two hours the antagonists grappled at close quarters, but neither side could make headway. Then disaster struck the British. A powder magazine in the bastion exploded, killing and maiming hundreds. With their casualties at nearly 900, the survivors struggled back to the British lines.

Drummond's force was considerably weakened, but he refused to give up. The bombardment continued, and skirmishing between the fort and the British batteries added daily to the casualty lists. In September, 1,500 New York militiamen crossed the Niagara and reinforced the U.S. garrison. The aggressive Jacob Brown, who returned to command to replace the wounded Gaines, decided to force the issue. On 17 September, Brig. Gen. Peter B. Porter and Col. James Miller led two columns out of Fort Erie. In a

torrential rainfall, the Americans fell upon the three British batteries, capturing two of them and spiking the guns. The Americans suffered over 500 casualties, the British 600. Drummond despaired of capturing the fort and withdrew northward.

In October, Maj. Gen. George Izard crossed over into Canada with the Right Division of several thousand trained regulars. Although he greatly outnumbered Drummond's army, he decided not to press the fight, and early in November, Izard withdrew all U.S. forces to the New York shore. The last Americans to leave blew up Fort Erie, leaving nothing of use to the British. The fort remained in ruins until 1937, when Canada restored it to its wartime appearance.

—*Richard V. Barbuto*

See also: Brown, Jacob J.; Drummond, Gordon; Drummond, William; Gaines, Edmund Pendleton; Izard, George; Ripley, Eleazar Wheelock; Scott, Winfield; Vincent, John

Further Reading

Owen, David A. *Fort Erie: An Historical Guide.* N.p.: The Niagara Parks Commission, 1986.

Whitehorne, Joseph. *While Washington Burned: The Battle for Fort Erie.* Baltimore, MD: The Nautical and Aviation Publishing Company of America, 1992.

ESSEX, VOYAGE OF THE

See Porter, David, Jr.

ESSEX DECISION

A prominent maritime law case prior to the War of 1812, the *Essex* Decision restricted neutral shipping under provisions of the so-called Rule of 1756. The decision exacerbated tensions between the United States and Great Britain and contributed to several economic countermeasures adopted by the U.S. government between 1806 and 1809.

In the four years after 1803, when a new round of warfare broke out between Great Britain and France, U.S. exports doubled to more than $100 million. Initially, U.S. trade with the two nations operated under the provisions of Jay's Treaty and the Convention of 1800, but both belligerents soon adopted increasingly severe restrictions on neutral trade. Under the Rule of 1756, the British government had claimed that neutral ships could not trade with certain colonies during wartime if that trade had previously been restricted during peacetime. This ruling related primarily to the French and Spanish West Indies colonies. In the 1790s, John Jay had agreed to this interpretation in his negotiations with the British. This rule remained in force until 1802, when a British Admiralty Court rendered a decision in the case of the *Polly.* That decision interpreted the Rule of 1756 in a manner more favorable to the United States.

The *Polly* had sailed from the United States to Spain with a cargo of sugar and cocoa from the Spanish West Indies. It was seized en route by a British naval vessel, but an Admiralty Court ruled that the *Polly's* voyage had not violated the Rule of 1756, since the cargo had initially been brought to the United States from the Spanish colonies. While in port at Marblehead, Massachusetts, the cargo was unloaded, customs duties were paid, and the ship was then reloaded and sailed for Spain. Surprisingly, the British court ruled in favor of the "broken voyage" concept, by which goods could be "re-exported" from the United States to European ports. Although this procedure increased costs, the reexport trade still proved profitable for U.S. shippers. "When war was renewed [in 1803]," Samuel Flagg Bemis has noted, "neutrals took like ducks to water to this lucrative trade." By 1805 the value of reexported foreign goods surpassed the value of exported domestic goods, an imbalance that continued for the next two years.

Complaints from British companies mounted in the three years after the *Polly* case, as they realized that U.S. shippers were simply carrying goods for the French and Spanish. "It was little use," according to Reginald Horsman, "to sweep the French from the seas if the Americans could immediately take their place." Publication of James Stephen's pamphlet, *War in Disguise, or The Frauds of the Neutral Flags,* led to growing demands for a judicial remedy. The Admiralty Court responded with a second ruling in May 1805, known as the *Essex* Decision.

The *Essex,* a U.S. ship seized en route from Salem to Havana, had actually begun her voyage in Barcelona. In this instance the court allowed the seizure. It ruled that goods could only be "neutralized" by shipping them through a neutral country if the import duty was actually paid. Previously it was common practice for this duty to be remitted if the goods were eventually reexported. Americans fumed at this new interpretation of a "continuous voyage," with James Madison calling it a "new and shameful depredation," but the decision stood.

In the aftermath of the *Essex* Decision the British navy seized perhaps 300 or 400 U.S. ships involved in the reexport trade, though British courts eventually released most

of these. The new Whig government that took office in 1806 proved to be more sympathetic to the United States and moved to reverse the *Essex* Decision. When a May 1806 decree established a blockade of northern Europe, it also essentially relaxed restrictions on the reexport trade. Still, the ruling had strained relations between the two countries. In its aftermath, James Monroe and William Pinkney tried to negotiate with Great Britain on the issues of impressment and the reexport trade. Congress adopted the Non-Importation Act but delayed its implementation pending the results of the negotiations.

In December 1806, the two nations signed a treaty that in part pledged British allowance of the reexport trade under certain conditions, such as the payment of nominal duties when breaking a voyage in a U.S. port. Despite other British concessions, Jefferson did not submit the treaty for ratification, primarily because of continued questions about impressment. By the next year, new Orders in Council issued by the British government, coupled with the attack on the *Chesapeake,* led to a U.S. response in the form of the Embargo Act. The *Essex* Decision of 1805 had set in motion the economic measures and countermeasures between Great Britain and the United States that culminated in war seven years later.

—*David Coles*

See also: Berlin Decree; Embargo Act; Impressment; Milan Decree; Monroe, James; Orders in Council; Pinkney, William; Trade Restrictions

Further Reading

Bailey, Thomas A. *A Diplomatic History of the American People.* 9th ed. Englewood Cliffs, NJ: Prentice-Hall, 1974.

Bemis, Samuel Flagg. *A Diplomatic History of the United States.* 3d ed. New York: Henry Holt, 1950.

Horsman, Reginald. *The Causes of the War of 1812.* Philadelphia: University of Pennsylvania Press, 1961.

Perkins, Bradford. *Prologue to War: England and the United States, 1805–1812.* Berkeley: University of California Press, 1961.

Spivak, Burton. *Jefferson's English Crisis: Commerce, Embargo, and the Republican Revolution.* Charlottesville: University of Virginia Press, 1979.

ESSEX JUNTO

The *Essex Junto* was a term first used by John Hancock to describe a group in Essex County, Massachusetts, during the American Revolution. Pres. Thomas Jefferson also used the term to identify his political enemies from the Bay State. Original members included Massachusetts chief justice Theophilus Parsons, Sen. Timothy Pickering, and former representative Fisher Ames. During the War of 1812, Federalist opponents of the Madison administration composed the Junto.

During the War of 1812, the Essex Junto called for a new union of the original thirteen states. The secessionist proposal was sponsored by John Lowell, a wealthy patrician from Roxbury and a founder of the Massachusetts General Hospital, the Athenaeum, and other old Boston institutions. Son of Judge John Lowell and Sarah Higginson, "Jack" Lowell led the New England Federalist opposition to "Mr. Madison's War." Shortly after the June 1812 declaration of war, Lowell published two powerful antiadministration pamphlets accusing Madison of refusing to pursue a reasonable peace settlement. The pamphlets were entitled *Mr. Madison's War* and *Perpetual War: The Policy of Mr. Madison.*

Lowell's attack took on substantive shape in early 1813. He proposed a plan for a new federal constitution and presented it as an ultimatum to the original thirteen states. His proposal was published in a pamphlet entitled *Thoughts in a Series of Letters, in Answer to a Question respecting the Division of the States by a Massachusetts Farmer.* Lowell not only emulated the persona assumed by Pennsylvanian John Dickinson when he had drafted letters opposing British taxation policy in the 1760s, he also relied upon the Virginia and Kentucky Resolves of 1798.

Lowell's pamphlet argued that the Louisiana Purchase violated the compact theory of the Constitution and that the newly elected congressmen from western states posed a threat to New England's commercial interests. A separation of the West, he insisted, "must take place, and the sooner the better." In Lowell's view, to have New England recover its "ancient prosperity" and unite "the original thirteen states . . . appears to be the last hope of our country." He proposed expelling the West from the Union.

In addition to receiving backing from some of the Essex Junto, including Sen. Timothy Pickering, Lowell's proposal received support from antiwar Federalists Gouverneur Morris of New York and Charles Carroll of Maryland. All of Boston's Federalist newspapers except one promoted the proposal as a platform for the proposed Hartford Convention. The most enthusiastic paper was Maj. Benjamin Russell's *Columbian Centinel.* It endorsed the secessionist idea in a series of articles called "The Crisis." A January 1813 piece proclaimed: "We are plunged into a war without a sense of enmity, or a perception of sufficient provocation; and obliged to fight the battles of a cabal which, under the sickening affectation of republican equality, aims at trampling into the dust the weight, influence, and power of commerce and her dependencies." Outside of New England, moreover, Baltimore's *Federal Republican,* briefly chased from that city by prowar mobs, published from Georgetown, D.C., an open letter to President Madison. In it the newspaper pleaded with him to "do immediate justice to the claims of New England. . . . Do you imagine that a people thus injured, insulted, abused, and libeled, can possibly feel towards you any sentiment but that of deep and fixed detestation?"

The Essex Junto's power culminated at the Hartford Convention, December 1814 to January 1815. With the exception of Pickering, however, the few remaining members of the Junto, such as Harrison Gray Otis, George Cabot, Joseph Lyman, and Benjamin Hazzard, opposed secession. Instead, the convention passed a series of measures calling for constitutional amendments that would repeal the three-fifths clause, reserve officeholding for native citizens, institute a single-term presidency, and require a two-thirds vote of Congress to admit new states, enact restrictions on commerce, or declare war.

The Essex Junto's earlier secessionist proposal was so obviously self-serving that the Hartford Convention never took it seriously. Nevertheless, the efforts of the Junto revealed for a time the strength of antiwar sentiment in Massachusetts as well as the rest of New England.

—*Charles F. Howlett*

See also: Federalist Party; Hartford Convention
Further Reading

Borden, Morton. *Parties and Politics in the Early Republic, 1789–1815.* New York: Thomas Y. Crowell, 1967.
Morison, Samuel Eliot. "Dissent in the War of 1812." In *Dissent in Three American Wars,* ed. Samuel Eliot Morison, Frederick Merk, and Frank Friedel. Cambridge: Harvard University Press, 1970.

ESSEX VERSUS *ALERT*
13 August 1812

The *Essex* was a U.S. Navy frigate rated at 32 guns and armed almost exclusively with 32-pounder carronades. She was therefore a very powerful vessel at close quarters. On 3 July 1812, she sailed under Capt. David Porter from New York for Bermuda. On arrival there the *Essex* encountered seven British troopships escorted by only one warship, the 32-gun frigate HMS *Minerva* (Capt.

Richard Hawkins). Hawkins refused battle and endeavored to protect the convoy, but Porter succeeded in cutting out one of the troopships and capturing her 200 soldiers. Porter sent her off with a prize crew.

During the next month the *Essex* took seven additional prizes. On 13 August, while in the North Atlantic, her seamen sighted a Royal Navy sloop, the HMS *Alert* (Capt. T.L.O. Laugharne). Porter pretended to be a merchantman endeavoring to escape. As the *Alert* came up, Laugharne discovered his mistake too late. Rated at 16 guns, the *Alert* was armed with 20 18-pounder carronades. Porter described the resulting action in these words: The *Alert* "ran down on our weather quarter, gave three cheers, and commenced an action (if so trifling a skirmish deserves the name) and after eight minutes, struck her colours, with but water in her hold, much cut to pieces and three men wounded."

Porter ordered the *Alert* disarmed (her guns were thrown overboard), shifted his prisoners to her, and sent them into Halifax with Laugharne's signed agreement to the parole of an equal number of Americans.

The *Essex* returned to New York on 7 September.

—*Spencer C. Tucker*

See also: Porter, David, Jr.
Further Reading
Donovan, Frank. *The Odyssey of the* Essex. New York: David McKay, 1969.
Long, David F. *Nothing Too Daring: A Biography of Commodore David Porter, 1780–1843.* Annapolis, MD: Naval Institute Press, 1970.
Porter, David. *Journal.* 2 vols. New York: Wiley and Halstead, 1815. Reprint, 1970.

ESSEX VERSUS *PHOEBE* AND *CHERUB*

28 March 1814

On 28 October 1812, the U.S. Navy frigate *Essex* (32 guns, commanded by Capt. David Porter) left the Delaware on a long and highly successful cruise in the Pacific. On 12 January 1814, after taking 16 prizes, she made land at Valparaíso, Chile. She then had a crew of 255 men and was sailing in company with one of her prizes, renamed the *Essex Junior*, with a crew of 60 men. The *Essex* was armed almost exclusively with carronades. She had 17 32-pounder carronades and only six long 12-pounders.

The *Essex Junior* had 20 guns—ten long 6-pounders and ten 18-pounder carronades.

On 8 February, the U.S. ships were anchored in neutral Valparaíso Harbor when the British frigate *Phoebe* (36 guns, Capt. James Hillyar and 300 men) accompanied by the *Cherub* (18 guns, Capt. Thomas T. Tucker, 140 men) arrived. The *Phoebe* had 15 long guns: Thirteen were 18-pounders, one a 12-pounder, and one a 9-pounder. She also had eight carronades: seven 32s and one 18. The *Cherub* had two long 9-pounders and 11 carronades: nine 32s and two 18-pounders.

Apparently Hillyar first attempted to take the *Essex* by coup de main. He brought the *Phoebe* to about 15 feet from the *Essex*, but the Americans were ready to repel a boarding attempt. Indeed, Porter had Hillyar's vessel at his mercy, but Hillyar assured Porter he meant nothing hostile and Porter allowed him to haul away. Later the two captains met on shore, and Hillyar assured Porter he had no intention of breaking Chilean neutrality.

The British warships then began a blockade, however. On 27 February, the *Phoebe* fired a weather-gun, which those aboard the *Essex* took as a challenge. Porter took the crew from the *Essex Junior* aboard and sailed out to meet the *Phoebe*. Hillyar refused the hazard, however, and ran down to the *Cherub* several miles distant. Although in number of guns the two frigates were closely matched, their armaments were in fact quite different. The *Essex*'s carronades were suited only for short-range action, whereas the *Phoebe* had mainly long guns. To the Americans it appeared that Hillyar was determined that if the two warships fought, it would be in circumstances of his choosing.

Porter, meanwhile, was laying plans to leave the harbor. He hoped to draw off the two British warships to chase the *Essex*, allowing the *Essex Junior* to escape. He had already discovered that the *Essex* was faster than the *Phoebe* and the even-slower *Cherub*, so he had no worry about his own vessel. A storm on 28 March unexpectedly moved up Porter's flight when the *Essex* parted her port cable, so he got her under way. Just as she exited the bay a heavy squall struck, causing her to lose her main top mast. Porter tried to regain the harbor, but a shift in the wind and his ship's crippled condition made this impossible. He anchored just off shore in a small bay some 3 miles from Valparaíso. As soon as Hillyar saw the *Essex*'s damaged condition, he prepared for an attack that would, in effect, violate his promise to respect Chilean neutrality.

The Americans prepared for action. Their carronade armament required vessel speed, so all knew they had virtually no chance of success. The British began the engagement about 4:00 P.M., before Porter was able to set springs on the *Essex*'s cables. Three times the American got out the springs, and three times they were shot away as soon as they were hauled taut. The two British warships stood off to sight their long-range guns and thus remained beyond the reach of the U.S. guns. In the process, the *Phoebe* and *Cherub* inflicted terrible punishment on the *Essex*. Most U.S. casualties occurred during this initial pounding.

After about five minutes, the Americans were able to get some long guns into the stern ports to fire at the rigging of the British warships. At 4:30, the two Britons hauled off to repair damage, but they soon returned, again positioning themselves out of carronade range to fire their long guns. At 5:20, Porter cut his cable, set what sail he could, and tried to close with his antagonists. The two British ships, however, hauled off out of carronade range and continued to fire their long guns. Unable to close, Porter tried to make the shore with the intention of burning rather than surrendering his ship, but the wind shifted and the British attack continued. The *Essex* was reduced to the sporadic firing of a long 12, and finally she caught fire. When some of her powder exploded, hurling many of her crew overboard, the ship could not continue the fight.

The Americans fought courageously but at high cost. Of 255 men aboard the *Essex* when the battle began, 58 were killed, 66 wounded, and 31 drowned. Twenty-four made it to shore, and a lucky 76 emerged unscathed. At 6:20, the *Essex* surrendered, and the British took possession. British losses were light. The *Phoebe* and *Cherub* together had five killed and ten wounded, a disparity in casualties explained by the British ability to fire ten shots for every one from the Americans.

The British repaired the *Essex* at Valparaíso and then sailed her to Britain, where she was taken into the Royal Navy. The *Essex Junior* was disarmed, and most of the U.S. prisoners embarked in her for New York.

This engagement considerably tarnished the reputation of the carronade and reinforced the conclusion that vessels should not be armed exclusively with them. Ironically, that was a point that Porter had made in vain to his superiors when he had assumed command of the *Essex*.

—*Spencer C. Tucker*

See also: Hillyar, James; Porter, David, Jr.
Further Reading
Donovan, Frank. *The Odyssey of the* Essex. New York: McKay, 1969.
Long, David F. *Nothing Too Daring: A Biography of Commodore David Porter, 1780–1843*. Annapolis, MD: Naval Institute Press, 1970.
Porter, David. *Journal*. 2 vols. New York: Wiley and Halstead, 1815. Reprint, 1970.

EUSTIS, WILLIAM
1753–1825
U.S. secretary of war

A prominent Massachusetts politician of the late 1700s and early 1800s, William Eustis served as secretary of war from 1809 through the first six months of the War of 1812. Unprepared for this position and roundly criticized for the nation's lack of military preparedness, he resigned in December 1812.

Born in Cambridge, Massachusetts, on 10 June 1753, Eustis, the son of a well-known physician, entered Harvard at the age of 14. He graduated in 1772 and subsequently studied medicine under the tutelage of Dr. Joseph Warren. Upon the outbreak of the Revolution, Eustis joined the patriot cause, enrolling first as a militiaman at Lexington and then performing duties as a surgeon. Attached to an artillery unit stationed at Cambridge, Eustis was present at Bunker Hill and later served as a senior camp surgeon. When hospital appropriations were exhausted, Eustis used his own funds to operate the facility for "many months." The young doctor stayed in the army until the war's end, when he entered private practice in Boston. During 1786 and 1787, Eustis was surgeon with the expedition organized to put down Shays's Rebellion.

While continuing his medical practice, Eustis also became active in politics as an anti-Federalist. He served in the Massachusetts state legislature from 1788 to 1794, and in 1800 he ran for Congress as a Republican, narrowly defeating his Federalist opponent, Josiah Quincy. Two years later he won a close reelection fight against John Quincy Adams. In 1804, the two candidates ran again, but this time Adams was victorious.

In March 1809, James Madison nominated Eustis, described by a biographer of the president as an "ardent Republican and physician of high repute," to the position of secretary of war. "I transmit the Commission," the president wrote to the new secretary, "with a hope that I shall have the pleasure of learning that your Country will have the benefit of your services in that important station." Eustis replied: "I will come to the duties of the office with such means and talents as I possess and with the hope that . . . there may arise no just cause for censure from the public and no regret on your part that the appointment has been thus bestowed." Eustis's loyalty and Madison's desire to shore up Republican support in Federalist-dominated New England evidently overcame concerns about the nominee's lack of military administrative experience.

William Eustis

Modern historians have not been kind to Eustis. William Hassler called him "a pathetic appointment" with little experience, who "was selected to head the War Department in order to give geographical balance to the ticket. He was totally unfit for the onerous position." James Jacob, biographer of Gen. James Wilkinson, referred to Eustis as "essentially a military tinker," with "a second-rate mind that dwelt on petty things." Believing that Eustis was more concerned with politics than with his position, Jacob described the secretary as "incompetent."

Critics charged that the secretary overly concerned himself with minor administrative details and displayed almost an obsession with reducing costs. For example, during his administration Eustis abandoned early experiments with horse-drawn light artillery because of the expense. He personally examined even the smallest requests for expenditures. Russell Weigley concludes that Eustis proved "even more singlemindedly devoted to thrift" than his parsimonious predecessor, Henry Dearborn.

Disputes with several generals also limited Eustis's effectiveness. The new secretary immediately became embroiled in a bitter dispute with Gen. James Wilkinson. In the last months of Jefferson's administration some 2,000 troops were sent under Wilkinson's command to increase the defenses of New Orleans. As the sick list lengthened, Eustis urged the reluctant general to move his camp to a new lo-

cation. When Wilkinson finally did establish a new camp, it was downriver at Terre aux Boeufs, a location that was even more unhealthy. During the summer of 1809, Eustis pleaded and finally demanded that Wilkinson move to higher ground. The secretary only exacerbated the situation, however, by questioning supply expenditures that might have eased the troops' suffering. Although the troops did move by late summer, Wilkinson's force had lost over 1,000 men to disease and desertion by early 1810. Two years after this incident with Wilkinson, Eustis clashed with Brig. Gen. Wade Hampton. The secretary initially accepted the general's challenge to a duel, but the two were able to settle their differences peacefully.

Like many Republicans, Eustis displayed little enthusiasm for the newly established military academy at West Point. He "did nothing to encourage the appointment of new cadets," though he did establish regulations for the academy, including rigorous entrance requirements that remained in effect for years. Eustis initially planned to send cadets into the regular army as enlisted men where they could compete for commissions, but he ultimately agreed to give cadets preference for regular army commissions. Political favoritism often overrode military competence when selecting officers for the army, with choice appointments given to loyal Republicans.

Despite his many critics, Eustis did make some improvements in the United States' defenses. In late 1809, he reported to Madison that new seaboard fortifications were "in many parts completed, furnished with cannon and capable of affording a respectable defense." The secretary of war added that small arms production had increased in both quantity and quality. He admitted, however, that the army's effective force was "in some way diminished by sickness & other casualties" as well as by the resignation of a number of veteran officers. Eustis pushed for the reestablishment of the quartermaster general and the commissary general of purchases as well as a commissary general of ordnance. Delays in congressional approval and the conflicting responsibilities of these positions caused confusion that lasted through the early months of the War of 1812.

Despite grandiose prewar plans for enlarging the ranks of the regular army, when war was declared in June 1812 the army consisted of fewer than 7,000 troops in scattered garrisons commanded by officers of generally poor quality. There was no commanding general, so Eustis was forced to oversee operations in nine separate military districts, and the army's logistical system was badly in need of overhaul. The military's poor performance in the first six months of the war, including disaster on the northwestern and failure on the northern frontiers, severely damaged Eustis's reputation with Congress and the public. "It was typical of his performance," writes Russell Weigley, "that on the day war was declared, he ordered Brigadier General William Hull to hurry from Dayton to take command at Detroit but neglected to inform [him] that war had begun." He also failed to notify Maj. Gen. Henry Dearborn, who commanded along the Canadian frontier, of the boundaries of his command, an omission that created confusion and delay in U.S. operations. The loss of Detroit, Mackinac, and Fort Dearborn in the Northwest, coupled with defeats along the Niagara Frontier and the failure of the movement against Montreal, displayed all too clearly the ineptness of Eustis and other military leaders.

Despite increasingly vociferous calls for Eustis's removal from Republicans and Federalists alike, Madison retained his secretary of war through the election of 1812. In September, James Monroe sent the president a letter from Sen. William Crawford that predicted that the president "must be content with defeat and disgrace in all his efforts during the war" if Eustis and Secretary of the Navy Paul Hamilton remained in office. Madison evidently considered the possibility of shuffling the cabinet and placing Monroe in the War Department, but in the end he remained loyal to the beleaguered secretary. "Much as Eustis might deserve dismissal," writes Irving Brant, "Madison was hardly to be charged with either cowardice or electioneering . . . in standing by a cabinet officer whose retention was a one hundred per cent political liability."

Upon Madison's reelection, Eustis himself recognized the need for new leadership in the War Department. The president might still have kept him in office, but the secretary "capitulated to congressional criticism of him for want of energy." On 3 December 1812, Eustis submitted his letter of resignation to Madison. The president, undoubtedly relieved, accepted the resignation while praising the secretary's efforts under "difficulties peculiarly arduous and trying." James Monroe temporarily assumed responsibility for running the War Department in addition to his position as secretary of state. The president eventually selected New York's John Armstrong as a permanent replacement, a not altogether popular or successful choice.

Two years after Eustis's resignation, Madison appointed him envoy extraordinary and minister plenipotentiary to the Netherlands, a position he held until 1818. Upon his return to the United States, Eustis ran for Congress and was elected to a vacated seat in Massachusetts. While in Congress, he three times ran unsuccessfully for the Massachusetts governorship. He did not seek reelection in 1822, but the next year he ran again for governor and this time defeated Federalist Harrison Gray Otis. Upon Eustis's elec-

tion, former president Madison wrote to his old cabinet member: "I congratulate you very sincerely on this event, with every wish that your administration may be as happy to yourself as I am confident it will be propitious to the welfare of those who have called you into it." In 1824 Eustis won reelection to a second term in office. Early the next year, he developed pneumonia, from which he died on 6 February 1825.

Several years after Eustis's death, Madison provided a sympathetic view of the secretary's wartime services: "I am tempted to do him the justice of saying that he was an acceptable member of the Cabinet, that he possessed an accomplished mind, a useful knowledge of military subjects . . . and a vigilant superintendance of subordinate agents; and that his retreat from his station, proceeded from causes not inconsistent with these endowments. With the overload of duties . . . and the refusal to him of assistants asked for who were ridiculed as crutches for official infirmity, no minister could have sustained himself." During "ordinary times," Madison concluded, "Eustis w[oul]d have satisfied public expectation." If the War Department had been properly organized with an adequate staff, "the result w[oul]d have been very different."

Of course Eustis, as well as Madison and Jefferson, deserves criticism for the poor condition of the military at the outbreak of the war. Eustis's lack of administrative ability and his failure to engender confidence in his leadership made his failure virtually inevitable.

—*David Coles*

See also: Dearborn, Henry; Hull, William; Madison, James; Wilkinson, James

Further Reading

Clary, David A., and Joseph W.A. Whitehorne. *The Inspector General of the United States Army, 1777–1903*. Washington, DC: Office of the Inspector General and Center of Military History, 1987.

Hassler, Warren W., Jr. *With Shield and Sword: American Military Affairs, Colonial Times to the Present*. Ames: Iowa State University Press, 1982.

Porter, G. W. "A Sketch of the Life and Character of the Late William Eustis." *Lexington Historical Society Proceedings* 1 (1890): 101–109.

Stagg, J. C. A. *Mr. Madison's War: Politics, Diplomacy, and Warfare in the Early American Republic, 1783–1830*. Princeton: Princeton University Press, 1983.

Weigley, Russell F. *History of the United States Army*. New York: Macmillan, 1967.

F

FARRAGUT, DAVID GLASGOW
1801–1870
U.S. naval officer

Born James Glasgow Farragut in Tennessee to George Farragut, a naval officer, and Elizabeth Stine Farragut, the younger Farragut and his four brothers and sisters moved to New Orleans with their parents in 1807. His mother died a year later on the same day as Comdr. David Porter, Sr., an elderly houseguest. The commander's son, Comdr. David Porter, Jr., was in charge of naval forces in New Orleans. In gratitude for the kindness to his father, Porter offered to take young James Farragut into his home to ease the family's burden. James later adopted the name David in honor of his benefactor.

Porter supervised Farragut's education for the first two years of his guardianship and then in 1810 secured him a commission as a midshipman at the age of nine. The child officer soon saw his first sea duty when Porter was given command of the USS *Essex* (46 guns) in 1811.

When war started with Great Britain in 1812, Farragut continued to serve aboard the *Essex* as Porter harassed British merchant ships in the Atlantic. When a British crew from one of the *Essex*'s prizes plotted to take over the ship, young Farragut overheard the plan and immediately alerted Porter, foiling the attempt.

The most exciting service Farragut saw in the war was in early 1813 when Porter took the *Essex* around Cape Horn to make her the first U.S. warship to ply the Pacific Ocean. The *Essex* spent most of her time wreaking havoc among British whalers. When in the summer of 1813 the ship captured the *Alexander Barclay*, Porter had more prizes than officers to take them to Valparaíso, Chile. The *Barclay* was put under the command of twelve-year-old Midshipman Farragut.

After disposing of their prizes, the Americans set sail for the Marquesas Islands, where officers and crew enjoyed both the beautiful scenery and accommodating island women.

Farragut and the other young midshipmen, however, were kept aboard ship most of the time, away from temptation.

When the expedition returned to Chile in early 1814, Farragut was aboard the *Essex* when it was attacked by HMS *Phoebe* and HMS *Cherub*. During the battle, Farragut conveyed messages between officers, assisted gunners, and carried powder. When Porter finally surrendered, Farragut became a prisoner of war just like the other survivors.

British captain James Hillyar paroled the prisoners and sent them to the United States. As a paroled prisoner, Farragut could not serve again aboard a warship until he was officially exchanged. He received word of his exchange in November 1814 and was assigned to USS *Spark*, but the war ended before he saw further service.

Following the war, Farragut served in the Mediterranean. After achieving the rank of lieutenant he served again under Porter in the West Indies. During the 1830s, he commanded several vessels on different stations. He was in the Gulf of Mexico during the Mexican-American War. Farragut's most important duty of his naval career occurred during the Civil War, when he secured the naval approaches to New Orleans in 1862 and Mobile Bay in the fall of 1864. As a result of these achievements, Farragut became the first admiral in U.S. naval history. He continued in the navy until his death from a stroke in 1870.

—*Jeanne T. Heidler and David S. Heidler*

See also: *Essex* versus *Phoebe* and *Cherub*; Porter, David, Jr.
Further Reading
Lewis, Charles L. *David Glasgow Farragut*. 2 vols. Annapolis, MD: U.S. Naval Institute, 1941–1943.

FEDERALIST PARTY

The opposition party in the Age of Jefferson was the Federalist Party. Although strongest in New England, the party had significant support in the middle states and upper South and a smattering of followers in the West. Led by Josiah Quincy, Harrison Gray Otis, and James Lloyd in New England, Rufus King and James A. Bayard in the middle states, and Charles Cotesworth Pinckney and John Marshall in the southern states, the Federalist Party opposed the Republican policy of confrontation with England. The Federalists favored the Monroe-Pinkney Treaty of 1806 (an Anglo-American agreement that the United States never ratified), condemned the restrictive system of embargo and nonintercourse (which Federalists argued undermined U.S. prosperity and government revenue), and opposed the drift toward war with England.

Except for two brief periods, one in the summer of 1812 (before party opinion had solidified) and the other in the fall of 1814 (when the war appeared to be defensive), Federalists presented a united front against the War of 1812. Throughout the war, New England Federalists insisted that the best way to bring the war to a speedy end was to oppose it, using every legal means available. Although Federalists in the middle and southern states were more cautious and less outspoken, in general they followed New England's lead.

Federalists opposed the war for a variety of reasons. For one thing, they saw it as a party war designed to further the interests of Republicans and to silence the opposition—a view that was reinforced by the Baltimore riots of 1812 and the refusal of the administration to take Federalists into the cabinet during the crisis of 1814. Federalists were also disillusioned by the government's refusal to limit the war to the high seas and to include France in the reprisals, by the failure of the government to repeal the restrictive system after war had been declared, and by the adoption of wartime taxes that discriminated against the North. Federalists also feared that the war would throw the nation into the arms of Napoleon, whom they described as the "the great destroyer," the "monster of human depravity," and "the arch-fiend who has long been the curse and scourge of the European World." The initial protests against the war, particularly in New England, often expressed greater fear of a French alliance than of the war itself.

Even after the danger of a French alliance had receded, Federalists continued to oppose the war because they considered it an "offensive" war aimed at Canada. Although willing to support a war to protect U.S. commerce or to defend the nation's frontiers, they refused to sanction the conquest of Canada. "Let it not be said," Congressman Morris Miller of New York told the Republicans in 1813, "that we refuse you the means of defense. For that we always have been—we still are ready to open the treasure of the nation. We will give you millions for defense; but not a cent for the conquest of Canada—not the ninety-ninth part of a cent for the extermination of its inhabitants."

Even if the invasion of Canada succeeded, Federalists were convinced that the war would do more harm than good. "Whether we consider our agriculture, our commerce, our monied systems, or our internal safety," declared the Alexandria (Virginia) *Gazette*, "nothing but disaster can result from it." Nor did Federalists expect to win any concessions from the British, certainly not on an issue as vital as impressment. "No war of any duration," said James A. Bayard, "will ever extort this concession."

In sum, Federalists saw the War of 1812 as a costly, futile, and partisan venture that was likely to produce little good and much evil. In their eyes, it was the wrong war against the wrong enemy fought in the wrong place at the wrong time. The best way to bring the conflict to an end, most Federalists agreed, was to oppose it. Hence they wrote, spoke, and preached against the war; they discouraged enlistments in the army and subscriptions to the war loans; and they vigorously condemned all who supported the war and worked for their defeat at the polls.

In Congress, Federalists voted as a bloc on almost all war legislation. They unanimously opposed the declaration of war in June 1812 (voting 33 to 0 in the House and 6 to 0 in the Senate), and thereafter they voted against almost every proposal to recruit men, raise money, foster privateering, or restrict trade with the enemy. The only war measures they supported were those they considered defensive—mainly bills to increase the navy and to build coastal fortifications.

In the House, there were 305 roll-call votes on war-related measures between 1 June 1812 (when President Madison sent his war message to Congress) and 13 February 1815 (when news of the peace treaty reached Washington). Federalists achieved an index of relative cohesion on these measures of 94.4 percent, meaning that on the average war measure almost 95 percent of House Federalists voted together. In the Senate, there were 227 roll-call votes on war-related measures, and here Federalists achieved a cohesion of 92.5 percent. A cohesion of 70 percent is considered a sign of party solidarity, so the record of the Federalists is extraordinary—surely the most remarkable record of bloc voting in any war in the nation's history.

Even though Federalists everywhere opposed the war, those in New England went the farthest. Because they were the dominant party, Federalists there did not have to worry about persecution or violence from an outraged majority. Moreover, they shared an abhorrence of the war—frequently grounded on religious principles—that was unmatched elsewhere (except perhaps in Maryland, where the Baltimore riots had radicalized the party).

Federalists in New England were also able to use the machinery of state and local government to obstruct the war effort. In Hartford, Connecticut, Federalists sought to end loud demonstrations by army recruiters by adopting a pair of city ordinances that restricted public music and parades. In New Bedford, Massachusetts, Federalists denounced privateering and voted to quarantine all arriving privateers for 40 days—ostensibly on medical grounds. And in Boston, the Massachusetts legislature threatened to sequester federal tax money if militia arms due to the state under an 1808 law were not delivered.

New England Federalists made their opposition felt in other ways. In Massachusetts, after a Republican paper denounced Federalists for applauding naval victories in a war they opposed, Josiah Quincy sponsored a resolution in the state senate declaring that "in a war like the present . . . it is not becoming a moral and religious people to express any approbation of military or naval exploits, which are not immediately connected with the defense of our sea coast and soil." The senate adopted this resolution, and it remained on the statute books until 1824, when Republicans finally succeeded in expunging it.

In Connecticut, Federalists were accused of aiding the enemy in the "blue-light affair." In late 1813 a squadron of ships under Stephen Decatur tried to slip out of New London harbor at night but was driven back by the British fleet. Decatur later complained that someone had signaled the British by flashing blue lights. Whether the signals were given by a British spy or a U.S. citizen or came from some other source is unknown, but Republicans were quick to fix the blame on Federalists. Connecticut Federalists demanded a congressional investigation, but there was no way of ascertaining the truth. By then "blue-light Federalist" had already entered the political lexicon as a term of opprobrium.

The most persistent source of conflict between New England and the federal government was over the control and deployment of the militia. This was no small matter because the militia played such a vital role in the nation's defense. The militia problem, in turn, raised the larger issue of who was responsible for New England's defense. Was it the federal government, or was it the states? Federalists never found a satisfactory answer to this question.

The first clash over the militia took place in the summer of 1812. On 22 June, four days after the declaration of war, Brig. Gen. Henry Dearborn, the army's ranking officer in New England, ordered out 41 companies of militia in Massachusetts, 5 companies in Connecticut, and 4 in Rhode Island. The War Department was sending the regulars in New England to the northern frontier and wanted the militia to garrison the empty forts that would be left behind. But to facilitate deployment and control, Dearborn asked for *detached* companies without a full complement of officers. This assured that the regular officer in charge of each post would retain control and would not be outranked by a militia officer.

All three governors—Caleb Strong of Massachusetts, Roger Griswold of Connecticut, and William Jones of Rhode Island (no relation to the secretary of the navy of the same name)—refused to meet the requisition. Acting with the full support of their councils (and in the case of Massachusetts, with the approval of the state supreme court as well), the governors grounded their refusal on the Constitution. Strong and Griswold argued that, internal disorders aside, the militia could not be called out unless the country were invaded or were in imminent danger of invasion and that no such contingency existed.

Moreover, since the states were constitutionally charged with appointing the militia officers, the Connecticut council and the Massachusetts court held that their troops could not serve under regulars. Rhode Island, however, did not raise this objection, doubtless because Dearborn's order called for a suitably high-ranking state officer to accompany the troops. Governor Jones merely said that the militia would be called out when, in his opinion, the Constitution required it.

The three governors refused to comply with Dearborn's request both to protest the war and to insure that they retained control over their militia. Convinced that the assault on Canada was unjust and unwise, they were unwilling to subject their militia to the rigors of garrison duty in support of the venture. Moreover, rumors were rife that if the militia were federalized, they would be marched to Canada. Already citizen soldiers from New York, Pennsylvania, and the western states were being called up for service on the northern frontier, and New Englanders feared that their militia would meet the same fate. It was to disassociate themselves from an unjust war, then, and to retain control over their only means of defense that New England officials refused to comply with Dearborn's request.

Even though New England leaders were uncooperative in 1812, they had no objection to calling out their militia when the enemy actually threatened. In different ways, too, each state tried to resolve the command problem. Connecticut officials were the least flexible. They were unwilling to place their militia under U.S. officers under any circumstances. To assure control, they simply assigned a high-ranking state officer to any troops called into service. Massachusetts and Rhode Island officials were more cooperative and tried to compromise whenever possible. But in the end their compromises broke down, and they found themselves in much the same position as Connecticut. Since the federal government refused to pay and supply militia serving under state officers (and did not have the funds to pay and supply many militia serving under U.S. officers), the states had to shoulder this burden in the last months of the war.

To deal with mounting defense costs as well as other problems, New England Federalists summoned the Hartford Convention, a regional conference that met in the winter of 1814–1815. Although the report of the Hartford Convention called for state nullification of unconstitutional federal laws, its tone was generally moderate. The report recommended securing federal tax money for defense measures and adopting seven constitutional amendments to protect New England's position in the Union and prevent a recurrence of the most destructive Republican policies.

The War of 1812 ended before any serious confrontation could take place between state and federal officials over the recommendations of the Hartford Convention. Even so, it left the Federalist Party indelibly tainted with disloyalty, if not treason. Federalists never lived down the notoriety of the Hartford Convention, which contributed to the party's decline in the postwar era.

—*Donald R. Hickey*

See also: Baltimore Riots; Dearborn, Henry; Decatur, Stephen, Jr.; Hartford Convention; Militia Controversy, The New England; Militia in the War of 1812; Quincy, Josiah

Further Reading

Adams, Henry. *History of the United States during the Administrations of Jefferson and Madison.* 9 vols. New York: Charles Scribner's Sons, 1889–1891.

Banner, James M., Jr. *To the Hartford Convention: The Federalists and the Origins of Party Politics in Massachusetts, 1789–1815.* New York: Alfred Knopf, 1970.

Broussard, James H. *The Southern Federalists, 1800–1816.* Baton Rouge: Louisiana State University Press, 1978.

Hickey, Donald R. *The War of 1812: A Forgotten Conflict.* Urbana: University of Illinois Press, 1989.

Morison, Samuel Eliot. *The Life and Letters of Harrison Gray Otis, Federalist, 1765–1848.* 2 vols. Boston: Houghton Mifflin, 1913.

FINANCING THE WAR OF 1812

Although the War of 1812 made heavy financial demands on the nation for four years, it did not last nearly as long as the earlier war against Great Britain. The cost of the war for the free population was just under $15 per capita, roughly one-fifth of the comparable figure for the War for Independence. Military expenditures were nearly $95 million, of which $82 million, or 85 percent, was borrowed money. The per capita addition to the outstanding national debt was slightly less than half the comparable figure in 1790.

When Secretary of the Treasury Albert Gallatin sought to borrow money from the private sector in 1812, he met the first in a series of sharp rebuffs. His worst fears had come true. Three years earlier, in 1809, Gallatin had warned Congress not to reject an application for recharter from the First Bank of the United States because in an emergency the Treasury might need the national bank's assistance in funding extraordinary governmental expenditures. The federal government had been generally free of routine bank debt for nearly a decade, he observed, but those favorable conditions might not last indefinitely.

Congress authorized the issuance of $11 million in new bonds at 6 percent interest in March 1812, three months before it actually declared war. Optimists believed new debt could be placed at relatively low interest rates—meaning around 6 percent or lower—given U.S. government securities' gilt-edged status that generally resulted from the implementation of the Hamiltonian funding program in the early 1790s. U.S. obligations had a solid international reputation as well, with over half of the outstanding bonds held by foreigners. The United States was one of the few nations that had followed a consistent policy of paying off substantial amounts of its national debt for over a decade; less debt reduced the interest drain on budgets and lowered the risk of default. So the outlook seemed reasonably good for generating a strong demand for U.S. government bonds at modest interest rates. But uncertainties surrounding the war altered the investment climate.

As in the past, the Treasury Department attempted to manage the first bond sale without the assistance of private underwriters. The Treasury began accepting subscriptions starting in May, but only $6.2 million of the initial offering was taken—$4.2 million by banks for their long-term loan portfolios and a mere $2 million by individuals. Meanwhile, requests for military expenditures kept pouring in. Under different circumstances, Gallatin might have given greater consideration to the possibility of paying more than 6 percent interest or perhaps offering to sell bonds at discount prices in an effort to attract more investors, but those two options were rejected by Madison and his closest advisers. The president insisted on borrowing at relatively inexpensive rates or pursuing other financing alternatives.

When the terms offered to long-term investors were insufficiently remunerative to float the entire $11 million issue, Madison instructed Gallatin to ask Congress for permission to pursue an option that had not surfaced at the federal level since 1780: the issuance of some form of inconvertible fiat paper to meet the pressing demands of military suppliers. In this case, the secretary was not anticipating the emission of a huge volume of non-interest-bearing paper money with no redemption dates. He certainly did not want to recreate the disreputable continental currency of the revolutionary era. Instead, Gallatin proposed short-term debt instruments fairly similar to the one- and two-year treasury notes issued by the colony of Massachusetts as early as 1751. The exact plan called for the issuance of negotiable treasury bills that were legal tender in public, but not private, transactions, with maturity dates of one year or less and carrying an interest rate of 5.4 percent, a shade below the yields on long-term U.S. bonds.

In June 1812, Congress authorized $5 million in treasury bills to cover the shortfall from the bond sale. Over the course of the war, the government issued a total of $36.7 million in treasury bills, although no more than $17.6 million were outstanding on any given date. Most were issued in denominations of $20, $100, and $1,000. There were exceptions, however. In 1815, the Treasury issued about $2.75 million in treasury bills in smaller denominations ($3, $5, $10) and bearing no interest. These small bills, little different than the continental currency of the 1770s, immediately entered the money stock, thereby helping to fuel inflationary expectations and push prices higher. Small bills constituted less than 4 percent of the Treasury's total indebtedness, however, and their overall impact was fairly modest. Unlike continental currency, the purchasing power of these small bills held up fairly well, since holders had the option of converting these monies at face value into long-term government bonds paying 7 percent interest.

Meanwhile, Gallatin tried again in early 1813 to float another debt issue. In light of the shortfall in 1812, military indecisiveness, and the opposition of many wealthy New Englanders to the war, the prospects were not encouraging. Congress authorized up to $16 million, and it allowed the Treasury to pay a commission of 0.0025 to private agents who solicited bond sales if outside help was deemed necessary. This provision opened the door to more aggressive marketing. In response to its appeal for funds—the traditionally passive system of merely announcing a subscription date—the Treasury had received applications for only about one-third of the sum required through the end of March. That left $10 million unsold. Gallatin then invited interested private parties to submit proposals that indicated the terms under which they would be willing to purchase the remainder of the issue. The secretary put everything on the table for discussion, including higher interest rates, discount purchase prices, call privileges, and other features.

During the first week of April 1813, Gallatin engaged in negotiations with representatives of a syndicate of underwriters and investors. The three principals were Stephen Girard in Philadelphia, John Jacob Astor in New York, and David Parish, the agent of an international banking house who had resided in Philadelphia since 1806. The son of the senior partner in Parish & Co., a firm headquartered in Hamburg, Germany, David Parish was the chief initiator and organizer of the U.S. syndicate. He was presumably familiar with the techniques of forming syndicates and underwriting large issues of government securities, and he transferred those skills to the U.S. capital market.

Gallatin traveled from Washington to Philadelphia in early April to work out the details with Parish and Girard. The syndicate agreed to assume responsibility for marketing the remaining $10.1 million of 6 percent bonds at a discounted price of $88, which produced a current yield to investors of 6.8 percent. Girard and Parish ended up taking $3.1 million each, and Astor assumed responsibility for $1.5 million, for a total of $7.7 million. To complete the transaction, the principals recruited several independent firms—at least seven and possibly up to 12—in New York and Philadelphia (and perhaps one or two in Baltimore) to act as junior members of the syndicate. Altogether these junior participants sold around $2.4 million in bonds to various customers.

This precedent-setting transaction benefited all participants. The principal organizers—Girard, Parish, and Astor—assumed responsibility for marketing $7.7 million in government bonds to investors on terms deemed acceptable, and they earned $11,510 in commission fees for their services. Seven other firms received another $6,130 in commissions, a modest 0.0025 of face value, for handling $2.4 million in bond subscriptions, all of which were completed within the month. Treasury secretary Gallatin had reason for satisfaction as well. With the cooperation of private underwriters, he was able to avoid the embarrassment of a second unsuccessful or unduly prolonged fund-raising campaign. Moreover, with total commissions of $17,600 paid to syndicate organizers and subcontractors, the cost of marketing these bonds was a mere fraction of 1 percent, 0.0017 to be exact, of the face value of the bonds that were unsubscribed when the syndicate entered the picture.

The U.S. government thus experienced its first involvement with financiers performing essentially investment banking functions in April 1813. Fortunately, the venture was reasonably successful. This association between government and underwriters was a singular event, however, in the context of financing the War of 1812. Despite the success of the 1813 public offering, the participation of underwriters was not repeated. During the next two years, the

Treasury stuck to the former practice of managing the distribution of new securities without the assistance of outside financiers.

Gallatin left the post of treasury secretary in May 1813, soon after the conclusion of negotiations with the syndicate. He was succeeded first by Secretary of the Navy William Jones (later president of the Second Bank of the United States), who served as acting treasury secretary through February 1814, then by George Campbell through October 1814, and then by Alexander Dallas. Jones managed to sell $8.5 million in 6 percent bonds at $88 in August 1813, the same terms established by the syndicate three months earlier. Thereafter, treasury secretaries had difficulty raising sufficient funds in the capital market to cover military expenditures on equally favorable terms. They resorted to a mix of short-term treasury notes plus occasional sales of long-term bonds to keep the government afloat.

In early 1814, Congress authorized a bond issue totaling $25 million, but Secretary Campbell worried about the difficulties he would likely encounter if he attempted to raise such a large sum in a single public offering and decided on an incremental approach. He sought bids on an initial $10 million loan at 6 percent in May. Applications for $11.9 million at a range of prices poured in, demonstrating that the Treasury had substantial drawing power even without the assistance of loan contractors.

Campbell agreed to sell $9.2 million at a subscription price of $88, which produced a current yield of 6.8 percent to investors, and summarily rejected applications for the additional $2.7 million submitted at lower prices. In order to sell the $9.2 million, the Treasury agreed that, if any of the remaining $15.8 million of the $25 million congressional authorization was sold later at a price below $88, then current subscribers would be entitled retroactively to the same consideration. In other words, they would receive some form of rebate either in the form of cash or additional securities. The general success of this public offering primarily resulted from a single subscription for $5 million—more than half the issue—from Jacob Barker, a wealthy New York merchant.

Secretary Campbell tried to raise another $6 million in August 1814, but the British threat to the nation's capital made the timing inopportune. Investors submitted subscription applications for only $2.8 million, and over four-fifths were at prices yielding 7.5 percent or greater. Campbell accepted subscriptions for $2.5 million at $80, but the transaction netted only $1.3 million because the Treasury was required to adjust the accounts of Barker and others who had subscribed in May.

The military setbacks in the late summer of 1814, exemplified by the British burning of public buildings in Washington and the threat to Baltimore, were reflected in the market value of outstanding U.S. government securities. Government bonds paying 6 percent interest traded at from $75 to $85, which produced yields ranging from 7 to 8 percent.

When George Campbell resigned in October 1814, Madison invited Alexander Dallas to become secretary of the treasury. Dallas soon solicited bids on a supplemental loan of $3 million. He focused his attention on commercial banks rather than individuals and placed the loan at the nominal price of $80 in November, the same figure his predecessor had settled for in August. The proceeds realized were actually far less than the nominal figure, however, since payment was largely in the form of banknotes from institutions that had temporarily suspended convertibility into specie. Their banknotes passed at discounts averaging 15 percent of face value, which meant that the net price realized by the Treasury was little more than $65 in *real* terms, which produced a current yield of over 9 percent to investors. The acceptance of these financial conditions was the low point in the Treasury's wartime funding operations. The status of the nation's credit had not been so questionable in over a quarter-century, since the prevailing financial disarray on the eve of the constitutional convention of 1787. But the gloom of 1814 was short-lived.

Following the announcement of the signing of the Treaty of Ghent and news of General Jackson's victory in New Orleans early in 1815, the market for government securities began to revive. Prices rose and by the spring of 1815 the yields on outstanding issues had fallen from 9 percent to 7 percent. Secretary Dallas sought subscriptions for an issue of $12 million at 7 percent interest in March 1815 and adamantly refused to consider all bids of less than $95, a price that yielded 7.4 percent to investors. Dallas had to face the consequences of his rigid pricing policies, however, by way of an undersubscribed issue. Only $9.3 million in new securities were sold that year at $95. The Treasury accepted payments in unconvertible banknotes that passed at discounts as much as 10 percent below face value, so the real cost of borrowing may have risen above 8 percent. The $2.7 million shortfall in sales was not seriously missed as events unfolded. With the rebound in foreign trade after the war, customs duties started to climb in mid-1815 and jumped to $36 million in 1816, a sum slightly greater than the total amount collected in the four previous years combined. The budget surplus in 1816 exceeded $17 million, and most of the excess revenue went to retire maturing treasury notes. By 1817, current yields on government bonds had fallen to 6.5 percent or less, matching their predominant level from 1790 to 1810.

Although the federal government failed to raise all the

funds it wanted in the capital markets from 1812 to 1815 at the 6 to 8 percent interest rates it considered acceptable, the record of the Treasury Department was fairly respectable, given extenuating circumstances such as the liquidation of the First Bank of the United States. The Treasury's performance far outdistanced that of its counterpart during the American Revolution. One critical difference was that Congress in 1812 did not need to rely on state legislatures to share the responsibility of raising troops and financing the war effort.

No market for long-term securities, stocks or bonds, had existed prior to 1790, but by the 1810s the capital market was functioning sufficiently well that Congress was able to avoid the option of resorting to the wholesale issuance of fiat monies to generate purchasing power. Of the $80 million added to the national debt during the war years, about $60 million, or 75 percent, arose as a result of the direct sale of government securities to U.S. investors, both to individuals and to financial services firms such as commercial banks and insurance companies. By comparison, less than 15 percent of the cost of the War for Independence had been financed by the flotation of debt issues, and approximately half of that total had come from French and Dutch sources rather than domestic investors. The average interest rate paid to attract investors for the five major bond flotations combined was 7.1 percent. It was a reasonably respectable rate given the absence of a national bank to provide bridge loans between issue dates. If the interest rate of 5.4 percent associated with short-term treasury notes is included in the calculations, the cost of all the money borrowed by the federal government to fight the War of 1812 averaged about 6.8 percent. All things considered, Alexander Hamilton himself would have been hard pressed to have performed much better than the four treasury secretaries—Gallatin, Jones (acting), Campbell, and Dallas—who held office from 1812 to 1816.

Most of the slowness in filling subscription lists was not because of a dearth of potential investors but because the Madison administration sought to float its bonds at a fraction of a percent below prevailing yields on government bonds in secondary markets. The government was determined to borrow money at extremely favorable rates irrespective of market conditions. The strong attachment to a maximum allowable rate of 6 percent interest on government bonds, with 8 percent the absolute outside limit, caused the government to muddle through several years of fiscal uncertainty.

That rigidity is more important in explaining the tribulations at the Treasury Department during the war years than the absence of a national bank. To view the situation from a different perspective, if from 1812 to 1815 the Treasury Department had followed the same procedures that its modern counterpart routinely employs in capital markets today, then most of the difficulties Gallatin, Jones, Campbell, and Dallas encountered in selling the $80 million in U.S. securities likely would never have arisen. In short, the Treasury could have conducted auctions of its debt obligations without preconditions, agreeing in advance to accept whatever interest rates emerged. Yet by trying to save their fellow taxpayers relatively modest sums in interest payments over the next decade or so, the four treasury secretaries only made life unnecessarily difficult for themselves and other influential decisionmakers in the Madison administration. With the exception of August 1814, when the British captured Washington, the Treasury probably could have raised all the money it required throughout the war if the Madison administration had been more flexible in the management of its interest rate and bond pricing policies.

—*Edwin J. Perkins*

See also: Astor, John Jacob; Barker, Jacob; Campbell, George W.; Dallas, Alexander; Gallatin, Albert

Further Reading
Adams, Donald, Jr. "The Beginning of Investment Banking in the United States." *Pennsylvania History* (1978): 99–116.
———. *Finance and Enterprise in Early America: A Study of Stephen Girard's Bank*. Philadelphia: University of Pennsylvania Press, 1978.
Hammond, Bray. *Banks and Politics in America from the Revolution to the Civil War*. Princeton: Princeton University Press, 1957.
Perkins, Edwin J. *American Public Finance and Financial Services, 1700–1815*. Columbus: Ohio State University Press, 1994.
Walters, Raymond, and Philip G. Walters. "The American Career of David Parish." *Journal of Economic History* (1944): 149–166.

FITZGIBBON, JAMES
1780–1863
British army officer

Born on 16 November 1780 at Glin, Limerick, Ireland, the son of a farmer and weaver, Fitzgibbon enlisted at age 15 in the Knight of Glin's Yeomanry and soon became a sergeant. In 1798, he joined the Tarbert Infantry Fencibles, then the 49th Regiment, and fought at Egmond aan Zee, Holland (1799). He also fought as a marine at

Copenhagen (1801), for which he received the Naval General Service medal. In 1802, he went to Quebec with Lt. Col. Isaac Brock's 49th regiment. Fitzgibbon became a sergeant major in 1802, ensign and adjutant in 1806, and lieutenant in 1809. He resigned in 1812 to study for promotion, but war intervened.

Fitzgibbon escorted St. Lawrence River batteaux to Kingston in August 1812, and in January 1813 he brought 45 sleighs from Kingston to Niagara to replenish the garrison's stores. He was at Fort George when Gen. Henry Dearborn's forces attacked in May 1813 and retreated with the army to Burlington. Fitzgibbon led a company in the counterattack at Stoney Creek on 6 June 1813. He then operated with 50 chosen men in advance of the army from the De Cou house, near Beaver Dams, to observe U.S. movements. When Lt. Col. Charles Boerstler moved to Beaver Dams, his force of 500 was ambushed by 400 Caughnawaga Indians, who won the battle through Fitzgibbon's ruse. Although he had only 46 rank and file, Fitzgibbon bluffed Boerstler into believing that the Americans were greatly outnumbered. Boerstler surrendered 462 officers and men to Fitzgibbon on 24 June. For this cunning act, Fitzgibbon received a gold medal from his fellow officers and was promoted to captain in the Glengarry Light Infantry Fencibles in October 1813. His dragoons observed U.S. movements near Fort George for most of 1813, but his activities for the remainder of the war did not approach the notoriety of his feat at Beaver Dams.

Fitzgibbon went on half-pay from 1816 to 1825. He dabbled in land claims from 1819 to 1821 and became colonel of militia in 1826. As a Tory and prominent mason, he supported the Family Compact. In 1827, he was appointed clerk of the Upper Canadian House of Assembly and became justice of the peace, chairman for the Court of Quarter Sessions, register of the Court of Probate, commissioner of customs, a member of the building committee for Upper Canada College, and member of the Board of Health for York after the 1832 cholera epidemic. Reformers attacked his inveterate office-holding.

Fitzgibbon was a peacemaker among Irish immigrants, urging the Orange and Catholic Irish to bury their differences and not each other, though he jailed rioters at York in 1833. On 4 December 1837, as acting adjutant general of militia, Fitzgibbon suppressed the rebellious population that marched on Toronto. He resigned because of his treatment by Lt. Gov. Bond Head. In 1838, Fitzgibbon became judge advocate and in 1841 clerk of the Legislative Council of the Province of Canada. In 1846, when the Council retired him from his office, he issued *An Appeal to the people of the late province of Upper Canada*, but nothing happened. Embittered, Fitzgibbon left for England and re-

mained as a military knight at Windsor Castle, where he died on 12 December 1863 at age 83.

—*Frederick C. Drake*

See also: Beaver Dams, Battle of; Boerstler, Charles G.; George, Fort; Stoney Creek, Battle of

Further Reading

Cruikshank, Ernest A., ed. *The Documentary History of the Campaign upon the Niagara Frontier in the Year 1813.* Welland, Ont.: Lundy's Lane Historical Society, 1902.

Fitzgibbon, James. *An Appeal to the People of the Late Province of Upper Canada.* Montreal: N.p., 1847.

Fitzgibbon, Mary A. *A Veteran of 1812: The Life of James Fitzgibbon.* Toronto: William Briggs, 1894. Reprint, 1972.

Johnson, J. K. "Colonel James Fitzgibbon and the Suppression of Irish Riots in Upper Canada." *Ontario History* 58 (1966): 39–55.

Jones, F. L. "A Subaltern of 1812: Fitzgibbon." *Canadian Army Journal* 9 (1955): 59–68.

Mallory, Ebid L. *The Green Tiger: James Fitzgibbon, Hero of the War of 1812.* Toronto: McClelland, 1976.

FLORIDA

At the time of the War of 1812, Florida was composed of the two Spanish colonies of East and West Florida. Spain had regained both provinces from the British in 1783, following British defeat in the Revolutionary War in North America. Spanish authority continued to maintain a tenuous hold into the early nineteenth century, centering on enclaves surrounding administrative posts, such as St. Augustine and Pensacola. The remainder of this nominally Spanish region was often free of any direct European control and was viewed as a relatively lawless no man's land. The population of both Floridas was small in number and more often than not was Indian or Anglo-American in background.

The role of East and West Florida in the war was influenced by three interrelated outside events that led to the colonies' being pulled into the conflict. The first of these factors involved the invasion and subsequent occupation of Spain by the armies of Napoleon Bonaparte from 1808 to 1813, which exacerbated the weakness and vulnerability of the Floridas and left them open to the nations that were fighting one another in North America. As a result of the French occupation of Spain, many Spaniards resorted to a particularly vicious form of guerrilla warfare against the French occupiers. They were aided in their cause by a

British army, led by the duke of Wellington, that began attacking the French in Spain from its base in Portugal. In this atmosphere of violence and insurrection there was no single, central Spanish government. Instead, whatever authority existed was carried out by a number of local juntas, with the junta in Cadiz having a vague jurisdiction over the Spanish colonies. Thus, by 1812, Spain had been in political chaos for years, with a series of local governments allied loosely with the British against a common enemy.

Because of this absence of central authority, the Spanish colonies around the world were increasingly left to their own devices. In much of Spanish America this eventually led to independence movements. In the little backwater provinces of East and West Florida, however, it simply meant a lack of men, supplies, and superintendence. Both colonies were nearly helpless outposts trying to survive in the face of growing U.S. power and to cope with British pressure to use Spanish territory as a stage from which to conduct the war. Indeed, it is possible that the British alliance with the juntas in Spain may have encouraged a continuation of such a relationship in the Floridas. The impact of the so-called Peninsular War in Spain, therefore, was critical to events that unfolded in Spanish Florida during the War of 1812.

The second factor was the overall course of the war in North America. The Floridas became a focal point for both the British and the Americans by war's end because of military stalemates in other theaters. The U.S. inability to conquer Upper or Lower Canada led to a sense of frustration and to an enhanced interest in the Spanish provinces. By the same token, British armies seemed incapable of successfully invading the United States from Canada or of prosecuting a winning campaign. The British looked for other fronts to open and turned to a strategy that led to peripheral attacks on Washington and Baltimore on Chesapeake Bay. The next point of invasion was the Gulf of Mexico and the southern United States, with New Orleans as the obvious target. It was hoped that this strategy would help to reduce U.S. pressure on Canada and keep the U.S. army off balance. The first step in this plan was to gain a foothold in Spanish West Florida.

The third factor was the Creek War of 1813 and 1814, which was an attempt by a faction of Creek Indians known as Red Sticks to challenge the encroachment of the United States onto their lands. A series of armed clashes culminated in the Battle of Horseshoe Bend on 27 March 1814, at which U.S. forces virtually defeated the Red Stick Creeks. The Creek War had gone far in militarily destabilizing the region and brought U.S. forces close to Spanish Florida sooner than the British had anticipated. In addition, many Americans had for years blamed the Spanish

and the British for arming and inciting the Indians. This attitude was reinforced when Indian refugees from the war filtered down into West Florida and clustered around Pensacola as a haven and a source of supplies.

All of these events had by 1814 caused increased interest in East Florida and especially in West Florida. In short, these two isolated enclaves of Spanish neutrality had begun to draw Indian, British, and U.S. forces into their political vacuum. Consequently, the Floridas were caught up in a war that was none of their concern or doing. As the focus of the war shifted to the south, they became a part of the last months of the conflict and a springboard for the campaign that led to the Battle of New Orleans in January 1815.

The Americans had actually begun the process of encroachment against West Florida years before the war. In 1803, following the acquisition of the Louisiana Purchase from France, the United States put forward the claim that part of the colony west of the Perdido River had been included in the purchase. This included the town of Mobile. These claims were denied by Spanish authorities, but their ability to withstand U.S. pressure was limited. Filibustering from the United States began soon after 1803 and first came to fruition during the war in 1813. Before then, the Americans controlled only that part of West Florida that fell between the Mississippi and Pearl Rivers, an area known as the Florida Parishes. On 15 April 1813, however, the government ordered Gen. James Wilkinson to occupy Mobile and eventually annex all of the region up to the Perdido River (the present-day western border of the state of Florida). This action was accomplished with little Spanish resistance, and it left Pensacola, the capital of West Florida, as the only significant Spanish settlement in the colony.

Though not as strategically important, East Florida had also received U.S. attention and had suffered an armed incursion just before the War of 1812 in an incident known as the Patriot's War. In March 1812, Gen. George Mathews of Georgia moved into northeast Florida with 70 to 80 men and announced the beginning of a rebellion against Spanish rule. He was hoping to gain support from the Anglo-American planters living in East Florida. Believing that he would receive tacit support from Pres. James Madison, Mathews organized a provisional government and attempted to lay siege to the Castillo de San Marcos, Spain's fortress in St. Augustine. But the Spanish governor refused to surrender, and the invaders had neither the men nor the siege equipment necessary to take the Castillo. The Americans withdrew to the north of the St. Johns River, prodded by Spanish troops and Seminole Indians who opposed U.S. annexation. The invasion failed to gather significant local support, and soon the U.S. Senate repudiated the entire adventure, forcing Madison to follow suit. U.S. forces, however, stayed on the north Florida coast near the St. Marys River for another year before withdrawing.

After war was declared against Great Britain in June 1812, President Madison tried to secure congressional authorization to invade and occupy East Florida. He claimed such a move would forestall any British intervention into the area. In anticipation of congressional approval, Madison called for a force of 1,500 men from the governor of Tennessee to march into Florida in October. Tennessee and Georgia greeted the action with enthusiasm because both states believed Spanish Florida was the source of Indian depredations and a haven for runaway slaves from the southern states. Unfortunately for those two states and for Madison, Congress did not cooperate. Although permission was granted for the seizure of part of West Florida, as noted earlier, Congress refused any such authorization for East Florida. Madison was blocked by a coalition of Federalists and anti-Madison Republicans. New orders were issued to the Tennessee militia, who had already begun their long march south, to disband and to go back home.

Meanwhile, the war had arrived in West Florida because of the military importance of Pensacola and its fine harbor. The British strategy of invading the Gulf Coast was about to be put into operation, and the Americans, already in the area because of the Creek War, realized the importance of the Gulf to their defenses. In May 1814, Gen. Andrew Jackson was given command of the U.S. forces in the Gulf region, and he was well aware of Pensacola's place in the overall military planning on the southern front.

The British arrived first in August 1814. Maj. Edward Nicholls of the Royal Marines had originally been sent to the mouth of the Apalachicola River, east of Pensacola, to open a supply post for the Indians. On 14 August, he moved into Pensacola with 100 to 200 men. Spanish governor Don Mateo Gonzales Manrique feared an imminent U.S. invasion, so he reluctantly permitted the British to occupy both the town and its fortress, Fort Barrancas. Nicholls proceeded to control movement into and out of Pensacola and demanded command of the Spanish garrison should Jackson threaten the city. After an ill-conceived attack by Nicholls's troops on U.S.-held Mobile ended in failure, the Spanish governor began to distance himself from his increasingly unwanted British protectors. The British were now seen as an embarrassing violation of Spanish neutrality who would almost certainly bring on a response from the United States. Furthermore, British high-handedness and arrogance regarding the "liberation" of Spanish slaves and property were a growing source of resentment within Pensacola.

The British role in West Florida was not dissimilar to that being played by Britain in Spain itself, a role that also had created friction between the two countries. In a sense, West Florida had become something of a smaller version of the British intervention into the Iberian Peninsula, only this time the common threat was the United States, not France, and the British would leave the Spaniards to fend for themselves in the end. Ironically, British troops now arriving on the Gulf Coast were often veterans of the Peninsular War.

Spanish officials refused Nicholls the authority he wanted, so he took his force out of Pensacola and joined the men already in Fort Barrancas. Jackson arrived outside the town on 6 November with an army of 4,000 men and attacked the next day. Implementing a deft maneuver around the town's northern perimeter, Jackson surprised the Spanish garrison and the small British fleet in the harbor by attacking the town from the east, rather than the west as expected. The 500-man garrison put up only a token defense, and Governor Manrique soon surrendered the town. The British responded to this development by blowing up Fort Barrancas and evacuating the area. They sailed east to the mouth of the Apalachicola River and reestablished themselves at Prospect Bluff. From there they could supply Indian allies and maintain a presence on the coast.

Jackson moved most of his men first to Mobile and then to New Orleans, where he defeated the British Army on 8 January 1815. He also detailed a force of 1,000 men, led by Maj. Uriah Blue, to pursue the Indians into West Florida and, if possible, to take the British post at Prospect Bluff. This foray to protect Jackson from enemy raids out of Florida had a difficult time. Short of supplies from the beginning, the men fought a few small battles and burned several Indian villages, but they inflicted no serious damage before returning to their base. Prospect Bluff was not even threatened, let alone taken. Although Blue did keep the enemy from harassing Jackson from the Florida sanctuary, the British could count substantial achievements. They had drawn U.S. soldiers away from the New Orleans area at a crucial time and had cut communications between Mobile and Georgia. Furthermore, the Indians maintained their freedom of action, a fact that led to Jackson's 1818 invasion into Spanish West Florida to subdue them.

Following their defeat at New Orleans, the British returned eastward to launch a successful attack against Fort Bowyer, which guarded the entrance to Mobile Bay. Thus, the last fight of the War of 1812 occurred in what had been, as recently as 1813, West Florida. The British remained at Prospect Bluff on the Apalachicola River to support their Creek allies until June 1815.

The War of 1812 had a significant impact on the Floridas. It signaled the beginning of the end of Spanish rule, and it provided a major push toward annexation by the United States. Much of old West Florida was absorbed by the United States during the war. The part that remained in Spanish hands faced increased U.S. encroachment. Specifically, the seizure of Pensacola by Jackson in November 1814 pointed to the eventual end of any recognized Spanish authority.

The Spanish government was aware of its own relative weakness following the Napoleonic wars, and obviously U.S. raids and increased settlement by Americans in both of the Floridas would ultimately result in outright annexation to the United States. Madrid's policy, therefore, was to play for time, hoping for a negotiated settlement before the United States simply took the peninsula. U.S. expansionism likely would have forced Spain to negotiate a cession in any event, but the War of 1812 certainly accelerated the process. The Adams-Onís Treaty signed on 22 February 1819 and ratified by Spain in February 1821 ceded both Floridas to the United States. Florida became a U.S. territory in July 1821.

Finally, because of the battles fought at Pensacola and New Orleans and the occupation of parts of West Florida, many Americans, particularly in the South, were able to see the war as a victory for the United States. For them it had ended with a string of triumphs. In part because of the Floridas, it was possible for people to ignore the defeats that had taken place on other fronts in the war and to view the peace settlement at Ghent as something more than just an arrangement based upon the status quo antebellum.

—*Eric Jarvis*

Further Reading
Coker, William S., and Thomas D. Watson. *Indian Traders of the Southeastern Spanish Borderlands: Panton, Leslie and Co. and John Forbes and Co., 1783–1847.* Gainesville: University Presses of Florida; Pensacola: University of West Florida Press, 1986.
Coles, Harry L. *The War of 1812.* Chicago: University of Chicago Press, 1965.
Covington, James W. *The Seminoles of Florida.* Gainesville: University Presses of Florida, 1993.
Hawk, Robert. *Florida's Army: Militia, State Troops, National Guard, 1565–1985.* Englewood, FL: Pineapple Press, 1986.
Heidler, David S., and Jeanne T. Heidler. *Old Hickory's War: Andrew Jackson and the Quest for Empire.* Mechanicsburg, PA: Stackpole Books, 1996.
Owsley, Frank L., Jr. *Struggle for the Gulf Borderlands: The Creek War and the Battle of New Orleans, 1812–1815.* Gainesville: University Presses of Florida, 1981.
Rucker, Brian R. "In the Shadow of Jackson: Uriah Blue's Expedition into West Florida." *Florida Historical Quarterly* (January 1995).

FLOURNOY, [JOHN] THOMAS
1775–1857
U.S. Army officer

Noted more for his ineptitude and fastidious temperament than for his military competence, Flournoy was a marginally significant commander of the War of 1812 era. Information about [John] (some documents include the name "John," whereas others do not) Thomas Flournoy's early life and career is very sketchy. Besides stating his birth in North Carolina in 1775, extant military records provide no additional information about his family history or education. Documents show that during the early 1800s, Flournoy practiced law in Augusta, Georgia. Legal differences with Judge George Walton (1741–1804), chief justice of Georgia's Supreme Court, resulted in a duel between Flournoy and Judge Walton's nephew, John Carter Walton.

Commissioned a brigadier general on 18 June 1812, the date that the War of 1812 began, Flournoy soon found himself defending a vast frontier. He took a prominent, if indecisive, part in the Creek War of 1813–1814 in Alabama and neighboring territories. Named to succeed Gen. James Wilkinson as commander of the Seventh Military District headquartered at New Orleans, Flournoy proved to be almost as much of an enigma as the man whom he replaced. He was apparently incapable of getting along with anyone.

Military reductions by the Jeffersonian Republicans had reduced preparedness, so wartime exigencies of June 1812 required rapid military expansion and deployment. Amateurism flourished, and Flournoy's inflated rank irritated many seasoned commanders who criticized his background and lack of military experience. His earliest responsibilities involved training Georgia and South Carolina recruits and overseeing defensive measures taken along the Georgia coastline. Even in this limited capacity, he encountered profound difficulties because he treated backwoods militiamen as seasoned regulars.

The Creek nation overlapped boundaries of the Sixth Military District, commanded by Maj. Gen. Thomas Pinckney at Charleston, South Carolina, and the Seventh District, commanded by Flournoy at New Orleans. Subsequent confusion surrounding appropriate military jurisdiction hampered effective management of the impending conflict in the region. Communication between the two headquarters was almost impossible because of the British blockade and Indian troubles, leading Secretary of War John Armstrong to believe that the condition required a unified command. Accordingly, Armstrong placed Pinckney in charge of the entire region, conspicuously infringing upon Flournoy's authority and likely bruising his ego.

Flournoy underestimated the Creeks and the potential danger of war before it broke out in July 1813 and refused to reinforce the wilderness outposts in any significant way. After the defeat at Burnt Corn (27 July 1813), the Creek War looked like a serious affair, and the entire Mississippi territorial militia joined the conflict. Brig. Gen. Ferdinand L. Claiborne, the militia commander, had no troops in reserve for offensive action against the Indians, and though he appealed to Flournoy for reinforcements, he received no help. Flournoy initially declined to recruit Choctaws as regular or volunteer troops against the Creeks and only after tardy reconsideration decided to permit it. He misread the tactical situation, hoping to avoid open warfare with the Creeks even after the Fort Mims disaster (30 August 1813) and persisting in the belief that the Indians would settle down to a civil war among themselves. Thus, he was slow to permit his forces to invade Creek territory, waiting until Andrew Jackson's Tennessee militia entered the field.

Flournoy's unyielding dependence upon protocol and regulation often impaired his judgment. He feuded with David Holmes, governor of the Mississippi Territory, over the proper administrative relationship between regular forces and militia. Unwilling to tolerate any hint of irregularity, Flournoy was so obstinate as to delay the addition of militia to his command, thus reducing his potential force in the field. Later, when Maj. Thomas Hinds's Mississippi Dragoons protested their demeaning assignment of guarding isolated settlements against Indian attack, Flournoy responded irrationally. He dismissed from federal service this entire group of aristocratic cavalrymen from the Natchez District for what he called their insubordination. This action infuriated leading citizens, earning Flournoy few friends in the Seventh Military District.

The disaster at Fort Mims certainly accentuated serious questions about Flournoy's leadership. Apparently, most victories against the Creeks occurred in spite of, rather than because of, his efforts. President Madison wisely disregarded Secretary of War Armstrong's suggestion to promote Flournoy to major general. Had that promotion occurred, Flournoy would have been the chief U.S. commander at the Battle of New Orleans, with Jackson a subordinate. Louisiana officials believed that Flournoy's in-

competence and his contemptuous attitude only enraged local residents against national service.

Not surprisingly, Flournoy held the Creoles of Louisiana in contempt. In official communications with the War Department, he described Louisiana's residents as people who "have no respect for the laws—& are ready at times to oppose those who do." He also suggested that Louisiana's people would trade with the British without hesitation and that "not one person in twenty . . . would take up arms in its [the United States] defence." Not surprisingly, Louisiana militia enlistments remained low, and few residents volunteered to serve in the regular army under his command.

Flournoy resigned from the army 13 September 1814 when General Jackson succeeded him as commander of the Seventh Military District. This assignment had a profound influence upon future U.S. success in the Battle of New Orleans. The conventional wisdom of many local officials was that Louisiana's inhabitants would not have fought well, if at all, under Flournoy's command, but these residents fought valiantly under Jackson.

Receiving a postwar assignment in 1820 as U.S. commissioner to treat with the Creek Indians, Flournoy lived along the frontier for years in the Alabama territory. He retired from this post upon the Creek removal in 1836. Having lived for several years in Eufala, Alabama, Flournoy died in North Carolina on 24 July 1857.

—*Junius P. Rodriguez*

See also: Armstrong, John; Burnt Corn, Battle of; Claiborne, Ferdinand L.; Creek War; Mims, Attack on Fort; Pinckney, Thomas

Further Reading
Clark, Thomas D., and John D.W. Guice. *Frontiers in Conflict: The Old Southwest, 1795–1830.* Albuquerque: University of New Mexico Press, 1989.

Halbert, H. S., and T. H. Ball. *The Creek War of 1813 and 1814.* 1895. Reprint, Tuscaloosa: University of Alabama Press, 1995.

Owsley, Frank L., Jr. *Struggle for the Gulf Borderlands: The Creek War and the Battle of New Orleans, 1812–1815.* Gainesville: University Presses of Florida, 1981.

FLOYD, JOHN
See Georgia

FORSYTH, BENJAMIN
d. 1814
Lieutenant colonel, U.S. First
Regiment of Riflemen

Benjamin Forsyth was a master of the rough-and-tumble irregular warfare that characterized combat along the border between Canada and the United States. Born in North Carolina, Forsyth spent some time in state politics before entering active military duty in 1809 as a captain in the Regiment of Riflemen. In July 1812, his company was the first regular U.S. unit to appear at Sacket's Harbor. Until his death in 1814, Forsyth remained on the frontier of New York, leading his expert marksmen from the front in battles and numerous skirmishes.

Forsyth quickly earned a reputation as an intrepid fighter. In September 1812, he led a successful raid on the town of Gananoque on the St. Lawrence River. The War Department recognized his ability and promoted Forsyth to major in January 1813. In command of U.S. forces at Ogdensburg, Forsyth led another successful raid against Elizabethtown in February, taking 52 prisoners in the process. The British, however, were not to be attacked with impunity. Lt. Col. George MacDonnell, in many ways Forsyth's nemesis, led a surprise attack against Ogdensburg on 21 February and, after a sharp house-to-house fight, forced the outnumbered riflemen to abandon the town.

Forsyth and his battalion were called westward; on 27 April 1813, he and his men were in the first wave of the attack on York. Under accurate fire as their boats approached the shore, Forsyth and his men nonetheless pushed the defenders back, securing the beach for the infantry following close behind. The following month Forsyth's riflemen again led an amphibious assault against Fort George. Landing on a narrow beach 2 miles from the fort, Forsyth's riflemen and several light infantry companies under the command of Lt. Col. Winfield Scott fought a desperate battle on the water's edge. Reinforced by the second wave, Scott pushed into the fort and, with Forsyth and his riflemen in the forefront, pursued the withdrawing British several miles until recalled. For his distinguished service, Forsyth was breveted lieutenant colonel.

In March 1814 Forsyth was with Maj. Gen. James Wilkinson's abortive advance into Lower Canada. Sent to outflank the British position at La Colle Mill, Forsyth and his riflemen missed the battle and Wilkinson's defeat. In April, Forsyth earned promotion to the permanent rank of lieutenant colonel.

Benjamin Forsyth died in a skirmish on the Canadian border. His brigade commander had ordered a small party of riflemen to lure the British out of the village of Odelltown. Forsyth, with the rest of his riflemen, was to feign a further retreat, enticing the British into an ambush by the remainder of the U.S. brigade. All went according to plan until Forsyth, rather than withdrawing, turned and opened fire on his attackers. The British returned fire, cutting down the gallant Forsyth. Sensing a trap, the British withdrew to their original position.

Forsyth was blamed for the failure of the mission. His reputation for personal bravery and leadership by example were balanced by criticisms that he acted rashly and was lax in disciplining his men. In many regards, Benjamin Forsyth exemplified the prototypical U.S. frontier soldier—resourceful, fearless, determined, and deadly with a rifle. His native North Carolina honored him in 1849 when it created Forsyth County.

—*Richard V. Barbuto*

See also: George, Fort; Ogdensburg, Battle of
Further Reading
Lemmon, Sarah. *Frustrated Patriots: North Carolina and the War of 1812.* Chapel Hill: University of North Carolina Press, 1973.

FORT
See individual sites by name, e.g., Amanda, Fort

FORT JACKSON, TREATY OF
9 August 1814

The Treaty of Fort Jackson did not completely end the Creek War (1813–1814), but it did reduce the level of hostilities in the Mississippi Territory. The chief negotiator of the treaty was Maj. Gen. Andrew Jackson, commander of the U.S. Seventh Military District. While negotiating with tribal elders, Jackson ignored the conciliatory terms drafted by Secretary of War John Armstrong and imposed his own brutal demands. As a result, on 9 August 1814, the Creek Nation ceded more than half of its land (over 22 million acres) to the United States. Jackson's land grab not only increased the United States' wealth and security on the southern frontier but also signaled a shift in focus. In

Louisiana and the Mississippi Territory, the new threat became Great Britain rather than hostile natives.

The immediate cause of the Treaty of Fort Jackson was the Battle of Horseshoe Bend. When General Jackson discovered over 1,000 warriors encamped on the Tallapoosa River, he mounted an attack. By Jackson's own account, "the *carnage was dreadfull.*" At the conclusion of the battle, approximately 800 tribesmen lay broken and spent, as did the power of the Creek Nation. Secretary of War Armstrong subsequently chose Maj. Gen. Thomas Pinckney, commander of the Seventh Military District, and Creek Indian agent Benjamin Hawkins to negotiate a suitable peace with tribal leaders. The selection of Pinckney and Hawkins was highly unpopular in Tennessee, where frontier leaders wanted huge tracts of native land and feared the two negotiators would not ask for them. Their fears almost came true in April 1814, when General Pinckney offered tribal leaders conciliatory terms. The United States, for example, wanted to annex an unspecified amount of native land as "a just indemnity" for its losses. It also expected the right to build military posts and trading facilities in tribal areas. The Creeks, in turn, would have to yield up those who had instigated hostilities and agree to restrictions on trade with foreign nations.

Andrew Jackson thought Pinckney's terms were too lenient. Like other frontiersmen, he argued that the Creeks should turn over all their land west of the Coosa River and north of the Alabama River. Jackson's personal opinion suddenly mattered when Secretary of War Armstrong appointed Jackson to succeed General Thomas Flournoy as commander of the Seventh Military District, which included Louisiana, Tennessee, the Mississippi Territory, and most of the Creek Nation. As the new chief negotiator with the Creeks, General Jackson ignored the temperate terms first offered by Pinckney; he wanted to break the Creek Nation forever. As a result, and on his own initiative, Jackson made harsh demands on native leaders. He wanted land (over 22 million acres), including territory that belonged not only to hostile tribesmen but also to those who had fought along with whites or at least remained neutral.

Jackson's demand was implacable and unfair, but the only other option he offered to the shocked tribesmen was to move to Florida and join the British or Spanish. Fear rather than loyalty kept the Creek Nation in place, and on 9 August 1814, 35 tribal elders signed the Treaty of Fort Jackson. These leaders, however, were accommodationists who had no standing with either the war faction of the Creek Nation or even the British. As a result, neither of those two entities ever recognized the validity of the treaty, a fact that became significant at the conclusion of the War of 1812.

Article Nine of the Anglo-American Treaty of Ghent stipulated that the United States had to restore the rights and lands (as they existed in 1811) of those Native American tribes that had allied themselves with the British during the War of 1812. Since an arguably limited and unrepresentative number of Creek leaders had signed the Treaty of Fort Jackson and since Creek settlements near the Gulf Coast finally allied themselves with Great Britain in late 1814, the British argued that the first treaty was null and void and that the Creek Nation deserved the return of its land. Some in Washington agreed, but Andrew Jackson and his fellow frontiersmen won the debate. The United States formally claimed that since the Creeks became nonbelligerents on 9 August 1814, they were not in a state of war at the time of the signing of the Treaty of Ghent. Article Nine, therefore, did not apply to them. Not surprisingly, Andrew Jackson and his allies used this "logic" to etch in stone the provisions of a 22-million-acre land grab.

—*Peter R. Faber*

See also: Creek War; Ghent, Treaty of; Horseshoe Bend, Battle of; Jackson, Andrew

Further Reading

Heidler, David S., and Jeanne T. Heidler. *Old Hickory's War: Andrew Jackson and the Quest for Empire.* Mechanicsburg, PA: Stackpole Books, 1996.
Owsley, Frank L., Jr. *Struggle for the Gulf Borderlands: The Creek War and the Battle of New Orleans, 1812–1815.* Gainesville: University Presses of Florida, 1981.

FOSTER, AUGUSTUS JOHN
1780–1848
British minister to the United States

Augustus J. Foster was born on 1 December 1780, the second son of John Thomas Foster, member of Parliament for Ennis in the Irish House of Commons, and Lady Elizabeth Hervey. After his widowed mother married the duke of Devonshire, Foster became secretary of legation in Naples.

As His Majesty's envoy and minister plenipotentiary to the United States, Foster replaced chargé d'affaires John Philip Morier on 30 June 1811. On 23 April 1812, Foster alerted Viscount Castlereagh, secretary of state for foreign affairs, to the likelihood of some incident "either on the frontier of Canada, or off this Coast calculated to create considerable irritation among Americans." Foster consulted Secretary of State James Monroe about impressment and the

British Orders in Council, but he continued to believe that a majority in Congress wished for some incident that would provoke war. He warned Sir George Prevost that feelings were "very inflammatory." Foster reported over 140 vessels leaving New York in one week with supplies for Wellington's Peninsula army and issued licenses to such vessels, but after the war vote passed Congress, Foster's recall was inevitable.

Prior to his return to England on 18 August 1812, however, Foster received word in Halifax that the Orders in Council had been repealed. His conveyance of this information and the hope that it might mean a possible cessation of hostilities prompted a temporary armistice between Sir George Prevost and U.S. Maj. Gen. Henry Dearborn. Foster's optimism, however, proved groundless.

Back in England, he became member of Parliament for Cockermouth and on 1 May 1814 became minister plenipotentiary to Copenhagen, where he served for ten years. He was in Turin from 1824 to 1840 and from that place retired. He married Albinia Jane Hobart in 1815. In 1822 he became a member of the privy council, was knighted, and was awarded the GCH in 1825 and a baronetcy in 1831 Foster committed suicide on 1 August 1848 by cutting his throat at Branksea Castle, near Poole, Dorset.

—*Frederick C. Drake*

See also: Castlereagh, Viscount, Robert Stewart
Further Reading
Davis, Richard B., ed. *Jeffersonian America: Notes on the United States of America Collected in the Years 1805–6–7 and 11–12 by Sir Augustus Foster, Bart.* San Marino, CA: Huntington Library, 1954.

Foster, Vere, ed. *The Two Duchesses: Georgiana, Duchess of Devonshire, Elizabeth, Duchess of Devonshire.* New York: Charles Scribner's Sons, 1898.

Perkins, Bradford. *Prologue to War: England and the United States, 1805–1812.* Berkeley and Los Angeles: University of California Press, 1964.

Tinksom, Margaret B. "Caviar along the Potomac: Sir Augustus John Foster's Notes on the United States, 1804–1812." *William and Mary Quarterly*, 3d ser., 8 (1951): 69–107.

Willson, Beckles. "Foster Fails to Avert War." In *Friendly Relations: A Narrative of Britain's Ministers and Ambassadors to America, 1791–1930.* Boston: Little, Brown, 1934.

FOXALL, HENRY
1758–1823
Cannonfounder

Henry Foxall was the most important figure in cannon manufacture in the United States from 1798 to 1815. Born in West Bromley, Monmouthshire, England, on 24 May 1798, Foxall learned the iron trade in nearby Birmingham. In 1794 he became superintendent of an ironworks near Dublin, Ireland; a short time later he took a similar post at Carrick-on-Shannon.

In 1796, Foxall moved to Philadelphia, where in partnership with Richard Morris he established the Eagle Foundry on the Schuylkill River. Within a year he was casting cannon for the navy. In 1800, Foxall ended his association with Morris and established a new cannon foundry—the Columbian (or Columbia)—at Georgetown outside Washington. It was in operation from 1801 to 1849. In 1810 its annual production capacity was some 300 guns.

Foxall was the first in the United States to produce effective boring machinery for cannon manufacture. Competitors copied his methods and even hired away his workers. During the period of Foxall's ownership, the foundry cast long guns, carronades, and mortars as well as shot for both the army and navy. He also cast the Columbiad, a short type of heavy cannon, which some believe was the first heavy ordnance of distinctly U.S. design. Probably it was named for his foundry.

The Columbian Foundry escaped destruction during the 1814 British raid on Washington, but in 1815 Foxall sold the firm and returned to England for an extended visit. He was mayor of Georgetown from 1821 to 1823, then again visited England, where he died at Handsworth, near Birmingham, on 11 December 1823.

—*Spencer C. Tucker*

See also: Columbiad
Further Reading
Davis, Madison. "The Old Cannon Foundry above Georgetown, D.C., and Its First Owner, Henry Foxall." *Records of the Columbia Historical Society, Washington, D.C.* 2 (1908): 38–40.

FRENCH CANADIANS

For French Canadians, the War of 1812 represented a rare period of political and ethnic calm. In the face of possible U.S. invasion, the various classes that made up French Canadian society joined together to express their loyalty to the British king and their support for the continuation of British rule.

The French, who made up the majority of the population in the colony of Lower Canada, had just gone through a difficult period of political discord prior to 1812. Immediately before the war the mood began to change, however, partly resulting from the arrival of a new governor, George Prevost, a Swiss-born, bilingual officer of the British army with previous colonial administrative experience. He successfully lessened the ethnic divisions within the colony and used conciliation to create a province ready to resist any U.S. encroachment.

The political tone of the colony was improved also by the infusion of Army Bills, paper money issued by the government of Lower Canada and backed by the British treasury. The bills helped to revitalize the sagging economy by creating a paper currency that circulated throughout colonial society. In addition, this innovation put money into the government coffers through tariffs collected from increased imports. Thus, as a whole, the improved political and economic situation of French Canadians during the war went far in enhancing their feelings of unity and loyalty.

More important than these factors, however, were the French Canadians themselves, who for varying reasons wanted to prove that they were as loyal as their English-speaking fellow colonists. The Roman Catholic clergy, for instance, saw themselves as defenders of established order against the revolutionary, secular forces of the United States. As the self-proclaimed leaders of French Canadian society, the clergy urged obedience to the British crown and fidelity to the concepts of tradition and hierarchy. Another elite group, the landholding seigneurial class, also supported the monarchical principle (no matter who the monarch was) and was particularly anxious to recapture the old military glories for which the class was once famous. At least one of its number, Charles-Michel de Salaberry, managed to do so by winning the Battle of Châteauguay (26 October 1813) and thwarting the only serious U.S. invasion of Lower Canada during the war.

Once the war began, the vocal and politically active French Canadian professional class called for a moratorium on political disagreements with the English-dominated colonial government. Fearful that U.S. democracy and materialism would undermine and ultimately destroy their traditional way of life, this group favored British institutions as the surest guarantee of French cultural survival.

Finally, the largest segment of the French Canadian population, the peasant habitant farmers of the St. Lawrence Valley, were also opposed to the Americans. The invaders were seen as a direct threat to their rural heritage and to the seigneurial system of landholding. The last thing that the habitants wanted was a wave of rapacious, landgrabbing Yankee settlers who would cause overcrowding and increased land shortages. To prevent this, the peasants demonstrated their support for the British government in

a practical way—by responding enthusiastically to militia calls to defend Lower Canada.

Thus, the common unifying factor in the response of all these groups, who rarely agreed about most matters, was the fear of Americanization. To all classes of French Canadians, Americans represented a political, social, and economic threat. French Canadians therefore remained loyal to their government and united in a common cause, something that could not be said about either the English-speaking colonists in British North America or, for that matter, the U.S. population to the south.

Following the war, political strife soon returned to Lower Canada, and many members of the French professional class moved toward accepting U.S. viewpoints. Soon issues again divided the colony into English and French factions, alienating the government and the governed. In 1837, this growing division exploded into outright rebellion. But during the years 1812 to 1814, French Canadians of all classes and outlooks pulled together and, more significantly, joined with the British colonial administration against the common enemy. The war, therefore, proved to be a brief respite from the endemic Canadian problem of having two nations within one state.

—*Eric Jarvis*

See also: Châteauguay, Battle of; Prevost, George
Further Reading

Oullet, Fernand. *Economic and Social History of Quebec, 1760–1850.* Toronto: Gage Publishing, 1980.
———. *Lower Canada, 1791–1840: Social Chance and Nationalism.* Toronto: McClelland and Stewart, 1980.
Trofimenkoff, Susan Mann. *The Dream of Nation: A Social and Intellectual History of Quebec.* Toronto: Macmillan of Canada, 1983.

FRENCH CREEK
1–2 November 1813

As part of Gen. James Wilkinson's advance on Montreal, Gen. Jacob Brown occupied positions along French Creek at the end of October 1813. Because Commodore Isaac Chauncey had not succeeded in bottling up the British in Kingston, a British flotilla and infantry detachment were also in the vicinity. In the midst of miserable weather—the Canadian winter was coming early—Brown discovered that the British were preparing to descend on his position, so he placed three 18-pounders on high ground west of the creek. When the British attempted to assail Brown late on 1 November and early the following day as well, the U.S. battery proved accurate and decisive. In repulsing this British attack, Brown lost only two men, with four others receiving wounds.

Wilkinson and the main body of the army arrived by 4 November, and the Americans continued their progress, though harassed and stalked at every turn by the British. Ultimately, the entire campaign was abandoned short of any substantive gain.

—Jeanne T. Heidler and David S. Heidler

See also: Brown, Jacob J.; Wilkinson, James

FRENCHTOWN, BATTLES OF
18 and 22 January 1813

Following the surrender of Detroit in the summer of 1812, Pres. James Madison organized the Northwestern Army commanded by Maj. Gen. William Henry Harrison. He thought he could win back the critical outpost by a winter campaign and sent Brig. Gen. James Winchester and an advance party of untrained regulars and volunteers, mostly from Kentucky, to establish a base camp at the Maumee River Rapids (modern Perrysburg, Ohio). Against Harrison's orders, but at the request of local citizens whose village had been pillaged and occupied by the British and Indians, Winchester advanced to the hamlet of Frenchtown (modern Monroe, Michigan). There he dispersed a small British detachment on 18 January 1813.

Learning of this dangerous threat to his security, Col. Henry Procter, commander of British forces in the Detroit River region, quickly organized a counterattack. He gathered troops from Fort Malden, most from the 41st Foot and local militiamen, and a body of Indians led by the Wyandot chief Roundhead. Procter crossed the Detroit River to Brownstown, bringing his artillery with him over the ice. His total force was approximately 1,300 compared to Winchester's 934. Winchester failed to provide adequate security and dispersed his troops throughout the village situated on the River Raisin.

On 22 January, a combination of artillery fire and Indian attack surprised and crushed the hastily formed U.S. right. Winchester was captured as he tried to join his forces from his comfortable farmhouse quarters some distance from the battlefield. Even though his left wing was giving a good account of itself, Winchester surrendered the whole

force to avoid a massacre of his troops. Of the Americans engaged, only 33 escaped death or capture. When Procter withdrew 25 miles to Brownstown (modern Trenton, Michigan), he left wounded prisoners in Frenchtown under Indian guard. The Indians executed between 30 to 60 (depending upon the source) of these men. The U.S. press called it the River Raisin Massacre.

The brief engagement (sometimes called the Battle of the River Raisin) had important consequences. It forced Harrison to cancel his winter offensive. Instead, he began construction of Fort Meigs at the Maumee Rapids and awaited the outcome of Oliver Hazard Perry's efforts to eliminate British control of Lake Erie. "Remember the River Raisin" became a western rallying cry and aided recruiting efforts for Harrison's 1813 campaign that ended with the Battle of the Thames.

General Winchester's conduct infuriated frontiersmen and increased anti–regular army sentiment in the West. Procter received a brigadier generalship, but his inability to control the Indians brought severe censure upon him by many of his own officers as well as his opponents.

—David Curtis Skaggs

See also: Harrison, William Henry; Winchester, James
Further Reading
Carter-Edwards, Dennis. "The War of 1812 along the Detroit Frontier: A Canadian Perspective." *Michigan Historical Review* 13 (1987).
Darnell, Elias. *A Journal Containing an Accurate and Interesting Account of the Hardships . . . of . . . Kentucky Volunteers and Regulars Commanded by General Winchester in the Years 1812–1813 . . .* Philadelphia: Lippincott, Brambo, 1854.
McAfee, Robert B. *History of the Late War in the Western Country.* Lexington, KY: Worsley & Smith, 1816.
Richardson, John. *Richardson's War of 1812.* Ed. Alexander C. Casselman. Toronto: Historical Publishing, 1902.

FRIGATE, EVOLUTION OF THE

A major naval development of the seventeenth century was the differentiation between merchantmen and men-of-war. The advent of standing navies demanded that ships be designed and built for the main purpose of fighting; no longer would lumbering merchantmen be made over to serve a naval purpose in an emergency. Throughout the century, there was emphasis on and continued growth in the size of ships of the line. So much emphasis was placed on the multidecked monsters that by the beginning of the next century navies were looking around for other specialized types of ships to perform lesser functions at smaller cost.

Although the term *frigate* had been used in a variety of ways in the seventeenth century, it was not until the middle third of the eighteenth that it came to be applied to the specific warship type next inferior to the ship of the line. The type seems to have originated with the French about 1740 and to have come to English notice with their capture of the privateer "fregat" *Tygre* later that same decade. She carried 26 9-pounders on her main deck and was a fast sailor. So impressed was the Royal Navy that her lines were taken off and used as the basis for their first two "frigates" (of 28 guns), *Unicorn* and *Lyme,* each of which reflected variations on the *Tygre* pattern.

In general terms, the British designs were stoutly built vessels, well suited to the British preference for slugfests. The French had built their frigates with heavy armament but with the speed both to overhaul a prey and to escape an unexpectedly tough opponent. The British construction meant that their frigates could withstand and perform better in heavier weathers; too, they carried heavier rigs.

Of the first two British frigates, *Unicorn* was built more closely to the privateer's pattern and had a beakhead bulkhead. *Lyme* was innovative in that her bow timbers were taken right up to the forecastle deck, marking the introduction of the round bow in the type. This change meant that *Lyme* could better withstand end-on fire and also permitted the fitting of hawse holes at the gundeck level, providing drier, healthier conditions on the berthing deck.

Like the growth among liners mentioned earlier, the frigates grew in power rather rapidly, soon leaving their 24- and 28-gun ratings for 32; 36; and 38, which later came to be the most popular rate in the Royal Navy in the Napoleonic wars. And not only did the number of guns increase; so, too, did their caliber. The 28-gun frigate carried 9-pounders and 3-pounders, but the 32s had 12-pounders and 6s, and the 38s had 18s and 12s. By the end of the eighteenth century, HMS *Endymion,* carrying 26 24-pounders and 18 32-pounder carronades, was in service. Naturally, frigate size had grown apace: *Lyme* (1748), 581 tons; *Pallas* (1756), 718 tons; *Endymion* (1797), 1,277 tons. In January 1794, when the United States had become sufficiently aroused by the depredations of Barbary pirates against Yankee merchantmen to begin congressional debate on the subject, Philadelphia shipbuilder Joshua Humphreys wrote a letter to Robert Morris that evidently found its way to Capitol Hill, for its warship design philosophy clearly was that later espoused by the legislators:

[A]s our navy must for a considerable time be inferior in numbers, we are to consider what size ships will be most formidable . . . ; such [as] Frigates as in blowing weather would be an overmatch for double deck ships, and in light winds to evade coming to action. . . . Ships built on these principles will render those of an enemy in a degree useless, or require a greater number before they dare attack our ship. Frigates, I suppose, will be the first object and none ought to be built less than 150 feet keel to carry 28 32-pounders or 30 24-pounders on the gun deck and 12-pounders on the quarterdeck. These ships should have the scantlings equal to 74's. . . . As such ships will cost a large sum of money they should be built of the best materials that could possibly be procured.

Five months later, Humphreys was formally employed as the first naval constructor, with William Doughty and expatriate Englishman Josiah Fox as clerks who copied his frigate designs for distribution to building yards. These three produced many of the U.S. Navy warship designs from gunboat to ship of the line through the War of 1812.

Humphreys's best-known product is USS *Constitution,* 145 feet on keel and, although rated as a 44, originally armed with 30 24-pounders, 16 18-pounders, and 14 12-pounders. Her final price of $302,718.84 represented a 260 percent cost overrun from original appropriations, but her service to the nation in the Quasi-War with France, the Barbary Wars, the War of 1812, and beyond made her a bargain.

—*Tyrone G. Martin*

Further Reading

Chapelle, Howard I. *The History of the American Sailing Navy.* New York: Bonanza Books, 1949.

Howard, Dr. Frank. *Sailing Ships of War, 1400–1860.* New York: Mayflower Books, 1979.

Martin, Tyrone G. *A Most Fortunate Ship.* Annapolis, MD: Naval Institute Press, 1997.

FULTON, ROBERT
1765–1815
Naval inventor; civil engineer

Robert Fulton was born on 14 November 1765 in Little Britain, Lancaster County, Pennsylvania, son of Robert Fulton and Mary Smith. The younger Fulton acquired a reputation as a painter before leaving for England in 1786, yet his real fame came as an inventor. He invented

Robert Fulton

and on 20 July 1807, at the third attempt, he blew up another brig in New York Harbor. In August 1807, Fulton's *Clermont* began her inaugural voyage from New York to Albany for Robert Livingston. Fulton's plans for large steam warships found little favor among naval officers in 1814, but he did build a steam-powered floating battery for New York Harbor named the *Demologus*, though its completion came too late for any service in the war. After Fulton's death on 24 February 1815, the ship was renamed the *Fulton*.

—*Frederick C. Drake*

See also: Demologus; Torpedoes
Further Reading
Baldwin, Hanson W. "Fulton and Decatur." *United States Naval Institute Proceedings* 71 (1936): 231–235.
Dickinson, Henry W. *Robert Fulton—Engineer and Artist—His Life and Works.* New York: John Lane, 1913.
Fredriksen, John C., comp. *Free Trade and Sailors' Rights: A Bibliography of the War of 1812.* Westport, CT: Greenwood Press, 1985.
Hutcheson, Wallace S., Jr. *Robert Fulton: Pioneer of Undersea Warfare.* Annapolis, MD: Naval Institute Press, 1981.
O'Connell, Robert L. *Sacred Vessels: The Cult of the Battleship and the Rise of the U.S. Navy.* Boulder, CO: Westview Press, 1991.
Parsons, William B. *Robert Fulton and the Submarine.* New York: Columbia University Press, 1912.
Roland, Alexander. *Underwater Warfare in the Age of Sail.* Bloomington: Indiana University Press, 1978.
Sutcliffe, Alice C. *Robert Fulton and the* Clermont*: The Authoritative Story of Robert Fulton's Early Experiments, Persistent Efforts and Historic Achievements.* New York: Century, 1909.
Thomson, David W. "Robert Fulton's Torpedo System in the War of 1812." *United States Naval Institute Proceedings* 70 (1946): 1207–1217.

canal machinery, a double inclined plane for raising canal boats, a power shovel for digging channels, and cast iron aqueduct spans. Fulton first pursued his experiments in 1797, envisioning a steam-powered fleet, a submarine, and torpedoes as a system of defense for England. In 1797, Fulton tested a torpedo in France and in 1800 and 1801 a three-man submarine (the *Nautilus*) in the Channel. In 1803, he and his patron, Robert Livingston, demonstrated a steamboat and suggested to Napoleon that such vessels could carry an army to England.

Fulton returned to England and, encouraged by William Pitt, achieved success on 15 October 1805 when his torpedo devices blew up a 200-ton brigantine. The Royal Navy was more alarmed than impressed. The first lord of the Admiralty thought Fulton's devices "a mode of warfare which they who commanded the seas did not want, and which, if succeeded, would deprive them of it." In October 1806, Fulton returned to the United States,

G

GAINES, EDMUND PENDLETON
1777–1849
U.S. officer

Born in Virginia to James Gaines and Elizabeth Strother Gaines, Edmund Pendleton Gaines moved as a child with his parents to North Carolina and then to Tennessee. After some volunteer service in the Indian wars of the 1790s, Gaines received a commission as an ensign in the U.S. Army in 1797. Following a quick promotion to lieutenant, Gaines served in the southwest, rising to captain by 1807 and assuming command of Fort Stoddert. One of his most important acts while serving in that area was to make the arrest of Aaron Burr and to serve as a witness at Burr's trial.

Shortly after Burr's trial, Gaines took a leave of absence from the army to study law and see if he preferred a civilian career. Impending war with Great Britain, however, saw him back in service and brought promotion to major and then lieutenant colonel. By 1813, he had risen to the rank of colonel. During the war, in addition to his many combat assignments, Gaines was a vocal critic of the supply system, blaming the bad or nonexistent rations rather than battle injuries for causing more deaths.

Gaines served in several theaters, starting in the southwest. From there he moved to the northwest under Maj. Gen. William Henry Harrison. During the invasion of Canada in the fall of 1813, Gaines was Harrison's adjutant general and performed duties with such distinction that he was promoted to brigadier general in January 1814.

Transferred to Sacket's Harbor on Lake Ontario in early 1814, Gaines was placed in command of that town by Maj. Gen. Jacob Brown while Brown took the bulk of the army on the Niagara River campaign. In April, Gaines's intelligence sources warned of increased British activity at Kingston that possibly portended an attack on Sacket's Harbor. Gaines immediately sent word to Brown, who had yet to cross the Niagara River and so returned promptly with part of his army. The Americans then learned that the British did not intend to move in that direction. Brown ordered Gaines to begin construction of gunboats, to cooperate with Commodore Isaac Chauncey to disrupt British communications on the St. Lawrence River, and to stand ready with Chauncey to cooperate with Brown's movements on the Niagara.

While Brown commenced his movement into Canada, British Adm. Sir James Yeo's squadron positioned itself to make naval movements out of Sacket's Harbor difficult. The British move and Chauncey's illness meant that cooperation between Sacket's Harbor and Brown's campaign was unlikely. When Brown reached Lake Ontario, however, he sent word to Chauncey asking again for his cooperation. On 23 July, Brown received a letter from Gaines informing him of the difficulties at Sacket's Harbor and that there would be no help coming from that quarter. Following the campaign, a bitter dispute arose between Brown and Chauncey regarding the latter's lack of cooperation. During the controversy, Gaines took Brown's part to criticize Chauncey's inactivity.

Because Major General Brown had received several serious wounds at Lundy's Lane to close his Niagara campaign, Gaines was summoned from Sacket's Harbor at the end of July to assume command of the U.S. forces at Fort Erie. He arrived and took command on 5 August 1814. The first task confronting Gaines was that of correcting the old fort's weakness. Knowing that the British were close by and receiving reinforcements daily, he immediately set to work strengthening and expanding the existing fortifications and adding new ones. As his men frantically hammered and sawed, Gaines watched the British under Gen. Sir Gordon Drummond move into position to begin bombarding the fort. The British artillery opened up on 13 August. Gaines sensed the British would try to storm the fort, so he inspected the old and new works on the night of 14 August. As it happened, his inspection occurred just hours before the British launched their attack after midnight on 15 August. Repulsed at all three points of their attack, the British brought in more heavy artillery to extend the siege. Gaines's official reports of the battle of the 15th noted the overwhelming success of the U.S. defenders. He and others had heard some British officers shout to their men as they stormed the fort not to give the Americans quarter.

Drummond began a heavier artillery barrage, bringing in additional and heavier guns to bomb Gaines into submission. On 28 August, one of the British shells crashed through the roof of Gaines's room, severely injuring him and forcing his evacuation. General Brown returned to the fort to assume command because of Gaines's injuries. For his actions in the defense of Fort Erie, Gaines received a brevet promotion to major general. In addition, Congress commissioned a medal be struck in his honor, and he was awarded swords by the states of Tennessee, Virginia, and New York.

Gaines's injuries prevented any further active service during the war. After his recovery, Gaines received orders from Secretary of War James Monroe to report to Maj. Gen. Andrew Jackson at New Orleans to aid in the defense of that city, but Gaines received these orders too late to take part in the Battle of New Orleans.

Following the war Gaines remained in the army, serving under Jackson in the South and participating in Jackson's invasion of Spanish Florida in 1818. He participated in the early stages of the Second Seminole War, but age and disagreements with the War Department prevented him from seeing action in the Mexican-American War. He died in New Orleans of cholera in 1849.

—Jeanne T. Heidler and David S. Heidler

See also: Brown, Jacob J.; Erie, Fort; Harrison, William Henry; Sacket's Harbor, New York

Further Reading

Silver, James W. *Edmund Pendleton Gaines: Frontier General.* Baton Rouge: Louisiana State University Press, 1949.

GALES, JOSEPH
1786–1860
U.S. journalist

The son of Joseph Gales and Winifred Marshall Gales, English-born Joseph Gales came to the United States with his father in 1795. He spent the remainder of his childhood in Philadelphia, Pennsylvania, and Raleigh, North Carolina. His mother, a well-read woman, educated him in the classics and works of contemporary political philosophy. His father, a printer/journalist by occupation (he had had to flee England because of his criticism of the government) taught his son his trade.

In 1807, the younger Gales began reporting on Congress for the Washington *National Intelligencer.* As the only full-time reporter covering the Senate, he sat next to the vice president during all sessions. In 1810, Gales became the owner of the paper and in 1812 entered into a partnership with his brother-in-law, William W. Seaton. As the official paper of the Madison administration, the *National Intelligencer* strongly supported the move toward war, and Gales used its pages to praise Madison's handling of the conflict after it began. Giving tangible substance to their confidence in the administration, Gales and Seaton joined the army at the onset of hostilities and served in the Washington area throughout the war. The two also alternated days in the city in order to print the paper as a daily.

One of the favorite topics of Gales's editorials throughout the war was British Adm. Sir George Cockburn. Cockburn had an especially bad reputation in Chesapeake Bay country because of his raids on towns along its shores. Gales never missed an opportunity to emphasize what he portrayed as the depravity of Cockburn's actions. Cockburn, who habitually read U.S. newspapers for information about the U.S. war effort, took particular offense at what he believed were unfair attacks produced by the man he derisively referred to as "Josey." When the British took Washington, D.C., in August 1814, Cockburn was determined to have his revenge on "Josey" Gales's newspaper.

After some difficulty in finding the *Intelligencer's* offices, Cockburn finally came to the proper building. His first impulse was to burn it to the ground, but after hearing the pleas of two elderly ladies that their neighboring home would also be destroyed, Cockburn resolved to sack only the interior. As British soldiers destroyed Gales's library, press, and other equipment, Cockburn reportedly insisted that the soldiers take special effort to obliterate all of the *c*'s in the newspaper's type racks so that Gales could no longer write about Cockburn. Gales's housekeeper saved his residence from destruction by posting a For Rent sign outside.

Following the war Gales continued to operate the *National Intelligencer* until his death in 1860. Much of the paper's space covered congressional proceedings. In 1816 his press also began publishing the *Register of Debates in Congress,* the *Annals of Congress,* and the *American State Papers.*

—Jeanne T. Heidler and David S. Heidler

See also: Cockburn, George

Further Reading

Ames, William E. *A History of the* National Intelligencer. Chapel Hill: University of North Carolina Press, 1972.

Lord, Walter. *The Dawn's Early Light.* New York: W. W. Norton, 1972.

GALLATIN, ALBERT

1761–1849

Secretary of the treasury, 1801–1813;
commissioner to Ghent, 1814

"Stop the Wheels of Government".

Albert Gallatin

Born into a prominent Swiss family on 29 January 1761, Abraham Alfonse Albert Gallatin was orphaned at a young age. Raised by a distant relative, he enjoyed the benefits of private instruction, a classical education at the Academy of Geneva, and the intellectual enlightenment of his birth city. Yet an increasingly liberal outlook put Gallatin in conflict with his aristocratic Genevan heritage. Insisting that "he would never serve a tyrant," Gallatin spurned the offer of a lieutenant colonelcy of Hessian troops during the American Revolution.

Nevertheless, the prospect of future opportunity led him to cross the Atlantic in the summer of 1780. Following a stint as a Harvard tutor, he turned to land speculation on the western frontier and established his home, Friendship Hill (now maintained by the National Park Service), along the banks of the Monongahela River in Fayette County, Pennsylvania. In October 1789, the estate became the final resting place for the former Sophia Allegre, whom Gallatin had married but five months earlier.

Friendship Hill never became the idyllic sanctuary that the youthful Gallatin had envisioned. He was increasingly frustrated by the cultural isolation of frontier living, but as a highly educated Swiss immigrant he gained in influence among neighbors who were all struggling trans-Appalachian newcomers. Gallatin's keen intellect, world ken, and belief in the rights of the common citizen garnered the respect of his Fayette County associates, who did not seem to mind that his words were laced with a thick French accent. In August 1788, they appointed Gallatin to attend a statewide meeting in Harrisburg to consider amending the federal Constitution, and the following year they made him a delegate to the state constitutional convention in Philadelphia. He returned to the state capital following his election to the lower house of the Pennsylvania Assembly in 1790. There he became "the laboring oar" for innumerable committees and first demonstrated an unusual aptitude for understanding public finance. Support from anti-Hamiltonians in the Assembly resulted in his election to the U.S. Senate in February 1793.

That summer, before taking his seat in the Senate, Gallatin proposed marriage to Hannah Nicholson, daughter of James Nicholson, a retired naval officer of Revolutionary War distinction. They wed in November and remained united for more than 55 years. Gallatin's tenure as senator, however, lasted less than three months. Gallatin had raised Federalist ire while serving in the Pennsylvania statehouse, and hostile forces immediately called Gallatin's citizenship into question. The Democratic Republican was voted out of office along strict party lines but not before he had attempted to hold Alexander Hamilton and the Treasury Department accountable to Congress. Returning to a Pennsylvania frontier soon engulfed by the Whiskey Rebellion, Gallatin gallantly fought both to preserve the union and to redress what he thought was an unjust excise tax. His moderating presence prevented widespread violence and resulted in his election to the House of Representatives in 1794.

By 1797, Gallatin was the recognized leader of the Republican minority in the lower chamber. Although he took an interest in foreign affairs, his focus remained public finance. Within days of being seated in Congress, Gallatin successfully gained the establishment of a house standing committee on finance that later became the committee of ways and means. His influential *A Sketch of the Finances of the United States* criticized Federalist finance policies that had increased the public debt. Remembering the concerns of his frontier constituency, Gallatin became one of the primary authors of the compromise Land Act of 1796. Though many of his financial reform efforts were initially rebuffed, opportunities once again arose when Thomas Jefferson became president and appointed Gallatin as his secretary of the treasury in May 1801.

The new secretary lost no time in attacking a public debt that exceeded $80 million. He concluded that by annually designating $7.3 million of federal income toward payment of principal and interest, the debt in theory would be extinguished by 1817. Future debt, Gallatin envisioned, could then be prevented through economy of federal expenditures, specific congressional appropriation legislation, and strict financial accountability practices. However, such radical reforms faced serious challenge even in the Republican-controlled Congress. Through dogged effort in the opening months of his secretaryship, Gallatin succeeded in gaining the annual debt reduction appropriation but failed to secure federal financial accountability oversight for the Treasury Department. The excise tax, against which he had long fought, he now believed necessary in order to reduce the national debt. The tax was repealed, however, at Jefferson's request.

Perhaps Gallatin's greatest civic asset was an ardent nationalism during a period of zealous regional, state, and local prejudice. Because his propositions were based upon reason and not the emotions of the moment, his cabinet influence steadily extended well beyond strictly Treasury matters. Not surprisingly, Gallatin's foreign birth was attacked and his allegiance questioned by politicians whose regional agendas were restrained by the secretary's steadfast national fidelity. Creative financing facilitated the Louisiana Purchase and eased the burden of the Barbary War. For the latter, a temporary increase in ad valorem duties on imports, known as the Mediterranean Fund, was enacted in March 1804. However, support for the Bank of the United States, which Gallatin deemed critical to expedite Treasury transactions in an expanding nation, gained for him the animosity of many within his own party. Indeed, the bank issue would haunt Gallatin throughout much of his lifetime.

Following admission of Ohio into statehood and the opening of the Indiana Territory, Gallatin sought to accelerate settlement by means of a reduction to 160 acres of the minimum land tract purchase. To compensate for short-term Treasury revenue losses, the secretary recommended prompt payment to prevent long-term indebtedness. Furthermore, he declared public works spending as in the national interest and laid out his vision in an insightful 1808 internal improvement plan. Development of the transportation network in the United States, he contended, would bind regions together in more perfect union. Unfortunately, the specter of local interest gained renewed vigor following the 1807 *Chesapeake-Leopard* incident, the issuance of British Orders in Council, and Napoleon's Berlin and Milan decrees.

Gallatin then had the unenviable task of enforcing Jefferson's embargo while at the same time seeking its repeal on the basis that it was fiscally unsound (the act resulted in a treasury deficit for the first time in the secretary's tenure). As the possibility of war loomed, Gallatin tried to ready the nation's finances to meet the crisis. Yet his unequivocal support for rechartering the Bank of the United States provided another cause for bitter partisan politics during "Mr. Madison's War." As a consequence, the United States had difficulty remaining solvent throughout the Anglo-American contest. Personally, his stand destroyed Gallatin's opportunity for higher public office. Fettered by political attacks questioning his fitness to serve, the secretary successfully issued the first U.S. treasury notes when loans from state-chartered banks failed to fill the war chest.

In many ways, the exigencies of war brought Gallatin's statecraft to the fore. Besides diligently working treasury issues, he energetically assisted James Monroe in overseeing all aspects of the war effort following the demonstrated incompetence of the secretaries of war and navy. By the spring of 1813, however, Gallatin sought relief from what had become a thankless task in guiding the Treasury Department. He requested and was appointed envoy extraordinary of a U.S. delegation, which included John Quincy Adams and James A. Bayard, established to explore possible peace mediation by Alexander I of Russia. Unfortunately, internal jealousies prevented Senate ratification of Gallatin's nomination, though he had already departed for Russia. Later, his name was left off the commission established for direct negotiations with Great Britain, since the president believed Gallatin would return to his cabinet post. Undeterred by this apparent affront, Gallatin set off from St. Petersburg as a private citizen in January 1814 for the harsh overland journey west. He was belatedly named a commissioner after George W. Campbell officially replaced him as secretary of the treasury. Following a brief sojourn in London, during which he informally corresponded with Lord Castlereagh, Gallatin arrived in Ghent in July 1814 and quickly became the main U.S. contributor to the peace talks. Not only did he frame most responses to British demands, but his national outlook, calming presence, and willingness to compromise won over friend and foe alike. The subsequent peace treaty left virtually all issues unresolved, but Gallatin's primary concern had been a quick conclusion to the negotiations.

With peace, Gallatin remained in Europe with Adams and Henry Clay to reestablish commercial ties with the British. After many delays, a convention that essentially returned to an economic status quo antebellum was signed in July 1815. Rejecting the offer of his former treasury post, Gallatin served seven years as minister to France. Although he and his family delighted in the cosmopolitan Parisian surroundings, Gallatin was frustrated by a lack of progress in resolving Franco-American affairs that had been disrupted by Bonaparte. His successful negotiations with the British in 1818, renewing the commercial treaty, proved to be the highlight of his mission: Resolution of the matter of the boundary between Canada and the United States in the northern Great Plains and temporary agreement on the occupation of the Oregon country reduced potential friction between the two nations. Returning to the United States in 1823, he reluctantly became William Crawford's vice presidential running mate before being asked to withdraw from the ticket when the folly of his nomination became apparent.

Gallatin concluded public life with a diplomatic appointment to London in 1826. Negotiations on renewal of trade, impressment, occupation of the Oregon Territory, the boundary dispute between Maine and New Brunswick, navigation of the St. Lawrence River, and other issues met with both success and failure. Without Gallatin, most experienced at dealing with the British, the mission would likely not have been as positive in outcome. In November 1827 the diplomat embarked upon an active private life in New York City, his wife's hometown, after forsaking once and for all life along the Monongahela.

Financial acumen led to his selection in 1831 as president of longtime friend John Jacob Astor's new National (later Gallatin) Bank of New York, where the sage continued to influence national fiscal policy. Through well-reasoned expositions, often printed in pamphlet form for wide distribution, Gallatin examined such 1830s issues as the high protective tariff, paper money, and bimetal currency. The Jackson administration took particular issue with his support for the Second Bank of the United States. Gallatin's persistence, however, in fighting for a return to specie payment paved the way for national recovery following the Panic of 1837. Finance remained but one of his private pursuits.

Egalitarian beliefs made Gallatin an early leader in the movement to establish what ultimately became New York University. Interest in the folkways of aboriginal peoples, piqued decades earlier by naturalist Alexander von Humboldt, led to Gallatin's founding of the American Ethnological Society in 1842 and his becoming known as the "father of American ethnology." Gallatin's scholarly writings became recognized internationally for their importance to the field. He was also active in the leadership of the New York Historical Society.

Gallatin's death on 12 August 1849 at the home of daughter Frances in Astoria, on Long Island, New York, brought the Jeffersonian era to a close. His intellect, integrity, dedication to republican principles, and long pub-lic service make Gallatin one of the most important, though ill-remembered, figures of the early republic.

—*William E. Fischer, Jr.*

See also: Adams, John Quincy; Bayard, James Asheton; Clay, Henry; Financing the War of 1812; Ghent, Treaty of
Further Reading
Adams, Henry, ed. *The Writings of Albert Gallatin*. 3 vols. Philadelphia: Lippincott, 1879.
Ewing, Frank E. *America's Forgotten Statesman, Albert Gallatin*. New York: Vantage Press, 1959.
Gallatin, Albert. *The Papers of Albert Gallatin*. Philadelphia: Historical Publications, 1969.
Thornbrough, Gayle, ed. *John Badollet and Albert Gallatin: Correspondence, 1804–1836*. Indianapolis: Indiana Historical Society, 1963.
Walters, Raymond, Jr. *Albert Gallatin: Jeffersonian Financier and Diplomat*. New York: Macmillan, 1957.

GALUSHA, JONAS
See Chittenden, Martin

GARDNER, CHARLES KITCHEL
1787–1869
U.S. officer

Born in New Jersey to Thomas Gardner and Sarah Kitchel Gardner, Charles Gardner grew up in Newburgh, New York. After briefly studying medicine, Gardner received an ensign's commission in the Sixth Infantry Regiment in 1808. Before the War of 1812, he served both in New York and in Louisiana. During this period he gained experience as an adjutant. After the war commenced, though he served briefly as a captain in the Third Artillery, his earlier training gained him a transfer to Washington, D.C., in 1813, where he served as an assistant in the adjutant general's office.

Later in 1813, after a promotion to major, he transferred to Sacket's Harbor and the 25th Infantry Regiment. He participated in Gen. James Wilkinson's abortive invasion of Canada late in that year and fought in the Battle of Chrysler's Farm. In 1814, he served under Brig. Gen. Jacob Brown at Sacket's Harbor and Buffalo. He was promoted in that year to colonel and served as Brown's adjutant general.

While serving in that position, Gardner participated in the taking of Fort Erie in July 1814. During that campaign, Brown and Brig. Gen. Eleazar Ripley began a dispute regarding Ripley's conduct that lasted beyond the war.

Following the war, Gardner became embroiled in this quarrel, taking Brown's part. The deed made an enemy of Ripley, who charged Gardner with cowardice and conduct unbecoming an officer and a gentleman. Though the ensuing court-martial found Gardner guilty of the second offense, it declined to punish him, claiming that the entire affair stemmed from personal differences between the officers.

Gardner resigned from the army in 1818 and embarked on various careers, including journalism and diverse jobs in government. He retained his interest in the military and over his lifetime wrote a number of works on infantry drill and regulations. Later in life he compiled a dictionary of army officers from 1789 to 1853.

—Jeanne T. Heidler and David S. Heidler

See also: Brown, Jacob J.; Erie, Fort; Ripley, Eleazar Wheelock
Further Reading
Gardner, Charles K. *Trial by Court-Martial.* Boston: N.p., 1816.

GEORGE, FORT

Constructed during the period 1796 to 1799 to replace Fort Niagara, which had been turned over to the United States by Jay's treaty of 1794, Fort George was Gen. Isaac Brock's principal British headquarters on the Niagara Frontier as war began in 1812. It was a log-and-palisade fort with several bastions and ravelins, built on high ground on the Niagara River's west bank, overlooking the channel mouth, and upstream from the United States' Fort Niagara on the eastern bank. U.S. officers, dining with their British counterparts, first heard the news of war in the fort, finished their meal, and were escorted across the river.

The first action against Fort George came from Fort Niagara. An artillery barrage set buildings on fire with hot shot on 13 October 1812. The powder magazine, then containing 800 barrels of powder, received a direct hit on the roof. A small party of engineers under Captain Vigoreux bravely doused the fire by scaling the roof, tearing off the metal coverings, and extinguishing the blaze in the support timbers with buckets of water.

On 27 May 1813, a combined expedition of 2,500 men, 13 ships, and 180 batteaux under Gen. Henry Dearborn

and Commodore Isaac Chauncey captured Fort George by driving out Brig. Gen. John Vincent's 1,000 defenders. For seven months U.S. forces retained possession and refortified the fort, intending to use it as a bridgehead for an attack along the peninsula toward the British headquarters at Burlington Heights. The plan was thwarted after the British night counterattack at Stoney Creek (6 June 1813), the Battle of the Forty, and the Battle of Beaver Dams (24 June), which confirmed the inability of U.S. forces to break out of their enclave. U.S. troops were besieged in the fort for the summer. It was left in command of a skeleton force under Gen. Winfield Scott when General Wilkinson's troops moved down Lake Ontario, and it then became the base for William Henry Harrison's western army in October and November 1813, also en route to Sacket's Harbor.

In December 1813, as New York brigadier general George McClure withdrew from Fort George, he burned the town of Newark but left Butler's barracks and Fort George standing, a piece of military and social stupidity that led Pres. James Madison to repudiate his action. McClure's action nevertheless provoked instant reprisals from the British. Lt. Gen. Sir Gordon Drummond waged a hard-hitting winter campaign that captured Fort Niagara on 29 December 1813 and burned the Niagara Frontier settlements.

Thereafter, both Fort George and Fort Niagara remained in British possession, providing them with control of the only safe river anchorage at the western end of Lake Ontario. Moreover, British possession of the forts denied that anchorage to Commodore Chauncey's immeasurably strengthened 1814 squadron. In fact, this British dominance of the Niagara River denied Chauncey any anchorage, a fact of palpable importance that prevented Chauncey and Maj. Gen. Jacob Brown from coordinating their efforts. This failure in turn effectively undermined Jacob Brown's Niagara Frontier campaign against Fort George in July 1814. In mid- to late summer 1814, the fort became the main garrison headquarters for Sir Gordon Drummond's British army of 2,500 to 3,000 men operating in defense of the frontier. In August, Drummond sallied forth from Fort George to besiege Jacob Brown's army in Fort Erie.

Peace meant sharp reductions of the military establishment. In the 1820s, Fort George was abandoned. Between 1871 and 1965, the Canadian army used the plains outside the fort for annual exercises. The stone powder magazine, built in 1796, is the only original building still standing, and the current fort is a reconstruction not built on the lines of the original. Open to the public since 1950, it became a Canadian national historical park in 1969.

—Frederick C. Drake

See also: Brown, Jacob J.; Chauncey, Isaac; Dearborn, Henry; Drummond, Gordon; McClure, George; Newark, Upper Canada; Vincent, John

Further Reading

Allen, Robert S. "A History of Fort George, Upper Canada." *Canadian Historic Sites* 11 (1974): 61–93.

"Capture of Fort George." *Portfolio* 4 (1817): 3–8.

Coleman, Margaret. *The American Capture of Fort George, Ontario.* Ottawa: Department of Northern and Indian Affairs, 1977.

Cruikshank, Ernest A. *The Battle of Fort George.* Niagara Falls, Ont.: Niagara Historical Society, 1904.

Fort George. Ottawa: Parks Canada, 1979.

Montross, Lynn. "An Amphibious Doubleheader." *Marine Corps Gazette* 42 (1957): 131–140.

Wilson, John P. *Fort George on the Niagara: An Archaeological Perspective.* Ottawa: National Historic Parks, 1976.

GEORGIA

The state of Georgia, bordering on Spanish Florida to the south, two large Indian nations to the northwest (Cherokee) and west (Creek), and a large coastline, was in a particularly vulnerable position as war approached in 1812. Many Georgians, however, saw the advent of hostilities as an opportunity rather than a threat. With war imminent with Great Britain, Georgians saw the possessions of Britain's ally, Spain, as ripe for the picking.

Georgians had been moving into northeastern Florida for years. Others simply used the prairies of north Florida to graze livestock and moved freely over the rather fluid border. Less upstanding citizens took advantage of the unguarded border to make raids, primarily against the Seminoles of north Florida. They stole cattle and other possessions, then retreated into Georgia.

In early 1812, Pres. James Madison secretly encouraged former Georgia governor George Mathews to organize a rebellion of the Georgians in north Florida. Taking 80 Georgians with him, Mathews began what would be called the Patriot's War with the clandestine assistance of U.S. regulars at St. Marys, Georgia, and U.S. naval forces off the coast. These so-called rebels declared that East Florida was no longer a possession of Spain, seized Amelia Island, and laid siege to St. Augustine.

As the United States entered the war with Great Britain in the summer of 1812, things fell apart for the patriots. The Spaniards in St. Augustine refused to surrender control of the fortifications around the city, the Seminoles became increasingly hostile, and the Madison administration

began to rethink its actions regarding Florida in light of the larger conflict it now had to prosecute.

Still, Georgia remained enthusiastic about the project, and Gov. David Mitchell began raising militia to supplement the forces already in Florida. The Georgia and Tennessee militias that marched into Florida, however, seemed to be far more interested in Seminole plunder than in attacking Spaniards, and when Congress voted against a resolution to annex Florida in early 1813, the entire scheme unraveled.

By 1813, Georgians were looking more to the west than the south, as the Creek Indians descended into civil war. The Creeks in west Georgia and the Mississippi Territory (now Alabama) had been increasingly uneasy since the U.S. government had forced them to accept the construction of a road through their nation. Originating at the westernmost white settlements of Georgia, the road was completed in 1810. By then those Creeks who had opposed its construction and had resisted Creek agent Benjamin Hawkins's acculturation plans for the nation were brimming with resentment. When Tecumseh visited the Creeks in 1811, a large part of the nation was more than willing to listen to his pleas for unity among native peoples.

Several incidents within the Creek nation in 1812 indicated a rising hostility between those Creeks who supported Hawkins's plans and those Creeks, sometimes referred to as Red Sticks, who did not. When the Creek civil war erupted in 1813, many Georgians feared that it would spill over onto their frontier settlements. They blamed Hawkins for not controlling the situation and then complained when initially he would not let Georgia militia march into the Creek nation to suppress the violence. For many Georgians, the Creek civil war presented an excellent opportunity to seize that part of the Creek nation within the borders of their state.

Not until the Red Sticks attacked Fort Mims in August 1813, however, was the Georgia militia allowed to march against the Creeks. The attack prompted Maj. Gen. Thomas Pinckney, commander of the Sixth Military District, to call out surrounding state militias to end the Creek War. In Georgia, militia brigadier general John Floyd commanded the state's contingent of 950 militiamen who assembled at Fort Hawkins (the Creek Agency) in September 1813. Pinckney's original plan called for Floyd to march his men to the conjunction of the Coosa and Tallapoosa Rivers to rendezvous with the Tennessee militia marching there under Maj. Gen. Andrew Jackson. Supply shortages prevented both expeditions from reaching the rendezvous point. The dearth of supplies and the ineffectual supply system plagued the Georgians throughout the Creek War.

Floyd and his men remained at Fort Hawkins for two months, waiting for enough rations to march into the Creek Nation. While at Fort Hawkins, Floyd tried to hone the training of his raw militia, but this activity combined with the lack of victuals only darkened the men's mood. Adding insult to these injuries, many Georgians began criticizing Floyd and his men for remaining idle, even implying that cowardice kept them from moving against the Creeks.

Sniped at by the public, Floyd also had an exasperating time dealing with the state government. Governor Mitchell and his successor, Gov. Peter Early, withheld militia to guard what they feared would be an exposed Georgia frontier. Commanding 500 such militiamen, Maj. Gen. David Adams operated north of Floyd's position, but he encountered few Red Sticks.

By mid-November Floyd had stockpiled rations to last about 20 days and prepared to march into the Creek nation. He moved his men to the Chattahoochee River, where he was joined by about 400 Allied Creeks under William McIntosh. After building Fort Mitchell at the Chattahoochee, Floyd and his Indian allies moved out of Georgia toward the Red Stick town of Autosse. Floyd's force approached the town on the Tallapoosa River on the morning of 29 November, discovering that actually two towns were in close proximity. Floyd hoped to surround both towns, but his failure to do so caused the battle to dissolve into fierce hand-to-hand fighting. Ultimately, most of the Red Sticks fled into the brush. Some of Floyd's men gave chase to catch the wounded and kill them. In all, the Red Sticks lost about 200 dead and an undetermined number of wounded; the Americans suffered 11 killed and 54 wounded. General Floyd was among the wounded.

With supplies again running out, Floyd marched his men back to Fort Mitchell. Red Sticks staged an attack on Floyd's rear guard, but the Georgians fought it off and made their way safely back to the Chattahoochee. At Fort Mitchell, while recovering from his wounds, Floyd coped with chronic supply problems. He had to wait six weeks before he could plan another invasion of the Creek Nation. With his force's enlistments expiring on 22 February 1814, the most Floyd could hope for was a raid against the Red Sticks. A coordinated campaign was out of the question. Even his modest plans depended on his receiving rations.

When food finally arrived, Floyd set out in mid-January with about 1,200 militiamen and 600 Creeks. The Georgians constructed Fort Hull about 40 miles west of Fort Mitchell and left a small garrison there. Floyd moved out again, establishing a fortified camp on Calabee Creek. Before dawn on 27 January 1814, Red Sticks attacked this camp, catching Floyd's men by surprise. In a ferocious engagement that stretched into daylight, the Georgians gradually repelled the Red Stick attack. His losses severe (26 dead and 143 wounded), Floyd had to retreat first to Fort Hull and then to Fort Mitchell, leaving the field to the Red Sticks.

As Andrew Jackson penetrated deeper into the Creek Nation in the early months of 1814, the Georgia militia remained on the Georgia frontier, guarding it against attack from fleeing Red Sticks. By the spring of 1814, alarms spread that the British would land a major force on the Gulf Coast of Florida to threaten the southern frontier of Georgia. Militia forces remained to guard against that possibility. In the summer of 1814, rumors became reality when the British navy landed forces under Maj. Edward Nicholls on the Apalachicola River. Nicholls rallied the defeated Red Sticks and beckoned Georgia slaves to flee their masters. The Georgia frontier stayed nervous and on alert for the remainder of the War of 1812. Though Nicholls never became the nemesis that Georgians expected, his presence kept approximately 3,500 militia, regulars, and Allied Creeks tied down on the Georgia frontier.

While Georgians watched Nicholls's activities on the gulf in the fall and winter of 1814, another threat materialized along the Georgia coast. Vice Adm. Sir Alexander Cochrane left the Chesapeake to begin the New Orleans campaign, but he had left Rear Adm. Sir George Cockburn to continue raids in the bay to distract U.S. forces from British activities in the Gulf of Mexico. After a few weeks of pillaging, however, Cockburn was under orders to make his way down the coast to begin similar activities along the Georgia and South Carolina shores. Cochrane hoped that Cockburn would prevent those states from sending reinforcements to New Orleans.

Rumors of Cockburn's movements reached coastal Georgia before he did, primarily because Cockburn was delayed by the wait for additional Royal Marines. By the time he did arrive, he did not know that the United States had already won the Battle of New Orleans. When Cockburn landed in mid-January on Cumberland Island, Georgia, he enthusiastically commenced his raiding, taking both St. Marys and Brunswick, Georgia, on the coast and then moving into the interior. Georgia was alarmed more by Cockburn's proclamations to slaves than by his raids. Cochrane had prepared documents for Cockburn promising freedom to any slaves who joined the British. When Cockburn and his raiders threatened Savannah, Gov. Peter Early took 2,000 Georgia militiamen to strengthen the defenses of that city. The Treaty of Ghent, however, put an end to the business, and the feared slave uprising never materialized.

Though no major battles of the War of 1812 occurred in Georgia, the state experienced much turmoil during the conflict. Georgia did not realize the territorial gains it had envisioned, but ironically, thanks to the efforts of the Tennessee forces under Andrew Jackson and to the Treaty of Fort Jackson imposed on the Creeks, Indian lands in Georgia came increasingly under state control.

—*Jeanne T. Heidler and David S. Heidler*

See also: Autosse, Battle of; Calabee, Battle of; Cockburn, George; Creek War; Hawkins, Benjamin; Jackson, Andrew; Mathews, George; McIntosh, William; Nicholls, Edward; Patriot War

Further Reading

Owsley, Frank L., Jr. *Struggle for the Gulf Borderlands: The Creek War and the Battle of New Orleans, 1812–1815.* Gainesville: University Presses of Florida, 1981.

Pratt, Julius. *Expansionists of 1812.* New York: Macmillan, 1925. Reprint, Gloucester, MA: Peter Smith, 1957.

Elbridge Gerry

GERRY, ELBRIDGE
1744–1814
Governor of Massachusetts; vice president of the United States

The son of Thomas Gerry and Elizabeth Greenleaf Gerry, Elbridge Gerry was born in Massachusetts. He entered Harvard in 1758 and earned a master of arts. For his master's thesis, he argued the question of whether or not Americans could evade paying the stamp duties imposed by Parliament and remain loyal subjects of the king. He believed that they could. Though upon graduation Gerry began a career as a merchant, his thesis—his final work of his college career—foretold a lifelong intense interest in politics.

During the 1760s and 1770s, Gerry was involved in the political protests against British measures and developed a reputation in Massachusetts as a radical on these issues. Once the Revolution began, he remained active in Massachusetts politics and became so well known by 1776 that he was sent to the Continental Congress. He strongly supported the Declaration of Independence. Following the war, Gerry worried about the country's losing its republican virtue. He became convinced that some factions in the government favored monarchy and might use the army to establish it. Except in times of national emergency, Gerry opposed a standing army as antithetical to the country's interests.

Gerry's growing prestige resulted in his selection to rep-

resent Massachusetts at the Convention in 1787 that drafted the Constitution of the United States. After using his influence to prevent many centralizing proposals, Gerry still thought the final document granted too much power to the national government. He initially refused to sign it, but after the Constitution was ratified by the requisite number of states, he pledged to support the new government.

Elected to the First Congress, Gerry served two terms before the growing partisanship in Congress so disillusioned him that he returned to Massachusetts. The election of his old friend John Adams to the presidency in 1796, however, convinced him that there was hope for the government, and he returned to public life. Appointed by President Adams to serve as one of the three commissioners to smooth turbulent relations with France, Gerry left for Paris in 1797 to begin one of the most controversial periods in his life. The French government, through three consecutive emissaries (dubbed X, Y, and Z in subsequent official reports), indicated that a bribe would be necessary to commence negotiations.

Gerry alone among the Americans (John Marshall and Charles Cotesworth Pinckney were the other two) resisted breaking off the talks in the XYZ Affair. Believing that foreign policy's only purpose was to serve the national interest, he was acting on the conviction that it was not in the United States' best interest to go to war with France. When

Pinckney and Marshall refused to deal further with the French, however, Gerry's attempt to continue talks led to charges at home that he was a Francophile and a tool of the French government. On his return to the United States in 1798, Gerry was stung by the criticism levied against him and disturbed by the government's militant response to the XYZ Affair. What agitated him more was his fear that the new, larger military would be used to put down domestic opposition to government policy. For that reason, the previously unaffiliated Gerry became an ardent Democratic Republican.

Following the election of Thomas Jefferson as president, Gerry became the leading Republican in Massachusetts, but by 1804 he was removing himself from public life. Occasionally he wrote letters to political leaders, advising them on certain policies, but otherwise he showed no interest in returning to public office. That changed in 1809, however, when Gerry became convinced that New England Federalists intended to dissolve the Union. In 1810, he successfully ran for governor against Federalist Christopher Gore in an exceedingly nasty campaign. Perhaps because of Gerry's desire to heal campaign wounds, his first administration from 1810 to 1811 was quite moderate. Also, the Massachusetts legislature's virtually even division between Republicans and Federalists dictated a middle course. Some believed, though, that the old nonpartisan Gerry had resurfaced.

Gerry's reelection in 1811 proved otherwise. Republicans gained firm control of both houses of the legislature, and Gerry's second term thus donned a partisan cloak. Fueling political hostility in Massachusetts during Gerry's second term was Federalist anger over the decision to admit Louisiana as a state. The disaffected were already talking about secession when the renewal of nonintercourse against Great Britain threatened the region's economic well-being. Gerry and the Republicans in the legislature responded to this growing hostility by adding to it. Gerry replaced most Federalists in state offices with Republicans, and the Republicans in the legislature redrew most of the state legislative districts in Massachusetts to perpetuate Republican dominance. No evidence suggests that such redistricting was advocated by Gerry—it had been done in other states—but the practice in Massachusetts had produced a map with eccentric district boundaries that resembled a salamander. Thereafter such a practice would be called gerrymandering. Even if he had no role in this episode, Gerry did nothing to stop what many regarded as excessive Republican partisanship. Believing the Federalists were disloyal, he did not think they deserved consideration. When Federalists newspaper editors criticized him, Gerry charged them with libel. Thus, in Massachusetts a poisoned political climate existed even before war with Great Britain.

Gerry and the Republicans were turned out of office in 1812, victims of their perceived abuse of power. Yet Gerry's support for the Madison administration and his national reputation gained him the Republican nomination for vice president in 1812 and his subsequent election in the fall. As usual then and since, Vice President Gerry wielded little power, but he continued to speak out against people he viewed as disloyal. He also took his job as presiding officer in the Senate seriously. He persistently worked to secure military and government positions for his family and Massachusetts Republicans.

Perhaps the most important time of his vice presidency came in the summer of 1813, when Congress was not in session and he had no real duties to perform. In previous years, when Congress had adjourned for the summer, the vice president would ceremoniously step down as presiding officer. Congress then had elected a president pro tem, the person next in line of succession if both the president and vice president died. In the summer of 1813, Madison was very ill. Gerry also was in bad health, but when it came time to follow custom and step aside as presiding officer, he refused. Later he explained that since it was quite possible that both he and Madison could have died that summer, he had wanted to prevent the administration's enemies in Congress from choosing a successor.

Gerry was an old man, and even limited duties began to tax his health by the end of 1814. On 23 November 1814, he apparently suffered a heart attack and died at his boarding house.

—*Jeanne T. Heidler and David S. Heidler*

See also: Federalist Party; U.S. Congress
Further Reading
Billias, George Athan. *Elbridge Gerry: Founding Father and Republican Statesman.* New York: McGraw-Hill, 1976.

GHENT, TREATY OF
24 December 1814

Ending a war in which U.S. military successes were few and problematic, the so-called Peace of Christmas Eve proved to be a resounding diplomatic victory for the beleaguered republic. Though British envoys refused to concede the fundamental issues that had brought about hostilities in 1812, they accepted a treaty that left both the United

States and its honor intact. Even though the specific provisions of the Treaty of Ghent suggested a more ambiguous verdict, most Americans celebrated the treaty's signing as a confirmation of nationality and a vindication of the republican experiment.

Pres. James Madison began the search for a diplomatic resolution to hostilities shortly after the U.S. declaration of war in June 1812. U.S. peace overtures began, Madison noted, when "the sword was scarcely out of the scabbard." In late June, Jonathan Russell, U.S. chargé d'affaires in London, proposed an armistice in return for Britain's renunciation of impressment and the Orders in Council. As the Orders had already been rescinded, the British were disinclined to concede anything more. Though Britain did not authorize general reprisals against the United States until October, and even offered an armistice to Gen. Henry Dearborn in Canada, impressment remained an insurmountable obstacle.

The next opportunity for peace came through Russian intermediaries in March 1813. Though the Russian offer of mediation was snubbed by the British, President Madison authorized a delegation consisting of Federalist senator James A. Bayard, Secretary of the Treasury Albert Gallatin, and minister to Russia John Quincy Adams to pursue the matter. The British were adamant that the Russians be excluded, as there were continental calculations involved, and finally acceded to Anglo-American negotiations in January 1814. Despite the bellicose tone of the British press, intimations of pending punitive operations against the Americans, and the burning of public buildings in the U.S. capital in August 1814, circumstances increasingly favored the U.S. envoys. With the defeat of Napoleonic France in April, the British government was increasingly desirous of ending the North American war because it had become a constant drain on their hard-pressed treasury. Given the situation, envoys from both nations gave consideration to a site for serious talks. The initial choice of Gothenburg, Sweden, was rejected in favor of Ghent, Belgium.

At Ghent the U.S. delegation was joined by Kentucky's Henry Clay, a War Hawk from an expansionist-minded frontier state. Whatever their diversity in temperament and tactics, an exceptional group of men formed the U.S. delegation. Because Britain's top diplomats were required at the Congress of Vienna, men of diplomatic second rank were dispatched to Ghent. They included the Admiralty lawyer Dr. William Adams, the Royal Navy's Lord Gambier, and Colonial Office undersecretary Henry Goulburn, who was charged with insuring Britain's interests in Canada. The British commissioners dallied, hoping additional military successes would improve their position, so Adams was the first to arrive in Ghent on 24 June 1814. Soon joined by

his colleagues, Adams found little to admire in them and particularly disdained the all-night card games hosted by the hard-drinking Clay.

Negotiations began on 8 August 1814, with the Americans having learned only recently that their government had decided to drop the impressment issues. The close of the Napoleonic wars ended the outrageous practice, so it was no longer an active issue. Meeting alternately in each party's hotel, the envoys turned to issues almost as daunting, however. The initial British terms were, at first hearing, altogether unacceptable. In addition to requesting U.S. territory in the Maine district of Massachusetts and in Minnesota, the British envoys insisted on the creation of an Indian barrier state in the Old Northwest and naval disarmament on the Great Lakes.

From the British perspective, these provisions were a reasonable means of attaining the fundamental objective of Canadian security. U.S. designs on Canada were no secret, and the British produced two U.S. annexationist proclamations issued in 1812 as evidence. Indeed, while at Ghent the U.S. envoys with difficulty dissuaded Adams from pressing yet another claim on Canada. The British hoped that the proposed Indian reservation would deter expansionist Americans from forcing Indian land cessions in the Northwest and also would create a buffer zone between the United States and British Canada. As Canadians had no annexationist goals, the demilitarization of the Great Lakes would make unlikely any U.S. advance into Canada, with no attendant threat to the United States.

The U.S. delegation saw the terms as an egregious encroachment on the sovereignty of the United States that would establish an unenforceable obstacle to fuller U.S. settlement and a threat to the 100,000 white settlers in the region. When the delegation rejected these British terms, the talks seemed hopelessly deadlocked. In reality, the British envoys had exceeded their instructions by making the Indian barrier a nonnegotiable point and were actually engaging in some preliminary probing. In October, the British asked the Americans for their basic terms, well knowing that regional differences among the delegates would weaken unity on the U.S. commission. The British believed that time was on their side, as the end of the European war would permit the deployment of reinforcements to North America. The burning of Washington, D.C., in August seemed to vindicate this strategy.

Although the Americans were buoyed by news of continuing British losses at sea, the need for peace became increasingly urgent as autumn dragged on. When the British made a new offer in October based on each side's retaining territory held at war's end, the U.S. envoys balked and merely dispatched a truce ship across the Atlantic to apprise the Madison administration of the latest developments. Now events worked in the Americans' favor, as British officials glumly pondered the possibility of another U.S. campaign. The duke of Wellington, asked to assume command of a renewed military effort, agreed but made clear his belief in the futility of further efforts and noted that, given the current situation, Great Britain could not justifiably make any territorial demands on the United States. Wellington's gloomy assessment convinced the British government to drop the territorial demands. This breakthrough left only issues involving U.S. rights to the Newfoundland fisheries and British rights to navigation on the Mississippi River.

The final treaty took shape in the month before Christmas Eve 1814. The document made no reference to the maritime issues that had put the two powers at war in 1812. Rather, its provisions restored the status quo antebellum. Both nations agreed to evacuate territories belonging to the other. Confiscation of enemy property was forbidden, and all prisoners were to be returned as rapidly as feasible. Both parties agreed to make peace with the Indians and to restore such possessions and rights as they had enjoyed in 1811. There was an additional pledge to cooperate in the suppression of the slave trade. Disputes over the boundary between Canada and the United States were to be settled at a future time by joint commissions. Hostilities were to cease when both countries had ratified the treaty.

The fortunes of war continued to fluctuate in the interim before ratification. U.S. naval commander Stephen Decatur was bested by the Royal Navy outside New York in January 1815, but in early February, the news of Andrew Jackson's victory at New Orleans reached Washington. The British invaders, however, continued their depredations elsewhere along the Gulf Coast. Ultimately, both nations received news of the treaty with relief, if not celebration. Despite Federalist mutterings that the treaty failed to gain a single Republican war aim, Congress ratified the document on 15 February 1815. Though there were complaints in the British press that the upstart Americans had not been given a more thorough beating, the British government, faced with the difficulties of European peace, was glad to end the conflict.

The War of 1812 came to an official end at 11:00 P.M. on 17 February 1815. Though the provisions of the treaty might not have fully reflected it, most Americans considered the war a victory. The United States of America had fought the world's mightiest empire to a standoff, which was in itself something of a victory. The larger triumph came in the clear assertion of U.S. nationality and Britain's implicit acknowledgment of complete U.S. independence

through the Treaty of Ghent. As of 1815, for the first time in its brief existence, the American Republic was secure.

—*Blaine T. Browne*

See also: Adams, John Quincy; Bayard, James Asheton; Clay, Henry; Gallatin, Albert; Goulburn, Henry; Impressment; Orders in Council; Russell, Jonathan

Further Reading

Engleman, Fred L. *The Peace of Christmas Eve.* New York: Harcourt, 1960.

Johnson, Paul A. *The Birth of the Modern: World Society, 1815–1830.* New York: HarperCollins, 1991.

Updyke, Frank A. *The Diplomacy of the War of 1812.* Baltimore, MD: Johns Hopkins University Press, 1915.

GIBSON, JAMES
1781–1814
U.S. officer

Born in Delaware in 1781, James Gibson entered the U.S. Military Academy in 1806, before a formal class system had been instituted. Cadets matriculated at their own pace, and Gibson completed his course of study in two years, graduating in 1808. Upon graduation, he immediately received a commission as a lieutenant of the Light Artillery Regiment. By May 1810, he had achieved the rank of captain.

When war started with Great Britain, Captain Gibson saw early action on the Niagara Frontier. At the Battle of Queenston on 13 October 1812, he was among the regulars trapped on the Canadian side of the river who surrendered to the British. Many of these stranded Americans were being killed by Indian allies of the British. Attempts at surrender thus inviting only murder, Gibson accompanied Lt. Col. Winfield Scott and Capt. Joseph Totten, carrying a sword on which was tied Totten's white cravat. While trying to find a British officer to whom they could surrender the U.S. army, the three were accosted by two warriors. The officers fought off the Indians with their swords until British soldiers effected a rescue. The three Americans were then allowed to surrender to British protection their remaining countrymen.

Within a few months, Gibson had been exchanged and in April 1813 was promoted to major. Again on the Niagara Frontier, Gibson earned the rapid promotions typical of wartime and by July 1813 had become a colonel and was appointed the inspector general of the Ninth Military

District. Occupying that position until February 1814, when he became the colonel and commander of the Fourth Rifle Regiment, Gibson was in the Northern Army's Left Division as the campaign season of 1814 began. By summer's end, Gibson's Fourth Riflemen made up part of the Fort Erie garrison.

In August 1814, the British began a heavy bombardment of the fort, and by mid-September the fort had become almost untenable. Gibson's regiment made up part of the force ordered by Commander of the Army of the Niagara Maj. Gen. Jacob Brown to take the British batteries with a sortie under the overall command of Maj. Gen. Peter Porter of the New York Volunteers. Gibson led men from his Fourth Riflemen and a detachment from the First Rifle Regiment to secure the batteries on the British right. Moving out at 12:00 noon on 17 September, the force was in position to attack by 3:00 P.M. Gibson led his men in the attack on the first British battery and took it easily. The British artillerymen at the second battery, alerted by the firing at the first, put up a stiffer fight. Gibson fell mortally wounded in the otherwise successful attack on the second British battery. He died the following day.

—*Jeanne T. Heidler and David S. Heidler*

See also: Erie, Fort; Queenston, Battle of

GILES, WILLIAM BRANCH
1762–1830
U.S. senator

Born to William Giles and Ann Branch Giles, William Branch Giles attended Hampden-Sidney College and graduated from the College of New Jersey (Princeton). After studying law with George Wythe, Giles enter the practice of law before beginning his political career in the House of Representatives in 1790. In Congress, Giles almost immediately gravitated to the supporters of Thomas Jefferson and James Madison, becoming a staunch Democratic Republican.

During the presidency of Thomas Jefferson, Giles could be counted on to champion administration programs in the House and then after 1804 in the Senate. He supported the election of James Madison in 1808, yet soon after Madison took office Giles became increasingly vocal in his opposition to many administration measures. Most of this opposition stemmed from his growing dislike for Jefferson's and now Madison's secretary of the treasury, Albert Gallatin.

As war approached with Great Britain, Giles joined the faction known as War Hawks, urging an increase in government spending for the military. Perhaps his desire for a stronger military establishment led him to gravitate toward that faction of Democratic Republicans known as the Invisibles. This group, led by Samuel Smith of Maryland, had several things in common—all advocated heavy military spending in order to prosecute a war vigorously, all disliked Albert Gallatin because they thought his financial policies prevented military preparedness, and most disliked James Madison.

When Congress began increasing war measures in the winter of 1811–1812, the administration opposed enlarging the regular army, preferring instead to rely on the militia if war came. Responding in Congress to the administration's position, Giles urged reliance on regulars and persuaded his colleagues to raise the authorized strength of the army from 10,000 to 35,000.

Once the war commenced, Giles and the Invisibles never wasted an opportunity to attack any measure they even suspected Gallatin was behind. When Madison nominated Gallatin as part of the peace commission to travel to Russia to accept Czar Alexander's offer of mediation, Giles and the Invisibles condemned the appointment and secured Gallatin's rejection.

By the fall of 1814, Giles and his faction had become so distressed at the country's military weakness that they began to work for significant increases in the militia and regular army establishments. As a member of the Senate Military Affairs Committee, Giles reported two bills to the Senate to accomplish these goals. The first bill actually tried to compromise on a stronger militia conscription measure proposed by Secretary of War James Monroe. It called for the conscription of 80,000 militiamen for two years to serve in their state or in an adjoining state under state officers. The second bill increased the amount of land granted to regular recruits from 160 acres to 320 acres. It also lowered enlistment age to 18 without parental permission. The first bill never passed, but the second did, with the amended stipulation that recruits under 21 years could change their minds within four days of enlisting.

Giles and the other Invisibles could not know that as they were finally realizing some of their goals for a stronger military, the war was coming to an end. In light of that development, their constant carping at the administration began for some to resemble disloyalty. Perhaps this perception defeated Giles's return to the 14th Congress. He left the Senate in March 1815.

For the next decade Giles remained relatively inactive in politics, but in the 1820s he became a very strong supporter of states' rights, continuing that effort until his death in 1830. He wrote prolifically on the topic and returned to political office as governor of Virginia in 1827 to thwart what he described as the increasingly centralizing power of the federal government. He had come to believe that such measures as the tariff and internal improvements threatened the rights of Virginia. Giles thus followed the path of many southerners whose nationalism during the War of 1812 gradually eroded in subsequent years. In the Senate, he had fought hard to make the nation physically strong, but he spent his last years fighting against a strong national government.

—*Jeanne T. Heidler and David S. Heidler*

See also: Gallatin, Albert; Monroe, James; Smith, Samuel; War Hawks
Further Reading
Anderson, Dice Robins. *William Branch Giles: A Study in the Politics of Virginia and the Nation from 1790 to 1830.* Gloucester, MA: Peter Smith, 1965.

GILMAN, JOHN TAYLOR
1753–1828
Governor of New Hampshire

John Taylor Gilman was born in Exeter, New Hampshire, to Nicholas Gilman and Ann Taylor Gilman. After attending public school, John Gilman worked with his father in the latter's shipbuilding and merchant enterprises. The younger Gilman became involved in New Hampshire politics during the American Revolution. Toward the end of the Revolution, he served in Congress. Following the war, he returned to New Hampshire politics and to running his late father's businesses. Between 1794 and 1805, Gilman served as the Federalist governor of New Hampshire. He lost the election in 1805 because the growing number of New Hampshire Democratic Republicans raised questions about the ethics of only allowing one bank, of which Gilman was president, to incorporate in the state.

Following his defeat, Gilman remained active in state politics and unsuccessfully ran for governor again in 1812. Undeterred, he ran again and was elected in 1813. Gilman had been a vocal opponent of the War of 1812, but as a governor he took his state's defense seriously. Unlike many of his Federalist counterparts in New England, he had to conciliate a state almost equally divided between Federalists and Democratic Republicans.

In the spring of 1814, rumors of a British threat to

John Taylor Gilman

Portsmouth, New Hampshire, prompted many to deduce that the British menace stemmed from the federal government's building the warship USS *Washington* in the shipyards there. Gilman called up 1,500 militiamen to meet the emergency, but he refused to allow the men to serve under regular army officers. Responding to Gilman's action, the federal government refused to supply any men, and Gilman petulantly sent his militia home. Another and apparently a more serious threat occurred in late summer, so on that occasion Gilman relented and allowed the men to serve under regulars.

Gilman might have cursed the political burdens imposed by a state council dominated by his political opposition, but at the end it saved him from the political folly of his fellow New England governors. The Democratic Republican majority on the council refused to send delegates to the Hartford Convention. As a result, Gilman would be spared the sort of embarrassing suspicions about his patriotism that were leveled at others. He retired from politics soon after the war.

—*Jeanne T. Heidler and David S. Heidler*

See also: Federalist Party; Hartford Convention
Further Reading
Plumer, William. "John Taylor Gilman: A Sketch." *Early State Papers of New Hampshire* 22 (1893): 830–835.

GLASGOW, GEORGE
d. 1820
British Army officer

George Glasgow was the senior British artillery officer in the Canadas for almost 14 years. He entered the Royal Artillery as a cadet in 1771 and was gazetted a second lieutenant in 1774. He took almost 20 years to reach the rank of captain, and there are no records to show he ever served outside England during the period. In 1794, he finally was posted to command an artillery company, which was then stationed in Quebec. His eventual promotion to lieutenant colonel in 1801 left him the effective chief of the Royal Artillery in Canada. By the time he reached the rank of major general in 1811, he had already served in Lower Canada longer than any other senior British officer.

During the war, Glasgow never participated in a combat operation, but he held several important administrative posts. In June 1812, Gen. Sir George Prevost entrusted Glasgow with the defense of Quebec. From 14 June to 25 September 1813, Glasgow served as the president administering the government of Lower Canada while Prevost was occupied in Upper Canada. During the entire war, Glasgow also retained administrative control of all Royal Artillery units and was primarily responsible for the support and training given by his regulars to the militia artillery.

Glasgow returned to England in August 1815 and retired after 44 years of military service—21 of which had been spent in Canada. About a year before his death, he received one final promotion, becoming a lieutenant general in 1819.

—*David T. Zabecki*

See also: Prevost, George
Further Reading
Duncan, Francis. *History of the Royal Regiment of Artillery.* Vol. 2. London: John Murray, 1873.
Kane, John. *List of Officers of the Royal Regiment of Artillery.* London: Royal Artillery Institution, 1890.
Laws, M.E.S. *Battery Records of the Royal Artillery: 1716–1859.* London: Royal Artillery Institution, 1952.

GORDON, JAMES ALEXANDER
1782–1869
British Navy captain

James Alexander Gordon entered the navy in 1793 aboard the HMS *Arrogant.* Gordon saw extensive duty against the French at L'Orient and at the battles of Cape St. Vincent and the Nile. In 1800, he was promoted to lieutenant aboard the HMS *Bordelais.* His heroism in Cuban waters earned him the command of the HMS *Racoon* (1804). Gordon cruised the West Indies until assignment at Newfoundland. In 1807, and for the next four years, Gordon saw action in the Adriatic Sea against the Spanish and French. On 13 March 1811 at the Battle of Lissa, Gordon captured the *Pomone* and had his leg shot off at the knee. For his performance in this contest, he was awarded a gold medal. In a later engagement, Gordon lost an arm and returned to England to recuperate. In 1812, he was appointed to HMS *Seahorse* and joined Sir Alexander Cochrane in Chesapeake Bay.

In August 1814, Gordon aboard the *Seahorse* led a squadron of two frigates and five smaller vessels up the Potomac in conjunction with Maj. Gen. Robert Ross's advance on the U.S. capital. Gordon's mission was to destroy any Potomac River fortifications and secure an escape route if Ross's British troops were cut off from their transports on the Patuxent River. Gordon took Fort Washington without a fight and sailed on to undefended Alexandria, Virginia. Alexandria's town fathers surrendered after a brief attempt to negotiate, not knowing that a U.S. force was but 10 miles away. Gordon destroyed all of Alexandria's military installations and seized 21 small vessels in the harbor, but he left the village intact in exchange for needed supplies.

Fearing entrapment, Captain Gordon departed Alexandria 1 September and sailed downstream. The rest of his squadron followed with 21 prize vessels and their decks bulging with 13,786 barrels of flour, 757 hogsheads of tobacco, and tons of cotton, tar, beef, and sugar. A U.S. attempt to take the grounded HMS *Devastation* failed, but the ironic situation of U.S. naval officers commanding shore batteries turned the river into something of a gauntlet for the returning Gordon to run. On the Virginia side of the river, shore batteries directed by naval officer David Porter at White House bluff exchanged a spirited fire with the British squadron. Gordon weighted his ships to port so his starboard guns fired higher, and thus his 63 guns easily outmatched Porter's 13, and the squadron sailed by in triumph. Farther downriver on the Maryland side, Capt.

Oliver Hazard Perry had placed guns at Indian Head. Unfortunately for the Americans, only one gun was capable of doing effective harm to the British ships, and it soon ran out of ammunition. After 6 September, Gordon continued down the Potomac River without incident to rejoin the rest of the British fleet on 9 September, temporarily anchoring in the Patuxent before sailing for Annapolis and Baltimore.

Because of his extensive wartime contributions James Gordon was appointed to the command of HMS *Madagascar*. He also saw service aboard HMS *Meander* and HMS *Active* that took him to both the Mediterranean and the North Atlantic. Sir James Gordon's naval service ashore included appointments as superintendent of Plymouth Hospital (1828), superintendent of Chatham dockyard (1832), and lieutenant-governor and governor of Greenwich Hospital (1840–1869). His promotions included vice admiral (1848), admiral (1854), and admiral of the fleet (1868). James Gordon was knighted by the Crown.

—*William A. Paquette*

See also: Chesapeake Bay Campaign, 1813–1814; Cochrane, Alexander; Perry, Oliver Hazard; Porter, David, Jr.; Washington, Fort
Further Reading
Lord, Walter. *The Dawn's Early Light.* New York: W. W. Norton, 1972.
Marshall, John. *Royal Naval Biography.* 4 vols. London: Longman, Hurst, Rees, Orme, and Brown, 1823–1835.

GORE, CHRISTOPHER
1758–1827
U.S. senator

Christopher Gore

Born in Boston, Massachusetts, Christopher Gore graduated from Harvard College in 1776 and practiced law in Boston for several years before entering state politics during the Confederation period. During George Washington's administration, Gore became involved in diplomatic affairs and was sent by the administration to Great Britain in 1796 to negotiate trade concessions. He remained a commissioner to Great Britain until 1803, when he was formally given the title of U.S. chargé d'affaires, a position he held for a year before returning to Boston.

Back in the United States, Gore reentered private practice but also became active in Massachusetts Federalist politics. He was elected governor in 1809. His opposition to the growing hostility between the United States and Great Britain caused his popularity in antiwar New England to grow, and his strong hostility to the war once it started was probably responsible for his selection as one of Massachusetts's U.S. senators in 1813.

Gore's ties to extreme antiwar sentiment in Massachusetts and his respectable reputation as a U.S. statesman abroad made him an important source of information for Federalist moderates in Congress. In 1813, he quietly reported a growing movement among radicals in New England to dissolve the union, information that may have dissuaded New England investors from helping to finance the war. Some members of Congress viewed Gore as a moderate, but there was no mistaking his sectionalism when he voted in Congress or expressed his views toward the war. When the Hartford Convention met in the fall of 1814, Gore supported the effort to bring the views of this important minority before the nation. When the final report of the convention was issued, he praised it as thoughtful and wise.

In 1816, Gore retired to private life, devoting much of his remaining years to the affairs of Harvard College. He died in Waltham, Massachusetts.

—*Jeanne T. Heidler and David S. Heidler*

See also: Federalist Party; Hartford Convention
Further Reading
Banner, James M., Jr. *To the Hartford Convention: The Federalists and the Origins of Party Politics in Massachusetts, 1789–1815.* New York: Alfred Knopf, 1970.

GOULBURN, HENRY
1784–1856
British statesman; diplomat

Henry Goulburn was born on 19 March 1784, the eldest son of Munbee Goulburn and Susannah, daughter of William Chetwynd, fourth Viscount Chetwynd. He was educated at Trinity College, Cambridge, receiving a bachelor of arts in 1805 and a master of arts in 1808.

On 27 February 1810, he became undersecretary for the Home Department in Spencer Perceval's administration and in August 1812 succeeded Robert Peel as undersecretary for war and the colonies. When the U.S. government intimated readiness to enter into peace negotiations, Goulburn was appointed a British negotiator at Ghent in 1814 with Admiral Lord Gambier and Dr. William Adams, a Cambridge jurist. Goulburn was reluctant to accept and only consented when allowed to take his wife and eldest son, ill with "infantile fever," to Ghent. He presented the British position on impressment, establishment of a separate Indian state, and revisions to the 1783 boundary between the United States and the British North American provinces.

Goulburn contended that the United States had distracted Britain from its struggle with Napoleonic France, and he wrote a private memorandum stressing that the Americans' real object of the war had been "the conquest of the Canadas." He reported to Lord Bathurst in the Colonial Office, who opposed concessions, and Lord Castlereagh in the Foreign Office, who desired a reasonable peace. Goulburn also continued talks with the U.S. delegation after negotiations had seemingly stalled.

Goulburn presented the government's defense of the treaty in the House of Commons debate, and the favorable vote of 128 to 37 confirmed Goulburn's work. He later became chancellor of the exchequer in the duke of Wellington's and Robert Peel's governments. He died on 12 January 1856.

—*Frederick C. Drake*

See also: Bathurst, Henry, Third Earl Bathurst; Castlereagh, Viscount, Robert Stewart; Ghent, Treaty of
Further Reading
Adams, Henry, ed. *The Writings of Albert Gallatin.* 3 vols., Vol. 1, p. 629. Philadelphia: J. B. Lippincott, 1879.
Barker, George Fisher Russell. "Henry Goulburn." *Dictionary of National Biography.* Vol. 8, pp. 283–285. London: Oxford University Press, 1937–1938.
Engelman, Fred. *The Peace of Christmas Eve.* London: Hart-Davis, 1962.
Jones, Wilbur Devereux, ed. "A British View of the War of 1812 and the Peace Negotiations." *Mississippi Valley Historical Review* 45 (1958–1959): 482, 485–486.
Perkins, Bradford, *Castlereagh and Adams.* Berkeley and Los Angeles: University of California Press, 1964.

GRIFFITH, EDWARD
1760s–1832
British rear admiral

Little is known about Edward Griffith's ancestry and birth except that he was the nephew of Adm. Sir John Colpoys and entered naval service in 1778 aboard the *Royal George.* From 1778 to 1812, Edward Griffith saw continuous duty in either Europe or the East Indies, was raised to the rank of rear admiral (August 1812) while commanding the North Sea Fleet, and had his naval career rated by his peers as useful and praiseworthy.

The British Admiralty sent Rear Adm. Edward Griffith to Halifax, Nova Scotia, in 1813 to take over the construction and repair of ships from an overburdened Adm. Sir John Borlase Warren. Griffith's task became more difficult when a hurricane hit Halifax on 12 November, beaching over 50 ships and damaging all those that remained afloat. Warren immediately went south, as did many of the damaged ships for repair, leaving Griffith with 16 vessels to keep the U.S. Navy confined to New England ports.

On 1 September 1814, Griffith and Sir John Sherbrooke arrived at Penobscot Bay, Maine, with 2,000 regular soldiers. The approaching British flotilla caused the U.S. garrison to evacuate Castine. Griffith's objective was to capture the U.S. frigate *Adams,* under repair at Hampden. He sent an expeditionary force within 3 miles of Hampden, and on 3 September he put to flight 1,400 U.S. militia and captured 20 U.S. guns with only ten casualties on the British side. The *Adams* was burned by Capt. Charles Morris, and the town of Hampden surrendered.

After the capture of Hampden the British expedition continued up the Penobscot River, taking the town of

Bangor without a fight. On 9 September, the British returned downriver to Castine and took possession of the settlement of Machias. Further advances inland became unnecessary when U.S. forces in Washington County of the Maine district between the Penobscot River and Passamaquoddy Bay surrendered on 13 September. Two days later, Griffith officially proclaimed the resumption of trade between New England and New Brunswick and Nova Scotia. A second proclamation on 21 September appointed a military governor for the "British" territory in Maine. When no further hostile acts continued in Maine against the British, Griffith noted that the people of Maine were too busy resuming trade to worry about a war they did not want.

On 18 October 1813, Griffith wrote to first secretary of the Admiralty John W. Croker to acknowledge that British owners of merchant vessels were recruiting seamen for their ships from a Halifax prison on Melville Island. This approach was new with the War of 1812, but Griffith maintained that without recruiting prisoners of war for sea duty, trade between Halifax and London would be impossible. The Admiralty disapproved of this practice, however, so Griffith pledged to discontinue it.

From 1814 until 1817 and again from 1819 to 1821, Griffith commanded the British fleet at Halifax and Nova Scotia. Appointed to the rank of vice admiral in 1821, he returned to England and retired. Upon the death of his uncle, Admiral Colpoys, Edward Griffith gained the permission of King George III to adopt both the name and arms of the Colpoys family. Vice Adm. Edward Griffith Colpoys died in 1832.

—*William A. Paquette*

See also: Castine, Maine; Hampden, Maine; Morris, Charles; Sherbrooke, John Coape

Further Reading

Harvey, D. C. "The Halifax-Castine Expedition." *Dalhousie Review* 18 (1938): 207–213.
Stanley, George F. "British Operations on the Penobscot in 1814." *Journal of the Society for Army Historical Research* 19 (1940): 168–178.

GRISWOLD, ROGER
1762–1812
Governor of Connecticut

Born to Matthew Griswold and Ursula Wolcott Griswold in Lyme, Connecticut, Roger Griswold gradu-

ated from Yale, studied law, and became a practicing attorney by the age of 21. After brief service in the Connecticut state legislature, Griswold was elected to the U.S. House of Representatives in 1794. Already active in Federalist Party politics in Connecticut, Griswold became an active supporter of the Washington administration in Congress. When Thomas Jefferson was elected president in 1800, Griswold and his fellow Federalists found themselves in the opposition.

Griswold became one of the leading spokesmen for the Federalists in Congress and never wasted an opportunity to reprove the Republicans for what he viewed as their destructive policies. As early as 1804, Griswold apparently flirted with a conspiracy to establish a New England confederacy. After leaving Congress in 1805, Griswold again briefly practiced law but then returned to Connecticut politics, first as lieutenant governor and then, beginning in 1811, as governor of the state. Griswold, like most Federalists, believed the War of 1812 an unjust and unnecessary war. As governor of Connecticut, he had the opportunity early in the conflict to dramatize his displeasure.

Brig. Gen. Henry Dearborn, the senior ranking regular officer in New England when hostilities commenced, called out portions of the Connecticut, Massachusetts, and Rhode Island militias within a week of the declaration of war. He intended to use the men to garrison frontier forts throughout New England so that he could use the regulars assigned to those forts for an invasion of Canada. Griswold and the other governors refused to comply. Griswold insisted that Dearborn's request violated the U.S. Constitution. Dearborn could not place men into federal service under regular officers, said Griswold, unless the country were in danger of invasion.

The issue of when and by whom militias could be called would continue to plague the administration, as would the question of whether the militia should serve under regular officers. The entire debate regarding authority over the state militias had only entered its first stage when Griswold died suddenly in October 1812.

—*Jeanne T. Heidler and David S. Heidler*

See also: Connecticut; Federalist Party; Militia Controversy, The New England

Further Reading

Banner, James M., Jr. *To the Hartford Convention: The Federalists and the Origins of Party Politics in Massachusetts, 1789–1815*. New York: Alfred Knopf, 1970.
Hickey, Donald R. "New England's Defense Problem and the Genesis of the Hartford Convention." *New England Quarterly* 50 (December 1977): 587–604.

GRUNDY, FELIX
1777–1840
Tennessee congressman, 1811–1814

Felix Grundy was a noted criminal lawyer and a state legislator in both Kentucky and Tennessee as well as a jurist in Kentucky. Grundy was born in what is now West Virginia. The family later moved to Pennsylvania and then to Kentucky. He studied at an academy headed by Dr. James Priestly and then read law and was admitted to the Kentucky bar in 1795. He married Ann Phillips Rodgers, and the couple had eight children. While in Kentucky he served in several public offices, including commonwealth attorney, delegate to the state constitutional convention (1799), delegate to the U.S. House of Representatives (1800–1805), and associate justice and then chief justice of the state Supreme Court of Errors and Appeals (1806–1807). He resigned his last post and moved his family to Nashville, Tennessee, chiefly for financial reasons. He arrived there in January 1808 and opened up his law practice.

Grundy prospered in Tennessee, a fact that allowed him to run successfully for Congress in the 1810 election. He entered the 12th Congress along with such other notable young Republicans as Henry Clay and John C. Calhoun and immediately became identified with the faction known as the War Hawks because of their spirited calls for a more aggressive foreign and military policy.

The Tennessee congressman became a lightning rod for attacks by aggrieved New England Federalists who believed the Republicans' aggressive policy was meant to ruin New England's commercial ties with England. One New England Federalist openly declared that responsibility for the War of 1812 rested with "James Madison, Felix Grundy, and the Devil." A minister in Boston advocated disunion, saying that there was "nothing to lose but Thomas Jefferson, James Madison, Albert Gallatin, and Felix Grundy." Grundy, the arch War Hawk, did not temper his attacks on New England for dissenting from Republican policies of economic coercion, and he was especially critical of New England's opposition to the war. When New England congressmen sought to prevent the raising of taxes necessary to fund the war and of troops to fight it, Grundy declared Federalists guilty of "moral treason." It was a sharp charge that cut deeply.

No doubt Grundy's vehemence stemmed from his talents as a superb advocate and lawyer, but he was also a spokesman for frontiersmen; he himself had lost three

Felix Grundy

brothers to Indian attacks. He reflected his Tennessee constituents' impatience with the "pacific character" of a national policy embodied by the embargo and only defensive actions against the Indians. Those efforts had failed, he believed, and "something must be done," or the nation would "lose our respectability abroad, and even to cease to respect ourselves." On the House Foreign Affairs Committee, Grundy supported the Madison administration's war policies and took that advocacy to the floor of Congress. When the committee's chairman, John C. Calhoun, could not publicly defend measures required to fund the war effort, Grundy assumed the duty of presenting and defending the Committee's recommendations to the full House.

Felix Grundy insisted that war with England was necessary "to secure national independence, individual liberty, and a permanent security of property." The position made the Tennessean a primary spokesman for a more vital and forceful national policy, a precursor of the so-called Shirtsleeves Diplomacy of the Hero of New Orleans, Andrew Jackson, when he became president. Grundy had defined the best case for war and had become the most vocal proponent of his region's viewpoint. As a Nashville newspaper put it in advocating his reelection, "If the war is just, he has been its advocate . . . he was a man of talents that were the envy and scourge of the enemies." Grundy later served as a U.S. senator (1829–1835, 1839–1840) and U.S. attorney general (1836–1839).

—*Thomas H. Winn*

See also: War Hawks
Further Reading

Parks, Joseph H. *Felix Grundy: Champion of Democracy.* Baton Rouge: Louisiana State University Press, 1940.

Watts, Steven. *The Republic Reborn: War and the Making of a Liberal America.* Baltimore, MD: Johns Hopkins University Press, 1987.

GUNBOATS

In the decade before the War of 1812 the United States constructed some 174 gunboats. In June 1812, 62 of them were in service. The program originated with Pres. Thomas Jefferson, who with the support of Republican majorities in Congress opposed a large navy of big ships for the United States. He wanted a force essentially limited to coastal defense and, as a result, cut the size of the navy by two-thirds, gutting the fleet put together during the Quasi-War with France. As Jefferson observed, "Gunboats are the only water defence which can be useful to us, and protect us from the ruinous folly of a navy."

Gunboats were favored because of their success in shoal-water operations during the Barbary wars and the belief that they would be sufficient for defending U.S. harbors against an aggressor. Proponents of the gunboats expected them to be less expensive to maintain than larger vessels (they could be laid up until needed), and their building could be parceled out to the party faithful. A policy of relying on gunboats, however, ignored the possibility of a loose blockade and virtually prevented the U.S. Navy from taking the offensive at sea.

The gunboats, known only by number, were narrow-built vessels 40 to 60 feet in length and 50 to 100 tons burden. Generally they were either sloop or schooner rigged and armed with one or two long 24- or 32-pounder guns, though some had up to five guns. Smaller gunboats carried one 18- or 24-pounder long gun on a pivot mount. Larger gunboats had two long 32-pounders on slide or swivel mounts and several howitzers, or small swivels, on their rails.

Whatever their supposed advantages, gunboats were not economical. Even though they cost far less to build per unit than larger warships, they were far more expensive to maintain. One gun on a gunboat cost $12,096 a year compared to $2,333 on a frigate. Yet contrary to what many scholars have written, the Jeffersonian gunboats did achieve some successes. Too late to participate in the Tripolitan War, they were subsequently the major line of coastal defense. In peacetime they helped to prohibit traffic in slaves and to enforce the nation's trade laws, and they served as receiving vessels, tenders, hospital ships, lighters, and transports for men and supplies.

During the War of 1812 the gunboats did not fulfill the role originally envisioned for them. They did, however, convoy coastal vessels, particularly along the southern coast; they played prominent roles in the taking of Mobile (the only permanent territorial gain of the war) and the reduction of the Barataria pirates; and in the Battle of Lake Borgne they delayed the British advance on New Orleans. They also had some success in protecting U.S. coastal shipping from enemy cutting-out operations and captured some enemy tenders. After the war, gunboats assisted in actions that helped bring Florida into the United States, and a few took part in the West Indian campaign to eradicate piracy.

The gunboats also served as a naval school for young officers such as James Lawrence, James Biddle, Lawrence Kearny, Jacob Jones, John Percival, and Thomas ap Catesby Jones. The record here is mixed, however. Gunboat service did provide command experience for junior officers, but it did not produce the skills acquired on and needed for larger vessels. Gunboats spent most of their time in harbors and coastal shoal waters and thus precluded men from learning blue-water seamanship. Their commanders were often poor role models for new officers, and because there was usually only one officer on board a gunboat, service aboard such vessels impeded the professionalism that develops when officers serve together. Indeed, most senior officers believed that gunboat service encouraged vices. Much of this criticism is valid, but no doubt the desire of many young officers for transfer to frigates had something to do with wanting greater creature comforts as well as the prestige of service on the larger ships.

The traditional view of the gunboats as totally worthless is largely the work of Mahanian naval historians such as Fletcher Pratt. Their exaggerated criticisms reflect their frustration that the United States did not have a big-ship navy. Yet it was that lack of larger ships, not the failure of the gunboats, that made the new nation so powerless at sea in the War of 1812. Concentrating on gunboats simply turned out to be a poor approach for the United States. But it is hard to agree with some writers who assert that had the United States possessed more frigates and some ships of the line, the War of 1812 might not have occurred. It would have taken expenditures far above those appropriated for gunboats to avert the War of 1812, and even this assumes no preemptive British attack and other factors remaining constant.

That the U.S. Navy was negligible played into the hands of those in Britain who pursued an aggressive maritime policy toward the United States. It was primarily that policy that brought the U.S. declaration of war in 1812. But this is not so much a condemnation of gunboats as it is an argument in favor of a strong navy. The experience of the Jeffersonian gunboat navy did show the need for a strong defense-in-being as a deterrent to attack. It is also true that

without public support, the costly alternative policy of a big-ship navy could not have been adopted. Such support was lacking even as late as the beginning of the war.

Most of the gunboats were sold off soon after the war. By 1822, only No. 158 remained in service.

—*Spencer C. Tucker*

See also: Jones, Thomas ap Catesby
Further Reading
Tucker, Spencer C. *The Jeffersonian Gunboat Navy.* Columbia: University of South Carolina Press, 1993.

H

HALIFAX, NOVA SCOTIA

The English founded Halifax as a military outpost in the summer of 1749 at a harbor the French had called Chebucto. By 1812, mercantile, agricultural, and administrative activity had developed to the point that the city's population of 10,000 constituted a community as well as a garrison, although Halifax was Britain's only year-round North American naval base. The War of 1812 underscored the city's strategic importance to the defense of the remnants of Britain's New World empire.

Halifax crouched along the west shore of the narrows separating Chebucto Bay from the Bedford Basin. Behind the dockyards and warehouses sprawled some ten blocks of shops, taverns, brothels, inns, houses, government buildings, and congregational-style churches. The royal dockyards sat north on the narrows. Above the Brunswick street barracks and the town clock the dilapidated Vaubanesque fortress atop Citadel Hill looked west onto stone fences that enclosed cleared farmland, woodlots, and trails that crisscrossed the peninsula to the Northwest Arm. Block houses, bastions, Martello towers, and batteries in various states of repair on islands and the mainland constituted the defensive installations.

The *Nova Scotia Royal Gazette* announced on 1 July 1812 that "the madness which has for many years pervaded the European continent, has at length reached this Hemisphere" in the form of a formal U.S. declaration of war by James Madison's administration. But Haligonians heard cannon only when vessels entered or left port. The Royal Navy, New England's virtual neutrality, and the lack of blue-water U.S. sea power rendered the city safe, even from privateers. The Nova Scotia Assembly nevertheless immediately voted £42,000 to refurbish "decayed" Fort George on the hill and several "ruinous" barracks and storehouses. War expenses eventually totaled £108,095, but largely unspent appropriations more than offset the ultimate paper debt of £6,978. The city gained, rather than lost, financially from the War of 1812.

Merchants and officials personally profited, but although work was more plentiful and wages higher, 25 percent of Haligonians still depended upon poor relief for their daily bread. Merchants finagled licenses from officials to trade with enemy Boston, about three days' journey by sea. Smugglers throve in the Bay of Fundy. The city's Marine Insurance Association increased rates sharply because privateers infested maritime waters, but Enos Collins nevertheless reputedly acquired £30,000 from wartime profits in 1814 alone. Much business came from marine seizures. British warships and privateers escorted some 700 captures to local Vice Admiralty courts. Richard Uniacke, the advocate general, collected £50,000 in fees. The royal dockyard and private merchants regularly sold seized and condemned goods at public auctions. This trade dominated the newspapers, although Haligonians usually expressed greater interest in the Napoleonic campaigns in Europe than in the battles in the wilderness far to the west.

From Halifax, Britain launched naval raids and established the blockade on the New England coast. Adm. Sir John Borlase Warren arrived in September 1812 to command Jamaica, the Leeward Islands, and local stations. HMS *Shannon* brought the battered USS *Chesapeake* into the harbor on 6 June 1813, an event witnessed by cheering crowds on the docks and rooftops. November lists showed 106 armed vessels in port, including 13 74-gun battleships. Men-of-war came and went constantly to be refitted, cruised for privateers, convoyed, or blockaded. The 1814 Chesapeake Bay expedition, raiders bound for Thomaston and St. George, Maine, and Sir Thomas Hardy's substantial fleet that captured Eastport and occupied much of eastern Maine from July 1814 to June 1818 all used Halifax as a staging center.

Many French and U.S. prisoners sat out at least part of the war in Halifax. Captured officers roamed freely on parole. Hulks in the harbor and prisons built on Melville Island and the sparsely settled Dartmouth shore held the rank and file. Haligonians occasionally attended bazaars put on by the Melville Island inmates, who sold carved toothpicks, model warships, and other handicrafts to help support themselves. Some prisoners found private jobs, and others labored on public projects such as roads to outports. A resident U.S. agent worked with British officials to manage cartel vessels from Boston that took captured Americans back to the United States.

The community also experienced the uglier side of the war. Perhaps as many as 10,000 soldiers and sailors swamped the city's resources. Rough at the best of times, Halifax taverns, brothels, and streets became unsafe at night. Merchants installed iron shutters to protect their wares and families. Soldiers, however violent they might be toward civilians, were largely immune from prosecution in a garrison city under martial law. For example, five civilians were stabbed with bayonets in a January 1813 Market Wharf brawl, and Gov.-Gen. Sir George Prevost pardoned the only soldier convicted of murder. Press gangs could sweep the town with little notice. The government, military, and civilians all competed for provisions and accommodations. Prices rose, hitting hardest those least able to pay. A smallpox epidemic erupted in 1814 because diseases spread rapidly in the crowded, dirty, and unhealthy wartime conditions.

Despite the war, peacetime activities continued. Land surveyors laid out plots; schools were built; a dancing academy opened; theaters produced plays. Kings College sought a schoolmaster. Haligonians feared that wartime prosperity would wither when on 3 March 1815, they heard of the peace of Christmas Eve concluded at Ghent. But it took two years for the excess troops to pack up and leave, the dockyards to idle, and the backlog of captured goods to clear local warehouses. By 1818, though, a depression settled in, and the War of 1812 was truly over for Halifax.

—*Reginald C. Stuart*

See also: *Chesapeake* versus *Shannon*; Hardy, Thomas Masterman; Prevost, George; Warren, John Borlase

Further Reading

Akins, Thomas Beamish. *History of Halifax City.* Halifax, 1895.

"American Vessels Captured by the British during the War of 1812." *The Records of the Vice-Admiralty Court at Halifax.* Salem: The Essex Institute, 1911.

Lohnes, Barry J. "The War of 1812: The British Navy, New England and the Maritime Provinces of Canada." Master's thesis, University of Maine at Orono, 1971.

Martell, James. "Halifax during and after the War of 1812." *Dalhousie Review* 23 (October 1943): 289–304.

Nova Scotia Royal Gazette (1812–1815)

Piers, Harry. *Evolution of the Halifax Fortress 1749–1928*, ed.

G. M. Self. Publication No. 7. Halifax: Public Archives of Nova Scotia, 1947.

Raddall, Thomas. *Halifax: Warden of the North.* Rev. ed. Toronto: McClelland and Stewart, 1974.

HALL, AMOS

?

U.S. militia officer

A New York militia officer, Hall served under militia general George McClure until that officer's unpopularity forced his removal in December 1813. McClure relinquished command to Hall at Batavia on Christmas day. Hall left for Buffalo immediately because of the threat of a British invasion in that quarter. He arrived there the following day.

Hall immediately established his headquarters between Black Rock and Buffalo so he could respond in several directions. What he found there, though, was a collection of disorganized militia units alarmed by rumors that a British offensive under Gen. Sir Gordon Drummond was imminent. Over the next 24 hours, Hall frantically tried to organize his forces and place them at the likely and most defensible points of attack.

Drummond placed his men in position to attack outside Black Rock on 29 December. The New York militia guarding the bridge across Shogeoquady Creek were routed that night. A messenger immediately took the news to Hall's headquarters, and the general immediately sent out an urgent call to all available militia. This effort proved ineffective; the second party of militia sent out by Hall that night ran almost at first sight of the advancing British. At dawn on 30 December, Hall had 800 fewer men than the night before.

Undaunted, Hall started for Black Rock at first light on 30 December with his 1,200 remaining men. As he approached the British position, Hall sent his right flank against the British left, and for a short time his men put up a good fight. When the British threatened to envelop his entire army, however, Hall ordered a retreat. This order panicked some of the men, who ran pell-mell through Buffalo, putting the civilians there into a panic as well. Hall was able to rally enough of his force to cover the retreat of the civilians. He had suffered approximately 140 casualties in 24 hours.

Although Hall was blamed by many for the disaster at Black Rock, he suffered under the same handicaps as many other militia commanders in similar circumstances, most notably the lack of regular support for his militia troops. In the short time he had, Hall did everything he could but in the end was unable to control the panic of his raw, untrained troops. In early 1814, congressman-turned-general Peter B. Porter replaced Hall as militia commander on the northern frontier.

—Jeanne T. Heidler and David S. Heidler

See also: Black Rock, New York; Buffalo, New York; Drummond, Gordon; McClure, George; Porter, Peter Buell.
Further Reading
Dorsheimer, William. "Buffalo during the War of 1812." Buffalo Historical Society Publications 1 (1879): 185–229.
Hall, Amos. "Militia Service of 1812–1814 as Shown by the Correspondence of Major General Amos Hall." Buffalo Historical Society Publications 5 (1902): 26–62.
"Papers Relating to the Burning of Buffalo and to the Niagara Frontier during the War of 1812." Buffalo Historical Society Publications 9 (1906): 311–406.

HALL, JAMES
1783–1868
Newspaper editor and author

James Hall sought to create and publish a literature of the West of his times. Through his newspapers and magazines, he and other writers presented the frontier west of the Ohio River Valley in the first half of the nineteenth century. Hall's first actual experience with the West came in the War of 1812.

Born in Philadelphia on 29 July 1783, James Hall was one of nine children born to John and Sarah Ewing Hall. He grew up in an intellectual family and gained most of his early education from his mother. When the war began, Hall was reading the law with his uncle, John Ewing. Hall's brother John Elihu Hall was a staunch Federalist and was severely beaten in a riot in Baltimore, where he edited an antiwar newspaper. James Hall did not share his brother's antiwar fervor, however, and he joined the militia as the war came closer to Philadelphia. Enlisting as a second lieutenant in the Second Artillery, Hall joined the army of Maj. Gen. Jacob Brown in Buffalo for the summer 1814 invasion of Canada. Hall's wartime experiences included fighting in the Battle of Lundy's Lane and acting as a messenger for General Brown during the siege of Fort Erie. His service was creditable and provided material for two stories, "The Bearer of Despatches" and "Empty Pockets," which were published in the Port Folio edited by his brother.

Hall resigned his commission in 1818 and lived in the Midwest until his death on 5 July 1868. He was the editor of several newspapers and magazines that sought to popularize the West and western writers.

—Kurt E. Leichtle

HAMILTON, PAUL
1762–1816
Governor of South Carolina; secretary of the navy

Paul Hamilton was born on 16 October 1762, the son of Archibald and Rebecca (Brunford) Hamilton and the sole surviving child after his two brothers died. He left school at 16 and joined a militia company fighting at Savannah, Georgia, and Camden, South Carolina, and with guerrilla units in the American Revolution. His marriage to Mary Wilkinson brought him 23 slaves, and he became an indigo planter on Edisto Island and a rice planter in St. Paul's Parish, both in South Carolina. From 1787–1789, he served as a member of the South Carolina assembly, then became a state senator in 1794 and again in 1798–1799. He was the comptroller of finance from 1800–1804 before becoming governor in 1804.

Hamilton became Pres. James Madison's secretary of the navy on 7 March 1809. Detractors accused him of being an alcoholic, claiming that he was usually inebriated by the afternoon, but Hamilton possessed considerable acumen that they overlooked. He characterized the attack on the Chesapeake as "inhuman and dastardly" and expected his commanders to conduct their forces based upon principles of strict and upright neutrality "and support, at any risk and cost, the dignity of your flag." His navy was restricted by congressional economizing supported by Secretary of the Treasury Albert Gallatin. Though navy yards were in disrepair and vessels were laid up, Hamilton helped to establish naval hospitals in 1811.

Impending war scarcely wakened the Congress. When the House naval committee reported on 5 March 1812, Hamilton's requests for ten frigates and 12 74-gun ships failed by 62 to 59 and 76 to 33 votes, respectively. Of the 79 members who would vote for the declaration of war in June 1812, 53 had voted against Hamilton's requests for new vessels the previous January. However, Congress did appropriate money to refit three frigates in ordinary reserve and construct dockyards. As war approached, Hamilton's senior naval captains—John Rodgers, William Bainbridge, and Stephen Decatur—disagreed over strategy. Yet the navy's squadrons were ready to sail following the declaration of war. And from June to December 1812, Hamilton's navy was organized into small frigate squadrons that under his orders achieved the high point of U.S. success in single-ship actions: the frigate *Constitution* destroyed the *Guerrière*, the frigate *United States* captured the *Macedonian*, the frigate *Essex* captured the sloop *Alert*, the *Constitution* captured the frigate *Java*, and the sloop *Hornet* destroyed the *Peacock*.

Hamilton devised the strategy of contesting for the Canadas by controlling the lakes and appointed Commodore Isaac Chauncey to command the Great Lakes station. A shipbuilding program was also instituted for Lake Erie and Lake Champlain. Although Chauncey gained temporary control of Lake Ontario in late November 1812, U.S. armies' failures at Detroit (Michigan Territory), Queenston (Upper Canada), La Colle (Lower Canada), and the Upper Niagara undermined the achievement.

Attacked in Congress, Hamilton resigned his post and retired. Ironically, under his secretaryship the U.S. Navy achieved its greatest successes, and never again in the war did such favorable conditions prevail. Hamilton acquitted himself reasonably well, though his historical reputation has suffered. The president apparently appreciated Hamilton's efforts at the time. Madison's letter of 31 December 1812 accepting Hamilton's resignation was much kinder than the one he sent to Secretary of War William Eustis, who also resigned in December.

Hamilton died on 30 June 1816.

—*Frederick C. Drake*

See also: Chauncey, Isaac; Decatur, Stephen, Jr.; Rodgers, John
Further Reading
Maloney, Linda. "The War of 1812: What Role for Sea Power?" In *In Peace and War: Interpretations of American Naval History, 1775–1978*, Kenneth J. Hagan, ed. Westport, CT: Greenwood Press, 1978, 46–62.
McKee, Christopher. *A Gentlemanly and Honorable Profession: The Creation of the U.S. Naval Officer Corps, 1794–1815.* Annapolis, MD: Naval Institute Press, 1991.
Paullin, Charles Oscar. "American Naval Administration under Secretaries of the Navy Smith, Hamilton and Jones, 1801–14." *Proceedings of the U.S. Naval Institute* 32 (1906).

HAMPDEN, MAINE

This village on the Penobscot River fell to the British in September 1814. The British campaign formed part of the strategy to occupy as much of northern New England as necessary to secure uninterrupted communication between Halifax and Quebec. Implementing this task became the responsibility of Sir John Coape Sherbrooke, the lieutenant governor of Nova Scotia, who planned initially to move on Machias on the east bank of the Penobscot. Sherbrooke assembled a sizable force that included HMS *Dragon* and *Bulwark* (both 74-gun ships), several cruisers and transports, and a land force of 3,500 men. Rear Adm. Edward Griffith commanded the fleet; Sherbrooke, with Maj. Gen. Gerard Gosselin, commanded the embarkation force.

Sherbrooke and Griffin changed the mission's objective, however, after receiving word that the USS *John Adams* (28 guns) had made port at Hampden. A detachment under Capt. Robert Barrie of the *Dragon* would now ascend the Penobscot, with Lt. Col. Henry John commanding land forces, to bag the U.S. ship. It is doubtful that the British knew the *Adams* was at Hampden for hull repairs, having run hard aground off Isle au Haute. Her commander, Capt. Charles Morris, had heeded his worries about the ship's vulnerability to dash to Hampden. Once there, he put the *Adams's* guns ashore for defense.

After capturing Castine, Maine, on 1 September, the British sent the detachment under Barrie and John up the river. Contrary winds and the vagaries of the Penobscot impeded the flotilla's progress, and finally at Frankfort, Barrie had to leave the deep-draft *Dragon* and continue with a gaggle of ship's boats to complete the journey to Bald Hill, near Hampden. Lieutenant Colonel John's land forces, making their way up the river from below Soadabscook Stream, were plagued by poor visibility as a Maine mist settled over the area.

Messengers from Castine rushed to Hampden with the news of the British advance. Militia sent to take the measure of the British clashed with lead elements of John's infantry, only briefly slowing their fumbling but inexorable advance. Meanwhile, both Morris and Brig. Gen. John Blake braced to defend the merchant wharves and ships tied to them on the Penobscot. As Massachusetts militia gathered, Hampden's citizens expressed only wavering resolve to resist the British. The defeatism infuriated Morris, but more important, it seems to have immobilized Blake. His preparations consisted solely of exposing inexperienced militia to harm's way by wasting an entire night with inactivity instead of erecting breastworks.

The result the next morning was an American disaster. As the infantry and boats emerged from the fog, the only real resistance they encountered came from the *Adams's* shore-bound cannon, ably manned by her officers and crew. Otherwise, the militia panicked and fled, unnerved in part by Barrie's Congreve Rockets. Finally, Morris ordered his men to safety, but only just barely, after setting fire to the *Adams*. The British claimed Hampden at the light cost of one dead and eight wounded. The loss of Hampden opened the Maine coast to British depredations, starting with Bangor, and Penobscot River shipping fell prey to plunder.

Brigadier General Blake doubtless could have done more, but given the inexperience of his forces, the irresolution of the community, the general disaffection of New England, and the formidability of British forces, Hampden's fate was probably foreordained. A court of inquiry would acquit him of misconduct, but popular opinion branded him a coward at best.

—*Jeanne T. Heidler and David S. Heidler*

See also: Castine, Maine; Griffith, Edward; Maine, District of; Morris, Charles; Sherbrooke, John Coape

HAMPTON, VIRGINIA

Hampton, a southeastern Virginia seaport founded in 1610 at the mouth of the James River on the north shore of Hampton Roads, was sacked and burned by the British on 26 June 1813, four days after the British were defeated at Craney Island. The U.S. victory at Craney Island, Virginia, one of the few land victories for the United States, spared both the cities of Norfolk and Portsmouth and Portsmouth's Gosport Navy Yard with its fledgling navy.

Their defeat at Craney Island made the British more determined than before to score a land victory. British attention was turned toward Hampton, a community of questionable value to them, which was only 10 miles from Craney Island by sea and was protected by 450 relatively raw recruits. Adm. Sir George Cockburn instructed his 2,500 men to go ashore under the leadership of Gen. Sir Sidney Beckwith. British troops entered Hampton from the rear, at a distance of 2 miles to the north at Celey's Plantation.

The Battle of Hampton was over within a matter of hours because many of the untrained U.S. recruits fled, leaving their guns and the colors of the James City Light Infantry behind for Beckwith and his men to confiscate. The U.S. forces were outgunned and outnumbered. The British sustained five killed, 33 wounded, and ten missing, and the Americans suffered 30 casualties, a third of which were later believed to have returned to their homes. Yet it was not the Battle of Hampton that was so historically significant but what occurred the next day, after a relatively quiet evening under British occupation.

On 26 June, British soldiers—particularly the Canadian Chausseurs or Chausseurs Britanniques (French prisoners enlisted in British service and wearing green uniforms)—went on a rampage of burning, looting, pillaging, and raping. The U.S. commander, Maj. Stapleton Crutchfield, reported to Virginia governor John Barbour in Richmond on 28 June that the "unfortunate females of Hampton who could not leave the town were suffered to be abused in the most shameful manner." Later, British Lt. Col. Charles Napier wrote that during the Hampton incident, "every horror was perpetrated with impunity (by our troops)—rape, murder, pillage—and not a one was punished." One Hampton resident, a man named Kirby, was killed, his wife shot in the hip, and the family dog murdered. What the British did not steal, they burned.

The U.S. government sent Thomas Griffin and Robert Lively to investigate the charges. A report was filed, and Virginia's governor formally protested the actions in Hampton to Adm. Sir John Borlase Warren, the British squadron commanding officer aboard the HMS *San Domingo*. Warren claimed that the behavior at Hampton was a reprisal for Americans shooting at a helpless British crew floundering on a barge and for U.S. cruelty at Craney Island. Any sexual misconduct was blamed on the French unit and later was dismissed as unsubstantiated. British newspapers violently disagreed, however, and vigorously condemned the violations perpetrated on innocent U.S. civilians.

Some claim the sacking of Hampton, Virginia, inflamed U.S. resentment and stiffened U.S. resolve at the defense of New Orleans two years later. After the capture of Hampton, the British fleet remained in Chesapeake Bay until the end of 1813. Cockburn then pushed up the James, York, and Potomac Rivers. In some ways, the taking of Hampton foreshadowed scenes at Washington a year and a half later in 1814.

—*William A. Paquette*

See also: Craney Island, Battle of; Cockburn, George; Napier, Charles (British army officer)

Further Reading

Emmerson, John C., Jr., comp. *War in the Lower Chesapeake and Hampton Roads Area, 1812–1815, as Reported in the Norfolk Gazette and Publick ledger and the Norfolk and Portsmouth Herald.* Portsmouth, VA: N.p., 1946.

HAMPTON, WADE
1751–1835
U.S. Army officer

Wade Hampton (I) was born in Halifax County, Virginia, in May 1751. In the late 1760s, his father Anthony Hampton removed the family to Spartanburg District, which was then on the South Carolina frontier. In July 1776, several Hamptons were killed while defending their farmstead from Cherokee warriors. Wade and several of his siblings survived this fierce melee.

When the American Revolution broke out, he joined a company of dragoons that had formed in Spartanburg District. By 1778, Hampton was a commissioned captain in the American Continental Army. He made his reputation as a daring cavalry officer while serving under Maj. Gen. Thomas Sumter. Hampton was promoted to the rank of full colonel for battlefield heroism at the Battle of Eutaw Springs.

Immediately following the Revolution, Hampton served several consecutive terms in the South Carolina General Assembly. In 1788, he bought a large tract of land in the lower Richland District near the outskirts of Columbia, the new state capital. On Woodlands Plantation, he became among the first inland planters in South Carolina to cultivate short staple cotton extensively as a cash crop.

In the autumn of 1787, Hampton was a delegate to the state convention to consider ratifying the U.S. Constitution, and he was a member of the Anti-Federalist faction that voted against the document. In 1795, Hampton was elected to the U.S. House of Representatives as a Jefferson Republican. During a decade of service in that chamber, he often aligned with a doctrinaire states' rights faction led by John Randolph of Roanoke, Virginia. After refusing to seek reelection in 1805, he retired to private life in South Carolina.

In October 1808, he renewed his commission with the regular U.S. army. Within a year, Hampton had been promoted to a brigadier generalship; moreover, he was ordered to replace Maj. Gen. James Wilkinson as commandant of U.S. forces in Louisiana. During a stormy change of command in New Orleans, the two men became bitter per-

Wade Hampton

sonal enemies. Hampton's chief military aide in Louisiana was Capt. Winfield Scott. It was during this tour of duty that Hampton, a tireless land speculator, acquired several sugar plantations along the lower Mississippi River.

By the time war was declared against Great Britain in 1812, General Hampton had been assigned command of all coastal fortifications around Norfolk, Virginia. Elevated to major general in July 1813, Hampton assumed command of an army stationed near Plattsburg, New York, in the Ninth U.S. Military District. He was later superseded as senior officer by James Wilkinson, however, who was supposed to direct a pending military incursion into Canadian territory. Hampton never attempted to conceal his profound contempt for his superior.

Hampton also became embroiled in a noisy public dispute with Gov. Martin Chittenden of Vermont. This Federalist governor, a fiery antiwar advocate, refused to cede control of his state's militia to Hampton. Chittenden especially opposed the inclusion of the Vermont Brigade in the expedition to capture Montreal. In any event, the invasion in the fall of 1813 proved a logistical fiasco, and U.S. troops never came near to achieving the occupation of Montreal. Virtually all observers attributed this U.S. setback to Wilkinson's general military incompetence.

Although Hampton conducted his part of the campaign as well as resources permitted, Wilkinson sought to make him the scapegoat for its ultimate failure. A subsequent review by Secretary of War John Armstrong exonerated Hampton of all wrongdoing, but in the meantime Hampton had resigned his commission and returned to South Carolina.

Hampton spent his final two decades concentrating upon his plantation properties located throughout the Deep South. By 1830, he was considered among the wealthiest men in the United States. Although he did not serve in any public office, Hampton was definitely a political power broker in his native state. Hampton died at Woodlands on 4 February 1835, following a short illness. He was interred in the family plot at Trinity Episcopal Churchyard in Columbia.

—*Miles S. Richards*

See also: Armstrong, John; Chittenden, Martin; Scott, Winfield; Wilkinson, James

Further Reading

Maynard, Virginia S. *The Venturers: The Hampton, Harrison, and Earle Families of Virginia, South Carolina, and Texas.* Easley, SC: Southern Historical Press, 1981.

Wolfe, James Harold. *Jeffersonian Democracy in South Carolina.* Chapel Hill: University of North Carolina Press, 1940.

HANSON, ALEXANDER CONTEE
1786–1819
U.S. journalist and politician

Born to a prominent Maryland family in Annapolis, Alexander Hanson graduated from St. John's College at the age of 16 and for a brief time pursued a legal career. In 1808, he changed to newspaper publishing because he felt that career afforded the best opportunity to spread the Federalist message in Maryland. He called his newspaper the *Federal Republican*, published it in Baltimore, and began its run with an attack on Pres. Thomas Jefferson's embargo. He so incensed Democratic Republicans in the city that his militia company court-martialed him for inciting mutiny. Though acquitted, Hanson would remain an unpopular figure among opposition leaders throughout the prewar period.

As the country approached war in 1812, Hanson's editorials criticizing James Madison's administration became more biting. Hanson received threats after every issue. Democratic Republican anger exploded two days after the de-

Alexander Contee Hanson

claration of war, when the *Federal Republican* attacked Madison as a French puppet. That night a mob destroyed the newspaper office and its contents. Following this attack on Hanson's operation, mobs continued to roam the city of Baltimore for weeks.

To avoid losing another set of equipment, Hanson shifted his publishing activities to the home of his partner, Jacob Wagner of Georgetown, D.C. Hanson, however, still maintained an office in Baltimore in a house on Charles Street, from which he wrote the paper and supervised its distribution. To protect his operation, a group of Federalist friends, including Revolutionary War hero Henry "Light-Horse Harry" Lee, offered their services as guards.

On 27 July, the first issue since the attack in June was circulated. In it Hanson included an editorial that attacked the mobs of Baltimore as the unwitting dupes of Democratic Republican politicians. Inevitably, the ugly scenes of the previous month were to be repeated. People began gathering outside the house on Charles Street before dark, and by evening, the mob began throwing rocks and other debris at the house, breaking windows and scarring the outside. At one point, one of the house's defenders aimed a warning shot above the crowd, but instead of scattering the mob the shot enraged it. As the mob stormed the house, breaking down the front door, the defenders fired, killing one man. The mob retreated outside to set up an informal siege.

The militia and municipal authorities had been alerted to the violence, but most of the militia refused to respond to the call. Finally in the early hours of the morning of 28 July, a small militia cavalry unit appeared, under the command of Maj. William Barney. After assuring the mob that he was on its side, Barney entered the house to begin negotiations. While he conducted talks with both sides, someone in the crowd fetched a cannon, brought it down the street and pointed it at Hanson's office. Barney rushed to the men manning the artillery piece as they were being urged to fire. He persuaded them to wait while he returned to the house.

After several hours of tense negotiations, the defenders of the house agreed to surrender if Barney could guarantee them protection and ensure that the house would be untouched. Hanson counseled caution, not believing that Barney could guarantee any of these things, but he was overruled by the others. Under guard on the morning of 28 July, Hanson and his friends were marched to the Baltimore County jail. Although some in the crowd continued to throw things at and generally harass the departing Federalists, the remainder of the mob set about wrecking the house on Charles Street.

During the day, mobs continued to rove through the city. Although most people in the city believed that as soon as night fell the jail would be a target, the few militiamen guarding that facility were allowed to go home. Authorities also denied the imprisoned Federalists' requests that they be allowed to go home to fend for themselves or at least be given arms. Before sunset, a crowd gathered at the jail. Mayor Edward Johnson arrived to calm the angry mob, but his fellow citizens merely pushed him out of the way as they stormed the jail. Someone in the jail opened the door for them as they prepared to knock it down, and the crowd pushed into the cell area. Hearing the commotion outside and fearing the worst, the prisoners had extinguished lights in the hope that they could melt into the rabble and escape. This strategy worked for a few, but 12 of them, including Hanson and Lee, were grabbed by the mob.

For the next several hours the crowd took turns clubbing, gouging, stabbing (with small knives), and pouring hot candle wax on the 12 Federalists. One of the victims died, one was ultimately tarred and feathered, and the rest were left for dead. Doctors arrived to minister to the wounded. Both Lee and Hanson were so badly hurt that they never fully recovered from their wounds. They died within a year of one another, Lee in 1818 and Hanson in 1819.

In the time left to him, Hanson would not be silenced. By August, he was publishing his paper again, safely from Georgetown now, but still distributing it in Baltimore. Hanson and his fellow defenders of Charles Street were brought to trial for manslaughter stemming from the death on the night of 27 July, but a jury in Annapolis acquitted them. In fact, the backlash in Maryland against the Baltimore mob was so great that Hanson was elected to Congress and took his seat in March 1813. He then took his anti-Madison campaign to the national arena, angrily castigating the administration for the tremendous debt the war had caused.

By the fall of 1814, however, Hanson showed signs of mellowing. When the British terms for peace—an Indian buffer zone, loss of territory along the northern border, and an end to U.S. fishing rights in some Canadian waters— were published in the United States, Hanson rose in Congress to urge stout resistance to them. He advocated a fight to the finish to force the British to offer better terms.

Following the war, Hanson resigned his seat but returned to Congress to fill the term of a departing Maryland senator. Within a short time, however, his attendance became irregular due to his bad health. He died at his country estate at the age of 33.

—Jeanne T. Heidler and David S. Heidler

See also: Antiwar Sentiment; Baltimore Riots; Lee, Henry
Further Reading
Testimony Taken before the Committee of Grievances and Courts of Justice: Relative to the Late Riots and Mobs in the City of Baltimore. Annapolis, MD: Jonas Green, 1813.

HARDY, THOMAS MASTERMAN
1769–1839
British naval officer

Born on 5 April 1769 at Portisham, Dorsetshire, second son of Joseph and Nanny Hardy, Thomas Masterman Hardy entered the navy as a midshipman in 1781 and fought at the battles of St. Vincent (14 February 1797) and Copenhagen (1801). He became captain of HMS *Victory* in Lord Horatio Nelson's blockade of Toulon and was with Nelson when he died at Trafalgar. He became a baronet in

Thomas Masterman Hardy

1806 and served under Sir George Cranfield Berkeley at Halifax, 1806–1809, and at Lisbon, 1809–1812. He married Berkeley's daughter, Louisa Emily, at Halifax in December 1807.

In August 1812, he was ordered to take *Ramillies* (74 guns) to join Adm. Sir John Borlase Warren and patrol Long Island Sound. On 25 June 1813, off New London, his vessel was the target of an explosive device placed under flour barrels on board a captured sloop, the *Eagle*. The detonation killed ten but missed the *Ramillies*. Later a U.S. attempt to fasten a torpedo to her hull failed. Hardy removed his vessels from New London and threatened to burn coastal towns in retaliation. In July and August 1814, his forces mounted raids against Eastport and the Passamaquoddy Islands, Maine district, and on 11–12 August 1814 against Stonington, Connecticut.

After the war, Hardy commanded the Royal Navy's South American station until 1824. He was appointed rear admiral on 27 May 1825, then Lord of the Admiralty after 1830. He received the GCB on 13 September 1831 and succeeded Sir Richard Keats as governor of Greenwich Hospital in 1834. Promoted to vice admiral on 10 January 1837, Hardy died on 20 September 1839.

—*Frederick C. Drake*

Further Reading
Annual Register 81 (1839): 365.
Gentleman's Magazine. 1839, Part ii, 650.
Howarth, David. *Trafalgar: The Nelson Touch.* London: World Books, 1970.
Laughton, James Knox. "Sir Thomas Masterman Hardy." In *Dictionary of National Biography.* Vol 8. London: Oxford University Press, 1937–1938: 1243–1245.
Marshal, John. *Royal Naval Biography.* 12 vols. London: Longman, Hurst, Rees, Orme, 1823–1830.
Warner, Oliver. *A Portrait of Lord Nelson.* Harmondsworth, Middlesex: Penguin, 1958.

HARPER, JOHN ADAMS
1779–1816
U.S. congressman

Born in Derryfield, New Hampshire, John A. Harper was admitted to the New Hampshire bar in 1802 and, while engaged in private practice, became active in state Democratic Republican politics. He served as the clerk of the state senate for three years and then entered the state house of representatives. Beginning in March 1811, he began serving in the 12th Congress, where he was associated with the War Hawk faction. When Speaker of the House Henry Clay packed crucial committees with fellow War Hawks, he gave Harper an important position on the House Foreign Relations Committee.

When Pres. James Madison submitted his annual message to Congress on 5 November 1811, Clay referred much of it to the Foreign Relations committee. As a member of the committee, Harper was responsible for the committee report, which condemned British actions in much stronger terms than had the president.

As the country moved toward war in the spring of 1812, Harper confided to friends in May 1812 that he was convinced that the House would receive a strong war message from the president during the following month. In anticipation of this message, the House passed a resolution calling all absent members to assemble in Washington by 1 June.

After the declaration of war, Harper remained a strong supporter of the administration, even when it promoted unpopular measures. Because some parts of the country continued to trade food directly or indirectly with the British, Harper offered a resolution in Congress on 6 November 1812 to place an embargo on certain items. Military setbacks had made the war so unpopular, however, that the resolution was voted down.

As the war became increasingly unpopular in his native New England, Harper's actions in support of the Madison administration did little to endear him to his constituents. The elections for the 13th Congress in the fall of 1812 saw Harper defeated. He returned to New Hampshire and persisted in his support for the administration. He died soon after the war in Meredith Bridge, New Hampshire.

—Jeanne T. Heidler and David S. Heidler

See also: U.S. Congress; War Hawks
Further Reading
Egan, Clifford L. "The Path to War in 1812 through the Eyes of a New Hampshire 'War Hawk.'" *Historical New Hampshire* 30 (1975): 147–177.

William Henry Harrison

HARRISON, WILLIAM HENRY
1773–1841
U.S. officer

Born in Virginia to Benjamin Harrison and Elizabeth Bassett Harrison, both from prominent Virginia families, William Henry Harrison attended Hampden-Sidney College and had embarked upon the study of medicine when his father's death allowed him to pursue the career of his choice. Entering the First U.S. Infantry Regiment in 1791 as an ensign, Harrison served near present-day Cincinnati. At the commencement of Anthony Wayne's campaign against the northwestern Indians, Harrison obtained a position as the general's aide and was present at the Battle of Fallen Timbers. The following year, 1795, he was one of the signers of the Treaty of Greenville.

Harrison resigned from the army in 1798 to accept the position of secretary of the Northwest Territory. In 1799, he became the territorial delegate to Congress. While there, he influenced Congress to divide the region into the territories of Indiana and Ohio. At the age of 27, he became the territorial governor of Indiana.

As governor, one of Harrison's primary goals was to extinguish Indian title to as much land in the Northwest as possible. He negotiated several treaties with various tribes to extend U.S. control gradually westward. Although these activities made him popular with white westerners, the slow but steady diminution of Indian lands excited suspicion from the growing nativist movement led by Tecumseh and his brother Tenskwatawa (the Prophet). The Treaty of Fort Wayne in 1809, which alienated a large part of Indian land in the Northwest, so angered Tecumseh that he responded to Harrison's invitation to discuss their differences by bringing 400 heavily armed warriors to Vincennes in August 1810. After this tense meeting accomplished nothing—it nearly came to blows—fear mounted in the territory as Indian attacks on frontier settlements increased. When another meeting between Tecumseh and Harrison in July 1811 ended badly, Harrison began planning a military expedition against Prophet's Town, the nativists' settlement on Tippecanoe Creek.

Harrison had already been corresponding with the Madison administration about his need for more military forces to meet the Indian threat; now, he increased those pleas, insisting that he needed regulars to crush the Indian confederation. By early fall 1811, he believed he had the necessary militia and regulars to make his strike.

Tecumseh traveled south during the late summer of 1811 to recruit southern Indians to his confederacy, so he was away from Prophet's Town when Harrison's force approached it in early November. The Indians in the town, however, were well aware of Harrison's intentions. Before dawn, while the white soldiers slept in their camp just a few miles away from the Indian town, Tenskwatawa directed a surprise attack on Harrison's army. The ensuing Battle of Tippecanoe on 7 November 1811 swung back and forth until Harrison's men finally fought off the Indian attack. Facing the modern weapons of Harrison's army, the Indians had to abandon the area following the battle, and Harrison directed the destruction of Prophet's Town the following day.

Though anything but a smashing victory for Harrison, the Battle of Tippecanoe won him a national reputation. The battle did nothing to end Indian attacks on the frontier; in fact, if anything they became more frequent. The only possible benefit from the engagement for whites was the discrediting of Tenskwatawa in some Indian eyes: the Prophet had promised that he would prevent the whites' bullets from killing Indians.

Following the battle, Harrison returned to Vincennes to resume his duties as governor. The job was becoming more taxing as war loomed with Great Britain and threatened to revive Indian hostilities. Harrison continued to warn the administration about the potential danger of Indian attacks, especially when it became apparent that Tecumseh's confederation had increased its contacts with British forces in Canada. Harrison's warnings did not go unheeded. In the spring of 1812, before war had been declared, the War Department began to increase the military presence in the Northwest and appointed the governor of the Michigan Territory, William Hull, to command in that theater. After war was declared and Hull ignominiously surrendered Detroit, Secretary of War William Eustis began searching for Hull's replacement. His first choice was regular Brig. Gen. James Winchester, but he was unpopular with the militia forces in the theater. Kentuckians especially wanted Harrison to receive the command, and while they lobbied furiously to that end, they made Harrison the major general of the Kentucky militia, even though he did not live in the state. Should a question of rank arise, thought the Kentuckians, Harrison as a major general would take precedence over the brigadier general Winchester. Such support made Harrison's choice inevitable, and on 17 September 1812 the administration bowed to it, giving Harrison the command of all military forces in the Northwest. He was already on the march with the Kentucky militia when he received the appointment. Assembling a large enough force, particularly of militia with sufficient terms of enlistment to warrant a fall 1812 campaign, seemed impossible. Therefore, Harrison contented himself with raiding hostile Indian towns.

One such raid in force was commanded by Brigadier General Winchester and ended in disaster. On 22 January 1813, Winchester was forced to surrender to a superior British-Indian army on the River Raisin. Following the surrender, a number of Winchester men, especially his wounded, were killed by the Indians. This incident led to the use of the rallying cry "Remember the Raisin!" by the military forces in the Northwest for the remainder of the war.

As Harrison's campaign season approached in early 1813, he received good and bad news from the War Department. His regular commission to command the Northwest had been as a brigadier general, but Congress had approved his promotion to major general. At the same time, however, the new Secretary of War John Armstrong, in an effort to save money, had decided to give priority to the northern theater. Armstrong sent instructions to Harrison to maintain a defensive posture. Not wanting this changed policy to cost him ground, Harrison began the construction of a series of forts to guard against British expansion.

In the spring of 1813, Harrison constructed Fort Meigs at the rapids of the Maumee River as part of these defensive efforts. The British under Col. Henry Procter and his Indian allies under Tecumseh tried to take Fort Meigs in May 1813. Procter seriously outnumbered Harrison, but on 5 May a relief party under Kentucky militia brigadier general Green Clay bolstered U.S. numbers. Although about half his force was killed or captured trying to take the British batteries, Clay was able to lead the remainder into the fort. Procter, who lost one of his batteries to a sortie from the fort, abandoned the siege on 9 May. Later attempts by Procter to take Fort Meigs and Fort Stephenson in the summer would also fail.

The early August attempt on Fort Stephenson resulted in one of the more romantic episodes of the war in the Northwest. Twenty-one-year-old Maj. George Croghan commanded the fort and disobeyed Harrison's order to evacuate the position if the British attacked. Croghan's successful repulsion of Procter gained him the admiration of his commander and of a nation in grave need of heroes.

In the meantime, Harrison had been busy. To secure the surrounding area, he had left Fort Meigs shortly after the British lifted their first siege. Throughout the summer of 1813, in fact, Harrison moved around quite a lot, though he spent much of his time at Cleveland to cooperate with Commodore Oliver Hazard Perry on Lake Erie. Harrison was so anxious to see Perry gain control of Lake Erie that when the young commodore complained that his squadron was seriously undermanned, Harrison loaned him Kentucky riflemen as well as men in his army who had maritime experience.

When Perry defeated the British on 10 September, Procter did as Harrison had hoped: he pulled his forces out of the Northwest, retreating into Canada. Harrison wanted to seize the opportunity for pursuit, so he sent out a call to all surrounding state and territorial militia. The largest response came from Kentucky, with forces personally led by

Gov. Isaac Shelby. Still, Harrison feared that even with these reinforcements his delay in starting would prevent him from catching Procter. As he began the pursuit on 2 October, Harrison did know that Procter had tried to allay Tecumseh's anger with promises that they would stop somewhere along the Thames River to make a stand against the Americans.

For the first two days, Harrison's army only skirmished with Procter's rearguard, primarily his Indian allies. On 4 October, though, Harrison believed that the entire British army had stopped outside Chatham, Upper Canada, to do battle, so he called up and prepared his army for the engagement. The force in front of him was mostly Tecumseh's Indians, who were dispersed by Harrison's artillery.

The following day, 5 October, at Moraviantown, Upper Canada, Harrison caught up with the main British army. This time it was the British army that was easily dispersed, while Tecumseh's Indians put up the stiffest resistance. In the Battle of the Thames (sometimes called the Battle of Moraviantown), Tecumseh was killed, but most of the British army escaped. Still, the battle proved decisive, ending immediate British threats to the Northwest and forever breaking Tecumseh's confederation.

Following the Battle of the Thames, Harrison remained in command in the Northwest, but he could not get along with Secretary of War John Armstrong. Perhaps because of his own military experience during the Revolutionary War, the secretary alienated his commanders in the field both by countermanding their orders and by issuing his own instructions directly to their subordinates. By the spring of 1814, with no future campaigns in sight, Harrison was so angered by these inept habits that he resigned his commission.

For the remainder of the war, Harrison occupied himself as a commissioner to the northwestern Indians, negotiating the treaties of Greenville and Spring Wells. After the war, Harrison entered Congress briefly, became active in Ohio politics, and served part of a term in the U.S. Senate. He also served a tumultuous year as minister to Colombia, where he inappropriately interfered with internal Colombian affairs.

When he returned from Colombia, Harrison retired to his farm in Ohio. His popularity from the war had never abated, and a number of people encouraged him to enter the presidential race of 1836. Though the existence of three Whig candidates in that year prevented any one of them from winning, Harrison's respectable showing convinced him and his followers that he could win in 1840. The next four years were spent preparing a party mechanism to rival the highly organized Democratic organization, and that, with the failed economy of Martin Van Buren's adminis-

tration, won Harrison the election of 1840. What President Harrison would have accomplished was never to be known. He became ill during his first month in office and died on 4 April 1841.

—Jeanne T. Heidler and David S. Heidler

See also: Chatham, Upper Canada; Clay, Green; Croghan, George; Meigs, Fort; Procter, Henry; Stephenson, Fort; Tecumseh; Thames, Battle of the; Tippecanoe, Battle of; Winchester, James

Further Reading

Cleeves, Freeman. *Old Tippecanoe: William Henry Harrison and His Time.* New York: Charles Scribner's Sons, 1939.

Creason, Joe C. "The Battle of Tippecanoe." *Filson Club Quarterly* 36 (1962): 309–318.

HART, NATHANIEL GRAY SMITH
1785–1813
Kentucky militia officer

Nathaniel G.S. Hart, known as "Nat," was born in Hagerstown, Maryland, the second son of Col. Thomas Hart. The family moved to Lexington, Kentucky, in 1794, where Colonel Hart acquired wealth operating a ropewalk, nail plant, and blacksmith shop and engaging in a large retail and wholesale mercantile business. Nat Hart's father died in 1808 and his older brother shortly afterward. Hart, however, opened his own ropewalk and also made a fortune in the mercantile business. He studied law with Henry Clay, who married Hart's sister, Lucretia.

In 1812, Hart at age 27 raised a company as part of the Lexington Light Infantry (originally organized in 1788). Henry Clay commented at the time that these 100 were "as fine fellows as ever shouldered a musket." Mustering at Georgetown in August 1812, Hart and the light infantry marched northward to join the Northwestern Army.

William Henry Harrison detached about 1,200 troops (mostly Kentuckians, including Hart's company) under the command of Brig. Gen. James Winchester. Winchester's troops captured Frenchtown on the River Raisin (near present-day Monroe, Michigan), on 18 January 1813. Four days later Gen. Henry Procter counterattacked with 597 British soldiers and 800 Indians. After sustaining heavy losses, Winchester surrendered. Five hundred Kentuckians were among the captives, including Hart, who had been wounded in the knee. Capt. William Elliot, a British officer who had been a classmate of Hart's at Princeton and who had visited Hart in Lexington, where Elliot had been cared for during an illness, promised Hart protection. Elliot said he would send a carryall to convey Hart to Elliot's quarters at Fort Malden, but when the pledges proved empty, Hart paid an Indian $600 to guide him to the British fort.

On the way, they clashed with a band of drunken Indians, and a musket ball knocked Hart from his horse. The Indians used their tomahawks on him. Other captives met similar fates, and Hart's body was among the many mutilated corpses left by the wayside to be scavenged by dogs and hogs. Kentuckians were slow to forgive Harrison, blaming him for not coming to the aid of Winchester and purposefully allowing the sacrifice of the Kentucky troops.

Hart left two sons, Thomas and Henry. His wife, Anna Maria Gist (stepdaughter of Gov. Charles Scott), whom he had married in 1809, died in 1818. That same year, Hart's remains were moved first to a cemetery in Monroe, Michigan, and then transferred to Detroit; they were reinterred at the State Cemetery at Frankfort in 1834.

—*Harry M. Ward*

See also: Frenchtown, Battles of; Harrison, William Henry
Further Reading

Clift, G. Glenn. *Remember the Raisin! Kentucky and Kentuckians in the Battles and Massacre at Frenchtown, Michigan Territory, in the War of 1812.* Frankfort, 1961; reprint, Baltimore: Genealogical Publishing, 1995.

Collins, Lewis, revised by Richard H. Collins. *History of Kentucky.* 2 vols. Covington, KY: Collins and Co., 1874.

Dunn, C. Frank. "Captain Nathaniel G.S. Hart." *Filson Club Historical Quarterly* 24 (1950): 28–33.

Hopkins, James F., ed. *The Papers of Henry Clay.* Vol. 1. Lexington: University of Kentucky Press, 1959.

HARTFORD CONVENTION

15 December 1814–5 January 1815

The climax of Federalist opposition to the War of 1812 was the Hartford Convention, a regional conference held in the Connecticut state capital near the end of the war. Although generated by the frustrations of the War of 1812—particularly the problem of providing for local defense—the Hartford Convention was also an attempt to deal with long-term problems growing out of the Virginia dynasty's domination of national politics.

A feud with the federal government over the deployment and control of the militia was the catalyst for the Hartford Convention. Throughout the war, the New England governors were reluctant to place their militia under U.S. officers, fearing that they would lose control over their only means of defense. By the fall of 1814, this dispute, combined with an empty federal treasury, had forced the New England states to finance their own defense measures.

More and more frequent British raids along the region's long and exposed coast drove these costs steadily upward. In Massachusetts the total reached $850,000; in Connecticut, $200,000; and in Rhode Island, $50,000. Because the federal tax burden was heavy and still growing and the British blockade had thrown the region into a depression, new state taxes were especially unpalatable. Nor could state officials borrow the money they needed. The suspension of special payments elsewhere in the nation had created a credit squeeze in New England that dried up bank funds.

Facing this crisis, Governor Caleb Strong of Massachusetts summoned the state legislature to a special session in the fall of 1814. This body recommended a convention to air the region's grievances and resolve its problems. Connecticut and Rhode Island soon endorsed the proposal. Massachusetts appointed 12 delegates to attend the convention; Connecticut, seven; and Rhode Island, four. Although New Hampshire and Vermont declined to take part in the proposed convention, two counties from each selected delegates, and three of the four delegates were seated by the convention. In all, 26 delegates took part in the convention.

Despite pleas in the New England press for secession and a separate peace, most of the delegates taking part in the Hartford Convention were determined to pursue a moderate course. Only Timothy Bigelow of Massachusetts apparently favored extreme measures, and he did not play a major role in the proceedings. When asked what the result of the convention was likely to be, Massachusetts hothead Josiah Quincy replied: "A GREAT PAMPHLET!"—a prediction that proved remarkably accurate.

The Hartford Convention held its deliberations in secret. At the opening session, George Cabot of Massachusetts was unanimously chosen president, and Theodore Dwight, editor of the *Connecticut Mirror*, was chosen secretary. No log of the debates was kept, and no one ever revealed their content. The only record was Dwight's barebones journal. Harrison Gray Otis of Massachusetts was the driving force behind the deliberations. The final report of the convention, which was published on 6 January 1815, was largely his work.

About half of the report was devoted to war-related issues: the defense problem, a federal law that authorized the enlistment of minors in the army, and federal proposals to draft men into the army and navy. To finance local defense measures, the report recommended that the states seek authority from the national government to use federal tax money collected within their borders. To deal with proposals to fill the ranks of the army and navy by conscripting adults and enlisting minors, the report—in its only radical proposal—recommended state nullification.

The other half of the report was devoted to New England's long-term problems. To resolve these problems, the report recommended seven constitutional amendments. These would require a two-thirds vote in Congress to declare war, interdict trade with foreign nations, or admit new states to the Union; limit embargoes to 60 days; repeal the three-fifths rule for apportioning direct taxes and representation in Congress; bar naturalized citizens from holding federal office; limit presidents to a single term; and prohibit the election of a president from the same state twice in succession.

These amendments represented a catalog of New England's grievances over the previous decade. They struck at the overrepresentation of white southerners in Congress, the growing power of the West, the trade restrictions and the war, the influence of foreigners (like Albert Gallatin), and the Virginia dynasty's domination of national politics. Federalists hoped that the adoption of these amendments would restore New England's influence in the Union and prevent a recurrence of those policies they considered destructive of the region's vital interests.

Although the report of the Hartford Convention recommended the nullification of federal laws, otherwise the tone of the document was moderate. The report expressly opposed any "irrevocable" step that might lead to disunion and recommended instead "a course of moderation and firmness." Even if New England's grievances were not redressed, the report simply called for another convention to be convened in June 1815, or sooner if necessary.

Massachusetts and Connecticut formally approved the convention report and endorsed the constitutional amendments. Both states also nullified the minor enlistment law (the only one of the proposed recruitment measures that was actually adopted by Congress), although Massachusetts judiciously waited until after the war was over and recruiting had been suspended.

Both states sent emissaries to Washington to seek federal tax money to finance local defense measures. On their way to the nation's capital, the emissaries learned of Andrew Jackson's victory at New Orleans, and news of the Treaty of Ghent soon followed. This effectively killed their mission.

Although the Hartford Convention was essentially a victory for moderation, few people remembered it that way in the rush of events at the end of the war. Instead, the very term "Hartford Convention" became a synonym for dis-

loyalty and treason, and the Federalist Party, which rapidly declined after the war, never lived down its notoriety.

—*Donald R. Hickey*

See also: Antiwar Sentiment; Cabot, George; Militia Controversy, The New England; Otis, Harrison Gray; Strong, Caleb

Further Reading

Banner, James M., Jr. *To the Hartford Convention: The Federalists and the Origins of Party Politics in Massachusetts, 1789–1815.* New York: Alfred Knopf, 1970.

Hickey, Donald R. *The War of 1812: A Forgotten Conflict.* Urbana: University of Illinois Press, 1989.

Morison, Samuel Eliot. *The Life and Letters of Harrison Gray Otis, Federalist, 1765–1848.* 2 vols. Boston and New York: Houghton Mifflin Company, 1913.

HARVEY, JOHN
1778–1852
British army officer

John Harvey was born on 23 April 1778, the son of a poor and an obscure Anglican clergyman. In spite of his background, Harvey procured an ensignship in the 80th Foot on 10 September 1794. He served in the Netherlands and on the French coast from 1794 to 1796 and was promoted to lieutenant at the Cape of Good Hope in 1796. He subsequently served in Ceylon from 1797 to 1800, in Egypt in 1801, and in the Marathas campaigns in India, from 1803 to 1806. On 9 September 1803, he was appointed a captain. On 16 June 1806, he married Lady Elizabeth Lake, daughter of his commanding officer, with whom he would have five sons and one daughter. Harvey returned to England in September 1807, was promoted to major on 28 January 1808, and served until June as an assistant quartermaster general. In July 1808, he joined the Sixth Royal Garrison battalion in Ireland. After earning promotion to lieutenant colonel on 25 June 1812, he sailed to Upper Canada as deputy adjutant general to Brig. Gen. John Vincent.

Harvey displayed considerable individual courage in his most daring contribution to the war, the night action at Stoney Creek, Niagara Peninsula, on 6 June 1813. Counterattacking with 700 men, he repulsed the threat by John Chandler and William Winder's 4,000-strong army at Burlington Heights. For this deed and his subsequent collaboration with naval commander Sir James Lucas Yeo to harass the retreating U.S. forces, Harvey was praised in dispatches by Vincent. Harvey also fought at Chrysler's Farm (November 1813), Oswego (May 1814), Lundy's Lane (July 1814), and Fort Erie (August 1814). Remarkably, he remained unscathed until the battle at Fort Erie, where he was at last wounded.

After the war he received a knighthood in 1824 and was promoted to colonel in May 1825, major-general in January 1837, and lieutenant general in November 1846. As a Crown commissioner (December 1825–June 1826), he investigated the price for which Crown lands should be sold in Canada. In 1828, he became inspector general for police in Leinster, Ireland.

Beginning in April 1836, Harvey built a successful second career as a peacemaking governor of four different colonies: he was appointed lieutenant governor of Prince Edward Island (April 1836), governor of New Brunswick (May 1837), lieutenant governor of Newfoundland (September 1841), and lieutenant governor of Nova Scotia (August 1846). He died on 22 March 1852 following a stroke.

—Frederick C. Drake

Further Reading
Buckner, Philip. "Sir John Harvey." In *Dictionary of Canadian Biography*. Vol. 7: *1836–1850*. Toronto: University of Toronto Press, 1979: 374–384.
Hannay, James. *History of New Brunswick*. Saint John, NB: J. A. Bowes, 1909.
MacDonell, Malcolm. "The conflict between Sir John Harvey and Chief Justice John Gervase Hutchinson Bourne." *Canadian Historical Association Report* (1956): 45–54.
Maclean, D. F. "The Administration of Sir John Harvey in Nova Scotia, 1846–1852." Master's thesis, Dalhousie University, Halifax, 1947.
McNutt, W. S. "New Brunswick's Age of Harmony: The Administration of Sir John Harvey." *Canadian Historical Review* 32 (1951): 101–125.
United Service Gazette and Naval and Military Chronicle. London: 10 April 1852.
Wood, H. F. "The Many Battles of Stoney Creek." In *The Defended Border: Upper Canada in the War of 1812*, Morris Zaslow, ed. Toronto: Macmillan of Canada, 1964: 56–60.

HAVRE DE GRACE, MARYLAND, ATTACK ON
3 May 1813

In the spring of 1813, Adm. Sir John Borlase Warren directed Rear Adm. Sir George Cockburn to penetrate the rivers of Chesapeake Bay and disrupt trade between Philadelphia and Baltimore. Using escaped slaves as guides, Cockburn carried out a number of hit-and-run operations along the bay. In late April, he ordered a British barge force up the Elk River, and on 29 April a land party went ashore at Frenchtown, where it burned some stores and five bay schooners. The British then went up the Susquehanna River to attack Havre de Grace, Maryland, which lay astride the Baltimore-to-Philadelphia road.

Citizens there had mounted an around-the-clock watch for several days, but Cockburn delayed his approach to lull the defenders. Guided by the escaped slaves, Cockburn then approached at night as Havre de Grace slept. At dawn on 3 May, he surprised the town in an attack with some 150 marines. A Congreve Rocket killed one American in the brief skirmish that followed. The British then burned up to 40 of the 60 houses in the town and most buildings at Samuel Hughes's nearby cannon foundry. These works, known as the Cecil Company, were one of the three cannon foundries in the United States with machinery for boring and finishing guns from solid castings. Although the British spiked 35 of the 24- and 32-pound cannon, most of the latter were later drilled out and made serviceable.

The British then turned their attention to the Sassafras River, where they destroyed and looted Georgetown and Fredericktown after overcoming resistance. The expedition of some 15 warships sailed back down the bay on 12 May 1813.

—Spencer C. Tucker

See also: Maryland
Further Reading
"Conflagration of Havre de Grace." *North American Review* 5 (1817): 157–163.

HAWKINS, BENJAMIN
1754–1816
Creek Indian agent

Born to Philemon Hawkins and Delia Martin Hawkins in North Carolina, Benjamin Hawkins attended the College of New Jersey (Princeton) but left there during the American Revolution to serve as a French interpreter for Gen. George Washington. During the Confederation period, he served several terms as a representative from North Carolina to Congress. When the new government was organized under the Constitution, Hawkins was chosen to be

Benjamin Hawkins

one of the first senators from North Carolina. A good friend of the Washington administration, he lost favor in an increasingly Jeffersonian North Carolina and was not reelected for a second term.

Throughout the 1780s, as a resident of a state with a large Indian population, Hawkins had been interested in Indian affairs and had served on several treaty commissions to various tribes. Following his defeat in the 1795 Senate race, Hawkins was appointed by President Washington to negotiate a treaty with the Creek Nation. His success led Washington to offer him the position of agent to the Creeks. Leaving a handsome estate and his disapproving family, Hawkins accepted the appointment and moved to the Creek Nation, where he would spend the remainder of his life.

From the very beginning of his time among the Creeks, Hawkins saw his mission as making the Indians more acceptable to their white neighbors. By doing so he hoped to prevent in the South the frictions that always had led to Indian war. To accomplish the goal, he tried to

remake Creek society and government in a white image. The existence of a Creek confederation of towns made his job easier.

The Creeks were a sedentary, agricultural people who supplemented their livelihoods with commercial hunting. By the time Hawkins arrived in the nation, the impact of overhunting was already being felt, and the subsequent economic hardships combined with the pressures of white settlement to heighten tensions in the nation. Hawkins's efforts to transform the Creek people thus contributed to a division in the nation between the Lower Creeks in its eastern part near the Chattahoochee River and the Upper Creeks almost due west.

The Lower Creeks, living closer to white settlements in Georgia and trading extensively with them, appeared more receptive to Hawkins's acculturation plan. The Upper Creeks, however, watched their hunting grounds shrink because of white expansion and consequently saw accommodation with the U.S. government as the heart of their problems. U.S. initiatives to build roads through the Creek Nation only increased the tensions and divisions between the Upper and Lower towns.

By 1811, many Upper Creeks were angry over the dominant influence of Hawkins on the Creek National Council and were disturbed by their changing circumstances. They listened to religious prophets who blamed Creek problems on the abandonment of native ways and the acceptance of Hawkins's authority. When Tecumseh visited the Upper Creeks in the fall of 1811, there was little Hawkins could do to prevent the great Shawnee's message from being heard.

During the next two years, he did try, with limited success, to keep the uneasiness among the Creeks confined to the nation. He was afraid that an Indian war would undo all his work of the previous 15 years. Yet having the Creek Council send out "law menders" to execute perpetrators of attacks on whites only divided the nation more. Finally in the summer of 1813, divisions between the Creeks erupted into open warfare when some Upper Creeks known as Red Sticks attacked and besieged the Upper Creek capital of Tuckabatchee, home of headman Big Warrior.

The Red Sticks were named after the custom of sending a certain number of sticks to a town to designate the number of days until an event; if those sticks were red, the event was a war. Some Upper Creeks, including Big Warrior, refused to join the Red Sticks in what was initially a civil war between supporters of and opponents to Hawkins's acculturation plan. Still, even after open warfare erupted, Hawkins tried to restrict the civil conflict to the nation. Shortly after the attack on Tuckabatchee, a group of Red Sticks led by Peter McQueen were returning from Spanish

Pensacola with gunpowder when Mississippi Territorial Militia attacked them. In revenge, Red Sticks led by Red Eagle (William Weatherford) struck Fort Mims, a shelter for white settlers and mixed-blood Creeks in the southern part of what is now Alabama. Most of the fort's inhabitants were killed. The attack on Fort Mims brought calls throughout the South for militia to put down the Creek War. Benjamin Hawkins could only watch, hoping that his worst fears would not be realized, as white soldiers marched into the Creek Nation.

Partly to demonstrate that only a small portion of his charges had engaged in hostilities against the United States, Hawkins spent much of the Creek War organizing groups of Lower Creeks to aid militia and regular forces in defeating the Red Sticks. Many of these forces, led by such Creeks as William McIntosh, provided invaluable aid to the campaigns of John Floyd and Andrew Jackson.

When the Red Sticks were dealt their most devastating blow by Jackson at Tohopeka (Horseshoe Bend), Hawkins had reason to hope that his experiment could now continue in peace. He received word that he and Maj. Gen. Thomas Pinckney had been appointed to negotiate the final peace treaty with the Creeks. Both agreed with the War Department that the Creeks should lose land only to the extent necessary to pay the cost of the war. Their appointments, however, angered land-hungry people in the South who considered Pinckney and Hawkins too inclined toward lenience. Georgians and Tennesseans especially protested, and lobbying efforts commenced to replace the two men. Considered the softer, Hawkins's role was first reduced to a consultative one. Then Andrew Jackson received a regular major general's commission, and he replaced Pinckney. When Jackson returned to the Creek Nation, he instructed Hawkins to assemble all Creek leaders at Fort Jackson on 1 August. Hawkins nervously complied, aware that Jackson's peace terms would likely be quite different from those agreed upon by Hawkins and Pinckney.

As the Creek leaders, only one of whom was a Red Stick, met with Jackson on 1 August, they and Hawkins were dumbfounded by Jackson's terms. Jackson dictated to the Creeks that they would relinquish to the United States 23 million acres, almost half their nation. Over the next few days before signing the treaty, the Creeks implored Hawkins to change Jackson's mind, but he helplessly told them the matter was beyond his control. On 9 August 1814, the Treaty of Fort Jackson was signed.

Hawkins knew better than to confront the powerful Jackson on this or any other issue. As the military commander in the area, Jackson had the power to renew the war against the Creeks and thereby extract even more land. Hawkins did send protesting letters to the War Depart-

ment that harshly criticized Jackson's behavior, but even this small gesture was fruitless. Jackson supporters later removed the letters from War Department files.

Hawkins spent the remainder of the War of 1812 marshaling the resources of the Creek Nation against a new threat on the Gulf Coast. The British had landed a party of Royal Marines under Maj. Edward Nicholls at the mouth of the Apalachicola River. Up the river at Prospect Bluff, Nicholls built a fort and sent out a call to the Creek Indians to join the British in a war against the United States. Red Stick survivors flocked to the call and now threatened frontier Georgia with a renewal of the Creek War. Hawkins organized units of Lower Creeks, primarily under McIntosh, to guard against this menace. Though the danger of English-sponsored depredations was largely illusory, after the war Nicholls remained on the Gulf Coast, insisting that Article IX of the Treaty of Ghent negated the Treaty of Fort Jackson. He and Hawkins exchanged letters on this subject, with the U.S. agent insisting that Nicholls was wrong. It must have galled Hawkins to defend the validity of the Treaty of Fort Jackson.

After Nicholls finally left in the summer of 1815, the frontier calmed somewhat, and Hawkins resumed his work with the Creeks. The presence of Nicholls's fort, however, proved to be a gathering point for runaway slaves and disaffected Red Sticks, again disrupting the frontier. Hawkins was preparing an expedition of Lower Creeks against the fort at Prospect Bluff when he became ill and suddenly died in June 1816.

—*Jeanne T. Heidler and David S. Heidler*

See also: Creek War; Jackson, Andrew; McIntosh, William; Red Sticks; Weatherford, William
Further Reading
Heidler, David S., and Jeanne T. Heidler. *Old Hickory's War: Andrew Jackson and the Quest for Empire.* Mechanicsburg, PA: Stackpole Books, 1996.
Pound, Merritt B. *Benjamin Hawkins: Indian Agent.* Athens: University of Georgia Press, 1951.

HAWKINS, WILLIAM
1799–1819
Governor of North Carolina

Born at Pleasant Hill, North Carolina, on 10 October 1777 to Philemon Hawkins, Jr., and the former Lucy Davis, William Hawkins hailed from a prominent family that included his uncle Benjamin Hawkins, U.S. Creek Indian agent. William was a lawyer by education, but he spent about two years with his uncle at the Indian agency in Georgia before completing legal studies in Philadelphia. He was elected to the lower house of the North Carolina legislature for two consecutive terms beginning in 1804 and again from 1809 to 1811. In 1811, the legislature elected him governor, a post he held throughout the War of 1812.

Hawkins favored the declaration of war against Britain and consistently supported the Madison administration during the conflict. He successfully held at bay a small antiwar faction in North Carolina while keeping the militia at the ready, and mustered the state's forces when Madison called up the country's militia. When the British under Adm. Sir George Cockburn conducted a raid at Ocracoke on 12 July 1813, landing to capture Portsmouth, Hawkins personally led troops to New Bern. Despite the British departure from North Carolina, he was vigilant about the state's coastal defense for the remainder of the war.

After the war, his uncle Benjamin's death in 1816 required Hawkins to travel frequently to Georgia to help resolve the family estate. While on one such journey, he died in Sparta, Georgia, on 17 May 1819.

—*Jeanne T. Heidler and David S. Heidler*

See also: Hawkins, Benjamin
Further Reading
Lemmon, Sarah McCulloh. *Frustrated Patriots: North Carolina and the War of 1812.* Chapel Hill: University of North Carolina Press, 1973.

HAYNE, ARTHUR P.
d. 1867
U.S. officer

Born in South Carolina, Arthur P. Hayne entered the army in 1808 as a first lieutenant of the Light Dragoons. By 1809 he had risen to captain; he was promoted to major in 1813 and colonel in 1814. In 1814, he served under Maj. Gen. Andrew Jackson as the general's aide and inspector general.

Hayne accompanied Jackson on the march that culminated in the taking of Spanish Pensacola in November 1814. While in Pensacola, Jackson received the pleas of the citizens of New Orleans begging him to bring his army there. Jackson sent Colonel Hayne ahead to inspect the defenses of New Orleans and ready a report for Jackson's arrival.

Hayne departed in mid-November 1814. Upon his arrival in New Orleans, he traveled to the mouth of the Mississippi, where he decided it was impractical to establish batteries to stop the British from entering the river. His reports recommended that Jackson depend on Fort St. Philip as his first line of defense against the British advance.

Hayne continued to advise Jackson about New Orleans's defenses after the general arrived on 1 December. He remained attached to Jackson's command until the end of the war and remained in the army after it. He remained Jackson's friend, often informing him about public opinion and the state of the army after the general entered politics. In 1836, Hayne resigned his commission to become an Alabama planter. He died in Alabama in 1867.

—*Jeanne T. Heidler and David S. Heidler*

See also: Jackson, Andrew; New Orleans, Battle of; Pensacola, West Florida
Further Reading
"Journal of the Defense of New Orleans." *Niles' Weekly Register* 7 (1814–1815): 374–379.

HENRY, JOHN
1776?–1853
British agent

John Henry was born in Ireland, emigrated to New York when he was 21, and served briefly as an officer in the U.S. Army until about 1800. He then lived in Cambridge, Massachusetts, where he apparently knew prominent figures such as Elbridge Gerry. By the time he moved to Windsor, Vermont, some two years later, Henry had married and fathered two daughters. He studied law at Windsor and continued his associations with eminent social and political people. In 1805, he moved again, this time to Montreal, where he was to begin a relationship with British authorities that would eventually place him at the center of a controversy known as the Henry-Crillon Affair.

Between 1808 and 1809, Henry was employed by the governor-general of Canada, Sir James Craig, to travel around the northern United States gauging political sentiments in that region. Henry reported in letters to Craig, assessing anti-British feelings and offering his opinions about the likelihood of war between the United States and Great Britain. Evidently, Henry was also to explore the possibility of recruiting disaffected Federalists to the British cause.

When Henry returned to Canada, he requested that Craig pay for his services, and when the governor remitted only a fraction of what Henry thought he was owed, he departed for Great Britain to press his claims. Having no better luck with the Foreign Office, Henry sailed for Boston in 1811. On the voyage, he met a man claiming to be a French nobleman, the Comte Edouard de Crillon, who was actually a commoner named Soubiran. The Frenchman, after hearing Henry's tribulations, suggested that they sell Henry's papers to the U.S. government. Henry agreed, and during the early months of 1812, he remained in Boston while Soubiran traveled to Washington to negotiate with Pres. James Madison and Secretary of State James Monroe. The three eventually arrived at the sum of $50,000, which Madison and Monroe obtained by committing the government's entire secret service fund.

With this newfound wealth, Henry soon left the country. The Madison administration thought it had purchased valuable information to discredit Federalist opponents in New England and to foment national anger against the British. Yet copies of Henry's letters contained little to incriminate any specific Federalists, so publishing the documents hurt Madison and Monroe more than their opponents, especially when the price for them was revealed. The letters did have the effect, however, of further inflaming public opinion against the British.

Henry's career following this episode continued its strange and exotic course. He became an agent for King George IV in 1820, with the task of compiling a dossier on Queen Caroline for the king's divorce. He also maintained some ties with his old New England friends, especially Henry Cary, who bequeathed an annuity to Henry's heirs, evidently for kindness shown to Cary during the financial exigencies caused by the embargo of 1807. In any event, Henry's enjoyment of material comforts and his familiarity with the highest echelons of European society suggest that his covert services to the British crown did not end with his investigation of Caroline. Henry died in 1853 after many years of residence in Paris.

—*Jeanne T. Heidler and David S. Heidler*

Further Reading
Morison, Samuel Eliot. "The Henry-Crillon Affair." In *By Land and by Sea: Essays and Addresses by Samuel Eliot Morison.* New York: Alfred A. Knopf, 1954: pp. 265–286.

HILLABEE MASSACRE, CREEK TERRITORY
18 November 1813

During Andrew Jackson's 1813 campaign against the Creek Indians, considerable jealousy existed between Jackson, who commanded the West Tennessee Militia, and Gen. John Cocke of the East Tennessee forces. Their rivalry, in no small measure, led to the Hillabee Massacre on 18 November. Jackson's campaign against the Creeks to that date had been remarkably successful and had culminated in a major U.S. victory at the Battle of Talladega. This battle had all but crippled the Creeks' ability to continue the war and had seriously weakened their morale. A significant number of Creek warriors at Talladega were from the Hillabee towns along the Tallapoosa River in present-day Cherokee County, Alabama, and both Jackson and Cocke contemplated marching against these towns to retaliate for the Hillabee Creeks' role in the war.

Realizing that they were hopelessly outgunned and that their efforts against Jackson's army were futile, on 17 November the principal chiefs of the several Hillabee towns dispatched a released prisoner named Robert Grierson (sometimes spelled Grayson) to Jackson to ask for terms. Grierson informed the general that the Hillabee Creeks had been so badly beaten at Talladega that they were willing to abandon the war altogether. Jackson at once agreed to stop the fighting if the Hillabees would surrender the main instigators of the war and return all property—including, of course, slaves—that had been seized from white settlers. Grierson assured Jackson that the Hillabee chiefs would agree to his terms and that their participation in the war would end. Early the following morning, Jackson sent a message to General Cocke informing him of the Hillabees' capitulation and suggesting that their two armies unite in a final campaign against the remaining Creek resistance.

But Jackson's message to Cocke was useless, for Cocke had already ordered that the Hillabee towns be destroyed. He had previously learned of Jackson's success at Talladega, and not wishing to leave all of the glory to the West Tennesseans, Cocke determined that the Hillabees had to be punished for their role in the war. Consequently, he ordered Gen. James White to take the field with cavalry and a small detachment of Cherokee allies under Col. Gideon Morgan. White's first targets were the towns of Little Oakfusky and Genalga, both of which were left smoldering and abandoned.

During the early morning hours of the 18th, White sent part of his cavalry and all of Morgan's Cherokees to surround the principal town and prepare to attack the village at dawn. The Creeks of Hillabee, believing that the Americans had accepted their peace offer and would not attack, were caught completely by surprise when White's soldiers and the Cherokee warriors opened fire at first light. In the brief battle that followed—during which the Creeks showed little if any resistance—64 Creek warriors were killed and 29 were taken prisoner. White also forced 237 Creek women and children to return with him to Fort Armstrong, where General Cocke eagerly awaited news of the battle.

General Jackson was incensed that Cocke had taken the offensive without first coordinating his movements with the West Tennessee Militia. Of course, Cocke had no way of knowing that Jackson had made peace with the Hillabees just one day previous to White's attack. Nevertheless, had the two men been able to join forces earlier, the massacre could have been avoided. The remaining Hillabee Creeks who had escaped the massacre felt altogether betrayed by Jackson and thereafter resolved to fight to the death. These Creeks were indeed some of the last combatants of the Creek War.

General Cocke resisted joining forces with Jackson until just ten days before the majority of his 1,450 soldiers' terms had expired. Jackson, who experienced chronic supply shortages throughout the entire campaign against the Creeks and could hardly provide for more men, immediately dismissed the East Tennesseans and summarily sent Cocke back to Tennessee in quest of badly needed supplies. Jackson was from then on the supreme commander during the Creek War, and it was he who led the U.S. forces against the remaining hostile Creeks.

—Robert Saunders, Jr.

See also: Cocke, John; Creek War
Further Reading
Owsley, Frank Lawrence, Jr. *Struggle for the Gulf Borderlands: The Creek War and the Battle of New Orleans, 1812–1815.* Gainesville: University Presses of Florida, 1981.

HILLYAR, JAMES
1769–1843
Royal Navy officer

Born on 29 October 1769 at Portsea to James Hillyar, a navy surgeon, Hillyar served from 1779 to 1801 with Admiral Hotham in the Mediterranean, with Lord Hood aboard *Victory,* and as a lieutenant on *Aquilon* in March 1794. Hillyar fought at the famous 1st of June battle in 1794 and served off Barcelona during September 1800 and in gunboats at Aboukir Bay during March 1801. He achieved the rank of post-captain on 29 February 1804 and served with Lord Nelson off Toulon and Cádiz. As captain of the *Phoebe* (36 guns), he took part in the captures of Mauritius in December 1810 and Tamatave and Java in September 1811.

In 1813, Hillyar undertook a secret mission "to annihilate any [American] settlement . . . on the Columbia River . . . and . . . neighboring Coasts." Sailing with the sloops *Cherub* (18 guns) and *Racoon* (18 guns) to South America, Hillyar dispatched the *Racoon* under Capt. William Black to the northwest coast of North America in February 1814. Hillyar then, in company with the *Cherub,* blockaded the U.S. naval frigate *Essex* in Valparaíso, Chile. In spite of Hillyar's promise to respect Chilean neutrality, he finally moved to engage the *Essex* when, crippled by a storm while trying to escape, she sought refuge in Chilean coastal waters.

The *Essex* was rated at 32 guns, but she was carrying 46 that could throw a broadside of 676 pounds. The *Phoebe* also was carrying 46, with a broadside of 488 pounds, but both her and the *Cherub*'s guns (broadside of 348 pounds) carried a much longer range than those of the U.S. ship did. In the ensuing action on 28 March 1814, the *Phoebe* and *Cherub* cut *Essex* to ribbons at long range. Of the *Essex*'s 255-man crew, 58 were killed, 65 wounded, and 31 missing, with 161 taken prisoner. On the *Phoebe,* 4 were killed and 7 wounded; on the *Cherub,* 1 was killed and 3 were wounded. Hillyar returned to England, anchoring the *Phoebe* and *Essex* at Plymouth on 13 November 1814.

—Frederick C. Drake

See also: *Essex* versus *Phoebe* and *Cherub*; Porter, David, Jr.
Further Reading
Hussey, John A., ed. *The Voyage of the "Racoon": A "Secret" Journal of a Visit to Oregon, California and Hawaii, 1813–1814* [by Francis Phillips]. San Francisco: Book Club of California, 1958.
Long, David F. "David Porter: Pacific Ocean Gadfly." In *Command under Sail: Makers of the American Naval Tradition 1775–1830*, James C. Bradford, ed. Annapolis, MD: Naval Institute Press, 1985: 173–198.
Mahan, Alfred Thayer. *Sea Power in Its Relations to the War of 1812.* 2 vols. Boston: Little, Brown, 1905.
Porter, David. *Journal of a Cruise Made to the Pacific Ocean . . . 1812, 1813 and 1814.* 2 vols. Philadelphia: Bradford and Inskeep, 1815.

"Sir James Hillyar" (obituary). *Annual Register* 85 (1843): 279–280.

HINDMAN, JACOB
d. 1827
U.S. officer

Jacob Hindman was born in Maryland. He entered the U.S. Army in May 1808 as a second lieutenant in the Fifth U.S. Infantry. He made first lieutenant two years later, and on 2 July 1812 he transferred to the Second U.S. Artillery as a captain. During the U.S. attack on Fort George in May 1813, Hindman was reportedly the first American to reach the Canadian side of the river. He then commanded a company in an infantry assault on the fort to capture its guns before the evacuating defenders could spike them. At Stoney Creek the following month, Hindman again commanded an artillery company fighting as infantry, which was not at all uncommon for U.S. artillery to do during the War of 1812.

On 26 June 1813, Hindman became the major of the Second Artillery and held that position until the regiment was merged into the Corps of Artillery on 12 May 1814. Under the new Corps of Artillery, Hindman was one of its 12 battalion commanders. Hindman's 300-man unit was probably the only battalion of the Corps of Artillery that fought as a battalion during the war. During the 1814 Niagara Campaign, Hindman's company commanders included Nathan Towson, Thomas Biddle, John Ritchie, and Alexander Williams. All four companies were armed with 17-pounders.

Hindman was the senior artilleryman during the U.S. defense of Fort Erie. While most of his company commanders commanded batteries in the outer works, Hindman commanded the line of guns in the fort itself. When 100 Royal Artillerymen seized one of the fort's bastions in the early hours of 15 August 1814, Hindman led an unsuccessful assault to dislodge them. Hindman later received a brevet promotion to lieutenant colonel for "gallant conduct in the defense of Fort Erie."

Hindman was the best and perhaps the only truly effective U.S. artillery battalion commander of the War of 1812. Yet, he was overshadowed by his subordinate, Nathan Towson. At the end of the war, Hindman received one more brevet to colonel on 17 May 1815, for "meritorious services." While Towson went on to more prominent achievements, Hindman remained a major in the Corps of Artillery. He stayed in that position until the artillery reorganization of 1 June 1821, when he became the major of the newly organized Second U.S. Artillery. Ironically, the colonel of that regiment was Nathan Towson. Hindman was still holding the position of major when he died on 17 February 1827.

—*David T. Zabecki*

See also: Artillery
Further Reading

Armstrong, John. *Notices of the War of 1812.* New York: Whiley and Putman, 1840.
Birkhimer, William E. *Historical Sketch of the Organization, Administration, Materiel, and Tactics of the Artillery of the United States Army.* Washington, DC: Chapman, 1884.
Heitman, F. B. *Historical Register of the United States Army.* Washington, DC: National Tribune, 1890.
Powell, William. *List of the Officers of the Army of the United States, 1777–1900.* New York: L. R. Hammersley, 1900.

HOLCROFT, WILLIAM
1778–1858
British officer

William Holcroft entered the Royal Military Academy at Woolwich as a gentleman cadet on 5 January 1795 and moved out on 4 April of the following year as a second lieutenant in the Royal Artillery. He served in Sir Eyre Coote's 1798 expedition to Flanders, where he was both mentioned in official dispatches and taken prisoner. In 1807, as a captain lieutenant, he participated in the siege of Copenhagen.

On 4 June 1808, Holcroft received his promotion to captain and assumed command of a company of the Royal Artillery's Fourth Battalion, which was then stationed at Montreal. Shortly after that his company moved to Quebec, where it remained until June 1812. When the company transferred to Kingston, just a few weeks before the start of the War of 1812, it was the only Royal Artillery company in Upper Canada. In July, the unit moved to a forward position on the U.S. border at Fort George.

For most of the next two years, Holcroft's company constituted the whole of the Royal Artillery in Upper Canada and the far west. True to the Royal Artillery's motto, "Ubique," it was everywhere, however. The first three months of the war saw the company conducting split operations across a 200-mile front. A sergeant, two gunners, and two 6-pounders from Holcroft's company supported the

British attack on Fort Michilimackinac, Michigan Territory, in July. At about the same time, Lt. Felix Troughton took three 6-pounders, two 3-pounders, and a detachment of 25 men from the company to Detroit with Gen. Isaac Brock.

Holcroft, meanwhile, stayed at Fort George with his remaining gunners and trained the militia artillery units Brock had put under his direction. When Gen. Stephen Van Rensselaer attacked at Queenston Heights, Upper Canada, that October, Holcroft and his two 6-pounders moved down from Fort George with the British reinforcement column and took up a forward position where they could engage the U.S. boats coming across the river. Using spherical case (shrapnel) shot for the first time in the war, Holcroft's gunners sank at least three boats and silenced a U.S. battery on the opposite side of the river. With Holcroft's guns dominating the crossing site, few additional U.S. troops got across, and those already on the far shore were cut off. Winfield Scott and his force of 950 on the Canadian side of the river later surrendered to Maj. Gen. Roger Sheaffe. Holcroft received a brevet promotion to major for his role at Queenston Heights.

Holcroft was Gen. John Vincent's artillery commander during the U.S. attack on Fort George in May 1813. The garrison mounted only eight guns and two mortars, which were manned by the militia artillery under Holcroft's general direction. Holcroft's regulars manned five 6-pound field pieces positioned to the front of the fort. On the morning of 26 May, the Americans opened up from Fort Niagara with 25 guns and mortars firing red-hot shot and shell. The following day, an additional 51 guns from 16 U.S. naval vessels joined the cannonade. Heavily outnumbered and outgunned, Vincent abandoned Fort George and withdrew his forces to Burlington. Holcroft's company formed part of the rearguard during the retreat.

During the British attack at Stoney Creek in June, Holcroft and a small group of his artillerymen accompanied the assaulting party. Their mission was to turn any captured guns on the Americans, but the totally surprised U.S. troops fled too quickly into the darkness. Holcroft's men did capture four guns and nine horses with harnesses. They dismounted and spiked two of the guns, and took a 6-pounder and a 5.5-inch howitzer back to the British camp.

Holcroft's last action of the war came in December 1813, when he commanded his company during the British night attack on Fort Niagara. A few days later, Holcroft returned to England on sick leave, but his company remained in the Niagara Peninsula and participated in the siege of Fort Erie.

In June 1815, Holcroft's company left Canada after serving there for 24 years. In February 1816, the company moved to the Woolwich garrison, but that May, Holcroft exchanged companies with Capt. J. Brome of the Third Battalion and joined his new unit in France. Holcroft's new company remained in France until November 1818, when it too moved back to Woolwich. Holcroft retained command of that company until his retirement on 22 July 1821. He died at Sevenoaks on 30 January 1858.

On 28 September 1816, the Board of Ordnance awarded Holcroft's company the honor title "Niagara," declaring that it was "in consideration of the gallantry and good conduct shown by that company in the capture of Niagara, on 19 December 1813, and during the whole of the subsequent campaign in the Niagara frontier." In the British army today, Holcroft's company is represented by 52 (Niagara) Field Battery, Royal Artillery.

—*David T. Zabecki*

See also: Artillery; Sheaffe, Roger Hale; Stoney Creek, Battle of; Vincent, John

Further Reading

Browne, James Alex. *England's Artillerymen*. London: Hall, Smart, and Allen, 1865.

Duncan, Francis. *History of the Royal Regiment of Artillery*. Vol. 2. London: John Murray, 1873.

Homfray, Irving L. *Officers of the British Forces in Canada during the War of 1812*. Welland: Tribune Print, 1908.

Hughes, Maj. Gen. B. P. *Honor Titles of the Royal Artillery*. Woolwich: Royal Artillery Institute, 1974.

Kane, John. *List of Officers of the Royal Regiment of Artillery*. 4th ed. London: Royal Artillery Institute, 1890.

Nicolson, G.W.L. *The Gunners of Canada*. Toronto: McClelland and Stewart, 1967.

HOPKINS, SAMUEL
1753–1819
U.S. militia officer; congressman

Born to Dr. Samuel Hopkins and Isabella Taylor Hopkins in Albemarle County, Virginia, Samuel Hopkins began his military career during the American Revolution. Serving under George Washington in New Jersey, New York, and Pennsylvania, Hopkins was made lieutenant colonel of the Tenth Virginia Regiment in 1779 and was captured in the siege of Charleston, South Carolina, in 1780. Soon exchanged, he served the remainder of the war as the colonel of the First Virginia Regiment.

Following the Revolution, Hopkins settled near the Green River in Kentucky. Before the outbreak of the War of 1812, he was active in Kentucky state and Democratic

Republican politics and supported the policies of the Jefferson and Madison administrations.

War with Great Britain in 1812 made Hopkins's military experience valuable to his adopted state. Kentucky governor Isaac Shelby placed Hopkins, now a brigadier general, in command of an irregular force of Kentuckians gathering at Fort Vincennes. Eventually Hopkins's ranks would swell to over 4,000 poorly trained and equipped volunteers. Ordered by the commander of the Northwestern Army, Maj. Gen. William Henry Harrison, to assume command of Indiana and Illinois territorial forces, Hopkins began planning an expedition against Kickapoo and Peoria Indian villages on the Illinois River.

Hopkins gathered 2,000 mounted riflemen for a march to Fort Harrison and then crossed the Wabash River in the middle of October 1812. From the start of this expedition, morale among the poorly trained, undisciplined volunteers was low. Poor guides and prairie fires set by the Indians caused spirits to plummet further, and the men finally demanded a retreat. Hopkins dismally followed his men back to Fort Harrison, where he discharged them.

Not wanting to end his military career on such a note, Hopkins recruited another force of approximately 1,200 men and marched them in early November 1812 against Prophet's Town, Indiana Territory. Finding this place and two other villages deserted, Hopkins ordered their destruction. After brief skirmishes with the few Indians in the vicinity, bad weather and poor supplies forced the army to return to Fort Harrison. Hopkins could claim this expedition, at least, as a limited success, and he chose to retire from military service.

Beginning in 1813, Hopkins spent the remainder of the war as a congressman from Kentucky. In Congress, he championed an energetic prosecution of the war. He retired following the war and died at his home in Henderson, Kentucky, in 1819.

—*Jeanne T. Heidler and David S. Heidler*

Further Reading
Gilpin, Alec R. *The War of 1812 in the Old Northwest.* East Lansing: Michigan State University Press, 1958.

HORNET VERSUS PEACOCK
24 February 1813

The 18-gun U.S. Navy sloop *Hornet*, commanded by Capt. James Lawrence and carrying a complement of 144 men, set sail for the South Atlantic with the 44-gun frigate *Constitution* (Commodore William Bainbridge) on 26 October 1812. She blockaded the Brazilian port of Bahia, where the treasure-laden 18-gun sloop *Bonne Citoyenne* was anchored, from 13 December 1812 to 24 January 1813, when the British warship *Montagu* (74 guns) arrived to lift the blockade. The *Hornet*, greatly outgunned, was driven into the harbor and escaped that night in the darkness. The *Constitution* had previously returned to the United States.

The *Hornet* then prowled the northern coast of Brazil for a month and captured several merchantmen. On 24 February, while chasing another British brig off the mouth of the Demerara River, she came upon the anchored brig *Espiegle* (18 guns). While the *Hornet* positioned to attack this new foe—the *Espiegle* was behind a bar—the Royal Navy brig *Peacock* (18 guns), under Capt. William Peake and with a crew of 122 men, bore down upon her. In a lopsided 15-minute engagement, the *Hornet* gained a favorable position and so damaged the *Peacock* (which had been previously employed as a yacht) that she began to sink. Every effort was made to save the *Peacock*, but in the end she took nine Britons and three Americans down with her.

Total British casualties were estimated at 21 dead, including the captain, and 30 wounded. U.S. losses were four dead and two wounded. The *Hornet* then set sail for the United States. Her officers were each awarded a silver medal, and Captain Lawrence a gold medal by an act of Congress.

—*Robert J. Bunker*

See also: Lawrence, James
Further Reading
Barnes, James. *Naval Actions of the War of 1812.* New York: Harper and Brothers Publishers, 1896.
Gleaves, Albert. *James Lawrence: American Man of Energy.* New York: G. P. Putnam's Sons, 1904.
Peabody Museum of Salem. *"Don't Give Up the Ship": A Catalogue of the Eugene H. Pool Collection of Captain James Lawrence.* Salem: Peabody Museum, 1942.

HORNET VERSUS PENGUIN
23 March 1815

The U.S. sloop *Hornet*, rated at 18 guns (Master Commandant James Biddle, 142 men), along with the 18-gun sloop *Peacock* and brig *Tom Bowline*, a storeship, ran the blockade of New York harbor on 22 January 1815. They were on a course toward Tristan da Cunha to rendezvous with the frigate *President* (44 guns), which had left earlier and, as yet unknown to them, had been captured by the British.

The *Hornet* arrived at Tristan da Cunha on 23 March 1815, about a week after the *Peacock* and *Tom Bowline*, which had been driven away by a storm. Upon the *Hornet's* arrival, a sail was discovered, which turned out to be the brig HMS *Penguin* (18 guns) under Capt. James Dickenson and with a crew of 132 men. This brig was on a special mission to hunt down the U.S. privateer *Young Wasp*.

The two vessels soon engaged in a 22-minute action early that afternoon. Superior Yankee gunnery may have prompted the *Penguin* to ram the *Hornet*, thus entangling the two ships. Neither side boarded, however, and the *Hornet* lurched ahead, tearing apart the foremast and bowsprit of the *Penguin* as the two vessels separated. It was during this entanglement that Commandant Biddle was seriously wounded when he attempted to confirm that the British had surrendered.

The *Hornet* then maneuvered into position to discharge another broadside into the now disabled *Penguin* as she struck her colors. British losses were 14 killed and 28 wounded; U.S. losses were one killed and ten wounded. The *Penguin* was scuttled soon after this action. The contest took place after the war had formally ended and was the last true naval combat of the War of 1812.

—*Robert J. Bunker*

Further Reading

Long, David Foster. *Sailor-Diplomat: A Biography of Commodore James Biddle, 1783–1848*. Boston: Northeastern University Press, 1983.

HORSESHOE BEND, BATTLE OF
27 March 1814

The Battle of Horseshoe Bend was the climactic act in the Creek War between the United States and elements of the Creek Nation. Having raised a militia army composed of mostly Tennessee and Georgia volunteers, Tennessee militia major general Andrew Jackson and John Coffee had pushed deep into Creek country, inflicting serious defeats on the warring Red Sticks at Tallushatchee on 3 November and Talladega on 9 November 1813. The militiamen had crushed the military strength of the Indians, having killed or captured nearly 500, and Jackson made plans to finish off the enemy Creeks in the coming months. Jackson discovered, however, that most of his men would be leaving for home within days, their terms of enlistment having expired. Low on supplies and with his troops departing, Jackson had to retreat to Fort Strother on the Coosa River to regroup and await reinforcements before delivering his planned knockout blow. During the winter of 1813–1814, Jackson's army dwindled to just 150 men.

Meanwhile, Red Sticks under William Weatherford (Red Eagle) and Josiah Francis regained their strength and began to threaten Jackson's position, while other Red Sticks constructed a stronghold town at Tohopeka in a horseshoe-shaped bend of the Tallapoosa River. The Indians numbered some 1,500 warriors altogether, including some African American slaves.

In early January 1814, Jackson began receiving reinforcements. A contingent from Tennessee allowed him to lash out at the Creeks, defeating them at Emuckfau on 22 January and at Enitachopco Creek on 24 January. Meanwhile, a brigade of Tennessee mounted militia under the command of Gen. John Coffee arrived, as did volunteers from Georgia, Cherokees and Creeks allied with the United States, and the 600-man 39th U.S. Infantry. This new army numbered nearly 4,000 men. Jackson ordered his troops underway for Tohopeka in late February.

The Red Sticks had prepared their defenses well. Warriors had constructed a breastwork of dirt and pine logs across the neck of land on the horseshoe bend peninsula, including firing steps and loopholes. Behind this defense, the Indians had built their village but had been careful to keep the dense tangle of underbrush and briers in place. The terrain itself aided the defense: a series of ravines and stands of pine covered the site, providing many fallback positions. The only weakness lay to the rear—the Tallapoosa River—but its swift and deep currents deterred a serious approach from that direction. Satisfied that any attack would have to come from the direction of the breastwork, the Red Sticks had lined their canoes along the riverbank, should retreat become necessary.

Jackson's army arrived in the vicinity of Tohopeka in the third week of March. Allied Indians reported the defensive layout of the Red Stick citadel, remarking on the vulnerable river approach. Jackson ordered Coffee to lead his men and the allied Indians across the river to block the Red Stick escape route, while he led the remaining militia and the 39th Infantry into position opposite the log wall. Jackson sent messengers in to request the removal of women and children, but Red Sticks rejected the offer. Meanwhile, enterprising Cherokee auxiliaries swam the Tallapoosa and paddled away in the Red Stick canoes. The Red Sticks, now stranded, secreted their wives and families among the huts of Tohopeka, then grimly moved to man their defenses.

Jackson began the battle in earnest at about 10:00 A.M. with an ineffective bombardment of the Red Stick breastwork. Meanwhile, General Coffee's Indians sent showers of flaming arrows into the village, setting the town ablaze. After two hours, Jackson unleashed the 39th Infantry, which conducted a bayonet charge against the Red Stick stronghold. After severe hand-to-hand fighting, the Indians abandoned their wall, with the Americans in close pursuit. The Creeks made several stands among the pines and ravines, but gradually gave ground until they were pinned against the Tallapoosa River. Surrounded, the remaining Red Stick warriors attempted to flee, many being killed while swimming the river.

Casualties were appalling and were made worse by the systematic killing of Red Sticks for hours after the actual battle. The Red Sticks lost 917 people—almost all of their warriors. U.S. troops captured more than 300 women and children. Jackson's army fared better, with 47 killed and 159 wounded among the regulars and militia; his Indian allies had 23 killed and 47 wounded.

The major fighting in the Creek War ended with this battle. U.S. troops raided other Creek towns until remaining Red Sticks surrendered that summer or fled to Florida. On 9 August 1814, Creeks—including allies and enemies—signed the Treaty of Fort Jackson, which ceded some 23 million acres of Creek territory to the United States. Horseshoe Bend not only provided the Americans with a much-needed morale boost, but it also added luster to Andrew Jackson's growing national reputation.

—*Donald S. Frazier*

See also: Creek War; Fort Jackson, Treaty of; Jackson, Andrew; Red Sticks
Further Reading
Heidler, David S., and Jeanne T. Heidler. *Old Hickory's War: Andrew Jackson and the Quest for Empire.* Mechanicsburg, PA: Stackpole Books, 1996.
Owsley, Frank Lawrence, Jr. *Struggle for the Gulf Borderlands: The Creek War and the Battle of New Orleans, 1812–1815.* Gainesville: University Presses of Florida, 1981.

HOUSTON, SAM
1793–1863
U.S. officer, politician

Born on 2 March 1793 in southwestern Virginia, Sam Houston moved as a teenager to Blount County, Tennessee. Farming, with its incessant chores, both irritated

Sam Houston

and bored him, and he occasionally ran away to live among the Cherokees in the years leading up to the War of 1812.

Upon the declaration of war against Great Britain, Houston briefly served in the Tennessee militia. Later, he joined the Seventh U.S. Infantry in Knoxville, then transferred to the 39th U.S. Infantry. In this regiment, Houston advanced to the rank of third lieutenant and served from 1813 to 1814 in East Tennessee. In 1814, this unit reinforced Andrew Jackson's army, which was forming to fight the Red Stick faction of the Creek Nation. Traveling from Fort Strother, the 39th U.S. Infantry along with Creeks, Cherokees, and militia from Georgia and Tennessee pushed the Red Sticks into their stronghold on the banks of the Tallapoosa River at Tohopeka, or Horseshoe Bend. In a savage, day-long battle, Ens. Sam Houston received several serious wounds but emerged as one of the heroes of the fight, having led several charges against Red Stick positions. His injuries kept Houston out of the rest of the war, but his heroism brought him to the attention of Andrew Jackson, who became Houston's political mentor.

Houston successfully parlayed his battlefield reputation into success in state politics, starting in 1818; he went on to serve two terms in the U.S. Congress, starting in 1824. In 1827, Tennesseans elected Houston governor.

His future appeared bright until 1829, when he resigned his office after his marriage of only four months disintegrated under mysterious circumstances. Houston went on a drinking binge and disappeared into the West. He settled with his old friends among the Cherokees who had previously been removed to Indian Territory (now Oklahoma). Here, Houston took an Indian wife and pursued private life while earning two Cherokee names: "The Raven" in polite company and "Big Drunk" behind his back. Before long, Houston began serving in a political role for his adopted people, going to Washington, D.C., as their advocate.

In 1832, after one such trip, Houston returned to the Cherokee Nation and then abandoned not only his native trappings but his Cherokee family as well by moving into Texas, then a part of the Mexican state of Coahuila. By 1833, he had become politically active in the Anglo-Texican dispute with the Centralist government of Mexico and, upon the opening of hostilities, received appointment to general of the forces of the Republic of Texas. In that capacity, Houston won the Battle of San Jacinto on 21 April 1836, although he also received a wound in his ankle that nearly proved fatal. Texans elected Houston president to two nonconsecutive three-year terms in 1836 and again in 1842. His policy, while in office, was to maintain a caretaker government until the United States could annex the republic.

In between terms, he married Margaret Lea in 1840 and would eventually father eight children. When Texas became a state in 1846, Houston went to Washington, D.C., as one of its senators, where he served until 1859. In 1860, Houston won election as governor of Texas, but secessionists removed him from that office at the time of Texas's secession in 1861. Houston then retired to his home in Huntsville, Texas, where he died.

—*Donald S. Frazier*

Further Reading

Bruce, Henry. *Life of General Houston, 1793–1863.* New York: Dodd, Mead, 1891.

Houston, Samuel. *The Autobiography of Sam Houston.* Norman: University of Oklahoma Press, 1954.

James, Marquis. *The Raven: A Biography of Sam Houston.* Indianapolis: Bobbs-Merrill, 1953.

Kinney, Joseph Lair. "The Life of Samuel Houston." Master's thesis, Lafayette College, 1934.

Smith, Beatrice Merle. "Sam Houston in Tennessee." Master's thesis, University of Tennessee, 1932.

Wright, Frances Fitzpatrick. *Sam Houston, Fighter and Leader.* Nashville: Abingdon Press, 1953.

HUGHES, CHRISTOPHER
1786–1819
Lawyer; soldier; diplomat

Born in Baltimore, Hughes attended the College of New Jersey and later studied law. He served as captain of artillery at Fort McHenry, 1812–1813. On 2 February 1814, Pres. James Madison appointed him secretary of the joint mission to negotiate a treaty of peace and commerce with Great Britain. He sailed on 25 February aboard the frigate *John Adams,* with two commissioners, Henry Clay and Jonathan Russell, and attaché William Shaler. After the *John Adams* landed at Gothenburg, Sweden, on 11 April 1814, Hughes briefly visited London.

Hughes arrived at Ghent on 7 July and initiated contact with British agent Anthony St. John Baker to propose a meeting between British and U.S. representatives. From 9 July until 24 December 1814, when the treaty was signed, the U.S. ministers employed Hughes as the recording secretary for their sessions. Hughes referred to himself as "the fly on the coach wheel." He broke down weeping before Henry Clay when he discovered he was not only not commended for his work but was not even mentioned in the dispatches to Madison's government.

Hughes and Henry Carroll, Clay's private secretary, each took copies of the treaty to the United States. Hughes journeyed via Paris to inform U.S. minister William Harris Crawford and sailed from Bordeaux. He arrived at New London, Connecticut, on 1 March 1815 and learned that Carroll had arrived aboard the British sloop of war *Favourite* on 11 February to deliver his copy. Hughes subsequently had ten days of discussions with Madison and Secretary of State James Monroe. He later served as a diplomat in Central America.

—*Frederick C. Drake*

Further Reading

Dunham, Chester G. "Christopher Hughes, Jr. at Ghent, 1814." *Maryland Historical Magazine* 66 (fall 1971): 288–299.

———. "The Diplomatic Career of Christopher Hughes." Ph.D. dissertation, Ohio State University, 1968.

Engleman, Fred L. *The Peace of Christmas Eve.* New York: Harcourt, Brace and World, 1962.

Reeves, James S., ed. "A Diplomat Glimpses Parnassus: Excerpts from the Correspondence of Christopher Hughes." *Michigan Alumnus* 41 (1934): 189–201.

Whitely, Emily S. "Between the Acts at Ghent." *Virginia Quarterly Review* 5 (1929): 18–30.

HULL, ISAAC
1773–1843
U.S. Navy officer

A Connecticut Yankee and son of a Revolutionary brigadier general, rotund Isaac Hull went to sea at an early age and already had qualified as a ship's master by 1798. He accepted a proffered commission as a lieutenant in the then-forming U.S. Navy in March of that year and was assigned to the USS *Constitution*. During nearly four years on the frigate, he rose from fourth to first lieutenant, serving on the *Constitution* throughout the Quasi-War with France.

Detached from the *Constitution* in April 1802, he next became first lieutenant of the light frigate *John Adams* but soon was ordered to command the schooner *Enterprise*. He sailed her to the Mediterranean, then exchanged commands with Stephen Decatur, taking over the brig *Argus*. Promoted to master commandant in May 1804, he was one of Commodore Edward Preble's "boys" and in early 1805 provided the naval command component in the successful taking of Derne, Libya, by General William Eaton. Ordered home later that year after peace had been gained, he was promoted to captain in April 1806.

With the increased activity for the navy during James Madison's administration, Hull gained command of the frigates *Chesapeake* and *President* successively, but in June 1810 exchanged commands with Commodore John Rodgers when his senior indicated he preferred the *President* to the *Constitution*. Hull took his new command to northern Europe on a diplomatic voyage in 1811 and returned in time to have his ship overhauled just before the war broke out on 18 June 1812.

Under orders to join Rodgers at New York, Hull sailed from Chesapeake Bay early in July and in the middle of the month found himself pursued by a British squadron off the New Jersey coast. Exhibiting imaginative seamanship that included having oarsmen in boats tow and kedge the becalmed *Constitution*, he outwitted and finally outdistanced his pursuers in a chase that lasted nearly three days. With the British between him and New York, he headed for Boston, where he expected to find orders awaiting him.

Boston provided Hull with more supplies, but no orders awaited him. Deciding to get to sea before the British could bottle him up in that port, he headed for Canadian waters early in August. After causing a considerable stir off the Gulf of Saint Lawrence by destroying enemy merchant ships not yet aware that war had been declared, Hull headed for the Bermuda area. There he planned to stalk British ships homeward bound from the West Indies.

On 19 August 1812, he met HMS *Guerrière* (38 guns), a frigate. In a battle lasting nearly four hours from first shot to last, Hull managed to pound his foe to pieces in a clumsily fought engagement that gave Hull all the luck. The captain himself apparently realized this, for his published action report glossed over much of the fight and made it appear he had won in just 35 minutes! The public was thrilled, Hull was lionized, and Congress awarded him a gold medal. For the remainder of the war, he was content to command navy yards.

In the postwar years, like most of his contemporaries, Hull remained ashore, either at a navy yard or on the Board of Naval Commissioners. In the mid-1820s, he commanded the Pacific Squadron on the west coast of South America for three years and in the late 1830s, the Mediterranean Squadron for another three. He returned home in poor health, fatter than ever and going blind. He died ashore in Philadelphia in 1843. The Hulls (he married Ann McCurdy Hart in 1813) had no children.

Five ships in the U.S. Navy have been named for Commodore Hull.

—*Tyrone G. Martin*

See also: *Constitution* versus *Guerrière*

Further Reading
Fowler, William M., Jr. *Jack Tars and Commodores*. Boston: Houghton Mifflin Company, 1984.
Maloney, Linda M. *The Captain from Connecticut: The Life and Naval Times of Isaac Hull*. Boston: Northeastern University Press, 1986.
Martin, Tyrone G. *A Most Fortunate Ship*. Annapolis, MD: Naval Institute Press, 1980. Reprinted Norwalk: Easton Press, 1990.
———. "Isaac Hull's Victory Revisited." *The American Neptune* 47 (winter 1987): 14–21.

HULL, WILLIAM
1753–1825
U.S. general; governor of Michigan Territory

Born on 24 June 1753, William Hull graduated from Yale College at age nineteen. His distinguished Revolutionary War record included action at White Plains, Trenton, Princeton, Saratoga, Monmouth, and Stony

Point. Ending his service as a lieutenant colonel, he helped organize the Society of Cincinnati after the war. A strong Republican, Hull was named governor of Michigan Territory by Pres. Thomas Jefferson in 1805. His tenure in this office was marked by his winning land concessions from the northwestern Indians and earning their enmity.

With war imminent in March 1812, Hull proposed to Secretary of War William Eustis that a strong force be dispatched to Detroit with the intent of defending Michigan from the British and the Indians, gaining control of Lake Erie, and conquering Upper Canada. Despite these confused objectives and misgivings about Hull's fitness, Pres. James Madison offered Hull the rank of brigadier general and command of a "North Western Army." Leaving Washington on 9 April, Hull, who retained his position as governor, spent much of May raising and training an army of 1,200 Ohio militiamen organized into three regiments and commanded by Cols. Duncan McArthur, James Findlay, and Lewis Cass. Hull's force was soon augmented by 800 regulars of the Fourth U.S. Infantry, veterans of Tippecanoe, under Lt. Col. James Miller.

From the beginning, Hull's army was plagued by tensions between the regulars and the militia, by squabbles among the ranking colonels over precedence, and by distrust in the capabilities of their leader. Suffering from the residual effects of a stroke in 1811 and aged 59, Hull cut an unimpressive figure. An eyewitness characterized the general as a "short, corpulent, good natured old gentleman, who bore the marks of good eating and drinking." In one particularly embarrassing episode, Hull lost control of his horse, which bolted across the front of his army drawn up for review.

On the move in early June, Hull's force advanced slowly as it cut a road from Urbana through the Ohio wilderness. To safeguard his supply route, Hull built blockhouses, although manning their garrisons weakened his army. To speed his march, Hull dispatched much of his baggage and his military papers by the schooner *Cuyahoga* to Detroit; unfortunately, the British captured this vessel with its invaluable intelligence.

Hull reached Detroit on 5 July; one week later, he entered Canada. Despite the refusal of about 200 Ohio militiamen to cross the Detroit River, Hull's army outnumbered the British defenders by a two-to-one margin. His vainglorious proclamation of 12 July further weakened the British defenders by inducing about 500 Canadian militia to desert, and Cass soon advanced to within 4 miles of the key British position, Fort Malden.

Despite this promising beginning, the U.S. offensive stalled. Hull failed to follow up his initial successes and instead spent two weeks drilling his troops and readying his artillery for an assault on Malden. Concerned that his supply line, which stretched for 200 miles, might become vulnerable to attack by Indians in northern Ohio and to harassment by British naval vessels along the Lake Erie shoreline, Hull further weakened his drive by sending out two detachments to meet an expected relief column. But Hull's units were driven back to Detroit by the British and Tecumseh's raiders. Then, on 29 July, Hull learned of the fall of the U.S. garrison at Michilimackinac. Fearing an Indian onslaught, Hull abandoned his offensive on 8 August, pulled his command back to Detroit, and contemplated further retreat to Ohio. Hull's troops, disheartened by his retrograde steps, threatened mutiny; some of the Ohio officers circulated a petition "requesting the arrest and displacement of the General."

Unfortunately for Hull, his British opponents received strong reinforcements when the energetic Isaac Brock reached Amherstburg on 13 August. Brock crossed into U.S. territory 3 miles below Detroit and, playing on Hull's fears of Indian atrocities, demanded the surrender of the Detroit garrison. Hull rejected Brock's initial demand and, in a final, futile effort to prevent defeat, sent out McArthur and Cass to meet and bring in the relief column.

Increasingly concerned about the fate of the many civilians in the fort (including his daughter and her two children), Hull broke down physically and mentally. Perhaps under the influence of liquor or drugs, his speech became incoherent; he stuffed wads of chewing tobacco into his mouth until spittle ran down his clothing; and he crouched low as he moved about the fort.

Without consulting his officers, on 16 August Hull surrendered the garrison, including the McArthur and Cass detachments. He later claimed that a shortage of powder and "only a few days' provisions" forced him to capitulate. In fact, Brock found at Detroit rations adequate for almost a month's resistance, 5,000 pounds of gunpowder, 33 cannon, and 2,500 muskets. In the words of an authority, "Hull's surrender was one of the most disgraceful episodes in the military history of the United States." His capitulation opened the entire Northwest to enemy incursions.

Although Brock allowed the 1,600 militiamen to return home, Hull and the 582 U.S. regulars were sent as prisoners to Quebec. Paroled, Hull then faced court-martial in 1814 for neglect of duty, cowardice, and treason. The court found Hull guilty of the first two indictments and sentenced him to death but recommended mercy because of his "revolutionary services and his advanced age." President Madison approved the verdict and recommendation. Hull remains the only U.S. general officer ever condemned to death.

Hull wrote two exculpatory works: *Defence of Brig. Gen.*

Wm. Hull (1814) and *Memoirs of the Campaign of the Northwestern Army of the United States: A.D. 1812* (1824). To his credit, Hull was generous in these books to his troops and subordinate officers. Following the war, Hull lived with his family in Newton, Massachusetts, until his death on 29 November 1825. His nephew, Isaac Hull, won fame as commander of the frigate *Constitution* in its famous victory over HMS *Guerrière* on 19 August 1812, three days after William Hull's surrender of Detroit.

—*Malcolm Muir, Jr.*

See also: Detroit, Surrender of
Further Reading
Bender, Mark L. "The Failure of General William Hull at Detroit in 1812 and Its Immediate Effects upon the State of Ohio." Master's thesis, Kent State University, 1971.
Gilpin, Alec R. *General William Hull and the War on the Detroit in 1812.* Ann Arbor: University of Michigan, 1949.
Hull, William. *Memoirs of the Campaign of the North Western Army in the Year 1812: Addressed to the People of the United States.* Boston: Boston Statesman, 1824.
Rauch, Steven J. "The Eyes of the Country Were upon Them: A Comparative Study of the Campaigns of the Northwestern Army Conducted by William Hull and William Henry Harrison, 1812–1813." Master's thesis, Eastern Michigan University, 1992.

HUMPHREYS, JOSHUA
1751–1838
Philadelphia shipbuilder; designer of U.S. frigates

Joshua Humphreys began his experience with warships during the Revolutionary War, with the 1775 conversion of five merchant ships to warships for the Continental Navy. He is also credited with the design of the three classes of 13 frigates (five of 32 guns, five of 28 guns, and three of 32 guns). One of these ships, the *Randolph,* was built at the Wharton and Humphreys shipyard in 1776.

One letter signifies his major contribution to the six famous frigates of the late 1790s and early 1800s. This letter, dated 6 January 1793 and addressed to Sen. Robert Morris, conveyed his reasons for building large frigates armed with 24-pounders, as opposed to building frigates with 18-pounders, as the British did. Though inferior in numbers, these ships' size, armament, and construction would overmatch those of a European enemy. The ships would be built with timbers equal in dimensions to those of a 74-gun ship. The six frigates so constructed contributed greatly to the beginnings of the U.S. Navy.

A drawing of a 44-gun frigate, *Terrible,* attributed to Joshua Humphreys, was used as the basis for copies sent to yards building the frigates. Also, the incorporation of live oak in their construction added to the strength and durability of the ships. Live oak came from the fever-ridden tidelands of Georgia. Timothy Pickering, secretary of war (January 1795–January 1796), introduced a note of irony when he stated that had the difficulties encountered in obtaining these timbers been fully known, only two of the six frigates would have been completed.

—*Richard Eddy*

See also: Frigate, Evolution of the
Further Reading
Carson, Hampton L. *The Humphreys Family of Haverford and Philadelphia.* Lancaster: Wickersham Press, 1922.
Paullin, Charles O. "Early Naval Administration under the Constitution." *U.S. Naval Institute Proceedings* 32 (1906).
Smelser, Marshall. *Congress Founds the Navy, 1787–1798.* Notre Dame, IN: University of Notre Dame Press, 1959.
Symonds, Craig. *Navalists and Anti-Navalists: The Naval Debate in the United States, 1785–1827.* Newark, DE: University of Delaware Press, 1980.

I

ILLINOIS TERRITORY

The Illinois Territory, established in 1809, included the present-day states of Illinois and Wisconsin. The territory's white settlers were in a particularly precarious position during the War of 1812 for the following reasons: the territory's geographical location on the far frontier caused problems of communication and of supply; the region contained a substantial number of Indians who were not reconciled to white encroachments on their land; in 1810, the area had a population of only 12,282 settlers, with almost all of them being situated in the territory's southern portion in a narrow strip along the Mississippi River; and there was an insufficient regular army force to provide protection.

Unrest among the tribes had been increasing during the first decade of the 1800s, partly due to the growing influence of the Shawnee brothers, Tenskwatawa (the Prophet) and Tecumseh. Bands of Potawatomi recently had moved down the Illinois River to establish villages at and near Peoria, where Chief Main Poc, an adherent of Tenskwatawa, held sway. Kickapoo villages were also located there near Lake Michigan. In 1811, the deterioration of relations between the Indians and whites accelerated. Several Americans were killed by raiding parties, and property was stolen.

The Battle of Tippecanoe, in present-day Indiana, technically was a victory for the military force led by Indiana territorial governor William Henry Harrison. Nevertheless, it served only to heighten Indian animosity and further unrest throughout the region north of the Ohio River. The Kickapoo in particular raided homesteads in the Illinois Territory during the winter and spring of 1812, the most notorious incident being the massacre of the O'Neal family near Peoria. In April 1812, Potawatomi warriors struck farms in southeastern Illinois on the Wabash River, killing 14 whites.

Illinois territorial governor Ninian Edwards, whose previous military experience was limited to peacetime militia activities, was in charge of military operations during the war's first year. Forts and blockhouses were constructed to combat the Indian threat, and companies of mounted rangers and militia were raised to patrol between the forts and in advance of the settlements. Fort Russell, built near present-day Edwardsville, served as a military headquarters. During the spring of 1812, Edwards had 2,000 men eligible for militia duty, but that number was decreasing daily as many citizens headed east for safety.

During the summer of 1812, the focus briefly shifted north to the Chicago area, where Fort Dearborn was situated in an exposed and dangerous position. After Gen. William Hull, who was at Detroit, sent orders to evacuate Fort Dearborn, Capt. Nathan Heald began the long journey to Fort Wayne on 15 August with 54 regulars and 12 militia, plus women and children. A large Indian force, composed primarily of Potawatomi, killed the majority of soldiers and some of the women and children a short distance from Fort Dearborn. On the following day, 16 August, General Hull's surrender of Detroit to the British and Indians marked the low point of the war in the West for the United States.

Determined to regain the offensive in the Illinois Territory, Americans planned a two-pronged campaign against the increasing number of hostile warriors gathered at the villages near Peoria. Gen. Samuel Hopkins was to march with 2,000 Kentucky volunteers up the Wabash River to Fort Harrison and then westward across the prairies to the Illinois River, while Governor Edwards and Col. William Russell were to lead Illinois militia and U.S. Rangers north from Fort Russell. Hopkins's troops, however, refused to continue after they had traveled six days from Fort Harrison. In the meantime, Edwards and Russell departed Fort Russell on 18 October with less than 400 militia and U.S. Rangers. After destroying two Kickapoo villages on a branch of the Sangamon River, they made an early morning attack on a Kickapoo and Potawatomi village in which they claimed to have killed 24 to 30 Indians. Following this action, the Indians abandoned the Peoria area and established new villages to the north.

In March 1813, Edwards reported additional murders of settlers to the secretary of war and stated that he had between 300 and 400 militia volunteers patrolling on horseback. In addition, 17 small forts were constructed along the dangerous frontier between the Mississippi and Kaskaskia Rivers. By April, Indian raiding had become particularly intense in the Kaskaskia area.

Also in March 1813, Benjamin Howard, governor of the Missouri Territory, was appointed brigadier general in the regular army with responsibility for Missouri and Illinois territories. During September 1813, Howard sent 1,300 troops up the Illinois River to Peoria, where Fort Clark was built. Patrols from the fort reduced the number of raids against the settlements and kept the hostile warriors concentrated to the north.

In June 1814, William Clark, the newly appointed governor of Missouri, led an army of 260 regulars and militia northward and established Fort Shelby at Prairie du Chien, in what is now Wisconsin. This post subsequently was retaken and was renamed Fort McKay by the British and Indians in July. In the meantime, a U.S. force of approximately 100 regulars and rangers commanded by Maj. John Campbell was en route by water from St. Louis to reinforce Prairie du Chien. On 21 July, these boats were attacked by Sac, Fox, and Kickapoo Indians several miles above the mouth of the Rock River, near present-day Rock Island, Illinois. The troops were forced to retreat with considerable losses. General Howard then sent Maj. Zachary Taylor up the Mississippi River on 6 September with 350 troops, but Taylor was also forced to turn back after engaging a superior force of Indians and a detachment of British artillery near the mouth of the Rock River.

With this action, the major fighting of the War of 1812 in the Illinois Territory ended. Throughout the region, an extended period of peace would follow, only to be interrupted briefly by the limited Winnebago War in 1827 and by the Black Hawk War in 1832.

—*Robert J. Holden*

See also: Detroit, Surrender of; Edwards, Ninian; Harrison, William Henry; Tippecanoe, Battle of; Wayne, Fort

Further Reading

Edmunds, R. David. *The Potawatomis, Keepers of the Fire.* Norman: University of Oklahoma Press, 1978.

Gilpin, Alec R. *The War of 1812 in the Old Northwest.* East Lansing: Michigan State University Press, 1958.

Hagan, William T. *The Sac and Fox Indians.* Norman: University of Oklahoma Press, 1958.

McAfee, Robert B. *History of the Late War in the Western Country: Comprising a Full Account of All the Transactions in That Quarter, from the Commencement of Hostilities at Tippecanoe, to the Termination of the Contest at New Orleans on the Return of Peace.* 1816. Reprint, Bowie, MD: Heritage Books, 1994.

Reynolds, John. *My Own Times: Embracing Also the History of My Life.* Chicago: Fergus Printing Company, 1879.

IMPRESSMENT

One of the major stated causes for the U.S. declaration of war against Great Britain, impressment was the practice of stopping U.S. merchant vessels to seize suspected deserters from the Royal Navy. It was a practice as old as the Royal Navy, but the British Admiralty had especially resorted to impressment early in the French revolutionary wars, when desertions threatened to deprive British ships of sufficient crews. British seamen often could not resist the better pay and softer conditions enjoyed by U.S. sailors either in the merchant marine or in the U.S. Navy.

Yet the Royal Navy took few pains to distinguish between U.S. citizens and British deserters disguising themselves as such. Casting their impressment net ever wider, Royal Navy officers adhered to a principle of inalienable British citizenship that disregarded U.S. naturalization papers. In any event, many such naturalization documents were forgeries, easily obtained and hence casually dismissed by Royal Marines searching U.S. crews. Impressment netted perhaps as many as 6,000 sailors from U.S. merchant shipping. The result was that the British most likely impressed a significant number of actual U.S. citizens while reclaiming deserters. The numbers were immaterial, however, for the U.S. reaction to one violation was as reflexive as to 100. Outraged honor was to make "sailors' rights" as important as "free trade" among the frictions that led to war.

The most notorious case of impressment was the *Chesapeake-Leopard* Affair, in which four sailors were removed from a U.S. naval vessel in June 1807. The resulting tumult nearly caused war with Britain five years earlier than its actual occurrence. The British government disavowed the *Leopard*'s action, ordered the complete cessation of waylaying U.S. naval ships, and subsequently had the Royal Navy exercise greater care in searching U.S. merchant vessels. Yet the return of two of the *Chesapeake* sailors (one of the four was a Briton who was executed for desertion, and the other, an American, died in a Halifax hospital) was delayed until 1811, thus reviving the 1807 incident and reanimating the impressment debate in such a way as to have it figure prominently as a spur to war.

Consequently, impressment was more a perceived problem in the years immediately preceding the War of 1812, but circumstances such as those surrounding the *Chesapeake* incident kept the issue alive and troublesome nonetheless. Both Madison's and Congress's explanations for going to war in 1812 listed it with neutral rights violations as the main British transgressions. When the British repealed the Orders in Council at almost the same time as the U.S. declaration, only the doctrine of impressment officially remained as an obstacle to peace. The British refused to abandon the doctrine, however. In the summer of 1814, U.S. peace commissioners at Ghent finally removed the U.S. demand that Britain formally forsake impressment, mainly because its practice had assuredly ceased upon the conclusion of the European war. Thus, the Treaty of Ghent would not contain any mention of impressment, even though it had been one of the two main causes for U.S. belligerence two and half years earlier.

—*Jeanne T. Heidler and David S. Heidler*

See also: Chesapeake-*Leopard* Affair
Further Reading

Frater, Daniel A. "Impressment in the 18th Century Anglo-American World." Master's thesis, Queens College, New York, 1995.

Jackson, Scott Thomas. "Impressment and Anglo-American Discord, 1787–1818." Ph.D. dissertation, University of Michigan, 1976.

Thompson, David Scott. "'This Crying Enormity': Impressment as a Factor in Anglo-American Foreign Relations." Master's thesis, Portland State University, 1993.

Zimmerman, James F. *Impressment of American Seamen.* New York: Columbia University Press, 1966.

INDIANA TERRITORY

The general peace that prevailed throughout the region north of the Ohio River following the U.S. victory in the 1794 Battle of Fallen Timbers began to deteriorate during the first decade of the 1800s. Contributing to this situation was Indiana territorial governor William Henry Harrison's aggressive land acquisition activity through treaty making. Another factor was the growing antipathy toward the Americans of the Shawnee brothers, Tenskwatawa (the Prophet) and Tecumseh, who were rising to prominence during this period. In 1808, the Prophet moved his headquarters from Greenville in western Ohio to the Tippecanoe River in Indiana Territory, where he established Prophet's Town, near present-day Lafayette, Indiana. This growing assemblage of angry warriors from many tribes presented an ominous situation for Harrison.

During 1810 and 1811, raiding became common in both the Indiana and Illinois territories. These incursions prompted Harrison's Tippecanoe campaign. While Tecumseh was attempting to rally the Indians south of the Ohio River, Harrison departed Vincennes with a force of 1,000 regulars, militia, and volunteers in late September 1811. Stopping to build Fort Harrison at present-day Terre Haute, they arrived on 6 November at Prophet's Town. Arranging to confer with the Indians the next day, Harrison set up camp nearby.

At 4:00 A.M. on 7 November 1811, the Indians attacked. Harrison quickly rallied the troops and successfully held his ground. Charge and countercharge followed, with the Americans eventually remaining in possession of the field. Harrison's army suffered 60 killed and twice that number wounded. The Indian losses were unknown. The Indians abandoned Prophet's Town, and Harrison destroyed it the next day.

Following Harrison's narrow victory in the Battle of Tippecanoe, the Indians resumed their raids on the frontier settlements during the ensuing spring of 1812, and even the inhabitants of Vincennes believed they were threatened. Many of the settlers from the outlying areas fled southward; the remainder erected forts and blockhouses. Small contingents of regular army soldiers garrisoned at Fort Knox near Vincennes, Fort Wayne at the present-day city of that name, and Fort Harrison at what is now Terre Haute could provide only a minimal amount of protection. Because of the Indiana Territory's relatively sparse population, its territorial militiamen were used throughout the war primarily for defense; offensive operations within the territory were performed by regular army troops and militia from Kentucky and Ohio.

Encouraged by the capitulations of Fort Michilimackinac, Fort Dearborn, and Fort Detroit soon after war was declared, the Indians launched a major offensive throughout the Indiana Territory during the late summer of 1812. On 3 September, a raiding party attacked the small settlement of Pigeon Roost, in present-day Scott County, killing 24 men, women, and children.

The next day, a large force of Potawatomi, Winnebago, Kickapoo, Shawnee, and Miami Indians attacked Fort Harrison. After the Indians had set fire to one of the blockhouses, Capt. Zachary Taylor rallied his garrison's 50 men. While successfully fighting the flames, they managed to keep the Indians at bay with well-directed gunfire.

Fort Wayne, around which hostile Indians had been collecting since late August, was struck on 5 September. An estimated 500 warriors, primarily Ottawa and Potawatomi tribesmen, assailed the fort several times before settling in for a siege. Learning of the beleaguered fort, Governor

Harrison, with a brevet rank of major general in the Kentucky militia, led a force of more than 2,000 troops to the post's relief. Finding that the warriors had dispersed, Harrison sent detachments to destroy the nearby Indian villages and food supplies.

Soon afterward, Harrison learned of his appointment as brigadier general in the regular army, with the responsibility for retaking Detroit. Prior to moving toward Lake Erie, Harrison made arrangements for the protection of the Indiana Territory. Col. William Russell was placed in command of the regular army troops, including U.S. Rangers. During October, Samuel Hopkins, general of the Kentucky militia, led a force of 2,000 mounted Kentucky volunteers to Vincennes and then further along the Wabash River to Fort Harrison, Indiana Territory. His orders were to march from there north and west to the Indian villages on the Illinois River in the Peoria region. Then he was to coordinate an attack in conjunction with forces led from Illinois Territory settlements. Hopkins's troops, however, refused to proceed further after they had traveled six days on the Illinois prairies.

Returning to the Indiana Territory with his troops, Hopkins reorganized his force. With 1,200 Kentucky infantry militia and a small contingent of regulars, plus 50 mounted rangers and scouts, he left Fort Harrison on 11 November. Moving up the Wabash, his men destroyed deserted villages. On 22 November, a contingent of the army suffered the loss of 18 men killed and wounded in an ambush. Cold weather forced the command to march south to Vincennes.

Unwilling to leave an unknown number of potentially hostile warriors behind his lines, in December 1812 Harrison sent Lt. Col. John B. Campbell with 600 regular army and militia troops from western Ohio into Indiana Territory to attack the Indians on the Mississinewa River southwest of Fort Wayne. After the soldiers destroyed three villages on 16 December, the Indians launched a surprise charge upon the U.S. camp just before dawn the next morning. This offensive was repulsed after hard fighting and considerable casualties had occurred on both sides. Campbell's troops slowly made their way back to Ohio in bitterly cold weather.

Early in 1813, Indiana Territory acting governor John Gibson ordered a chain of blockhouses built north of the line of settlement and garrisoned by militia. Patrols were conducted by the militia and U.S. Rangers. Small-scale raiding by the Indians started in February, much of it in the vicinity of the little settlement of Vallonia, approximately 90 miles east of Vincennes. Two expeditions were sent from Vallonia during June and July to destroy the Indian towns throughout that area. The second and larger force,

led by Colonel Russell, marched 500 miles and burned numerous villages, but it saw no Indians.

By the summer of 1813, most of the hostile Indians had departed the Indiana Territory. The major focus of the War of 1812 in the West henceforth would occur to the northeast and to the northwest of the Indiana Territory.

—*Robert J. Holden*

See also: Harrison, William Henry; Hopkins, Samuel; Miami Indians; Tecumseh; Tenskwatawa; Tippecanoe, Battle of

Further Reading

Anson, Bert. *The Miami Indians*. Norman: University of Oklahoma Press, 1970.

Barnhart, John D., and Dorothy L. Riker. *Indiana to 1816: The Colonial Period*. Indianapolis: Indiana Historical Bureau, 1971.

Cleaves, Freeman. *Old Tippecanoe: William Henry Harrison and His Times*. New York: Charles Scribner's Sons, 1939.

Gilpin, Alec R. *The War of 1812 in the Old Northwest*. East Lansing: Michigan State University Press, 1958.

McAfee, Robert B. *History of the Late War in the Western Country: Comprising a Full Account of All the Transactions in That Quarter, from the Commencement of Hostilities at Tippecanoe, to the Termination of the Contest at New Orleans on the Return of Peace*. 1816; reprint, Bowie, MD: Heritage Books, 1994.

INDIANS
See individual nations by name

INGERSOLL, CHARLES JARED
1782–1862
Lawyer; congressman; historian

Born in Philadelphia, Ingersoll was a scion of a prominent New England family. His grandfather, Jared Ingersoll (1722–1781) was a Loyalist, and his father, Jared Ingersoll (1749–1822) was a national political figure. A prominent lawyer, the father had been a delegate to the Constitutional Convention of 1787 and was later Gov. DeWitt Clinton's running mate against Madison in the election of 1812. Initially a Federalist, Charles Ingersoll was to become a strong supporter of both Jefferson and Madison, as well as, later, a Jacksonian Democrat.

In 1796, he entered Princeton but failed to graduate. Educated by private family tutors, he was admitted to the

Pennsylvania bar at the age of 20 in 1802. Before establishing one of the most extensive legal practices in Philadelphia, he undertook a European tour. This tour left a deep impression upon him, and on his return to the United States he rejected the politics of his father and became a staunch supporter of Jefferson. He favored war against Britain following the *Chesapeake-Leopard* Affair in 1807 and penned some of the earliest American pamphlets promoting the choice for war, a war he would term the "second edition of American independence."

His first pamphlet, *A View of the Rights and Wrongs, Power and Policy, of the United States of America*, was published in November 1808. Rejecting the pro-British attitude of the Federalists, the work reviewed the historical rights of neutral commerce. As he explained to Rufus King, Ingersoll wrote that it was his wish to put country before party, and he was critical of the Federalist tendency to admire everything English at the expense of the United States. The work was widely read, and Ingersoll followed it with another in 1810 defending the U.S. character and extolling national self-respect in the strangely titled *Inchiquin, the Jesuit's Letters*. Revealing himself as the author to James Madison, Ingersoll declared that he desired to reverse the "want of self-respect" he found among his countrymen following his return from Europe. Though widely attacked by the *British Quarterly Review*, the pamphlet helped win him the Republican nomination for the Pennsylvania State Assembly, a race he lost amid the bitter Philadelphia city politics of 1811. In the autumn of the following year, however, he won the seat for the First Congressional District of Pennsylvania.

Taking his seat in May 1813, Ingersoll proved a strong supporter of energetic prosecution of the war. He defended bills to encourage enlistments, to raise revenue by increased taxation, to charter a national bank, and even to institute militia conscription. His prominence as a War Hawk soon won him congressional recognition; he became a member of the Foreign Relations Committee as well as the chairman of the Judiciary Committee. An able orator, he challenged Daniel Webster in his first set debate in January 1814, an exchange that won him the hatred of Webster.

When U.S. military defeats led to Republican political reverses, Ingersoll lost his seat in 1814. Returning to his Philadelphia law practice, he remained active in state politics. In 1830–1831, he served for one term as a state assemblyman. Losing a bid for the U.S. Senate, he also unsuccessfully ran for Congress in 1836 and 1838. As a nationalist, he initially supported the Bank of the United States, but having later embraced Jacksonian Democracy, he came to reject the bank's interference in national politics.

In 1840, he again won election to the House and kept his seat until 1849. Noted for his championing of causes

that were unpopular among his constituents, he was a voice for moderation during the rising abolitionist crusade against the South. As chairman of the Committee of Foreign Affairs from 1843 to 1847, he proved to be an ardent annexationist regarding Texas and supported James Polk over the Oregon boundary dispute.

Ingersoll wanted to write a history of the War of 1812, but the pressure of his legal practice and later congressional career prevented its completion. He had frequently contacted Madison with the project in mind, and in May 1836, just before Madison's death, he visited the former president to collate opinions and sources for such a history. An admirer of the Scottish historian Thomas Carlyle, Ingersoll finally published a four-volume history of the war under two separate titles: *Historical Sketch of the Second War between the United States of America and Great Britain*, two volumes published in 1845 and 1849; and *History of the Second War between the United States of America and Great Britain*, two volumes published in 1852.

Ingersoll's style will perhaps strike the modern reader as somewhat turgid, but his work is noteworthy for providing a contemporary analysis of the war's causation. A year before his death, he published his political *Recollections*, but his work on the dispute with Britain over the Oregon and Maine boundaries remained unpublished at the time of his death. A man of outstanding ability, a sound orator, and a constant patriot who championed causes unpopular with his constituents, Ingersoll died on 14 May 1862.

—*Rory T. Cornish*

See also: Clinton, DeWitt
Further Reading
Avery, Lillian Drake. *A Genealogy of the Ingersoll Family in America, 1629–1925: Comprising Descendants of Richard Ingersoll of Salem, Massachusetts, John Ingersoll of Westfield, Mass., and John Ingersoll of Huntington, Long Island*. New York: Grafton Press, 1926.

Meigs, William M. *The Life of Charles Jared Ingersoll*. Philadelphia: J. B. Lippincott, 1897.

IROQUOIS, THE SIX NATIONS OF THE

The Iroquois entered into the War of 1812 and quit it for their own reasons: to preserve their lands and their prosperity in a conflict that threatened both. The Iroquois Confederacy, which had reached its height of power in the seventeenth century with the subjugation of all neighboring tribes, was clearly in decline by 1812. The Treaty of Paris of 1783 left the Iroquois straddling the new international border. They distrusted both the British and the Americans.

Although most Iroquois still occupied portions of their traditional lands in central New York, several settlements existed in Lower and Upper Canada. Fewer than 3,000 Iroquois resided in a handful of villages in Lower Canada. After the American Revolution, the Iroquois chief, Thayendanegea, whose English name was Joseph Brant, brought hundreds of his followers into Upper Canada to escape the retribution of the new U.S. government. Brant settled his people, mostly Iroquois but with a sprinkling of Delawares and others, black and white as well as native, on a grant of land along the Grand River just west of the Niagara Peninsula. By the start of the War of 1812, the Grand River settlement was home to 1,800 people, who lived in log cabins rather than the traditional longhouses. On the U.S. side, most Iroquois lived along the Finger Lakes, but the Niagara Frontier was home to two settlements—the Tuscarora village perched atop the Niagara escarpment and the large Seneca reservation along Buffalo Creek. These New York Iroquois, like those in Canada, had adopted some European ways, particularly in cultivation and animal husbandry.

Because their villages were in areas long overhunted, the Iroquois depended upon government gifts of iron tools, cloth, and food for their survival. Still, they could take pride in the knowledge that the Iroquois Confederacy had never been conquered. Although Britain and the United States might claim sovereignty over the land, it was clear to the Iroquois that they were an independent nation who, if they chose to fight, would do so under their own war chiefs and as independent allies.

The British were eager to secure an alliance with the Canadian Iroquois. Even before war was declared, Isaac Brock approached the Grand River Indians for assistance. Teyoninhokarawen, whose English name was John Norton, was the acknowledged leader, and he wholeheartedly supported the British cause. He feared Americans and worried that they could gain control of Upper Canada. Yet not all Grand River Indians saw any advantage in risking their lives for the British, particularly when so many of the U.S.-born residents of the province openly supported a U.S. victory. Nonetheless, a hard core of Grand River warriors followed Norton throughout the war.

In June 1812, Little Billy, a chief of the New York Iroquois, pleaded with his Grand River cousins for Iroquois neutrality. He argued that the Iroquois cause could not be furthered by alliance with either the British or Americans,

who had both proven to be inconstant allies. The Iroquois on both sides of the Niagara River reached an agreement. Norton could fight for the British and the New York Iroquois would maintain their neutrality. In no event would Iroquois fight Iroquois. The U.S. government initially supported Iroquois neutrality, but the Seneca feared that this policy would change if the Americans were denied a quick victory.

The Iroquois concept of warfare was so foreign to European custom that it was scorned by many whites. Because the native economy remained at a subsistence level, the death of a warrior was calamitous for his extended family, and the loss of a large number of adult males could prove disastrous for the community. A warrior would fight to prove his courage, but he saw no point in dying. After demonstrating his bravery in a single encounter, he would feel no duty to remain for the duration of a long campaign. Central to Iroquois justice was the imperative to avenge death, which could lead to a widening circle of vengeance. A band of natives might join a white expedition with only the motive to avenge a killing. After exacting retribution, the party would return to its village, much to the consternation of the white commander. Thus a native warrior, faithful to the logic of his own world, appeared both fierce and ill-disciplined to his European or U.S. allies.

Nevertheless, the Iroquois contribution to the British war effort was substantial. The Grand River Indians terrified the Americans on Queenston Heights, and this played no small part in their surrender. In 1813, Iroquois warriors were present in small numbers at the battles for York and Fort George and at Chrysler's Farm and Châteauguay. Five hundred Iroquois, mostly from Lower Canada, surrounded and forced the surrender of a larger body of U.S. regulars at Beaver Dams in June. The U.S. commander mentioned his fear of massacre as his reason for quitting the fight.

Then, in July, the British raided Black Rock. This was too close to Seneca land, and when Young King, a Seneca chief, led his warriors to repulse the British, the Iroquois truce quickly unraveled. The New York Iroquois declared a defensive war against the British; they would fight to defend U.S. territory. Some Seneca volunteered to cross into Canada and in August, near Fort George, the inevitable happened—New York Iroquois clashed with warriors from Grand River. The truce was over.

In December, when the British launched their attacks along the Niagara Frontier, Canadian Iroquois burned the Tuscarora village. The Seneca of western New York sought revenge, and in July 1814, 600 Iroquois under their chief Sagoyewatha, known to whites as Red Jacket, invaded Canada as part of Jacob Brown's Left Division. On 5 July, in the forest opposite Chippewa Plain, Iroquois fratricide was frightful. Over 80 Iroquois from both sides died in those woods, largely killed by each other. The extent of the bloodletting induced an enduring peace within the Iroquois nation. Except for a few small bands that continued to fight, the Six Nations of the Iroquois withdrew from the war, their Confederacy intact.

—*Richard V. Barbuto*

See also: Niagara Campaigns
Further Reading

Benn, Carl. "Iroquois Warfare, 1812–1814." In R. Arthur Bowler, ed., *War along the Niagara.* Youngstown, NY: Old Fort Niagara Association, 1991: 61–76.

Horsman, Reginald. "The Role of the Indian in the War." In Philip P. Mason, ed., *After Tippecanoe: Some Aspects of the War of 1812.* East Lansing: Michigan State University Press, 1963: 60–77

Parker, Arthur C. "The Senecas in the War of 1812." In *Proceedings of the New York State Historical Association*, vol. 15. Albany: New York State Historical Association, 1916: 78–90.

Stanley, G.F.G. "The Significance of the Six Nations' Participation in the War of 1812." *Ontario History* 55 (1963): 215–231.

ISLE AUX NOIX

This small island south of Montreal, close to the U.S. border, was a key element in the defensive strategy of Sir George Prevost, governor-general of Canada. Situated on the upper Richelieu River, Isle aux Noix's fortifications were built during the French and Indian War and the Revolutionary War and rebuilt in the War of 1812. The base constituted a plug in the Champlain bottle and a threat to the communications of any U.S. force using the Champlain Valley to attack Montreal. Approaches to Montreal were also guarded by forts at St. John's and Chambly.

On 2 June 1813, British gunboats operating from Isle aux Noix captured two U.S. sloops, *Growler* and *Eagle.* Lt. Sidney Smith commanded the *Growler*, and Sailing Master Jarius Loomis and Midshipman Horace Sawyer the *Eagle.* Having advanced over the Canadian border and into the Richelieu River to chase British gunboats, they proceeded as far as Ash Island 6 miles downstream and fought a spirited engagement before being overwhelmed by artillery, gunboats, and musket fire from British forces under the command of Maj. George Taylor of the 100th regiment, the British commander at Isle aux Noix. Each sloop carried 11 guns; a total of 12 18-pounders and 10 32-pounders, and had a combined crew of 112 men, including 34 infantrymen under Capt. Oliver Herrick and Ens. Worthington Dennison. The garrison at the British fort suffered three men wounded, one severely, and the attacking forces lost one killed and eight severely wounded. The British officers applauded the Americans' gallant struggle but thought Smith imprudent to hazard the dominion of Lake Champlain by risking an engagement in the narrows before the Isle aux Noix's batteries.

Furthermore, the action opened the way for a counterattack on U.S. lake bases and merchant shipping in late July and early August. Maj. Gen. Roger H. Sheaffe ordered Thomas Everard, with 50 seamen from HMS *Wasp* at Quebec and 30 from the troopship *Dover,* to join Lt. Col. John Murray and 940 men at Isle aux Noix. They were to create a diversion from Isle aux Noix and to destroy public buildings, military stores, and vessels at Plattsburg, New York, and Burlington, Vermont.

Isle aux Noix was also the key shipbuilding center for British efforts on Lake Champlain, employing a master shipbuilder and several carpenters, who were aided by troops cutting timber. The operation attracted considerable trade from Vermont timber merchants. While the British were planning the Murray-Everard raid, they also arranged to build another vessel at the Isle. When Simmons, the master builder from Montreal, came to Isle aux Noix to assess the value of the two U.S. sloops, he informed Everard that it should be possible to complete a 16-gun brig at the site in six weeks. Major General Sheaffe, in command at Montreal while Prevost was visiting Kingston, also thought two gunboats would be a useful addition, but finding officers and crews for them posed the chief obstacle. In late 1813, Capt. Daniel Pring arrived to command the naval forces at the Isle, and eventually the construction of a larger vessel—a small frigate—was authorized. It was still under construction when U.S. forces entered into a shipbuilding race for the control of Lake Champlain. The Battle of Lake Champlain on 11 September 1814 was the result.

By the beginning of February 1815, Master Commandant Thomas Macdonough suspected that the British at Isle aux Noix were planning to build another naval force. Timber for three frigates, three brigs, and several gunboats was being collected, and as additional carpenters arrived there, Macdonough tried to discover if the timber was being prepared for shipment to Lake Ontario or for use on Champlain. The British frigate's frames were partially up when news of peace came.

Nevertheless, Macdonough employed local builder Matthew Sax to watch the British at Isle aux Noix and report on their progress. Sax visited the British site and recounted seeing "preparations for the next Campaign[.] they have 12 New Gallies on the Stocks of a large Size and 3 Large Vessels. the Keels laid and the Stem and Stern posts up." Once peace came to the border in March 1815, he revealed that "all is now stoped [*sic*] they did not expect to be on the Lake till Sept." Isle aux Noix remained as a defensive fortification guarded by Fort Lennox.

—*Frederick C. Drake*

Further Reading

Bellico, Russell P. *Sails and Steam in the Mountains: A Maritime and Military History of Lake George and Lake Champlain.* New York: Purple Mountain Press, 1992.

Charbonneau, Andre. *The Fortifications of Ile aux Noix: A Portrait of the Defensive Strategy on the Upper Richelieu Border in the 18th and 19th Centuries.* Canadian Heritage Parks Canada, 1994.

Crisman, Kevin J. *The Eagle: An American Brig on Lake Champlain during the War of 1812.* Shelburne, VT, and Annapolis, MD: New England Press and Naval Institute Press, 1987.

Wood, William H. *Select British Documents of the Canadian War of 1812.* Vol. 2. Toronto: Chaplain Society, 1920–1928: 221–225, 229–230.

IZARD, GEORGE
1776–1828
U.S. officer

George Izard was born to Ralph Izard and Alice De Lancey Izard outside of London, England. Izard's parents were Americans living in England for a short time when he was born. At age seven Izard came to the United States, where he received his primary and secondary education before returning to Europe for a military education. He was commissioned a second lieutenant in the U.S. Army in 1797. He rose to the rank of captain before resigning his commission in the midst of Pres. Thomas Jefferson's military cuts.

At the beginning of the War of 1812, Izard was commissioned a brigadier general in command of New York City. When no threat to the city seemed imminent, he moved his force to New York's northern border with Canada. In January 1814, he was promoted to major general and became the ranking general on the Canadian frontier. Yet, with this elevation in rank and status came almost constant conflict with Secretary of War John Armstrong.

In the spring of 1814, Izard spent his every waking moment preparing the Lake Champlain area, particularly around Plattsburg, for what he was sure was an impending British invasion along that traditional route. With the aid of Brig. Gens. Alexander Macomb and Thomas A. Smith, Izard drove his forces to complete massive fortifications around Plattsburg. He also effectively coordinated his activities with the naval commander on the lake, Capt. Thomas Macdonough. Macdonough's force successfully drove off a small British flotilla in May after being alerted to its presence by Izard.

Soon word reached Izard of the impending invasion by Sir George Prevost at the head of 15,000 British veterans of the Napoleonic campaigns. Izard had approximately 7,500 men to defend against this force, and he accelerated the construction of redoubts and trenches around Plattsburg. As Izard awaited the arrival of the British, however, he received an incredible order from the War Department. Armstrong had become concerned about Maj. Gen. Jacob Brown's precarious situation on the Niagara Frontier. Therefore he ordered Izard to take 4,000 men to the Erie frontier as a diversion for Brown. Izard explained his hazardous position in a series of letters to Armstrong, but the secretary refused to reverse his order. Izard turned over command of his remaining men to Macomb and departed for Sacket's Harbor, thus missing one of the great U.S. victories of the war.

Izard marched his men over 400 miles as British forces retreated before him. Though his army was larger than most in the region, it was still too small to make an effective invasion of Canada. Armstrong, dismissed from office because of the capture of Washington, publicly criticized Izard's inactivity and possibly provoked Izard's exasperated resignation. Following the war, Izard attempted to redeem his reputation by publishing his correspondence with Armstrong.

Izard's last public role was to serve as territorial governor of Arkansas from 1825 until his death in 1828.

—*Jeanne T. Heidler and David S. Heidler*

See also: Niagara Campaigns
Further Reading

Izard, George. "The War of 1812 in Northern New York: General George Izard's Journal of the Châteauguay Campaign." *New York History* (April 1995): 173–200.

Manigault, George Edward. "The Military Career of General George Izard." *Magazine of American History* (June 1888): 462–478.

J

JACKSON, ANDREW
1767–1845
Lawyer; general;
seventh president of the United States

A grandson of Hugh Jackson, a merchant of Carrickfergus, Ireland, Andrew Jackson was the third son of Scots-Irish immigrants. Leaving County Antrim in 1765, his parents Andrew and Elizabeth Hutchinson Jackson followed several of their relatives to the Waxhaws Region, which straddled North and South Carolina. Worn out after just two years of farming the thin red soil of the region, Andrew Jackson, Sr., injured himself lifting a too-heavy load and died in March 1767, just before the birth of Andrew, Jr. The family moved to the Lancaster district in South Carolina, where they lived with Elizabeth Jackson's relatives. Receiving something of a rudimentary education, the young Andrew grew into a wild and reckless adolescent. In both his speech and attitudes, he exhibited a fierce temper and a deep hatred of the British. This latter attitude was fostered by his formidable mother and his own experiences in the American Revolution.

In May 1780, the Waxhaws Region was ravaged by British regulars and Carolina Tories under the notorious Lt. Col. Banastre Tarleton. Jackson's two older brothers, Hugh and Robert, quickly joined the patriot forces, and young Andrew had his first taste of combat at the age of 13, in August 1780 at the battle of Hanging Rock. Both brothers were to die in the Revolution, and Andrew, who acted as a courier for Col. William R. Davie, was captured by British dragoons. Refusing to clean the boots of a British officer, he was assaulted by the officer. For the rest of his life he carried a scar on his face, the result of a deep gash caused by the British officer's sword. Jackson nearly died of smallpox during the war but was nursed back to health by his mother, who later died while nursing U.S. prisoners in Charleston in 1781. Jackson thus lost all his immediate family during the Revolution.

Left a small inheritance by his Irish grandfather, he lived a dissolute life until he quickly dissipated his means. Then at age 17, he began to study law. Neither a noted scholar nor an avid reader, Jackson nevertheless was admitted to the North Carolina bar in September 1787 at the young age of 20. His chosen career would lead him to Tennessee, to his involvement in the War of 1812, and eventually to the presidency.

One of Jackson's old gambling friends, John McNairy, was appointed to the superior court of the western district of North Carolina, an area that would include the future state of Tennessee. After McNairy appointed him public prosecutor, Jackson settled in the frontier village of Nashville and quickly made a name for himself. He fought his first duel and fell in love with Rachel Donelson Robards, a member of a prominent Scots-Irish frontier family. Their marriage in August 1791 gave rise to gossip that would plague their happiness for the rest of their lives: at the time of the marriage Rachel was still technically married to her first husband, Lewis Robards. In January 1794, Jackson formally remarried her after her divorce from Robards was finalized. Jackson was understandably sensitive about the issue, and his impetuous impulses to defend his wife's honor resulted in violent attempts to protect her name, using both the rituals of the dueling code and the impromptu brawl.

As a rising young lawyer with growing political connections in the territory, Jackson attended the Tennessee Territory Constitutional Convention in January and February 1796. He became the first congressional representative from Tennessee in October 1796. Jackson never felt comfortable in Philadelphia. Moody, angry, and homesick, he was remembered by Thomas Jefferson as a man of dangerous passions and an uncontrollable temper. When his political mentor William Blount was removed from the Senate because of his involvement in the so-called Blount conspiracy—a plot to seize Spanish lands in the southwest—Jackson took Blount's place in the U.S. Senate, but business reverses forced his resignation in a year's time.

In February 1802, Jackson finally won election to a position he had long coveted, major general of the Tennessee

Andrew Jackson

militia, but he would see little action early in his career. An enthusiastic supporter of the Louisiana Purchase of 1803, he hoped to be appointed the area's territorial governor but was passed over. The rebuff soured his relationship with Jefferson, and Jackson increasingly allied himself with the anti-Jefferson faction in the Republican Party. He flirted with the vague plans of another anti-Jeffersonian, Aaron Burr, and was drawn into his conspiracy to conquer Mexico and Florida. When he became aware that Burr was aiming to divide the republic and not extend it by these conquests, Jackson drew back. After Burr's arrest, though, Jackson made no secret of his conviction that the real culprit in the "Burr Conspiracy" was Gen. James Wilkinson. The circle of blame in Jackson's mind widened to include the Jefferson administration, which prosecuted the scapegoat Burr while protecting the master plotter Wilkinson. The memory of Jackson's behavior in this episode would naturally hurt his chances for military advancement when the War of 1812 broke out.

Delighted by Pres. James Madison's decision for war against the British, Jackson immediately offered to be dispatched to the Canadian front. When months passed without word from the administration, Jackson believed that his involvement with Burr had made his loyalty suspect.

Expecting a British attack upon the Gulf Coast, however, Madison called for 1,500 Tennessee volunteers. Tennessee governor Willie Blount, a political ally of Jackson, filled in Jackson's name on a blank commission for a major general commanding U.S. volunteers. With no previous military experience to speak of, Andrew Jackson, at the age of 46 and not in the best of health, launched himself upon a military career in 1813. It was less than glorious at first.

Ordered to Natchez, Mississippi, to await orders from his old enemy Gen. James Wilkinson, who was commanding New Orleans, Jackson arrived, only to find instructions to halt his advance. When he received further orders on 15 March 1813 to disband his army and return home, Jackson, in a fury, ignored his orders and led a forced march back to Nashville during a harsh winter. By sheer force of personality, Jackson kept his command intact and so stoically endured the rigors of the march that his men dubbed him "Old Hickory." He had yet to engage any enemy, but Nashville welcomed him as a hero. The legend was already beginning.

Divisions in the Creek Indian nation would finally provide Jackson with national fame. The War of 1812 aggravated existing frictions in the Creek Nation. Many older, more conservative Creek headmen wanted to continue a policy of accommodation with the United States, but many others wanted to use British aid to block U.S. westward expansion into their homelands. Influenced by Tecumseh, these warriors, called Red Sticks, began a civil war within the nation. When, under Red Eagle (William Weatherford), these Red Sticks killed more than 250 pro-U.S. Creeks and their white allies at Fort Mims on 30 August 1813, southern white attitudes toward the southern tribes hardened. The Tennessee state legislature reacted immediately and called for 5,000 volunteers to put down the hostile Creeks. In October 1813, these volunteers, under Maj. Gen. John Cocke in eastern Tennessee and Jackson in western Tennessee, pushed into Creek territory. The first campaign of the Creek War, a war that would merge into the larger War of 1812, called for the two Tennessee armies to meet with a Georgia army under Maj. Gen. John Floyd and a western column of Mississippi volunteers and regulars under Brig. Gen. Ferdinand L. Claiborne. With plans to rendezvous where the Coosa and Tallapoosa Rivers flowed together to form the Alabama River, all four converging armies were supposed to kill any Red Sticks encountered, burn villages, destroy crops, and build blockhouses to secure the territory.

Jackson initially planned a more decisive and lasting campaign. Hoping to build a road as he marched, he intended to push on to Mobile, from where he could invade Spanish Florida. Leaving Fayetteville, Tennessee, on 10 October 1813, he established a supply base at Fort Deposit, crossed the Coosa River and established another base at Fort Strother in modern-day Alabama. On 3 November 1813, Jackson's friend and lieutenant Gen. John Coffee destroyed the important Upper Creek settlement of Tallushatchee, killing over 200 Red Sticks. Believing that Fort Mims had been avenged, Jackson's army in three columns marched south to reach the friendly Creek village of Talladega, then under attack by Red Eagle. Deploying his force into a crescent shape on 9 November 1813, Jackson attacked. His plan was simple: when Red Eagle's 1,000 Red Stick warriors attacked the infantry in the center of the line, the cavalry on the flanks would snap shut, encircle the Red Sticks, and destroy them. The plan nearly worked, but when the infantry line began to fragment, Red Eagle and over 700 of his followers escaped.

Aggressive as ever, Jackson intended to continue the offensive and destroy the survivors. He was hindered, however, by the action of General Cocke, a political rival. Unwilling to enhance the military reputation of Jackson, Cocke slowed his advance and delayed joining Jackson to destroy the Hillabee townships, unaware that Jackson had made peace with their inhabitants. Meanwhile, Jackson's troops were short of supplies and, in due time, mutinous. With their term of enlistment coming to an end, Jackson kept his force together by yet another fearful show of temper but was forced to retreat to Fort Strother. When Cocke finally did arrive, many of his troops' terms of enlistment were coming to an end as well. Although more than 1,000 Red Sticks had been killed and much of the Creek food supply had been destroyed, this first Creek campaign ended inconclusively.

By January 1814, Jackson could report only 400 effectives at Fort Strother, but when 800 new 60-day recruits under Col. William Carroll arrived as reinforcements, Jackson decided to reopen the campaign. By March, Jackson commanded 4,000 troops and was determined to break the Red Stick resistance. On 27 March 1814, he bombarded the breastworks of Tohopeka (Horseshoe Bend), and his troops stormed the township. Caught between a deadly crossfire and with the Tallapoosa River at their backs, the Red Sticks were trapped. With a loss of 49 soldiers, Jackson inflicted horrific casualties upon the hostile Creeks; some 800 were cut down and survivors were scattered. Having won one of the most decisive battles of the War of 1812, Jackson destroyed Red Stick villages along the west bank of the Tallapoosa, establishing Fort Jackson in the heart of Creek territory in April 1814.

The Creek campaigns established Jackson's reputation as a general. On 18 June 1814, he accepted a regular commission of major general in the U.S. Army and the posi-

tion of military commander of the Seventh Military District. Believing that the hostile actions of the Red Sticks had forfeited all Creek territorial rights, he forced 35 friendly Creek chiefs to accept the controversial Treaty of Fort Jackson on 9 August 1814. Ignoring all protests, Jackson made the Creeks cede 23 million acres to the United States, a demand that stiffened Red Stick resistance and antagonized previously friendly Creeks on the eve of the British invasion of the Gulf Coast.

Jackson's appointment coincided with the British defeat of Napoleon in Europe, an event that then allowed London to concentrate on ending the War of 1812 on favorable terms. Reinforcements were sent to Sir George Prevost in Canada, a large raiding force under Maj. Gen. Robert Ross was dispatched to the Chesapeake, and the British planned their major thrust against the Gulf Coast. With Spanish help, it was hoped, British Indian allies could be supported and U.S. expansionism halted. Concerned over the growing power of the United States, the Spanish governor of Florida, Don Mateo González Manrique, forfeited his neutral rights by inviting the British to land at Pensacola and establish a supply base for the Creeks at Apalachicola. Aware of the growing threat to the South, Jackson quickly sent a force to Mobile to strengthen Fort Bowyer and defend the port. When the British naval attack was repulsed on 16 September 1814, Jackson had thwarted British plans and focused British attention on the capture of New Orleans, a much more difficult military operation.

Correctly believing that an attack on New Orleans from the southern land approaches was folly, Jackson remained convinced that Mobile continued to be the chief British target. In a punitive measure designed to weaken the British buildup, Jackson, without orders, invaded and captured Pensacola on 7 November 1814. After castigating Governor Manrique with a display of his fabled fury, Jackson scattered the hostile Creeks and returned to Mobile to await the expected British attack. Only after it had failed to materialize was Jackson persuaded that New Orleans was the likely British target. It was almost too late, however, and he set off to the Crescent City with urgency, arriving there on 1 December 1814.

The undefended city was vacillating between panic and resignation. Jackson set up his headquarters at 106 Royal Street and enlisted any help he could find, including that of the Baratarian buccaneers under the Lafitte brothers—"hellish banditti" in Jackson's initial estimation—and over 600 of the city's free black population. Jackson proclaimed martial law, waited for reinforcements, and refused to entertain any notions of surrendering the city.

Lying 100 miles upstream from the mouth of the Mississippi, New Orleans was not easily approachable by water, for such an advance would be hampered by Forts St. Philip and St. Leon. Jackson deduced that the British attack would have to come from the east, through Lake Borgne and Lake Pontchartrain, so he prepared a defensive line accordingly. On 13 December 1814, the British flotilla was sighted at the entrance to Lake Borgne. After the British quickly gained control of the lakes, they took advantage of Jackson's failure to block many of the water passages to the city, establishing a forward position 12 miles from New Orleans.

Yet Jackson was a lucky commander because his British counterpart, Maj. Gen. John Keane, was a cautious man. Keane ignored his subordinates' advice to storm the city's defenses, an action that probably would have succeeded before 22 December. Instead, Keane decided to wait for the reinforcements on the way with the new, overall commander, Lt. Gen. Sir Edward Pakenham. The initiative on 22 December 1814 shifted to Jackson, who, aggressive as ever, was about to change the course of U.S. history.

Unaware of the British forces' strength, Jackson attacked on 23 December and blunted the British advance. While Jackson continued to strengthen a defensive line along the Rodriguez Canal, Pakenham arrived on Christmas Day, 1814. An Irishman as brave as Jackson and the brother-in-law of the Duke of Wellington, Pakenham was not considered one of the brightest lights in the British army, but he did have a clear conception of what his primary object was in this campaign. Aware of the peace discussions then taking place in Ghent, Belgium, Pakenham wanted to take the city as soon as possible and thus strengthen the British diplomatic position. He probed the U.S. position in some force on 28 December; made a superhuman effort to bring up his artillery; and on the evening of 7 January 1815 dispatched a strike force under Col. William Thornton to the west bank of the Mississippi, to capture a U.S. battery there and train it on Jackson's right flank. If this was perhaps the only intelligent maneuver Pakenham ordered, he nullified its merits the next day by launching his own frontal assault without waiting for Thornton, who had been delayed, to get into position.

At dawn on 8 January 1815, the British forces marched in line toward Jackson's position. Initially the British were protected by a low-lying mist, but at a crucial moment it began to clear and exposed them to a deadly U.S. small arms and artillery fusillade. The result was a disaster for the British. In an action that lasted perhaps 30 minutes, both Pakenham and Gen. Samuel Gibbs were killed. General Keane was wounded, and over 2,000 British soldiers, out of an attacking force of just over 5,000 men, became casualties. Witnessing this catastrophe, Maj. Gen. John Lambert, in charge of the British reserve line, called off the as-

sault against the eastern portion of Jackson's line and eventually pulled Thornton's troops back across the Mississippi. Maintaining a defensive line until 15 January, Lambert finally withdrew to his transports. Jackson had won the Battle of New Orleans.

Frequently mentioned is the notable irony of Jackson's greatest victory occurring after the peace at Ghent had been signed on 24 December 1814. Yet this does not lessen the importance of the U.S. victory at New Orleans. According to terms in the Treaty of Ghent, the peace would not officially obtain until the document was ratified. Before this happened in February 1815, the British had dispatched additional troops both to Canada and the Gulf Coast. The British government sent Anthony St. John Baker to New York, expecting news of a British victory at New Orleans to greet him there. He was instructed to renegotiate as he saw fit in light of new developments. Meanwhile, General Lambert, unaware of the peace, captured Fort Bowyer and began a siege of Mobile. When Baker arrived in New York City on 11 February 1815, however, he learned of Pakenham's defeat and abandoned any plans for renegotiation. The final peace treaty was formally ratified by the Senate on 17 February 1815. Jackson's exploits convinced many Americans that they had won the war with a resounding triumph over Wellington's veterans.

Jackson may not have won the war with his victory at New Orleans, but he had made possible the avoidance of any ambiguity regarding Louisiana. Pakenham had arrived carrying a commission as the new governor of Louisiana as well as a personnel list for a new British-Spanish civil government to be established in the region. A British victory at New Orleans might have meant European control of the mouth of the Mississippi. Such a circumstance would have direly impeded U.S. expansion to the southwest.

Jackson and his army returned to a heroes' welcome in New Orleans on 21 January 1815, but even as his reputation achieved greater and wider luster, the Crescent City was soon to adjust its attitude about the "Hero of New Orleans." Concerned by continuing British activity, Jackson refused to lift martial law, a decision that provoked considerable resentment among the city's citizens.

Although Article IX of the Treaty of Ghent called for the restoration of all Indian lands to their boundaries before the war, Jackson believed the new treaty was not applicable to the Creeks because they had made a separate peace at Fort Jackson. Their forcible removal from the lands ceded at Fort Jackson thus continued. As Creeks fled to or were forced into Florida, they overcrowded lands inhabited by Seminole cousins. Continuing Indian hostility stemming from the War of 1812 thwarted peace in the South. Spanish authorities could not control Indians who used Florida as a base to raid Georgia, and U.S. authorities could not stop squatters in the Fort Jackson cession area from plundering Indians in Florida. The growing instability and increasing unrest on the southern frontier meant that Jackson's campaigning days were not over.

Jackson's controversial invasion of Spanish Florida in 1818, ostensibly to chastise Indians there, is known as the First Seminole War, but it was mainly directed against Spanish control of West Florida. He hanged two British agents he believed responsible for inciting the Indians, but most important, he captured Spanish garrisons at St. Marks and Pensacola. Jackson's behavior troubled many in Washington—he had made war on Spain without congressional authorization—but it reinforced his popularity on the frontier. Supported by Pres. James Monroe and Secretary of State John Quincy Adams, Jackson escaped congressional censure even as his actions exposed Spanish weakness in Florida and obviously persuaded Spain to cede the province to the United States.

In a military career marked by only three major campaigns, the "Hero of New Orleans" had broken the resistance of the southern tribes to U.S. expansion, secured Louisiana for the republic, added Florida to the United States, and greatly increased western prestige and power in the United States. Without the War of 1812, it is unlikely that Andrew Jackson would have gained the presidency. His reentry into national politics would coincide with a vast movement known as Jacksonian Democracy, a populist campaign that Jackson never understood but that he supported because it supported him. The most successful of all U.S. generals of the War of 1812, Andrew Jackson would translate that success into political invincibility.

—*Rory T. Cornish*

See also: Creek War; Fort Jackson, Treaty of; Horseshoe Bend, Battle of; New Orleans, Battle of
Further Reading
Basset, John S., and J. Franklin Jameson, eds. *The Correspondence of Andrew Jackson.* 7 vols. Washington, DC: Carnegie Institution of Washington, 1926–1935.
Brown, Wilburt S. *The Amphibious Campaign for West Florida and Louisiana, 1814–1815: A Critical Review of Strategy and Tactics at New Orleans.* University, AL: University of Alabama Press, 1969.
Heidler, David S., and Jeanne T. Heidler. *Old Hickory's War: Andrew Jackson and the Quest for Empire.* Mechanicsburg, PA: Stackpole Books, 1996.
Owsley, Frank L., Jr. *Struggle for the Gulf Borderlands: The Creek War and the Battle of New Orleans, 1812–1815.* Gainesville: University Presses of Florida, 1981.
Remini, Robert V. *Andrew Jackson and the Course of American Empire.* New York: Harper and Row, 1981.
Watson, Harry L. *Liberty and Power: The Politics of Jacksonian America.* New York: Hill and Wang, 1990.

JACKSON, FORT

Located 12 miles north of present-day Montgomery, Alabama, on the east bank of the Coosa River just north of where it joins the Tallapoosa River, Fort Jackson was situated on a site first occupied by the French in 1717 as a buffer to British expansion. Under French maintenance, it had a garrison of about 40 men. Originally named Fort aux Alibamos, it later was renamed Fort Toulouse. Ceded to the British in 1763, it was not regarrisoned and fell into disrepair.

During the Creek War of 1813–1814, Andrew Jackson used the site as a base camp. After defeating the Red Stick Creeks at Horseshoe Bend (Tohopeka) on 27 March 1814, Jackson marched south to the site of Toulouse and had his soldiers erect a fort there. The new structure was named Fort Jackson, and here the Creeks were compelled to sign the Treaty of Fort Jackson on 9 August 1814. The treaty deprived both Allied and Red Stick Creeks of about 23 million acres of land in Georgia and present-day Alabama.

The fort afterward served as a rendezvous for troops moving to the defense of New Orleans. From 1815 to 1817, it was garrisoned by regular army troops to control the frontier and supervise settlement of the Fort Jackson cession area. Afterward, the fort fell into ruin. It is now a part of the Alabama state park system.

—*Charles H. Bogart*

Further Reading
Grant, Bruce. *American Forts.* New York: E. P. Dutton, 1965.

JACKSON, FRANCIS JAMES
See Non-Intercourse Act

JACKSON, JOHN GEORGE
1777–1825
U.S. congressman

John George Jackson experienced a typical frontier childhood. He was born on 22 September 1777 to George and Elizabeth Jackson in Bush's Fort in western Virginia. On the frontier, John George learned skills such as hunting, surveying, and tracking. Like most other frontiersmen of the time, one of his greatest concerns was that of the Indian threat. Rumors of the British supplying Indian raids would later affect his views toward war with Great Britain.

Jackson followed in the footsteps of his father's political career. Traveling with his father, who was first elected to the House of Representatives from Virginia in 1795, he saw parts of the country outside Virginia, such as Philadelphia and Washington. In 1801, Jackson married Mary "Molly" Payne, the sister of Dolley Madison. This connection to a prominent political family helped Jackson's social standing in Washington and made for a uniquely bellicose political career. He was elected to the U.S. House of Representatives, serving from 1803 through 1810, when he resigned. During his service in the House, his defense of Madison would see him fight duels with John Randolph, Josiah Quincy, and Joseph Pearson, the last of these leaving both Pearson and Jackson grimly wounded.

Like most western politicians of the time, Jackson favored a hard stance against Great Britain. In April 1808, he voted to eliminate smuggling through Canada and Florida by increasing the size of the army. During the House debate on the 1809 Non-Intercourse Act, Jackson attempted to keep a clause allowing the issuance of letters of marque and reprisal. Later in the debate, he tried to insert a clause authorizing the military to capture British land adjacent to the United States. In an effort to preserve Pres. James Madison's war powers, however, Jackson helped defeat an amendment to Macon's Bill No. 2 that would have required the president to have the U.S. Navy convoy U.S. ships.

Like most War Hawks, John George Jackson helped move the country toward a confrontation with Great Britain. Influenced by his frontier experiences and armed with political connections to President Madison, Jackson used his voice in Congress to support legislation that helped lead to the War of 1812.

—*John Newbill*

See also: War Hawks
Further Reading
Davis, Dorothy. *John George Jackson*. Parsons, WV: McClain Printing Company, 1976.

JAMAICA

The island of Jamaica, a British possession, played a relatively minor role in the War of 1812 until the last year of the war. Because of its proximity to the Florida coast and because of British traders' presence on the Florida Gulf Coast, however, rumors abounded throughout the war that the British intended to use Jamaica as a base of operations for an attack on the southeastern United States.

In the fall of 1814, these rumors proved true. The British chose Jamaica as the rendezvous for their European veterans and the naval and land forces under Vice Adm. Sir Alexander Cochrane, which were coming from their campaign in Chesapeake Bay. When Cochrane arrived at Negril Bay on 18 November, he learned that the planned campaign was an open secret throughout Jamaica. Furthermore, a New Orleans merchant illegally doing business in Jamaica had immediately sailed to Pensacola to give the information to Maj. Gen. Andrew Jackson, commander of the U.S. occupation forces there. Cochrane consequently decided not to wait for Gen. Edward Pakenham's continental forces; instead he hurried to New Orleans, hoping to arrive there before Jackson could move his army. To augment his land forces, Cochrane took with him to New Orleans approximately 1,000 black Jamaican troops. The prospect that the British would use Jamaican troops in the southern United States had terrified U.S. southerners since the beginning of the war.

Cochrane departed Jamaica on 26 November, just a few days before Pakenham's arrival in Jamaica. When Pakenham did reach Jamaica with his 10,000-man army, he could not let his men rest from the sea voyage but had to embark almost immediately, arriving off the Florida Gulf Coast on 5 December.

Though British islands in the Caribbean like Jamaica were always good places from which to conduct operations against French and U.S. shipping in the West Indies, they were never fully utilized to launch military campaigns against U.S. soil.

—*Jeanne T. Heidler and David S. Heidler*

See also: Cochrane, Alexander; New Orleans, Battle of; Pakenham, Edward
Further Reading
Owsley, Frank Lawrence, Jr. *Struggle for the Gulf Borderlands: The Creek War and the Battle of New Orleans*. Gainesville: University Presses of Florida, 1981.

JEFFERSON, THOMAS
1743–1826
Third president of the United States, 1801–1809

Thomas Jefferson

The War of 1812 was a conflict that Thomas Jefferson, author of the Declaration of Independence, Republican party leader, vice-president, and president, watched from afar as his chosen successor James Madison conducted it. No longer a maker of policy, Jefferson in 1812 had already assumed the role of revered elder statesman as "the sage of Monticello." And yet, "Mr. Madison's War," as well as the years preceding it, can hardly be separated from the statecraft of Thomas Jefferson.

Throughout Jefferson's two terms as president, he had tried with only limited success to navigate a course between the great warring powers of Britain and France that would protect both U.S. commerce and U.S. sovereignty. Although Jefferson achieved foreign policy triumphs, such as the purchase of Louisiana from France, increasingly foreign affairs would be dominated by the maritime problems caused by the Napoleonic wars. Though desiring a balance of power between the two, Jefferson considered Great Britain the greater threat. With his concurrence, Congress in the spring of 1806 passed an act prohibiting the importation of certain British goods, but buoyed by seemingly encouraging negotiations that James Monroe and William Pinkney conducted with the British, Jefferson asked for a delay on its enforcement. The treaty negotiated by the U.S. ministers, however, contained no concessions from Great Britain regarding impressment. Displeased, Jefferson refused to submit it to the Senate for consideration.

The inability of the United States to reach an understanding with Great Britain greatly increased the chances for conflict between the two countries, but the United States was ill-prepared for such an event. Jefferson, realizing the danger to the United States, advocated a series of military measures to improve the nation's readiness, but he met with little cooperation from Congress. The cornerstones of the Jeffersonian defense plan, outlined in 1805–1806, were fortification of seaport cities, a large gunboat navy, a reorganization of the state militias on the basis of classification by age, and the building of six 74-gun ships of the line. With a reliance on gunboats and militia, Jefferson hoped to keep military expenditures relatively low and to avoid increasing the size of the peacetime army. Congress appropriated a small sum ($150,000) for fortifications and another sum to build 50 gunboats (eventually 180 boats would be built during Jefferson's term of office). It refused to vote funds for the 74-gun ships, and its decision on militia classification, a proposal likely to be unpopular with the people as well as one that took power away from the states, was similarly negative. With only the gunboat policy receiving adequate support from Congress and the utility of those craft highly questionable, Jefferson's defense policy was simply unsuccessful.

It was against this background of failure in military reform that the greatest clash with Great Britain during Jefferson's tenure in office occurred, when the HMS *Leopard* fired upon, then boarded, the USS *Chesapeake* on 22 June 1807, killing some sailors and impressing others. This incident caused great public outcry in the United States, with a strong feeling for war erupting across the country. Jefferson took immediate measures, such as calling out militia to defend the coasts, but he was still faced with the question of how to deal with Great Britain. Though support for war was high, the ability of the United States to conduct it was low—the U.S. Army numbered only a few thousand men, widely scattered, and the Navy consisted only of a few frigates and some smaller craft.

From the beginning, Jefferson's actions were circumspect. While meditating on military or economic retaliation, he dispatched a vessel to Great Britain to receive an official explanation but did not immediately call Congress into session. Rather, he solicited advice on military measures from government heads, including Secretary of the Treasury Albert Gallatin, Secretary of War Henry Dearborn, and Gen. James Wilkinson. Jefferson also embarked upon other military preparations in the fall of 1807, including the collection of supplies for possible military campaigns. The country's military incapacity increasingly made the economic option more desirable to Jefferson, however, and in December he advocated to Congress a policy of embargo, which would shut down U.S. commerce to the European powers. The only significant military measure resulting from the *Chesapeake* incident was a significant increase in the size of the peacetime army in April 1808. Unfortunately for the United States, most of the new military forces were significantly diminished in 1809–1810, when they were sent to New Orleans to protect that city from a British threat that never materialized. The embargo proved equally ineffective, damaging U.S. commerce far more than anything else.

In 1809, Jefferson left office and returned to Monticello, leaving his successor Madison to cope with increasingly difficult foreign relations. Jefferson kept in touch with most major figures in the Madison administration but rarely offered Madison advice. His mood rose and fell with the apparent successes and failures of U.S. foreign policy, but he grew increasingly pessimistic about the chances of avoiding war. By the spring of 1812, Jefferson felt war was inevitable.

When war came, as it soon did, Jefferson's support for it was extremely strong, yet his optimism concerning the United States' military prospects initially was quite unrealistic. In the summer of 1812, he went so far as to predict that the conquest of Canada "will be a mere matter of marching." Events soon proved Jefferson wrong, but the former president remained steadfast in his support for James Madison, tending to put the blame for debacles on subordinates instead. After William Hull surrendered Detroit, Jefferson felt that the general should be shot for cowardice and treachery and that Stephen Van Rensselaer, who had mismanaged affairs at Queenston Heights in October 1812, should be broken "for cowardice and incapacity." Hull's surrender, wrote Jefferson that fall, "was followed by cases of surprise, of cowardice, of foolhardiness and of sheer imbecility, by which bodies of men were successively lost as fast as they could be raised." As frustrated as Jefferson was with the army, he rejoiced in the successes of the navy, repeatedly exclaiming his delight with that arm's victorious ship-to-ship fights with the British.

During the war, Jefferson tended to refrain from offering suggestions to Madison, though he was more outgoing with James Monroe. In 1813, Jefferson outlined a plan of taxation and borrowing to finance the war that he discussed with his son-in-law John W. Eppes, at the time chair of the House Ways and Means Committee, and James Monroe. Monroe supported these measures, but congressional opinion favored reviving the national bank. On occasion Jefferson did solicit appointments for acquaintances or relatives. Many of his kin did serve in the war, including his son-in-law Thomas Mann Randolph.

During the years 1812–1815, Jefferson followed the war closely, but he was also heavily involved in other matters. He had experimented with nail production, but the war cut off his supply of iron and forced him to close down for the duration. Other ventures included the building of a gristmill, cloth manufacture, and sheep raising. The war years marked other important events as well, including the process of reestablishing a friendship with former political opponent John Adams, which had begun in 1811. In 1814, the British invaded Chesapeake Bay, setting fire to the Capitol in the process and destroying the Library of Congress. Jefferson offered his own library of almost 6,500 books to Congress at a price of its asking, thus founding the modern Library of Congress.

Continued prosecution of the war was important to Jefferson, and he was dismayed to learn that the peace negotiations at Ghent in 1814 had set aside the issue of impressment and were focusing on a return to the status quo antebellum. Jefferson argued repeatedly that any agreement could be no more than a temporary truce unless the question of impressments was settled. Nevertheless, upon hearing in February 1815 of Andrew Jackson's great victory at New Orleans and the news of peace shortly thereafter, Jefferson became more ebullient. He ended the war as optimistically as he had begun it, asserting that if the war had gone on, the United States would have taken Quebec and Halifax.

Jefferson's relationship to the War of 1812 is a complex one. His foreign policy and military policy initiatives while president kept the United States out of war but did little to prepare the country for the eventuality of a military conflict. Though Jefferson was unsuccessful in winning recognition of U.S. neutral rights, it is hard to imagine what a successful policy might have been, given the power and intransigence of the belligerent European nations. The United States' problems were linked to events outside the control of Jefferson, his successor, or anyone else.

—Mark Pitcavage

See also: Embargo Act
Further Reading
Cunningham, Noble E., Jr. *In Pursuit of Reason: The Life of Thomas Jefferson.* Baton Rouge: Louisiana State University Press, 1987.
Malone, Dumas. *Jefferson and His Time: The Sage of Monticello.* Boston: Little, Brown, 1981.
Mapp, Alf J., Jr. *Thomas Jefferson: Passionate Pilgrim.* Lanham, MD: Madison Books, 1991.
Peterson, Merrill D. *Thomas Jefferson and the New Nation.* London: Oxford University Press, 1970.
Stuart, Reginald C. *The Half-way Pacifist: Thomas Jefferson's View of War.* Toronto: University of Toronto Press, 1978.

JESUP, THOMAS SIDNEY
1788–1860
U.S. officer

Thomas S. Jesup was born on 16 December 1788 in Virginia. The family moved to Kentucky, where Thomas's father, James, died when his son was four years old, leaving a family of five with little means of support. The boy had little formal education but learned to read early and read widely and became well informed over the years. When conflict with Great Britain threatened, he applied for a commission in the army. Without military experience, at age 19, he became a second lieutenant on 3 May 1808 in the Seventh Infantry Regiment. Only 22 months later, on 1 December 1809, he advanced to first lieutenant.

It was his misfortune to be an officer in the 2,000-man army that Brig. Gen. William Hull surrendered at Detroit on 16 August 1812, virtually without a fight. Jesup considered Hull's capitulation cowardly. While he was a prisoner in Canada, he was promoted on 20 January 1813 to captain, and three months later, after his parole, he was commissioned major.

The bloodiest combat service of his 52 years in the army took place during July 1814. At the Battle of Chippewa on 5 July, his regiment protected Winfield Scott's vulnerable left wing. When ammunition was exhausted, he did not retreat but ordered a bayonet charge that routed the foe. He was brevetted lieutenant colonel. At Lundy's Lane on 25 July his regiment, the 25th Infantry, worked its way to the British rear, capturing Gen. Phineas Riall, the commander, and some of his staff. Jesup was hit hard four times. He became colonel by brevet.

Jesup recovered slowly from his severe wounds. When he was well enough, he was ordered to Connecticut, os-

tensibly to recruit but actually to observe the actions of the Hartford Convention during December 1814. The town of Hartford, firmly antiadministration, passed a resolution excluding the U.S. Army from its limits. Jesup replied that if the town tried to enforce its ordinance he would resist it by force. Hartford reconsidered.

Following the War of 1812 Congress cut the army to 10,035 men, one third its wartime size, but Jesup was retained as a regular (not brevet) lieutenant colonel in command of the Third Infantry Regiment. Secretary of War John C. Calhoun established a permanent general staff with Jesup as a quartermaster general and ranked as a brigadier general, effective 8 May 1818. Ten years later, for faithful service in grade he reached major general by brevet, his highest rank.

Jesup would subsequently serve in wars against the Creek and Seminole Indians and in Mexico under Gen. Zachary Taylor. In almost every instance, controversy and quarrels marked his career after the War of 1812. During the Mexican-American War, his life lost most of its joy with the death of his wife of 24 years in April 1846, leaving six children aged from six to 23.

In the 1850s Jesup strongly supported the Union but also believed in states' rights. Before he had to choose sides in the coming sectional contest, he died on 10 June 1860, six months before secession. His 42 years as quartermaster general remain the longest tenure of any staff officer in U.S. history.

—*John K. Mahon*

Further Reading
Kieffer, Chester L. *Maligned General: The Biography of Thomas Sydney Jesup.* New York: Presidio Press, 1979.

JOHNSON, RICHARD MENTOR
1780–1850
U.S. officer; politician

Richard Mentor Johnson's long and varied life began in the frontier settlement of Beargrass, Kentucky, the site of modern Louisville. The son of Virginians Robert and Jemima Johnson, Richard spent his boyhood in a frontier setting that offered little in the way of formal education but no doubt helped prepare him for the later rigors of his military service. At age 15, Richard began the study of Latin as an introduction to legal studies at Transylvania University.

Richard Mentor Johnson

Equipped with this relatively sparse educational background, Johnson was admitted to the bar in 1802. In 1804, pursuing a path fairly common among ambitious men in the early republic, Johnson gained election to the state legislature. A subsequent election in 1806 advanced him to the U.S. House of Representatives, where he would serve until 1819.

As a Republican congressman, Johnson was an ardent supporter of Pres. Thomas Jefferson's much-maligned embargo policy. As the crisis with Great Britain grew during James Madison's presidency, Johnson naturally gravitated to the militant Republican faction known as the War Hawks. Adamant about resisting Britain's provocations and injuries, the War Hawks abandoned the long-extant policy of peaceful coercion and advocated war against Britain in spring 1812. The desired declaration of war in June, however, presented Johnson and other Republicans with a dilemma. Empowering the federal government with the authority necessary to prosecute the war effectively would contradict Republican principles regarding small government. Congressman Johnson, together with many of his colleagues, took solace in their belief that a republican people would rise to the occasion. Yet the military defeats of 1812 forced Republicans like Johnson to acknowledge that a larger national military establishment would have to be authorized.

Though Johnson retained his congressional seat throughout the war, he was quickly drawn into military service. Appointed an aid to Gen. William Henry Harrison in late summer 1812, Johnson dedicated himself to raising 500 Kentucky volunteers to serve as mounted infantry. Johnson quickly advanced from major of a battalion to colonel of a regiment as defenses were organized for the northwestern frontier. His initial military experiences were brief, however, because he returned to Washington for the second session of Congress in November 1812.

Johnson came back to Congress with a much clearer conception of the military situation. He was impressed by the men's enthusiasm but appalled by their poor equipment and supplies. Nonetheless, he put before the House a resolution proposing a major campaign against the hostile northwestern Indians, believing that they would be most vulnerable in the dead of winter. Though the House agreed, General Harrison countered that winter would be the most difficult season to locate large concentrations of Indians. The plan was dropped.

In late February 1813, Johnson received authorization to organize a regiment of mounted volunteers in Kentucky. Though he undertook the assignment enthusiastically, he feared that Harrison would be reluctant to utilize the volunteers. Indeed, coordination with the regular army proved most frustrating during the spring, especially as Kentuckians grew alarmed over reports of Indian massacres of U.S. troops. Johnson fretted over his men's morale. In early June, his mounted regiment arrived at Fort Wayne, Indiana Territory, where his orders were to patrol the northwestern frontier and interdict small raiding parties. Under instructions to remain no longer than three days in any one spot, Johnson complied, though he respectfully questioned War Department orders that put his men where he felt they would be of little use. He wanted to join the main army and aid in the recapture of Detroit.

After a portion of Johnson's men returned to Kentucky for fresh horses in July, the regiment reassembled at Great Crossings, Kentucky, in mid-August with hopes of helping to force Canadian defensive lines around Lake Erie. News of a signal U.S. naval victory reached the men in September and prefigured their march to Fort Meigs. From there Johnson's regiment embarked on 25 September for the River Raisin and Detroit. During the journey, the troops passed through the site of a January 1813 Indian massacre of Americans. No doubt this fueled their desire for vengeance.

The opportunity for retribution came on 5 October, when Johnson's regiment, together with regular army troops, pursued British and Indian forces up the Thames River. In the famous engagement that followed, Johnson established a reputation as an innovative and courageous officer and as the probable instrument of Tecumseh's death.

In the battle, Johnson's men dismounted and pursued their Indian opponents into thick brush and met in hand-to-hand combat. Johnson remained mounted, receiving severe wounds in his hip and thigh, but he was spared by the thick smoke that prevented more accurate fire from the Indians. In the last stage of the battle, Johnson fought and ultimately killed an Indian chief presumed to have been Tecumseh.

The Battle of the Thames proved to be a critical event of the War of 1812, and Colonel Johnson would be remembered and rewarded for his role in it. He continued an active political career in the House and later in the Senate (1819–1829), with a brief interim spent in the Kentucky legislature. A supporter of Henry Clay in the 1824 presidential election, Johnson quickly gave his allegiance to Andrew Jackson following charges of a "corrupt bargain" between Clay and John Quincy Adams. Losing his Senate seat in 1829, Johnson was again elected to the House. From that position he generally supported the policies of President Jackson, which probably predisposed Jackson to recommend that Johnson join the Martin Van Buren ticket in 1836 as the vice-presidential candidate.

Johnson's exploits in the War of 1812 provided rich potential for exaggeration in 1836. As the ostensible slayer of Tecumseh, Johnson already enjoyed considerable fame, but campaign literature multiplied his war wounds far beyond what any human body could have endured. William Emmons's election-year *Authentic Biography of Colonel Richard M. Johnson* had Johnson overcoming three-to-one numbers on the battlefield and sustaining 25 gunshot wounds. Nonetheless, the much-wounded Colonel Johnson was said to have killed Tecumseh with a pistol shot even as the howling savage raised his tomahawk to strike. Some critics complained that killing Tecumseh hardly qualified Johnson for the vice presidency, but the more devastating charges involved his black mistress Julia Chinn. Though Chinn had died several years before, the mulatto children produced by the couple were an enduring target for those wishing to denounce Johnson as a "racial amalgamator." Johnson failed to gain a majority of electoral votes and became the only vice president elected by the Senate.

After an inconspicuous vice presidency, Johnson retired briefly before being elected once again to the Kentucky legislature in 1850. Though many expected him to take up his lifelong interest in education once again (he had supported numerous efforts to establish military academies and Indian schools), Johnson died about two weeks after assuming his last representative post in November 1850. Always a bachelor, he left only two daughters by Julia Chinn.

—*Blaine T. Browne*

See also: Tecumseh
Further Reading

Emmons, William. *Authentic Biography of Colonel Richard M. Johnson of Kentucky.* New York: H. Mason, 1833.
Meyer, Leland W. *Life and Times of Colonel Richard M. Johnson of Kentucky.* New York: Columbia University Press, 1932.

JONES, JACOB
1768–1850
U.S. Navy officer

Born in the Gap, Delaware, tall, lantern-jawed Jacob Jones studied to be a doctor and, when that profession did not suit him, tried clerking in a law office. That, too, palled, and in 1799 he became a midshipman in the new U.S. Navy. He was older than his peers by more than a decade. He served in the frigate *United States* and in the armed ship *Ganges* during the Quasi-War and became a lieutenant in 1801. In the Barbary War, he had the misfortune to be first lieutenant in the frigate *Philadelphia* when Capt. William Bainbridge rashly ran her aground and had to surrender her to the Tripolitan pirates. Nineteen months as a prisoner of war followed.

Following several years on the New Orleans station, Jones was promoted to master commandant in 1810 and given command of the brig *Argus*. The following year, he commissioned the sloop *Wasp* and in 1812 defeated HMS *Frolic* in a vicious fight that left both ships disabled. In that condition, he was captured by a British battleship, then exchanged, promoted to captain, and awarded both a congressional gold medal and command of the recently captured British frigate *Macedonian*. The British blockade prevented him from taking her to sea for the remainder of the war, but immediately thereafter, he sailed to the Mediterranean in the squadron sent to put down Algerine piracy.

Jones was squadron commander in the Mediterranean from 1821 to 1824, with *Constitution* as his flagship. He followed this with two years on the Board of Naval Commissioners and then was the commander of the Pacific Squadron until 1829. The remainder of his career was served ashore, including command of the Baltimore station, and, at the time of his death, command of the Naval Asylum at Philadelphia. Jones was married three times, and his only child, a son by his second wife, was a Marine officer with Commodore Matthew Calbraith Perry when that officer opened Japan to western relations in 1853–1854.

Jacob Jones

Four ships in the U.S. Navy have been named for Commodore Jones.

—*Tyrone G. Martin*

See also: *Wasp* versus *Frolic*
Further Reading
Dudley, William S., ed. *The Naval War of 1812: A Documentary History*. Washington, DC: Naval Historical Center, 1985.
Guttridge, Leonard F., and Jay D. Smith. *The Commodores*. New York: Harper and Row, 1969.
Martin, Tyrone G. *A Most Fortunate Ship*. Annapolis, MD: Naval Institute Press, 1997.
Tucker, Glenn. *Dawn Like Thunder*. Indianapolis: Bobbs-Merrill Company, 1963.

brother Thomas ap Catesby entered the College of William and Mary. After a year, Roger moved to Richmond, where he remained until January 1809, when he received an appointment in the marines. Commissioned a second lieutenant, and promoted to first lieutenant six months later, Jones remained with the marines until early July 1812; he resigned from the marines upon the declaration of war and joined the army as a captain.

In late May 1813 while serving with the Third Regiment of Artillery, he participated in the joint army-navy attack on Fort George. Days later, in early June, Jones was with U.S. forces that retreated in the face of a British counterattack at nearby Stoney Creek. For his distinguished gallantry and conduct with Gen. Jacob Brown at the Battles of Chippewa and Lundy's Lane in July 1814, he was brevetted to major. While serving with Gen. Peter Porter in mid-September 1814, Jones distinguished himself in a sortie that held Fort Erie and was brevetted to lieutenant colonel. From August 1813 until June 1815, he also served as assistant adjutant general.

After the war Jones became an aide-de-camp to General Brown before being appointed adjutant general of the army with the rank of colonel in August 1818. He remained in that position until his death on 15 July 1852, ultimately achieving the rank of brigadier general and holding the position longer than any other officer. For meritorious conduct in performing his duties during the Mexican-American War, he was brevetted to major general.

—*Gene A. Smith*

Further Reading
Heitman, Francis B. *Historical Register and Dictionary of the United States Army*. Baltimore, MD: Genealogical Publishing, 1903.
Hughes, J. Patrick. "The Adjutant General's Office, 1821–1861: A Study in Administrative History." Ph.D. dissertation, Ohio State University, 1977.
Jones, Lewis Hampton. *Captain Roger Jones of London and Virginia*. Albany, NY: J. Munsell's Sons, 1891.

JONES, ROGER
1789–1852
U.S. officer

Born in Northumberland County, Virginia, Roger Jones was the son of Catesby Jones and Lettice Tuberville, farmers. In 1800, because of his father's death, he and

JONES, THOMAS ap CATESBY
1790–1858
U.S. Navy officer

Born on 24 April 1790 in Northumberland County, Virginia, he was the son of Catesby Jones and Lettice Tuberville, farmers. In 1800, because of his father's death, he and brother Roger entered the College of William and Mary. After a year, they moved to Richmond, where Jones studied rhetoric and oratory until, in November 1805, his uncle Meriwether Jones obtained a midshipman's warrant in the U.S. Navy for him. He remained in Richmond until the *Chesapeake-Leopard* Affair of June 1807, after which Secretary of the Navy Robert Smith ordered him into service at Norfolk.

In the spring of 1808, Jones was transferred to the gunboat flotilla at the New Orleans station on the Gulf of Mexico. Until the outbreak of war, he confronted pirates, smugglers, privateers, and those violating the country's slave trade law, as well as an inhospitable climate and a strange culture. Although the war raged for two and a half years, the most significant action for the gunboat flotilla at New Orleans occurred in the last half of 1814. In September, Commodore Daniel Todd Patterson and Col. Robert Ross, wanting to break the power of the Baratarian pirates led by Jean and Pierre Lafitte, attacked their encampment at Barataria Bay. During the melee, according to Patterson, Lieutenant "Jones distinguished himself by boarding one of the schooners which had been fired and extinguishing the fire after it had made great progress; a quantity of powder being left in her open cabin, evidently designed to blow her up."

On 14 December 1814, Jones, commanding five gunboats and 175 men on Lake Borgne, confronted 40 barges and more than 1,000 British personnel commanded by Vice Adm. Alexander Cochrane. For over two hours Jones and his flotilla, unable to retreat because of unfavorable tides and winds, fought in a desperate contest before each of the vessels succumbed to British numerical superiority. During the battle, Jones received a near-fatal wound in his right shoulder, which affected him the remainder of his life. Although the gunboat battle on Lake Borgne still raises controversy, Jones's defense bought Andrew Jackson's army time and provided information about the proposed British invasion route. Captured in the Battle of Lake Borgne, Jones remained a prisoner on the island of Bermuda until February 1815, when he was exchanged.

The remainder of Jones's controversial career included three cruises to the Pacific: one in 1826 in which he established diplomatic relations with Tahiti and the Hawaiian Islands; a second in 1842 in which he mistakenly seized Monterey, California, believing the United States and Mexico were at war; and a third in 1849 in which his squadron faced the anarchy and chaos of the California gold rush. Additionally, in the 1830s he served as inspector of ordnance for the navy, in which post he experimented with and tested new types of weapons. In 1836, Pres. Andrew Jackson appointed him commander of the South Seas

Exploring Expedition, but poor health and political intrigue forced him to resign. Jones achieved the rank of captain before being court-martialed in 1851; he was subsequently dismissed from the service. He spent the rest of his life on his farm outside Washington, D.C. He died on 30 May 1858.

—*Gene A. Smith*

See also: Baratarian Pirates; Lake Borgne, Battle of
Further Reading

Bradley, Harold W. "Thomas ap Catesby Jones and the Hawaiian Islands, 1826–1827." *Hawaiian Historical Society Report* 39 (1931): 17–30.

Bradley, Udolpho Theodore. *The Contentious Commodore: Thomas ap Catesby Jones of the Old Navy, 1788–1858*. Ph.D. dissertation, Cornell University, 1933.

Clericus. "Biographical Sketch of Thomas ap Catesby Jones." *Military and Naval Magazine of the United States* 3 (1834): 27–34.

Eller, E. M., W. J. Morgan, and R. M. Basoco. *The Battle of New Orleans: Sea Power and the Battle of New Orleans*. New Orleans: Battle of New Orleans, 150th Anniversary Committee of Louisiana, 1965.

Gapp, Frank W. "'The Kind-Eyed Chief': Forgotten Champion of Hawaii's Freedom." *Hawaiian Journal of History* 19 (1985): 101–121.

Jones, Walter, Richard Coxe, and Joseph H. Bradley. *Review of the Evidence, Findings, and Sentence of the Naval Court Martial in the Case of Comm. Thomas ap Catesby Jones*. 1851.

McKee, Christopher. *A Gentlemanly and Honorable Profession: The Creation of the U.S. Naval Officer Corps, 1794–1815*. Annapolis, MD: Naval Institute Press, 1991.

Smith, Gene A. "The War That Wasn't: Thomas ap Catesby Jones' Seizure of Monterey." *California History* 66 (1987): 104–113, 155–157.

Tucker, Spencer C. *The Jeffersonian Gunboat Navy*. Columbia: University of South Carolina Press, 1993.

JONES, WILLIAM
1760–1831
Merchant; congressman;
secretary of the navy

Born in Philadelphia, William Jones spent part of his early life as a boatyard apprentice in the Moravian community of Bethlehem on the Lehigh River. During the early years of the American Revolution, he participated at the Battles of Trenton in December 1776 and Princeton in January 1777. Before the war ended, he served with

Thomas Truxtun on the privateer *St. James* and as a first lieutenant in the Continental Navy. He was both wounded and captured twice. From 1790 to 1793, he resided in Charleston, South Carolina, serving in the city's militia artillery and working as a merchant engaged in the Charleston-to-Philadelphia coastal trade. In 1793, he returned to Philadelphia, resumed his mercantile activities, and became active in politics. Elected as a Republican to the 7th Congress in 1801, he served a single term before returning to his commercial ventures, which included the opium trade with China.

On 12 January 1813, Jones accepted Pres. James Madison's appointment to replace Paul Hamilton as secretary of the navy. Ironically, he had refused the same appointment in 1801. Upon assuming the duties of office, he found a precarious situation. During Jefferson's presidency, an antinavy Congress had implemented the defensively oriented gunboat program to protect the nation's ports rather than build seagoing ships to protect commerce at sea. Yet, during the first six months of the war, the country's few seagoing ships won a series of dramatic, although unimportant, victories. This prompted a public outcry for more seagoing vessels and convinced Britain to blockade U.S. ports. Jones responded in the only feasible manner: he concentrated the available gunboats at crucial ports, sent the nation's capital vessels and privateers against British commerce, and provided support for building a naval force on the Great Lakes.

Even though Jones believed the gunboats to be a waste of resources, they were virtually the only naval defense the nation possessed. On 30 March 1812, Congress had directed that the craft be placed in ordinary until times of emergency. Jones instead ordered that they remain in commission; be outfitted for service; and be concentrated in New York, New Orleans, and the Delaware and Chesapeake Bays as well as along the coast of Georgia to discourage British operations.

Understanding the navy's weakness, Jones reluctantly chose to undertake single-ship campaigns of *guerre de course*. To maximize the use of U.S. vessels, he instructed his captains to proceed with caution to designated cruising grounds, to capture or destroy enemy commerce, and most important, to avoid battle with larger enemy ships. He also advocated privateering as a means to disrupt British commerce further.

Jones realized the importance of the northern lakes as a British route of invasion, and he sent experienced officers, crews, guns, and ammunition to bolster U.S. positions on Lakes Erie, Ontario, and Champlain. Moreover, the department supported the construction of additional vessels, increased the number of marines to be used as an am-

phibious force, modified recruiting procedures, and raised the pay for seamen on the lakes to $15 a month in an attempt to make the service more appealing. These reforms helped establish naval superiority and allowed for successful operations. Ultimately the victories on Lake Erie by Oliver H. Perry and on Lake Champlain by Thomas Macdonough secured the northern frontier.

Jones's most unsuccessful service was in defending Washington, D.C. Sharing responsibility for the city's defense with Secretary of War John Armstrong, Jones positioned Commodore Joshua Barney's gunboats in Chesapeake Bay to confront and harass British operations. Barney's forces successfully prevented a landing until 19 August 1814, when they were overwhelmed by 23 capital vessels. Taking the cannon from their gunboats before setting them afire, Barney's men joined army and militia forces trying to protect the city. Knowing the capital to be vulnerable, Jones had removed the Navy Department's records, equipment, and valuables to a safe place; when the British approached the city on 24 August 1814, he ordered the Navy Yard and the almost-completed frigate *Columbia* burned. After the British had sacked the city, Jones and Commodore John Rodgers led a spirited counterattack as the British evacuated from nearby Alexandria, Virginia.

In addition to his wartime activities, Jones worked diligently to reorganize the routine duties of the department. He sought additional civilian personnel and an increased number of officers to run the office more effectively, requested that the department standardize its shipboard equipment and ordnance, solicited Congress to create a naval board to assist the secretary with complicated technical matters, and insisted that the department explore the possibility of applying new technologies. Most of his requests, however, went unanswered. Claiming his personal resources were exhausted, he resigned in September 1814, but he did not relinquish the office until 1 December.

From January 1813 to December 1814, Jones also served as acting secretary of the treasury. His success in that position, combined with his friendship with succeeding treasury secretary Alexander James Dallas, resulted in his election as the first president of the Second Bank of the United States in July 1816. He held the presidency until January 1819, when he was forced to resign because of financial mismanagement and fraud. This disgraceful episode subsequently colored his earlier exemplary service as secretary of the navy. During his later years, Jones operated a successful shipbuilding company and served as collector of customs for Philadelphia. He died on 6 September 1831 in Bethlehem, Pennsylvania, from yellow fever.

—*Gene A. Smith*

Further Reading

Dudley, William S., ed. *The Naval War of 1812: A Documentary History*. Washington, DC: Naval Historical Center, Department of the Navy, 1984.

Eckert, Edward K. "Early Reform in the Navy Department." *American Neptune* 33 (October 1973): 231–245.

———. *The Navy Department in the War of 1812*. Gainesville: University Presses of Florida, 1973.

———. "William Jones: Mr. Madison's Secretary of the Navy." *The Pennsylvania Magazine of History and Biography* 96 (April 1972): 167–182.

Owsley, Frank L., Jr. "William Jones." In Paolo Coletta, ed., *American Secretaries of the Navy*. Vol. 1. Annapolis, MD: Naval Institute Press, 1980: 93–98.

Paullin, Charles Oscar. "Naval Administration under Secretaries of the Navy Smith, Hamilton, and Jones, 1801–1814." *United States Naval Institute Proceedings* 32 (December 1906): 1289–1328.

K

KEANE, JOHN
1781–1844
British army officer

Born on 6 February 1781, John Keane entered the British army as an ensign in 1793 and served at Gibraltar in 1799 and 1804 and in Egypt from 1800 to 1803. He was also in Ireland, Bermuda, and Martinique in 1809. In April 1813, as brevet colonel, he joined the Duke of Wellington's army, headed a brigade of the third division, and fought at Vitoria, the Pyrenees, Nivelles, Nive, Vie Bigorre, and Toulouse.

Promoted to major general on 14 June 1814, Keane sailed with reinforcements from Garonne and joined Sir Alexander Cochrane's fleet in the attack on New Orleans in late December 1814. Keane's 1,800 troops formed the advance and repulsed a strong attack by Andrew Jackson. On Christmas Day 1814, he was superseded by Sir Edward M. Pakenham and Samuel Gibbs, who had arrived with additional troops. On 2 January 1815, he received a KCB with gold cross and two clasps for Martinique and the Peninsular battles. In the British defeat of 8 January 1815, Keane commanded the third brigade, left column, and was twice severely wounded.

In 1815 he joined Wellington in Paris and commanded the Ninth Infantry Brigade of the army of occupation. He later commanded in Jamaica from 1823 to 1830; was appointed commander in chief at Bombay in 1833; headed the army of the Indus at the taking of Ghuznee, Cabul, on 23 July 1839; and became lieutenant general on 22 July 1839. On 19 December 1839 he received the thanks of Parliament and a peerage. Keane died on 26 August 1844.

—*Frederick C. Drake*

See also: New Orleans, Battle of
Further Reading
Gleig, George R. *The Campaigns of the British Army at Wash-ington and New Orleans in the Years 1814–1815*. London: John Murray, 1836, 1847.

KEARNY, STEPHEN WATTS
1794–1848
U.S. officer

Born to Philip Kearny and Susanna Watts Kearny, Stephen Watts Kearny was born in Newark, New Jersey. He briefly attended Columbia College but received a commission as a first lieutenant in the 13th Infantry Regiment as war loomed in March 1812.

During the summer of 1812, Kearny and the 13th were stationed at Buffalo, New York, but moved to the Niagara River to participate in the planned attack on Queenston. When the regulars at Lewiston, New York, crossed the Niagara on 13 October, Kearny was among them, and as the day's fighting wore on, he found himself under one of the few regular officers left standing, Capt. John Wool. Kearny followed Wool, who led the scaling of Queenston Heights. When British reinforcements arrived, Kearny suffered minor wounds in the final fighting and was one of the many Americans captured at Queenston.

While en route to Quebec, where they were to be imprisoned, Lt. Col. Winfield Scott and Lieutenant Kearny plotted their escape. Renewed vigilance by their guards forced them to abandon the plan, however. In early 1813, Kearny and many of the other officers were loaded aboard a ship and taken to New York City to be exchanged.

After being exchanged, Kearny was promoted to captain. Though commended for his gallantry at Queenston, he was placed on recruiting duty, an activity that he apparently engaged in for the remainder of the war. His repeated requests for a combat assignment went unanswered.

Following the war, Kearny, who would remain in the army for the remainder of his life, served most of his duty on the western frontier. He was in the ill-fated Yellowstone expedition of 1825, was in present-day Wisconsin during the Winnebago War, and ultimately became the colonel of the First Regiment of Dragoons. As a new brigadier general in 1846, Kearny led the expedition in the first year of the Mexican-American War that captured Santa Fe and New Mexico and established a U.S. government in California. After putting down an attempt by Mexicans to retake California, he was transferred to Vera Cruz to serve as governor of that city until the U.S. evacuation of Mexico. Shortly after his return to St. Louis, he died of a disease contracted in Vera Cruz.

—*Jeanne T. Heidler and David S. Heidler*

See also: Queenston, Battle of; Scott, Winfield
Further Reading
Clarke, Dwight L. *Stephen Watts Kearny; Soldier of the West.* Norman: University of Oklahoma Press, 1961.

KENNEDY, JOHN PENDLETON
1795–1870
Maryland militia private

John P. Kennedy's role in the War of 1812, while minor, provides one of those colorful vignettes that bring any conflict alive for later generations. Born in Baltimore to prosperous merchant John Kennedy and his wife Nancy Pendleton Kennedy, the young Kennedy graduated from Baltimore College in 1812. During the war, he enlisted as a private in the Maryland Fifth Baltimore Light Dragoons, an elite unit made up of the younger gentlemen of Baltimore.

Called out when the British threatened Washington, D.C., in August 1814, the Fifth initially performed well at the Battle of Bladensburg on 24 August, but when it was in danger of being flanked by the attacking British, it joined the rout. During the engagement, Private Kennedy fought alongside his compatriots but did so in great pain. When called from his bedroll in the predawn hours of the 24th, he had been unable to find his boots. As a last resort, he remembered that he had packed his dancing shoes for the victory ball after the expected repulse of the British. He struggled into these thin-soled pumps and joined the remainder of the regiment to stop the British.

Kennedy fought and marched the entire day in these shoes, and when his regiment began its flight, he ran in them. As he fled on perhaps the sorest feet on the battlefield, he encountered one of his friends, James McCulloch,

wounded and lying on the side of the road. Rather than leave McCulloch to the British, Kennedy lifted him onto his shoulder to carry him away. Also lugging his musket proved impossible, so Kennedy gave it away and continued the retreat. Before the war ended, the Fifth and Kennedy had a chance to redeem themselves in the defense of Baltimore.

Following the war, Kennedy studied law and went into private practice. He also began dabbling in the writing of fiction and soon was recognized as one of the United States' most important novelists. Also involved in politics, Kennedy served as a Whig Congressman in the 1830s and 1840s and as Pres. Millard Fillmore's secretary of the navy from 1852 to 1853. He died in Newport, Rhode Island, in 1870.

—*Jeanne T. Heidler and David S. Heidler*

See also: Bladensburg, Battle of
Further Reading
Bohner, Charles H. *John Pendleton Kennedy, Gentleman from Baltimore.* Baltimore: Johns Hopkins University Press, 1969.

KENTUCKY

A colonial charter gave Virginia claim to the transmontane area called Kentucky. After considerable exploration, the first permanent settlements were founded in 1775, but their future was in doubt as the British and their Indian allies attacked the isolated settlements. Such early settlers as Daniel Boone, James Harrod, and Benjamin Logan resisted valiantly, and George Rogers Clark relieved some of the danger by his audacious invasion of the Illinois country. Virginia organized Kentucky County in December 1776, then split it into three counties in 1780.

The population increased even during the Revolutionary War; its growth after the war was phenomenal. "Heaven is a Kentucky of a place," one enthusiastic settler exalted, and thousands of immigrants poured through the Cumberland Gap or floated down the Ohio River to secure a piece of that paradise. In 1790, when Kentucky was still a part of Virginia, the district had a population of 73,677. Twenty years later the total was 406,511, and Kentucky was the seventh most populous state in the Union. Slavery existed in Kentucky from the early days of exploration, and in 1810 slaves made up about 20 percent of the population.

Separation from Virginia required the concurrent consent of both Virginia and the United States, and Kentuckians endured years of frustrating delays before attaining statehood on 1 June 1792. Isaac Shelby, a Revolutionary War hero who had moved to Kentucky in 1783, was elected governor. Among the state's major concerns were the Indian problems in the Old Northwest territory and the urgent need for unrestricted use of the Mississippi River to market surplus crops. Many Kentuckians were dissatisfied with the nation's handling of these problems, and as political parties formed in the 1790s the state became a Jeffersonian Republican stronghold.

In 1798, when the Republicans wanted to protest against the Federalists' Alien and Sedition Acts, Thomas Jefferson secretly wrote the Kentucky Resolutions that emphasized states' rights. Most Kentuckians were delighted with Jefferson's election to the presidency in 1801, and John Breckinridge, who had sponsored the Kentucky Resolutions in the legislature, became one of the administration's leaders in the Senate. When he was appointed attorney general in 1805, the West had its first cabinet member. After Breckinridge's death in 1806, Henry Clay became Kentucky's major spokesman on the national scene.

Although far distant from the ocean, Kentuckians were indignant over British and French violations of U.S. neutrality in the early years of the nineteenth century. Some irate citizens believed that Great Britain intended to crush the commerce of her former colonies. The *Chesapeake-Leopard* Affair in 1807 created demands for war to preserve national honor, and only a few Federalists, such as the intrepid Humphrey Marshall, dared challenge the prevailing sentiment. Under the able leadership of Tecumseh, the Indian tribes north of the Ohio River became aggressive again, and many Kentuckians believed that the British were responsible for their unrest. Some citizens wanted war to gain additional territory, particularly the area known as Upper Canada. Dissatisfied with the futile efforts of Jefferson and James Madison to gain concessions through economic pressure, Kentuckians led in the growing demand for war. John Pope was one of the few state leaders who dared oppose it.

After war was declared in June 1812, Kentucky carried much of the burden of its conduct in the Northwest. The state's support, however, varied with such factors as leadership and the general course of hostilities. Both militia and volunteers disliked long campaigns, the legislature seldom provided adequate support, and federal assistance was often inadequate and slow. State pressure helped William Henry Harrison get the northwestern command, and Kentuckians played a major role in his campaigns, although there were instances of wavering resolve and at least one mutiny. Kentucky nonetheless provided many of the supplies used by the western armies, including a considerable amount of gunpowder.

By early 1814, even such stalwarts as Governor Shelby, who had been reelected in 1812 to be a war governor, were in favor of seeking peace. Once victory was achieved at the Battle of the Thames, the state's interest in the war slackened. The 2,500 militia sent to New Orleans in late 1814 were so poorly equipped that Gen. Andrew Jackson was shocked. Told that many were not even armed, he replied, "I have never seen a Kentuckian without a gun and a pack of cards and a bottle of whiskey in my life!"

Before word arrived in Kentucky of the New Orleans victory, Shelby called for 10,000 adequately supplied men to serve in Louisiana. News of the victory there was greeted with joy; yet the reaction to the peace settlement reached at Ghent was mixed. The British made no concessions on neutral rights, and land conquests reverted to pre-war boundaries. Many Kentuckians, however, saw the result as a triumph in a second war for independence. It enhanced the legend of the Kentucky fighting man, for Kentucky had made a notable contribution to the war. Some 3,800 Kentuckians had enlisted in the regular army, and 21,905 had served as volunteers or in the active militia. Of the 1,876 Americans killed in battle, some 1,200 were Kentuckians. Kentucky provided the nation with 4.6 percent of the troops who fought in the war and 64 percent of the men killed in action.

—Lowell H. Harrison

Further Reading

Clark, Thomas D. *A History of Kentucky.* Lexington: University Press of Kentucky, 1960.

Hammock, James Wallace, Jr. *Kentucky and the Second American Revolution.* Lexington: University Press of Kentucky, 1976.

KERR, JOSEPH
1765–1837
Army contractor; militia general; U.S. senator

Joseph Kerr (pronounced Car) was born in Kerrtown (now Chambersburg), Pennsylvania. He migrated to Ohio in 1792, where he became a prominent manufacturer and shipper.

In the fall of 1812, he was appointed a brigadier general of mounted volunteers, but his active service was very brief and did not involve combat. His most important role was that of army supply contractor. He was twice employed by the federal government to provision its northwestern armies—first during Maj. Gen. William Hull's 1812 campaign and later during Maj. Gen. William Henry Harrison's operations on the Upper Sandusky River in 1812–1813. Kerr fulfilled these obligations conscientiously, but his honesty and patriotism brought him to the brink of bankruptcy. In both instances, late payments from Washington forced him to mortgage his own property to pay local farmers. Although Kerr blamed his financial difficulties solely on the War Department, his own account books and correspondence indicate that spoilage due to insufficient salt and the price gouging of local gristmill owners contributed to his losses.

The Ohio legislature later elected Kerr to the U.S. Senate to fill a vacancy. He served from 10 December 1814 to the final adjournment of the 13th Congress on 3 March 1815. While in Washington, Kerr opposed the reestablishment of a national bank because he believed that "incorporated bodies" would ultimately destroy free government. He favored federally issued paper money as the solution to the nation's wartime financial problems.

After the war, Kerr moved to Tennessee and Louisiana, where he died in 1837 at Providence in present-day East Carroll Parish.

—*Michael S. Fitzgerald*

Further Reading

Barlow, William R. "Ohio's Congressmen and the War of 1812." *Ohio History* 72 (1963): 175–194, 257–259.

Dickore, Marie P., ed. *General Joseph Kerr of Chillicothe, Ohio.* Oxford, OH: Oxford Press, 1941.

Gilmore, William E. "General Joseph Kerr." *Ohio Archaeological and Historical Society Publications* 12 (January 1903): 164–166.

"Joseph Kerr." Kathryn A. Jacob and Bruce A. Ragesdale, eds. *Biographical Dictionary of the United States Congress, 1774–1989.* Washington, DC: U.S. Government Printing Office, 1989.

KEY, FRANCIS SCOTT
1779–1843
Author of "The Star-Spangled Banner"

Francis Scott Key was born in Frederick County, Maryland, on 1 August 1779. He was educated at St. John's College in Annapolis as a lawyer and practiced first in Frederick and, from 1802, in Georgetown in the District of Co-

Francis Scott Key

lumbia. In that year he married Marie Tayloe Lloyd. They had 11 children.

At the beginning of the War of 1812, Key was a successful lawyer in Georgetown. The writing of "The Star-Spangled Banner" came about as a result of the British attack in Chesapeake Bay in the summer of 1814. When the British withdrew, after their temporary occupation of Washington, D.C., they took with them an American physician, Dr. William Beanes, of Upper Marlboro, Maryland. Key was asked to obtain the release of Dr. Beanes and, together with an U.S. agent for prisoners, went to the British fleet in Chesapeake Bay and arranged for Beanes's freedom.

While Key was with the fleet, the British began their attack on Baltimore by bombarding Fort McHenry on the night of 13–14 September. The fort successfully resisted the British attack, and on the following morning, when Key saw the U.S. flag still flying over the fort, he wrote the poem that was to become famous as "The Star-Spangled Banner." When he was released from the British fleet, the poem he had written was printed in the form of a handbill entitled "Defence of Fort M'Henry." It quickly became popular and was set to the music of the British drinking song, "To Anacreon in Heaven." In this form it spread throughout the nation, although Congress did not adopt it as the official U.S. national anthem until 1931.

Key wrote other poems, and a collection of them was published in 1857, but his fame rested on the poem he wrote while watching the British bombardment of Fort McHenry. He continued a successful career as a lawyer, serving near the end of his life as district attorney in Washington, D.C. Appropriately, he died in Baltimore on 11 January 1843.

—*Reginald Horsman*

See also: Beanes, William; Star-Spangled Banner, The
Further Reading
Key, Francis Scott. *Poems of the Late Francis S. Key.* New York: R. Carter, 1857.
Smith, Francis Scott Key. *Francis Scott Key: Author of the Star Spangled Banner.* Washington, DC: Key-Smith, 1911.

KING, RUFUS
1755–1827
U.S. diplomat; senator

Rufus King was a talented attorney, Federalist Party leader, diplomat, state and national legislator, soldier, and unsuccessful candidate for governor of New York as well as vice president and president of the United States. He served as either a senator or diplomat under all of the first six presidents of the United States. His greatest public accomplishment was his work drafting and gaining support for the ratification of the U.S. Constitution. King was considered to be one of the finest orators of the Early Republic.

Rufus King was born in Scarboro, Massachusetts (now Maine), on 24 March 1755. He was the eldest son of Capt. Richard King and his first wife. Richard King was a successful merchant, lumberman, land owner, and conservative Loyalist. In the period immediately before the American Revolution, radical mobs burned some of his properties and attacked the King home. Richard King died soon afterward, and these events may, in part, explain Rufus King's later disdain of democracy, so often associated with violent mobs. When the Revolutionary War fighting started in 1775, King was a student at Harvard College. At Harvard his studies were interrupted by the events of the war, but he was able to graduate in 1777 and start his legal studies with a prominent attorney in Boston.

A year later in 1778, he joined the militia as a major and served as Gen. John Glover's aide-de-camp as part of Gen. John Sullivan's unsuccessful attempt to regain control of Newport, Rhode Island. He fought in one battle and then returned to the study of law after his one month of service

Rufus King

ended. King was admitted to the Massachusetts bar in 1780. He soon became a successful attorney and served as justice of the peace. He was elected to the Massachusetts General Court's House of Representatives and served there in the last days of the Revolutionary War.

In 1784, Rufus King was elected to the Confederation Congress, which met in New York City. While living in New York, he married Mary Alsop, the daughter of a wealthy merchant, in 1786. The marriage was for love, money, and political connections in New York. King continued to represent Massachusetts in the Confederation Congress and the Constitutional Convention, and his district in the state legislature until 1788, when he changed his official residence to New York.

In New York City, he started a successful law practice, and his political career prospered. King was elected to the New York State Assembly, and ten days later that legislature selected him as the state's first U.S. senator. King became a friend of Alexander Hamilton, the first secretary of the treasury, and the two were leaders of the Federalist Party in New York. King was important in implementing the Federalist program, introducing many of Hamilton's programs as bills in the U.S. Senate. King and his wife were active socially and in a number of charitable, Episcopal Church, and educational activities. When Mary Alsop King's father died, the Kings became independently wealthy, and he became a gentleman farmer on Long Island when he was not in Washington or overseas.

When King's senatorial term ended, he was appointed minister to England, where he served successfully under Pres. John Adams and Pres. Thomas Jefferson. While in the United Kingdom, King made many English friends and successfully dealt with the British government. Many authorities, however, consider King to have been overly sympathetic to the English and hostile to the Irish and French during his overseas service and afterward. When he returned to New York, his brand of moderate Federalism was out of favor, and he spent his time farming, advising other Federalists, and practicing law part-time. King reentered national politics when he ran unsuccessfully with Charles Cotesworth Pinckney as his party's vice-presidential candidate in 1812. When war was declared he was out of office, but his diaries and voluminous correspondence provide much information about the period immediately prior to and during the War of 1812. King was a keen judge of personalities, and his insights suggest that he was not sympathetic to Madison's leadership or to what he perceived as the expansionist reasons for declaring war.

He was elected again to the U.S. Senate in 1813 and, until the British occupation of Washington, remained skeptical about the war. He often tried to embarrass the president in foreign policy and fiscal matters relating to the conduct of the war. Naturally, he did not want military defeat, but he did want to discredit the Republican Party and return the Federalists to power. After the British occupation of Washington, however, King became an active supporter of the war. He opposed the secessionists in the Federalist Party and did not participate in the Hartford Convention.

King resigned from the Senate to run for president and was the last Federalist candidate for that office when he unsuccessfully opposed Secretary of War James Monroe in 1816. He also failed in his bid for the governorship of New York, but he was reelected to the Senate in 1818. Serving out that term, he thus became the last of the Founding Fathers to hold elective office. Highly respected, he received honorary doctorates from Williams, Dartmouth, Harvard, Columbia, and the University of Pennsylvania. His participation in the Constitutional Convention, successful diplomacy with England, and role as leader of the loyal Federalist opposition during the War of 1812 were his greatest accomplishments. King died on 29 April 1827.

—*George E. Frakes*

Further Reading

Brown, Dorothy M. "Embargo Politics in Maryland." *Maryland Historical Magazine* 58 (1963): 193–210.

Ernst, Robert. "The Aftermath: Rufus King, Violence, and the Reputation of the New Republic." *Journal of Long Island History* 10 (1973): 14–28.

———. *Rufus King, American Federalist.* Chapel Hill: University of North Carolina Press, 1968.

King, Rufus. *The Life and Correspondence of Rufus King, Comprising His Letters . . .* New York: Da Capo Press, 1971.

KING, WILLIAM RUFUS DEVANE
1786–1853
U.S. congressman

Born near Monks Crossroads in Sampson County, North Carolina, on 7 April 1786, William Rufus Devane King was formally educated at Grove Academy (in Duplin County), Fayetteville Academy, the Preparatory School at the University of North Carolina, and the University of North Carolina. He studied law in Fayetteville and returned to his native county to practice.

A dedicated Republican, King was elected to the North Carolina House of Commons in 1808 and 1809. He served as solicitor of the Fifth Circuit of the state Superior Court, 1809–1810. He was elected to the 12th Congress from the fifth district in 1810. In the special session called by Pres. James Madison to meet in November 1811, King, at the age of 25, was likely the youngest member of Congress and North Carolina's leading War Hawk. In December, he supported increasing the size of the standing army of the United States, contending that he was "at all times willing to make not only pecuniary sacrifices, but to expose my person in vindicating the rights and interests of my country." Among those rights was that of carrying "in our own ship the produce of our country to any quarter." Great Britain had tested U.S. patience to the point that "forbearance had ceased to be a virtue." King denied that the approaching war with that country was one of conquest and averred that the extension of the boundaries of the United States would make the country too large. Still, simply as a wartime expedient, Canada would undoubtedly have to be conquered. As for British impressment, King emphasized that he "had rather that fast-anchored isle . . . should be swept from the catalogue of nations than submit that one American—one natural born citizen—should, at her will be torn from his family, his country" and subjected to "the most horrid slavery." Voting in favor of the declaration of war in June 1812, King continued to support the war effort. His position was endorsed by his constituents, who re-elected him to the 13th and 14th Congresses.

King resigned his seat in the House in November 1816 to become the secretary of the United States legation to the Court of Naples and the Two Sicilies and to the Russian court in St. Petersburg. Returning to the United States, he moved to Alabama in 1818. He attended the Alabama Constitutional Convention the next year and served in the U.S. Senate, 1819–1844; he was president pro tempore, 1837–1841. After serving as U.S. minister to France, 1844–1846, King was sent back to the Senate from 1848 to 1852. He was elected vice president of the United States in 1852 and sworn into office in March 1853 in Cuba, where he had gone to try to recuperate from tuberculosis. Back in Alabama, he died on 18 April 1853 at his plantation, King's Bend, without ever assuming his duties in Washington. He was buried in Selma, Alabama. King never married.

—Charles H. Bowman, Jr.

Further Reading

Dameron, E.S.W. "William Rufus King." *University of North Carolina Magazine* 20 (1903): 317–322.
Strange, Robert. *Eulogy on the Life and Character of William Rufus King: Delivered in Clinton on the 1st Day of June, 1853.* Raleigh: N.p., 1853.

KINGSBURY, JACOB
d. 1837
U.S. officer

From Connecticut, Jacob Kingsbury entered the U.S. Army under the Articles of Confederation and rose to the rank of first lieutenant, First U.S. Infantry Regiment, in September 1789. Steadily rising in rank through the 1790s, Kingsbury survived army cuts under Pres. Thomas Jefferson and had attained the rank of colonel by August 1808.

As war loomed in the spring of 1812, Colonel Kingsbury commanded the First Infantry headquartered at Fort Detroit. When the governor of the Michigan Territory, William Hull, initially declined the War Department's offer of a general's commission and the command of the anticipated invasion of Canada from Detroit, Secretary of War William Eustis ordered Kingsbury to recruit an army in Ohio and march it to Detroit to command the invasion.

When these orders arrived, Kingsbury was on leave in the East due to ill health and consequently could not accept the command. When the war started, however, his health had significantly improved, and he requested that he be restored to command. By that time, Hull had been persuaded to accept the command. Following Hull's disastrous surrender of Detroit to the British, Kingsbury refused to join the chorus of condemnation directed toward the governor.

Later in the war, Kingsbury was transferred to the command of New Haven, Connecticut, presumably because of that state's difficulty in working with regular officers. After the War Department had transferred Brig. Gen. Henry Burbeck from Connecticut because of his difficulties with local officials, it assumed that appointing a native of the state might overcome the state's refusal to allow militia to serve under regular officers. As a Federalist and a native, Kingsbury did not press the issue as his predecessors had done and his successors would do. When the British threatened New Haven in the summer of 1814, however, the War Department determined that more senior leadership was needed, and Kingsbury was replaced by Brig. Gen. Thomas Cushing.

With the army reduction at the end of the war, Kingsbury was discharged from the service. He died on 1 July 1837.

—Jeanne T. Heidler and David S. Heidler

See also: Connecticut; Detroit, Surrender of; Hull, William

KINGSTON, UPPER CANADA

On Lake Ontario, Kingston lies at the junction of the Cataraqui River and Lake Ontario. Originally founded by the French as Fort Frontenac, it became a headquarters for naval squadrons in the French and Indian War and began to grow after the passage of the Inland Navigation Act in 1788 and the decision to build a naval dockyard there in 1789. The supplies for the upper country passed along the St. Lawrence River and then through Kingston, usually by bateaux. Large lake vessels seldom went down the river, though they could easily have reached Prescott, in present-day Ontario. Shipbuilding continued to attract capital and labor skills. The shipbuilding trade brought money, trade, and skilled artisans to the town, and adequate customs collection arrangements were made in the town after 1791, when Upper Canada was divided from the old province of Quebec. Rum became a standard item to barter in Kingston's trade. After 1809 the Durham boat, bigger than the bateaux, with flat bottoms made of heavy oak, began to deliver bigger cargoes. Bateaux continued in use in the Bay of Quinte, and schooners ran regularly to Sacket's Harbor on the U.S. shore. A cross-lake smuggling trade existed.

By 1812, Kingston was the most important town on Lake Ontario. A wooden scow ferry crossed the Cataraqui River to link the naval settlement with Kingston. The town's location controlled the approaches of vessels along the lake to where it narrowed into the upper reaches of the St. Lawrence River. From Kingston, trade and troops could venture west, south, or east to Montreal. In 1812, the authorities ran a palisade wall west to Sydenham Street, across Princess or Store Street, to Raglan Road, then northeast to the Cataraqui River. Two log blockhouses were built, one on Princess Street and the other on Montreal Street. The waterfront was guarded by three batteries. On Mississauga Point, a battery of six 24-pounders in a log casement and covered by earthworks was built. On the shore opposite at Point Frederick, another battery covered by earthworks with a line of *cheveaux de frise* (a palisade fence covered by iron spikes) was erected. Inside was a blockhouse with heavy artillery that commanded both bays. On the eastern side of this point was the Royal Navy dockyard. Later, in 1813, a battery of six 24-pounders, protected by logs and earthworks, was built at the entrance to Navy Bay on the eastern side, along with a blockhouse.

On the eve of the War of 1812, Kingston had about 1,200 people who lived in about 190 wooden and stone houses, a number of shops, three hotels, about 20 taverns, a courthouse, two churches (St. George's on King Street and St. Joseph's on William and Bagot Streets), a jail, advanced naval yards and wharves for merchants, and a newspaper (the Kingston *Gazette*) published by Stephen Miles and Charles Kendall. The newspaper reprinted a number of articles from the Federalist press of the United States that were critical of the Jeffersonians and Madisonian Democratic Republicans. Yet merely because the Kingston *Gazette* drew a good deal of its articles from those sources did not mean that there was an alliance between a Kingstonian elite and New England and New York Federalists.

In November 1812, Kingston was bombarded by Commodore Isaac Chauncey's squadron of a dozen converted war schooners. Led by the brig *Oneida*, Chauncey chased the Canadian Provincial Marine vessel *Royal George* from a midchannel anchorage to the protection of batteries and a wharf defended by the small Kingston garrison of regulars and militia. With a gale blowing up, Chauncey had to haul

out of the harbor entrance and claw off a developing lee shore. It was the first and last attack on Kingston in the war. Over the winter Gov.-Gen. Sir George Prevost made a visit. A group of Royal Navy officers and men led by Sir James Lucas Yeo arrived in May, and Kingston became the launching pad for a raid on Chauncey's base at Sacket's Harbor, New York. In 1813, the population of Kingston swelled to 5,000 troops and naval personnel. A small theater was operated by the naval officers, and a naval hospital was opened.

In 1814, huge quantities of military supplies arrived and were organized at the dockyard by Capt. Richard O'Conor. One or two artificers strikes occurred but were of short duration. Shipbuilders came in from Quebec and England to build larger ships. The frigates *Prince Regent* and *Princess Charlotte* were launched and operational by April 1814. Kingston geared up for an attack on the U.S. base at Oswego, New York, which was successfully carried out on 6 May 1814, and thereafter large quantities of captured goods flowed into the town. Between April and September 1814, the ship of the line *St. Lawrence* was built, and at the end of the war plans were drawn up at Kingston for two 90-gun ships, which would have carried at least 112 guns (90 fixed guns plus others in the bow or stern). Supplies were ordered, and artificers engaged in Quebec were sent to Kingston to work on them. Peace brought an economic depression, but the ships were maintained under a new commodore and a garrison was retained in the town.

The old fleet was kept in existence after the war in Kingston Dockyard until it deteriorated to the point at which it was no longer serviceable. A huge building known as the stone frigate, now part of the building of the Royal Military College, housed the sails, rigging, and supplies. The *St. Lawrence* was later sold, and the rest of the fleet was abandoned, part of it in Navy Bay and the remainder around Point Henry in Deadman Bay, where the timbers still lie. Kingston retained the flavor of a garrison town well into the late nineteenth century.

—*Frederick C. Drake*

Further Reading

Dolan, George R. "The Past and Present Fortification at Kingston." *Ontario Historical Society Papers and Records* 12 (1914): 72–80.

Errington, Jane. "British American Kingstonians and the War of 1812." *Historic Kingston* 32 (January 1984): 35–45.

———. "Friends and Foes: The Kingston Elite and the War of 1812: A Case Study in Ambivalence." *Journal of Canadian Studies* 29 (spring 1985): 58–79.

Preston, Richard A. "The History of the Port of Kingston." *Ontario History* 56 (1954): 201–211.

Spurr, John W. "The Royal Navy's Presence in Kingston, Part I: 1813–1836." *Historic Kingston* 25 (March 1977): 63–77.

———. "The Royal Navy's Presence in Kingston, Part II: 1837–1853." *Historic Kingston* 26 (March 1978): 81–96.

———. "Sir James Lucas Yeo: A Hero of the Lakes." *Historic Kingston* 30 (March 1981): 30–45.

Stacey, Charles P. "The American Attack on Kingston Harbour." *Canadian Army Journal* 5 (August 1951): 2–14.

———. "Commodore Chauncey's Attack on Kingston Harbour, November 10, 1812." *Canadian Historical Review* 32 (June 1951): 126–138.

———. "The Ships of the British Squadron on Lake Ontario 1812–1814." *Canadian Historical Review* 34 (December 1953): 311–323.

———. Stanley, George F.G. "Kingston and the Defence of British North America." In Gerald Tulchinsky, ed., *To Preserve and Defend: Essays on Kingston in the Nineteenth Century.* Montreal and London: McGill-Queen's University Press, 1976: 83–101.

Stanley, George F.G., and Richard A. Preston. *A Short History of Kingston as a Military and Naval Centre.* Kingston: Royal Military College, 1950.

KNOX, FORT

Vincennes, capital of the Indiana Territory from 1800 to 1813, was one of the most important frontier settlements. Three military posts named Fort Knox were built in or near Vincennes and were garrisoned by small contingents of regular army troops during the three decades following the Revolution. The first Fort Knox (1787–1803) in Vincennes was, for a time, the westernmost post on the far frontier. A combination of relative peace with the Indians and troubles between civilians and soldiers in Vincennes led the army to abandon the fort and to build another one at a new location.

The second Fort Knox (1803–1813) was erected 3 miles north of Vincennes. For much of the fort's existence, it consisted of a few buildings without a palisade wall. During most of this time, it served primarily as a symbol of U.S. authority and aided Indiana Territorial Governor William Henry Harrison in his administration of the territory. By 1809, however, the situation began to change as the Shawnee brothers, Tecumseh and Tenskwatawa (the Prophet), gained increasing influence over the more bellicose warriors in the region. In 1811, as hostilities appeared imminent, Capt. Zachary Taylor of the Seventh Infantry Regiment was assigned to the command of the post. Harrison wrote to the secretary of war as follows: "In the short time he has been Commander, he has rendered the Garrison defensible—before his arrival it resembled anything but a place of defence."

As a result of Harrison's request for additional troops, 400 soldiers of the Fourth Regiment arrived in Vincennes during September 1811. On 26 September, Harrison, with a combined force of 1,000 regular army soldiers, Indiana militia, and Kentucky volunteers, departed Vincennes and Fort Knox on their march to confront the hostile Indians at Prophet's Town, near present-day Lafayette, Indiana, on the Tippecanoe River. He left behind a small contingent of regular army soldiers at the fort. Two months later, the fort served as a hospital for many of the soldiers who had been wounded during the Battle of Tippecanoe.

The October 1811 construction of Fort Harrison (approximately 55 miles north of Vincennes at present-day Terre Haute) and the fort's successful defense against an attack in September 1812 helped to keep Fort Knox and Vincennes safe from assault during the war's critical first year. During this time, Vincennes saw considerable activity. Many of those from the outlying settlements sought safety in the town, which soon became an armed camp. The Fourth Regiment left Vincennes in May to join William Hull's ill-fated campaign at Detroit, leaving a small number of Seventh Regiment troops assigned to Fort Knox.

To provide closer protection for Vincennes, the second Fort Knox was abandoned in 1813, and most of its wood was floated downstream for construction of the third Fort Knox (1813–1816). This structure was located within the town. As it turned out, this Fort Knox was unnecessary. The conflict had moved northeast and northwest of Vincennes for the remainder of the war.

—*Robert J. Holden*

Further Reading

Crawford, Mary M., ed. "Journal of Mrs. Lydia Bacon." *Indiana Magazine of History* 40 (1944): 376–386.

Gray, Marlesa A. *The Archaeological Investigations of Fort Knox II, Knox County, Indiana, 1803–1813.* Indianapolis: Indiana Historical Society, 1988.

Watts, Florence G. "Fort Knox: Frontier Outpost on the Wabash, 1787–1816." *Indiana Magazine of History* 62 (1966): 51–78.

L

LA COLLE MILL, BATTLE OF
30 March 1814

Coming out of winter quarters at French Mills in the early spring of 1814, Maj. Gen. James Wilkinson heard that 2,500 British soldiers had fortified a position at La Colle Mill. In anticipation of the long-awaited campaign against Montreal, Wilkinson decided to send his 4,000-man army against this British position.

After crossing into Canada on the morning of 30 March, Wilkinson's army scattered the British pickets and moved on the mill. Approaching the British main army at about 3:00 P.M., Wilkinson and his officers noted the strength of the British position. The stone mill had been converted into a strong fortification. In addition to the mill, the British occupied a barn and a blockhouse, all on the opposite side of La Colle Creek from the U.S. army. To add to the strength of the position, the British had dug entrenchments, had cut down trees along the only road approach to the mill, and had the benefit of melting snow, which made the surrounding landscape muddy and swampy.

Still, in spite of these obstacles, Wilkinson ordered his men and artillery to begin firing at the mill when they reached a distance of 250 yards. The firing did little to no damage to the thick stone walls of the mill, and to add to Wilkinson's woes, the British began receiving reinforcements shortly after the fighting began.

These fresh British troops planned to push back the Americans by staging a sortie across the only bridge spanning La Colle Creek. After repeated attempts to cross the bridge to attack the U.S. battery failed, the British reinforcements retreated to their blockhouse.

Wilkinson, however, still could do no damage to the mill and decided to withdraw. In the battle, the Americans suffered 254 casualties; the British, 61. Though he did not yet know it, Wilkinson had been relieved of command a week before and would see no more combat in the War of 1812.

—Jeanne T. Heidler and David S. Heidler

See also: Wilkinson, James
Further Reading
Gosling, D. C. "The Battle of La Colle Mill, 1814." *Journal of the Society for Army Historical Research* 47 (1969): 169–174.

LACOCK, ABNER
1770–1837
U.S. congressman and senator

Born in Virginia to William and Lovey Lacock, Abner Lacock moved with his family to Pennsylvania when he was a young child. Essentially self-educated, Lacock entered public life in 1796 as a justice of the peace for Beaver, Pennsylvania. He spent the first decade of the nineteenth century in the Pennsylvania legislature, first in the lower house and then in the senate. During his time in the legislature, he became involved in the divisions within the Democratic Republican Party in that state, acquiring a number of enemies along the way.

In 1810, Lacock was elected to Congress and spent the next two years as part of the growing faction of War Hawks. He, like his colleagues, urged the institution of military measures that would better put the country on a war footing. In addition, he also argued in favor of redressing the country's grievances against Great Britain through war.

After war was declared, the Pennsylvania legislature elected Lacock to the U.S. Senate. He served as a member of that body from 1813 until 1819. During the War of 1812, his most visible activity was his attempt to block the appointment of his Pennsylvanian political rival Alexander Dallas to replace Albert Gallatin as secretary of the treasury. Finally, by the fall of 1814, with the finances of the nation in a shambles, he acquiesced in Dallas's appointment.

Following the war, Lacock spent his remaining years in the Senate advocating the nationalist measures of the Madison and Monroe administrations. After leaving the Senate, Lacock remained active in Pennsylvania politics but spent most of his time promoting the construction of canals to aid the commerce of the state.

—*Jeanne T. Heidler and David S. Heidler*

Further Reading
Houtz, Harry E. "Abner Lacock." Master's thesis, University of Pittsburgh, 1937.

LAFITTE, JEAN
1780?–1826?
Pirate, privateer

The youngest of three boys (Alexandre Frederic, 1771; Pierre, 1776), Jean Lafitte was probably born in or near Bayonne, France. Some sources list his birthplace as Port-au-Prince, Haiti, and others as the Spanish Pyrenees. Conflicting stories about his origins compound the mystery of his early life. He may have resided in the West Indies with his grandmother, and he may have been taught by tutors until he was 14; he supposedly attended a private school on Martinique and gained some military training on Saint Christopher. Married in 1800 to Christina Levine of St. Croix, he and Pierre probably migrated to Louisiana with the Creole exodus from Santo Domingo in the aftermath of the 1804 slave rebellion. Although some accounts claim that the Lafitte brothers arrived in Louisiana as early as 1802, the earliest confirmed report of Pierre Lafitte was as captain of an armed French privateer in 1804; Jean was not officially listed as a privateer until 1812.

Some assert the brothers opened a blacksmith shop in New Orleans upon arrival. If so, it probably only served as a front for their more profitable privateering and smuggling operations. Between 1807 and 1810, Lafitte supposedly acquired warehouses in New Orleans, Donaldsonville, and at Barataria and became the spokesman for the privateering/smuggling association based on the Louisiana island of Grand Terre. This group, under Lafitte's leadership, boasted an operation at Grand Terre that by 1810 included 40 warehouses, slave pens, a hospital, residences, a fort with cannon, and an estimated force of between 3,000 and 5,000 men. They plundered U.S., English, Spanish, and neutral merchantmen, disregarding international neutrality laws to hijack any vessel that could yield a profit, especially Spanish slave ships bound for Cuba. The organization's elaborate network consisted of ships, warehouses, and distribution depots that stretched from the Gulf of Mexico to the Crescent City.

Lafitte's illegal businesses prospered prior to the War of 1812, generating the wealth to build a sizable warehouse at the Temple, an ancient Indian site south of New Orleans that became his distribution center. Lafitte's audacity prompted Louisiana governor William C.C. Claiborne to authorize an expedition against the Baratarians. In November 1812, U.S. dragoons commanded by Capt. Andrew Hunter Holmes ambushed several Baratarian pirogues loaded with contraband. Jean Lafitte was taken prisoner in the struggle and later released on bond. In October 1813, revenue officials unsuccessfully attacked a Baratarian cargo, and a federal agent was killed in the struggle. Claiborne then issued a $500 reward for Lafitte's capture. In January 1814, Lafitte advertised a slave auction at the Temple, and customs agent John B. Stout was killed while trying to stop the event.

On 3 September 1814, Royal Navy captain Nicholas Lockyer, commanding the sloop *Sophie*, delivered dispatches to Jean Lafitte proposing an alliance between the Baratarians and British forces. Should Lafitte have accepted, he would have been rewarded with money, land, a pardon for past offenses, and a captaincy in the British army. Telling the British he needed time to consider the proposal, Lafitte secretly communicated the plans to Governor Claiborne, who forwarded copies to Gen. Andrew Jackson. In spite of Lafitte's professed loyalty to the United States, Master Commandant Daniel Todd Patterson and Col. Robert Ross led a joint army-navy expedition against the pirate encampment at Barataria on 16 September 1814. The U.S. force encountered little resistance and seized several privateers and prizes, as well as 80 prisoners.

Even though U.S. forces sacked his base, Lafitte refused to help the British. Jackson, who initially refused assistance from the "hellish banditti," learned of British plans and the defeat of the U.S. gunboats on Lake Borgne on 14 December and immediately realized New Orleans needed the pirates' defensive help. As British forces prepared their assault, the Louisiana legislature passed a resolution providing amnesty for any Baratarian who aided in New Orleans's defense. Jean Lafitte offered his services to Jackson, serving as a topographic adviser and guide on the general's volunteer staff. Contrary to rumor, Lafitte was not at the battle on 8 January 1815. He was delivering a letter on the Left Bank.

The Lafitte brothers were pardoned by Pres. James Madison in February 1815 for their services at the Battle of New Orleans. Afterward, Jean Lafitte became involved in privateering and filibustering against the Spanish, using Galveston, Texas, as a base. His new operations grew into an extensive network for smuggling and the slave trade and soon resembled his former establishment at Barataria. In

1819, several of Lafitte's associates from Galveston were convicted of piracy and hanged in New Orleans. Although tarnished by the accusations of piracy, Lafitte remained in charge at Galveston until he was expelled in 1820.

The rumors of Lafitte's demise are as abundant as those about his early life. One story claims that Jean Lafitte moved to the Yucatan Peninsula in 1821 and died there of fever in 1826. Another account, however, charges that Lafitte, alias John Lafflin, traveled extensively in Europe and lived a long life in the U.S. Midwest, supposedly dying on 5 May 1851 in Alton, Illinois.

—*Gene A. Smith*

Further Reading

Arthur, Stanley Clisby. *Jean Lafitte, Gentleman Rover*. New Orleans: Harmanson, 1952.

De Grummond, Jane Lucas. *The Baratarians and the Battle of New Orleans*. Baton Rouge: Legacy Publishing, 1961.

———. *Renato Beluche: Smuggler, Privateer and Patriot, 1780–1860*. Baton Rouge: Louisiana State University Press, 1983.

Faye, Stanley. "The Great Stroke of Pierre Lafitte." *Louisiana Historical Quarterly* 23 (1940): 733–826.

Gayarre, Charles. "Historical Sketch of Pierre and Jean Lafitte: The Famous Smugglers of Louisiana." *Magazine of American History* 10 (1883).

Vogel, Robert C. "Jean Lafitte, the Baratarians, and the Historical Geography of Piracy in the Gulf of Mexico." *Gulf Coast Historical Review* 5 (1990): 63–77.

LAKE BORGNE, BATTLE OF

14 December 1814

To defend New Orleans, Master Commandant Daniel Todd Patterson had five gunboats, Nos. 5, 23, 156, 162, and 163 (3 to 5 guns and carronades each); the sloop of war *Louisiana* (16 guns); the *Carolina* (15 guns and carronades); and two schooners, the *Sea Horse* and *Alligator* (1 gun each). More gunboats at New Orleans might have foiled the British attack altogether. As late as December 1811, 26 had been there.

Patterson declined Gen. Andrew Jackson's suggestion that he move his squadron to Mobile because he was certain the British would attack New Orleans. Patterson instead positioned his gunboats to delay the British. All U.S. ground forces were not yet in place, so it was essential that the navy buy as much time as possible. Because Patterson kept his largest warships at New Orleans, where they could

work with ground forces, he gained Jackson two valuable weeks.

There were a number of approaches to New Orleans. One was the route Jackson expected—by land from Mobile. Others were via Barataria Bay to the west or the Mississippi River, and Lakes Borgne and Pontchartrain to the east. As Patterson predicted, British admiral Alexander Cochrane chose the Lake Borgne route. Its chief liability was its shallow water. The British troops would have to be transported in small boats and barges.

Patterson ordered five of his six gunboats (Nos. 5, 23, 156, 162, and 163) to Lake Borgne under the command of Lt. Thomas ap Catesby Jones. Jones also had the *Sea Horse* and *Alligator* for detached service. To transport 7,000 men across Lake Borgne, through the Rigolets, and into Lake Pontchartrain, Cochrane first had to defeat the U.S. gunboats.

Over the period from 8 to 12 December, most of the British vessels arrived in Mississippi Sound and concentrated near Cat Island. The British then transferred troops from the larger transports into shallower draft vessels, which were escorted by gun brigs as they entered Lake Borgne. There they discovered the U.S. gunboats, but as the shallow-draft brigs moved to attack, they ran aground.

Patterson had ordered Jones to delay the enemy as long as possible and then retreat to the Rigolets. There was a fort there (Petites Coquilles) that could support him, and Jones would either "sink the enemy, or be sunk." A stand at the Rigolets would also impose a longer advance on the British boats.

On the morning of 13 December, Jones sighted a flotilla of barges headed for him. Westerly winds blowing for several days had made the water in the lakes very low, so Jones ordered his men to lighten the gunboats by jettisoning anything "that could be dispensed with." By 3:30 that afternoon, the tide had increased sufficiently to allow the gunboats to get under way for the Petites Coquilles. That same evening the *Sea Horse*, on detached service, beat back several British boat attacks before her captain was forced to destroy her.

Jones's hope of getting his gunboats to the Petites Coquilles proved futile in the absence of any appreciable wind and the running of a strong ebb tide. At 1:00 A.M. on 14 December, he ordered the gunboats to anchor at the west end of the Malheureux Islands passage, there to give the enemy "as warm a reception as possible." He arranged his force in "close line abreast" athwart the channel. They were anchored at the stern with springs on their cables and boarding nets triced up. The Americans spotted the British boats at daybreak. Soon after first light the British boats, in three divisions under the overall command of Capt.

Nicholas Lockyer, weighed anchor and moved toward the Americans. The British took the *Alligator*, which was southeast of the U.S. force and trying to join it. At about 10:00 A.M., Lockyer ordered the flotilla to anchor just beyond the range of the U.S. long guns. The men had rowed 36 miles and were now given a much-needed rest and breakfast.

Jones said his force numbered 182 men and 23 guns. He estimated British strength at 1,200 men in 45 boats: 40 launches and barges, each with a carronade; two launches or barges with one long gun; and three gigs with small arms only. Yet the odds were not as overwhelming as they seemed. The U.S. gunboats were larger and stationary, and they had heavy, long guns (15 of them, as well as eight carronades) that were able to engage at longer range.

At 10:30, the enemy weighed anchor, formed up in line abreast, and made for the U.S. line. The British had to row against a strong 3-knot current, the same impediment that had worked against the Americans earlier. The current also broke the U.S. battle line, however, when Nos. 156 and 163 dragged their anchors and moved about 100 yards eastward in front of the others. This fragmenting of the battle worked very much to the British advantage.

When the enemy was within range, the Americans opened with their long guns, but the British boats were such small targets that little damage was done. At 10:50, the British opened fire along their entire line and the action became general. For the next two hours, the British used their superior numbers to take the U.S. vessels by storm; the chief weapons on both sides were pistols, cutlasses, and boarding pikes.

The turning point in the battle was the British capture of No. 156 at about 12:10, after the Americans had beaten back several attacks and inflicted heavy casualties on the British, which included a wounded Captain Lockyer. Jones was also wounded and forced to go below. Their superior numbers finally gave the British control of the gunboat's deck and subsequently the vessel. After taking No. 156, they turned her guns against the other gunboats. The battle continued for another half hour with No. 163 the next gunboat taken, followed by Nos. 162, 5, and 23.

Both sides exhibited tenacity and courage in the battle. The Americans lost 6 killed, 35 wounded, and 86 captured. In their official report of the action the British acknowledged 17 killed and 77 wounded, many mortally.

The Battle of Lake Borgne was as close as the U.S. Navy's gunboats came during the entire war to fulfilling their promise. They bought a vital delay in the British army advance upon New Orleans that allowed Jackson more time to strengthen defensive positions. Ultimately, on 8 January 1815, the British army suffered defeat in its land

assault on New Orleans, and a week later the British retreated to their ships and sailed away.

—Spencer C. Tucker

See also: Gunboats; Jones, Thomas ap Catesby; New Orleans, Battle of
Further Reading
Brown, Wilburt S. *The Amphibious Campaign for West Florida and Louisiana.* University, AL: University of Alabama Press, 1969.
Eller, E. M. *Sea Power and the Battle of New Orleans.* N.p.: 1965.

LAKE CHAMPLAIN, BATTLE OF
11 September 1814

Recognized for its strategic importance as a north-south invasion corridor, Lake Champlain had been a center of martial activity long before the War of 1812 refocused attention upon its waters. Both sides in the Anglo-American conflict built naval squadrons on the lake in an effort to secure lines of supply and communication as a precursor for offensive land operations. Yet, throughout much of 1813 and on into the following year, the lake's New York and Vermont shorelines witnessed only indecisive actions as the belligerents fought more vigorously in the western and southern theaters. Control of the lake became imperative once British reinforcements, freed from the European fray, began arriving in Canada during the summer of 1814.

Sir George Prevost, governor-general of Canada, planned to use these battle-hardened veterans for a late-season offensive to isolate New England from the remainder of the United States. Crucial for the success of the campaign was the capture of the U.S. stronghold at Plattsburg, New York, which the governor-general sought to reduce through a combined land and water assault. Unfortunately for Prevost, his Lake Champlain naval squadron was still being fitted out as it was ordered to weigh anchor and move south. The British flotilla consisted of four ships and 12 armed gunboats, all under the command of George Downie. His flagship, the 37-gun frigate *Confiance*, was the most potent vessel plying the lake. Other British ships were the brig *Linnet*, with 16 guns, and the sloops *Chubb* and *Finch*, each mounting 11 cannon. All galleys carried a long gun as well as a carronade.

Opposing the British was Thomas Macdonough's comparable U.S. squadron of four ships and ten armed gun-

Due to its strategic location, both the British and the Americans wanted control of Lake Champlain. The decisive American victory under Thomas Macdonough is depicted in this 1816 engraving by B. Tanner.

boats, most of which had been constructed at Vergennes, Vermont, under the direction of shipbuilders Noah and Adam Brown. The Browns were earlier involved in the building of Oliver Hazard Perry's Lake Erie squadron. Macdonough's flagship, the corvette *Saratoga*, mounted 26 guns. The brig *Eagle* carried 20 cannon, and the schooner *Ticonderoga* held 17. The smallest ship in the U.S. flotilla was the sloop *Preble*, with a complement of 7 guns. Galleys were a mixed bag, with six mounting 2 guns and four carrying 1 gun each. Essentially evenly matched in number, the British held an advantage in long-range gunnery, whereas the U.S. strength lay in short-range carronade.

With the British requiring a quick victory to carry the campaign toward Albany, Macdonough weighed his options, then decided to let the British come to him. Using the configuration of Plattsburg Bay and the prevailing winds to his advantage, the U.S. naval commander anchored his ships bow to stern across a confined stretch of water between Cumberland Head and the shoals surrounding Crab Island at the southern entrance to the bay. Unable to maneuver effectively in the narrows from leeward, the British squadron would be forced to give up its long-gun advantage and close with the Americans. To offset his own inability to put to sail as the fight developed, Macdonough rigged anchors and cables to provide limited maneuverability for what now amounted to a floating battery.

To engage the Americans, Downie had to turn his squadron into the wind as it rounded Cumberland Head. Attacking bows on would expose the length of his ships to punishing broadsides as they sailed into position. Yet with few options available and under orders to attack, Downie decided to concentrate the fire of *Confiance*, *Linnet*, and *Chubb* against the two largest U.S. ships, *Saratoga* and *Eagle*. He intended for his flagship *Confiance* to turn hard to port and anchor across the bow of *Saratoga*. *Finch* and 11 galleys were to strike at *Ticonderoga* and *Preble*. Prevost had also promised land-based artillery support once he had routed the Americans at Plattsburg.

Downie's plan quickly came apart. The wind turned fickle and halted the British advance, forcing him to anchor more than 300 yards from the U.S. flagship. The contest quickly turned general, with broadside after broadside exchanged between combatants. Casualties mounted and included Downie, who was mortally wounded early in the battle. At the van of the British line, the outgunned *Chubb* was soon crippled by concentrated fire from *Eagle's* carronades. Drifting helplessly toward the powerful broadside of *Saratoga*, the British sloop struck her colors. However, to the rear the small *Preble* was no match for *Finch* and the closing British gunboats. Raked by grapeshot and canister and soon to be boarded, the U.S. sloop cut her cable and maneuvered toward shore. *Finch* then drew up with *Ticonderoga*. The heated exchange that followed shattered both ships, with *Finch* ultimately running aground on the shoals off Crab Island, where it subsequently surrendered.

At the van of the U.S. line, *Eagle*, her starboard broadside pounded into near total submission, cut her cable and slipped into an anchorage between and to port of *Saratoga*, now on point, and *Ticonderoga*. From that position, the brig's fresh broadside could only strike *Confiance*, leaving the U.S. flagship exposed to withering fire from both the British frigate and *Linnet*. As *Saratoga's* starboard broadside was pummeled into uselessness, Macdonough gave the order to wind ship, or turn her around on her anchor cable. Slowly the corvette's port cannon were brought to bear upon *Confiance*, which was unsuccessfully attempting the same maneuver. Barely afloat, the shattered frigate struck its colors, as did *Linnet* not long after.

Though the Americans had achieved victory, the outcome remained uncertain until the closing moments of more than two hours of battle, thereby validating the tactics employed by both naval commanders. Perhaps the finest compliment was one veteran British sailor's assertion that Trafalgar "was a mere flea bite in comparison" to the Champlain action.

When word arrived of the British naval disaster, Prevost moved to lift his siege of Plattsburg. Deprived of secure lines of supply and communication and deep in hostile territory late in the campaigning season, the British commander had no option but to withdraw to Canadian sanctuary. The U.S. naval victory on Lake Champlain and the successful defense of Plattsburg were quite possibly the most decisive actions of the war and influenced the outcome of peace negotiations soon to be concluded at Ghent.

—*William E. Fischer, Jr.*

See also: Downie, George; Macdonough, Thomas; Plattsburg, Battle of

Further Reading
Burdick, Virginia Mason. *Captain Thomas Macdonough: Delaware Born Hero of the Battle of Lake Champlain.* Wilmington: Delaware Heritage Press, 1991.

Crisman, Kevin James. *The* Eagle, *an American Brig on Lake Champlain during the War of 1812.* Shelburne, VT, and Annapolis, MD: New England Press and Naval Institute Press, 1987.

———. *The History and Construction of the United States Schooner* Ticonderoga. Alexandria, VA: Eyrie Publications, 1983.

Everest, Allan S. *The War of 1812 in the Champlain Valley.* Syracuse, NY: Syracuse University Press, 1981.

Lewis, Dennis M. *British Naval Activity on Lake Champlain during the War of 1812.* Plattsburg, NY, and Elizabethtown, NY: Clinton County Historical Association and Essex County Historical Society, 1994.

Mahan, Alfred T. *Seapower in Its Relation to the War of 1812.* 2 vols. Boston: Little, Brown, 1919.

Muller, Charles Geoffrey. *The Proudest Day: Macdonough on Lake Champlain.* New York: Curtis Books, 1960.

Stahl, John M. *The Battle of Plattsburg: A Study in and of the War of 1812.* Argos, IN: Van Trump, 1918.

LAKE ERIE CAMPAIGN
1813

On 8 February 1813, U.S. Navy master commandant Oliver Hazard Perry received orders to proceed to Sacket's Harbor, New York, for duty on the Great Lakes under Commodore Isaac Chauncey. Arriving at Erie, Pennsylvania, in March, Perry thus set in motion the Lake Erie Campaign.

During the spring and early summer of 1813, Perry supervised the construction, assembly, equipage, and manning of a potent naval squadron to challenge the Royal Navy and Canadian Provincial forces that were based at the Amherstburg Navy Yard on the Detroit River. The crown naval forces under Royal Navy commander Robert Heriot Barclay, an experienced and a talented officer with significant service in the Napoleonic wars, endured significant shortfalls in trained sailors and logistical support. Although Perry enjoyed a secure route for men and materials along the East Coast through New York and the safety of Pittsburgh, Barclay had no reliable overland route. Once Perry's squadron began active operations in mid-August, the British lost their water route. Barclay labored under additional disadvantages, including inferiority in ships, men, and guns. His largest vessel, the corvette HMS *Detroit*, carried only 20 experienced seamen. British soldiers, Canadian militia, and merchant marines composed the bulk of

The standoff on Lake Erie finally ended when the Royal Navy was faced with starvation. Here, American commander Oliver Hazard Perry abandons the USS Lawrence in a daring move and rows half a mile to the USS Niagara through enemy fire.

his crews. Although the Royal Navy vessels had a 63-to-54 advantage in guns, Perry's ships carried many 32-pounder carronades, compared to Barclay's 24-pounders and smaller long-barreled cannon. The cannon's effective range was twice that of the carronade, but the weight of metal at shorter range gave Perry a profound advantage.

All U.S. sailors and marines assigned to the Great Lakes reported to Chauncey's headquarters before detachment to Perry, so top-quality sailors were usually siphoned off to the Lake Ontario forces. Manning a full ship required 720 men, but Perry had only 400 by mid-August, including nearly 100 inexperienced soldier-volunteers. Despite crew shortages, the work of building progressed (supervised by Master Mariner Daniel Dobbins), resulting in the launching of four gunboats by late May and two brigs in early June. By August, Perry's force stood ready to challenge Barclay with a squadron of ten warships formed around the newly launched sister brigs USS *Lawrence* and USS *Niagara.*

To disrupt the U.S. building program, Barclay sailed from Amherstburg on 15 June with three ships to attack the Presque Isle shipyard; however, fog disrupted the oper-

ation. Unwilling to press an attack against the fortifications and blockhouses guarding the harbor entrance, Barclay returned to Amherstburg. He established a close blockade of Presque Isle in mid-July to induce Perry to sortie and fight. Yet on 29 July, Barclay broke off the blockade and returned to Long Point, the station at the mouth of the Detroit River. Perry was thus able to move his squadron unopposed over the Presque Isle sandbar into the open lake. It remains unclear why Barclay did not persist in his blockade. The possibility of a sudden lake storm perhaps influenced his decision, but it is more likely that he realized the futility of maintaining a close blockade against a much stronger opposing force. He apparently did not want to bring Perry to action until the completion of the *Detroit* and the arrival of reinforcements.

Taking advantage of Barclay's withdrawal, Perry moved his squadron over the sandbar between 1 and 4 August. Guns and heavy equipment had to be removed to lighten the larger ships, and an ingenious floating dock or "camel" was constructed to lift the brigs over the shallow entrance. On 4 August, Barclay returned to Presque Isle but declined to attack when he realized that the Americans were clear of the harbor. The fourth thus emerged as the critical day of the campaign. Barclay's failure to maintain the blockade or to fight once it was loosened allowed Perry to clear the bar and conduct lake operations. A close blockade might have kept Perry bottled up in harbor for the remainder of the sailing season, allowing for the gradual reinforcement of royal forces. Yet in the absence of such a blockade, an attack on 4 August would likely have inflicted grave damage on Perry's stripped and degunned ships.

Perry received reinforcements from two sources in mid-August. Sensitive to the necessity of controlling the lake, Gen. William Henry Harrison, commanding U.S. Army forces in Ohio, sent soldier-volunteers to man Perry's warships. Master Commandant Jesse Duncan Elliott also arrived at Presque Isle with 100 officers and sailors. A dispute with Chauncey over the quality of men sent to him induced Perry to request a transfer. When Secretary of the Navy William Jones refused the request, Perry resolved to conduct the campaign with the available men. Perry placed Elliott in command of the *Niagara* and raising his flag on the brig *Lawrence*, got underway from Presque Isle on 12 August for the eventual conquest of Lake Erie.

The U.S. squadron anchored in Sandusky Bay, Ohio, on 16 August. A council of war onboard the *Lawrence* with General Harrison decided that Perry would operate out of Put-in-Bay on Bass Island in the western end of Lake Erie to disrupt British supply lines and instigate a general engagement whenever possible. From this forward base, Perry could observe British movements and support Harrison's army 30 miles away.

From Put-in-Bay, Perry conducted two reconnoiters to the Amherstburg area on 24 August and 1 September, despite the crippling effects of a "lake fever" epidemic. To counter U.S. attempts to force the entrance of the Detroit River, Barclay anchored several ships across the mouth. Perry declined to attack the defensive anchorage. Several factors drove Perry's decision. Fort Malden and the floating batteries at Amherstburg were formidable, the river ran swiftly there, winds were frequently fickle, and the narrow channel would restrict his squadron's ability to maneuver. Nonetheless, the presence of the Royal Navy force, considerably strengthened by the launching and commissioning of the *Detroit* in August, convinced Perry that the British squadron would have to be nullified prior to an amphibious invasion.

To improve his firepower, Barclay transferred guns from Fort Malden to the ships and floating batteries. He thus created a mix of various gun calibers that required differently prepared powder cartridges and shot. Barclay drilled the gun crews twice daily, but a powder shortage limited live firing practice. Additionally, faulty firing mechanisms required many guns to be touched off by shooting a pistol at the vent.

By early September, the supply situation had become critical at Amherstburg. Only a few day's flour remained, and although the summer wheat harvest was in, neither of the local mills operated. The commissary officer at Fort Malden had no cash to purchase the local meat and vegetables or to pay the men. On 6 September, Barclay received some 30 officers and sailors from the troopship HMS *Dover* at Quebec, but no other reinforcements arrived. By 9 September, the storehouse held only one day's rations. Barclay had to act. Faced with starvation, he decided to draw Perry into a general fleet action.

At 3:00 P.M. on 9 September, the Royal Navy Lake Erie Squadron weighed anchor. Barclay's strategy to nullify the U.S. numerical advantage included a running battle in which the British would stand off using long-range cannon. The U.S. heavy carronades had an effective range of only 400 yards. At sunrise on 10 September, a lookout on the *Lawrence* sighted the British, and Perry committed his squadron to combat. The British force consisted of the 300-ton corvette HMS *Detroit* (11 guns), the 200-ton corvette HMS *Queen Charlotte* (17 guns), the 96-ton schooner *Lady Prevost* (13 guns), the 75-ton brig *General Hunter* (10 guns), the 60-ton sloop *Little Belt* (3 guns), and the 35-ton schooner *Chippeway* (1 gun). Opposing Barclay, the U.S. squadron consisted of the 260-ton brigs USS *Lawrence* and USS *Niagara*, each with 20 guns; the 85-ton *Caledonia* (3 guns); the 65-ton schooner *Somers* (2 guns); the 50-ton sloop *Trippe* (1 gun); and the 50- to 60-ton gunboats *Tigress*, *Porcupine*, *Scorpion*, and *Ariel*, each mounting 1 to 4 guns.

In the early morning, Barclay held the weather gauge, but by 10:00, the wind changed and blew from the southeast in a light breeze. This undid Barclay's long-range strategy and gave the Americans the wind advantage. Perry's battle plan called for the *Lawrence* and *Niagara* to lay alongside the *Detroit* and *Queen Charlotte* respectively, with smaller ships engaging an opposite equivalent enemy. By 10:00 the *Lawrence* cleared for action, and Perry hoisted his battle ensign, a dark blue flag displaying Capt. James Lawrence's last words, "Don't give up the ship." Barclay opened fire at 11:45 A.M. at a range of 2,000 yards. At 11:55, Perry signaled to close the range and engage assigned opponents. The deeper-draft gunboats fell behind in the light winds, but Perry took the tactical risk of a premature engagement. Gradually, all of his ships maneuvered into line except the *Niagara*, which shortened sail and lagged behind for over two hours. Failing to engage the *Queen Charlotte*, the *Niagara* allowed her to concentrate fire on Perry's flagship.

The *Lawrence* received the brunt of British broadsides and soon became a derelict with 83 of 103 crewmen killed or wounded and all guns disabled. At 2:30 P.M., Perry fired the *Lawrence's* last operable gun, struck the battle ensign, and transferred his flag to the *Niagara* in one of the most dramatic moments in naval history. He rounded up four unwounded crewmen and, standing in the stern of the ship's cutter—a small boat—with the battle ensign, defied British sharpshooters and rowed the half-mile to the *Niagara*. Commandant Elliot then embarked in the cutter to direct the gunboats as Perry took charge of the relatively undamaged brig.

The senior officer left aboard the *Lawrence* struck her colors, but Barclay had neither the men nor undamaged boats to take possession of the prize. Two crippling wounds forced Barclay to go below, leaving Lt. George Inglis in effective command. In the British ships, five of six commanding officers and four first officers lay dead or wounded, thus placing less experienced junior officers in charge. When the *Niagara* moved forward to get windward of the disabled *Lawrence*, the *Queen Charlotte* drew up under the stern of the badly mauled *Detroit* to pass ahead and engage Perry. Inglis attempted to wear ship (pivot 180 degrees) to engage the starboard side guns against the *Niagara*. With her damaged sails, spars, and rigging, the *Detroit* turned too slowly, however, and the *Queen Charlotte's* bowsprit became entangled in the *Detroit's* mizzen mast. As British sailors desperately hacked away at the enmeshed rigging, Perry sailed across the bow of the *Detroit*, breaking the British line, and raked the enemy with effective carronade broadsides at less than 100 yards. By 3:00, unable to return effective fire, both the *Queen Charlotte* and the *Detroit* surrendered. They were followed by the *General Hunter* and the *Lady Prevost*. The other British ships attempted to flee but were quickly overhauled and captured.

In the Battle of Lake Erie, the Royal Navy suffered casualties of 41 killed and 94 wounded, compared to the U.S. Navy's 27 killed and 96 wounded. In late September, Harrison invaded Canada, capturing Amherstburg and Detroit, and defeating the royal forces at Moraviantown. Perry's victory on the water allowed for conquest on land. To Harrison, Perry had written within an hour of the last broadside one of the most memorable dispatches in naval history: "We have met the enemy and they are ours—Two Ships, two brigs, one schooner and one sloop." To the secretary of the navy, he reported, "It has pleased the Almighty to give to the arms of the United States a signal victory over their enemies on this lake."

—*Stanley D.M. Carpenter*

See also: Barclay, Robert Heriot; Dobbins, Daniel; Elliott, Jesse Duncan; Harrison, William Henry; Lawrence, James; Malden, Fort; Perry, Oliver Hazard

Further Reading

Dillon, Richard. *We Have Met the Enemy: Oliver Hazard Perry, Wilderness Commodore.* New York: McGraw-Hill, 1978.

Malcomson, Robert, and Thomas Malcomson. *HMS Detroit: The Battle for Lake Erie.* Annapolis, MD: Naval Institute Press, 1990.

Welsh, William J., and David C. Skaggs. *War on the Great Lakes: Essays Commemorating the 175th Anniversary of the Battle of Lake Erie.* Kent, OH: Kent State University Press, 1991.

LAKE ONTARIO

Lake Ontario formed part of the border between British North America and the United States. All war supplies to support British settlements in the West passed over its waters or along its shores; thus the fight to control Lake Ontario figured prominently in the war. Lake Ontario also saw the largest naval arms race of the war, although that contest did not result in a decisive battle.

Lake Ontario bisected the theater of operations that Americans called the Northern Frontier, leaving an invasion route on each side. In the east was the Lake Champlain–Richelieu River valley leading toward Montreal. The western route into Canada traversed the Niagara Peninsula. The lake itself was a broad waterborne avenue of invasion in its own right. Depending upon the wind and weather, a fleet could move an army the length of the lake in three days or cross it in one. That same army would take 18 days or longer to march around the northern shore of the lake. Whoever controlled the lake held a potentially decisive advantage, and both the United States and Britain saw the benefit of conducting raids against weakly defended naval yards or supply depots.

The configuration of Lake Ontario favored the British. They enjoyed two excellent harbors: Kingston and York (modern-day Toronto). Because Kingston was closer to Montreal and therefore more easily supplied, the British chose it as their major naval base. The British also controlled Burlington Bay and the Bay of Quinte, which served as refuges for British vessels chased by the U.S. fleet. In contrast, the Americans had only Sacket's Harbor, New York, which became their naval base on Lake Ontario. The mouth of the Niagara River was adequate as a sheltered haven; however, it was useless unless both Forts George and Niagara were in friendly hands.

In winter, ice on the lake posed tactical possibilities. Boats of all sizes were useless. In a long, cold winter, it was possible to cross the ice between Kingston and Sacket's Harbor. Although both sides recognized the potential, neither took advantage of the lake ice. Lake Ontario was generally ice-free by early April, several weeks before the St. Lawrence River was completely open. Thus, the Americans could begin operations west of Kingston in earnest before the British could bring reinforcements from Montreal or Quebec.

The British supply line ran up the St. Lawrence and across the full length of the northern shore of the lake to Burlington Bay or to the Niagara River. The U.S. supply line ran by water and short portages from Albany to Oswego, New York, at the mouth of the river by that name. From there, supplies moved east to Sacket's Harbor or west to the Niagara Frontier. The roads encircling Lake Ontario were dirt tracks, difficult when dry and nearly impassable to wagons when wet. Water travel, in contrast, was on the average six times faster than land travel and correspondingly less expensive.

The U.S. Navy was outnumbered in vessels seven to one on Lake Ontario at the outset of hostilities. However, the Americans rebounded quickly by buying up civilian schooners and sending naval guns, seamen, and carpenters to Sacket's Harbor. The commander there, Commodore Isaac Chauncey, was a skillful organizer, and he set about the business of out-building the British. In this regard, the Americans held an advantage because the British received guns, cordage, sails, and sailors from Britain itself, there being few to spare at Halifax. At the beginning of the war, the British naval force on Lake Ontario was called the Provincial Marine, and it was a transport service for the army rather than a fighting force. When Chauncey sailed in November, he destroyed a schooner of the Provincial Marine, captured three merchant boats, and chased the largest Provincial Marine vessel, the *Royal George* with 22 guns, into Kingston Harbor.

In April 1813, Chauncey joined the army in a successful raid on York. The Americans captured a ship there and carried off naval supplies intended for the British fleet on Lake Erie. The following month, Chauncey cooperated with the army in a joint attack on Fort George. As a result, the Americans now had a safe haven at the mouth of the Niagara River. However, while Chauncey and the fleet were away, a Royal Navy force under Sir James Yeo from Kingston raided Sacket's Harbor. Though ultimately unsuccessful, Yeo's attack came close to destroying the U.S. shipyard. Chauncey, learning how vulnerable his base was, refused to cooperate further with the army in joint operations. Instead, he single-mindedly focused his efforts on

out-building the Royal Navy, and when the circumstances favored him, he planned to offer Yeo battle with his entire fleet. The outcome of one decisive battle, thought Chauncey, would determine the war on the lake.

Yeo was pleased to take up the arms race, but like Chauncey, he was unwilling to join battle unless the circumstances were favorable—and that time never came. Circumstances were never quite right to convince either commander that he enjoyed enough advantage to justify the considerable risk. The loss of Lake Ontario to either side would mean losing the ground war along the margin of the lake. That would affect the war on all the Great Lakes and in the upper Mississippi Valley. If the British lost on Lake Ontario, all of Upper Canada was forfeit. With the stakes so high, it is perhaps understandable that both sides settled for the tediousness of a shipbuilding war. The effort consumed hundreds of cannon and thousands of sailors, carpenters, and marines. Each ship launched was larger than the one before. Soon, vessels as large as any ship of the line were being assembled in the frontier boatyards of Kingston and Sacket's Harbor.

The final year of the war saw little action. Yeo raided Oswego with some success in May. His attempt to deprive Chauncey of guns for his largest ship failed when his raiders were ambushed along the Big Sandy Creek later that month. Chauncey's refusal to sail in July contributed to the failure of Jacob Brown's army to recapture Fort George. With the U.S. flotilla in harbor, Yeo was free to transport hundreds of troops up the lake to challenge Brown at Lundy's Lane and at Fort Erie. In August, when Chauncey deemed his fleet superior to the Royal Navy, he blockaded Yeo in Kingston. Although Chauncey offered battle, Yeo refused. Then in September, Yeo launched the *St. Lawrence,* which carried 102 guns on three decks. With this immense ship, the Royal Navy controlled the lake for the remainder of the year. Taking up the challenge, Chauncey's shipwrights began construction of two vessels, the *Chippewa* and the *New Orleans,* each carrying more and larger guns than the *St. Lawrence.* Neither vessel was launched because the war ended in December. For all the fighting and building on and around Lake Ontario, the border shifted not one jog.

—*Richard V. Barbuto*

See also: Chauncey, Isaac; George, Fort; Niagara Campaigns; Sacket's Harbor, Battle of; Sacket's Harbor, New York; Yeo, James Lucas
Further Reading
Cruikshank, Ernest A. "The Contest for the Command of Lake Ontario in 1814." In *Ontario Historical Society Papers and Records* 21 (1924): 99–159.

Thatcher, Joseph M. "A Fleet in the Wilderness: Shipbuilding at Sacket's Harbor." In R. Arthur Bowler, ed., *War Along the Niagara*. Youngstown, NY: Old Fort Niagara Association, 1991, 53–59.

Winton-Claire, C. "A Shipbuilder's War." In Morris Zaslow, ed., *The Defended Border*. Toronto: Macmillan of Canada, 1964, 165–173.

See also: Bowyer, Fort; New Orleans, Battle of
Further Reading
Brown, Wilburt S. *The Amphibious Campaign for West Florida and Louisiana, 1814–1815: A Critical Review of Strategy and Tactics at New Orleans*. Mobile: University of Alabama Press, 1969.

LAMBERT, JOHN
1772–1847
British army officer

The second of five sons of Royal Navy captain Robert Lambert, John Lambert was commissioned an ensign, First Foot Guards, on 27 July 1791. He fought at Valenciennes, Lincelles, and Dunkirk, Flanders, in October 1793; saw duty during the Irish Rebellion of 1798; served in the New Holland expedition from 1799 to 1800 and in Portugal; and fought at La Coruña, Spain, from 1808 to 1809 and at Walcheren, the Netherlands, in 1809. In 1811, he joined Wellington's army with the Third Battalion, First Foot Guards, and commanded a brigade in the Sixth Division. He was promoted to major general on 4 June 1813 and fought at Nivelles, Nive, Orthes, and Toulouse.

After Gen. Robert Ross's death at Baltimore, Lambert was ordered to replace him but eventually was superseded by Sir Edward Pakenham. Lambert arrived off New Orleans on 1 January 1815 with the fusiliers and Forty-third Regiment, which formed the reserve in the battle that occurred on 8 January 1815. After Pakenham's death and the wounding of Generals John Keane and Samuel Gibbs, Lambert became the senior general. He called off the attack on Andrew Jackson's line and ordered the troops back to the ships. He reported that the service of the army and navy since landing had been arduous beyond anything he had ever witnessed.

Lambert conducted the last land operation of the War of 1812 by capturing Fort Bowyer, near Mobile. He then returned to England and would quickly see service on the continent. At Waterloo, he commanded the Tenth brigade, which sustained two-thirds casualties at La Haye Sainte. He had already received a cross and a KCB on 2 January 1815, but his service in the final battle with Napoleon saw Lambert commended by the Duke of Wellington and decorated by Parliament and the Russian and Austrian governments. Lambert died on 14 September 1847.

—*Frederick C. Drake*

LAWRENCE, JAMES
1781–1813
U.S. Navy officer

James Lawrence was born in Burlington, New Jersey, on 1 October 1781. He entered the U.S. Navy as a midshipman in September 1798 and served on various ships before earning promotion to sailing master in September 1801 and lieutenant in April 1802. During the Quasi-War with France he served in the *Ganges, New York,* and *Adams;* from 1801 to 1802, he was on the *New York* in ordinary at the Washington Navy Yard; and from 1802 to 1805, he was aboard the *Enterprise* in the Mediterranean. Lawrence was second in command to Lt. Stephen Decatur during the daring 16 February 1804 raid into Tripoli Harbor to burn the captured frigate *Philadelphia.* He remained in the Mediterranean until 1808, with the exception of a brief return to the United States from February to April 1805. Lawrence commanded Gunboat No. 6 in the Mediterranean from 1805 to 1806. Immediately after her Atlantic crossing, the British stopped No. 6 off Cádiz. Lawrence was conferring with Admiral Collingwood aboard his flagship when a British boarding party removed two seamen from the gunboat. Lawrence protested, but there was nothing he could do about it. Subsequently his second in command was shipped home, but Lawrence was exonerated of any blame in the affair.

In 1807 Lawrence was in gunboat duty at New York, where he commanded No. 29. He subsequently served on other warships and was promoted to master commandant in November 1810.

As commander of the sloop *Hornet* (18 guns), Lawrence sailed with Commodore John Rodgers in June–August 1812. During an independent cruise in the West Indies in February 1813, the *Hornet* took the brig *Resolution* with $23,000 in specie aboard. On February 24, the *Hornet* engaged and defeated the Royal Navy brig *Peacock* (18 guns, commanded by Capt. William Peake). Superior gunnery and heavier ordnance decided the issue in favor of the Americans. Despite efforts to save her, the *Peacock* sank.

Promoted to captain in March 1813, Lawrence received

command of the frigate *Chesapeake* (38 guns). On 1 June 1813, with an inexperienced crew, Lawrence unwisely sailed the frigate out of Boston harbor to accept a challenge from Capt. Philip Broke of the British frigate *Shannon* (38 guns) for a one-on-one duel. Broke was perhaps the best frigate captain in the Royal Navy, and he commanded a well-trained and seasoned crew. The battle that followed was brief (15 minutes), and the British were victorious. Lawrence, mortally wounded, achieved immortality as he was being carried below with his appeal, "Don't give up the ship." The British took the *Chesapeake* into Halifax, where Captain Lawrence was buried with full military honors. Although he was undoubtedly a capable and courageous officer, Lawrence was also rash, a characteristic that cost the U.S. Navy its first frigate defeat in the War of 1812 and Lawrence his life.

—*Spencer C. Tucker*

See also: *Chesapeake* versus *Shannon*
Further Reading
Gleaves, Albert. *James Lawrence, Captain, U.S. Navy: Commander of the Chesapeake*. New York: Putnam, 1904.
Post, Waldron K. "The Case of Captain Lawrence." *United States Naval Institute Proceedings* 62 (July 1936): 969–974.
Purcell, Hugh D. "Don't Give Up the Ship," *United States Naval Institute Proceedings* 91 (May 1965): 82–94.

LAWRENCE, WILLIAM
d. 1841
U.S. officer

Born in Maryland, William Lawrence entered the U.S. Army in 1801 as a second lieutenant in the Fourth U.S. Infantry. He was promoted to first lieutenant in the Second Infantry in 1804 and had achieved the rank of captain in that regiment by the outbreak of the War of 1812.

Serving primarily in the South during the war, Lawrence, promoted to major in April 1814, commanded approximately 130 men of the Second Infantry in August 1814, when Maj. Gen. Andrew Jackson visited Mobile to inspect its defenses. Expecting a British attack out of Pensacola on that town, Jackson ordered Lawrence and his men to garrison Fort Bowyer, which guarded the entrance to Mobile Bay.

Lawrence arrived at the fort in early September and immediately went to work strengthening the little fort's weak defenses and preempting British seizure of the dunes overlooking the position. Not quite finished with his work, Lawrence looked out over the walls of the fort on 12 September to observe a force of about 130 British marines and several hundred Indians under the command of Maj. Edward Nicholls approaching Fort Bowyer from the rear. That evening four British warships appeared within sight of the other side of the fort.

The following morning, Nicholls began firing on the fort with a howitzer, to no effect. Lawrence's own guns prevented the British land force from moving too close to the fort and prevented the small boats launched from the warships from adequately sounding the channel leading into the bay. Things remained relatively quiet the next day, but from the British movements in the afternoon Lawrence discerned that a coordinated attack would likely occur on 15 September.

About noon on 15 September the British ships began moving into position to enter the channel. Lawrence called his officers together to discuss the circumstances under which they thought it would be appropriate to surrender. The group decided that they should fight until they had no hope of victory and then surrender only if the British officers promised that private property would be respected, that the officers would be allowed to keep their arms, that the survivors would be protected from the Indians, and that they be treated as befitted prisoners of war.

At about 4:00 P.M., the British ships began firing. The fort returned fire while at the same time firing at the British marines and Indians to their rear, who were discharging the howitzer and a 12-pounder that had been brought up. In the late afternoon, the British flagship HMS *Hermes* was disabled and floated dangerously close to the fort at a point where Lawrence ordered the concentration of his guns. To prevent the ship from falling into U.S. hands, the *Hermes* was set on fire and later exploded when its magazine caught fire.

At about the same time the U.S. flag was shot away from atop the fort, leading the marines and Indians to suppose that the Americans were surrendering. As they charged closer to the fort, Lawrence let loose several rounds of grapeshot, dispersing the attackers in all directions. Shortly thereafter, the British decided to abandon the attack.

Lawrence's defense of Fort Bowyer against an attacking force over five times the size of his garrison greatly helped recruiting in the South, something that would be of tremendous benefit to Andrew Jackson in his upcoming defense of New Orleans. At the same time, Lawrence's action demoralized the British Indian allies and probably led to a decrease in the number moving down to the British base at Apalachicola. For his efforts, Lawrence was commended by General Jackson, brevetted a lieutenant colonel, and presented with a sword by the city of New Orleans.

Lawrence remained in command at Fort Bowyer until the end of the war. Before the peace of Ghent arrived in the United States, however, the British in the gulf made one last attempt to take Mobile. In February 1815, Gen. John Lambert landed about 5,000 men behind Fort Bowyer. Having learned from Nicholls's mistake, Lambert brought with him heavy artillery, with which he opened up on the fort on 11 February. After only a short time, Lawrence surrendered his garrison of 375 men, but before Lambert could launch an attack on Mobile, word arrived that peace had been made.

Following the war, Lawrence remained in the army. He achieved the rank of lieutenant colonel in 1818 and colonel in 1828. He resigned his commission in 1831 and died in 1841.

—*Jeanne T. Heidler and David S. Heidler*

See also: Bowyer, Fort; Jackson, Andrew; Lambert, John; Mobile, Battles of; Nicholls, Edward; Seminole Indians
Further Reading
Brown, Wilburt S. *The Amphibious Campaign for West Florida and Louisiana, 1814–1815.* Tuscaloosa: University of Alabama Press, 1969.
Coker, William S. "The Last Battle of the War of 1812: New Orleans? No, Fort Bowyer!" *Alabama Historical Quarterly* 43 (1981): 42–63.

LEAVENWORTH, HENRY
1783–1834
U.S. Army officer

Henry Leavenworth was born in Connecticut but grew to manhood and practiced law in Delhi, New York. He was commissioned a captain in the 13th U.S. Infantry in April 1813 but after a few months was transferred to the 25th Infantry. In August 1813, Leavenworth was promoted to major and with promotion came another transfer, this time to the Ninth Infantry. The spring of 1814 found Henry Leavenworth marching under Maj. Gen. Jacob Brown toward the Niagara Frontier at the head of 200 troops.

At Buffalo, Leavenworth's battalion came under Brig. Gen. Winfield Scott's grueling training program. The Ninth drilled up to ten hours a day, six days each week. On 30 June, four companies, mostly new recruits, of the 22nd Infantry marched into camp. Since their colonel was still en route, Brown entrusted Leavenworth with command of the untrained newcomers. Three days later, Brown's division crossed the Niagara River and seized Fort Erie. The Americans pressed northward with Scott's brigade in the vanguard. On 5 July, Scott met the British in open combat on Chippewa Plain. Leavenworth's battalion led the brigade across Street's Creek bridge and directly into the fire of a battery of the Royal Artillery. Leavenworth's men deployed into line and covered the position of Scott's other two battalions. The British and U.S. lines closed to musket range and opened a terrible fire with neither side inclined to withdraw from the fray. Leavenworth's men loaded and fired with the precision and steadiness that resulted from their intensive training and confidence in their leaders. A cannon shot severed the leg of one of Leavenworth's company commanders, Capt. Thomas Harrison, but he refused to be carried from the field until the battle was won. In the face of such determination and superior marksmanship, the British broke. Leavenworth had brought about 550 men with him into battle; he reported 111 casualties.

Twenty days later, Leavenworth was again at the head of his battalion, this time at Lundy's Lane. Scott, somewhat outnumbered, impetuously threw his brigade against a British line on the crest of a gentle rise. Much of the ensuing battle was fought after darkness had fallen, and, like Chippewa, neither side would admit defeat. Scott's brigade suffered heavily. Scott himself was seriously wounded, as were the other battalion commanders. Command of the brigade devolved upon Leavenworth, the least wounded of the U.S. officers. Leavenworth kept his diminished brigade in the fight until he was ordered to withdraw.

Henry Leavenworth received two brevet promotions for his heroic service in Upper Canada in July 1814. After the war, he was retained on active duty and sent out West. Learning the Dakota (Sioux) language, he established a reputation as an able negotiator with the Plains Indians. In 1827, he founded a permanent fort on the Missouri River that today bears his name.

While on an expedition in 1834, brevet Brigadier General Leavenworth fell from his horse while chasing buffalo; he developed a fever and died. Four days later, orders arrived announcing his promotion to the permanent rank of brigadier general. Henry Leavenworth was well respected by officers and enlisted soldiers alike and displayed significant qualities as a tactician, disciplinarian, negotiator, and leader.

—*Richard V. Barbuto*

See also: Chippewa, Battle of; Lundy's Lane, Battle of; Scott, Winfield
Further Reading
Parker, Henry S. *Henry Leavenworth, Pioneer General.* Fort Leavenworth, KS: N.p., n.d.

LEE, HENRY
1756–1818
Virginia politician

Henry Lee was born in Westmoreland County, Virginia, into one of the state's most distinguished families. Educated at Princeton, Lee managed his father's extensive business interests, served in the Continental Army as a major, and during the American Revolution was given command of a separate cavalry corps of three companies. Henry Lee thus earned the nickname of "Light-Horse Harry." During the Revolution, his bravery in attacking the British garrison at Pawlus Hook won him a gold medal from Congress. For the remainder of the war, Lee served under Gen. Nathanael Greene, distinguishing himself at the battles of Guilford Courthouse, Augusta, Eutaw Springs, and the siege of Ninety-Six.

After the war, Henry Lee pursued a political career that included such roles as appointment to the Congress until the Constitution was adopted, membership in the Virginia legislature (1789–1791), governor of Virginia (1791–1794), and member of Congress (1799–1801). Lee also commanded the forces sent to suppress the Whiskey Rebellion (1794) and gave the funeral oration for George Washington, which included the famous line "First in war, first in peace, first in the hearts of his countrymen."

Lee's private life was less successful. His financial affairs were a confusion that landed him in debtor's prison in 1809. When the War of 1812 broke out, Henry Lee had turned to writing recollections of past service, just completing his two-volume *War in the Southern United States*. On 27 July 1812, he was in Baltimore on a visit to Alexander Hanson, editor of the *Federal Republican* and a staunch Federalist who opposed the war and printed denunciations of Pres. James Madison's policy. Hanson's printing office had been destroyed by an unruly mob, but the editor moved the paper's office and continued his criticisms.

"Light-Horse Harry" Lee and other Federalist Revolutionary War officers were in Baltimore to defend Hanson. The new office was attacked, and in the resulting melee, Lee was taken for dead and left on the street. Found insensible, Lee was carried to the security of a jail, but that too was attacked, leaving Henry Lee severely injured. He never recovered his health. Lee eventually sailed for the West Indies to recuperate. Longing to return home, Lee set sail but got only as far as Cumberland Island, Georgia, where he died at the home of General Greene's daughter (1818).

Henry Lee

Lee's remains were eventually interred with his son's, Gen. Robert E. Lee, in Lexington, Virginia.

—*William A. Paquette*

See also: Baltimore Riots; Hanson, Alexander Contee
Further Reading
Chase, Philander D. "The Early Career of 'Light Horse Harry' Lee." Master's thesis, Duke University, 1968.
Templin, Thomas E. "Henry 'Light Horse Harry' Lee: A Biography." Ph.D. dissertation, University of Kentucky, 1975.

LETTER OF MARQUE

The letter of marque authorized the practice of seizing certain ships. That same practice, in the absence of such authority as provided by a letter of marque, would have been piracy.

The pirate acted outside the law of nations (or international law) by treating ships as targets of opportunity regardless of their nationality. The privateer, however, acted under a commission—the letter of marque—provided by a recognized sovereign power. Such a commission sanctioned the taking of prizes but only under strictly defined rules. Specifically, the letter of marque designated its holder as a "private ship of war" and gave permission to seize enemy vessels, their crews, and their cargoes. The privateer would then submit the captured vessel to a prize court, usually situated in a port of the privateer's sponsor. Under a complicated set of rules, the prize court would determine if the seizure was a valid prize of war (a vessel of an enemy power duly noted in the letter of marque) or an invalid capture. If the privateer had acted within the stipulations of the letter of marque, the captured vessel was condemned, meaning it and its value were the property of the privateer.

The letter of marque was originally a way of commissioning reprisals against a nation whose judicial system had proven unresponsive to a private complaint. By the eighteenth century, however, the letter of marque had become a way for nations to wage war on an enemy's maritime commerce at little or no expense. Even without a large navy, the United States' reliance in the War of 1812 on privateers allowed it to mount a highly destructive campaign on British shipping. And because a successful privateer could produce spectacular profits for captains, crews, and investors, such enterprises were spurred by tangible rewards as well as patriotism.

—*Jeanne T. Heidler and David S. Heidler*

See also: Privateering

LEVY, URIAH PHILLIPS
1792–1862
U.S. Navy officer

A fourth- or fifth-generation American Jew, Uriah Levy's career was marked by acrimony due to his Jewishness as well as his abrasive personality. He eventually rose in the U.S. Navy to command of the Mediterranean squadron, in spite of six courts-martial and two courts of inquiry.

Born in Philadelphia on 22 April 1792, he began his sailor's life as a cabin boy on coasting vessels. By October 1811, he was one-third owner and master of the schooner *George Washington*. Levy entered U.S. naval service as a sailing master three months after the War of 1812 began. His first service was on board the sloop *Alert,* which was sta-

tioned in New York Harbor. In June 1813, he shifted to the brig *Argus*, as a volunteer acting lieutenant. The *Argus* set sail for France to transport William H. Crawford, the U.S. minister to France.

The day before the *Argus* was defeated by the British *Pelican*, Levy had been given command of a prize ship. When he attempted to run the prize into a French port, the vessel was recaptured by a British frigate. Levy was held in prison in England for 16 months before he was repatriated. While he was on a cartel (prisoner exchange) ship bound for Norfolk, Virginia, news was received on board that the War of 1812 had ended.

—*Henry S. Marks*

See also: Argus versus *Pelican*
Further Reading
Marcus, Jacob Rader. "Uriah Phillips Levy." In *Memoirs of American Jews.* Vol. 1, *1775–1865.* Philadelphia: Jewish Publication Society of America, 1955: 76–116.
Wyllie, John C. "Uriah Phillips Levy." In *Dictionary of American Biography.* Vol. 6. New York: Charles Scribner's Sons, 1936: 203–204.

LEWIS, MORGAN
1754–1844
New York political leader; U.S. officer

Born to Francis Lewis and Elizabeth Annesley Lewis, Morgan Lewis graduated from the College of New Jersey at the young age of 19 and pursued a legal career before serving as an officer in the American Revolution. During this conflict, he married Gertrude Livingston, allying himself with the Livingston family in New York politics. This association proved important following the Revolution in securing Lewis's appointment as New York attorney general in 1791 and subsequently a seat on the New York Supreme Court. He rose to become its chief justice in 1801.

In 1804, Lewis became embroiled in an ugly campaign when he received the nomination for governor from New York Democratic Republicans. His opponent was Aaron Burr, who had been nominated by a conspiratorial group of New York Federalists. Burr perhaps intended to join with these supporters to bring about a northeastern confederation. Whether or not they would have succeeded remains in dispute, and their early plans nonetheless were foiled by the election of Lewis. Lewis owed his victory at least partly to the actions of Alexander Hamilton: Hamilton's attacks on Burr would lead to the duel that ended with Hamilton's death and that tarnished Burr's reputation.

Lewis's political career suffered because of his inability to deal effectively with the ambitions of the Clinton-Livingston faction. He temporarily left politics, then returned briefly before entering military service at the beginning of the War of 1812. He started the war as a member of the New York state senate but soon entered the military as a quartermaster general. By 1813, he had risen to the rank of major general, serving first on the Niagara Frontier. In 1814, he received command of New York City and its environs. He supervised the defense of the city after receiving news of Washington, D.C.'s destruction. Through the fall of 1814, he accepted into service militia forces in the area of the city and directed the construction of fortifications to meet any British threats.

In addition to his activities in New York City, Lewis spent much of his time negotiating for the release of U.S. prisoners, frequently covering the expenses of such activities with his own money. He ended the war with a distinguished if unexciting record. His failure to gain a major combat command has generally been attributed to political difficulties. Following the war, he spent his remaining 32 years in public service and died in New York City.

—*Jeanne T. Heidler and David S. Heidler*

LEWIS, WILLIAM
d. 1825
U.S. officer

William Lewis, a native of Virginia, entered the U.S. Army at a young age and served as a captain in Arthur St. Clair's army when it suffered its dreadful defeat in 1791. Lewis remained in the army for another six years, resigned his commission in 1797, and went to live in Kentucky. When the war with Great Britain began in June 1812, Lewis received a commission as a lieutenant colonel of the Kentucky Volunteers.

When William Henry Harrison received command of the Army of the Northwest upon William Hull's surrender of Detroit, Lewis commanded one of the volunteer regiments attached to Harrison's command at Cincinnati. Shortly afterward, Lewis's regiment was placed under the command of Brig. Gen. James Winchester in the latter's advance toward the Michigan Territory.

While the army was stopped at the rapids of the Maumee River, Winchester received instructions from Harrison not to advance too quickly against the British in Michigan. Yet at the same time he received pleas from the inhabitants at Frenchtown on the River Raisin that they were in imminent danger of attack from the British and their Indian allies. Winchester sent Lewis in command of almost 600 men in advance of the main army on 17 January 1813 to discern the situation at Frenchtown.

As Lewis approached the River Raisin on the afternoon of 18 January, he spotted a small force of British and Indians on the other side of the river. He ordered his men into battle formation and, after crossing the river, easily dispersed the enemy, chasing them for several miles before returning to Frenchtown. His pursuit and reports from the inhabitants nearby convinced him that British reinforcements were en route, so he sent word back to Winchester to bring up the remainder of the army.

Leaving a small force at the rapids, Winchester advanced quickly, arriving the next day. Most of his army followed on 20 January. The army rested the following day while scouts attempted to learn the position of the British forces. When the army retired for the night on 21 January, however, Winchester and Lewis had no idea that Col. Henry Procter and a larger force of British regulars and Indians was preparing to attack.

As the U.S. army began to stir in its camp between 4:00 and 5:00 A.M. on 22 January, the British and Indians attacked. Lewis and the other officers tried vainly to rally the panicked soldiers, but the British and Indians divided the Americans into small groups and quickly tore the little army to pieces. Winchester, captured early, was persuaded to surrender on the condition that the wounded and prisoners would be protected from the Indians. By the time the surrender took place, Lewis too had been captured. Winchester, Lewis, and most of the healthy officers and men were marched off to Canada, while Procter abandoned the wounded to his Indian allies.

Lewis spent the next year as a prisoner of war in Quebec. After his exchange in the spring of 1814, he did not see significant action for the remainder of the war. Following the war, he eventually moved to Arkansas Territory, where he died in 1825.

—*Jeanne T. Heidler and David S. Heidler*

See also: Frenchtown, Battles of; Harrison, William Henry; Winchester, James
Further Reading
Au, Dennis. *War on the Raisin.* Monroe, MI: Monroe County Historical Commission, 1981.
Clift, G. Glenn. *Remember the Raisin!* Frankfort, KY: Kentucky Historical Society, 1961.

LEWISTON, NEW YORK, DESTRUCTION OF
18 December 1813

In December 1813, the British invaded the United States at several places along the Niagara River. The attackers intended these moves as raids to destroy property and war supplies and as revenge for the U.S. destruction of Newark, Upper Canada. British brigadier general Phineas Riall commanded one prong of the assault, with Lewiston, New York, and the surrounding villages as its objective.

Lewiston had served as headquarters for the U.S. Army during its attack across the river at Queenston the year before, so it seemed a fitting target for British retaliation. As Riall moved across the northern end of the river on 18 December, a larger British force under Maj. Gen. Sir Gordon Drummond prepared to move across to the south to destroy the towns of Black Rock and Buffalo. On the U.S. side, militia forces were alerted to the possibility of such a coordinated action and had established a system of alarms to warn townspeople of a British approach. In the case of Lewiston, the alarms were never sounded.

As the British marched toward Lewiston at dawn on 18 December, most of the citizens were still in bed. Many of the militia in the vicinity ran at the approach of Riall's men, also failing to alert the people that the town was being invaded. Mrs. Solomon Gilette was surprised by three of Riall's Indian allies while she was milking her cows. On the approach of the Indians, her ten-year-old son ran, and Mrs. Gilette hurried to the house with her three younger children. As she moved into the street and headed toward the house with the three children in tow, Indians shot and scalped her seven-year-old son before a British officer could stop the killing. On the other side of town, Mr. Gilette, captured by the British, watched helplessly as Indians shot and scalped his nineteen-year-old son. In all, about ten civilians were killed by Riall's Indian allies in Lewiston. All but one were scalped, and one was decapitated. The remainder ran to safety when a handful of militia arrived to guard their retreat.

After the evacuation of the town, Riall ordered all buildings destroyed. Once he was assured that the town was irretrievably sacked, Riall burned villages nearby and then moved back across the Niagara.

—*Jeanne T. Heidler and David S. Heidler*

See also: Buffalo, New York; Drummond, Gordon; Riall, Phineas

Further Reading
Cruikshank, Ernest A. *Drummond's Winter Campaign, 1813.* Welland, Ont.: Lundy's Lane Historical Society, 1898.

LITTLE PRINCE
d. 1828
Lower Creek headman

Little Prince (Tustunnuggee Hopoi) was a powerful leader in the Creek National Council. He fought to preserve the political independence of the Creek Nation and played a significant role in the outbreak of the Creek War of 1813–1814.

In 1812, Creek headman Little Warrior led a war party that killed white settlers on the Duck River in Tennessee, one of many such attacks during the time of the Red Stick spiritual revolt against Anglo-American influence. At the insistence of Benjamin Hawkins, the U.S. agent, the Creek National Council ordered the execution of the killers. The killing of Little Warrior and his allies precipitated retaliatory attacks by the Red Sticks that provoked a Creek civil war. Little Prince, Big Warrior, and William McIntosh organized southeastern native support for the war against the Red Sticks, and these forces combined with Andrew Jackson's army to defeat the nativist Creeks at Horseshoe Bend.

After the war, Little Prince resisted the increasing pressures brought by Georgia and the United States to force the Creeks to remove to the West. As a leader of the National Council, he ordered the execution of William McIntosh for his violation of a Creek law prohibiting the sale of national lands to the United States. Despite this opposition to the cession of Creek lands, Little Prince soon after approved the Treaties of Washington and Fort Mitchell, agreements that provided for the sale of remaining Creek territory in Georgia.

—*Tim Alan Garrison*

See also: Creek War; Hawkins, Benjamin

Further Reading
Dowd, Gregory Evans. *A Spirited Resistance: The North American Indian Struggle for Unity, 1745–1815.* Baltimore: Johns Hopkins University Press, 1992.
Green, Michael D. *The Politics of Indian Removal: Creek Government and Society in Crisis.* Lincoln: University of Nebraska Press, 1982.
Griffith, Benjamin W., Jr. *McIntosh and Weatherford, Creek Indian Leaders.* Tuscaloosa: University of Alabama Press, 1988.

LIVERPOOL, ROBERT BANKS JENKINSON, SECOND EARL OF
1770–1828
British prime minister

Liverpool was educated at Charterhouse and Christchurch College, Oxford. He was in Paris in 1789 and saw the beginnings of the French Revolution. From the first he was a determined opponent of the Revolution and French expansion. Entering Parliament in 1790 as a supporter of William Pitt the younger and the Tories, he won a place in the government for the first time in 1793. Thereafter, he was continually in office until 1827, except for one brief interval in 1806. He rose steadily in importance the whole time, until he was obliged to withdraw from politics toward the end of his life. Much of his political career was devoted to managing Britain's efforts to deal with the military consequences of the French Revolution and the success of Napoleon.

After his father became the first Earl Liverpool in 1796, Robert was known, by courtesy, as Lord Hawkesbury. As foreign secretary in the Addington ministry (1801–1804), he negotiated the unsuccessful Peace of Amiens (1801) with France that quickly broke down. He served as the head of the Home Office in the last Pitt administration (1804–1806) and, after Pitt's death, in the weak, divided government of the ill and aged Lord Portland (1807–1809). In December 1808, on the death of his father, he succeeded him as Earl of Liverpool. In this period of extreme political fragmentation and partisanship, Liverpool and his colleagues were regarded with some contempt as feeble disciples of Pitt.

On the fall of the Portland ministry in 1809, Liverpool supported his colleague Spencer Perceval as prime minister, serving briefly as foreign minister and then as secretary for war and the colonies. His energies at the War Office were devoted unstintingly from the first to the support of Wellington's army in Spain, which eventually began to have some success against the French. When Perceval was assassinated (May 1812), Liverpool became prime minister by default because he was the most experienced member of the government who was acceptable to all the Tory factions. Unable to bring any of the opposition Whigs into the government, his ministry was a shaky Tory one without a broad base of support and as deeply divided as its predecessor. Surprisingly, it lasted 15 years.

After taking office on 8 June, Liverpool acted almost immediately to repeal the Orders in Council (24 June) that had caused so much friction with the United States. He hoped to eliminate the problem posed by the deteriorating relations with the United States so that there would be no distraction in concentrating the government's attention on its first priority, the defeat of Napoleon. Before the repeal of the Orders in Council could be implemented, however, the U.S. Congress had already declared war.

Liverpool deplored the outbreak of the war with the United States, but once it began the conflict had only secondary importance for British policymakers locked in a life-and-death struggle around the globe with Napoleon. Although British commerce suffered from U.S. privateering and Liverpool's government was embarrassed by unexpected military and naval setbacks in North America, he and his colleagues did not allow themselves to be distracted from the principal threat confronting them. Though the Whig and radical opposition harassed the government in Parliament for their failures in North America, Liverpool was determined that only after Napoleon had been defeated would he allow the focus of attention to be shifted to the U.S. problem.

Liverpool believed that no one in Britain desired a war with the United States, and he was eager to make peace promptly, provided that reasonable terms could be found. If negotiations failed, a far more substantial military effort would have to be attempted against the Americans. During the final stages of the war against France in early 1814, Liverpool was able to begin increasing the military pressure on the United States. But only in the spring when Napoleon was forced to abdicate, ending the European fighting, was Britain fully free to deal with the U.S. problem. Liverpool and Viscount Castlereagh, the foreign secretary, were then able to devote more attention to the U.S. war, although their principal concerns were focused on forging a durable and secure peace in Europe in the complex negotiations at Vienna.

The British army, including some of Wellington's battle-hardened veterans from the Spanish peninsula and the bulk of the Royal Navy, had become fully available for service in North America. Peace negotiations with the Americans seemed to be making no progress. By September, Liverpool feared that he had reached the limits of the concessions he could afford. In November, he offered the U.S. command to his best general, the triumphant Wellington, in the event a diplomatic settlement could not be reached. He hoped news of the offer would put additional pressure on the U.S. diplomats to reach a settlement.

It is not clear if Liverpool actually intended to send Wellington to North America. For his part, Wellington had advised the government to take a softer negotiating line, especially to abandon any claims for territorial gains, thereby to facilitate a prompt peace. Before the duke had to make up his mind about whether to accept the command, peace was concluded at Ghent on 24 December 1814. Liverpool was fortunate because a few months later Napoleon unexpectedly returned from exile to take up arms again. The British had Wellington on hand rather than in the United States, and he was able to command the troops in the final and definitive victory of the European war at Waterloo (June 1815). For Liverpool, the U.S. war had always been a regrettable accident and frequently an annoyance and an embarrassment, but always it had been a secondary concern.

—*S. J. Stearns*

See also: Castlereagh, Viscount, Robert Stewart
Further Reading

Gash, Norman. *Lord Liverpool: The Life and Political Career of Robert Banks Jenkinson, second Earl of Liverpool, 1770–1828.* London: Weidenfeld and Nicolson, 1984.

Petrie, Charles. *Lord Liverpool and His Times.* London: J. Barrie, 1954.

Edward Livingston

LIVINGSTON, EDWARD
1764–1836
U.S. congressman, senator, and diplomat

Edward Livingston was one of his generation's greatest legal minds and served in public life as a noted attorney, elected official, and diplomat. Born in Columbia County, New York, into a family of renowned statesmen, Edward was the youngest son of Margaret (Beekman) and Robert R. Livingston the elder. His brother, Chancellor Robert R. Livingston, helped draft the Declaration of Independence and negotiated the Louisiana Purchase in 1803, and his sisters' marriages into prominent families furthered well-established kinship connections. In 1779, Livingston entered the junior class at the College of New Jersey (now Princeton) and graduated in 1781. Adept at philosophy, poetry, and languages, Livingston further studied French and German from private tutors before deciding to study law. He read cases for three years in Albany under John Lansing's direction and often sparred intellectually with fellow students including Alexander Hamilton, Aaron Burr, James Kent, and Egbert Benson. Livingston passed the bar in 1785 and practiced law for nine years before beginning his political career.

In 1794, New York residents elected Livingston to the U.S. House of Representatives, where he served for six years. Though the Livingston family had supported ratification of the Constitution, disappointment over the lack of gratitude in the Federalist Party's dispersion of political patronage convinced the influential New York dynasty to support the Jeffersonian Republican camp. Although Livingston was one of six New York congressmen who voted consistently with Jeffersonian Republican policies, conventional wisdom held that he did so without great conviction. Eventual legal difficulties with Thomas Jefferson widened the political rift between the two men.

Despite lukewarm ideological convictions, Livingston initiated a strongly nationalistic legislative agenda and achieved much success in his initial congressional career. He introduced a measure to revise the U.S. penal code, but though this bill foreshadowed later accomplishments, Congress tabled the freshman legislator's measure. Livingston supported legislation to protect U.S. seamen victimized by the naval impressment of foreign powers. Accordingly, he bitterly opposed ratification of Jay's Treaty (1794), which did little to ease the captives' plight. In a more partisan squabble, he sided with Jefferson when the Congress voted in 1801 to break the electoral tie between Jefferson and Aaron Burr, despite his long-standing friendship and professional association with fellow New Yorker Burr.

Livingston willingly left the Congress in 1801 but found himself appointed U.S. attorney for the district of New York as a result of Jefferson's victory. Shortly thereafter, he also won election as mayor of New York, and he held both full-time posts simultaneously. As mayor, he presided during the infamous yellow fever epidemic of summer 1803, and unafraid of personal risk, he continued at his posts until stricken by illness. The unfortunate embezzlement of government funds by a city clerk during the mayor's convalescence triggered Livingston's resignation, self-imposed exile, and lifetime of debt. The mayor assumed full responsibility for his subordinate's crime and promised full restitution of the stolen funds. He sold his New York property to provide partial payment on the debt, and he labored for 23 years paying off the remainder plus interest.

Livingston moved to New Orleans in February 1804, shortly after the United States took possession of the Louisiana Territory. He hoped to distance himself from the New York fiasco and begin rebuilding a broken career by establishing a legal practice. In what proved to be an ingenious investment strategy, Livingston accepted payment for his services in land, in lieu of money, from clients who were cash-poor but land-rich. In time, Livingston's property increased in size, and Louisiana's land value appreciated. Undoubtedly, his most controversial acquisition was Batture Sainte Marie, the ground between the levee's crest and the Mississippi River. Since this was prime real estate in a developing port city, Livingston faced litigation from state and federal authorities who sought to acquire the title to this property. After decades of lawsuits and appeals, Livingston finally won the case, but full compensation came to his family only after his death.

Livingston enjoyed a certain popularity in Louisiana. Since some U.S. policies seemed arbitrary and harsh to many Louisiana Creoles, Livingston drafted a memorandum to the national government demanding a redress of local grievances. Closer than many to the local temper, Livingston urged Jefferson to retain as much as possible of French and Spanish law in the new territory's code. Later, Gen. James Wilkinson tarnished Livingston's reputation in Louisiana in 1806 with unfounded accusations that the New York exile was a conspirator in the Burr affair. Though Livingston and Burr were friends and Burr had been a creditor to Livingston during difficult times, no connection existed between the two regarding Burr's nefarious plans for the southwest. The combined effects of Livingston's New York fiscal problems, the continuing Batture Sainte Marie litigation, and Wilkinson's allegations caused Pres. Thomas Jefferson to distance himself from his one-time ally. It would take years before the two statesmen could patch up their strained relationship.

During the War of 1812, Livingston offered his services in various capacities. Always a champion of the navy, he supported construction of frigates by selling timber from live oaks on his Louisiana properties. After the British approached the pirate Jean Lafitte to entice him to aid them against the Americans at New Orleans, Livingston used his professional connections as Lafitte's attorney and his influence as chairman of the Committee on Public Defense to attain the Baratarians' support. The pirates promised Livingston $20,000 in exchange for their certain acquittal on trade law violations, and he judiciously encouraged their public-spirited enlistment in the U.S. cause. Several months later, the Baratarian pirates received an official pardon from Pres. James Madison in appreciation of their meritorious service to the nation during the War of 1812.

Livingston knew Gen. Andrew Jackson from their service together in Congress, and each man held the other in esteem. When Jackson arrived at New Orleans in December 1814, Livingston served his friend as aide-de-camp, military secretary, interpreter, and confidential adviser. In this capacity, he not only drafted Jackson's important orders and proclamations but also conducted sensitive negotiations regarding prisoner exchanges.

Louisiana residents elected Livingston to the state legislature in 1820, where he initiated a sophisticated campaign to revise the state's penal law code. From the Louisiana state legislature, Livingston won election to the U.S. House of Representatives in 1822. He represented the New Orleans district for six years until his election to the U.S. Senate in 1829. In 1826, Livingston completed paying $100,014.89 to the national treasury to satisfy the earlier disappearance of $43,666.21 of government funds from New York.

In March 1831, upon Martin Van Buren's resignation, Pres. Andrew Jackson offered Livingston the cabinet position of secretary of state. Despite being a Jackson supporter, as a probank politician in an antibank administration, Livingston found it increasingly difficult to function effectively within the cabinet. He resigned as secretary of state and subsequently accepted appointment as minister plenipotentiary to France in 1833. He spent two years in Paris negotiating an accord to guarantee compensation involving U.S. spoliation claims dating back to the Napoleonic wars.

Livingston returned to the United States in 1835 and retired to "Montgomery Place" in New York, where he died on 21 May 1836. John Randolph recognized the troubling paradox of Livingston's life with the caustic assessment, "So brilliant, yet so corrupt, which like a rotten mackerel by moonlight, shines and stinks." Unfortunately, his genius in law did not transfer into management of personal finances, and Livingston lived much of his life a debtor. Almost a prisoner to money, his eagerness to secure wealth often made his private actions seem avaricious and his motives suspect. Nevertheless, Livingston's universal command of the law and his brilliant efforts at codification were remarkable achievements, unparalleled in his lifetime.

—*Junius P. Rodriguez*

See also: Baratarian Pirates; Lafitte, Jean; New Orleans, Battle of
Further Reading
Hatcher, William B. *Edward Livingston: Jeffersonian Republican and Jacksonian Democrat.* University: Louisiana State University Press, 1940.
Hunt, Carleton. *Life and Services of Edward Livingston: Address of Carleton Hunt, May 9, 1903.* New Orleans: J. G. Hauser, 1903.
Hunt, Charles Havens. *Life of Edward Livingston.* New York: D. Appleton, 1864.

LOUISIANA

Admitted into the Union in 1812, Louisiana was named in 1682 by Francois Robert de La Salle to denote the entire Mississippi River basin in honor of King Louis XIV. Successful settlement of the area comprising the present state of Louisiana did not occur until 1718, with the establishment of New Orleans. Although it was controlled by France until 1763, by Spain from 1763 to 1800, and again nominally by France from 1800 until the U.S. purchase of the territory in 1803, Louisiana was crucial to the development and settlement of North America because it commanded the great Mississippi watershed.

After the Treaty of Paris of 1783, which provided independence for the United States with the Mississippi River as its western boundary, Louisiana became even more important. During the Confederation period and Pres. George Washington's administration, negotiations were conducted with Spain to settle the question regarding navigation and the right of deposit on the Mississippi River. Pres. Thomas Jefferson's administration finally settled the Mississippi question when the government purchased Louisiana from France in April 1803 for $15 million and carved from the southeastern corner the Territory of Orleans. This area comprised the present-day state minus the district east of the Mississippi River known as Spanish West Florida. During the first decade of the nineteenth century,

Louisiana, with its capital at New Orleans, became the primary commercial center of the West and the focus of various notorious schemes of disunion, one of which was the Aaron Burr conspiracy.

The Louisiana territory increased in size in September 1810 as residents from the Baton Rouge district, situated north of New Orleans on the east bank of the Mississippi River, declared independence from Spanish rule. The following month Pres. James Madison instructed Governor William C.C. Claiborne to take possession of the district for the United States. Even though the move was legally questionable, the Spanish did not take action to regain the area. In early April 1812, Louisiana was admitted into the Union amid the fervor for war with Britain; by mid-May Congress approved a resolution dividing West Florida at the Pearl River, with the western half incorporated into the new state and the eastern half into the Mississippi Territory.

With the beginning of the War of 1812, New Orleans took on new importance because it was the nation's only naval station on the Gulf Coast. Also, if the city were taken by British forces, the country would lose not only control of the Gulf Coast but also access to the interior rivers of the Mississippi watershed. Thus, New Orleans specifically and Louisiana generally became key to the survival of the country. Fortunately for the United States, British operations aimed at Louisiana did not occur until late 1814. Master Commandant Daniel Todd Patterson, commanding the New Orleans naval station, perceived that New Orleans was exposed to several possible routes of attack from the water, including Bayou La Fourche, Barataria Bay, River Aux Chenes, Bayou Terre Aux Boeufs, the Mississippi River itself, and three routes via Lake Borgne.

Bayou La Fourche, a deep, narrow stream running from the Mississippi River north of New Orleans to the Gulf of Mexico, would not serve as a British route of attack because of its length, narrowness, and ease of obstruction. Barataria Bay, 70 miles west of the mouth of the Mississippi, with numerous channels running north to the river across from New Orleans, was also unfeasible unless the British procured experienced pilots familiar with the narrow, shallow, treacherous passages. River Aux Chenes and Bayou Terre Aux Boeufs, small streams running almost from English Turn and emptying into the Gulf of Mexico just east of the river's mouth, were also winding, narrow, and easily defended.

The main channel of the Mississippi River provided a possible alternative and, in hindsight, was probably the best route a British attack could have taken since it provided the only place where deep-draught vessels could be used; its shallow mouth (generally less than 14 feet deep), however, denied access to large ships. A strong current also forced vessels to make a long beat upstream, leaving them exposed to fire from the river's banks. Since this was the most viable route of attack, Fort St. Philip had been constructed about 30 miles from the river's mouth and Fort St. Leon 70 miles upstream. Moreover, Fort St. Leon commanded English Turn, an S-shaped turn where sailing vessels had to wait for a change in wind before proceeding upstream. While it was possible to sail upriver, the time spent tacking and waiting for favorable winds left the enemy exposed to a constant barrage.

Considering the possible routes and the U.S. defense, Lake Borgne became the most feasible alternative for a British attack. Also, the saltwater estuary provided three possible approaches. The first was through Lake Borgne's Rigolet's Pass into Lake Pontchartrain. This avenue, combined with the Bayou St. John, would have permitted the English to move by water within 2 miles of New Orleans. But this route necessitated using many light, shallow-draft vessels that the British had problems securing. It also was guarded by Fort Petites Coquilles, which the British believed to have over 500 men and 40 guns. The second alternative was through Lake Borgne to the Plain of Gentilly. From there British troops could use the Chef Menteur Road to march to the city. This avenue, because of its accessibility, was defended by both men and artillery, and a pitched battle there would have allowed the Americans to fall back and construct other lines of defense well away from the city.

The last route, and ultimately the one chosen by the British in December 1814, called for using Bayou Bienvenu, which drained the area east of New Orleans and stretched from Lake Borgne to within 1 mile of the Mississippi River. From there an enemy could proceed north 9 miles along the river levee, a narrow strip of land through the region's sugar plantations, toward New Orleans. Although this approach appeared to be the path of least resistance, it too was fraught with obstacles. The route was more shallow than expected, thus prohibiting British ships from entering the estuary or providing gunfire support to cover their barges' advance. Furthermore, the distance from Cat Island at the mouth of Lake Borgne to Bayou Bienvenu was 62 miles, and it took 36 hours of hard rowing to reach. But the most serious obstacle, according to one British participant, was the five U.S. gunboats that commanded the shoal waters.

Geography as well as U.S. defenses determined the British approach in their attack on New Orleans in December 1814–January 1815. But although geography limited British approaches, it enhanced Gen. Andrew Jackson's defenses. The resultant Battle of New Orleans demon-

strated the preeminence of Louisiana's geography as well as its importance for future U.S. development.

—Gene A. Smith

See also: Baratarian Pirates; Mississippi River; New Orleans, Battle of

Further Reading

Ainsworth, W. L. "An Amphibious Operation That Failed: The Battle of New Orleans." *United States Naval Institute Proceedings* 71 (February 1945): 193–201.

Brown, Wilburt S. *The Amphibious Campaign for West Florida and Louisiana. 1814–1815: A Critical Review of Strategy and Tactics at New Orleans.* University: University of Alabama Press, 1969.

Eller, E. M., W. J. Morgan, and R. M. Basoco. *The Battle of New Orleans: Sea Power and the Battle of New Orleans.* New Orleans: Battle of New Orleans, 150th Anniversary Committee of Louisiana, 1965.

Latour, A. Lacarriere. *Historical Memoir of the War in West Florida and Louisiana in 1814–15.* 1816; reprint, Gainesville: University Presses of Florida, 1964.

McClellan, Edwin N. "The Navy at the Battle of New Orleans." *United States Naval Institute Proceedings* 50 (December 1924): 2041–2060.

Owsley, Frank L. *Struggle for the Gulf Borderlands: The Creek War and the Battle of New Orleans, 1812–1815.* Gainesville: University Presses of Florida, 1981.

Tucker, Spencer C. *The Jeffersonian Gunboat Navy.* Columbia: University of South Carolina Press, 1993.

LOVELL, JOSEPH
1788–1836
U.S. medical officer

Born in Boston, Massachusetts, to James S. Lovell and Deborah Gorham Lovell, Joseph Lovell graduated from Harvard Medical School in 1811. One month before the U.S. declaration of war against Great Britain, he entered the U.S. Army as the regimental surgeon for the Ninth Infantry. Being one of the few medical school–trained physicians in the army, he quickly gained recognition for his superior medical knowledge and organizational skills. He established several hospitals in the northern theater, including one in Burlington, Vermont, and another in Williamsville, New York, that became models for military hospital organization.

Following the war, he rose to the position of surgeon general, primarily because of the service he rendered during the War of 1812 and his efforts immediately following the war to improve the health of the average soldier. His death in this position in 1836 followed a distinguished career dedicated to the organization of the medical corps and the health of the U.S. Army.

—*Jeanne T. Heidler and David S. Heidler*

See also: Medicine, Army

LOWNDES, WILLIAM
1782–1822
South Carolina congressman

Born to Rawlins Lowndes and his third wife Sarah Jones Lowndes in Colleton County, South Carolina, William Lowndes spent part of his early life in school in England. After entering into legal and farming careers, he entered public service in 1806 as a member of the South Carolina General Assembly. He grew increasingly critical of what he saw as Presidents Thomas Jefferson's and James Madison's weak response to British violations of U.S. trade. He believed that by hampering U.S. industry with first the embargo and later the various forms of nonintercourse, the United States was weakened more than its enemies were. Instead, he advocated first in South Carolina and later in 1810 as a member of Congress that the United States use its resources to increase the strength of the army and navy.

Lowndes entered the historic 12th Congress as one of a group of young congressmen who would become known as the War Hawks. Like many freshmen congressmen in the 12th Congress, Lowndes garnered appointments generally reserved for more senior men. The new speaker of the House, Henry Clay, appointed him second chair on the Committee of Commerce and Manufactures and fourth chair on the Committee on Military Affairs. In spite of these senior positions, Lowndes rarely spoke in debate, but he soon developed a reputation for quiet reflection and for courteous, measured debate. Though they considered him a friend of the administration, his fellow congressmen quickly learned that he voted his conscience rather than for party loyalty. Still, he could generally be counted on to vote for increases in military spending, even before the declaration of war, because he saw preparedness as the United States' greatest safeguard.

After the declaration of war in June 1812, Lowndes considered leaving Congress to accept a field commission, but

his fragile health finally discouraged him. Although he did not take the field himself, he kept abreast of military affairs, particularly in the South, through his father-in-law, Thomas Pinckney, commanding general of the Southern Department. In Congress, he concerned himself throughout the war with securing sufficient funding to protect the South Carolina coastline.

In the 13th Congress, Lowndes's activities and responsibilities grew when, in December 1813, Speaker Clay appointed him the chairman of the Committee on Naval Affairs. In that capacity, Lowndes worked hard to bring bills before Congress to strengthen naval organization and to encourage shipbuilding.

Lowndes suffered considerable financial reverses because of the war, and his health was chronically bad, but he tirelessly attended all sessions of Congress during the conflict. He was sitting in Congress when word arrived of the signing of the Treaty of Ghent, and Lowndes joined his fellow congressmen in eagerly departing for home as soon as the last business was completed.

Lowndes spent the seven years remaining to him in Congress, continuing his reputation for quiet, mature deliberation that won him the admiration of political enemies as well as friends. In May 1822, poor health forced his resignation. He died a few months later at sea, having sought recuperation in a voyage to Europe.

—*Jeanne T. Heidler and David S. Heidler*

See also: U.S. Congress
Further Reading
Vipperman, Carl J. *William Lowndes and the Transition of Southern Politics, 1782–1822.* Chapel Hill: University of North Carolina Press, 1989.

LUNDY'S LANE, BATTLE OF
25 July 1814

Lundy's Lane was the climactic battle of the last U.S. invasion of the Niagara Peninsula. It was also the conflict's bloodiest and most violent engagement.

The campaign that culminated at Lundy's Lane began in early July 1814, when the U.S. commander Jacob Brown crossed the frontier into Upper Canada and easily captured Fort Erie. He then moved his army northward along the Niagara River and fought a sharp battle against the British at Chippewa on 5 July. Failing to receive the expected naval support and supplies from Commodore Isaac

British and American troops were almost on top of each other at the Battle of Lundy's Lane. This painting gives the sense of brutality of what may have been the bloodiest battle in the war.

Chauncey, Brown had to abandon further offensive action and withdraw southward. The fear of a possible raid on his supply base at Fort Schlosser, New York, however, led him to send Gen. Winfield Scott's brigade back north to draw away the enemy. Scott ran directly into a British force, commanded by Gen. Phineas Riall, forming up on Lundy's Lane just to the west of Niagara Falls. Soon Gen. Gordon Drummond, commander of all British troops in Upper Canada, arrived with reinforcements, and Brown countered by supporting Scott with the remainder of his army.

The focus of the ensuing battle was on a small hill that straddled the lane. The British had placed cannon on the crest, and it was this position that the Americans tried to carry in the early evening and night of 25 July. Their first attempt was a maneuver around the British left flank that was halted by regulars and Canadian militia. In the meantime, on the other side of the line and in enveloping darkness, the British mistakenly fired into one of their own units, the Glengarry Light Infantry, as it approached the battlefield from the southwest. The unit, however, suffered only a small number of casualties.

Unable to outflank the enemy, the Americans began the deadly business of attempting to seize the hill with frontal attacks. After repeated assaults, it was finally taken at approximately 9:00 P.M. Drummond then ordered counterattacks to regain the position. The exchange of musket and cannon fire was now at extremely close range. The Americans soon began to run out of water and ammunition, and Brown ordered them to pull back from the hill, leaving the guns to the enemy. At midnight, fearing yet another attack, British troops on the hill started dragging in the bodies of dead horses to form a makeshift breastwork.

The Americans, however, did not attack again. Instead, they withdrew from the field and eventually moved all the way back to Fort Erie, throwing baggage and equipment into the river as they departed. Drummond's force was so thoroughly exhausted that it could not pursue. The casualties remained on the battlefield, and British troops heard the screams of the wounded throughout the night. The next day soldiers ate their breakfasts surrounded by corpses. In places, the British and U.S. dead were only a few yards apart. Many of these bodies were gathered together and burned on the field in a mass pyre. Catherine Lundy opened her house 1 mile east from the battlefield to serve as a hospital for the most direly wounded.

The British held the hill at the end of the fighting, and the U.S. withdrawal was unqualified. The grim nature of the fight occasioned comment even among battle-hardened veterans of the European war. Lundy's Lane produced the highest casualty figures of any encounter during the war. Of the nearly 3,000 British troops involved, 81 were killed and another 562 were wounded, a casualty rate of 21 percent. The 2,100 Americans engaged fared even worse, with 171 killed and 573 wounded, a rate of 35 percent. Such losses were comparable to those sustained in battles fought in Europe. Phineas Riall, Winfield Scott, Jacob Brown, and Gordon Drummond were all wounded. Scott's injuries were severe enough to end his participation in the war. The Battle of Lundy's Lane was fought with a ferocity that rivaled anything seen in the Napoleonic contest.

—*Eric Jarvis*

See also: Niagara Campaigns
Further Reading
Cureton, Janet. "Catherine Lundy at the Battle of Lundy's Lane." *McLeans* (October 1960).
Graves, Donald E. *The Battle of Lundy's Lane: On the Niagara in 1814.* Baltimore, MD: Nautical and Aviation Publishing Company of America, 1993.

LYON, MATTHEW
1750–1822
U.S. congressman

Born in Ireland, Lyon came to the American colonies in 1765 as an indentured servant. For the first few years of his life in America, he lived in Connecticut but moved to Vermont after serving his indenture. During the Revolutionary War, he served under Ethan Allen, Richard Montgomery, and Arthur St. Clair. Following the war, Lyon became an important businessman in Vermont and became increasingly involved in Vermont politics. In 1797, Lyon was elected to the House of Representatives as a Democratic Republican.

As a New England Democratic Republican among Federalists, Lyon was a rarity, and he was not popular among the other congressman from his region. Since Vermont was still regarded as a frontier area, Lyon was sometimes ridi-

culed by New England Federalists as rough and crude. One such incident resulted in violence. In January 1798, while the House was debating President John Adams's recommendations that the country's defenses be strengthened, Roger Griswold of Connecticut responded to Lyon's opposition by insulting Lyon's performance during the Revolution. Lyon spat tobacco juice in Griswold's face. Congressman Griswold stewed over this insult for two weeks and then attacked Lyon with a cane, prompting a general brawl in the House. The ensuing investigation by Congress resulted in no official action, though Lyon would carry the nickname "spitting Lyon" for the remainder of his life.

Lyon's vocal criticism of the Adams administration gained him more than just a lashing with a cane. In the summer of 1798, he was charged with violation of the Sedition Act, tried in the fall, and sentenced to a fine and four months in jail. His constituents responded to his conviction by reelecting him to Congress. He immediately returned to Congress following his release.

In 1801, Lyon and his family moved to Kentucky, where Lyon became an important businessman and political figure. In 1803, he was elected to Congress from his new state and became known as a staunch supporter of the Jefferson administration. He defended the president against the verbal assaults of the Federalists as well as those of Democratic Republicans such as John Randolph. During the war scare of 1808 that followed the *Chesapeake-Leopard* Affair of 1807, Lyon believed that the best way to protect U.S. rights was to go to war with Great Britain. Between 1808 and 1811, however, he became less sure, particularly because those who most urged war also advocated an invasion of Canada.

By 1811, Lyon questioned the wisdom of a land war to protect free trade. His stand cost him election to the 12th Congress. Lyon then spent the war years trying to save his business activities and writing to prominent political figures concerning his views on the war. Ironically, he used his acquaintance with many New Englanders to urge the region's loyalty to the Union.

Following the war, Lyon's business failures compelled him to accept a government appointment as a factor to the Cherokees in Arkansas in 1820. He died there in 1822.

—*Jeanne T. Heidler and David S. Heidler*

See also: Griswold, Roger
Further Reading
McLaughlin, James Fairfax. *Matthew Lyon, the Hampden of Congress: A Biography.* New York: Wynkoop Hallenbeck Crawford, 1900.

M

MACDONNELL, GEORGE
See Ogdensburg, Battle of

MACDONOUGH, THOMAS
1783–1825
U.S. Navy officer

Of all the U.S. naval officers who won fame in the War of 1812, few were more deserving than Thomas Macdonough. At Plattsburg Bay on 11 September 1814, the 30-year-old Macdonough guided his undergunned and outmanned flotilla to a crushing victory against a British squadron. The destruction of the enemy's fleet in this bay on Lake Champlain preserved northern New York from invasion and so made the British far more amenable to U.S. demands at the peace talks in Ghent. Macdonough's triumph not only testified to his skills as a tactician and leader, but it was also a tribute to his education and training as a young officer.

Macdonough was born near Middletown, Delaware, in 1783, the sixth of ten children. His father was a physician and Revolutionary War veteran who went on to achieve prominence in Delaware politics. Both parents died when he was young, leaving Macdonough an orphan at age 11. Nonetheless, his father bequeathed Thomas an important legacy: the patronage of some powerful political friends. While still in his teens, Macdonough parlayed his family connections into a midshipman's commission in the country's infant navy. He embarked on his new career in 1800, assigned to a berth in the converted merchantman *Ganges*.

Macdonough's first cruise almost turned out to be his last. While serving on the *Ganges* in the West Indies, Macdonough came down with yellow fever. After surviving this misfortune, he narrowly escaped becoming a casualty of the reduction in navy ordered by Congress in 1801. Only

the timely intercession of another family benefactor prevented his name from being stricken from the navy's list. So instead of receiving notice of his dismissal, Macdonough found himself ordered to join the *Constellation*. The frigate was part of Commodore Richard Morris's squadron, which was being readied for service against the Barbary States in the Mediterranean.

Macdonough departed the United States aboard the *Constellation* in 1802, still largely a novice at his chosen profession. By the time of his homecoming in 1806, however, three-plus years of foreign duty had turned him into a seasoned, accomplished officer. He was fortunate at the outset to serve on the *Constellation* with Capt. Alexander Murray. The Navy Department did not have a high opinion of Murray's qualities as a fighting captain, but Murray was one of the navy's most conscientious commanders when it came to mentoring the young midshipmen in his charge. Under his tutelage, Macdonough received a thorough education in seamanship, navigation, and gunnery.

During his long stint in the Mediterranean, Macdonough also had the good luck to fall under the influence of two other dynamic individuals, Edward Preble and Stephen Decatur. In an autobiographical fragment composed in the 1820s, Macdonough recalled those exciting months with Preble battling the Barbary corsairs as "the school where our navy received its first lessons." Shortly after the arrival of Preble's squadron on the Mediterranean station in 1803, Macdonough was transferred to the schooner *Enterprise*, commanded by Decatur. This assignment marked the beginning of a lifelong friendship between the two. Macdonough was at Decatur's side when the latter pulled off two of the most celebrated exploits of the Barbary conflict: the destruction of the *Philadelphia*, a U.S. ship that had been captured by pirates, in February 1804 and the capture of two Tripolitan gunboats the following August. Macdonough was rewarded for his part in these actions with a promotion to acting lieutenant.

The years that followed Macdonough's return to the United States in 1806 were desultory ones for the navy—and naval officers. Although Macdonough received confirmation of his lieutenant's commission in January 1807, the

Thomas Macdonough

prospects for further advancement looked bleak. Macdonough remained on active duty in a variety of posts until 1811, when he took a furlough from the navy to captain a merchant ship bound for the East Indies. The voyage was so profitable that he immediately asked for another leave of absence. When Secretary of the Navy Paul Hamilton balked at this second request, Macdonough tendered his resignation. The onset of war with Great Britain rendered the dispute moot, however, and in late June Macdonough notified the Navy Department that he was ready to return to service.

He was initially posted as first lieutenant on the *Constellation*, which was then fitting out at the Washington Navy Yard. Upon arriving in Washington, though, Macdonough saw that the frigate was still months away from readiness. Disappointed, he arranged a transfer to Portland, Maine, where he was given command of a division of gunboats. He had scarcely settled in at Portland when he received new orders. In September 1812, Hamilton directed the 28-year-old lieutenant to take charge of all U.S. naval vessels on Lake Champlain.

During the first three years of the Revolutionary War, Lake Champlain and its environs had been the scene of several major U.S. and British offensives. In 1812, however, the theater was something of a backwater. Arriving at Burlington, Vermont, in October, Macdonough discovered that the sum total of the warships at his disposal consisted of a pair of leaky gunboats and three sloops that the army had been using as transports. Fortunately, this meager force was as much as the British could assemble at their end of the lake.

During the winter of 1812–1813, Macdonough scrounged what naval stores he could to bolster the fighting capabilities of his tiny flotilla. He added more guns to the sloops *Growler* and *Eagle*, increasing their armament to 11 cannon each. Obtaining qualified sailors to man these vessels, however, posed more of a problem, and Macdonough found that soldiers drafted from the army made poor substitutes. A serious blunder during the summer of 1813 gave Macdonough further cause to worry. In early June, his subordinate, Lt. Sidney Smith, allowed the *Growler* and *Eagle* to stray too far down the Richelieu River in pursuit of some enemy gunboats. The British managed to capture both sloops, a coup that instantly reversed the balance of naval forces on the lake. Undaunted, Macdonough immediately set out to redress his losses. News of his promotion to master commandant on 24 July provided gratifying evidence of the Navy Department's continued confidence in him. By 6 September, he was back on the lake in force, at the head of a squadron of three sloops and two gunboats. The campaigning season wound down with the Americans once more in control of the waterway.

The situation on Lake Champlain acquired new urgency in 1814 as both the Americans and the British stepped up the pace of naval construction. By the time Macdonough sortied from his base at Vergennes, Vermont, in May, he had two new ships under his command, the *Saratoga* (26 guns) and the *Ticonderoga* (17 guns), to go along with his three existing sloops and six gunboats. Still not satisfied, he urged the Navy Department to approve construction of an additional brig or schooner. His advice was accepted, and on 11 August the *Eagle* (20 guns) was launched, a mere 19 days after the laying of her keel at Vergennes.

Macdonough spent most of the summer patrolling the lower end of the lake, keeping an eye on enemy movements along the Richelieu River. By the end of August, it had become clear that a major British offensive was imminent. Sir George Prevost, the governor-general of Canada, had amassed an army of more than 10,000 men on his side of the border. Prevost had also assembled a powerful naval flotilla consisting of a frigate, two sloops, and a brig to escort his troops up the lake. Mindful that the odds might be against him, Macdonough resolved not to rush rashly into battle under conditions that favored his opponent. "'Tis better to save a force by retiring from a superior foe than to lose it even by hard fighting," he wrote Gen. George Izard in June. Accordingly, upon hearing on 1 September that the British squadron had entered the lake, Macdonough retreated to Plattsburg Bay. Over the next few days, he plotted his strategy, taking great care to ensure that when the enemy did finally appear, the circumstances would be decidedly in his own favor.

Macdonough's planning paid off almost to perfection. The British squadron rounded Cumberland Head on the morning of 11 September. Finding the Americans anchored in a north-south line across the bay, the British naval commander Capt. George Downie responded much as Macdonough hoped he would. Downie allowed himself to be drawn into a short-range slugging match in which the Americans could make the most of their numerous carronades. Macdonough had also had the foresight to prepare a kedge anchor on his flagship, *Saratoga*. At the decisive moment in the battle, he used the preset kedge to pivot his ship and bring a fresh broadside to bear on the British. Shortly after accomplishing this maneuver, the *Saratoga* battered both the 37-gun *Confiance* and another British vessel into submission. The engagement ended with all of Downie's fleet save for some gunboats in U.S. possession.

Macdonough's victory at Plattsburg Bay was the high point of his career. In addition to receiving a promotion to captain and a medal from Congress, he also netted over $22,000 in prize money. He would later remark, "In one month from a poor lieutenant I became a rich man." The years after 1815, however, were not a happy time for Macdonough. He had contracted tuberculosis during his many months of service on the lake, and he would be dogged by ill health for the remainder of his life. After the war, his frail condition limited him primarily to shore commands. In 1824, he did return to active duty as captain of the *Constitution*, but before he could finish his cruise, infirmity compelled him to turn the frigate over to another captain and take passage on a merchant ship headed back to the United States. He died en route on 10 November 1825 at the age of 41.

—*Jeff Seiken*

See also: Lake Champlain, Battle of
Further Reading

Eckert, Edward K. "Thomas Macdonough: Architect of a Wilderness Navy." In James C. Bradford, ed., *Command under Sail: Makers of the American Naval Tradition*. Annapolis, MD: Naval Institute Press, 1985

Everest, Allan S. *The War of 1812 in the Champlain Valley*. Syracuse, NY: Syracuse University Press, 1981.

Macdonough, Rodney. *Life of Commodore Thomas Macdonough, U.S. Navy*. Boston: Fort Hill Press, 1909.

MACKINAC ISLAND
See Michilimackinac, Fort

MACOMB, ALEXANDER
1782–1841
U.S. Army officer

Born in Detroit, Alexander Macomb was exposed to army life at that isolated post at a young age. He moved to New York as a child and as a young man joined the New York Rangers to protect the Canadian frontier of that state. This further taste of military life convinced him to seek a commission in the U.S. Army. After becoming a lieutenant, he moved to the southwest, where he served under Maj. Gen. James Wilkinson. Macomb was promoted to captain in 1805 and to major in 1808. As an engineering officer, his primary responsibility before the outbreak of the War of 1812 was to supervise the construction of frontier fortifications.

Immediately before the war, Macomb served as inspector general of the army. He found it a frustrating position because of the lack of organization in most of the frontier posts. Because of the army's inefficiency, Macomb could not calculate its actual strength as war loomed.

At the beginning of the war, Macomb moved to artillery, where he distinguished himself and consequently rose in rank. By early 1814, he was recognized as one of the emerging young officers who were quickly replacing the older generation of generals who had commanded during the first two years of the war. In January 1814, along with some of these other younger officers, Macomb received a promotion to brigadier general. Two months later, he witnessed the last battle of one of the older generation, James Wilkinson, at La Colle Mill, Lower Canada. In that battle of 30 March 1814, Macomb commanded the reserve and did not see significant action.

With the forced retirement of Wilkinson and his replacement by Maj. Gen. Jacob Brown, Macomb was stationed at Plattsburg on Lake Champlain, under the immediate command of Maj. Gen. George Izard. In August 1814, Secretary of War John Armstrong erroneously mistook the British actions in Canada to indicate a massive attack along the Niagara River, and the secretary ordered Izard to take 4,000 of his less than 8,000 men to Sacket's Harbor, New York. After unsuccessfully protesting this order, Izard left Plattsburg at the end of August. Within two days, a 10,000-man British army under Gen. Sir George Prevost invaded the United States and, in cooperation with the British fleet on Lake Champlain, marched toward Plattsburg.

Macomb frantically began strengthening his defenses, knowing that his little army was outnumbered by more than two to one. To add to his problems, Macomb's approximately 3,400 men consisted of fragments of various units, with very little coherent organization. To delay the British march, Macomb sent out skirmishers daily, but they had little effect on the British advance. Finally, on 6 September, he dispatched a larger U.S. force to Beekmantown, New York. Though overwhelmed by British numerical superiority, this detachment fought a gallant rearguard action all the way back to the Saranac River within sight of Plattsburg.

When Prevost reached the Saranac later that day, he halted to await the remainder of his army and artillery, as well as the arrival of the British fleet, so that they could coordinate the attack. This delay stretched into five days as the Americans on their side of the Saranac watched the British carefully erect their batteries. To boost morale, on the night of 9 September 1814 Macomb sent a 50-man raiding party across the river to spike the guns of one of the British rocket batteries. The raid succeeded, and the party returned safely to U.S. lines. Macomb also used the delay in British action to send out calls to all local militia to reinforce his lines. A large contingent of Vermont militia surprised everyone by answering this call. Previously, the Vermonters had been reluctant to participate in campaigns. To demonstrate how much their effort was appreciated, Macomb personally greeted the units as they marched into the U.S. camp.

On the morning of 11 September, the coordinated British attack commenced, with the naval forces moving against the U.S. fleet and Prevost's army assaulting the two bridges across the Saranac. While one of the bridges held, the British under Gen. Sir Frederick Robinson stormed across the other. Waiting for reinforcements before advancing on the town, Robinson heard that the British fleet had been defeated and shortly thereafter received General Prevost's order to withdraw. Without naval support, Prevost feared that surrounding militia would soon cut his communication and supply lines; by 12 September he was already on the way back to Canada. Prevost carried out the retreat so quickly that Macomb had no idea that it was taking place until late on the twelfth.

For his actions in defending Plattsburg, Macomb was voted a gold medal by Congress and was awarded a sword by the state of New York. The president rewarded his actions by giving him a brevet promotion to major general.

Following the war, Macomb commanded briefly at Detroit but was shortly promoted to chief engineer and was headquartered in Washington, D.C. Upon the death of Maj. Gen. Jacob Brown in 1828, Macomb was appointed commanding general of the army. He held that position until his death in Washington in 1841.

—Jeanne T. Heidler and David S. Heidler

See also: Izard, George; La Colle Mill, Battle of; Plattsburg, Battle of; Wilkinson, James

Further Reading

Richards, George H., ed. *Memoir of Alexander Macomb, the Major-General Commanding the Army of the United States.* New York: McElrath, Bangs, 1833.

MACON, NATHANIEL
1758–1837
U.S. congressman

Born on Shocco Creek in what is now Warren County, North Carolina, on 17 December 1758, Nathaniel Macon was a dedicated soldier, state legislator, congressman, and U.S. senator. He attended an "old field school" in his neighborhood and in 1774 entered the College of New Jersey (now Princeton University), where he remained two years. His Revolutionary War career was short but extraordinary. After serving briefly in the New Jersey militia, Macon returned to North Carolina to study law. He enlisted as a private in 1780 in the North Carolina Line, refusing a commission. The next year he was elected to the state senate and thus began his long public career. Macon was often active thereafter in either the upper or lower house of the state legislature. He was elected in 1786 to the Confederation Congress, but he declined to serve. He opposed both the Philadelphia Convention and the federal Constitution that it produced. In 1791 Macon took a seat in the U.S. House of Representatives, where he represented the Sixth Congressional District until December 1815, when he was sent to the U.S. Senate. He stayed in the Senate until December 1828. In the national election of 1824 he received 24 electoral votes for vice president.

An ardent Republican, Macon was elected Speaker of the House in 1801 and continued in that office until 1807.

His preference for James Monroe over James Madison in the upcoming presidential election of 1808 cost him the speakership. By the time war clouds were gathering, Macon chaired the important committee on foreign relations and reported two bills bearing his name, although not his endorsement. Macon's Bill No. 2, passed in May 1810, gave President Madison the authority to suspend trade with either France or Great Britain, should the other forgo interfering with U.S. commerce.

Managing and directing much legislation, Macon was possibly the most powerful man in the House in the years 1809–1811. In the latter year, he generally supported military preparedness, but he opposed commissioning ships for the navy but not putting them into service and allowing merchant vessels to arm themselves. His philosophy was that when "people are prepared for war they are sure to fight. I do not wish to carry this imitation of England too far. To support her army and navy, her people are kept poor. Our people pay enough taxes. . . ." He voted against a bill passed in January 1812 that raised 25,000 troops and 50,000 volunteers. He did vote in April for an embargo and in May for the House resolution that war be declared against Great Britain: "Our affairs are in such a state that we must try what has been called the last resort of kings. I have made up my mind on the subject, and whenever we are ready to declare war, I shall vote for it." He explained that he voted for war in June mainly to protect sailors' rights.

While supporting the declaration of war, Macon was nevertheless ambivalent about providing troops, ships, and fortifications. On 13 January 1813, he delivered an impressive speech on the new army bill, in which he voiced a marked interest in territorial expansion: "For one, I am willing to have Canada and Florida, and have them you must before many years." He asserted that no one objected more to a standing army in peacetime than he, but "we are at war, and that ought to be carried on by regular soldiers. . . . This war is like every thing else which has been done—to begin it was wrong, to continue it is wrong, to make a bad treaty to get peace will undoubtedly be wrong."

Appointed chairman of the congressional committee to report on British conduct in the war, Macon's committee found the enemy in various violations of the rules of war. He requested on 22 July that the secretary of the navy supply "a copy of [U.S. Navy] Captain [Isaac] Chauncey's letter, or an extract of it, which gives the account of the scalp found above the chair of the Speaker of the legislature of Upper Canada."

Macon supported the loan bill of 1814 against which his colleague William Gaston had inveighed. At the same time, he described the war as one that was being fought "for the rights of the poor and not for the property of the rich." He informed the secretary of the treasury on 31 March that Pres. James Madison had just recommended to Congress the repeal of the Non-Intercourse Act, a measure that Macon opposed and against which he had voted.

After the war, Macon entered the U.S. Senate (president pro tempore, 1825–1827). When his career of 37 years in Congress ended, he retired to Buck Spring, his plantation in Warren County. His political advice was often sought. The last major activity of his long life occurred at the state constitutional convention of 1835, where he was unanimously elected president of that body. He died at his plantation on 29 June 1837 and was buried on the grounds. In 1783, he had married Hannah Plummer, with whom he had two daughters and a son.

—*Charles H. Bowman, Jr.*

See also: U.S. Congress
Further Reading
Ashe, Samuel A., ed. *Biographical History of North Carolina from Colonial Times to the Present.* 7 vols. Greensboro, NC: C. L. Van Noppen, 1906.
Dodd, William E. *The Life of Nathaniel Macon.* Raleigh, NC: Edwards and Broughton, 1903.
Macon, Nathaniel. *A Speech Delivered by Nathaniel Macon, in the House of Representatives of the United States. January 13, 1813.* N.p., n.d.
Wilson, Clyde. "Nathaniel Macon." *Dictionary of North Carolina Biography.* Vol. 4. Chapel Hill: University of North Carolina Press, 1991: 185–187.
Wilson, Edwin M. "The Congressional Career of Nathaniel Macon." *James Sprunt Historical Monographs.* Chapel Hill: University of North Carolina Press, 1900.

MACON'S BILL NO. 2
1 May 1810

Macon's Bill No. 2 (officially titled "An Act concerning the commercial intercourse between the United States and Great Britain and France. . . .") concluded a series of laws to avoid war with Britain and France by attempting economic coercion. Pres. James Madison's first annual message (29 November 1809) called upon Congress to deal with Britain after the collapse of negotiations. After a speech by Nathaniel Macon (1758–1837) on 1 December supported a prohibition on vessels from countries that restricted U.S. merchantmen, the House of Representatives formed a nine-member select committee on foreign relations. Macon became its chairman. He reported a bill

(19 December), later called the "American Navigation Act," that among other things prohibited importation of British and French goods except in U.S. ships.

The Non-Intercourse Act (1 March 1809) was generally considered dead: congressmen reported stores that had paid no customs duties having shelves nevertheless filled with British goods. After extensive and repetitive debate, the American Navigation Act passed the House on 29 January 1810, but the Senate amended it out of existence on 22 February. The House then voted to recommit the bill to the same committee. At the end of March, with nothing done, John Randolph moved to repeal the nonintercourse law, deriding it as "a scarecrow . . . a toy, a rattle."

Macon reported a new bill on 7 April 1810. Macon did not support the measure in debate and believed the cabinet had originated it—he had been visiting Secretary of the Treasury Albert Gallatin during April. Although James Madison seemed to suggest in a letter to Jefferson (23 April 1810) that the legislature acted on its own, in fact Madison's written account of his firing of Secretary of State Robert Smith in late March 1810 describes cabinet consultations on the Macon bills. The same document justifies the practice of the executive influence on individual legislators to effect legislation.

The gist of "Macon's" bill (Section 1) repealed the Non-Intercourse Act and instructed the president (Section 3) to impose key sections of that act on either Britain or France if the other abandoned or significantly modified their restrictions against U.S. shipping. On 18 April, Richard M. Johnson of Kentucky succeeded in amending the bill to include a 50 percent tariff on these belligerents' ships. The Senate version dropped this amendment, however, and debate resumed. Several congressmen confessed to confusion over the meaning of the amendments and, having experienced five months of debate, probably over the meaning of the bill itself.

The House accepted the Senate's version on 1 May 1810. Essentially, the bill prohibited belligerents' warships (except in cases of emergencies and delivery of dispatches) from entering U.S. waters and opened trade with both powers until one or the other eased its restrictions. Should that happen, the president should reimpose the Non-Intercourse Act of 1809. Both Macon and Madison privately expressed their opinion that the bill represented a desire of congressmen "to do something."

On 5 July 1810, Napoleon hinted at the withdrawal of the Berlin and Milan Decrees in a letter to the Duc de Cadore. On 5 August 1810, Cadore wrote the U.S. minister to the same effect. Madison accepted this letter as a revocation of the decrees and issued a proclamation on 2 November 1810 imposing nonintercourse with Great Britain,

effective 2 February 1811. In spite of warnings that Napoleon was insincere and in the face of continued French depredations on U.S. shipping, the administration remained adamant in its position. It was thus charged that Macon's Bill No. 2 effectively made the United States an unwitting participant in Napoleon's Continental System.

—*James Edward Scanlon*

See also: Barlow, Joel; Berlin Decree; Cadore Letter; Diplomacy; Macon, Nathaniel; Milan Decree; Napoleon I; Trade Restrictions

Further Reading
Adams, Henry. *History. . . . the First Administration of James Madison.* 2 vols. New York: Charles Scribner's Sons, 1890.
Ambler, Charles H., ed. "Nathaniel Macon Correspondence." *John P. Branch Historical Papers* 3 (1910): 27–93.
[Annals of Congress]. *Debates and Proceedings . . . 11th Congress.* Washington, DC: Gales and Seaton, 1853.
Madison, James. *Letters and Other Writings.* 4 vols. Vol. 2: *1794–1815.* New York: R. Worthington, 1884.

MADISON, DOLLEY PAYNE
1768–1849
First Lady of the United States

Dolley Payne was born in North Carolina, but her parents returned to their home in Virginia when she was an infant. Her family being Quakers, she led a simple life. Perhaps to be near other Quakers, Dolley Payne's family moved to Philadelphia when she was 15. In 1790, she married her first husband and had two sons over the next three years. In 1793, her husband and youngest son died during the Philadelphia yellow fever epidemic. Soon after her husband's death, Dolley Payne Todd met Congressman James Madison, and they married in 1794.

Over the next few years, Dolley Madison became a talented and popular hostess, a quality that she would carry to the new capital of Washington, D.C., in 1800. After she became First Lady in 1809, her invitations were the most sought-after in the capital.

During the war, Dolley Madison continued her official duties as hostess, trying to maintain some semblance of civility during an otherwise uncivil time. Her crowning moment came during the British march on Washington in August 1814. Her bravery and coolness in this crisis earned her the admiration of the nation.

Dolley Payne Madison

As the British approached the capital on 22 August, President Madison left in search of Gen. William Winder, the overall commander of the district's defenses. Before his departure, the president left all cabinet papers in his wife's care, instructing her that if the British broke through to Washington, she was to take them with her. Mrs. Madison then spent two anxious days waiting for news. Meanwhile, she had her carriage prepared so that she could leave at a moment's notice; she packed the papers and had them placed in the carriage. Busy with these chores, she also noticed a growing stream of militiamen retreating through the streets of Washington. She also watched, with considerable chagrin, the 100 men left to guard the president's mansion simply melt away.

Dolley Madison spent the night of 23 August alone, except for a few loyal servants. She had planned a dinner party for the next evening, but in the morning the regrets began coming in as most of the capital's residents elected to flee the city. By afternoon, she could hear distant cannon, and several friends arrived, urging her to escape. Her sister also came to add her voice. As Dolley Madison hurriedly packed as much silver and other valuable objects as she

could carry, she insisted that she would not leave until she was assured that someone would save the Gilbert Stuart portrait of George Washington. That task required removing the massive painting from its frame. Finally, after the frame was broken to extract the picture, Dolley Madison entered her carriage for her journey to Virginia. President Madison met her at a roadside inn that evening.

Following the war and the retirement of her husband, Dolley Madison spent the rest of her husband's life as the mistress of their plantation, Montpelier. After his death, she moved to Washington, where she spent the remainder of her life as a revered matriarch of the republic.

—*Jeanne T. Heidler and David S. Heidler*

See also: Barker, Jacob; Madison, James
Further Reading
Madison, Dolley. *Memoirs and Letters of Dolley Madison, Wife of James Madison, President of the United States.* Boston and New York: Houghton, Mifflin, 1888.

MADISON, JAMES
1751–1836
Fourth president of the United States

James Madison, Jr., was born on 16 March 1751 in Port Conway, Virginia, the eldest of 12 children born to Orange County planter James Madison, Sr., and his wife, Nelly Conway Madison. He grew up at Montpelier, the family home he would inherit upon his father's death in 1801.

Rather than attend the College of William and Mary, the choice of most aristocratic Virginians of that time, Madison enrolled at the College of New Jersey (now Princeton University) in 1769. While at Princeton, Madison was greatly influenced by its president, John Witherspoon, and was immersed in the writings of Enlightenment thinkers such as James Hutchinson, David Hume, Adam Smith, and Montesquieu, among others. Intellectually inclined and gifted, Madison completed four years of study in two, graduating with a baccalaureate in 1771. He stayed at Princeton for an additional year of study, however, before returning to Montpelier exhausted and ill. The experience foreshadowed the periodic bouts of illness and depression that would afflict him throughout his life. Indeed, he was to fall ill for an extended period during the War of 1812.

Unenthusiastic about being a planter in a backwater, Madison's interest in political events found fertile ground

James Madison

in the advent of revolutionary resistance to Great Britain. He was certainly influenced by his prestigious father's involvement in various activities. Though family connections helped pave the way for early appointments, including one as a colonel in the Virginia militia, Madison exhibited little ardor for a military career. He seems to have discovered his gift for politics and philosophical debate with his election in 1776 to the Virginia Convention, where he helped write the Virginia Constitution and Declaration of Rights. In October 1776, as a member of the newly created Virginia House of Delegates, Madison began his long and important association with fellow Virginian Thomas Jefferson. Although in 1777 Madison was not reelected to the House of Delegates, ostensibly because he refused to reward voters with whiskey, he was elected by his colleagues to a seat on the Council of State.

In December 1779, Madison was elected to the Continental Congress in Philadelphia, and served from March 1780 until December 1783, shortly after the conclusion of the Revolutionary War. Returning to Virginia, he was again elected to the House of Delegates and became the foremost spokesman in the assembly to call for the convening of the Annapolis Convention, the meeting that would lay the groundwork for the Constitutional Convention in Philadelphia. When the Constitutional Convention opened on 25 May 1787, preliminary work done by Madison and the Virginia delegation was evident in the so-called Virginia Plan, also known as Madison's Plan, a proposal that advocated a stronger national government. Although many compromises followed, Madison was clearly the guiding intellectual force behind the Convention. His notes of the debates provide the most complete and authoritative record of what happened at the Constitutional Convention between May and September 1787.

His role in the ratification process was equally crucial. Along with fellow Federalists Alexander Hamilton and John Jay, Madison wrote 29 out of a series of 85 essays for several New York newspapers. Collectively known as *The Federalist Papers*, these essays are regarded as some of the most important documents in U.S. political history. And as a member of the newly created House of Representatives in 1789, Madison would take up the task of writing a Bill of Rights for the Constitution, which would fulfill a promise made by Federalists to allay the fears of opponents in various ratifying conventions. Approved by both houses of Congress on 25 September 1789, the amendments composing the Bill of Rights were subsequently ratified by three-fourths of the states by December 1791. Madison's contributions at the Constitutional Convention, in the ratification process, and to the Bill of Rights secure forever his place among U.S. statesmen.

Philosophical and political differences between George Washington's Secretary of the Treasury, Alexander Hamilton, and Madison would help spur the development of political parties in the United States. Hamilton's financial plans that would have expanded federal power forced Madison to move gradually into opposition and to become a strict constructionist with respect to constitutional interpretation. Within a decade of the founding of the constitutional government, Federalists would contend with Democratic Republicans (or simply Republicans) led by Jefferson and Madison.

Issues associated with the French Revolution also increased political partisanship. In January 1793, France declared war on Great Britain and called upon the United States to honor treaty obligations under the Franco-American alliance of 1778. Hamilton was pro-British in his sympathies, but Madison and Jefferson believed that the United States should be committed to France. President Washington, fearing that U.S. involvement in the European war would be adverse to U.S. interests, proclaimed neutrality in 1793, a move that Madison opposed.

As British commercial measures and British support for Indians along the western frontier produced an increasingly belligerent climate, Madison believed, as did Jefferson, that a policy of peaceable economic coercion could best challenge the British practice of seizing U.S. ships. Yet when Federalist John Jay negotiated Jay's Treaty in 1795, it appeared to Madison and Jefferson—as well as to the French government—as nothing more than a pro-British measure.

Madison resolved to retire from Congress when his term expired in March 1797. He had married in 1794 the widow Dolley Payne Todd, an outgoing Quaker, who would delight Washington society until her death in 1849. She and Madison were extremely devoted to each other, and he likely longed for the tranquillity of his Virginia home. The main factor influencing his decision to retire from Congress, however, was probably the death of his brother Ambrose and the need to assume greater responsibility for his aging parents at Montpelier.

The serene life of a devoted family man and gentleman farmer did not last long, though. In 1798 repressive legislation sponsored by the Federalists in Congress, collectively known as the Alien and Sedition Acts, sought, among other things, to muzzle Republican critics of the government. Madison collaborated with Jefferson to draft a protest in the form of the Virginia and Kentucky Resolutions, with Madison writing the former. Adopted by the Virginia and Kentucky legislatures, these resolves attacked the Alien and Sedition Acts as violations of the First Amendment of the Constitution. In the election of 1800, many nominal Federalists deserted Federalist candidates to vote Republican. Thomas Jefferson defeated incumbent president John Adams to become third president of the United States on 4 March 1801.

Viewing the election of 1800 as the "Revolution of 1800," and no less significant than the revolution of 1776, Jefferson and the Republicans sought to undo much of what the Federalists had done and to redirect the nation along a path that more accurately reflected the traits of a representative republic. Asked to become secretary of state in the new administration, James Madison served for two terms. In doing so, he joined a cabinet that included Albert Gallatin, who was to Jefferson what Hamilton had been to Washington. Together, Madison and Gallatin were Jefferson's most important advisers, and, as secretary of state, the former was positioned to succeed Jefferson as president when the time came. Madison supported the purchase of Louisiana from France in 1803 and, along with Secretary of the Navy Robert Smith and Gallatin, convinced the president that a constitutional amendment was not necessary for the United States to acquire the territory.

The greatest challenges that confronted Madison were the consequences of the bitter struggle between France and Great Britain. Standing apart from this contest, the United States sought to continue in lucrative trade as a neutral carrier. When the Peace of Amiens of 1802 gave way to re-

newed war between the belligerents in 1803, U.S. ships and seamen were again subjected to depredations from both the British and the French. Like Jefferson, Madison believed that the rest of the world was so dependent upon U.S. trade and resources that a denial of that trade would force the offending powers to rescind their obnoxious policies. So confident were they in the efficacy of peaceable economic coercion that when the U.S. warship *Chesapeake* was boarded by British sailors from the *Leopard* and U.S. sailors were removed by the British in June 1807, the president and the secretary of state moved to implement their theory of peaceable economic coercion in the form of the Embargo Act of 22 December 1807. This law closed U.S. ports and prevented U.S. ships from leaving those ports and caused enormous economic dislocation in coastal communities. Madison's association with the policy of peaceable economic coercion while also pursuing policies to reduce the army and navy caused him to come under severe criticism not only from Federalists but also from Republicans. When the Embargo Act failed to achieve its desired effects, and when it looked as though the Republican Party would be irreparably split if the Embargo were continued, it was repealed on 1 March 1809, just three days before Jefferson left office. For Jefferson, as well as for Madison, the repeal of the Embargo Act and its replacement with the face-saving, watered-down Non-Intercourse Act, was a personal and political embarrassment.

Jefferson wanted Madison to succeed him as president, but the political damage of the Embargo had injured Republican unity. Although not an official candidate, James Monroe, who thought that his diplomatic efforts had not been adequately supported by Madison and Jefferson and felt some pique that Jefferson had demonstrated a preference for Madison, allowed his name to be circulated as a presidential contender. This estranged the two men whom Jefferson referred to as the two "principal pillars" of his happiness. As the election season approached, not only did Monroe seem a genuine threat to Madison, but so too did the powerful political machine in New York, which backed Vice Pres. George Clinton. Support for Clinton reflected a growing distaste for the "Virginia Dynasty" and increasing eastern hostility toward the Embargo because of its disastrous economic consequences. Madison's opponents were unable to agree upon a suitable alternative, however and thus could not profit from opposition to his nomination within Republican ranks. In the end, in order to prevent the Federalists from benefiting from a Republican split, most of the party came together to support Madison's election. Nevertheless, he would never command the personal or political loyalty that Jefferson had, even in his home state of Virginia.

Madison was elected by the Electoral College on 7 December 1808 and was sworn in on 4 March 1809. From the beginning of his presidency, Madison confronted opposition not only from Federalists but from members of his own party, who associated him with Jefferson's failed policies toward France and England. Also, Madison proved singularly incapable of treading surely through the political maze created by the personality conflicts and contentious ambitions of subordinates. Madison's first choice for secretary of state was Albert Gallatin, the two-term secretary of the treasury in Jefferson's administration. Although few could deny that Gallatin had handled Treasury ably, many in Congress believed that his diligent pursuit of fiscal restraint had left the country so inadequately prepared militarily that its security was seriously jeopardized. Secretary of the Navy Robert Smith, who enjoyed prominent political connections, had defended the navy by challenging Gallatin's economies. When covert efforts to oust Smith from the cabinet were attributed to Gallatin, overt enmity between the two had ensued.

During the early days of March 1809, Madison thus found himself in a dilemma. If he continued to push for Gallatin's confirmation to become secretary of state, he would do so at the risk of producing a Republican schism. Determined, however, to retain Gallatin in the cabinet, Madison succumbed to pressure from Smith's allies (sometimes dubbed the "Invisibles"), which included his powerful brother Sen. Samuel Smith of Maryland, and asked Robert Smith to assume the position of secretary of state. The controversy left Gallatin bitterly resentful toward the Smith brothers, and these strong feelings intensified the growing divisions both within the cabinet and the Republican Party. Robert Smith nonetheless sought to work with his cabinet colleague, though on principle he would continue to oppose Gallatin's economic policies. Yet, the foremost supporter of military and naval preparedness had been rewarded with the state department, and Gallatin's pique only increased at having been denied the position. This incident marked the beginning of Madison's troubles. Gallatin considered Smith incompetent and fought incessantly with him and his brother. The Smiths, for their part, found allies in Wilson Cary Nicholas, William Branch Giles, Michael Leib, and newspaper publisher William Duane, among others.

Madison must be held largely accountable for divisions in his cabinet, which were not confined simply to this group. Thinking he was wholly dependent upon Gallatin, Madison sided with him rather than build a consensus. Jefferson had been able to keep the feud between Gallatin and Smith from boiling over in public. Neither inclination nor ability enabled Madison to diffuse the volatile situation between the two most important men in the cabinet. In fact, the president merely exacerbated the growing tensions within his cabinet and the party. These factors, and perhaps his desire to heal the rift between himself and James Monroe, convinced Madison by March 1811 of the need to remove Smith as secretary of state. The threat of impending war convinced most Republicans to close ranks; otherwise, the consequences of Smith's firing might have doomed Madison's presidency.

While Madison contended with divisions in the Republican Party and attacks from Federalists, the Non-Intercourse Act as a substitute for the failed Embargo showed no signs of forcing either Britain or France to repeal policies obnoxious to U.S. neutral rights. Secretly, however, the new British minister to the United States, David M. Erskine, was pleased with the passage of the Non-Intercourse Act, which he saw would benefit England, and he expressed this view to his superior in London, George Canning. In subsequent negotiations involving Erskine, Madison, and Smith, disputes still stemming from the *Chesapeake-Leopard* Affair were disposed of, and the negotiators also agreed to terms that, among other things, provided for the repeal of the British Orders in Council, those measures designed to curb trade by neutrals with France.

The Erskine Agreement of 18 and 19 April 1809 set the withdrawal of the Orders in Council for 10 June 1809. On 19 April, Madison issued his proclamation that restored trade with Great Britain, effective 10 June 1809. The restoration of trade was thus to be simultaneous to the suspension of the January and November 1807 Orders in Council, as promised by Erskine. Although Madison may have been hasty in issuing his proclamation, the administration saw a low-risk opportunity to escape from its predicament. For a few weeks following Madison's proclamation, the nation was more unified than it had been for a long time. Many U.S. vessels that had been bottled up in port raced for the British Isles.

It was all for nothing. On 22 May 1809, Canning received Erskine's dispatches and immediately disavowed them. Canning recalled the discredited minister and replaced him with the notorious Francis James "Copenhagen" Jackson, an appointment that did not bode well for Anglo-American relations. Finally, on 9 August, the president, supremely embarrassed by the entire matter, issued another proclamation, this one restoring the Non-Intercourse Act against Great Britain.

The subsequent Jackson mission failed to resolve the United States' difficulties with Britain, and when pessimistic reports from U.S. Minister to France John Armstrong about French policies toward the United States were received, some in Congress sought legislation that at least had the appearance of resisting the policies of the great powers for the sake of honor. What emerged was Macon's Bill No. 2, named after Nathaniel Macon of North Carolina. This latest law reopened U.S. trade with all the world, including Britain and France. If, however, either Britain or France agreed to respect U.S. rights, either by revoking or modifying their edicts before 3 March 1811, the president could again apply nonintercourse to the nation that had not done so. This would be done after three months had elapsed, thereby allowing the violating nation to follow the example set by its rival.

Macon's Bill No. 2 was the last congressional measure aimed at counteracting infringements of France and Great Britain through commercial pressure. Each year since 1806 had witnessed a new experiment in peaceable economic coercion. After the Embargo Act, however, each subsequent act represented a weakening faith in the policy until Macon's Bill No. 2 marked the last step before admitting the failure of commercial restrictions as a substitute for war.

Napoleon in France saw an opportunity to exploit the U.S. position to his advantage. Through Minister John Armstrong, the French government announced in what became known as the Cadore Letter of August 1810 that the hated Berlin and Milan Decrees were revoked in regard to the United States and that they would cease to have effect after November 1810. Yet, Napoleon actually had no intention of mitigating France's policy toward neutral U.S. commerce, and subsequent events clearly confirmed this. In spite of evidence available at the time that the French decrees were still in force, Madison issued a proclamation on 2 November declaring that "it has been officially made known to this Government that the said edicts of France have been so revoked as that they ceased, on the said first day of the present month, to violate the neutral commerce of the United States." Though reports from Armstrong's successors in France, Jonathan Russell and Joel Barrow, further confirmed that the French repeal was counterfeit, Madison nevertheless allowed nonintercourse with Great Britain to be reinstated on 2 February 1811. When he did so, he committed the United States to Napoleon's Continental System against Great Britain, which was likely to draw the country into war with that nation.

More than likely, Madison followed this course in part because he had already suffered a great deal of humiliation over the Erskine Agreement. He simply refused to admit that he might be wrong again. Furthermore, he hoped that by giving the appearance of accepting the French revocation of their decrees, he could persuade the British to follow suit. From Madison's perspective, if the United States delayed or haggled, the emperor might change his mind and swing back to enforcing the decrees he had so tena-

ciously supported. In 1810, however, Madison was discouraged about the prospects of a British repeal under the ineffectual terms of the Non-Intercourse Act, so he took consolation in the course dictated by Macon's Bill No. 2.

His inability to craft a viable policy reveals the president's predicament. In one sense, the unifying function expected from the president as party leader was in James Madison simply not forthcoming. In fairness to him, however, the approach of war with England was not the president's sole responsibility, for he was limited by time and circumstance to reactive gestures as he tried to cope with the aggressive policies of the world's two greatest powers. The war that eventually broke out between the United States and Great Britain owes as much to the state of British politics as it does to any other factor.

Nor was this all. Events not related to commerce also spawned anti-British sentiment in the United States. Westerners incorrectly believed that British agents in Canada were responsible for Indian resistance to U.S. settlement in the Old Northwest. Southerners saw a reason to acquire Spanish Florida: if war broke out, Britain might seize the Floridas and use them as a base of operations against the United States. President Madison had already sought to occupy West Florida, and he secretly supported the actions of Americans in the region to separate it from Spain, thereby allowing for its annexation to the United States. In January 1811, Madison sent Congress a secret message asking for the authority to seize East Florida. He stated that he "could not see, without serious inquietude, any part of a neighboring territory, in which they [the United States] have in different respects so deep and so just a concern, pass from the hands of Spain into those of any other foreign Power." On 15 January, Congress responded with an act authorizing the president to take possession of East Florida, ostensibly to prevent a power other than Spain from gaining control of it. Though these efforts prior to the War of 1812 would prove abortive, Madison was not blind to the benefits of expansionism that would create "an empire for liberty."

Such domestic and international problems confronting Madison at the end of his first term were highlighted by the rise of a new group of southern and western leaders in the Republican Party. They were young, vocal nationalists who found it contemptible that the United States was being subjected to national humiliation at home and abroad. Dubbed "War Hawks," they were led by such men as Henry Clay of Kentucky, John C. Calhoun of South Carolina, and William H. Crawford of Georgia. They urged the annexation of the Floridas and Canada and the suppression of the Northwest Indians. They were insulted by the British policy of impressment and the maritime infringements of both Britain and France. Electing 34-year-old freshman Henry Clay as Speaker of the House of Representatives, the War Hawks would control the important committees, and from that forum they demanded that the Madison administration take a stand for national honor. Jefferson's policy of peaceable economic coercion was failed and weak, they believed, and they pressed Madison to declare war on Britain, if not also on France.

Ironically, when Madison forwarded his war message to Congress on 1 June 1812, it was without the knowledge that Spencer Perceval's assassination had brought in a new British government intent upon suspending the Orders in Council as applied to the United States. In a sense, Jefferson's and Madison's faith in peaceable economic coercion was being vindicated, albeit too late. For some time, British merchants and manufacturers had sought reconciliation with the United States, and public opinion had turned against continuing the Orders in Council. By the time that Madison learned of the British government's actions, the U.S. decision for war had already been taken. Had news of the repeal of the orders been received before the vote for war, it most certainly would have been prevented.

Increasingly goaded by the War Hawks, Madison reluctantly but resolutely bowed to the pressures within his party for war against Britain. In asking for war against Great Britain, Madison cited British violations of U.S. neutral rights, impressment, and incitement of Indians, but other factors also contributed to the impetus for war. Many Americans recognized the perceived benefits that would come from the acquisition of British Canada and Spanish Florida, and for the War Hawks, going to war for national honor, among other things, was fully justifiable.

The decision for war within the Congress was far from unanimous, however, and this lack of unified purpose would almost prove disastrous as the country grew even more gravely divided during the contest. In the 79 to 49 House vote for war on 4 June, all Federalists voted against war, but, ominously, nearly a quarter of Republicans also voted against it. The vote divided along sectional as well as party lines. Even though they had seen trade seriously hurt by the abusive policies of Britain, New England Federalists opposed war, believing that conflict with Britain would be even more unfortunate. These states were dominated by Federalists, whose anti-French bias tended to incline them to the British by default. The West and Deep South voted solidly for war. In the Senate, debate continued for two weeks, until on 17 June the vote was 19 to 13 in favor of war along party lines. On 18 June 1812, President Madison signed the declaration of war.

The next 31 months would prove trying for the young nation as the war brought military disaster and political division. His enemies called it "Mr. Madison's War," and he entered it with optimism, perhaps convinced that a simple vote for war would prod Britain into productive negotiations. Military embarrassments quickly eliminated whatever expectation there may have been about a quick resolution with a minimum of sacrifice. As commander in chief, Madison was at a disadvantage. He was unfamiliar with the actual conduct of war and apparently unaware that it could be wretched and ugly, costly in both men and money. Madison believed that it could be waged in gentlemanly fashion with certain rules prevailing. Such ignorance about the rigors of war, however, was representative of the nation and certainly of Congress. Having voted for war in June, the national legislature adjourned without really providing for military necessities.

The initial strategy was to seize Canada, but U.S. military planners overestimated their ability to conquer Canada, and the early results were demonstrations of U.S. ineptitude and poor leadership. On 16 August 1812, Maj. Gen. William Hull surrendered his army of more than 2,000 men to a smaller British force at Detroit. Other failures followed, all most galling because the British were preoccupied by the war in Europe, thus paying little attention to activities in North America. The U.S. Navy fared better. In August, Capt. Isaac Hull's *Constitution* defeated HMS *Guerrière* after a fierce battle, and U.S. privateers succeeded in destroying or capturing British merchant vessels. Such victories, however, were facilitated in part by Britain's inability to spare warships for the U.S. contest while still fighting Napoleon in Europe.

In the midst of these mixed achievements, the 1812 election was held, the outcome of which would reveal that Madison was by no means wholeheartedly supported. A faction of antiwar Republicans nominated New York's De-Witt Clinton, who was endorsed by the Federalists. Nevertheless, Madison won reelection with 128 electoral votes to Clinton's 89. With his reelection secured, Madison sought to reinvigorate the military command with new appointments. William Eustis resigned under congressional pressure as secretary of war on 3 December 1812. Seeking a replacement, Madison hit upon Gen. John Armstrong of New York, a Revolutionary War veteran, former senator, former minister to France, and then currently in charge of the defenses of New York City. Armstrong's appointment would also put a New Yorker in the cabinet, thus helping to secure the support of that state for the war effort. Offered the position on 14 January 1813, Armstrong accepted. Yet he was not without his detractors, Monroe chief among them. During the closing days of the American Revolution, Armstrong had drafted the infamous Newburgh Addresses suggesting that discontented officers depose the civilian government. Even if Armstrong had outgrown such impulses, he still was noted for being caustic, and at times he would flirt with insubordination toward the president.

In February 1813, Armstrong increased the number of general officers to eight major generals and 16 brigadier generals. The two senior major generals were Henry Dearborn and Thomas Pinckney. With the exception of William Henry Harrison, who was 40, the other major generals were advanced in age and lacking in vigor. The new brigadiers, however, added youth to the upper ranks with such men as Zebulon Pike, George Izard, Duncan McArthur, Lewis Cass, and William Winder. Benjamin Howard and Thomas Parker were, in fact, the only brigadiers who had fought in the Revolutionary War. Other appointments by Armstrong demonstrated his ability to recognize talent, and many officers appointed by him played important military roles in the country's history up to the outbreak of the Civil War.

In 1813, Canada remained as impenetrable to U.S. invasion as it had the previous year. Oliver Hazard Perry destroyed a British fleet on Lake Erie in September and thus gained naval supremacy that allowed William Henry Harrison to score another victory on 5 October 1813 over a combined British and Indian force at the Battle of the Thames. Yet the Madison administration's main focus on assailing Kingston, Upper Canada, and Montreal fell prey to quarrels among U.S. commanders and stubborn British resistance. Meanwhile, the British adopted a policy of coastal raiding that visited the hardships of war on citizens along the Atlantic seaboard, especially in Chesapeake Bay country.

In 1814, Madison would find that the character of the war changed radically. Napoleon's defeat left the British free to direct greater attention to the war with the United States, and the result was an offensive on three fronts: the Canadian frontier, Chesapeake Bay, and New Orleans. Little had been done to bolster the defenses of Washington, D.C., mainly because Secretary Armstrong did not think the capital was militarily significant. Armstrong believed that Baltimore would be the objective of any British assault, and he felt comfortable applying stark economies that prevented the construction of elaborate defenses of Washington.

When the British increased their activity in Chesapeake Bay during the spring of 1814, a nervous Madison called a cabinet meeting on 1 July to discuss defensive measures. From these discussions and over Armstrong's objections, a new military district—the Tenth—was created on the Potomac River, and Brig. Gen. William Winder was selected to command it. This force was to comprise about 3,000 men, 1,000 of whom were regulars. Armstrong suspected that his rival, Secretary of State James Monroe, who had

consistently criticized Armstrong's lack of defensive preparations for the district, had actually been behind the president's actions. At this crucial moment, Madison watched helplessly as Armstrong and Monroe quarreled over almost everything, especially about when to call out the militia.

On 22 August, desperate to stop the British advance on Washington, Madison and members of the cabinet rode out to Bladensburg, Maryland, to assess the situation. Though total U.S. forces outnumbered the British, they were no match for the battle-seasoned veterans of the European war. The battle on 24 August became a U.S. rout, and the president ordered his cabinet to withdraw. In Washington, the heroic aplomb of the president's wife Dolley saved as many documents, furnishings, and artifacts as possible from the president's house, including the large Gilbert Stuart portrait of George Washington. Dolley had already departed when Madison returned from the disaster at Bladensburg. The difficult decision was made not to defend Washington, and he paused at the executive mansion briefly before himself leaving for Virginia. Unopposed, the British army entered Washington, and that evening Rear Adm. Sir George Cockburn and fellow British officers dined at the abandoned president's house before ransacking and burning it. A similar fate befell the Capitol and other public buildings. The British then withdrew and by August 30 were back on the decks of Royal Navy ships.

President Madison had already returned to the devastated city on the evening of 27 August 1814 to begin the work of reassembling his cabinet and restoring the government. Armstrong, condemned now by many for failing to provide for the defense of Washington, was confronted directly by Madison. Although Armstrong irritably threatened to resign, Madison wanted to avoid giving the impression that his government, so recently scattered, was now falling apart, and he suggested that his secretary of war take a leave from his duties. Armstrong was en route from Washington to his New York home when he paused in Baltimore on 4 September to bitterly pen his resignation anyway.

When Madison accepted Armstrong's resignation, he removed Monroe's most serious rival. The secretary of state had consistently interfered in the operations of the war department, and though Monroe's advice and action during the August crisis had been occasionally confused, his visible presence throughout the fiasco had enhanced his reputation. When Madison hesitated to fill the war department vacancy, Monroe directly requested the job on 25 September. Madison complied, and Monroe became secretary of war while simultaneously serving as acting secretary of state. With the president's house in ashes, the Madisons moved into Col. John Tayloe's Octagon House, in which they resided until the executive mansion was rebuilt.

It hardly looked it at the time, but Madison's fortunes in the war would only improve from the nadir marked by the sack of Washington. The British offensive on Lake Champlain was repulsed at Plattsburg, New York, on 11 September 1814, and the British assault on Baltimore three days later, by the same forces that had descended on Washington, was turned away after the failure of the extended bombardment of Fort McHenry.

Also, although Madison's popularity plummeted in August following the British torching of the capital, his resolve and activities shortly after the disaster gradually caused some critics to amend their opinions. His sixth annual message to Congress, with his honest appraisal of events and assessment of obstacles still confronting the country, was a commendable performance, but he privately despaired over the outcome of the war, as did others. Originally incensed by Republican policies that had severely hurt trade, disaffected New England Federalists were now angry at having their communities occupied and harassed by British troops. Convinced that continuing the war courted disaster, these Federalists convened at Hartford, Connecticut, on 15 December 1814. The meeting would only recommend changes the Federalists felt necessary to produce equitable conditions for their section, but the Madison administration feared it would turn into a move for disunion.

Yet Madison was delivered on 8 January 1815, when Gen. Andrew Jackson sustained a tremendous U.S. victory over the British at New Orleans. News of Jackson's victory changed the entire U.S. perception of the War of 1812 almost overnight. Americans either forgot—or dismissed the fact—that the U.S. capital was in ashes, that its navy was mostly bottled up under a tight British blockade that also strangled the coast, and that the British occupied parts of New England.

Within two weeks of Jackson's triumph at New Orleans, news came from Ghent that a peace treaty had been signed on 24 December 1814 by the U.S. and British delegations there. The timing could not have been worse for emissaries from the Hartford Convention, who had arrived in Washington to press their demands on Madison, who studiously ignored them. As well-wishers passed through the Octagon House, Federalist delegates, led by former Congressman Harrison Gray Otis, found themselves in an embarrassing and awkward position. With nationalism running rampant after the victory at New Orleans and the glorious news from Ghent, the perceived disloyalty of the Federalists proved to be their death knell as a party.

The news from Ghent was not completely unexpected, but the journey to the Christmas Eve peace had been a long and difficult one. A negotiated settlement had been proposed as early as 1812 in an offer by Czar Alexander I of Russia to mediate between the United States and Great Britain. President Madison, not even waiting to hear if the British government had accepted the offer, reacted favorably. In late May 1813, the president named Secretary of the Treasury Albert Gallatin and James A. Bayard, a prominent Federalist senator from Delaware, to be special envoys. They were to join the U.S. minister to Russia, John Quincy Adams. To the list of nominees for diplomatic appointments was added the name of Jonathan Russell, Madison's designee to be minister to Sweden.

The British government refused the Russian mediation offer, but in November 1813 the British foreign secretary Lord Castlereagh proposed to the United States that the two countries begin direct negotiations. Although the Senate had previously rejected Russell's nomination to become U.S. minister to Sweden and refused to confirm Gallatin's diplomatic appointment as well, it now reversed itself. With the British offer to negotiate directly with the Americans, Bayard and Gallatin, along with John Quincy Adams, were joined by Russell and Henry Clay of Kentucky, Speaker of the House of Representatives. The Flemish town of Ghent was selected as the meeting place for the negotiations.

Although many factors, such as impressment and a violation of U.S. neutral rights, had helped to provoke war between Great Britain and the United States in the first place, in the end, the Treaty of Ghent called for the status quo antebellum. Central to the successful conclusion of these negotiations was the Madison administration's decision in the summer of 1814 to drop demands that the British renounce impressment. Equally important for the future, also, were the clauses that called for mixed arbitration commissions to resolve boundary disputes along the northeastern borders with British North America.

Madison's last two years in office were relatively easy compared to the previous six. Farmers prospered as prices shot up and imports increased, which had a positive impact on the treasury. U.S. exports rocketed from $45,000 in 1815 to $65,000 in 1816 and to more than $68,000 in 1817. And Madison, one of the foremost opponents of expanding federal power, came to view some basic Federalist programs—a national bank, tariffs, and measures for strengthening permanent military and naval establishments—as desirable and necessary.

On 4 March 1817, Madison's sometime close friend and ally, James Monroe, became president, and Madison departed Washington for Montpelier in Orange County, never again to leave Virginia. In spite of the negative light in which Madison was viewed by so many during the war, its successful conclusion forced a reassessment of his performance as president. Even his old adversary John Adams spoke positively of Madison's presidency with these words: "Notwithstanding a thousand faults and blunders, his Administration has acquired more glory, and established more Union than all three Predecessors, Washington, Adams and Jefferson put together." Actually, as president, Madison made serious errors of judgment, and if not for fate or luck, the results of the War of 1812 could have been devastating. Nevertheless, by the time he left Washington, circumstances had made the presidency a much stronger office than the one he had assumed eight years earlier.

He spent his many remaining years managing his 5,000-acre estate, indulging his reading and other intellectual interests, and playing the role of elder statesman. Like Jefferson, former President Madison was exceptionally hospitable and graciously entertained the numerous guests who flocked to visit the Sage of Montpelier for advice and conversation. He died at Montpelier on 28 June 1836 and was buried in the family cemetery. Although his legacy as president is mixed, his role in bringing about the Constitution with its Bill of Rights cannot be overestimated. He, along with Jefferson, embodied the best philosophical views of the nation, and he left an indelible legacy for future generations to study and emulate.

—*Thom M. Armstrong*

See also: Armstrong, John; Bladensburg, Battle of; Federalist Party; Gallatin, Albert; Jefferson, Thomas; Madison, Dolley Payne; Monroe, James; Pinkney, William; Washington, British Capture of

Further Reading

Adams, Henry. *A History of the United States of America during the Administrations of Thomas Jefferson and James Madison.* 9 vols. New York: Charles Scribner's Sons, 1891–1892.

Bradford, Melvin E. "James Madison: Political Philosopher, Planter, Virginia Statesman, and Fourth President of the United States." In Melvin E. Bradford, ed., *Founding Fathers.* Lawrence: University Press of Kansas, 1994.

Brant, Irving. *James Madison.* 6 vols. Indianapolis: Bobbs-Merrill, 1941–1961.

Brown, Roger H. *The Republic in Peril: 1812.* New York: W. W. Norton, 1971.

Ketcham, Ralph. *James Madison: A Biography.* Charlottesville: University Press of Virginia, 1971; reprint ed., 1992.

Lowell, John. *Mr. Madison's War: A Dispassionate Inquiry into the Reasons Alleged by Mr. Madison for Declaring an Offensive and Ruinous War against Great Britain: Together with Some Suggestions as to a Peaceable and Constitutional Mode of Averting That Dreadful Calamity.* Boston: Russell and Cutler, 1812.

Madison, James. *The Papers of James Madison: Presidential Series.* Vol. 3, 3 November 1810–4 November 1811, J.C.A.

Stagg, Jeanne Kerr Cross, Susan Holbrook Perdue, eds. Charlottesville and London: University Press of Virginia, 1996.

———. *The Writings of James Madison Comprising His Public Papers and His Private Correspondence, Including Numerous Letters and Documents Now for the First Time Printed.* 9 vols. New York: G. P. Putnam's Sons, 1900–1910.

McAuley, R. Bryan. "President James Madison and the War Congress of 1812." Master's thesis, Southwest Texas State University, 1995.

McCoy, Drew R. *The Last of the Fathers: James Madison and the Republican Legacy.* Cambridge and New York: Cambridge University Press, 1991.

Rakove, Jack. *James Madison and the Creation of the American Republic.* New York: HarperCollins, 1990.

Rutland, Robert A. *James Madison: The Founding Father.* New York: Macmillan, 1987; reprint, Columbia: University of Missouri Press, 1997.

Stagg, J.C.A. *Mr. Madison's War: Politics, Diplomacy, and Warfare in the Early Republic, 1783–1830.* Princeton: Princeton University Press, 1983.

MAINE, DISTRICT OF

The Maine district of Massachusetts, in close proximity to British Canada, was naturally vulnerable to attack during the War of 1812. That the British claimed territory in northern Maine added to the threat. The position of this part of the United States projecting into Canada obstructed land communications between Halifax, Nova Scotia, and Quebec, and by 1814, the British government had determined that U.S. cession of part of this area would be a condition for a peace settlement.

In June 1814, the British government issued orders to the governor of Nova Scotia, Sir John Sherbrooke, to launch a campaign against northern Maine. On 11 July 1814, Adm. Sir Thomas Hardy transported 1,000 men under Lt. Col. Andrew Pilkington to Eastport on Moose Island. The 85-man garrison of Fort Sullivan surrendered, and Hardy declared the area a part of Great Britain.

On 1 September 1814, the conquest continued when Adm. Edward Griffith took Sherbrooke and 2,500 men to Castine. The defenders blew up the town's defenses and retreated. Sherbrooke then set about conquering all of the territory along the Penobscot River up to Bangor. To prevent his ship from falling into British hands, Capt. Charles Morris burned the USS *John Adams* in port at Hampden. When the British were finished, they controlled the northern 100 miles of Maine coastline.

The impact of this conquest was considerable. The Madison administration was shocked to learn that the people of Maine seemed little concerned with their change of status. Moreover, the region had been considered a stronghold of Democratic Republicanism in New England. Nevertheless, two-thirds of the people in the conquered area took an oath of allegiance to the British crown. Further, the occupation of this territory allowed the British to increase smuggling from the United States to Canada.

Seeking some solace, James Madison and his cabinet hoped that this invasion of New England at least would motivate New Englanders to support the war effort. Although many coastal New Englanders feared British plans to extend their activities down the coastline, this threat did not increase New England's martial spirit. Instead, inhabitants placed added pressure on the government in Washington to reach a peace settlement with the British.

Ironically, the British presence in this disputed territory actually complicated the peace process. The actual occupation of territory they hoped to gain in the negotiations made the British negotiators at Ghent more reluctant than ever to conclude a settlement that did not include northern Maine. Several of the U.S. commissioners actually considered meeting the demand, but Massachusetts native John Quincy Adams refused to consider the proposal.

British demands for the territory and the fear that the Hartford Convention meeting in the fall of 1814 might lead to radical actions in New England led the administration to plan the reconquest of northern Maine. The military expedition, it was hoped, would serve the dual purpose of retaking U.S. territory while awing the delegates to the Hartford Convention. When it came time to raise this army, however, the governor of Massachusetts, Caleb Strong, refused to cooperate. There was some evidence that he or someone close to him even leaked news of the plan to the New England press. In any event, the publication of the plan obviously alerted the British in Maine, so the administration abandoned it.

When the final peace was signed at Ghent, most of the disputed territory was returned to the United States. The disposition of the remainder was left to a later commission.

—*Jeanne T. Heidler and David S. Heidler*

See also: Castine, Maine; Hampden, Maine; Hardy, Thomas Masterman; Sherbrooke, John Coape

Further Reading

Kilby, William. "A New England Town under Foreign Martial Law." *New England Magazine* 14 (1894): 685–695.

Stanley, George F. "British Operations on the Penobscot in 1814." *Journal of the Society for Army Historical Research* 19 (1940): 168–178.

MALDEN, FORT

Amherstburg, Upper Canada, was a thriving river town in 1812, only a bit smaller than nearby Detroit. Its strategic value was threefold: much of the trade bound for the upper Great Lakes passed through or nearby, Fort Malden could close down traffic by land or river, and one of Upper Canada's two navy yards was located there.

Fort Malden was built between 1797 and 1799, after the British were forced to vacate Detroit. It was continually improved and updated and underwent expansion during the war scare of 1807–1809. Four massive bastions with an advanced redoubt faced the river, and the whole was surrounded by ditches and pickets. One hundred and fifty loopholes supplemented the 20 mounted cannon. The powder magazine had walls 5 feet thick and a strong roof. At the outbreak of war, Capt. Adam Muir commanded the 41st Regiment of Foot there; together with a Royal Artillery detachment, the garrison numbered about 300. The fort's commander was Lt. Col. Thomas St. George of the 63rd Regiment. Nearby, the navy yard was home port for three large warships and a number of merchant vessels. In addition, the fort could call on the Upper Canada militia and more than 4,000 Indian warriors.

St. George learned of the declaration of war on 28 June 1812 and promptly took steps to secure the Detroit River. He dispatched militia to Sandwich and stopped the ferry traffic and thus anticipated Gen. Isaac Brock's orders (received on 1 July) to prepare for an offensive against Detroit. A week later, however, outlying forces retreated to the fort under U.S. fire. On 7 July, U.S. brigadier general William Hull was authorized to attack Fort Malden. During the next several weeks his plans to do so met several unexpected obstacles, notably the defection of the Wyandots and the Battle of Brownstown. In the meantime, on 26 July Col. Henry Procter took over the command at Fort Malden. On 7 August, learning of the approach of fresh British troops from Niagara, Hull called off the attack. That same day the British launched a quick and psychologically effective attack against Detroit. Nearly the entire garrison, with the ships from the navy yard, took part in the capture of Detroit on 15 August.

Not until after the Battle of Lake Erie did Fort Malden again occupy center stage. Knowing that he could no longer defend the Detroit River region, General Procter called a council with his Indian allies at the fort on 18 September 1813. Here Tecumseh made his famous pledge to stand by his British friends. He offered to defend Amherstburg while the British regulars retreated toward the Thames, but Procter persuaded the Indians to depart with him before the Americans could arrive to attack the fort. Oliver Hazard Perry's fleet landed William Henry Harrison's army at the abandoned fort on 27 September, and soon after the Americans began their fateful pursuit toward the Thames. From then until 1815, the area was in U.S. hands. Because of the large number of troops stationed in the area, a second, temporary camp—Fort Covington—was constructed just outside Amherstburg. Under the *uti possidetis* proposal made at Ghent in October 1814, Fort Malden would have remained in U.S. hands, but it was returned to the British under the provisions of the Treaty of Ghent.

—*Thomas S. Martin*

See also: Brock, Isaac; Hull, William; Procter, Henry; Thames, Battle of the

Further Reading

Calloway, Colin G. *Crown and Calumet: British-Indian Relations, 1783–1815.* Norman: University of Oklahoma Press, 1987.

Gilbert, Bil. *God Gave Us This Country: Tekamthi and the First American Civil War.* New York: Atheneum, 1989.

Gilpin, Alec R. *The War of 1812 in the Old Northwest.* East Lansing: Michigan State University Press, 1958.

MARKLE, ABRAHAM
?
Canadian-American raider

Abraham Markle was one of a number of men along the New York–Canadian border who took advantage of the wartime conditions to plunder citizens on both sides of the border. Born in the United States, Markle moved to Newark, Upper Canada, as a young man for the cheaper land and economic opportunities of that frontier area. When the war started, he joined a group of former U.S. citizens who attacked his Canadian neighbors out of purported loyalty to the United States.

Markle was present at and participated in some of the more notorious examples of U.S. atrocities against Canadian civilians, most notably the burning of Newark in December 1813 and the plundering and burning of Port Dover in May 1814.

In order to discourage such activities, the Canadian government rounded up a number of Markle's compatriots and tried them for treason. Markle was tried in absentia

and convicted. Eight fellow raiders were captured, tried, and hanged as an example to others.

Markle lost his considerable landholdings outside of Newark to forfeiture and could not return to Canada. He moved to Indiana, where he lived out his life in obscurity.

—*Jeanne T. Heidler and David S. Heidler*

See also: Newark, Upper Canada; Port Dover, Destruction of
Further Reading
Berton, Pierre. *Flames across the Border: The Canadian-American Tragedy, 1813–1814.* Boston: Little, Brown, 1981.

MARYLAND

Aristocrats, pirates, rioters, and runaway slaves all played a part in Maryland's wartime social and military conflicts. Baltimore, Maryland's largest city, erupted in violence four days after the 18 June 1812 declaration of war and experienced anti-Federalist riots throughout the war's first summer. Baltimore grew rapidly as a commercial port during the Napoleonic wars, becoming the United States' third-largest city with 50,000 residents in 1815, and its citizens strongly resented British restrictions on neutral shipping. Baltimore's vocal Federalist minority viewed James Madison's Republican administration as pro-Irish, pro-French, and generally a threat to the hierarchical social order. That order was run by wealthy Baltimoreans and their downstate planter allies, many of whom had family ties to leading Baltimore Federalists.

On 22–23 June, a Republican mob destroyed the presses of the *Federal Republican,* the leading antiwar newspaper in the city, and chased its editor, Alexander Contee Hanson, out of town. In late July, Hanson returned to Baltimore from exile in Georgetown and took up residence in a fortified house on Charles Street. Angry at Hanson's presence and his armed guards, a mob besieged Hanson's garrisoned home on the night of 27 July. Unable to hold the house, Hanson, Revolutionary War hero Henry "Light-Horse Harry" Lee, and other Federalist notables accepted a militia escort to the relative safety of the city jail. Militia protection proved halfhearted when a mob of several hundred artisans and shopkeepers, a mix of native-born citizens and immigrants, stormed the jail and beat the prisoners. As women shouted "kill the Tories," rioters killed another Revolutionary War hero, Gen. James M. Lingan, and maimed others, including Hanson and Lee.

The Baltimore Riots polarized state politics and strengthened Federalist support among southern Maryland tobacco planters. That fall Federalists won a majority in the state legislature, and planter-dominated Montgomery County elected Hanson to Congress. Maryland Federalists supported the war more than New England Federalists, but they remained critical of Madison's administration, and many individuals in southern Maryland offered little resistance to the British during the naval campaigns of 1813 and 1814. Conversely, Baltimore merchants and artisans who already resented England's squeeze on shipping became fiercely committed to the Republican Party and the war.

When war broke out, Baltimore merchants turned to privateering to make up for commerce lost to British blockades. Maryland, and particularly Baltimore, took full advantage of Madison's issuance of letters of marque and reprisal against enemy vessels. More than 100 privateering vessels sailed from Maryland, mostly from Baltimore, and they captured one-third of the 1,345 British ships taken during the war. The sleek "Baltimore Clipper," which crammed narrow hulls with as many sails as possible, proved ideal for the hit-and-run tactics of privateers. As Baltimore's plunder rose to more than $16 million, the number of people pursuing opportunities as captains and crews of privateering vessels created a labor shortage in more conventional pursuits.

Privateering and the exposed character of the Chesapeake coast made Maryland an inviting target for British naval operations. On 4 February 1813, Adm. Sir George Cockburn entered Chesapeake Bay under orders to blockade it and Delaware Bay. Reinforcements eventually gave Cockburn more than 70 vessels and 2,500 land troops with which to harass the Chesapeake coast. British operations varied from small plunder parties that raided valuable coastal tobacco plantations to full-scale assaults on ports like Norfolk, Virginia. In the fall of 1813, Cockburn established a base on Kent Island, from which he tried to influence Maryland's elections in favor of the Federalists. Although U.S. troops, as in Norfolk, occasionally stopped Cockburn, poorly organized and demoralized militia generally failed to protect tidewater farmers from British depredations.

In the summer of 1813, Commodore Joshua Barney, a Revolutionary War hero and a veteran of the U.S. and French navies, devised a plan for the Chesapeake Bay's defense and volunteered to lead the proposed Chesapeake Flotilla. Desperate to break British control of the bay, Madison granted Barney, who began the war as a Baltimore privateer, command of a makeshift fleet of river barges. Barney's squadron could not match Cockburn at sea but had the advantage of shallow drafts in navigating Chesapeake Bay tributaries and thwarting British raiding parties. By the spring of 1814, the Chesapeake Flotilla had

checked Cockburn's plundering operations along the upper reaches of the Maryland coastline.

Cockburn's raiders left a mixed legacy of outrageous behavior and fair treatment. Generally, when British raiding parties met resistance, as they did at Havre de Grace, they treated the area as hostile and resorted to burning homes and seizing property. When individual Marylanders made peace with the British, as happened frequently in the Federalist tidewater counties, Cockburn paid them for needed supplies and provided commercial opportunities for tobacco planters and farmers whose livelihoods British blockaders originally had threatened.

Cockburn's campaign in Chesapeake Bay softened Maryland's defenses to the point that British strategists seeking to "chastise the savages" in the United States viewed the state as a prime target for operations in the summer of 1814. Adm. Sir Alexander Cochrane, commander of the Royal Navy's Atlantic Squadron, with the help of Gen. Robert Ross, commander of 5,000 British army veterans of the Napoleonic wars, led a combined force of navy, army, and marines to Chesapeake Bay in August. More concerned with inflicting punishment and diverting attention from the Canadian front than with occupying territory, Cochrane's invasion of Maryland brought about the destruction of the Chesapeake Flotilla and the sack of Washington, D.C., in late August. At the "Bladensburg Races" of 24 August, as the battle for Washington came to be known, Ross's veterans routed U.S. militia and went on with little resistance to take Washington that evening. After burning the White House and other government buildings, Ross took his leave of the capital, retracing his steps through southern Maryland to rejoin Cochrane's fleet.

Baltimore's privateering and its prowar riot marked it for further British retribution. Yet, unlike the defenders of the national capital, Baltimoreans put aside local rivalries and organized all military personnel under the command of Maj. Gen. Samuel Smith, a longtime Maryland politician. Following the sack of Washington, D.C., Smith quickly prepared Baltimore to repel the British attack. His 10,000 to 15,000 militia dug extensive earthworks along the eastern land approach to the city, and Fort McHenry and a line of sunken ships impeded access to the harbor.

At 3:00 A.M. on 12 September 1814, Ross landed 4,200 soldiers at North Point, east of the city, and proceeded inland. Halfway to Baltimore, the British encountered 3,200 militiamen who slowed their advance and killed Ross in the process. Artillery helped the British carry the field and inflicted some of the 214 U.S. casualties, but the English paid a high price in the death of Ross and the loss of 340 soldiers. The next day, British troops reached the entrenched city limits. Lacking naval support and unwilling to assault fixed positions, Ross's replacement, Col. Arthur Brooke, retreated to the safety of the fleet.

Meanwhile, Cochrane tried to soften Baltimore's defenses through a naval bombardment of Fort McHenry. On 13 and 14 September, British mortars pounded Fort McHenry with over 1,500 rounds but inflicted little damage on the fort or its gigantic flag, which inspired Francis Scott Key to compose "The Star-Spangled Banner" while watching the bombardment from a ship in the harbor. Cochrane had loaded 1,500 men aboard barges for an assault on the southwestern entrance to the city, but shore batteries forced them to retire. Following his defeat at Baltimore, Cochrane left Chesapeake Bay and sailed south to an even more disastrous loss at New Orleans.

Some 2,000 Maryland slaves ran away to the British ranks during Cochrane's invasion because of the admiral's ambiguous proclamation that all Americans had "a choice of either entering into His Majesty's Sea or Land forces, or being sent as FREE Settlers, to the British possessions in North America or the West Indies." More inspired by military self-interest than humanitarianism, Cochrane's proclamation succeeded in enlisting at least 300 runaway slaves into British ranks and encouraged hundreds more to seek freedom aboard his ships. Perhaps to counter British propaganda, white Baltimoreans made much of African American participation in the city's defense.

Despite enforcement efforts, Maryland's militia laws depended on voluntary support during the war. Republican, prowar Baltimore turned out most of its able-bodied adult men for military service, but Federalist planters in southern Maryland more frequently shirked their obligation to the militia, and consequently regiments rarely went into battle at full strength.

By curtailing commerce, the war stimulated industrial development in Baltimore. Merchants whose ships had been idled by the British blockade invested surplus capital in steam-powered mills in central Baltimore and began meeting domestic consumer demand with their own manufactures rather than British imports. By the end of the war, Baltimore was on the way to becoming a mixed industrial and commercial center, more similar to the northern seaports of Boston, New York, and Philadelphia than to exclusively mercantile southern ports like Charleston, Mobile, and Savannah. In so doing, Baltimore moved closer to the North's industrial, free-labor society, while the Eastern Shore and the southern tidewater remained committed to the South's slave plantation economy.

—*Frank Towers*

See also: Baltimore, Battle of; Baltimore Riots; Bladensburg, Battle of; Cockburn, George; Smith, Samuel

Further Reading

Browne, Gary L. *Baltimore in the Nation, 1789–1861.* Chapel Hill: University of North Carolina Press, 1980.

Cassell, Frank A. "The Great Baltimore Riot of 1812." *Maryland Historical Magazine* 70 (fall 1975): 241–259.

Lord, Walter. *The Dawn's Early Light.* New York: W. W. Norton, 1972.

Shomette, Donald G. *Flotilla: Battle for the Patuxent.* Baltimore: Calvert Marine Museum Press, 1981.

MASON, JEREMIAH
1768–1848
U.S. senator

Born in Connecticut to Jeremiah Mason and Elizabeth Fitch Mason, the younger Mason graduated from Yale in 1788, studied law, and settled in Portsmouth, New Hampshire, in 1797. Over the next few years, Mason became one of the best attorneys in New Hampshire. His services were sought by people all over the state. He was acknowledged by his younger rival in town, Daniel Webster, to have had a tremendous impact on Webster's legal style and view of the law.

Like Webster, Mason also became active in Federalist politics in New Hampshire. Like most Federalists, Mason opposed the United States' move toward war with Great Britain during the James Madison administration, and once the war began, he disagreed with the methods used to prosecute it.

His opposition led him to accept election to represent New Hampshire in the U.S. Senate in 1813. Mason believed that the administration and the Democratic Republicans in Congress had behaved irresponsibly in leading the country into war, but more important, he agreed with his fellow Federalists that the methods used to finance the conflict unnecessarily discriminated against New England and that the ways in which the administration prosecuted the war invited disaster.

By the fall of 1814, however, he had come to the conclusion that the crisis the country found itself in required cooperation between parties. In a speech before the Senate on 16 November 1814, Mason recognized that the nation faced a serious crisis. The complexion of the war had changed since the publication of what seemed to be inflexible and unreasonable demands of the British negotiators at Ghent. Mason did not pretend to have a solution, but he implied in his speech that if the country were to overcome the tremendous financial and military challenges ahead, everyone would have to work together.

Following the war, Mason remained for a while in the Senate, but the decline of the Federalist Party caused him to resign his seat in 1817. Returning to his legal practice and state politics, Mason's reputation in New England continued to grow. In his later years he moved to Boston, where he died in 1848.

—*Jeanne T. Heidler and David S. Heidler*

See also: Webster, Daniel
Further Reading
Fish, Frank L. "Jeremiah Mason." *American Law Review* 53 (1919): 269–284.

MATHEWS, GEORGE
1739–1812
U.S. agent to Spanish Florida

Garnering much praise for heroics during the Revolutionary War, Mathews enjoyed a long and successful political career, serving as Georgia's governor from 1787 to 1789 and again from 1793 to 1796. After the turn of the century, however, as diplomatic relations between England and the United States deteriorated to the brink of war, George Mathews's activities in East Florida throughout 1811 and 1812 sparked an international crisis that could well have involved the United States in a war with Spain.

In 1811, Congress and the Madison administration appointed Mathews and John McKee of Georgia agents of the nation, authorized to receive any territory in Spanish Florida that might come under U.S. control. After negotiations for the acquisition of West Florida broke down, Mathews set his sights on acquiring East Florida, where discontent with Spanish domination among the English-speaking population led to a minor insurrection known as the "Patriot War." Like many Georgians who believed Spanish Florida to be little more than a haven for runaway slaves and who greatly prized Florida land, Mathews was determined to assist the rebels and to wrest East Florida from Spain.

Mathews convinced the administration that acquiring East Florida would be a matter of indirectly aiding the insurrectionists. As a result, Col. Thomas Adams Smith was ordered to advance to Point Petre, Georgia, with 250 regulars, ostensibly to provide protection for the rebels—who by this time had declared their independence from Spain, had drafted a constitution, and had petitioned the Madison administration to formally annex East Florida. Five

gunboats and the sloops *Wasp* and *Nautilus* under the command of Capt. Hugh Campbell were ordered to patrol the coastline off the Georgia-Florida border. The two sloops were positioned at the mouth of the St. Marys River. Though Campbell was under no orders to assist the insurgents in any manner whatsoever, on 11 March 1812 Mathews convinced Campbell to station two gunboats off the coast of Amelia Island to pressure the Spanish officials at Fernandina into surrendering the town.

Meanwhile, Mathews ordered Smith's forces at Point Petre to join him in an assault on Fernandina. On 14 May, Mathews and his band of 250 "patriots" crossed the St. Marys River into Spanish Florida and within two days had advanced onto Amelia Island. The Spanish commandant at Fernandina, Justo Lopez, had sufficient forces in town to oppose Mathews's army, but he was concerned that Campbell's gunboats, which had their guns trained on the town, would open fire. Lopez sent word to Campbell, inquiring whether he intended to use force. Campbell responded that he was not predisposed to fire on the city, yet he could not ignore the pleas of the patriots hopeful of ceding the island to the United States. Under such terms, Lopez had no alternative but to surrender the town to Mathews. On 19 March, Fernandina was formally surrendered to the patriots, whose force soon numbered over 800 men after reinforcements from Georgia arrived.

The patriots—under Mathews's leadership—then left Fernandina for an even larger prize: St. Augustine. Meanwhile, in Washington, the president was under extreme pressure from the British and Spanish embassies and also from New England Federalists who vehemently disagreed with the administration's foreign policy, to explain the events in East Florida. Madison could not admit that he had had anything to do with Mathews's invasion, and he disavowed all knowledge of the expedition. Upon learning that the patriots intended to attack St. Augustine, the president summarily dismissed Mathews for exceeding his orders. Incensed over his dismissal, Mathews determined to go to Washington and reveal the full extent of his mission and how the administration was largely responsible for the entire affair. But he died of fever in Augusta, Georgia, and official knowledge of his activities and of the Madison administration's role in the Patriot's War died with him.

—*Robert Saunders, Jr.*

See also: Florida; Georgia; Patriot's War; St. Augustine, Florida
Further Reading
Gilmer, George R. *Sketches of Some of the First Settlers of Upper Georgia, of the Cherokees, and the Author.* New York: D. Appleton, 1855; reprint, Americus, GA: Americus Book Co., 1926.

Knight, Lucian Lamar. *Georgia's Landmarks, Memorials, and Legends*. 2 vols. Atlanta: Byrd Printing, 1914.

Patrick, Rembert W. *Florida Fiasco: Rampant Rebels on the Georgia-Florida Border, 1810–1815*. Athens: University of Georgia Press, 1954.

MCARTHUR, DUNCAN
1772–1839
Ohio politician; U.S. officer

A Pennsylvania frontiersman who served in Josiah Harmar's expedition in 1790, McArthur settled in Ohio in 1796, serving in the Ohio legislature from 1804 to 1812. A longtime militia officer, he rose to the rank of major general in 1808. In the spring of 1812, his men elected him colonel of one of three Ohio volunteer regiments raised to accompany Gen. William Hull's expedition to Detroit. McArthur spent much of his time in this command arguing with his fellow officers, first with Cols. John Gano, James Findlay, and Lewis Cass over which colonel was most senior; then with the regular army officers; and later still over the merits of Hull as a commander. He and the other Ohioans were particularly critical of Hull as the campaign progressed, and at times they were openly insubordinate. Though more active than Hull, McArthur demonstrated no particular military skill in the skirmishes around Detroit and Fort Malden. Away from Detroit when Hull surrendered the fort (16 August 1812), the isolated McArthur had to surrender as well.

Paroled, McArthur returned to Ohio, where he was elected to the U.S. House of Representatives in late 1812. In early 1813, he was appointed colonel and then brigadier general of the 26th U.S. Infantry. Resigning his congressional seat, McArthur (along with Cass, who had been similarly commissioned) spent the spring of 1813 trying to recruit soldiers for the army, with only limited success. In May 1813, he collected 330 men to aid William Henry Harrison, besieged at Fort Meigs by British major general Henry Procter, but Procter withdrew. In July, when the British tried a second time to take Fort Meigs, McArthur again came to the aid of Harrison and the fort, calling out the entire Second Division, Ohio militia (though he was no longer a militia officer), but the British again withdrew. By then, McArthur had officially received word of his exchange and accompanied Harrison's expedition into Canada in the fall of 1813, but he was left behind to garrison Detroit. In the winter of 1813–1814, McArthur testified at the court-martial of William Hull and served at the

abortive trial of James Wilkinson that was disbanded when Wilkinson objected that the court was not composed solely of general officers.

Reverting to his old habits of criticism, McArthur also joined other westerners in a campaign of words against Harrison. When Harrison resigned on 11 May 1814, McArthur received command of the Northwestern Army. However, by this time, the far western theater had become a peripheral part of the war, and McArthur was given few resources. His only noteworthy achievement was a raid into Upper Canada in the fall of 1814—made with 650 mounted volunteers and 70 Indians—that had little strategic impact.

After the war, McArthur served in a variety of political offices, including the governorship of Ohio, and amassed a great fortune. As a military officer, McArthur proved energetic, but he was too willing to engage in bickering with fellow Americans. In any event, he never received an opportunity to demonstrate his capacity or incapacity for military command.

—*Mark Pitcavage*

See also: Cass, Lewis; Harrison, William Henry; Hull, William; Meigs, Fort
Further Reading
Cramer, Clarence Henley. "The Career of Duncan McArthur." Ph.D. dissertation, Ohio State University, 1931.
McDonald, John. *Biographical Sketches of General Nathaniel Massie, General Duncan McArthur, Captain William Wells, and General Simon Kenton*. Cincinnati: E. Morgan, 1838.

MCCLURE, GEORGE
1770–1851
U.S. officer

George McClure was born near Londonderry, Ireland, in 1770. At the age of 20, he migrated to the United States, bringing with him a chest of carpenter's tools and a few extra clothes. During his third year in the country, he responded to an advertisement inviting carpenters to work at Bath on the northwestern frontier of New York. He built houses with crews of men at Bath in an ambitious, remote development.

On his own time he tried anything that promised a profit. He bought land at 25 cents an acre, shipped barrel staves and flour by water, and drove cattle overland to the populated east. He built a flour mill, a sawmill, and even a carding machine. Since wheat was too bulky to ship profitably, he established a distillery and shipped whiskey instead.

McClure also found time for public affairs, serving first as a justice of the peace and later as a judge. Most important with regard to the War of 1812 was his rise in the New York militia to the rank of brigadier general.

In September 1813, commanding a brigade of 2,000 militiamen, he reported to Gen. James Wilkinson at Fort George, Canada, which was held by U.S. forces. He urged attacking Burlington Heights at the head of Lake Ontario, but the War Department instead transferred the regular troops eastward to Kingston to attack Montreal via the St. Lawrence River. This shift left McClure in command at Fort George with 60 sick regulars, 40 volunteers, and a band of Canadians who favored the United States. When a British column advanced against Fort George, McClure and a council of his subordinates decided that they had to abandon the fort. McClure alone added that they should also destroy the village of Newark, lying 1 mile away toward the lake. He had permission from the War Department to do this if necessary.

Newark had a population of 400 and, from an earlier era of prosperity, 300 buildings. At dusk on 10 December 1813, with the temperature at zero and snow deep on the ground, McClure sent men to notify the inhabitants that they had until noon the next day to leave. Thus on 11 December, he detailed three companies under a Canadian turncoat to burn the town. They burned it to the ground, except for one usable barrack and 1,500 standing tents. McClure then crossed the river and made his way to Buffalo to raise volunteers and entreat the administration to send regulars. He described the militia as little better than an "infuriated mob." The militia in return refused to serve under him. He turned command over to Amos Hall.

The British avenged Newark several times over. They captured Fort Niagara, inflicting heavy casualties, devastated the small towns on the U.S. side of the river, and finally burned Black Rock and Buffalo. The Niagara Valley passed entirely under their control.

George McClure is mentioned in most histories of the War of 1812 because of the burning of Newark. His military career was over, but he overcame the onus of that destruction. He served as sheriff of Steuben County, New York, and later in the New York legislature for three terms. He moved to Elgin, Illinois, in 1834 and was a respected citizen there until his death in 1851.

—*John K. Mahon*

See also: Black Rock, New York; Buffalo, New York; Hall, Amos; Newark, Upper Canada; Wilkinson, James

Further Reading

Kirby, William. *Annals of Niagara*. New York: Macmillan, 1927.

Mahon, John K. *War of 1812*. Gainesville: University Presses of Florida, 1972.

McClure, George. *Causes of the Destruction of the American Towns on the Niagara Frontier, and Failure of the Campaign of the Fall of 1813*. Bath, NY: Printed by Benjamin Smead, 1817.

McMaster, G. H. *History of the Settlement of Steuben County, New York*. Bath, NY: Underhill, 1853.

MCDOUALL, ROBERT
1774–1848
British army officer

McDouall was the second son of John McDouall, a magistrate in Stranraer, Scotland. He purchased an ensigncy in the 49th Foot on 29 October 1797 and a lieutenant's position in the Eighth Foot on 1 November 1797. He came to Canada in 1810 with the Eighth (King's) Regiment of Foot, after 14 years of service in Egypt (1801), Copenhagen (1807), and Martinique, West Indies (1809). Appointed as aide-de-camp to Sir George Prevost in summer 1812, he was present during the attack on Sacket's Harbor in May 1813. He took instructions to Brig. Gen. John Vincent and claimed to have suggested the counterattack at Stoney Creek that occurred on 6 June 1813. After promotion to major in the Glengarry Light Fencibles on 24 June, he conveyed dispatches to England and was brevetted lieutenant colonel on 29 July. He returned to Canada toward the end of 1813.

At the end of 1813, Prevost selected McDouall as commandant for Michilimackinac (Mackinac Island). He took 90 of the Royal Newfoundland Regiment, 21 sailors under Lt. Newdigate Poyntz of the Royal Navy, 11 artillerymen, four field guns, and shipwrights safely across the ice of Lake Simcoe, along the 9-mile portage from Kempenfelt Bay to the head of the Nottawasaga River. There his men built bateaux. Setting out on 25 April 1814, McDouall brought 29 of 30 bateaux through the ice from Nottawasaga Bay to Michilimackinac on May 18. He lost only one boat and saved its crew and contents before the ice crushed it. Lt. Andrew Bulger remembered that the party moved through "fields of ice and in almost constant and at times terrific storms." The supply effort rescued the garrison that had been on half rations since March 1814.

At Michilimackinac, McDouall relieved Capt. Richard

Bullock of the 41st Regiment. Poyntz irritated McDouall, however, by assuming command of all water craft. McDouall dispatched a force of Michigan Fencibles, Indians, and Voyageurs under William McKay to recapture Prairie du Chien, at the junction of the Fox and Mississippi Rivers in Wisconsin. That post had been taken by U.S. forces in June 1814, but the British recaptured it on 20 July 1814.

With 140 troops and several hundred Indians, McDouall successfully defended Mackinac Island on 4 August from the attack of 770 U.S. troops and marines under Lt. Col. George Croghan. When the North West Company schooner *Nancy* was burned at Nottawasaga River by Commodore Arthur Sinclair's forces, her commander Lt. Miller Worsley led a spirited night attack on the two schooners *Scorpion* and *Tigress,* with his sailors and troops provided by McDouall. His force captured one schooner on 5 September and the other three days later.

When peace brought the mutual restoration of all forts to their original occupiers, McDouall regretted the return of Michilimackinac. It was restored 18 July 1815, and the British moved to nearby Drummond Island. McDouall commanded there until the garrison was reduced in June 1816. He was promoted to colonel in July 1830 and major general in November 1841. In February 1847, he became a Companion of the Order of the Bath. Never married, he died 15 November 1848.

—*Frederick C. Drake*

See also: Croghan, George; Michilimackinac, Fort; Prairie du Chien; Prevost, George; Sacket's Harbor, Battle of; Sacket's Harbor, New York

Further Reading

Allen, Robert S. "Robert McDouall." In *Dictionary of Canadian Biography.* Vol. 7, *1836–1850.* Toronto: University of Toronto Press, 1979: 556–557.

Bulger, Andrew. *An Autobiographical Sketch.* Bangalore, India: Regimental Press, 1865.

Cruikshank, Ernest A. "An Episode of the War of 1812: The Story of the Schooner *Nancy.*" *Ontario Historical Society Papers and Records* 9 (1910): 76–129.

Wood, William H. *Select British Documents of the Canadian War of 1812.* 3 vols. in 4. Toronto: Champlain Society, 1920–1928.

MCHENRY, FORT

This fortification, more than any other location in the United States, came to symbolize the U.S. experience in the War of 1812. After the fort withstood a bombardment on 13 September 1814, Francis Scott Key was moved to pen the words to "The Star-Spangled Banner," which, in 1931, became the national anthem of the United States. The fort, like the nation itself, stood up to a fierce attack but emerged intact.

The United States built Fort McHenry in the late 1790s as a defensive bastion protecting the inner harbor of Baltimore, Maryland. Situated on Whetstone Point, the fortification mounted 20 guns and covered most approaches to the city by way of the Patapsco River. To its east was the Northwest or Harbor Branch, to its west the Ferry Branch, and to the south the main channel. Designed by John Jacob Ulrich Rivadi, Fort McHenry was made of masonry and dirt fill, a typical construction in Sébastien Vauban's style of five bastions protected by an outer work fronting the river.

In the War of 1812, Fort McHenry became the locus for the defense of Baltimore. With Fort Covington to the west on the Ferry Branch and a small battery on the opposite bank of the Northwest Branch, the post would have to protect the city from the Royal Navy. Vice Adm. Alexander Cochrane, commanding some 45 warships and transports, planned to capture Baltimore after his successful raid up the Potomac River in August. Landing four regiments of infantry at North Point to carry the city's land defenses, Cochrane intended for about 20 ships to provide covering fire from the Northwest Branch. He assumed Fort McHenry could be reduced without much trouble.

The British troops went ashore on 12 September 1814 but ran into trouble on North Point, making the close support of the Royal Navy imperative. Accordingly, Cochrane dispatched 16 ships toward Whetstone Point, ordering them to drop anchor some 2 miles from Fort McHenry, out of range of the U.S. guns. Beginning about midday, the British warships pounded away at the U.S. position, using, among other munitions, shells ("bombs bursting in air") and Congreve Rockets ("rockets' red glare"). The long range of the attack reduced British accuracy and, after nearly 16 hours of shelling, Fort McHenry remained relatively undamaged.

Cochrane tried to carry the fort by amphibious assault on the night of 14 September, but his landing party lost its way in a fog. Instead of landing in the fort's rear, whaleboats loaded with Royal Marines came under fire from Fort Covington and the battery on the Northwest Branch, which killed many and drove the rest back to the fleet. The British abandoned their campaign against Baltimore the next day and withdrew.

After the War of 1812, Fort McHenry was maintained off and on as a federal military installation through World

War I. In 1925, Congress designated Fort McHenry and its surrounding grounds a national park, changing its status to national monument and historic shrine in 1939.

—*Donald S. Frazier*

See also: Armistead, George; Artillery; Baltimore, Battle of; Beanes, William; Brooke, Arthur; Cochrane, Alexander; Hughes, Christopher; Key, Francis Scott; Maryland; Napier, Charles (British naval officer); Smith, Samuel; Upper Marlboro, Maryland
Further Reading
Lord, Walter. *The Dawn's Early Light.* New York: W. W. Norton and Company, 1972.

MCINTOSH, WILLIAM
1775?–1825
U.S.-allied Creek

William McIntosh, also known as Tustennugee Hutkee (White Warrior), was born on the banks of the Chattahoochee River in Coweta, Georgia. His parents were the Scotsman William McIntosh, a Tory captain in the British army in the American Revolution, and a Creek woman of the powerful Wind Clan.

By the time of the War of 1812, McIntosh, as a member of the prestigious Wind Clan, had become one of the leaders of the Lower Creeks who allied with Americans against Red Stick Creeks during the Creek War of 1813–1814. McIntosh and some 450 of his Creek warriors contributed significantly to Gen. John Floyd's victory over the Red Sticks at the Battle of Autosse on the Tallapoosa River on 29 November 1813, and later aided Andrew Jackson at the battle at Horseshoe Bend (Tohopeka). He then signed the Treaty of Fort Jackson (9 August 1814) in four places (once for himself and three times as proxy for his uncle and two other chiefs). This treaty ceded 23 million acres of Creek lands in Georgia and Alabama to the United States and further exacerbated the hostilities among Creeks.

In July 1816, McIntosh and 200 Creek warriors joined Col. Duncan L. Clinch in an attack on a fort at the mouth of the Apalachicola River, which had been outfitted by the British near the end of the war. When the British left in 1815, a force composed primarily of fugitive slaves had occupied the stronghold. Clinch and McIntosh ravaged the surrounding countryside before being joined by a U.S. naval expedition whose cannon fire demolished the fort.

McIntosh subsequently served in Jackson's Seminole campaign of 1818, leading as many as 2,000 warriors.

In the 1820s, McIntosh cooperated with his cousin, Georgia governor George M. Troup, and federal government officials in their efforts to acquire Indian lands in Georgia, Alabama, and Mississippi. McIntosh profited handsomely for his influence in facilitating the treaties and accumulated considerable wealth in both land and money. His main residence was on the bank of the Chattahoochee River in what later became Carroll County, Georgia. It consisted of a large two-story house, which also served as a tavern, and a plantation worked by slaves. Big Warrior and the Upper Creeks, however, strongly opposed the cession of tribal lands, and the Creek National Council threatened death to anyone ceding Creek land without the Council's permission. Nevertheless, McIntosh signed several treaties, including the second Treaty of Indian Springs (1825), which ceded all remaining Creek lands in Georgia and a portion of those in eastern Alabama to the United States in exchange for $400,000 and equivalent tracts in the Arkansas River country. Many of those who signed this treaty were McIntosh's relatives or mixed bloods, and only a few exercised much influence among the Creeks. In response, the Creek National Council, already embittered by the recent death of Big Warrior, ordered the execution of McIntosh.

The former Red Stick Menewa led a band of some 200 Upper Creeks from the Tallapoosa country to McIntosh's plantation on the Chattahoochee River. They attacked on the night of 30 April–1 May 1825, burning the house and shooting McIntosh when he emerged. The attackers then dragged him by his feet away from the house and stabbed him with a knife.

—*Charles H. McArver, Jr.*

See also: Big Warrior; Creek War; Fort Jackson, Treaty of; Horseshoe Bend, Battle of; Little Prince; Seminole Indians
Further Reading
Bonner, James C. *The Georgia Story.* Oklahoma City: Harlow Publishing Corporation, 1961.
Heidler, David S., and Jeanne T. Heidler. *Old Hickory's War: Andrew Jackson and the Quest for Empire.* Mechanicsburg, PA: Stackpole Books, 1996.
Jones, Mary K., and Lily Reynolds, eds. and comps. *Coweta County Chronicles for One Hundred Years.* N.p., 1928; reprint, Easley, SC: Southern Historical Press, 1978.
Owsley, Frank L. *Struggle for the Gulf Borderlands: The Creek War and the Battle of New Orleans, 1812–1815.* Gainesville: University Presses of Florida, 1981.

MCKAY, WILLIAM
See Prairie du Chien

MCNEIL, JOHN
1784–1850
U.S. officer

Born in New Hampshire, John McNeil received a commission as an ensign in his state militia in 1801 and quickly rose to captain of his own company. Before the start of the War of 1812, he accepted a commission as a captain of the 11th U.S. Infantry Regiment. In 1813, he was promoted to major.

As commander of the 11th Regiment, McNeil, along with Maj. Henry Leavenworth's Ninth Infantry Regiment, occupied the center of Brig. Gen. Winfield Scott's brigade as it neared the British position at the Chippewa River on 5 July 1814. In the middle of a parade review, Scott realized that the British under Brig. Gen. Phineas Riall were advancing on his position. Riall moved forward quickly because he was under the mistaken impression that McNeil and Leavenworth's men were militia (they were clad in light blue rather than the traditional dark blue uniforms). When he attacked the center of the U.S. line, Riall expected it to break and run.

The engagement became heavy, and McNeil worked tirelessly to keep his regiment together. He knew that Scott would move to exploit any weakness in the British line. When Scott finally found his salient, he ordered McNeil to stage a bayonet charge at one point while Leavenworth went in at another. The 11th and the Ninth did not stop chasing the British forces until Riall had them back across the Chippewa.

With General Scott, and in command of the 11th Regiment on the return march along the Niagara from Lake Ontario, McNeil was part of the small force that encountered the British at Lundy's Lane on 25 July 1814. This little core held out for hours waiting for reinforcements to be brought up by Maj. Gen. Jacob Brown. The force became so pressed that the 22nd Regiment started to run, but McNeil rode his horse into their path and ordered them back into action. After rallying these troops, McNeil had his horse shot from under him as he suffered wounds in both legs. These injuries eventually forced him from the field. He would never have complete use of his right leg again.

His wounds, however, did not prevent him from re-maining in the army after the war. Serving in a variety of posts in the West, McNeil achieved the rank of colonel before resigning his commission in 1830. He died in Washington, D.C., in 1850.

—Jeanne T. Heidler and David S. Heidler

See also: Chippewa, Battle of; Lundy's Lane, Battle of; Scott, Winfield

MCQUEEN, PETER
1780?–1820
Red Stick Creek

Like many other Creek Indian chieftains, Peter McQueen was the son of a Scottish trader and a Creek woman. He was an Upper Creek Red Stick who commanded the Tallassees, part of the confederacy that went to war against the accommodationist Creeks in 1813. McQueen was greatly influenced by Tecumseh and the Creek prophets who declared that the Creeks must break off all relations with the whites.

Peter McQueen was the primary cause of the first major action of this campaign. During the initial war council in June 1813, he strongly supported a war against the Americans, as recommended by northern Indians. He believed that both the Spanish and British would provide the Creeks with arms and ammunition to support their cause. McQueen based this on the Malden letter from the British to the Spanish at Pensacola, authorizing them to provide the Creeks with arms. In July 1813, he headed for Pensacola with a large party of warriors to obtain powder and ammunition.

The Spanish governor in Pensacola was hesitant to provide McQueen with supplies because Spain was not at war with the United States. He finally provided the Creeks, however, with half a ton of gunpowder and enough ammunition for five rounds per man. Meanwhile, news of McQueen's visit to Pensacola had reached Americans at Mobile, Alabama. Militia colonel James Caller gathered about 200 men and set out after McQueen. On 27 July 1813, the Americans came upon McQueen's column halted astride Burnt Corn Creek, about 80 miles north of Pensacola. Caller's men stormed the Indians, forcing them across the creek, but when his untrained militia stopped to plunder the wagons, McQueen had time to regroup. The Red Sticks struck back, sending the militia fleeing into the woods. Although McQueen lost most of his supplies and

20 men, his victory increased the Red Sticks' confidence and gave them a unifying cause for war.

McQueen then summoned warriors from 13 towns to wage an attack against Fort Mims in retribution for the U.S. attack on his column at Burnt Corn Creek. William Weatherford (Red Eagle) joined forces with McQueen. Some believe McQueen forced Weatherford to join the warring party by holding his family hostage. Whatever the case, McQueen and Weatherford set out for Fort Mims, where they overwhelmed a large force of Americans in what became a massacre of all but a few of the fort's inhabitants. This so incensed Americans that it led to U.S. intervention in the Creek War.

Peter McQueen continued to command various groups of warring Indians throughout the next nine months. He assisted in turning back Andrew Jackson's column at Emuckfau Creek, forcing the Tennessean to abandon his advance. After Jackson's crushing victory over the Red Sticks at Horseshoe Bend, McQueen fled to Florida in 1814 and continued fighting. He allied himself with the British in Florida and after the War of 1812 ended, he continued to fight Jackson during the First Seminole War. McQueen died on an unknown island on the east coast of Florida in 1820.

—*John M. Keefe*

See also: Creek War; Red Sticks
Further Reading

Griffith, Benjamin W. *McIntosh and Weatherford, Creek Indian Leaders.* Tuscaloosa: University of Alabama Press, 1988.

Halbert, H. S., and T. H. Ball. *The Creek War of 1813 and 1814.* Chicago: Donohue and Henneberry, 1895.

Heidler, David S., and Jeanne T. Heidler. *Old Hickory's War: Andrew Jackson and the Quest for Empire.* Mechanicsburg, PA: Stackpole Books, 1996.

Owsley, Frank L. *Struggle for the Gulf Borderlands: The Creek War and the Battle of New Orleans, 1812–1815.* Gainesville: University Presses of Florida, 1981.

Rowland, Dunbar. *Andrew Jackson's Campaign against the British, or the Mississippi Territory in the War of 1812.* New York: Macmillan Company, 1926.

Wright, J. Leitch. *Creeks and Seminoles.* Lincoln: University of Nebraska Press, 1986.

MCREE, WILLIAM
1787–1833
U.S. officer

Born in North Carolina, William McRee attended the U.S. Military Academy and graduated in 1805. Having attained the rank of major by the commencement of hostilities with Great Britain, McRee became the chief engineer of the Northern Army beginning in 1813, serving primarily on the Niagara Frontier.

When Maj. Gen. Jacob Brown began his campaign along the Niagara in the spring of 1814, Brown consulted McRee frequently regarding the best places to cross the river at Fort Erie and approaches to the attack on that position. Following the successful attack on Fort Erie, McRee accompanied the army to Lake Ontario and back, serving as Brown's primary engineering adviser. On the return to Fort Erie, McRee accompanied General Brown to the battlefield at Lundy's Lane on 25 July and offered Brown the advice that if the Americans were to hold their position there, it would be necessary to take the British hilltop battery overlooking the main U.S. force. Brown immediately ordered Col. James Miller to take a party to capture the battery. This attack, after suffering severe casualties, was successful.

When Brown was evacuated to Sacket's Harbor after suffering injuries at Lundy's Lane, McRee remained with the army at Fort Erie to aid the new commander, Brig. Gen. Edmund Pendleton Gaines, in preparing Fort Erie's defenses. The two worked closely together for the first two weeks of August 1814, strengthening and adding to the decrepit fort, so that when the British attacked shortly after midnight on 15 August, the defenders were able to repulse the assault. In his official report of the battle, Gaines gave McRee a large part of the credit for the U.S. defense of Fort Erie.

Following the war, McRee was part of a large group of U.S. officers who traveled to Europe to inspect fortifications and study engineering techniques. He resigned his commission in 1819 and became U.S. surveyor general. He died in St. Louis, Missouri, in 1833.

—*Jeanne T. Heidler and David S. Heidler*

See also: Brown, Jacob J.; Erie, Fort; Gaines, Edmund Pendleton; Lundy's Lane, Battle of
Further Reading

Cruikshank, E. A., editor. *The Documentary History of the Niagara Frontier, 1812–1814.* 9 volumes. Welland: Lundy's Lane Historical Society, 1896–1908.

MEDICINE, ARMY

Although Secretary of War William Eustis was a physician, when war began in June 1812, the U.S. army was ill-prepared to provide even basic medical services.

Medical supplies were inadequate, their procurement procedures were described as "wanton waste," and some surgeons were not even competent. The situation had not been much improved six months later, when Gen. John Armstrong replaced Eustis. By then, the number of regiments had been nearly doubled, necessitating the recruitment of many more trained surgeons to meet the statutory requirement for one surgeon and two surgeon's mates per regiment. (Militia regiments often recruited volunteer surgeons from among their neighbors, but records of their services are virtually nonexistent for the War of 1812.)

When Congress reorganized the general staff on 3 March 1813, it created the posts of physician and surgeon general and apothecary general, both to be filled by civilians. Pres. James Madison outlined their specific duties two months later. The new regulations specified minimum professional qualifications for army surgeons. They were to be assigned by the physician and surgeon general, who was also to appoint hospital stewards and nurses and to manage the stores, instruments, and medicines acquired for the Medical Department by the army's Purchasing Department. The apothecary general was to assist with procurement. The regulations also established pay scales and perquisites for the surgeons and precluded them from engaging in private practice while on active duty. Eustis had divided the country into nine administrative districts (a tenth, centered in Washington, D.C., was created on 2 July 1814). Madison specified that the senior surgeon in each district was to direct both the regimental and army general hospital surgeons within his district.

On 11 June 1813, Dr. James Tilton, who had become familiar with military medical needs during the Revolution, was appointed physician and surgeon general. He devised new procedures based on observations he had made from 1777 to 1781. Although he concluded that the army's overall health was good after touring Northern District military hospitals, he tried to improve hospital services by requiring greater attention to cleanliness, to increased discipline, and to avoidance of hospital overcrowding. He sought to monitor the army's health by requiring submission of periodic hospital reports, but few such summaries actually reached his desk. Tilton also tried to centralize purchasing procedures, but they remained as disorganized as before, and doctors in the field claimed that the drugs sent by the Medical Department did not meet their actual needs.

Dr. Francis LeBaron, who had been a naval surgeon's mate during the Quasi-War with France, was made apothecary general; he had been doing the same job unofficially—and with considerable frustration—since February 1812. He devised a standard medicine chest designed to serve a 900-man regiment for a year, but army surgeons, protesting that such chests were too large to move, forced him to prepare smaller ones weighing only 160 pounds for field use, as well as storage chests that weighed 120–200 pounds.

The army relied chiefly on two traditional hospital types: relatively permanent general hospitals built well behind the lines (at Brownville, Buffalo, Greenbush, Lewiston, Malone, Plattsburg, Sacket's Harbor, and Williamsville, New York; Burlington, Vermont; Detroit, Michigan; Greenleaf's Point [now Fort McNair], on Capitol Hill, and at Norfolk, Virginia, in the Washington area; and at New Orleans, Louisiana) and flying hospitals, analogous to today's mobile field hospitals, for use on the front lines. Tilton's earlier experience had taught him that flying hospitals should be nonautonomous emergency branches of general hospitals. Army and navy surgeons sometimes cooperated when necessary, as they did after the Battle of Lake Erie and perhaps at Sacket's Harbor, but it is not known whether the two services competed for their medical supplies.

The most important army surgeon in the field was probably Dr. James Mann (1759–1832) of New York. As medical director of the Northern Army, he managed the hospitals at Greenbush, Malone, and Plattsburg and a temporary one at Fort Niagara. His postwar memoir provides a clear picture of the medical problems faced by the army and of how they were treated. In general, he explicitly followed the military surgical precepts of Napoleon I's surgeon in chief, Baron D. J. Larrey (as laid out in his *Memoires de Chirurgie Militaire*).

Unlike Tilton, Mann thought that morbidity was unacceptably high among U.S. soldiers. He blamed it on their dirtiness and intemperance, on bread contaminated with plaster of Paris (calcium sulfate, but it has no known toxicity), and water contaminated with human excrement. He also imputed the men's indolence, observing that many soldiers had been easy to recruit because they were unemployed but were not paid enough by the army to encourage any better performance. Mann was particularly concerned about men who had been poisoned by the mercurial drugs customarily prescribed for their venereal diseases, about deaths caused by overly zealous administration of antimonial drugs to fever victims, and about the high prevalence of dysentery and pneumonia among the troops. His book contains detailed clinical descriptions of many surgical cases, especially amputations, as well as autopsies of pneumonia victims. Mann may also have introduced the modern usage of the ambulance to U.S. medicine.

The War of 1812 contributed less than most other wars to medical knowledge, probably because it was relatively short-lived, because few academic physicians were involved, and because there were so few battles and therefore few opportunities to improve surgical skills. Dr. Henry Huntt, however, did report one of the earliest cases of excision of the head of the humerus (in *American Medical Recorder*). In addition, army surgeons performed a surprising number of autopsies, but only a few were reported in the medical literature. Although Tilton had helped protect the Continental Army against smallpox and although LeBaron urged that the new U.S. army be vaccinated, there is no good evidence that it was done systematically on a large scale. In any event, however, the army suffered no epidemics of the dreaded illness, but the usual camp diseases remained prevalent throughout the war. Army surgeons often argued over which drugs were best for specific illnesses, but they all relied on similar medical reasoning.

Throughout the war, army surgeons probably did the best they could in the face of congressional ambivalence over drug procurement policies and adequate funding. On 3 March 1815, Congress abolished Tilton's position (but not LeBaron's), perhaps realizing that the post had not really helped the national cause, though Tilton's sensible regulations had never been adequately implemented. Not until 1818 was a Medical Department, fully empowered to collect the data it needed, permanently imposed on the U.S. Army.

—*J. Worth Estes*

See also: Beaumont, William; Tilton, James
Further Reading

Gillett, Mary C. *The Army Medical Department 1775–1818.* Washington, DC: Center of Military History, U.S. Army, 1981.

Huntt, Henry. *American Medical Recorder* 1 (1818): 365–366.

———. "An Abstract Account of the Diseases Which Prevailed among the Soldiers, Received into the General Hospital, at Burlington, Vermont, during the Summer and Autumn of 1814." *American Medical Recorder* 1 (1818): 176–179.

Larrey, Baron D. J. *Memoires de Chirurgie Militaire.* 5 vols. Paris: J. Smith, 1812.

Mann, James. *Medical Sketches of the Campaigns of 1812, 13, 14. . . .* Dedham, MA: H. Mann and Co., 1816.

Niles' Weekly Register 7, no. 24, 11 February 1815.

Phalen, James M. "Surgeon James Mann's Observations on Battlefield Amputations." *Military Surgeon* 87 (1940): 463–466.

Waterhouse, Benjamin. *Circular Letter from Dr. Benjamin Waterhouse to the Surgeons of the Different Posts in the Second Military Department.* Cambridge, MA: N.p., 1817.

MEDICINE, NAVAL

The medical practice in the U.S. Navy and the entire service suffered during most of the War of 1812 because of the lack of full-time leadership at the head of the department and the financial problems facing the nation.

Paul Hamilton, who had served as secretary of the navy since May 1809, resigned from that office on 31 December 1812. William Jones of Pennsylvania became secretary on 19 January 1813. He had hardly learned his naval duties when he was asked to take over the Treasury Department as well while Albert Gallatin, the secretary of that department, was in Europe on a peace mission. Early in 1813, Jones sent a report to the House of Representatives on the state of the nation's finances, which indicated that nine direct and indirect taxes were necessary to balance the budget and maintain the credit of the country. Not all of the tax proposals were adopted, and those that were began to be collected by the end of the year. Jones estimated that the taxes approved would raise only about two-thirds of the funds required. The shortfall would have to be made up by a loan. As a result of these factors, Jones drew up a budget for the army and navy that required a maximum of economy and efficiency from March through December 1813. Discouraged by the outlook in the nation's and his personal financial affairs, Jones wanted to resign from the government in December 1813, but he was induced by Pres. James Madison to stay on for another year.

With the declaration of war against Great Britain in June 1812, the U.S. Navy faced problems on the medical front. There were few surgeons who had any experience in dealing with war wounds. Those who had served in previous wars were senior men who were assigned to shore installations. There was also no adequate hospital system. In 1804, a marine hospital that was supposed to serve the sick of the merchant service, navy, and marines had been built on ground acquired from the navy yard at Charlestown, Massachusetts. Navy and marine commanders soon found, however, that there were problems connected with its use, especially the lack of a disciplined environment and lax security.

In the latter case, convalescents were able to desert with relatively little difficulty. As a result, the navy and marines made their own hospital arrangements in the navy yard: the navy made use of a house that was fitted up as best as could be arranged for the care of the sick, and the marines usually set aside a room or two for the sick. Patients in the two services were cared for by the surgeons and surgeon's mates assigned to the navy yard.

Other navy yards in New York, Philadelphia, Washington, and Norfolk had similar arrangements. Plans were underway to build a new hospital in Washington to improve the health care arrangements there, but before this could be done, the war began. The result was that the navy's hospital facilities onshore, which were not adequate for the proper care of the sick during peacetime, now had to adjust to the demands of war.

At sea, health care aboard frigates was normally provided by a surgeon and a surgeon's mate. Each morning sick call was held at the mainmast on the berth deck (the third one down), and the surgeon or the mate (or both) listened to health complaints and made determinations about treatments. The goal was to have a list of the sick in the captain's hands as soon as possible, ideally by 8:00 A.M.

To restore the health of members of the crew, a doctor might resort to cathartics or drugs used to stimulate the intestinal tract, so that disease-producing materials would be eliminated. Calomel (mercurous chloride), castor oil, and jalap were among the drugs used for this purpose. Other common remedies were tonics or drugs that were believed to strengthen body tissues weakened by disease. Peruvian bark, Virginia snakeroot, and several spices were common tonics. Peruvian bark, which is now known to contain quinine, was widely used as a tonic in the treatment of malaria and other types of fever. Emetics, especially ipecac and tartar emetic (antimony potassium tartrate) were used to empty the stomach. Diuretic salt (potassium acetate) was used to increase the secretion and flow of urine. Diuretics were also used to promote the absorption of fluid by vessels throughout the body so that it could be eliminated via the kidneys. Diaphoretics, such as antimony salts, were drugs that stimulated increased perspiration.

Opium was administered in pill form or in alcohol solutions such as laudanum to control diarrhea, relieve pain, and induce sleep. Astringents, such as lime water, were believed to condense the solids of arteries and nerves to reduce abnormal losses of heat and fluid.

Severely ill patients might be treated with blistering agents or by bleeding. A blister was raised by applying an alcohol solution of cantharides (powdered Spanish flies) directly to the skin so that pus and other noxious materials could escape from the body into the blister fluid. Bleeding was performed only if the patient's pulse was full and strong. Between 8 and 20 ounces of blood might be removed at one time, but the average was about 12 ounces.

Men with minor problems would be bandaged or given medicines, and if they were able to work, they were returned to duty. Others who were not fit to work but who needed minimal care might be excused from duty and allowed to rest in their hammocks. Still others who required more continuous treatment and observation were assigned to sick bay, a roughly triangular area in the bow of the ship. In a frigate, the sick bay was located on the berth deck. Medications were dispensed by the surgeon's mate with the assistance of enlisted helpers who were called loblolly boys. There were no portholes or sources of light other than candles, and the only source of ventilation was an open hatch farther back. Some attempts were made both before and after the war to improve the ventilation in ships by means of a system of pipes and hand-operated bellows, but with mixed results. The only other solution was to rig a wind sail to divert wind down the hatch. This might bring some relief to those on the gun or berth deck, but it was of little help on the orlop deck (the fourth deck down).

When a frigate was preparing for battle, the surgeon's assistants would collect and stack mess chests to form an operating table and lay out the instruments in the cockpit. This was an area in the center of the ship on the orlop deck. It was regarded as an area less subject to the motion of the ship and relatively safe from enemy shot. In the USS *Constitution* the cockpit measured 13 feet by 8 feet and had an overhead of 4 feet 10 inches. The area was lit by overhead lanterns containing as many candles as the surgeon could procure. During a battle, the wounded men were carried from the spar deck to the cockpit for treatment. While awaiting the care of the physician, they were laid on the deck adjacent to the cockpit. In ships smaller than frigates, naturally there were fewer decks and smaller crews, so the size of the space allotted for medical purposes was much reduced.

When he examined the patient, the surgeon had to determine the nature of the injury and what could be done. For men with shattered limbs, the usual solution was amputation. Wounds in abdominal and thoracic cavities were generally regarded as untreatable. In such cases, the patient was made as comfortable as possible until he died. Others might be suffering from broken bones, lacerations, or gunshot wounds. In such cases the bones were set, the wounds were cleaned (a process that included the removal of musket balls or fragments of metal or wood), bleeding was stopped, and the wound was bandaged.

After a battle, the sick bay usually could not accommodate all the injured. Overflow cases might be placed on the gun deck or in the officers' wardroom. In most of the high seas ship-to-ship battles in the War of 1812, U.S. medical men had to deal with the wounded only for a few days until they were landed at a naval hospital in the United States or, if that was too great a distance to sail, at a hospital in a neutral country. The loss of records from such hospitals makes it virtually impossible to determine the rate of recovery of the wounded or whether some men later died of their wounds. Shortly after the battle between the *Constitution* and the *Guerrière*, wounded British prisoners were sent to the marine hospital at Boston, and the U.S. wounded went to the hospital in the navy yard. Following the battle between the *United States* and the *Macedonian*, the majority of the wounded were British, so Capt. Stephen Decatur put a prize crew on the *Macedonian*, transferred the five wounded Americans to it, and sent it to Newport, Rhode Island. There the arrival of over 70 wounded put a strain on the local hospital facilities, so the naval commander at that port rented a few rooms to accommodate the care of the wounded and sent the overflow to the gunboats stationed there. A civilian, Dr. Edward T. Waring of Newport, was placed in charge of the wounded.

The war put a strain on the medical men assigned to gunboats guarding various ports. Here the problem was not war wounds but fevers, digestive disorders, respiratory illnesses, sprains, ruptures, broken bones, pneumonia, and other illnesses that were characteristic of peacetime duty. In New York, Commander Jacob M. Lewis reported that both British prisoners and U.S. sick were being transferred to his gunboat flotilla, so that his force had become a combination of hospital and prison ship. Soon there was not enough room, and some of the sick died for want of proper medical attention. Lewis appealed for help to the commandant of the navy yard and to the surgeon at the base. Receiving no reply to his appeals, he hired a civilian physician with naval experience and put his name on the ship's books so he could be paid. Later, when Secretary of the Navy William Jones heard about this arrangement, he was outraged at the assumption of authority by Lewis. He promptly ended the services of the civilian physician and made the New York gunboat flotilla subordinate to Decatur. Surviving medical records suggest, however, that most of the sick in the various settings recovered.

A concern about the prompt treatment of men assigned to the gunboats operating in Delaware Bay led Surgeon Edward Cutbush at the Philadelphia Navy Yard to suggest that a temporary hospital be established at New Castle, Delaware. This was authorized by Secretary Hamilton, and Cutbush rented a small house that could accommodate 15 patients. For a time after that, Cutbush was obliged to commute between Philadelphia and New Castle, a 48-hour journey, to treat his patients. He therefore asked the secretary for help in attending to the men at New Castle. When none was forthcoming, Cutbush hired a civilian doctor in New Castle who was paid the same salary as that of a surgeon's mate.

Not until November 1812 did the Navy Department send Cutbush a newly commissioned surgeon's mate to help him. The new doctor was William L. Whittelsey, whom Cutbush considered too young and inexperienced to be of much help. About this time the commandant of the Philadelphia Navy Yard recommended that the hospital in New Castle be closed and the patients transferred to Philadelphia. Cutbush expected this to take place in the spring of 1813, but in November 1812, Capt. David Porter transferred nine invalids from the frigate *Essex* to the hospital. This caused additional problems for Cutbush. He recommended that the men be discharged from the service, but this could not be done until their accounts had been received, and the *Essex* had since sailed. The men also needed clothing, and Cutbush was not authorized to issue any. After the men were transferred to Philadelphia, they left their sick quarters at night for drinking binges, returning inebriated the next morning. Finally for the good of the service, the secretary authorized Cutbush to discharge these men. For the remainder of the war, the navy medical officers in Philadelphia were involved in the routine care of the sick in the area and the examination of recruits.

In the spring of 1813, Cutbush was transferred to the Washington Navy Yard. Upon his arrival he found Surgeon's Mate Henry Huntt treating men suffering from an undiagnosed illness that began with colds, sore throats, a redness in the eyes, and a pain in the right nipple. Within 48 hours these symptoms included a fever, increased pain in the breast, and frequently delirium. Huntt was giving his patients doses of calomel and tartar emetic, applying a large blister to the breast, and following with a warm bath. About the third day, he treated his patients with calomel and opium and alternated with wine, Peruvian bark, and Virginia snakeroot. Bark and snakeroot were often used in treating fevers. At night, patients were given a drug to kill the pain. After six or seven days of such treatment, most patients recovered. In two instances, however, the patients complained of a great pain in the right nipple, a symptom accompanied by a cough and difficult respiration. Huntt thought that these men had pleurisy, so he bled them. The patients then experienced cold in their extremities, a faltering pulse, and violent delirium followed by death within a few hours.

By the time these cases had been resolved, new problems emerged. In June 1813, Huntt had 140 cases of what he thought was pneumonia. The illness came on suddenly and was accompanied by cold skin, a feeble pulse, loss of energy, and difficulty in breathing. Wine, brandy, and aromatics were given to the patients, followed by a hot blister to the chest and the application of heat to the extremities. Huntt did not believe that his patients could stand the normal purgatives, but in some instances he used a gentle purge. After such treatments, Huntt was pleased to see that 134 of his 140 patients recovered.

A similar outbreak took place in one of the ships at the navy yard. In these instances, the sickness was frequently accompanied by vomiting and diarrhea and a cold, clammy sweat. Of 22 cases, seven died, but one of these men had suffered from a pulmonary infection for some time.

In August 1814, after the British had captured Washington and burned some public buildings before returning to their ships, Secretary Jones learned that there were wounded marines and men from Commodore Joshua Barney's gunboat force at the Bladensburg battlefield. He ordered Cutbush to send a doctor to investigate the situation. Cutbush reported that a surgeon's mate had been sent to the battlefield and that five wounded men had been transferred to the hospital facilities at the navy yard. Four others could not be moved, and these were under the care of the army in a temporary hospital. Later, when the army dismantled its hospital, arrangements had to be made to provide quarters and medical attention for these men. Jones authorized Cutbush to do what was necessary.

While reporting to the secretary about the wounded at Bladensburg, Cutbush gave Jones an indication of his own problems. There were 37 patients in the navy yard hospital, 24 of these wounded. Cutbush had to dress the wounds of these men twice a day as well as care for the sick. Surgeon's Mate Huntt had resigned a year earlier, so Cutbush desperately needed an assistant. Jones sent him a surgeon and a surgeon's mate to help with the work, and gradually the patients recovered, allowing Cutbush to return to a more normal routine.

At the Norfolk Navy Yard, the hospital was on the second floor of a frame building. The sick received treatment there as did the small number of wounded from the battles near the city in 1813. During the Battle of Craney Island, Surgeon's Mate William Turk amputated two legs at the thigh, an experience that prompted him later to complain to Secretary Jones about the poor quality of the tourniquets received from the medical stores at Washington.

In North Carolina, Surgeon's Mate E. D. Morrison found himself caring for the sick in the gunboats at Ocracoke Inlet and at Beaufort, which were more than 100 miles apart by road. As a result, he had to rent a horse and spend time on the road between his assignments. While he was attending to the sick at Ocracoke during the winter of 1812–1813, the men in the gunboats at Beaufort became ill with dysentery and pleurisy. After one man died, the commander at Beaufort hired a civilian physician to care for the sick, and he authorized the purchase of the necessary medicines. When news of this arrangement reached Secretary Jones, he demanded explanations. After they were made he urged the utmost vigilance in guarding against abuses and in regulating expenditures.

At Charleston, South Carolina, the annual outbreak of fever in the summer of 1812 brought an increase in the pa-tient load of Surgeon George Logan but no deaths. There was a great need for a hospital for the clinically sick, but there were no funds available for this purpose. In 1813, the marines were transferred to quarters in the navy yard and the sailors to a barracks at Hampstead. At the end of 1814, the barracks were transferred to the army, and new arrangements became necessary. The corporation of Charleston agreed to make two large rooms in the city hospital available for the sick of the navy. The steward of the hospital would keep order among the patients and direct the nurse and the cook on matters relating to their care. In lieu of rent, the Navy Department was to pay the steward a moderate sum each quarter. Under these arrangements, nine clinically sick patients were sent to the hospital. Other sick seamen were sent to a gunboat, which had been converted into a hospital ship.

A similar solution was applied in Savannah, Georgia. The sloop *Troup*, which was unfit for use as a cruising vessel, was converted into a hospital ship at the suggestion of Secretary Jones. In mid-October 1813, Jones was informed that during the previous three months there had never been less than 30 patients in the ship and that the number had now risen to 45. The nature of the illnesses was not reported. Later, when Jones wanted to move the ship to Wilmington, North Carolina, he was told that between sickness, desertion, and the discharge of men whose time had expired, there were too few able-bodied men on the station to navigate the schooner. Subsequently the secretary decided that the cost of providing hospital care to the men assigned to six armed barges at Sunbury, Georgia, was too high, and he ordered the sick sent to Savannah.

Farther south, at St. Marys, Georgia, there were additional health problems. Surgeon William Dandridge died in July 1812, leaving Surgeon's Mate William Baldwin with over 20 sick men to care for. When he overcame that crisis and was promoted, he secured the services of a civilian physician, Dr. Seaborn Jones Saffold, as his mate. Baldwin asked Secretary Jones to appoint Saffold surgeon's mate, pointing out that in addition to his qualifications, he was a native of the area. Instead, Jones sent Surgeon's Mate Hyde Ray to St. Marys. He did not work out, and in August 1814 Jones commissioned Saffold as a surgeon's mate.

The War of 1812 brought increased attention to the defenses on Lakes Erie and Ontario. Commodore Isaac Chauncey was given the responsibility for creating the naval forces to defend these lakes. Accordingly, he proceeded to Sacket's Harbor, New York, on Lake Ontario, where men who had gone ahead of him were transforming that location into an important base. To assist him with the medical aspects of his command, Chauncey turned to Dr. Walter W. Buchanan of Columbia College, who had served as a surgeon in the navy during the Quasi-War with France. Other naval medical officers were also ordered to Sacket's Harbor. In addition, army units were assembling at the base in anticipation of a campaign against British forces in Canada. A hospital was established at the base, and Buchanan attended the sick at the hospital as well as in the squadron of ships that were eventually stationed there. In general, most of the sick of the navy were treated in their ships, and only the more serious cases were sent to the hospital onshore. During the winter months, the ice on the lake prevented any naval activity. In March 1813, Chauncey reported to Secretary Jones that sickness had taken its toll among the marines assigned to him. The ships on Lake Ontario and Lake Erie required 300 marines in addition to those needed as guards, but Chauncey had only 39 marines who were fit for duty. The previous January, he was obliged to ask the army for sentinels for his squadron. Chauncey asked that 200 marines be sent to him by the spring.

When spring came, Buchanan and his medical colleagues had their hands full in caring for those who were wounded in the U.S. attack on York, Upper Canada, and in the British assault on Sacket's Harbor. That summer more than 25 percent of the crew in Chauncey's flagship was on the sick list, and aboard the ship *Madison*, 80 percent of the crew was ill. For the squadron as a whole, the sick list fluctuated between 10 and 20 percent of the force. Fortunately there were few deaths. The maneuvers and countermaneuvers that Chauncey and the British squadron engaged in never resulted in a naval battle, but throughout the war, Buchanan and his medical colleagues had to deal with routine medical problems.

In the meantime, another naval force had been built at Presque Isle on Lake Erie under the supervision of Oliver Hazard Perry. Medical officers were also being sent to that lake. Among them was a newly commissioned surgeon's mate named Usher Parsons. The diary that he kept of his service on the lake provides some glimpses into the medical environment on that front. Ordered to the naval base at Black Rock, near Buffalo, New York, in 1812, Parsons treated the health problems of sailors there, mainly fevers and dysentery, as well as the army wounded from the Battle of Queenston. Additional wounded arrived in November 1812 following an attack on an enemy position that was not supported with reinforcements. During the winter of 1812–1813, Parsons had a number of cases of pleurisy, which he treated by bleeding his patients. January brought other ailments, including three cases of pneumonia. In late February, Parsons noted in his diary that of the 25 men on the sick list, there were not more than two to whom the same treatment could be applied. March and April 1813 saw his sick list rise from 33 to 51 before dropping to 25.

Parsons was too busy at this time to record the complaints or the treatments. Many cases seem to have been related to dysentery. Summer brought more cases of diarrhea, dysentery, and fevers, and the sick list reached 70 on July 6. Perry himself was sick with what was called "lake fever," but he forced himself to continue the work of building his ships. The number of men on the sick list made it necessary to establish a new hospital in the county courthouse on Presque Isle. Later two additional hospitals were built in the area. These were probably simple wooden structures or tents that provided some shelter from the elements.

When the ships were completed and moved to the lake, Parsons was assigned to Perry's flagship, the *Lawrence*. Illness continued to plague the command. Between 2 and 5 September 1813, Parsons's patient load rose from 26 to 57, and four days later it reached 87. This was because the other medical men attached to the squadron were absent or ill. British and U.S. squadrons fought the battle of Lake Erie on 10 September, and during the fight Parsons was the only medical officer on duty in Perry's force. Out of a crew of 150, 31 were sick before the battle. During the engagement, seven were killed and 63 wounded. Working steadily and ignoring the noise and destruction in the ship, Parsons put tourniquets on the wounds and amputated six legs. The amputees were laid on the berth deck to recover. Four of them subsequently died from their wounds or from cannonballs crashing through the hull. Parsons himself narrowly escaped death. Through it all he did what he had to do immediately to save a life. The wounded were given cordials or alcoholic liquors and anodynes containing opiates that deadened the pain and allowed them to sleep. Years after the battle, Parsons realized that by delaying the operations until the patient's system had recovered from the shock of the injury, he had saved many lives.

Although the fighting ended in the afternoon of 10 September with a U.S. victory, there was no slackening in the demands for medical attention. Parsons had little time for sleep. By 12 September, he had finished dressing all the wounded in the *Lawrence*, and he now turned his attention to the 23 wounded in the *Niagara*. The next day the effects of his intense labor caught up with him, and Parsons became ill. Fortunately there were others who were ready to help with the wounded, including two British surgeons and two army doctors from Gen. William Henry Harrison's command. When he felt well enough, Parsons prepared an official report on the wounded. The battle had cost the Americans 27 killed and 96 wounded, and 22 of the dead and 61 of the wounded were aboard the *Lawrence*. British losses were 41 killed and 96 wounded.

Ten days after the battle, Parsons was able to resume his duties. The wounded were transported by ship to Presque

Isle, and the Americans were placed in the temporary hospital in the courthouse. The British wounded were treated in two of the captured ships that were brought to Presque Isle. Parsons continued to care for the wounded in the courthouse until the end of the year, when he was promoted and given a new assignment. He was assisted by a prominent local physician, Dr. John C. Wallace, who had earlier served as a medical officer in the army. Of the 96 men under the care of these two physicians, only three died.

In the summer of 1814, British military and naval forces invaded New York State by way of the Lake Champlain route. At Plattsburg, the British naval squadron was defeated by one under the command of Commodore Thomas Macdonough. The British lost more than 80 killed and 100 wounded, in contrast to Macdonough's casualties of 52 killed and 58 wounded. The U.S. wounded were cared for by the army's 33rd Infantry Regiment surgeon, Dr. John Briggs, who was in Macdonough's flagship during the battle. Additional care was provided by another army doctor named Stoddart and by navy surgeon's mate Gustavus R. Brown.

Late in 1814, the British launched a campaign to capture New Orleans. When they reached Villeré Plantation, 8 miles below the city, they found Andrew Jackson's men waiting for them behind bales of cotton. Some navy sailors served with Jackson's men, and the *Louisiana* used its 16 guns to protect the U.S. flank. Three navy medical officers served as volunteers with the army. One of these acted as the superintendent of the general hospital.

In addition to their service at sea and in shore installations, navy medical officers provided health care to the U.S. and British prisoners of war who were exchanged by means of cartel ships. The health of the Americans who were released was often poor, and the doctors assigned to the cartel ships did all that they could to provide some relief.

As near as can be ascertained from incomplete records, it seems likely that there were at least 300 combat-related deaths, that various diseases killed as many as 300, and that accidents accounted for at least another 100 deaths, not counting deaths on two ships that were lost after the formal ending of the war.

At the end of the war, there were 53 surgeons and 75 surgeon's mates on the rolls of the navy. Of this number, 14 surgeons and 68 mates were appointed during the war. The largest increase came in July 1813, when 22 were commissioned as mates and eight were promoted to surgeon. The demand for experienced medical men resulted in the promotion of 18 surgeon's mates to surgeon during the course of the conflict. Six surgeons and two mates died during the war but none as the result of enemy actions. Despite the war and the shortage of medical men at various stations, the secretary accepted the resignations of two surgeons and six mates.

—*Harold D. Langley*

Further Reading

Estes, J. Worth. *Dictionary of Protopharmacology: Therapeutic Practices, 1700–1850*. Canton, MA: Science History Publications, 1990.

Goldowsky, Seebert J. *Yankee Surgeon: The Life and Times of Usher Parsons, 1788–1868*. Boston: Francis A. Countway Library of Medicine, 1988.

Langley, Harold D. *Medicine in the Early U.S. Navy*. Baltimore: Johns Hopkins University Press, 1995.

MEIGS, FORT

Following the defeat and massacre of U.S. troops under the command of James Winchester at Frenchtown in January 1813, William Henry Harrison ordered the building of a fortification on a bluff overlooking Ohio's Maumee River rapids. The south bank location was strategic, affording a strong defensive position against British incursions into the Ohio country as well as providing a staging area for future U.S. offensive operations into Michigan Territory and Canada. Named in honor of Ohio's governor Return J. Meigs, the site was surveyed by chief engineer Charles Gratiot, with Eleazer Wood supervising construction. When Harrison departed the fort and Wood was assigned to assist with the rebuilding of Fort Stephenson at Lower Sandusky, Ohio, construction languished under militia general Joel Leftwich. With Wood's return, the large earth-and-timber-palisaded fortification, which included seven blockhouses and five artillery batteries along its perimeter, was completed by late April to enclose an area of almost 10 acres. The effort came none too soon, for a 2,000-strong British invasion force under the command of Henry Procter had departed Fort Malden and established a base camp downriver near the ruins of Fort Miami. Accompanying the combined force of British regulars and Canadian militiamen were more than 1,000 Indians led by Tecumseh.

Outnumbered, Harrison sent a messenger to Green Clay, whose 1,200 Kentucky militiamen were advancing from Defiance, Ohio. On 1 May, the British began their siege with ineffectual artillery fire against the well-built palisades. As Clay neared the fortification, he received instructions from Harrison to divide his men. The main force, under second in command William Dudley, successfully spiked the British batteries on the north side of the Maumee River but failed to disengage and enter the U.S. stockade as ordered. Dudley's detachment then disintegrated under a stiff British counterattack. On the south bank, Clay's column drove off assaulting Indians, while a detachment from the fort succeeded in spiking a British battery that had been established to the east of the stronghold. Without quick victory, Indians and Canadian militia began to leave the field. Procter, fearing that his lines of communication were endangered, lifted the siege and withdrew.

Clay assumed control of Fort Meigs from Harrison and, unlike Leftwich, maintained his command in a state of readiness. In late July 1813, Procter returned to the Maumee with a British force that included between 3,000 and 4,000 Indians. Though surprised at the sudden appearance of the numerically superior enemy, the Americans were prepared when the siege began on 21 July. Having encircled the stockade, Procter then sought to lure a U.S. detachment into the open by feigning battle along the Sandusky Road with an imaginary U.S. relief party. Clay, fearing ambush and realizing his strength lay behind the ramparts of Fort Meigs, overruled his officers and refused to send men out of the stockade. Unable to deceive the enemy and unwilling to risk a direct assault against the well-organized U.S. position, Procter marched his forces to do battle against the seemingly less formidable Fort Stephenson.

With the threat to interior Ohio diminished by British defeat at Lower Sandusky, Harrison ordered a smaller stockade built to replace the expansive fortification at the Maumee River rapids. By early September 1813, a new Fort Meigs, roughly 150 feet square with corner blockhouses and surrounding ditch, was completed. Ohio militiamen then maintained the stronghold until it was finally abandoned in May 1815. The original fort has been reconstructed by the Ohio Historical Society.

—*William E. Fischer, Jr.*

See also: Clay, Green; Harrison, William Henry; Procter, Henry; Tecumseh; Wood, Eleazer Derby

Further Reading

Gilpin, Alec R. *The War of 1812 in the Old Northwest.* East Lansing: Michigan State University Press, 1958.

Lindley, Harlow, ed. *Fort Meigs and the War of 1812: Orderly Book of Cushing's Company, 2nd U.S. Artillery, April, 1813–February, 1814, and Personal Diary of Captain Daniel Cushing, October, 1812–July, 1813.* Columbus: Ohio Historical Society, 1975.

"Mapping of Fort Meigs, The." *Northwest Ohio Quarterly* 58 (1986): 123–142.

Nelson, Larry L. *Men of Patriotism, Courage, and Enterprise:*

Fort Meigs in the War of 1812. Canton, OH: Daring Books, 1986.

MEIGS, RETURN JOHNATHAN
1765–1825
Governor of Ohio; postmaster general

Born in Connecticut, Return J. Meigs graduated from Yale and entered upon a career in law in Middletown, Connecticut. In 1802, he was appointed the chief justice of the state supreme court but held that position for only a year. In 1803, Pres. Thomas Jefferson appointed him to command all military forces in the upper Louisiana Territory. Shortly thereafter, he moved to the Michigan Territory, where he served for a short time as a judge before moving to Ohio. In 1808, he became U.S. Senator from Ohio but resigned that position to become governor in 1810.

As war loomed with Great Britain in 1812, Meigs still held the position of governor of Ohio, and in early 1812, he became increasingly concerned about the security of the state. Indian attacks north of the Ohio River had accelerated since William Henry Harrison's campaign against Prophet's Town the previous November, and Meigs repeatedly wrote to Washington insisting that the Madison administration assign more importance to the defense of the Northwest. In March, Pres. James Madison responded to Meigs's pleas by authorizing the governor to call up volunteers to be placed under the command of Michigan territorial governor William Hull. Hull was to take the Ohio troops to Detroit, seen by most as the first line of defense for the entire Northwest.

On 6 April 1812, Meigs sent out the call for volunteers to assemble at Dayton at the end of the month. Hull arrived in early May, but because he was awaiting the arrival of regular troops, he did not take command of the Ohio volunteers until 25 May. On the appointed day, the troops were paraded with much pomp and then lined up by regiment for patriotic exhortations by both Meigs and Hull. Hull did not know that by turning over these volunteers, Meigs had saddled him with a controversy involving seniority among the Ohio colonels that Meigs had been unable to solve.

Hull marched off to disaster, while Meigs continued to organize his militia forces in case they would be needed in the coming campaign. After the war started, Meigs heard that Hull had retreated out of Canada and was in jeopardy, so the governor began preparations to take his militia to Detroit's aid. Before he could depart, however, news arrived of Hull's surrender. Meigs became especially vigilant in seeing to the security of Ohio's now exposed frontier.

To improve frontier defenses, Meigs and Kentucky governor Isaac Shelby supported the appointment of William Henry Harrison over James Winchester to command all forces in the Northwest. Both governors believed that Harrison would have more success with the militia forces in the region than the unpopular regular officer Winchester. Ultimately the governors' efforts prevailed, and Harrison received the appointment. Perhaps in gratitude for Meigs's labors, Harrison named the fort at the rapids of the Maumee River Fort Meigs.

When in the spring of 1813, Meigs heard that Harrison was in need of additional men, he personally marched part of the Ohio militia to rendezvous with Harrison on the Lower Sandusky in May. When Meigs arrived, however, Harrison mistakenly believed that he had enough men and sent the governor and his force home. Harrison, planning his invasion of Canada, discovered he did not have as many men as he had thought, so he sent a call to Kentucky and Ohio for additional militia forces. Meigs, incensed at the considerable and pointless expense the state had borne the previous spring, sent word to Harrison that Ohio troops would be sent to him only if Harrison paid them in advance. Lacking such resources, Harrison refused the services of Ohio in the upcoming campaign. Ironically, it was this campaign that resulted in the Battle of the Thames and security for Ohio for the remainder of the war.

In 1814, President Madison appointed Meigs to the position of postmaster general. Following the war, he would accept several government appointments, including agent to the Cherokee Indians. Meigs returned to Ohio upon leaving the Cherokee agency and died there in 1825.

—*Jeanne T. Heidler and David S. Heidler*

See also: Harrison, William Henry; Hull, William; Meigs, Fort; Ohio
Further Reading
Knopf, Richard C. *Return Johnathan Meigs and the War of 1812.* Columbus, Ohio: Anthony Wayne Board, 1957.

MERRITT, WILLIAM HAMILTON
1793–1862
Canadian militia officer

Born in Upper Canada, William H. Merritt was educated in Newark, studied surveying, and was running a farm and store by the age of 16. When the war with the United States began, he joined the Niagara Light Dragoons, which were organized by his father, and served in that unit until it was abolished in the spring of 1813. Shortly thereafter, Gen. John Vincent made Merritt the captain of the 50-man Provincial Dragoons.

In his new position, Merritt's primary job was to act as a scout for British forces on the Niagara Peninsula and to ferret out Canadian turncoats who were helping the Americans. Because of the wide variety of his assignments, Merritt saw action in a number of engagements. He accompanied the retreat of the British from Fort George in May 1813, commanded his party of horsemen at the Battle of Stoney Creek on 6 June 1813, and was sent back to the battlefield the next day to look for the missing General Vincent.

Perhaps one of the most disturbing engagements in which Merritt had a part occurred on 8 July 1813, when he was sent with a party of Indians back to the vicinity of Fort George to retrieve medicine that the British had hidden nearby. When his Indian allies happened upon a party of about 40 U.S. soldiers, they killed or captured all of them. The surviving Americans begged Merritt to save them from the Indians, but there was nothing he could do to prevent his allies from killing them all.

Throughout the remainder of 1813, Merritt continued his scouting activities and was one of the first military men on the scene in Newark after the Americans had burned the town in December 1813. With the Americans temporarily out of Upper Canada, Merritt had little to do until Jacob Brown's invasion in the spring of 1814. Merritt joined the British forces that rushed to the Niagara Frontier and participated in the Battle of Lundy's Lane during Brown's retreat to Fort Erie. Merritt was captured during the battle, however, and did not see combat again for the remainder of the war.

Following the war, Merritt became a prominent Canadian businessman. He promoted canal construction in Canada and eventually became an important political figure. He served as the president of the Executive Council of the Province of Canada and on the Legislative Council of Canada.

—*Jeanne T. Heidler and David S. Heidler*

See also: George, Fort; Lundy's Lane, Battle of; Newark, Upper Canada; Stoney Creek, Battle of; Vincent, John
Further Reading
Merritt, Jedediah. *Biography of the Honorable William H. Merritt, M.P., of Lincoln, District of Niagara.* St. Catherines, Ont.: E. S. Leavenworth, 1875.

MIAMI INDIANS

The Miami tribe probably originated in Wisconsin but was living between the upper Wabash and Great Miami Rivers, Ohio, by the early nineteenth century. They were also called Twightwee ("call of the crane") and originally were divided into six distinct lineages that were sometimes mistaken for separate tribes. The Wea and Piankashaw sects were the only ones remaining by 1812. The Piankashaw mostly dwelt in the lower Wabash Valley, where they were in frequent contact with the Illinois tribes and with Spanish and English traders from the Mississippi River. The Wea lived farther up the Wabash and often worked with the Shawnee, Wyandots, and Ottawas. They controlled the strategic Tippecanoe Valley, gateway from the Ohio country to the upper Great Lakes region. From the European point of view, the Miamis could limit or stop communications between Louisiana and Canada and could block the westward movement of settlers coming down the Ohio, especially if they cooperated with the Shawnee. In the last half of the eighteenth century, they became dependent on the Shawnee; during the Revolution the British solicited the support of their chief, Little Turtle, and the Americans strove to keep them neutral.

In the decades before the War of 1812, the Miami were widely regarded as the chief obstacle to white expansion in the Northwest. Little Turtle masterminded the defeats of Josiah Harmar and Arthur St. Clair before he was superseded in the Ohio country by Blue Jacket. Twenty-five Miamis were among the warriors gathered at Fort Dearborn in August 1812, but they refused to join Nathan Heald's attack on the Potawatomi on the shore of Lake Michigan (15 August). In the fall of 1812, William Henry Harrison attacked Miami villages on the Mississinewa River because he regarded them as a threat to U.S. supply routes. In December, some of the villages were burned by Lt. Col. John B. Campbell, who was operating out of Greenville.

An undetermined number of Miami warriors followed Tecumseh to Canada in 1813. Once Henry Procter began his retreat from Amherstburg, the Miamis, many Wyandots, and Delawares abandoned the British and offered to make peace with Harrison. Thus the tribe as a whole was able to participate in the general Indian armistice signed by Harrison on 14 October, after Tecumseh was killed at the Battle of the Thames. At the Greenville treaty conference (8 July 1814), they pledged loyalty to the United States. A considerable number of Miami warriors continued to fight for the British, however. Although the United States made a separate treaty with the Miami after the war, their military and strategic importance was then practically nil. Most of the tribe eventually settled in northeastern Oklahoma, but some remain in Indiana and Ohio.

—*Thomas S. Martin*

See also: Harrison, William Henry; Tecumseh; Thames, Battle of the

Further Reading

Anson, Bert. *The Miami Indians.* Norman: University of Oklahoma Press, 1970.

Calloway, Colin G. *Crown and Calumet: British-Indian Relations, 1783–1815.* Norman: University of Oklahoma Press, 1987.

Gilpin, Alec R. *The War of 1812 in the Old Northwest.* East Lansing: Michigan State University Press, 1958.

MICHIGAN TERRITORY

Created as a separate territory in 1805, Michigan was still sparsely populated during the War of 1812. Governor William Hull, the territory's first and, as of 1812, only governor, oversaw an area around Detroit and a small strip of land in the eastern part of the territory. When the war began, the territory contained not quite 5,000 white inhabitants and an undetermined number of Indians.

In September 1811, Governor Hull took an extended trip to his home in Massachusetts and while there learned of the Battle of Tippecanoe. Concerned about what this renewal of open hostilities between Indians and whites in the Northwest portended for Michigan, he traveled to Washington to urge Pres. James Madison to increase the defenses of the territory. He especially insisted that the defenses around Detroit be strengthened and recommended the addition of U.S. naval forces on Lake Erie. The people of Michigan, along with acting governor Reuben Attwater, added their voices with a memorial to Washington asking for more regulars and fortifications.

In March 1812, President Madison bowed to part of these demands (the staunch Democratic Republican Madison was not yet prepared to spend money on ships for Lake Erie) by authorizing Hull to raise an army in Ohio and march it to Detroit. The call went out to Governor Return Johnathan Meigs in March to muster Ohio volunteers for Hull to collect when he passed through Ohio on the way back to Michigan. In the meantime and after much hesitation, Hull agreed to take command of the army in the Northwest.

The war had not yet erupted with Great Britain, yet preparations were well underway, not only for the defense of Michigan but also for a possible invasion of Upper Canada. President Madison informed Hull while the latter was in Washington that in the event of war, Hull and his army were to serve as one of three prongs of an offensive against Canada. He was to be ready to move when word of the declaration arrived in Michigan.

Hull arrived in Ohio in early May and took command of the Ohio volunteers on 25 May 1812. Following the arrival of regulars in June, he marched his army to Detroit. By then, the British at Fort Malden had heard about the declaration of war of 18 June and were more than prepared when he slowly began his invasion of Canada in July 1812. Hull's caution, perhaps born of his advanced age, persuaded him that the British in Upper Canada were far stronger than they were, and he retreated to Detroit. The British under Gen. Isaac Brock followed and began a siege of Detroit. Following Hull's surrender of the town, fort, and his army on 16 August 1812, the Michigan Territory effectively fell under British control.

General Brock issued a proclamation to the Michigan Territory asserting British control over it and calling on all citizens to relinquish public property in return for guaranteed safety of their private property. Brock then departed, leaving command of the territory to Col. Henry Procter. Over the next year, Procter used Michigan as a base of operations for offensives into the remainder of the Northwest. Constantly concerned over the security of the territory, Procter ordered a number of U.S. citizens, particularly some living in Detroit, out of the region.

From the beginning of British occupation of the Michigan Territory, the U.S. military forces in the Northwest had as their goal to reclaim it. When William Henry Harrison assumed command of the Army of the Northwest, he began the construction of a string of forts to establish a supply and communication line for a campaign against the British in Michigan.

In January 1813, Brig. Gen. James Winchester, hoping to dislodge the British from at least part of the territory, advanced against Harrison's instructions to the River Raisin to protect the inhabitants of Frenchtown. After scattering a small British and Indian force at the river on 18 January 1813, Winchester's army was surprised by a larger British and Indian army under Procter on 22 January. Much of Winchester's army was killed or captured, and many of the U.S. wounded and prisoners were later killed by Procter's Indian allies.

Winchester's attempt to regain a foothold in Michigan was the last U.S. attempt to retake the territory until Oliver Hazard Perry gained control of Lake Erie in September

1813. Following Perry's victory, Procter retreated into Upper Canada, allowing the United States under Harrison to reoccupy the territory. At the end of September, Harrison reestablished civil government in Michigan before beginning his pursuit of Procter into Upper Canada. The subsequent defeat of the British and the death of Tecumseh at the Battle of the Thames made the Michigan Territory fairly secure for the remainder of the war.

On 29 October 1813, President Madison appointed Lewis Cass the new governor of Michigan Territory. During the last year of the war, Cass and the military commanders in the territory sent out patrols and raids from Detroit, keeping the Northwest free of major combat during that time.

—Jeanne T. Heidler and David S. Heidler

See also: Brock, Isaac; Detroit, Surrender of; Frenchtown, Battles of; Harrison, William Henry; Hull, William; Procter, Henry; Tecumseh; Thames, Battle of the; Tippecanoe, Battle of; Winchester, James

Further Reading
Hamil, Fred C. "Michigan in the War of 1812." *Michigan History* 44 (1960): 257–291.

MICHILIMACKINAC, FORT

The British garrisoned Fort Michilimackinac, in present-day Michigan, after defeating the French in the French and Indian War (1763). The fort soon became the gathering place for western tribes to bring in furs and receive presents distributed by the British Indian department. Two years after Jay's Treaty of 1794, Britain turned Fort Michilimackinac over to the United States. On 17 July 1812, the garrison there of 54 U.S. troops commanded by Lt. Porter Hanks, ignorant of the declaration of war, was surprised by a force of British regulars, voyageurs, and Indians from St. Joseph's led by Capt. Charles Roberts. Hanks capitulated. Because Gov.-Gen. Sir George Prevost believed its influence extended to New Orleans and the Pacific, the British repaired the fort. Throughout 1813–1814, however, the garrison was usually on half rations as Indian appetites placed an enormous strain on sutlers' supplies.

On 26 July 1814, a combined U.S. army-navy expedition of five ships and 760 troops, led by Commodore Arthur Sinclair, naval commander on Lake Erie, and Lt. Col. George Croghan, the hero of Fort Stephenson, arrived to retake Michilimackinac. By May 1814, the new British commander, Lt. Col. Robert McDouall, Glengarry Regiment, an 18-year veteran, had brought reinforcements consisting of 90 men from the Royal Newfoundland Regiment, several shipwrights, 21 sailors under Lt. Newdigate Poyntz of the Royal Navy, 11 artillerymen, four field guns, and 29 bateaux of supplies for the half-starved garrison. McDouall divided his small forces to send a party to recapture Prairie du Chien (Wisconsin) that had been taken by a U.S. force. That left him with 140 regular troops.

Michilimackinac's fur-trading had continued even during the war. The well-connected fur trader John Jacob Astor of New York sent a vessel, authorized by Prevost as a cartel under the French flag, into the upper lakes to retrieve furs his agent Toussaint Pothier had stored there and return them to Buffalo. Arthur Sinclair, fearing spies, was most irritated by the Astor gambit.

The U.S. attack commenced on 4 August 1814 on an island that Sinclair regarded as "by nature as strong as Gibraltar; being a perpendicular Rock on three sides and an impenetrable forest intersected with deep ravines, apparently formed by a volcanic eruption, on the fourth." The British had two forts, one commanding the other, the lowest of which was over 100 feet above the water. The attack was repulsed by a creditable defense mounted by McDouall's garrison of 140 men and Indian allies, none of whom suffered casualties. Croghan's attacking force lost 12 dead, including Maj. Andrew Hunter Holmes and Capt. Thomas Van Horne of the 19th Infantry; 59 wounded, of whom seven later died; and two missing. Sinclair reported that Croghan's force was onshore about two hours and "came off with nearly one tenth man killed or wounded." The northern Indians remained with the British until peace was restored, and the fort was returned when U.S. forces gave up Fort Malden, Amherstburg.

—Frederick C. Drake

See also: Croghan, George; McDouall, Robert; Prairie du Chien
Further Reading
Andrews, Roger. *Old Fort Mackinac on the Hill of History.* Menominee, WI: Herlad-Leander Press, 1938: 123–145.
Cruikshank, Ernest A. "The Capture of Mackinac, 1812," and "The Defence of Mackinac." *Canadian History Readings* 1 (1900): 158–163, 195–201.
Dunnigan, Brian. "The Battle of Mackinac Island." *Michigan History* 59 (1975): 239–254.
———. "The British Army at Mackinac, 1812–1815." *Reports in Mackinac History and Archaeology* 7 (1980).
Havinghurst, Walter. *Three Flags at the Straits: The Forts of Mackinac.* Englewood Cliffs, NJ: Prentice-Hall, 1966: 115–130.
Kellogg, Louis Phelps. "The Capture of Mackinac in 1812."
Proceedings of the State Historical Society of Wisconsin 60 (1912): 124–145.
Schermerhorn, Hazel Fenton. "Mackinac Island under French, English and American." *Michigan History Magazine* 14 (summer 1930): 367–380.
Van Fleet, J. A. *Old and New Mackinac.* Ann Arbor: Courier Steam Printing, 1870.

MILAN DECREE

Responding to what he characterized as illegal blockades of the European coast from Brest to the Elbe, Napoleon I issued economic decrees from the capitals of conquered countries to enforce continental economic conformity. From Berlin, he declared a blockade of the British Isles on 21 November 1806, which prohibited any exportation of English goods to the Continent through any port under French control. The British government's response was to issue additional Orders in Council that increased blockades and stipulated that France and her allies would have no trade but through Britain. Royal Navy captains and commanders were authorized to visit, search, and bring into port for the assessment of tariffs all vessels, including neutral or allied ones, transporting goods to continental ports and markets controlled by Napoleonic forces.

Napoleon retaliated with a decree, issued in Milan on 17 December 1807, stating that vessels visited or inspected by British men-of-war, with ship's papers endorsed by Royal Navy officers, or that had touched at a British port, were to be seized as English, whatever their flag.

Napoleon's economic warfare utilized the Continent's economic resources against the British. Initial responses included the Austrian government's suing for peace and Napoleon's Tilsit agreement with Russian czar Alexander I on 25 June 1807. The decree fell heavily on neutral traders, especially the United States. Eventually such economic warfare caused a serious break in 1812 between Napoleon and Alexander I; by then the United States was at war with Britain.

—Frederick C. Drake

See also: Berlin Decree; Cadore Letter; Diplomacy; Napoleon I
Further Reading
Crouzet, François. "Bilan de l'économie britannique pendant les guerres de la Révolution et de l'empire." *Revue Historique* 234 (1965): 71–110.
———. "Groupes de pression et politique de blocus: Remar-

ques sur les origines des Ordres en Conseil de novembre 1807." *Revue Historique* 228 (1962): 45–72.

———. *L'Economie Britannique et le Blocus Continental, 1806–1813*. 2 vols., 2nd ed. Paris: Economica, 1987.

———. "Wars, Blockade, and Economic Change in Europe, 1792–1815." *Journal of Economic History* 24, no. 4 (1964): 567–588.

Harvey, A. D. "European Attitudes to Britain during the French Revolutionary and Napoleonic Era." *History* 63 (1978): 356–365.

Hecksher, Eli F. *The Continental System: An Economic Interpretation*, ed. H. Westerguard, trans. C. S. Fearenside. Oxford: Clarendon Press, 1922.

Vandal, Albert. *Napoleon et Alexander 1er: L'alliance russe sous le premier empire*. Vol. 2. Paris: Plon, 1891–1896: 441–445.

MILITIA CONTROVERSY, THE NEW ENGLAND

In April 1812, the Democratic Republican majority in the U.S. Congress enacted various legislation to mobilize the nation for war with Great Britain. One of these measures authorized Pres. James Madison to raise 100,000 militiamen from the respective states. Although within New England this requirement was quite unpopular, one-fifth of those proposed forces was to be supplied by the five states of the region.

On 22 June 1812, four days after the formal declaration of war, Maj. Gen. Henry Dearborn, commander of the First U.S. Military District, sent requisition dispatches to the governors of Massachusetts, Connecticut, and Rhode Island. He requested that their states jointly muster 41 militia companies, which would join his command in Providence, Rhode Island. But Dearborn soon learned that none of those state governments intended to comply. Governor Caleb Strong of Massachusetts spearheaded this campaign to obstruct the national war effort.

Strong was the titular leader of the Federalist Party in Massachusetts in 1812. An adroit politician, Strong knew that antiwar sentiments were vehement in Massachusetts, so he felt confident in assuming an obdurate stance. On 5 August, Strong wrote to Secretary of War William Eustis, stating his reasons for refusing Dearborn's requisition. The governor began with the disingenuous statement that he was surprised that the Madison administration thought a muster was needed. It was his belief that the British did not possess sufficient military forces to mount a major invasion into New England from Canada. Moreover, none of the states from his region intended to launch a similar incursion into Canadian territory.

Strong and his advisers also argued that the Massachusetts militiamen lawfully could be commanded only by state militia officers. Accordingly, these troops would not be placed under the authority of the federal War Department. Strong believed that if he ceded control of the militia to national officials, he would be powerless to prevent its being dispatched elsewhere, including Canada.

The Massachusetts constitution required that the governor solicit a definitive written opinion from the state's highest court when confronting an important legal or constitutional problem. Consequently, Strong submitted two questions to the justices of the Massachusetts Supreme Court. First, he asked if any of the exigencies cited in Article I, Section 8 of the federal Constitution applied in the present situation. Second, the governor inquired whether the militia, once in federal service, could be commanded by any national official other than the president of the United States.

Chief Justice Theophilus Parsons, Justice Samuel Sewell, and Justice Isaac Parker collaborated on the final opinion. All three were associated with the ultraconservative wing of the Federalist Party. Their finding strongly reflected the states' rights sentiments ascendant among New England Federalists by the 1810s.

Parsons and his colleagues opened the treatise with the comment that their state constitution vested with the governor the ultimate power of command over the militia. They conceded that the national government had the right to activate such troops when any of three explicit constitutional exigencies existed, to wit: suppressing insurrections; maintaining domestic tranquillity; and repelling foreign invasions. The Massachusetts Supreme Court did not believe any of these emergencies were operative. Moreover, neither Madison nor Congress possessed an inherent discretionary power to determine if such conditions existed. The justices declared that under most circumstances the militia could only be commanded by state officers. The sole exception was when the president of the United States assumed personal command over forces in the field. But they did not concede that Madison (or any other U.S. president) was empowered to delegate such authority to a designated military subordinate.

Governor Strong conveyed this ruling to the Massachusetts General Court (state legislature), where it was well received. This opinion by Parsons and his colleagues served as the intellectual basis for their state's continued refusal to place the militia under national control throughout much of "Mr. Madison's War."

Unlike his counterpart in Massachusetts, Governor William Jones of Rhode Island did not use any refined legal argument when refusing to comply with Dearborn's requisition. For instance, he made no issue over Rhode Island troops serving under federal officers. In his 22 August 1812 letter to Eustis, Jones declared that the militia would be mobilized only after he was personally satisfied that the constitutional grounds sanctioning such an action actually existed.

In late August, Governor Roger Griswold of Connecticut summoned the state legislature into special session to discuss this same issue. A select legislative committee prepared a written summary that became the state's official position for the next several years. These lawmakers refused to accept the proposition that Connecticut militiamen would become "standing troops" in a national army. Those soldiers were an important symbol of state sovereignty. Like many other New Englanders, the members of the Connecticut General Assembly suspected that Madison had ulterior motives for summoning the militia. The various state divisions, they thought, would be used in a forthcoming invasion of Canada. Accordingly, Griswold and the majority of the state legislators would not allow their troops to participate in an "offensive war."

In August 1812, the state governments of Massachusetts, Rhode Island, and Connecticut refused to commit their militia forces into federal service. In essence, they believed that the War of 1812 was a costly policy mistake and sought to remain aloof from all its adverse effects. Since these states believed that any invasion into British Canada was unjustified, they refused to subject their "citizen soldiers" to the rigors of an overland northern march during the late autumn months. Of course, many living New Englanders bitterly recalled the abortive American invasion into Quebec Province in late 1775, the first year of the Revolution. Strong and others were determined to avoid another such martial fiasco in 1812.

—*Miles S. Richards*

See also: Chittenden, Martin; Griswold, Roger; Jones, William; Militia in the War of 1812; Strong, Caleb

Further Reading

Banner, James M., Jr. *To the Hartford Convention: The Federalists and the Origins of Party Politics in Massachusetts, 1789–1815.* New York: Alfred Knopf, 1970.

Morison, Samuel Eliot. *The Life and Letters of Harrison Gray Otis, Federalist, 1765–1848.* 2 vols. Boston and New York: Houghton Mifflin Company, 1913.

MILITIA IN THE WAR OF 1812

Both the United States and Britain relied heavily on militia and volunteer forces during the War of 1812.

The United States used militia out of necessity. In one sense, it was the only way to provide the necessary number of men to prosecute the war. Yet the reliance on militia stemmed mainly from the long-held belief that the citizen soldier was the best protection against threats to the republic that might be posed by a large regular military establishment.

In the United States, dependence on militia as the first line of defense had been a controversial subject since the end of the American Revolution. When a group of George Washington's officers at Newburgh, New York, touted a military coup as a way to redress grievances against Congress, the perceived threat posed by the so-called Newburgh Conspiracy caused many in the government to advocate the complete elimination of a regular military establishment. Even when military necessity on the frontier brought about the creation of a small regular force, the militia remained the country's primary mode of defense.

Before the War of 1812, critics argued that the lack of training and the states' continued control of militia forces made them virtually useless in an actual war. These critics worked tirelessly—though not very effectively—in the two decades before the war to bring about some type of reform of the system. Henry Knox, secretary of war under President Washington, attempted to bring about a classification of militia by age. He also proposed establishing a system of standardized, routine training and having the federal government supply weapons. The best that Congress would do was pass the Uniform Militia Act of 1792, which required every state to maintain militia forces consisting of all able-bodied free males between the ages of 18 and 45, with no provision for any classification by age. This act provided no means for enforcement, and each militiaman was expected to provide his own arms. For those who viewed centralized government with growing suspicion, especially those who would become the Democratic Republicans, the Uniform Militia Act was a victory. For military preparedness, however, it was an empty gesture.

When Thomas Jefferson became president in 1801, he gradually came to see the need for a more organized, efficient military establishment. The tense world situation during the latter part of Jefferson's first term became full-blown European war during his second. Confronting the possibility of U.S. involvement in the conflict, Jefferson recommended to Congress at the end of 1805 that it adopt a classification system for state militias, dividing them into four age categories, with those men between the ages of 21 and 25 expected to serve the most frequently. Although the Senate passed a bill incorporating the president's suggestions, the measure never came to a vote in the House. The most the House was willing to give the president toward strengthening the military was to renew its 1803 authorization for him to instruct governors to hold militia quotas in readiness.

As relations with Great Britain worsened, Jefferson's successor James Madison had similar difficulties persuading Congress to grant him greater latitude over state forces. In 1810, Congress ignored his request for funds for training militia officers. In January 1812, he failed to move through Congress a measure that would have allowed him to raise 50,000 volunteers from the states. Enough senators objected to what they viewed as the president's attempt to bypass state control of the militia that the bill was voted down. As war loomed in the spring of that year, federal recruiting officers often found themselves competing with their militia counterparts for the same people, resulting in tremendous hostility between the two groups. Some militia officers refused to allow federal recruiters near militia encampments.

Militia service was of much shorter duration than regular service, so most men naturally preferred it. Consequently, throughout the war the government had to rely on militia not only to supplement regulars but frequently to serve instead of them. Even when militiamen performed well, reliance on them proved to be a serious handicap to U.S. operations. Their short enlistments made adequate preparation and execution of long-distance campaigns virtually impossible. Madison and his secretaries of war urged Congress to give them more flexibility in the use of militia and greater control over those forces that were called up. The best Madison could get from Congress was a measure at the end of 1813 that gave the president more power to punish militiamen who did not fulfill their terms of service.

Secretary of War James Monroe nevertheless disregarded congressional reluctance to impinge upon state control of militia when, in the fall of 1814, he tried to get Congress to implement some form of conscription from the militia. Monroe apparently believed that patriotic enthusiasm would outweigh congressmen's concern for their constituents. He proposed a measure to organize all militiamen between 18 and 45 into 100-man groups and then conscript four men from each group into existing units. He offered as an alternative that all state militias be classified by age and that the president be given the power to conscript parts of each class. Congress disliked both options and refused to enact either of them. Thus the U.S. militia remained essentially unchanged in organization throughout the war, and the national government lacked any effective mechanism to compel state militias to cooperate with regular forces.

This lack of centralized control was probably most felt in New England, where the governors of Massachusetts, Rhode Island, Connecticut, and occasionally Vermont refused to allow their militias to serve under regular officers.

At the beginning of the war, they even refused to call up their militias at the request of regular officers. These disputes remained unresolved at the war's end. The New England militia were among the best-trained in the nation, and their failure to provide support to the northern campaigns partially contributed to the failure of U.S. offensives in that theater.

The performance of the militia was mixed. The lack of training and discipline among the men was sometimes a problem. Yet frequently poor leadership from officers in both militia and regular ranks was responsible for the militia's poor performance in battles and campaigns. Early in the war, many regular general officers were overly cautious and knew little about leading militia forces. However, some of the most successful officers to emerge during the war came from state militias. Leaders like William Henry Harrison, Andrew Jackson, and Jacob Brown demonstrated that not only could militia be effectively utilized, but also that they could actually be the backbone of a campaign.

In spite of these successes, the overall impression at the end of the war was that reliance on militia had been a failure and that such reliance should be avoided in the future. Militia failures would be recited so often that they became a litany: the militia had not reinforced the regulars at Queenston in October 1812; the Kentucky militia had perpetrated a massacre after a lamentable performance at the Battle of Frenchtown in January 1813; and the centerpiece was reference to the infamous "Bladensburg Races" of August 1814 that opened Washington to British occupation and destruction. Easily forgotten then were militia achievements in the Creek War, the enthusiastic support of militias for William Henry Harrison's campaign into Canada in October 1813, and the performance of the militia forces at Baltimore (many of whom just a month before had run away at Bladensburg) in September 1814.

Given the political climate of the United States, the lingering fear of professional armies, and lack of conscription, the U.S. government had no choice during the War of 1812 but to rely on its militia forces. The British in Canada were in a similar position, though for different reasons. The British were really fighting two completely different wars between 1812 and 1814. The war in Europe commanded most of Great Britain's attention and manpower, so the British had no choice but to use Canadian militia forces in their war against the United States.

Militia forces in Canada had a long history that stretched back to the earliest days of New France. By the eighteenth century, these forces had fallen into a disorganized state and were not utilized much during the French and Indian War. Following the American Revolution, the British attempted to reorganize and recreate militia forces in Canada as a first line of defense along the border with their erstwhile southern colonies, now calling themselves the United States.

During the period immediately preceding the War of 1812, various British officers such as Isaac Brock worked especially hard to organize Canadian militia units, with mixed results. Those units formed out of areas settled by Loyalist refugees from the United States proved to be the most enthusiastic. Units from other areas suffered from widespread desertions and even saw some of their number enlist in the U.S. invasion force when William Hull entered Canada. Even with these problems, almost half of Brock's army that invaded the United States and secured the surrender of Detroit consisted of Canadian militiamen.

With the repeated attempts by the United States to stage an invasion of Canada, desertion proved to be the biggest problem afflicting the British use of militia forces. Pleas from home that were either urgent or routine beckoned men away from the field. For example, the simple necessities of farm chores during the fall harvest season meant that no British commander could ever be sure that he would have adequate militia units to repel a U.S. attack.

To solve the desertion problem, the British decided to recruit long-term volunteers whose choice to enlist would make them less likely to desert. Also, they could be more adequately trained than short-term militiamen. In February 1813, what was referred to as a Volunteer Militia Battalion was created to serve for the duration of the war. The only problem then became persuading men that this type of service was worthwhile. Recruiting remained stubbornly slow, though this battalion did see valuable service, especially in Brig. Gen. John Vincent's efforts to keep the U.S. invading force bottled up around Fort George in the summer of 1813.

Like those of the United States, Canadian militia forces were present in virtually every major engagement of the War of 1812. In addition to their combat duty, they also provided a number of other invaluable services to the British cause in Canada, ranging from garrison duty to fortification construction and repair. Both the United States and Great Britain, sometimes quite reluctantly, relied on militia in the War of 1812. To the British, this reliance stemmed entirely from necessity because of the tremendous drain on British military resources brought on by the Napoleonic wars. The United States, on the other hand, although certainly needing militia forces to sustain the war effort, used these men also because of the continued belief that a large regular establishment threatened the security and ideals of the republic.

—*Jeanne T. Heidler and David S. Heidler*

See also: Baltimore, Battle of; Bladensburg, Battle of; Brock, Isaac; Detroit, Surrender of; Frenchtown, Battles of; George, Fort; Harrison, William Henry; Hull, William; Jackson, Andrew; Militia Controversy, The New England; Monroe, James; Queenston, Battle of; Vincent, John

Further Reading

Mahon, John K. *History of the Militia and the National Guard.* New York: Macmillan, 1982.

Stanley, George F. G. "The Contribution of the Canadian Militia during the War." In Philip P. Mason, ed., *After Tippecanoe: Some Aspects of the War of 1812.* East Lansing: Michigan State University Press, 1963: 28–48.

MILLER, JAMES
1776–1851
U.S. officer

James Miller was born 25 April 1776, in Peterborough, New Hampshire. After attending Williams College, he studied law and was admitted to the bar in his native state in 1803. Gaining some military experience by serving as a captain in the New Hampshire militia, Miller was commissioned a major in the Fourth Regiment of U.S. Infantry in 1808. Promoted to lieutenant colonel in 1810, he remained in the East until 1811 when the regiment, commanded by Col. John P. Boyd, was ordered to Vincennes, Indiana Territory. There Miller and the regiment joined the militia and volunteer force being formed by Indiana territorial governor William Henry Harrison, who planned to move his force against the Indians at Prophet's Town on the Tippecanoe River near present-day Lafayette, Indiana. Miller was unable to participate in the Battle of Tippecanoe due to illness.

During the spring of 1812, the Fourth Regiment was ordered to Ohio to join Brig. Gen. William Hull on his march to Detroit. Boyd had returned east, leaving Miller in command of the regiment. War was declared while the army was en route. On 12 July 1812, the U.S. army crossed from Detroit into Canada. A detachment under Ohio militia colonel Lewis Cass and Miller opened the road to the British at Fort Malden near Amherstburg, but Hull ordered the detachment to return. There followed nearly a month of inactivity that allowed the initiative to swing toward the British.

On 8 August, Miller was dispatched with 600 men to open communications south of Detroit to the River Raisin at present-day Monroe, Michigan, where provisions were being brought. On the ninth, at approximately 4:00 P.M., as the Americans reached the Indian village of Maguaga, the advance troops were ambushed by a British and Indian force of approximately 525 men. Miller brought up the remainder of his troops and led a charge. The British soon withdrew from the conflict, leaving their Indian allies (under the control of the Shawnee leader Tecumseh) to contest the field with the Americans. Finally the Indians were forced to withdraw, with the Americans in pursuit. Instead of immediately pushing onward to the River Raisin, Miller requested reinforcements and additional provisions. Hull then sent orders directing the force to return to Detroit.

The militia officers by now were convinced of Hull's incompetence. They tried to persuade Miller, who, next to Hull, was the most senior regular army officer present, to remove the general and assume command. Miller, however, was unwilling to take this drastic measure. In the meantime, British major general Isaac Brock moved his force up, surrounded Detroit, and called for the fort's surrender. Fearing a massacre by the Indians, Hull capitulated on 16 August. Miller was paroled and in 1813 was exchanged for a British officer. He spent the remainder of that year participating in the futile U.S. campaign against Montreal.

In 1814, Miller was promoted to colonel of the 21st Regiment and was involved in the Niagara campaign. After capturing Fort Erie and routing the English and Indians at Chippewa, the Americans confronted the British at Lundy's Lane on 25 July. During the battle, Miller was ordered by Maj. Gen. Jacob Brown to take a hill from enemy artillery that was threatening the U.S. force. Miller responded with a reply that was to become famous: "I'll try, sir." Leading 300 men, Miller advanced and in furious hand-to-hand fighting drove the British from the hill. The capture of this fortified position and its retention during repeated counterattacks constituted the battle's pivotal point.

After the Americans held their ground without dispute for an hour, General Brown ordered a withdrawal, falling back to Fort Erie. After being reinforced, the British army laid siege to the fort on August 3. On September 17, Brown ordered a sallying attack upon the British lines, with Miller commanding the right column. Miller's attack, in combination with that of the other corps, carried the whole line of British entrenchments and forced them to abandon the siege.

The United States rewarded Miller for his part in the campaign. On 3 November 1814, Congress voted Miller a gold medal bearing his likeness; his famous words, "I'll try, sir"; and the names of the battles of Chippewa, Niagara, and Fort Erie. He had previously received a brevet promotion to brigadier general on 25 July 1814. Miller later served as Arkansas's first territorial governor and as the collector of the port of Salem, Massachusetts. He died the morning of 4 July 1851 at his farm in Temple, New Hampshire.

—*Robert J. Holden*

See also: Boyd, John Parker; Cass, Lewis; Chippewa, Battle of; Erie, Fort; Harrison, William Henry; Indiana Territory; Lundy's Lane, Battle of; Prophet's Town
Further Reading
Holden, Robert J. "General James Miller, Collector of the Port of Salem, Massachusetts, 1825–1849." *Essex Institute Collections* 104 (1968).

MILLER, JOHN
1781–1846
U.S. officer

Born in Virginia, John Miller moved to Ohio as a young man, where he established a newspaper, the *Western Herald*. Rising to prominence in Ohio, he became an officer in the state militia and rose to the rank of general. When the War of 1812 started, he received an appointment as a regular colonel commanding the 19th U.S. Infantry, stationed in the Northwest.

In the early spring of 1813, Maj. Gen. William Henry Harrison ordered Miller to Fort Meigs to take command of that post. Shortly after issuing these orders, Harrison learned that the British intended to take Fort Meigs. Harrison considered this post near the rapids of the Maumee River to be key to the future control of Lake Erie and what he hoped would be his eventual invasion of Canada. Even though he was about to lose a large part of his militia forces because their terms would soon expire, he set out for Fort Meigs at the end of March, signing up men from other posts as he went.

Harrison caught up to Miller, who had also accumulated additional regulars and militia on the march, and they both entered the fort on 12 April. At the time of their arrival, the fort's defenses were still under construction, a task hampered by the recurring British-allied Indians' raids in the area. Over the next few weeks, both officers supervised the completion of the works, finishing just as the British under Col. Henry Procter and his Indian allies under Tecumseh arrived opposite the fort on the other side of the Maumee.

For the next few days Harrison, Miller, and the garrison watched as the British erected their batteries. When Procter called for the fort's surrender, Harrison refused. On the night of 4 May, word reached the fort that Kentucky militia brigadier general Green Clay was bringing 1,200 Kentuckians down the river the next day. Harrison decided to take advantage of these surprise reinforcements. He sent word to Clay to use part of his force to take the British batteries on the other side of the river. In the meantime, Harrison hoped to use Clay's arrival as a distraction for Miller's sortie against a battery threatening the northern end of the fort.

Initially Clay's attack went well, but the British-Indian counterattack overwhelmed it; most of Clay's men were captured or killed. While this action was happening, however, Colonel Miller led 350 men out of the fort, took the targeted British battery, captured about 40 prisoners, spiked the guns, and retreated to the fort before the British were able to mount a counterattack against his force. Procter lifted the siege on 9 May.

For the remainder of the war, Miller continued to serve in the Northwest. In August 1814, Brig. Gen. Duncan McArthur in Detroit, after inspecting the defenses there, ordered Miller to strengthen the defenses at the old British fortifications at Fort Malden because of recent Indian activity on both sides of the Detroit River. That done, McArthur gave Miller command of the entire region while the general engaged in a raid deep into Canadian territory. While in command at Detroit and Fort Malden, Miller sent out raiding parties to communities within striking distance to destroy enemy supplies in the region.

Miller remained in the army following the war. Sent to Missouri, he realized the economic opportunities in the territory, resigned from the army in 1818, and settled there. Rising quickly in the estimation of his fellow citizens, Miller was elected governor in 1825. As governor until 1832, he championed what he saw as the needs of the West, including federal assistance for roads and river transportation. After leaving the governorship, he served three terms in the U.S. House of Representatives, where he also worked to improve the economic situation of the western states. He retired from Congress in 1842 and died in Missouri in 1846.

—*Jeanne T. Heidler and David S. Heidler*

See also: Harrison, William Henry; McArthur, Duncan; Meigs, Fort

MIMS, ATTACK ON FORT
30 August 1813

Tensions within the Creek Nation had been increasing for several years before the outbreak of the War of 1812. One faction of Creeks, known as Red Sticks, had been arguing against further accommodation with white Americans, while other Creeks accepted the encouragement of U.S. Creek Agent Benjamin Hawkins to adopt the white lifestyle.

By the summer of 1813, those tensions had erupted into civil war among the Creeks, and whites on the periphery of the Creek Nation feared that they would be attacked as hostilities escalated. After Mississippi Territorial Militia attacked a group of Red Stick Creeks led by the warrior Peter McQueen at Burnt Corn Creek on 27 July 1813, most of the settlers and non–Red Stick Creeks in Alabama moved into blockhouses or fortified towns.

The respectable showing made by Peter McQueen and his men at Burnt Corn helped Red Stick recruiting. These new recruits, eager to avenge what they saw as the unprovoked attack at Burnt Corn, planned to attack some of the forts in lower Alabama. Fort Mims, an isolated post built by the mixed-blood Samuel Mims, drew the Red Sticks because it was isolated and contained mixed bloods and other Creeks who did not support the Red Sticks as well as white settlers. William Weatherford (Red Eagle), a mixed-blood Red Stick leader, organized the assault.

In preparation for a possible attack, Fort Mims was reinforced with 120 Mississippi Territorial Militia under Maj. Daniel Beasley. The remainder of the inhabitants of the fort consisted of approximately 180 white, Creek, and mixed-blood men, women, and children. The fort also contained an undetermined number of black slaves. In spite of knowledge about possible Red Stick intentions, Major Beasley did not take many precautions. The few scouting parties he sent out were not very vigilant. The day before the attack, two slave boys ran into the fort, claiming to have seen large numbers of painted Indians, but scouts sent to investigate made only a cursory search of the area. Beasley then had the two slaves whipped for lying. Some reports allege that Beasley was drunk just hours before the attack.

At noon on 30 August 1813, while most of the fort's occupants were having their midday meal, the Red Sticks attacked. The gate gaped open, propped by (and now blocked by) sand that had built up along its edges. The sentries quickly surmised what was happening and shot the first few warriors who entered the gate. Major Beasley tried to shut the door, but he could not move the gate against the sand. He was still struggling with it when he was killed.

To add to the panic, the Red Sticks were firing through the fort's portholes, situated 4 feet above the ground. Once Red Sticks were in control of most of these portholes, the remainder of the approximately 750 attackers rushed into the fort. Inhabitants scattered in various places and buildings could not mount a unified defense. As the Red Sticks

An officer offers protection to a woman at Fort Mims during a Red Stick retaliation. This attack left almost 350 wounded or dead and triggered a panic that eventually led to greater U.S. involvement in the Creek War.

set fire to buildings, survivors of this first attack collected in two of the few remaining standing structures. Weatherford directed his men to repeatedly attack these buildings, forcing their occupants into tighter and tighter quarters. Finally, the Red Stick noose snugged too tight for the beleaguered inhabitants to load and fire their weapons. Realizing the impossibility of the situation, about a half-dozen defenders cut their way through the walls of the fort and ran for safety.

The killing of those remaining then proceeded in earnest. Some reports had Weatherford begging his men to spare the women and children, to no avail. When a relief party arrived several weeks later, it found 247 corpses of defenders, mingled with approximately 100 Red Stick dead.

News of the attack on and massacre at Fort Mims rapidly traveled the country. Nervousness turned into panic on the frontier, and calls went out to surrounding state governments to intervene with the object of ending the fighting and avenging the attack on Fort Mims. Several

states, Tennessee most notably, activated their militias, and the United States thus transformed the Creek civil war into the Creek War. The result for the Creeks would be destruction of their countryside and the forcible cession of 23 million acres of their land to the United States.

—*Jeanne T. Heidler and David S. Heidler*

See also: Burnt Corn, Battle of; Creek War; Fort Jackson, Treaty of; Hawkins, Benjamin; McQueen, Peter; Red Sticks; Weatherford, William

Further Reading

Braund, Kathryn E. Holland. *Deerskins and Duffels: The Creek Indian Trade with Anglo-America, 1685–1815.* Lincoln: University of Nebraska Press, 1993.

Owsley, Frank Lawrence, Jr. *Struggle for the Gulf Borderlands: The Creek War and the Battle of New Orleans, 1812–1815.* Gainesville: University Presses of Florida, 1981.

MISSISSIPPI RIVER

Called the "Father of Waters," the Mississippi River measures 2,470 miles from headwaters to mouth and drains 1,257,000 square miles, or the entirety of land between the Appalachian and Rocky Mountains. It became the United States' western boundary with ratification of the Treaty of Paris in 1783. Even so, the country did not gain full navigation rights to the river until ratification of Pinckney's Treaty (the Treaty of San Lorenzo) with Spain in 1795. In October 1802, the Spanish Intendant at New Orleans, acting under royal orders, closed the river to all U.S. commerce. This action prompted Pres. Thomas Jefferson to send James Monroe to negotiate with both France and Spain to settle the Mississippi question; the Louisiana Purchase of 1803 resulted, ensuring U.S. control of this vital lifeline.

Commanding the Mississippi watershed was the most important city of the Gulf South—New Orleans, located about 105 miles north of the mouth of the river and surrounded by swamps, marshes, shallow lakes, and bayous. The swampy terrain surrounding New Orleans demonstrated the importance of the Mississippi River as the artery that connected the city to the outside world. Though the river was a deep-water estuary, any vessel with more than a 14-foot draft could not enter because of sandbars at the river's mouth. Moreover, a strong current forced vessels to make a long beat upstream, leaving them exposed to attack from the river's banks. Because the river was the most obvious and viable route of attack against New Orleans, the U.S. government had constructed Fort St. Philip about 30 miles from the river's mouth and Fort St. Leon 70 miles upstream. Fort St. Leon commanded English Turn, an S-shaped turn where sailing vessels had to wait for a change in wind before proceeding upstream. Thus, it was possible to sail upriver, but the time spent tacking and waiting for favorable winds would leave an enemy flotilla exposed.

While these conditions provided advantages for a military force guarding against an invasion via the river, they inconvenienced merchants by leaving them exposed. Given these circumstances, British forces approached New Orleans in December 1814, not by the river but rather via Lake Borgne to the east of the city. After defeating the U.S. gunboats stationed on Lake Borgne, British troops proceeded via Bayou Catalan (or Bayou Bienvenu) to the eastern bank of the Mississippi River, 9 miles south of New Orleans. Commander of the New Orleans naval station Master Commandant Daniel Todd Patterson, working in cooperation with the two forts and shore batteries, used the converted merchant sloop *Louisiana* and schooner *Carolina* in the Mississippi to cover land attacks along the river, and prepared gunboats and fire ships to discourage an assault via the river. These preparations forced the English to funnel their forces along a narrow strip of land on the east bank, which ran north toward the city. Gen. Andrew Jackson strengthened his defenses accordingly, putting the British at a severe disadvantage.

—*Gene A. Smith*

See also: Lake Borgne, Battle of; Louisiana; New Orleans, Battle of

Further Reading

Ainsworth, W. L. "An Amphibious Operation That Failed: The Battle of New Orleans." *United States Naval Institute Proceedings* 71 (February 1945): 193–201

Brown, Wilburt S. *The Amphibious Campaign for West Florida and Louisiana. 1814–1815: A Critical Review of Strategy and Tactics at New Orleans.* University: University of Alabama Press, 1969.

Eller, E. M., W. J. Morgan, and R. M. Basoco. *The Battle of New Orleans: Sea Power and the Battle of New Orleans.* New Orleans: Battle of New Orleans, 150th Anniversary Committee of Louisiana, 1965.

Latour, A. Lacarriere. *Historical Memoir of the War in West Florida and Louisiana in 1814–15.* N.p., 1816; reprint, Gainesville: University Presses of Florida, 1964.

McClellan, Edwin N. "The Navy at the Battle of New Orleans." *United States Naval Institute Proceedings* 50 (December 1924): 2041–2060.

Owsley, Frank L. *Struggle for the Gulf Borderlands: The Creek War and the Battle of New Orleans, 1812–1815.* Gainesville: University Presses of Florida, 1981.

Tucker, Spencer C. *The Jeffersonian Gunboat Navy.* Columbia: University of South Carolina Press, 1993.

MISSISSIPPI TERRITORY
See Creek War

MISSOURI TERRITORY

Integrated into the United States by the Louisiana Purchase (1803), the Missouri Territory was an isolated, lonely frontier on the westernmost reaches of the country. Far removed from the focus of the War of 1812, the territory was subject to Indian raids, combated by the efforts of local militia. Most Indians in the region, tied to both Americans and the British through the fur trade, allied with the British when the war started. The exception was the Osage tribe, which had established links to the United States with treaties four years earlier. Others, however, joined in the spiritual revival started by Tecumseh and Tenskwatawa (the Prophet), and after William Henry Harrison destroyed Prophet's Town following the 1811 Battle of Tippecanoe, anti-American sentiments among Indians noticeably increased.

When war was declared in June 1812, the U.S. Army had less than 250 regulars west of the Mississippi River, so Missouri Territory relied almost exclusively on ill-equipped and frequently unpaid militia for defense. The federal government did raise some ranger units, constructed blockhouses, and put up some fortifications at larger settlements such as St. Louis, but the territory was in the main bereft of consistent defense.

In 1813, Pres. James Madison appointed the explorer William Clark territorial governor of Missouri. Up to that time, Clark had been the superintendent of Indian affairs in St. Louis and had been nominally a subordinate of Brig. Gen. Benjamin Howard. In 1814, Clark accompanied a squadron of gunboats conveying regular and militia forces to Prairie du Chien, but after initial success, the U.S. garrison there proved too weak to hold against renewed British efforts in the area.

Fighting in Missouri essentially occurred in coincidence with the War of 1812, more merging with it than actually being caused by it. A continuation of Indian hostilities that predated the war with Britain, violence on the Missouri frontier continued after that war was ended by the Treaty of Ghent. Clark's task after the War of 1812 became ending the Missouri Indian wars. He accomplished this with the Treaty of Portage des Sioux in the summer of 1815. Although angry whites in the territory regarded the treaty's terms as far too indulgent and would punish Clark politically for his leniency toward the Indians, the treaty restored peace, encouraged immigration into the territory, and made possible statehood at the end of the decade.

—*Jeanne T. Heidler and David S. Heidler*

See also: Clark, William; Prairie du Chien
Further Reading

Foley, William E. *A History of Missouri*. Columbia: University of Missouri Press, 1971.

Gregg, Kate. "The War of 1812 on the Missouri Frontier." *Missouri Historical Review* 33: 3–22, 184–202, 326–348.

Houck, Lewis. *A History of Missouri*. 3 vols. Chicago: R. R. Donnelly and Sons, 1908.

MITCHELL, GEORGE E.
See Oswego, New York

MOBILE, BATTLES OF
12–15 April 1813; 14–15 September 1814;
8–11 February 1815

Mobile was assailed in three separate battles during the War of 1812. The first began when Secretary of War Henry Dearborn instructed Gen. James Wilkinson, commander of U.S. forces in the Southwest, to take possession of West Florida, including the city of Mobile. In late March 1813, Wilkinson ordered Capt. John Shaw, commander of the New Orleans naval station, to send gunboats to occupy Mobile Bay and disrupt the city's communications with Pensacola. Wilkinson also directed Col. John Bowyer, stationed 40 miles north at Fort Stoddert, to move his troops in position to attack the Spanish at Fort Charlotte at Mobile. U.S. vessels and troops from both New Orleans and Fort Stoddert arrived near the city on the morning of 12 April; by noon the Americans were prepared for an attack. The presence of a force of more than 600 men surprised Spanish captain Don Cayetano Perez and convinced him to negotiate the city's surrender. Three days later, on 15 April 1813, Spanish forces evacuated Mobile, never to return.

After the battle, Wilkinson chose to move the city's primary defense 30 miles southeast to Mobile Point, a 4-mile-wide sandy peninsula that commanded the entrance to Mobile Bay. Capt. Rueben Chamberlain oversaw construction of the fort until June 1813, when Gen. Thomas Flournoy ordered Bowyer to finish the bastion, which would be known as Fort Bowyer. Reinforced with cannon from nearby Fort Charlotte, the position served as Mobile's primary defense until early July 1814, when Flournoy ordered its evacuation. Less than one month later, however, Gen. Andrew Jackson, learning that British forces intended to attack the city, sent Maj. William Lawrence with 160 men to reoccupy the position. Over the next month, Lawrence and his men added wooden batteries and acquired additional guns in preparation for an attack.

The British arrived at Mobile Point on 12 September 1814; over the next two days Capt. Sir William H. Percy of the Royal Navy and Col. Edward Nicholls of the Royal Marines amassed four ships carrying 78 cannon and 600 men and a land force of 72 marines and 180 Indians. Percy chose to postpone the attack while British representatives unsuccessfully negotiated with the Baratarian pirates for their support. The opening salvos of the attack occurred two days later on 14 September, when Nicholls's land force moved within 800 yards of Fort Bowyer and commenced firing. The Americans responded, driving the British back. The following day Nicholls's men approached Fort Bowyer again, only to deplete their ammunition before retreating.

On 15 September, as Nicholls made his land approach, Percy's ships conducted a simultaneous attack from the water. At 4:30 P.M., the British flotilla anchored in a broadside position and began firing on Fort Bowyer. A lucky U.S. shot cut the bow spring cable of Percy's flagship, HMS *Hermes*, and the current drove her bow abreast of the fort, where for 20 minutes she suffered a devastating pounding. The disabled *Hermes* ran aground in shoal waters, and Percy destroyed her to prevent a U.S. capture. The remainder of British forces retreated to Pensacola; official British casualties were 27 killed, 45 wounded, and the destruction of one ship. U.S. losses were four killed and five wounded.

The last battle of Mobile occurred one month after the British debacle at New Orleans and after the Treaty of Ghent had officially ended the conflict. On 28 January 1815, British forces landed on Dauphin Island off Mobile Bay and began preparing for another attack on Fort Bowyer. British ships arrived off the island on 6 February. Even though Gen. Andrew Jackson had anticipated a British attack against New Orleans before the end of 1814, he had also understood the strategic importance of Mobile and Fort Bowyer. In November, Jackson had increased the fort's complement to almost 400 men. Yet even with increased strength, now-brevetted Lieutenant Colonel Lawrence reported his position as precarious because of the vulnerable landward approach.

On the morning of 8 February about 1,400 British troops disembarked 3 miles east of Fort Bowyer. Maj. Gen. John Lambert and his staff concluded that an infantry assault would be useless, but they believed artillery could effectively reduce the bastion. Beginning on the evening of 8 February and continuing for the next two days, British forces faced heavy U.S. fire while trying to position their cannons. By the morning of 11 February, however, the British artillery was ready.

Before starting any attack, General Lambert sent brevet major Harry Smith, under a flag of truce, to offer terms of surrender. Lawrence realized that Fort Bowyer, without casemates to protect the wounded or the powder magazine and without landward ramparts, could only be held at a great cost of lives. Facing these circumstances, Lawrence reluctantly accepted British terms and surrendered on 11 February 1815, two days before news of the Treaty of

Ghent reached the Gulf Coast. Even though the British had taken Fort Bowyer, Mobile was spared an attack because the war had ended.

—*Gene A. Smith*

See also: Bowyer, Fort; Flournoy, [John] Thomas; Lambert, John; Lawrence, William; Nicholls, Edward; Percy, William Henry

Further Reading

Coker, William S. "The Last Battle of the War of 1812: New Orleans? No, Fort Bowyer!" *Alabama Historical Quarterly* 43, no. 1 (1981): 43–63.

Owsley, Frank L. *Struggle for the Gulf Borderlands: The Creek War and the Battle of New Orleans, 1812–1815.* Gainesville: University Presses of Florida, 1981.

MONGUAGON, BATTLE OF
9 August 1812

After William Hull's retreat to Detroit following the U.S. defeat at Brownstown, Hull sent a party out to open communication lines and to bring in the supply train commanded by Capt. Henry Brush. On 8 August, Hull dispatched Lt. Col. James Miller with about 600 men.

Before reaching Brownstown, at the abandoned Indian town of Monguagon on the afternoon of 9 August, Miller was attacked by a combined British-Indian force of 350 to 400 men under the command of Canadian militia captain Adam Muir and Tecumseh. When the U.S. advance was fired on, it uncharacteristically held its position, which allowed time for the remainder of the force to reach its position and begin a steady defense. To complicate things for the British, they accidentally fired on their own Indian allies, creating chaos in their lines. The British and their allies ended up retreating in different directions. The Americans chose to pursue the Indians.

Although it was a U.S. victory, the Battle of Monguagon did not succeed in opening the supply and communication lines that Hull had hoped for. Miller was injured in the battle, and his men were short of rations. Even when a relief party arrived under Duncan McArthur, little could be done short of abandoning the wounded before Hull surrendered Detroit on 16 August.

—*Jeanne T. Heidler and David S. Heidler*

See also: Brownstown, Battle of; Detroit, Surrender of; Hull, William; McArthur, Duncan; Miller, James

Further Reading
Bishop, Levi. "The Battle of Monguagon." *Michigan Pioneer* 6 (1884): 466–469.

MONROE, JAMES
1758–1831
Secretary of state; secretary of war

James Monroe played a central role in the War of 1812. Serving as secretary of state and twice as secretary of war, he helped fashion the Madison administration's policies and thus deserves some recognition for their achievements as well as their shortcomings.

James Monroe was born in Virginia on 28 April 1758. He grew up in modestly comfortable surroundings and attended the College of William and Mary. The American Revolution interrupted his studies, and he was commissioned a lieutenant in the spring of 1776. Monroe saw action in a number of engagements and was severely wounded at the Battle of Trenton. Gen. George Washington took notice of the young officer's performance, marking his zeal and devotion to duty. In 1778, Monroe resigned his commission and returned to Virginia. His subsequent service in the Virginia militia proved less successful.

As the Revolution drew to a close, Monroe became Thomas Jefferson's protégé. The Sage of Monticello encouraged Monroe to study law. Achieving some level of local prominence, Monroe conducted a variety of activities before serving in the Confederation Congress in 1783. He married Elizabeth Kortright on 16 February 1786. That same year, he opened his law office in Fredericksburg, Virginia. Though skeptical of the new federal Constitution, he served in the newly created U.S. Senate in 1790.

Between 1794 and 1811, Monroe held a variety of posts abroad and in the Virginia state government. Monroe began a stormy term as U.S. minister to France in 1794. Suspecting that Monroe had fallen under the influence of his hosts, Pres. George Washington recalled him in the fall of 1796, and Monroe sailed for home in the spring of 1797. In 1799, he was elected governor of Virginia. Early in 1803, President Jefferson dispatched him to France to assist Robert Livingston in securing the purchase of New Orleans, subsequently consummated as the Louisiana Purchase, which doubled the United States' land area.

Monroe was sent to Great Britain later in 1803 as the U.S. minister. During the next several years, he labored to solve disputes with Britain and Spain, but with limited success. In December 1806, Monroe and special envoy

James Monroe

William Pinkney signed the Monroe-Pinkney Treaty with the British. Although it offered Americans commercial concessions, it did not resolve the thorny impressment issue. No British government would be willing to relinquish the right of impressment, but the failure to secure this point caused Jefferson to withhold the treaty from Senate consideration in 1807. The action deeply offended Monroe, who returned to Virginia to nurse his wounded pride.

Anti-Jeffersonian Republicans, hoping to exploit the rift between Monroe and Jefferson, encouraged Monroe to run for president in 1808, but he mounted only a halfhearted attempt. Soon afterward, he was elected to the Virginia legislature. In January 1811, he again became Virginia's governor but held this position for only two months. That spring, Pres. James Madison dismissed James Ross, his inept secretary of state, and offered Monroe the post. Trying to mend a breach of nearly four years but insisting that he would actually direct foreign policy, Monroe reconciled with Madison (Jefferson's former secretary of state) and accepted on 29 March 1811. On 6 April, Monroe assumed his duties as secretary of state.

He immediately confronted rapidly deteriorating relations with Britain. Nearly 20 years of war in Europe had degenerated into a life-or-death struggle between Britain and France. Both sides interfered with U.S. shipping, and the British insistence on impressment continued to be a sore point. Napoleon I had attempted to manipulate U.S. opinion so as to drive a wedge between Britain and the United States. By 1811, the threat of war was growing.

During the summer of 1811, Monroe and Madison concluded that war was inevitable unless the British yielded substantial concessions by year's end. One last opportunity arose on 2 July 1811, when British minister Augustus J. Foster reached Washington, D.C. During the next few months, Monroe held numerous discussions with Foster. The secretary of state sought to impress upon Foster that London had to repeal the Orders in Council and end impressment. Foster, for his part, pressed the Americans to repeal their Non-Intercourse Act, which threatened to choke off Anglo-American trade. Foster argued to Monroe that French failure to revoke their decrees in fact made U.S. nonintercourse with Great Britain discriminatory. Monroe, after failing to obtain appropriate assurances from the French minister to the United States, Louis Sérurier, dodged Foster's arguments by trying to draw legal distinctions between the British and French actions. By December 1811, Monroe had made it plain that British intransigence would mean war.

Congress had begun meeting that November. On 5 November, Madison sent Congress a message calling for military preparations. The 12th Congress's angry young men, eager for war with Britain, would become known as the War Hawks. Under their influence, the belief that war was inevitable rose rapidly within both houses of Congress. Ultimately, only some of Madison's proposals were enacted, but Monroe worked tirelessly behind the scenes to garner support for the administration. He developed a good working relationship with Henry Clay, the new Speaker of the House. In the spring of 1812, Monroe proposed a 60-day trade embargo against Britain, later extended to 90 days. It was intended as a final warning.

Monroe's efforts extended outside Congress as well. In April, several editorials written by Monroe that called for war appeared in the *National Intelligencer*. At the same time, Monroe and Madison appeared convinced that war with France was unnecessary, even though the French also were violating U.S. neutral rights. Both men seemed deceived by Napoleon's duplicitous diplomacy, a circumstance noticed by the British. Some observers then and since have suggested that Monroe's pro-French bias blinded him to diplomatic realities.

Monroe viewed the approaching war with considerable optimism, a sentiment held by many Americans. He believed the British, preoccupied in Europe, lacked the capability to strike at the United States. Monroe considered the possibility of seizing Canada rapidly and using it as a bargaining chip during peace negotiations. Yet, he also believed that initially the country should engage mainly in a maritime war, until it was better prepared for land operations. Confining his territorial aspirations to Florida, the secretary of state had no desire to retain the vast British colony. Accordingly, he used U.S. agents in an attempt to seize Spanish East Florida, but he remained sufficiently removed from the operation to disown it when it failed. Meanwhile, Monroe took some part in the preparation of the House of Representative's war report, although the extent of his contributions is a matter of dispute. Monroe's prior efforts helped win acceptance for Madison's war message, which passed quickly in the House and was finally approved in the Senate on 17 June 1812.

Both Madison and Monroe expected the British to capitulate once they learned war had been declared, so Monroe continued discussions with Foster even after the declaration. Instead, news arrived from London in several weeks that the British had repealed the Orders in Council on 16 June, two days prior to the U.S. declaration of war. Foster by then had taken his leave to return home, but he paused briefly in Halifax, hoping that the repeal of the Orders in Council would stop hostilities. The hope proved futile.

After the war had started, Monroe felt restlessly deskbound. He eagerly sought a field command in a U.S. Army chronically short of trained officers, but Madison feared the political implications of giving Monroe a rank higher than those of more experienced officers. Meanwhile, William Eustis's management of the War Department proved increasingly inept. By year's end, Eustis's incompetence finally forced Madison to accept his resignation and temporarily appoint Monroe acting secretary of war. During the two months Monroe served as acting secretary at the War Department, he pushed through Congress a military expansion program and drew up plans for an invasion of Canada. He hoped that with the declining fortunes of the senior officer corps, when it came time to implement the plan, Madison would be willing to give him command of the operation. When John Armstrong assumed the position of secretary of war on 13 February 1813, Monroe resumed his State Department duties that had been temporarily monitored by Richard Rush. In time, Monroe and Armstrong would perceive each other as rivals for the presidency. Consequently, Armstrong worked successfully to prevent Monroe from receiving a military command.

Back in the State Department, Monroe carefully watched for any sign of British peace feelers. Russian foreign minister Count Nicholas Romanzoff offered Russian mediation to U.S. minister John Quincy Adams. As soon as this overture reached Washington in February 1813, Madison and Monroe instantly accepted it without awaiting either congressional or British response. Madison appointed Albert Gallatin, who was tired of his duties at the Treasury Department, and Sen. James Bayard to join Adams in St. Petersburg. The vast distances obviously reduced Monroe's control over negotiations to sending instructions to diplomats and then awaiting news of developments. The British rejected Russian mediation, pressing instead for direct negotiations. At the same time, news reached Washington of Napoleon's massive defeat in Russia and the ensuing collapse of his empire in central Europe. The imminent end of the European war meant that Britain would have considerable resources to send to the United States. When British foreign secretary Lord Castlereagh sent Monroe a note on 4 November 1813 calling for direct talks, Monroe received the note on 30 December 1813 and notified Castlereagh of the president's acceptance on 5 January 1814. Soon afterward, Henry Clay was dispatched to Europe to join Bayard, Gallatin, Adams, and the U.S. chargé d'affaires in London, Jonathan Russell, as the U.S. commissioners.

While Monroe awaited news of the opening of negotiations in Europe, the rivalry between him and Armstrong intensified. When the invasions of Canada from New York failed during the winter of 1813, Monroe urged Armstrong's removal. During 1813 and early 1814, the British also staged raids in Chesapeake Bay, underscoring Washington's vulnerability to attack. Armstrong insisted the British could never target the capital, but Monroe and other officials in the administration fretted about such a possibility. At Monroe's instigation and against Armstrong's advice, Madison on 2 July 1814 established a new military district encompassing Washington, D.C., and the Potomac River under the command of Gen. William Winder. Yet Monroe's prodding resulted in only a few improvements to the city's defenses, and U.S. forces in the area were hastily assembled and poorly trained. In August 1814, when a British fleet entered Chesapeake Bay and landed British troops on Maryland's shores to begin their march on Washington, Monroe himself rode the countryside to ascertain the invasion force's intentions. The British reached Bladensburg, Maryland, on 24 August to find a hodgepodge U.S. force assembled to meet them. Monroe, playing the gifted amateur, likely contributed to U.S. disorganization by changing the placement of certain militia units without telling the commanders on the field. Given such chaos, British victory was all but inevitable.

As the British marched on the capital, Monroe helped evacuate Washington and especially aided in the rescue of some government documents. The British reached Washington on 24 August and spent the night burning many of the city's public buildings. The following day, they returned to their boats and were back on their ships by 30 August. Monroe was one of the first officials to return to the charred U.S. capital on 27 August, and soon he was to have additional duties. Armstrong was widely blamed for the destruction of the capital and resigned on 4 September. Madison asked Monroe to become the acting secretary of war while retaining his post at the State Department. Monroe held both posts for nine months, but immediately the War Department consumed his attention because of the need to bolster Baltimore's defenses. The successful repulse of the British there in September was due in part to Monroe's more capable administration of the War Department.

Monroe wanted to retain the War Department post for the remainder of the conflict, and he pressured Madison to submit his name to the Senate for confirmation. Reluctantly, Madison agreed, and Monroe thus occupied State (as acting secretary because Madison could not find a suitable replacement) and War until news of the Treaty of Ghent arrived.

The negotiations at Ghent had been facilitated by Madison and Monroe's decision in the summer of 1814 to remove the resolution of the impressment issue as a sine qua non for a peace settlement. Yet in the fall, the British had stalled the talks by insisting on territorial adjustments along the Canadian border and the creation of an Indian buffer state. The publication of these demands in the United States had the effect of uniting the nation behind the war effort. The combination of U.S. determination and British difficulties at the Congress of Vienna finally broke the negotiation deadlock.

While Monroe's peace commissioners labored at Ghent, the new secretary of war faced several difficulties at home. He received word in September that Armstrong's movement of troops away from Lake Champlain luckily had not spelled disaster: the British invasion there had been repulsed. Still, with more British troops freed from the fighting in Europe, Monroe believed that the numbers of U.S. regulars would have to be augmented to continue the war. He urged Congress to aid his recruiting by lowering the minimum age of enlistment without parental permission to 18 and to increase the monetary and land bounty for new recruits. Monroe also wanted Congress to implement limited conscription. The extreme unpopularity of this last proposal meant that Monroe could secure only the first two recommendations. While these issues were being debated, Monroe grew increasingly concerned for the security of New England, where these measures had proven most unpopular. Afraid of the secessionist potential of the Hartford Convention, Monroe ordered military commanders in the Northeast to suppress rebellion if necessary.

Monroe also devoted considerable time during late 1814 to campaigns in the Southwest. U.S. forces there, commanded by Maj. Gen. Andrew Jackson, were short on supplies and long on responsibility, especially in having to protect a vast area. The possibility of a British invasion along the Gulf Coast posed profound challenges to Jackson and Monroe, but Jackson's obsession with Spanish Pensacola most excited Monroe's fear about the security of New Orleans. From Washington, Monroe communicated with Jackson on a frequent basis, providing him with whatever men, supplies, and instructions he could. Jackson responded with voluminous reports on his force's operations. When a British Army attacking New Orleans was defeated on 8 January 1815, both men could take credit.

Monroe's labors slackened as peace approached. The news of the Treaty of Ghent reached Washington on 13 February 1815, the official copy arriving the next day. The Senate ratified the Treaty on 16 February 1815; the previous day, Monroe had quit his War Department duties. By the summer, he was haggard and ill. Desperately needing rest, he vacationed for most of the summer, planning for the future, especially in contemplation of his candidacy for the presidency.

Monroe's work during the War of 1812 helped to reconcile him with the Democratic Republican leadership he had alienated prior to the war. This made possible his election to the presidency in November 1816. Madison, for one, was delighted that Monroe would succeed him, thereby continuing the so-called Virginia Dynasty. Thus, on 4 March 1817, James Monroe, the last Revolutionary War veteran to live in the White House and the first of several political beneficiaries of the last war with Britain, took the oath of office as president of the United States.

—*James C. Biedzynski*

See also: Diplomacy; Madison, James
Further Reading
Ammon, Harry. *James Monroe: The Quest for National Identity.* New York: McGraw-Hill, 1971.
Ketcham, Ralph. *James Madison.* New York: Macmillan, 1970.
Rutland, Robert Allen. *The Presidency of James Madison.* Lawrence: University Press of Kansas, 1990.
Styron, Arthur. *The Last of the Cocked Hats.* Norman: University of Oklahoma Press, 1945.

MONROE-PINKNEY TREATY
signed 31 December 1806
See Monroe, James; Pinkney, William

MONTREAL

Even before war erupted between the United States and Great Britain in June 1812, Montreal, Lower Canada, concerned the U.S. government. During nonintercourse with Great Britain, first in 1809 and then after the implementation of Macon's Bill No. 2, the British used Montreal as a base to smuggle their manufactured goods into the United States. Because the St. Lawrence made it easier for Americans along the lakes to trade with Montreal than with U.S. cities, the British always had a market for their goods in the United States.

Partly because of the trade emanating from there and the belief that Quebec's fortification made attack on that place impractical, U.S. war plans, even before the declaration of war, concentrated on Montreal. Pres. James Madison became convinced that securing Montreal would bring about the fall of Upper Canada. Concentration on Montreal, however, ignored the political realities of strong western support for war and westerners' desires to strike at British bases in the Northwest. Westerners believed that British agents in the West were responsible for recent Indian unrest, and their political influence forced Madison immediately before the commencement of hostilities to modify his plan to include offensives from Detroit and across the Niagara River. Still, because Madison believed that securing Montreal would seriously damage British trade, the city remained an important focus of the war effort for the first year and a half of the contest.

Early in the war, Henry Dearborn commanded the northern front, with a primary goal of launching an offensive against Montreal. Dearborn, however, suffered a number of difficulties, not the least of which were his own inadequacies, in implementing the government's plan. First, his command was divided between Lake Champlain and the Niagara Frontier, and he was expected to stage offensives across both. Second, in order to invade Canada to strike at Montreal along the traditional Lake Champlain/Richelieu River route, he needed to augment his force with New England militia. Most of the New England governors refused to supply their militias, leaving Dearborn undermanned for an invasion. He made one last effort to raise a force at the end of 1812, but again he could not raise enough men.

When John Armstrong became secretary of war in February 1813, he tried to shift administration policy away from Montreal to Kingston, the primary British port on Lake Ontario. Armstrong believed that if Kingston fell into U.S. hands, the United States would be able to move down the St. Lawrence to Montreal without worrying about the British presence in their rear. Armstrong could not convince President Madison to give up an offensive on Montreal in 1813, so the secretary simply began planning a two-pronged offensive.

The object of these offensives was to strike at Montreal via the Lake Champlain invasion route while a second navy-army force secured Kingston and then moved down the St. Lawrence to join the other army. Armstrong gave command of the Lake Champlain front to Maj. Gen. Wade Hampton; the army at Sacket's Harbor was given to Maj. Gen. James Wilkinson with vague instructions that Wilkinson should have seniority over the entire operation. Both men so despised one another that cooperation between the two was unlikely.

When the time came to begin the campaign in the fall of 1813, Wilkinson balked at moving against Kingston first, arguing with Armstrong that he could move immediately on Montreal down the St. Lawrence. Armstrong eventually conceded, and Wilkinson began the campaign, harried most of the way by British gunboats and infantry out of Kingston. Finally stopping to drive off his pursuers at Chrysler's Farm in November 1813, Wilkinson failed miserably and decided to go into winter quarters at French Mills, New York.

Hampton, too, had stopped well short of Montreal. After moving briefly into Canada along the Châteauguay River, Hampton was repulsed at the Battle of Châteauguay by far inferior numbers on 26 October 1813. He moved back to New York and set up winter quarters.

Thus ended the only major campaign whose object was to take Montreal. Toward the end of the war, Secretary of War James Monroe and Maj. Gen. Jacob Brown held talks in Washington to plan another offensive against Montreal, but the war ended before they could implement the project.

—*Jeanne T. Heidler and David S. Heidler*

See also: Armstrong, John; Châteauguay, Battle of; Chrysler's Farm, Battle of; Dearborn, Henry; Hampton, Wade; Militia Controversy, The New England

Further Reading

Sellar, Gordon. *The U.S. Campaign of 1813 to Capture Montreal.* Huntington, Quebec: Gleaner Office, 1914.

Suthern, Victor J. "The Battle of Châteauguay." *Canadian Historic Sites* 11 (1974): 95–150.

MORAVIANTOWN
See Thames, Battle of the

MORRIS, CHARLES
1784–1856
U.S. Navy officer

Connecticut-born Charles Morris's distinguished naval career began 1 July 1799, when he was appointed a midshipman in the U.S. Navy. He saw duty aboard the *Congress* and the *Constitution*. Morris was one of 70 volunteers sent to recapture the *Philadelphia*, which had fallen into Tripolitan hands, and was the first man of his party to reach the quarterdeck of that ship (in 1804). Morris, along with Stephen Decatur, shared the honors for the capture and the destruction of the *Philadelphia*. His subsequent successful bombardments of Tripoli led to his 1807 appointment as a lieutenant aboard the *President*.

In July 1812, Charles Morris was appointed first lieutenant under Isaac Hull of the *Constitution* and was present in the first naval engagement of the War of 1812 on 19 August between the *Constitution* and HMS *Guerrière*. Shot through the body without receiving damage to any vital organs, Morris won promotion to captain in 1813 for his bravery. Promoted to lieutenant commander in 1814, Morris was given command of the frigate *John Adams* (28 guns). Morris cruised his ship off the U.S. and Irish coasts, capturing ten British vessels and damaging British commerce.

Morris was forced to place the *John Adams* into Penobscot Bay, Maine, for repairs; there the vessel came under attack from the British in September 1814. Morris made land preparations to defend his ship in case the British attacked. The ship's cannon were sent ashore, obstructions were placed in the river, and the militia called up. Yet, a heavy British attack by Rear Adm. Edward Griffith on 3 September forced Morris to burn the *John Adams* rather than let it fall into enemy hands. He divided his men into small parties and marched them to Portland. A naval board of inquiry cleared Morris of any wrongdoing.

After the war, Charles Morris's naval career included action in Algiers (1815), the Caribbean (1817), and Buenos

Aires (1819–1820). He was appointed to the Board of Naval Commissioners in 1823 and held the position until 1827. As commander of the *Brandywine*, Morris conveyed Lafayette back to France. Charles Morris was commander of the Boston Navy Yard (1827–1832), naval commissioner until 1841, and commander of the Brazil and the Mediterranean squadrons (1841–1844). From 1851 until his death in 1856, Charles Morris was chief of naval ordnance and hydrography in Washington, D.C. Morris gave more than 50 years to promoting the growth and development of the U.S. Navy. At the time of his death, he was regarded as the foremost authority on the navy as it existed before the Civil War.

—*William A. Paquette*

See also: Griffith, Edward; Hampden, Maine

Gouverneur Morris

MORRIS, GOUVERNEUR
1752–1816
U.S. statesman and diplomat

A French-speaking American of Huguenot descent, Morris was born in Morrisania, New York, to a wealthy landed family. Educated at King's College (later Columbia University), he was admitted to the bar in 1771. In the same year, he started a legal practice in New York.

Morris was active in public office intermittently from 1775 to 1776, when he served in New York state's revolutionary-era Provincial Congress and assisted in the drafting of its first constitution in 1776. In 1787, Morris was elected as a Pennsylvania delegate to the Constitutional Convention in Philadelphia and supervised the final draft of that document. He served as U.S. minister to France from January 1792 until August 1794, when his open hostility to the French Revolution prompted the French to demand his recall. Filling an unexpired term in the Senate (1800–1803), he sided with the Federalist Party but was too independent to follow the party line consistently. He was not returned in March 1803, but he continued to play an important role in public affairs.

Morris was a strong supporter of England in her crusade against France, as revealed in a letter to an English friend in 1807: "You stand alone, and those who ought to side with you keep aloof." He grieved that the United States had not become Britain's "firm and useful ally." Not surprisingly, Morris vehemently contested the Embargo Act (1807) as a preposterous attempt to frighten England. Nevertheless, he was opposed to war, arguing in 1808 that U.S. involvement in protecting foreign seamen on U.S. merchant ships was "downright madness."

Initially he thought war could be averted, but when it threatened, he recommended to DeWitt Clinton that a convention of northern political parties be called to recommend eliminating the three-fifths slave apportionment so favorable to the South. He condemned the war as the work of "the inland States under the Pretext of protecting Commerce and Seamen but for the avowed Purpose of conquering Canada with the obvious Intention of scattering Millions among their Constituents."

Once war began, Morris did not relent in his opposition. Only two weeks into war he wrote: "If Peace be not immediately made with England, the Question of Negro Votes must divide this Union." A committee for peace was formed, and several meetings were held in Morrisania during August 1812. This committee, composed of extreme Federalists such as Rufus King and John Jay, formulated a number of antiwar resolutions. These included a demand for the establishment of committees of correspondence between the states and the creation of a northern confederation. A huge meeting of the "Friends of Liberty, Peace and Commerce" adopted the resolutions in New York on 18 August. Under the pseudonym "An American," Morris published in the 29 August issue of the New York *Herald* an "Address to the People of the State of New York." In it he promoted the secession of the northern states.

The signing of the Treaty of Ghent ended hopes of a separate confederation. Morris died two years later on 6 November 1816, a disappointed man who had lost much faith in the country he had helped establish.

—Leigh Whaley

Further Reading

Kline, Mary-Jo. *Gouverneur Morris and the New Nation 1775–1788*. New York: Arno Press, 1978.

Mintz, Max, M. *Gouverneur Morris and the American Revolution*. Norman: University of Oklahoma Press, 1970.

Morris, Anne Cary. *Diary and Letters of Gouverneur Morris.* 2 vols. New York and London: Charles Scribners/Kegan and Paul, 1888, 1889.

Swiggett, Howard. *The Extraordinary Man Mr. Morris*. Garden City: Doubleday, 1952.

MORRISON, JOSEPH WANTON
1783–1826
British army officer

In 1813, Joseph Morrison was commanding the 89th Regiment, observing the activity and movement of U.S. forces along the St. Lawrence River. The U.S. objective was to join forces at Longue Salte Rapids and advance on the road to Montreal. In November, when near-blizzard conditions halted the movement of both armies, Morrison set up headquarters at the home of John Chrysler. About 1 mile away, the Americans were at Cook's Tavern. Morrison carefully surveyed Chrysler's Farm to best utilize its terrain, should he do battle there with the Americans.

Morrison's soldiers included the 89th Regiment, a militia battalion from Lower Canada, volunteer riders from the Provincial Dragoons, and Mohawk Indians. On the morning of 11 November 1813, Morrison positioned 450 of his regulars behind an extended log fence. Directly to the right, he staggered the remaining regulars along the road to Montreal that ran parallel to the St. Lawrence River. Further in front, he placed three companies of Canadians to perform as a skirmish line. Scattered throughout the woods were the Mohawk Indians. One of the Mohawks accidentally discharged his musket in the direction of the Americans, and the battle began.

U.S. general John Boyd outnumbered the British forces by about three to one. U.S. infantry arranged in a line of three columns charged across the snow-covered field but were so badly managed that they were repulsed. Morrison's stand left the Americans no choice but to withdraw, and shortly afterward, they abandoned their march on Montreal. Morrison would receive a medal and thanks from the Lower House Assembly of Canada.

Morrison and the 89th Regiment also participated in the Battle of Lundy's Lane on 25 July 1814, supporting Gen. Phineas Riall. They also assisted Gen. Thomas Pearson and Gen. Gordon Drummond's 800 British regulars. Morrison's forces suffered in excess of 200 casualties, and he sustained such a severe wound in his arm that it ended his service during the War of 1812. Morrison died on 15 February 1826.

—Gary L. Morrison

See also: Boyd, John Parker; Chrysler's Farm, Battle of; Lundy's Lane, Battle of

Further Reading

Way, Ronald L. "The Day of Chrysler's Farm." *Canadian Geographical Journal* 62 (June 1961): 185–217.

N

NANTUCKET ISLAND, MASSACHUSETTS

Located 30 miles off the coast of Massachusetts, Nantucket Island was vulnerable to the British throughout the War of 1812. Yet until 1814, the small island managed to maintain its security. The biggest problem faced by the island's fishing community was obtaining food and other necessities from the mainland or other sources. When enacting a new Embargo Act in 1813, Congress realized the difficulties afflicting Nantucket and exempted it from the Embargo's restrictions on importing food and fuel. It did not hurt that the island also contained a Democratic Republican majority.

Even the exemption did the islanders little good by the summer of 1814. The British began increasing their naval activities in New England waters, and food shortages on the island reached a critical level in August. Island leaders opened negotiations with British admiral Sir Alexander Cochrane. In return for the island's declaration of neutrality and its promise to pay no more U.S. taxes, Cochrane allowed the islanders to import food from the mainland with the understanding that they would also sell some of that food to Cochrane's fleet. Because of this agreement, the tradition developed that Nantucket made peace with the British four months before the U.S. government.

—*Jeanne T. Heidler and David S. Heidler*

See also: Cochrane, Alexander
Further Reading
Horsman, Reginald. "Nantucket's Peace Treaty with England in 1814." *New England Quarterly* 54 (1981): 180–198.

NAPIER, CHARLES
1782–1853
British army officer

Born in London to Col. George Napier and Lady Sarah Bunbury Napier, Charles Napier spent most of his childhood in Ireland. He received a commission as an ensign in 1794. Promoted to lieutenant colonel by June 1811, Napier served with distinction in the Peninsular Campaign and was wounded several times. Transferred to the U.S. theater, he arrived in Bermuda in September 1812.

In the spring of 1813, Napier commanded a brigade under Gen. Sir Thomas Sydney Beckwith in its move to join forces with Adm. Sir George Cockburn in Chesapeake Bay. Napier commanded part of the landing force that attempted and failed to take Craney Island, which guarded the approach to Norfolk, and led the initial land force in the successful subjugation of Hampton, Virginia. Napier was one of the few officers who tried to restrain his men from engaging in rape and murder in Hampton on 26 June 1813. Later he lamented the terrible excesses committed there and decried the lack of punishment meted out to the perpetrators.

Following this raid into Chesapeake Bay, Napier and his 102nd Foot were detached from Beckwith's army to accompany Cockburn on raids along the Carolina coasts. Once again, he found the looting side of the campaign to be distasteful. He believed that a British-instigated slave rebellion in the South would be far more expedient.

Longing for real military glory, Napier requested and received a transfer back to the European war but arrived after the abdication of Napoleon. When he learned, while at home, of the return of Napoleon from Elba, once again he arrived on the continent too late to participate at Waterloo.

Following the war, Napier remained in the army and served in a variety of posts, including Greece. He gained his greatest fame, however, during several tours in India in the 1840s, suppressing local rulers and cementing British control there. He returned to Great Britain in 1851.

In 1852, Napier caught a cold while serving as a pallbearer at the Duke of Wellington's funeral. His health never recovered, and he died in 1853.

—*Jeanne T. Heidler and David S. Heidler*

See also: Cockburn, George; Craney Island, Battle of; Hampton, Virginia

Further Reading

Butler, William F. *Sir Charles James Napier.* London: Macmillan, 1890.

Napier, William B. *The Life and Opinions of General Sir Charles James Napier.* 4 vols. London: J. Murray, 1857.

NAPIER, CHARLES
1786–1860
British naval officer

Born in England to Charles Napier and Christian Hamilton Napier, the younger Napier entered the British navy in 1799. He served in various theaters throughout the Napoleonic wars, including in the West Indies from 1807 to 1809 and in the Mediterranean in 1811. Given command of HMS *Euryalus,* he joined the British convoy to Chesapeake Bay in the summer of 1814.

In the Washington, D.C., campaign of August 1814, Napier and the *Euryalus* were part of the squadron commanded by Capt. James A. Gordon that made its way up the Potomac as Gen. Robert Ross and Adm. Sir George Cockburn traveled overland. Stopping at Fort Washington on 24 August, Napier ordered *Euryalus's* guns opened up on the U.S. position. Much to his surprise, however, the U.S. garrison under Capt. Sam Dyson, rather than returning fire, blew up the fort and retreated, leaving the way open to Alexandria. Napier continued on with Gordon to that wealthy city and participated in the confiscation of much of the public and private property there.

On the way back down the Potomac, the *Euryalus* ran aground. Napier, eager to join the fighting about to commence at Baltimore, ordered the ship's artillery removed to float the vessel off the sandbar. While the process was underway, he took one of the smaller boats and a small crew to Baltimore. He arrived almost too late to participate in the attempt to take the city.

Just as the British forces on land and water were about to abandon the attempt on Baltimore, Adm. Alexander Cochrane decided to make one more attempt at a diversion for the land forces. Cochrane chose the intrepid Captain Napier to command the attempt. Napier was to lead a flotilla of 20 small boats to the west of Fort McHenry and then, at a rocket signal to be given at 2:00 A.M. on 14 September, stage a diversionary attack on the land forces there to draw off some of the defenders from North Point.

As his boats tried to find their way in the darkness after midnight, 11 of them lost their way and never made it to the rendezvous. Napier led the other nine into position, but they were spotted by Americans on shore, who opened fire. Napier returned fire for a while, but the British on North Point never began their attack, so he withdrew to the British ships. The British land forces had already decided to abandon the offensive.

Following the war, Napier traveled extensively and, for a while, became a successful businessman. Because of financial reverses, he returned to active naval service in 1829 and, beginning in 1833, hired his services to the Portuguese navy. In later life, he returned to British service and entered Parliament. He died in England in 1860.

—*Jeanne T. Heidler and David S. Heidler*

See also: Baltimore, Battle of; Chesapeake Bay Campaign, 1813–1814; Cochrane, Alexander; Gordon, James Alexander; McHenry, Fort

Further Reading

Napier, Elers. *The Life and Correspondence of Admiral Sir Charles Napier.* 2 vols. London: Hurst, Blackett, 1862.

NAPOLEON I
1769–1821
Emperor of the French

Born Napoleone Buonaparte on 15 August 1769 of a minor noble family in Ajaccio, Corsica, one year after its reunion with France, Napoleon received a military education at the College of Autun, the Military School of Brienne, and the Ecole Militaire. In 1785, he graduated as a sublieutenant of artillery and was posted to a regiment at Valence. With the reorganization of the army in 1791, he was promoted to the rank of lieutenant. After his successful defeat of the British at Toulon in 1793, Bonaparte was promoted to general of the brigade. He saved the republic by subduing a serious uprising in Paris in 1795 with the famous "whiff of grapeshot" and was duly rewarded with an appointment to command the Army of Italy. During

1796–1797, he defeated larger Austrian armies and compelled all of France's continental opponents to peace. He also established several Italian republics under the umbrella of France.

By then, only Britain remained at war with France. To defeat the British, the French government planned to interdict the British trade route to India. Napoleon undertook an Egyptian campaign, but Nelson destroyed the French fleet in 1798 at Aboukir.

Deserting his army, Napoleon returned to France, where he launched a successful coup d'état to overthrow the republic in 1799. Upon seizing power, he made himself first consul for life (1800) and later emperor (1804). Napoleon's military successes, particularly the defeat of Austria at Marengo, guaranteed his power.

Internally, Napoleon carried out significant reforms, many of which laid the foundations of the modern French state. In 1800, he created the Bank of France, and by 1802 the budget was balanced. He espoused a policy of national reconciliation, using both persuasion and force. His concordat with Pope Pius VII in 1801 pacified Roman Catholics. He centralized local government by appointing prefects and mayors, and he actively participated in the drafting of a French law code, the Napoleonic Code (1804). To reward military excellence, he founded the Legion of Honor (1802). Finally, he created the *lycées* and organized schools and teachers into an Imperial University (1806), which administered all levels of education.

Although Europe was at peace in 1802, Napoleon's expansionist policies led to a renewal of warfare the next year. Abandoning schemes to reestablish a French empire in the New World, he sold Louisiana to the United States and used the money to finance his new war against the British. Napoleon overran Hanover and threatened Austria and Russia by proclaiming himself king of Italy in 1805. The Austro-Russian alliance was defeated at the battles of Ulm and Austerlitz (1805). With the Treaty of Pressburg (December 1805), he expanded the kingdom of Italy by adding Venice and Dalmatia. The next year brothers Joseph and Louis were made kings of Naples and Holland and Napoleon himself president of the Confederation of the Rhine. Prussia and Russia allied against Napoleon but were unable to defeat him at the battles of Jena-Auerstadt (1806), Eylau, and Friedland (1807). The Peace of Tilsit made Czar Alexander I an ally of Napoleon and expanded the latter's control over continental Europe. The kingdom of Westphalia under brother Jérôme and the Duchy of Warsaw governed by ally king Augustus of Saxony were added to the empire.

By this time, Napoleon, at the peak of his power over continental Europe, was in a position to launch economic warfare against Great Britain, a nation he was unable to defeat by conventional means. The Continental Blockade that Napoleon initiated in 1806 and that lasted until his downfall in 1814 was his attempt to paralyze Britain through the destruction of her commerce. Through the Berlin and Milan Decrees of 1806 and 1807, which closed European ports to British commerce, Napoleon hoped to break Britain's merchant marine. Britain retaliated with the Orders in Council (January and November 1807) ordering a naval blockade of all European ports obeying Napoleon's decrees and requiring all neutral ships bound there to submit to searches. Colonial and overseas merchandise could not reach Europe except through British ports. This led to quarrels with neutrals over maritime rights and eventually to the United States' decision to declare war on Britain in 1812.

The French started seizing U.S. ships in 1807, and in March 1810 with the Decree of Rambouillet, Napoleon captured large numbers of U.S. ships trying to enter the ports of the French empire. This development was so serious that French captures actually outnumbered those made by the British (approximately 519 to 389). Napoleon adopted a hostile attitude toward U.S. commerce because he did not regard the United States as an independent nation. At the same time, Britain seized hundreds of U.S. merchantmen and interrupted the sale of agricultural products abroad; British impressment forced U.S. seamen into service under the Union Jack, thereby disregarding U.S. interests.

The Continental System was not a complete success for France. Britain continued to trade with neutral and allied nations such as Sweden, Denmark, Spain, Portugal, and Russia. Further, states directly controlled by Napoleon did not wish to undermine their commerce. Holland was notorious for smuggling. French officials breached their own laws. By 1809, Napoleon himself agreed to allow trade that was nominally banned, provided his treasury benefited at Britain's expense.

Napoleon's obvious chicanery was evident in his baiting of the Americans with his sly and false response to Macon's Bill No. 2, which was passed by the U.S. Congress in 1810. Pres. James Madison accepted Napoleon's offer, made in the Cadore letter, that he would annul his decrees against neutral shipping if Britain removed the Orders in Council or if the Americans coerced the British into respecting French rights. Napoleon did not keep his word. The French decrees were not lifted until May 1812.

In 1812, Napoleon set off to punish the Russians for leaving the Continental System. The Russian campaign ended in humiliating retreat from Moscow and defeat at the hands of a united Europe at Leipzig in October 1813.

Napoleon abdicated on 6 April 1814 and was exiled to Elba. In March 1815, after escaping from Elba and returning to France, Napoleon returned to power. The European allies outlawed him, and when he attacked them in Belgium, he was defeated at Waterloo and abdicated a second time on 22 June in favor of his son. He was exiled to St. Helena in the south Atlantic, where he died on 5 May 1821.

General, first consul, and later emperor of the French, Napoleon is remembered first for the military expansion of the French empire. He was also one of the most enlightened monarchs of all time, who left a lasting mark on French institutions and much of western Europe. Yet, his economic war against Britain and the British response to it prompted depredations against neutrals, especially the United States, that led to the War of 1812.

—Leigh Whaley

See also: Berlin Decree; Cadore Letter; Impressment; Macon's Bill No. 2; Milan Decree; Orders in Council; Rambouillet Decree

Further Reading

Chandler, David. *The Campaigns of Napoleon.* London: Weidenfeld and Nicolson, 1967.

Lefebvre, Georges. *Napoleon: From 18 Brumaire to Tilsit, 1799–1807,* trans. Henry F. Stockhold. New York: Columbia University Press, 1969.

Markham, Felix. *Napoleon.* London and New York: Weidenfeld and Nicolson/New American Library, 1963, 1964.

Thompson, J. M. *Napoleon Bonaparte: His Rise and Fall.* Oxford: Basil Blackwell, 1990.

Tulard, Jean. *Napoleon, the Myth of the Saviour,* trans. Teresa Waugh. London: Weidenfeld and Nicolson, 1984.

NATIONAL ANTHEM

See Star-Spangled Banner, The

NATIONAL INTELLIGENCER

See Gales, Joseph

NAVAL ORDNANCE

Heavy warship guns during the War of 1812 were muzzle loaders, and virtually all larger ones were made of iron. Guns were denominated by the weight of their solid shot rather than by the diameter of their bore, as is now the custom. Projectiles consisted of solid shot, explosive shell, and—for close action—canister and grape. All weighed approximately the same as a solid ball. The most common projectile for engaging another vessel was solid shot. In close actions, guns might be double-, even triple-shotted.

Most guns of the War of 1812 were long guns, but there were also carronades as well as small howitzers carried in the fighting tops of larger vessels and utilized as antipersonnel weapons. Also in the latter category were small guns of cannon form, known as swivels, which were mounted on the rails of smaller vessels. Howitzers and swivels were normally not counted as part of a ship's armament rating.

The carronade was the most important innovation in naval ordnance made at the end of the eighteenth century. It was a short, light gun of large bore that was used extensively in the War of 1812. It was named for the Carron Company of Scotland, which produced the first prototype in 1776. The lightness of the carronade enabled it to be employed where a heavier gun could not be supported, such as on the poop or forecastle. The savings in weight made it especially popular for smaller vessels, and in fact it became the principal armament of brigs. Generally speaking, the carronade replaced the small, 4- to 12-pounder, long guns on board naval vessels. Although in the smaller ships there was a shift to carronades, in the larger vessels the long gun remained in favor—although there, too, some carronades were included.

The true carronade had no trunnions but was mounted on its bed by means of a bolt through a loop cast on the underside of the piece. All carronades were short, only about seven calibers in length. Royal Navy carronades weighed about 50 to 60 pounds of metal for every pound of shot. U.S. Navy carronades were closely patterned after those of the Royal Navy but were heavier, 60–70 pounds per 1 pound of shot. This was in contrast to as much as 150 to 200 pounds per 1 pound of shot in long guns. The carronade used approximately one-third of the powder charge of its counterpart long gun. Owing to its low muzzle velocity, the windage on the carronade could be sharply reduced. The ball fired by the carronade moved at relatively slow velocity but produced a large irregular hole and considerable splintering (wooden splinters were the chief cause of casualties in ship battles during the age of sail).

The carronade was ideally suited for close action, but it had its disadvantages. One was its excessive recoil; another was that because it was so short, its burning powder might ignite its own ship's side or rigging. Its chief weakness, however, was its lack of range. Carronades were employed at point-blank, which meant about 450 yards for a 68-

pounder and 230 yards for a 12-pounder. If the fighting was at long range, the carronade was a liability, as was revealed during the War of 1812.

By the War of 1812, carronades had replaced the smaller long guns in the U.S. Navy and were also placed on the upper decks of frigates. The heavier U.S. frigates carried 32-pounder carronades; the *President* was the only U.S. frigate to carry 42-pounders.

The U.S. Navy retained a preference for the long gun for pursuit and as the main armament, but on many smaller U.S. vessels carronades formed the entire armament. In a battle fought at close quarters, 32-pounder carronades on the *Wasp* inflicted heavy damage on HMS *Frolic*, also armed largely with carronades. The same was true in the victory won by the *Hornet* over HMS *Peacock*, another contest in which carronades were the principal armament.

The War of 1812 also revealed the carronade's fatal weakness and heralded its demise. Although a formidable weapon at close range, at longer range the carronade was no match for long guns, even those of smaller caliber. British carronade-armed vessels on Lakes Erie and Ontario were at a decided disadvantage when they confronted U.S. long-range guns. Commodore Sir James Yeo reported on 12 September 1812 that the Americans had been able to engage the British at long range with their long 24- and 32-pounders, but the British had been unable to close to employ their carronades.

Late in the war, the tables were turned on the U.S. Navy when the frigate *Essex*, armed almost exclusively with carronades, was defeated at long range by the British warships *Phoebe* and *Cherub*, both armed with long guns. This engagement considerably tarnished the reputation of the carronade and reinforced the conclusion that vessels should not be armed exclusively with them.

In positioning ordnance, the heaviest guns were mounted on the lower or gun decks to aid in vessel stability. In addition, one or more long pieces, known as chase guns, were mounted on the top deck forward to engage the enemy at long range in pursuit.

The biggest gun at sea during the war was the 68-pounder carronade carried by some British ships of the line. On the U.S. side, the largest guns in general use were the 24-pounder long gun and the 32-pounder carronade, although 32-pounder long guns and 42-pounder carronades did see naval service.

U.S. guns of this period were of many patterns and nationalities, including a substantial number purchased from Britain during the Quasi-War with France. In addition, during the War of 1812 there was considerable swapping of ordnance between army and navy, the bulk of it in loans from the navy to the army. For all these reasons, it is difficult to identify with any precision the exact types of guns carried by a particular vessel.

In design, U.S. naval ordnance tended to follow British patterns (the Americans did accept French practice in omitting the chase astragal). Trunnions, the lugs that held the gun in its carriage, were also located on the center line, whereas those of British guns were below. The standard length of U.S. Navy long guns was 18 shot diameters, but this varied widely; chase guns, which had the greatest range, were always the longest; lower deck guns were the shortest. U.S. guns also tended to be somewhat heavier in proportion to shot weight than their British counterparts. The ideal weight of long guns was considered to be approximately 200 pounds of metal per 1 pound of shot. A comparison of naval cannon (the longest, or chase guns) and carronades is shown in Table 1.

Range of guns varied according to powder charge and

Table 1

	Length (ft-in)	Weight (lbs.)	Powder Charge (lb.-oz.)	Bore Diameter (inches)	Shot Diameter (inches)
68-pdr carronade	5-2	4,032	6-0	8.05	8
42-pdr long gun	10-0	7,504	14-0	7.018	6.684
42-pdr carronade	4-3.5	2,492	4-8	6.85	6.684
32-pdr long gun	10-0	6,496	10-11	6.41	6.105
32-pdr carronade	4-0.5	1,918	4-0	6.25	6.105
24-pdr long gun	10-0	5,824	8-0	5.824	5.547
24-pdr carronade	3-7.5	1,456	3-0	5.67	5.547
18-pdr long gun	9-6	4,704	6-0	5.292	5.04
18-pdr carronade	3-3	1,008	2-0	5.14	5.04
12-pdr long gun	9-6	3,808	4-0	4.623	4.403
12-pdr carronade	2-2	654	1-8	4.5	4.403
9-pdr long gun	9-6	3,388	3-0	4.2	4
6-pdr long gun	9-0	2,688	2-0	3.668	3.498
4-pdr long gun	6-0	1,372	1-5	3.204	3.053
3-pdr long gun	4-6	812	1-0	2.913	1.775

elevation. For example, in 1812 the shot for a long gun charged with powder one-third of the weight of the ball and at an elevation of 2 degrees would reach 1,200 yards on the first graze. A charge of one-quarter and the same elevation would propel the shot to 1,000 yards for a first graze (double-shot with the same charge and elevation would reach only 500 yards). At 7 degrees elevation and a charge of one-quarter, a single shot would reach 2,020 yards at first graze.

The largest U.S. vessels to take part in the war were frigates. Generally, U.S. frigate armament was in advance of its British counterparts. While the Americans had 24-pounders on the gun decks, the British mounted mainly 18-pounders.

Guns of U.S. naval vessels during the War of 1812 ranged from 24-pounder long guns and 32-pounder carronades on the larger frigates, and 12- and 18-pounder long guns and 18- and 24-pounder carronades on the smaller frigates, to 9-pounders on sloops of war and 6-pounders on the smaller brigs and schooners. Armament also varied widely from ship to ship, even those of the same class, for individual captains had their own preferences, and there were frequent changes in regulations.

Theodore Roosevelt probably erred in his observation that U.S. ordnance was not as good as that of the British and was more likely to burst. Several guns did burst aboard U.S. vessels during the war: a bow-chaser gun burst on board the *General Pike*; another burst on board the frigate *President* when she was chasing the British frigate *Belvidera*. Despite these accidents, U.S. naval ordnance was generally as good as that of the British. Certainly, superior U.S. gunnery and tactics were important factors in the early U.S. victories at sea.

Of new gun designs during the war, on the U.S. side there was the Columbiad. The British also had the Congreve gun, designed by Sir William Congreve in 1814. It appeared in only one class: a 24-pounder, 7 feet, 6 inches in length, weighing approximately 4,592 lbs. It had a plain, tapered muzzle and the first ring cascable. Its relatively smooth exterior form and single-curved breech may have influenced subsequent designs of General Millar in England and Lt. John A. Dahlgren in the United States.

Table 2 illustrates representative armament for U.S. vessels (note that rate does not correspond to actual number of guns carried).

—*Spencer C. Tucker*

See also: Cannon, Naval; Columbiad

Further Reading
Tucker, Spencer C. *Arming the Fleet: United States Navy Ordnance in the Muzzle-Loading Era.* Annapolis, MD: Naval Institute Press, 1989.
———. "The Carronade." *Naval Institute Proceedings* 99 (August 1973): 65–70.

Table 2

Type	Rate	Armament
Frigate	44	52 guns: 30 long 24-pdrs, 2 long 24-pdr bow chasers, 20 32-pdr carronades
Frigate	38	49 guns: 28 long 18-pdrs, 1 long shifting 18-pdr, 20 32-pdr carronades
Ship sloop	18	20 guns: 18 32-pdr carronades, 2 18-pdrs
Brig	16	18 guns: 16 24-pdr carronades, 2 12-pdrs
Brig	14	16 guns: 16 18-pdr carronades
Brig	12	14 guns: 12 18-pdr carronades, 2 9-pdrs
Gunboats/Galleys		usually 1 to 2 guns, long 18- to 32-pdrs, or carronades

NAVAL STRATEGY, GREAT BRITAIN

While Anglo-American relations deteriorated, Great Britain was also engulfed in the titanic wars of the French Revolution and Napoleon. This contest involved operations all over the world, including India, the East Indies, and the West Indies, and against not only powerful France, but, on occasion, Spain, the Netherlands, several Italian states, Austria, Prussia, Denmark, and Russia. British naval superiority was overwhelming, especially after the French-Spanish defeat at Trafalgar in 1805, but the naval obligations of such a vast conflict were more than demanding. During the first year of the War of 1812, the Royal Navy's North American squadron was so low in priority that its modest forces included only one ship of the line and about 30 others and was not reinforced until 1813. In fact, during this first year, the British Admiralty was so embarrassed by the poor performance against U.S. frigates on the high seas that it ordered its forces to avoid one-on-one clashes with U.S. Navy ships.

Because they dominated the Northwest territories and the central United States, the Great Lakes absorbed a considerable amount of the British naval effort. After building

A satirical depiction by Charles del et Sculp of British efforts to recover after major naval losses on the Great Lakes in 1813 and 1814.

the necessary warships, Britain planned to use combined land and naval forces to defeat the Americans on and around Lakes Champlain, Erie, and Ontario. Although the British enjoyed numerous advantages at the outset, ultimately their extensive efforts were to fail, especially at the Battle of Lake Erie in September 1813 and the Battle of Lake Champlain the following year.

In addition, the British implemented an extensive blockade of the U.S. coast. In 1813, the Royal Navy's North American squadron was significantly reinforced with up to ten ships of the line, 38 frigates, and 52 other vessels. In addition to establishing a convoy system to protect British shipping from U.S. privateers and naval forces, the Royal Navy's predatory methods crushed U.S. trade, especially that of New England merchants, and facilitated reinforcement of British forces conducting amphibious operations throughout the area. In New England, bankruptcy loomed, the region was alienated from the rest of the country, and calls for secession were heard. In other areas, there was plunder and elimination of coastal trade.

The British had gained much experience in combined army-navy operations against the French and their allies during the European wars. Several amphibious operations were planned against the Americans, in Chesapeake Bay, the Maine district of Massachusetts, the southern Atlantic coast, and the Mississippi Territory and Louisiana coasts in the Gulf of Mexico. These targets were selected in part to distract the Americans from further forays into Canada, but other objectives included destruction of U.S. war production, elimination of U.S. merchant shipping and privateers, and retribution for attacks and depredations against Canadian towns and cities, especially the capital of Upper Canada at York (later Toronto). From 1813 to the end of the war, British army and naval forces carried out raids and attacks on U.S. coastal areas, harassing private citizens and destroying government and war production facilities. Adm. Sir George Cockburn led amphibious attacks in Chesapeake Bay country during 1813. The following year, the British presence greatly increased when Adm. Sir Alexander Cochrane brought a large fleet into the bay. After land forces under Gen. Robert Ross had sacked Washington, Cochrane and Ross tried unsuccessfully to reduce Baltimore. In late 1814, while Cockburn continued operations along the southern coast, Cochrane ferried forces to New Orleans. Although the Royal Navy would clear Lake Borgne of U.S. gunboats, the land assault on the Crescent City ended in disaster.

The strategy of coastal raiding drew mixed responses. The only real success of the strategy occurred in the Maine district, where the British assault on Castine, Hampden, Bangor, and Machias accomplished the concrete objective of securing communications between Halifax and Montreal. Otherwise, the policy was either controversial or ineffectual. Many Britons condemned the vandalism that frequently accompanied such operations, as in the sack of Hampton, Virginia, or at Washington, D.C. Occurring in the same season as the British defeat on Lake Champlain, the failures of campaigns against Baltimore and New Orleans were serious setbacks. When the British cabinet sought advice from the Duke of Wellington, even proposing that he take command of the U.S. war, he bluntly declared that Britain could only triumph by controlling the Great Lakes. Wellington did not favor coastal raiding. There was little enthusiasm for continuing the war under these circumstances.

The U.S. Navy's early success on the high seas was the result of Britain's preoccupation with the European war. By the conclusion of that conflict, the Royal Navy's blue-water preponderance had stopped U.S. victories in that setting. Yet the strategic importance of the Great Lakes and Lake Champlain made the Royal Navy's coastal strategy more a costly distraction from, rather than a positive contributor to, larger British objectives in North America. U.S. commanders Oliver Hazard Perry on Lake Erie in 1813 and Thomas Macdonough on Lake Champlain in 1814 accomplished far more of substance than Cockburn ever did in Chesapeake Bay or Cochrane did on Lake Borgne. In many respects, British naval strategy was a reflection of the British government's persistent opinion that the U.S. war was a marginal event, a particle literally on the edge of the vast Napoleonic canvas.

—Jeanne T. Heidler and David S. Heidler
—Eugene L. Rasor, contributing

See also: Baltimore, Battle of; Chesapeake Bay Campaign, 1813–1814; Cochrane, Alexander; Cockburn, George; Downie, George; Lake Borgne, Battle of; Lake Champlain, Battle of; Lake Erie Campaign; Warren, John Borlase; Yeo, James Lucas; and ship battles by name

Further Reading

An Inquiry into the Present State of the British Navy Together with Reflections on the Late War with America, Its Probable Conse- *quences, &c. &c. &c.* London: C. Chapple, printed by W. M'Dowall, 1815.

Dudley, William S. "Naval Historians and the War of 1812." *Naval History* 4 (spring 1990): 52–57.

Dundonald, Thomas Cochrane. *Message from the President of the United States, Transmitting a Correspondence between Admiral Cockrane* [sic] *and the Secretary of State, in Relation to an Order of the Former to Destroy and Lay Waste the Towns on the Coasts of the United States.* Washington City: Printed by Roger C. Weightman, 1814.

Lewis, Dennis M. *British Naval Activity on Lake Champlain during the War of 1812.* Plattsburg, NY, and Elizabethtown, NY: Clinton County Historical Association and Essex County Historical Society, 1994.

Norie, J. W. *The Naval Gazetteer, Biographer, and Chronologist Containing a History of the Late Wars, from their Commencement in 1793 to Their Conclusion in 1801; and From their Re-commencement in 1803 to Their Final Conclusion in 1815; and Continued, as to the Biographical Part, to the Present Time.* London: J. W. Norie and Co., 1827.

Patton, Philip. *The Observations of an Admiral on the State of the Navy, and More Particularly as it is Connected with the American War.* Fareham, Hampshire: N.p., 1813.

NAVAL STRATEGY, UNITED STATES

A decisive fleet action never was a consideration for a nation whose entire navy was smaller than some British squadrons. As has always been the case with the weaker side in a conflict, ways had to be found and means adopted that, to the greatest extent possible, resulted in some sort of equalization of forces in at least some areas of confrontation. One bright spot in the picture for U.S. naval planners at the outset of the War of 1812 was the fact that Great Britain was in a monumental struggle with Napoleonic France. Britain could not bring more than a small portion of its power to bear on the upstart across the Atlantic. The best hope for the U.S. leadership was to devise a strategy that would so annoy the British that they would settle the matters at issue between the two nations in order to concentrate once again on Napoleon.

Congress, ever eager to wield power but not directly empowered to conduct any war, sought to impose through legislation its collective will on the direction of the war. Initially, it would not increase the size of the navy and would limit high seas action to a privateering effort. The real attraction for many senators and representatives was Canada. The army would be expanded (14 times!) to conquer that British colony so that it could be used as a bargaining chip in negotiations, either to settle points of difference or provide compensation for perceived wrongs of interference with free trade and impressment of U.S. seamen. That done, if Britain did not sue for peace, it at least would be denied a convenient staging area for operations against the United States. Congress ignored whether such forces necessary to conquer Canada could be recruited, as well as considerations of the time and expense of mobilizing, outfitting, and training such a force for combat operations. Many Americans thought that fighting both in North America and in Europe would eventually wear Britain down.

In the months preceding the war, the executive, too, regarded Canada as an alluring target for land operations. All agreed that *some* sort of offensive plan was mandatory. Even Secretary of the Navy Paul Hamilton believed that the U.S. Navy was too small to have any impact against the British; he thought that the navy should be maintained in port as a sort of "fortress in being." He was supported in this notion by Secretary of the Treasury Albert Gallatin, long the foe of the seagoing (and expensive) navy. Accident intervened to alter this idea.

Capt. William Bainbridge, having newly returned from an extended furlough during which he had engaged in merchant voyages, was in Washington, D.C., in February 1812 seeking an active assignment. When he learned of the idea of keeping the warships in port as floating defensive batteries, he was filled "with infinite regret and mortification." He shared his concern with Capt. Charles Stewart, also in town seeking a new assignment, and instantly found a kindred spirit. No doubt motivated as much by thoughts of fame and glory denied as by patriotism, the two drafted a letter to Hamilton. This forceful document stressed, among other things, that the navy never again would find public support if it were kept in port and therefore was adjudged "useless during a period of national peril." It was their recommendation that the navy adopt the *guerre de course*, or warfare against the enemy's commerce, causing Britain the loss of gold and goods and requiring the dissipation of its naval forces to bring raiders to bay.

Among other senior naval officers, Commodore Stephen Decatur likewise favored a widespread raiding concept that would employ ships singly and in pairs. Commodore John Rodgers, senior naval officer on active service and commander of the most powerful squadron in the navy, not surprisingly proposed a squadron to raid British commerce all the way to England, while other, lesser units would individually harass British trade in the West Indies (then a prime trade area) and occasionally unite to strike at homeward-bound merchant convoys.

Pres. James Madison came down on the side of his naval officers. His position, succinctly stated, was to secure victories, even at the cost of ships, because the ships could be replaced.

When war came, one way or another, all the naval officers got their way. Rodgers was first off the mark with his squadron and raided (with small effect) all the way to England. In their turn, Bainbridge, Stewart, Decatur, and others went on single-ship or small-unit cruises that repeatedly gained the headlines. British shipping interests were pained, and British naval officers were embarrassed. On that level, the strategy was a complete success.

As for affecting the outcome of the war, the high seas effort had little impact. Instead, it was the navy's support of the army's often-abortive efforts toward Canada that bore important fruit. Defeats of British naval forces on Lakes Erie and Champlain, combined with the preservation of the status quo antebellum on Lake Ontario, preserved the United States' northern border and led the British to be more amenable in the peace negotiations at Ghent.

—*Tyrone G. Martin*

See also: Bainbridge, William; Decatur, Stephen, Jr.; Hamilton, Paul; Lake Champlain, Battle of; Lake Erie Campaign; Naval Strategy, Great Britain; Privateering; Rodgers, John; Stewart, Charles; and ship battles by name

Further Reading

Forester, C. S. *The Age of Fighting Sail*. Garden City: Doubleday and Company, 1956.

Long, David F. *Ready to Hazard*. Hanover: University Press of New England, 1981.

Mahan, Alfred T. *Sea Power in Its Relation to the War of 1812*. 2 vols. Boston: Little, Brown, 1905.

Paullin, Charles O. *Commodore John Rodgers, 1773–1838*. Annapolis, MD: Naval Institute Press, 1967.

NEW HAMPSHIRE

Not as heavily Federalist as its neighbors Massachusetts, Connecticut, and Rhode Island, New Hampshire was divided among Federalist opponents of the war and Democratic Republican supporters of it. The governor of the state in the first year of the war, William Plumer, a Democratic Republican, responded to Brig. Gen. Henry Dearborn's request for militia in the first days of the war by sending the requested men to aid in the proposed invasion of Canada. This action put him at odds with his counterparts in the aforementioned states, who decried his action as unconstitutional. Federalists throughout New England, including those within New Hampshire, condemned Plumer not only for supplying the militia but also for allowing it to serve under federal regular officers. Plumer probably also increased his unpopularity among certain people in the state by trying to prohibit smuggling across the New Hampshire border into Canada.

The strong reaction to Plumer's actions and the growing unpopularity of the war led to his loss to Federalist candidate John Taylor Gilman in the gubernatorial election of 1813. The Democratic Republicans still controlled the state executive council, indicating the persistently divided nature of New Hampshire politics.

Gilman immediately reversed Plumer's policy of allowing New Hampshire militia to serve under regular officers. When Gilman called out militia in early summer 1814 to protect Portsmouth against the Royal Navy, the federal government refused to supply these forces unless they served under a regular officer. Gilman responded to Washington's action by sending his militia home, but as the British threat stretched down the coast toward Portsmouth (where the USS *Washington* was under construction), Gilman called out 1,500 men at the end of the summer. New Hampshire militia brigadier general John Montgomery sent word to his men that every tenth militiaman should report to Portsmouth, and he immediately set about to strengthen tiny Fort Sumner, which guarded the harbor.

By the fall of 1814, it appeared that Portsmouth and the remainder of New Hampshire were out of danger. This may partly explain the state's apathy toward Massachusetts's call for New England states to send delegates to the Hartford Convention. Officially, the state government took no action regarding the invitation, though two counties sent Benjamin West and Mills Olcott to the convention as delegates.

New Hampshire was a politically divided state, but it probably contributed more to the war effort than its New England neighbors. Its strong Federalist contingent also helped to promote the divisiveness that characterized the War of 1812 in the United States.

—*Jeanne T. Heidler and David S. Heidler*

See also: Dearborn, Henry; Federalist Party; Gilman, John Taylor; Hartford Convention
Further Reading
Wade, Arthur P. "The Defenses of Portsmouth Harbor, 1794–1821." *Historical New Hampshire* 33 (1978): 25–51.
Watts, Emma C. "New Hampshire in the War of 1812." *Granite Monthly* 30 (1901): 357–366.

NEW JERSEY

In the spring of 1812, New Jersey Federalists hoped the imposition of the 90-day embargo in April and the threat of war would provide them with issues for the fall elections. From 1807 to 1812, Federalists had raised foreign policy issues, but with the exception of 1808 (because of the embargo), they failed to successfully exploit the weaknesses of Republican foreign policy. Responding to the new crisis, Federalists organized a series of antiwar meetings in May and June. They got a jump on their political opponents by organizing a state convention. About 60 to 70 members attended a May meeting in Trenton, where they railed against war, taxes, standing armies, and drafting the militia. This anticipated the positions Federalists took in the fall election. At the meeting, Federalists called upon the faithful to elect delegates to the Fourth of July convention and adopted the title Friends of Peace, the name they used throughout the 1815 elections.

When Congress voted to declare war on 18 June 1812, both Federalists and Republicans were surprised that the majority of the state's congressional delegation voted against war. New Jersey's two senators and six congressmen were Republicans, but they split over the 1812 presidential race. Sen. John Lambert and Reps. Jacob Hufty, Thomas Newbold, and George C. Maxwell supported DeWitt Clinton, and they voted against war. Sen. John Cordit and Reps. Lewis Condict, James Morgan, and Adam Boyd favored the reelection of James Madison, and with the exception of Boyd, they voted for war. Boyd broke with the other Madison supporters and voted against war because he agreed with the Clintonians that the United States was militarily unprepared.

After the declaration of war, Republicans condemned the antiwar votes as pressure built for conformity to the party line. Many New Jersey Republicans had reservations about going to war, including party kingpin James Wilson, but the New Jersey Republican Party rallied behind the president and the decision for war. Antiwar Republicans were read out of the party. However, Federalists praised the antiwar Republicans and used the Fourth of July convention to denounce the war and call for a nonpartisan peace coalition.

By the fall of 1812, Federalists, Clintonians, and other antiwar Republicans like Boyd joined together in a peace coalition. Evidence of a Clintonian-Federalist alliance appeared as early as May, when Clintonian Republican James Sloan, former leader of the Gloucester Democratic Association, attended an antiwar Federalist meeting. In

September, the Federalist nominating convention nominated three Federalists and three antiwar Republicans to run for Congress. Meanwhile, in New York City, John Pintard met with New Jersey Federalists attending the Federalist national convention. Pintard, a Clintonian Republican with family ties to New Jersey Federalists, sought to cement the alliance and ensure the nomination of Clintonian presidential electors if the Federalists took control of New Jersey.

Foreign policy became the dominant issue in the 1812 election. While the Federalists railed against the war and the militia draft, Republicans denounced the Federalists and their allies as the Tories of the War of 1812. Because the Republicans realized that many New Jerseyans opposed the war, they argued that President Madison had chosen war because no other option existed. As a means of drumming up support for the war, Republicans whipped up Anglophobia and wrapped themselves in the Revolutionary War legacy. This provided a way to legitimize the War of 1812 and to discredit the opponents of the United States' second Anglo-American conflict. Republicans also turned the Anglo-American conflict into a struggle between republicanism and monarchy. By appealing to the public's faith in republicanism, the Republicans hoped to justify the war, generate public support, and discredit criticism of the war.

Despite all the Republican efforts, the Federalists won a majority on the New Jersey council (7 to 6) and assembly (23 to 17) for the first time in a decade. Republicans attributed their defeat to fraud, intrigue, divisions within Republican ranks, and better Federalist organizations in Monmouth and Hunterdon counties, the two swing counties. Federalists saw their victory as a repudiation of the war, and eventually even the Republicans admitted that opposition to the war played a key role in the Federalist victory. The coalition with Clintonians in Hunterdon helped the Federalists carry the county, and divisions within Republican ranks also aided in Monmouth. Opposition to the war led to a surge of antiwar Quaker and Dutch voters supporting the Federalists in Gloucester and Middlesex counties. Even in counties that remained Republican, their majorities dropped as Republicans expressed their dissatisfaction by remaining home. Many Republicans abandoned the party in 1812. The movement away from the Republican Party was a protest against the war.

The campaign for the presidency coincided with the New Jersey legislative contest. Both Clintonian Republicans and Federalists believed that if the two groups united they could carry the state. They hoped to capitalize on the dissatisfaction with Madison in New Jersey. Even the prowar Republicans did not show as much enthusiasm for Madison as they had in 1808. However, fearing that the Republicans might still win the election for presidential electors, the Federalists decided after their October triumph to alter the election law. They postponed the 3–4 November congressional election to 12–13 January 1813 and eliminated the direct election of presidential electors. Instead, the legislature would pick the electors. It chose eight pro-Clinton electors.

The 1813 congressional election was fought on foreign policy issues, with the Republicans having the additional issue provided by the change in the electoral laws. Although the Federalists maintained their coalition with the Clintonians, they dropped two of three Republicans from their slate. The new election laws divided the state into three districts, each electing two congressmen. Republican strength was concentrated in the northern district and Federalist in the southern, with the central district up for grabs. The election results confirmed the drift away from the Republicans. They carried the northern district, but despite a hotly contested race in the central district, the Federalists won it and the southern district.

With Federalists in control of the legislature, they elected Aaron Ogden governor for 1812–1813. He pursued a moderate course on war-related issues. Ogden cooperated with the federal government and New York governor Daniel Tompkins to protect New York City, and he favored additional expenditures to defend the state. But he supported the legislature's antiwar resolutions and removed prowar Republicans from state office. His administration also opposed using the militia to invade Canada.

The issues in the 1813 election for state legislature repeated those of 1812, but the Republicans also charged that the Federalists had inadequately protected the state from British raiding parties. This time Republican appeals to patriotism, republicanism, and the Revolution succeeded. Both Monmouth and Hunterdon counties went Republican, and the party gained a 31-to-22 majority in the state legislature.

Although historians have discounted the impact of the war on New Jersey, British warships captured coasting vessels, and raiding and foraging parties burned ships, replenished their water supplies, and seized cattle. These incursions began in March 1813 and lasted until the fall of 1814. The raids scared some voters into believing the Republicans could better defend the state. Republicans also benefited from the return of some Clintonians to the fold and from public resentment over the changes in the election laws.

Republicans won again in 1814 and the composition of the legislature remained about the same, but Federalists picked up votes throughout the state. The Republican majority in Hunterdon was halved, and Monmouth's dropped from 300 to 45. A 150-vote difference in the election would have given the Federalists control, and they won 48 of the congressional votes. Continuation of the war and the militia draft aided the Federalists. However, the crisis created by the British attack on Washington, D.C., and the state's general prosperity overcame enough public dissatisfaction with the draft and the embargo of December 1813–April 1814 to allow the Republicans to remain in power.

In the fall 1815 election, the Republicans solidified their control of the state, and the swing toward the Federalists disappeared. These election results suggest that a majority of New Jerseyans accepted the Republican view of the war as a victory and identified with the Republican themes of Anglophobia and republicanism. The previous Federalist victories in October 1812 and January 1813, as well as the near-Federalist victory in 1814, represented a protest vote against Madison's foreign policy and not a realignment of the state's politics.

—Harvey J. Strum

See also: Clinton, DeWitt
Further Reading

Fee, Walter. *The Transition from Aristocracy to Democracy in New Jersey, 1789–1826.* Somerville, NJ: Somerset Press, 1933.

Lee, Francis. *New Jersey as a Colony and as a State.* 4 vols. New York: Publishing Society of New Jersey, Winthrop Press, 1902.

Pasler, Margaret, and Rudolph Pasler. *The New Jersey Federalists.* Rutherford, NJ: Fairleigh Dickinson University Press, 1975.

Prince, Carl. *New Jersey's Jeffersonian Republicans: The Genesis of an Early Party Machine, 1789–1817.* Chapel Hill: University of North Carolina Press, 1967.

Strum, Harvey. "New Jersey Politics and the War of 1812." *New Jersey History* 105 (fall/winter 1987): 37–69.

NEW LONDON, CONNECTICUT

This Connecticut port became a center of blockading activity and trade during the war. In October 1812, New London ladies produced a tumultuous welcoming ball for Stephen Decatur and the frigate *United States* after her capture of the frigate *Macedonian.* After taking both vessels to New York, Decatur brought them and the *Hornet* out in May 1813 but was driven into New London in June 1813. The presence of these ships guaranteed that the town would be blockaded, and on 7 June, a squadron com-

manded by Sir Thomas Masterman Hardy in *Ramillies* (74 guns) and Capt. Dudley Oliver in *Valiant* (74 guns), with attached frigates, sealed the port. Fearing an attack, Decatur took his vessels upstream 6 miles, leaving the river's entrance guarded by Fort Trumbull on the western bank and Fort Griswold on the eastern one. The local militia so reluctantly mounted a guard that Decatur believed his vessels were safeguarded more by the difficulties of the channel than by the strength of the fortifications.

New London was reported "full of apprehension." Benjamin Tallmadge thought the 74-gun ships might try to enter the harbor, while the Madison administration regarded New London as a home of "Blue-Light" Federalists, turncoats who used blue lantern signals to warn the British squadron about escape attempts by the *United States* and *Macedonian.* In November 1813, Decatur thought that if his ships dropped down to a mooring nearer the river's entrance the British might attack, so the U.S. frigates and New London remained blockaded for the remainder of the war. Meanwhile, British blockaders traded freely with the New London inhabitants

—Frederick C. Drake

See also: Connecticut; Decatur, Stephen, Jr.; Hardy, Thomas Masterman; Tallmadge, Benjamin
Further Reading

Goldenberg, Joseph A. "Blue Lights and Infernal Machines: The British Blockade of New London." *Mariner's Mirror* 61 (November, 1975): 385–397.

Niles' Weekly Register, vol. 4: 227, 245, 263, 293, 309, 325.

NEW ORLEANS, BATTLE OF
8 January 1815

Rumors abounded from the beginning of the War of 1812 that the British planned to land on the Gulf of Mexico's coast and wage a campaign against the southern United States. When the Creek War started in western Georgia and the Mississippi Territory in 1813, many white Americans incorrectly assumed that the Creeks had been encouraged in their attacks by the British. Not until 1814, however, did the British possess the manpower and the resources to plan a campaign on the gulf.

By the time the British began landing preliminary forces on Florida's Gulf Coast in the summer of 1814, Maj. Gen. Andrew Jackson had already defeated the hostile Creeks at Tohopeka (Horseshoe Bend). Before the summer was out,

The Battle of New Orleans and the death of Lt. Gen. Sir Edward Pakenham. It was mainly because the British waited for Pakenham and his troops, giving American defenders time to prepare, that they failed to take the city.

he had dictated the Treaty of Fort Jackson to the Creek Nation, wresting from them 23 million acres and ending British hopes that Indian allies would be of much help to them in their southern campaign. Still, in August 1814, the British advance forces established a base on the Apalachicola River and at Spanish Pensacola. Using Pensacola as a staging area, British land and naval forces, as well as some Indian allies, attempted and failed to take Mobile in September 1814.

British actions in Florida and against Mobile correctly convinced Jackson that the British planned larger operations in the gulf. Adm. Sir Alexander Cochrane planned to complete his operations in Chesapeake Bay, rendezvous with British veterans of the European wars at Jamaica, and stage a major invasion of the Gulf Coast before the end of 1814. Originally, Cochrane's plan called for Gen. Robert Ross to command the land forces in the assault on the gulf, but Ross's death in the Baltimore campaign required his replacement with Lt. Gen. Sir Edward Pakenham.

Although Jackson suspected the impending arrival of a large British land-and-sea force, he did not know where on the Gulf Coast it was headed or what its major target would be. Partially to satisfy his and westerners' ambitions regarding the remainder of West Florida and also to remove a possible base of operations for the British, Jackson decided in the fall of 1814 to take Spanish Pensacola. As the British withdrew from the town rather than fight Jackson's superior force, they blew up the town's fortifications, making the town useless as a base either to themselves or Jackson. While at Pensacola, however, Jackson learned of the arrival of Cochrane at Jamaica and of the impending arrival of more British land forces there. He also learned from a New Orleans merchant who had been visiting the island at the time of Cochrane's arrival that the target of the British operation was New Orleans. Jackson left Pensacola immediately for New Orleans, anxiously hoping to reach the city before Cochrane. Jackson arrived in the city with his army on 1 December 1814.

Surrounded by swampy wetlands, New Orleans, located about 150 miles north of the Gulf of Mexico, had at least seven possible approaches for an attacking army. All of them presented problems to an attacker, but providing a defense for all of the possible approaches was equally, if not more, difficult. When Jackson arrived in New Orleans, Col. Arthur P. Hayne, who had been sent ahead, provided him with detailed reports on possible defensive strategies for New Orleans. Based on Hayne's recommendations, Jackson decided to stage his first line of defense at Fort St. Philip on the Mississippi. Farther upriver, Jackson also strengthened the defenses at English Turn. In case the British veered into any of the many streams off the river, Jackson dispatched Louisiana militia well acquainted with the terrain to watch for British activities in these quarters. Guarding the approaches via Lake Borgne or Lake Pontchartrain was left to the naval gunboats under the command of Commander Daniel Todd Patterson.

The defense of the city itself was left primarily to militia units made up of the inhabitants of New Orleans. The British had hoped that the Creoles' disaffection with the United States would cause them to help or at least not hinder the invasion. Yet, French hatred of the British and animosity toward their use of slaves and black troops alienated wealthy Creoles of New Orleans and the surrounding plantations. Though ill-trained and poorly armed, these militia forces, Jackson's regulars, and militia units arriving from Tennessee and Kentucky provided Jackson with an army that was large, if nothing else.

Jackson's ammunition shortage was partly solved by his decision to accept the help of Jean Lafitte and the Baratarian pirates. Not only did Lafitte and his men provide Jackson's army with much-needed supplies, but they also supplied intelligence about possible British approaches and combat experience during the actual fighting.

In the meantime, Cochrane had departed Jamaica on 26 November, not waiting on the remainder of the land forces under Pakenham to arrive from Europe. Knowing that informants had alerted the Americans about the intended invasion, Cochrane hoped to arrive in New Orleans before Jackson. The transparency of his plans was not Cochrane's only problem. He had not received the shallow-draft landing craft he had requested, so he had to adjust his approach to the city accordingly.

Cochrane left word in Jamaica for Pakenham to follow him to Chandler Island immediately. Arriving there on 8 December, Cochrane had the area scouted and decided to land his forces at Bayou Bienvenu. Thomas ap Catesby Jones's gunboat squadron on Lake Borgne would have to be destroyed first, however. After a running battle of several hours, Jones's entire squadron and, consequently, Lake Borgne fell to the British on 14 December. Control of the lake increased the number of possible British approaches to New Orleans and further complicated Jackson's defenses. Cochrane immediately began landing his forces at Bayou

Bienvenu and sending scouts into the interior to determine possible routes. Commanded by Maj. Gen. John Keane, the landing force moved in from Pea Island, completing the operation by 23 December and establishing headquarters at Villeré Plantation. Keane and Cochrane did not know how many men Jackson had defending the city, so they waited for Pakenham and his forces before attacking New Orleans.

Jackson intended to attack them before they were fully organized. Commander Patterson could support Jackson from the Mississippi with two vessels, so Jackson left part of his force to guard other approaches while marching his available forces to Villeré Plantation. He attacked the British on the night of 23 December. Patterson commenced the engagement by firing into the British encampment; his bombardment was the signal for the attack on the British right and advanced position. Both U.S. assaults pushed the British back, but the redcoat line held, and low visibility forced a U.S. withdrawal. Jackson then pulled his men back to the Rodriguez Canal. When an advance unit of Louisiana militia attacked Keane's rear the following morning, it confirmed the British belief that Pakenham was crucial to the main assault on the city. The U.S. attacks on 23–24 December had done little besides buy Jackson time to strengthen his defenses, but in doing that, they had done much to win the Battle of New Orleans.

Patterson's two ships on the Mississippi continued to pester the British encampments as Pakenham arrived on 25 December and began unloading his troops. The British brought heavier guns forward to silence the U.S. vessels, finally destroying one and forcing the other's retreat. Meanwhile, Jackson had put his extra time to good use, building up his defenses on the north side of the Rodriguez Canal and destroying in front of it any cover the attacking British might use. The Americans erected four batteries, augmented by two navy 24-pounders. When Pakenham attacked in two columns on the morning of 28 December, Jackson's right flank was flush against the Mississippi River, guarded on that flank by Commander Patterson's remaining ship, the *Louisiana*, and protected on the left by an impenetrable cypress swamp. The *Louisiana* proved effective in preventing the British from turning the U.S. right flank, though one British column came close to breaking through. Pakenham called off the attack, however, to bring up more artillery. Three days would pass before he had what he considered enough ordnance for another offensive.

Pakenham also wanted Cochrane to create a diversion in Lake Pontchartrain and near the mouth of the Mississippi to draw off some of Jackson's defenders. Cochrane obliged, and Jackson did divert some men to those locations, but time rather than numbers had become important in this campaign. While Cochrane mounted a sham menace and Pakenham unloaded and hauled artillery, Jackson braced his positions even beyond their strength of 28 December. He also had time to bring in more artillery, including naval guns, to double the number of his batteries from four to eight.

On the morning of 1 January 1815, Pakenham opened up with his extra artillery, and Jackson returned fire with his enlarged batteries. Jackson's guns scored devastating hits on the British batteries as the British guns overshot their marks or had their cannonballs buried in the abundant mud Jackson had been able to put on his breastworks. After a brief infantry assault failed, Pakenham and his colleagues suddenly seemed uncertain about how to proceed. While they mulled over the possibilities, Jackson received reinforcements. He used these troops, primarily Kentuckians, to deepen his defenses. The fact that many of the 2,250 men who came in on 2 January were unarmed posed some problems, but Jackson scrounged up weapons. He placed his forces into three lines, comforted by the protection his daunting artillery now provided them.

Pakenham also received reinforcements with the arrival of Maj. Gen. John Lambert and 2,000 men. Cochrane persuaded Pakenham to let the Royal Navy ferry a detachment under Col. William Thornton to the west bank of the Mississippi to capture naval batteries there under Commander Patterson. Thornton then was to turn these guns on Jackson's line. Cochrane began transporting the force on the night of 7 January, but otherwise it proved late in almost every regard. Thornton successfully carried the U.S. batteries on the west bank, but not until the British main assault had been defeated.

Because Jackson's right would be imperiled by Patterson's captured batteries on the west bank and possibly left unprotected by the potential sinking of the *Louisiana*, Pakenham hoped that a massive frontal assault bolstered by Lambert would be successful. Pakenham moved up a large battery of 18-pounders and had his men prepare bundles of sugarcane to throw in the canals guarding Jackson's lines. They planned to place ladders across them to reach Jackson's breastworks.

All the plans seemed overly complicated to Pakenham's officers and men. After weeks of failure, they apparently had little faith that yet another attack would succeed. Still, on 8 January, Pakenham's approximately 8,000 men arranged in four columns gave the look of an imposing force. There were problems, however. Anxious to strike before full light, Pakenham did not make sure that his men were in proper order. The men who were supposed to bring the sugarcane bundles and ladders had not carried them

the entire distance, so soldiers initially reaching the canals could not cross them. And to make everything worse, the main British column under Maj. Gen. Sir Samuel Gibbs was to attack the U.S. left flank because the British had incorrectly surmised that was Jackson's weakest point. It was actually the strongest section of the U.S. line.

Once in motion, the entire British battle plan simply disintegrated. Gibbs could not make any headway against the U.S. left flank, and the fog and darkness that Pakenham had hoped would mask his movements against the U.S. right flank began to lift. Exposed to Jackson, as well as to Patterson's still-secure batteries on the west bank, this British column was cut to pieces. The greatest damage to the British lines, however, was probably done by Jackson's artillery on the east bank and the rifle- and musket-wielding infantrymen. Waiting steadily as the British came resolutely within range, they opened up with volley after volley of murderous fire. The debate about the relative effectiveness of Jackson's riflemen versus the muskets of the average infantryman in the U.S. lines may never be settled, but it misses the larger point in any event. Most of Jackson's force was probably armed with muskets, but that did not matter. The combined firepower of artillery, rifles, and muskets turned the plain before the Rodriguez Canal into a charnel pen. When the smoke cleared, the U.S. defenders of New Orleans beheld a grotesque scene. Almost 300 British soldiers, including General Pakenham, lay dead, mingled with 1,262 wounded. Many additional British soldiers had played dead to escape the carnage, and the Americans would eventually round up 484 prisoners. The American losses were six killed and seven wounded in Jackson's main lines on the east bank.

Colonel Thornton had captured Patterson's batteries across the river. Although some among the British contemplated following up on this small and now insignificant victory, General Lambert, now in command, had seen enough. He pulled Thornton back, and the Americans reoccupied those positions. Lambert gave Cochrane the chance to reduce Fort St. Philip so that naval forces could be brought up the Mississippi, but more than a week's bombardment could not force the fort's surrender. Lambert would not repeat the mistakes of the previous weeks—he withdrew his army. On his way out of the gulf, Lambert stopped to attack Fort Bowyer that guarded the approaches to Mobile. He successfully captured the fort, but news of the Treaty of Ghent arrived before he could make an attempt to take the city.

The British campaign against New Orleans failed for several reasons, but probably the most important one was the amount of time given to Andrew Jackson and the U.S. defenders to prepare a defense of the city. Also, the British never exploited their strengths, such as applying numerical superiority to the right places at the right times. When the major British attack came on 8 January, British morale was low and organization and timing poor, but the redcoats were still buoyed by an ineffable arrogance as they faced what they believed to be an inferior enemy. At the end of that day, that belief was as dead as Edward Pakenham.

—*Jeanne T. Heidler and David S. Heidler*

See also: Artillery; Baratarian Pirates; Cochrane, Alexander; Hayne, Arthur P.; Jackson, Andrew; Jones, Thomas ap Catesby; Keane, John; Lafitte, Jean; Lake Borgne, Battle of; Lambert, John; Louisiana; Pakenham, Edward; Patterson, Daniel Todd; Pensacola, Battle of; Pensacola, West Florida; Villeré Plantation

Further Reading

Owsley, Frank Lawrence, Jr. *Struggle for the Gulf Borderlands: The Creek War and the Battle of New Orleans.* Gainesville: University Presses of Florida, 1981.

Reilly, Robin. *The British at the Gates: The New Orleans Campaign.* New York: G. P. Putnam's Sons, 1974.

NEW YORK

At the beginning of 1812, Republicans dominated New York politics. George Clinton, serving as vice president, and his nephew DeWitt Clinton controlled the Republican Party. When the Republicans ousted the Federalists in 1801, the Republicans began to war among themselves for control, however, and this continued from 1801 through the War of 1812. In 1804, the Clintonians united with the followers of the Livingston clan, headed by Robert R. Livingston, to defeat Aaron Burr and the Burrites. With the elimination of Burr as a political force after the 1804 election, the Clintonians and Livingstons began a war for power. In 1807, the Clinton faction won the assembly races and elected their candidate, Daniel Tompkins, as the governor of New York

Remnants of the Burr and Livingston factions in New York City joined with other anti-Clinton Republicans to gain control of the Tammany Society, Burr's own political vehicle. In 1811, they attempted to prevent the election of DeWitt Clinton as lieutenant governor, but they failed. Yet, George Clinton's death combined with DeWitt Clinton's aspiration to become president in 1812 provided an opportunity for the anti-Clinton coalition to challenge Clinton's control of the party. The Tammany-Livingston coalition supported President James Madison and the War of 1812 to destroy DeWitt Clinton, gain control of the party, and obtain federal patronage from the grateful president.

In the spring of 1812, New York Republicans received a rude shock when the Federalists gained a majority of the state assembly in the spring election. Congress had imposed a 90-day embargo, and the threat of war appeared real. Federalists denounced both the embargo and war. Clintonians did not directly attack the embargo but criticized the timing of the measure because Congress had passed the law before New York merchants and farmers could sell their stocks of wheat, flour, corn, and rye. Anti-Clinton Republicans identified with the president and Congress and used these remarks by Clintonians to undermine their base of support among rank-and-file Republicans.

When Congress voted for war, only three New York congressmen and Sen. John Smith voted for war. Seven Republicans and four Federalists in the House of Representatives joined with Republican senator Obadiah Gernan against war. With the exception of Samuel Mitchell of New York City, the antiwar Republicans were Clintonians. The Clintonians thought they had learned the lessons of the spring 1812 election. Voting for embargo and war would ensure Federalist control of New York. Moreover, the country was totally unprepared for war, and New York might become a battleground if the British invaded from Canada, as they had during the Revolution.

Throughout the summer and fall of 1812, Federalists denounced the war as immoral, unjust, and partisan. In addition, Federalist leaders decided to quietly back DeWitt Clinton's challenge to the president's reelection. On 5 August 1812, Clinton met with Rufus King, John Jay, and Gouverneur Morris and assured the Federalists of his break with Madison and his support for a nonpartisan Peace Party. Despite the opposition of Rufus King, who distrusted Clinton, Federalist leaders decided to indirectly back Clinton at their national convention in New York City in September 1812. Meanwhile, Clinton dared not openly identify with the Federalists because it would alienate his prowar Republican supporters, like the New York City Irish. Therefore, Clinton walked a political tightrope in 1812. His challenge to Madison and his criticism of the war decision cost him the support of Governor Tompkins. Although he obtained Federalist support, Clinton could not win enough prowar Republicans to his banner to defeat Madison in 1812.

As a result of reapportionment, New York held special congressional elections in December 1812. Campaigning on the slogan of "Friends of Peace, Liberty, and Commerce," Federalists denounced the war and the use of the militia to invade Canada and called for a negotiated end to the war. During the election, the coalition of Clintonians and Federalists fell apart, except in New York City and, to a lesser extent, Albany County. Republicans sought to rally the public behind the president and the flag, but the appeals to patriotism did not work. New Yorkers sent 19 Federalists, one Clintonian, and seven prowar Republicans to Congress. As a result of the election, the Federalists gained 14 seats and sent the largest antiwar delegation to Congress.

As soon as the state legislature met in 1813, confrontation developed between prowar Republicans and the Federalists. The governor wanted to loan the federal government $500 to help finance the war, and the Republican majority in the state senate passed prowar resolutions. Since the Federalists controlled the assembly, they killed the loan bill and drafted a series of antiwar resolutions that neutralized the impact of the Senate's resolutions.

The war issue reemerged during the spring legislative and gubernatorial elections in 1813. Federalists nominated Stephen Van Rensselaer to challenge Governor Tompkins, who ran for a third term. Tompkins's compliance with presidential requests to call out the militia to aid in the conquest of Canada came under Federalist censure. During the campaign, Federalists attacked the war and praised the Federalist governors of Connecticut, Rhode Island, and Massachusetts for their resistance to presidential requests to call out the militia. Federalists sought to gain political mileage from the widespread resistance to militia service in New York.

Meanwhile, the Republican legislative caucus that nominated Tompkins for governor dropped DeWitt Clinton from the ticket as lieutenant governor. Outraged, his followers issued an antiwar and anti-Tompkins election address. Federalists permitted Clinton to retain the appointed position of mayor of New York City, but his alliance with the Federalists and his attempt to sabotage the reelection of Tompkins destroyed his position in the Republican Party for the duration of the war. Tompkins emerged as the new leader of New York Republicans.

Tompkins won the 1813 gubernatorial election by a vote of 43,324 (52%) to 39,718 (48%). His majority had dropped in half from 1810, and his reelection was hardly a ringing endorsement for the war, especially since the Federalists retained a majority in the assembly. Western New York, benefiting from soaring farm prices because of the demand created by troops stationed on the Niagara Frontier, aided Tompkins's reelection, whereas Clinton's flirtation with the Federalists made him a pariah to state Republicans. As in 1807 with Morgan Lewis and 1804 with Burr, whenever a Republican leader appeared to be openly courting Federalists, the Republican rank and file abandoned that leader.

Throughout 1812 and 1813, New Yorkers revealed their hostility to the war, not only in the elections but also in their refusal to serve in the militia, their reluctance to invade Canada, and in widespread smuggling. All along the northern frontier of the state, from Lake Champlain to Oswego, New Yorkers shipped cattle, hogs, flour, grain, candles, soap, butter, cheese, leather, and potash to the Canadians. Widespread evasion of the militia draft in 1812 led Governor Tompkins to urge the establishment of special courts to try militia delinquents, but New Yorkers remained just as determined to resist militia service in 1812–1813. Even many of the militia who answered the governor's call demonstrated some reluctance to fight. Repeatedly, the militia refused to cross the border into Canada.

In late December 1813, the war came to New York when the British burned Buffalo and neighboring settlements. The following spring, Congress removed its latest embargo on trade. These two events enabled the Republicans to win two-thirds of the state assembly seats and 21 of 27 congressional seats in the spring 1814 elections. Two Clintonian Republican leaders, Solomon Southwick and Philip Van Cortlandt, ran for the state senate and Congress, respectively. Both lost, once again demonstrating that rank-and-file Republicans would not vote for Republicans linked with Federalists. A few prominent Federalists, notably Cyrenius Chapin of Buffalo, had split from the party early in the war, but no open division took place until the 1814 election. A group of prowar Federalists led by former Secretary of the Treasury Oliver Wolcott, Jr., Gulian C. Verplanck, Hugh Maxwell, and Thomas Morris formed the American Federalist Party (known as the "Coodies") and ran a separate assembly slate in New York City, but they won less than 1 percent of the vote. The Tammany Society adopted them, and they soon merged into the Republican Party.

Even though the war ended before the 1815 election, it emerged as the major issue. Federalists emphasized conscription, taxes, and the futility of the war. Republicans justified the war, because the war proved that a republican government could wage war and the U.S. citizen-soldier could defeat the trained armies of Europe. Federalists picked up 22 seats in the assembly, which equalled the numbers of seats won by the Republicans. The Republicans, to gain a majority, disqualified one of the Federalists and obtained a 64-to-62 majority. This result reflected the deep divisions the war created in New York. No other state entered the war as divided as New York, and no state left the war as politically split.

—Harvey J. Strum

See also: Clinton, DeWitt; Tompkins, Daniel D.

Further Reading
Everest, Allan S. *The War of 1812 in the Champlain Valley.* Syracuse: Syracuse University Press, 1981.
Strum, Harvey. "New York's Antiwar Campaign." *Peace and Change* (spring 1982): 7–18.

NEW YORK CITY

Seriously injured by the Embargo and Non-Intercourse Acts, New York, a city of approximately 100,000 people in 1812, anticipated the war with a certain amount of dread. The city's political establishment, divided between Democratic Republicans and Federalists, was complicated by its being a stronghold of Clintonians, followers of DeWitt Clinton. These were nominally Democratic Republicans, but they often allied with New York Federalists.

Paramount to most people in the city were trading interests. Evidence of this view became apparent when word leaked out that Congress and Pres. James Madison would be imposing a trade embargo effective 4 April 1812. More ships left New York harbor in the five days between the leak and implementation than any other port in the country.

For a time after the declaration of war, however, trade from New York City flourished as grain and other foodstuffs found their way from the port to the armies fighting on the Spanish Peninsula. Consequently, New Yorkers relaxed and enjoyed the naval triumphs of the fall of 1812 probably as the residents of no other city did. Tremendous celebrations greeted returning hero Isaac Hull after his *Constitution* defeated the *Guerrière,* and Stephen Decatur enjoyed similar demonstrations after the triumph of the *United States* over the *Macedonian.*

Even after Britain's Orders in Council extended a blockade up to New York City (still leaving New England ports unblockaded so that they could supply the British in Canada), the city did not suffer economic hardship. The use of New York City as the major military supply base in the North insured that the city's merchants would continue to prosper throughout the war. Therefore, the city turned out in force in September 1813, when the remains of the *Chesapeake*'s gallant captain James Lawrence entered the city for his massive public funeral there. The procession made its way up Manhattan Island along a circuitous route to Trinity Church, where Lawrence's remains were finally laid to rest.

Until the summer of 1814, the war had only impinged upon New York City's economy. That insularity came to an end, however, with increasing British activity along the New England coast that threatened to move down to New York. Concerned citizens then noted that the city's defenses had been neglected over the past two years. Mayor DeWitt Clinton set about to strengthen the city and mobilize its inhabitants. In early August, Clinton published an address asking the people to help federal authorities prepare the city against attack. On 9 August, a massive citizens' meeting selected a Committee of Defense to direct the activities of the city. At the same time, Brig. Gen. Joseph Swift began supervising the construction of breastworks and fortifications on Brooklyn Heights. Thousands of New Yorkers helped with the various construction projects around the city. News of the fall of Washington, D.C., at the end of August only accelerated these activities.

On 31 August, 6,000 soldiers paraded through the city, and on 2 September, New York City's militia joined that of surrounding areas as it was mustered into service under Maj. Gen. Morgan Lewis. Stephen Decatur, bottled up in the harbor, commanded the naval preparations there. By October 1814, New York City presented to the British an almost impregnable defense, built and manned largely by its own citizens.

Although it possessed an almost Byzantine political structure that defied labels like Democratic Republican and Federalist and its citizens were early divided in their opinions regarding the war, New York City made an important contribution to the war effort as a supply base and a model of citizen mobilization.

—Jeanne T. Heidler and David S. Heidler

See also: Clinton, DeWitt; Decatur, Stephen, Jr.; Hull, Isaac; Lawrence, James; Lewis, Morgan; Swift, Joseph Gardner
Further Reading
Apgar, Wilbur E. "New York's Contribution to the War Effort of 1812." *New York Historical Society Quarterly* 29 (1945): 203–212.

NEWARK, UPPER CANADA

At the start of the War of 1812, the town of Newark (now called Niagara) had a population of approximately 620 people. It had been the capital of the British colony of Upper Canada from 1792 until 1797, when the seat of government was moved to York (now called Toronto) for military reasons. Newark's location at the Lake Ontario end of the Niagara River, caught between British Fort George and U.S. Fort Niagara, made it vulnerable to crossborder attack and enemy occupation.

By the end of 1813, Americans were in possession of both Newark and Fort George. The entire region was under the control of the New York militia, commanded by Gen. George McClure. The regular forces had been sent east to participate in an attempt to capture Montreal.

McClure had previously received authority from Secretary of War John Armstrong to destroy Newark if doing so was necessary to defend Fort George. Newark's citizens were to have ample warning to allow them to pack what they could carry and evacuate the town. McClure, however, did not follow the intent of these instructions. Because of growing British strength in the area and faced with militiamen who had not been paid and whose terms of service were nearly expired, he decided to abandon Fort George and return to New York.

As part of this withdrawal on 10 December 1813, Mc-Clure abruptly notified the inhabitants of Newark that their town would be put to the torch and that they had one half-hour to gather their possessions and leave. Despite the fact that the fort was not going to be defended and that the citizens of the town had done nothing during the occupation to warrant reprisals, their homes and businesses were to be destroyed on very short notice.

The job was assigned to a band of Canadian irregulars who had transferred their allegiance to the U.S. side earlier in the war. They were led by Joseph Willcocks, a former member of the Upper Canadian assembly for the Niagara District. As a result of this group's work, over 400 people stood in subzero temperatures to watch Newark go up in flames. McClure later explained that his decision was based on military necessity, but little proof of this claim was ever provided. In fact, one of his own officers resigned to protest the burning, and the U.S. government eventually disavowed the action.

The British commander in Upper Canada, Canadian-born Gordon Drummond, soon put into motion a plan for revenge. Drummond's men crossed the Niagara River on the night of 18 December and seized Fort Niagara. The British then proceeded down the New York side of the river and burned the towns of Lewiston, Black Rock, and Buffalo. Thus, the burning of Newark was the first incident in a growing spiral of violent reprisals along both sides of the frontier that scarred the last stages of the war.

—*Eric Jarvis*

See also: Black Rock, New York; Buffalo, New York; Drummond, Gordon; George, Fort; Lewiston, New York, Destruction of; McClure, George; Niagara Campaigns; York, Battle of

Further Reading
Craig, Gerald M. *Upper Canada: The Formative Years, 1784–1841.* Toronto: McClelland and Stewart, 1963.
Morton, Desmond. *A Military History of Canada.* Toronto: McClelland and Stewart, 1985.
Sheppard, George. *Plunder, Profit and Paroles: A Social History of the War of 1812 in Upper Canada.* Montreal: McGill-Queen's University Press, 1994.

NIAGARA CAMPAIGNS
1812–1814

The shores of the Niagara River were the scene of considerable fighting during the War of 1812, as U.S. invasions and British raids repeatedly traversed this water border separating the two belligerents. The Niagara River is a 37-mile-long strait connecting Lake Erie to Lake Ontario. The river is cut perpendicularly by an escarpment about 7 miles south of Lake Ontario. In its rapid northward course, the river spills over Niagara Falls and flows between the walls of a deep gorge for nearly 6 miles. The combination of rapids, falls, and unapproachable shores limited the places both armies could safely cross a military force. The British guarded the southern end of the river, with Fort Erie opposite the villages of Buffalo and Black Rock, New York. At the northern mouth of the river, British Fort George and the village of Newark stood across the water from the U.S. Fort Niagara. The goal of seizing Canada drew repeated U.S. attempts to cross the river and clear the British from the Niagara Peninsula. Every attempt failed, and the armies were either driven back by the British or withdrawn when they could not be sustained on the Canadian shore.

By October 1812, New York militia major general Stephen Van Rensselaer had gathered 6,000 militia and regulars on the Niagara Frontier. About 1,650 of the U.S. regulars were under the command of Brig. Gen. Alexander Smyth at Buffalo. Smyth, a regular, refused to subordinate himself to Van Rensselaer. The Americans—both regulars and militia—were inadequately trained and equipped and poorly disciplined. They were opposed by Maj. Gen. Isaac Brock, who commanded 1,600 regulars and militia. Brock was assisted by several hundred Indian warriors under their leader, John Norton.

On 13 October, Van Rensselaer struck at the village of Queenston at the base of the escarpment. Despite the fire from several shore batteries, the Americans gained the top of Queenston Heights. Brock, whose courage and

A soldier's wife helps in the American campaign to seize Canada, known as the Niagara Campaigns. None of the repeated attacks were very successful, though not due to lack of persistence.

charisma were unsurpassed, led a counterattack to regain the heights. He was killed at the front of his men, and the assault collapsed. Despite the initial U.S. success, Van Rensselaer could not persuade or threaten all the available militiamen to cross the river to reinforce their comrades. On Queenston Heights, Lt. Col. Winfield Scott frantically tried to put the Americans in a defensive posture to withstand the expected British counterattack. That afternoon, Maj. Gen. Roger Hale Sheaffe attacked and pushed the Americans against the edge of the gorge. Scott surrendered over 1,000 Americans, many of whom had abjectly avoided combat by hiding in the woods. Up to that time, many Canadians believed that defense against the Americans was ultimately futile. The Battle of Queenston reversed the mood of defeatism that had heretofore paralyzed British preparations.

Smyth replaced Van Rensselaer, who resigned after the defeat. Smyth concluded that Van Rensselaer's mistake was crossing his troops in waves. The militiamen remaining on the friendly shore could, at any time, invoke their consti-

tutional right not to serve outside the United States. Smyth decided to build enough boats to cross 3,000 men in a single wave. On 28 November, at Buffalo, Smyth began embarking his men. The boats filled slowly and at midafternoon Smyth, claiming that only 1,200 men were in boats, ordered his troops to return to their camps. The men, discontented and murmuring, disembarked. On 1 December, Smyth again ordered the men into the boats and, again citing insufficient participation, canceled the crossing and the campaign. Many of the men reacted furiously, firing their weapons wildly. Smyth departed Buffalo and was later dropped from the rolls without the spectacle of a court-martial. Although there is no denying Smyth's inability to lead, his venture was doomed by widespread sickness among his troops and rampant desertion by hundreds of New York and Pennsylvania militia.

The third U.S. attempt to seize the Niagara Peninsula came on 26 May 1813. In an operation planned by Oliver Hazard Perry and Winfield Scott and commanded by Maj. Gen. Henry Dearborn, thousands of U.S. regulars transported by Commodore Isaac Chauncey's fleet landed on the shores of Lake Ontario just west of Fort George. Protected by naval gunfire, the Americans defeated several hundred British and Canadians who made a determined but futile stand in front of the fort. The British commander, Brig. Gen. John Vincent, ordered the fort evacuated and withdrew his weakened division from the line of the Niagara River.

The Americans made two attempts to find and defeat Vincent. On 6 June, the British conducted a night attack, which threw back a superior force of Americans camped at Stoney Creek. Encouraged by this success, Vincent moved closer to Fort George, loosely encircling the fort. The Americans sent out a strong raiding party under the command of Col. Charles G. Boerstler to capture a British strong point at Beaver Dams. Boerstler's 700 regulars were surrounded in the forest by 500 Indian warriors on 24 June. Terrorized at the prospect of a massacre, Boerstler surrendered his command. With this second victory, Vincent closed in on Fort George. Secretary of War John Armstrong redirected the next U.S. invasion away from the Niagara River and toward the city of Montreal. U.S. regulars departed Fort George for Sacket's Harbor, leaving the defense of the Niagara River in the hands of the militia.

On 11 July, Lt. Col. Cecil Bisshopp led a successful British raid on the naval yard at Black Rock. The British were chased out of U.S. territory by militiamen and New York Iroquois. The New York Iroquois, unlike their Grand River brothers, had maintained their neutrality in what they considered to be a white man's conflict. The raid at Black Rock prompted the Iroquois in U.S. territory to declare a defensive war against the British. About 140 formed a company of U.S. volunteers and saw action in August against the Grand River Iroquois, which shattered the uneasy peace between the two Iroquois groups.

In December, militia brigadier general George McClure, despairing of reinforcements, decided to abandon Fort George. Claiming that the British would use the nearby village of Newark as shelter for their troops once the Americans left, McClure ordered the burning of that unoffending town. Over 400 civilians were roused from their houses in a snowfall to watch their homes and possessions go up in flames. British reaction to this violation of the rules of war was quick and deadly. Lt. Gen. Sir Gordon Drummond arrived on the Niagara River soon after McClure departed. Drummond launched a two-week offensive that captured Fort Niagara and burned virtually every structure on the U.S. side.

The last year of the war witnessed the hardest fighting on the Niagara. Maj. Gen. Jacob Brown, commanding a division composed of regulars, volunteers, and New York Iroquois, embarked from Buffalo on 3 July 1814 and seized Fort Erie. Pushing north, he confronted the strong British position behind the Chippewa River. On 5 July, Maj. Gen. Phineas Riall came out from behind the Chippewa and attacked toward the U.S. camp. He was confronted by Brig. Gen. Winfield Scott's brigade of regulars. In a short, sharp, bloody contest, the Americans broke the British line and forced their retreat. Scott's well-trained regulars won a victory that went a long way toward reestablishing the army's self-confidence.

The British withdrew to Fort George, and Brown followed closely. He expected that Commodore Isaac Chauncey and his fleet would soon appear, carrying heavy guns with which to batter down the walls of Fort George. Chauncey, more interested in fighting a decisive battle with the Royal Navy, failed to appear. Unwilling to storm the fort without adequate artillery support, Brown withdrew to the Chippewa battlefield. General Drummond arrived, bringing with him heavy reinforcements. Moving toward the Americans, the British occupied a gentle rise along Lundy's Lane on 25 July 1814. Brown, unsure of British intentions, sent Scott forward to develop the situation. Finding the British drawn up for battle, Scott launched an attack, which began the bloodiest battle of the war up to that time. Brown, Scott, Drummond, and Riall were all wounded in a seesaw battle fought at close quarters long into the night. With his division running out of ammunition and exhausted, Brown ordered a withdrawal to their camp to continue the contest after a few hours' rest. When the Americans approached the British line the following morning, it was stronger than before. With Brown and Scott evacuated to Buffalo, Brig. Gen. Eleazar Ripley withdrew the U.S. forces to Fort Erie. Drummond followed slowly, determined to eject the invaders from Canadian soil.

The British opened the siege of Fort Erie on 4 August. Command of the fort fell to Brig. Gen. Edmund Pendleton Gaines (Ripley had lost Brown's confidence by not continuing the attack at Lundy's Lane on 26 July). On 15 August, Drummond launched a determined but unsuccessful night assault, which cost the British over 900 casualties, far exceeding U.S. losses. In September, Brown reassumed command, and on 15 September he ordered a sortie, which captured two of the three British batteries before withdrawing in the face of a strong counterattack. Many of the U.S. attackers were New York militiamen who redeemed themselves after their disgrace at Queenston Heights. The sortie broke the back of the British siege, and on 21 September, Drummond withdrew behind the Chippewa.

U.S. major general George Izard arrived on the Niagara

Frontier early in October with 3,500 trained regulars. Chauncey had ceded control of Lake Ontario to Royal Navy commodore Sir James Yeo. Thus Izard was in the same strategic situation as was Brown in July; military action on the Niagara, however successful, was ultimately futile without control of the adjoining lake. In a halfhearted offensive, Izard pushed the British out of Cook's Mills on Lyon Creek before destroying Fort Erie and returning to the U.S. shore in November. News of the peace reached the Niagara region that winter, signaling an end to the struggle for control of Canada.

—Richard V. Barbuto

See also: Beaver Dams, Battle of; Bisshopp, Cecil; Black Rock, New York; Boerstler, Charles G.; Brock, Isaac; Brown, Jacob J.; Buffalo, New York; Chauncey, Isaac; Chippewa, Battle of; Cook's Mills, Battle of; Dearborn, Henry; Drummond, Gordon; Gaines, Edmund Pendleton; George, Fort; Iroquois, The Six Nations of the; Izard, George; Lundy's Lane, Battle of; McClure, George; Montreal; Newark, Upper Canada; Perry, Oliver Hazard; Queenston, Battle of; Riall, Phineas; Ripley, Eleazar Wheelock; Sacket's Harbor, Battle of; Sacket's Harbor, New York; Scott, Winfield; Sheaffe, Roger Hale; Smyth, Alexander; Stoney Creek, Battle of; Van Rensselaer, Stephen; Vincent, John

Further Reading

Babcock, Louis L. *The War of 1812 on the Niagara Frontier.* Buffalo: Buffalo Historical Society, 1927.

Graves, Donald E. *The Battle of Lundy's Lane.* Baltimore: Nautical and Aviation Publishing Company of America, 1993.

Whitehorne, Joseph. *While Washington Burned: The Battle for Fort Erie.* Baltimore: Nautical and Aviation Publishing Company of America, 1992.

NICHOLLS, EDWARD
1779–1865
Royal Marine officer

The son of John Nicholls, Edward Nicholls was born in Coleraine, Ireland, and in 1795, at the age of 16, received a commission as a Royal Marine second lieutenant. By the outbreak of the War of 1812, he had achieved the rank of brevet major. His primary service during that war was on the coast of Spanish West Florida.

In August 1814, Nicholls arrived with a party of marines at the mouth of the Apalachicola River. He had been proceeded by Capt. George Woodbine earlier in the summer. Woodbine had prepared the way for this larger British presence by sending out a call to Creek Indians and slaves in Georgia and the Mississippi Territory to join the British against the United States. At the end of March, Andrew Jackson had defeated the Red Stick faction of the Creeks at Tohopeka (Horseshoe Bend), and the survivors were receptive to the calls sent out by the British.

When Nicholls arrived at Woodbine's base on the Apalachicola at Prospect Bluff, he found about 1,500 Creeks and runaway slaves. After starting a fort at the Bluffs, Nicholls departed for Spanish Pensacola on 14 August, accompanied by 200 marines. Spanish governor Don Mateo González Manrique was concerned that the British in his town would invite retaliation from the Americans. The weakness of his garrison, however, prevented him from actively resisting the British presence. In any event, it did not look as though the British would be staying long. Nicholls assured the governor that all they needed was a staging area for an attack against the Americans at Mobile. After securing that town, the British would be moving there.

Nicholls and a British naval squadron under Capt. William Percy started for Mobile on 12 September. Part of the force of marines and Creeks went overland. Due to illness, Nicholls traveled aboard one of Percy's ships. In the attack on Fort Bowyer, which guarded the approach to Mobile, the British failed to capture the fort and Nicholls was severely wounded, losing the sight in his right eye. The defeated British returned to Pensacola, much to the chagrin of Governor Manrique.

Nicholls's actions on the Gulf Coast at Pensacola and certainly at Mobile had caught the attention of Maj. Gen. Andrew Jackson, who by September had decided to remove Pensacola as a base of operations for the British. Nicholls, hearing of Jackson's plans, tried to strengthen the defenses at Pensacola in preparation. The townspeople and Manrique offered no assistance, again worried that Nicholls's presence invited a U.S. invasion. The lack of cooperation so exasperated Nicholls that he threatened to level the town if anyone tried to surrender to Jackson.

The inhabitants of Pensacola, as well as Jackson and the Americans, viewed Nicholls with increasing alarm because he promised both Spanish and U.S. slaves that if they helped the British, they would be rewarded with freedom. Apparently the Royal Marine was combining his strong antislavery views with his need for additional manpower. In any case, when Jackson approached the city in November 1814, Nicholls quickly learned that even slaves laboring for freedom were useless without Spanish assistance. He did not have the men to withstand Jackson's assault. In disgust, Nicholls blew up the fortifications protecting the harbor and retreated to the Apalachicola. Jackson occupied the town and from there moved to the defense of New Orleans.

Back at Prospect Bluff, Nicholls saw his numbers continue to swell. He used these new recruits to complete the fortification he called Fort Apalachicola. The area especially served as a haven for runaway slaves, a matter of increasing alarm to slave owners in the Southwest. Several expeditions were planned against Nicholls's position, and though none of them reached the objective, Nicholls on the Gulf Coast effectively preoccupied some regulars and large numbers of militia on the southern frontier. His numbers alone attracted considerable notice: by the end of 1814, Nicholls had over 2,000 people at Prospect Bluff.

When the war ended, Nicholls remained at the bluff. British forces retreating from the gulf left him well supplied and armed, and Spaniards at Pensacola still lacked the men to dislodge him. When Nicholls received a copy of the Treaty of Ghent ending the war, he believed there was more reason to remain in West Florida. He would act as a negotiator for the Creek Indians who had fled the United States.

Article IX of the Treaty of Ghent guaranteed that all lands taken from Indians during the War of 1812 would be returned to them at war's end. Nicholls interpreted this article to mean that the land cession contained in the Treaty of Fort Jackson that ended the Creek War was void. The U.S. interpretation of Article IX was that only land taken from Indians with whom the United States was still at war would be returned. Since the United States had made a separate peace with the Creeks, they were not seen as being covered by the Treaty of Ghent. Nicholls regarded that as a disingenuous interpretation of the treaty. Trying to convince someone of the error of the U.S. interpretation, he began a letter-writing war with Creek agent Benjamin Hawkins in the spring of 1815.

Debate continues about why Nicholls fought so tenaciously for what he viewed as Creek rights, even after the War of 1812 ended. One interpretation holds that he truly believed the Creeks were victims and that after making so many promises to them, he felt obliged to keep at least some of them. Another interpretation is that Nicholls, completely misjudging the British government's commitment to Indian rights in North America, hoped to secure an appointment as British agent to the Creeks. Perhaps his aid combined elements of both motives.

Whatever Nicholls's reasons, in the summer of 1815, he took the Creeks' case directly to the British government. On his own initiative, he concluded a treaty of alliance between the Creeks in Florida and the British government and then departed, treaty in hand, for London. A Creek prophet, Josiah Francis, accompanied him. On arriving in London, Nicholls quickly confronted the reality of postwar diplomacy when the British government refused to discuss his treaty and would not officially receive Josiah Francis as an emissary of the Creeks.

Nicholls among the Creeks was a further illustration of how white contact, even if altruistic, wronged these Indians. He had left a fort full of arms and supplies for their protection, but the presence of this fort and the hundreds of runaway slaves it contained so unnerved Americans that the following year, a joint U.S. army-navy expedition attacked it and blew it up.

Nicholls never returned to the Creeks. He continued in the army for the next 20 years. After his retirement, he accepted several posts as governor of British possessions. He died in Kent in 1865.

—*Jeanne T. Heidler and David S. Heidler*

See also: Bowyer, Fort; Creek War; Fort Jackson, Treaty of; Ghent, Treaty of; Hawkins, Benjamin; Horseshoe Bend, Battle of; Jackson, Andrew; Mobile, Battles of; Pensacola, Battle of; Pensacola, West Florida; Percy, William Henry; Prospect Bluff, West Florida

Further Reading
Boyd, Mark F. "Events at Prospect Bluff on the Apalachicola River." *Florida Historical Quarterly* 16 (1937): 55–93.
"Documents Relating to Colonel Edward Nicholls and Captain George Woodbine in Pensacola in 1814." *Florida Historical Quarterly* 10 (1931): 51–54.
Heidler, David S., and Jeanne T. Heidler. *Old Hickory's War: Andrew Jackson and the Quest for Empire.* Mechanicsburg, PA: Stackpole Books, 1996.
Owsley, Frank L. "Jackson's Capture of Pensacola." *Alabama Review* 19 (1966): 175–185.

NILES' WEEKLY REGISTER

Printer, essayist, and editor Hezekiah Niles apprenticed in Philadelphia; began his journalistic career in 1794 in Wilmington, Delaware; and became editor of the *Baltimore Evening Post* in 1805 after his literary venture, the *Apollo,* failed. Niles was by then a staunch Jeffersonian and first published his *Weekly Register* on 7 September 1811. He mixed his Anglophobia and biases into a paper of integrity that reflected the fierce partisanship of his times.

Niles reprinted public documents, speeches, and statistics, as well as reports cribbed from other papers, to support James Madison's foreign policy and then the War of 1812. Niles painted Britain as an international tyrant, saddled with monarchism and awash with corruption. Of all the U.S. grievances, impressment struck him as the most outrageous. Commercial seizures seemed to him less significant because of New England's trade patterns. Through 1812 he became progressively more bellicose, encouraged congressional militants, and declared on 18 April that the United States had a choice between "war or submission."

Editors during the war gleaned news where they could. The *Register*'s reporting was therefore broad but haphazard. Niles himself interviewed soldiers and travelers from combat zones as well as politicians. He reprinted clippings from Montreal and Quebec papers and speeches and proclamations by provincial officials, all of which gave Americans a window on the war from behind enemy lines. He also published excerpts from George Heriot's *Travels in Canada* and a Jesuit report on the Detroit region from the French period. He argued that the Canadas would join the United States. Prewar "American emigrants as well as the dissatisfied French descendants" would welcome U.S. invaders, and Canadians would not support their own government. He anticipated a swift victory, but he denied the United States had begun a war of conquest.

His editorials fumed over defeats and domestic dissent. William Hull had "surrendered" Detroit to Isaac Brock. News of smuggling led him to insist that "the Treasury Department must be put upon the war establishment—the whinings of the dealers have been so much attended to, that smuggling and treason have almost passed for virtues." He labeled Vermont an ally of Britain when the state's governor seemed lukewarm about the war.

Niles muted his stridency by 1814, when the war remained stalled. Provincials had defended their homes after all, and Sir George Cockburn's campaigns in Chesapeake Bay suggested that the United States could not even defend her own coasts. When the terms of the Treaty of Ghent arrived, he shouted, "Long live the republic! All hail! Last asylum of oppressed humanity." Postwar nationalism thus succeeded wartime patriotism, although Niles never lost his Anglophobia or his belief that Britain was jealous of U.S. maritime success.

—*Reginald C. Stuart*

Further Reading

Luxon, Norval. "*Niles's Weekly Register*": *News Magazine of the Nineteenth Century*. Baton Rouge: Louisiana State University Press, 1947.

Mitchell, Broadus. "Hezekiah Niles." In *Dictionary of American Biography*. Vol. 7, ed. Dumas Malone. New York: Charles Scribner's Sons, 1936: 521–522.

Niles' Weekly Requester. Vol. 1 (September 1811) to Vol. 8 (September 1815).

Rutland, Robert A. *The Newsmongers: Journalism in the Life of the Nation 1690–1972*. New York: Dial Press, 1973.

NON-INTERCOURSE ACT
1 March 1809

By January 1809, the 1807 Embargo Act had failed to defeat either Great Britain's Orders in Council or Napoleon's Berlin and Milan Decrees. Although the Whig opposition in Great Britain argued that the Orders in Council were driving the United States into Napoleon's camp, the ruling Tory government viewed them as an unqualified success; Thomas Jefferson's self-imposed embargo had eliminated both U.S. commercial competition for British markets and aid to Napoleon's government. The embargo also failed to unify the nation behind the Republican Party. Jefferson's Federalist critics vehemently charged that it was directed primarily against their economic interests, and in the 1808 election, they doubled their representation in the House of Representatives.

On 1 March 1809, the lame-duck Congress substituted the Non-Intercourse Act for the Embargo Act. Whereas the Embargo Act had prohibited any U.S. vessel from sailing to any foreign port, the Non-Intercourse Act forbade U.S. trade with Great Britain, France, and their colonies. In addition, the act authorized the president to suspend U.S. trade restrictions in favor of the belligerent that repealed its decrees first. Pres. James Madison notified both Great Britain and France that the United States would restore trade with the nation that eliminated its trade restrictions against the United States. Moreover, he warned of potential U.S. retaliatory action against the nation that failed to follow suit.

George Canning, Great Britain's foreign secretary, regarded the Non-Intercourse Act as an opportunity to draw the United States closer to Britain. He instructed David M. Erskine, Britain's minister to the United States, to offer Madison's administration repeal of the Orders in Council for the withdrawal of all trade restrictions against Great Britain and the continuation of those restrictions against France. In addition, Canning insisted that the United States renounce all trade with France's colonies not open to U.S. trade in time of peace and therefore accept the Rule of 1756, which stipulated that trade not permitted in time of peace would not be permitted in time of war. Finally, Canning instructed Erskine to demand that the United States allow the Royal Navy to enforce the Non-Intercourse Act by seizing U.S. ships attempting to trade with France or its colonies.

In April 1809, Erskine met with U.S. Secretary of State Robert Smith. Erskine considered Canning's instructions as mere suggestions. He assured Smith that if the United States renounced trade with France, Great Britain would revoke the Orders in Council. Erskine and Smith agreed that since the Non-Intercourse Act outlawed trade with France, it was unnecessary to issue a statement declaring that the United States both renounced trade with France and acknowledged the Rule of 1756. Additionally, they agreed that it was both insulting and unnecessary to issue a public statement declaring that the Royal Navy would enforce the Non-Intercourse Act. The U.S. Navy, they argued, could enforce its nation's laws.

Madison welcomed the Erskine Agreement. On 19 April 1809, he issued a proclamation reestablishing trade with Great Britain, effective 10 June 1809. However, Canning was unwilling to accept the Erskine Agreement. He recalled Erskine on 30 May, and on 21 July repudiated the agreement. Great Britain would not revoke the Orders in Council without a U.S. declaration explicitly stating acceptance of Canning's three demands. On 9 August 1809, Madison therefore issued a second proclamation restoring nonintercourse with Great Britain. Nevertheless, 90 percent of U.S. ships reached British ports.

The new British minister, Francis James Jackson, took a much harder line toward the Americans. He argued that the misunderstandings in the Erskine Agreement were solely the United States' fault. After a month of Jackson's belligerent and accusatory statements, Madison, on the advice of his cabinet, refused to receive him. In April 1810, Canning recalled Jackson to Great Britain. However, rather than leave the United States, Jackson remained for another year, financially supporting Madison's Federalist opponents.

In May 1810, Congress replaced the unenforceable and unsuccessful Non-Intercourse Act with Macon's Bill No. 2, which declared U.S. commerce open to all the world. If either Great Britain or France ceased restrictions against U.S. shipping before 3 March 1811, the act authorized the president to revive nonintercourse with the other power.

The Non-Intercourse Act was a turning point in Anglo-American relations. Britain's acceptance of the Erskine Agreement may have averted war between the two countries. Although it is not clear why Canning wrecked the Erskine Agreement, his actions certainly increased American feelings of hostility and anger toward Great Britain.

—*John E. Grenier*

See also: Cadore Letter; Canning, George; Diplomacy; Embargo Act; Macon's Bill No. 2
Further Reading
Brown, Roger H. *The Republic in Peril: 1812.* New York: Columbia University Press, 1964.
Carr, Albert Z. *The Coming of War: An Account of the Remarkable Events Leading to the War of 1812.* Garden City, NY: Doubleday and Company, 1960.
Horsman, Reginald. *The Causes of the War of 1812.* Philadelphia: University of Pennsylvania Press, 1962.
Perkins, Bradford. *Prologue to War: England and the United States 1805–1812.* Berkeley: University of California Press, 1961.

NORFOLK, VIRGINIA

At the beginning of the nineteenth century, Norfolk was a thriving center of maritime commerce. Strategically situated on the Elizabeth River just inside Chesapeake Bay, the town enjoyed a flourishing trade with the northern states, Europe, and the West Indies. By 1807, its merchants were exporting between five and seven million dollars' worth of grain, tobacco, naval stores, and other goods yearly. This burgeoning commercial activity also proved a boon to Norfolk's shipbuilding industry. During the 1790s and the first decade of the 1800s, local contractors turned out hundreds of vessels, including the frigate *Chesapeake,* launched in 1799. In 1800, the Navy Department selected neighboring Gosport as the site for one of its six federal shipyards.

The 1807 embargo brought an abrupt end to Norfolk's boom times. Even after the measure was replaced by the less restrictive Non-Intercourse Act in 1809, trade revived only partially. Norfolk's citizens blamed most of their economic woes on the French and their own government. A February 1811 article in the Norfolk *Gazette and Public Ledger* warned that the town's seaborne livelihood would wither away if Napoleon and Madison persisted in their present policies. Two months later an angry mob vented its frustrations by setting fire to a French privateer's vessel anchored in the Elizabeth River.

Not surprisingly, given the direction that public sentiment was running, Norfolk greeted the news of the country's declaration of war against Great Britain in 1812 with little enthusiasm. Although the town had responded with indignation and outrage to the *Leopard*'s attack on the *Chesapeake* in 1807, tempers had cooled over the intervening years. Moreover, Norfolk fully appreciated the dangers that war with Britain portended. It had felt the sting of British wrath once before, when it was burned to the ground by Lord Dunmore in 1776. Now, in 1812, with its coastal defenses in poor condition and only four of its ten gunboats ready for service, the town's prospects hardly seemed brighter.

As it turned out, the first eight months of the war passed almost without incident. The flow of commercial shipping into and out of the harbor remained steady, if somewhat thinner in volume. But Norfolk's reprieve ended with the New Year. In the spring of 1813, the British clamped a tight blockade across the mouth of Chesapeake Bay, throttling Norfolk's trade. At the same time, the town also began to attract the direct attention of the Royal Navy. In February, the frigate *Constellation* was forced to take refuge under the guns of Fort Norfolk after failing to slip through the British blockade. Anchored in the channel and supported by gunboats on either flank, the *Constellation* foiled several attempts to cut her out. The danger to Norfolk increased appreciably in mid-March, with the arrival in Hampton Roads of three ships of the line and several smaller vessels under the command of British rear admiral Sir George Cockburn. Cockburn ended up bypassing Norfolk in favor of a destructive raid into the upper reaches of the bay. But the Royal Navy returned in force to Hampton Roads in June. This time, the British, led by Adm. Sir John Borlase Warren, set their sights on the *Constellation* and Norfolk's extensive shipyard facilities.

Norfolk had not been idle, however, in the months since the British threat first materialized. A mixed force of militia and volunteers was scraped together and assigned to the command of Gen. Robert B. Taylor. Sailors and marines from the *Constellation* also turned out for the defense of the town. The river immediately below Norfolk was stoutly protected by Forts Nelson and Norfolk. Taylor also fortified Craney Island at the mouth of the Elizabeth River, and 20 gunboats deployed in a crescent formation guarded the main channel to the east.

Warren struck on 22 June, launching a two-pronged attack against the U.S. positions on the mainland and Craney Island. Both assaults were handily repulsed. Realizing that further operations against Norfolk would be fruitless, Warren elected to withdraw and carry on his depreda-tions elsewhere. The U.S. victory at Craney Island represented a minor triumph for Jefferson's pluralistic vision of national defense. The battle demonstrated that coastal batteries, gunboats, and militia could, under the right conditions, provide effective security against attack. Of course, the officers and crew of the *Constellation* also deserved a share of credit for the happy outcome.

Although British warships continued their marauding cruises up and down Chesapeake Bay for the remainder of the conflict, the danger of a direct attack on Norfolk receded. The return of peace in 1815, however, did not bring with it the economic windfall that Norfolk merchants anticipated. Britain's refusal to open its West Indian carrying trade dealt the town's shipping concerns a serious blow. Overseas trade with Europe also declined. By 1850, Norfolk had settled firmly into the ranks of minor U.S. seaports.

—*Jeff Seiken*

See also: Cockburn, George; Craney Island, Battle of; Hampton, Virginia; Warren, John Borlase

Further Reading

Tucker, Spencer C. *The Jeffersonian Gunboat Navy*. Columbia: University of South Carolina Press, 1993.

U.S. Navy Department. *The Naval War of 1812: A Documentary History*. Ed. William S. Dudley. Two vols. to date. Washington, DC: Government Printing Office, 1985–.

Wertenbaker, Thomas J. *Norfolk: Historic Southern Port*. 2nd ed. Marvin W. Schlegel, ed. Durham, NC: Duke University Press, 1962.

NOVA SCOTIA
See Halifax, Nova Scotia

O

OGDENSBURG, BATTLE OF
22 February 1813

On 6 February 1813, Maj. Benjamin Forsyth left Ogdensburg, New York, to stage a raid on Elizabethtown, Upper Canada, to rescue some British deserters and Americans who had been captured by the British on U.S. soil. All of these men were confined in the jail at Elizabethtown, and Forsyth's spies told him that only a small British garrison guarded the prisoners. Forsyth crossed the ice of the St. Lawrence River, surprised the British garrison, and took both the garrison and its prisoners back to Ogdensburg. For this daring act, Forsyth was brevetted a lieutenant colonel.

The British immediately began planning retaliation for this raid, and Gov.-Gen. Sir George Prevost placed Lt. Col. George (known as "Red George") MacDonnell in command of the offensive against Ogdensburg. MacDonnell set out across the ice of the St. Lawrence on the morning of 22 February with his own Glengarry Light Infantry Fencibles, King's Regiment, Royal Newfoundland Corps, Canadian militia, and Indian allies arranged in two columns, around 800 men total.

Forsyth, outnumbered more than two to one, had warning from his spies of MacDonnell's approach and attempted to arrange most of his men around the only fortifications near the town, while placing some of his militia and artillery on the outskirts of town. In the meantime he sent word to Gen. Henry Dearborn asking for reinforcements, but Dearborn was unwilling to supply them.

MacDonnell's right flank, as it came across the ice, consisted of the Glengarry Light Fencibles and some Canadian militia. The right flank attacked Forsyth's fortifications, while the left moved toward the town. Forsyth was able to repel the right flank, but the left pushed through the light defenses of the town and then turned to the right toward Forsyth's position. MacDonnell demanded Forsyth's surrender and was refused, but after a brief exchange, Forsyth realized the impossibility of his situation and retreated.

MacDonnell then set about to destroy the town's fortifications, while the militia forces and Indians looted the town. Ogdensburg remained unfortified for the remainder of the war, but when the townspeople returned, they made a handsome profit for the next two years trading with the British in Canada.

—Jeanne T. Heidler and David S. Heidler

See also: Dearborn, Henry; Forsyth, Benjamin; Prevost, George
Further Reading
Raudzens, George. "Red George MacDonnell, Military Savior of Upper Canada?" *Ontario History* 62 (1970): 199–212.

OHIO

The first state organized out of the original Northwest Territory, Ohio had entered the Union less than a decade before hostilities with Great Britain erupted in June 1812. Although its population had grown rapidly following the U.S. victory at Fallen Timbers in 1794 and already approached a quarter of a million people, popular opinion was divided over entry into the conflict. Many citizens feared the state's vulnerability to military incursion from Canada as well as to hostile Indian attacks. Others relished war as an opportunity to destroy remaining Indian resistance in the aftermath of Tippecanoe. Seeking to quell fears along the United States' largely defenseless northwestern frontier, Pres. James Madison authorized Ohio governor Return J. Meigs, Sen. Thomas Worthington, and Rep. Jeremiah Morrow to hold council with regional Indian leaders at Piqua, Ohio, in August 1812: their goal was to obtain pledges of neutrality in the Anglo-American contest. Unfortunately for the Ohio delegation, the rapid fall of Forts Michilimackinac, Dearborn, and Detroit to British aggression proved more persuasive than words. Suddenly, the failure of the state legislature to authorize Governor Meigs's requests for preparedness measures during the winter and spring of 1812 loomed ominously in the face of such disastrous setbacks so close to home.

Ohio's militia regiments, with an 1808 federally authorized strength of 2,384, were inadequately manned, trained, and equipped to defend the state from invasion. More men were needed to reinforce besieged Fort Wayne in Indiana Territory and adequately garrison Forts Adams, Loramie, Murrys, and St. Mary's in northwestern Ohio. William Henry Harrison's Northwestern Army regulars moved into the state, but sickness and desertion soon reduced U.S. military effectiveness and did little to instill popular confidence north of the Ohio River. To blunt an anticipated 1813 British campaign, Harrison began construction of Fort Meigs at the Maumee River rapids and sent forces to assist with the strengthening of Fort Stephenson at Lower Sandusky. These two vanguards of the state's defensive cordon were put to the test in the most decisive actions held on Ohio soil, with U.S. forces repulsing the British advance. Further hostile ambitions against Ohio were checked by the U.S. naval victory on Lake Erie.

When Meigs left the state capital of Chillicothe in March 1814 to become Madison's postmaster general, the ensuing campaign for governor demonstrated that party factionalism remained strong. Acting governor Othneil Looker took issue with Thomas Worthington's Senate vote against declaring war, and Duncan McArthur, Harrison's replacement as commanding general of the Northwestern Army, accused Worthington of keeping him in the military to prevent his election bid. Though Worthington won easily, his emergency attempts to reorganize the Ohio militia and strengthen the state's frontier fortifications were rebuffed by the legislature. Fortunately, the war ended before Ohio's defenses were again put to the test.

With peace came the ignoble removal of the Indians from north of the Ohio River. No longer threatened, Ohio entered a period of general prosperity. Internal improvements, especially with regard to land and water transportation routes, enabled the state's population to exceed 500,000 by 1820 and close in on one million a decade later, as Americans pushed the frontier ever westward.

—*William E. Fischer, Jr.*

See also: Dearborn, Fort; Detroit, Surrender of; Harrison, William Henry; Indiana Territory; Lake Erie Campaign; McArthur, Duncan; Meigs, Fort; Meigs, Return Johnathan; Michilimackinac, Fort; Stephenson, Fort; Wayne, Fort; Worthington, Thomas

Further Reading

Brown, Jeffrey P. "The Ohio Federalist, 1803–1815." *Journal of the Early Republic* 2 (1982): 261–282.

Gilpin, Alec R. *The War of 1812 in the Old Northwest.* East Lansing: Michigan State University Press, 1958.

Utter, William T. *The Frontier State, 1803–1825.* Columbus: Ohio Historical Society, 1942.

ORDERS IN COUNCIL
January and November 1807, April 1809, September 1811

The British Orders in Council were a succession of decrees intended to control neutral trade with European ports. The first orders were issued on 7 January and 11 November 1807 as retaliatory measures against Napoleon's Berlin Decree of 21 November 1806, which had proclaimed the British Isles to be in a state of blockade by land and sea. The January orders banned neutral trade from ports controlled by Britain's enemies, and those of November, which were more rigorous, not only forbade maritime trade between ports controlled by France and her allies, but compelled all neutral ships to call at British ports or be subjected to a search by British authorities. All vessels were liable to capture and confiscation. In addition, the British ordered neutral ships to pay duties and obtain licenses for trade with enemy ports. The use of restricting trade on the seas was a measure that the British, as a superior naval power, had often used in the past to destroy an enemy's shipping.

In response to the orders, Napoleon issued the Milan Decree of 17 December 1807. It extended to neutrals the embargo on British products or items destined for Britain. By this time, French maritime trade had been seriously disrupted. The French blamed the British for starting the commercial warfare with the Fox Blockade of May 1806, which had enforced a blockade from Ostend to the Seine. In defending the orders, the British pointed to the much more sweeping Berlin Decree.

The British had no intention of stopping all trade to the Continent, as is revealed by the remarks of Prime Minister Spencer Perceval: "The object of the Orders in Council was not to destroy the trade of the Continent, but to force the Continent to trade with us." With this purpose in mind, Britain actually lessened the extent of her blockade and reduced transit duties. In addition, the British distributed thousands of licenses that permitted trade with Europe. These licenses were issued to British subjects and European neutrals. France ignored the licensing system and also compromised the Continental Blockade when it served her interests.

The British authorized U.S. goods to be transported directly from the United States to the Continent. Although Americans continued to ship goods that were not manufactured in the United States to the European Continent through a variety of measures (by acquiring a British license, carrying dual papers, or bribing French officials), U.S. losses under the restrictions were high. From 1807 to 1812, approximately 900 U.S. ships were seized by either Britain or France.

Napoleon had hoped to acquire the United States as an ally. The orders annoyed neutral nations, particularly the United States, which was already infuriated with the Royal Navy's practice of impressment. The British bombardment of the USS *Chesapeake* on 22 June 1807 provoked Jefferson into banning British warships from U.S. waters. Although the timing seemed perfect for a Franco-American alliance, Napoleon's decision on 18 September 1807 to confiscate British merchandise from neutral ships foiled the hope. Jefferson, frustrated with both belligerents, asked Congress for and got an Embargo Act on 28 December 1807. It prohibited U.S. ships from trading with Europe and banned the importation of goods manufactured in England in an attempt to force England and France to terminate their controls. The Embargo Act had more serious consequences for the U.S. economy, however, than it had for either of the warring nations. Napoleon reacted to the U.S. embargo with the Decree of Bayonne, 17 April 1808, ordering that U.S. vessels entering European ports should be sequestered. Congress repealed the Embargo Act in March 1809 and replaced it with the Non-Intercourse Act, which reopened trade with all countries except Britain and France and their colonies. It was equally ineffective in gaining concessions. Britain reissued its Orders in Council in April 1809. U.S. commerce was greatly hurt by these acts, and consequently in May 1810, Americans resumed trading with the belligerents under the terms of Macon's Bill No. 2.

In August 1810, Napoleon offered to lift the blockade of the United States if the British revoked their Orders in Council. This measure was popular in the United States, which responded by declaring that nonintercourse with Britain would recommence if the orders were not revoked by February 1811. Rather than annulling previous orders, the British issued new ones on 6 September 1811. This final order prohibited the United States from selling salt fish to the West Indies and inflicted onerous levies on everything else brought into the United States. It was intended to favor Canadian–West Indian trade at the expense of the Americans.

By this time, the British were in a deep economic reces-

sion. Only the renewal of U.S. trade could revive the economy. Particularly hard hit were the manufacturing districts, which petitioned Parliament for a repeal of the orders and the restoration of friendly relations with the United States. On 16 June 1812, Henry Brougham, who had led the campaign to rescind Britain's orders, introduced a motion in Parliament demanding their repeal. He claimed that Napoleon had finally withdrawn his decrees, citing the St. Cloud Decree of 28 April 1811, in which Napoleon had announced their "definitive repeal." The French had produced this document on 11 May 1812 in response to the British declaration that they would withdraw the orders if the French provided proof of repeal. It was common knowledge that this document was a fraud and had not existed before May 1812.

Finally, in reply to Brougham's motion, the orders were repealed on 16 June 1812. The British were so confident their repeal would improve relations between the United States and Britain that Foreign Secretary Castlereagh told U.S. chargé d'affaires Jonathan Russell that British officials continued to hold "great hopes . . . of the favorable effects" that the repeal of the orders would have on U.S. policy. But it was all too late. On 1 June, Madison had asked Congress for a declaration of war against Britain. He cited a long list of complaints against Britain that included impressment, harassment of U.S. coasts, blockades, and a renewal of Indian warfare. Without doubt, during the commercial struggle, Britain had yielded nothing, and her refusal to cancel the orders was a primary factor in provoking a declaration of war by the United States.

—*Leigh Whaley*

See also: Bathurst, Henry, Third Earl Bathurst; Berlin Decree; Canning, George; Castlereagh, Viscount, Robert Stewart; *Chesapeake-Leopard* Affair; Embargo Act; Macon's Bill No. 2; Milan Decree; Napoleon I; Non-Intercourse Act; Perceval, Spencer; Russell, Jonathan

Further Reading
Horsman, Reginald. *Causes of the War of 1812.* New York: Octagon Books, 1972.
Stagg, J.C.A. *Mr. Madison's War.* Princeton: Princeton University Press, 1983.

OSWEGO, NEW YORK

Oswego, on Lake Ontario, was an important point along the U.S. supply line. Before the war, this robust commercial village was the primary port in the trade with

York and Kingston in Upper Canada. The road network north and west of Albany was notoriously bad, particularly in the spring, when melting snow and rains turned the trails into rivers of mud. The easiest and cheapest mode of transport was by water. War supplies forwarded from Albany went west along the Mohawk River. With short portages, the water route continued across Lake Oneida and down the Oswego River to the village of Oswego. From there, coastal vessels moved cargo either east to the naval base at Sacket's Harbor or west toward the Niagara Frontier. An impediment along this route was Oswego Falls, about 8 miles upriver from Oswego. A set of rapids rather than a true waterfall, this obstacle nonetheless forced captains to unload their cargoes. Skilled pilots then ferried the cargoes through the rapids and down to Oswego. During most of the war, large quantities of food, salt, and war supplies sat above the falls or at Oswego awaiting shipment.

In the spring of 1814, Sir James Yeo, commander of the Royal Navy on the Great Lakes, perceived that he was losing the naval arms race on Lake Ontario. The loss of his Lake Erie squadron to Oliver Hazard Perry the previous year had devastating effects on the British war effort in western Upper Canada. The stakes were even higher on Lake Ontario. If the Americans controlled the lake, it would be nearly impossible to supply British forces west of York. Yeo and his superior, Lt. Gen. Gordon Drummond, devised a plan to impede construction of the U.S. fleet at Sacket's Harbor by raiding Oswego and capturing the supplies there. When Commodore Isaac Chauncey became aware of the danger, he asked his army counterpart, Maj. Gen. Jacob Brown, for assistance. Brown sent Lt. Col. George E. Mitchell and a battalion of artillerymen fighting as infantry to Oswego. After a forced march of 150 miles, Mitchell and nearly 400 of his men arrived on 30 April. They found the remains of the Revolutionary War fort situated on a rise overlooking Oswego and the lake. The wooden pickets still in place were rotten; the few guns remaining were unmounted. This shocking scene symbolized U.S. unpreparedness even after nearly two years of war. Mitchell's men made some improvements, but the arrival of Yeo's squadron on 5 May forced the Americans to stop their work.

Yeo bombarded the decrepit fort from the guns of his ships. He then landed nearly 800 infantry, sailors, and Royal Marines, who stormed the old fort. Mitchell's men put up a stalwart defense until he ordered them to fall back to Oswego Falls. The most important war supplies, heavy guns to arm the ships nearing completion at Sacket's Harbor, were at the falls, not in Oswego. The British, unaware of the guns upriver, were content with the capture of 2,400

barrels of food and salt. Both sides claimed victory. Mitchell was proclaimed a hero for his courageous fight at Oswego and his success in keeping the guns in U.S. hands. Yeo captured enough food to feed British forces in Upper Canada for two weeks and enough salt to preserve thousands of barrels of meat. The raid on Oswego slowed down Chauncey's shipbuilding program for vital weeks. Oswego saw no more action in the war. Its role as an important commercial center diminished with the opening of the Erie Canal.

—Richard V. Barbuto

See also: Brown, Jacob J.; Chauncey, Isaac; Drummond, Gordon; Kingston, Upper Canada; Lake Ontario; Sacket's Harbor, Battle of; Sacket's Harbor, New York; Yeo, James Lucas

OTIS, HARRISON GRAY
1765–1848
U.S. politician

Born in Boston to Samuel Allyne Otis and Elizabeth Gray Otis, Harrison Gray Otis graduated from Harvard College in 1783 and began the practice of law in Boston in 1786. During the 1790s, Otis became a prominent member of Boston's Federalist Party and, after serving in the Massachusetts legislature, was sent to the U.S. House of Representatives in 1797. Otis served for the duration of the John Adams administration and was known as a strong supporter of the president, but partly because of the move of the capital to the raw wilderness of Washington, D.C., he did not seek another term in 1800.

Following his return to Boston, Otis remained active in Massachusetts Federalist politics, serving in the lower and upper houses of the state legislature. At the same time, Otis remained in touch with members of the party outside Massachusetts and New England. Though ardently supportive of measures to enhance the position of New England in national affairs, Otis's contacts with Federalists outside the section as well as his interest in the national party set him apart from the more radical sectionalists within the Boston political elite.

Even so, when the Jefferson administration began implementing policies that Otis found especially harmful to his section (such as the embargo), he quickly spoke out against these measures. When the country moved toward war with Great Britain in 1812, Otis opposed the declaration of war, and when the declaration came, he expressed the belief that it should be treated like any bad law—the people should work for its legal repeal.

One of the ways that Otis believed this goal could be accomplished was to defeat James Madison in the election of 1812. Knowing that a Federalist candidate did not have a chance in the election, Otis advocated Federalist support of the Democratic Republican candidacy of New Yorker De-Witt Clinton. Though he was unable to convince fellow Federalists formally to endorse Clinton, the instructions the party ultimately gave to its members were that they should vote for someone other than the current office-holders, which clearly implied that Clinton was the better choice for the party.

Although this plan did not succeed, Otis continued to work against the Madison administration and its war policy. Certainly not a secessionist, Otis nevertheless gained a reputation as an eloquent spokesman for his section. During the summer of 1814, he came to believe that the New England states needed to meet to discuss their common concerns. His reputation for moderation together with his devotion to the interests of Massachusetts gained him a place on the state's delegation to the Hartford Convention in December 1814.

At the convention, Otis quickly assumed the most prominent leadership role of all of the delegates. He spoke often and persuasively for the resolutions that emerged, but he was also seen by radicals as too moderate to effect substantial concessions from the government in Washington.

When the delegates completed their deliberations, Otis served as the primary author of the report and was chosen as one of the three commissioners from the convention who would take the demands to Washington, D.C. On the way, Otis learned of the Treaty of Ghent, and when he arrived, the administration officially refused to consider the convention's demands.

Following the war, Otis's reputation was somewhat redeemed due to his cooperation with the Monroe administration. He served briefly in the U.S. Senate but returned to Massachusetts politics because his defense of the actions of the Hartford Convention prevented him from achieving real power in that body. With the demise of the Federalist Party, Otis became a Whig in later years. He died in Boston in 1848.

—*Jeanne T. Heidler and David S. Heidler*

See also: Embargo Act; Federalist Party; Hartford Convention
Further Reading
Morison, Samuel Eliot. "The Life and Correspondence of Harrison Gray Otis." Ph.D. dissertation, Harvard University, 1915.

P

PAKENHAM, EDWARD
1778–1815

Born at Longford Castle, County Westmeath, Ireland, on 19 April 1778, Edward Michael Pakenham, second son of Baron Longford, grew up in the privileged world of the eighteenth-century British aristocracy, which guaranteed him early advancement in his military career. His exceptional tactical acumen and leadership qualities, however, earned him elevation to general officer rank. Following a limited basic education, Pakenham received a lieutenant's commission in the 92nd Regiment of Foot on 28 May 1794. Within days, he purchased a captaincy and by 6 December acquired the rank of major in the 33rd (Ulster) Light Dragoons.

His rapid rise continued throughout the wars of the French Revolution. As a major in the 23rd Light Dragoons, he served in Ireland during the Irish Rebellion of 1798 (June to October). Promoted to lieutenant colonel (October 1798), he commanded a battalion of the 64th Regiment of Foot (Staffordshire Regiment) in the Danish-Swedish West Indian Islands expedition of 1801. During the capture of the island of St. Lucia, he received the first of his two battlefield wounds (both in the neck at the same spot) on 22 June 1803 and returned to Britain to convalesce. As a brevet colonel in 1805, he commanded the First Battalion of the Seventh Royal Fusiliers and participated in the Copenhagen Campaign of 1807 and the capture of Martinique in 1809.

Tall, handsome, and precise in dress and manners, Pakenham conducted himself in accordance with the gentlemanly concept of warfare common to the preindustrial era. During the New Orleans campaign, he wrote a personal letter to Gen. Andrew Jackson protesting that nighttime raids and the killing of British pickets were barbaric, ungentlemanly warfare. Jackson replied that he was engaged in repelling an invasion of his country and was therefore not concerned with Pakenham's concept of gentlemanly

ethics. Although Pakenham dominated fellow officers with his physical traits and strong personality, he nonetheless commanded respect and was socially liked by fellow officers. In 1806, Arthur Wellesley, the future Duke of Wellington, married Pakenham's sister Catherine, thus establishing an enduring familial and professional relationship.

The major thrust of British operations in the last years of the Napoleonic wars occurred in the Peninsular Campaign of 1809–1814. Pakenham joined his brother-in-law as deputy adjutant general (March 1810) and then as a brigade commander in Sir Brent Spenser's First Division. Pakenham's brigade, composed of the Second Battalion of the Seventh Royal Fusiliers and the Cameron Highlanders, fought at Bussaco (27 September 1810) and Fuentes de Onoro (May 1811). His excellent generalship earned him the local rank of major general.

Sir Thomas Picton, wounded at Badajoz on 6 April 1812, personally selected Pakenham to command his Third Division at the Battle of Salamanca on 22 July 1812. When the French weakened their center while attempting to position themselves between the British and Badajoz, Wellington ordered the Third Division to assault the French line. Pakenham attacked with such alacrity and effectiveness that he thoroughly defeated the French forces. For his martial accomplishments, Pakenham received a promotion to the permanent rank of major general and command of the Sixth Division, which he led to victory at the Battle of the Pyrenees in 1813. A Knighthood of the Bath followed in September 1813 in recognition of his war service, later upgraded to Knight of the Grand Cross of the Order of the Bath (GCB) just days before his death in battle.

Although he opposed the war in the United States, he accepted command of the British North American army on the death of Maj. Gen. Robert Ross near Baltimore. The army departed from Chesapeake Bay to capture New Orleans, but adverse winds delayed Pakenham's arrival from Europe via Jamaica, so he did not join his command until it had already debarked and opened the campaign. The army operated on a narrow neck of land flanked by the Mississippi River and a swamp. After several unproductive attempts to breach Jackson's defensive line, Pakenham resolved to attack on both sides of the river simultaneously. The assault on 8 January 1815 started before key units assumed their positions, and a battlefield disaster ensued. When the 44th Regiment broke and ran, Pakenham attempted to rally those Peninsular veterans by riding forward, shouting to the cowering men, "Shame! Shame! Remember, you're British! Forward, gentlemen, forward!"

As he approached the U.S. lines, the enemy riflemen ceased fire, but the artillery did not. A cannonball struck him in the shoulder, and another knocked him from his horse. Mounting his aide-de-camp's horse, Pakenham again rode toward the enemy lines. Two bullets struck him in the throat and chest. He issued his final orders for the reserve to be brought into action as the aide carried him back and laid him under an oak tree. His final words were: "lost for the lack of courage."

His troops placed his remains in a rum cask for transport home, and legend says that his organs were buried under a pecan tree, which never again bloomed. The rum cask was put on the wrong ship, an error discovered only after the sailors complained of a foul taste in their grog. In honor of Sir Edward, a public subscription raised the funds to pay for the erection of a life-size statue of him and his second in command, Samuel Gibbs, also killed in action, in the South Transept of St. Paul's Cathedral in London.

—*Stanley D.M. Carpenter*

See also: New Orleans, Battle of

Further Reading

Barthorp, Michael. *Wellington's Generals*. London: Osprey, 1978.

Brooks, Charles B. *The Siege of New Orleans*. Seattle: University of Washington Press, 1961.

Carter, Samuel. *Blaze of Glory: The Fight for New Orleans, 1814–1815*. London: Macmillan, 1971.

Fortescue, J.W. *A History of the British Army* Vol. 10. London: Macmillan, 1920.

PARKER, PETER
1785–1814
Royal Navy officer

Peter Parker was born in 1785, the eldest son of Adm. Christopher Parker and grandson of Admiral of the Fleet Sir Peter Parker, 1721–1811. He was a relative of Lord

Peter Parker

Byron, who wrote a touching eulogy on the occasion of Parker's death in 1814. He was an aggressive, dashing naval officer, noted as overly reckless, a ruthless disciplinarian, and a spoiled child of patronage. As was the practice for young aristocrats at the time, Parker first appeared on the books of the Royal Navy at age eight. In 1803, he was serving aboard HMS *Victory*, and at the time of the battle of Trafalgar in 1805, he was in the ship that took the message to Lord Nelson that the French-Spanish fleet was underway.

During the War of 1812, Capt. Sir Peter Parker commanded the frigate HMS *Menelaus* (38 guns). He was under the command of Adm. Sir Alexander Cochrane, commander of the British North American squadron based at Halifax, Nova Scotia. Participating in Sir George Cockburn's raids of Chesapeake Bay country, Parker earned a reputation for dashing arrogance and whimsical destruction that secured for him among Chesapeake inhabitants a hatred rivaling that leveled at Cockburn. During the British assault on Washington, D.C., in 1814, Parker was sent to the upper bay to divert U.S. attention and scout the defenses of Baltimore. His observations were to prove of some value to Cochrane when the British moved upon Baltimore in September, but the diversionary operation was to be Parker's last. After dark on 30 August 1814, he led a force of 134 marines and sailors ashore against alerted U.S. militiamen on the Maryland Eastern Shore near Caulk's Field. Parker and 14 others were killed, and 27 were wounded.

Parker's death put a check on marauding operations ashore by forces from British frigates and sloops. His body was carried to England, where he was buried in St. Margaret's Church, next to Westminster Abbey.

—Eugene L. Rasor

See also: Caulk's Field, Battle of; Chesapeake Bay Campaign, 1813–1814; Cochrane, Alexander; Cockburn, George; Maryland

PARSONS, USHER
1788–1868
U.S. Navy surgeon

Born on 18 August 1788 in Alfred, Massachusetts (Maine District), Parsons was apprenticed to Dr. Abiel Hall, Sr., for four years and then studied briefly with the eminent Boston surgeon Dr. John Warren. Unable to find a suitable opening after being licensed, Parsons joined the U.S. Navy as a surgeon's mate on 10 July 1812.

Assigned to the USS *Lawrence,* he was the only surgeon available for duty at the Battle of Lake Erie on 10 September 1813. While treating about 100 casualties of that action (including at least seven amputations and one trephination), Parsons realized that delaying major surgery on battle victims until they had recovered from the initial traumatic shock would improve their chances of survival. That was a novel idea at the time, but his overall surgical mortality rate was a remarkably low 3 percent. Although promoted to full surgeon in 1814, Parsons saw no more major action during the war. He reported the details of his combat cases in the *Journal of Medicine and Surgery,* and his other publications and his diaries provide valuable eyewitness accounts of Perry's victory.

He was with Perry again on the *Java* in 1815–1817 and managed to retain his naval appointment while touring European and U.S. medical centers. In 1820, he published the first of five editions of his influential medical vade mecum for ships, *The Sailor's Physician.* A year later he settled in Providence, Rhode Island, married Mary Jackson Holmes in 1822, and resigned from the navy on 23 April 1823. Parsons taught at Brown University's short-lived medical school and was active in local and national medical affairs until he died in Providence on 1 December 1868.

—J. Worth Estes

See also: Medicine, Army; Medicine, Naval
Further Reading
Goldowsky, Seebert J. *Yankee Surgeon: The Life and Times of Usher Parsons, 1788–1868.* Boston: Countway Library of Medicine, 1988.
Parsons, Usher. *Journal of Medicine and Surgery* 7 (1818): 316.

PATRIOT WAR
1811–May 1814

By European standards, Spain owned Florida in 1810, but the United States lusted for it, Britain was determined to keep the United States out of it, and the Florida Indians thought of it as their homeland. The Madison administration, asserting that West Florida was part of the Louisiana Purchase, annexed that portion of it between the Perdido and the Mississippi Rivers, from the Gulf of Mexico northward to the 31st parallel.

Pres. James Madison was obsessed with acquiring Florida. Accordingly, he pushed through Congress on 15 June 1811 a secret resolution to absorb Florida if some responsible authority willingly transferred it. He found a trustworthy agent to promote the acquisition in Gen. George Mathews, an honored veteran of the Revolutionary War, twice governor of Georgia, and at the time of this episode 72 years old. Mathews never received positive written instructions on his mission, but he was convinced by talks with the president and Secretary of State James Monroe that he was carrying out national policy.

He concluded that a small, easy revolution against Spain would be necessary to place leaders in control who would then offer Florida to the United States. Then he conferred with men of property and position who had interests on both sides of the border. A group of them organized and called themselves the Patriots. Their first object was to conquer St. Augustine. The U.S. government kept two gunboats and one brig afloat in Spanish waters and 150 professional soldiers on Spanish ground, yet neither Capt. Hugh Campbell at sea nor Col. Thomas Adam Smith on land had positive orders to aid the Patriots. Without direct U.S. military help, the Patriot force could not capture the stone castillo at St. Augustine. On 13 March 1812, the Patriots were at most able to take Fernandina on Amelia Island. Declaring Fernandina their capital, the Patriots from that place declared the independence of East Florida. They next offered the area between the St. Marys and the St. Johns Rivers to General Mathews, who accepted it on behalf of the United States. On 26 March, the Patriots summoned the Spanish governor to surrender St. Augustine. He scorned their threat. Next, on 10 July, they drew up a constitution for East Florida and elected John Houston McIntosh, a wealthy American who had sworn allegiance to the king of Spain, to be the director.

By this time, the Madison administration realized that war with Great Britain was imminent. Since Spain and Britain were allies against Napoleon, an adventure in Florida would be even more hazardous. Madison determined to sacrifice General Mathews "for the public good." Monroe initiated this immolation on 4 April, when he wrote to Mathews that the measures he had adopted to gain possession of Amelia Island and parts of the mainland were not authorized by the nation's laws. The government never intended to wrest Florida from Spain by force, asserted Monroe. To soften the shock, he added that the general's error had sprung from commendable zeal. Mathews was relieved as agent, and David B. Mitchell, the governor of Georgia, was appointed in his place. Mathews started for Washington to vindicate himself and reveal the government's duplicity, but he died on 30 August en route.

On 19 June 1812 (one day after the declaration of war against Britain), the House of Representatives resolved to consider occupation of all of Florida, but when the Senate disagreed, 16 to 14, Monroe wrote Mitchell to remove the troops. His letter strongly implied, though, the hope that Mitchell, for the good of the nation, would not actually follow these instructions. Perhaps he could make it appear that he, not the government, was responsible for the continued occupation of East Florida. Mitchell understood the hint. The troops stayed.

Because many of their slaves escaped to Florida and a happier relationship with the Indians, inhabitants of the southeastern United States were perpetually indignant at Spain and the Florida Indians. Spain could not control the Seminoles, and there were recurring clashes between Georgians and Florida Indians. Two major incursions of militia into Florida occurred, one by Georgia in the fall of 1812 and the other from Tennessee in February 1813. These expeditions were neither requested nor directed by the Patriots.

Early in 1813, the Madison administration made a second attempt to get Congress to authorize the acquisition of Florida. When the Senate once again refused, Monroe ordered Gen. Thomas Pinckney, who had replaced Mitchell, to withdraw the U.S. armed forces from Florida. This time there was no oblique suggestion that the government would be secretly happy if the troops remained. The Patriots, still vigorous, pleaded with Pinckney to protest the removal, but instead he firmly carried it out.

By the fall of 1813, the Patriots were led by Buckner Harris, a bold, turbulent man, whom General Mathews had not thought respectable enough to be part of the leadership. Harris's goal was to found a U.S. colony on Seminole land. He knew that the last resort to draw the United States into the imbroglio was to keep Florida in constant turmoil. He sent out foraging parties to confiscate any property that could be sold for cash, regardless of who owned it. Also, he threatened those men who would not support the Patriots.

The Patriots established a nucleus for their colony by building a blockhouse in the heartland of the Seminoles. Here, on 25 January 1814, 150 of them constituted a legislature and created the District of Elotchaway of the Republic of East Florida. The new polity sent a minister to Washington, D.C., to offer itself to the United States. Secretary of State Monroe rejected their entreaty because Spain and the United States were at peace.

Without U.S. or Spanish support, neither the Patriot colony nor the Patriot cause could survive. Harris, however, unwilling to acknowledge this, scouted widely in the Alachua region, sometimes alone. A party of Indians caught and killed him on 5 May 1814. The settlers at the blockhouse lost hope and fled back into the United States. Thus ended the Patriot War.

—*John K. Mahon*

See also: Florida; Mathews, George
Further Reading
Patrick, Rembert W. *Florida Fiasco: Rampant Rebels on the Georgia-Florida Border, 1810–1815.* Athens: University of Georgia Press, 1954.

PATRIOTIC SONGS

The cultivation of U.S. nationalism during the War of 1812 was aided by the writing, publishing, and performing of patriotic songs. Overwhelmingly dedicated to the celebration of ephemeral naval heroes and individual engagements, most of these songs have been forgotten by all except historians. One song, however, has claimed a much larger role than originally intended by its author, Francis Scott Key (1779–1843). Written in 1814, "The Defense of Fort M'Henry," otherwise known as "The Star-Spangled Banner," was proclaimed the national anthem of the United States on 3 March 1931.

Francis Scott Key was a Maryland-born attorney. In September 1814 he was aboard an enemy ship in Chesapeake Bay persuading the British to free their captive, Maryland doctor William Beanes. Although Key's mission was successfully completed, neither he nor his negotiating companion and the government's representative, John Skinner, were allowed ashore because the British were planning the bombardment of Fort McHenry. Throughout the night of 13–14 September 1814, Key watched the attack that was to inspire his poem.

"The Star-Spangled Banner" was set to the tune "To Anacreon in Heaven," a popular drinking song and the theme for the Anacreontic Society. The composer is unknown, although the possibilities have been narrowed to one of two English Chapel Royal composers, Samuel Arnold (1740–1803) or John Stafford Smith (1750–1836). It is highly likely that Key had the tune in mind when he wrote the words, especially as he had written for this music before. In 1805, he had written "The Warrior's Return" to celebrate the exploits of naval hero Stephen Decatur.

Indeed, many lyrics were sung to the tune "To Anacreon in Heaven," including J. R. Calvert's "Columbia Victorious," also written in praise of Stephen Decatur, and Joseph Hutton's "Battle of the Wabash," written about the Battle of Tippecanoe (4 November 1811). It was quite common for patriotic words to be set to well-known tunes, frequently English in origin. In some cases, "Rule Britannia" was as popular a choice as "Yankee Doodle."

Patriotic songs were performed at public and private entertainments. "The Defense of Fort M'Henry" was probably first performed somewhat spontaneously by an actor, Ferdinand Durang, on the street outside a tavern in Baltimore. Dinners and theaters, however, were more commonly the chosen venues for the formal presentation of patriotic songs, which were offered both as tributes to successful naval heroes and to boost national feeling for the war. In New York, for example, on 30 December 1812, a subscription dinner for 500 guests was hosted by the mayor to honor Stephen Decatur, Isaac Hull, and Jacob Jones. The *Boston Patriot* reported that during the evening, "the company was electrified by the sudden exposure of two superb transparent Paintings." One depicted naval battles and the other the American eagle holding three crowns emblazoned with the names of the guests of honor and their ships. A series of patriotic toasts was interspersed with songs, duets, and tunes including "Decatur, Hull and Jones Are Here," "Hull's Victory," and "Decatur's Victory." In some cases, such as at the Holliday Street Theater in Baltimore in 1813, patriotic songs formed part of an integrated program of entertainment that included an opera entitled *The* Constitution *and the* Wasp, the unveiling of a portrait of Isaac Hull, and dancing as well.

Patriotic songs were published widely. They were printed as broadsides in newspapers and as sheet music in songbooks. Some songbooks were quite specialized, such as the 1813 volume *The Columbian Naval Melody*, subtitled *A Collection of Songs and Odes, Composed on the Late Naval Victories and Other Occasions.* Other songbooks, *The American Star* being one, contained a selection of various songs popular in the United States during the war, some of which had patriotic content. Some collections drew patriotic material from the Revolutionary period; however, the vast majority of songs published in these books were written in response to the War of 1812 and dealt specifically with contemporary engagements.

Patriotic songs of the War of 1812 almost always had a naval theme. Undoubtedly, U.S. success at sea compared with the army's lackluster performance on land encouraged this. Furthermore, the first largely reported naval victory, that of the *Constitution* over the *Guerrière* on 19 August 1812, occurred quite soon after war was declared. Naval victories were especially sweet, given Britain's reputation as the most powerful seafaring nation in the world. Added to this, free trade and sailors' rights (the end of impressment) had been asserted as justifying the declaration of war. "Kidnapped Seamen" addressed impressment in graphic terms to illustrate one of the causes of the war. Songs provided an opportunity to reinforce these maritime arguments, to boast about naval success, and to boost nationalism. The most famous exception was Samuel Woodworth's "The Hunters of Kentucky," which celebrated the U.S. victory in the Battle of New Orleans (1815).

Songs usually recounted the story of a single engagement in a stylistically simple fashion. "The *Constitution* and *Guerrière*"; "Huzza, for the American Tars," or "Hull and Victory"; "Huzza for the *Constitution*"; "The Sovereignty of the Ocean"; and "Hull's Victory" all celebrated the defeat of the *Guerrière* by the *Constitution* under the command of Isaac Hull. The *Hornet* over the *Peacock*, the *Wasp* over the *Frolic*, the *United States* over the *Macedonian*, and the *Constitution* over the *Java* were similarly treated. The five naval engagements between August 1812 and February 1813, plus the actions on Lake Erie (also in 1813), provided the material for most patriotic songs.

A small number of songs were general in approach and not tied to particular events or individuals. "Columbia," "Patience Exhausted," "Columbia's Exhortation," "The American Star," and Edwin C. Holland's "National Song" all addressed the war as a declaration of U.S. pride and as an obligatory defense of independence. Very few songs dealt with the tragedies, horrors, or hardships of war. Battles were described in detail, but it was usually the enemy whose "decks were with carnage and blood delug'd o'er."

Songwriters used current naval victories to encourage nationalism by creating links with previous heroic deeds related to the Revolution and juxtaposing the names of naval heroes such as Isaac Hull (1773–1843); William Bainbridge (1774–1833); Stephen Decatur, Jr. (1779–1820); and Jacob Jones (1768–1850) with George Washington. For example, in J. R. Calvert's "Columbia Victorious" (again, sung to the tune "To Anacreon in Heaven"), Dame Amphitrite searches the archives to find where heroism is recorded and finds the name of Washington. She announces that "here Decatur I'll place / On the page which the deeds of brave Washington graced." Similarly, in "Columbia's Exhortation," the British foe is said to

Wither beneath these western skies,
As erst before great Washington,
Their spirit faints, their courage dies.

Apologists for the War of 1812 had long argued that this conflict was merely round two of the Revolution. There was much nationalistic mileage to be gained by an association in song between the heroes and sentiments of the Revolutionary War and the current conflict. In "The Question," the War of 1812 is seen as the naval extension of the Revolution. Rights won in independence would now be achieved in maritime freedom through battles "on the main." This theme was particularly evident in songs written for Fourth of July celebrations. In "Ode for the Fourth of July, 1812," Americans were exhorted to capture the spirit of the revolutionary patriots in the prosecution of a new war against an old foe.

Britain that enslav'd your fathers,
Stretches now the yoke on you;
Know you still the stubborn spirit,
That your patriot fathers knew?

The nationalistic content of these songs was particularly important because the War of 1812 was not widely popular. Geographic and political divisions were acute. Not surprisingly, songs heavily emphasized the need for national unity. Political factions, such as in the song "Let Feds, Quids and Demo's," were asked to come together to support the nation and its principles. Division was portrayed as a British ploy to weaken U.S. resolve to wage an effective war.

Patriotic songs of the War of 1812 were the vehicles whereby the victories of the U.S. navy were translated into expressions of popular acclaim. The advantages of capturing or destroying a British vessel were multiplied through the patriotic effects of propaganda in song.

—*Jennifer Clark*

See also: Beanes, William; Key, Francis Scott; McHenry, Fort; Star-Spangled Banner, The

Further Reading
Clark, Jennifer. "The War of 1812: American Nationalism and Rhetorical Images of Britain." *War and Society* 12 (1994).
Kouwenhoven, John A., and Lawton M. Patten. "New Light on 'The Star-Spangled Banner'?" *Musical Quarterly* 23 (1937).
Lawrence, Vera Brodsky. *Music for Patriots, Politicians, and Presidents: Harmonies and Discords of the First Hundred Years.* London: Macmillan, 1975.
Sonneck, Oscar George Theodore. *The Star Spangled Banner.* New York: De Capo, 1969.
Spaeth, Sigmund. *A History of Popular Music in America.* London: Phoenix House, 1948.

PATTERSON, DANIEL TODD
1786–1839
U.S. Navy officer

Born on 6 March 1786 in Long Island, New York, Daniel Todd Patterson was the son of John Patterson, a former collector of customs in Philadelphia, and Catherine Livingston. Little is known about his early life, but at age 13 Patterson signed up as an acting midshipman aboard the sloop *Delaware* and sailed on two West Indian cruises during the Quasi-War with France. Warranted a midshipman in August 1800, he sailed against the Barbary pirates in March 1803 aboard the *Constellation*. Transferring to the *Philadelphia* the following May, he suffered the humiliation of capture when that ship ran aground and surrendered to the Tripolitans on 31 October 1803; Patterson remained a prisoner for 19 months. After his release, he transferred to the gunboat flotilla at the New Orleans station on the Gulf of Mexico, where he remained from January 1806 to June 1807.

He was promoted to lieutenant in the spring of 1808 and again sent to New Orleans. In 1810, while commanding 12 gunboats operating from Natchez, Mississippi, he participated in the U.S. occupation of Baton Rouge, Louisiana. Until the outbreak of war, he confronted pirates, smugglers, privateers, and those violating the country's slave trade law. In July 1813, Patterson was promoted to master commandant, and he assumed command of the station five months later. The most significant action for the New Orleans flotilla occurred in the last half of 1814. In September, Patterson and Col. Robert Ross, wanting to break the power of the Baratarian pirates led by Jean and

Pierre Lafitte, successfully attacked and destroyed their encampment at Grand Terre.

Patterson, realizing that New Orleans was virtually undefended, reported in June 1814 to Secretary of the Navy William Jones that the British had established a base at the mouth of the Apalachicola River. Believing New Orleans to be their objective, he refused Andrew Jackson's request in early September to send the naval force to Mobile. He intended to defend New Orleans by using the converted merchant sloop *Louisiana* and schooner *Carolina* in the Mississippi River to cover land attacks along the river. Some of his gunboats would support Fort St. Philip downriver, and fire ships would be used to disperse an enemy assault via the river. Most of his gunboats would be stationed on the bays and estuaries east of the city to prevent an attack along those avenues.

On 14 December 1814, five U.S. gunboats to the east on Lake Borgne confronted 40 barges and over 1,000 British forces commanded by Vice Adm. Alexander Cochrane. Although the gunboats succumbed to British numerical superiority, Patterson's decision to station the craft in the waters east of the city provided Jackson's army with time and information concerning the proposed British invasion route. On 23 December, while commanding *Carolina* on the Mississippi River, Patterson conducted a bombardment against British forces preparing to assault the city. After losing *Carolina* to enemy fire on 27 December, he transferred to *Louisiana*, mounted cannon on the east and west banks of the river, and continued to inflict casualties on the British. When the main British attack began on the east bank on 8 January 1815, Patterson, commanding a battery on the west bank, provided continuous fire before eventually being overrun by the enemy. Nonetheless, his forces maintained control of the river, which contributed significantly to Jackson's victory.

Patterson, promoted to captain in February 1815, remained on the New Orleans station until 1824, when he gained command of the *Constitution*, then on duty in the Mediterranean. In 1828, because of his friendship with Jackson, he became one of three navy commissioners and served in that position until 1832. Afterwards, he returned as commander of the Mediterranean squadron until 1836; his last appointment was as commandant of the Washington Navy Yard, where he remained until his death on 25 August 1839.

—*Gene A. Smith*

See also: Baratarian Pirates; Lafitte, Jean; New Orleans, Battle of
Further Reading
Ainsworth, W. L. "An Amphibious Operation That Failed: The Battle of New Orleans." *United States Naval Institute Proceedings* 71 (February 1945): 193–201.

Little, James D., Jr. "The Navy at the Battle of New Orleans." *Louisiana Historical Quarterly* 54 (spring 1971): 18–29.

McClellan, Edwin N. "The Navy at the Battle of New Orleans." *United States Naval Institute Proceedings* 50 (December 1924): 2041–2060.

Patterson to the Secretary of the Navy, 20 January 1815. *Niles' Weekly Register* 7 (18 February 1815): 389.

Tucker, Spencer C. *The Jeffersonian Gunboat Navy.* Columbia: University of South Carolina Press, 1993.

PATUXENT RIVER, BATTLES OF
June–August 1814

Commodore Joshua Barney commanded the U.S. flotilla on the upper Chesapeake Bay. On 25 May 1814, he left Baltimore with part of his flotilla, consisting of the sloop *Scorpion*, 13 barges, Gunboats No. 137 and 138, a galley, and a lookout boat. Barney established a base of operations in the Patuxent River, which flows into the bay at a point some 60 miles below Baltimore and some 20 miles above the Potomac. Although Barney's force was hardly a significant threat to their operations, the British were nonetheless anxious to destroy the only U.S. force of any significance in the Chesapeake Bay area and the only impediment to a sudden descent against Washington, D.C.

The Patuxent River was navigable by small boats some 40 miles from its mouth to a point about 15 miles by land from the city of Washington. Large vessels could enter the river but could not go far upstream, so the British would have to rely on small boats. The Americans would be able to use militia forces on land to help defend the flotilla. For these reasons, any hopes the British had of destroying the U.S. naval force rested on a combined land and water operation. For the British, such an operation had the advantage of masking their intention of a quick strike at the national capital. Their base at Tangier Island, across the bay from the mouth of the Potomac, enabled them to keep Barney's force under observation.

On the morning of 1 June, Barney's force left the Patuxent River with the aim of reaching the Potomac River. The Americans spotted two enemy schooners that promptly made signals and fired their guns, apparently to summon a 74-gun vessel under sail to come up and send barges to their assistance. With the 74-gun vessel in position to cut off the flotilla from the Potomac, Barney made the signal "for Patuxent." After exchanging fire with the leading

British schooner, the Americans managed, by late afternoon, to make it without damage to the mouth of the river.

Barney's force retreated 3 miles up the Patuxent as the enemy's 74-gun ship, large schooner, and barges closed off the mouth of the river. The two smaller schooners disappeared and soon returned with reinforcements in the form of a razee and a brig. Barney now retreated 2 miles farther upriver to St. Leonard's Creek. From here, at 5:00 A.M. on 8 June, one British ship, a brig, two schooners, and 15 rowing barges were spotted moving up the Patuxent. Barney's flotilla retreated 2 miles up the creek, formed in line abreast, and prepared for action. Early on 9 June 1814, as the larger enemy vessels lay at anchor at the mouth of St. Leonard's Creek, the British sent barges up the creek. U.S. fire fell short, and British rockets from a barge passed over the Americans.

Leaving the *Scorpion* and gunboats at anchor, Barney attacked with his 13 barges, whereupon the British withdrew. A second British assault, largely with rockets, occurred that afternoon with more success. The British kept beyond the range of U.S. shot and hit one U.S. barge with a rocket, killing one man and wounding several.

Barney was determined to launch a counterattack. Next day, the Americans disabled the *St. Lawrence* (13 guns), one of the schooners at the mouth of the creek. The British had to run her ashore to keep her from sinking. Other British boats were damaged, and U.S. shot also raked one of the small schooners. In turn, a U.S. gun burst and Barney lost a galley, leaving him with 12 barges and 450 men.

The British landed men on the banks of the Patuxent. Barney, meanwhile, had little militia support, in large part because of British threats (subsequently carried out) to set fire to any deserted houses. His flotilla was trapped. Secretary of the Navy William Jones hoped that the barges might be transferred to the bay by land, but this proved impossible. He then instructed Barney to try to drive the British from the mouth of the creek and move up the Patuxent. At 4:00 A.M. on 26 June, Barney took the offensive in conjunction with land units of artillery, marines, and militia against two frigates, the *Loire* and *Narcissus*, guarding the mouth of the creek. After a two-hour engagement, the British vessels got under way and moved downriver. Barney's boats then left the creek and moved upriver. The U.S. flotilla had suffered 11 killed and wounded. Barney abandoned his two gunboats, Nos. 137 and 138, in the creek; later the British set fire to them.

There was no way for Barney to get his force out of the river. Even if the flotilla had been able to leave the Patuxent, Barney knew it would be "difficult if not impossible" to get up the Potomac or up the bay, and nothing short of Baltimore would bring safe haven "or give us the means of

acting as occasion may require against the enemy." The British retained the initiative.

Beginning in early July, the British built up their forces at the mouth of the Patuxent. Counting forces of Rear Adm. Sir George Cockburn already on hand, Vice Adm. Sir Alexander Cochrane had at his disposal 20 warships, including four ships of the line, and a large number of transports and store ships. British ground strength was more than 4,000 men, including a battalion of 700 marines.

To distract the Americans from the real intent of his operations, Cochrane detached two squadrons of frigates—one up the Potomac River and the other up the bay to a point above Baltimore. At noon on 19 August, the main British force started up the Patuxent. Cochrane was able to mask the descent on Washington by making it appear that Barney's flotilla was the target. British troops landed at Benedict, Maryland, 25 miles from the mouth of the river, and on 20 August began the march along the west bank of the Patuxent, flanked by light British vessels on the river. The U.S. flotilla was cornered at Pig Point, abreast of Upper Marlboro. Barney foresaw the inevitable result and, to save his men, abandoned his boats on 21 August, leaving a few men to destroy them at the last minute. This was done on 22 August 1814, just as the British approached.

—*Spencer C. Tucker*

See also: Barney, Joshua; Chesapeake Bay Campaign, 1813–1814; Cochrane, Alexander; Cockburn, George; Upper Marlboro, Maryland
Further Reading
Shomette, Donald. *Flotilla Battle for the Patuxent.* Solomons, MD: Calvert Marine Museum Press, 1981.

PEACOCK VERSUS EPERVIER
29 April 1814

The *Peacock* was a U.S. Navy 18-gun sloop that carried 166 men and was commanded by Master Commandant Lewis Warrington. She was named after Capt. James Lawrence's prize taken off Demerara in February 1813. Built in New York, the *Peacock* escaped through the British blockade in March 1814 and set sail for St. Marys to deliver supplies and secretly rendezvous with the frigate *President* (44 guns) that, unknown to Warrington, had not made it through the blockade.

The *Peacock* was cruising the Bahamas in search of the Jamaica convoy when she happened upon a small convoy out from Havana on 29 April 1814. This convoy was escorted by the 18-gun British brig *Epervier* (Capt. Richard H. Wales, 128 men) carrying $118,000 in specie. Even though outclassed by the *Peacock*, the *Epervier* turned to fight, which allowed the few merchantmen in the convoy to escape. The ships traded a broadside that crippled them both, but the *Epervier* sustained far more damage. In a forty-five-minute action during which the British crew refused to board the *Peacock* and British gunnery was totally ineffectual, the *Epervier* took a forty-five roundshot in the hull and surrendered. British losses were eight killed and 15 wounded, but the Americans suffered only two wounded.

Warrington was then able to bring his prize into Savannah past two British frigates by means of a ruse. Congress awarded him a gold medal for his victory, and the *Peacock* was reoutfitted to set sail for British home waters, where she took 14 prizes before returning home again in October 1814.

—*Robert J. Bunker*

See also: Peacock versus *Nautilus*; Warrington, Lewis

PEACOCK VERSUS NAUTILUS
30 June 1815

The U.S. sloop *Peacock*, rated at 18 guns (Capt. Lewis Warrington, 166 men), and the brig *Tom Bowline* arrived at Tristan da Cunha on 23 March 1815 shortly after the *Hornet*, a sister ship to the *Peacock*, had defeated and scuttled the British 18-gun sloop *Penguin*. The *Tom Bowline* was soon thereafter converted into a cartel ship and took the British prisoners from the *Penguin* to Rio de Janeiro.

The *Penguin* and the *Hornet* waited for the frigate *President* (44 guns), suspected as having been captured, until 13 April, when they set sail for the Cape of Good Hope. Early in their journey, they were pursued by the British ship of the line *Cornwallis* (74 guns), which forced them to flee and become separated. After a long and harrowing chase, the *Hornet* barely escaped and set sail for home, while the faster *Peacock* easily outdistanced her pursuer and continued for the Indian Ocean.

The *Peacock* rounded the Cape of Good Hope and captured four valuable Indiamen crewed by 291 men. She then entered the Straits of Sunda and, on 30 June, encountered the 14-gun East India Company brig *Nautilus* (Lt. Charles Boyce, 80 men) off the Fort of Anjier. Warrington demanded that the *Nautilus* surrender, but she

would not because, as her commander stated, the war had ended. Thinking this claim to be a ruse to allow the *Nautilus* to escape under the guns of Anjier, Warrington attacked and broadsides were exchanged. The *Nautilus* immediately struck her colors; six men were killed and eight wounded. The *Peacock* suffered no losses. Upon receiving confirmation of the peace the next day, Warrington gave up his prize and set sail for the United States. The *Peacock* was the last U.S. Navy warship to return home.

—*Robert J. Bunker*

See also: Peacock versus *Epervier*; Warrington, Lewis

PENNSYLVANIA

Rent by factions within the Democratic Republican Party in the state, Pennsylvania nevertheless strongly sustained the U.S. war effort during the War of 1812. The state supported entering the war: 14 of the 16 members of the state's congressional delegation voted for the declaration. When the governors of Massachusetts, Connecticut, and Rhode Island refused to supply militia to the federal government in the summer of 1812, the Pennsylvania state legislature resolved that the declaration of war had been a national necessity and that the governors' actions were dangerous to national security.

Perhaps one of the reasons the state endorsed the actions of the Madison administration was that throughout most of the war, the state fared very well economically. Philadelphia was one of the most important government supply depots, and those supplies traveled overland to Pittsburgh and points west. Merchants and bankers of the city correspondingly prospered. Construction in Philadelphia and other communities boomed, and real estate prices went up.

All of this prosperity, however, could not heal the deep factional wounds that afflicted the state's politics. After the so-called Philadelphia Junto led by Philadelphia *Aurora* editor William Duane and Sen. Michael Leib criticized the Madison administration for not going far enough to prosecute the war effort (primarily as a way of attacking in-state rival and Secretary of the Treasury Albert Gallatin), Pres. James Madison's supporters such as Alexander J. Dallas refused to join the administration because of the potential attacks from vicious opponents.

To complicate the political situation in the state further, Gov. Simon Snyder, the leader of the "Snyderites" in Pennsylvania politics, disliked Madison and Secretary of War

John Armstrong, a Pennsylvania native. The anti-Madison forces in the state, including the Philadelphia Junto, tried to throw the state's electoral vote to DeWitt Clinton in the presidential election of 1812 but were foiled by the mainstream Democratic Republicans.

With the exception of the Philadelphia Junto, whose main opposition was to Gallatin, none of these groups formed a cohesive faction. Different men floated in and out of different groups, depending on the circumstances and the enemies of the moment. This situation was illustrated when Secretary of War Armstrong attempted to expand his influence in the state and weaken political rival Albert Gallatin through the appointment of Gallatin's archenemy William Duane as adjutant general of the Fourth Military District. Nevertheless, some of the factionalism abated during the crisis months of the fall of 1814, when Sen. Abner Lacock dropped his opposition to Alexander Dallas so that the country could have a competent secretary of the treasury. The different factions also found common cause through efforts to move the national capital to Philadelphia after the burning of Washington, D.C., in August 1814.

The state was far more united militarily than it was politically. When Oliver Hazard Perry established his naval base at Presque Isle on Lake Erie, the state responded by supplying men and supplies. Men also were supplied to Maj. Gen. William Henry Harrison's campaigns in the neighboring Northwest. To the east, when Adm. Sir George Cockburn invaded Delaware Bay, volunteer artillery and infantry companies were formed to strengthen Fort Mifflin and the defenses around Philadelphia.

When the British invaded the Chesapeake region en masse in the summer of 1814, Governor Snyder began mustering militia and calling for volunteers. Very few made it to the defense of Washington or Baltimore, but by the end of August, camps had been established southwest and southeast of Philadelphia to guard the approaches to the city. Most of these forces were placed under the command of Brig. Gen. Thomas Cadwalader and remained in service almost until the end of the war.

Pennsylvania felt very few direct effects from the fighting in the War of 1812, but as one of the wealthiest and most populous of the states, its contributions to the war effort were essential. Even though the state was politically divided before and during the conflict, general support for the war meant that Pennsylvania's impact was crucial.

—*Jeanne T. Heidler and David S. Heidler*

See also: Dallas, Alexander; Duane, William; Gallatin, Albert; Lacock, Abner; Presque Isle; Snyder, Simon

Further Reading
Sapio, Victor. *Pennsylvania and the War of 1812.* Lexington: University of Kentucky Press, 1970.

PENSACOLA, BATTLE OF
7 November 1814

The Battle of Pensacola took place within the complex maneuverings conducted by the British and the Americans on the southern front during the latter part of the war. Pensacola was the capital of the truncated and enfeebled Spanish province of West Florida. By 1814, it had become a magnet for a number of diverse groups who viewed it as a strategically important place. Indians, searching for a haven following their defeat by the Americans in the Creek War, began to gather in its environs for protection and supply. The British wanted to gain a foothold on the Gulf Coast and wanted to control the town's excellent harbor for their own purposes. The Americans, in turn, grew increasingly concerned about the presence of the Indians and the possible designs of the British.

Andrew Jackson was given command of the U.S. gulf region in May 1814. He believed that Pensacola was the most important military site in the region, and he correctly assumed that the British were also aware of the town's significance for any proposed incursion into the southern United States. Jackson was determined to foil any such plan by seizing Pensacola from the neutral Spanish. His superiors in Washington, however, were opposed to such a move for fear of inciting a war with Spain. In October, the secretary of war ordered Jackson to refrain from any offensive action against West Florida. The message arrived after he had completed his invasion.

The British, meanwhile, had already arrived in Pensacola on 14 August. Between 100 and 200 men under the command of Maj. Edward Nicholls of the Royal Marines landed there. He had been sent by Vice Adm. Sir Alexander Cochrane to take the town and to supply arms to the Indians gathered in and around it. The move was to be the first step in the larger plan to secure Mobile and eventually attack New Orleans. Once having landed at Pensacola, the British simply occupied the town and its major fortification, Fort San Carlos de Barrancas, with the halfhearted compliance of the Spanish governor, Don Mateo González Manrique. Nicholls did not permit anyone to enter or leave the town without authorization and threatened Manrique with Pensacola's destruction if its Spanish inhabitants inclined toward submission to the

Americans. Following an unsuccessful attack on Mobile by Nicholls on 12 September, Manrique refused to cooperate any further. The British left Pensacola to its fate and moved all of their men into Fort Barrancas just before the Americans arrived.

Jackson and his army of some 4,000 men appeared before the city on 6 November. They had marched from U.S.-held Mobile to the western side of Pensacola. Jackson then used 500 of his men to attack the town from the west as a feint, while slipping the bulk of his army northward completely around the town to arrive on its east side. This maneuver surprised both the Spanish authorities and the British troops in the fort. Amazingly, Jackson had even managed to move his force unseen by the British fleet of seven ships, commanded by Commodore James Gordon, that had earlier arrived in the harbor.

Jackson attacked on 7 November 1814, and after a brief resistance by the Spanish garrison of 500 men, Governor Manrique surrendered Pensacola to the Americans, much to the disgust of Nicholls and Gordon. Following the fall of Pensacola, the British threatened to level the town with the guns of the fleet but decided instead to fire rounds into the dock area and then blow up Fort Barrancas and its powder magazine. They also destroyed the village of San Carlos de Barrancas and a small fort on Santa Rosa Island before sailing eastward to the mouth of the Apalachicola River, where they established an outpost. At the same time, Jackson, having secured the town, moved most of his troops west to Mobile and then on to the defense of New Orleans, satisfied that he had accomplished the strategic goals that he had set out for himself.

Thus, as a military engagement, the Battle of Pensacola did not amount to much, but it did have a significant impact on the course of the war's final months. As a result of Jackson's attack, the British were prevented from using Pensacola and its harbor as a jumping-off place for their planned invasion. By gaining control of the city, Jackson altered the military balance on the Gulf Coast, foreshadowing his victory over the British outside New Orleans on 8 January 1815.

—*Eric Jarvis*

See also: Florida; Jackson, Andrew; Nicholls, Edward; Pensacola, West Florida; Percy, William Henry

Further Reading

Coker, William S., and Thomas D. Watson. *Indian Traders of the Southeastern Spanish Borderlands: Panton, Leslie and Co. and John Forbes and Co., 1783–1847.* Gainesville and Pensacola: University Presses of Florida and University of West Florida Press, 1986.

Heidler, David S., and Jeanne T. Heidler. *Old Hickory's War: Andrew Jackson and the Quest for Empire.* Mechanicsburg, PA: Stackpole Books, 1996.

Owsley, Frank L. *Struggle for the Gulf Borderlands: The Creek War and the Battle of New Orleans, 1812–1815.* Gainesville: University Presses of Florida, 1981.

PENSACOLA, WEST FLORIDA

The second-oldest city in Spanish Florida, Pensacola is situated on the northern shore of Pensacola Bay. The bay made Pensacola important in the history of the Gulf of Mexico, for it provides the best harbor on the entire gulf, having at low water, on the bar, 21 feet. The bay and the city are protected by the island of Santa Rosa, which fronts the entire bay. The western point of Santa Rosa, called Point Siguenza, forms the eastern entrance to the bay. There are red bluffs on the mainland opposite Santa Rosa, three of which, located near the entrance to the bay, are called the Barrancas.

Pensacola is also strategically located so as to protect commerce in the upper Gulf of Mexico and prevent encroachment into the region. Spain's first attempt to establish settlement on the bay, in 1559, was abandoned two years later. Successful colonization was not to come until 1698, when Fort San Carlos de Austria was constructed, located on the mainland just inside the bay. By the early 1800s, Spanish control over both East and West Florida was ebbing, and the underlying causes of the War of 1812 had long been in motion. Spain wished to protect the Floridas; U.S. frontiersmen in the Southwest wished for an aggressive campaign against the Spaniards for several reasons; and Great Britain continued to supply Indian nations of the Southwest with arms and ammunition to check U.S. expansion. The two major causes of U.S. resentment against the Spaniards were the haven afforded runaway slaves by the Florida Indians and Spanish aid to Indian groups, particularly the Creek Nation, in resisting expansion in the Southwest.

The British firm of John Forbes and Company, successors of Panton, Leslie, and Company, had been the principal supplier of trade and military goods to the Indians and maintained its center of operation in Pensacola. The failure of many Creek leaders to pay debts owed to Forbes and Company caused the firm's managers, John and James Inerarity, to discontinue much of the firm's declining trade with the Creeks. If the Creeks were to continue to provide a buffer against further U.S. expansion aimed at West Florida, the Spanish governor in Pensacola would have to provide the arms and ammunition. Thus, to the Americans, a successful expansion would necessitate the acquisition of West Florida and Pensacola, its capital.

When the War of 1812 began, Pensacola could claim a population of barely 1,000. In 1812, the town was declared a municipality under a liberal constitution adopted in Spain. There was some argument as to whether Pensacola met the minimum population of 1,000 inhabitants. The most important new official was the *alcalde* (an official who combined the functions of mayor and justice of the peace). This new form of government proved unworkable. The *alcalde* began to challenge the governor of West Florida for power. The controversy was eliminated when Pensacola was again operated as a military garrison. Spain had at most 400–500 soldiers stationed in West Florida, principally at Pensacola, and because the Napoleonic wars had thrown Spain into chaos, it could not do more for its overseas colonies.

Spain was officially neutral in the conflict between the United States and Great Britain. It continued, however, to rely on British economic and military assistance to the Indians in the U.S. Southwest in an attempt to protect the Floridas. As early as November 1812, the British began to show interest in planning for military movement into the Gulf of Mexico, using Florida as a base to attack U.S. territory. New Orleans was their chief target because capturing that city would throttle the trans-Appalachian West and possibly sever this region from the United States. Yet Pensacola had its place in British schemes. Pensacola Bay was of strategic importance to the British and could be utilized to organize aid to the Indian nations in the Southwest. The Spanish position also favored militarily aiding the Creek Nation because the failure to do so might mean the Creeks would turn against the Spanish and capture Pensacola in retaliation. Governor of West Florida Don Mateo González Manrique provided the Creeks with munitions, with the captain general of Cuba giving full approval. Indeed, part of a regiment to reinforce Pensacola had been sent from Cuba.

Great Britain decided to provide military support to the Creeks several months after the Spanish decision to support them. A British ship was sent to Pensacola to ascertain the status of the southern Indians, only to learn that the anti-American Red Stick faction had been almost annihilated by U.S. troops led by Andrew Jackson at the Battle of Horseshoe Bend on 27 March 1814. Jackson had marched against the Creeks as a result of the slaughter of Americans at Fort Mims. When about 900 starving and defenseless Creeks streamed into Pensacola seeking haven, the Spanish feared reprisals by the Americans. Manrique was no happier about the arrival of British troops in Pensacola, but there was little he could do to resist.

The first area that had been occupied by the British was near the mouth of the Apalachicola River. George Woodbine, a former trader, was appointed British agent to the Creeks, with a brevet rank of captain of Royal Marines. After establishing a base on the Apalachicola, Woodbine moved his headquarters to Pensacola. Maj. Edward Nicholls also arrived in West Florida, taking 200 marines, field artillery, and other military equipment to Pensacola in August 1814. The British misbehaved, however, refusing to cooperate with their Spanish hosts, expropriating slaves, and threatening to destroy Pensacola if the Spaniards would not make preparations for the city's defense against the Americans.

Following his victory at Horseshoe Bend, Andrew Jackson had been appointed major general in command of the Seventh Military District. After dictating the Treaty of Fort Jackson to the Creek Nation, he moved to strengthen U.S. defenses at Mobile. He waited in vain for the U.S. government to give him instructions to occupy Pensacola, and finally in early November he took the initiative to advance on the town with about 4,000 men. Jackson reached Pensacola on 6 November and demanded that the Spanish force the British to leave. When he was rebuffed, he stormed the town. There were only two forts in the Pensacola area when Jackson attacked. Both were constructed of earth and logs or timber. Fort San Miguel was within Pensacola and had been reconstructed by Spaniards in 1783. Fort San Carlos, on the Barrancas, guarded the harbor mouth. At one time a blockhouse had existed on the western tip of Santa Rosa Island, but it had been destroyed in a hurricane in 1752 and was never rebuilt. Jackson's forces moved in three columns and met only limited opposition. Fort San Miguel and the town were surrendered to Jackson on 7 November 1814, but only after the British had retired, destroying Fort San Carlos and spiking its cannon. Since the fortifications had been disabled and the British had departed, the town held no strategic importance. Jackson evacuated Pensacola to head for Mobile and eventually to New Orleans.

This ended the role of Pensacola in the War of 1812. The town never recovered from its capture by Jackson during the second period of Spanish control. By 1818, its population had declined to about 400 inhabitants, and once again it would fall into Old Hickory's hands.

—*Henry S. Marks*

See also: Creek War; Florida; Jackson, Andrew; Nicholls, Edward; Pensacola, Battle of; Percy, William Henry
Further Reading
Heidler, David S., and Jeanne T. Heidler. *Old Hickory's War:*

Andrew Jackson and the Quest for Empire. Mechanicsburg, PA: Stackpole Books, 1996.

Mahon, John K. "British Strategy and Southern Indians: War of 1812." *The Florida Historical Quarterly* 44 (April 1966): 285–302.

McAlister, L. N. "Pensacola during the Second Spanish Period." *The Florida Historical Quarterly* 37 (January-April 1959): 281–327.

Owsley, Frank L., Jr. "British and Indian Activities in Spanish West Florida during the War of 1812." *The Florida Historical Quarterly* 46 (October 1967): 111–123.

PERCEVAL, SPENCER
1762–1812
British prime minister

As a younger son of John Perceval, Earl of Egmont, and Catherine Compton Perceval, Spencer Perceval had to choose a profession and opted for the law. After gaining a reputation for his knowledge of the law and using his family connections, Perceval secured minor government appointments. Rising in political circles as his legal practice expanded, Perceval entered Parliament in 1796.

Over the next decade, Perceval gained a reputation as one of the best debaters in Parliament and, as a result, was much sought-after by various factions when controversial measures were being considered. In this way, Perceval acquired a number of very important alliances and was in a position in 1809 to step into the prime ministership upon the illness of the Duke of Portland.

As Perceval formed his ministry, U.S. minister to Great Britain William Pinkney had hopes that this new government would prove to be more flexible regarding the Orders in Council than the previous one. Within a short time, however, both Pinkney and Pres. James Madison came to see the Perceval government as more intractable than Portland's government. In fact, Perceval never had any intention of withdrawing the Orders in Council because he sincerely believed that they were the only way of guaranteeing the continuation of British trade on the Continent.

With the renewed illness of George III and the move toward the establishment of a regency for George, Prince of Wales, in 1810, Pinkney hoped that the prince would want to form a new ministry when he assumed power. The future regent's dislike for Perceval was no secret, and neither was his closeness with Parliamentary Whigs, who favored a more conciliatory attitude toward the United States. Factionalism within both British parties prevented a change

with the establishment of the regency, and as a result, Pinkney decided to return to the United States.

As the United States moved closer to war with Great Britain over violations of its trading rights, word from Great Britain and the Perceval ministry was that there would be no change in British policy. Things did change, however, when Perceval entered Parliament on 11 May 1812 and was shot in the chest by an angry petitioner. He died almost immediately. The new ministry under Lord Liverpool was inclined toward accommodation with the United States but could not form a government until 8 June. By the time word reached North America of the revocation of the Orders in Council, the United States had already declared war.

—*Jeanne T. Heidler and David S. Heidler*

See also: Liverpool, Robert Banks Jenkinson, Second Earl of; Orders in Council; Pinkney, William
Further Reading
Jones, Wilbur D. *The American Problem in British Diplomacy.* Athens: University of Georgia Press, 1974.

PERCY, WILLIAM HENRY
1788–1855
British naval officer

William Henry Percy, the sixth son born to the Earl of Beverly, entered the British navy in 1801, was assigned to HMS *Lion,* and saw service in China. In 1802, Henry Percy was transferred to HMS *Medusa,* commanded by acting lieutenant Joscelline Percy, his older brother. On 2 May 1810, Percy was promoted to commander and in 1811 assigned to HMS *Mermaid,* a troop transport ship.

On 21 March 1812, Henry Percy was promoted to captain, assigned to HMS *Hermes* (20 guns), and saw duty off the coast of North America. During the War of 1812, Percy approached the Spanish governor of West Florida at Fort San Miguel about recruiting the Seminole Indians as a fighting force against the United States. Percy also made an unsuccessful attempt to lure the pirate Jean Lafitte into joining the British side.

In August 1814, Captain Percy's squadron, including the HMS *Hermes, Sophia, Carron,* and *Anaconda,* arrived at Pensacola. Aboard ship was Royal Marine major Edward Nicholls, who wanted to make Pensacola his military base of operations against the United States. Percy refused unless the Spanish agreed. Unknown to both Percy and Nicholls, the Spaniards at Pensacola had already reluctantly turned Pensacola over to British brevet marine captain George Woodbine. With Pensacola as the British base of operations, Percy was reassured that the British could successfully take Mobile Bay if they controlled Fort Bowyer at the bay's entrance.

The news that Andrew Jackson had recently strengthened Fort Bowyer did not alter Percy's conviction that the fort was vulnerable. On 12 September, Percy's flotilla set sail for Mobile Bay, where Nicholls and his marine detachment went ashore. Adverse winds and tides prevented Percy from giving Nicholls's detachment adequate sea support. On 15 September, Percy sailed into Mobile Bay with four ships and bombarded the fort for three hours, but it gave no sign of surrender. The *Hermes* was so severely damaged that Percy burned the ship rather than let it be taken. Nicholls was severely wounded, but Percy rescued him while withdrawing from Mobile Bay. In the battle for Fort Bowyer, Captain Percy had 162 men killed and 72 wounded, compared to only four killed and four wounded among the fort's U.S. defenders.

Henry Percy's career at sea ended with the conclusion of the War of 1812. Back in England, he was appointed commissioner of excise, elected a member of parliament from Stamford, and retired in 1846 a rear admiral. He died in 1855.

—*William A. Paquette*

See also: Baratarian Pirates; Bowyer, Fort; Lafitte, Jean; Mobile, Battles of; Nicholls, Edward

PERRY, OLIVER HAZARD
1785–1819
U.S. Navy officer

Born on 20 August 1785 at South Kingston, Rhode Island, at 14 Perry went to sea as a midshipman under his father's command. He, his father, and all three of his brothers were career officers in the U.S. Navy. At various times, he had the good fortune to serve under Edward Preble, James Barron, Charles Morris, and John Rodgers, all of whom saw promise in him and helped him advance. Through them and through his own diligence, he learned gunnery and seamanship but also skill as a flutist, horseback rider, and fencer. He also read widely.

Oliver Hazard Perry

While serving in the Mediterranean, Perry became a lieutenant at 17. Five years later, he was chosen to build 17 of Thomas Jefferson's gunboats. At the age of 24, he received command of the schooner *Revenge*. She struck rocks and broke apart off the Rhode Island coast on 2 February 1811. He was suspended from command pending a hearing but was exonerated and returned to duty.

When the United States declared war on Great Britain on 18 June 1812, Perry was stationed at Newport, Rhode Island, commanding the squadron of gunboats that he had built. As there was no glory to be won there, he regularly petitioned his superiors to send him where there was action. Finally orders came for him to report to Capt. Isaac Chauncey, commander on the Great Lakes. Chauncey sent him on to Lake Erie to build brigs, collect some small boats already afloat, and gain control of the lake.

Perry arrived at Presque Isle in bitterly cold weather on 27 March 1813. The wood to build two brigs was in standing trees, and other needed materials had to come a long distance from Pittsburgh or Philadelphia. Skilled craftsmen were scarce, but on hand to direct the construction was Noah Brown, an expert in shipbuilding. Perry's experience in building gunboats also helped him. With characteristic determination, he drove construction forward in spite of fearfully cold weather and lapses in his own health.

Perry had other serious problems. His brigs would draw 2 more feet of water than was over the bar at the mouth of Presque Isle's otherwise excellent harbor. There were five small vessels 80 miles eastward at Black Rock, New York, that were essential to the squadron Perry was trying to form but immobilized by the British guns at Fort Erie. Additionally, Great Britain had a squadron already on Lake Erie, commanded by Capt. Robert Barclay, that could block the brigs at Presque Isle and prevent the Black Rock vessels from joining Perry there.

Luck favored Perry, however: the British had to evacuate Fort Erie, freeing the Black Rock vessels, and somehow Barclay failed to intercept them as they crept the 80 miles along the shoreline to Presque Isle. To get the *Lawrence* and *Niagara* over the bar, Perry had to unship their guns and put them on a device called a camel to lift them across to open water. While Perry was in the middle of this awkward process, Barclay's squadron appeared 1 mile offshore. Perry then demonstrated the audacity that marked him as a combat commander. He sent two small vessels straight at the British flotilla, blazing away with such long guns as they had. Barclay thought he saw the entire U.S. contingent over the bar and in open water, so he sailed away.

During the second week of August 1813, Master Commandant Jesse Duncan Elliott arrived with 100 men and reported to Perry. With this reinforcement and the two brigs in deep water, Perry sailed westward with seven vessels to attack the foe.

Captain Barclay could not maintain his force any longer without the supplies piling up at Long Point, 150 miles away. Also, Sir George Prevost, overall commander in Canada, kept urging him to sail out and fight. Accordingly, Barclay left his base and sailed into open water. He had an advantage in long guns, but his broadside was only 459 pounds to Perry's 896. Perry's lookouts sighted Barclay 9 miles west of the new U.S. base in the Bass Islands. Perry ordered each ship to engage her equivalent the following day, 10 September 1813. He would command from the *Lawrence*, hoisting a battle flag emblazoned with the late James Lawrence's last command, "Don't Give Up the Ship."

For his part, Barclay had decided to concentrate 35 of his 63 guns on Perry's *Lawrence*. His long guns could punish her before she was close enough to reply. Thus, for two and one-half hours *Lawrence* suffered severe damage. Only 19 of the crew of 142 remained fit for duty. Perry, however, in ordinary seaman's clothes, stood the entire time by the mainmast without receiving a scratch. The *Lawrence*, though, was dead in the water.

The *Niagara*, commanded by Elliott, had not engaged the *Queen Charlotte* as directed, nor had Elliott done more than fire a few shots with the *Niagara*'s long guns. Finally, Elliott moved to within half a mile of the *Lawrence*, and Perry, with five sailors, audaciously passed from the *Lawrence* to the *Niagara* in a rowboat across water churned by enemy bullets. He boarded the undamaged vessel and took command. The words that passed between him and Elliott will never be known. Elliott went off to rally the small boats, while Perry turned *Niagara* through the British line to rake their ships with both port and starboard broadsides. In fifteen more minutes the battle was over, with all British ships captured or sunk. Perry dispatched news of the victory to Maj. Gen. William Henry Harrison with the opening words, "We have met the enemy, and he is ours."

This victory on 10 September 1813 laid Canada open to invasion from the west and radically changed the course of the war. Perry's ships carried Harrison's army across the lake to Canada, and Perry joined the army in the successful pursuit of the retreating foe. The Battle of Lake Erie was very small, involving only 15 vessels, 117 guns, and 1,000 men, yet it ranks as one of the decisive actions in U.S. history.

For some reason, ten days after his victory Perry asked to leave the lake theater. Permission granted, he transferred the command to Elliott and left for the East Coast. Isaac Hull, among others, considered that he had abandoned his post, but his journey east was a triumphal tour. He was involved in shore defense around Washington and then given command of the *Java* while she was being built. It would be a troubled and an unhappy command. He took the ship to sea, where it was discovered that rotten timbers had been used in her. He quarreled with the captain of marines aboard *Java* and became so provoked that he struck him in the face with his stick. He was tried for this clear breach of regulations and was punished with a private reprimand, but he had to reckon with marine honor as well. In 1818, he met the captain in a duel. At eight paces, Perry stood with his hands at his side, refusing to fire. His antagonist fired but missed, so with honor satisfied, the duel ended without bloodshed.

Perry had spoken well of Jesse Elliott in his official report of the Battle of Lake Erie. "At such a moment," he said later, "there was not a person in the world whose feelings I would have hurt." Yet a rumor circulated that Elliott had shirked in the fight. He repeatedly demanded more favorable notice from Perry without success. As time went on, he even claimed that he, not Perry, had made victory possible. By 1818, Perry had lost patience and denounced him. When Elliott challenged him to a duel, Perry declined because of Elliott's ungentlemanly conduct. Instead, he filed an official set of charges against Elliott, but nothing ever came of them.

In 1819, Perry sailed up the Orinoco River with two warships to find the newborn government of Venezuela and negotiate with it. He had stood for two and a half hours under a rain of bullets without injury on Lake Erie, but no charm could save him from the murderous mosquitoes of the Orinoco. At the mouth of the river, he died of yellow fever on 23 August 1819.

He left behind a beloved wife whom he had married in 1811, three sons, and a daughter. Because the Battle of Lake Erie had made him a naval hero for all time, the United States awarded liberal pensions to his survivors.

—*John K. Mahon*

See also: Barclay, Robert Heriot; Black Rock, New York; Chauncey, Isaac; Elliott, Jesse Duncan; Harrison, William Henry; Lake Erie Campaign; Presque Isle

Further Reading

Dillon, Richard. *We Have Met the Enemy: Oliver Hazard Perry, Wilderness Commodore.* New York: McGraw-Hill, 1978.

Mahon, John K. "Oliver Hazard Perry." In James C. Bradford, ed. *Command under Sail: Makers of the American Naval Tradition 1775–1830.* Annapolis, MD: Naval Institute Press, 1985.

PETER, GEORGE
1779–1861
U.S. officer

George Peter was one of the most significant U.S. artillerymen in the years just prior to the War of 1812. He was born on 28 September 1779 in Georgetown, in what was then Maryland. On 12 July 1799, he was commissioned a second lieutenant in the Ninth U.S. Infantry and was discharged the following June. On 16 February 1801, he reentered the U.S. Army as a second lieutenant in the Corps of Artillerists and Engineers. He made captain in November 1807 and assumed command of the company that today is the U.S. Army's Fourth Battalion, Third Air Defense Artillery. In May 1808, Peter transferred to the newly formed Regiment of Light Artillery. He was the senior ranking captain in that regiment, with Winfield Scott the next senior. The Regiment of Light Artillery was supposed to be a horse artillery unit, similar to what most of the European armies were then starting to field. But in the years before the War of 1812, only one company was ever mounted, and that lasted only a few months. As the senior captain of the regiment, the command of that company fell to Peter.

The equipment for Peter's mounted company was based on the French Gribeauval pattern and manufactured by the artillery artificers at Fort McHenry. At the direction of Secretary of War Henry Dearborn, Peter conducted a series of demonstrations for the Congress on 4 July 1808. Covering a distance of 3 miles with two 6-pounders at a gallop, Peter's troops halted, unlimbered, and fired the national salute. Then they relimbered, returned to the starting point, and fired a second salute. The entire exercise lasted only 22 minutes. Earlier that day, Peter had made the route march from Baltimore to Washington at an average speed of 6 miles per hour. Even by World War I standards, that would have been good time for field artillery. By the standards of 1808, it was dazzling speed.

On 24 December 1808, Dearborn ordered Peter to test the long-range durability of his equipment by marching his company to New Orleans. Traveling overland and by river flatboat, Peter reached his objective late the following March, with his guns and carriages in serviceable condition. By all expectations, the tests had been successful and should have shown the powerful potential of mobile light artillery. But by the time Peter's company reached New Orleans, a new administration was in office. New Secretary of War William Eustis ordered the company dismounted and the horses sold as an unnecessary expense. Peter resigned his commission in protest on 11 June 1809.

When the British attacked Washington in August 1814, George Peter was a District of Columbia militia major in command of a light company equipped with 6-pounders. The Company of Georgetown Artillery was one of the few militia units to fight well at Bladensburg. On 22 August, Peter's company was part of the small force sent to Nottingham to reconnoiter and harass the British. Later that day, the force was pulled back to the Wood Yard, outside Washington. The next day, a force of about 300 under Peter (including his company) was again sent against the British, now at Upper Marlboro. The Americans skirmished with the British advance guard just outside Marlboro and were driven back toward Old Fields, Maryland. On 24 August, Peter's guns supported the U.S. units in the third defensive line covering Turncliffe's Bridge. When Peter first arrived in the area, he was directed to a firing position by Francis Scott Key, who, as an aide to Gen. Samuel Smith, was one of the many civilians helping to confuse U.S. military efforts that day. (Key had only recently been a quartermaster lieutenant in Peter's company.) Peter did not like his new placement because he felt he had no room to maneuver. Ignoring Key's instructions, Peter situated his guns in a different position.

During the battle, Peter's battery covered the left flank of the five large naval 18-pounders under Commodore

Joshua Barney that held the middle of the road to Washington. When Robert Ross's troops first tried to come across Turncliffe's Bridge, they were caught in a withering cross fire from Barney's and Peter's batteries. Three times Peter's guns contributed to Barney's repulses of the British frontal attacks. But Gen. William Winder then arrived on the scene. He had hopelessly tried to halt the flight of the U.S. first and second defensive lines. Seeing Peter struggling to hold his ground on the left and believing Barney could not continue to hold the right, Winder ordered a retreat. Peter disregarded the order at first, but with his supporting infantry gone, he too was forced back, leaving Barney's naval battery alone on the field.

After the War of 1812, Peter served three terms in Congress and two terms in the Maryland state legislature and also served as the commissioner of public works for the state of Maryland. He died on 27 June 1861 in Montgomery County, Maryland.

—*David T. Zabecki*

See also: Artillery; Bladensburg, Battle of; Upper Marlboro, Maryland
Further Reading
Armstrong, John. *Notices of the War of 1812.* New York: Whiley and Putman, 1840.
Birkhimer, William E. *Historical Sketch of the Organization, Administration, Materiel and Tactics of the Artillery, United States Army.* Washington, DC: Chapman, 1884.
Downey, Fairfax. *The Sound of the Guns.* New York: David McKay, 1955.
Heitman, F. B. *Historical Register of the United States Army.* Washington, DC: National Tribune, 1890.

PHOEBE VERSUS *ESSEX*
See *Essex* versus *Phoebe* and *Cherub*

PIKE, ZEBULON MONTGOMERY
1779–1813
U.S. officer

Zebulon Montgomery Pike

Zebulon Montgomery Pike, explorer and career soldier, was born 5 January 1779 at Lamberton, New Jersey, into a family with a military tradition. His ancestor Capt. John Pike had distinguished himself in the early Indian wars, and his father Maj. Zebulon Pike had served gallantly in the American Revolution and was present at Arthur St. Clair's defeat. After receiving his commission in 1792, the elder Pike moved his family from western Pennsylvania, where Zebulon had attended several common schools, to the Ohio frontier. Then Captain Pike assumed command of Fort Washington, where his 14-year-old son first fell under the influence of Gen. James Wilkinson, his father's commander and a Spanish spy.

Aspiring to be like the dashing Wilkinson and his father, young Pike enlisted in the army at the age of 15. Following brief service in his father's company, he ferried supplies from Fort Washington to the garrisons along the Miami River for "Mad" Anthony Wayne. From 1795 to 1799, Pike distributed commodities to garrisons along the Ohio and Mississippi Rivers, learning command skills and acting as an agent for private contractors. Mature beyond his years, Pike was commissioned as an ensign in the Second Infantry in 1799, was promoted to first lieutenant a year later, and was made captain while he was in Mexico.

On his own time, Pike supplemented his inferior education by studying French, Latin, Spanish, mathematics, and general science. In March 1801, he eloped with his cousin Clarissa Brown against her father's will. Although they had five children, only one daughter, Clarissa, survived Pike.

Pike's greatest fame would rest on his exploits as an explorer. He undertook two expeditions, the second being the more famous and, ironically, the more troubled. Both expeditions were sponsored by Gen. James Wilkinson, whom Thomas Jefferson appointed governor of recently purchased Louisiana. Pike's 1806–1807 journey through the heartland to the front range of the Rocky Mountains, the arid Southwest, and into Spanish territory was beleaguered by both Spanish and U.S. suspicions about its motives and intentions. In Pike's absence, the revelations about Aaron Burr's shadowy conspiracy had resulted in Burr's arrest. Wilkinson's involvement with Burr was a matter of open speculation, so Pike's expedition, ordered on Wilkinson's personal authority, was suspect as well. Furthermore, Pike's adamant defense of Wilkinson brought suspicion upon himself. Apparently, the young captain truly believed that he had gathered intelligence for the U.S. government's use in the event of war with Spain. Upon Pike's request, however, the secretary of war exonerated him and praised his service. Pike's unpolished report, published in 1810, dramatically shaped western expansion by first describing the Great Plains as "sandy deserts" and pointing out New Mexico's enormous trade possibilities.

Promoted to major in 1809 and then to lieutenant colonel in 1810, Pike served as a battalion commander in the Sixth Regiment and then as deputy quartermaster general at New Orleans under his old friend General Wilkinson. Upon the general's removal, Pike was ordered to the Fourth Massachusetts Regiment in Mississippi Territory and was given command of the troops at Baton Rouge in April 1811. The troops Pike trained there distinguished themselves at the Battle of Tippecanoe. In February 1812, when bandits harassed peaceful settlers in the neutral ground between the Arroyo Hondo and the Sabine River, Louisiana, Pike's troops quickly captured the outlaws and burned their camps.

When war was declared against Great Britain in 1812, Pike was promoted to colonel in the new 15th Regiment and ordered to the Lake Champlain frontier. In October 1812, Colonel Pike marched his 600 men overland from Albany to Plattsburg to participate in Maj. Gen. Henry Dearborn's planned offensive against Montreal. Although Dearborn abandoned his plan and went into winter quarters, Pike obtained permission to advance into Canada. After crossing into Quebec, on 21 November, Pike encountered a small body of Canadian and Indian troops. Exchanging a few shots, the Canadians retreated into a swamp, leaving their barracks and blockhouses to be burned by Pike's men. On their way back to the border, Pike's men mistakenly exchanged fire with another U.S. force, wounding five, two mortally.

As part of the spring invasion of Canada at Kingston and York, in March 1813, Pike, who was promoted to brigadier general that month, marched his men to Sacket's Harbor, New York, where he assumed command of Fort Tompkins and became inspector general of the Northern Army. In ill health, Major General Dearborn ordered Pike to conduct the attack upon York, the weaker of the two Canadian shipbuilding centers and capital of Upper Canada. Personally working out the plan of attack, Pike gave strict orders that personal property be respected and forbade plundering under penalty of death.

From the deck of the *Madison*, General Pike directed the landing of the 1,700-man invasion force on the morning of 27 April. Watching Maj. Benjamin Forsyth's riflemen fight their way ashore, Pike and his staff leapt into their boat, landing in time to lead the next charge up the bank. Once all the troops had landed and formed ranks, Pike personally led the advance through the woods and stormed the western battery under the covering fire of Isaac Chauncey's flotilla. As British general Roger H. Sheaffe withdrew his regulars and began destruction of the military stores, General Pike led the U.S. forces to within 600 feet of Fort York.

Anticipating a surrender, Pike ordered a halt while his artillery was being brought up and the fleet's guns were finishing off the fort. While Pike sat interrogating a captured militiaman, the fort's grand magazine suddenly exploded. Charged by several hundred barrels of gunpowder and a vast amount of ammunition, the deafening explosion sent huge columns of fire and smoke upward along with enormous boulders, beams, and other debris that crushed almost everything within 300 yards. More than 100 men were killed or maimed. Pike was struck in the chest by a huge boulder, which crushed his ribs and tore a large hole in his back.

Passing command to Col. Cromwell Pearce, Pike told his men, "Push on my brave fellows and avenge your general." While he was being carried back to the *Madison*, Pike heard his men's joyful shouts as they raised the Stars and Stripes over the remains of the fort. As he lay upon his cot in great pain and unable to speak, he motioned for the captured British flag to be placed under his head just before he died. When the *Madison* reached Sacket's Harbor, he was buried in an iron casket at Fort Tompkins, "with stately pomp."

—*Michèle Butts*

See also: Chauncey, Isaac; Dearborn, Henry; Sheaffe, Roger Hale; Wilkinson, James; York, Battle of

Further Reading

Cumberland, Barlow. *The Battle of York*. Toronto: William Briggs, 1913.

Hollon, W. Eugene. *The Lost Pathfinder: Zebulon Montgomery Pike.* Norman: University of Oklahoma Press, 1949.

Humphries, Charles W. "The Capture of York." *Ontario History* 51 (winter 1959): 1–24.

Jenkins, John S. *The Generals of the Last War with Great Britain.* Auburn, NY: Derby, Miller and Co., 1849.

Niles, John M. *The Life of Oliver Hazard Perry with Appendix...a Biography of General Pike.* Hartford: Oliver D. Cooke, 1821.

Quaife, Milo M. *The Yankees Capture York.* Detroit: Wayne State University Press, 1955.

Terrell, John Upton. *Zebulon Pike: The Life and Times of an Adventurer.* New York: Weybright and Talley, 1968.

PINCKNEY, THOMAS
1750–1828
U.S. officer

Born in Charleston, South Carolina, to Charles Pinckney and Elizabeth Lucas Pinckney, Thomas Pinckney spent much of his childhood and youth in Great Britain, where he was educated at Oxford University and studied law. He did not return to South Carolina to live until 1774. After beginning the practice of law in Charleston, Pinckney became involved in the protests that would result in the American Revolution. He served with distinction as an officer in the Revolution, was wounded at Camden, and was present at Cornwallis's surrender at Yorktown.

Following the war, he returned to the practice of law and became involved in South Carolina politics. Beginning in 1787, he served two years as the governor of South Carolina and in 1791 became the Washington administration's minister to Great Britain. In 1795, he became a special negotiator to Spain, where he concluded the Treaty of San Lorenzo (known as Pinckney's Treaty in the United States), which set the southern boundary between the United States and Spanish Florida and opened up the Mississippi River and New Orleans to U.S. trade. He returned to the United States in 1796.

Upon his return, Pinckney stood for election as the Federalist candidate for vice president but lost to Thomas Jefferson. He then served for four years in the House of Representatives. Though a Federalist, he did not always support Federalist initiatives, including the Quasi-War with France and the Sedition Act. He retired from public life in 1801.

The approach of war with Great Britain in 1812 meant that the nation was in desperate need of men with military command experience. For this reason, Secretary of War William Eustis gave Pinckney a commission as a brigadier general and second in command to Henry Dearborn. When John Armstrong assumed the duties of Secretary of War the following year and divided the country into military districts, Pinckney was promoted to major general and given command of the Sixth Military District.

The Sixth District consisted of North Carolina, South Carolina, and Georgia, and except for the occasional coastal raid like those perpetrated by Adm. Sir George Cockburn in the summer of 1813, the primary activity in that district was the Creek War of 1813–1814. When this conflict erupted in the summer of 1813, it fell within the jurisdiction of both the Sixth District and the Seventh Military District commanded by Maj. Gen. Thomas Flournoy. This circumstance presented the problem of divided command and made coordination of military activities virtually impossible. As a result, Secretary of War Armstrong attempted to solve the problem by placing the entire war under the command of Pinckney. Rather than solving the problem, however, this decision only angered Flournoy to such an extent that he withheld valuable support for the war and eventually resigned his command.

Still, the unity of command produced by Armstrong's move allowed Pinckney to proceed with a plan to bring about the subjugation of the Red Stick Creeks. He hoped to bring about a three-pronged invasion of the Creek country from the Mississippi Territory, Tennessee, and Georgia. These three forces were to converge at the confluence of the Coosa and Tallapoosa Rivers and drive the enemy before them into the arms of the other converging armies. Problems of communication, transportation, supply, and short militia enlistments prevented the realization of this plan as Pinckney envisioned it.

Constantly disappointed, particularly with the failure of the Georgia militia under John Floyd to engage in anything other than raids from their base on the Chattahoochee River, Pinckney nevertheless tried to ensure that, should his hoped-for convergence ever take place, enough supplies would await the armies once they reached their destination. When Floyd's militia's terms finally expired in early 1814, Pinckney arranged for their places to be filled by new militia forces out of the Carolinas, but by that time he had become convinced that Tennessee militia major general Andrew Jackson's expedition could succeed where Floyd's militia had failed. As a result, Pinckney continued his efforts to guarantee that Jackson would have the supplies to continue his campaign. Also to aid Jackson's offensive, Pinckney dispatched the 39th Infantry Regiment to participate in the campaign. Pinckney was very gratified to learn that all of these efforts resulted in the overwhelming defeat of the Red Sticks at Tohopeka (Horseshoe Bend) on 27 March 1814.

Upon learning of Jackson's victory, Pinckney left his headquarters in Charleston for Jackson's headquarters at Fort Jackson. Assuming command of the army there, Pinckney instructed Jackson to send out parties to continue rounding up Red Sticks. At this time Pinckney also received an appointment from the War Department to act, along with Creek agent Benjamin Hawkins, as the negotiator of a peace treaty with the Creeks. These appointments greatly angered westerners, particularly in Tennessee, who considered both Pinckney and Hawkins too forgiving of the Creeks. This impression was confirmed when Pinckney released his terms for peace (those given to him by the War Department), which called for a land cession from the Creeks only large enough to compensate the United States for the cost of the war. Pinckney's and Hawkins's opponents eventually secured their removal and replacement by Jackson, who extracted from the Creeks the very harsh Treaty of Fort Jackson.

Though Pinckney never saw combat service during the War of 1812, he was one of its few early opponents to serve for the duration. He probably owed this circumstance more to the lack of attention paid to the South by the War Department than anything else. Nevertheless, Pinckney proved himself to be an able administrator during the Creek War, making the best of an almost complete reliance on militia.

Following the war, Pinckney again retired from public life. He spent most of the remainder of his life trying to develop more efficient farming techniques that would preserve the soil of the South. He died in Charleston in 1828.

—*Jeanne T. Heidler and David S. Heidler*

See also: Creek War; Flournoy, [John] Thomas; Fort Jackson, Treaty of; Georgia; Hawkins, Benjamin
Further Reading
Pinckney, Charles C. *Life of General Thomas Pinckney.* Boston: Houghton, Mifflin, 1895.

PINKNEY, WILLIAM
1764–1822
U.S. diplomat; attorney general; militia officer

Born in Annapolis, Maryland, to Jonathan Pinkney and Ann Rind Pinkney, William Pinkney, because of the Tory sentiments of his father, was reduced to poverty at a young age and consequently received little formal education. As a teenager, he espoused the cause of independence and thus made influential friends who helped him enter the study of law in 1783. In 1786, at the age of 22, he began the practice of law in Harford County, Maryland.

Pinkney quickly established himself as one of the rising young lawyers in the state. He entered politics, was elected to the U.S Congress in 1788, and remained a member of the House of Representatives under the new Constitution. Cementing his rise in Maryland society was his marriage to Ann Maria Rodgers, sister of Commodore John Rodgers.

Leaving Congress in 1792, Pinkney returned to his law practice and Maryland government. Beginning in that year, he served on the state executive council and in 1795 was elected to the state legislature. His legal expertise, however, gained him the attention of Pres. George Washington, who in 1796 appointed Pinkney to the commission to Great Britain to settle U.S. claims, beginning his long diplomatic career.

Pinkney remained in Great Britain until 1804, when he returned to practice law in Baltimore. He also continued his interest in his state's government by accepting appointment as state attorney general. His tenure in that position was not a long one. His legal opinions regarding the British revival of the Rule of 1756 gained him the attention of Pres. Thomas Jefferson and, in spite of Pinkney's Federalist politics, led the president to offer him a position as a commissioner to Great Britain to aid U.S. minister James Monroe in negotiating a treaty there.

Pinkney's acceptance of Jefferson's appointment caused some Federalists to view him as a traitor to the party, and perhaps their attitude contributed to his decision, on his return, to move to the Democratic Republican Party. In addition, his fellow commissioner James Monroe saw Jefferson's appointment of another commissioner as an indication of lack of confidence. As a result, when Pinkney arrived in London on 24 June 1806, Monroe greeted him coolly. The two quickly developed a good working relationship, however.

Pinkney had left for Great Britain with high hopes. The death of Prime Minister William Pitt the Younger in January 1806 led many in the United States to conclude that the British might change their maritime policy toward the United States. The appointment of Charles James Fox, a old friend to the United States, as foreign secretary expanded that hope. Even if Fox had been so inclined, however, the war with Napoleon and the political situation in Great Britain made a change of policy difficult; Fox's death in September 1806 made it impossible.

Still the U.S. commissioners persevered, and the British negotiators did not seem unbending. The one issue on which the British would not yield, however, was the one point that Jefferson had instructed his commissioners must be included in any treaty—the British abandonment of impressment. Rather than conclude no treaty at all, Pinkney and Monroe decided to violate their instructions and reach an agreement omitting the issue of impressment.

The Monroe-Pinkney Treaty, which the commissioners signed with their British counterparts on 31 December 1806, reinstituted the practice of the broken voyage, which the British had disavowed in the *Essex* Decision; prohibited U.S. commercial restrictions on British trade for ten years; bound the United States to disobey Napoleon's Berlin Decree, which had been issued in November of that year; granted the United States trade concessions; and contained a British guarantee not to search ships within 5 miles of U.S. shores.

When the treaty arrived in the United States, President Jefferson chose not to submit it to the Senate. He found the omission of the impressment issue very disturbing and privately lamented his commissioners' failure to follow instructions. Monroe, who had returned to the country shortly after the treaty's arrival, took the president's actions as a personal affront. The more practical Pinkney remained in Great Britain as U.S. minister, hoping to conclude a more appropriate agreement.

Over the next four years and through a succession of ministries, the British government refused to reopen negotiations. A glimmer of hope appeared briefly in 1810, when a regency was established under George, Prince of Wales. Pinkney hoped that the change in government would mean a change in ministries and perhaps a change in policy, but both ministry and policy remained the same. Therefore in early 1811, he announced to the British that since that government had not seen fit to appoint a new minister to the United States, it was inappropriate for the United States to maintain a minister in London. When the British attempted to remedy this situation by appointing Augustus John Foster as minister to the United States, Pinkney asked if this action signaled a reopening of talks. When he was told it did not, he left for the United States in May 1811. Before he departed, he sent a message to the Madison administration that Foster had no power to negotiate a settlement with the United States.

Upon his return to the United States, Pinkney received from Pres. James Madison appointment as U.S. attorney general. In that position, he gained national renown for his legal knowledge and the leadership that he demonstrated in the country's legal community.

As a member of Madison's cabinet, Pinkney strongly supported the government's preparations for war. When the House of Representatives began debating war in June 1812, Pinkney drafted the war bill eventually passed by that body. After the official declaration of war on 18 June 1812, Pinkney wrote the proclamation issued by the president announcing the war to the nation.

Once the war began, Pinkney advised the president on several issues regarding presidential war powers under the Constitution. He was especially incensed by the actions of the governors of Massachusetts, Connecticut, and Rhode Island concerning the use of state militia and recommended to the administration and members of Congress the enactment of a sedition law to prosecute those who obstructed the war effort. His advice was not heeded.

By the end of 1813, Pinkney's legal practice in Maryland was suffering and his role in the cabinet declining. There was also a move afoot to require the attorney general to reside in Washington, D.C., which would have hurt his legal practice even more. Therefore, in January 1814 he resigned and returned to private life.

Pinkney's role in the War of 1812, however, had not come to an end. As a major of riflemen in the Maryland militia, he commanded 160 men at Bladensburg on 24 August 1814 as the British marched on Washington. In that engagement, he was seriously wounded.

Immediately following the war, Pinkney served briefly in Congress until 1816, when Madison appointed him minister to Russia. He returned to the United States in 1818. He took a seat in the U.S. Senate in 1819 and continued his legal practice, arguing several cases before the Supreme Court (including *McCulloch* v. *Maryland*) over the next few years. At the time of his death in 1822, he was universally regarded as the greatest lawyer in the United States.

—*Jeanne T. Heidler and David S. Heidler*

See also: Berlin Decree; *Essex* Decision; Impressment; Jefferson, Thomas; Monroe, James; Rodgers, John
Further Reading
Hagan, Horace H. "The Greatest American Lawyer." *Case and Comment* 22 (1916): 87–96.

PLATTSBURG, BATTLE OF
11 September 1814

A natural gateway to the United States exists along the Richelieu River–Lake Champlain line. It was used as an invasion route by Gen. John Burgoyne in 1777 and would be used by the British again in 1814. The British plan was to invade the United States to move closer to their food supplies and increase territorial gains. This southward movement culminated in the Battle of Plattsburg.

Upon Napoleon's abdication in 1814, England moved large numbers of troops from Spain to Canada. By August, Maj. Gen. Sir George Prevost had almost 17,000 of the Duke of Wellington's veterans assembled in the Quebec and Montreal areas. These land forces, supported by a British fleet on Lake Champlain, were designated for the invasion of the United States. That operation appeared all the easier for the British because Secretary of War John Armstrong had ordered Maj. Gen. George Izard, commander of U.S. forces at Plattsburg, New York, to move the bulk of his forces to Sacket's Harbor. Izard departed on 23 August 1814, leaving Brig. Gen. Alexander Macomb in command of the 3,500 men remaining at Plattsburg. Fortunately, Izard had established a defensive position in the southern part of Plattsburg on the peninsula between the Saranac River and Lake Champlain. With water protecting three flanks, the Americans constructed three forts (Brown, Moreau, and Scott) and two blockhouses to protect the open end of their position.

After discovering British intentions, Macomb called on the governors of Vermont and New York for volunteers. Soon 2,500 Vermonters and 800 New Yorkers were en route to Plattsburg. These would be joined on 3 September by Lt. Thomas Macdonough and his fleet of three warships, the *Saratoga, Ticonderoga*, and *Preble;* the sloop *Eagle;* and ten gunboats.

By 5 September, the British had neared Plattsburg and divided into two columns to move on the town. Maj. John Wool and 300 regulars ambushed the inland column, while Macdonough's gunboats harassed the shore column. However, both British columns persevered, arriving in Plattsburg after suffering more than 200 casualties. The Americans held these forces in check by occupying their prepared defenses and destroying the bridges across the Saranac. Prevost ordered an immediate assault but then canceled it when he could not find a suitable ford.

Prevost then decided to await the arrival of the British fleet. He planned to have Maj. Gen. Thomas Brisbane's brigade of 3,500 pin down Macomb's force, while Maj. Gen. Frederick Robinson would cross the Saranac a few miles upstream from the bridges with 2,500 men. Maj. Gen. Manley Power's brigade of 3,500 would follow Robinson. As Robinson turned the U.S. flank, Brisbane would attack forward. All this would be predicated on the British naval attack on Lake Champlain. Capt. George Downie arrived on 9 September with the British fleet, which consisted of the *Confiance, Linnet, Chubb, Finch*, and 12 gunboats. The British were then ready for battle.

Macdonough knew that he was outgunned at long range, so he anchored his ships to force the British to come within carronade range. At 9:00 A.M. on 11 September, the British approached, and the *Saratoga* scored the first hit on the *Confiance*. The British responded with a broadside that killed or wounded 40 seamen aboard the *Saratoga*. In the first 15 minutes, Downie was killed aboard the *Confiance*. The battle then raged along the entire line with the *Eagle* crippling the *Chubb*. An hour later, the *Ticonderoga* sent the *Finch* aground on the shoals of Crab Island. Next, the British gunboats put the *Preble* out of action. At the front end of the line, the *Eagle* was out of action, exposing the *Saratoga* to devastating fire. With most of their exposed guns damaged, the Americans appeared defeated. However, Macdonough swung the *Saratoga* to bring a fresh broadside against the British. Lt. James Robertson, having succeeded Downie in command, tried the same maneuver but failed. At 10:30 A.M., the *Confiance* struck her colors and the battle ended in a U.S. victory.

The British land forces began their attack in concert with the naval action. Brisbane was stopped at the bridges, while Robinson made better progress at the ford. After being driven back several times, Robinson succeeded in bringing most of his forces across the river. Before he could advance, however, Robinson received orders from Prevost to withdraw, a decision made after the news of the British defeat on the lake. Prevost did not think he could hold Plattsburg without control of the lake. Early the next morning, the British began their retreat into Canada with a loss of over 2,000 men, compared to 150 for the Americans.

This U.S. victory—what Winston Churchill would call "the most decisive engagement of the war"—shattered any hopes of British gains in the north. It was also to affect favorably U.S. negotiations for peace at Ghent. Coming at a time when the nation reeled under the sack of the national capital, the triumph at Plattsburg helped maintain morale during the final days of what had been a dark summer for the Americans.

—*John M. Keefe*

See also: Downie, George; Izard, George; Lake Champlain, Battle of; Macdonough, Thomas; Macomb, Alexander; Wool, John Ellis

Further Reading

Bierne, Francis F. *The War of 1812*. New York: E. P. Dutton, 1949.

Elting, John R. *Amateurs to Arms! A Military History of the War of 1812*. Chapel Hill: Workman Publishing Company, 1991.

Muller, Charles G. *The Proudest Day: Macdonough on Lake Champlain*. New York: John Day, 1960.

PLUMER, WILLIAM
1759–1850
Governor of New Hampshire
See New Hampshire

PORT DOVER, DESTRUCTION OF
15 May 1814
See Campbell, John B.

PORTER, DAVID, JR.
1780–1843
U.S. Navy officer

David Porter, Jr.

The son of David Porter, Sr., a naval officer, and Rebecca Gay Porter, David Porter, Jr., was born in Massachusetts. The younger Porter entered the navy in 1798 as a midshipman and saw combat aboard USS *Constellation* during the Quasi-War with France. He was promoted to lieutenant the following year and was wounded and captured in the war with Tripoli.

After his return to the United States he was promoted again, this time to master commandant, and transferred to the command of naval forces at New Orleans. Following that assignment, in 1811 he once again put to sea as the commander of the frigate USS *Essex* (46 guns), which was stationed in the Atlantic. Once war was declared against Great Britain in June 1812, he was recommended for promotion to captain, which occurred in July 1812.

During the first months of the war, the *Essex* continued to patrol the Atlantic, protecting U.S. merchant ships and harassing British trade. During the late summer and fall of 1812, Porter and his crew captured nine British prizes. In the late fall, Porter received instructions to rendezvous, if possible, with USS *Hornet* and USS *Constitution* in the Atlantic. When the rendezvous did not take place, Porter decided to take the *Essex* into the Pacific to harry British whalers.

In early 1813, Porter began the difficult passage around Cape Horn and, after suffering through dreadful weather, finally sailed into the Pacific and made for Valparaíso, Chile. After stopping for supplies, Porter set sail for the Galapagos Islands, gathering prizes as he sailed. In the Galapagos, Porter continued to wreak havoc on the British whaling fleet, converting one of his prizes into the *Essex Junior*, arming his new companion ship with 26 captured naval guns.

From the Galapagos, Porter set sail for the Marquesas Islands. He moved that far into the Pacific not only because his activities had put most British whalers to flight, but also because he heard that a Royal Navy squadron under Capt. James Hillyar was prowling to stop Porter's depredations. In the Marquesas, Porter cut quite a swath. After establishing his base on Nukahiva, he and his men proceeded to make both love and war, the one with accommodating Marquesas women, the other with rival native groups. Porter capped his activities in the Marquesas by claiming Nukahiva for the United States and renaming it Madison Island. President Madison never officially took notice of this action.

With rested men and resupplied ships, Porter left the Marquesas in December 1813. Dragging his men away from their island paradise (and new loves) proved difficult, however, and Porter had to suppress several attempted mutinies as he departed the islands. In mid-January, the *Essex* and *Essex Junior* arrived off Chile and made for Valparaíso.

Porter hoped to encounter HMS *Phoebe* (46 guns) under Captain Hillyar. Porter's exploits in the Pacific had gained him a wide reputation, but nothing could match the acclaim U.S. naval officers received by defeating a British warship.

At Valparaíso, Porter did not have to wait long for Hillyar to find him. When the *Phoebe* entered the harbor, she was forced to move by the *Essex* in such a way that the U.S. ship could have opened fire and disabled the British ship before it could come about. Porter chose not to fire in Chile's neutral port and instead sent word to Hillyar challenging him to a one-on-one duel in international waters. Hillyar refused the challenge and, after resupplying his ship, moved out of the harbor along with HMS *Cherub* (26 guns) to wait for Porter to leave.

Porter attempted to slip between the British ships on 28 March 1814, but a sudden storm toppled his topmast and forced him into a small bay outside of Valparaíso harbor. Even though the *Essex* was still in Chilean territorial waters, Hillyar closed to just beyond Porter's range with both British ships. Unable to maneuver, Porter took a withering fire for several hours before finally surrendering his ship and what was left of his crew. Shortly afterward, Hillyar paroled Porter and the survivors of the *Essex* and sent them to New York aboard the *Essex Junior*.

Upon his return to the United States, Porter broke his parole by traveling to the Washington area, where he engaged in the last phase of the campaign on the Potomac River. He attempted, without success, to stop the British withdrawal from Alexandria, Virginia. Porter saw no additional action in the War of 1812. He was given command of the new steamship *Fulton*, but that vessel was not completed until after the war.

For a time after the war, Porter served on the Board of Naval Commissioners, advising the Madison and Monroe administrations on naval affairs. Following this service, he commanded U.S. naval forces in the West Indies. While there, he became involved in a dispute with Spanish officials in Puerto Rico and was recalled to the United States. His subsequent court-martial and suspension left him so embittered that he resigned from the navy and accepted an offer from the Mexican government to head its navy. His service there ended unhappily, and he returned to the United States. He ended his life a diplomat in the service of the United States, dying in Turkey in 1843.

—*Jeanne T. Heidler and David S. Heidler*

See also: Essex *versus* Alert; Essex *versus* Phoebe *and* Cherub; Hillyar, James

Further Reading
Long, David F. *Nothing Too Daring: A Biography of Commodore David Porter, 1780–1843.* Annapolis, MD: Naval Institute Press, 1970.

PORTER, MOSES
1755–1822
U.S. officer

When the War of 1812 started, Moses Porter was one of the United States' most experienced artillery officers. He was known in the U.S. Army as "Old Blowhard," primarily because of his fondness for using colorful language. Born in Danvers, Massachusetts, in 1755, Porter entered military service in May 1775 as a private in Capt. Samuel Trevett's company of Col. Richard Gridley's Regiment of Massachusetts Artillery. Henry Burbeck was a lieutenant in that same unit, and Porter would go through almost 40 years of his career as an artilleryman one step behind Burbeck.

Porter served at Bunker Hill with Trevett's company, which was the only unit of Gridley's regiment to fight well in that battle. In January 1777, Porter received a commission as an ensign in the Sixth Massachusetts Infantry. That April, he transferred back to the artillery as a second lieutenant in the Third Continental Artillery, where Burbeck later became his company commander. He served with that unit for the remainder of the Revolutionary War, fighting at Brandywine, Germantown, and Monmouth. Porter mustered out of the Continental service in November 1783.

When the United States started to rebuild its virtually disbanded army, Porter joined the U.S. Battalion of Artillery as a lieutenant on 20 October 1786. In 1791, he made captain, and the following year, he took command of a newly formed artillery company of the Third Sublegion near Fort Wayne, Indiana Territory. Under Porter, that unit participated in Gen. "Mad" Anthony Wayne's 1794 expedition against the northwestern Indians. Today Moses Porter's company of artillery is the U.S. Army's Fourth Battalion, First Field Artillery. It is the oldest element of the First Field Artillery, and Porter is considered the father of that regiment.

When Porter became the major of the Corps of Artillerists and Engineers in May 1801, Burbeck was already that unit's lieutenant colonel and commandant. In April 1802, the artillery and the engineers split into separate organizations. Porter retained his majority in the new Regiment of Artillerists and still served under Burbeck as the regiment's colonel. The U.S. Army formed the Regiment of Light Artillery in April 1808, but it did not appoint a colonel for it until almost four years later. On 12 March 1812, just three months before the outbreak of the war, Moses Porter was promoted from major directly to colonel and appointed the first and only colonel of the Regiment of Light Artillery.

In the early part of the war, Porter served on the Canadian frontier. During the attack on Fort George in May 1813, he commanded the artillery field train. When Secretary of War John Armstrong started pressuring Gen. Henry Dearborn to resign in July 1813, Porter was among the group of officers, including Winfield Scott, Abraham Eustis, and John Wool, that initially supported Dearborn. On 10 September 1813, Porter received a brevet promotion to brigadier general "for distinguished service in the campaign of 1813."

When Gen. James Wilkinson was preparing for his march on Montreal, Armstrong wrote to him at Fort George on 22 September 1813, ordering that "our old friend Moses Porter is to succeed you in command of the fort and its dependencies." Wilkinson disregarded the order, apparently feeling he needed Porter with him as his artillery commander. The following month, Wilkinson issued a field order assigning Porter command of all artillery troops and materiel in his army. Armstrong later maintained that had his orders been followed, Fort George would not have been lost.

Porter's appointment as overall artillery commander for Wilkinson's army was the only time during the War of 1812 that a senior U.S. officer was given command of all the artillery on the field. Unfortunately, it did not last long. Porter started to experience the health problems that would plague him for the rest of his career. He was forced to withdraw from active field operations, and near the end of 1813, he assumed command of the Ninth Military District, which covered New York and Vermont.

At the start of 1814, Moses Porter was the fourth-ranked substantive colonel in the U.S. Army. That year he became the commanding general of the Fifth Military District, headquartered at Norfolk, Virginia. When the Tenth Military District was formed in July to direct the defense of Washington, D.C., against the expected British attack, Armstrong recommended that the command should go to Porter, "whose whole life may be said to have been military." Pres. James Madison, for his own reasons, selected Brig. Gen. William H. Winder instead, the nephew of Maryland's Federalist governor.

Following the war, Porter remained in command of the Regiment of Light Artillery. In September 1818, he was ap-

pointed president of a board of officers responsible for establishing a uniform system of artillery materiel for the U.S. Army. Because of his lingering health problems, however, he never actually served on the board. In June 1821, the Corps of Artillery and Porter's Regiment of Light Artillery were consolidated and reformed as four new numbered artillery regiments. Most of the companies from the Light Artillery went to the new First Artillery Regiment, and Porter became its first colonel. He was still serving in that position when he died in Cambridge, Massachusetts, on 14 April 1822.

—David T. Zabecki

See also: Artillery; Burbeck, Henry
Further Reading
Armstrong, John. Notices of the War of 1812. New York: Whiley and Putman, 1840.
Birkhimer, William E. Historical Sketch of the Organization, Administration, Materiel and Tactics of the Artillery, United States Army. Washington, DC: Chapman, 1884.
Downey, Fairfax. The Sound of the Guns. New York: David McKay, 1955.
Heitman, F. B. Historical Register of the United States Army. Washington, DC: National Tribune, 1890.

PORTER, PETER BUELL
1773–1844
U.S. congressman; militia officer

Born in Connecticut to Joshua Porter and Abigail Buell Porter, Peter B. Porter graduated from Yale, studied law, and moved to western New York to open his first practice, all by the time he was 22. On the New York frontier, Porter quickly rose to prominence among his fellow pioneers, until his association with the Aaron Burr faction in New York politics temporarily put him in disrepute with fellow Democratic Republicans.

Porter quickly overcame this unfortunate association and began rebuilding his political fortunes as he increased his wealth through a variety of business enterprises. After moving to Black Rock, New York, on the Niagara Frontier, Porter became involved with mercantile and transportation interests and began his congressional career as a strong supporter of the Madison administration.

In Congress, Porter identified with the faction of young Republicans known as War Hawks, and at the commencement of the 12th Congress in November 1811, Speaker

Peter Buell Porter

Henry Clay appointed him to the powerful post of chairman of the House Foreign Relations Committee. In this position, Porter spoke enthusiastically for greater military preparations. When he read the report of his committee to the House on 29 November 1811, he spoke belligerently about British violations of U.S. neutral rights and called for increasing the size of the military through recruiting, activation of militia, and naval construction. Porter made it clear in his comments on the report that he saw such preparations as a prelude to war. He also repeatedly suggested throughout the winter of 1811–1812 that the seizure of Canada was the best means to achieve U.S. goals.

Porter became increasingly vocal in his calls for increased military preparedness. In January 1812, he proposed a bill that would raise 50,000 volunteers, with the officers for these new units appointed by the president. When the Senate, ever sensitive to state prerogatives regarding the militia, changed the appointment procedures to have them occur in the states, Porter urged the creation of a 20,000-man provisional army. Congress rejected his proposal.

In the spring of 1812, Porter was so distressed by what he saw as the lack of military preparation that he began to cool on a quick declaration of war. Following the declaration in June, Porter continued his criticism of the government's lack of preparation and was particularly disturbed by the vulnerability of Black Rock and his home there. This concern intensified when news arrived of the surrender of Detroit. By that time, Porter had assumed the rank of brigadier general in the New York militia and had traveled to the Niagara Frontier to offer his services.

During the fall of 1812, Porter served under Maj. Gen. Alexander Smyth, and like other officers in Smyth's command, Porter became disillusioned with the ability of his commander. Finally, when Smyth failed to launch the planned invasion of Canada, Porter marched his men home in disgust. A war of words followed, with Porter publicly criticizing Smyth and questioning his courage in the aborted campaign. Smyth responded by implying that Porter's only interest in the campaign stemmed from his stake in government supply contracts for the army. A duel resulted on 12 December at Grand Island in the Niagara River. Neither participant was hit.

Porter continued to criticize the prosecution of the war in 1813, still urging an invasion of Canada along the Niagara Frontier as the best way to prevent a British invasion there. When such a U.S. invasion did take place in the summer of 1813, Porter urged a more vigorous use of the resources. During the winter of 1813–1814, he finally took matters into his own hands and began a zealous recruiting campaign in New York.

During the spring of 1814, he put these efforts to practical use when his brigade comprised part of Winfield Scott's division of Maj. Gen. Jacob Brown's army. Porter's brigade consisted of approximately 600 New York and Pennsylvania volunteers and about 400 Seneca Indians. Following the crossing of the Niagara River and the taking of Fort Erie, Porter proceeded north under Scott. When on 5 July the division encountered the British near the Chippewa River, Scott believed that the British force detected in the woods to the left of his position was only a skirmishing party, and he sent Porter forward with his brigade to flush them out. Porter discovered, however, that Brig. Gen. Phineas Riall's entire force lay in front of him, and consequently Porter was forced to flee back to Scott's position. The Battle of Chippewa ensued, in which Porter's brigade participated in forcing the British retreat.

Porter's brigade was conspicuous in its bravery throughout the remainder of the movements on the Niagara Peninsula, including the Battle of Lundy's Lane. But following Maj. Gen. Jacob Brown's retreat to Fort Erie, Porter was sent to recruit reinforcements. In September, Porter entered Fort Erie with 2,000 volunteers just as Brown was planning a sortie against the besieging British artillery. Brown gave Porter command of the attack on the British right, a foray scheduled for 17 September. He captured British batteries 3 and 4, a success that led in part to the British withdrawal. For his actions in the sortie, Porter was awarded a gold medal by the U.S. Congress.

One of Porter's last military actions of the war occurred

when Secretary of War James Monroe authorized him in January 1815 to ready his volunteers to suppress violence in New England, should any arise because of the Hartford Convention. Porter readied his force, but the anticipated violence did not materialize.

Following the war, Porter briefly continued his congressional career before accepting an appointment as one of the commissioners to implement the Treaty of Ghent's boundary provisions. Following this duty, Porter engaged very little in public affairs except for a brief stint (1828–1829) as Pres. John Quincy Adams's secretary of war. He died at his home on the Niagara in 1844.

—Jeanne T. Heidler and David S. Heidler

See also: Chippewa, Battle of; Erie, Fort; New York; Scott, Winfield; Smyth, Alexander
Further Reading

Grande, Joseph A. "The Political Career of Peter Buell Porter, 1797–1829." Ph.D. diss., Notre Dame University, 1971.

PRAIRIE DU CHIEN

This British post and settlement of 100 settlers in 30 houses was situated on the east bank of the Mississippi River, north of the confluence with the Wisconsin River. It exerted considerable influence over the Indians west of Lakes Michigan and Superior. Despite U.S. raids into Indian country in September 1812 and 1814, Oliver Hazard Perry's victory on Lake Erie, and William Henry Harrison's success at the Battle of the Thames, the western Indians remained British allies. Forts Osage and Madison had to be abandoned by U.S. troops in the fall of 1813.

In 1814, U.S. forces raised by the new governor of Missouri Territory William Clark, Zachary Taylor, and Lt. Joseph Perkins of the U.S. 24th Infantry attacked Prairie du Chien with troops and three gunboats. Led by the *Governor Clark*, this force easily captured the undefended British post on 2 June. The Americans hastily constructed Fort Shelby at Prairie du Chien and mounted six cannon there, but it was later recaptured by a British and Indian party from Michilimackinac on 28 June. The British force under brevet lieutenant colonel William McKay and bombardier James Keating consisted of nearly 140 voyageurs and troops and 530 Menominee, Sioux, Puants, Winnebago, Follesavoines, and Sauks. As his supporting gunboats were driven away, Perkins's small garrison of 61 troops of the U.S. Seventh Regiment and 135 militia volunteers capitulated on 19 July, after a two-day artillery exchange.

Strong U.S. relief forces sallied forth from St. Louis on 19 July and again on 5–6 September. Though they enjoyed considerable keelboat support, they were turned back by Sauk, Renards, Kickapoo, and Fox Indians at Rock River rapids. Prairie du Chien remained in British hands until the peace was restored.

—Frederick C. Drake

See also: Clark, William; Taylor, Zachary
Further Reading

Allen, Robert S. "Canadians on the Upper Mississippi: The Capture and Occupation of Prairie du Chien during the War of 1812." *Military Collector and Historian* 31 (1979): 118–123.

———. *His Majesty's Indian Allies: British Indian Policy in the Defence of Canada, 1774–1815.* Toronto and Oxford: Dundurn Press, 1992: 158–159.

Anderson, Thomas. "Personal Narrative of Capt. Thomas G. Anderson: Early Experiences in the Northwest Fur Trade and the British Capture of Prairie du Chien, 1814." *Wisconsin Historical Society Collections* 9 (1880–1881):136–261.

Brymer, Douglas. "Capture of Fort McKay, Prairie du Chien, in 1814." *Wisconsin Historical Society Collections* 9 (1880–1881): 254–270.

Clark, James. *The British Leave Wisconsin: The War of 1812.* Madison: State Historical Society of Wisconsin, 1955.

Dunnigan, Brian Leigh. "The Michigan Fencibles." *Michigan History* 57 (winter 1973): 277–295.

Legler, Henry E. "The Capitulation of Prairie du Chien." *Leading Events in Wisconsin History: The Story of a State.* Milwaukee: Sentinel, 1898: 144–152.

McDougall, Robert. *Correspondence of Lt. Col. Robert McDouall and Col. McKay Relative to the Capture of Fort McKay, Prairie du Chien, 1814.* Canadian Public Archives Report, 1857.

"Prairie du Chien Documents." *Wisconsin Historical Society Collections* 9 (1880–1881): 262–281.

Pratt, Julius W. "Fur Trade Strategy and the American Left Flank in the War of 1812." *American Historical Review* 40 (January 1935): 246–273.

Quaife, Milo M. "An Artilleryman of Old Fort Mackinac." *Burton Historical Collection Leaflet* 6 (January 1928): 33–48.

———. "A Forgotten Hero [James Keating] of Rock Island." *Journal of the Illinois State Historical Society* 23 (January 1931): 652–663.

Steffen, Jerome O. *William Clark: Jeffersonian Man on the Frontier.* Norman: University of Oklahoma Press, 1977.

PRESIDENT VERSUS ENDYMION
15 January 1815

In January 1815, the U.S. squadron in New York consisted of the 44-gun frigate *President* (Commodore Stephen Decatur), the 18-gun sloops *Hornet* (Capt. James Biddle) and *Peacock* (Capt. Lewis Warrington), and the supply brigs *Macedonian* and *Tom Bowline*. The blockading British squadron was composed of the 56-gun razee *Majestic* (Capt. John Hayes), the 42-gun frigate *Endymion* (Capt. Henry Hope), the 38-gun frigate *Pomone* (Captain Lumly), and the *Tenedos* (Captain Parker), which joined this force on 13 January. The entire U.S. squadron planned to slip out past the British warships and later assemble at Tristan da Cunha for a cruise to the East Indies.

On 14 January, a strong gale blew the blockading squadron off the coast. That evening, the deeply laden *President*, with the *Macedonian* in company, attempted to run the blockade. In the darkness, the *President* grounded on the channel bar for an hour and a half, which resulted in severe damage. Unfavorable winds kept her from returning to port, so she continued on and ran into the British squadron. It was no accident: Hayes had anticipated Decatur's attempt and had set out to intercept any blockade-running U.S. warships while his squadron resumed its station off the coast.

An hour before first light on 15 January, the *President* was sighted and pursued by three of the British warships. At dawn, the *Majestic* and *Endymion* were astern, the *Pomone* on the port, and the *Tenedos* starboard of the unlucky U.S. frigate. The *President's* speed was critically impaired because of her damage. The *Majestic* led the chase, but a shift in the wind that afternoon favored the *Endymion*. Decatur tried to lighten the *President* as the *Endymion* gained on her, but by midafternoon, the *Endymion* was firing her bow chasers and was being answered by the *President's* stern guns. By late afternoon, the British frigate was on the *President's* starboard quarter, where she could fire without being fired upon. As the pounding became intolerable, Decatur maneuvered to force the *Endymion* to come abreast of the *President* or face a bow rake. The two ships then ran side by side, and a cat-and-mouse game ensued for a couple of hours, wherein the *Endymion* would harry the U.S. warship while always keeping a respectful distance. Finally, the *President* was able to leave the *Endymion* dead in the water with her sails shot from her yards.

Three hours later, at an hour before midnight, the *Pomone* and *Tenedos* caught up to the still-fleeing *President*.

The damage wrought by two broadsides from the *Pomone*, which were not returned by Decatur, finally caused him to strike his colors and surrender, a decision that has resulted in much controversy. The *Endymion* and the *Majestic* arrived on the scene much later. In this battle, the *President*, with a crew of 450, lost 24 killed and 55 wounded, and the *Endymion*, with a crew of 350, lost 11 killed and 14 wounded.

—*Robert J. Bunker*

See also: Decatur, Stephen, Jr.
Further Reading
MacKenzie, Alexander Slidell. *Life of Stephen Decatur: A Commodore in the Navy of the United States.* Boston: C.C. Little and J. Brown, 1846.

PRESIDENT–LITTLE BELT INCIDENT
16 May 1811

Concerned about another *Chesapeake-Leopard* Affair and the interruption of U.S. commerce by British and French ships, Secretary of the Navy Paul Hamilton issued orders in June 1810 to the U.S. Navy's two major squadrons to protect U.S. merchantmen and to defend the honor of the country, even if this meant using force. About a year later, the HMS *Guerrière* impressed a U.S. sailor off the coast of New York, whereupon Secretary Hamilton ordered Commodore John Rodgers, commander of the frigate USS *President*, to sail into the area to discourage such activity.

Rodgers sailed from Annapolis on 14 May, and two days later, at about 1:00 P.M., he was off Cape Henry when his lookouts spotted a sail on the horizon. After chasing the unidentified vessel for seven and a half hours, the *President* came within hailing distance of her quarry. Following a return of hails, the unknown ship fired at the *President*, and Rodgers ordered return fire. Although Rodgers attempted to hail the ship during the engagement, his efforts proved useless; within 15 minutes the unknown vessel had sustained considerable damage.

The next morning Rodgers dispatched his doctor to the crippled ship and discovered her to be the sloop of war HMS *Little Belt*. The British ship had 32 killed and wounded but declined Rodgers's offer for assistance. When Secretary Hamilton learned of this incident, he ordered a court of inquiry to determine if Rodgers had been at fault.

Despite contradictory British reports of the event, the court exonerated Rodgers and stated that the *Little Belt* had initiated the action. This event fueled anti-British sentiment as the United States moved closer to war.

—*R. Blake Dunnavent*

See also: Rodgers, John
Further Reading
Bradford, James C. *Command under Sail: Makers of the American Naval Tradition, 1775–1850.* Annapolis, MD: Naval Institute Press, 1985.
Fowler, William M. *Jack Tars and Commodores: The American Navy, 1783–1815.* Boston: Houghton Mifflin, 1984.
U.S. Navy Department. *The Naval War of 1812: A Documentary History.* Vol. 1, *1812,* ed. William S. Dudley. Washington, DC: U.S. Government Printing Office, 1985.

PRESQUE ISLE

Presque Isle, on the southern shore of Lake Erie, had attracted both the British, who maintained a fort there from 1753 to 1763, and the French. Settlers arrived in spring 1795, and a town was laid out. Erie became a port for small schooners after 1800, when the town's population was 81; there were 656 people in what is now the city of Erie, Pennsylvania, and 1,468 in the county. Shipbuilding developed, but the town's growth was stimulated by the salt trade between Pittsburgh and Onondaga, New York, and downlake shipping of provisions from Detroit. By 1812, Erie had 400 to 500 people, and travel to Pittsburgh took three days.

In September 1812, Erie shipmaster Daniel Dobbins informed Pres. James Madison and Secretary of the Navy Paul Hamilton that Presque Isle (Erie) was a safe place for shipbuilding. Presque Isle harbor, formed by a huge sandy peninsula, was almost 3 miles long and 1 mile wide. Another sandbar across the entrance joined the mainland to the end of the peninsula at a depth of 4–6 feet and effectively denied entry to deep-draft vessels. Raising vessels to cross it, however, was within the technological capability of the age to solve. On 11 September 1812, Dobbins was authorized to begin construction of three or four gunboats.

Dobbins engaged shipwright Ebenezer Crosby of Buffalo and corresponded with Commodore Isaac Chauncey. By December 1812, the first four gunboats were commenced at Presque Isle from a draft provided by Commodore Thomas Tingey at the Washington Navy Yard. At the end of December, Chauncey arrived at Presque Isle with New York shipbuilder Henry Eckford and found its harbor "large and capacious," easily defended, and, except for the bar, superior to Black Rock, New York, on the Niagara River.

Chauncey disapproved of the size of Dobbins's gunboats and ordered two of them lengthened by 10 feet to make them safer. Carpenters were sent from New York and Sacket's Harbor, and contracts were signed for two brigs of 300 tons each. Eckford procured the services of Noah Brown of Brown, Bell and Company of New York City, who between December 1812 and June 1813 superintended the construction of the gunboats *Ariel, Porcupine, Tigress,* and *Scorpion* (launched in April and May 1813) and two large brigs, *Lawrence* and *Niagara* (launched in June). Oliver Hazard Perry arrived on 27 March 1813 and brought in heavy artillery from Buffalo. His purser, Samuel Hambleton, noted that Erie was destitute of defense, and Perry contacted Gen. David Mead of the Pennsylvania militia and Pennsylvania governor Simon Snyder, who ordered 1,000 men under Gen. Rees Hill to provide protection. A contingent of 14 U.S. marines under Lt. John Brooks arrived, as did seamen sent by Chauncey.

Perry sailed from Lake Erie in August 1813 to a new base at the Middle Sister Island before his battle of 10 September. Erie continued as the home base for the squadron under Commodore Arthur Sinclair in 1814 and as a supply camp for forces reinforcing Buffalo, New York, and Fort Erie in 1814.

—*Frederick C. Drake*

See also: Brown, Noah; Chauncey, Isaac; Dobbins, Daniel; Lake Erie Campaign; Perry, Oliver Hazard; Snyder, Simon
Further Reading
Altoff, Gerard T. *Deep Water Sailors, Shallow Water Soldiers.* Put-in-Bay, OH: Perry Group, 1993.
Metcalf, Clarence S. "Daniel Dobbins, Sailing Master, U.S. N. Commodore Perry's Right Hand Man." *Inland Seas* 14 (winter 1958): 88–96; 14 (fall 1958): 181–191.
Muller, Mary H. *A Town at Presque Isle: A Short History of Erie, Pennsylvania to 1980.* Erie, PA: Erie County Historical Society, 1991.
Reed, John Elmer. *History of Erie County, Pennsylvania.* 2 vols. Topeka-Indianapolis: Historical Publishing Company, 1925.
Rosenburg, M. *The Building of Perry's Fleet on Lake Erie, 1812–1813.* Harrisburg, PA: Pennsylvania Historical and Museum Commission, 1968.
Severance, Frank H., ed. "Career of Daniel Dobbins Now for the First Time Compiled from Original Documents, Including Also 'The Dobbins Papers,' 'Early Days on the

Lakes,' and 'Episodes of the War of 1812,' written by Captain William W. Dobbins from the Papers and Reminiscences of His Father." *Publications of the Buffalo Historical Society* 8 (1905): 257–379.

PREVOST, GEORGE
1767–1816
Governor in chief and British commander in North America, 1811–1815

Sir George Prevost was born in New Jersey on 19 May 1767, the eldest son of Maj. Gen. Augustine Prevost, a Swiss-born officer, who served with distinction in the British army. He was educated in England and on the Continent in accordance with his father's intention that George should take up an army career. He entered the 60th Regiment of Foot (the Royal Americans) in 1779, transferred to the 47th, then the 25th, and back to the 60th in 1790 with the rank of major. He married Catharine Anne Phipps in 1789, and they had five children.

In 1794, he was promoted to the rank of lieutenant colonel, in 1798 to colonel, and then to brigadier general. He commanded the troops on Barbados and then on St. Lucia, where he also served as lieutenant governor. After a brief return to England, he was sent to Dominica as captain general and governor. In 1803, he won praise from his commander for his service as second in command of an expedition that recaptured St. Lucia and Tobago. In 1805, his stubborn defense of Dominica stopped a French invasion. He gained the rank of major general and returned to England, where he remained until 1808, when he was sent to Nova Scotia as lieutenant governor with the local rank of lieutenant general.

During his three-year term, he not only achieved political success, but he also gained further military distinction by his service in 1809 as second in command of an expedition that captured the French colony of Martinique. With this background of political and military success and with a reputation as a bold and decisive combat leader, he appeared well qualified to take full control of Canada at a time of growing danger of war between Great Britain and the United States. Furthermore, he had successfully governed a French-speaking population in St. Lucia, so it seemed likely that this bilingual military hero might well conciliate the political and religious leaders of French Canada, who had been alienated by the previous governor, Sir James Craig.

Promoted to the rank of lieutenant general on 4 July 1811, he took command of the British forces in North America and was sworn in as governor in chief that October. He first won the support of French Canadian political leaders and of the Roman Catholic hierarchy, and then turned his attention to preparing the colony for war. He gained from the assembly a stronger militia law and, after the outbreak of war, its guarantee of Army Bills. Paper money was not regarded as a viable form of currency, but these bills proved to be an exception. Thus, the British government was provided with a stable currency to meet wartime expenses, and British North America did not suffer the currency deflation that hampered the U.S. war effort. By 1815, the total issue of Army Bills would reach the sum of £3,441,993, and they would be fully redeemed by 1817. Whether or not Prevost devised this answer to expected financial problems, he deserves credit for winning strong support from the highly skeptical French Canadians.

Among other preparations that he made were the appointment of Maj. Gen. Isaac Brock to Upper Canada and the approval to raise two new colonial corps, the Glengarry Light Infantry Fencibles and the Provincial Corps of Light Infantry (Canadian Voltigeurs). Throughout the war, he would urge Britain to send more reinforcements and supplies and would meet most of the requests from commanders in Upper Canada for help. Yet, this vigorous policy contrasted sharply with his own nonaggressive strategy and timid battlefield generalship.

Initially, he believed that the United States should not be attacked and that Upper Canada was indefensible. The events of 1812 seemed to change his mind about the latter view, but he continued to prefer passive defense and negotiating truces to aggressive action. When he led in combat, he seemed unwilling to take any risks or to accept heavy casualties.

When he learned in August 1812 about the repeal of the Orders in Council, he sent Col. Edward Baynes to negotiate a truce with Maj. Gen. Henry Dearborn, the U.S. commander in chief. The resulting cease-fire allowed both sides to send reinforcements and supplies upriver unmolested, but its disadvantage for the British was that it prevented Brock from carrying out his attack on Sacket's Harbor, New York. The truce ended on 4 September and did nothing to restore civil relations. In April 1814, Prevost responded positively to Secretary of State James Monroe's suggestion for a cease-fire by sending Colonel Baynes to negotiate and by cautioning Lt. Gen. Gordon Drummond against undertaking any offensive actions. No truce resulted, and when he later learned of the offer, Lord Bathurst, the British colonial secretary, instantly spurned it.

The first time Prevost led troops in combat in the War of 1812 was during a raid on Sacket's Harbor on 28–29 May 1813. Although Colonel Baynes was in nominal command, Prevost seems to have made the significant decisions. He called off the first attempt to land, thus losing the advantage of surprise. The assault went in on 29 May, but he cut it short, apparently because of the lack of naval artillery support. The U.S. defenders had set fire to their own barracks, to a frigate under construction, and to naval stores, but the blazes were extinguished before much damage was done. The harm would have been greater and more significant had Prevost allowed the raid to proceed at the risk of heavier British losses.

The next and last occasion that Prevost led troops in combat was against Plattsburg in September 1814. He crossed the frontier into New York on 3 September at the head of 10,351 men, including veterans of Wellington's Peninsular Campaign. From 6 through 11 September, he held them on the north bank of the Saranac River across from their objective, while he waited for the naval squadron under Capt. George Downie to arrive. When it sailed into Plattsburg Bay early on the morning of 11 September, Prevost did not attack when the naval battle commenced but waited until it was almost ended before allowing his troops to advance. As soon as he learned of Downie's defeat—which was total—Prevost canceled the assault and retreated hastily toward Canada.

Opponents of Prevost's conciliatory political program were now joined by critics of his military conduct. Prevost's career in Canada ended under a cloud; he was recalled to England to defend himself against charges made by Sir James Yeo, commander of the British naval forces on the lakes. The government accepted Prevost's explanation, but when a later naval court-martial decided that Prevost had urged Downie to attack prematurely and had then failed to provide the promised support on land, he requested another court-martial to clear his name. He died in London on 5 January 1816 before it was held. At that time, there were supporters as well as critics of his conduct, but the subsequent prevalent view has been unfavorable to Prevost. More recent writing includes well-argued defenses of his policies, but any conclusive consensus is unlikely.

—*Wesley B. Turner*

See also: Dearborn, Henry; Downie, George; Drummond, Gordon; Plattsburg, Battle of; Yeo, James Lucas
Further Reading

[Brenton, E. B.] *Some Account of the Public Life of the Late Lieutenant-General Sir George Prevost, Bart., Particularly of His Services in the Canadas; Including a Reply to the Strictures on His Military Character, Contained in an Article in the* Quarterly Review *for October, 1822.* London: T. Cadell and T. Egerton, 1823.

Christie, Robert. *Memoirs of the Administration of the Colonial Government of Lower-Canada by Sir James Henry Craig, and Sir George Prevost: From the Year 1807 until the Year 1815, Comprehending the Military and Naval Operations in the Canadas during the Late War with the United States of America.* Quebec: N.p., 1818.

Hitsman, J. M. "Sir George Prevost's Conduct of the Canadian War of 1812." *Canadian Historical Association Report* (1962): 34–43.

Stanley, G.F.G. *The War of 1812. Land Operations.* Ottawa: National Museums of Canada, 1983.

"PRIDE OF BALTIMORE"

See Privateering

PRIVATEERING

Privateering is the wartime raiding of enemy commerce by privately armed vessels licensed by letters of marque. America possessed a long tradition of privateering that dated back through the colonial wars, the Revolution, and the Quasi-War with France. In this manner, a generation of future naval leaders such as Joshua Barney, Stephen Decatur, David Porter, and John Rodgers acquired their initial training. The United States resorted to privateering throughout the War of 1812 with brilliant success. During this time, the U.S. Navy numbered only 23 vessels mounting 556 guns. These ships captured 254 enemy craft. By comparison, 517 privateers were authorized, representing an aggregate of 2,893 guns; privateers took 1,345 British prizes. They inflicted an estimated $45.5 million of damage on British commerce, as well as taking 30,000 prisoners. U.S. privateers were so active in British home waters that insurance rates for crossing the Irish Sea rose an unprecedented 13 percent. For families and individuals associated with U.S. shipping interests, privateering was a source of immense personal fortune and an agent of social mobility.

The distribution of U.S. privateers ranged along the entire Atlantic seaboard. Massachusetts was the largest contributor with 150 vessels, followed by Maryland with 112, New York with 102, Pennsylvania with 31, New Hampshire with 16, Maine with 15, Connecticut with 11, Rhode Island with 10, Virginia with 9, Louisiana with 7, and Georgia with 7. The cities of Portsmouth, Boston, Salem,

Bristol, New York, Philadelphia, Baltimore, and Charleston were all leading privateer havens and reaped a financial windfall. Baltimore's notoriety was such that in 1814 the British attempted its capture, largely to eliminate sailors such as Thomas Boyle. Generally, the Royal Navy was hard-pressed to contain these swarms of sleek, speedy raiders, which could usually outrun warships with ease. A convoy system, similar to those used in World Wars I and II, was arranged, which cut down losses of valuable ships and cargoes. The privateers were not always so fortunate, however, and their crews constituted the majority of prisoners at Dartmoor and other facilities.

The most successful U.S. privateer vessel in the War of 1812 was the *Yankee* of Bristol, Rhode Island, a brig weighing 168 tons, mounting 14 cannon, and carrying a complement of 120 men. *Yankee* completed six cruises, ranging from Nova Scotia to West Africa and into the chops of the English Channel, under such experienced captains as Oliver Wilson, Elisha Snow, and Thomas Jones. She took 40 prizes, including nine ships, 25 brigs, five schooners, and a sloop. By war's end, *Yankee* had seized an estimated $5 million worth of property, and deposited at Bristol alone goods valued at $1 million. Owner James De Wolfe consequently became one of the richest men in Rhode Island.

Another significant commerce raider was the *America* of Salem, owned by the influential Crowninshield family. This vessel, at 350 tons, with 20 cannon and a crew numbering 150, was somewhat large for a privateer. Fortunately, she possessed an enormous spread of canvas that made her one of the fastest sailing ships of the day. *America* completed four cruises under captains Joseph Ropes and James W. Cheever and netted 21 prizes worth $1,100,000. If property destroyed at sea had been brought home, this amount probably would have doubled. In all, the *America* garnered $600,000 in profit for the Crowninshields.

Farther south, Baltimore was home port to two famous vessels commanded by Thomas Boyle. The first was the *Comet*, a 16-gun schooner that secured 27 captures in several cruises. Boyle subsequently transferred to a new 16-gun schooner, the *Chasseur*, which proceeded to take an additional 53 prizes. Boyle's most daunting feat occurred on 30 August 1814, when he mockingly declared the British Isles under a state of blockade. In two years, Boyle amassed a personal fortune of over $1,000,000 and the *Chasseur* became popularly heralded as the "Pride of Baltimore." Other vessels possessing its sleek, low lines were hereafter referred to as Baltimore Clippers.

The most celebrated battle involving an U.S. privateer happened in the port of Fayal in the Azores. On 26 September 1814, the *General Armstrong* of New York put into the Azores following a successful cruise. A British squadron of three ships soon arrived and violated Portuguese neutrality by attacking. U.S. captain Samuel C. Reid skillfully repulsed several attempts at boarding and inflicted 173 casualties, himself sustaining a loss of two killed and nine wounded. The *General Armstrong* was subsequently scuttled to avoid capture, but the crew escaped and took refuge on neutral soil. Consequently, the British squadron spent three weeks repairing itself at Fayal before proceeding with reinforcements destined for Adm. Sir Alexander Cochrane's squadron. This delay allowed the Americans to consolidate their defenses at New Orleans well ahead of Cochrane's arrival. Reid subsequently sued the British government for its breach of neutrality, and at the conclusion of a celebrated case that lasted 70 years, his son was awarded damages in 1882.

Privateering as practiced in the United States was a unique blend of patriotism and profit seeking. The War of 1812, however, was the last conflict to witness its use on such a vast scale. Aside from occasional outbreaks during the Spanish-American Wars of Independence, privateering fell into decline and was outlawed by most nations in 1856. The United States, following a spate of Confederate activity, finally renounced it in 1865.

—*John C. Fredriksen*

See also: Boyle, Thomas; Letter of Marque; Reid, Samuel Chester

Further Reading

Garitee, Jerome R. *The Republic's Private Navy: The American Privateering Business as Practiced by Baltimore during the War of 1812.* Middletown, CT: Wesleyan University Press, 1977.

Gillmer, Thomas C. *Pride of Baltimore: The Story of the Baltimore Clippers, 1800–1990.* Camden, ME: International Marine, 1992.

Mouzon, Harold Alwyn. *Privateers of Charleston in the War of 1812.* Charleston: Historical Commission of Charleston, SC, 1954.

Stivers, Reuben Elmore. *Privateers and Volunteers: The Men and Women of Our Reserve Naval Forces, 1766 to 1866.* Annapolis, MD: Naval Institute Press, 1975.

Winslow, Richard Elliott. *Wealth and Honour: Portsmouth during the Golden Age of Privateering, 1775–1815.* Portsmouth, NH: P. E. Randall, 1988.

PRIZE COURTS

See Letter of Marque

PROCTER, HENRY

1763–1822
British officer

The most controversial British officer during the War of 1812, Henry Procter commanded the British Right Division on the Detroit frontier and served as military governor of Michigan Territory from 17 August 1812 until 24 September 1813. He was largely responsible for the destruction of three U.S. armies in a row, but he is best remembered for his alleged mishandling of the Thames campaign.

Born in Ireland, Procter was the son of an army surgeon and appears in records in 1781 as an ensign in the 43rd Regiment on service in New York during the closing phases of the Revolutionary War. Although he gained his early commissions through purchase (lieutenant in 1781, captain in 1782, and major in 1795), his subsequent promotions came through merit. His promotion to lieutenant colonel of the 41st Regiment on 9 October 1800 marked his long association with that corp.

Procter came to Canada to join his regiment in 1802 with another lieutenant colonel, Isaac Brock of the 49th Regiment. They became the principal officers who, with their respective regiments, formed the backbone for the defense of Upper Canada during the first year of war. Additionally, they were committed to the acquisition of Michigan Territory as an Indian homeland. For this purpose, Brock (now a major general as well as military commander in Upper Canada) arranged for Procter to assume command on the Detroit frontier upon the anticipated outbreak of hostilities with the United States.

In the years prior to the war, Procter was repeatedly recognized by senior commanders for his "indefatigable industry" in transforming the 41st Regiment (in Canada since 1799) from a unit of garrison invalids to a fighting formation ready for field operations. Promoted to colonel in 1810, Procter commanded at Fort George on the Niagara River when war broke out. Brock immediately sent him to take charge of operations in the West, where Brig. Gen. William Hull had already occupied British soil at Sandwich, Upper Canada (present-day Windsor).

On arriving at Fort Malden (at Amherstburg) on 26 July 1812, Procter immediately undertook offensive measures. With the assistance of Tecumseh, he secured the support of the previously neutral Wyandot warriors on the U.S. side of the Detroit River. Then, with the assistance of this influential and strategically located nation, he severed Hull's supply line to Ohio at the engagements of Brownstown (5 August 1812) and Maguaga (9 August 1812). Fearful of isolation and encirclement, Hull abandoned his positions in Upper Canada. Procter promptly occupied Sandwich and constructed artillery batteries in preparation for a bombardment of Hull's stronghold, Fort Detroit.

Brock joined Procter with reinforcements on 13 August 1812 and, from U.S. correspondence captured at Brownstown, learned of the dissension within the U.S. army and the wavering resolve of its commander. Under Brock's command, the combined force crossed the Detroit River and secured the bloodless surrender of the entire Northwestern Army (16 August 1812). Brock unilaterally "ceded" the vast Michigan Territory to Britain and installed Procter as governor before hastening back to Niagara for the next U.S. attack. His death at Queenston Heights some weeks later deprived Procter of committed support to operations in the West.

In September 1812, Procter prepared for offensive operations by exploring northern Ohio as far as the Miami River rapids. While there, he learned of the massacre of the Fort Dearborn garrison (15 August 1812) and sent most of his disposable force up the Miami River to avert a similar occurrence at Fort Wayne, which was besieged by the Wabash tribes. This column made a rapid but orderly retreat after colliding with a superior force under Brig. Gen. James Winchester, who was advancing toward Detroit.

On 18 January 1813, Winchester's wing of 1,000 men suddenly rushed forward and, after driving off its garrison, occupied Frenchtown. Three days later, Procter counterattacked with his combined force of regulars, militiamen, mariners, and Indian warriors. After a bloody action, most of the Americans became casualties. With his own regulars badly cut up, Procter withdrew from his exposed position to Amherstburg, leaving the badly wounded Americans at Frenchtown. Some dozens of these were subsequently murdered by frenzied warriors, an atrocity for which the U.S. press held Procter responsible. Nonetheless, the British commander was appointed brigadier general for shattering the second Northwestern Army. The legislatures of Upper and Lower Canada, then in session, passed votes of thanks to Procter.

Resuming his strategy of beating the enemy piecemeal in the spring, Procter attacked Maj. Gen. William Henry Harrison's newly constructed base at Fort Meigs, Ohio. Although he failed to dislodge the Americans, he ambushed and destroyed a relief column of 800 Kentucky volunteers (5 May 1813). Once again thwarting U.S. offensive operations, Procter was promoted to major general on 4 June 1813.

Despite his successes to date, Procter's strategic position

Though Henry Procter was undoubtedly a superior leader, his brutal reputation is displayed in this political cartoon of the time.

became progressively weaker. U.S. assaults at York, Upper Canada, and Fort Niagara disrupted the flow of reinforcements, naval supplies, and provisions, so that the large concentration of Indian warriors in the area grew dissatisfied. In addition, a superior naval squadron under Master Commandant Oliver Hazard Perry was nearing completion at Erie. To man the inferior British vessels, Procter was joined by Royal Navy lieutenant Robert Heriot Barclay and a mere handful of seamen. Their combined efforts to secure the loan of additional regulars with which to destroy Perry's vessels were frustrated by the intervention of Procter's superior, Maj. Gen. Francis de Rottenberg.

In response to the demands of the large assembly of warriors around Amherstburg, Procter made another inconclusive attempt on Fort Meigs in July 1813. Before recrossing Lake Erie, he led the allied force against the smaller Fort Stephenson. In an unsuccessful assault on this position (2 August 1813), the British force sustained several dozen casualties. Back at Amherstburg, Procter learned that Perry had emerged onto Lake Erie with his superior flotilla, thereby cutting off the vital supply route to Fort Malden.

In a desperate bid to reopen his communications, Procter placed all his fort guns on Barclay's vessels, along with one-fourth of his regulars as marines and gunners. Inferior in broadsides, tonnage, and crews, Barclay's vessels engaged the enemy on 10 September 1813, and after a furious action of three hours, the entire British squadron was captured. This decisive engagement left the British position on the Detroit frontier untenable. With great difficulty Procter convinced Tecumseh to accompany the retreat, but most of the warriors believed that the British were abandoning their interests.

Facing overwhelming numbers of the enemy on land and sea, Procter destroyed public facilities at Detroit and Amherstburg before beginning his retreat to the Thames River. Harrison's mobile corps of 3,000 men (one-third of them mounted) overtook the ponderous British column within 2 miles of Moraviantown. Procter's exhausted and demoralized force (430 regulars and 600 warriors under Tecumseh) was completely defeated, and Tecumseh was killed at the head of his warriors. Procter escaped immediately after his lines collapsed, closely pursued by U.S.

horsemen. Two weeks later, he conducted the remnant of his command to the British lines on Lake Ontario. The censure of his superiors resulted in a court-martial that, in early 1815, found Procter "deficient in energy and judgment" during the campaign. His sentence of suspension of rank and pay for six months was reduced by the Prince Regent to a public reprimand, sufficient to end a promising career. Procter returned to England that year, and his name disappeared from the Army List after 1816. He lived in quiet semiretirement until his death at Bath, England, in 1822 at the age of 59.

Procter's long years of distinguished service in Canada had earned him considerable popularity. The neglect to which his command was subjected and his rough treatment at the hands of Gov.-Gen. Sir George Prevost generated a public outcry. In 1815, a series of anonymous articles entitled *Letters of Veritas* appeared in the *Montreal Herald,* harshly criticizing the alleged mishandling of the war effort in the West by Governor-General Prevost. Procter himself broke his public silence shortly before his death with an article in the *London Quarterly Review,* in which he attributed the loss of the Detroit country to Prevost's "imbecility of judgment." His nephew, Maj. George Procter, also authored an account of his uncle's ordeal on the frontier in a book entitled *Lucubrations of Humphrey Ravelin.* This work emphasized the tragedy of the expropriated "red children of the lake and forest."

Traditional U.S. writings frequently associate Procter with the barbarities committed by his allies, ignoring Procter's attempts to save captives in Indian hands. Modern interpretations increasingly recognize Procter's contributions and view his final defeat as the consequence of Prevost's strategic mismanagement, leaving Procter's division with a forlorn hope overwhelmed by sheer mass and its commander victimized as a political scapegoat. Nonetheless, Procter's legacy has remained conclusively stained, primarily because of the writings of one of his teenaged subalterns, a gentleman volunteer named John Richardson, who gained posthumous fame as Canada's first novelist. Incensed that Procter afforded him only the same recognition as his son (Henry Procter, Jr.) at the first siege of Fort Meigs, Richardson took every opportunity to criticize his former commander. His biased criticisms were freely incorporated into most histories with little attempt at objective analysis.

Procter had married one Elizabeth Cockburn in 1792. They had four daughters and two sons. One of his daughters married his nephew George Procter, who was previously cited.

Henry Procter is frequently confused with another officer, Henry Adolphus Proctor, who also served in Canada during the War of 1812 and subsequently rose to the rank of major general.

—*Sandor Antal*

See also: Barclay, Robert Heriot; Brock, Isaac; Detroit, Surrender of; Hull, William; Lake Erie Campaign; Malden, Fort; Meigs, Fort; Michigan Territory; Prevost, George; Stephenson, Fort; Tecumseh; Thames, Battle of the

Further Reading
Cruikshank, Ernest A. *Documents Relating to the Invasion of Canada and the Surrender of Detroit.* Ottawa: Government Printing Bureau, 1912.
Dunnell, Remark. *Barbarities of the Enemy Exposed in a Report of the Committee of the House of Representatives of the United States, Appointed to Enquire into the Spirit and Manner in Which the War Has Been Waged by the Enemy, and the Documents Accompanying Said Report.* Worcester, MA: Isaac Sturtevant, 1814.
Hyatt, A.M.J. "Henry Procter." In *Dictionary of Canadian Biography.* Vol. 6, *1821–1835.* Toronto: University of Toronto Press, 1979.
Lauriston Victor. "The Case for General Procter." In Morris Zaslow, ed., *The Defended Border: Upper Canada and the War of 1812.* Toronto: Macmillan, 1964.
[Procter, George]. *Lucubrations of Humphrey Ravelin.* London: G. and W. B. Whittaker, 1823.
[Procter, Henry]. "A Canadian Campaign." *London Quarterly Review* 27 (April and July 1822).
Procter, Henry. *The Defence of Major General Procter Tried at Montreal upon Charges Affecting his Character as a Soldier.* Montreal: John Lovell, 1842.
Richardson, Major [John]. *The Letters of Veritas . . .* Montreal: W. Gray, 1815.
Sugden, John. *Tecumseh's Last Stand.* Norman, OK: University of Oklahoma Press, 1985.
Whitehorne, A. C. *A History of the Welsh Regiment.* Cardiff, Wales: Western Mail and Echo, 1932.

PROPHET'S TOWN

The fabled center of Tecumseh's planned confederation was founded in May or June 1808 and was located on the Wabash River in northern Indiana Territory, 2 miles below its confluence with the Tippecanoe River. Burnett Creek, site of the Battle of Tippecanoe, ran along the north side of the settlement. Another stream, which skirted the eastern edge, is now called Harrison Creek. The land had been offered to Tecumseh by the Kickapoo and Potawatomi leaders. Tecumseh himself probably chose the site and directed the early construction, but the town came to be identified with Tenskwatawa (the Prophet) because he governed there during his brother's long absences. Its grid street plan was quite unlike that of any other Indian town in the Northwest, and at its peak it housed several thousand inhabitants. On the eastern side stood an enormous "house of strangers" for visiting dignitaries, and at the center was a council house capable of seating five hundred people. Tenskwatawa's medicine lodge was also a sizable structure.

For the next three years, Prophet's Town was the nerve center of the vast and complex web of allied tribes in the Northwest. Whites were not normally allowed to visit; Tecumseh and his lieutenants traveled to Amherstburg or Vincennes when circumstances required. He and Tenskwatawa repeatedly claimed that they had moved to Tippecanoe to be closer to their great friend Gov. William Henry Harrison. In fact, Tenskwatawa visited Vincennes several times with a large following, perhaps in order to secure food for them from the whites. At the same time, Harrison found it easier to spy on Tecumseh; his agent Michel Brouillette was often in Tippecanoe. After the Treaty of Fort Wayne of 1809, the influence of the town spread farther west and north because many tribes were worried about this major land cession. The carefully worded diplomatic messages that passed between Prophet's Town and Vincennes in 1808–1811 make fascinating reading.

Harrison marched his army of regulars and militia up the Wabash River in October 1811. In November, Tecumseh was away, and Tenskwatawa tried to surprise this force with a predawn raid, but his warriors proved unequal to the challenge. Tenskwatawa escaped into the wilderness with about 200 other refugees. Harrison burned the village to the ground after his victory, and the survivors scattered into the forests. Later some followers of Tenskwatawa returned and tried to rebuild, but their settlement was destroyed in November 1812 by the Kentucky militia under Gen. Samuel Hopkins.

—*Thomas S. Martin*

See also: Harrison, William Henry; Hopkins, Samuel; Tecumseh; Tenskwatawa; Tippecanoe, Battle of

Further Reading

Calloway, Colin G. *Crown and Calumet: British-Indian Relations, 1783–1815.* Norman: University of Oklahoma Press, 1987.

Gilbert, Bil. *God Gave Us This Country: Tekamthi and the First American Civil War.* New York: Atheneum, 1989.

Gilpin, Alec R. *The War of 1812 in the Old Northwest.* East Lansing: Michigan State University Press, 1958.

PROSPECT BLUFF, WEST FLORIDA

Located in Spanish West Florida on the east side of the Apalachicola River about 25 miles inland from the Gulf of Mexico, Prospect Bluff became the site of the English fort known as British Post. In the spring of 1814, Maj. Edward Nicholls of the Royal Marines and Capt. George Woodbine, his Indian agent and chief recruiter, surveyed the site and selected the location as an ideal base for operations since it commanded transportation and communication routes along the Gulf Coast.

Constructed under Woodbine's supervision by Indian laborers from September to December 1814, the fort had an earthen parapet 120 feet in circumference, 15 feet high, and 18 feet thick. Lt. Robert Christie of the Royal Artillery surrounded the fort with a moat 14 feet wide and 4 feet deep and erected a double row of pine logs to serve as a palisade. Within the middle of the structure stood a 30-foot octagon-shaped powder magazine constructed of earth and logs. The position, situated on a cliff commanding the river in front, had a swamp to the rear, a large stream to the north, and a small creek to the south and was well protected from artillery. It was also defended by one 32-pounder, three 24-pounders, two 9-pounders, and two 6-pounders in addition to a howitzer and an abundance of small arms, which rendered the position virtually invulnerable to a landward approach.

After establishing a British presence, Nicholls promised weapons for any Indians who joined the British cause. Those assurances helped him recruit more than 1,100 Seminole and Red Stick Creek warriors, accompanied by 450 women and over 700 children. Additionally, he organized 400–500 runaway slaves into three companies of Negro Colonial Marines. Many of the blacks settled their families around the fort; the agricultural community supposedly contained pastures and fields extending more than 50 miles north and south along the river.

The British amply supplied the position with food, at least 3,000 stands of muskets, several cannon, other weapons, and a tremendous quantity of ammunition. Nicholls also distributed a considerable number of new weapons to his new allies in the area. All totaled, probably at least 6,000 stands of muskets, rifles, and carbines were either stored at Prospect Bluff or distributed nearby. Yet despite the quantity of arms and volunteers, the subsequent British attack on Fort Bowyer near Mobile failed miserably. Moreover, only a few recruits accompanied the expedition to New Orleans, where they witnessed the devastating British defeat.

British forces in the gulf did not learn of the Treaty of Ghent until February 1815. Article IX of the treaty stipulated that all lands held by Indians in 1811 would be returned, a provision that led Creeks to believe that the lands they had lost to the United States in 1814 under the terms of the Treaty of Fort Jackson would be restored. When the English evacuated the position, Nicholls negotiated a treaty unofficially promising British support for their lost lands. Failing that, Nicholls's agreement pledged that Britain would recognize and support an Indian state carved from part of East and West Florida. The government in London, however, later repudiated this treaty, and consequently the Creeks never received a restoration or compensation for lost lands.

The Indians also departed when the British evacuated. The fort became a haven for runaway slaves, who frightened U.S. planters to the north and served as a visible symbol of opposition. When these blacks subsequently organized a government and chose a military commander, Americans condemned the bastion, renamed Negro Fort, as an obstacle to peace in the region. In late July 1816, a U.S. joint army-navy expedition reduced the fort and the threat to slave property that it represented.

—Gene A. Smith

See also: Bowyer, Fort; Ghent, Treaty of; Nicholls, Edward; Red Sticks

Further Reading

Coe, Charles H. *Red Patriots: The Story of the Seminoles.* 1898; reprint, Gainesville: University Presses of Florida, 1974.

Covington, James W. "The Negro Fort." *Gulf Coast Historical Review* 5 (spring 1990): 79–91.

Dowd, Gregory Evans. *A Spirited Resistance: The North American Indian Struggle for Unity, 1745–1815.* Baltimore: Johns Hopkins University Press, 1992.

Dudley W. Knox. "A Forgotten Fight in Florida." *United States Naval Institute Proceedings* 62 (April 1936): 507–513.

Porter, Kenneth Wiggins. *The Negro on the American Frontier.* New York: Arno Press, 1971.

Southall, Eugene P. "Negroes in Florida Prior to the Civil War." *Journal of Negro History* 19 (1934): 77–87.

Wright, James Leitch. "A Note on the First Seminole War as Seen by the Indians, Negroes, and their British Advisors." *Journal of Southern History* 34 (1968): 565–575.

PUT-IN-BAY, OHIO

South Bass Island's 1,382 acres make it the third largest of 26 limestone islands in western Lake Erie. Known as Put-in-Bay, its protected cove was described by an early commentator as being "the BEST HARBOR between Buffalo and [Fort] Malden" at the mouth of the Detroit River. It was "deep enough at certain points, to admit vessels of 400 tons burthen to anchor within twenty yards of the shore." Frequently used by sailing vessels as a refuge from lake storms and a point from which a ship might wait for favorable winds to enter the Detroit River, Put-in-Bay was one of the best-known locations on Lake Erie. At the center of the island was the entrance to a cave containing an amphitheatre-like limestone cavern 170 feet by 40 feet in size and a deep pool of water; inside were the relics of centuries of Indian visitations to this sacred site. The island's flora included several hundred acres of oak, black walnut, red cedar, and honey locust forest, and its fauna not only included an abundance of deer and rattlesnakes but also an enormous variety of birds during migratory seasons.

South Bass Island's excellent anchorage and its convenience for observing British naval movements out of the Detroit River induced Capt. Oliver Hazard Perry to moor his fleet there from late August until late September 1813. It was from there that Perry sailed on 10 September 1813 to meet the British squadron commanded by Capt. Robert Heriot Barclay. After Perry's victory in the Battle of Lake Erie (sometimes called the Battle of Put-in-Bay), the U.S. fleet and its British prizes anchored there. Subsequently, it was at Put-in-Bay that Perry assembled over 80 bateaux loaded with 3,500 of Gen. William Henry Harrison's soldiers. His squadron escorted this expedition to near the mouth of the Detroit River, where on 27 September they were landed on a hostile shore. The Northwestern Army's invasion of Upper Canada (modern-day Ontario) eventually culminated in the U.S. victory at the Battle of the Thames. Some of the U.S. Navy vessels spent the winter of 1813–1814 frozen in Put-in-Bay's waters. After that, Put-in-Bay returned to its traditional use as a refuge for those sailing the lake.

—David Curtis Skaggs

See also: Barclay, Robert Heriot; Lake Erie Campaign; Perry, Oliver Hazard

Further Reading

Brown, Samuel R. *Views on Lake Erie.* Troy, NY: Francis Adancourt, 1814.

Langlois, Thomas Huxley, and Marina Holmes Langlois. *South Bass Island and Islanders.* Ohio State University, Franz Theodore Stone Laboratory Contribution no. 10. Columbus: Ohio State University, 1948.

Skaggs, David Curtis. "Joint Operations during the Detroit-Lake Erie Campaign, 1813." In William B. Cogar, ed., *New Interpretations in Naval History: Selected Papers from the Eighth Naval History Symposium.* Annapolis, MD: Naval Institute Press, 1989: 121–138.

Q

QUEBEC

Though considered, like Montreal, to be an economic key to crippling the British in Canada, Quebec was never considered a primary target during the War of 1812 because of its strong fortifications. By 1812, Quebec had certainly become one of the most important commercial centers in Canada and the British Empire. Many in the United States believed that by gaining control of the St. Lawrence River and the cities of Montreal and Quebec, the United States would gain control of Canada. Yet Montreal remained the primary target in Lower Canada, in spite of evidence that the defenses of Quebec had lapsed in recent years.

However, the British were concerned about Quebec's security and about the protection of communications between there and naval bases at Halifax, Nova Scotia. Therefore, the British secured the northernmost part of the Maine district in the summer of 1814, opening up land communication between Quebec and Halifax. The territory would become an important bargaining point in the negotiations at Ghent.

Toward the end of the war, new Secretary of War James Monroe began to see the importance of the St. Lawrence River. When the war ended, he was planning a campaign against Montreal that would be followed up in the fall of 1815 with a siege of Quebec. The war ended, however, before Quebec ever saw the first U.S. soldier.

—*Jeanne T. Heidler and David S. Heidler*

See also: Halifax, Nova Scotia; Maine, District of; Monroe, James; Montreal
Further Reading
Creighton, Don G. *The Commercial Empire of the St. Lawrence.* Toronto: Ryerson, 1937.

QUEENSTON, BATTLE OF
13 October 1812

Along the Niagara Frontier in the late summer and fall of 1812, command was divided between Maj. Gen. Stephen Van Rensselaer, an aristocratic New York militia officer, and Brig. Gen. Alexander Smyth, a regular officer with virtually no military experience. Van Rensselaer was placed in overall command of the front, but Smyth refused to cooperate with Van Rensselaer's plans. By the fall of 1812, Van Rensselaer had made plans to cross the Niagara River from Lewiston to Queenston, Upper Canada. He hoped that Smyth, to the north on the Niagara at Fort Niagara, would cooperate by staging a diversion against Fort George, but this was a forlorn hope.

Van Rensselaer placed his nephew, Col. Solomon Van Rensselaer, a former regular officer with combat experience, in command of the attack on Queenston. This action occasioned a good bit of grumbling among regular officers such as Lt. Col. John Chrystie and Lt. Col. Winfield Scott. Nevertheless, the date for the movement across the Niagara was set for the predawn hours of 10 October. When the men reached the boats, however, they discovered that their oars had inexplicably disappeared. Therefore, the attack was delayed for three days while new oars were acquired.

The British along the Niagara under Gen. Isaac Brock were unaware of the U.S. plans. Brock believed that when an attack came, it would come from Fort Niagara and be directed at Fort George, and therefore the bulk of his forces were at that post.

The advance force of the U.S. attack consisted of approximately 300 militiamen led across by Solomon Van Rensselaer and 300 regulars under Chrystie. They departed the U.S. shore at about 3:00 A.M. on 13 October in 13 boats. The crossing point was at a narrow part of the river plagued by numerous eddies that carried three of the boats, including the one carrying Chrystie, downstream. When the other ten boats arrived on the Canadian shore, the men were unloaded and the craft returned for additional troops.

The British on the rocks overlooking the river heard the Americans and immediately opened fire. The Americans fought their way to cover. In the initial attempts to find a way up the heights, Colonel Van Rensselaer was severely wounded and eventually had to be taken back across the river. With Chrystie still missing and other officers wounded, command devolved upon 23-year-old Capt. John Wool. The young Wool led his men to a sheltered position out of sight of the British guns and luckily came upon a path that led up to the rear of the British position.

In the meantime, General Brock had heard the firing at Queenston from Fort George, 7 miles away, and immediately led reinforcements south. When he arrived with his staff, he rode to the top of Queenston Heights to survey the situation. Just as he arrived, however, Captain Wool led his men over the top of the hill, an event so surprising that it caused Brock to flee the position.

Regrouping in Queenston while sending word to Fort George for more reinforcements, Brock arranged a charge on the heights. By this time, first light allowed Brock to ascertain the relatively small number of the Americans on the heights. He personally led the charge against this position and came close to overwhelming Wool's tiny band. When Brock fell mortally wounded, however, the attack temporarily stalled. His men regrouped and once again pressed their advantage. At one point, Wool's men were nearly pushed over the edge of the heights, but they held on and began driving the British back.

During a lull that followed this British attack, U.S. reinforcements began crossing the river, including General Van Rensselaer and Lieutenant Colonel Scott. Scott assumed command from Wool, who had been severely wounded several times in the earlier engagements. After surveying the situation, Van Rensselaer returned to the U.S. shore to bring over the remainder of the militia.

In the early afternoon, the fighting resumed. John Brandt led several hundred British-allied Iroquois against the U.S. left. Gen. Roger H. Sheaffe had brought up a large body of British reinforcements from Fort George and was using the Indian attack as a preliminary for the main British assault. General Van Rensselaer knew the British strength at Fort George would be brought to bear because Smyth had done nothing to hold them. He was thus frantically trying to move his remaining militia forces across the river to reinforce Scott's position. The presence of Indians on the British side, the sight of the returning U.S. wounded, and the militia's dislike of Van Rensselaer led them to refuse to cross. When Sheaffe began his main attack against the heights at about 4:00 P.M., he was quickly able to isolate the outnumbered defenders into small groups and cut them to

pieces. Many of the Americans who tried to surrender were killed by Brandt's Iroquois. Many chose to take their chances by either jumping from the heights into the river or trying to scale down the cliffs. To stop the carnage, Scott fought his way through Indians to find a British officer to whom he could surrender his entire force. In the end, the Americans lost approximately 90 killed, 100 wounded, and about 800 captured at Queenston.

The Battle of Queenston came on the heels of U.S. defeats all along the Canadian border. Unlike the ignominious surrender at Detroit, though, the battle produced a number of heroes, Scott and Wool most notably, who would find greater fame in future U.S. victories. For the British, the victory on the heights was at great cost because of the loss of the talented and irreplaceable Isaac Brock.

—Jeanne T. Heidler and David S. Heidler

See also: Brock, Isaac; Chrystie, John; Scott, Winfield; Sheaffe, Roger Hale; Smyth, Alexander; Van Rensselaer, Solomon; Van Rensselaer, Stephen; Wool, John Ellis

Further Reading

Compton, Smith C. *The Battle of Queenston Heights, U.C., October 1812: A Collection of Documents and Records Together with Factual Reports Dealing with the Events of the Day.* Toronto: McGraw-Hill, 1968.

Whitfield, Carol. "The Battle of Queenston Heights." *Canadian Historic Sites* 11 (1974): 9–59.

QUINCY, JOSIAH
1772–1864
U.S. congressman

Josiah Quincy was born in Braintree (later Quincy), Massachusetts, to Josiah Quincy and Abigail Phillips Quincy. His father died when he was very young. He received an excellent education, graduating from Harvard at 18 at the top of his class. He then began the study of law and opened his practice in 1793.

While engaged in his law practice, Quincy became involved in Massachusetts Federalist politics. He entered the state senate in 1804 and immediately set the tone of his political career by championing the rights of New England against the other sections of the Union. In the same year, his advocacy of his section's rights secured him election to the U.S. House of Representatives.

In Congress, Quincy became the spokesman for the increasingly unimportant New England states and the voice of opposition to trade retaliation against Great Britain. Like many of his section, he feared the growing power of the South and West at the expense of the Northeast and spoke against the admission of new western states (particularly Louisiana). He stated in Congress that if new states consisting of territory not a part of the original United States were admitted to the United States without the agreement of all original states, then those states that opposed such action would be justified in dissolving the Union. Quincy also resolutely opposed trade restrictions with Great Britain, believing it a greater good to help the British in their struggle against Napoleon than to defend U.S. maritime rights.

When the 12th Congress convened in November 1812, Quincy actually agreed with many of the War Hawks that increased military preparations were necessary. His reasons for this seeming turnaround were complex. Quincy believed that if war came, it was absolutely essential that the United States be placed on a greater defensive footing. However, he also believed that Congress and the president had no intention of declaring war. He did believe that the country's first line of defense should be the sea. He therefore supported increasing U.S. maritime strength. In a speech to Congress on 25 January 1812, Quincy ridiculed the War Hawks for talking about an invasion of Canada as the best way to protect maritime rights.

When Congress began seriously discussing a declaration of war in secret session in June 1812, Quincy, believing that public opinion would sway the body against war, moved that the debates be open. When the remainder of the House voted him down, Quincy began working on an address that most Federalists in Congress would endorse after the declaration of war. Circulated widely after the declaration, Quincy's address returned to the theme of preparedness, criticizing Congress and the president for entering a war for maritime rights with very few naval preparations.

When the 12th Congress reconvened for the last time in the fall of 1812, the military reverses of the late summer and fall gave Quincy and his fellow Federalists fresh cause for dissent. In one of his last speeches before Congress on 5 January 1813, Quincy criticized the Virginia dynasty and implied that the war was a conspiracy to ensure the succession of James Monroe to the presidency. Shortly afterward, he resigned his congressional seat and returned to Massachusetts.

Quincy then devoted much of his time to philanthropy and his farm in Quincy. He could not permanently escape political life, however, because the people of his district elected him to the Massachusetts state senate. The speeches he made there mirror many of the remarks he had made in Congress, particularly in regard to his fears for the declining influence of New England. His opposition to the war reached a new height in the summer of 1813, when he put forth a resolution in the state senate calling the war immoral and urging the state to refuse to praise any of the military actions associated with it. The resolution passed.

Even though many people supported Quincy's sentiments regarding the war, most Federalists considered him too radical and arrogant. Fear of his sentiments and his potential for disruption kept him from being selected as a Massachusetts representative to the Hartford Convention in the fall of 1814.

Following the war, Quincy remained active in Massachusetts politics, continuing for a while in the senate and then serving five terms as a reform mayor of Boston. Following his defeat for reelection in 1828, he served for over 15 years as the president of Harvard College. Afterward, he retired from public life and devoted himself to writing, though he occasionally spoke out even late in life on matters of public importance—including the need to support the Union during the darkest days of the Civil War. He died in Boston in 1864.

—*Jeanne T. Heidler and David S. Heidler*

See also: Embargo Act; Federalist Party; Hartford Convention; War Hawks

Further Reading

McCaughey, Robert A. *Josiah Quincy, 1772–1864: The Last Federalist.* Cambridge: Harvard University Press, 1974.

R

RAMBOUILLET DECREE
23 March 1810

Apparently as retaliation for the U.S. Non-Intercourse Act of 1809, Napoleon I issued the Rambouillet Decree on 23 March 1810. This decree ordered the seizure of all U.S. ships that entered French ports or ports of cities occupied by the French. Any U.S. ships already in French ports were also subject to seizure if they had entered the port after May 1809. Napoleon intended this decree, coupled with the Trianon Decree issued in August 1810, to force the United States to cease trading with the British. He combined these measures with the duplicitous Cadore Letter in August 1810, which promised to revoke the Berlin and Milan Decrees as they affected the United States.

—*Jeanne T. Heidler and David S. Heidler*

See also: Berlin Decree; Cadore Letter; Milan Decree; Napoleon I
Further Reading
Egan, Clifford L. *Neither Peace nor War: Franco-American Relations, 1803–1812.* Baton Rouge: Louisiana State University Press, 1983.

John Randolph

RANDOLPH, JOHN
1773–1833
U.S. congressman

Few U.S. politicians have garnered more notoriety than the controversial John Randolph of Roanoke. Born into a large slaveholding family in Prince George County, Virginia, Randolph attended the College of New Jersey (Princeton) and also the College of William and Mary for a time. He then studied law under Edmund Randolph in Philadelphia in 1790–1791 but spent most of the next decade managing his family's plantations. In 1799, Randolph successfully ran for a congressional seat and entered the U.S. House of Representatives, where he would spend much of the rest of his life. After the Jeffersonians swept into power in 1800, the still young Randolph became increasingly important as the floor leader of the Jeffersonians and as chair of the House Ways and Means Committee. His talents as a speaker were tremendous, causing a New England Federalist to remark that all other speakers he had heard dwindled into insignificance when compared to Randolph.

Initially somewhat politically flexible, Randolph's conservative political principles eventually put him on a collision course with the Jefferson administration. In 1805, Randolph made an open break, attacking the administration's handling of the Yazoo land claims in Georgia. By the following year, Randolph had assumed the leadership of the Republican opposition to Thomas Jefferson. Few in number but vocal, these southern congressman (called the Tertium Quids) were reactionary Republican agrarians who favored individual liberties and local government, political stances more appropriate for the Jeffersonians of the 1790s than those of the subsequent decade. Randolph's unstable temperament and his unwillingness to compromise ensured that his voice would often be a lone one crying in the wilderness, but nevertheless he proved to be a major problem for the Jefferson and Madison administrations.

Among Randolph's firmly held convictions was a determination that the United States not get involved in foreign wars, particularly "offensive" ones, which meant increasingly vocal opposition by the congressman as the United States drifted toward war with Great Britain from 1806 to 1812. The *Chesapeake-Leopard* Affair (22 June 1807), in which a British warship fired on and boarded a U.S. warship, heralded Randolph's opposition to military conflict. Immediately after the incident Randolph, along with most Americans, assumed the action meant war. "Now that the rupture has taken place," Randolph wrote, "I would act with the most determined spirit against the enemy, for so I consider England at this moment."

Yet, as the Jefferson administration failed to move immediately toward war, Randolph quickly resumed his former hostile stance, denouncing the administration for inaction, then reacting to Jeffersonian attempts at general military preparations not aimed at immediate war. These attempts, especially a call to raise the size of the peacetime army, offended Randolph's Republican principles, but he had no power to prevent them. With only a bare handful of supporters—sometimes not even that—he had the power to criticize and to embarrass but not to shape matters. His own suggestion that the whole of the militia be armed at government expense went largely unheeded. Similarly, Randolph supported an embargo as a war measure but not as an instrument of economic pressure.

In 1810, Randolph continued his crusade against peacetime military forces by moving for a reduction in size of the army and navy. Though his measure garnered significant support, the House adjourned without acting on it. The following Congress, the 12th, saw the primacy of the War Hawks, against whom Randolph immediately found himself in opposition as they tried to prepare for a military solution to the nation's problems with Great Britain.

During the session of 1811–1812, Randolph often found himself alone, but he used his considerable rhetori-

cal skills to great effect, arguing against military preparations on the grounds that the proposed war would be an offensive war, a war "of aggrandizement, of ambition," the purpose of which would be to conquer Canada. He mocked claims that the conquest of Canada would be easy and argued that war with Great Britain would only aid France. His sentiments at times echoed those of the Federalists, who had in early years been the subjects of his invective. Once again, Randolph found himself in a minority as Congress voted for war with Great Britain.

Randolph's violent opposition to the war caused a backlash that swept him out of office in 1813 for the first and only time, causing him to retire temporarily to his beloved plantation, Roanoke. The war years were not happy ones for Randolph; they were marked by crop failures and personal tragedies. Of the two nephews Randolph loved like sons, one suffered a mental breakdown and the other developed consumption (from which he would die in 1815). Randolph was unable to father children of his own (because of a peculiar illness suffered as a young man), so these blows affected him immensely, causing him to turn to religion for relief. In earthly matters, Randolph was as critical of the administration and of the war out of Congress as he was in it; his reaction to news of the U.S. victory on Lake Erie was to say that it would add another year to the life of the war. Nevertheless, he still took pains to distinguish his antagonism to the war from the views of the Federalists.

Despite his mighty opposition to the war, Randolph rallied to the flag upon hearing of the British sack of Washington, D.C., in August 1814. He traveled to Richmond and offered his services to the governor of Virginia. Assigned to the Virginia militia, Randolph served briefly until it was clear that the British would head north to Baltimore instead of south to Virginia. He then returned home. In late 1814, Randolph was reelected to Congress, but the war ended shortly after he resumed his place in the House. Randolph's subsequent career included many more terms as a representative and senator and diplomatic service as the U.S. minister to Russia, all marked by his lone-wolf political stances and his increasingly idiosyncratic behavior.

—*Mark Pitcavage*

See also: Virginia
Further Reading

Adams, Henry. *John Randolph*. Boston and New York: Houghton, Mifflin, 1883.

Bruce, William Cabell. *John Randolph of Roanoke, 1773–1833*. New York: G. P. Putnam's Sons, 1922; reprint, New York: Octagon Books, 1970.

Dawidoff, Robert. *The Education of John Randolph*. New York: W. W. Norton, 1979.

Garland, Hugh A. *The Life of John Randolph of Roanoke*. New York: D. Appleton and Co., 1859.

Kirk, Russell. *John Randolph of Roanoke: A Study in American Politics*. Indianapolis: Liberty Press, 1978.

RATES

For about a century, warships had been categorized into three broad types and six rates in a system largely devised by the Royal Navy and accepted by the world's navies. Largest of the types was the ship of the battle line, or "liner," from which the modern word "battleship" stems. The ship of the line was a ship-rigged warship having two or more covered gun decks. Next in size was the frigate, also a ship-rigged unit, but with only one covered gun deck. The smallest type was the sloop of war, whose rig varied but all of whose armament was carried on the open, upper deck.

The six "rates" specified originally in the Royal Navy had to do with the number of long guns a ship was designed to carry. The first four rates all identified ships of the line in decreasing power of armament: a "first rate" in 1812 carried 100 or more guns; a "second rate," 90–100; a "third rate," 60–90; and a "fourth rate," 50–60. (By 1812, fourth-rate ships were considered too weak to fight in the line of battle, and only a few remained in the British inventory.) Frigates of 30–44 guns constituted the "fifth rate," and ships meriting a "post-captain" and armed with 20–30 guns were "sixth rates."

In the War of 1812, the Royal Navy included ships of all six rates; the U.S. Navy had only fifth- and sixth-rate ships. By this time, too, the rating system as originally arranged was falling into disarray: the advent of the lighter carronade in 1779, which permitted a ship to carry more guns higher up, resulted in most ships carrying greater numbers of guns than their rate indicated. (USS *Constitution*, for example, rated 44 guns, never carried fewer than 52 during the war.)

—*Tyrone G. Martin*

See also: Cannon, Naval; Frigate, Evolution of the; Naval Ordnance; Ship Types
Further Reading
Falconer's Marine Dictionary (1780). Newton Abbot: David Charles Reprints, 1970.
Gardiner, Robert, ed. *The Line of Battle*. Annapolis, MD: Naval Institute Press, 1992.
Lavery, Brian. *Nelson's Navy*. Annapolis, MD: Naval Institute Press, 1989.

RED JACKET
1750?–1830
Seneca warrior

Red Jacket, born near present-day Buffalo, New York, was a Seneca warrior and leader known to his people as Sagoyewatha. As a young man, he fought with the British in the American Revolution and after that war very adamantly resisted cessions of more land to the United States. He received his English name from the red coat presented to him by a British officer at the end of the Revolution.

In spite of his earlier alliance with the British and his fears regarding U.S. land hunger, he used his considerable oratorical skills at the beginning of the War of 1812 to convince the Seneca to ally themselves with the United States. Red Jacket, despite his advanced years, fought with the U.S. army in New York, especially distinguishing himself at the Battle of Chippewa in July 1814. In that engagement, Red Jacket and his warriors were attached to New York militia major general Peter Porter. On the left of Jacob Brown's army, Porter and his men were sent against what initially was considered to be a small body of British in a wooded area. Porter advanced Red Jacket and the Seneca into the woods to determine the British positions, only to discover that a large part of the main British force was deployed there. Though repulsed in this initial skirmish of the battle, the Seneca redeemed themselves in the eventual U.S. victory.

After the war, Red Jacket sank into alcoholism and lost a great deal of influence among his people. He died near Buffalo in 1830.

—*Jeanne T. Heidler and David S. Heidler*

See also: Chippewa, Battle of; Porter, Peter Buell
Further Reading
Kolecki, John H. "Red Jacket: The Last of the Senecas." Master's thesis, Niagara University, 1950.

RED STICKS

Antiassimilationist Creeks in present-day Alabama, the Red Sticks were drawn mainly from the Upper Creek townships, numbered perhaps as many as 4,000, and proved to be a formidable enemy to the United States in the War of 1812. Decisively defeated by Gen. Andrew Jackson in 1814, they continued to inspire further resistance to U.S. expansionism among the southern tribes. The name "Red Stick" evidently derived from the Creek practice of counting down days to an important event (such as the advent of war) by removing sticks from a red stick bundle.

The Creeks were a Muskogean-speaking people loosely united in a confederacy of perhaps 60 townships. After more than two centuries of contact with white civilization, many held firm to their traditional religious beliefs. Remaining neutral during many colonial wars, they had sided with Britain during the American Revolution. Following the Peace of Paris in 1783, many of the townships remained influenced by the anti-American Spanish in Florida as well as the British traders located there. In the 1780s and 1790s, the half-Scottish chief Alexander McGillivray attempted to centralize Creek government and create an intertribal alliance in the South to resist U.S. expansion, but he failed. After the turn of the century, militants were disillusioned with the policy of accommodation followed by the Creek National Council and the extensive land grants made by it between 1802 and 1805, and they were especially angered by a road constructed from Georgia into the white settlements in Alabama, which was completed in 1810. A war band under Little Warrior followed Tecumseh north after his visit in 1811 and took part in the River Raisin massacre of January 1813. Returning south, the Red Sticks attacked a number of isolated white settlements, actions that led the U.S. agent to the Creeks, Benjamin Hawkins, to demand that the Creek National Council punish them. Little Warrior's execution by Creek "law menders" ignited a tribal civil war, which led to the Creek War, 1813–1814, and General Jackson's involvement in the southern campaigns of the War of 1812. In this ever-growing conflict, the Red Stick Creeks were led by a number of mixed bloods, including the prophet Josiah Francis and the war chieftains Peter McQueen and William Weatherford, also known as Red Eagle.

Promised arms by the Spanish, McQueen led a Red Stick band to Pensacola in July 1813. They were ambushed at Burnt Corn Creek by Mississippi militia under Col. James Caller upon their return, which led the Red Sticks under Red Eagle to attack and destroy Fort Mims on 30 August 1813. The massacre of the garrison, which included U.S.-allied Creeks and white militiamen, roused the South against the Red Sticks. Maj. Gen. Thomas Pinckney, who commanded the Sixth Military District, organized an expedition against them under Brig. Gen. John Floyd. While Floyd moved west from Georgia, another expedition of Mississippi volunteers and regular troops under

Brig. Gen. Ferdinand L. Claiborne inflicted a serious defeat upon the Red Sticks under Francis's command at the Holy Ground on 23 December 1813.

Alarmed by Red Stick activity, the legislature of Tennessee called up 2,500 volunteers, and while Brigadier General Floyd succeeded in building a series of forts in the Creek homeland, General Jackson turned the Upper Creek townships into a charnel house. Defeated by a detachment of Jackson's forces under John Coffee at Tallushatchee on 3 November 1813 and again at Talladega on 9 November, the Red Sticks made a last desperate stand at Horseshoe Bend on 27 March 1814. Poorly armed, they were slaughtered; of the 1,000 present, 800 were killed.

Red Stick activity during the War of 1812 was to have disastrous consequences for the whole Creek Nation. By the Treaty of Fort Jackson on 9 August 1814, U.S.-allied Creek leaders were forced to cede some 23 million acres to the United States. Many Creeks would thus join their Seminole cousins after the British arrived in some force at the Apalachicola River in August 1814. The remaining Red Sticks there took little part in the engagements along the Gulf of Mexico.

The memory of the Red Stick opposition, however, would continue to inspire militant nativism. A former young Red Stick, Osceola, would prove to be one of the prominent leaders of the Seminole resistance during the Second Seminole War, 1835–1842.

—*Rory T. Cornish*

See also: Big Warrior; Burnt Corn, Battle of; Creek War; Fort Jackson, Treaty of; Hawkins, Benjamin; Horseshoe Bend, Battle of; Jackson, Andrew; Little Prince; McQueen, Peter; Nicholls, Edward; Patriot War; Seminole Indians; Weatherford, William

Further Reading

Dowd, Gregory Evans. *A Spirited Resistance. The North American Indian Struggle for Unity, 1745–1815*. Baltimore: Johns Hopkins University Press, 1992.

Heidler, David S., and Jeanne T. Heidler. *Old Hickory's War: Andrew Jackson and the Quest for Empire*. Mechanicsburg, PA: Stackpole Books, 1996.

Owsley, Frank L., Jr. *Struggle for the Gulf Borderlands: The Creek War and the Battle of New Orleans, 1812–1815*. Gainesville: University Presses of Florida, 1981.

Wright, J. Leitch. *Creeks and Seminoles: Destruction and Regeneration of the Muscogulge People*. Lincoln: University of Nebraska Press, 1986.

REID, SAMUEL CHESTER
1783–1861
U.S. privateer captain

Born on 25 August 1783 in Norwich, Connecticut, Samuel Chester Reid was the son of John Reid and Rebecca Chester Reid. His father was a lieutenant in the Royal Navy who, after being captured, decided to join the Americans in their struggle for independence. When he was 11 years old, Reid went to sea and was subsequently captured by a French privateer and imprisoned on the island of Guadeloupe for six months. After his release, he joined the U.S. Navy, where he served as acting midshipman on the USS *Baltimore* during the Quasi-War between the United States and France. Later, at the age of 20, he became the master of the brig *Merchant* out of New York.

During the War of 1812, he commanded the privateer *General Armstrong*, a ship with nine guns and a crew of 90. On 26 September 1814, the ship was at anchor in the port of Fayal, in the Azores, arranging for the delivery of water and provisions, when three British warships entered the harbor. These ships, the *Plantagenet* (74 guns), the *Rota* (38 guns), and the *Carnation* (18 guns) were under the command of Commodore Edward Lloyd and were en route to Jamaica to join the British assault on New Orleans. Late that afternoon, Reid and J. B. Dabney, the U.S. consul at Fayal, discussed the arrival of the British warships. While they conferred, the British ships began moving toward the *General Armstrong* and anchored close by. Dabney assured Reid that the British had not violated the neutrality of Portugal, and he did not think they would do so now. Yet when Reid noticed signal flags and other activity in the British ships, he was convinced that preparations for an attack were underway. He therefore moved his ship closer to the Portuguese fort.

As Dabney went ashore, four boats full of armed men had set out from the *Carnation,* apparently with the intention of seizing the *General Armstrong*. Reid hailed them, and when they failed to respond, he opened fire on the boats. The British returned the fire. In the exchange, the British suffered about 20 killed or wounded to the Americans' one killed and one wounded. Surprised by the ferocity of the attack, the British returned to their ship. On the beach, the Portuguese governor and Consul Dabney, as well as a large group of citizens, had watched the battle. The governor, noting that Fayal was a neutral port, warned the British against any further hostilities.

Reid then moved his ship closer to the beach and moored it broadside to the harbor. He had extra gunports cut into the starboard side and shifted his guns in anticipation of a new assault. After midnight, the British renewed the attack with about 400 men in boats. Despite heavy fire, the British reached the ship, boarded it, and engaged in hand-to-hand combat. The fight lasted about 40 minutes before the British retired. It was estimated that the British lost between 175 and 250 men killed and wounded, compared to the Americans' two killed and seven wounded. But the *General Armstrong* had sustained heavy damage, and Reid set about making repairs. Dabney asked to meet with Reid onshore, and there Dabney told Reid of the governor's warning and the British response. Commodore Lloyd had said that he intended to destroy the U.S. ship even if he had to blow up Fayal in the process. Furthermore, Lloyd threatened to level the town if the fort attempted to protect the U.S. vessel.

Since it was likely that the ship would eventually be taken, Dabney suggested that Reid scuttle it and bring his crew ashore. Reid agreed. At first light, he sent his dead and wounded ashore, along with most of the personal gear of the crew. At dawn, the *Carnation* moved toward the U.S. brig. A 42-pounder "Long Tom" gun in the *General Armstrong* put holes in the hull of the enemy ship, tore up its rigging, and shot off its foretop mast before the *Carnation* moved out of range. While temporary repairs were being made in the *Carnation*, Reid noticed considerable activity in the other British ships. Realizing that it was only a matter of time before the whole British force would be upon him, he moved quickly to scuttle his ship. Masts were cut away and holes were blown in its bottom before it was abandoned. The British nevertheless managed to board the *General Armstrong* and take off some provisions before burning it.

For the next several days, the British buried their dead and made repairs on the *Carnation*. They also checked the U.S. crew for any deserters from the British service. It was not until the evening of 4 October 1814 that the squadron sailed. As a consequence, Lloyd reached Jamaica ten days behind schedule. Had his force arrived on time, it would have participated in the campaign against New Orleans, where it might have made a difference in the outcome.

News of Reid's fight against heavy odds reached the United States and thrilled his countrymen. When he returned home, the New York legislature presented him with a sword, and New York City merchants gave him a silver service. After the war, Reid served as the harbormaster of New York, and in that capacity he improved the pilot boat service of the port, managed to get a lightship stationed off Sandy Hook to improve navigational safety, and published a signal code for U.S. vessels.

Reid's most lasting but least remembered service was to standardize the design of the U.S. flag. In 1795, Congress had authorized a flag of 15 stars and 15 stripes. Admittance of states to the Union since that time threatened to make official flags look rather awkward. Accordingly, Congressman Peter H. Wendover of New York introduced a resolution in the House of Representatives to appoint a committee to inquire into altering the flag. A committee was appointed and in January 1817 it reported a bill. While the matter was before the committee, Wendover called on Reid, who was in Washington at the time, and asked the captain to design a flag that would allow for the increase in the number of states without destroying the character of the flag. Reid recommended that the number of stripes be reduced to 13 to represent the original states, and that the stars representing all the states be placed in the form of one great star in the canton. The committee adopted Reid's suggestion, but the bill was not acted upon before Congress adjourned. Wendover introduced a new resolution in the next Congress, and another committee was appointed.

A new bill was introduced in January 1818. This time there was no mention of a great star design. Reid's suggestion of limiting the stripes to 13 was retained, however. The bill provided for a flag of 20 stars in a blue field or canton and stipulated that a new star would be added to the flag on the Fourth of July following a state's admission to the Union. This bill passed both houses of Congress and was signed into law by Pres. James Monroe on 4 April 1818. A few days after the passage of this law, Mrs. Reid made a new flag, and the captain sent it to Representative Wendover to be raised over the U.S. Capitol. The stars in this flag were arranged in the form of a single large star. In practice, flags used by the army and navy and government agencies had the stars arranged in horizontal rows. Merchant ships and various civilian organizations used flags with the more distinctive star arrangement.

Reid lived to see the Union grow to 34 states and then be threatened by the secession of six southern states following the election of Pres. Abraham Lincoln in 1860. He died in New York City on 28 January 1861.

—*Harold D. Langley*

Further Reading

Furlong, William R., and Byron McCandless. *So Proudly We Hail: The History of the United States Flag*. Washington, DC: Smithsonian Institution Press, 1981.

Preble, George H. *History of the Flag of the United States of America*. 2d rev. ed. Boston: A. Williams and Co., 1880.

Reid, Samuel Chester. *The New York Telegraph and Signal Book*. New York: Published by the author, 1822.

Reid, Samuel Chester, Jr. *The Case of the Private Armed Brig of War Gen. Armstrong*. New York: Banks, Gould and Co., 1857.

Roosevelt, Theodore. *The Naval War of 1812*. Vol. 2. New York: G. P. Putnam's Sons, 1904.

RHEA, JOHN
1753–1832
U.S. congressman

Born in Ireland to Joseph Rhea and Elizabeth McIlwaine Rhea, John Rhea moved with his family to Pennsylvania as a teenager. The family later moved to Maryland and then to Tennessee in 1778. John Rhea served briefly in the American Revolution, but during that conflict enrolled in the College of New Jersey (Princeton) and graduated in 1780.

After the Revolution, Rhea became involved in North Carolina politics while Tennessee was still a part of that state and represented his county at the Tennessee state constitutional convention and in the state legislature afterward. In 1803, he began a long career as a U.S. congressman.

In Congress, Rhea consistently supported Democratic Republican initiatives, though he remained, even as some in the party changed, a strict constructionist of the Constitution. As such, he voted with the majority in refusing to renew the charter of the Bank of the United States in 1811.

An ardent expansionist, Rhea supported the territorial ambitions of many of the War Hawks. As a Democratic Republican of the old school, he opposed a large navy, but he wanted to fight the British for U.S. rights on land. During the War of 1812, he advocated annexing the Canadas to the United States.

Following the war, Rhea, except during 1815–1817, continued his congressional career. During that time, he became embroiled in a controversy between his old friend Maj. Gen. Andrew Jackson and the Monroe administration regarding Jackson's unauthorized behavior during his invasion of Spanish Florida. In later years Jackson asserted, almost certainly erroneously, that Rhea had sent him an authorization from Pres. James Monroe to seize Florida from Spain. By the time this controversy surfaced regarding the so-called "Rhea letter," Rhea was in his dotage and could not remember either the circumstances or the letter.

—*Jeanne T. Heidler and David S. Heidler*

See also: Jackson, Andrew; Tennessee; War Hawks

Further Reading

Hamer, Marguerite B. "John Rhea of Tennessee." *East Tennessee Historical Society Publications* 3 (1932): 35–44.

Heidler, David S., and Jeanne T. Heidler. *Old Hickory's War: Andrew Jackson and the Quest for Empire*. Mechanicsburg, PA: Stackpole Books, 1996.

RHODE ISLAND

The War of 1812 solidified Federalist control of Rhode Island. In 1811, the Federalists put up their own gubernatorial candidate for the first time since 1806. They nominated William Jones, a state representative from Providence, to challenge the popular Republican governor, James Penner. Campaigning on the theme of "no Embargo or Non-Intercourse Laws," Federalists succeeded in electing Jones and winning a majority in the legislature. Rhode Island was unusual because it held elections for the state legislature twice a year, and in the summer 1811 election, the Federalists retained their control.

The spring 1812 election turned into a rematch between Penner and Jones in the gubernatorial race. Both Federalists and Republicans turned the election into a referendum on war. Republicans appealed to patriotism and identified their opponents with the hated British; they claimed that electing Republicans to the governorship and state legislature would strengthen the Madison administration's negotiations with the British. Meanwhile, Federalists campaigned against war and urged voters to send a message to President Madison with a vote for the Federalists. During the campaign, Congress had imposed a new embargo on trade, and the Federalists made the most of the new commercial restrictions. The new embargo combined with the threat of war led to the reelection of Jones and a Federalist majority in the legislature.

After the election, the state legislature sent a petition to Congress urging the repeal of the embargo and opposing war. Of course, Rhode Island's petition did not deter Congress from declaring war. When news of the war reached Providence on 24 June 1812, the town went into "mourning" to signify its opposition. Most shop owners closed their stores for the day. Flags on public buildings and on ships in the harbor were lowered to half-mast. To drown out the chiming of all the church bells against the war, prowar Republicans shot off cannon, and other Republicans threatened to use a hemp collar if antiwar protests continued.

Later in the summer, Reps. Richard Jackson, Jr., and Elisha Potter, both Federalists, ran for reelection. Both had entered Congress in 1808 during a Federalist resurgence because of Rhode Islanders' opposition to the embargo. While Jackson and Potter campaigned as the peace candidates, Republicans lashed out at their opponents as the British faction in the United States. Voters, however, demonstrated their support for Federalists by reelecting Jackson and Potter with a larger majority than in 1810. It was a Federalist landslide. They increased their majority in the state house of representatives and carried 23 of the state's 31 towns. When voters again went to the polls for presidential electors, DeWitt Clinton electors carried the race in Rhode Island, where only six towns voted for Madison.

Discouraged by the string of Federalist victories, local Republicans did not run a candidate against Governor Jones in 1813. Federalists won all state offices and retained sizable majorities in the legislature in both the April and August elections. In 1814, James Fenner ran as a token Republican challenger to Jones—the governor won reelection with 77 percent of the vote. During the summer of 1814, Republicans made a greater effort to regain control of the state. The Federalists succeeded, however, in retaining control of the legislature and electing James Mason and John Boss, Jr., to Congress over their Republican challengers Nehemiah Knight and John D'Wolf.

The period between the declaration of war and the news of peace represented the nadir of Republican political fortunes in the state. During the war, the Tammany Societies went into decline as their membership plummeted. In the two years prior to the war, the Tammany Societies had played an important role in Rhode Island politics as a Republican auxiliary, but the war seriously crippled them. Both the weakness of Tammany and regular Republican organizations reflected the widespread opposition to the war in the state. Voters en masse defected from the Republican Party for the duration of the war.

Republicans also watched helplessly while some of their fellow citizens traded with the enemy. The British naval presence off the New England coast was both a threat and an opportunity. For many Rhode Islanders, it provided a chance to make up for the losses the war created. Shipowners in Newport and Providence traded with the British, and Providence customs collector Thomas Coles admitted the existence of widespread smuggling in early 1814. Moreover, because of their exposed position, Block Island residents declared their neutrality in the War of 1812, and British vessels stopped at the island for water, cattle, sheep, poultry, and other supplies. Smuggling continued until the end of the war.

Another manifestation of Rhode Island's opposition to the war was the position taken by Governor Jones and the state legislature. Governor Jones refused President Madison's request to call out the militia, and the legislature approved the governor's actions. The governors of Massachusetts and Connecticut also refused the president's request. Repeatedly, Governor Jones expressed his distaste for the war, and the state legislature voted in 1814 against assuming the state's share of a federal tax to help finance the war. In November 1814, the legislature approved sending delegates to the Hartford Convention as a means of putting pressure on the president to end the war.

Although Governor Jones and the legislature opposed the war, they were necessarily forced to make preparations to defend the state. After the declaration of war, the federal government removed most of the army troops stationed at Fort Adams and Fort Wolcott, and the governor hesitated to use militia troops to man the forts. The federal government refused his appeals for the return of the army.

When three British frigates appeared off Point Judith in the fall of 1812, Rhode Island inhabitants panicked, but the British did not attack. Several months later, in April 1813, a British squadron stationed near Block Island began cruising near Newport. The state distributed arms and ammunition to the local militia in case the British attacked, and the governor sent a small militia detachment to man Fort Adams. Citizens of Newport organized nightly patrols, and local banks sent their money to interior towns for safekeeping. Newport was never the object of a British attack during the War of 1812, but Narragansett Bay was the site of several ship burnings by the British.

A few antiwar Rhode Islanders, such as Newport customs collector William Ellery, did not believe that the British would attack because of the state's extensive illegal trade with British ships off the coast. By the summer of 1814, however, most Rhode Islanders were less sure of British intentions. Citizens of Warren, Newport, and Providence appealed to the legislature to provide for the defense of their communities. Partially in response to these appeals, Governor Jones arranged with the Madison administration to raise a state corps of 550 men, but only 150 volunteered. To make up the remainder, Governor Jones called out four companies of the militia to defend Newport and sent five other companies to aid in the defense of Stonington, Connecticut. Local residents in Providence formed a committee of defense to raise funds and provide volunteers for the construction of fortifications around the town, but the British never landed in Rhode Island (except for Block Island) during the war.

Although both Republicans and Federalists rejoiced at the end of the war, both parties used the war one last time during the spring 1815 election. The end of the war did not mean an immediate gain for the Republicans, and the Federalists retained control of the state in 1815. A Republican tide swept through New England in 1816, and the Federalists narrowly won the 1816 elections. By 1817, the Republicans finally regained control of the state. The Federalist resurgence in Rhode Island during the embargo and War of 1812 reflected Rhode Islanders' opposition to the foreign policies of the Republican Party. Federalist strength peaked during the War of 1812, and in 1812–1813 it looked as though the Republicans were heading for political oblivion in the state, but they bounced back as the memory of the war faded.

—*Harvey J. Strum*

Further Reading
Allen, Samuel. "Federal Ascendancy of 1812." *Narragansett Historical Register* 7 (1889): 381–384.

Fowler, William M. *William Ellery: A Rhode Island Politico and Lord of Admiralty.* Metuchen, NJ: Scarecrow Press, 1973.

Jernegan, Marcus. *Tammany Societies of Rhode Island.* Providence: Preston and Rounds, 1897.

Livermore, S. T. *History of Block Island.* Block Island Committee, 1961.

RIALL, PHINEAS
1775–1850
British army officer

Riall had joined the army as a lieutenant, 92nd Foot, in 1794 and through purchase and seniority had risen to major general by 1813. He was apparently a brave, bordering on rash, officer, but aside from minor campaigning in the West Indies, he lacked real combat experience. In July 1813, Riall was posted to Canada with Lt. Gen. Gordon Drummond and assigned to the Montreal theater. Shortly upon arriving, he accompanied Drummond to the Niagara Frontier, the scene of recent U.S. depredations. In concert with Drummond, Riall helped direct punitive measures, commencing with the capture of Fort George on 18 December 1813. Thereafter Riall's force, consisting of 500 regulars and a like number of Indians, laid waste to the settlements of Lewistown, Youngstown, and several Indian villages before returning to Canada. On the night of 30 December, he recrossed to the U.S. side, defeated large militia contingents, and burned Buffalo and Black Rock, New York. This last act concluded British retaliatory measures, after which Drummond departed for York. In his absence, Riall assumed command of British forces along the Niagara Frontier, with headquarters at Fort George.

On 3 July 1814, the U.S. Left Division under Maj. Gen. Jacob Brown crossed the Niagara River and captured Fort Erie. Riall quickly gathered 1,500 soldiers and pushed south to confront the invaders. Given the past performance of enemy troops, the general anticipated an easy victory. On 5 July he crossed Chippewa Creek and attacked the U.S. camp, only to encounter the well-trained First Brigade of Gen. Winfield Scott, 1,200 strong. Riall's light troops dispersed Gen. Peter B. Porter's militia from the adjoining woods, but Scott expertly turned both British flanks on the open field and drove them off. Riall's losses were 415 to Scott's 302. Had Brown been more tactically adept, the entire British force might have been taken, but Riall extricated his men and fell back to Fort George.

The Americans pursued in a leisurely way, and on 20 July they commenced a loose siege of Fort George. Riall, however, managed to slip away into the Niagara Peninsula, where he awaited reinforcements. When the Lake Ontario squadron of Commodore Isaac Chauncey failed to appear, General Brown fell back behind the Chippewa River. On 24 July, Riall's 1,000 men shadowed the Americans as far south as Lundy's Lane, where the British forces awaited the arrival of General Drummond. On the evening of 25 July, the British position was suddenly attacked by Scott's brigade and Riall, under orders not to engage, precipitously fled. Fortunately for the British, Drummond made his appearance, countermanded Riall's retreat, and gave battle. In the ensuing fray, Riall was seriously wounded and, while being moved to the rear, fell prisoner to a company of the U.S. 25th Infantry. He was subsequently evacuated to Buffalo, endured the amputation of his left arm, and convalesced in the same room as General Scott. Riall was the highest-ranking British prisoner taken by the Americans, and the British lack of a U.S. prisoner of similar rank delayed his exchange until December 1814.

After the war, Riall returned to England, where he was appointed governor of Grenada. Despite his wounds, he remained active in military affairs and became lieutenant general in 1841. He remains best known to Americans for having uttered the legendary statement, "Those are Regulars, by God!" when confronted by the gray-coated soldiers of Scott's brigade at Chippewa.

—*John C. Fredriksen*

See also: Black Rock, New York; Brown, Jacob J.; Buffalo, New York; Chauncey, Isaac; Chippewa, Battle of; Drummond, Gordon; Erie, Fort; George, Fort; Lewiston, New York, Destruction of; Lundy's Lane, Battle of; Niagara Campaigns; Porter, Peter Buell; Scott, Winfield

Further Reading

Cruikshank, Ernest A., ed. *Documentary History of the Campaign upon the Niagara Frontier.* 9 vols. Welland: The Tribune, 1896–1908.

Fredriksen, John C. "Niagara, 1814: The American Quest for Tactical Parity in the War of 1812 and Its Legacy." Ph.D. dissertation, Providence College, 1993.

Graves, Donald E. *The Battle of Lundy's Lane: On the Niagara in 1814.* Baltimore: Nautical and Aviation Publishing, 1993.

RIGS

Ships in the War of 1812 were powered by wind and sail. The way in which the sails were organized—number of masts, pattern of sails, and so on—was called their "rig." There were four principal rigs:

1. *Full-rig:* The ship was given three masts—fore, main, and mizzen—on each of which were arranged four-sided ("square") sails suspended from horizontal "yards" attached to the masts perpendicular to the ship's centerline. Additional sails were attached between the foremast and the bowsprit protruding out ahead of the ship and on booms pivoting aft of the mizzenmast (the spanker or driver). All warships of the first five rates were so rigged.

2. *Brig:* A ship with two masts—fore and main—each rigged with square sails, headsails, and a spanker.

3. *Schooner:* A ship with two masts—fore and main—each rigged primarily with sails pivoted on the after sides of the masts and supported by booms and with headsails; some were also fitted with square sails on one or both masts in positions above the fore-and-aft sails, but on the forward sides of the masts.

4. *Sloop:* A single-masted ship fitted with a main sail pivoted on the after side of the mast and supported by booms and with headsails; it might also be fitted with a square sail in a position above the fore-and-aft sail, but on the forward side of the mast.

Confusingly, warships of the sixth rate generically were termed "sloops of war." They might, however, have been fitted with any of the foregoing rigs, although, even more confusingly, few actually had a sloop rig. The single-mast sloop rig was to be found most often among the smaller, unrated units of a navy.

—*Tyrone G. Martin*

See also: Rates; Ship Types

Further Reading

Chapelle, Howard I. *The History of American Sailing Ships.* New York: W. W. Norton, 1935.

Harland, John. *Seamanship in the Age of Sail.* Annapolis, MD: Naval Institute Press, 1987.

Kemp, Peter, ed. *The Oxford Companion to Ships and the Sea.* Oxford: Oxford University Press, 1988.

Lees, James. *The Masting and Rigging of English Ships of War, 1625–1860.* Annapolis, MD: Naval Institute Press, 1984.

The Visual Encyclopedia of Nautical Terms under Sail. New York: Crown Publishers, 1978.

RIPLEY, ELEAZAR WHEELOCK

1782–1839

U.S. officer

Maj. Gen. Eleazar Wheelock Ripley served with particular distinction during the War of 1812. He was born in Hanover, New Hampshire, on 15 April 1782. His father, Rev. Sylvanus Ripley, was a professor of divinity at Dartmouth College and died on 5 February 1787. After his father's death, Eleazar Ripley's mother encouraged him to pursue an education. In 1800, he graduated from Dartmouth College and proceeded to study law. As a Massachusetts state senator, Ripley advocated war with Great Britain, despite popular sentiment against the hostilities within that state.

In March 1812, Ripley began his military career with a commission as a lieutenant colonel from Pres. James Madison. Just before the declaration of war against Great Britain, Ripley was put in charge of detachments in and around Portland, Massachusetts. From September to October, he marched his unit more than 400 miles to Plattsburg, New York, and the following March he was promoted to colonel.

Soon after his promotion, Colonel Ripley led his unit to Sacket's Harbor, New York. During the battle at Sacket's Harbor, a magazine explosion caused many casualties, among them Ripley. Ripley nevertheless pursued a fleeing British commander. After the battle, Ripley's regiment was put in charge of guarding the town and protecting personal property, a task that had him working without sleep for three days and nights.

Ripley had a minor role in the capture of Fort George in May, and soon he was back at Sacket's Harbor. He became so ill that he did not regain his strength until mid-July, but he continued training new recruits for his unit.

Ripley's greatest fame would come from his actions at the Battle of Lundy's Lane. By then a general, he commanded a brigade that rescued Gen. Winfield Scott's right flank. To increase the effectiveness of the brigade's fire, Ripley gave orders to shoot at the enemy at a range of no more than 20 paces. Virtually every assault on Ripley's position was repelled, and meanwhile one of his regiments captured several British artillery pieces on a hill overlooking the battlefield.

Ripley resigned his commission in 1820 and began practicing law in New Orleans. He supported Andrew Jackson in the election of 1828 and became a state senator in 1832. He was elected to the U.S. House of Representatives in 1834 and 1836. Illness prevented him from serving out his second term in Congress, and he finally died on 2 March 1839.

—John P. Newbill

See also: Lundy's Lane, Battle of; Sacket's Harbor, Battle of
Further Reading

Baylies, Nicholas. *Eleazar Wheelock Ripley.* Des Moines: Brewster and Company, 1890.

Fredriksen, John C. *Officers of the War of 1812.* Lewiston, New York: Edwin Mellan Press, 1989.

RITCHIE, THOMAS

1778–1854

U.S. journalist

Born in Tappahannock, Virginia, to Archibald Ritchie and Mary Roane Ritchie, Thomas Ritchie enjoyed an affluent childhood because of his merchant father's wealth and his mother's prominent social position. Ritchie thus became a member practically by default of the "Richmond Junto," the group that virtually controlled Virginia politics. Acquainted with law and medicine through cursory study, he was also well-versed in the writings of prominent Enlightenment thinkers. He founded the Richmond *Enquirer* with his cousin Spencer Roane, and by the outbreak of the War of 1812, Ritchie had been the editor of the newspaper for eight years, establishing himself as a constant Jeffersonian both intellectually and politically.

Ritchie was a staunch supporter of Thomas Jefferson's policy of privileging commercial restrictions over military preparedness. Although Ritchie briefly succumbed to the general fury over the *Chesapeake-Leopard* Affair in 1807, going so far as to call for a greatly enlarged army to invade Canada, he ultimately endorsed the Embargo Act of 1807 and eschewed the quixotic challenge of James Monroe to

James Madison's 1808 presidential candidacy. Remaining loyal to Madison, he condemned Federalist attacks on the president and in 1810 supported the reimposition of trade sanctions against Great Britain when Napoleon cleverly manipulated the terms of Macon's Bill No. 2 to France's advantage.

When war was declared in June 1812, Ritchie joined the patriotic chorus that condemned the Federalist press, especially Alexander C. Hanson's Baltimore-based *Federal Republican*. Through the *Enquirer*, Ritchie lauded U.S. military successes while downplaying setbacks. With the return of peace in 1815, he reflected the dramatic shift in Democratic Republican philosophy regarding the military. Convinced that the Treaty of Ghent merely marked a respite from British aggression, he joined other erstwhile opponents of the military establishment to advocate a permanent regular army and an enlarged navy.

Ritchie remained active in public affairs for the remainder of his life, notably as a Jacksonian Democrat who opposed both Henry Clay's centralizing nationalism and John C. Calhoun's aggressive sectionalism. Remaining to the end an adherent to the Jeffersonian doctrines of state ascendancy and national unity, Thomas Ritchie died on 3 July 1854.

—Jeanne T. Heidler and David S. Heidler

See also: Virginia
Further Reading
Ambler, Charles Henry. *Thomas Ritchie: A Study in Virginia Politics*. Richmond, VA: Bell, Book and Stationery Co., 1913.
Mutersbaugh, Bert Marsh. "Jeffersonian Journalist: Thomas Ritchie and the Richmond *Enquirer*." Ph.D. diss., University of Missouri, 1973.

ROBERTS, JONATHAN
1771–1854
U.S. congressman and senator

The son of Jonathan Roberts and Anna Thomas Roberts, Jonathan Roberts grew up in Montgomery County, Pennsylvania. He spent his young adulthood farming but was quickly attracted to local and then national politics. After terms in both houses of the state legislature, where he grew to maturity as an ardent Democratic Republican, Roberts entered the U.S. House of Representatives as a War Hawk.

When the question of war was put before the House in June 1812 and opponents to the declaration, especially the Federalists, sought to delay the vote with an adjournment, Roberts proposed to the House that members' pay should be discontinued during any adjournment. The ensuing debate led directly to a vote on the question of war. Over the next two years, Roberts became one of the strongest administration men in Congress. When Pres. James Madison came under attack for the conduct and the financing of the war, Roberts wrote a series of letters, which were published in his home state's newspaper *Aurora*, defending the president. In Congress, by resolutely defending Albert Gallatin, Roberts also took on the "Invisibles," that faction of anti-administration Republicans led by Maryland senator Samuel Smith.

When Gallatin vacated his position as secretary of the treasury, Roberts privately criticized the selection of George Washington Campbell as his successor. Roberts, like so many others in and out of Congress, did not feel that Campbell possessed the necessary financial skills to assume such a role in such a desperate time. By the time Campbell, too, realized his incapacity, Roberts had been chosen by the Pennsylvania legislature to assume one of Pennsylvania's Senate seats, a position he would hold until 1821.

Following Roberts's departure from the U.S. Senate, he remained active in Pennsylvania politics. Because of his antipathy for Andrew Jackson and his support for the Second Bank of the United States and internal improvements, Roberts became a member of the Whig Party in the 1830s. He died in Montgomery County in 1854.

—Jeanne T. Heidler and David S. Heidler

See also: Campbell, George W.; Pennsylvania; U.S. Congress; War Hawks
Further Reading
Champagne, Raymond W., and Thomas J. Rueter. "Jonathan Roberts and the War Hawk Congress of 1812." *Pennsylvania Magazine of History and Biography* 115 (1980): 434–449.

ROBINSON, FREDERICK PHILIPSE
1763–1852
British army officer

The fourth son of Col. Beverley Robinson and Susannah Philipse of New York, Robinson joined his father's Loyal American regiment as an ensign during the

Revolutionary War in February 1777. He fought at Horseneck in March 1779 and was wounded and captured at Stoney Point in July 1779. In 1793, he fought at the capture of Martinique, St. Lucia, and Guadeloupe. As a major general (promoted 4 June 1813), he commanded a brigade, fifth division, in Spain, at Vittoria (Gamarra Mayor), San Sebastian, the passage of the Bidassoa, Secoa, Nivelles, Nive, and the blockade of Bayonne in 1814. He was wounded twice.

In June 1814, Robinson commanded four infantry regiments consisting of 3,750 men that joined Sir George Prevost's advance into New York to seize Plattsburg in September. Robinson's troops were ordered to force the Saranac River and storm the forts guarding its mouth. His light troops had made the crossing when Prevost recalled him after learning that Capt. George Downie's squadron had been defeated. Disgusted with Prevost's inept leadership, Robinson broke his sword.

From November 1815 to June 1816, he was provisional governor of Upper Canada. He later commanded in the Windward and Leeward Islands in the West Indies until 1821 and was governor of Tobago. On 27 May 1827 he was promoted to lieutenant general. He received the Knight Commander of the Bath on 2 January 1815 and a Grand Cross in 1838. He died in Brighton on 1 January 1852, the soldier with the longest service in the British army.

—*Frederick C. Drake*

See also: Downie, George; Lake Champlain, Battle of; Plattsburg, Battle of; Prevost, George

Further Reading

Lloyd, Ernest Marsh. "Sir Frederick Philipse Robinson." *Dictionary of National Biography*. Vol. 17. London: Oxford University Press, 1937–1938: 11–13.

Preston, Richard A. "The Journals of General Sir F. P. Robinson, G. C. B." *Canadian Historical Review* 37 (December 1956): 352–355.

Stanley, George. *The War of 1812: Land Operations*. Ottawa: National Museums of Canada and Macmillan, 1983.

RODGERS, JOHN
1772–1838
U.S. Navy officer

A Marylander, John Rodgers went to sea at the age of 13, apprenticed for five years to a merchant captain. By 1793, he was a qualified master himself. In March 1798, he accepted a lieutenant's commission in the new U.S. Navy and reported for duty aboard the frigate *Constellation*. In February 1799, then sailing the Caribbean during the Quasi-War with France, his ship defeated the French frigate *L'Insurgente*. Rodgers, as first lieutenant, was made prize master and sailed the ship safely back to the United States, where she was brought into service as the *Insurgent*. Rodgers was promoted to captain in March and given command of the ship *Maryland*, where he stayed until 1801, when the war ended and he resumed merchant service.

In 1802, Rodgers returned to active duty as commander of the light frigate *John Adams*, a unit of the Mediterranean squadron. He and his ship remained in that sea until the fall of 1803, when he returned to the United States. He returned to the Mediterranean in the spring of 1804 in command of the frigate *Congress*, as the navy expanded its forces in the Barbary War. Rodgers took command of the heavy frigate *Constitution* in November and eventually became de facto squadron commander. In that capacity, he successfully concluded a peace treaty with Tripoli and parallel negotiations with Tunis and Algiers. He returned home in the summer of 1806. That fall, he married Minerva Denison of Connecticut.

Rodgers next commanded the New York station and then the northern squadron on the United States coast. Upon the outbreak of the War of 1812, he immediately went to sea on the first of four wartime cruises. On the first two of these, he led a squadron. The cruises, from the Caribbean to Norway, netted nearly two dozen captures, including one small warship and a packet carrying $175,000 in gold and silver specie. Although each of his cruises did the enemy some damage, Rodgers never managed to win a frigate action, which would have captured the public's imagination. Indeed, the muted criticism of his lack of martial success was especially galling to the navy's senior active officer.

Shortly after the war ended, a Board of Naval Commissioners was created as a professional staff to assist the secretary of the navy in carrying out his responsibilities. John Rodgers was appointed its first president, and except for two years as commander of the Mediterranean squadron in the mid-1820s, he spent the remainder of his career in that post. He left active service in 1837 and died the following year.

John and Minerva Rodgers had 11 children. For at least five generations to follow, there was at least one male descendant in the U.S. armed forces. There have been three ships named for John Rodgers in the U.S. Navy.

—*Tyrone G. Martin*

Further Reading

Fowler, William M., Jr. *Jack Tars and Commodores.* Boston: Houghton Mifflin, 1984.

Guttridge, Leonard F., and Jay D. Smith. *The Commodores.* New York: Harper and Row, 1969.

Martin, Tyrone G. *A Most Fortunate Ship.* Chester: Globe Pequot Press, 1980.

Paullin, Charles O. *Commodore John Rodgers, 1773–1838.* Annapolis, MD: Naval Institute Press, 1967.

RODNEY, CAESAR AUGUSTUS
1772–1824
U.S. attorney general; militia officer

Born in Dover, Delaware, to Thomas Rodney and Elizabeth Fisher Rodney, Caesar Rodney grew up in Wilmington, Delaware, graduated from the University of Pennsylvania, and entered the practice of law in 1793. As a young lawyer, Rodney became involved in Delaware politics, serving in the state legislature from 1796 until 1802. He was elected to the U.S. House of Representatives as a Democratic Republican in that party's rout of the Federalists in 1802. In Congress, he became a strong advocate of administration policies, including Pres. Thomas Jefferson's attempt to purge the federal judiciary of Federalists.

As a reward for his loyalty and as an indication of his rise in legal circles, Rodney was appointed U.S. attorney general by President Jefferson in early 1807. The president found Rodney's services valuable in the upcoming controversy regarding the embargo in 1808. When state leaders and legal minds in New England questioned the constitutionality of the embargo, Rodney wrote the opinion that Jefferson instructed federal officials to use in enforcing the measure.

With the implementation of nonintercourse under Pres. James Madison, Rodney remained on as attorney general. While still supporting the legality and constitutionality of trade restrictions, Rodney, along with Secretary of the Treasury Albert Gallatin, urged President Madison to increase the enforcement measures of those restrictions. Rodney believed that for nonintercourse to be effective, especially against the British, the number of enforcement officials would have to be increased and their power expanded in search and seizure methods. Rodney resigned his position as attorney general in December 1811 to return to private life.

During the War of 1812, Rodney continued his private practice but also spent much of his time as an officer in the Delaware militia. Commissioned a captain of artillery in 1813, he rose to the rank of major by the end of the war.

Following the war, Rodney continued his state political career, but under the presidency of James Monroe he was increasingly called upon for diplomatic service in South America. In 1818, he served as one of the envoys sent to the newly declared republics of South America to report on their status. After a brief stint in Congress, Rodney was appointed U.S. minister to Argentina in 1823. He died the following year in Buenos Aires.

—Jeanne T. Heidler and David S. Heidler

See also: Embargo Act; Jefferson, Thomas; Madison, James; Non-Intercourse Act

Further Reading

Ryden, George H. *Biographical Sketches of Caesar Rodney, Thomas Rodney, and Caesar A. Rodney.* Dover, DE: Delaware Historical Society, 1943.

ROSS, ROBERT
1766–1814
British army officer

Born at Rostrevor, County Down, Ireland, Robert Ross studied at Trinity College in Dublin before embarking on a military career. Commissioned an ensign in the 25th Foot in 1789, he rose steadily through the ranks, becoming lieutenant in the Seventh Fusiliers in 1791 and captain four years later. Army reductions forced Ross into a prolonged period on half-pay, but in 1799 he joined the 20th Foot as major. That year the regiment took part in the Duke of York's Anglo-Russian expedition in Holland. In September, Ross was severely wounded during his first engagement, a sharp action that preceded the First Battle of Bergen.

In 1801, after being brevetted lieutenant colonel for his services in Holland, Ross was ordered to Egypt, where he participated in the capture of Alexandria. He assumed command of the regiment in 1803. A strict disciplinarian, Ross drilled his men relentlessly, and his diligence paid off. The regiment played a conspicuous role in Gen. Sir John Stuart's 1806 amphibious attack on Calabria, earning for Ross a gold medal for the Battle of Maida.

Promoted to the full rank of lieutenant colonel in 1808, Ross transferred with his regiment to the Iberian Peninsula. He distinguished himself throughout Sir John Moore's retreat to Coruña and in the successful defense of that city,

Robert Ross

garnering a second gold medal. In July 1810, Ross received a brevet promotion to colonel. In 1812, after an extended period of reorganization and drill in Ireland, the regiment returned to Spain to take part in Wellington's final offensive. The following spring, Ross received command of a fusilier brigade and, in June, a promotion to major general. His brigade distinguished itself at Pamplona and at Sorauren, where Ross had two mounts shot from beneath him. In the February 1814 Battle of Orthez, Ross was seriously wounded while personally leading his men into heavy fire. This ended Ross's participation in the Peninsular War, for which he received another gold medal, the thanks of Parliament for Orthez, and the Peninsula Gold Cross.

With the situation on the peninsula well in hand, British authorities freed four brigades of "Wellington's Invincibles" for service in North America: three for duty in Canada, and one, an expeditionary force, to operate along the U.S. coast. The latter was entrusted to Ross. In June 1814, Ross embarked with his new brigade, consisting of the Fourth, 44th, and 85th Foot. At Bermuda, Ross's command was augmented by the 21st Foot and a contin-

gent of Royal Marines, bringing his total forces to 4,500. In August, the expedition, under the overall command of Vice Adm. Sir Alexander Cochrane, sailed for Chesapeake Bay to unite with Rear Adm. George Cockburn's naval squadron, which had long harassed the U.S. coastline.

The mission, ostensibly a diversion to draw attention from ongoing operations in Canada, carried the expressed goal of high-profile retaliation for U.S. outrages committed in Canada and on the frontier. After entering Chesapeake Bay unopposed, the expedition sailed up the Patuxent River in Maryland. On 19 August, Ross's command debarked at Benedict, 40 miles south of Washington. Admonished to avoid extended operations away from the support of Cochrane's ships and having no cavalry, Ross moved judiciously along the riverbank, maintaining contact with Cockburn's squadron that was sailing up the Patuxent in search of Commodore Joshua Barney's U.S. flotilla.

Meeting only light opposition, Ross reached Nottingham on 21 August 1814 and Upper Marlboro the following day. That day, Barney ordered the destruction of his flotilla and led his sailors toward the threatened capital. Cockburn, who knew the area well, left his flagship to join Ross. Aware of his orders but spurred on by Cockburn, Ross resolved to move on Washington, 25 miles distant. At Bladensburg on 24 August, Ross's advance met 6,500 U.S. militia under Gen. William Winder and 400 of Barney's sailors. Ross attacked impetuously with about 1,500 veterans, gaining a quick victory. The militia broke with little provocation, although Barney's sailors and a handful of regular troops afforded some resistance. Despite its success, Ross's brigade suffered 300 casualties. Ross himself, always at the front, had a horse shot from under him.

That evening Ross reached Washington, characteristically leading the reconnoitering party that entered the capital. He escaped injury when shots fired from a private building killed his mount. The British met no further opposition as they filed into the city, which had been hurriedly abandoned by government officials. Throughout the night and into the following day, Ross's soldiers sacked and burned the Capitol, President's House, National Archives, Supreme Court, Library of Congress, Treasury Building, and almost all other public property. They also completed the destruction of the shipyard begun by fleeing Americans. Ross issued orders to respect all private property, but the building from which the shots had been fired was torched, as were other properties from which people offered resistance. For the most part, Ross proved as good as his word. British soldiers and sailors were flogged for looting, and officers frequently intervened on behalf of citizens. Ross apparently took little pleasure in the event. The British returned to Benedict, where they reembarked on 30 August.

Cochrane, along with Ross and Cockburn, selected nearby Baltimore as the next target. On 12 September, Ross landed his force at North Point. As the warships sailed on to attack Fort McHenry, Ross began the 12-mile march to Baltimore. Ross's column, the general again in the vanguard, soon encountered U.S. resistance. Riding back to hasten his army's approach, Ross was shot from his horse. A projectile had passed through the general's right arm and entered his chest. He was found conscious on the road by his oncoming soldiers. After transferring command to Col. Arthur Brooke, Ross was placed in a cart for transport. He died before reaching the coast. Although the expedition continued briefly, it was abandoned before reaching Baltimore.

A handsome man of good humor and soldierly bearing, Ross was a popular commander. Although a strict disciplinarian, he continually shared with his men the hardships of campaigning and the dangers of battle. His loss was a severe blow to the British. Robert Ross was buried in Nova Scotia.

—David Coffey

See also: Baltimore, Battle of; Barney, Joshua; Bladensburg, Battle of; Brooke, Arthur; Cochrane, Alexander; Cockburn, George; McHenry, Fort; Patuxent River, Battles of; Upper Marlboro, Maryland; Winder, William H.

Further Reading

Elting, John. *Amateurs, to Arms! A Military History of the War of 1812*. Chapel Hill: Algonquin Books of Chapel Hill, 1991.

Lloyd, Alan. *The Scorching of Washington: The War of 1812*. Washington, DC: Robert B. Luce, 1974.

Lord, Walter. *The Dawn's Early Light*. New York: W. W. Norton, 1972.

ROYAL NAVY

See Naval Strategy, Great Britain

RUSH, RICHARD
1780–1859
U.S. comptroller of the treasury and attorney general

Born to the famous physician Benjamin Rush and Julia Stockton Rush in Philadelphia, Richard Rush entered the College of New Jersey (Princeton) at the age of 14. Following his graduation, he studied law and began his prac-

Richard Rush

tice in 1800. Perhaps because of his youth, his reputation as a lawyer and an orator was slow in developing, but as tension between the United States and Great Britain began to increase with the *Chesapeake-Leopard* Affair of 1807, he became more visible in public life.

By that year, Rush had become increasingly involved in the labyrinth that was Pennsylvania Democratic Republican politics and began also to speak on national issues, gaining him the notice of political figures such as James Madison. Rush's political star rose even higher in Pennsylvania by 1811, when he was named the state's attorney general. He held that position for only a few months; late in the year Pres. James Madison, in an attempt to gain the backing of the supporters of Gov. Simon Snyder ("Snyderites"), of which Rush was one, appointed him comptroller of the treasury. With supporters of DeWitt Clinton making a bid for Pennsylvania's electoral votes, Madison hoped to gain the support of one of the more important factions in Pennsylvania politics.

Even though he was not a member of Madison's cabinet in the early years of the War of 1812, Rush was active in government councils concerned with the war. During the summer and fall of 1812, he wrote editorials in the *National Intelligencer* defending the administration's decision to go to war and deflecting criticism of its conduct.

In early 1814, Madison had to replace Secretary of the Treasury Albert Gallatin, who had been appointed to serve on the peace commission to Europe. He offered the position to Rush, who refused because there was no national bank to stabilize the economy. Ironically, Rush had been one of the most vocal critics of a national bank when the Bank of the United States was not rechartered in 1811.

As it happened, because of the resignation of William Pinkney, Madison also needed an attorney general, and he offered that position to Rush. The young lawyer accepted the appointment. Rush's primary activity was to supervise the compilation and issuance of the *Laws of the United States*. In the cabinet, he participated in all deliberations regarding war policy and the peace negotiations getting under way in Ghent. He was the only cabinet member who did not want to abandon the demand that the Royal Navy renounce impressment as a condition of peace.

When Washington was threatened by the British invasion later in the summer, Rush remained close to President Madison in the latter's survey of the military situation, and when the president decided to evacuate the city, Rush accompanied him to Virginia. When the two returned to Washington after the British evacuation, Rush suggested to Madison that the president issue a proclamation to the American people reassuring them that the U.S. government controlled the capital and decrying the barbarity of the British actions in Washington. Rush hoped that such an address would stir the nation's patriotism, but the document Rush drafted did little to reassure the country. Later that fall, when the House of Representatives investigated the defense and fall of Washington, Rush served as the president's spokesman.

Following the war, Rush acted as secretary of state in the early months of the James Monroe administration because John Quincy Adams was still in Great Britain. He negotiated the Rush-Bagot Agreement demilitarizing much of the Great Lakes and, upon Adams's arrival in the United States, received the appointment of minister to Great Britain. He has been assessed as one of the most successful ministers the United States has sent to that country.

For the remainder of his life, he held a number of public appointments, including secretary of the treasury under John Quincy Adams and minister to France under James K. Polk. Returning to the United States in 1849, Rush retired from public life, although he was often asked for and willingly gave his opinions on the events of the day. He died at his home in Philadelphia in 1859.

—Jeanne T. Heidler and David S. Heidler

See also: Gallatin, Albert; Madison, James; Pinkney, William; Snyder, Simon
Further Reading
Powell, John H. *Richard Rush, Republican Diplomat.* Philadelphia: University of Pennsylvania Press, 1942.

RUSSELL, JONATHAN
1771–1832
Merchant; diplomat; politician

Born in Providence, Rhode Island, on 27 February 1771, Jonathan Russell studied law at Rhode Island College (now Brown University); however, rather than practice law following graduation from college in 1791, he chose to enter the world of business and Republican Party politics. Because of his skill as an orator, numerous editions of his 1800 Fourth of July speech were published, and his efforts as Republican Party leader in his native state were rewarded by his being named collector of the port of Bristol, Rhode Island, by the newly elected Republican president, Thomas Jefferson. In the 1808 election, Russell threw his support behind the presidential candidacy of James Madison and wrote a pamphlet in support of Madison's bid to succeed Jefferson.

In 1810, Madison named Russell chargé d'affaires in Paris upon the departure from France of John Armstrong, who, as U.S. minister to France, had spent six years protesting Napoleon Bonaparte's decrees against U.S. shipping. Although Armstrong had left for the United States during the summer of 1810 believing that the French government had indeed rescinded its offensive decrees with respect to U.S. shipping, Russell soon learned that French assurances of the repeal were not forthcoming. On the contrary, evidence soon revealed that Napoleon had not abandoned his Continental System but in reality had imposed a new system of regulations directed against England and the products of its colonies. President Madison, however, chose to ignore this evidence and issued a proclamation on 2 November 1810 stating that France had indeed revoked or modified her decrees and had thus ceased to tamper with the commerce of the United States. In issuing this proclamation, Madison hoped to force Great Britain into repealing its repressive Orders in Council. For Madison, the repeal of the French decrees promised an extrication from the dilemma of a shameful peace or possible war with both belligerent powers.

In November 1811, Joel Barlow arrived in Paris to replace Russell, who became chargé d'affaires in London. He took the place of U.S. minister William Pinkney, who had left London in early 1811, having failed in his efforts to force a repeal of the Orders in Council. Unsuccessful in convincing the British government of France's genuine repeal of its Berlin and Milan Decrees, Russell was pessimistic as to the United States' ability to avoid war. When war was subsequently declared by the United States in June 1812, Madison immediately sought, using Russell in London, to negotiate an armistice. He told Russell to say that if the British would repeal their Orders in Council and their practice of impressment, the Americans would agree to bar British sailors, the mainstay of Britain's war against France, from joining U.S. vessels. Ironically, unknown to President Madison and Congress, the British government had actually suspended the Orders in Council; thus one of the major U.S. conditions had already been fulfilled. On the issue of impressment, however, British Foreign Secretary Lord Castlereagh would not budge. Other conditions conveyed by Russell to Castlereagh included the dismissal of impressed seamen, spoliations, and an abandonment of paper blockades. Unable to reach agreement, Russell's correspondence with Castlereagh ended on 19 September, and the American left England. Shortly thereafter, the British government ordered general reprisals against the United States, thus shattering any illusions that an armistice would be quickly implemented.

In March 1813, following an offer by Czar Alexander I of Russia to mediate between the United States and Great Britain, President Madison, not waiting to hear if the British government had accepted, reacted favorably. In late May, the president named Secretary of the Treasury Albert Gallatin and James A. Bayard, a prominent Federalist from Delaware, to be special envoys. They were to join U.S. minister to Russia John Quincy Adams. To the list of nominees for diplomatic appointments was added the name of Jonathan Russell, Madison's designee to be minister to Sweden. However, Federalists in the Senate, most of whom had opposed the war with Great Britain, sought to embarrass the Madison administration. Russell's nomination was opposed because of the perception that he had been eager for war as chargé d'affaires in London and because of suspicions about his activities as chargé d'affaires in Paris. His nomination was subsequently referred to a select Senate committee in mid-June 1813. On 9 July, the Senate rejected Russell's nomination by a vote of 22 to 14, on the grounds that it was "inexpedient" to send a minister to Sweden.

The British government refused the Russian mediation offer, but in November 1813, Lord Castlereagh proposed to the United States that the two countries begin direct negotiations for peace. Although the Senate had previously rejected Russell's nomination to become U.S. minister to Sweden, it now reversed itself. With the British offer to negotiate directly with the Americans, Bayard and Gallatin, along with Adams, were joined by Russell and Henry Clay of Kentucky, Speaker of the House of Representatives. The Flemish town of Ghent was selected as the meeting place for the negotiations.

The U.S. peace commission comprised some of the ablest men in the United States at the time. With more than enough ego to go around, the ability of the five men to work together was seriously challenged. Historians generally assign to Russell a less significant role in the five months of negotiations that commenced on 8 August 1814 and led to the signing of the Treaty of Ghent on Christmas Eve, 1814. One of the major sticking points in the negotiations, which clearly revealed personal and political divisions between the U.S. negotiators, was Adams's willingness to agree to British navigation of the Mississippi in return for access to Newfoundland fisheries. Russell staunchly opposed this concession and tended to support the position of his close friend Henry Clay on this and other issues. Although many factors, such as impressment and a defense of neutral rights, had helped to bring about war between the two countries, in the end, the Treaty of Ghent provided for the status quo antebellum. Important for the future, however, were clauses that called for mixed arbitration commissions to resolve disputes about the northeastern boundary with British North America.

Upon concluding the signing of the Treaty of Ghent, Russell returned to his post as minister to Sweden, where he served until being recalled by Pres. James Monroe in 1818. From 1821 to 1823, he was a member of the House of Representatives from Massachusetts, where he had relocated, and became chairman of the House Committee on Foreign Affairs. He was a bitter enemy of Secretary of State John Quincy Adams, whom he blamed when he did not receive another diplomatic appointment after Sweden. Russell's personal animosity for the secretary of state was to be the former's downfall. In 1822, he sought to discredit Adams, particularly among the western supporters of Clay, by revealing that during the Ghent negotiations Adams had been willing to allow British navigation of the Mississippi in return for concessions over the fisheries. Russell, however, had resorted to altering copies of his own documents, a fraud that Adams easily exposed. Russell was discredited politically for the rest of his life. Russell died in Milton, Massachusetts, on 17 February 1832.

—Thom M. Armstrong

See also: Adams, John Quincy; Armstrong, John; Barlow, Joel;

Castlereagh, Viscount, Robert Stewart; Ghent, Treaty of; Orders in Council; Pinkney, William

Further Reading

Bemis, Samuel Flagg. *John Quincy Adams and the Foundations of American Foreign Policy.* New York: Alfred A. Knopf, 1949.

Brant, Irving. *James Madison.* Vols. 4 and 5. Indianapolis: Bobbs-Merrill, 1941, 1961.

Egan, Clifford L. *Neither Peace nor War: Franco-American Relations, 1803–1812.* Baton Rouge: Louisiana State University Press, 1983.

Engleman, Fred L. *The Peace of Christmas Eve.* New York: Harcourt, Brace, World, 1962.

S

SACKET'S HARBOR, BATTLE OF
28–29 May 1813

Shortly after Sir James Lucas Yeo and a party of 450 Royal Navy officers and seamen arrived at Kingston, Ontario, in May 1813, Gov.-Gen. Sir George Prevost, commander-in-chief in the Canadas, decided to attack Commodore Isaac Chauncey's Lake Ontario naval base at Sacket's Harbor, New York, while Chauncey was engaged in joint operations against York (Toronto) and Fort George at the western end of the lake. Prevost later informed the Duke of York that the situation in Upper Canada was becoming "extremely critical," and the movement against Sacket's Harbor was a diversion to relieve pressure on Brig. Gen. John Vincent's Fort George garrison.

There is little doubt that Yeo's arrival inspired confidence in Prevost. On 24 May, he informed Vincent at Burlington that the British squadron was ready "to dispute the ascendancy on Lake Ontario with the enemy." The squadron consisted of the new ship *Wolfe* carrying carronades, four 68-pounders, and 14 18-pounder long guns; the *Royal George* (22 guns); the brig *Moira*; and the schooners *Prince Regent* (renamed as the *General Beresford*) and *Sir Sidney Smith* (the former merchant schooner *Simcoe*). All were well manned. Yeo rightly surmised that "the possession of Upper Canada must depend on whoever can maintain the naval superiority on Lake Ontario," but he was not as confident of success in the endeavor as was Prevost. He judged Chauncey's vessels "very superior both in number and the complete way they are equipped." Chauncey had the *Madison*, which mounted 20 32-pounder carronades and six long 12-pounder guns; the brig *Oneida*, with 18 24-pounders; and 16 smaller vessels, each carrying a long 32-pounder gun. Some had four and others six carronades. Chauncey also had a large ship with 30 guns, the *General Pike*, that was being prepared for launch at Sacket's Harbor.

After a reconnaissance revealed the absence of all of Chauncey's vessels, Prevost and Yeo planned to attack Sacket's Harbor with the garrison of Kingston commanded by Col. Edward Baynes. About 900 soldiers altogether, the garrison included the Grenadier company of the 100th Regiment, a section of Royal Scots, two companies of the Eighth (King's) Regiment, four of the 104th Regiment, and two of the Voltigeurs Canadiens; they embarked aboard the squadron and 33 small boats. At 10:00 P.M. on the night of 27 May, the troops left. Two 6-pounders, their gunners, and a company of the Glengarry Light Infantry were boarded on a light schooner to be towed ahead to land the guns in time. The British hoped to reach Sacket's Harbor at daybreak on 28 May, where they intended to burn the new ship under construction on the stocks and all the public stores.

Though it was raining hard, the men were kept in the boats in the hope of landing the troops before U.S. forces could oppose them. They arrived in the vicinity of Sacket's Harbor at 1:00 A.M., but the current began to scatter them from their regular order. They had to pull for the point of daybreak debarkation: Baynes had planned to land in the cove formed by Horse Island, a wooded 24-acre island 1 mile southwest of the harbor, but he found it well defended by rifle and musketry as well as by a field piece situated in the woods. He thus sent the boats to the other side of Horse Island for disembarkation.

The fleet was prevented from nearing the fort until evening, however, because of "light and adverse winds" all day, though it captured 12 of 19 supply barges coasting down the southern shore from Oswego to Sacket's Harbor. The absence of a pilot who knew the depth of the river approaching the harbor seriously hurt their chances. So for a day, the British squadron stood off the harbor in adverse winds while U.S. militia poured into Sacket's Harbor.

Militia major general Jacob Brown watched the British vessels. The back of Sacket's Harbor was on the open lakeside. Horse Island was connected to the mainland by a sand and gravel causeway about 4 feet wide. Brown arranged his troops to face this causeway, with 500 militia in the first line and about 400 regulars arranged in a second, and steadying, line. Prior to the attack, he arranged with Lt. Wolcott Chauncey to burn U.S. vessels if the British vessels or forces were not repulsed. In addition, Brown planned a final stand near the south side of the harbor, where a redoubt called Fort Volunteer had been prepared.

British forces faced about 1,500 troops, together with some dragoons, artillery, and militia and some seamen from two schooners that had run up the river. The British landed on Horse Island under covering fire from the *Beresford,* the *Sidney Smith,* and the gunboats. Again, because of their ignorance about water depth, the large vessels did not approach to provide an adequate covering fire, so they stood offshore from noon till night headed up to a steady 4- to 5-knot breeze. Yeo believed that a bar stretched entirely across the bay and would not admit a deep-draught vessel; having no pilot, he would not venture closer. The schooners could not get up in time to support the British attack, and the U.S. resistance was so stout that the British had no time to wait for their artillery to come up. The circumstances would prove to be a fatal weakness for the attacking forces.

The daybreak disembarkation came under a destructive fire of cannon and musketry. From the woods around the harbor, riflemen picked off some of the invaders. The Grenadiers of the 100th Regiment forced the causeway in the face of a 6-pounder, rushing it between the gun's first and second discharges. The U.S. militia broke and fled through the woods. Once across the causeway, the British forces divided round a hill. Colonel Young of the Eighth (King's) Regiment took half to the left, and Maj. William Drummond of the 104th Regiment took half to the right. The left side was densely wooded and more stubbornly contested, but the British finally cleared it with the joint detachments. The defenders retreated to the blockhouse, against which the British found that their artillery had little effect. Also, the fire of their schooners and gunboats under William H. Mulcaster had helped clear the woods, but it was ineffective against the redoubts. Mulcaster thought that "the contemptible Gun Boats which alone could approach the shore, found it impossible to destroy almost impenetrable Block houses, and regular Batteries." Adverse winds and the British leaders' caution prevented the squadron from coming close enough to employ its heavy guns, and on these points would turn the fate of the battle.

Prevost judged the fire from the woods on his right flank as "heavy and destructive," but he watched as his troops incredibly persevered to capture three 6-pounders. Soon the storehouses were in flames, but Prevost observed that his supporting ships were too far offshore to pound the blockhouses or silence the U.S. elevated batteries. Houses had been set on fire in the vicinity of the fort, but the attackers could breach neither the major blockhouses nor the fort itself. The British took up a position on the crest of a small hill they had captured earlier. They loaded the brass 6-pounders they had seized, as well as four officers and 150 soldiers who had been taken prisoner. Baynes and Prevost reluctantly ordered the troops to fall back from what Baynes of the Glengarry Light Infantry described as "a beaten enemy, whom a small band of British soldiers had driven before them for upwards of three Hours, through a country abounding in strong positions of defence."

Prevost conducted a general withdrawal. Baynes calculated that the retreat was performed at leisure and in perfect order, "the Enemy not presuming to show a single soldier without the limits of his Fortress." In contrast, Major General Brown, who was defending the town, wrote that had Prevost not "retreated most *rapidly* under the guns of his vessels, he would never have returned to Kingston." Brown did not mention in his official report that his militia had fled, his forces had been driven back for three hours toward the fort, and the British artillery had not been seriously brought into play. Yet neither Baynes nor Prevost could really claim that Brown's forces were completely beaten: their guns were still firing at the British in position on the hill as they waited to reembark. Mulcaster thought the skirmish "slightly disastrous."

About one-third of the British force was killed or wounded before it got to the blockhouses and batteries defending the port. Of the naval force, only one seaman was reported killed, and one midshipman, John Johnston, and four seamen were wounded. Out of 900 engaged in the attack, the British lost 48 killed, 195 wounded, and 16 missing—casualties totaling 259 or 28 percent. Brown's forces lost 21 killed, 84 wounded, and 26 missing, for a total of 131 casualties, mostly regulars who had borne the brunt of the action, though all of his militia casualties were not known. Maj. William Swan of the Second Regiment of Infantry put them at no more than 25, for the militia had fled after the first volley. Total U.S. casualties were probably 156, or just over 10 percent, but the British also took 154 prisoners with them to Kingston, bringing the U.S. total losses to 310. The attacking force thus lost 2.5 men to every 1.5 men the defenders lost, or, counting prisoners, 2.5 to 3. The British force returned to Kingston on 30 May, landing guns and prisoners.

At Sacket's Harbor, the old schooner *Gloucester,* captured by Chauncey at York, and the *General Pike* had been set on fire, but the flames on the latter were doused as the British withdrew. When Chauncey arrived later from his attack on Fort George, he found that his vast pile of naval stores, including those captured at York, had been burned. Work on the *Pike* would be delayed three to four weeks. The loss of canvas was a serious inconvenience, and his sail makers remained idle until Chauncey could get more canvas from New York.

Arthur Sinclair, who arrived at Sacket's Harbor to take command of the *General Pike* as Chauncey's senior post-captain, later analyzed Yeo and Prevost's attack on the base. He believed the British goal was not so much to draw U.S. troops back to Sacket's Harbor from Niagara but to destroy the *General Pike*. Sinclair surmised that Prevost, unable to secure the object of tipping the naval balance, had ordered a return to Kingston, fearing that he might be trapped in the harbor if Chauncey's vessels full of troops returned from the head of the lake. Had the action been pushed for another hour, or had he taken an adequate amount of artillery, Prevost would have been able to deny Chauncey the use of the *General Pike* altogether.

The attack on Sacket's Harbor was a tactical repulse for the British, but it redefined the strategic roles of Chauncey and Yeo. It arrested Chauncey's single-minded concentration on war at the Niagara Peninsula end of the lake and required his immediate and rapid return to Sacket's Harbor. As he returned to harbor, his new opponent, whom he now knew to be Yeo, took his squadron up the lake to relieve the pressure on the British military forces that had been pressed back to Burlington, Vermont. In this he was successful. The Niagara Peninsula campaign, thus far tilted against the British by the energy of Chauncey's and Dearborn's moves at York on 27 April and Fort George on 27 May, slowly swung against the Americans for most of the remainder of the summer.

When he was offshore at Sacket's Harbor, Yeo had seen the state of preparation of the *General Pike*. As soon as he returned to Kingston after the raid, he proposed laying down a new vessel to counter the *Pike*. The naval warfare thus began to become an issue of building, and in that the British eventually succeeded in thwarting Chauncey's plans.

—*Frederick C. Drake*

See also: Baynes, Edward; Brown, Jacob J.; Chauncey, Isaac; Prevost, George; Yeo, James Lucas

Further Reading

Brown, Jacob. "Letters to Daniel B. Tompkins: Battle of Sacket's Harbor." *Boston Public Library Bulletin* 8 (1903): 72–76.

Ellison, David. "David Wingfield and Sacket's [*sic*] Harbor." *Dalhousie Review* 52 (1972): 407–413.

Hitsman, J. Mackay. *The Incredible War of 1812: A Military History*. Toronto: University of Toronto Press, 1972.

Preston, Richard A. "The First Battle of Sacket's Harbor." *Historic Kingston* 2 (1963): 3–7.

Stanley, George. *The War of 1812: Land Operations*. Ottawa: National Museums of Canada and Macmillan, 1983.

Wilcox, Orlando B. "Sacket's Harbor and the War of 1812" and "The War of 1812." *Jefferson County Historical Society Transactions* 1 (1886–1887): 23–31, 97–100.

Wilder, Patrick, *The Battle of Sacket's Harbor*. Baltimore: Nautical and Aviation Book Company, 1994.

Wood, William H. *Select British Documents of the Canadian War of 1812*. Vol. 2. Toronto: Chaplain Society, 1920–1928.

SACKET'S HARBOR, NEW YORK

Sacket's Harbor is situated on the eastern shore of Lake Ontario, on land owned before the War of 1812 by Augustus Sacket, a lake trader, revenue officer, and smuggler of potash and pearl ash to Montreal, Lower Canada. Sacket's Harbor was small but well protected and was 40 miles by water from the main British base of Kingston. A long promontory, later called Ship House or Navy Point, sloped down from a low hill to enclose Black River Bay. Opposite the spit was a low island. Between the two, the harbor could accommodate several vessels while launching others. Timber was abundant, and the bay was well suited to serve as a naval base.

Before the war, the wealthy Kingston merchant Richard Cartwright admitted, "I am very well acquainted with Mr. [Augustus] Sacket, who is an intelligent and respectable man and of a character quite foreign to that of a visionary Projector." Sacket, a collector of revenue for the Treasury Department, informed Secretary of the Treasury Albert Gallatin that he wished to resign rather than risk his life enforcing the law. Sacket's Harbor then became a haven for smuggling, and networks of new "embargo roads" sprang up as farmers took their carts and wagons toward the border. Sacket asked $5,000 for the land on which the U.S. Navy later built its war vessels. Lt. Melancthon Taylor Woolsey in 1809 recommended that if the department intended to establish a navy yard on the lake, Sacket's Harbor was the most eligible of any site for an arsenal and dockyard. Woolsey, in fact, thought Sacket's Harbor was "the only place suitable on the American side," but he believed the $5,000 Sacket had asked was $4,000 more than its value, "as it can never be of great value to an individual." The water depth of ten to 13 feet was impressive, and an eminence within 150 yards was later fortified to command the harbor and the whole bay. Woolsey's selection would become the main U.S. naval base on either ocean or lake, the site of more naval construction than anywhere else during the War of 1812. Here in 1814 was launched the *Superior*, the largest ship in the U.S. Navy.

The base was attacked on 19 July 1812 by a small Canadian Provincial Marine squadron, and on 28–29 May 1813 a British combined force of troops and ships attacked but was repulsed. Sacket's Harbor undoubtedly was the most important naval post offered to any U.S. Navy officer. The naval commander there, Commodore Isaac Chauncey, generated more letters to the secretary of the navy than any other naval officer in the war, and he ordered more ships built at Sacket's Harbor than were built in any other port or harbor in the Union from January 1812 to January 1815. The harbor also became an important army base under Gen. Jacob Brown and later James Wilkinson and George Izard, a tradition that would continue well into the twentieth century, when Sacket's Harbor was a major recruiting and training barracks for the U.S. Army until World War II.

—*Frederick C. Drake*

See also: Chauncey, Isaac; Sacket's Harbor, Battle of; Woolsey, Melancthon Taylor

Further Reading

Brown, Jacob. "Letters to Daniel B. Tompkins: Battle of Sacket's Harbor." Boston Public Library *Bulletin* 8 (1903): 72–76.

Ellison, David. "David Wingfield and Sacket's [*sic*] Harbor." *Dalhousie Review* 52 (1972): 407–413.

Hitsman, J. Mackay. *The Incredible War of 1812: A Military History.* Toronto: University of Toronto Press, 1972.

Preston, Richard A. "The First Battle of Sacket's Harbor." *Historic Kingston* 2 (1963): 3–7.

Stanley, George. *The War of 1812: Land Operations.* Ottawa: National Museums of Canada and Macmillan, 1983.

Wilcox, Orlando B. "Sacket's Harbor and the War of 1812" and "The War of 1812." *Jefferson County Historical Society Transactions* 1 (1886–1887): 23–31, 97–100.

Wilder, Patrick, *The Battle of Sacket's Harbor.* Baltimore: Nautical and Aviation Book Company, 1994.

SALABERRY, CHARLES-MICHEL D'IRUMBERRY DE

1778–1829
British army officer

The eldest son of Ignace-Michel-Louis-Antoine d'Irumberry de Salaberry and Françoise-Catherine Hertel de Saint-Françoise, Charles-Michel d'Irumberry de Salaberry was born on 19 November 1778 in Beauport, Quebec, and enlisted in 1792 in the 44th Foot. He fought with the 60th Foot in 1794 at Saint-Dominique, Guadeloupe, and Martinique. He became a captain-lieutenant in 1799 and a captain in the First Battalion in June 1803. He joined the Fifth Battalion, 60th Foot, under Col. Francis de Rottenburg in 1806 and served in Ireland in 1808. He was brigade major of de Rottenburg's light infantry brigade at Walcheren in 1809, contracted Walcheren fever, and returned to England in October. Posted to the Canadas in June 1810 as aide-de-camp to de Rottenburg, Salaberry was promoted to brevet major on 2 July 1811 and commissioned lieutenant colonel of militia, commanding the Voltigeurs Canadiens, on 1 April 1812. He was a strict, demanding officer.

On 27 November 1812, Salaberry commanded the advance guard at La Colle Mill that repulsed Henry Dearborn's northern attack. In August 1813, his Voltigeurs covered the return of the Murray-Everard raid against Plattsburg and Burlington, Vermont. In October, believing himself held back by Prevost, Salaberry contemplated leaving the army.

On 21 October 1813, Gen. Wade Hampton advanced with 3,000 men via the Châteauguay River, and Gen. James Wilkinson, with 8,000 men, moved down the St. Lawrence River from Sacket's Harbor toward Montreal. Salaberry commanded 510 Voltigeurs Canadiens, five battalions of the select embodied militia, and some sedentary militia, about 1,700 troops total. At Allen's Corners on the Châteauguay River, he stationed 250 Voltigeurs, the Canadian Fencibles, and some Indians, with about 1,400 militia under Lt. Col. Richard John MacDonnell in reserve in four even lines of entrenchments (abatis). A company of sedentary militia and some of the Third Battalion select embodied militia were sent across the river. Hampton's right flank of 1,000 troops crossed the Châteauguay and advanced toward Salaberry's position. Hampton's flank force bogged down in thickets and tangled paths, however, and after four hours of fighting, Hampton retreated. Wilkinson went into winter quarters at French Mills, New York.

Salaberry became a folk hero, and Châteauguay became a source of pride to the population of Lower Canada. On 3 March 1814, Salaberry learned that Prevost had recommended him as inspecting field officer of militia. He retained his position as lieutenant colonel of the Voltigeurs. In 1816, he received the Châteauguay medal, and in June 1817 learned he was nominated a Companion of the Order of the Bath.

In 1815, Salaberry became a justice of the peace for the district of Quebec and later Montreal, for Trois-Rivières and Saint-François in 1821, and for the district of Gaspé in 1824. In February 1819, he joined his father on the legislative council of Lower Canada. He married Marie-Anne-

Julie Hertel de Rouville, daughter of Jean-Baptiste-Melchior Hertel de Rouville, and they had four sons and three daughters. Salaberry became seigneur of Saint-Mathias, amassed a large estate, and interested himself in transportation schemes. He died in Chambly, Lower Canada, after suffering a stroke on 27 February 1829.

—*Frederick C. Drake*

See also: Châteauguay, Battle of; Hampton, Wade; La Colle Mill, Battle of

Further Reading

Carman, Francis A. "Châteauguay and De Salaberry: An Account of the Famous Campaign from De Salaberry's Own Letters." *Canadian Magazine* 42 (1913): 23–28.

Dale, Allen. "Châteauguay." *Canadian Geographic Journal* 11 (1935): 33–41.

Grenon, Hector. *Canadian Battles: De Salaberry's Victory at Châteauguay.* Ottawa: National Defence Headquarters Library, 1943.

Guitard, Michelle. "Irumberry de Salaberry, Charles-Michel D'." *Dictionary of Canadian Biography.* Vol. 6, *1821–1835.* Toronto: University of Toronto Press, 1979: 341–345.

Stanley, George. *The War of 1812: Land Operations.* Ottawa: National Museums of Canada and Macmillan, 1983.

Sulte, Benjamin. *La Bataille de Châteauguay.* Quebec: R. Renault, 1899.

Suthern, Victor. "The Battle of Châteauguay." *Canadian Historic Sites* 11 (1974): 95–150.

schooners; and one stationary ship, the *Centurion* (50 guns), with lower deck guns removed. The *Africa,* under Capt. John Bastard, was so leaky she needed a refit.

When the Admiralty combined the Halifax, Jamaica, and Leeward Islands stations into a single command in September, Sawyer was relieved of command, his ill health forcing his return to England. In April 1813, he satisfied the Admiralty about the measures he had taken on his initiative before the war and was appointed commander in chief at Cork, Western approaches. In 1815, Sawyer became Knight Commander of the Bath. On 7 July 1792, he married Maria Louisa, daughter of John Lloyd, clerk of the cheque at the Plymouth Yard, and he died at Bath on 13 November 1834.

—*Frederick C. Drake*

Further Reading

Drake, Frederick C. *The War of 1812: Naval Operations.* Hull, Quebec: Canadian Museum of Civilization, forthcoming.

Lohnes, Barry J. "British Naval Problems at Halifax during the War of 1812." *Mariner's Mirror* 59 (August 1973): 317–333.

Marshall, John. *Royal Naval Biography.* Vol. 1. London: Longman, Hurst, Rees, Orme and Brown, 1823: 337–339.

Padfield, Peter. "Criticism." *Mariner's Mirror* 59 (November 1973): 453–454.

"Sir Herbert Sawyer Obituary." *Annual Register, 1834.* London: Baldwin and Cradock, 1835: Appendix to Chronicle: 245–246.

SAWYER, HERBERT
1765–1834
British naval officer

Sir Herbert Sawyer, the eldest son of Adm. Sir Herbert Sawyer (1731?–4 June 1798), had served with his father in the American Revolution and had a distinguished career in frigates and 74s in the 1790s. He was promoted to post-captain on 3 February 1789 and rear admiral on 2 October 1807 and became second in command at Portsmouth. When promoted to vice admiral on 31 July 1810, he was posted in the HMS *Africa* (64 guns) to command the Halifax, Nova Scotia, squadron. In January 1812, Sawyer had received cautionary orders to inform his commanders to promote no acts that might further strain relations between Great Britain and the United States. Anticipating war, nonetheless, he sailed for Halifax from Bermuda on 11 June 1812. His squadron consisted of 25 older ships that included the *Africa,* five frigates; ten sloops; four brigs; four

SCOTT, HERCULES
?–1814
British army officer

Hercules Scott was appointed brevet lieutenant colonel of the 103rd Regiment of Foot on 13 August 1813, with his new rank taking effect on 4 June 1814. His regiment was stationed at Coteau-du-lac on the St. Lawrence River and fought against James Wilkinson's descent toward Montreal in November 1813. In the 1814 spring campaign, Scott's 600-strong regiment was stationed at Twenty Mile Creek in mid-July 1814 and made a forced march to join Phineas Riall's division at Lundy's Lane. Scott's arrival and participation in the night action helped to turn back Winfield Scott's and Eleazar Ripley's attacks in the late evening. The regiment lost six killed, 46 wounded, and seven missing. Scott had a horse shot from under him.

During the siege of Fort Erie in August, Scott wrote to his brother on 12 August that the siege guns were "not ad-equate to the reduction of the place." In Gordon Drummond's attack on the fort on 15 August 1814, Scott's regiment and two companies of the First Royal Scots Regiment on the left formed the third column, attacking the Douglass Battery manned by the veteran U.S. Ninth Regiment on the U.S. right flank. Scott had a premonition about his death, and he was indeed killed by a shot in the forehead. His regiment had 370 men killed, wounded, or missing; and 14 out of 18 officers present were killed or wounded. Col. J. Le Coteur recollected on 29 September 1869 that Scott was "a most amiable officer and gallant officer; indeed there were no two more heroic men [Scott and William Drummond, nephew of Sir Gordon] in our army."

—Frederick C. Drake

See also: Drummond, William; Erie, Fort; Lundy's Lane, Battle of

Further Reading

Cruikshank, Ernest A., ed. The Documentary History of the Campaign upon the Niagara Frontier in the Year 1814. Welland, Ont.: Lundy's Lane Historical Society, 1905.

Homfray, Irving, L. Officers of the British Forces in Canada during the War of 1812–15. Welland, Ont.: Welland Tribune print, 1908.

SCOTT, WINFIELD
1786–1866
U.S. officer

Winfield Scott was arguably the most accomplished soldier to serve in the U.S. Army prior to the Civil War. His experience in the War of 1812 substantially affected his development as a general officer, for the conqueror of Mexico City learned his trade on the Canadian-U.S. border. Born in Virginia, Scott practiced law until 1808, when he was commissioned a captain in the artillery. His sharp tongue earned him a court-martial conviction in 1810. Scott had stated that Brig. Gen. James Wilkinson was as guilty of treason as Aaron Burr. Partisanship was rampant in an officer corps that was not yet professionalized, and Scott's indiscretion resulted in his release from active duty for one year. Scott possessed more than his fair share of arrogance and ambition and was often too free with criticism of his superiors. On the positive side, his nat-

ural leadership abilities were combined with physical courage, indomitable will, and aggressiveness approaching recklessness, which won the confidence and respect of his officers and men.

As preparations for war began in 1812, Scott was promoted to lieutenant colonel and ordered to the Niagara Frontier. At the Battle of Queenston, Scott crossed the Niagara River after the first wave had landed and joined the mixed force of regulars and militia atop Queenston Heights. The officer in command, a militia general, turned direction of the battle over to Scott. All was confusion. Iroquois warriors allied to the British were sniping at the Americans, who were terrified that defeat would bring massacre. At 6 foot, 5 inches, and broad-shouldered, Scott was an imposing presence on the battlefield. He restored order and inspired the men to fight on. Yet, the British counterattack proved too powerful, and Scott negotiated a surrender. While waiting to be marched off into captivity, Scott was very nearly murdered by two natives who were incensed that none of the many shots fired at the U.S. leader during the battle had found their mark. Scott fought off his attackers and was assisted in time by his guards.

Scott was exchanged, and in March 1813, he was promoted to colonel of the Second Regiment of Artillery. Scott joined Maj. Gen. Henry Dearborn's army at Fort Niagara in May and helped to plan the next major operation—a joint army-navy attack on Fort George. Scott worked hand-in-hand with Oliver Hazard Perry to coordinate the assault. The routes of the landing craft were marked, as were positions for naval craft to deliver effective covering fire. On the morning of 27 May, Scott was in the lead boat of the first wave of Americans heading for shore. Behind him on Lake Ontario were over 100 small craft crammed with soldiers, and nearby stood 16 larger vessels firing countless rounds at the opposing British batteries.

Musket balls churned up the water around him as Scott landed and scurried up the 12-foot embankment. Near the top, he was challenged by a Canadian soldier with a bayonet. Losing his footing, Scott tumbled downward. He jumped to his feet, rallied his men, and attacked again. The fighting at the shoreline was desperate; the outnumbered British were determined to stop the invaders on the beaches. After several critical moments, the next wave landed, and the weight of the U.S. attack pushed back the defenders. But the battle had only begun, and the British formed a firing line on the meadow beyond the embankment. They stood their ground until nearly destroyed by the increasing number of Americans. The British commander, Brig. Gen. John Vincent, despairing of salvaging the day, ordered the fort 2 miles away abandoned. Scott, in the front of the fight, launched a pursuit. The first American to enter the fort, he personally broke a burning trail of gunpowder leading to a magazine and seized the British colors. Chasing the retreating British, he stopped only after receiving a second order to cease his pursuit. Scott's prestige soared, in contrast to the reputations of many general officers whose caution or lack of skill became evident during the remainder of 1813. During Wilkinson's abortive fall offensive, Scott fought under Jacob Brown in the army advance guard and therefore missed the decisive battle at Chrysler's Farm.

Pres. James Madison recognized Scott's potential with promotion to brigadier general in March 1814, and Scott rode into Buffalo and into U.S. military lore in the spring of that year. Scott's training program at Buffalo was hard, exacting, and exceedingly effective. Tattered uniforms falling off their backs, Scott's soldiers drilled up to ten hours each day, six days each week. When payday gave a few soldiers the means to desert, Scott respected the decision of the court-martial and carried out the executions of the few unfortunate enough to be caught. He spared a young soldier's life, but only after the lad had stood before the firing squad whose weapons were loaded with blanks. Scott enforced high standards of camp sanitation, discipline, dress, and military courtesy. His officers were delighted to serve under him because they knew their leader was a fighter and a skilled tactician.

Scott and his brigade crossed the Niagara River on 3 July 1814 and two days later accomplished a feat of arms that had eluded the U.S. army since the beginning of the war. On Chippewa Plain, Scott and his brigade soundly defeated British regulars in a battle in which neither side possessed an advantage of position or numbers. Maneuvering and firing with speed and precision, Scott's brigade demonstrated the effectiveness of his rigorous training program. The nation and the army drew immense satisfaction from Scott's victory. Twenty days later, Scott and his brigade came upon a large British force drawn up for battle along Lundy's Lane. Rather than waiting for reinforcements, he attacked the larger force. Advancing into heavy fire, Scott's men were chewed up, but not before they had captured a British general and his staff. Severely wounded, Scott had fought his last battle of this war. When Brown appeared with the rest of the U.S. army, he picked up the fight and fought the British to a standstill in a hand-to-hand brawl that lasted well into the night.

Scott's career was long and productive. He reformed infantry tactics and other aspects of army administration. His campaign in Mexico, unparalleled in U.S. military experience, demonstrated his genius as a battle captain. At the height of his fame, Scott was nominated for the presidency in 1852 but was defeated. Having devised a strategy for the Civil War based on the economic strangulation and military division of the Confederacy (known derisively in the newspapers as the Anaconda Plan), he retired from the army in 1861. Scott had served as a general officer for 47 years. He lived long enough to see the nation reunited; its winning strategy had employed the general lines of the plan he had proposed before his retirement.

—*Richard V. Barbuto*

See also: Brown, Jacob J.; Chippewa, Battle of; George, Fort; Lundy's Lane, Battle of; Queenston, Battle of; Riall, Phineas

Further Reading

Elliott, Charles W. *Winfield Scott: The Soldier and the Man.* New York: Macmillan, 1937.

Scott, Winfield. *Memoirs of Lieutenant General Scott.* 2 vols. New York: Sheldon and Company, 1864.

Smith, Arthur D. Howden. *Old Fuss and Feathers: The Life and Exploits of Winfield Scott.* New York: Greystone Press, 1937.

SECORD, LAURA INGERSOLL
1775–1868
Canadian patriot

Born in Massachusetts to Thomas Ingersoll and Sarah Whiting Ingersoll, Laura Ingersoll moved with her parents to Upper Canada as a child because of her father's business failures. The family settled near Queenston, where Laura met and married James Secord, a member of a family of Loyalists from the American Revolution who had settled in Queenston.

At the start of the War of 1812, James Secord was a sergeant of the First Lincoln Militia serving under Isaac Brock on the Niagara Frontier. At the Battle of Queenston in October 1812, Secord was seriously wounded, and word was sent back to his wife in the town. She made her way to the battlefield, and according to tradition, arrived just as some U.S. soldiers were about to kill her wounded husband. She placed herself between the Americans and her husband, but before the Americans could do anything to her or her husband, U.S. captain John Wool arrived to prevent the atrocity.

In early June 1813, during the U.S. occupation of Queenston, Secord suffered the indignity of having U.S. officers quartered in her home. One night she overheard the officers talking about a plan to surprise Lt. James Fitzgibbon's small force at Beaver Dams. By convincing the sentries outside of town that she was going to visit her sick

Laura Ingersoll Secord

brother at St. David's, Secord was able to leave town and walk the 20 miles to Fitzgibbon's position to warn him of the impending attack.

A great deal of debate still exists as to whether or not Laura Secord's warning resulted in the ambush that brought about the U.S. defeat at Beaver Dams on 24 June 1813. Some reports have Fitzgibbon learning of the impending attack from other scouts before Secord arrived. Whatever the case, a patriotic Canadian woman's walk through unknown, dangerous territory captured the imagination of the Canadian people then and now, and Laura Secord became a national heroine as a result. A monument was erected to her bravery on Queenston Heights. She died at the age of 93 in Chippawa, Ontario.

—*Jeanne T. Heidler and David S. Heidler*

See also: Beaver Dams, Battle of; Brock, Isaac; Queenston, Battle of; Wool, John Ellis

Further Reading

Ingraham, George. "The Story of Laura Secord Revisited." *Ontario History* 57 (1965): 85–97.

Moir, John. "An Early Record of Laura Secord's Walk." *Ontario History* 51 (1959): 105–108.

SEMINOLE INDIANS

By the early nineteenth century, the term "Seminole" had become the generic term to describe all Florida Indians. Most of the Indians then living in Florida were descendants of Creek Indians who had migrated from the Mississippi Territory or Georgia or recent Creek arrivals. During the War of 1812, the number of Creek immigrants increased because of the large number of refugees from the Red Stick faction of the Creek Nation.

By 1812, the Seminoles were concentrated in East Florida, primarily in the Alachua prairie, and in West Florida near Pensacola and along the Gulf Coast. Even before the outbreak of the War of 1812, the Seminoles felt the impact of the impending conflict. In the east, the Seminoles were affected in the spring of 1812, before the United States declared war on Great Britain, when a group of Georgians and U.S. citizens living in north Florida declared themselves the Patriots and began an attempt to wrest control of East Florida from the Spanish authorities there.

When the Spaniards asked for Seminole aid in the so-called Patriot War, the Indians tried to maintain neutrality in what they saw as a white man's war. Yet, the Seminole Maroons, communities of black Seminoles who lived among the Indians as either slaves or allies, found the U.S. intervention in Florida a disturbing development. The belief, probably accurate, that the white Americans would attempt to enslave the maroons convinced these black Seminoles that they should resist the U.S. invasion. The Patriots did not help their cause by threatening the Seminoles with violence rather than courting them with promises of friendship. By the middle of the summer of 1812, Seminole raiding parties began attacking U.S. positions.

At the same time that the Madison administration was distancing itself from the Patriot War, U.S. forces began attacking Seminole towns in Florida in retaliation for attacks on Patriots. In the fall of 1812, Georgia militia invaded Florida to attack Seminole towns and were soon followed by a major expedition of Tennessee militia under Col. John Williams and regulars. Invading Alachua in the winter of 1812–1813, these forces devastated Seminole food supplies and demonstrated the weakness of the Seminole position. Most eastern Seminoles left the area. The largest migration, to new towns along the Suwannee River farther west, occurred under the leadership of Chief Bowlegs. By the War of 1812, the Patriot War experience had convinced eastern Seminoles that the United States was their enemy, and they arrived in their new homes just as another group of enemies of the United States began arriving just to their west in Spanish West Florida.

During the winter of 1813–1814, the Creek War to the north encouraged Red Stick Creek migrations into Florida. With the defeat of the Red Sticks at Tohopeka (Horseshoe Bend) by Andrew Jackson on 27 March 1814, the trickle of Red Sticks became a flood. On 11 May 1814, two British ships, HMS *Orpheus* and HMS *Shelbourne*, arrived in Apalachicola Bay. Their commander, Capt. Hugh Pigot, promised aid to his Seminole friends and began unloading arms and food. When Captain Pigot departed, he left behind a party of Royal Marines under Capt. George Woodbine, which quickly established a base and rendezvous point for Seminoles up the Apalachicola River at Prospect Bluff.

Recruiting of Seminoles at Prospect Bluff was initially slow, but more Red Sticks poured in. By August, Woodbine had approximately 1,000 warriors. That month, Royal Marine major Edward Nicholls arrived to take command of this British foothold on the Gulf of Mexico. Nicholls continued to send out calls to Seminoles and slaves in the South and then moved over to Spanish Pensacola in preparation for a joint British-Seminole move against Mobile. This expedition failed in September 1814, and Nicholls and his Seminole allies moved back to Pensacola.

The British-Seminole presence in Pensacola, along with the increasingly fortified base at Prospect Bluff, convinced Maj. Gen. Andrew Jackson of the need for a U.S. expedition into Florida. While sending his Indian allies against the Seminole settlements around Prospect Bluff, Jackson took his army to Pensacola in November 1814. The movements toward Prospect Bluff never reached their destination, but Jackson succeeded in taking Pensacola. Nicholls and his Seminole allies fled back to Prospect Bluff.

Although a few Seminoles (mostly refugee Red Sticks) accompanied the British expedition against New Orleans, most remained in Florida during that campaign in order to pin down militia forces in the Southeast. With raids into Georgia, the Seminoles effectively prevented large numbers of militiamen from being dispatched to Jackson's aid in Louisiana.

Following the War of 1812, the Seminoles (especially refugee Red Sticks) to a large extent considered themselves to be still at war with the United States. This view gained a large number of converts among the Seminoles when it became apparent that the United States did not intend to honor Article IX of the Treaty of Ghent, the section requiring that the United States return Indian lands taken during the war. Major Nicholls, who remained in Florida

for several months after the arrival of the treaty, encouraged the Seminoles in the belief that they were entitled to reclaim all of the land in southern Georgia and in the Mississippi Territory that had been ceded in the Treaty of Fort Jackson, which supposedly ended the Creek War.

Nicholls wrote letters to U.S. officials, particularly Creek agent Benjamin Hawkins, urging compliance with Article IX, but to no effect. Finally frustrated in his efforts, Nicholls on his own initiative concluded a treaty of alliance between Great Britain and the Seminoles and carried his case back to London. The British government, having no desire to renew the conflict with the United States, ignored Nicholls and his treaty.

U.S. attacks on Seminole settlements during the Patriot War and the immigration of Red Stick Creeks into Florida (which made them Seminoles in the eyes of the United States) resulted in continuing hostility between the Seminoles and the United States following the War of 1812. This hostility, combined with repeated raids by U.S. citizens into Florida to steal slaves and livestock, kept the border between the United States and Spanish Florida in turmoil and led directly to the First Seminole War of 1818.

—*Jeanne T. Heidler and David S. Heidler*

See also: Creek War; Nicholls, Edward; Patriot War; Prospect Bluff, West Florida

Further Reading

Heidler, David S., and Jeanne T. Heidler. *Old Hickory's War: Andrew Jackson and the Quest for Empire.* Mechanicsburg, PA: Stackpole Books, 1996.

SEVIER, JOHN
1745–1815
Tennessee governor; congressman

John Sevier, first governor of and congressman from Tennessee, was born near New Market, Virginia, on 23 September 1745. His father, Valentine Sevier, farmed, traded, and ran a tavern. After attending school in Fredericksburg and Staunton, John, the oldest son, became a partner in his father's business. By the time the entire Sevier family moved to the Holston River valley in 1773, John was already an active land speculator and tavern keeper in his own right.

When Sevier moved to the Watauga settlement in North Carolina in 1776, his neighbors elected him delegate to the Provisional Congress of North Carolina. That same year militia Lieutenant Colonel Sevier of Washington District began making his reputation as an "Indian fighter." Adamantly opposing Great Britain in the Revolutionary War, Sevier's militiamen joined those from North Carolina and Virginia in defeating Maj. Patrick Ferguson's Tory army at King's Mountain in 1780 and in aiding Gen. Nathanael Greene in the Carolinas in 1781.

After the Revolution, the Watauga settlers formed the State of Franklin and chose Sevier as governor. As Franklin disintegrated, Sevier negotiated with Spain for aid and commercial privileges. When the separation movement failed, in 1788 the settlers elected Sevier to the North Carolina Senate. As Greene County's representative, Sevier voted in favor of ratification of the U.S. Constitution at North Carolina's convention. He was elected to represent North Carolina's western districts in the 1st U.S. Congress, where he voted for the Bank of the United States and the compromise on the national capital but opposed Hamilton's excise tax and federal assumption of state debts.

Upon creation of the Tennessee Territory, Sevier retired from Congress, and Gov. William Blount appointed Sevier to his legislative council. When Tennessee entered the Union in 1796, Sevier was elected its first governor and served until 1801. Despite Andrew Jackson's opposition and accusations of land fraud, Sevier was elected governor again in 1803. After resolving land issues with North Carolina and the federal government, Sevier again worked to acquire additional Cherokee land and to attract new immigrants. When HMS *Leopard* attacked the USS *Chesapeake* in June 1807, Governor Sevier protested this "outrage," as he had British impressments and confiscations, and placed the state's militia quota on standby in the event of war. When his last term as governor ended in 1809, Sevier was elected state senator without opposition.

With his election to the 12th Congress in 1811, Sevier became identified with national politics, but he retained a "provincial attitude." He generally supported the Democratic Republican administration when its measures coincided with the interests of his East Tennessee constituents. Holding his peers' and the president's respect, Sevier served as pallbearer for two vice presidents. He frequently dined with Speaker of the House Henry Clay as well as with Pres. James Madison. Although he served on several committees, Sevier did not play a leading role in policy making and appears not to have made any speeches. Nevertheless, he made it clear to his colleagues that in regard to Anglo-American relations, "war or submission [was] the only alternative."

As war measures came before the House, Sevier almost always voted with the War Hawks and praised highly the aggressive actions of his fellow Tennessee congressman Felix Grundy. Sevier voted against a salt tax because it would adversely affect his western constituents, but he later changed his vote to support the administration. Although he joined other western representatives to oppose the building of new frigates, Sevier voted in favor of nine other war measures, including increasing the regular army, arming merchantmen, raising new taxes, and instituting a new embargo. On 4 June 1812, Sevier joined his peers from the West and the South in voting for the declaration of war with Great Britain and ardently supported the war effort thereafter.

At the close of the 13th Congress, President Madison appointed Sevier one of three commissioners authorized to run and survey the boundary with the Creeks established by the Treaty of Fort Jackson. While he was completing this service during the summer of 1815, Sevier's constituents reelected him to Congress. On 24 September, the old Tennessee statesman died in his tent and was buried with military honors on the east bank of the Tallapoosa River near Fort Decatur in Alabama.

—*Michèle Butts*

See also: Grundy, Felix; Tennessee

Further Reading

DeWitt, John H., ed. "Journal of John Sevier." *Tennessee Historical Magazine* 5 (1919): 156–194, 232–264; and 6 (1920): 18–68.

Driver, Carl S. *John Sevier: Pioneer of the Old Southwest.* Chapel Hill: University of North Carolina Press, 1932.

Gilmore, J. R. *John Sevier as a Commonwealth-Builder.* New York: Appleton, 1894.

Hatzenbuehler, Ronald L. "The War Hawks and the Question of Congressional Leadership in 1812." *Pacific Historical Review* 45 (1976): 1–22.

Heiskel, S. G. "'Diary,' or Journal of John Sevier." *Andrew Jackson and Early Tennessee History.* Vol. 2. Nashville: Ambrose Printing, 1920.

Henderson, William A. *"Nolachucky Jack," Lecture of William A. Henderson to the Board of Trade of the City of Knoxville.* Knoxville: Press and Herald, 1873.

Horsman, Reginald. "Who Were the War Hawks?" *Indiana Magazine of History* 60 (2): 121–136.

Sevier, Cora Bales, and Nancy S. Madden. *Sevier Family History, with the Collected Letters of General John Sevier, First Governor of Tennessee, and 28 Collateral Family Lineages.* Washington, DC: Kaufman, 1961.

Sevier, George W. "General John Sevier, a Sketch by His Son." *Tennessee Historical Magazine*, 2nd ser., 1 (1930–1931): 207–214.

Temple, Oliver P. *John Sevier, Citizen, Soldier, Legislator, Governor, Statesman, 1744–1815.* Knoxville: Zi-po Press, 1910.

Turner, Francis M. *Life of General John Sevier.* New York: Neale, 1910.

Walker, William A., Jr. "Martial Sons: Tennessee Enthusiasm for the War of 1812." *Tennessee Historical Quarterly* 20, no. 2: 20–37.

Wilkie, Katherine E. *John Sevier, Son of Tennessee.* New York: Messner, 1958.

SHANNON VERSUS CHESAPEAKE

See *Chesapeake* versus *Shannon*

SHAWNEE INDIANS

By 1812 the Shawnee, an Algonquian-speaking people, were few in number. Because of their resistance to continued white westward expansion, however, they were to play a significant role in the War of 1812. One of their war chiefs, Tecumseh (1768–1813), and his brother Tenskwatawa (the Prophet) were both in the vanguard of a nativist renaissance that helped inflame Indians living on the western frontier.

Originating in the woodlands of Pennsylvania, the Shawnee had constantly been forced to migrate westward and by the eighteenth century were located in Ohio, Missouri, and along the Tallapoosa River, Alabama. By then, lacking ancestral tribal lands, their own sense of tribal identity was fractured. Consisting of many bands or village groupings, they had nonetheless forged many intertribal links: Tecumseh, for example, was half Creek. Yet because the Shawnee included the Chillicothe, Piqua, Kispoko, and Mequashak bands, the Shawnee found it hard to follow a consistent tribal policy. Not all would follow the militant stand of Tecumseh. During the American Revolution, many initially followed the neutral policy of Cornstalk, and during the War of 1812, some of the Ohio Shawnee followed a similar policy advocated by Black Hoof. Tecumseh, however, dreamed of an organized intertribal confederation, and his ideas influenced other tribes, especially the Creek Nation, whose militant group was known as the Red Sticks.

Following the French and Indian War (1756–1763), the tribes of the old Northwest underwent a religious, evangelical renaissance, a rebirth of traditional ways sparked by increasing white pressure on their lands. When Chief Logan's Shawnee wife was murdered, Shawnee resistance on the volatile frontier erupted into open war. In Lord Dunmore's War (1774), the militant Shawnee bands were defeated at Point Pleasant on the Ohio River. This defeat initially led them to follow Cornstalk's policy of neutrality during the first few years of the Revolution. His murder by Americans in Kentucky, however, made many of the Shawnee side with the British after November 1777. In a vicious frontier war, they held their own against U.S. forces under Gen. George Rogers Clark. Betrayed by their British allies at the Peace of Paris in 1783, which ceded all territory east of the Mississippi to the United States, some Shawnees under Blue Jacket continued the fight. The northwestern tribes were not defeated until 1794 at Fallen Timbers. When the Treaty of Greenville in 1795 forced them to cede most of Ohio to the United States, Tecumseh refused to accept the treaty.

Between 1795 and 1812, the tribes continued to experience a religious revivalism that advocated a return to traditional ways and a rejection of white culture. Prominent in this movement was Tenskwatawa (1775–1836), who foresaw a coming apocalyptic struggle with the United States. Increased white pressure on tribal lands, especially the Treaty of Fort Wayne in 1809 that forced the northwestern tribes to surrender 3 million acres, hardened Indian resistance. Tecumseh warned Indiana Territory governor William Henry Harrison not to occupy this land. While Tecumseh was in the South attempting to create a pan-Indian confederacy with the Creeks, Chickasaws, and Choctaws, Governor Harrison attacked the militant Shawnee and their followers at Prophet's Town. In a confrontation known as the Battle of Tippecanoe (7 November 1811), Harrison scattered the militants and discovered British-made arms in their settlement. This further inflamed U.S. public opinion and convinced many westerners that war against Britain was inevitable.

Forced by necessity to ally with the British, the militant Shawnee helped Maj. Gen. Isaac Brock capture Detroit in August 1812. Although some Shawnee were partially responsible for the massacre at the River Raisin in January 1813, Tecumseh himself was not present. He did, however, take part in the unsuccessful siege of Fort Meigs in May 1813 and was vocal in the opposition against a planned British retreat to Toronto. It was during this retreat that the Anglo-Indian force under Col. Henry Procter was pursued and caught by Gen. William Henry Harrison. At the Battle of the Thames on 5 October 1813, the British ran while the Shawnee and their militant allies initially stood their ground. Yet when Tecumseh was slain, it broke their spirit, and they also ran from the field. Five months later, Gen. Andrew Jackson defeated the militant Red Stick Creeks at Horseshoe Bend in Mississippi Territory on 27 March 1814. This U.S. victory effectively ended organized Indian resistance east of the Mississippi during the War of 1812.

Some militant Shawnee followed Tenskwatawa into

exile outside Toronto, while the neutral bands remained in Ohio under Black Hoof. In 1817, the Treaty of Miami Rapids severely reduced the Ohio Shawnee holdings to land around the village of Wapakoneta. In 1826, Tenskwatawa returned to Ohio and followed a policy of accommodation, leading some of the Shawnee to the Kansas River valley. Black Hoof, it seems, also went through a change of heart, rediscovering some of the militancy of his youth. Throughout the 1820s and early 1830s, he resisted U.S. attempts to relocate his people west of the Mississippi. Against Black Hoof's wishes, but with Tenskwatawa's blessings, the surviving Shawnee began a poorly provisioned trek to the Kansas River. Some would survive the trip and would later continue to oppose white expansion.

—*Rory T. Cornish*

See also: Prophet's Town; Red Sticks; Tecumseh; Tenskwatawa; Tippecanoe, Battle of

Further Reading

Dowd, Gregory Evans. *A Spirited Resistance: The North American Indian Struggle for Unity. 1745–1815*. Baltimore: Johns Hopkins University Press, 1992.

Edmunds, R. David. *Tecumseh and the Quest for Indian Leadership*. Boston: Little, Brown, 1984.

SHEAFFE, ROGER HALE
1763–1851
British officer

Born on 15 July 1763, Sir Roger Hale Sheaffe was the third son of William Sheaffe, a Bostonian deputy collector of customs, and Susannah Child. Sheaffe became a protégé of the Duke of Northumberland during the American Revolution when Northumberland, colonel of the Fifth Foot, purchased a commission for Sheaffe as an ensign in the regiment in May 1778.

Sheaffe served in Ireland for six years and, after July 1787, in Quebec. He was at Montreal in 1788, Detroit in 1790–1792, and Fort Niagara until 1796. He was promoted to captain in May 1795. Returning to England in September 1787, he purchased a majority in the 81st Foot in December. In March 1798, he became a junior lieutenant colonel in the 49th Foot, with Isaac Brock as the senior lieutenant colonel. Sheaffe served in Holland in 1799, in the Baltic campaign in 1801, and in Upper Canada during the summer of 1802. There he was with Isaac Brock and the 49th at York and Fort George, where he earned a reputation for harsh discipline and Brock's censure.

In 1808, Sheaffe was promoted to brevet colonel and in 1811, to major general. In July 1812, Sir George Prevost appointed him to the army staff in the Upper Provinces, which again placed him under Brock's command. He took command at Fort George on 18 August because Brock had departed to assail William Hull at Detroit. After Brock's triumphant return, U.S. general Stephen Van Rensselaer attacked Queenston on 13 October. Brock was killed attempting to recapture the redan battery on the heights. Sheaffe brought reinforcements from Fort George in the afternoon, performed a brilliant flanking movement, joined troops from Chippewa as well as Indian allies, and won a decisive victory, capturing 900 prisoners. He received a baronetcy for Queenston Heights, a battle popularly associated with Brock.

Sheaffe succeeded Brock as military commander and on 20 October as president and civil administrator of Upper Canada. He transferred his headquarters to York and wrestled with inefficient army departments. On the Niagara Frontier, his forces near Fort Erie repulsed Brig. Gen. Alexander Smyth's futile attempt to invade Canada on 28 November. During 1812–1813, Sheaffe was concerned over ensuring naval supremacy on the lakes and proposed that additional vessels be fitted out at Kingston, York, and Amherstburg. In early winter 1813, he fell ill, and Prevost ordered Brig. Gen. John Vincent to Fort George. Sheaffe opened the Upper Canadian legislature on 25 February 1813 and prorogued it on 13 March 1813. His assembly recognized Army Bills as legal tender in Upper Canada, authorized him to prohibit the export or distillation of grain, and compensated disabled militiamen and widows and children of those killed in action. An $18 bounty for joining the army was offered, and the militia was reorganized.

When Henry Dearborn and Isaac Chauncey attacked York with 3,000 troops and 13 war vessels on 26–27 April 1813, they drove Sheaffe's 600 regulars and as many militia out of York. When the fort's magazine exploded, Gen. Zebulon Pike and 250 of his troops were killed. Sheaffe retreated to Kingston. From a strategic point of view, he saved his force, but he had surrendered the town, and for that he was heavily criticized by leading political figures, including the powerful Rev. John Strachan.

During fighting in the Niagara Peninsula in June, Prevost authorized Sheaffe to impose martial law if necessary, but Sheaffe declined, arguing that he did not possess constitutional powers. After the U.S. retreat to Fort George from Stoney Creek, Upper Canada, on 6 June, Prevost removed Sheaffe and replaced him with Maj. Gen. Francis de Rottenburg. Prevost informed Earl Bathurst, Secretary of

State for War and the Colonies, that Sheaffe had lost the confidence of the Province. Yet, William Dummer, a member of the provincial legislature, considered that Sheaffe had been "sacrificed to Ignorance and Jealousy." When Sheaffe commanded the reserve troops in the Montreal District, Prevost criticized him for indifference in discharging duties and not informing Prevost of his plans. Orders to recall him were sent from England in August 1813, and he left in November.

He was appointed to the army staff on 25 March 1814. After the war, Sheaffe and his family lived in Penzance and then Worcester, and, in 1817, moved to Edinburgh. He was later recalled and promoted to lieutenant general in 1821. He became colonel of the 36th Foot in 1829 and was promoted to general in 1838. His two sons and four daughters born to Margaret Coffin, whom Sheaffe had married on 29 January 1810, all died before him. He died in Edinburgh on 17 July 1851.

A competent professional, Sheaffe fell afoul of Sir George Prevost even when successfully applying Prevost's defensive strategy.

—*Frederick C. Drake*

See also: Queenston, Battle of; Strachan, John
Further Reading

Boase, George Clement. "Sir Roger Hale Sheaffe." *Dictionary of National Biography*. Vol. 17. London: Oxford University Press, 1937–1938: 1393.

Severance, Frank H. "Documents Relating to the War of 1812: The Letter-Book of Gen. Sir Roger Hale Sheaffe." *Buffalo Historical Society Publications* 17 (1913): 271–381.

Stacey, Charles P. *The Battle of Little York*. Toronto: Historical Board, 1963.

Stanley, George. *The War of 1812: Land Operations*. Ottawa: National Museums of Canada and Macmillan, 1983.

Weekes, W. M. "The War of 1812: Civil Authority and Martial Law in Upper Canada." *Ontario History* 48 (1956): 147–161.

Whitfield, Carol. "The Battle of Queenston Heights." *Canadian Historic Sites: Occasional Papers in Archaeology and History* 11 (1975): 10–59.

Whitfield, Carol M., and Wesley B. Turner. "Sir Roger Hale Sheaffe." *Dictionary of Canadian Biography*. Vol. 8, *1851–1860*. Toronto: University of Toronto Press, 1979: 793–796.

Wood, William H. *Select British Documents of the Canadian War of 1812*. 3 vols. in 4. Toronto: Chaplain Society, 1920–1928.

SHELBY, ISAAC
1750–1826
Governor of Kentucky

Born near North Mountain in present-day Washington County, Maryland, on 11 December 1750, Isaac Shelby received a limited education before the family moved to the Holston River area about 1772. His military career began with the Point Pleasant campaign of 1774. By 1775, he was surveying land in Kentucky for himself and others. Active in the Revolutionary War, he earned fame for his participation in the 1780–1781 southern campaigns, particularly for his role at the Battle of King's Mountain on 7 October 1781. Shelby served in the North Carolina legislature before moving to Kentucky in 1783. On 19 April 1783, he married Susannah Hart, with whom he had 11 children. Active in a variety of public and private enterprises, he helped achieve statehood for Kentucky and in 1792 was elected the state's first governor. In 1796, he retired to a comfortable private life.

The probability of war with Great Britain led to a public demand that he resume state leadership, and in 1812 he won an easy election. Winning the war in the West was his major concern, and consequently he paid little attention to domestic concerns. The state's militia law was revised to make men between the ages of 18 and 45 subject to military duty, and Shelby worked to secure the northwestern command for William Henry Harrison, in whom he had confidence and with whom he worked harmoniously. The disastrous defeat at the River Raisin on 22 January 1813, Shelby wrote Harrison, "has filled the state with mourning," but it induced Shelby to take command of the force raised in Kentucky. He wanted 10,000 to 15,000 men instead of the "half-way measures" that had produced defeat, and he pushed the organization and dispatch of troops, notably the mounted regiment commanded by Richard M. Johnson. On 20 July 1813, Harrison asked Shelby to help restore "complete tranquility" to the frontier. Although Shelby's command would be nominal, "I have such confidence in your wisdom," Harrison cajoled, "that you in fact would 'be the guiding Head and I the hand.'"

Shelby led some 3,500 mounted volunteers to Harrison's aid, although uncertainties about pay led to some decline in the initial martial ardor. At the Battle of the Thames on 5 October 1813, Shelby directed reinforcements to back Richard M. Johnson's attack against the British and Indian positions. In little over an hour, Tecumseh was killed, the Indians were dispersed, Gen. Henry

Procter was in flight, and over 600 of his soldiers were prisoners. With British resistance broken, the U.S. army withdrew to U.S. soil. Shelby returned to Kentucky, and by 4 November 1813, the Kentucky volunteers were discharged. In 1818, Congress awarded Shelby a gold medal for his services. In 1814, Harrison asked Shelby to negotiate peace settlements with the Indian tribes in the Northwest Territory. He refused because the state constitution forbade his holding an "office of trust or profit of the United States" while serving the commonwealth.

Shelby followed closely the course of the war on other fronts. He was especially concerned over the lack of success elsewhere and the opposition of New England Federalists to the war. "We are literally a house divided against itself," Shelby complained, and he admitted privately that perhaps peace should be negotiated. Like most Kentuckians, the governor believed that the state had fulfilled her major contribution, and Kentucky's war effort consequently slackened. In 1814, Shelby declared that 1,000 militiamen requested at Detroit would not be allowed to leave the state until the War Department promised to pay them.

Difficulties were encountered that fall when troops were requested for New Orleans. Shelby described most of those who went as being "composed by drafts and substitutes from amongst the poorer kind of citizens," and they were without adequate equipment, including rifles. Shelby asked the General Assembly to provide 10,000 militiamen for service in Louisiana, but this proposal was abandoned when news came of the New Orleans victory and the successful peace negotiations at Ghent.

When he left office in 1816, Shelby returned to his "Traveller's Rest" home, where he died on 18 July 1826. Active in public service, he joined Andrew Jackson in 1818 to negotiate with the Chickasaw Indians for a tract of land west of the Tennessee River. Solid, dependable, possessed of good judgment of both men and issues, Isaac Shelby was to Kentucky much of what George Washington was to the new nation.

—*Lowell H. Harrison*

See also: Harrison, William Henry; Johnson, Richard Mentor; Kentucky; Thames, Battle of the

Further Reading

Beasley, Paul W. "The Life and Times of Isaac Shelby, 1750–1826." Ph.D. dissertation, University of Kentucky, 1968.

McAfee, Robert Breckinridge. *History of the Late Wars in the Western Country.* Lexington, KY: Worsley, Smith, 1816.

Wrobel, Sylvia, and George Grider. *Isaac Shelby: Kentucky's First Governor and Hero of Three Wars.* Danville, KY: Cumberland Press, 1974.

SHERBROOKE, JOHN COAPE
1764–1830
British army officer

Sir John Coape Sherbrooke was a very experienced soldier-administrator. He became an ensign in the Fourth Regiment of Foot on 7 December 1780, a lieutenant on 22 December 1781, and captain of the 85th Foot in March 1783. When this regiment disbanded, Sherbrooke obtained a captaincy in the 33rd Foot, at Sydney, Cape Breton island, where he served from 1784 to 1786. War with France in 1793 brought promotion to major (30 September 1793) and lieutenant colonel (24 May 1794). He fought at Ostend, Flanders, and then in India, at Calcutta in April 1796, in the Mysore War of 1799, and in the siege of Seringapatam. Ill health required his return to England in January 1800, and in July 1803 he commanded the Fourth Battalion of Reserve at Norman Cross in Cambridgeshire.

After promotion to major general on 5 January 1805, Sherbrooke commanded the Sicilia Regiment from February 1807 to June 1808. A fellow officer, Henry Bunbury, thus characterized Sherbrooke: "A short, square, hardy little man... hot as a pepper, and rough in language, but with a warm heart and generous feelings, true, straight forward, giving vent to his detestation with boiling eagerness." In the early Peninsular campaign, he was second in command to the Duke of Wellington, who labeled him "a very good officer, but the most passionate man I think I ever knew." He fought at Oporto and Talavera and received the KCB in September 1809. In May 1810, he returned to England.

On 4 June 1811, he became a lieutenant general and lieutenant governor of Nova Scotia, with a commission taking effect on 19 August 1811. He married Katherine Pyndar on 24 August 1811 and brought her and her sister to Halifax, arriving on 16 October. He served five years as governor and commanded the British army forces in the Atlantic provinces. He ordered the restoration of the Citadel, the main fortifications in Halifax, and the Point Pleasant Martello Tower. Four other martellos were built at Fort Clarence, Georges Island, Maugher Beach, and York Redoubt during the war. In February 1812, he called for a respectable defense force of militia.

When news of war was confirmed on 27 June, Sherbrooke informed London and Sir George Prevost at Quebec. On 3 July, he proclaimed that war on defenseless citizens would serve no good purpose and urged his people not to molest Americans, their goods, and unarmed coasting vessels, or the property and persons of U.S. inhabitants living close to the provinces' borders, as long as they abstained from molesting Canadians. Sherbrooke established blockhouses and batteries in a dozen Nova Scotia outports, ordered guns mounted on sloops in harbors, and took steps to raise small militia detachments to resist landings from U.S. privateers, but no one could have protected the isolated coast from random privateer landings. Sherbrooke issued licenses to Nova Scotia privateers, who captured over 200 vessels during the war.

After October 1812, the British government authorized Sherbrooke to countersign trading licenses. Under Sherbrooke's proclamation of quasi-neutrality, Halifax and Saint John and Saint Andrew, New Brunswick, became prosperous, and their merchants welcomed the navy's presence. Halifax also became a replenishment center to provision armed forces along the St. Lawrence River.

In 1814, Sherbrooke was ordered to attack the coast of Maine. Thomaston and St. George west of Penobscot Bay were captured, along with four vessels in the river. On 11 July, Eastport and the Passamaquoddy Islands were raided. Fort Sullivan was captured and renamed Fort Sherbrooke, and Stonington was bombarded on 11–12 August. Sherbrooke planned the Penobscot expedition. Maj. Gen. Gerard Gosselin, with the 29th, 62nd, and 98th Regiments, sailed with Rear Adm. Edward Griffith, 11 war vessels, and ten transports carrying 2,500 troops to attack Castine on 1 September. Belfast, Bucksport, Frankfort, and Hampden fell. The U.S. frigate *John Adams*, trapped upstream, was attacked; her captain, Charles Morris, burned her. After taking Bangor and Castine, the expedition returned. A secondary force occupied Machias, 77 miles to the east, after a tedious night march. On 18 September, the expedition returned to Halifax. Castine was occupied for eight months.

On 10 April 1816, Sherbrooke was commissioned governor in chief of British North America and left Halifax on 27 June. He arrived in Quebec on 12 July, replacing Sir George Prevost, who had been recalled to England for court-martial. Sherbrooke worked well with Bishop Joseph-Octave Plessis and appointed him to the Council in 1818. He resolved problems with the assembly, which voted his civil list. In 1817, Sherbrooke became ill and wanted to resign. Then on 6 February 1818, he suffered a severe stroke and resigned immediately, leaving for England in August. He died in Calverton, Nottinghamshire, on 14 February 1830.

—*Frederick C. Drake*

See also: Castine, Maine; Griffith, Edward; Halifax, Nova Scotia; Hampden, Maine; Maine, District of; Morris, Charles; Stonington, Connecticut, Bombardment of

Further Reading

Burroughs, Peter. "Sir John Coape Sherbrooke." *Dictionary of Canadian Biography*. Vol. 6, *1821–1830*. Toronto: University of Toronto Press, 1979: 712–716.

Copp, Walter Ronald. "Military Activities in Nova Scotia during the War of 1812." *Collections of the Nova Scotia Historical Society* 24 (1938): 57–58, 74.

———. "Nova Scotian Trade during the War of 1812." *Canadian Historical Review* 18 (1937): 141–155.

Gentleman's Magazine, January-June 1830, 558–559.

Harvey, D. C. "The Halifax-Castine Expedition." *Dalhousie Review* 18 (1938–1939): 207–213.

Lloyd, Ernest Marsh. "Sir John Coape Sherbrooke." *Dictionary of National Biography*. Vol. 17. London: Oxford University Press, 1937–1938: 70–71.

Martin, A. P. *Life and Letters of the Right Honorable Robert Lowe, Viscount Sherbrooke . . . with a Memoir of Sir John Coape Sherbrooke*. 2 vols. London: Longmans, Green, 1893.

Stanley, George. "The Castine Expedition." In *The War of 1812: Land Operations*. Ottawa: National Museums of Canada and Macmillan, 1983: 357–378.

Sutherland, David. "Halifax Merchants and the Pursuit of Development, 1783–1850." *Canadian Historical Review* 59 (1978): 1–17.

SHIP TYPES

Ship of the Line (Line of Battle Ship)

A ship of the line was a two- to four-decked, three-masted, square-rigged (each mast with crossyards) ship that carried 64 to 120 guns. It was rated according to the number of guns in its main battery (first-rate ships carried 100 guns or more). Ships of the line formed the main battle line. The three-decked first- and second-rate ships were dull sailors. The main ship of the Royal Navy in 1812 was the 74-gun ship. Lighter guns were carried on the upper decks; heavier ones on lower decks. The U.S. Navy had no ships of the line in active service during the war. Independence, the first of three ships of the line authorized by Congress in January 1813, was not launched until June 1814 and was commissioned in July 1815. Ships of the line being built on the Great Lakes were not completed by war's end.

Frigate

Frigates were two-decked, square-rigged ships. Heavier guns were below; lighter ones above. Large frigates carried 40 to 50 guns, and small ones, 26 to 38. Frigates performed scouting for fleet (reconnaissance) or detached service and were not part of the line of battle in a fleet action.

Brig

Brigs were comparable in armament to medium sloops. In the War of 1812, brigs were principally armed with the carronade. Examples of brigs and their armaments in the U.S. Navy during the war were the *Syren* (rated at 16) with 18 guns, 16 24-pounder carronades, and two long 12-pounders; the *Vixen* (a 14) with 16 18-pounder carronades; and the *Enterprise* (a 12) with 14 18-pounder carronades and two long 9-pounders.

The *Hornet* was an example of a large ship-rigged sloop, armed in 1813 with two long 12-pounders and 18 32-pounder carronades.

Sloop of War

A sloop was a single-masted vessel, generally carrying two sails. Sloops of war were any vessels with their guns on a single deck, usually the upper, uncovered (or weather) one. Sometimes guns were also mounted on the quarterdeck. The sailing rig might be that of a schooner (fore-and-aft sails on two masts) or the brig (square sails on two masts). The usual practice was to carry less sail on the foremast than on the main; the mainsail was extended by a gaff above and a boom below.

Sloops were usually commanded by a master commandant (U.S. Navy) or commander (Royal Navy). Ship-sloops (sometimes referred to as corvettes) were commanded by a junior captain.

Small sloops carried ten to 16 guns, and large sloops might have 18 to 24 guns.

The schooners *Hamilton* and *Scourge* are examples of smaller sloops. The two vessels went down in a sudden squall early in the morning of 3 August 1813 on Lake Ontario. They have been located in an excellent state of preservation, and plans are underway to raise and display them in a museum at Hamilton, Ontario. The *Hamilton* was 75 feet long and armed with eight 18-pounder carronades and a 32-pounder cannon on a swivel mount. The 60-foot-long *Scourge* had ten 6-pounder cannon.

Brigantine

Brigantines were two-masted vessels. They had square rigs to topgallants on the foremast, but were fore-and-aft rigged on the mainmast with a top mast; they were full-rigged ships (square sails on three masts).

Schooner

A schooner was a small watercraft employed on lakes, rivers, and coastal waters for dispatch and supply. It was fore-and-aft rigged on two masts. Some armed schooners were large, with eight to 14 guns.

Bomb Ketch

These specially designed vessels were known in England as bomb ketches, bomb brigs, bombards, or simply as bombs. A ketch was a two-masted, square-rigged vessel. The mainmast was nearly amidships and had a course-and-square topsail and a topgallant as well as a gaff sail. On the mizzenmast were the square sails of a ship and also a spanker. In general appearance, the ketch looked like a ship that was missing the foremast. This left the forward portion of the ketch essentially clear for the mortar(s). In both the British and the U.S. navies, they were given the names of volcanoes (such as Hecla or Etna) or names that were expressive of their might (such as Thunder or Infernal). There were four bomb ketches in the U.S. Navy in 1812, the *Etna, Spitfire, Vengeance,* and *Vesuvius*.

—*Spencer C. Tucker*

See also: Cannon, Naval; Frigate, Evolution of the; Naval Ordnance; Rates; Rigs

SHUBRICK, JOHN TEMPLER
1788–1815
U.S. Navy officer

Born in South Carolina to Thomas Shubrick and Mary Branford Shubrick, John Templer Shubrick was educated in Charleston and at Harvard College before beginning the study of law. He decided in 1806 upon a naval career, however, and received a commission as a midshipman. Assigned to the USS *Chesapeake,* Shubrick was aboard when that ship was attacked and boarded by HMS *Leopard* on 22 June 1807.

Before the outbreak of the War of 1812, Shubrick served aboard a variety of vessels and gained promotion to lieutenant one month before the declaration of war in June 1812. At the start of the conflict, he served aboard the *Constitution* under Capt. Isaac Hull. Present at both Hull's escape from an entire British squadron in July and then at the *Constitution's* victory over the *Guerrière,* Shubrick commanded a battery of guns in the latter engagement and gained the commendation of his captain for both his coolness under fire and his courage during the ferocious hand-to-hand fighting to which the desperate British had resorted.

Shubrick continued to serve aboard the *Constitution* until the end of the year and consequently fought under

Capt. William Bainbridge when the *Constitution* defeated HMS *Java* on 29 December 1812. Shortly after this engagement, Shubrick transferred to USS *Hornet*, commanded by James Lawrence. On 24 February 1813, after the *Hornet* had disabled HMS *Peacock*, Lawrence sent Shubrick aboard the British ship to determine damages. Shubrick reported that the *Peacock* was not salvageable, and Lawrence ordered it evacuated.

In port at Norfolk, Virginia, in June 1813, Shubrick participated in the defense of Norfolk when that city was attacked on 22 June 1813. In one of the preliminary naval engagements on 20 June, Shubrick commanded one of the U.S. gunboats that inflicted heavy damage on some of the British ships.

Before the end of the war, Shubrick served aboard the USS *United States*, USS *Constellation*, the *Constitution* again, and finally under Stephen Decatur aboard USS *President*. He was among the captured when that ship fell to a British squadron on 15 January 1815.

Following the war, Shubrick continued to serve under Decatur aboard the new USS *Guerrière* in the brief conflict with Algiers in June 1815. While in the Mediterranean in the summer of 1815, he received his first command, but his ship, the *Epervier*, went down with all aboard in the Atlantic on the way back to the United States.

—*Jeanne T. Heidler and David S. Heidler*

See also: Bainbridge, William; *Constitution* versus *Guerrière*; *Constitution* versus *Java*; Decatur, Stephen, Jr.; *Hornet* versus *Peacock*; Hull, Isaac
Further Reading
Cooper, James F. "John Temple Shubrick." In *Lives of Distinguished American Naval Officers*. 2 volumes. Philadelphia: Carey, Hart, 1846.

SMITH, JOHN COTTON
1765–1845
Governor of Connecticut

Born in Connecticut to the Reverend Cotton Mather Smith and Temperance Worthington Gale Smith, John Cotton Smith attended Yale College during the Revolutionary War and after graduation studied and entered the profession of law. During the 1790s, Smith became involved in Federalist politics in Connecticut, entering the state legislature in 1793. In 1800, he was elected to the U.S. House of Representatives and served almost three

terms there before resigning in 1806. He returned briefly to the state legislature before becoming lieutenant governor in 1811. He occupied that position when Gov. Roger Griswold died in 1812 and therefore became acting governor until he was elected in his own right the following year.

Like Griswold, Smith had opposed the United States' entry into the War of 1812, and like his fellow governors in Rhode Island and Massachusetts, he refused to allow Connecticut militia to serve under federal officers during the conflict. This stand became particularly awkward in the spring of 1813 when Stephen Decatur's squadron was blockaded in New London harbor, and the British threatened to land forces there to destroy the U.S. ships.

As the threat materialized, Smith called out the militia. To prevent them from falling under the authority of Brig. Gen. Henry Burbeck, the regular officer in New London, Smith ordered Connecticut militia major general William Williams to New London. At first, Burbeck complained little of serving under a militia officer, but by early 1814, he began to chafe under what he viewed as amateurish officership. He was transferred in May 1814.

Burbeck was replaced by Col. Jacob Kingsbury, who was sent to New London perhaps because he was a Connecticut Federalist and hence was expected to soothe feelings. As the threat to New London intensified again in the summer of 1814, Brig. Gen. Thomas Cushing was sent to replace Kingsbury. When Cushing persuaded the local militia officers to serve at his orders, Smith, sensing a betrayal of his principles, dispatched Connecticut militia Maj. Gen. Augustine Taylor to wrest command from Cushing. Cushing responded to this move by mustering the militia forces at New London out of federal service, hence leaving their upkeep to the state.

Cushing's move greatly distressed a state already convinced that the war had unduly hurt its economy. Smith, in an address to the legislature in October 1814, condemned the federal government for abandoning the defense of Connecticut. His remarks did much to convince the legislature to vote overwhelmingly to send delegates to the Hartford Convention. To the end of his life, Smith defended the actions of this body as appropriate, given the circumstances of the time.

Following the war, Smith remained as governor until 1817, when he was defeated for reelection. Following this election, he retired from political life.

—*Jeanne T. Heidler and David S. Heidler*

See also: Burbeck, Henry; Decatur, Stephen, Jr.; Hartford Convention; Kingsbury, Jacob; New London, Connecticut

Further Reading
"John Cotton Smith Papers." *Connecticut Historical Society Collections* 5 (1948–1954).

SMITH, JOSEPH
1790–1877
U.S. Navy officer

Born to Albert Smith, a shipbuilder, and Anne Eells Smith in Massachusetts, Joseph Smith grew up around ships. He developed a love of the sea that compelled him to seek a midshipman's commission in 1809. Before the outbreak of the War of 1812, he served aboard the USS *Chesapeake.*

Early in the war, he was detailed to Lake Champlain, where he served for the duration of the conflict. During the summer of 1813, he was promoted to lieutenant and began his service aboard the USS *Eagle,* commanded by Robert Henley. Smith aided his captain in preparing the ship for action and, during the Battle of Lake Champlain in September 1814, maneuvered the ship into position to effect the most damage to enemy ships. In spite of having sustained a severe wound early in the battle, he insisted on remaining on deck until the end of the battle. He was commended for his heroism and awarded a silver medal by Congress.

Following the war, Smith served aboard the USS *Constellation* during the brief war with Algiers in the spring and summer of 1815. Later in the decade he served aboard the USS *Guerrière* in the Mediterranean and, during the 1820s, aboard the same ship in the Pacific. In 1827, Smith attained the rank of commander and a decade later was promoted to captain. After commanding the Mediterranean squadron from 1843 to 1845, Smith returned to the United States, where he served for over 20 years as the chief of the Bureau of Navy Yards and Docks. After retirement, Smith remained in Washington, D.C., where he died in 1877.

—*Jeanne T. Heidler and David S. Heidler*

See also: Lake Champlain, Battle of

Further Reading
Forester, Cecil S. *The Age of Fighting Sail: The Story of the Naval War of 1812.* New York: Doubleday, 1966.
Washburn, H. C. "The Battle of Lake Champlain." *United States Naval Institute Proceedings* 40 (1914): 1365–1386.

SMITH, SAMUEL
1752–1839
U.S. congressman;
Maryland militia general

Samuel Smith, though perhaps more influential as a merchant and legislator, has become most famous for his resolute defense of the city of Baltimore in the War of 1812. Born in 1752 into a family of merchants, Smith was soon introduced to commerce. During the Revolutionary War, he served as an officer in the First Maryland Regiment of the Continental Army, participating in most of the campaigns of 1776–1778. After his resignation in 1779, Smith returned to the Maryland militia, where he commanded the Baltimore brigade and in which he was commissioned a general.

Smith also returned to commerce, assuming control of the family firm in 1784. He was on his way to becoming one of the richest men in Baltimore when he entered national politics in 1792, winning election to the House of Representatives. In Congress, Smith became associated with the Jeffersonians. After the Republicans swept into power in 1800, Thomas Jefferson offered Smith the secretaryship of the Navy, which Smith declined (though he did serve temporarily). In 1802, the Maryland legislature elected him to the Senate.

Initially a strong Jefferson supporter, Smith increasingly disagreed with the administration, primarily over maritime issues. Smith's relationship with Jefferson's successor, James Madison, was even less amiable; Smith antagonized Madison by opposing the president's choice of Albert Gallatin for secretary of state. Smith became one of the leading members of the "Invisibles," a term coined to describe a clique of Republican opponents of the Madison administration. In the congressional session of 1811–1812, Smith voted for most war measures asked for by Madison, primarily those to increase coastal defenses and the size of the navy. Smith argued for declaring war on both Great Britain and France but voted in support of Madison's declaration of war.

Once war began, Smith had military as well as legislative duties, inasmuch as he still commanded the militia of Baltimore. He began repairs on Fort McHenry, instituted regular militia drills, and built fortifications. British Adm. Sir George Cockburn blockaded Chesapeake Bay in early 1813, giving increasing importance to Smith's defensive preparations. Smith established a system of coast watchers and scouts and began a successful search for large cannon.

Samuel Smith

At the same time, the Royal Navy attempted to bombard Fort McHenry, which, if silenced, would allow the British to destroy Smith's line at Hampstead Hill. Cochrane bombarded the fort throughout 13 September, but the fort and its covering forts (Covington and Babcock) proved too strong. The following day, Cochrane rejoined the troop transports holding the unsuccessful British army and left for the West Indies. Although bravery and initiative in the defense of Baltimore were widespread, most of the credit for its successful stand must go to Smith, whose preparations, determination, and direction caused Baltimore to be so formidable an obstacle to British success at arms.

After the war, Smith resumed his congressional career, surviving financial disaster and political upheavals until he retired in 1833 at the age of 83. Even then, Baltimore called him back to service after a series of violent riots in 1835 to act as mayor, an office he held until shortly before his death. It was a fitting culmination to the career of a man who had given so much for his city.

—*Mark Pitcavage*

See also: Baltimore, Battle of; Chesapeake Bay Campaign, 1813–1814; Cochrane, Alexander; Cockburn, George; McHenry, Fort; Stricker, John; U.S. Congress; Winder, William H.

Further Reading

Cassell, Frank A. *Merchant Congressman in the Young Republic.* Madison: University of Wisconsin Press, 1971.

Lord, Walter. *The Dawn's Early Light.* New York: W. W. Norton, 1972.

Pancake, John S. *Samuel Smith and the Politics of Business: 1752–1839.* University: University of Alabama Press, 1972.

In April 1813, Cockburn showed up in front of Baltimore, causing a flurry of mobilization on the part of Smith and his Marylanders, but Cockburn did not possess the strength to do more than scare Baltimore. However, the following summer brought a British offensive under Adm. Sir Alexander Cochrane and Gen. Robert Ross aimed at Chesapeake Bay. These forces landed in Maryland, routed a U.S. army at the Battle of Bladensburg (24 August 1814), and burned Washington, D.C. The British command then decided to take Baltimore. Samuel Smith, receiving word of the British presence, immediately began preparations. He mobilized the militia of Baltimore, defeated a challenge to his authority by U.S. Army general William H. Winder, and ordered additional fortifications built. By early September, Smith had 15,000 men under his command.

The British, led by Ross (until his death), landed on 12 September with 4,000 soldiers and encountered a delaying force led by Gen. John Stricker. Stricker retreated to Hampstead Hill, a fortified position east of Baltimore, where Smith had stationed thousands of militiamen. Smith foiled a flanking maneuver and then positioned his troops so that a British frontal assault would be exposed to crossfire. Convinced the position was too strong to take, the British retreated on 14 September.

SMITH, THOMAS A.
1781–1844
U.S. officer

Born in Virginia to Francis Smith and Lucy Wilkinson Smith, Thomas Smith moved as a child with his family to Georgia. Early in his life, Smith decided on a military career, secured an appointment as an ensign, and then was commissioned a second lieutenant in 1803. Serving under Brig. Gen. James Wilkinson in New Orleans, Smith was sent to Washington with the information Wilkinson had implicating Aaron Burr in his various schemes.

By 1808, Smith had achieved the rank of captain and, by the outbreak of the War of 1812, was promoted to lieutenant colonel. Before the war started he was sent to Point Petre, Georgia, on the St. Marys River. Mathews had been given secret approval by the Madison administration to provoke a revolution against Spanish authority in East Florida by using U.S. immigrants there. Lieutenant Colonel Smith was authorized to use his regular forces at Point Petre to aid Mathews, in conjunction with U.S. naval forces off the coast.

Smith arrived in southeastern Georgia in the fall of 1811, but Mathews was not ready for the so-called revolution until early 1812. When Mathews and the Patriots, as the revolutionaries styled themselves, made their move in March 1812, Smith was temporarily away from Point Petre. His second in command, Maj. Jacint Laval, not privy to Smith's instructions, refused to allow the regulars to cross into Florida. Therefore the Patriots acted with the navy gunboats alone to secure the surrender of Fernandina. Upon his return, Smith marched his regulars into Florida and cooperated with the Patriots in the failed siege of the fortifications guarding St. Augustine.

Smith operated in northeast Florida for the next year, primarily protecting the Patriots as their expedition disintegrated. Following the evacuation of U.S. forces from Florida, Smith was transferred to the northern theater, where he would serve out the remainder of the war.

As one of the brigadier generals created in January 1814, Smith commanded one of the two brigades under Maj. Gen. George Izard on Lake Champlain through the summer of 1814. In June 1814, Smith was sent with his brigade to occupy a position 5 miles south of the Canadian border, as an advance defense against what Izard suspected would become a major invasion of the United States along Lake Champlain.

Although Izard's suspicion would later be confirmed, Secretary of War John Armstrong was more concerned for the campaign recently underway along the Niagara. Armstrong ordered Izard to take most of his regulars to Sacket's Harbor, New York, to prepare to cooperate with Maj. Gen. Jacob Brown. After protesting the foolishness of these instructions, Izard left one of his brigades under Brig. Gen. Alexander Macomb and took the remainder, including Smith's brigade, to Sacket's Harbor. Before the end of the war, Smith served in Izard's campaign along the northern Niagara.

After the war, with the army reduction of 1815, Smith reverted to the rank of colonel. He resigned in 1818 and remained in Missouri, the site of his last command, where he became a prominent planter. He died at his plantation in 1844. Fort Smith, Arkansas, was named in his honor.

—*Jeanne T. Heidler and David S. Heidler*

See also: Armstrong, John; Izard, George; Mathews, George; Patriot War; St. Augustine, Florida

Further Reading

Davis, T. Frederick. "United States Troops in Spanish East Florida, 1812–1813." *Florida Historical Quarterly* 9 (1930): 3–23, 96–116, 135–155, 279–298.

SMUGGLING

During the American Colonial era, all imperial governments were unable to control smuggling at home, let alone in their overseas possessions. The U.S. government thus inherited an ancient problem. During the War of 1812, geography abetted smuggling with British North American colonies north and south, as well as with Spanish and French colonies in the Caribbean. Winter facilitated illegal trade because frozen lakes and rivers provided new routes alongside established roads and trails.

The Madison administration tried to buttress the military campaign against Britain with economic sanctions. A 90-day embargo preceded the declaration of war, and an Enemy Trade Act was passed in July 1812. A December 1813 bill created a wide-ranging embargo, outlawed coastal trade, and tried to close off loopholes merchants had used to evade previous regulations. Congress repealed both measures in April 1814, but no replacement legislation passed until February 1815, and that expired two weeks later when the war officially ended.

Smugglers and the British conspired to defeat all these measures. An Order in Council of October 1812 authorized limited trade with the United States. Jonathan Hagar was one of three dozen U.S. merchants in Montreal who swore allegiance to the Crown simply to carry on trade. British premiums and payment in gold drew U.S. suppliers away from their own government and markets. The British blockade choked coastal trade in 1814, but when an expedition captured Castine, Maine, British officials created a conduit for New England maritime commerce. The revenues endowed what became Dalhousie University. In Halifax, Nova Scotia, port revenues increased by a factor of three during the war. In 1815, notably, these revenues dropped below 1812 levels. U.S. officials levied fines on smugglers they caught, and the revenues from that source exceeded those collected during the embargo of 1807–1809.

Wartime smugglers trafficked principally to Montreal and Halifax. Vermonters and New Hampshirites toted or drove goods over the border. John Howe, a spy and smuggler, used backpacks, fake coffins, sleighs with hollow sides, and false-bottomed boxes to transport illegal goods, and he bribed officers to look the other way. Smugglers sailed the Bay of Fundy and inland lakes. New Yorkers built special roads to the frontier; Ogdensburg traded with Prescott, across the St. Lawrence River, as though no war existed. Southern smugglers used Amelia Island, Spanish East Florida, as an entrepôt, and Lake Barataria pirates ran goods between New Orleans and the Gulf of Mexico.

Exports from the United States consisted mostly of food-stuffs and war supplies, but timber and potash were also traded in the north. David Parish of Ogdensburg marched meat on the hoof to profit from a threefold price rise in Upper Canada. Gov.-Gen. Sir George Prevost reckoned in 1814 that two-thirds of all the troops under his command lived on enemy beef. As a result, U.S. quartermasters in the northern theaters could not find fresh meat for their troops. Halifax received naval and other stores. Sir John Coape Sherbrooke issued special licenses to Yankee exporters, his naval vessels escorted smugglers into port, and he issued special passports so merchants could "recover" allegedly condemned cargoes. Because U.S. laws did not cover neutral vessels, Ramon Manzuco ran Vermont goods on Missiquoi Bay under the Spanish flag. In Chesapeake Bay, locals supplied blockading British warships. U.S. smugglers imported manufactures, woolens, and scarce specialties, such as tea and wines. British licenses and bills of exchange traded openly in Philadelphia and Boston, whose banks supplied specie to finance smuggling ventures.

Enforcement misfired, and Treasury Secretary Albert Gallatin permitted Americans to travel into British territory, explaining that they would simply smuggle if he denied them. Thus John Jacob Astor sustained his fur business with Canada during the war. Customs officers lacked troops, sympathetic courts refused to convict, and conspiracies of silence reigned. Even local militiamen smuggled. One ring included C. P. Van Ness, the Vermont collector of customs. Residents of Moose Island, Maine District, forced the removal of Col. George Ulmer for chasing Passamaquoddy Bay smugglers too vigorously in 1812. Gen. George Izard fumed futilely at Champlain Valley violations.

Smuggling was an open scandal throughout the War of 1812, widely reported in newspapers and discussed in Congress. Defiance of enemy trade laws reflected not simply profit seeking at times when potential rewards far outran risk of loss but also the primacy in many minds of local over central interests. Americans refused to let war interfere with business, and smuggling constituted a significant part of internal resistance against Mr. Madison's War.

—Reginald C. Stuart

See also: Trade Restrictions
Further Reading

Copp, Walter R. "Nova Scotia Trade during the War of 1812." *Canadian Historical Review* 18 (June 1937): 141–155.

Galpin, W. Freeman. "The American Grain Trade to the Spanish Peninsula, 1810–1814." *American Historical Review* 28 (October 1922): 29–33.

Hickey, Donald R. "American Trade Restrictions during the War of 1812." *Journal of American History* 68 (December 1981): 517–538.

Muller, H. N. "A 'Traitorous and Diabolical Traffic': The Commerce of the Champlain-Richelieu Corridor during the War of 1812." *Vermont History* 44 (spring 1976): 78–96.

Smelser, Marshal, ed. "Smuggling in 1813–1814: A Personal Reminiscence." *Vermont History* 38 (winter 1970): 22–26.

SMYTH, ALEXANDER
1765–1830
U.S. officer

One of the most controversial U.S. generals of the War of 1812, Alexander Smyth served as the army's inspector general during the early months of the conflict. He failed miserably on the Niagara Frontier during his sole attempt at active campaigning and suffered the indignity of having his position abolished by Congress.

A native of the Island of Rathlin off the Irish coast, Smyth was born in 1765 and was brought to Botetourt County, Virginia, by his father, an Episcopal minister, in 1775. He studied law and, at the age of 20, earned an appointment as deputy county clerk. Smyth married in 1791 and shortly thereafter moved to Wythe County, where he practiced law and fathered four children. A Republican, he served several terms in the Virginia House of Delegates and the state senate between 1792 and 1809.

Possibly, political connections helped Smyth receive a commission in July 1808 as colonel of the U.S. Army's Rifle Regiment. Three years later, he began preparation of a new army manual that was published in 1812 under the title *Regulations for the Field Exercise, Manoeuvres, and Conduct of the Infantry of the United States.* Army historians David Clary and Joseph Whitehorne note that Smyth's "reputation as the author of a drill manual apparently impressed [Secretary of War William] Eustis, or someone," but also conclude that "[i]t should actually have served as a warning. Smyth's regulations were merely an abridged translation of the French Army's infantry regulations of 1791, not wholly applicable to American practice."

Alexander Smyth

In June 1812, shortly after the outbreak of war with Great Britain, Congress authorized the reestablishment of an inspector general for the army. The following month, Secretary Eustis selected Smyth for the position, which also brought promotion to brigadier general. Perhaps selection of Smyth seemed sound, but his subsequent performance was extremely disappointing. Smyth apparently did little to improve the organization and discipline of the army. Instead, he lobbied for a field command, and Eustis awarded him one in September.

Placed in command of a brigade of 1,700 regulars, Smyth reached the Niagara Frontier in late September. He displayed little inclination to cooperate with his superior, Maj. Gen. Stephen Van Rensselaer, despite orders from the War Department to do so. On October 13, Van Rensselaer ordered U.S. forces across the Niagara River near Queenston Heights. U.S. regulars under Lt. Col. Winfield Scott fought well, but much of Van Rensselaer's militia refused to cross the river and join the attack. The result was a debacle in which nearly 1,000 Americans were captured. Several days before the battle, Van Rensselaer had specifically directed Smyth to send his regulars "with every possible despatch" to join in the assault, but Smyth evidently ignored the order.

After the defeat, Van Rensselaer asked to be relieved, and Secretary Eustis placed Smyth in command of the remaining forces on the Niagara. Over the next month, Smyth seems to have spent much of his time composing bombastic proclamations designed to inspire his troops and the New York populace. Instead, the declarations led to ridicule and contempt. On November 10, hopeful of gaining militia recruits, Smyth issued a proclamation that "accomplished little except to offend the Federalists, many of whom were in his ranks." "In a few days," the Irishman proclaimed, "the troops under my command will plant the American standard in Canada.... They will conquer or they will die." Smyth then questioned the patriotism of the population: "Will you stand by with your arms folded and look on this interesting struggle? Are you not related to the men who fought at Bennington and Saratoga?" He added, "I cannot give you the day of my departure. But come on, come in companies, half companies, pairs or singly."

Smyth next issued a circular to his "Army of the Centre." After calling for the protection of Canadian citizens and their property and noting that "[p]rivate plundering is absolutely forbidden," he added, "your rights as soldiers will be maintained; whatever is booty by the usage of war you shall have." The general urged his militia to remain loyal and concluded: "It is in your power to retrieve the honor of your country and to cover yourselves with glory.... Rewards and honors await the brave. Infamy and contempt are reserved for cowards.... [W]hen you attack the enemy's batteries let your rallying word be : 'The cannon lost at Detroit or Death.'" The pompous officer's critics ridiculed him as "Alexander the Great" and "Napoleon the Second."

In early November, Smyth informed the War Department of his readiness to cross the Niagara and assault Fort Erie within 15 days. The arrival shortly thereafter of 2,000 Pennsylvania militiamen increased his force to between 4,000 and 6,000 troops, although many of these citizen-soldiers proved unreliable. On 25 November, the general issued orders "to be ready to march at a moment's warning." Over the next two days, about 4,500 men gathered at Black Rock, New York, opposite Fort Erie, where boats to accommodate most of this force had been assembled.

Alerted to their opponent's plans, the British had already launched several heavy cannonades to disrupt the Americans, and this may have dampened Smyth's enthusiasm for the operation. Early on 28 November, an advance party of Americans destroyed several outlying batteries, but another failed to completely dismantle a bridge between Fort Erie and Chippewa. When daylight arrived, the main U.S. force began loading for the crossing. The operation moved slowly, and it was late afternoon before most of the troops had boarded. Smyth, who remained at his headquarters during the day, sent a surrender demand to the British commander, which was rejected. Concerned that he would not be able to land his full force before dark and aware that the British had assembled a force to contest his crossing, he ordered the troops to return to their camps.

On 29 November, Smyth ordered another assault for the next morning, commenting to his soldiers that "Neither rain, snow or frost will prevent the embarkation." He added, "To-morrow will be memorable in the annals of the United States." Nothing, however, was accomplished on 30 November. Smyth instead held a council of war with his officers, who urged him to delay an assault until the early morning darkness of 1 December and to move the crossing several miles downstream. The next day only 1,500 men, many of them ill, loaded their transports. Others, primarily militia, refused to embark at all. For hours, the men received no order to proceed, while Smyth again huddled with his officers. Finally, at dawn, the general ordered his frustrated men to disembark one last time. He was unwilling to attack with less than 3,000 men.

Smyth's decision infuriated many of his troops: "The officers broke their swords, [and] the men beat their muskets over stumps with rage." Their commander "for safety took lodgings in Buffalo," until a mob forced him to return to his camps, where he posted a heavy guard around his headquarters. Shots were allegedly fired into his tent, and a $1,500 reward placed on his head. Brig. Gen. Peter B. Porter ridiculed Smyth and, in the pages of the Buffalo Gazette, publicly charged him with "cowardice." A duel between the two officers subsequently occurred on Grand Island, but neither man was wounded in the affair. Smyth shortly thereafter asked for leave and "stole back to Virginia using back roads." In early March 1813, Congress abolished the office of inspector general, and Smyth, who did not have a position with a line unit, lost his commission. He petitioned for further service, pleading for the opportunity to "die, if Heaven wills it, in the defence of his country." Not surprisingly, the War Department took no action on his request.

After his removal from the service, Smyth returned to his law practice. Ultimately he reentered politics, serving terms in the Virginia House of Delegates during 1816–1817 and 1826–1827 and six terms in the U.S. House of Representatives between 1817 and 1830. The old politician-soldier died in Washington on 17 April 1830 and was buried in the Congressional Cemetery in that city.

In Smyth's defense, his army was in a poor condition in late 1812 to attempt offensive operations. Camp sicknesses were widespread, supplies proved inadequate, the militia's loyalty was questionable, and desertions had weakened his ranks. Nonetheless, the general did little to improve these conditions, and his overbearing attitude infuriated many of his own officers and men. Years later, Pres. James Madison noted that "[t]he advanced position in the service given to General Smyth was much to be regretted.... [with] his talent for military command... equally mistaken by himself and by his friends." Historians of the inspector general's office David Clary and Joseph Whitehorne call him "one of the strangest people ever to don a general's uniform in the American army."

—David Coles

See also: Erie, Fort; Niagara Campaigns; Queenston, Battle of; Van Rensselaer, Stephen
Further Reading
Biographical Directory of the United States Congress, 1774–1989. Washington, DC: Government Printing Office, 1989.
Clary, David A., and Joseph W. A. Whitehorne. The Inspectors General of the United States Army, 1777–1903. Washington, DC: Office of the Inspector General and Chief of Military History, 1987.
Cruikshank, Ernest, ed. The Documentary History of the Campaign on the Niagara Frontier, 1812. New York: Arno Press and the New York Times, 1971.
Johnson, Allen, and Dumas Malone, eds. Dictionary of American Biography. 10 vols. Reprint ed. New York: Charles Scribner's Sons, 1963–1964.
"Reminiscences of the Late War." Army and Navy Chronicle, February 19, 1835.
Severance, Frank H. "The Case of Brig. Gen. Alexander Smyth, as Shown by His Own Writings, Some of Them Now First Published." Buffalo Historical Society Publications 18 (1913).

SNYDER, SIMON
1759–1819
Governor of Pennsylvania

Born to Anthony Snyder and Maria Elizabeth Knippenburg Kraemer Snyder in Lancaster, Pennsylvania, Simon Snyder was trained as a young man to be a tanner, but after serving his apprenticeship, he moved to Northumberland County and established his own mercantile business. He also became increasingly involved in local politics, becoming a county judge and, from 1797 to 1807, a member of the Pennsylvania Assembly. In the lower house of that body, he served three terms as speaker.

In the Pennsylvania legislature, Snyder, the son of poor immigrants, became a leader of the Snyderites, a faction that sought to democratize Pennsylvania by reducing the power of the executive. Snyder unsuccessfully ran for governor in 1805 but won the office in 1811.

As governor, Snyder believed one of his primary obligations was to encourage manufacturing in the state. He was convinced that the problems with Great Britain stemmed from the United States' dependence on foreign trade for manufactured goods. If the United States became more self-sufficient, Snyder thought, then foreign wars could be avoided.

Once the War of 1812 began, however, he supported the administration's conduct of it. In 1813, Secretary of the Treasury Albert Gallatin sent Congressman Jonathan Roberts of Pennsylvania to visit the governor to discuss a Pennsylvania Assembly bill known as the "forty bank bill." Gallatin was concerned that such a bill would proliferate banks in Pennsylvania and encourage too much speculation, destroying an already delicate economy. On Roberts's urging, Snyder vetoed the bill, but the Assembly overrode the veto.

After leaving the governor's chair, Snyder returned to the state senate, where he died in office in 1819.

—*Jeanne T. Heidler and David S. Heidler*

See also: Pennsylvania
Further Reading
Derr, Emerson L. "Simon Snyder, Governor of Pennsylvania, 1800–1817." Ph.D. diss., Pennsylvania State University, 1960.

ST. AUGUSTINE, FLORIDA

Founded by the Spaniards in 1565, St. Augustine is the oldest European-settled city in the United States. It was the largest community in and the capital of Spanish Florida from its founding until 1763. For the next 20 years, it was the capital of the British colony of East Florida. In 1783, it became the capital of the Spanish colony of East Florida as a result of the Treaty of Paris ending the American Revolution.

The colony had prospered during the British period, but after it returned to Spanish rule the combination of events caused by the Napoleonic wars in Spain, diminished Spanish resources to support this isolated outpost of empire, and the revolutionary movements in Mexico and South America made St. Augustine's situation decline. With few troops stationed at St. Augustine's fort, the Castillo de San Marcos, the Spanish governor's ability to enforce law and order

in East Florida was minimal. Native Americans used St. Augustine as a trade center to obtain weapons that were sometimes used against Americans in Georgia and the new southwestern territories. This situation and the fact that black slaves escaped southward from the United States enraged many U.S. politicians in the first decade of the 1800s. To add to the frustration of U.S. authorities, the Spanish community of Fernandina on Amelia Island, only a few minutes' sail from the Georgia border, had become a center for smugglers and pirates. The authorities in St. Augustine lacked the resources to resolve these problems to the satisfaction of the Americans. When Spain and England joined together in a mutual defense treaty, the threat of East Florida becoming a base for hostile British forces or a center for the support of Indians and former slaves who might attack the southern frontier caused War Hawk representatives to advocate the conquest of East Florida and its capital. The presence of British trading companies in both St. Augustine and Pensacola, the capital of West Florida, was interpreted as further evidence of British agents agitating hostile forces without interference from the Spanish officials.

The concerns of Georgians were taken seriously by Pres. James Madison and members of Congress in 1811. The expansionist rhetoric of the War Hawks and the fear of British military activities benefited some unprincipled and opportunistic Georgians who wanted fertile new lands. Congress, meeting in a secret session on 11 January 1811—nearly 16 months prior to the declaration of war—passed a bill, which President Madison signed, authorizing him to purchase or militarily occupy East Florida. The first agent appointed to accomplish this objective was 72-year-old frontiersman George Mathews.

Mathews was a former Revolutionary War general, former governor of Georgia, and Democratic Republican politician who had been discredited in a land scandal. An aggressive individual, he never let the "fine points" of law or accepted international diplomacy stand in his way. When he was unable to negotiate a successful transfer of either West or East Florida from its Spanish governor, Mathews believed that Secretary of State James Monroe supported him in a covert operation to achieve his goal. He knew that the two governors of East Florida in 1811, Enrique White and, after March 1811, Juan de Estrada, would not cooperate, so Mathews planned a rebellion to accomplish annexation.

George Mathews secured the support of several influential Americans living in Spanish East Florida, as well as a number of Georgians, to create the "Republic of East Florida." Col. John Houston MacIntosh, an American planter in Florida, was the elected leader of the self-styled

"Patriots." Mathews believed that he could count on the support of the U.S. army and navy units in southern Georgia to back his insurrectionists. Mathews and McIntosh issued a proclamation in March 1812 promising citizenship and retention of office for any Spaniard who would cooperate. On 18 March, an "army" of 79 Patriots under the flag of the new republic marched to attack St. Augustine. The attack started badly when the U.S. Army forces did not materialize because a new commander on the Georgia frontier strictly followed written orders that did not appear to support starting a war with Spain. Mathews's small force reached St. Augustine, but the Spaniards there refused either to negotiate or surrender. Although the Spaniards had few soldiers and limited supplies when Mathews appeared, the massive Castillo was too strong a position for the Americans to attack. Mathews and his men camped just out of cannon range while a stalemate developed. Meanwhile, bowing to criticism by Federalists in the Senate and to British diplomatic pressure, President Madison repudiated George Mathews, and the bulk of the Americans retreated back to Georgia, leaving destruction in their wake.

Gov. David Mitchell of Georgia was then appointed as the agent to acquire East Florida, but he was equally unsuccessful in his negotiations. Mitchell, like Mathews, was also repudiated by President Madison. The remaining Patriots of the "Republic of East Florida" were still encamped near St. Augustine, but a reinforced Spanish army, with help from Seminole warriors, drove these Americans northward. In 1813, Madison appointed a third agent to deal with the Spaniards, Maj. Gen. Thomas Pinckney, the commander of the U.S. Army units in the Southwest. Tennessee militia volunteers wanted to invade East Florida, but Congress refused to support another U.S. invasion.

The last attempt to conquer East Florida came a few months later in January 1814, when a small army of 140 Georgians led by Buckner Harris attempted an independent invasion. This group did not have the support of the U.S. Army or of Congress, and the Georgians were defeated by a group of Seminoles and escaped slaves. In March 1814, a squadron of Royal Navy ships appeared at the mouth of the St. Marys River to protect St. Augustine from such invasions, and the English did considerable damage to the southern Georgia towns of Point Petre and Saint Marys. A new Spanish governor in St. Augustine, Sebastian Kindelan, protested the British action because he feared a major invasion by the U.S. army.

Peace was restored prior to any major attack on St. Augustine. The Spaniards still officially remained in control of East Florida, but they did not have sufficient forces to maintain order. In 1817, a group of pirates and soldiers of fortune occupied Amelia Island, and the Spaniards could not force them out. The United States ultimately occupied Amelia Island. When Gen. Andrew Jackson invaded West Florida in 1818, the fate of St. Augustine was sealed. The city passed into U.S. control on 16 July 1822, after the ratification of the Adams-Onís Treaty.

In 1822, St. Augustine became a district capital of one of the two parts of the new U.S. territory of Florida. After statehood in 1845, Tallahassee became the capital, and St. Augustine declined in importance. It was and is the county seat of St. Johns County. After the construction of the coastal railroad and paved roads, it became a tourist center and college city of 12,000 citizens, with the Castillo de San Marcos and part of its old town as a national park.

—*George E. Frakes*

See also: Florida; Mathews, George; Patriot War
Further Reading
Arana, Luis Rafael, and George R. Fairbanks. *The History and Antiquities of the City of St. Augustine, Florida.* Gainesville: University Presses of Florida, 1958.
Douglas, Marjory Stoneman. *Florida: The Long Frontier.* New York: Harper and Row, 1967.
Patrick, Rembert W. *Florida Fiasco: Rampant Rebels on the Florida Boundary.* Athens, GA: University of Georgia Press, 1954.
Patrick, Rembert W., and Allan Marriss. *Florida under Five Flags.* Gainesville: University Presses of Florida, 1967.
Schwaller, John Frederick. "Spanish Colonial Towns, from Aztec to Anglo." *Journal of Urban History* 11 (1985): 245–251.
Tebeau, Charlton W. *A History of Florida.* Coral Gables, FL: University of Miami Press, 1971.

ST. CLOUD DECREE
See Orders in Council

ST. JOSEPH, FORT

Situated on the southern point of St. Joseph's Island at the western end of Lake Huron about 45 miles northeast of Mackinac Island, Michigan, Fort St. Joseph was a combined military and North West Company post. British troops garrisoned it when they withdrew from Fort Michilimackinac, after turning that place over to the United States in 1796 under the terms of Jay's Treaty of 1794. St. Joseph's had a number of storehouses for the North West Company and thus became a rendezvous for the Indian fur canoe convoys arriving from Lake Superior and heading toward the French River en route to Ottawa and Montreal.

After the British captured Fort Michilimackinac on 17 July 1812, they abandoned their old military post of Fort St. Joseph, which retained its North West Company stores. In July 1814, a detachment of the Arthur Sinclair–George Croghan expedition commanded by Maj. Andrew H. Holmes arrived off the abandoned British fort on 20 July, after vainly looking for Matchedash Bay. It was seeking the annual fur convoy but missed it.

The detachment burned the old fort and blockhouse, captured the *Mink*, a North West Company trading schooner laden with flour from Michilimackinac and bound for St. Marys. The Americans also wrecked the *Perseverance*, a North West Company Lake Superior schooner, when they tried to bring her down the falls of the St. Marys River. St. Joseph's remained derelict until the British restored it, after Michilimackinac was returned to the United States under the terms of the Treaty of Ghent.

—*Frederick C. Drake*

Further Reading

Bayliss, Joseph, and Estelle Bayliss. *Historic St. Joseph's Island.* Cedar Rapids, IA: Torch Press, 1938.

May, George S. *War of 1812.* Mackinac State Historic Parks: Village Press, 1990.

ST. LAWRENCE RIVER

The St. Lawrence River, connecting the Great Lakes to the Atlantic, was Britain's lifeline to its Canadian provinces. Virtually all war materiel—uniforms, weapons, gunpowder, naval supplies—originated in Great Britain and was pushed across the Atlantic and up the St. Lawrence to Quebec. From Quebec upriver to Montreal, the St. Lawrence was readily navigable. Cargoes were transloaded to river schooners for this part of the voyage. Entirely within British territory, this stretch of river was also fairly easy to secure and was paralleled by a road of good quality. Between Montreal and Kingston at the foot of Lake Ontario, however, three sets of rapids impeded river traffic. Bateaux directed by skilled pilots could negotiate the rapids, although in some places crews stationed on the banks had to pull the vessels.

During the war, gunboats escorted convoys of bateaux. This security measure slowed down travel, and convoys typically took eight days to move from Montreal to Kingston. A road of uneven quality, often not more than a trail, paralleled this portion of the river. From Cornwall to Kingston, the St. Lawrence defined the international border, and the threat of U.S. forces cutting the British supply line was always present. From Kingston, cargoes were transloaded to larger craft and sailed up Lake Ontario. Icebound in January, the St. Lawrence River was not completely open to navigation until mid-May. Winter cargoes were moved by sleigh on frozen roads or, more frequently, remained under cover until the spring thaw.

The war increased the need for supplies in Upper Canada, and the bateaux service between Montreal and Kingston consumed growing numbers of crafts and men. The boatmen were usually made up of militia called from Lower Canada. With farmers taken from their fields for weeks at a time, food production in the province was always at risk. The convoy service required over 4,000 laborers and boatmen to keep the bateaux manned and the supply line functioning at full capacity. Virtually every household between Montreal and Kingston was affected, and the populace grew tired of the repeated requisitioning of all able-bodied males. Nonetheless, the war would have been lost without the backbreaking toil of the militiamen who kept the food and war supplies flowing upriver.

U.S. leaders understood that severing the St. Lawrence supply line was the surest way of seizing all of Canada above the cut point. However, Quebec, Montreal, and Kingston were well-defended cities. The few attempts to bisect the St. Lawrence ended in failure.

In November 1812, Maj. Gen. Henry Dearborn entered Lower Canada at the head of 5,000 poorly trained recruits. Heading toward Montreal, Dearborn withdrew after a brief and inconclusive skirmish. In 1813, the Americans considered attacking Montreal but believed the British defense there to be too strong. Instead, the Americans raided York and seized Fort George. Neither of these successes seriously impinged on the British position, and in the fall, Maj. Gen. James Wilkinson decided on a two-pronged advance on Montreal.

Maj. Gen. Wade Hampton set off in late October down the Châteauguay River with 3,000 troops, heading toward Montreal. Wilkinson departed Sacket's Harbor, New York, with nearly 8,000 men and pushed down the St. Lawrence River to link up with Hampton. On 26 October, Hampton's force was stopped cold by a smaller number of Canadians and allied natives. Two weeks later, Wilkinson's column fought an inconclusive battle at Chrysler's Farm in Canada. Upon learning of Hampton's defeat, Wilkinson called for a council of war, which recommended withdrawal. The 1813 campaign ended, and the British supply line had been only temporarily disrupted.

The following year, the strategic balance shifted with Napoleon's defeat in Europe. Pres. James Madison hoped to realize some important success before the arrival of thousands of British veterans of the Peninsular War. Madison directed the main attack across the Niagara Peninsula toward York. He also ordered his military forces to cut the St. Lawrence River by launching gunboats operating from a base secured on the river for that purpose. Maj. Gen. George Izard, in command at Lake Champlain, located a position on the U.S. side of the river from which guns could challenge all traffic. He procrastinated, however, in building batteries and other defenses, and Madison's plans came to nothing.

Many rationalizations are offered for the United States' inability to seize Canada—incompetent generals, reluctant militia, untrained regulars among them. Certainly high on the list was strategic confusion. Too often the United States aimed efforts west of Kingston, where local success could not be parlayed into strategic victory. On those few occasions when attempts were made to cut the exceedingly slender British supply line, the country trusted its success to generals who lacked the determination to press the fight to a decisive conclusion.

—*Richard V. Barbuto*

See also: Châteauguay, Battle of; Chrysler's Farm, Battle of; Dearborn, Henry; Hampton, Wade; Izard, George; Montreal; Wilkinson, James

Further Reading
Landon, Harry F. *Bugles on the Border: The Story of the War of 1812 in Northern New York.* Watertown, NY: Watertown Daily Times, 1954.
Stanley, George F.G. *The War of 1812: Land Operations.* Ottawa: National Museums of Canada and Macmillan, 1983.

ST. MICHAELS, BATTLE OF
10 August 1813

A small town on Maryland's Eastern Shore, St. Michaels was one of several communities targeted by Adm. Sir George Cockburn as he worked his way down Chesapeake Bay in the summer of 1813. Because of its shipbuilding industries, particularly that producing privateers used to evade the British blockade, St. Michaels's shipyards were an inviting target.

Alerted that Cockburn was moving south along the Eastern Shore, Gen. Derry Benson mobilized the Talbot County militia to defend the town. In addition to the militiamen coming in from neighboring towns, Benson had several artillery pieces at his disposal. He erected three batteries, one guarding the harbor and consisting of three 6-pounders and one 9-pounder placed on a point on the south side of the harbor entrance, another consisting of two 6-pounders guarding the land approach to the town from Chesapeake Bay, and a third consisting of two 6-pounders in town at the shipyard.

Capt. William Dodson commanded the harbor battery manned by Talbot County militiamen. It was from this position after midnight on 10 August 1813 that the British were first spotted, though they had muffled their oars to prevent detection until they were within range of the town. They had entered the Miles River aboard 11 barges, each armed with one 6-pounder.

Because they were so close to land when they were spotted, the British unloaded their men to march on the town. When these soldiers fired on Dodson's battery, most of his militiamen fled. Only Dodson and two others remained to man the guns, but before they took flight, they got off one round of canister that staggered the first wave of the attacking British.

Dodson then retreated to the town battery, which was soon supplemented by the battery guarding the land approach. With these guns, the Americans kept up a steady fire at the British landing party and the barges that was so withering it forced the soldiers back to their boats. The guns aboard the barges continued to fire at the town, but with so little effect that by dawn the entire force had begun to withdraw from the Miles River. One local tradition explains why the British did so little damage to the town: the townspeople, aware of the British approach, had darkened their houses and hung lanterns from the trees, causing the British to overshoot.

In the battle, the militia of Talbot County suffered no casualties, but the British had 29. St. Michaels was never seriously threatened with attack for the remainder of the war.

—*Jeanne T. Heidler and David S. Heidler*

See also: Cockburn, George
Further Reading
Bryon, Gilbert. *St. Michaels, the Town That Fooled the British.* Satern, MD: Eastern Publishing, 1963.

STANSBURY, TOBIAS
1756–1849
Maryland militia officer

Born in Maryland, Tobias Stansbury became an important figure in the Maryland Democratic Republican Party during the presidential administration of Thomas Jefferson. Virtually a perennial member of the state legislature, Stansbury also served for a time as the lower house's speaker. As was so often the case, Stansbury, a prominent figure in Baltimore, also commanded a brigade of that city's militia.

When the Baltimore riots erupted in the summer of 1812 over the publication of Federalist Alexander C. Hanson's *Federal Republican*, Stansbury refused to call out his brigade even after he was informed that the rioters had broken into the jail and were assaulting Hanson and his friends. Following the riots, the Maryland legislature appointed a committee to investigate, and that committee criticized Stansbury's conduct during the incident.

Such criticism from a largely Federalist body only endeared Stansbury more to the largely Democratic Republican people of Baltimore, and his position as an officer in the militia there was not threatened. Perhaps he wished later that it had been when the British began their campaign in Chesapeake Bay in the summer of 1814.

As the British marched toward Washington, D.C., in August 1814, the commander of the defense of the city, Marylander William Winder, sent a call out for militia forces to move toward Washington for its defense. Stansbury was dispatched with his Third Brigade, but as he marched toward the capital, he began receiving conflicting orders from Winder. At one point, he received orders to stop halfway to the capital until the British route was discerned. Within hours, he received new orders from Winder urging him to come as quickly as possible. Finally, Stansbury was told that he should stop within a few miles of the capital, at Bladensburg, and establish a defensive line there.

At Bladensburg, Stansbury awaited more Maryland militia forces, but by the afternoon of 23 August, he did not believe that he could hold his position. As Stansbury began falling back toward Washington, Winder sent him three separate orders to return to Bladensburg. Stansbury finally retraced his steps and began positioning his men opposite the town.

On the morning of 24 August, Stansbury had approximately 2,200 men. He positioned them, but he and his men had no idea that many reinforcements were on the way, so everyone was nervous. Stansbury established his first line with artillery so that it stretched from the Georgetown Road on its left down to the Washington Road on the right. He then positioned a second line to support the first in an orchard not too far behind. Soon, however, Secretary of State James Monroe arrived, and without Stansbury's knowledge, Monroe moved the second line. It was then situated so far back that it was no use to the first line, now feeling very alone and increasingly nervous. By the time anyone realized what Monroe had done, the British were already in sight, and it was too late to move the men again.

Initially Stansbury's militia seemed steady, but after the British launched their major attack, these men did what most of the militia at Bladensburg did—they ran. Stansbury threatened to shoot the fleeing men, but there were too many of them. Making matters worse, Stansbury's men fled along the Georgetown Road rather than toward Washington, thus losing any chance of establishing a defensive line closer to the capital. Eventually, most of them turned toward Baltimore and home. As the panicked men poured into Baltimore, the citizens there became convinced that the British were right behind them, and the town was thrown into panic as well. Stansbury could do little but follow.

Though not a major part of the action, Stansbury aided in the defense of Baltimore three weeks later, and most of his men redeemed themselves. Following the war, Stansbury remained active in Maryland politics and was a popular figure in Baltimore until his death.

—*Jeanne T. Heidler and David S. Heidler*

See also: Bladensburg, Battle of; Hanson, Alexander Contee; Monroe, James; Winder, William H.

Further Reading

Arnold, James R. "The Battle of Bladensburg." *Columbia Historical Society Proceedings* 37 (1937): 145–168.

Hickey, Donald R. "The Darker Side of Democracy: The Baltimore Riots of 1812." *Maryland Historian* 7 (1976): 1–14.

STAR-SPANGLED BANNER, THE

Raised over Fort McHenry at the entrance to the harbor of Baltimore, Maryland, during the War of 1812, the U.S. flag with 15 stars and 15 stripes is commonly referred to as the Star-Spangled Banner because it inspired a poem that was set to music under that title.

This flag had its origin in 1813, when the British navy was blockading the eastern seaboard of the United States and carrying out raids on coastal areas. Maj. George Armistead, the commander of Fort McHenry, expected that the British would soon attack Baltimore, and he wanted a large flag that would clearly mark the fort. He informed Maj. Gen. Samuel Smith, who was in command of the defenses of Baltimore, of his desire, and the general appointed a committee to take care of this request. The committee consisted of Brig. Gen. John Stricker, the commander of the Baltimore militia brigade; Commodore Joshua Barney of the U.S. Navy's local gunboat flotilla; and William McDonald, colonel of a Maryland regiment. These men called on Mrs. Mary Young Pickersgill, a widow who supported herself by making flags for Baltimore's merchant ships. They told her what was needed, and she agreed to make the flag. With the assistance of her 13-year-old daughter Caroline, Mrs. Pickersgill measured and cut the English-made wool bunting and the 15 five-pointed cotton stars. When the time came to assemble the flag, there was not enough room in her home to lay it out, so she secured the permission of a local brewer to spread it on the floor of his malthouse in the evening hours. Working by candlelight in the malthouse, Mrs. Pickersgill and her daughter constructed a flag that measured 30 by 42 feet. The flag was delivered in August 1813, and the bill for the work totaled $405.90.

Major Armistead waited a year before the fort was threatened. In 1814, British troops landed at Benedict, Maryland; marched overland; defeated a U.S. force sent to oppose them; and captured the city of Washington. After burning a few federal buildings, they returned to their ships. They then ascended the Potomac River and accepted the surrender of the city of Alexandria, Virginia. Retracing their route back down the Potomac River, the British ships were lying off the mouth of that river and contemplating their next move, when two American visitors arrived in a cartel ship under a flag of truce and were sent to Vice Adm. Sir Alexander Cochrane, the commander of the British squadron.

One of the visitors was well known to the British. He was John S. Skinner, a U.S. government agent for the exchange of prisoners of war. With him was Francis Scott Key, a lawyer from Georgetown in the District of Columbia. Their mission was to secure the release of Dr. William Beanes, a physician from Upper Marlboro, Maryland, who had been carried off by the invaders for his role in arresting and jailing British deserters and stragglers. Before leaving on this mission, Skinner had secured letters from wounded British prisoners of war describing their good treatment at the hands of the Americans. He also carried a letter from his superior, Gen. John Mason, the commissary general of prisoners, requesting the release of Beanes. Skinner and

Key dined with Cochrane and Maj. Gen. Robert Ross, who had ordered the seizure of Dr. Beanes. At first, Ross was unwilling to release the doctor, but the letters from the wounded British prisoners changed his mind. The Americans had accomplished their mission, but their return had to be postponed because they knew that the British had decided to attack Baltimore. Key, Skinner, and Beanes were placed on the flag-of-truce ship, which was anchored at Old Roads Bay on the Patapsco River, 8 miles below Fort McHenry. There they awaited the outcome of the British attack on Baltimore.

British troops under General Ross landed at North Point and advanced toward the city. Royal Navy bomb ships moved up the Patapsco River to within range of Fort McHenry. The navy was to bombard the fort in support of an attack by the army on U.S. fortifications on land. The first phase of the attack on Fort McHenry began on the morning of 13 September and ended about 9:00 P.M. The British ships were out of the range of Armistead's cannon, so he held his fire and waited for a possible landing of troops aimed at seizing the fort. At midnight, 20 boats carrying about 300 men set out from the British ships and headed for the Ferry Branch of the Patapsco River, west of Fort McHenry, where they were to anchor and await a signal. About 1:00 A.M., to divert attention from the boats, the British bomb ships resumed their attack on Fort McHenry. The night was pitch black, and it was raining heavily. Using muffled oars, the boats passed by Fort McHenry without being noticed. But about 2:00 A.M., the boats were detected by U.S. forces deployed at nearby Forts Babcock and Covington, and they opened fire. Realizing that they had been discovered, the British in the boats returned fire. The guns of Fort McHenry joined in the action.

According to plans, the British navy was to keep up its attack until the army began its assault on the U.S. positions to the east of Baltimore. It was now 3:00 A.M., and there were still no sounds of cannon or flashes of light to indicate that a land attack was in progress. The army commander had studied the U.S. defense positions and had decided against attacking them at night and in the rain. Shortly after 3:00 A.M., his troops began moving back toward North Point. About this same time, the British naval forces in the boats returned to their ships. The bombardment of Fort McHenry came to an end about 4:00 A.M., except for an occasional shot.

In the flag-of-truce ship, Key, Skinner, and Beanes had spent a restless night. They had heard the bombs, rockets, and cannon fire in the darkness, but in the predawn interval they did not know how to interpret the period of quiet. Had the fort or the city fallen to the enemy? The rain had stopped, but there were still dark clouds. About 5:50 A.M., there was sufficient light for Key to train a telescope on the fort. Just then, a breeze revealed that the U.S. flag was still flying over the fort. Key and his companions experienced feelings of relief and joy. They did not know that in the early moments of daylight, the fort's garrison had hauled down the rain-soaked flag that had been there all night and had replaced it with the dry one made by Mrs. Pickersgill.

By 8:00 A.M., the bomb ships began moving downstream, and the other ships followed. As the morning wore on, it became apparent to Key and his companions that the land attack on the city had also failed and that the British army was withdrawing as well. Looking again at the flag flying over the fort, Key was inspired. Taking a letter from his pocket, he began to write verses on the back of it.

When the British squadron was ready to sail, the flag-of-truce ship was released from detention and sailed for Baltimore. Arriving there on the evening of September 16, Key stopped at a hotel and that night revised the notes and draft of a poem commemorating the battle. The next morning, he took his poem to Judge Joseph H. Nicholson of Baltimore, who was married to Key's sister-in-law. Nicholson was so pleased by the poem that he recommended that it be printed. Presumably, Key gave the poem to Skinner, who took it to a newspaper office where it was printed and sold in the form of handbills under the title *The Defense of Fort M'Henry*. The handbill also contained 14 lines explaining how the poem had come to be written. The introduction was Nicholson's work, and it did not name Key as the author of the poem.

Copies of the handbill were soon in the hands of the Fort McHenry garrison, and newspapers elsewhere were soon publishing the poem as well. A newspaper in Frederick, Maryland, identified Key as the author of the poem a week after it was first printed. A month after the first printing, the poem was appearing with a new title, "The Star-Spangled Banner." There are indications that Key had the English drinking song "To Anacreon in Heaven" in mind when he wrote his poem. It was a well-known tune, and Key himself had used it earlier for another poem. The first known public singing of the new song took place at the theater on Holliday Street in Baltimore on the evening of 19 October 1814. A Mr. Hardinge sang "The Star-Spangled Banner" after the performance of the play *Count Benyowsky*.

The song was printed in various collections of national and patriotic tunes and grew slowly in popularity in the years following the War of 1812. By the middle of the century, the navy often used it as the national anthem in place of "Hail Columbia" when receiving heads of state aboard ships. During the Civil War, it enjoyed a great popularity. In 1889, the Navy Department ordered that the music be played during the morning color ceremony. This regulation

was amended in 1893 to include both the morning and evening color ceremonies. Army regulations published in 1895 stated that the song was to be played at every post and station when the flag was lowered during the retreat ceremonies at the end of the day. By 1916, both services regarded the song as the national anthem. Civilians were also urging that the song be officially designated as the national anthem. From time to time, resolutions with this goal were introduced in the U.S. House of Representatives and Senate, but none was acted upon. Leading this movement was the Maryland Society, United States Daughters of 1812, under the presidency of Mrs. Reuben Ross Holloway. With corresponding secretary Mrs. James B. Arthur, Mrs. Holloway approached many prominent persons and sought their support for the cause. In 1918, Maryland representative J. Charles Linthicum was asked to introduce a bill in Congress making "The Star-Spangled Banner" the national anthem. He did so, but the measure failed to gain much support. Linthicum introduced similar measures in every succeeding Congress. Other congressmen also introduced bills to designate the national anthem, without success. As time passed, other organizations added their support to the effort. Linthicum's bill finally passed in the House on 21 April 1930 and in the Senate on 3 March 1931. Pres. Herbert Hoover signed it into law that same day.

Meanwhile, the flag that inspired the song had taken on a special meaning. It was given to Armistead when he was relieved of his command of the fort in April 1818. Not long after the attack on Fort McHenry, one of the soldiers who was stationed there during the battle had died, and his widow asked Armistead for a piece of the flag to bury with him. Armistead granted her request. When Armistead died suddenly in 1818, the flag was bequeathed to his daughter, who had been born in the fort. She later became Mrs. William Stuart Appleton, and she bequeathed the flag to her son, Eben Appleton.

From time to time, the flag was put on public view. One such occasion was when the Marquis de Lafayette, hero of the Revolutionary War and aide to Gen. George Washington, visited Baltimore in August 1824. The flag was then displayed with one that had been used by Washington. In the 1870s, Commodore George Henry Preble was writing a history of the flag, and he borrowed it to photograph it for the first time. Before suspending it from a building in the Boston Navy Yard for the benefit of the photographer, Preble had a canvas backing sewed on the flag. This was still on it when it was returned to the owner, who kept it in a safe deposit box in New York City. In 1907 the owner, Eben Appleton, loaned the flag to the Smithsonian Institution for an exhibit. Five years later, he converted the loan to a gift with the stipulation that the flag never be removed from the museum for any reason. He wanted to make sure that any U.S. citizen who visited the Smithsonian would be able to see the flag.

Over the years, the size of the flag had been gradually reduced by cutting off pieces and giving them as keepsakes. When the flag was given to the Smithsonian, it was decided that it needed extensive conservation work before it could be placed on permanent display. Mrs. Amelia Fowler had done conservation work on flags for the U.S. Naval Academy, and she was asked to do the work on the flag from Fort McHenry. She assembled a group of experienced women, who removed the canvas backing from the flag and replaced it with unbleached Irish linen. The flag was attached to this new backing with a series of open button-hole stitches about 0.5 inch in length that interlocked horizontally and vertically. Linen tapes about 2 inches wide were sewn on the backing so that the flag could be hung without placing any strain on it. The flag was mounted horizontally in a large case and placed on exhibit in the Arts and Industries Building of the Smithsonian Institution.

With the adoption of a national flag code by Congress in 1942, the canton of the flag was not correctly displayed, but it was not considered feasible to change it. Later, when the new Smithsonian Museum of History and Technology was opened in 1964, visitors could see the flag correctly displayed in a vertical position. A text rail and photographs below the flag told its story.

The new arrangement subjected the flag to exposure to dirt and pollutants in the air, so after it was cleaned in 1984, a cover was placed over the flag to minimize its exposure to these elements. Each hour the cover was lowered, while a sound and light show related highlights of the history of the flag and played two different musical arrangements of "The Star-Spangled Banner."

A breakdown in the mechanism that raised and lowered the cover in 1994 made it necessary to remove that protection and create a new sound and light show. The flag was now exposed all the time, and a study of its condition indicated that some new cleaning was desirable. A Smithsonian conservator recommended that the old backing be removed and replaced with a new one. Exhibits and conservation specialists and some flag historians discussed the arguments for and against a new cleaning, the removal of the backing, and what might be done in the way of a new and better display arrangement. Yet budget cuts and staff reductions meant that nothing could be done about most of these recommendations unless a large sum of money was raised and allocated for this purpose. As of 1997, there were no public indications of how or when these things might be accomplished.

—*Harold D. Langley*

See also: Armistead, George; Baltimore, Battle of; Beanes, William; Key, Francis Scott; McHenry, Fort; Patriotic Songs

Further Reading
Elting, John R. *Amateurs, to Arms!: A Military History of the War of 1812.* New York: Da Capo Press, 1995.
Filby, P. W., and Edward G. Howard. *Star-Spangled Books.* Baltimore: Maryland Historical Society, 1972.
Lord, Walter. *The Dawn's Early Light.* New York: W. W. Norton, 1972.
Sheads, Scott S. *Fort McHenry.* Baltimore: Nautical and Aviation Publishing, 1995.
———. *The Rockets Red Glare: The Maritime Defense of Baltimore in 1814.* Centerville, MD: Tidewater Publishers, 1986.
Svejda, George J. *History of the Star Spangled Banner from 1814 to the Present.* Washington, DC: U.S. Department of the Interior, National Parks Service, 1969.

STEPHENSON, FORT

Originally built by Ohio militiamen under the direction of Col. Mills Stephenson in June 1812, this stockade-outpost was situated at the lowest ford of the Sandusky River at modern Fremont, Ohio (then known as Lower Sandusky). Abandoned by the Americans after the fall of Detroit, Fort Stephenson was burned and sacked by the British and Indians. In early 1813, the United States decided to rebuild it, and Gen. William Henry Harrison dispatched one of his engineers, Capt. Eleazer D. Wood, to supervise construction. On 15 July, Maj. George Croghan brought two companies of the 17th U.S. Infantry to garrison the post that Harrison believed was a prime target for a British-Indian raid from Fort Malden on the Detroit River. Croghan's only artillery piece was an eighteenth-century French 6-pounder naval cannon known as "Old Betsy." Following the failure of the second siege of Fort Meigs, Gen. Henry Procter was induced by the Indians to transfer his attack to Fort Stephenson. Procter and his troops of the 41st Foot, plus the Indians, arrived below the fort starting on 29 July.

Harrison had reservations about the utility of the post, given its vulnerability to artillery fire. He ordered Croghan to retire to Harrison's supply base at Camp Seneca, but before the order was received, Croghan found himself surrounded by the Indians. "We have determined to maintain this place," replied the young commander, "and, by heavens, we can." Harrison gave reluctant approval to this decision. Croghan refused to surrender to Procter on 1 August 1813, so the British commander determined to take the post by direct assault. A bombardment on 2 August that hurled over 500 cannonballs at the fort did little damage, but Procter decided his brave men could take Fort Stephenson by storm. Croghan had stopped firing "Old Betsy" during the bombardment, so the British thought that perhaps it had been disabled.

At 4:00 P.M. on 2 August, some 115 officers and men of the 41st Regiment led by Lt. Col. William Short assaulted the post. They were met by a hail of fire, particularly from "Old Betsy," which had been charged with a half-load of powder and a double-load of grapeshot. The combination was disastrous for the British. Even though some broke through the shot-filled ditch to the wall, they discovered that few comrades were able to join them. Also, their axes, necessary to open the wall, were not sharpened. The British had no ladders to scale the wall. By 4:30 P.M., it was all over. The British retreated to their encampment and subsequently began to withdraw towards the Detroit River.

British casualties were quite high: approximately 26 officers (including Colonel Short) and men died, 28 were wounded or captured, and 35 wounded had withdrawn from the field. Croghan's losses were 1 dead and 7 slightly wounded.

The consequences of this little engagement were substantial. It would be the last offensive British operation in the Lake Erie region for the remainder of the war. Both Procter's troops and his Indians began to grow discouraged, and desertion rates rose. Croghan became an immediate national hero and received a brevet promotion to lieutenant colonel. At 21, he was the youngest officer of that grade in the army. And the little outpost reconstructed under the direction of Captain Wood had withstood a siege and an assault, expanding the reputation of the young military academy at West Point, whose graduates like Wood did not have a single post they designed taken by the enemy throughout the war.

—*David Curtis Skaggs*

See also: Croghan, George; Meigs, Fort; Procter, Henry; Wood, Eleazer Derby

Further Reading

Bruce Bowlus. "A 'Signal Victory': The Battle for Fort Stephenson, August 1–2, 1813." *Northwest Ohio Quarterly* 63 (summer/autumn 1991): 43–57.
Clift, G. Glenn. "War of 1812 Diary of William B. Northcutt." *Register of the Kentucky Historical Society* 66 (1958): 325–344.
Richardson, John. *Richardson's War of 1812.* Toronto: Historical Publishing, 1902.

STEWART, CHARLES
1778–1869
U.S. Navy officer

Charles Stewart, born in Philadelphia, went to sea at 13 and had qualified as a master before accepting a lieutenant's commission in the new U.S. Navy in March 1798. Serving first aboard the frigate *United States* and the schooner *Enterprise,* in 1800 he became commander of the schooner *Experiment.* All of these ships saw service in the Caribbean during the Quasi-War with France, 1798–1801.

With the outbreak of the Barbary War, Stewart went to the Mediterranean as first lieutenant of the frigate *Constellation* in 1802 and then was given command of the new brig *Siren.* During his second Mediterranean tour (May 1803–September 1805), he was involved in the close blockade of Tripoli by Commodore Edward Preble and was commander of the operation that saw Stephen Decatur burn the captured U.S. frigate *Philadelphia* in that harbor in February 1804. He was promoted to master commandant later that year and captain a few months after his return to the United States in 1806.

After several years of humdrum duty in the latter part of the Jefferson administration, Stewart shuttled among several ship commands (three in 1812 alone) before settling aboard the *Constellation* at Norfolk in September 1812. The British blockade prevented him from getting to sea, and in the spring of 1813, he was transferred to the heavy frigate *Constitution* at Boston. British blockaders again stymied him until December, when he got to sea on a cruise shortened by the failure of one of his masts.

Stewart returned to Boston in April 1814 and was blockaded again until December. In November, he married Sarah Ford. On 20 February 1815, at sea again for two months some 180 miles from Madeira, he met the British light frigate *Cyane* and the corvette *Levant* together in a sunset and evening fight that saw him divide and conquer his enemies in a stunning display of ship handling and shooting. *Levant* subsequently was recaptured by the British, but *Cyane* was sailed back to the United States and taken into naval service. As was customary, Congress awarded Stewart a gold medal.

Stewart's subsequent service was punctuated by long periods of "awaiting orders." He commanded the Mediterranean squadron shortly after war's end and the Pacific squadron in the 1820s. From 1830 to 1833, he was on the Board of Naval Commissioners and later that decade

Charles Stewart

commanded the Philadelphia Navy Yard. Although briefly considered as a presidential candidate in 1840, he was not interested. In the 1840s, he was first commander of the Home squadron, 1841–1843, and beginning in January 1846 again commanded the Philadelphia Navy Yard for three years. That yard also was his to command from 1853 until 1860. Retired in 1861 as senior flag officer, he was made a rear admiral in July 1862. The following month, as the most appropriate man to perform a christening for the U.S. Navy, he christened the ironclad steamer USS *New Ironsides*. Occasionally consulted by national leaders on naval matters during the Civil War, Stewart passed away in 1869, having served for 71 years.

Admiral and Mrs. Stewart had two children. A grandson was the Irish nationalist Charles Stewart Parnell.

—*Tyrone G. Martin*

See also: *Constitution* versus *Cyane* and *Levant*
Further Reading
Cogar, William B. *Dictionary of Admirals of the U.S. Navy.* Vol. 1, *1862–1900.* Annapolis, MD: Naval Institute Press, 1989.
Forester, C. S. *The Age of Fighting Sail.* Garden City: Doubleday, 1956.
Guttridge, Leonard F., and Jay D. Smith. *The Commodores.* New York: Harper and Row, 1969.
Martin, Tyrone G. *A Most Fortunate Ship.* Chester: Globe Pequot Press, 1980. Reprint, Norwalk: Easton Press, 1990.

STEWART, ROBERT, VISCOUNT CASTLEREAGH

See Castlereagh, Viscount, Robert Stewart

STODDARD, AMOS
1762–1813
U.S. officer

Amos Stoddard was born in Woodbury, Connecticut. During the American Revolution, he enlisted in the Continental Army and served first in the infantry under Baron Friedrich von Steuben and later with the artillery. Following the war, he became a lawyer in Massachusetts, but he returned to the military in 1798 and was commissioned a captain in the First Regiment of Artillery. In 1807, he was promoted to major.

After the United States purchased the Louisiana Territory from France, Stoddard was appointed the first civil and military commandant of Upper Louisiana, holding the position from 10 March until 30 September 1804.

As tensions between the United States and Great Britain mounted during the opening decade of the nineteenth century, Stoddard saw that if the United States were to train an adequate number of artillery officers, the drill for artillery, based on a manual written shortly after the Revolution by Thaddeus Kosciusko, would have to be simplified. Stoddard completed his modified drill in 1810, and it served as the standard text for the military throughout the War of 1812.

Following the outbreak of the War of 1812, Stoddard served on the Detroit frontier under William Henry Harrison. He conducted a train of artillery to the Maumee River rapids on 2 January 1813 and assisted in the construction of Fort Meigs the following spring. He commanded the post's artillery during the first siege (29 April–7 May 1813) and was wounded by an exploding shell while directing the artillery at the grand battery on 1 May. He died of tetanus on 5 May 1813.

—*Larry L. Nelson*

Further Reading
Gilpin, R. Alec. *The War of 1812 in the Old Northwest.* East Lansing: Michigan State University Press, 1958.
Knopf, Richard C., ed. *Document Transcriptions of the War of 1812 in the Old Northwest.* 10 vols. Columbus: Ohio Historical Society, 1956–1962.
Nelson, Larry L. *Men of Patriotism, Courage, and Enterprise: Fort Meigs in the War of 1812.* Canton: Daring Books, 1986.

STONEY CREEK, BATTLE OF
6 June 1813

The Battle of Stoney Creek ended the first U.S. attempt to exploit U.S. victory at Fort George on 27 May 1813. Brig. Gen. John Vincent, having ordered his division to abandon Fort George in the face of Maj. Gen. Henry Dearborn's overpowering assault, drew back his forces from the line of the Niagara River to Burlington Heights, Upper Canada. From this position overlooking Burlington Bay, Vincent could protect the land supply line to Brig. Gen. Henry Procter in western Upper Canada. Dearborn, receiving reports that Procter was en route to Burlington to assist Vincent in regaining Fort George, decided to act first. He sent newly promoted Brig. Gen. William Winder to defeat the British before reinforcements arrived. Winder marched his troops westward along the shore of Lake Ontario. This avenue was cut at frequent intervals by creeks running north from the steep-sided Niagara escarpment into the lake. A convoy of supply boats traveling a parallel course sustained Winder's brigade.

Winder drew up to Burlington Heights and judged the British position too strong to be assaulted by his present force. Dearborn, learning of Winder's concern, dispatched Brig. Gen. John Chandler with reinforcements. Chandler, Winder's senior, was, like Winder, a political appointee. Their combined force camped west of Stoney Creek, 46 miles from Fort George, where it began preparations to attack the British. Vincent considered his situation. If he avoided battle and withdrew his division to York, he would abandon Procter, his native allies, and the western loyalists. If he was encircled in the fortifications on Burlington Heights, he risked defeat that would result in more battle losses as well as stranding Procter and the Indians. A careful reconnaissance of the U.S. camp revealed defects in the positioning of the troops. Vincent chose a bold course; he ordered Lt. Col. John Harvey to conduct a night attack against the U.S. camp. In the darkness, the element of surprise would compensate for inferior British numbers.

Attacking one hour before dawn, the British achieved only partial surprise; a blood-curdling yell delivered as the British advanced served as ample warning for the Americans, who were already apprehensive about a night attack. Losses were moderate on both sides, but the Americans lost both of their generals, who were captured in the confused struggle. The Americans fought back hard but were at a loss about what to do when the sun came up and the British had withdrawn. Command devolved to dragoon Col.

James Burn, who ordered his men to fall back upon their supply vessels at Forty Mile Creek. Demoralized, Burn's troops did not linger to bury their dead or to take their tents and camp equipment with them. Brig. Gens. John Boyd and Morgan Lewis joined Burn's command at the mouth of Forty Mile Creek, where Lewis assumed command.

A handful of Grand River Indians under John Norton appeared at the outskirts of the U.S. camp, giving Lewis the impression that he was faced by a much larger native contingent. Coincidentally, a Royal Navy squadron appeared offshore, chased off the supply boats, and fired into the U.S. camp. Rather than risk encirclement and defeat, Lewis ordered a return to Fort George. Vincent followed at a safe distance and closed in on Fort George in a loose ring. Harvey's audacious night attack at Stoney Creek saved the British position on Burlington Heights.

—*Richard V. Barbuto*

See also: Boyd, John Parker; George, Fort; Harvey, John; Lewis, Morgan; Vincent, John
Further Reading
Berton, Pierre. *Flames across the Border: The Canadian-American Tragedy, 1813–1814*. Boston: Little, Brown, 1981.
Stanley, George F.G. *Battle in the Dark: Stoney Creek, 6 June, 1813*. Toronto: Balmuir Book Publishing, 1991.

STONINGTON, CONNECTICUT, BOMBARDMENT OF
9–12 August 1814

For four days, beginning 9 August 1814, a large, heavily armed British naval squadron under the command of Commodore Sir Thomas Masterman Hardy bombarded the tiny seaport of Stonington, Connecticut. Hardy's ships included HMS *Ramillies* (74 guns), the frigate *Pactolus* (38 guns), the brigs *Dispatch* and *Nimrod* (both 18 guns), and the bombship *Terror*. In all, at least 50 tons of British ammunition were thrown into the village in the form of explosive shells, rockets, incendiary missiles, and cannonballs. Stonington fought back against this massed armed might as best it could, but the village was hopelessly outgunned.

The British had over 160 cannon, while the town could muster only two 18-pounders and a brass 6-pounder, all manned by local civilians. Despite the disparity in weight of metal, however, the village remained largely unharmed over the course of the battle. Of Stonington's 100 or so wooden houses, the British managed to destroy only four and to damage another 30–40. The record showed only a half-dozen U.S. wounded (none seriously) and no deaths. British deaths amounted to anywhere from two to 21, depending on who did the counting. Finally, on the fourth day, after everyone had banged away at each other for the better part of a week, Hardy pulled up anchor and sailed. He had utterly failed to achieve his goal.

The bombardment of Stonington was one of a series of British actions ordered in the late summer of 1814—including the attacks on Washington and Baltimore the following month—designed to distract the U.S. militia from the Canadian border and to force the army to pull troops back to the Atlantic coast. It is clear that Hardy, who had been Nelson's flag officer and who was known as a brave and resourceful officer, was anxious to avoid inflicting civilian casualties. He went to considerable efforts to mitigate the effect of his attack, including giving the inhabitants of Stonington an opportunity to leave town prior to commencing the bombardment. It is also apparent that he expected no opposition and was surprised by the brave response and almost foolhardy defiance of the townspeople.

The news of this curious little action caused a sensation throughout the United States. The story of courageous little Stonington was a refreshing break from the dreary reports arriving from other fronts, and Americans acclaimed it as a stunning victory, a modern Thermopylae, in which a handful of gallant Yankees held off the might of the British navy. In truth, Stonington's victory owed as much to Hardy's determination to spare civilian casualties as it did to the undoubted bravery of the townspeople.

—*James Tertius de Kay*

See also: Connecticut; Hardy, Thomas Masterman
Further Reading
Trumbull, James H. "The Defense of Stonington against a British Squadron, August 9th to 12th, 1814." Hartford: n.p., 1864.

STRACHAN, JOHN
1778–1867
Educator; clergyman; politician

John Strachan was born on 12 April 1778 in Aberdeen, Scotland, the son of John Strachan, a quarry overseer, and Mary Findlayson. He was the youngest survivor of six children, and his family decided to educate him for the ministry. He graduated in 1797 from King's College, Aberdeen, after having studied divinity at St. Andrews University. The death of his father in 1794, however, had left Strachan without family resources; his future appeared constricted to the post of village schoolmaster. He decided to take a teaching position in Upper Canada, where there was the prospect of becoming the mathematics instructor in an academy. This combination of ambition and initiative remained his dominant characteristic throughout his life.

Strachan arrived in Kingston, Upper Canada, in 1799. The promised academy never materialized, and as the end of his three-year contract approached, Strachan considered a number of possibilities. Most appealing was the prospect of a church position. In 1803, Strachan applied for the Anglican parish of Cornwall. On 22 May, he was ordained a deacon of the Church of England, and a year later, a priest.

The Church of England in Upper Canada then occupied an ambiguous position. Only a tiny percentage of the population actively supported the church. On the other hand, Anglicanism was the established church of the province. Stipends did not depend on the support of a congregation; rather, they came from the government and an English missionary society. The position in Cornwall thus offered Strachan a combination of social status and financial security. From 1803 to 1811, he worked to solidify both. To his stipend of £130 he added the profits of a private school. In 1807, he married a widow, Annie Wood McGill, whose annuity amounted to £300. In 1811, after much lobbying, King's College, Aberdeen, conferred on him an honorary doctorate in divinity.

The onset of the War of 1812 changed Strachan's career. Initially, Strachan had declined the offer of the rectorship of York (later Toronto), the provincial capital. Only after Sir Isaac Brock offered to add to it the position of chaplain to the garrison at a salary of £150 did Strachan accept. He arrived in the town shortly after the outbreak of the war and immediately became active. In 1812, he was one of the founders and president of the Loyal and Patriotic Society of Upper Canada, an organization that raised funds for militiamen and their families. When, in April 1813, Americans under Gen. Henry Dearborn and Commodore Isaac Chauncey captured York, Strachan was one of the citizens appointed to negotiate terms. He helped to draft the capitulation and personally lobbied Dearborn and Chauncey to sign and enforce it. In his clerical capacity, he attended to the men wounded in the battle. When Chauncey returned at the end of July, Strachan again negotiated with the U.S. commander, particularly about the return of books looted in the spring.

The war also allowed Strachan to become active in political affairs. With the frequent absences of Brock's successors as administrator, Strachan and such Anglican associates as William Allan and William Powell moved into greater prominence. John MacDonnell, the provincial attorney general, had been killed at the Battle of Queenston. Powell and Strachan secured the vacancy for John Beverley Robinson, a 23-year-old former student of Strachan's. Robinson in turn nominated Strachan to a commission to investigate disloyalty and disorder. In 1814, Gen. Francis de Rottenburg considered naming Strachan to the executive council, but the appointment was not made until September 1815.

Strachan's most permanent contribution to the war was, however, in the area of mythmaking. After the Battle of Queenston, he launched the legend that the Canadian militia, with only minimal assistance from the British army, had saved the colony. He articulated a rhetoric of antirepublicanism and anti-Americanism. After the war, he and men like Robinson and Allan formed the core of the York "Family Compact" that was devoted to the British connection and an established church. To this end, Strachan attempted to shape the emerging educational system of the colony. He and his associates were also involved in such political and entrepreneurial projects as the Bank of Upper Canada and the Welland Canal. Resentment against this group, and Strachan in particular, was a major factor in provoking the Upper Canadian Rebellion of 1837.

In 1839, Strachan became the bishop of Toronto. This marked his apogee. His influence waned in the 1840s and 1850s, and he became more and more exclusively concerned with issues of church governance in the colony. He died on 1 November 1867.

—*Michael McCulloch*

See also: York, Battle of
Further Reading

Bethune, Alexander Neill. *Memoir of the Right Reverend John Strachan.* London: H. Rowsell, 1870.

Fahey, Curtis. *In His Name: The Anglican Experience in Upper Canada, 1791–1854.* Ottawa: Carleton University Press, 1991.

Henderson, J.H.L., ed. *John Strachan: Documents and Opinions.* Toronto: McClelland and Stewart Limited, 1969.

———. *John Strachan, 1778–1867.* Quebec: Presses de l'Universite Laval, 1970.

STRICKER, JOHN
d. 1825
Maryland militia officer

A veteran of the Revolutionary War, Brig. Gen. John Stricker commanded the city of Baltimore brigade in the defense of that city in September 1814. Stricker had dispatched part of his force to the defense of Washington in August 1814, but like the other militia units at the Battle of Bladensburg, those men ran when their position was attacked by the British. The men returned to Baltimore, where they joined with the remainder of the brigade to defend their own city.

In preparation for the British attack, Stricker worked with the other militia officers in and around the city to plan for its defense. Stricker placed his men under the command of Maryland militia major general Samuel Smith, who planned to use Stricker's men as the first line of defense should the British land to the east at North Point. On the night of 11 September 1814, word reached the city that British ships had been sighted off North Point.

Smith immediately dispatched Stricker with about 3,200 men to establish a defense line to block the British advance on the city. Stricker advanced that night and camped at the place where he intended to make his stand the following day. On the morning of 12 September, Stricker deployed his men in three lines, with the first anchored on the right by Bear Creek and on the left by a swamp.

Stricker, knowing that the British had landed and had begun their march, expected an attack early in the morning. When such an attack did not materialize, he dispatched scouts about noon to ascertain the British position. These scouts returned to report that the British had stopped at the Gorsuch farm to eat the farmer's livestock and produce. Stricker then sent forward a group of cavalry and riflemen to provoke the British into a fight. These men approached the farm as the British were finally moving out, and it was one of Stricker's riflemen who mortally wounded British general Robert Ross.

In spite of the death of Ross, Stricker's men succeeded in bringing on the battle. Ross's successor, Col. Arthur Brooke, drove back the U.S. advance party and attacked Stricker's prepared position about 2:00 P.M. The battle raged back and forth for about two hours until the British attempted to turn the U.S. left flank. This maneuver caused a brief panic among Stricker's men that forced the general to abandon his position. He was, however, able to keep his men in good order as they began their retreat to the city's main defenses.

The retreat of Stricker's brigade caused a brief alarm in the city. Many inhabitants feared another Bladensburg, but the defenses planned by Smith and the other officers prevented a British advance into the city. Stricker and his men were placed along these defenses, where they remained until the British withdrew to their boats.

Following the war, Stricker continued to live in Baltimore, where he died in 1825.

—*Jeanne T. Heidler and David S. Heidler*

See also: Baltimore, Battle of; Bladensburg, Battle of; Brooke, Arthur; Ross, Robert; Smith, Samuel
Further Reading
Sanford, John L. "The Battle of North Point." *Maryland Historical Magazine* 24 (1929): 356–365.
Stricker, John. "General John Stricker." *Maryland Historical Magazine* 9 (1914): 209–218.

STRONG, CALEB
1745–1819
Governor of Massachusetts

Caleb Strong was born on 9 June 1745 in Northampton, Massachusetts, the scion of a family that had resided in New England for four generations. Despite chronically poor eyesight, the result of smallpox, he graduated from Harvard College in 1764 with high academic honors. After reading law in the offices of Joseph Hawley, he was admitted to the Massachusetts bar in 1772. That same year, he was elected a selectman of Northampton, which was the beginning of Strong's political career. Following the Boston Massacre of March 1770, Strong consistently supported those American colonials opposing the policies of the British Crown.

His poor vision precluded active military service during the American Revolution; therefore, he spent the war years serving as secretary of the Committee of Public Safety for Northampton. After 1777, Strong was a long-standing member of the Massachusetts General Court (state legislature). In 1778, he was elected a delegate to the constitutional convention of Massachusetts and became an influential member of the committee that drafted the state constitution. Preferring to remain in Massachusetts, in 1780 he declined to fill a seat in the Continental Congress.

In 1787, he was willing to join the Massachusetts delegation to the Constitutional Convention in Philadelphia. During the early sessions, Strong was often absent, tending to family business back home, but during the final months, he was a vocal participant in the debates. He was allied to the faction led by Alexander Hamilton of New York that wanted to create a strong central government.

He sympathized, however, with the positions of the smaller states on various issues, especially regarding the apportionment of representation in Congress. He was also supportive of his home state's political tradition of public officials standing in frequent elections. Accordingly, Strong endorsed the so-called Connecticut Plan, framed by Roger Sherman, that called for proportional representation, as well as biennial elections for the lower congressional house. Sherman's compromise further provided that all states be accorded equal strength in the upper chamber.

During the successful struggle to ratify the federal constitution in Massachusetts, Strong was a leader of the Federalist faction. The Massachusetts General Court in 1789 elected him to the U.S. Senate, where he became a loyal supporter of Pres. George Washington's policies. He was a key framer of various pieces of national legislation, most notably the Federal Judiciary Act of 1789. Strong was the sponsor of the bill that led to the establishment of a national bank, which had been proposed by Secretary of the Treasury Alexander Hamilton. In 1796, Strong resigned this seat to resume his legal practice back in Northampton.

Despite a professed desire to remain in private life, the erstwhile senator became quite active in Massachusetts state politics. Throughout this phase of his career, Strong was a staunch Federalist, although he was no blind follower of either Alexander Hamilton or John Adams. In 1800, Thomas Jefferson and his Democratic Republican party garnered a sweeping national electoral triumph; however, during that same election Strong was elected to the governorship of Massachusetts. Strong was regularly returned to that office until his retirement in 1807. Consequently, he was among the Federalists' most effective national spokesmen against the policies of the Jefferson administration. Certainly he was a vocal critic in 1807 of President Jefferson's embargo. Like most New Englanders, Strong knew that Britain was that region's most lucrative international trading partner.

For the same reason, the respective New England states firmly opposed the congressional declaration of war against the British in June 1812. Some months earlier, Strong had regained his old gubernatorial post as an antiwar candidate. To demonstrate his opposition to the conflict, he refused the request of Secretary of War William B. Eustis to cede his state militia to federal control. The governor argued that none of the explicit constitutional exigencies existed that justified Pres. James Madison's attempts to requisition the Massachusetts militia. Strong particularly opposed the notion that his state troops be used in any proposed U.S. invasions into Canada.

In September 1814, when a British naval flotilla threatened the Massachusetts coastline, Strong mobilized the militia independent of the Madison administration. Acting Secretary of War James Monroe bluntly informed Strong that his state would have to bear unilaterally all subsequent military defense costs. In an address to a special session of the Massachusetts General Court, Strong argued that the federal government had virtually abandoned the five New England states to their own collective resources. Accordingly, he endorsed the growing sentiment among local Federalist partisans that a regional convention be convened to discuss (among other issues) New England's status within the federal union.

Strong was also willing to consider that Massachusetts, as a sovereign entity, negotiate a separate peace agreement with the British. Although not an official delegate to the convention that met during December 1814 in Hartford, Connecticut, Strong was most supportive of its efforts. When news of the Treaty of Ghent reached North America in January 1815, however, any need to reconvene the Hartford Convention no longer existed.

Despite the inevitable and negative political backlash that engulfed the Federalist party in the postwar years, Strong retained his gubernatorial office until 1816. That year, sensing certain defeat, he refused to be the party's national presidential candidate. Because of declining health, Strong completely withdrew from active politics during his final years. On 7 November 1819, Strong died at his lifelong Northampton residence.

—*Miles S. Richards*

See also: Militia Controversy, The New England
Further Reading

Banner, James M., Jr. *To the Hartford Convention: The Federalists and the Origins of Party Politics in Massachusetts, 1789–1815.* New York: Alfred Knopf, 1970.

Beard, Charles A. *An Economic Interpretation of the Constitution of the United States.* New York and London: Free Press, Collier Macmillan, 1989.

Fischer, David Hackett. *The Revolution of American Conservatism: The Federalist Party in the Era of Jeffersonian Democracy.* New York: Harper and Row, 1965.

Kerber, Linda K. *Federalists in Dissent: Imagery and Ideology in Jeffersonian America.* Ithaca, NY: Cornell University Press, 1980.

STROTHER, FORT

As Gen. Andrew Jackson marched south into the Creek Nation in October 1813, it became necessary to establish fortified bases along his route of march. Jackson first established Fort Deposit 20 miles south of Huntsville, Alabama. Pushing farther south, he detached John Coffee to attack at Tallushatchee and then established Fort Strother. This fort would become Jackson's base of operations for his entire campaign against the Creek Indians.

Fort Strother was located at a point on the Coosa River known as Ten Islands. It was constructed on a defensible point on the right bank of the river. Jackson adopted the usual method of fortifying against Indian assaults by enclosing a large space within a line of strong timber pickets. Fort Strother was a square enclosure, with each side approximately 100 yards long, and was completed at the end of October 1813. It contained a blockhouse in each of the four corners. Inside the fort were eight small huts, a supply building, a hospital, and room for approximately 25 tents. At its maximum capacity, the fort held over 1,000 men.

Fort Strother became the center of Jackson's operations until the signing of the Treaty of Fort Jackson in August 1814. All of Jackson's attacks were launched out of Fort Strother and included his campaigns against Econochaca, Emuckfau, and Horseshoe Bend. The base was used to store supplies and provided protection for his entire army when it was not on campaign.

—*John M. Keefe*

See also: Creek War
Further Reading

Halbert, H. S., and T. H. Ball. *The Creek War of 1813 and 1814.* Chicago: Donohue and Henneberry, 1895.

Owsley, Frank Lawrence. *Struggle for the Gulf Borderlands: The Creek War and the Battle of New Orleans, 1812–1815.* Gainesville: University Presses of Florida, 1981.

Rowland, Dunbar. *Andrew Jackson's Campaign against the British, or the Mississippi Territory in the War of 1812.* New York: Macmillan, 1926.

SWIFT, JOSEPH GARDNER
1783–1865
U.S. officer

Born on Nantucket to Foster Swift and Deborah Delano Swift, Joseph Swift became a cadet in the Corps of Engineers in 1800 and, with the establishment of the U.S. Military Academy at West Point, entered the first class in 1802 and became its first graduate later that year. As a talented engineer-officer, Swift rose quickly in the corps, to first lieutenant in 1805, captain in 1806, major in 1808, and lieutenant colonel on 6 July 1812 and three weeks later to colonel and commander of the Corps of Engineers.

During his rise in rank, Swift also served a brief stint as commandant of cadets at West Point.

During the War of 1812, Swift served in a variety of posts, including that of chief engineer of the Army of the North during James Wilkinson's invasion of Canada in the winter of 1813. Before the campaign commenced, he conferred with both Wilkinson and Secretary of War John Armstrong regarding the best approaches to British fortifications and the city of Montreal. He was never able to use his plans, however, because Wilkinson's dispirited army never seriously threatened British positions.

Following the end of this campaign in the spring of 1814, Swift was transferred to New York City, where he was instrumental in the strengthening of that city's fortifications during the summer and fall of 1814. Because of British attacks on Washington, D.C., and Baltimore, the citizens of New York became convinced that they were a likely target for British aggression. They were more than willing to follow Swift's instructions in August and September 1814 in preparing New York for attack. Though such a British offensive never materialized, the citizens of New York remained forever grateful to Swift for his efforts, believing that his plans dissuaded the British from making the attempt.

Following the war, Swift remained the commander of the Corps of Engineers, but his authority was much diminished by the government's reliance on Gen. Simon Bernard, the French engineer. Unhappy over his ebbing influence, Swift resigned in 1818. For the remainder of his life, he would engage in engineering projects on the Great Lakes and in eastern railroad construction. He also worked again for the government on various harbors on the eastern seaboard. He died in Geneva, New York, in 1865.

—*Jeanne T. Heidler and David S. Heidler*

See also: New York City; Wilkinson, James
Further Reading
Walker, Charles E. "The Other Good Guys: Army Engineers in the War of 1812." *Military Engineer* (June 1978): 178–183.

T

TAGGART, SAMUEL
1754–1825
U.S. congressman

Born in New Hampshire to Matthew Taggart and Jane Anderson Taggart, Samuel Taggart graduated from Dartmouth College in 1774. After deciding on a ministerial career in the Presbyterian Church, Taggart moved to Massachusetts, where he combined a clerical and political life.

With the election of Democratic Republican Thomas Jefferson to the presidency, the vocal Federalist Taggart became increasingly interested in politics and stood for election to Congress in 1802. As the United States moved closer to war with Great Britain, Taggart, along with his fellow Federalists, became increasingly critical of Democratic Republican policies.

When the United States declared war in June 1812, Taggart theorized that there were far more opponents to the war than the vote indicated but that many who had voted for the declaration had been frightened into doing so by the War Hawks. Taggart was also one of the first Federalists to openly criticize the Madison administration's conduct of the war. In a speech before Congress in June 1812, Taggart outlined one of the primary objections of the Federalists during the war by chastising the administration for conducting what he saw to be an immoral war. He believed that to attack Canada to protect U.S. maritime rights unjustly punished the Canadian people because they had done nothing wrong, unless one were willing to extend British guilt to them through association.

For the remainder of the war, Taggart continued to be a vocal critic of the administration. Everything from military policy to cabinet appointments drew a generally negative opinion. Like many who questioned the fiscal responsibility of the administration, Taggart was especially critical of Pres. James Madison's appointment of George Washington Campbell to the position of secretary of the treasury in early 1814.

Following the war, Taggart continued to serve in congress for another two years before retiring in Massachusetts. He retired from the ministry in 1818 and died in Colerain, Massachusetts, in 1825.

—Jeanne T. Heidler and David S. Heidler

See also: Campbell, George W.; U.S. Congress; War Hawks
Further Reading
Hayes, George H., ed. "Letters of Samuel Taggart, Representative in Congress, 1802–1814." *American Antiquarian Society Proceedings* 33 (1924): 390–440.

TALLADEGA, BATTLE OF
9 November 1813

In the early phases of Tennessee militia major general Andrew Jackson's campaign against the Red Stick Creeks in the Creek War, he established a supply base at what he dubbed Fort Deposit on the Tennessee River. During the last week of October 1813, Jackson heard that Red Sticks intended to attack the U.S.-allied Creek town of Talladega. For that reason, Jackson decided to move south from Fort Deposit.

In advance of his main force, Jackson sent Brig. Gen. John Coffee's cavalry to destroy the Red Stick town of Tallushatchee, which Coffee accomplished on 3 November 1813. In the meantime, Jackson had moved forward and established Fort Strother, at which he received a message from Talladega on 7 November that the town was besieged. Leaving his sick behind because he believed that reinforcements and supplies would be arriving soon, Jackson set out that evening with 2,000 men for Talladega.

The following night Jackson was within a few miles of the besieged town. At the same time, however, he received word that the expected reinforcements and supplies would not be arriving at Fort Strother, leaving that position very vulnerable. Since he was within striking distance of his objective, Jackson decided to attack the Red Sticks outside of Talladega first and then move quickly back to Fort Strother.

On the morning of 9 November 1813, Jackson deployed his cavalry in front and positioned his infantry in two columns with the objective of encircling the Red Stick camps. Unfortunately for Jackson, the battle began before the envelopment was complete, and most of the Red Sticks were able to find the gap in his lines. When the battle ended, Jackson had suffered 95 casualties and found 299 dead Red Sticks. How many additional casualties the Red Sticks suffered out of their total force of approximately 1,000 was never determined.

Because of his supply shortage and the precarious position of Fort Strother, Jackson was unable to pursue the Red Sticks. These problems became so acute within a short time that Jackson was forced to march the bulk of his army back to Fort Deposit. He would not be able to engage in further campaigning until reinforcements arrived after the first of the year.

—*Jeanne T. Heidler and David S. Heidler*

See also: Coffee, John; Creek War; Deposit, Fort(s); Jackson, Andrew; Red Sticks; Strother, Fort
Further Reading
Owsley, Frank L., Jr. *Struggle for the Gulf Borderlands: The Creek War and the Battle of New Orleans, 1812–1815.* Gainesville: University Presses of Florida, 1981.

TALLMADGE, BENJAMIN
1754–1835
U.S. congressman

Benjamin Tallmadge was born in Brookhaven, New York, to Benjamin Tallmadge and Susannah Smith Tallmadge. He graduated from Yale in 1773 and enlisted at the outbreak of the American Revolution. By the end of the war, his bravery and skill in battle had won him the rank of brevet lieutenant colonel. Following the war, he went into business in Connecticut and entered politics. From 1801 to 1817, he served in the U.S. House of Representatives as a Connecticut Federalist.

A devoutly religious man, Tallmadge decried the turn toward war he feared the country was taking during the first Madison administration. A tremendous admirer of George Washington, under whom he had served during the Revolution, Tallmadge urged Congress to follow the first president's advice to prevent war by preparing for it. He did not see his recommendations acted upon, however, until the

country was within months of war. As he and many of his fellow Federalists lamented, it was too little, too late.

Retiring from Congress in 1817, he spent the remainder of his life in private and charitable pursuits, dying in Litchfield, Connecticut, in 1835.

—*Jeanne T. Heidler and David S. Heidler*

Further Reading
Hall, Charles S. *Benjamin Tallmadge.* New York: Columbia University Press, 1943.

TALLUSHATCHEE, BATTLE OF
3 November 1813

Following the massacre at Fort Mims, Alabama, by Red Stick Creek Indians in August 1813, an emotional call for volunteers went out to the surrounding states. The Tennessee legislature voted funds to equip a volunteer militia, and Andrew Jackson was selected as commander. Jackson led his army into Alabama in October 1813 and established his base camp at Fort Deposit, near present-day Huntsville. Eventually Jackson pushed his army southward to the Coosa River, which placed him in proximity to several Creek villages. Jackson instructed Gen. John Coffee to construct an advance base, Fort Strother, at the Ten Islands of the Coosa River. About 10 miles from Fort Strother was the northernmost Red Stick Creek village of Tallushatchee. Learning that hostile Indians had gathered there and considering the village's strategic threat to Fort Strother, Jackson ordered Coffee to take 1,000 men and destroy the village.

Pursuant to the orders, Coffee detailed 900 cavalry and friendly Indians and advanced to within 1.5 miles of Tallushatchee on 2 November 1813. On the following morning, he divided his force into two columns as it approached the village. The right column under Col. John Allcorn circled the village on the south side, while Col. Newton Cannon encircled the village on the north side. Coffee then sent a smaller force under Lts. E. Hammond and Andrew Patterson directly toward the village to draw the warriors to them. The Indians responded as Coffee expected, and they were easily overwhelmed by the forces that attacked them from all sides. The Creeks fired their muskets only once and reverted to bows and arrows. Davy Crockett, a participant in the battle, described women using bows and for the first time saw a man killed by an arrow. The Indians fought fiercely against the more numerous and better-armed Americans. The Indian cabins were burned, and many noncombatants chose to die with the warriors in the flaming structures. Coffee reported to Jackson that 186 warriors were killed, and others probably died in the surrounding brush. Eighty-four women and children were taken to Fort Strother as prisoners. Coffee's force suffered five dead and 40 wounded in the battle.

In addition to Coffee and Crockett, other participants in the battle or members of patrols visiting the battlefield in the hours following the carnage were Richard Keith Call (future governor of Florida); John Reid (Jackson's secretary and biographer); Sam Houston; and Cherokee scouts John Ross, Sequoyah, Selocta Chinnobee, Jim Fife, and the Ridge. Crockett, Reid, Call, Coffee, and John Walker, another participant, left written accounts or letters describing the brief battle at Tallushatchee Creek.

Jackson, in response to Coffee's initial account of the battle, notified the governor of Tennessee that his army had retaliated for the destruction of Fort Mims. The Battle of Tallushatchee was a primitive engagement ordered by Jackson to eliminate a threat to Fort Strother and to send a stern message to the Red Stick Creek warriors.

—*Phillip E. Koerper*

See also: Coffee, John; Creek War; Crockett, David "Davy"; Houston, Sam; Red Sticks; Strother, Fort

Further Reading

Basset, John S., and J. Franklin Jameson, eds. *The Correspondence of Andrew Jackson.* 7 vols. Washington, DC: Carnegie Institution, 1926–1935.

Buell, Augustus C. *History of Andrew Jackson.* 2 vols. New York: Charles Scribner's Sons, 1904.

Crockett, David. *A Narrative of the Life of David Crockett of the State of Tennessee.* Ed. James A. Shackford and Stanley J. Folmsbee. 1869; reprint, Knoxville: University of Tennessee Press, 1973.

Parton, James. *Life of Andrew Jackson.* 3 vols. Boston: Fields, Osgood and Company, 1870.

Reid, John, and John Henry Eaton. *The Life of Andrew Jackson.* Ed. Frank Lawrence Owsley, Jr. 1817; reprint, University: University of Alabama Press, 1974.

TANEY, ROGER BROOKE
1777–1864
Maryland Federalist

Born at Taney Place on the Patuxent River in Calvert County, Maryland, to Michael Taney and Monica Brooke Taney, Roger Taney was trained to be a lawyer from a young age. He began practicing law in 1799 and immediately entered Maryland politics with his election to the lower house of the state legislature in the same year.

As a Federalist, Taney was swept out of office with many of his party in the election of 1800. Shortly afterward he moved to Frederick, Maryland, where he practiced law for the next two decades. While in Frederick, he met and married Anne Key, the sister of Francis Scott Key. Taney established a lucrative legal practice and became a leading figure in the state Federalist Party. When the War of 1812 began, Taney's influence in the state party declined because he believed it his duty to support the war effort. His minority faction became known as "Coodies" and Taney, its leader, as "King Coody."

Taney differed from most of his fellow Maryland Federalists not only in his opinions about the war but also in his refusal to endorse Alexander C. Hanson's continued publication of the *Federal Republican.* After the Baltimore riots over this controversial antiwar publication and his serious injury, Hanson never forgave Taney for his lack of support and worked relentlessly until his death in 1819 to destroy Taney politically. In the meantime, Taney's stance regarding the *Federal Republican* probably cost him a congressional seat in the fall 1812 elections.

The British campaign in Maryland in 1814, however, changed the fortunes of the "Coodies." As Marylanders experienced the war firsthand on a large scale, seeking revenge for British depredations in the state became an important consideration. Those political figures who supported fighting the war to its fullest became increasingly popular.

Taney and his family were among those who experienced the war firsthand during the Washington campaign of August 1814. As the British moved up the Patuxent River, they stopped briefly at Taney Place, looting the property and destroying much of what they did not take. The family's finances never recovered from the devastation.

While the British looted Taney Place, Taney was in Frederick; yet as the British sat in Washington, Taney's wife urged him to rescue her brother's family. She feared that the British would move on Georgetown next, the home of her brother Francis Scott Key. Taney hastened to evacuate his wife's sister-in-law and her children before the town was overrun with British. Taney did not arrive there until after the British had started back to their ships, but just to be safe he took Mrs. Key and the children to Frederick. His brother-in-law was on his way to see the British to try to gain the release of Dr. William Beanes, who had been made their prisoner.

After Baltimore was successfully defended, the "Coodies" began ascending in Federalist politics in the state, and Taney intended to take advantage of the growing weakness of the opposition. Following the war, he was elected to the state senate, where he worked to further weaken extremists in the party. All this effort proved of little worth, however, as the Federalist Party rapidly died in Maryland.

With the demise of his party, Taney became a Jacksonian in 1824 and would remain a strong Democrat for the remainder of his life. Taney continued to work in state politics until 1831, when he was appointed Andrew Jackson's attorney general. He eventually moved over to the treasury, where he helped Jackson deal the death blows to the Second Bank of the United States. As a reward for his loyalty, Taney was nominated by Jackson to the Supreme Court in 1835. The Senate did not confirm the nomination, but on Chief Justice John Marshall's death, Jackson nominated Taney to that position, and this time a much-changed Senate confirmed him. He would be chief justice until his death in 1864 and hand down some of the most influential decisions in the history of the Supreme Court.

—Jeanne T. Heidler and David S. Heidler

See also: Hanson, Alexander Contee; Key, Francis Scott
Further Reading
Lewis, Walker. *Without Fear or Favor: A Biography of Chief Justice Roger Brooke Taney.* Boston: Houghton Mifflin, 1965.

TAYLOR, JOHN
1753–1824
U.S. political theorist

Born in Virginia to James Taylor and Ann Pollard Taylor, John Taylor of Caroline was orphaned at an early age and was reared by his cousin and uncle by marriage, Edmund Pendleton. After attending the College of William and Mary, Taylor studied law under his guardian. Taylor served as an officer in the Continental Army and the Virginia militia during the American Revolution, as well as in the Virginia House of Delegates.

Following the Revolution, Taylor retained his interest in politics, though primarily from a theoretical standpoint. During the 1790s, he became increasingly supportive of Thomas Jefferson and the Democratic Republicans, believing that the Federalists of that decade were moving too much toward a strong central government at the expense of individuals and the states. During this period through the presidency of Thomas Jefferson, Taylor served terms in the Virginia House of Delegates and was appointed to fill two unexpired terms in the U.S. Senate.

During Jefferson's first term, Taylor supported most of the administration's policies. By the second term, however, Taylor became increasingly associated with the group known as "Old Republicans," or Tertium Quids. Ostensibly led by John Randolph, this group grew increasingly suspicious of what they saw as the centralizing tendencies of Jefferson's second administration and generally blamed Jefferson's Secretary of State James Madison for what they believed to be a move toward Federalist policies. For this reason, Taylor strongly supported James Monroe's bid for the presidency against Madison in 1808.

Madison's administration confirmed Taylor's suspicions, especially as the country moved toward war with Great Britain in 1812. Taylor believed that Madison had defected to Federalism and that his efforts to embroil the country in a war were Madison's way of strengthening the central government. When Madison purchased the John Henry letters in the spring of 1812, Taylor believed the act was aimed at stirring up the mob for war.

Once the War of 1812 began, Taylor remained critical of the power accrued by the central government. Most of his reproaches remained relatively private, however, and were contained in his various correspondence to people such as Secretary of State James Monroe. He observed to Monroe at the end of 1812 that because of the military reverses in the summer and fall of 1812, the Madison administration had backed itself into a corner. The country could not possibly win the conflict outright but could not honorably extricate itself from it either.

Already interested in political theory and the author of a number of short treatises before the war, in 1814 Taylor published *An Inquiry into the Principles and Policy of the Government of the United States.* In this work, Taylor asserted that the presidency and the Senate had become too powerful and were in danger of creating an American aristocracy. He presented the elimination of patronage and a shortening of terms as one solution to this growing problem.

Though his writings during the war and afterward did little to influence public opinion (few people read them), Taylor continued to advocate limited government. In spite of its lack of appeal to his own generation, later generations would view his work as some of the most important works of political theory produced in the United States.

—Jeanne T. Heidler and David S. Heidler

See also: Henry, John; Jefferson, Thomas; Madison, James; Monroe, James

Further Reading

Hammond, Hans, ed. "Letters of John Taylor of Caroline." *Virginia Magazine of History and Biography* 52 (1944): 1–14, 121–134.

Shalhope, Robert F. *John Taylor of Caroline: Pastoral Republican.* Columbia: University of South Carolina Press, 1980.

TAYLOR, ZACHARY
1784–1850
U.S. officer

Zachary Taylor was a 40-year career soldier and war hero who was elected the 12th president of the United States in 1848 as the candidate of the Whig Party. He was born on 24 November 1784 near Orange Court House, Virginia. His father, Richard Taylor, was a planter, a College of William and Mary graduate, and an attorney. During the Revolutionary War, the older Taylor was a lieutenant colonel. Shortly after the end of that conflict, the Taylor family moved west to a plantation near Louisville, Kentucky. Unlike his father, Zachary Taylor had little formal education. Instead he received private tutoring and practical learning on the frontier plantation and in the Kentucky militia.

When he was 22 years old, he served as a volunteer lieutenant in an Indian war. Two years later, in 1808, Taylor received an appointment as a first lieutenant in the U.S. Army and was stationed in New Orleans. By 1810, Zachary Taylor had been promoted to captain and was transferred to the Indiana Territory. As Tecumseh and Tenskwatawa's influence increased, Taylor was placed in command of Fort Knox and later Fort Harrison. During the first year of the War of 1812, Zachary Taylor distinguished himself when his small detachment of 50 soldiers defeated an Indian army of 400 under the command of Tecumseh. In this engagement, he saved the important frontier community of Vincennes, Indiana. Later, Taylor won another victory defending Fort Madison.

Promoted to brevet major for his successes in 1813, Taylor spent most of the next year and a half recruiting troops; inspecting U.S. army and militia units; and campaigning against Indians in the Illinois, Indiana, and Missouri Territories. Later, in August 1814, he began offensive actions against British-allied Indian nations in what is now Iowa and Wisconsin. Taylor's offensive force of 330 soldiers moved north up the Mississippi River to attack Indian settlements on the Rock River west of Lake Michigan. At Rock River, Taylor's small army met a force of over 1,000 Indians, Canadians, and British armed with field artillery. The Americans lost the battle, and Taylor retreated southward down the Mississippi to the mouth of the Des Moines River, where he erected a small fortification named Fort Johnson. This was the last major battle of the war in the West. Although Taylor's forces were defeated, he retreated in an orderly manner and still had enough forces to protect St. Louis, Missouri, and most of the Illinois Territory. Since his position at Fort Johnson was an unprotected one, he later destroyed this fortification in October 1814 and withdrew his forces to St. Louis. At the end of the war in December 1814, he was placed in command of Fort Knox near Louisville, Kentucky.

After a brief period of civilian life, Taylor rejoined the army, where he remained for the next 35 years. In his post–War of 1812 career, Taylor distinguished himself as a frontier soldier during the Black Hawk, Second Seminole, and Mexican-American Wars. General Taylor's greatest fame came in the Mexican-American War, for his great victory at the Battle of Buena Vista and his masterful southward march from the Rio Grande River into the heart of Mexico.

Affectionately referred to as "Old Rough and Ready" by his soldiers and the public, Zachary Taylor retired from military service shortly after the Mexican-American War and settled briefly on a plantation in Louisiana prior to the 1848 presidential election. Taylor was elected president and served almost two years before his death in 1850.

His is considered to be a classic American success story, of a frontiersman who through hard work, courage, and determination achieved success in both his military and political careers.

—George E. Frakes

Further Reading

Allison, Joseph. *An Eulogy upon the Life, Character and Public Services of General Zachary Taylor: Delivered at the Commissioners' Hall, Spring Garden, July 29th, 1850.* Philadelphia: J. H. Jones, 1850.

Bauer, Karl Jack. *Zachary Taylor: Soldier, Planter, Statesman of the Old Southwest.* Baton Rouge: Louisiana State University Press, 1985.

Burnett, Kevin. "Tippecanoe and Taylor Too." *Journal of the West* 31 (1992): 44–50.

Dyer, Brainerd. *Zachary Taylor.* Baton Rouge: Louisiana State University Press, 1946.

Hamilton, Holman. *Three Kentucky Presidents—Lincoln, Taylor, and Davis.* Lexington: University Press of Kentucky, 1978.

———. *Zachary Taylor, Soldier of the Republic.* Hamden, CT: Archon Books, 1966.

Howard, Oliver Otis. *General Taylor*. New York: D. Appleton: 1892.

Lincoln, Abraham. *The Life and Public Service of General Zachary Taylor: An Address by Abraham Lincoln*. Boston: Houghton Mifflin, 1922.

Melville, Herman. *Authentic Anecdotes of Old Zack*. New Brighton, MN: K. Starosciak, 1973.

TECUMSEH
1768?–1813
Shawnee chief

Tecumseh was born in what is now the state of Ohio, probably near present-day Springfield. There is no reliable account of his childhood and youth, but in the early 1790s he began to participate in resistance to the Americans in the Ohio region. He served as a scout with the Indians who defeated Arthur St. Clair's expedition in November 1791 and fought in the Indian loss at the Battle of Fallen Timbers in August 1794.

In the years after Fallen Timbers, while U.S. settlers advanced in large numbers beyond the Ohio, Tecumseh lived in the Ohio/Indiana region and was still little known beyond his immediate surroundings. He was to come to prominence as a result of the way in which he, together with his brother Tenskwatawa (the Prophet), reacted to the extensive land cessions secured by the Americans in the years after Thomas Jefferson became president. In 1805, Tenskwatawa began to preach an Indian religious revival at Greenville, Ohio. He wanted the Indians to throw off the ways of the Europeans and return to the ways of their forefathers, arguing that this would enable them, with the support of the Great Spirit, to overcome the settlers who were taking their lands and destroying their way of life.

The Prophet's influence spread rapidly in the Great Lakes region, but in the following years his brother Tecumseh began to assume a leadership role in dealing with the U.S. demands for land in the region. In 1807–1808, when the British in Canada began to fear conflict with the United States and decided to renew their efforts to win Indian support in the event of any future war, they became anxious to enlist the support of the Prophet and his brother. At first the Prophet was their main hope, but from the summer of 1808, when Tecumseh visited the British at Fort Malden in Upper Canada, the British became increasingly interested in assisting and supplying Tecumseh's efforts to resist the advance of the U.S. frontier.

In these years, Tecumseh developed his idea of an Indian confederacy that would own its lands in common. He argued that no individual tribe had the right to cede land that in reality belonged to all the Indians. He began to travel widely to encourage Indian tribes to join his movement. Tecumseh had the most success among younger warriors, who from 1808 began to gather on the Tippecanoe River in northern Indiana. The two brothers had made this settlement the center of their activities.

The activities at Tippecanoe were viewed with great suspicion by Gov. William Henry Harrison of the Indiana Territory. Although the root causes of the movement lay in the relentless U.S. pressure for land, Harrison often placed the blame on the members of the British Indian Department across the Detroit River at Fort Malden. The British wanted to take advantage of the activities of Tecumseh and his brother, but they were not the prime movers.

After Harrison secured another land cession from the Indians through the Treaty of Fort Wayne in 1809, tensions increased, and Tecumseh began to take a more dominant role than his brother. In August 1810, Tecumseh and Governor Harrison met in dramatic fashion in Vincennes, and Tecumseh impressively spoke of the Indian desire to unite to resist the Americans and to retain their lands. That fall, Tecumseh again visited the British at Fort Malden and made it clear that he was ready to fight to resist U.S. demands.

When in the summer of 1811, Tecumseh again visited Harrison at Vincennes, he took with him several hundred of his warriors. A tense meeting resolved nothing, and on leaving the conference, Tecumseh traveled into the south to try to enlist Chickasaws, Choctaws, and Creeks to his cause. He won some supporters among the Upper Creeks, but in general he was not successful in winning the support of a large number of southern Indians.

While Tecumseh was away in the South, Governor Harrison had decided to take action against the center of resistance at Prophet's Town on the Tippecanoe River. In the fall of 1811, he led an army north, and when he camped close to the Indian settlement, the Prophet decided to attack. In the battle on 7 November, the Indians were dispersed and Prophet's Town was burned, but the Americans had suffered as many casualties as the Indians, and the Indian will to resist had not been destroyed.

When Tecumseh returned from the South and found his village in ruins, he set about rebuilding his confederacy and preparing for war against the Americans. In July 1812, when news of the U.S. declaration of war reached the Detroit frontier region, Tecumseh was already on the British side of the river with many of his warriors. He quickly began to take an important part in the conflict.

The U.S. general William Hull had crossed the Detroit

River in the expectation of attacking Fort Malden, but he was extremely concerned about his supply lines that linked Detroit with the U.S. settlements in Ohio. His concern increased considerably when, early in August, Tecumseh led warriors across the Detroit River and ambushed a U.S. force that was sent to provide an escort for the supplies. This helped to persuade Hull to withdraw his forces to Detroit. He also attempted to secure his supply lines by sending another, and larger, force to protect and open the route into Ohio. Again the Americans were ambushed, this time by a combined force of British regulars and Indians under Tecumseh. The U.S. force put up a strong resistance, but Hull recalled it to Detroit. When British general Isaac Brock then prepared to attack Detroit with a combined force of British troops and Indian warriors, Hull surrendered on 16 August. Brock had the highest opinion of Tecumseh's abilities.

Tecumseh and his Indian warriors continued to give important support to the British forces in the Detroit frontier region. In the spring and summer of 1813, along with other Indian chiefs, he led over 1,000 Indians to take part in the British sieges of Fort Meigs in northwestern Ohio. The sieges were unsuccessful, but on the first expedition a U.S. relief force was defeated. Tecumseh's reputation was enhanced following that engagement when he intervened to stop the killing of U.S. prisoners.

After the second siege of Fort Meigs, the British turned their attention to the U.S. Fort Stephenson in northern Ohio. Because the Indians were reluctant to attack entrenched positions and complained that the British could not reduce the fort with their guns, the unsuccessful attack on the fort on 2 August brought mutual recriminations between the British and their Indian allies.

In September 1813, the situation on the Detroit frontier changed decisively in favor of the Americans when Commander Oliver Hazard Perry defeated the British fleet on Lake Erie at the Battle of Put-in-Bay (or the Battle of Lake Erie). The British commander, Henry Procter, needed control of the lake to obtain supplies from the east. In addition to the British troops, there were now several thousand Indian warriors and their families in the area around Fort Malden. Expecting an attack from the U.S. general William Henry Harrison, Procter decided to retreat eastward.

When on 13 September Procter ordered the dismantling of Fort Malden, Tecumseh protested the decision with great anger. General Procter twice held meetings with Tecumseh to try to persuade him that the retreat was essential, but Tecumseh accused Procter of cowardice. The British retreat began in some confusion, both because of Procter's lack of leadership and because of the reluctance of the Indians to abandon the Detroit River region. Tecumseh and his Indian allies found it difficult to accept the argument that a naval victory on Lake Erie had made it essential that the British and Indian force should abandon its position.

In the course of the retreat eastward from Fort Malden, many Indians began to leave the British forces. Tecumseh and his close followers stayed, but Tecumseh was still angry at Procter's conduct. With the Americans in close pursuit, Procter decided to make a stand near Moraviantown on the River Thames. His force was now outnumbered and demoralized, and when on 5 October the Americans attacked, the British quickly broke ranks. On the British right flank, however, Tecumseh and his warriors put up a stern resistance before Tecumseh was killed.

How Tecumseh died and the fate of his body have been the subject of endless discussion. Although there was never any certainty, the most accepted version at the time was that Tecumseh had been shot by the commander of the Kentucky mounted militia, Col. Richard M. Johnson. The assumption that Johnson had shot Tecumseh helped the Kentuckian in his subsequent political career. There was also never any certainty about what happened to Tecumseh's body. The U.S. troops mutilated many of the Indian dead after the engagement, and it is possible that one of these bodies was that of Tecumseh. It is also possible that the Indians carried him off and buried him.

The Tecumseh confederacy collapsed with the death of its leader, but the fame of the Shawnee grew larger after his death. Legends were inserted into the story of his life, and fictional accounts were often allowed to impinge on the real Tecumseh. Little is known of his family life. It is believed that he married twice. The name of his first wife is unknown. By his second wife, Mamate, he had one son, Pachetha. Mamate died before Tecumseh became involved in the formation of his confederacy, and his son was brought up by his sister, Tecumpease. Tecumseh was respected by all who met him, as a leader, as an orator, and as a man.

—*Reginald Horsman*

See also: Brock, Isaac; Detroit, Surrender of; Harrison, William Henry; Hull, William; Indiana Territory; Johnson, Richard Mentor; Lake Erie Campaign; Meigs, Fort; Procter, Henry; Prophet's Town; Put-in-Bay, Ohio; Stephenson, Fort; Tenskwatawa; Tippecanoe, Battle of

Further Reading

Edmunds, R. David. *Tecumseh and the Quest for Indian Leadership*. Boston: Little, Brown, 1984.

Gilbert, Bil. *God Gave Us This Country: Tekamthi and the First American Civil War*. New York: Atheneum, 1989.

Goltz, Herbert. "Tecumseh: The Man and the Myth." Ph.D. dissertation, University of Western Ontario, 1973.

Sugden, John. *Tecumseh's Last Stand*. Norman: University of Oklahoma Press, 1985.

TENNESSEE

Tennessee played as prominent a role in the War of 1812 as any state in the union. Tennessee's congressional delegation boasted several prominent War Hawks, including Felix Grundy and John Sevier. Its senators and representatives voted unanimously in favor of declaring war, and the people of Tennessee needed little prompting to participate in the conflagration. They mobilized rapidly, undertook several campaigns against Britain's Indian allies, and contributed men and material to the rousing victory at New Orleans in January 1815. Most significant, Tennessee's Andrew Jackson emerged as the greatest hero of the war.

Tennesseans proved eager for confrontation during the Madison administration for several reasons. Not one of the original 13 states, Tennessee could claim little in the way of a Revolutionary War heritage. Although wartime land grants had paved the way for settlement, few of the state's prominent citizens played a significant role in the struggle for independence. The War of 1812 promised the young state and its citizens an opportunity to fight anew for freedom. Once again the enemy was a predatory Great Britain, and again the stakes were extremely high. Many Tennesseans believed that defeat might bring about the collapse of the U.S. republic.

Citizens of Tennessee greatly desired to defend the honor of the nation; patriotism and a strong sense of national pride ran deep on the frontier. Although few Tennesseans were directly affected by British maritime depredations—such as impressment and the confiscation of U.S. cargo on the high seas—many felt that U.S. honor had to be defended at all costs. In their numerous speeches, Congressmen Felix Grundy and John Sevier as well Gov. Willie Blount bristled with indignation at Britain's repeated slights to U.S. honor committed on the high seas. It seemed to matter little that no sea washed upon Tennessee's borders.

Although Tennesseans echoed Pres. James Madison's demand for freedom of the seas, their real interest lay in western lands. Ardent expansionists, the citizens of Tennessee immediately seized the opportunity presented by a war with England and its allies. Tennesseans had long harbored suspicions of British and Spanish intentions in the Mississippi Valley. Few residents needed convincing that European imperial ambitions ranged from Canada in the north to Florida in the south. As long as the English and Spanish possessed lands in the West, Tennessee's territorial ambitions were at risk. Many Tennesseans agreed with Andrew Jackson that the war presented a great opportunity to acquire western lands "indispensable to the prosperity" of the state and the nation.

Tennesseans well understood that it was neither the British nor the Spanish but their Indian allies who held in check the frontiersman's insatiable appetite for land. The War of 1812 promised the chance to upset the confederation of Indian tribes on the western frontier. Tennesseans readily believed that the British had encouraged the great Indian warrior Tecumseh and his followers to conspire against the United States. When Felix Grundy declared that "future ages would be proud to celebrate the day on which a virtuous Congress Declared War against imperial Britain," he well understood that Tennessee would celebrate the destruction of imperial Britain's Indian allies. When the United States declared war on England, the Creek Nation became fair game.

By far the major part of Tennessee's war effort manifested itself in Indian fighting. By 1813, Tennesseans were actively engaged in the Creek War, responding to the Red Stick attack on Fort Mims. At the ghastly Battle of Horseshoe Bend on 27 March 1814, Tennessee troops slaughtered 800 Creeks while losing only 45 of their own. Many Tennesseans made their military reputations by means of their dubious exploits against the Creeks. Both Sam Houston and Andrew Jackson, the latter labeled "tough as hickory" by his men during an abortive 1812 march by the Tennessee militia, utilized their military victories to catapult themselves to great political heights. Houston was elected the first president of the Republic of Texas in 1836, and Jackson rode his Indian triumphs and his command of U.S. forces at New Orleans all the way to the presidency of the United States.

The average Tennessean proved no less enthusiastic for war than the state's leaders. News of the declaration of war "produced lively beams of satisfaction from almost every countenance," a Knoxville newspaper editor wrote. When Governor Blount called for 1,500 volunteers in October 1812, more than 2,000 responded. After the Creeks attacked Fort Mims in August 1813, virtually all of Tennessee proved eager for retribution. By the time Jackson led his "volunteers" into the Battle of Horseshoe Bend, the Creek Nation had been ravaged. After the Treaty of Ghent, the Creeks never again presented much of a threat to the state of Tennessee. Tennesseans joined other Americans in settling the millions of fertile acres ceded by the Treaty of Fort Jackson.

When the news arrived almost simultaneously of Jackson's stunning victory at New Orleans and the signing of the Treaty of Ghent, Tennesseans celebrated with gusto. Although their national capital far off on the Potomac had been sacked and burned, Tennesseans chose to focus on great achievements closer to home. They had secured New

Orleans, had virtually eliminated any European threat in the west, and, most important, had opened for settlement vast areas of Indian land. Although the peace treaty stipulated a return to the status quo antebellum, Tennesseans knew better. In 1815, Tennessee was more secure than ever in its place on the frontier and in its position in the Union. For General Jackson and for the general populace, the War of 1812 was a ringing success.

—Peter S. Field

See also: Blount, Willie; Creek War; Grundy, Felix; Jackson, Andrew; New Orleans, Battle of; Sevier, John

Further Reading

Allen, Penelope, comp. *Tennessee Soldiers in the War of 1812: Regiments of Colonels Allcorn and Allison.* Chattanooga: Tennessee Society, United States Daughters of 1812, 1847.

Brown, Roger H. "The War Hawks of 1812: An Historical Myth." *Indiana Magazine of History* 60 (1964): 137–151.

Garret, William R., ed. "Report of General Andrew Jackson to Governor Willie Blount. 'Battle of Tehopiska or the Horseshoe.'" *American History Magazine* 4 (1899), 291–296.

Holland, James W. *Andrew Jackson and the Creek War: Victory at the Horseshoe.* Tuscaloosa: University of Alabama Press, 1969.

Owsley, Frank L., Jr. "The Role of the South in the British General Strategy in the War of 1812." *Tennessee Historical Quarterly* 31 (1972): 22–38.

———. *Struggle for the Gulf Borderlands: The Creek War and the Battle of New Orleans. 1812–1815.* Gainesville: University Presses of Florida, 1981.

Walker, William A., Jr. "Martial Sons: Tennessee Enthusiasm for the War of 1812." *Tennessee Historical Quarterly* 20 (1961): 20–37.

Young, Mary E. "The Creek Frauds: A Study in Conscience and Corruption." *Mississippi Valley Historical Review* 47 (1955): 411–437.

TENSKWATAWA
1775–1836
Shawnee prophet

Consulting the "Shawnee Prophet," Tenskwatawa.

Born in present-day Ohio and known as Lalawethika until he assumed the name Tenskwatawa in 1805, Tenskwatawa (known as "the Prophet" or "Shawnee Prophet" to whites) grew to adulthood during a difficult time for Indians of the Old Northwest. In the face of shrinking lands, disrupted societies, and increasing poverty, more and more Indian men turned to alcohol as a solution to their problems. Adding to the young Tenskwatawa's problems was the difficulty of growing up without a father, his own having died in battle shortly before his birth.

In his youth, Tenskwatawa seems to have led a directionless life. In his adolescence, many believed him to be a hopeless alcoholic. One day in 1805, perhaps because of alcohol poisoning, Tenskwatawa sank into a coma; when he later awakened, he claimed to have had an important vision. He had visited Heaven, he said, and had spoken with the "Master of Life." He had also visited Hell and had seen what happened to Indians who abandoned the old ways to adopt white customs, the most detrimental of which was drinking alcohol. He swore from that day forward never to drink again and took the name "Tenskwatawa," symbolizing his new status as a Shawnee holy man.

Thanks to his phenomenal charisma and singular speaking skills, Tenskwatawa's movement spread very quickly throughout the Shawnee towns and, by 1807, was attracting Indians throughout the Northwest. He preached a return to native customs and ways of subsistence and encouraged Indian brotherhood, a foreshadowing of his brother Tecumseh's movement for Indian political and military unity.

In 1808, Tenskwatawa established the center for his new faith at Prophet's Town in the Indiana Territory. From there and for a short time, he was able to convince William Henry Harrison, the governor of that territory, that his movement was friendly to the United States, but his anti-white rhetoric inspired many of his followers to begin attacking white settlements. By 1809, Harrison was convinced that the purpose of Tenskwatawa's movement was eventual war on the United States.

The Treaty of Fort Wayne, ceding 3 million acres to the United States, was negotiated between Harrison and chiefs opposed to Tenskwatawa's movement. It was a turning point for the efforts at Indian unity in the Northwest. When Tenskwatawa threatened the lives of the signatory chiefs and warned Harrison that the ceded land would never be settled by whites, he needed military and political unity to sustain his threats. Tecumseh would thus emerge as the leader of the movement because he could provide military leadership. Correspondingly, the influence of Tenskwatawa began to decline. As Tecumseh recruited followers in the South in the fall of 1811, Tenskwatawa saw all his remaining power ebb after he promised that his magic would protect warriors from white bullets while they attacked Harrison at Tippecanoe on 7 November.

During the War of 1812, the movement started by Tenskwatawa played a significant part in the British campaigns in the Northwest, though Tenskwatawa did not participate in the fighting there. Following the war, he fled to Canada, where he was supported by a British pension until 1826. He returned to the United States just in time to be caught up in the Indian removal of the 1820s and 1830s. He eventually moved to Kansas, where he died in 1836.

—*Jeanne T. Heidler and David S. Heidler*

See also: Harrison, William Henry; Prophet's Town; Tecumseh; Tippecanoe, Battle of

Further Reading

Edmunds, R. David. "Tecumseh, the Shawnee Prophet, and American History: A Reassessment." *Western Historical Quarterly* 14 (1983): 261–276.

THAMES, BATTLE OF THE
5 October 1813

The Battle of the Thames (known to Canadians as the Battle of Moraviantown) marked the end of 13 months of British control on the Detroit frontier during the War of 1812.

The British-Indian alliance had successfully repelled three U.S. advances at Detroit (16 August 1813), Frenchtown (22 January 1813), and Fort Meigs (5 May 1813). Subsequently, Washington directed Maj. Gen. William Henry Harrison to remain in a defensive posture until command of Lake Erie was assured. The U.S. victory at the Battle of Put-in-Bay (10 September 1813) prepared the way for Harrison's drive into Canada.

As a result of the situation on Lake Erie, British major general Henry Procter realized that his position at Amherstburg, Upper Canada, was untenable. With the loss of the British squadron, he also lost all his fort guns, 250 precious regulars, and any hope of reopening his supply route on the lake. Amherstburg was already destitute of provisions, and Procter could not hope to feed his regulars plus the large concentration of warriors who had settled in the region with their families. In northern Ohio, Harrison was poised for an attack on Canada, massing upwards of 6,000 fighters. He could now select the time and place to meet the inferior British force.

Despite the urgent reasons for a prompt retreat, Procter was delayed by the native confederacy, which equated strategic withdrawal with a broader abandonment of their interests by the British Crown. The native purpose had been to expel U.S. settlers from their ancestral lands northwest of the Ohio River, an aim openly and repeatedly endorsed by Isaac Brock, Procter, and other British officials. Procter did eventually convince Tecumseh, the Shawnee leader of the confederacy, to accompany a retreat for tactical and logistical reasons. It was agreed that the allies would fall back on the lower Thames, where they would make a stand. The specific destination of the retreat was unclear because neither Tecumseh nor Procter was familiar with the Thames country.

Upon learning of Harrison's landing below Amherstburg, Procter destroyed the public buildings on both sides of the river and began his retreat from Sandwich on 24 September 1813. In addition to the soldiers, settlers, and families, the retreat was encumbered by cattle, wagons, and boats loaded with impedimenta. The warriors did not accompany the retreat, and Procter halted the main party in an effort to induce them forward. About half the warriors under Tecumseh did eventually trek eastwards, but their families trailed behind, preventing the systematic destruction of all bridges. Incessant rains and "shocking bad" roads also impeded the retreat. While Procter was reconnoitering the heights at Moraviantown, the Americans were suddenly found to be in pursuit and strong in mounted infantry. Harrison had advanced with uncharacteristic speed,

However brief, the Battle of the Thames marked the first major U.S. land victory in the war. It was also the scene for the death of the famous Shawnee warrior Tecumseh, shown in the lower left corner.

with about 3,500 troops, mainly Kentucky volunteers. Col. Richard M. Johnson led the pursuit with his mounted regiment.

As the British column accelerated the march, Tecumseh and a body of warriors briefly contested Harrison's advance at Chatham on 4 October 1813. Procter rejoined the troops that day and directed them toward Moraviantown, where he had purchased the entire town for winter quarters. The rapid advance by Johnson's mounted regiment captured considerable stragglers and stores. Several British schooners and gunboats were found burning in the river, after having grounded in the shallows. On the morning of 5 October 1813, all the British reserve ammunition was captured in boats. Just 2 miles short of Moraviantown, the horsemen overtook the British main party in an exhausted, hungry, and dispirited state.

After deducting the captured stragglers, the sick, and the wounded at Moraviantown, Procter was able to field only 430 soldiers (mainly of the 41st Regiment). The number of warriors had dwindled to 600. Procter had only one 6-pounder gun on site, the remaining pieces having been positioned on the high ground of Moraviantown to cover a ford east of the village.

The ground Procter had selected to engage the Americans consisted of a wedge-shaped clearing in a beech forest. His regulars were drawn up across the narrow end of the opening to limit the frontage of his more numerous enemy. The British soldiers formed two extended lines about 250 yards apart. Their left was flanked by the Thames, with the 6-pounder planted on the road. The right of the British position was covered by the warriors who lurked in the thickets of a morass known as Backmetack Marsh. Procter's plan called for the British regulars and artillery to throw the attackers into confusion while the warriors turned their flank.

Facing the allied positions, Harrison commanded approximately 3,000 men. He decided to engage only the British regulars with Johnson's mounted men, while his infantry held the native warriors "in the air," leaving them unengaged unless they emerged from the marsh and advanced onto the open ground. Finding the frontage too constricting for 1,000 horsemen, Johnson led half his regiment across a small swamp to engage the warriors, leaving his brother James with the remainder to charge the British regulars.

As James Johnson's men advanced in column, a screening force of spies drew an irregular fire of musketry from the first British line. The mounted men got into motion and charged through both lines, taking most of the British force in the rear. The single British 6-pounder failed to fire because the horses were startled early in the action and dragged the artillery limber into the woods. The British officers attempted to reform their men, but they generally threw down their arms or escaped into the forest. The rapidity and weight of the U.S. charge had broken the effectiveness of the British line, leaving the men surrounded by a more numerous enemy. Despite wide disagreement among participating British officers about the duration of the battle, the small number of casualties and the consistent U.S. accounts indicate a very brief engagement of approximately three minutes. Procter briefly tried to rally the men, but the advancing horsemen drove him up the road to Moraviantown, along with his aides and a small mounted party. A body of mounted U.S. infantry continued to pursue Procter into the Longwoods Wilderness.

In the meantime, the warriors held their ground fiercely, concealed in the thick underbrush that suited their mode of warfare. Early in the action, they actually advanced on the U.S. left flank, led by Tecumseh, who was killed during the onslaught. Although the exact circumstances of his death remain uncertain, Richard Johnson is generally acknowledged as having slain the famous war chief. As additional reserves were brought up, the warriors yielded the field and dispersed after a half-hour engagement.

Both the U.S. and British sides sustained light casualties. The warriors left 33 bodies on the field and undoubtedly carried off others (possibly including that of Tecumseh), as was their custom. Harrison reported 601 British prisoners taken in the entire campaign.

On 17 October 1813, Procter led the remaining 235 men of his command into Ancaster (near Burlington on Lake Ontario). Gov.-Gen. Sir George Prevost immediately and publicly denounced Procter's role in the Thames campaign. He had him brought before a court-martial that, in early 1815, found Procter guilty of mishandling the campaign, ending a previously promising career with unforgiving finality.

The circumstances of Procter's defeat have not been adequately examined. Despite the general condemnations of his role, which focus on his errors in judgment, there is ample evidence to indicate that he was simply overwhelmed by events beyond his control. The core of his strength, the first battalion of the 41st Regiment, had been in Canada since 1799 and was due to return home just when war broke out. The soldiers had been dispersed in frontier posts in Upper Canada and were largely worn out by their arduous frontier duties. Because of wartime shortages in British North America, these men were the last consideration, situated at the end of a long supply line that was ruptured several times. In 1813, as a result of a provincial prohibition against the manufacture of spirits, the men were even deprived of alcohol. With their uniforms in rags and their pay six to nine months in arrears, it is not surprising that the soldiers did not give a better account of themselves. According to court-martial testimony, they could not even buy soap.

Similarly, Procter was exhausted. His pleas for materiel as well as naval and military support went unfulfilled and resulted in the naval defeat of his colleague Robert Heriot Barclay on Lake Erie, setting the stage for the events that followed. The difficult political question of the Indian alliance was left to him, a soldier, to resolve under trying circumstances. Even then, despite numerous warnings from Procter, his superiors showed poor understanding of the situation in the Detroit country, assuming that the starving warriors could be made agreeable to a "retrograde movement." In his despondent letters of September 1813, Procter wrote, "If poor Barclay and I had been attended to, our reverse would not have happened.... I hope I shall be fairly judged." Despite his numerous letters warning about the impending disaster, Governor-General Prevost withheld vital resources to the east, supplying Procter with little more than exhortations to meet the challenges with "fortitude."

Although magnified versions of Procter's disaster at Moraviantown caused widespread alarm in Upper Canada, prompting Prevost to direct the evacuation of the province west of Kingston, Harrison was unable to follow up his success. After burning the village of Moraviantown, he led his men back to Detroit. He discharged most of the Kentucky volunteers, left 1,000 regulars to garrison Fort Detroit, and delivered another 1,200 for operations on the Niagara Frontier. The animosity of Secretary of War John Armstrong resulted in Harrison's resigning his commission shortly thereafter. On hearing of Procter's reprimand, he commented, "My fate has been more hard than his." Nonetheless, Harrison went on to become president of the United States. Richard Johnson became vice president, largely on the basis of his legendary fight with Tecumseh.

As the first significant land victory of the war for the Americans, the Battle of the Thames prompted widespread jubilation in the republic. Michigan was restored to U.S. control, and the Western District of Upper Canada came under U.S. occupation until the end of the war. The Indian confederacy was definitively shattered, its great leader gone. British hopes for the establishment of an Indian buffer state in the Ohio country were finally derailed. The Old Northwest was opened up for wholesale settlement, and the longstanding struggles of the Americans with the natives were finally drawn to a close.

—*Sandor Antal*

See also: Harrison, William Henry; Johnson, Richard Mentor; Procter, Henry

Further Reading

Armstrong, John. *Notices of the War of 1812.* 2 vols. New York: Wiley and Putnam, 1840.

Byfield, Shadrach. "A Common Soldier's Account." In John Gellner, ed., *Recollections of the War of 1812: Three Eyewitness Accounts.* Toronto: Baxter Publishing, 1964.

Drake, Benjamin. *The Life of Tecumseh.* Cincinnati: Anderson, Gates and Wright, 1858.

Esarey, Logan, ed. *Messages and Letters of William Henry Harrison.* Vol. 2. New York: Arno Press, 1975.

Gray, Elma. *Wilderness Christians.* Toronto: Macmillan, 1956.

Lomax, D.A.N. *History of the Services of the 41st Regiment.* Davenport, UK: Hiornes and Miller, 1899.

McAfee, Robert Breckinridge. *History of the Late War in the Western Country.* Lexington, KY: Worsley and Smith, 1816.

Michigan Pioneer and Historical Society. *Historical Collections Volumes 15 and 16.* Detroit: Michigan Pioneer and Historical Society, 1909–1910.

Richardson, Major [John]. *The Letters of Veritas . . .* Montreal: W. Gray, 1815.

Sugden, John. *Tecumseh's Last Stand.* Norman: University of Oklahoma Press, 1985.

Wood, William. *Select British Documents of the Canadian War of 1812.* 3 vols. New York: Greenwood Press, 1968.

Young, Bennett H. *The Battle of the Thames.* Louisville, KY: John P. Morton, 1903.

THORNTON, WILLIAM
1779–1840
British officer

Sir William Thornton was born in Ireland, but little is known about his life before he received his commission in 1796. His military career rapidly advanced through the patronage of fellow Irish officer Lt. Gen. Sir James Craig, who had served during the American Revolution and, following a number of postings abroad, was appointed governor and captain general in British North America in August 1807. Thornton was regularly posted with Craig and was promoted to captain in 1803, major in 1806, and lieutenant colonel in 1811. Given command of the 85th Foot, Thornton led his regiment both in the Peninsular Campaign, where he was decorated and promoted to colonel, and in North America from 1814 to 1815. Arriving in the United States with Maj. Gen. Robert Ross, Thornton led the light brigade in the attack on Bladensburg on 24 August 1814.

Although his troops were exhausted by the heat of a Maryland summer, Thornton led the brigade through Bladensburg and attempted to rush the bridge over the Potomac River. It was a rash move, and he was initially repulsed. Yet he rallied his troops, forded the river, and outflanked the U.S. troops under Gen. Tobias Stansbury. Aided by the confusion caused by noisy but harmless Congreve Rockets, Thornton's attack forced the Americans to retreat, a retreat that turned into a rout. Badly wounded, he was left behind as the British army under Ross raided and burned Washington, D.C. Considered a prisoner of war, he was exchanged in October and joined the British forces collecting in Jamaica under Maj. Gen. John Keane.

This force embarked for Louisiana in November 1814, landing at Pine Island, Lake Borgne, in December 1814. Thornton commanded the advance guard, which established the British presence a few miles from New Orleans. During the attack on New Orleans under the new commander in chief, Sir Edward Pakenham, Thornton was charged with leading his brigade over the Mississippi River on the night of 7 January and taking a U.S. battery on the western bank. Thornton was then to train these guns on Jackson's right flank as the main British assault commenced on 8 January. Thornton was delayed, however, and when Pakenham launched his ill-fated frontal attack against Jackson's lines, Thornton had not yet begun to press his own attack. Finally putting the U.S. troops at the batteries to flight, Thornton's troops prepared to turn the captured artillery pieces against Jackson's flank. It was the only British success of the day, and Thornton was wounded in it. News of Pakenham's disaster finally reached Thornton, along with orders that his own attack was called off. Thornton's withdrawal signaled the end of one of the worst defeats in British military history.

Thornton returned to Britain in March 1815, and his later career was noteworthy. Serving in Ireland, he was promoted to major general in 1825, knighted in 1836, and advanced to lieutenant general in 1838. He never fully recovered from his wounds received in the United States, however, and his mind gradually tilted into such imbalance that he committed suicide in 1840. In their regimental orders, the 85th Foot paid tribute to his noble character and zeal. Buried in his local church at Greenford, Middlesex,

Thornton was one of the ablest British officers during the War of 1812.

—*Rory T. Cornish*

See also: Bladensburg, Battle of; New Orleans, Battle of
Further Reading
Reilly, Robin. *The British at the Gates: The New Orleans Campaign in the War of 1812.* New York: G. P. Putnam's Sons, 1974.
Williams, John S. *History of the Invasion and Capture of Washington.* New York: Harper's, 1857.

THORNTON, WILLIAM
1759–1828
Physician; superintendent of U.S. patents

Born in the Virgin Islands, Thornton moved to Scotland, where he graduated from Aberdeen University with a medical degree. He moved to the United States in 1787 and settled in Philadelphia. A Renaissance man, Thornton's interests moved beyond medicine to all manner of scientific and engineering pursuits, and he became famous for his winning design for the U.S. Capitol.

In 1802, his eclectic interests won him the appointment by Pres. Thomas Jefferson as the superintendent of U.S. patents. He occupied that position until his death in 1828. Never an efficient administrator, Thornton ran his office with little attention to detail, and inventions piled up in every corner of the building he shared with the Post Office on Eighth Street.

When news arrived in Washington of the approach of the British, Thornton loaded what he could onto a wagon and, with Mrs. Thornton, made his way to Georgetown on the afternoon of 24 August, just after the disaster at Bladensburg. The following morning, he heard from other refugees that the patent office had not yet been destroyed and decided to go back to the city to salvage some of his personal possessions in the office and what inventions he could carry.

He arrived almost simultaneously with the British party of soldiers sent to destroy the building. He made a lengthy speech to the officer in charge claiming that since most of the contents of the building were inventions sent in by private citizens, the building contained mostly private property. He also pointed out to the officer that to destroy inventions meant for the betterment of all people would be an act of barbarism. After consulting his superiors, the of-

ficer agreed to spare the patent office. His mission complete, Thornton rejoined his wife in Georgetown for the night but returned to the capital the next day.

When Thornton returned, he immediately observed that no other government officials had done so. He also noted that looters were making short work of what the British had left behind. As the only government official in the area, he organized guards for private and public property and arranged medical attention for wounded U.S. and British soldiers. When the mayor of Washington finally returned, Thornton publicly criticized the man for neglecting the protection of the city's property and citizens.

Two days later rumors began to spread that the British intended to return to the city. Thornton immediately made his way to whatever government officials he could find. Eventually locating President James Madison, Thornton expressed his belief that it would be better to send a message to the British surrendering in advance than to have the remainder of the city destroyed. Madison refused to consider the suggestion, so Thornton returned to his home for his sword to help defend the city. Luckily, the eccentric old gentlemen never had to use his sword.

Following the war, Thornton continued in his post at the patent office and became involved in a variety of philanthropic activities that included education for deaf children and the American Colonization Society. He died in Washington at the age of 69.

—*Jeanne T. Heidler and David S. Heidler*

See also: Bladensburg, Battle of; Washington, British Capture of
Further Reading
Thornton, Anna M. "Diary of Mrs. William Thornton: Capture of Washington by the British." *Columbia Historical Society Proceedings* 19 (1916): 172–182.

TILTON, JAMES
1745–1822
Surgeon general of the army

Born near Dover, Delaware, on 1 June 1745, James Tilton was apprenticed there to Dr. Charles Greenberry Ridgely before taking a medical degree at the University of Pennsylvania in 1771. In 1776, Tilton volunteered as a surgeon in the Delaware Regiment. From January 1777 to October 1780, he ran three Continental Army hospitals in New York and New Jersey, whereupon Congress solicited his advice on the optimal management of military hospitals. Promoted to senior hospital physician and surgeon for his efforts in reforming army medical care, Tilton managed a hospital in Virginia during the Yorktown campaign. After the war, he resumed his practice in Dover, served in the Continental Congress and in the Delaware House of Representatives, and was federal commissioner of loans for Delaware. About 1801, he retired to Wilmington.

In February 1813, Tilton expanded his 1781 report to Congress into a small book, *Economical Observations on Military Hospitals and the Prevention and Cure of Diseases Incident to an Army*. Its major messages were still pertinent years after the events he described. "It would be shocking to humanity to relate the history of our general hospital, in the years 1777 and 1778, when it swallowed up at least one half our army," he said. And he continued, "More surgeons died, in the American service, in proportion to their number, than officers of the line! A strong evidence this that infection is more dangerous, in military life, than the weapons of war."

Tilton's book was undoubtedly instrumental in his appointment, at the age of 68, to the newly created post of physician and surgeon general of the army on 11 June 1813. After touring many military hospitals, he issued sweeping new regulations for improving them in December 1814. Although his recommendations were often ignored, hospitals that did comply became recognizably more efficient.

When Tilton's position was abolished by Congress in June 1815, he retired again. Six months later one of his legs had to be amputated, but he survived another seven years, dying at Wilmington on 14 May 1822, at the age of 77.

—*J. Worth Estes*

See also: Medicine, Army
Further Reading

Paulshock, Bernadine Z. "'Let Every Reader Form His Own Conclusions': Dr. James A. Tilton's Case Report of a Delaware Woman Cured of Rabies." *Delaware History* 21 (1985): 186–196.

Saffron, Morris H. "The Tilton Affair." *Journal of the American Medical Association* 236 (1976): 67–72.

Thacher, James. *American Medical Biography*. Vol. 2. 1828; reprint, New York: Milord House, 1967: 129–141.

Tilton, James. *Economical Observations on Military Hospitals and the Prevention and Cure of Diseases Incident to an Army*. Wilmington, DE: J. Wilson, 1813.

Wooden, Allen C. "James Tilton, Outstanding Military Medical Administrator." *Delaware Medical Journal* 47 (1975): 429–441.

TINGEY, THOMAS
1750–1829
U.S. Navy officer

Thomas Tingey was born in London and lived most of his early life as a British subject, serving first in the British navy and then as a merchant officer. He immigrated to the United States as a young man and in the 1790s entered the U.S. Navy, becoming a captain by 1798. He fought in the Quasi-War with France and in 1800 was given command of the new Washington Navy Yard. He remained in that command until his death in Washington, D.C., in 1829.

During the War of 1812, Tingey was charged with managing the construction of new naval vessels. Three such ships, the frigate *Columbia*, the sloop *Argus*, and the schooner *Lynx*, stood either almost ready or ready for service when the British arrived in Washington on the night of 24 August 1814. Tingey had been alerted, as had all of Washington, and had received orders from Secretary of the Navy William Jones to burn the yard rather than allow its valuable contents to fall into British hands.

As refugees from the disastrous Battle of Bladensburg poured into the city, it became clear during the afternoon of 24 August that the British would soon be in the city. Tingey prepared to carry out his painful orders. A group of neighborhood women heard about the plans and begged him to reconsider, claiming that their homes would be consumed in the flames. Tingey promised to wait as long as possible, but he told the women he had no choice. He would have to burn the navy yard.

When Tingey received word shortly after 8:00 P.M. that the British had entered the city, the matches were set. The *Columbia* and *Argus* were destroyed with most of their supplies and equipment. As the fires burned brightly, Tingey entered a small boat and rowed to Alexandria. The following morning he rowed back to check on the damage, only barely missing a party of British soldiers just leaving the smoldering yard. Tingey was gratified to see that the *Lynx* had survived the fire and saw to her removal to safer waters before returning to Alexandria.

Captain Tingey returned shortly after the British evacuation and began salvaging what little was left from his life's work at the yard. He would spend the remainder of his life returning it to its model of naval order.

—*Jeanne T. Heidler and David S. Heidler*

See also: Washington, British Capture of
Further Reading
Peck, Taylor. *Roundshots to Rockets: A History of the Washington Navy Yard and U.S. Naval Gun Factory.* Annapolis, MD: Naval Institute Press, 1949.

TIPPECANOE, BATTLE OF
7 November 1811

In the years after 1805, Tenskwatawa (the Shawnee Prophet) and his brother Tecumseh encouraged Indian resistance to U.S. demands for land in the Old Northwest. Tecumseh argued that Indian lands were owned in common and that no individual tribe should make cessions, whereas his brother urged Indians to throw off European ways and win the favor of the Great Spirit. Tecumseh traveled widely to gain recruits to his confederacy, and from 1808, the followers of the Shawnee brothers gathered at Prophet's Town near the Tippecanoe River in northern Indiana Territory.

The governor of Indiana Territory, William Henry Harrison, was greatly concerned at the growth of Indian resistance, which threatened the governmental policy of the widespread acquisition of land in the Old Northwest. He also believed that Indian resistance owed much of its strength to the machinations of British Indian agents. The tensions in Indian-American relations increased sharply after September 1809. In that month, Governor Harrison persuaded Potawatomi, Miami, and Delaware chiefs to make another large land cession to the Americans. The cession increased Tecumseh's influence among the young tribesmen and aided the growth of his confederacy.

In the summers of 1810 and 1811, Tecumseh met with Harrison at Vincennes in Indiana Territory. At the first meeting, Tecumseh warned Harrison that no lands were to

Responding to U.S. pressure, Shawnee brothers Tecumseh and Tenskwatawa began gathering an Indian force at Prophet's Town. Although this painting depicts a resounding U.S. victory, the Battle of Tippecanoe served only to strengthen Native American resistance.

be sold without general Indian approval, and he threatened that the chiefs who had ceded lands at Fort Wayne would be killed. At the meeting in July and August 1811, the situation was extremely tense because Tecumseh arrived with several hundred warriors and Governor Harrison had assembled some 800 troops in Vincennes. Tecumseh told Harrison that he should not be disturbed by the confederacy, for in trying to unite the tribes, he had merely followed the example of the American states. He also announced that after the conference, he was going to the South to enlist more support.

Harrison, his concerns increasing, decided that he would take the opportunity of Tecumseh's absence to attack the center of his movement at Prophet's Town. In late September, Harrison moved north from Vincennes with over 1,000 troops. These were regulars and Indiana militia and Kentucky volunteers. He advanced with caution, delaying to build Fort Harrison on the site of present-day Terre Haute, Indiana.

On 6 November, as Harrison and his army moved close to Prophet's Town, Tenskwatawa sent messengers to say that he would meet on the following day to discuss Harrison's demands that the Indians disperse and hand over troublemakers. Harrison encamped close to the Indian village, but he was also preparing to attack if negotiations failed.

On his part, the Prophet had decided that he must attack to forestall Harrison. Early on the morning of 7 November, the Indians from Prophet's Town attacked the U.S. encampment, expecting that the Prophet's special powers would enable them to overcome the Americans. The battle was fiercely fought, and the Americans lost nearly 200 killed and wounded. It is likely that Indian casualties were about the same. Harrison, however, claimed a major victory because the Indians dispersed; Prophet's Town was deserted; and, after seizing food supplies, Harrison's troops burned the village. The Indians, however, were now more determined than ever to resist the Americans, and many were ready to join the British in the event of war.

When Tecumseh returned from the South, he found his village in ruins. He continued to recruit Indians to his cause and was with the British on the Canadian Detroit frontier at the outbreak of war. He fought with the British until his death at the Battle of the Thames in October 1813.

William Henry Harrison was later to make good use of the Battle of Tippecanoe to further his political ambitions. When he was elected president in 1840, with John Tyler as his vice president, voters were reminded of his early military career with his slogan "Tippecanoe and Tyler Too."

—Reginald Horsman

See also: Harrison, William Henry; Prophet's Town; Tenskwatawa

Further Reading

Cleaves, Freeman. *Old Tippecanoe: William Henry Harrison and His Time.* New York: Scribner's, 1939.

Edmunds, R. David. *The Shawnee Prophet.* Lincoln: University of Nebraska Press, 1983.

Gilpin, Alec R. *The War of 1812 in the Old Northwest.* East Lansing: Michigan State University Press, 1958.

Jacobs, James R. *The Beginnings of the U.S. Army, 1783–1812.* Princeton: Princeton University Press, 1947.

TIPTON, JOHN
1786–1839
Indiana militia officer

John Tipton was born in Tennessee to Joshua Tipton and Jennett Shields Tipton; his father was killed by Indians when he was seven years old. As a young man, Tipton accompanied his mother and siblings to Indiana Territory. At the age of 24, Tipton became a local justice of the peace. Increasingly, as Tecumseh and Tenskwatawa's Indian confederacy became stronger in the territory, Tipton spent much of his time as part of a patrolling group of Indiana riflemen, attempting to protect the outlying settlements.

When Indiana Territory governor William Henry Harrison planned his offensive against Prophet's Town in the fall of 1811, he asked that Tipton's troop of riflemen accompany the expedition. As a result, Tipton was present at what some people view as the opening of the war in the northwest. He kept a journal of his experience on the expedition.

During the War of 1812, Tipton, having been promoted to major, led a group of Indiana Territorial Rangers who patrolled the more isolated sections of the territory, operating out of settler-constructed blockhouses on the frontier. His primary activity involved responding to calls from settlers regarding Indian attacks by pursuing the raiding parties toward their towns.

On 18 March 1813, for example, Tipton's rangers received word that settlers had been attacked outside of one of the blockhouses known as Fort Vallonia. Tipton and his men set out in pursuit of the raiding party on 19 March. They caught up to them at an island (later named Tipton Island in his honor) in one of the local rivers. Tipton's men killed one Indian but were unable to locate the others. A month later, a similar raid occurred, and once again, Tipton set out in pursuit.

The activities of Tipton and his rangers were typical military actions along the northwestern frontier during the War of 1812. The surrender of Detroit to the British had left all Northwest settlements vulnerable, and much of the militia in the territories was occupied full-time in protecting the isolated settlements until the British abandonment of Detroit in the late summer of 1813.

Following the war, Tipton remained active in the Indiana militia, rising to the rank of major general of the Second Division in 1822. Tipton also became increasingly interested in politics and served in the U.S. Senate during part of the presidency of his good friend Andrew Jackson. He died shortly after completing his last term in the Senate.

—Jeanne T. Heidler and David S. Heidler

See also: Detroit, Surrender of; Harrison, William Henry; Indiana Territory; Prophet's Town; Tecumseh; Tenskwatawa; Tippecanoe, Battle of

Further Reading

Pershing, Marvon W. *Life of General John Tipton and Early Indiana Territory*. Tipton, IN: Tipton Club, 1900.
Tipton, John. "John Tipton's Tippecanoe Journal." *Indiana Magazine of History* 2 (1906): 170–184.

TODD, CHARLES STEWART
1791–1871
U.S. officer

Born in present-day Kentucky to Thomas Todd and Elizabeth Harris Todd, Charles Stewart Todd graduated from the College of William and Mary in 1809 and began the study of law. After admission to the bar, he opened his first practice in Lexington, Kentucky, immediately before the outbreak of the War of 1812.

Upon the declaration of war, Todd received a commission as an ensign in the Kentucky Volunteers. He served briefly as the quartermaster for Brig. Gen. James Winchester's brigade of the Army of the Northwest, but upon his promotion to captain, he was invited to serve as aide to commander of the Army of the Northwest William Henry Harrison. During his service under Harrison, which lasted until Harrison's resignation, Todd always drew the highest praise from the general. He accompanied the army in the campaign that resulted in the Battle of the Thames and, following the battle on 5 October 1813, was one of the officers dispatched by Harrison in pursuit of the British commander Brig. Gen. Henry Procter. The British general,

who some witnesses claimed began his retreat before his army, managed to outrun them.

After the Battle of the Thames, Todd became deputy inspector general for the Eighth Military District and, the following year, adjutant general for the same district. Later that year, he served as adjutant in Brig. Gen. Duncan McArthur's raids into Canada out of Detroit.

At the end of the war, Todd achieved the rank of colonel but left the service in June 1815 to resume his law practice. He served briefly in the Kentucky legislature after the war but in 1820 was sent to Colombia by Pres. James Monroe to discern the status of that new country. He returned to the United States and private life in 1823 but entered the political scene again in 1840 to campaign for his old mentor William Henry Harrison for president. He cowrote one of the campaign biographies. Shortly after President Harrison's death, Todd was appointed U.S. minister to Russia by Pres. John Tyler. Upon his return from that post, he tried his hand at a variety of tasks, including that of newspaper editor. After the Civil War erupted, Todd, at the age of 71, offered his military services to the United States. He died ten years later in Louisiana.

—Jeanne T. Heidler and David S. Heidler

See also: Harrison, William Henry; McArthur, Duncan; Thames, Battle of the

Further Reading

Griffin, G. W. *Memoir of Colonel Charles S. Todd*. Philadelphia: Claxton, Remsen, Haffelfinger, 1874.

TOMPKINS, DANIEL D.
1774–1825
Governor of New York

As the wartime governor of New York and later the vice president of the United States, a lawyer, a judge, an educational reformer, and a humanitarian, Daniel Tompkins was a popular leader who gained great respect from Presidents James Madison and James Monroe as well as the Republican Party as a whole.

Tompkins was born into a middle-class, tenant-farming family in Westchester County, New York, on 21 June 1774. During the 1780s, Tompkins's father served as a judge and state legislator and on the State Board of Regents. Tompkins followed his father's lead and developed an interest in politics while attending Columbia Law School. He practiced in New York City and became active in the Tammany

Hall faction of the Democratic Republican Party. As a party organizer, he was especially active in electing Thomas Jefferson to the presidency in 1800.

Tompkins benefited from his political connections and the expanding patronage of the Democratic Republican Party. Former governor George Clinton, who became vice president during Jefferson's second term, and New York City Mayor DeWitt Clinton were especially supportive. Tompkins received a series of appointments after 1801, serving as counselor in the Mayor's Court and the state Supreme Court, as commissioner of bankruptcy, and as justice of the state Supreme Court. He became a highly respected and popular circuit judge. In 1807, Tompkins was elected governor with the help of Tammany Hall's "Bucktail" Republicans and the Clintonians.

Because of his wartime leadership, Tompkins built a strong political base in both New York and Washington. On the day of his inauguration, New York City received word of the attack on the U.S. frigate *Chesapeake*. The response from Jefferson and Congress was the Embargo Act of 1807, which prohibited the departure of U.S. ships for foreign ports. Republicans were divided over the embargo. New York City merchants and shippers were hit hard by the embargo and rallied around DeWitt Clinton, who united Federalists and downstate Republicans to oppose the act. Clinton caused further problems for Tompkins when he promoted the nomination of his uncle, former governor George Clinton, for the presidency in 1808. Yet Tompkins's faction ultimately prevailed. He backed James Madison for the presidency, and eventually Tompkins's Republicans gained control of the state legislature. Despite being leaders of rival political factions, Clinton and Tompkins remained close friends during the war years.

As tension increased between the United States and Great Britain, Jefferson informed governors that the states would receive little aid from the federal government in the event of war. Tompkins upheld the embargo in New York and began to make defense plans for the state. New York City fortifications were constructed; 14,000 militiamen were put on the alert; and appointments were made to supervise militia operation. With monies in short supply, Tompkins personally contributed to the efforts from his own private funds. Despite financial hardships caused by the embargo and widespread opposition from downstate, Governor Tompkins remained loyal to the Jefferson and Madison administrations.

After the declaration of war in June 1812, he toured the state's fortifications, including remote sites in Oswego and Buffalo. He knew that New York City and the Niagara Frontier were particularly vulnerable. Militia leaders mistakenly assumed that large numbers of Canadians would join the fight against the British. Many of these commanders were political appointees with little or no military experience. Gen. Stephen Van Rensselaer was placed in charge of the Niagara Frontier with disastrous results. In 1813, Madison selected John Armstrong of New York to serve as secretary of war.

Politically, Tompkins continued to face opposition from Peace Republicans and Federalists, who dominated the assembly, but events in late 1813 helped to shift the political balance in his favor. Despite the victory of Commodore Oliver Hazard Perry in the Battle of Lake Erie in September, the western frontier was still in danger. Two devastating incidents took place in December. Fort Niagara was taken by surprise, and major ammunition stores were raided. Worse yet, the British attacked the villages of Black Rock and Buffalo on 30 December, burning them to the ground.

In 1814, Tompkins finally got the support he needed with the election of a Republican state legislature sympathetic to his views. The militia received pay raises, and enlistment procedures were streamlined. Yet funds were still in short supply. Because Tompkins placed the war effort above all else, he made decisions that later caused him great financial problems. He personally backed war notes issued in 1814 and made advances for military expenses from his own private funds. By March, the militia was better equipped and prepared for further British attacks. Madison was so impressed with Tompkins's efforts in New York that he invited him to be secretary of state in 1814. Tompkins felt that the continued defense of New York was a higher priority and respectfully declined. Under Madison's orders, Tompkins moved to New York City to command the Third Military District, a position he held until the end of the war in February 1815. During that time, U.S. forces at Plattsburg and on Lake Champlain repulsed the last British attempt to invade New York.

Tompkins was at the peak of his popularity following the war. In 1816, he ran for vice president with James Monroe, and they were elected in an overwhelming Republican victory. Tompkins remained active in New York affairs and participated in a powerful reform movement led by Martin Van Buren. They were opposed by a coalition of Federalists and conservative Republicans led by DeWitt Clinton, who wished to keep political power centered in the New York City area. Tompkins worked with Van Buren and upstate leaders to call for major constitutional revisions. Despite failing health and financial problems, Tompkins presided over the 1821 New York state constitutional convention. The new constitution democratized the state by expanding the franchise, eliminating property requirements, and shifting political power upstate.

Tompkins spent much of his later years attempting to put his finances in order. He had frequently advanced monies during the war for military operations and did not always have accurate records. In 1824, he finally received $60,000 as reimbursement for those expenses. Tompkins had also developed a serious drinking problem and was becoming less effective in Washington. After serving out his term as vice president, he retired from public life in 1824. He died in New York in 1825.

—*George D. Torok*

See also: Clinton, DeWitt; New York; New York City; Van Buren, Martin; Van Rensselaer, Stephen
Further Reading
Irwin, Ray W. *Daniel D. Tompkins: Governor of New York and Vice President of the United States.* New York: New York Historical Society, 1968.

TORPEDOES

Torpedo was the early term for an underwater mine. Such a device was not new in U.S. history. In 1777, David Bushnell had made the first attempt to explode gunpowder underwater against British warships at Philadelphia in the Delaware River. After the war, investigation of this concept continued in both Europe and in the United States. During the Napoleonic wars, Robert Fulton tried to interest the British in submarine-laid mines against the French and, when that was unsuccessful, to interest Napoleon in employing the same to attack the British! In 1805, he returned to the United States and presented plans for both a submarine and a moored mine. The navy provided funds, and in 1807 Fulton blew up a brig in New York harbor. It took several attempts, however, leading to a loss of faith in his plans. In 1810, Fulton carried out another experiment against a sloop. This was unsuccessful because the defenders were permitted to deploy

This 1813 political cartoon demonstrates the ideal British reaction to America's initial use of torpedoes, even though in reality the effect was less devastating.

a net. While admitting failure, Fulton pointed out the immobility such defensive schemes would impose on an enemy. He also noted that moored mines could close U.S. ports to an attacking force.

During the War of 1812, using mines provided by Fulton, in July 1813 Sailing Master Elijah Mix made six attempts to send paired torpedoes drifting into HMS *Plantagenet* (74 guns), then moored at Lynnhaven Roads near Norfolk, Virginia. On the seventh attempt, he got in proper position, but the mines, once set adrift, went off prematurely. Two torpedo craft were also employed on Long Island Sound. One went aground but was destroyed by U.S. citizens before the British could take her. A submarine built by a resident of Norwich, Connecticut, was taken to New London, where it made several attempts to secure a mine to the hull of another 74-gun vessel, HMS *Ramillies*.

During the war, Fulton himself made numerous proposals to the U.S. government to plant moored sea mines in U.S. harbors and to arm a harpoon system with mines for offensive purposes. As late as 1814, he was gathering equipment at the Washington Navy Yard for experiments that were, however, not performed.

—*Spencer C. Tucker*

See also: Demologus; Fulton, Robert
Further Reading

Hartmann, Gregory K., with Scott C. Truver. *Weapons That Wait: Mine Warfare in the U.S. Navy.* Annapolis, MD: Naval Institute Press, 1991.
Roland, Alex. *Underwater Warfare in the Age of Sail.* Bloomington: Indiana University Press, 1979.

TOWSON, NATHAN
1784–1854
U.S. officer

The U.S. artillery historian William Berkhimer once noted that Nathan Towson had the "good fortune... to be present with his company in almost every affair of importance on the northern frontier during the years 1812–14." Towson was born near Baltimore on 22 January 1784 and received his education in the public schools. When the U.S. Army expanded its artillery just prior to the start of the War of 1812, Towson gained a direct commission as a captain on 12 March 1812. He was assigned to command a company of the newly formed Second Regiment of Artillery. That company is presently the U.S. Army's Second Battalion, Second Air Defense Artillery.

Towson received three brevet promotions during the war. On 8 October 1812, Towson led the contingent of 50 soldiers in navy lieutenant Jesse D. Elliot's 124-man raiding party that captured the British brig *Caledonia* from under the guns of Fort Erie. The *Caledonia* became the nucleus of the U.S. flotilla on Lake Erie, and Towson was brevetted to major. A few days later, Towson commanded the U.S. guns that supported Winfield Scott's command in the crossing of the Niagara River to Queenston.

In July 1813, Towson participated in the attack on Fort George, Upper Canada, where he was wounded. At the Battle of Chippewa on 5 July 1814, Towson commanded one of the four companies in Maj. Jacob Hindman's artillery battalion. Directly supporting Scott's brigade, Towson's small battery of four 12-pounders engaged both the British infantry as well as a larger battery of the Royal Artillery. Towson lost one gun in the process but retaliated by scoring a direct hit on a British caisson. The resulting ammunition explosion completely disoriented the surviving British gun crews. Towson then moved his three remaining guns to enfilade the British lines and covered Henry Leavenworth's assault on the British left flank. Towson was brevetted a lieutenant colonel for that action.

Towson's company also supported Scott's brigade at the Battle of Lundy's Lane. When Capt. Thomas Biddle was wounded and Capt. John Ritchie was killed, the primary weight of the fire support requirement fell to Towson. This time, however, Towson's gunners received the worst of it because the British guns fired from high ground and the U.S. guns could not achieve sufficient elevation to return effective fire. According to Canadian sources, Towson lost 26 of the 37 men serving his three guns before the British battery was finally overrun by a flank attack from the 21st U.S. Infantry. Immediately following the battle, Towson was among the group of officers who opposed Gen. Eleazar Ripley's intention to cross back over to the U.S. side of the river.

Towson finished the war a colonel. He received his third brevet "for gallant conduct in the assault on Ft. Erie," where he commanded a battery of five long 24-pounders. Towson's position was a redoubt on Snake Hill, at the extreme southwest end of the line of defenses that ran from the fort. During the early morning hours of 15 August 1814, Towson's guns repulsed five British assaults. Firing canister, his battery put out such a continuous stream of fire that the British troops called it the "Yankee Lighthouse."

After the war, Towson was retained in the regular army. On 1 September 1818, he was appointed to an artillery materiel review board headed by Brig. Gen. Moses Porter. Because of illness, Porter never actually sat on the board, and Towson was its sole artilleryman. He served on the board until October 1819, when he was appointed paymaster general of the U.S. Army. On 1 June 1821, all U.S. artillery regiments were consolidated and reorganized into four new numbered regiments. Pres. James Monroe appointed Towson colonel of the new Second Regiment. The major of the new Second Artillery was Jacob Hindman, under whose command Towson had served in the old Second Artillery.

Towson held the command of the regiment for little less than a year. The Senate refused to confirm his appointment because it supported some of the older artillery colonels who were dropped out of the army in the reorganization. The president refused to accept the rebuff from the Senate, however, and a power struggle began that was dragged out for 11 years over the course of three different administrations. The Second Artillery went without a colonel for the entire period. Towson, meanwhile, was reappointed paymaster general on 8 May 1822, with the rank of colonel.

Towson was the U.S. Army's paymaster general for the remainder of his career—a terrible waste of a talented artillery commander. On 30 June 1834, he received a brevet promotion to brigadier general, and on 30 May 1848, he was brevetted to major general "for meritorious conduct in the war with Mexico." He died in Washington, D.C., on 20 July 1854.

—*David T. Zabecki*

See also: Artillery; Chippewa, Battle of; Hindman, Jacob; Lundy's Lane, Battle of

Further Reading

Armstrong, John. *Notices of the War of 1812.* 2 vols. New York: Wiley and Putnam, 1840.

Birkhimer, William E. *Historical Sketch of the Organization, Administration, Materiel, and Tactics of the Artillery of the United States Army.* Washington: Chapman, 1884.

Heitman, F.B. *Historical Register of the United States Army.* Washington: National Tribune, 1890.

Powell, William. *List of the Officers of the Army of the United States, 1777–1900.* New York: L. R. Hammersley, 1900.

TRADE RESTRICTIONS

Between 1806 and 1815, the United States employed a series of trade restrictions collectively known as the restrictive system. Initially, these measures were designed to force Great Britain and France, the leading belligerents in the Napoleonic wars, to show greater respect for neutral rights. Later, during the War of 1812, they became a vehicle for denying the British access to U.S. trade, both to undermine their war effort and, through economic pressure, to force them to the peace table.

The restrictive system had its origins in the era of the American Revolution. Americans employed nonimportation and nonexportation in the 1760s and 1770s to force the British to modify their tax and trade policies. Although these measures had only a marginal impact on British colonial policy, patriots such as Thomas Jefferson and James Madison interpreted history otherwise. Convinced that the United States held the key to British—and, to a lesser extent, French—prosperity, Republicans in the early national period were confident that economic sanctions would win greater recognition for neutral rights.

In the years before the War of 1812, the Republicans experimented with a broad range of trade restrictions. A partial nonimportation law in 1806 barred a select list of British manufactured goods from the U.S. market; a general embargo in 1807 prohibited all U.S. ships and goods from leaving port; a nonintercourse act in 1809 prohibited all trade with England and France and their colonies; and a second nonimportation law in 1811 barred all British ships and goods from U.S. ports.

These restrictions failed to achieve their aim. Britain and France continued to loot U.S. commerce and to violate other U.S. rights in the pursuit of victory. Even though England did repeal the Orders in Council in 1812, it was a concession that came too late to avert war.

The failure of the restrictive system played an important role in causing the War of 1812. By embracing trade restrictions, the Republicans committed themselves to winning concessions from Great Britain through coercion. When this policy failed, Republican leaders felt they had little choice but to increase the stakes by going to war.

Even though the restrictive system had always been defended as an alternative to war to uphold the nation's rights, the Republicans refused to abandon the system after war had been declared. As Thomas Jefferson's secretary of state, James Madison had been the chief architect of the restrictive system, and after becoming president he retained his faith in economic coercion. During the War of 1812 he repeatedly asked Congress to impose additional sanctions, both to undermine Britain's war effort and to step up the pressure on Britain's economy.

Most Republicans, including some of the War Hawks, shared the president's confidence in wartime restrictions. Henry Clay, for example, insisted in late 1812 that "if you cling to the restrictive system, it is incessantly working in your favor," and "if persisted in, the restrictive system, aiding the war, would break down the present [British] ministry, and lead to a consequent honorable peace." Other Republicans—particularly the South Carolina War Hawks and representatives from the northern commercial districts—disagreed. So too did the Federalists, who voted against almost every trade restriction proposed during the war.

Although Congress was less enthusiastic than the president, ultimately it adopted most of the trade restrictions that he requested. In early and mid-1812, the prorestrictionists in Congress beat back several attempts to repeal the Non-Importation Act of 1811. They added a limited enemy trade act in mid-1812, a law prohibiting the use of British licenses in mid-1813, and a general embargo in late 1813. Shortly thereafter, news arrived of Napoleon's defeat at Leipzig. This opened all of northern Europe to British trade, thus depriving the restrictive system of much of its effectiveness as a coercive instrument. Recognizing this, the president in early 1814 recommended that the Nonimportation Act and the embargo be repealed. Over the protests of diehard restrictionists, Congress complied with Madison's request. To prevent Americans from supplying British forces in the New World, however, Congress enacted a new and sweeping enemy trade law in early 1815. This measure never received a fair test because it expired with the restoration of peace shortly after it became law.

The trade restrictions adopted during the War of 1812 proved no more effective than those employed before the war. The British were far less dependent on the United States economically than Republicans imagined, and illegal trade flourished on every frontier. Americans smuggled British goods into virtually every U.S. port on the Atlantic and Gulf Coasts, and British goods flowed into the country from Canada. Americans also supplied British warships in U.S. waters and British troops in Canada, Chesapeake Bay, and elsewhere in the U.S. theater. Indeed, by the summer of 1814, the governor-general of Canada reported that two-thirds of the large and growing British army there was feasting on U.S. provisions. This trade knew no political or social barriers. Republicans and Federalists alike took part in the traffic and shared in the profits, which were often substantial.

The United States found it difficult to stamp out enemy trade during the War of 1812 because the customs department was woefully undermanned, and even the army and navy could not adequately police the vast and often inaccessible border regions. In the contest between government officials anxious to suppress enemy trade and those determined to make a profit, most of the advantages lay with the latter.

—*DonaPld R. Hickey*

See also: Embargo Act; Macon's Bill No. 2; Non-Intercourse Act; Smuggling

Further Reading

Adams, Henry. *History of the United States during the Administrations of Jefferson and Madison.* 9 vols. New York: Charles Scribner's Sons, 1889–1891.

Heaton, Herbert. "Non-importation, 1806–1812." *Journal of Economic History* 1 (November 1941): 178–198.

Hickey, Donald R. *The War of 1812: A Forgotten Conflict.* Urbana: University of Illinois Press, 1989.

TRIANON DECREE
5 August 1810

On the same day that the Duc de Cadore delivered a letter to U.S. minister to France John Armstrong, claiming that Napoleon had lifted the Berlin and Milan Decrees as they affected the United States, the emperor issued the Trianon Decree, instructing his officials to condemn U.S. ships already in French custody.

These instructions, of course, violated the spirit of the message delivered to Armstrong and demonstrated that Napoleon had no intention of lifting the restrictions on U.S. trade. What Napoleon apparently was trying to do, as indicated by the Rambouillet Decree of 23 March 1810, was to force the United States to cease trading with the British and trade exclusively with Napoleon and his allies.

—*Jeanne T. Heidler and David S. Heidler*

See also: Armstrong, John; Berlin Decree; Cadore Letter; Milan Decree; Napoleon I; Rambouillet Decree

Further Reading

Egan, Clifford L. *Neither Peace Nor War: Franco-American Relations, 1803–1812.* Baton Rouge: Louisiana State University Press, 1983.

TRIMBLE, ALLEN
1783–1870
Ohio militia officer

Born in Virginia to James Trimble and Jane Allen Trimble, Allen Trimble moved as a child with his parents to Kentucky and, as a young man, after his father's death, with his mother and siblings to Ohio. In Ohio, Trimble became involved in local politics.

When war erupted with Great Britain in 1812, Trimble had achieved sufficient prominence in the state to be given a colonel's commission in the Ohio militia and was attached to William Henry Harrison's Army of the Northwest. Harrison used these militia forces for a variety of tasks, primarily to guard the frontiers of the Indiana and Michigan Territories and Ohio from Indian raids.

In September 1812, Trimble participated in Harrison's relief of Fort Wayne. For the remainder of 1812, Trimble continued to patrol the Indiana frontier. In November, Harrison dispatched Trimble with about 500 men to destroy White Pigeon's Town in the Michigan Territory. The mission failed, primarily because about half of Trimble's men refused to travel that far from home. Trimble had to content himself with the destruction of a few villages west of Fort Wayne.

After the expiration of his militiamen's terms of service, Trimble tried to raise another regiment. The need for additional forces after Harrison's defeat of the British at the Battle of the Thames did not seem pressing, however, and Trimble's men were discharged almost as soon as he had raised them.

Following the war, Trimble became more active in state politics, serving in the lower and upper houses of the Ohio legislature from 1816 to 1825. He later served as governor of the state and became a leader of the Whig Party in Ohio.

—*Jeanne T. Heidler and David S. Heidler*

See also: Harrison, William Henry; Ohio; Wayne, Fort
Further Reading
Tuttle, Mary M., and Henry B. Thompson. *Autobiography and Correspondence of Allen Trimble, Governor of Ohio, with Genealogy of the Family.* Columbus, OH: N.p., 1909.

outbreak of the War of 1812, he received a commission as a major in the Ohio Volunteers.

Like most of the Ohio Volunteers, Trimble accompanied Brig. Gen. William Hull to Detroit in the summer of 1812 and was part of the army that Hull surrendered to the British in August of that year. Exchanged the following year, Trimble transferred from the Volunteers to the 26th U.S. Infantry in March 1813 and then to the 19th U.S. Infantry in May 1814.

Trimble accompanied the latter regiment when it was ordered to the Niagara Frontier in the summer of 1814, where he was part of the force occupying Fort Erie after the Battle of Lundy's Lane. Trimble and the 19th Infantry occupied the northeast portion of the fortifications at Fort Erie, and during the British attack on 15 August, Trimble participated in driving the British out after they had gained entrance into the bastion.

One month later, Maj. Gen. Jacob Brown placed Trimble and the 19th Infantry in the second division commanded by Col. James Miller, as part of the sortie against the British batteries on 17 September 1814. This division attacked the center of the British position, taking British batteries one and two. Trimble received a brevet promotion to lieutenant colonel for his bravery during the sortie.

After the war, Trimble remained in the army and went with his regiment to St. Louis and then New Orleans. He participated in Andrew Jackson's invasion of Spanish Florida in 1818 and resigned from the army the following year. Shortly thereafter, he was elected to the U.S. Senate from Ohio but became ill on a tour of the Northwest and died in 1821, soon after his return to Washington, D.C.

—*Jeanne T. Heidler and David S. Heidler*

See also: Brown, Jacob J.; Detroit, Surrender of; Erie, Fort; Hull, William; Jackson, Andrew; Lundy's Lane, Battle of
Further Reading
Tuttle, Mary M. "William Allen Trimble." *Ohio Archaeological and Historical Society Journal* 14 (1905): 225–246.

TRIMBLE, WILLIAM ALLEN
1786–1821
U.S. officer

Born in Kentucky to James Trimble and Jane Allen Trimble, William Allen Trimble attended Transylvania College before entering the practice of law. He moved from Kentucky to Pennsylvania before settling in Ohio. At the

TROUP, GEORGE M.
1780–1856
U.S congressman

Born in what is now Alabama to George Troup and Catherine McIntosh Troup, the younger Troup was educated in Georgia and New York before attending and graduating from the College of New Jersey (Princeton) in 1797. He returned to Georgia, where he studied and began practicing law and entered Georgia politics. He served for several years in the Georgia legislature before being elected to the U.S. House of Representatives in 1807.

During the *Chesapeake-Leopard* Affair with Great Britain, Troup advocated going to war with Great Britain but strongly supported the Embargo Act of 1807 as an alternative. During the years leading up to the War of 1812, Troup was increasingly associated with that faction of Democratic Republicans known as the War Hawks. He urged Congress to take stronger measures to prepare the country for war and especially recommended increased military spending on both the army and the navy.

Once the war began, Troup continued his aggressive stance, criticizing the Madison administration in the fall of 1812 for not prosecuting the war more vigorously. His interest in and frequent pronouncements on military affairs gained him the appointment as the chairman of the House Committee on Military Affairs in the 13th Congress. In this position, Troup continued to urge energetic, offensive actions on the part of the military, but when James Monroe assumed the position of secretary of war in the fall of 1814, Troup questioned some of the recommendations for strengthening the army made by the new secretary.

Particularly at issue was Monroe's request that Congress approve the classification of the state militias by age and then the conscription of members of some of the classes. Not only was this proposal seen as an infringement on state government's authority over their militias, but given the objections raised by New England to the federal use of militias throughout the war, the proposal was downright impolitic. Troup, ever the advocate of strengthening the armed forces, proposed instead that the president be authorized to call up additional volunteers to meet anticipated needs. As it happened, the end of the war did away with the need for more recruits.

Following the war, Troup served several terms in the U.S. Senate, as well as two terms as the governor of Georgia. In the latter position, he insisted on the implementation of the fraudulent second Treaty of Indian Springs, which ceded the remaining Creek Indian lands in the state to the United States. This treaty, negotiated with Troup's first cousin, Creek leader William McIntosh, resulted in the execution of the latter by the Creek Nation.

In his later life, Troup was an ardent advocate of southern rights. Before his death in 1856, he urged the South to be prepared to protect its interests, by force of arms if necessary.

—*Jeanne T. Heidler and David S. Heidler*

See also: McIntosh, William; Militia in the War of 1812; Monroe, James; U.S. Congress; War Hawks
Further Reading
Harden, Edward J. *The Life of George M. Troup.* Savannah, GA: E. J. Durse, 1859.

TUCKABATCHEE

One of the four principal Creek towns, Tuckabatchee stood on the Alabama River near the present site of the Fort Toulouse State Monument (at the confluence of the Coosa and the Tallapoosa Rivers, a most strategic location). It was a peace town and the repository of the Muskogee people's most sacred objects, seven mysterious round copper and brass plates. In the years before the War of 1812, the headman at Tuckabatchee was Efa Harjo (Mad Dog), a "medal chief" friendly to the United States. The town was the site of the famous council in which the old tribal government was abolished in favor of a new system designed by agent Benjamin Hawkins. Efa Harjo was elected first "speaker" of the confederation; he died early in 1812. In November 1811, Tuckabatchee was thrust into the center of the coming storm: Tecumseh himself appeared there, speaking to a great council of all the Creeks, urging them to join his alliance. He warned that the whites would devastate the land if they were not halted and promised that after he returned to Ohio, he would stamp his feet and cause the whole earth to shake as a sign that he spoke for the Great Spirit. A month later the great New Madrid earthquake shook the eastern half of North America, but evidently the Tuckabatchee people were not convinced; most did not join the rebellion. The influence of the chief man of the town, Tustunnuggee Thlucco, known to whites as Big Warrior, was greater than Tecumseh's.

Many Upper Creeks, however, led by the aged chief Opothle Micco, listened to the Shawnee's message. Thus Tuckabatchee was at the center of the Creek, or Red Stick, War of 1813–1814. The town declared neutrality but was besieged in the summer of 1813 by a Red Stick party. Approaching Tuckabatchee, the Red Sticks demanded the surrender of Big Warrior and Tustunnuggee Hopoi (Little Prince), headman of Coweta; speaking for all the besieged Creeks, the Micco (headman) of Cusseta refused. At that moment, some 200 warriors arrived from Cusseta and Coweta, enabling almost everyone in Tuckabatchee to escape before the town was burned. The Red Sticks then rampaged over the surrounding countryside, killing Indians, whites, and livestock. Hawkins and the allied chiefs decided to make a stand at Coweta, with the aid of some 200 Cherokees who had arrived too late to help Tuckabatchee.

In April 1814, Col. Homer Milton and Benjamin Hawkins erected Fort Decatur just across the Tallapoosa River from Tuckabatchee's ruins. This new post would anchor the chain of fortifications stretching back to the Georgia border and would play a crucial role in the final defeat of the Indian confederation. Tuckabatchee was later rebuilt and served as the venue for a number of councils before Creek removal.

—*Thomas S. Martin*

See also: Big Warrior; Creek War; Hawkins, Benjamin; Little Prince

Further Reading

Cotterill, R. S. *The Southern Indians: The Story of the Civilized Tribes before Removal.* Norman: University of Oklahoma Press, 1954.

Debo, Angie. *The Road to Disappearance.* Norman: University of Oklahoma Press, 1941.

Heidler, David S., and Jeanne T. Heidler. *Old Hickory's War: Andrew Jackson and the Quest for Empire.* Mechanicsburg, PA: Stackpole Books, 1996.

Henri, Florette. *The Southern Indians and Benjamin Hawkins, 1796–1816.* Norman: University of Oklahoma Press, 1986.

Owsley, Frank Lawrence, Jr. *Struggle for the Gulf Borderlands: The Creek War and the Battle of New Orleans, 1812–1815.* Gainesville: University Presses of Florida, 1981.

U

UNDERWOOD, JOSEPH ROGERS
1791–1876
Kentucky militia officer

Born in Virginia to John Underwood and Frances Rogers Underwood, Joseph Underwood spent most of his youth at the home of his uncle, Edmund Rogers, in Kentucky. He graduated from Transylvania College in 1811 and studied law until the outbreak of the War of 1812.

At the start of the war, Underwood volunteered as a private in the Kentucky militia but was soon elected one of the lieutenants of his company. Underwood's men were attached to the expedition under Kentucky militia brigadier general Green Clay that set out in early May 1813 to relieve Fort Meigs.

As Clay's boats approached Fort Meigs, Clay received a message to send part of his force to the bank opposite the fort to spike the guns of the British batteries. Underwood's company was in the lead boat and was part of the force that Clay sent to take out the British guns. The men easily accomplished their task but were lured into the nearby forest by a handful of Indians they saw at the edge of the woods. As they charged after this new target, they ran into a trap set by the Indians and were quickly killed, captured, or put to flight.

Underwood found himself in command of his company after his captain was severely wounded. He tried to rally his men to flee back to the British batteries to regroup, but as he made his way back, he received a musket ball in the back and was captured by a British soldier. The wound did not penetrate any organs, and as a result he could march to the enclosure where the British and Indians were keeping the prisoners. Upon arrival, Underwood, like the other prisoners, was forced to run a gauntlet of Indians who beat some of the prisoners to death before they could enter the enclosure. Underwood made it in safely, only then to witness the beginning of a systematic execution and scalping of some

Joseph Rogers Underwood

of the prisoners by their Indian captors. The massacre was ended when Tecumseh rode into the enclosure and threatened the Indians carrying it out.

Shortly afterward, Col. Henry Procter, the commander of British forces outside the fort, lifted the siege and paroled the militiamen who had been captured. Underwood returned to Kentucky and his new law practice.

After the war, Underwood became increasingly involved in Kentucky politics. After serving in the state legislature, he also served terms in the U.S. House of Representatives and Senate, where he was a prominent Whig. Though a slaveholder, he opposed secession and worked to keep Kentucky in the Union during the Civil War. He retired from public life during the war and died in 1876.

—*Jeanne T. Heidler and David S. Heidler*

See also: Clay, Green; Meigs, Fort; Tecumseh
Further Reading
Averill, James P. *Fort Meigs: A Condensed History of the Most Important Military Post in the Northwest, Together with Scenes and Incidents Connected with the Sieges of 1813.* Toledo: Blade Printing Company, 1886.
"Hon. Joseph R. Underwood." *American Review* 7 (1848): 609–614.

UNITED STATES VERSUS MACEDONIAN
25 October 1812

After refitting throughout September, the frigate USS *United States*, commanded by Commodore Stephen Decatur, Jr., set sail from Boston on 8 October 1812. Shortly after dawn on 25 October, the frigate HMS *Macedonian*, commanded by Capt. John S. Carden, and the U.S. lookouts spotted one another, and the warships approached to give battle. At 9:00 A.M., the two vessels maneuvered into position, and both ships exchanged a broadside at extremely long range with little success. Moments later, Decatur, realizing that Carden had mistakenly decided not to close, maneuvered within range of his 24-pounders and bombarded the *Macedonian* with his broadsides. Despite Carden's attempts to match Decatur's swift and accurate broadsides, the 18-pounders of the *Macedonian* could not overcome the superior firepower of the U.S. guns. Sometime after 9:30 A.M., Carden finally tried to close, but because of Decatur's ability to predict Carden's intentions, the *United States* sailed in and out of range of the 18-pounders while unleashing devastating broadsides at the *Macedonian*. With most of her starboard guns out of commission, extensive damage above and below decks, and terrible casualties, Carden surrendered the *Macedonian* to Decatur at 10:30 A.M.

The hour and a half engagement proved devastating for the *Macedonian*. The British ship sustained damage to her hull, mizzenmast, topmast, main yard, lower masts, and lower rigging. Only two of her starboard carronades remained operational, and two of her main deck guns were disabled. Above all, however, her crew of 301 suffered 36 dead and 68 wounded. By comparison, the *United States* had minor damage to her rigging and only 7 dead and 5 wounded.

—*R. Blake Dunnavent*

See also: Carden, John Surman; Decatur, Stephen, Jr.

UPPER MARLBORO, MARYLAND

Upper Marlboro was a major crossroads in Great Britain's August 1814 campaign against Washington, D.C. It was at Upper Marlboro on 22 August that Adm. Sir George Cockburn and approximately 400 marines and sailors joined 4,500 British army regulars commanded by Maj. Gen. Robert Ross. Ross debarked from the British naval force sent to "chastise" the United States under the command of Vice Adm. Sir Alexander Cochrane at Benedict, Maryland, on 19–20 August. In four days, Ross's veterans of the Napoleonic wars marched 30 miles west to Upper Marlboro and stood just 16 miles from the U.S. capital.

On 22 August, Cockburn's gun boats cornered U.S. commodore Joshua Barney's Chesapeake Flotilla at Pig Point near Upper Marlboro on the Patuxent River. Barney scuttled his fleet to prevent its capture. Although he was frustrated at Barney's escape and the lack of plunder, Cockburn had renewed confidence that U.S. forces could not effectively oppose professional British troops.

Unlike the battle-hungry Cockburn, Ross wavered in planning his next move from Upper Marlboro. Ross had yet to meet armed resistance. Annapolis, Baltimore, and Washington all represented viable targets, but separation from the main fleet without cavalry or artillery risked disaster. Cockburn, a veteran of hit-and-run warfare in Chesapeake Bay since 1813, wanted to crush U.S. morale by taking Washington. Aware of Ross's uncertainty, Cockburn rode to Upper Marlboro on 23 August and convinced the general that his troops could easily seize Washington. This meeting at Upper Marlboro crystallized British strategy in favor of the historic sack of Washington. Despite a strong showing by Barney's sailors, U.S. forces were routed at Bladensburg on 24 August, and the capital fell with minimal resistance that evening. After setting fire to the government buildings, Ross withdrew from Washington and again camped at Upper Marlboro on 27 August before rejoining Cochrane's ships on Chesapeake Bay.

Ross set up camp at Upper Marlboro, a small hamlet that housed the Prince George's County government, because it commanded high ground and contained the fine home of Dr. William Beanes. Ross took possession of the house for his headquarters. The night before British regulars arrived, a small U.S. force that included Secretary of State-turned-scout James Monroe fled the hamlet in fear of British troops. Dr. Beanes, a 65-year-old landowner, physician, and gristmill operator, was one of the few residents who remained to welcome Ross. As a Federalist, Beanes sufficiently loathed Madison's administration to avoid a futile defense of his home against several thousand British troops. Ross and Beanes got along well on 23 August 1814, but following the British sack of Washington, Beanes and other villagers arrested seven British stragglers whom they viewed as potential looters. Enraged at Beanes's apparent reversal of loyalties, Ross arrested him when the British reentered Upper Marlboro. It was to secure Beanes's release that Francis Scott Key wound up aboard a British transport ship to witness the early morning bombardment of Fort McHenry on 13 September and compose "The Star-Spangled Banner."

—*Frank Towers*

See also: Beanes, William; Bladensburg, Battle of; Key, Francis Scott; Star-Spangled Banner, The
Further Reading
Lord, Walter. *The Dawn's Early Light.* New York, W. W. Norton, 1972.
Shomette, Donald G. *Flotilla: Battle for the Patuxent.* Baltimore: Calvert Marine Museum Press, 1981.

U.S. CONGRESS

Under the provisions of the U.S. Constitution, the U.S. Congress has the exclusive authority to levy war. The national legislature thus assumed an important role in the war against Britain from its outset. Controversy has ever since clouded understanding of the congressional stand toward war and its alternatives.

After the election of Thomas Jefferson in 1800 and during the years leading up to the war, the Republican Party dominated Congress. In Jefferson's first term, Congress and the president enjoyed peace in Europe for the first time in ten years, a situation occasioned by the Peace of Amiens between France and Great Britain and their allies. Republicans in Congress, abandoning Federalist doctrines of preparedness as unnecessary, optimistically cut military spending and benefited from the significant tax cuts made possible by this and other economies. Purchasing Louisiana

(1803) and presiding over a burgeoning trade and diminishing debt made for good political and economic times, until the European war was revived in 1803. The beginning of this last phase of the Napoleonic contest was to throw Congress into a series of crises. Halting and floundering responses ultimately would end in war with Britain.

Following President Jefferson's lead, Congress legislated a series of commercial restrictions that were ineffective and politically divisive. Already cramped by French and British commercial strictures, the United States was outraged by the *Chesapeake-Leopard* Affair in June 1807. In Congress, the Federalist minority united with Republicans against British depredations on the high seas. Jefferson could have had war then, and Congress (like the country) would have given him more support than it would give to James Madison five years later. Yet Jefferson avoided war and instead applied the United States' imagined commercial leverage to coerce better behavior from both Britain and France. On the president's initiative, Congress passed the Embargo Act on 22 December 1807, but the country's resistance, especially in New England and among New York Republicans, caused its repeal 14 months later.

Neither James Madison's administration nor Congress abandoned commercial sanctions. Passing first the Non-Intercourse Act and then Macon's Bill No. 2, the 11th Congress struck out from administration guidance to craft its own version of economic coercion. Such congressional behavior was a result of growing frustrations with both a worsening commercial situation and Madison's passive leadership. Madison himself observed that Congress seemed unhinged as the system of commercial restrictions proved increasingly ineffective. In fact, Macon's Bill No. 2 put commercial restrictions into the realm of laughable absurdity because it was positively inclusive and only potentially restrictive. It opened commerce with all nations while promising to stop trade with the country that did not repeal restrictions when the other did.

The inability of both executive or legislature to cope with the British crown and the French emperor brought about a major turnover in congressional membership with the elections to the 12th Congress. The Republican majority grew in both the House and the Senate. The emergence of that voluble, influential faction of Republicans known as the War Hawks has often been seen as a turning point in congressional attitudes. Federalists had enjoyed a brief political renaissance during the dark days of the unpopular embargo, but the War Hawks would have their day in rousing the wounded feelings of national pride when the 12th Congress convened on 4 November 1811. Led in the House by the able Kentuckian Henry Clay (who would become speaker during this, his freshman term) and including such

527

luminaries as South Carolina's John C. Calhoun, William Lowndes, and Langdon Cheves and Tennessee's Felix Grundy, the War Hawks would be credited by many with goading a reluctant and irresolute Madison to the decision for war.

Yet the War Hawks were only a faction within the Republican Party in Congress, and their influence can be overly emphasized. Old Republicans led by Virginian John Randolph of Roanoke opposed the move to war, and Clintonians—the followers of New Yorker DeWitt Clinton—included many northern, commercially inclined Republicans who tended to see foreign policy through lenses very similar to those of the Federalists. Maryland senator Samuel Smith led a Republican faction called the "Invisibles" that included Virginian William Branch Giles and Pennsylvanian Michael Leib, whose anti-Madison stand stemmed from their fierce dislike of Secretary of the Treasury Albert Gallatin.

And, of course, there were the minority Federalists, whose numbers were slight but whose leaders were gifted, including such men as Massachusetts's Josiah Quincy and James Lloyd and Delaware's James A. Bayard. Early in the session, the Federalists tried to remove the onerous accusations of being reflexively pro-British. They followed Quincy's lead to support Republican military measures that pointed to war, thus hoping to embarrass Madison and his party by forcing the decision on war. Thus the 12th Congress oddly seemed of one mind for a while and enacted a war-preparation program that enlarged the army, readied the militia, and proposed ways to finance a war, should one occur. In the spring of 1812, however, the move for new taxes and the imposition of a new set of commercial sanctions consisting of a 90-day embargo and a Non-Exportation Act had driven the Federalists back into opposition.

Conventional Republican unity likely had as much to do with the favorable vote for war in 1812 as did the exceptional influence of any one faction, War Hawks included. The House of Representatives received James Madison's war message on 1 June 1812 and voted for war three days later, 79 to 49. Yet for all the haste in this decision, the vote marked significant divisions along both party and regional lines. The political establishment would never be so fractured again until the eve of the Civil War. The declaration was crafted with difficulty and passed only after occasionally acrimonious debate. There were defections from Republican unity, most notably John Randolph of Roanoke, who had years before broken with Jefferson in the belief that the president had deserted true Republican principles. Randolph now found Madison no more attractive in his positions. He condemned the coming contest as an act of considerable hypocrisy, born of expansionism disguised as a design to vindicate neutral maritime rights. Although he was answered with equal vehemence by War Hawk Felix Grundy, Randolph's voice carried: about a fourth of the Republicans either voted against or abstained from the war vote. Republicans who favored war revealed a regional demarcation, especially in the South and the West. This made for some irony in the claim that the fight was for "Free Trade and Sailors' Rights," especially since much opposition to war derived from those areas—New York and New England—that should have been most interested in protecting neutral rights. That these areas evinced the most stolid opposition to war has encouraged speculation ever since that the war was, as Randolph charged, a thinly veiled bid for territorial expansion. Yet the notion that the war was primarily about vindicating the national honor has endured the scrutiny of historians and in fact has emerged as the dominant interpretation of congressional voting behavior.

In any case, nothing could hide the truth that the country entered the war with a deeply divided national legislature. The Senate deliberated over the vote for two weeks before rendering a favorable decision on 17 June, but only just barely. The vote in the upper chamber was 19 to 13, an even more ominous portent of national disunity than had been exposed in the House. During the next two and a half years, matters would only get worse as congressional responses to the demands of the war would be hampered by declining Republican popularity and indefatigable Federalist hostility, especially centered in New England.

After adopting measures to maintain a modified restrictive system (U.S. trade with British forces on the Iberian peninsula was permitted, for instance), issuing $5 million in treasury notes, raising customs duties, and authorizing codes for privateers, the first session of the 12th Congress adjourned on 6 July 1812. By the time the second session opened on 2 November 1812, the 1812 congressional elections were already revealing the depth of Federalist disaffection and Republican vulnerability. The Republicans lost seats in commercial and maritime states such as New York and Massachusetts and suffered defeat in New Jersey and especially in Maryland as well, where reaction to the summertime violence against the Federalist press in Baltimore created an electoral recoil. It was a trend that would continue throughout the war: the 1814 congressional elections would further deplete Republican ranks and see defeated the leaders of the irascible Invisibles—Senate fixtures such as Samuel Smith, William Branch Giles, and Michael Leib.

Suffering through the military setbacks, declining economic fortunes, and increasing political discord of the second session, the 12th Congress seemed less golden by the time it stumbled to its adjournment on 3 March 1813. By then, the applause of many contemporaries who had lauded the 12th Congress as likely to take rank with the great Continental Congress of 1776 had been muted. The 13th Congress would sit for the remainder of the war in three sessions (24 May 1813–2 August 1813; 6 December 1813–18 April 1814; and 19 September 1814–3 March 1815), wrestling with the problems of adequately manning the armies, fashioning viable commercial policies, and paying for the conflict.

In the process, new quarrels greeted almost everything. The Senate sharpened its teeth to snap at Madison's diplomatic initiatives, rejecting by a vote of 22 to 14 Madison's nomination of the unpopular Jonathan Russell to become U.S. minister to Sweden. Worse was the Senate's 18 to 17 rejection of Albert Gallatin when Madison appointed him a peace commissioner to accompany James A. Bayard to Europe. Gallatin's opponents—they were led chiefly by the Invisibles—coyly explained that they could not support Madison's plan to have Gallatin's treasury duties assumed by Secretary of the Navy William Jones, but everyone knew that the real reason was Gallatin's unpopularity and Senate reaction to presidential presumption. In any event, such setbacks were acutely embarrassing to the administration and supremely humiliating to Gallatin, who by 1813 was a virtual patriarch of the Republican Party.

The House of Representatives, again with Clay as speaker, would prove equally if differently troublesome. Freshman Federalist Daniel Webster of New Hampshire habitually carved at the administration with his sharp tongue. He sought to embarrass Madison about his foreign policy with resolutions demanding information Webster claimed would reveal the president's partiality for Napoleon and uncover Napoleon's deceit toward the United States. As a result, the session was difficult and frequently roiling, making it remarkable that anything got done at all, and indeed not much was done at that: a new tax program was enacted, something that would become a staple of the war years; and privateers were more widely authorized.

Henry Clay resigned from the House and hence stepped down from the speakership on 19 January 1814 to accept an "important diplomatic mission," having been appointed by Madison to join the peace commission in Europe that was opening direct negotiations with Great Britain. Clay's House seat was filled by Joseph H. Hawkins, and the speaker's chair was conferred by a vote of 94 to 59 on South Carolinian and fellow War Hawk Langdon Cheves. The new speaker confronted an increasingly fierce Federalist minority during the second and third sessions of the 13th Congress, and debate often stalled in unpleasant insinuations about fidelity and patriotism.

The last two sessions of the 13th Congress addressed more thoroughly than its predecessors the rising demands of the war for manpower and money. Congress raised bounties to encourage recruiting for the army and adopted measures to extend the terms of soldiers' service. The delicate subject of militia cooperation was finally tackled when Congress passed procedures curtailing militia independence from federal authority. Manpower shortages chronically plagued the war effort, however, and in the closing months of the conflict Secretary of War James Monroe set forth a conscription bill. Congress defeated it but did enact over loud objections from New England new enlistment procedures that proffered hefty bounties and allowed for the enlistment of minors without parental consent. Congress also authorized the recruitment of 40,000 volunteers to serve under federal authority while providing for an additional 40,000 state troops to serve in local defense. Inasmuch as the Maine district was by then suffering from British coastal raids, this last part of the measure was mildly and uncharacteristically popular in New England.

In spite of its early and almost exclusive success in the war, the navy never basked in a budget matching the army's. Most congressmen believed that attempting to challenge the Royal Navy's preponderant strength would prove too costly. Congress thus confined itself to encouraging privateers by granting wide authority and offering sizable bounties for prisoners. When Congress appropriated funds for Robert Fulton to build a floating steam-powered battery, the gesture was regarded as experimental and thus dubious. The attitude meant such funding was by far the exception and never the rule.

Congress remained curiously attached to the notion of commercial sanctions against Britain even after the declaration of war. Such measures found application in legislation to curtail trade with the enemy, especially in a final embargo adopted in the closing months of the war. This embargo was so extensive that it rivaled that of 1807, not only in the criticisms it evoked but in its ineffectiveness as well. This futile gesture encouraged a renewed round of smuggling and only lasted some four months. Madison, like Jefferson, finally relented and requested that the commercial restrictions be repealed on 31 March 1814. Frustrated by military failure and widespread smuggling, the 13th Congress, just a month prior to its final adjournment, bolstered the Enemy Trade Act of 1812. The Enemy Trade Act of 1812 had sought to prevent trade with all of Britain except for Peninsular armies, but smuggling had mocked its provisions. In February 1815, the federal government was invested with enforcement powers so extensive that they were more obnoxious than anything prior. Yet they too were almost impossible to enforce.

By far, the most daunting task was paying for the war, and Congress proved most disappointing in trying to do so. The task of financing the war was complicated by Congress having allowed the Bank of the United States to lapse in 1811. The bank was a victim of anti-Hamiltonian Republican dogma resistant even to the advice of erstwhile bank opponent Albert Gallatin. In spite of his and other influential Republican voices, the bank was not renewed (Clay was an adamant enemy), and the country thus plunged into war without a central fiscal agent to control the government's finances or direct the public credit. Congress thus found itself adopting a series of measures that were marginally appropriate and only partially successful. The second session of the 13th Congress actually considered reviving the national bank, although it would have been a shadow institution limited only to the District of Columbia and having no branches. The initiative did not survive its critics, however, and finally fell prey to the false notion that peace was near at hand.

As debt mounted and the soundness of public credit declined, the third session of the 13th Congress considered proposals to issue paper money, impose additional taxes, and create a real national bank. Recently appointed Secretary of the Treasury Alexander Dallas promoted these last two suggestions, painting such a dire economic picture in his report to Congress that the legislature agreed to the taxes and to new paper notes. But opponents of the bank so altered its structure that Dallas and the administration finally opposed it, and Madison wielded the veto. An effort to revive Dallas's original proposal roughly coincided with the news of peace, and bank opponents were thus able to suppress it as unnecessary.

When it convened on 19 September 1814, the third session of the 13th Congress had abandoned the shell of the Capitol, recently burned in the British occupation of Washington in August. Congressmen met uncomfortably in the Patent Building, which had been spared the British torch by the intrepid intervention of Dr. William Thornton. After briefly considering the prospect of moving the capital from the District of Columbia, Congress made perhaps its most momentous decision of the war. It narrowly voted to rebuild Washington and keep the government there. The legislature's own library would be resurrected, starting with the purchase of bibliophile Thomas Jefferson's enormous private collection of books.

During the War of 1812, the U.S. Congress operated under the normal tensions and complications of a free political system that tolerates dissent, even in times of emergency. Always a contentious body—because, after all, politics is a contentious art—Congress sometimes avoided hard decisions and postponed difficult issues. Yet there were efforts to address recruiting problems, regularize federal-state relations in regard to the militia, and enact loans and taxes against financial exigency. Congress did not always cover itself in glory during the war, but neither did much of the rest of the country. In that, the national legislature fared no worse and sometimes a little better than might have been expected.

—Jeanne T. Heidler and David S. Heidler

See also: Federalist Party; Financing the War of 1812; Trade Restrictions; War Hawks

Further Reading
Annals of the Twelfth Congress, 1811–1812. Washington: Gales and Seaton, 1853.
Barlow, William R. "Congress during the War of 1812." Ph.D. diss., Ohio State University, 1961.
Bell, Rudolph M. "Mr. Madison's War and Long Term Congressional Voting Behavior." *William and Mary Quarterly* 36 (1979): 373–395.
Hatzenbuehler, Ronald L. *Congress Declares War: Rhetoric, Leadership, and Partisanship in the Early Republic.* Kent, OH: Kent State University Press, 1983.
———. "Party Unity and the Decision for War in the House of Representatives, 1812." *William and Mary Quarterly* 29 (1972): 367–392.
Johnson, Leland R. "The Suspense Was Hell: The Senate Vote for War in 1812." *Indiana Magazine of History* 65 (1969): 247–269.

V

VAN BUREN, MARTIN
1782–1862
New York politician

Though he would later reach considerably greater heights, during the War of 1812, Martin Van Buren was still a young state politician. Born in Kinderhook, New York, on the Hudson River, Van Buren studied law in the 1790s, then in the following decade associated himself with the New York Republican party. In 1807, Van Buren supported George Clinton's faction of New York Republicans, helping Daniel D. Tompkins win the governorship. A superior lawyer, Van Buren was well known when he ran for office himself and won a seat in the state senate in 1812.

Only a few weeks after his election, the War of 1812 began. In the years before the declaration of war, Van Buren had supported Republican measures against the British. Despite his junior status, Van Buren soon found himself one of the leading New York state politicians backing the war effort, along with Tompkins and Judge Ambrose Spencer. Van Buren took the lead in getting war-related measures through the state legislature (the lower house of which had a Federalist majority). Never content with passing measures for their own sake, he also used these political battles as a way to destroy support for the Federalists. At the same time, he performed other services, such as serving as a prosecutor in the court-martial of Gen. William Hull. Hull was sentenced to be shot for cowardice, but his sentence was later remitted. Van Buren also developed a close friendship with U.S. Army general Winfield Scott, who sometimes acted as a conduit between New York Republicans and the Madison administration.

Van Buren's efforts were in part responsible for the sweeping Republican success in the 1814 state elections. This represented a decided victory for Van Buren and Tompkins, which was soon followed by military victories on the Niagara Frontier and Lake Champlain. British successes in Chesapeake Bay, however, called for renewed ef-

Martin Van Buren

fort on the part of New Yorkers, who feared an attempt to take New York City. Tompkins called a special session of the legislature to meet and vote on defensive measures, in which Van Buren took the lead in proposing legislation (with advice from Aaron Burr) to activate 12,000 men from the militia. This "Classification Bill" passed, despite heated opposition; so did measures for raising militia pay, creating a brigade of marines, and authorizing privateering under state authority. Van Buren finished his War of 1812 career with an appointment to state attorney general.

Van Buren's later achievements as senator, vice president, and president were foreshadowed by the considerable political skills that he developed during the War of 1812. He had navigated through a mass of factions and parties to make himself one of the leading politicians in New York. And in so doing, Martin Van Buren became one of the individuals most responsible for the continuation of New York's contribution to the war effort, second only to Daniel D. Tompkins.

—*Mark Pitcavage*

See also: New York
Further Reading

Cole, Donald B. *Martin Van Buren and the American Political System.* Princeton: Princeton University Press, 1984.
Niven, John. *Martin Van Buren: The Romantic Age of American Politics.* New York: Oxford University Press, 1983.
Remini, Robert. *Martin Van Buren and the Making of the Democratic Party.* New York: Columbia University Press, 1951.

The anti-Clinton faction, led by Gov. Daniel D. Tompkins, supported the war measures of the Madison administration and consequently drew the wrath of the Clintonians. In an address published in April 1813, they accused Tompkins of being a puppet of the Virginia dynasty. Van Cortlandt signed that address.

In 1813, Van Cortlandt retired to private life. He took little part in political activities for the remainder of his life, though he was affiliated with the Whig Party in the 1830s and 1840s. He devoted much of the remainder of his life to his estates and banking.

—*Jeanne T. Heidler and David S. Heidler*

See also: Clinton, DeWitt; Tompkins, Daniel D.
Further Reading

Judd, Jacob. *Correspondence of the Van Cortlandt Family of Van Cortlandt Manor, 1800–1814.* Tarrytown, NY: Sleepy Hollow Press, 1980.

VAN CORTLANDT, PIERRE, JR.
1762–1848
U.S. congressman

Born in New York to a prominent New York family, Pierre Van Cortlandt graduated from Queen's College (Rutgers) in 1783 and began the study of law in the office of Alexander Hamilton. After practicing law for a short time, he retired to his estates. For a brief time during the presidential administration of James Madison, he became involved in New York and national politics because of his concern that Virginia was coming to dominate the national scene.

In 1811, he served in the New York legislature before being elected to the 12th Congress. For two years, Van Cortlandt was associated with that group of New York Democratic Republicans, known as the Clintonians, who supported the presidential aspirations of DeWitt Clinton. Along with their fear of the so-called Virginia dynasty, this group questioned the wisdom of a war against Great Britain, particularly if that war was going to be prosecuted on the New York–Canadian frontier.

This concern prompted Van Cortlandt to vote against the declaration of war in June 1812, a move that would subject him to considerable criticism from the anti-Clinton forces in New York. During the summer of 1812, he worked for the election of DeWitt Clinton to the presidency, believing that Clinton's election would mean that the war would not be prosecuted on the New York frontier.

VAN RENSSELAER, SOLOMON
1774–1852
New York militia officer

Solomon Van Rensselaer was born on 8 August 1774 into a powerful Dutch-American family in New York. He obtained a commission as cornet in the newly formed Light Dragoon Squadron in 1792. As such, he took part in the Battle of Fallen Timbers on 20 August 1794, in which a bullet tore through his lungs. He lived but had to miss active service for two years. His conduct had impressed Brig. Gen. James Wilkinson, who befriended him. Years later, Van Rensselaer spoke of the general as his best friend.

He became a captain in 1795; married a relative, Harriet Van Rensselaer, on 17 January 1797; and that same year intended to resign his commission. His friend General Wilkinson and Alexander Hamilton dissuaded him. That spring he marched his troop 600 miles to Knoxville in one month without a single loss. Although he was a harsh disciplinarian, he took good care of his men, horses, and equipment.

He advanced to major in 1799, but when the Jefferson administration reduced the army, it found his ardent Federalism unacceptable and honorably discharged him. The state of New York picked him up at once. As adjutant and major general of New York militia, he served under five governors, not all of his party, from 1801 into 1811, and from 1813 to 1821.

Like many Federalists, Van Rensselaer considered the Republican leadership to be criminally delinquent in its failure to prepare the nation for the war it had brought on. He opposed the War of 1812 but felt bound as a patriot to serve in it. His last and most honored military action took place in this war.

The Van Rensselaer patroon, Stephen, who was also a major general in the New York militia, was given command of the U.S. forces along the Niagara River in spite of his being a Federalist. He appointed his nephew, Solomon, with whom he had a strong bond, as colonel and his aide. Obliged to act rapidly, Stephen decided to cross the Niagara River from Lewiston, attack Queenston, and then take the heights 345 feet above it. Regular army officers craved command of the advance party, but the general gave it to Solomon, who was to lead 300 militiamen. Solomon wrote his wife, "I must succeed or you, my dear Harriet, will never see me again."

In the scramble up the steep cliff, Van Rensselaer was hit five times. He ordered the assault to continue, and then he lost consciousness. Weeks later when able to be moved, he went home on a stretcher to Albany, where he was welcomed as a hero. The wounds he received at Queenston and the Battle of Fallen Timbers advanced his later career, but not as a soldier.

From 1819 to 1822, Van Rensselaer was a U.S. congressman. But in 1822, the Republican administration awarded him the political plum of the postmastership at Albany, New York, in spite of his dogged Federalism. Even Andrew Jackson, influenced by Solomon's honorable wounds, reappointed him, but Pres. Martin Van Buren turned him out in 1839.

By 1839, he had become a Whig. Having served with William Henry Harrison in the army, he campaigned with and for him in 1840. Harrison restored him to the postmastership at Albany, but John Tyler, a turncoat Whig, removed him.

Harriet died in 1840, their son Rensselaer Van Rensselaer in 1850, and Solomon himself on 21 April 1852.

—*John K. Mahon*

See also: Queenston, Battle of; Van Rensselaer, Stephen
Further Reading

Bonney, Catharine V.R. *Legacy of Historical Gleanings*. 2 vols. Albany, NY: J. Munsell, 1875.

Van Rensselaer, Solomon. *A Narrative of the Affair at Queenston in the War of 1812*. New York: Leavitt, Lord, 1836.

VAN RENSSELAER, STEPHEN
1764–1839
New York militia officer

Stephen Van Rensselaer was the eighth and last of a family of wealthy Dutch and, later, Dutch-American patroons, large landowners in the Hudson River Valley in New York state. He was a Harvard graduate and a great supporter of education in New York. Van Rensselaer was an early regent and benefactor of what is now the State University of New York and the founder of Rensselaer Polytechnic Institute of Troy, New York. His great wealth and vast estates near Albany, the state's capital, made him an influential figure in New York politics for many years. A Federalist leader from upstate New York, Van Rensselaer served as a U.S. congressman, was elected to many terms in the state legislature, and was appointed president of the New York state constitutional conventions of 1801 and 1821. He also was lieutenant governor of New York from 1795 to 1801. Van Rensselaer was a leader of the commissions that were responsible for the construction of the Erie and Champlain Canals. In addition to these political offices, he served as a major general in the New York militia during the first year of the War of 1812.

Stephen Van Rensselaer was selected for this post by the Democratic Republican governor, Daniel D. Tompkins, in order to secure the support of New York Federalists for the war. When he was called to active service to protect the Niagara Frontier, he was a political appointee who had the great disadvantage of no prior military experience. Part of his mission was to protect northwestern New York; the other responsibility was to achieve the congressional War Hawks' goal of the annexation of Upper Canada. In the autumn of 1812, Stephen Van Rensselaer marched with 6,000 poorly trained militiamen to the Niagara River, where he was, in theory, the senior commander in the area. Since he knew very little about military matters, he appointed his nephew Col. Solomon Van Rensselaer, a seasoned war veteran, as his principal aide to give him guidance. Neither aristocratic officer could secure the support of the local citizenry or the regular army or navy officers in the area. In particular, Brig. Gen. Alexander Smyth of the U.S. Army was hostile to the idea of serving under a militia leader and refused to meet or to communicate with the Van Rensselaers. Their inability to conduct joint operations was to have disastrous results. Both the regulars and militia units were handicapped by problems of sickness, inadequate supplies, and a shortage of boats and larger ships to cross the rivers to invade Canada.

Pres. James Madison was dissatisfied with the lack of aggressive action in the summer of 1812 by the senior general on the northern front, Gen. Henry Dearborn. The disastrous surrender of Maj. Gen. William Hull, commander of U.S. forces in Detroit, made Secretary of War William Eustis and the president eager for a victory in the Niagara area. The fact that Dearborn and his British opponent had informally agreed to an armistice on 9 August 1812 also made U.S. leaders want a quick invasion before the British and Canadians could improve their defenses.

In October 1812, the lull ended and an invasion began. The combined militia and regular army (if they had cooperated) gave the U.S. forces nearly 7,200 men in the field, a significant numerical advantage over the British-Canadian forces. Confident of victory, Van Rensselaer ordered the invasion to start on 11 October 1812, but his poor logistical planning was made evident when there were not enough boats to carry his soldiers over the 250-yard-wide Niagara River to the Canadian shore. Again the next day, Van Rensselaer ordered another attack, and this time a night operation took the regulars and some of the militia assigned to Van Rensselaer to the Canadian side. Their goal was to take control of the Queenston Heights. This position would give the U.S. field artillery command of the entire area. The advance column of New York militia faltered, but a troop of regulars under the command of Col. Winfield Scott enabled the Americans to have a short-lived victory and command of Queenston Heights. The next day, 13 October, Stephen Van Rensselaer ordered his reserve units to cross the Niagara River to reinforce Scott's forces and to consolidate the victory. The timing was right because the British were outnumbered and had lost their commander, Gen. Sir Isaac Brock, the previous day. Unfortunately for Scott and Van Rensselaer's reputation, the militia refused to comply with his order to fight in Canada. Van Rensselaer exhorted them to attack. In his report of the battle, he later wrote, "To my utter astonishment I found that at the very moment when complete victory was in our hands, the ardor of the unengaged troops had entirely subsided. I rode in all directions; urged the men by every consideration to pass over, but in vain." Additional British and Canadian militia units arrived at Queenston Heights, and the larger enemy forces defeated Scott's small detachment. Many of the Americans on the Heights ran for the river, but the boatmen fled the scene, leaving the soldiers stranded. Many Americans drowned while attempting to swim the swift Niagara River or were captured. Winfield Scott was captured in the battle but was later exchanged for an enemy officer.

The result was a major defeat for the Americans. Canadian scholars believe that Upper Canada was saved by this battle, considered the greatest military victory in Canadian history. Stephen Van Rensselaer resigned his command and never again served in the war.

Stephen Van Rensselaer was a brave and patriotic gentleman, but he did not match the generalship of the British in this battle. He did not inspire his troops, lacked adequate plans, and had inadequate logistical support for his men. He has also been criticized for not coordinating with Brigadier General Smyth, who was a few miles away. If Smyth had brought up his regulars, U.S. victory very likely would have been achieved. Smyth took over command on the Niagara Frontier, but he was equally ineffective in the rest of 1812 and 1813.

—*George E. Frakes*

See also: Queenston, Battle of; Smyth, Alexander; Van Rensselaer, Solomon

Further Reading

Barlow, William. *The Character and Reward of a Just Man.* Albany: Packard, Van Banthusen and Co., 1839.

Barnard, Daniel D. *A Discourse on the Life, Services and Character of Stephen Van Rensselaer Delivered before the Albany Institute, April 15, 1839.* Albany: Hoffman and White, 1839.

Brown, Roger H. *The Republic in Peril: 1812.* New York: Columbia University Press, 1964.

Fink, William Bertrand. "Stephen Van Rensselaer: The Last Patroon." Ph.D. dissertation, Columbia University, 1950.

Gomola, Christopher Ira. "Bright Victory Wasted." *Military History* 7 (1990): 30–37.

VERMONT

Like other New England states, Vermont was home to a large number of Federalists who opposed the United States' going to war against Great Britain. The state, however, was fairly evenly divided between Democratic Republicans and Federalists, and at the start of the war, the Democratic Republicans controlled the governor's chair and the legislature. Therefore, when in 1812 Brig. Gen. Henry Dearborn sent out a call to New England states to supply militia to garrison the frontier with Canada, Gov. Jonas Galusha supplied the required troops. The state legislature also responded to the war by passing laws ending trade between the state and Canada.

These measures were very unpopular with Vermont Federalists, and with militiamen leaving the state and the economic effects of the interruption of trade increasingly felt, other citizens began to question the desirability of this war. When during the following fall, Maj. Gen. Wade Hampton requested more Vermont militia to participate in his invasion of Canada and Governor Galusha once again met the call, the voters responded in the fall of 1813 by electing Federalist Martin Chittenden governor and returning a Federalist majority to the state legislature.

Though Chittenden did not believe that state militia could constitutionally participate in a foreign invasion, he did not want to be held responsible for Hampton's failure. Therefore, he waited until Hampton's invasion had stalled before recalling the men. Some of the officers, however, refused to return, claiming that it would be unpatriotic to abandon the campaign.

The economic effects of the curtailment of trade with Canada were also addressed by the new Federalist government when the state legislature repealed the laws against trading with Canada. The Vermont courts also increasingly refused to enforce federal laws against such trade. One militia officer who tried to prevent smuggling was arrested.

The British invasion along Lake Champlain in late summer 1814 alerted many citizens of Vermont to their potential danger, and cooperation with the federal government's war effort increased. When Brig. Gen. Alexander Macomb, in command of the defense at Plattsburg, New York, requested militia forces from Governor Chittenden, the governor was at somewhat of a loss. He still believed that he did not have the power to send these forces out of the state, but he also realized the danger to Vermont if the British prevailed at Plattsburg. Therefore, he sent out a call to the Vermont militia encouraging the men to volunteer for federal service. This summons eventually produced approximately 2,500 men for the defense along Lake Champlain.

The threat to Vermont security posed by this invasion and the effective military response to that threat at the Battle of Plattsburg probably contributed to Vermont's less than enthusiastic response to Massachusetts's call for a convention of New England states. Once again, Governor Chittenden did not feel that he had the power to send delegates to the Hartford Convention, so he refused to do so. One Vermont town disagreed, however, and as a result Vermont had one delegate at the convention.

Although many people in Vermont supported the war, the farmers of this heavily agricultural state did not feel that they should have to lose their best customers because of it. Therefore, while Vermont supported the war effort with men and supplies to a greater extent than some of its New England neighbors, the people of Vermont continued to trade with the enemy throughout the conflict and rejected political leaders who tried to stop such practices.

—*Jeanne T. Heidler and David S. Heidler*

See also: Chittenden, Martin; Dearborn, Henry; Federalist Party; Hampton, Wade; Hartford Convention; Macomb, Alexander; Plattsburg, Battle of

Further Reading
Brynn, Edward. "Patterns of Dissent: Vermont's Opposition to the War of 1812." *Vermont History* 60 (1972): 10–27.

VILLERÉ PLANTATION

During the campaign that culminated in the Battle of New Orleans, the Villeré Plantation served as British headquarters from 23 December 1814 to 19 January 1815. Located approximately 9 miles southeast of New Orleans on the left-descending bank of the Mississippi River in St. Bernard Parish, the plantation known locally as "Conseil" was home to Maj. Jacques Philippe Villeré and his son. Built before 1753 as a simple French-style one-story structure encircled by a spacious gallery, the house sat upon blocks elevating it a few feet off the ground.

Although British scouts had previously selected the more spacious de La Ronde home to serve as army headquarters, unusually shallow levels in the connecting waterways forced a change of plans. Rather than risk the dangerous maneuver of portaging supplies, the British squadron instead navigated an intricate route from Lake Borgne into Bayou Bienvenu to Bayou Mazant and up the Villeré Canal. The British troops disembarked upon reaching dry land just to the rear of "Conseil."

By quickly storming the plantation, the British advance party surprised and seized an unsuspecting detachment of Louisiana militia. According to colorful local legend, Maj. René Philippe Gabriel Villeré eluded capture by jumping through a window to alert New Orleans authorities that the British had arrived. Upon learning of the situation, Gen. Andrew Jackson reportedly thundered, "By the eternal, they shall not sleep on our soil." Accordingly, Jackson ordered an immediate attack upon the enemy position.

The skirmish that ensued at the Villeré Plantation on 23 December, sometimes called the Night Battle of New Orleans, was strategically critical to the campaign. Jackson's sudden attack caught the British unprepared, undermanned, tired from the expedition, and ill-adjusted to their new surroundings. Yet, as seasoned veterans of the Napoleonic campaigns, British general John Keane's troops recovered from initial setbacks and fiercely engaged Jackson's forces on an often-confusing battlefield. The engagement pitted Jackson's 2,000 U.S. troops against the 1,680-man British advance party that had occupied the Villeré grounds earlier in the day. Costs were heavy to both sides: U.S. forces suffered 215 casualties in the battle, and the British lost 275 men. Although indecisive, this encounter made the British cautious, discouraging Keane from launching an immediate assault upon New Orleans. Jackson thus gained time to collect an army to defend the city.

Gen. Edward Pakenham arrived at the Villeré Plantation headquarters on Christmas Day, 1814, with additional soldiers, thus raising British troop strength beyond 4,000 men. Pakenham's decision not to attack directly allowed Jackson's men the time to construct an earthen rampart along the Rodriguez Canal, about 2 miles west of the Villeré property. That site would be the location of the main battle on 8 January 1815.

The British continued to occupy the Villeré home and its outbuildings until their evacuation from Louisiana. The plantation home survived the Battle of New Orleans, but it was later destroyed by fire. Today only a rectangular cluster of ancient live oaks remains to mark the site where the Villeré Plantation once stood.

—*Junius P. Rodriguez*

See also: Jackson, Andrew; Keane, John; New Orleans, Battle of; Pakenham, Edward
Further Reading
Owsley, Frank L., Jr. *Struggle for the Gulf Borderlands: The Creek War and the Battle of New Orleans, 1812–1815.* Gainesville: University Presses of Florida, 1981.
Roush, J. Fred. *Chalmette.* Washington: National Park Service, 1958.
Wilson, Samuel, Jr. *Plantation Houses on the Battlefield of New Orleans.* New Orleans: Battle of New Orleans, 150th Anniversary Committee of Louisiana, 1965.

VINCENT, JOHN
1765–1848
British officer

Born in Great Britain, Vincent entered the British army as a teenager in 1781. By the War of 1812, he had achieved the rank of brigadier general and was sent to Canada. When the United States began its invasion of the Niagara Frontier in May 1813 via Lake Ontario, Brigadier General Vincent commanded the British and Canadian forces there, which numbered approximately 1,800.

Vincent quickly realized that the U.S. landing force of about 4,000 men could overwhelm his smaller army and decided to retreat. He ordered the artillery pieces in Fort George spiked, the ammunition destroyed, and the fort evacuated. He then moved his little army south to Queenston and then west to a stronger position on the western end of Lake Ontario at Burlington Heights, Upper Canada. The U.S. army, had it been more aggressive, might have caught him in his flight, but the U.S. commanders cautiously maintained their positions along the Niagara River. As a result, Vincent was able to consolidate his position at Burlington Heights and receive reinforcements before the Americans began moving west along the lake.

During the first week of June 1813, two U.S. forces under Brig. Gens. John Chandler and William Winder joined forces and moved toward Vincent's position. Vincent's scouts informed him on the night of 5 June of the U.S. camp at Stoney Creek, about 10 miles away. A local youth had learned the U.S. sentries' countersign, and Vincent was armed with this information as he set out to surprise the U.S. camp.

In the predawn hours of 6 June 1813, Vincent's army surprised the Americans and fought a chaotic battle. Although neither side could claim a conclusive victory, Vincent was able to prevent the attack on his camps at Burlington Heights. In the midst of the night battle, however, Vincent was thrown from his horse and became lost in the countryside. He did not find his way back to his own lines until late the following day.

Later that year, Vincent, still in command along Lake Ontario, heard about the U.S. victory at the Battle of the Thames and grew concerned that William Henry Harrison would continue his pursuit of the defeated army there to the Niagara River. He concentrated as many of his forces as possible at Burlington Heights to meet the possible threat from the West. Harrison instead moved back to Detroit.

Though he had achieved the rank of major general by the end of 1813, Vincent asked to be relieved because of bad health. He departed Canada with a good reputation among his Canadian troops as well as his U.S. enemies, primarily among the latter because he was known for his efforts to restrain his Indian allies from killing prisoners.

Following the war, Vincent remained in the British army, eventually achieving the rank of full general in 1841. He died in London.

—*Jeanne T. Heidler and David S. Heidler*

See also: Chandler, John; George, Fort; Stoney Creek, Battle of; Thames, Battle of the; Winder, William H.

Further Reading

Cruikshank, Ernest A. "The Battle of Stoney Creek and the Blockade of Fort George." *Niagara Historical Society Transactions* 11 (1898): 15–31.

Johnson, Charles M. *The Battle for the Heartland: Stoney Creek, June 6, 1813.* Stoney Creek, Ont.: Pennell Printing, 1963.

VIRGINIA

Virginia, the largest of the states in area and in population at the time of the war, extended from the Atlantic Ocean–Chesapeake Bay to the Ohio River. Its geography rendered it vulnerable both to the British fleet and British-allied Indians. The land was far from uniform: the "sea sands" up to the fall line were the oldest area of settlement but were being abandoned owing to the exhaustion of the soil. Westward was the Piedmont, more fertile but with less access to transportation. Farther west was the Shenandoah Valley and beyond were the mountains that extend to the Ohio Valley. The state's population of 983,000 included 426,000 blacks, most of whom were slaves, a source of danger as well as wealth. Estimates of the time placed the militia at 80,000 men. Nearly that many would serve in the war—60,000 by October 1814. They were ill prepared for war, however, with training consisting of a meager two hours during one day in the spring and one day in the fall.

Virginians had controlled the presidency of the United States, except for four years, since 1789; a Virginian, John Marshall, had been chief justice of the U.S. Supreme Court since 1801. Its population gave Virginia the largest delegation in the House of Representatives (22). In spite of the influence of Thomas Jefferson and James Madison, in 1812 that delegation contained five Federalists who, paradoxically, represented opposite sides of the state along the Potomac and Ohio Rivers. The former region shared the Atlantic commercial world and favored a British connection. The latter, near the frontier but on a commercial waterway, perhaps preferred the domestic economic policies of the Federalists.

With regard to the bills leading to the war, the Federalist delegates generally voted against raising troops and taxes. Regarding the declaration of war, four Federalists voted against and one abstained, and one Republican, the irascible and eccentric John Randolph, joined them. In the congressional elections that fall, only one of the antiwar men (James Breckinridge) was returned to Congress. The commonwealth's constitution elected the governor by vote of the legislature, limited him to three one-year terms, denied him the veto power, confined his appointments to minor offices, and tied his executive powers to the 18-member Council of State, but did give him command of the militia. After Gov. G. W. Smith was killed in a theater fire in December 1811, the legislature elected Speaker of the House of Delegates James Barbour (1775–1842) governor on 3 January 1812.

In preparing for the war, the Virginians, being Virginians, began with Barbour's proclamation of January 1812 regulating uniforms (officers and special troops in blue coats; riflemen in purple linen hunting shirts; the main body of the militia in blue hunting shirts with red fringe). With war looming, in March 1812 Barbour called up 12,000 militia. In May, he toured the area of the James River and Norfolk and rather accurately predicted that the poor roads would hamper British operations along the James against Richmond. He also sensibly recommended that a fort be built at Craney Island to defend both Norfolk and the U.S. Navy Yard at Gosport. Virginians throughout the war would fret over shortages of gunpowder, ammunition, and tents (the absence of which was thought to be the principal cause of disease).

In September 1812 (after the fall of Detroit), a force of 1,500 Virginians was assembled and marched into Ohio to join the new army under William Henry Harrison. Although the Virginians were ordered to the support of Gen. James Winchester during the fiasco of the Battle of Frenchtown (or River Raisin), they saw no action and returned, to be disbanded the following May. The real ordeal appeared with the arrival in Chesapeake Bay (in early February 1813) of two British 74s and three frigates, which blockaded the USS *Constellation* in Norfolk. Within the year, the British would place 11 ships of the line, 33 frigates, 38 sloops, and a number of schooners in the bay. Their seamen numbered 8,200. The state legislature responded in February 1813 by raising an army of 1,000 men in addition to the militia; the latter continued to be called upon to defend the Tidewater area. In April 1813, the British captured four armed schooners in the Rappahannock River. On 22 June 1813, the British attacked the new fort at Craney Island with 3,000 men but were repulsed by 500 Americans there. Three days later, the British attacked Hampton by land and sea with 900–1,100 men and drove out the U.S. garrison. Some of the royal troops were in fact French nationals, and these were blamed by both Virginians and Englishmen for the plundering and assaults on persons. These attacks produced drafts of neighboring county militia by Gen. R. B. Taylor "for as many men as was consistent with their safety from the internal foe."

Between 18 and 24 July, the Americans made four attempts to sink the *Plantagenet* (74 guns) by using "torpedoes" contrived by Elijah Mix after an idea of Robert Fulton's. The torpedoes were, in fact, underwater metal-cased, clockwork-timed explosives carried by currents, three of which failed and the last of which detonated a few seconds too soon. For the remainder of the year, the British refrained from attacking fortifications (Norfolk had 3,000–4,000 militiamen in its garrison by early 1814) and contented themselves with daylight raids and plundering in Surrey County and Jamestown. The British were apparently unable to feed themselves by raiding, in part because the militia was sufficient to drive off smaller parties and in part because of the deserted nature of the country. Their supplies came from Bermuda (probably originating in Europe). Small raids were chronic, and the governor was besieged with appeals for help from nervous men in the river towns of Fredericksburg and Petersburg.

By April 1814, the British had taken over Tangier Island as a base, where they built houses, a hospital, and fortifications with cannon. Here they collected runaway slaves; 700 were reported there at one time in 1814. The black males were given a choice "to become blue Jackets, *take up arms* or join the working party." Women and children were to be sent to Bermuda and Halifax, Nova Scotia. The body of a black man was found in full British uniform after a raid on Pungoteague on the Eastern Shore. In May 1814, Adm. Alexander Cochrane formed a Corps of Colonial Marines of 200 blacks who later fought at Bladensburg, Maryland. All told, between 3,000 and 5,000 former slaves left Chesapeake Bay with the British. Most went to Nova Scotia, where 2,000 were left penniless on the docks of Halifax in early 1815. The Virginians believed some were sold by the British, possibly as indentured servants. From the Northern Neck came complaints that blacks "are flocking to the enemy from every quarter," and these ex-slaves passed on to the British a better working knowledge of the "passes and by-ways through our innumerable necks and swamps" than most U.S. soldiers had. Even in Lynchburg (far from the fighting), bankers feared a slave revolt and fretted about the militia's being called up to the theater of war.

When the British captured Washington, D.C., they also burned the fort at Alexandria, Virginia. The citizens consequently surrendered the town on August 29. Under the guns of six British ships, the Alexandrians gave up all commercial tobacco, flour, and merchandise in exchange for keeping their houses and home furnishings safe. The Alexandrians refused to allow 1,400 Virginia troops to enter the city. A Virginia force of 1,753 men assisted in the defense of Baltimore. The British defeat there, while help-

ing morale, did not end the war. In October, there was a raid on Northumberland County, and on 1 December the British hit Tappahannock, blowing up the local tannery, setting fire to the houses, and burning the Essex County courthouse. In December, the British fleet began slowly to withdraw from Chesapeake Bay from north to south, marking their departure with a raid in Hampton Roads to seize boats on 29 January 1815. When the militia army was disbanded in February 1815, the soldiers were sent home "without a cent of money to travel on."

The war was expensive for the state. By April 1814, Virginia had spent over $440,000, which it expected the federal government to repay. By the end of the conflict, the war debt would reach $2,000,000. The state levied a stamp tax on paper negotiated at banks in February 1813. This was not enough. For instance, the state assumed it could feed its men on 18 cents a day, but the real cost was 20 to 23. Assuming the cost at 20 cents, the 4,000-man garrison at Norfolk (July 1814) would have consumed about $292,000 a year for food alone. In January 1814, the legislature raised taxes by one-third and in October authorized borrowing $200,000 from the Farmers' Bank of Richmond.

As a source of troops for the U.S. Army, Virginia's rate of 285 enlistees per 10,000 ranked it tenth of 18 states whose rates are known. Just under 300 men enlisted in Virginia, of whom 46 percent were native Virginians. Recruiters preferred urban areas, of which Virginia had fewer than New England and the mid-Atlantic states, and it may be that the militia service at Norfolk and in the Chesapeake Littoral dimmed the luster of arms.

—James Edward Scanlon

See also: Chesapeake Bay Campaign, 1813–1814; Craney Island, Battle of; Hampton, Virginia

Further Reading

Bell, Rudolph M. "Mr. Madison's War and LongTerm Congressional Voting Behavior." *William and Mary Quarterly* 36 (July 1979): 373–395.

Butler, Stuart Lee. *A Guide to Virginia Militia Units in the War of 1812.* Athens: University of Georgia Press, 1988.

Cassell, Frank A. "Slaves of the Chesapeake Bay Area and the War of 1812." *Journal of Negro History* 57 (April 1972): 142–154.

Debates and Proceedings in the Congress of the United States...Twelfth Congress. Washington, DC: Gales and Seaton, 1853.

Dudley, William S., ed. *The Naval War of 1812: A Documentary History.* Vol. 1. Washington, DC: Naval Historical Center, 1985.

Flournoy, H.W., ed. *Calendar of Virginia State Papers* Vol. 10: 1 January 1808–31 December 1835. Richmond: n.p., 1892.

Foytik, Rodney C. "Aspects of the Military Life of Troops Stationed around the Norfolk Harbor, 1812 to 1814." *The Chesopiean* 22 (1984): 12–20.

Lowery, Charles D. *James Barbour: A Jefferson Republican.* University: University of Alabama Press, 1984.

Paulding, James Kirke. *Letters from the South: Written during an Excursion in the Summer of 1816.* 2 vols. New York: Eastburn and Co., 1817.

Stagg. J.C.A. "Enlisted Men in the United States Army, 1812–1815: A Preliminary Survey." *William and Mary Quarterly* 43 (October 1986): 615–645.

WAR HAWKS

War Hawks is the term used to describe the group of congressmen who, in the first session of the 12th Congress in 1811–1812, were most vocal in supporting the movement leading to a declaration of war against England.

Anglo-American relations, which had been extremely strained in the decade following the end of the American Revolution, experienced a rapprochement in the years after the signing of Jay's Treaty in November 1794. Difficulties were renewed after the coming to power of the Democratic Republican administration under Pres. Thomas Jefferson in 1811 and the intensification of the war in Europe after 1803. From 1806, the United States responded to British impressment and the widespread blockades imposed by both England and France with measures of economic coercion.

When these policies of economic coercion failed to produce a change in the policies of the European belligerents, and with Congress and the nation seemingly impotent, some politicians began to call for more decisive action, both to force England to recognize U.S. maritime rights and to redeem the national honor. Young Henry Clay of Kentucky, while in Congress to fill out an unexpired senatorial term, spoke in February 1810 of the necessity of resistance by the sword. He told the Senate that though both England and France had harmed the United States, England was the main aggressor, and England was vulnerable in Canada. Clay argued that an attack on this British province would redeem the national honor and exert pressure on the British.

In the 1810 congressional elections, almost half of the incumbents were defeated. There was now to be a core of congressmen who were prepared to follow Clay in his belief that the United States' honor and commerce could be protected by military action and that England could be hurt by an invasion of Canada. Although this group included some older congressmen, most War Hawks were younger Democratic Republicans, particularly from the West and South.

The Congress elected in 1810 did not take office until November 1811, and in the intervening period, the old 11th Congress merely demonstrated its ineffectiveness. Pres. James Madison, however, had reached the conclusion that war preparations were necessary, and the new Congress was greeted by a presidential message calling for a state of readiness against long-standing British aggressions. Congress, although bitterly divided, now organized itself in a manner to prepare for war. Although Henry Clay had never previously served in the House of Representatives and was only 34 years old, he was elected Speaker of the House, a position that at the time held the power of appointment to congressional committees. He made sure that those who were prepared to argue for war were strongly represented on the key committees. There were five War Hawks on the Foreign Relations Committee: Peter B. Porter (the chairman), John C. Calhoun, John A. Harper, Felix Grundy, and Joseph Desha; War Hawks Langdon Cheves and David R. Williams were chairmen of the Naval Committee and the Military Affairs Committee, respectively; and War Hawk Ezekiel Bacon was chairman of the Ways and Means Committee.

It took Congress from November 1811 to June 1812 to find the resolve and make the preparations necessary to declare war. In the debates that filled these months, some 21 members of the House were vocal enough in their pressure for action to be regarded as War Hawks: Clay, Richard M. Johnson, and Samuel McKee of Kentucky; Felix Grundy and John Rhea of Tennessee; George M. Troup of Georgia; Calhoun, Cheves, Williams, and William Lowndes of South Carolina; William Blackledge, William R. King, and Israel Pickens of North Carolina; Burwell Bassett of Virginia; Stephen Archer, Alexander McKim, and Robert Wright of Maryland; Adam Seybert of Pennsylvania; Peter B. Porter of New York; William Widgery of Massachusetts; and John A. Harper of New Hampshire. These men—12 of them from the South Atlantic states and five from the Mississippi Valley—differed greatly in their commitment and in their influence, but they generally argued for the necessity of war and, perhaps more important, generally cast their votes in favor of the necessary military and financial measures. They argued that U.S. commerce and U.S. honor were under attack by the British and that honor could be redeemed and pressure placed on the British by the invasion of Canada.

Those who spoke for action also gained the support of other Democratic Republicans, who, while not participating actively in the debates, voted fairly consistently for measures leading toward war. The war party consisted of some 60 Democratic Republicans who voted for most of the war preparations; among them were about 20 who were vocal in support of some action and who can be grouped as the War Hawks. They wavered on such issues as increasing the U.S. Navy and how the war would be paid for, but they generally agreed that the time for a peaceful response had passed. Ultimately, the vote for war passed by 79 to 49; all 79 were Democratic Republicans. To achieve this vote had been a difficult process, and in the winter of 1811–1812, the main burden of arguing for it had been carried by a group of some 20 Democratic Republicans, most of them from the South and West.

—*Reginald Horsman*

See also: U.S. Congress
Further Reading
Fritz, Harry. "The War Hawks of 1812." *Capitol Studies* 5 (spring 1977): 25–42.
Horsman, Reginald. *The Causes of the War of 1812.* Philadelphia: University of Pennsylvania Press, 1962.
———. "Who Were the War Hawks?" *Indiana Magazine of History* 60 (June 1964): 122–136.

WARREN, JOHN BORLASE
1753–1822
Royal Navy officer

Born on 2 September 1753, the fourth son of John Borlase Warren of Stapleford, Nottinghamshire, and his wife Anne of Little Marlow, England, Sir John Borlase Warren was educated at Emmanuel College, Cambridge, and graduated with a B.A. in 1773 and an M.A. in 1776. On 24 April 1771, he appeared as an able seaman on the books of HMS *Marlborough,* guardship, Medway, and he was rated midshipman on the *Alderney* sloop while still in residence at Emmanuel. Discharged from the *Alderney* on

17 March 1774, Warren stood for election to Parliament and was elected first from Little Marlow. He sat in four parliaments—1774 and 1780 for Marlow, 1796 and 1802 for Nottingham. At his father's death on 1 June 1775, the baronetcy was conferred on Warren.

During the American Revolution, Warren served aboard the frigates *Venus* and *Apollo* in December 1777 and, after 19 July 1778, as a lieutenant in *Nonsuch, Victory, Helena, Ariadne* (20 guns), and *Winchelsea* (32 guns). He was promoted to captain in 1781 and with peace went on half-pay. A tall man with robust features, he married Caroline, daughter of Lt. Gen. Sir John Clavering and Lady Diana West, in December 1780 and had three daughters and two sons. The elder son, a lieutenant in the Guards, was killed in Egypt, and his eldest daughter, Frances Maria, married to George Charles, the fourth Lord Vernon, became his sole heiress.

Warren had a distinguished career as a frigate captain during the French Revolution. Patrolling off Brest and the Channel Islands, his squadron captured three out of four frigates on 23 April 1794, for which he received a KB. He destroyed the French frigate *Voluntaire* (36 guns) and two 18-gun corvettes in August 1794 and large numbers of vessels along the French coast. He also convoyed the expedition of French royalists to and from Quiberon Bay in June 1794 and October 1795. In 1796, his frigate squadron captured 220 sail, including 37 naval vessels and the frigate *Andromache* (26 guns), for which the patriotic fund presented him with a sword valued at 100 guineas. Promoted on 10 October 1798 to command a squadron of three 74-gun ships and five frigates, with his flag in *Canada* (74 guns), Warren intercepted a French squadron that consisted of *Hoche* (74 guns) and eight frigates supporting a 5,000-strong French expedition to Killala Bay, Ireland. *Hoche* and three frigates were captured, and only two frigates and a schooner escaped. For this exploit, Warren was promoted to rear admiral on 14 February 1799 and received the thanks of the English and Irish parliaments. Subsequent service included action off Brest and Ferrol, the Bay of Biscay, and Cádiz, and the support of British troops in Egypt in 1801. In 1802, he became a member of the Privy Council and went to St. Petersburg as ambassador extraordinary to Czar Alexander I for the accession celebrations. After promotion to vice admiral on 9 November 1805, Warren, aboard his flagship *Foudroyant* (74 guns) and with his small squadron, captured the French ship *Marengo* (74 guns) and frigate *Belle Poule,* which were returning from the East Indies on 13 March 1806. Warren was appointed commander in chief of the Halifax station from November 1807 to July 1810 and was promoted to admiral on 31 July 1810.

On 3 August 1812, Warren was ordered to hoist his flag as admiral of the White fleet aboard the *San Domingo* (74 guns), "to unite the hitherto separate commands of the Halifax, Jamaica and Leeward Island Stations," and to direct the war against the United States. He arrived at Halifax on 26 September with authorization to propose an armistice to Secretary of State James Monroe on the basis that the U.S. government would revoke its hostile measures, but nothing developed from this initiative. Warren adopted a strategy of fighting a defensive war with limited blockading forces operating from Halifax and Bermuda. He proclaimed a selective blockade south of New York, combined with raids on the U.S. coast. He expected that this activity would keep U.S. militia employed in defending their own country and would relieve the pressure on the British North American provinces.

After corresponding with Gov.-Gen. Sir George Prevost, commander in chief of the British North American provinces, Warren recommended a naval force for the Canadian lakes. The Admiralty responded in March 1813, when Sir James Lucas Yeo and 440 officers and men were ordered out. Warren also sent three lieutenants—Robert Heriot Barclay, Daniel Pring, and Robert Finnis—while urging Prevost to commence a shipbuilding program.

Naval writers such as William James, Alfred T. Mahan, and Cecil S. Forester have usually underestimated Warren's achievements, partly because he called constantly for reinforcements, a detail that also irritated Secretary of the Admiralty John Wilson Croker. Yet, Warren's defensive arrangements meshed with Prevost's land strategy in 1812–1813. In 1813, he organized small squadrons that blockaded the main U.S. ports after February 1813, restrained "swarms of privateers," neutralized the raiding potential of the U.S. frigates and sloops, guarded the Caribbean convoys to Quebec and England, and organized raids under Rear Adm. Sir George Cockburn against Chesapeake Bay coastal towns. Essentially, Warren patrolled an extensive theater with limited resources until the downfall of Napoleon in Europe allowed reinforcements.

In March 1814, Warren was relieved when the Admiralty redivided the command into the original stations. His successor, Sir Alexander Inglis Forester Cochrane, conducted a more offensive strategy of combined operations. Warren protested the transfer to Lord Melville and delayed Cochrane's command for nearly a month until April 1814, which circumstance Cochrane protested vociferously to the Admiralty. Apart from the blow to his pride, Warren's concern over the loss of command may have arisen from a desire to capture more prizes along the U.S. coast. Warren returned to England aboard the *San Domingo* and received the GCB in 1815. He died on 27 February 1822 at Greenwich hospital while visiting Sir Richard Keats and is buried in the family vault in Stretton Audley, Oxfordshire. Warren's portrait was painted by John Opie, and a tablet commemorating him is in Attenborough Church, near Stapleford, Nottinghamshire. Warren's wife, Caroline, died at Stapleford in December 1839.

—*Frederick C. Drake*

See also: Barclay, Robert Heriot; Cochrane, Alexander; Croker, John Wilson; Naval Strategy, Great Britain; Prevost, George; Yeo, James Lucas

Further Reading

Anson, Walter. *The Life of Admiral Sir John Borlase Warren.* London: Wyman, 1912.

Drake, Frederick C. "Sir John Borlase Warren." *Dictionary of Canadian Biography.* Vol. 6: *1821 to 1835.* Toronto: University of Toronto Press, 1979: 802–804.

Dudley, William S., ed. *The Naval War of 1812: A Documentary History.* Vol. 2. Washington, DC: Naval Historical Center, 1992.

Forester, C. S. *The Age of Fighting Sail: The Story of the Naval War of 1812.* Garden City, N Y: 1956.

Laughton, John Knox. "Sir John Borlase Warren." *Dictionary of National Biography.* Vol. 20, *UB-WH.* London: Oxford University Press, 1937–1938: 869–872.

WARRINGTON, LEWIS
1782–1851
U.S. Navy officer

Born in Williamsburg, Virginia, on 3 November 1782, Lewis Warrington attended the College of William and Mary. He entered the navy as a midshipman on 6 January 1800, served in the West Indies and the Mediterranean, and became an acting lieutenant in November 1804 and lieutenant in 1805. When war commenced in 1812, he joined the *Congress* as first lieutenant, transferring the next year to the *United States.* He took command of the sloop *Peacock* (22 guns) and was promoted to master commandant.

On 18 April 1813, near the Bahamas, the *Peacock* disabled and captured the British brig *Epervier* (18 guns), commanded by Capt. Richard W. Wales. The *Epervier*'s broadside was 274 pounds; the *Peacock*'s 338 pounds. After the *Peacock* entered Savannah, Georgia, the citizens gave Warrington and his officers a public dinner on 14 May. Congress later granted him a gold medal and approved a resolution on 21 October 1814 to present the officers with silver medals and the midshipmen with swords.

In the controversial last U.S. ship action of the war on 1 July 1815 near Anjier Roads, Straits of Sunda, Warrington fired into the Bombay Marine brig *Nautilus* (14 guns), which had 108 pounds broadside and a crew of 80. His officers' diaries reveal that Warrington knew of the Treaty of Ghent before the action, though he later denied it. The commander of the *Nautilus*, Lt. Charles Boyce, while hailing to ask if Warrington knew of the peace, suffered dangerous thigh wounds and a shattered knee. A Navy Court of Inquiry exonerated Warrington. The U.S. Congress voted Boyce a life pension.

Warrington died on 12 October 1851.

—*Frederick C. Drake*

See also: *Peacock* versus *Epervier*; *Peacock* versus *Nautilus*
Further Reading

Aimone, Alan Conrad. "The Cruise of the U.S. Sloop *Hornet* in 1815." *Mariner's Mirror* 61 (November 1975): 377–384.

Harrington, Gordon K. "The American Naval Challenge to the English East India Company during the War of 1812." In Jack Sweetman et al., eds., *New Interpretations in Naval History*, selected papers from the Tenth Naval History Symposium, United States Naval Academy, 11–13 September 1991. Annapolis, MD: Naval Institute Press, 1993: 144–145.

James, William. *A Full and Correct Account of the Chief Naval Occurrences of the Late War between Great Britain and the United States of America*. London, T. Egerton, 1817.

Mindte, R. W., U.S.N. (Retd.). "Another Navy Rodgers." *American Neptune* 19 (July 1959): 213–226.

Paullin, Charles O. "The Cruise of the *Peacock*." In *American Voyages to the Orient, 1690–1865*. Annapolis, MD: Naval Institute Press, 1991: 19–23.

Sridharan, Rear Admiral K. *A Maritime History of India*. New Delhi: Government of India Publication Division,, 1982.

WASHINGTON, BRITISH CAPTURE OF

24 August 1814

Adm. Sir Alexander Forester Inglis Cochrane, British commander in chief, left Bermuda on 1 August 1814 with 20 warships and 30 transports to campaign in Chesapeake Bay. Aboard was Gen. Robert Ross's armed brigade of 2,500 troops, dispatched from France, and a regiment from Maj. Gen. Gerard Gossling's division. Cochrane was supported by three rear admirals, Captain of the Fleet Edward Codrington, Sir George Cockburn, and Pulteney Malcolm, who escorted the transports. On 19 August, the main force entered the Patuxent River and disembarked near Benedict, Maryland.

Cockburn's advance squadron attacked Commodore Joshua Barney's gunboat flotilla above Pig Point. Barney had been ordered by Secretary of the Navy William Jones to retreat toward Queen Anne's Town and, facing imminent destruction, Barney burned his flotilla. Cochrane also dispatched a frigate squadron to bombard Fort Washington, 10 miles below Washington, and another squadron toward Baltimore.

Pres. James Madison called for 6,000 Maryland troops to defend Washington, and on 21 August, Brig. Gen. Tobias Stansbury's 11th Brigade and two battalions of the Second and Ninth Brigades totaling about 2,000 men moved toward the capital. Barney's 500 seamen were available. Some 2,000 Baltimore militia and 5,000 Pennsylvania militia were alerted. Brig. Gen. William Winder, in command of regulars in the newly created Tenth Military District, fell back toward Washington and camped near Old Fields.

On 21 August, Ross's Light division reached Nottingham and the next day moved to Upper Marlboro, where it camped in the evening. Cockburn's armed launches and pinnaces guarded the river flank. Near Upper Marlboro, the British Light Brigade under Col. William Thornton aimed for Old Fields and dispersed 1,200 militia on the evening of 23 August. At daylight the next day, the brigade resumed its march to Washington via the Bladensburg Road. Ross's forces attacked Winder's, posted "on very Commanding Heights formed in two lines, his Advance occupying a fortified House which with Artillery covered the bridge over the Eastern Branch." About 1,000 men of Thornton's 85th Foot and the light companies of other regiments broke through, driving a wedge between Stansbury's and Winder's positions. The British lost 64 killed and 185 wounded, including Thornton. As Winder's defense crumbled, however, Ross's forces captured 10 guns and 220 stands of arms.

The two regiments of the Light Brigade rested for two hours and then advanced to Washington, which they reached at dusk. Citizens streamed out of the city to the north and west. Winder's troops joined the exodus. British skirmishers were fired on from two houses, which were promptly burnt, and Ross had two horses shot from under him. Finding no one with whom to negotiate to ransom the city, Ross judged it necessary to destroy the public buildings without delay, "so that the Army might retire without loss of time." The Capitol, Senate Chamber and House of Representatives, Treasury, War Office, and the

"President's Palace," as Pulteney Malcolm called it, were burned. Offices of the *National Intelligencer*, the Arsenal, the dockyard, and a ropewalk were destroyed. Winder's forces burned two bridges over the eastern branch of the river to prevent pursuit. The Washington naval dockyard, under the command of Capt. Thomas Tingey, the public shipping, and the naval stores were fired on orders from Secretary Jones. Tingey later estimated the naval yard's damages and losses at $678,210, with $260,454 recoverable. The British destroyed 194 pieces of heavy ordnance, 17 brass, and the remaining iron guns. Between 19 and 22 August, U.S. defenders lost 206 cannon, 500 barrels of gunpowder, 180,000 rounds of ammunition, 40 barrels of fine ground powder, and 20,000 stands of arms in the retreat.

Driven out of the capital and mortified at the debacle, Madison demanded the resignation of John Armstrong as secretary of war. James Monroe replaced him. Satires on "The Bladensburg Races" parodied the administration. James Rhea, brother of Congressman John Rhea of Tennessee, labeled the attack "a lasting Monument of disgrace to the nation at large."

Ross's troops retraced their steps to Benedict on 25 August and reembarked on 30 August. This fast-moving, impressive victory over a numerically superior but relatively untrained and hastily gathered force exposed the weakness of using uncoordinated militia for national military requirements. In ten days, British light troops marched 100 miles, won one battle and two skirmishes, destroyed the Chesapeake gunboat flotilla, burned the public buildings of Washington, humiliated the administration, and rejoined their supporting vessels, with a loss of less than 300 men.

—*Frederick C. Drake*

See also: Barney, Joshua; Cochrane, Alexander; Cockburn, George; Codrington, Edward; Ross, Robert; Stansbury, Tobias; Thornton, William; Washington, Fort; Winder, William H.

Further Reading

Bourchier, Lady, ed. *Codrington's Memoirs of Admiral Sir Edward Codrington.* London: Longmans, Green, 1873.

Cassell, Frank A. "Slaves in the Chesapeake Bay Area and the War of 1812." *Journal of Negro History* 57 (1972): 144–155.

Footner, Hulbert. *Sailor of Fortune: The Life and Adventures of Commodore Joshua Barney, USN.* New York: Harper's, 1940.

Gleig, George R. *The Campaigns of the British Army at Washington and New Orleans in the Years 1814–1815.* London: John Murray, 1836.

Lord, Walter. *The Dawn's Early Light.* New York: Norton, 1973.

Shomette, Donald G., and Fred W. Hopkins, Jr. "The Search

for the Chesapeake Flotilla." *American Neptune* 43 (January 1983): 5–19.

Skeen, C. Edward. "Monroe and Armstrong: A Study in Political Rivalry." *New York Historical Society Quarterly* 57 (April 1973): 120–147.

WASHINGTON, FORT

Fort Washington was the key military outpost in the Northwest Territory during the Indian wars of the early 1790s; it was largely superseded by the building of Fort Wayne at the headwaters of the Wabash River in 1794. Fort Washington was the staging area of the Indian campaigns led by Josiah Harmar, Arthur St. Clair, Charles Scott, James Wilkinson, and Anthony Wayne. From 1793 to 1794, Wayne stationed his troops at a nearby encampment called Hobson's Choice.

Maj. John Doughty, with 140 men from Fort Harmar, constructed Fort Washington in 1789. The site was located just across the Ohio River from the mouth of the Licking River. The fort was adjacent to Loantiville (founded in 1788, now called Cincinnati), with the site coming within the bounds of Cincinnati, from the riverfront east of Broadway. The fort, 180 feet square, had four timber-hewn blockhouses at different angles, and the outside grounds consisted of 15 acres. As the fort became obsolete, it was replaced by the Newport arsenal and barracks, also a federal installation, across the Ohio at Covington, Kentucky. This post, begun in 1803, was completed about 1807.

—*Harry M. Ward*

Further Reading

Knopf, Richard C., ed. *Anthony Wayne, A Name in Arms: Soldier, Diplomat, Defender of Expansion Westward of a Nation; the Wayne-Knox-Pickering-McHenry Correspondence.* Westport, CT: Greenwood Press, 1975.

Richard, Richard C. et al. "Fort Washington Re-Discovered." *Bulletin of the Historical and Philosophical Society of Ohio* 11: 1–12.

Smith, Allen W., comp. *Beginning at "The Point": A History of Northern Kentucky and Environs, the Town of Covington in Particular, 1751–1834.* Park Hills, KY: Smith, 1977.

WASP VERSUS AVON
1 September 1814

The *Wasp* was a U.S. Navy sloop rated at 18 guns and commanded by Capt. Johnston Blakely. She had earlier destroyed the British 18-gun sloop *Reindeer* in June and then spent seven weeks being refitted in L'Orient, France, before sailing again on 27 August 1814. The *Wasp* then proceeded to seize and destroy three more enemy ships, including one taken from a convoy and burnt in the presence of the 74-gun ship *Armada*.

On the evening of 1 September, the *Wasp* sighted four sails in the distance and pursued the ship most windward for almost three hours. Having caught up to this unknown brig, Blakely gave up his advantageous position and went on her lee bow to prevent her from joining up with her sister ships. After a minute's engagement on dark and windy seas, the ship surrendered. This vessel turned out to be the British 18-gun brig *Avon*, a fact that never became known to Blakely or his crew. The *Wasp* was in the act of taking possession of this ship when she was chased off by a quickly approaching brig that loosed a broadside into her rigging and by two more ships that appeared on the horizon. The *Avon* sank soon after with ten killed and 32 wounded. The *Wasp* suffered two killed and one wounded.

The *Wasp* then went on to capture several more ships, including the valuable brig *Atlanta*, bringing her total prizes to 13 British merchantmen worth 200,000 pounds sterling. She was lost with all on board while on her way toward the Spanish Main, sometime after being sighted on 9 October 1814 by the Swedish brig *Adonis*.

—*Robert J. Bunker*

See also: Blakely, Johnston; *Wasp* versus *Reindeer*
Further Reading
Barnes, James. *Naval Actions of the War of 1812.* New York: Harper and Brothers, 1896.
Mahan, A. T. *Sea Power in Its Relations to the War of 1812.* Vol. 2. Boston: Little, Brown, 1905; reprint, New York: Greenwood Press, 1968.

WASP VERSUS FROLIC
18 October 1812

The U.S. 18-gun sloop *Wasp* was commanded by Master Commandant Jacob Jones. Constructed in 1806, she was the first ship so named to serve in the war. Her sole action took place when she left Delaware Bay on 13 October 1812 on a course to intercept British vessels heading north from the West Indies. On 16 October, she encountered a strong gale, which carried away her jib-boom and two of her crew. The weather cleared the following day, and toward midnight several sails appeared in the distance. The *Wasp* shadowed these vessels.

On the morning of 18 October, the Royal Navy 22-gun sloop *Frolic* (Capt. Thomas Whinyates, 110 men) positioned herself between the *Wasp* and a convoy of six merchantmen, allowing them to flee. The *Frolic* had suffered heavy damage in the same gale that had lightly damaged the *Wasp*. In the ensuing broadsides, the sails and rigging of the *Wasp* were shot away, while the *Frolic* suffered serious hull damage. The two ships then ran foul of each other, which allowed the *Wasp* to rake the deck of the *Frolic* with such ferocious fire that she was turned into a charnel ship. Before Jones had time for another broadside, excited members of his crew boarded the *Frolic* without opposition and seized her.

The *Frolic* suffered 90 killed and wounded, and the *Wasp* had five killed and five wounded. Before Jones had time to capitalize on the victory, however, the 72-gun British ship *Poictiers* bore down on the two heavily damaged vessels and forced him to surrender.

—*Robert J. Bunker*

See also: Jones, Jacob
Further Reading
Barnes, James. *Naval Actions of the War of 1812.* New York: Harper and Brothers, 1896.
Frost, John. *The Pictorial Book of the Commodores: Comprising Lives of Distinguished Commanders.* New York: Nafis and Cornish, 1845.
Ringwalt, Roland. *Commodore Jacob Jones of the United States Navy.* In *Papers of the Historical Society of Delaware,* No. 44. Wilmington: Historical Society of Delaware, 1906.

WASP VERSUS REINDEER
28 June 1814

The *Wasp,* a U.S. Navy sloop rated at 18 guns, left Portsmouth, New Hampshire, on 1 May 1814 under the command of Capt. Johnston Blakely on a commerce-raiding cruise to the sea lanes west of the English Channel. This was a new ship, the second named *Wasp* to serve in the war, and she contained a crew of 173 men. By the end of June, she had taken seven British merchantmen in the North Atlantic.

On the morning of 28 June, the *Wasp* was chased by two warships, who were then joined by a third. The foremost vessel showed English colors and by midafternoon came within carronade range. This ship was the British 18-gun sloop *Reindeer* (Capt. William Manners, 118 men), which was greatly inferior to the *Wasp* in every respect.

The *Reindeer* opened an initial fire with a shifting 12-pound carronade, getting in four discharges before the vessels became locked in a severe action with grape and solid shot. Twice the crew of the *Reindeer* attempted to board the *Wasp* but were repulsed. Nineteen minutes after the first broadside, the battle was over, with the *Reindeer* wrecked. Captain Manners, the purser, and 23 others were killed, and 42 were wounded. Blakely had the prisoners removed and the crippled ship burned. Losses on the *Wasp* were five killed and 22 wounded.

For his gallantry, Congress voted Blakely a gold medal. The victorious *Wasp* then set sail for L'Orient, France, arriving on 8 July.

—*Robert J. Bunker*

See also: Blakely, Johnston; *Wasp* versus *Avon*
Further Reading
Barnes, James. *Naval Actions of the War of 1812.* New York: Harper and Brothers, 1896.
Frost, John. *The Pictorial Book of the Commodores: Comprising Lives of Distinguished Commanders.* New York: Nafis and Cornish, 1845.

WAYNE, FORT

Following the capitulations of Fort Michilimackinac, Fort Detroit, and Fort Dearborn during the summer of 1812, the U.S. garrison at Fort Wayne was in a precarious position on the exposed northern frontier. Eighteen years earlier, after his victory at the Battle of Fallen Timbers near present-day Toledo, Ohio, Gen. Anthony Wayne had marched westward into what is now Indiana to build Fort Wayne at the strategic portage between the Maumee and Wabash Rivers. Situated in the midst of the Miami Indians' country, the fort also was in proximity to the Ottawa, Wyandot, Shawnee, Delaware, and Potawatomi tribes. In addition to its military mission, Fort Wayne served as the site for an Indian agency and as a fur trade center.

After their capture of the three previously mentioned forts, the British and Indians decided to attack Fort Wayne and Fort Harrison, the latter at present-day Terre Haute, Indiana. Capt. James Rhea, the commander of Fort Wayne, learned on 19 August of the Fort Dearborn massacre at present-day Chicago, which had occurred four days earlier. Correctly believing his post to be in imminent danger, he sent urgent messages requesting help to supplement his garrison of 70 effective soldiers and four small cannon. At this point, however, Rhea began deteriorating physically and mentally.

An allied Indian warned interpreter Antoine Bondie of an impending attack, and Bondie informed Indian Agent Benjamin Stickney. When Stickney warned Rhea, the latter failed to make the appropriate preparations. The Indians, primarily Ottawa and Potawatomi, began gathering around Fort Wayne during late August. Numbering approximately 500, they killed an agency employee on 28 August. They then proceeded to loot the outlying buildings around the fort, while the garrison, following Rhea's orders, passively watched.

On 4 September, a group of warriors led by the Potawatomi chief Winnemac was allowed to enter the fort and to confer with Rhea. The captain, to the great surprise of all present, said to the chief, "My good friend I love you I will fight for you, I will die by your side."

The next morning, the Indians killed two soldiers outside the fort wall. That evening, under a flag of truce, Winnemac and other Indians again sought entry into the fort. They apparently hoped for an opportunity to attack the officers and nearby soldiers and to throw open the gate for the Indians outside the fort. Stickney limited the number of warriors admitted. He also made certain they were searched and were watched closely. Frustrated in their plans, the Indians departed.

A series of attacks upon the fort began almost immediately. The warriors tried to set it on fire with flaming arrows, but the garrison countered by keeping the roof wet with buckets of water. The Indians also fashioned two "cannon" from hollow logs and tried to bluff the garrison into surrendering. Because Rhea was continuously drunk, the defense was led by Lt. Philip Ostrander and Ens. Daniel Curtis.

William Henry Harrison, commanding by virtue of a brevet appointment as major general in the Kentucky militia, marched with a force of more than 2,000 men to the rescue of Fort Wayne, arriving on 12 September. The Indians besieging the fort melted away without a fight, having made a final effort to take the fort during the previous night. After being informed of Rhea's behavior, Harrison forced the captain to resign. He then sent detachments of troops to destroy the nearby Indian villages.

The British had not moved with speed or with determination to aid the Indians at Fort Wayne. Col. Henry Procter delayed until 14 September in sending Maj. Adam C. Muir with 1,100 Indians, militia, and regulars south from Detroit. While Muir's troops were moving up the Maumee River, the major learned of Harrison's relief of the fort. The British force then made a disorganized retreat when its scouts reported the continued advance of the U.S. army.

Fort Wayne did not play a significant role during the remainder of the war. During 1813, the major fighting would occur in the Lake Erie region.

—*Robert J. Holden*

Further Reading

Edmunds, R. David. *Tecumseh and the Quest for Indian Leadership.* Boston: Little, Brown, 1984.

Gilpin, Alec R. *The War of 1812 in the Old Northwest.* East Lansing: Michigan State University Press, 1958.

McAfee, Robert Breckinridge. *History of the Late War in the Western Country.* Lexington, KY: Worsley and Smith, 1816.

Woehrman, Paul W. *At the Headwaters of the Maumee: A History of the Forts at Fort Wayne.* Indianapolis: Indiana Historical Society, 1971.

WEATHERFORD, WILLIAM
1780–1824
Creek Indian chieftain

William Weatherford, the son of a Scottish trader and a Creek woman, was born in 1780 in what is now Montgomery County, Alabama. Although Weatherford never learned to read or write, he was considered very educated. He was also an excellent hunter, swimmer, horseman, and athlete. Weatherford, known as Red Eagle, was greatly influenced by Tecumseh, though he was equally at home with whites and Indians. Prior to the War of 1812, Weatherford was a Creek chieftain and a wealthy planter.

In June 1813, the prophets, Creek Indians claiming divine powers, assumed leadership in a Creek spiritual revival. Inspired by Tecumseh, they decided to break off all relations with the whites. William Weatherford did not initially want to join the warring faction because it would pit Creeks against Creeks, but he eventually did. His change of heart is variously explained. One source says he did it because his family was being held hostage. Another claims he joined to prevent atrocities and to hold the Creek Nation together. Whatever the reason, he joined the warring faction on 25 August 1813.

His first act was to join forces with Peter McQueen, another mixed-blood chieftain, in an attack at Fort Mims. Weatherford took command of 750 Indians and stormed the open gates of the fort during the noon meal on 30 August. He was instrumental in planning the attack and keeping the Indians in the fight throughout the day. After he was sure of victory, he attempted to stop the killing, but his fellow Creeks refused. They massacred almost all of the inhabitants of the fort. This incensed citizens of the United States, and thus began the war against the Creeks.

Weatherford quickly became the Creek military leader and planned to keep his army united and strike toward Tennessee or Georgia. His influence was weakened, however, by his attempt to restrain the massacre at Fort Mims, and the Red Sticks (as the aggressive faction was called) dissolved into small roving bands. Unable to maintain a cohesive body of warriors, Weatherford decided to establish a series of strong points throughout the Creek Nation. He would assemble warriors at each point and strike out at the advancing U.S. columns.

Weatherford suffered his first defeat in an attempt to defend the strong point at Econochaca, which was situated on a bluff overlooking the Alabama River. However, he was able to escape by leaping off a 30-foot cliff on his horse. Weatherford then used his central position to parry the advances of Brig. Gen. John Floyd from Georgia and Gen. Andrew Jackson from Fort Strother on the Coosa River. Weatherford's plan was to strike each army separately in order to interpose his army between the two converging columns. This way, he could unite his own forces, should they be defeated. His plan was a testimony to Weatherford's astute military capabilities.

On 27 January 1814, Weatherford led his men under the cover of darkness to a position surrounding Brigadier General Floyd's camp near Calabee Creek. Floyd was able to defeat the Indians and hold his ground. However, Floyd was forced to abandon his objective and retreat to Georgia. A similar action turned back Jackson's forces at Emuckfau Creek on 22 January. In both battles, Weatherford's forces were outnumbered by the better-trained and equipped Americans. After the battles at Emuckfau and Calabee, the remaining Creek warriors gathered at Tohopeka, the Horseshoe on the Tallapoosa River. There the approximately 1,500 Indians protected themselves with a line of breastworks. Jackson, with artillery and over twice as many Americans and allied Indians, was able to carry the works by storm. With the death of over 800 Red Sticks, they were greatly weakened, and Weatherford, who had not been at the Horseshoe, disappeared into the wilderness.

Mixed-blood leader of the Red Sticks William Weatherford boldly surrenders to Andrew Jackson after General Jackson's victory over the resistance group at Tohopeka.

Jackson would give no terms to the Creeks or accept their surrender until Weatherford was turned over to him. Instead of escaping to Florida, Weatherford boldly walked into Jackson's camp and surrendered. He offered his surrender only if Jackson agreed to care for the Creek women and children who were suffering from hunger. Jackson accepted his terms and offered Weatherford a full pardon.

Myths and legends surround this complex character. Although he apparently returned to his old home at Econochaca, he was forced to seek refuge with the U.S. army at Fort Claiborne. His safety again remained in question because many soldiers at Fort Claiborne had friends or family killed during the Fort Mims massacre, which was still blamed on Weatherford. Reports tell of his being smuggled out of camp to Jackson's headquarters and, after the signing of the Treaty of Fort Jackson on 9 August 1814, returning with Jackson to the Hermitage, Jackson's home in Tennessee. Weatherford remained there for perhaps a year before returning to Alabama and resuming life as a planter. He remarried for the third time in 1817 and died on 9 March 1824 from fatigue incurred in a bear hunt. He left a large family of children.

—*John M. Keefe*

See also: Big Warrior; Calabee, Battle of; Creek War; Econochaca, Battle of; Emuckfau Creek, Battle of; Georgia; Horseshoe Bend, Battle of; Jackson, Andrew; Little Prince; McQueen, Peter; Mims, Attack on Fort; Red Sticks; Strother, Fort

Further Reading

Brewer, W. *Alabama: Her History, Resources, War Record and Public Men.* Montgomery, AL: Barret and Brown, 1872.

Griffith, Benjamin W. *McIntosh and Weatherford, Creek Indian Leaders.* Tuscaloosa: University of Alabama Press, 1988.

Halbert, H. S., and T. H. Ball. *The Creek War of 1813 and 1814.* Chicago: Donohue and Henneberry, 1895.

Martin, Joel W. *Sacred Revolt: The Muskogees' Struggle for a New World.* Boston: Beacon Press, 1991.

Owsley, Frank Lawrence. *Struggle for the Gulf Borderlands: The*

Creek War and the Battle of New Orleans, 1812–1815. Gainesville: University Presses of Florida, 1981.

Rowland, Dunbar. *Andrew Jackson's Campaign against the British, or the Mississippi Territory in the War of 1812.* New York: Macmillan, 1926.

WEBSTER, DANIEL
1782–1852
U.S. congressman

Daniel Webster

Born in Salisbury, New Hampshire, the next to the youngest child of Ebenezer Webster and Abigail Eastman Webster, Daniel Webster rose from rural, middle-class origins to become one of the most powerful political figures in the United States. Before the War of 1812, he graduated from Dartmouth College; studied law under Thomas W. Thompson of Salisbury; and in 1807 opened his practice in Portsmouth, New Hampshire. In Portsmouth, Webster gained a statewide reputation as a public speaker and began his activities in Federalist Party politics.

In 1808, Webster published a pamphlet attacking Pres. Thomas Jefferson's embargo. Over the next few years, he remained an active opponent of Republican candidates but did so by working for other Federalist candidates. When war was declared in June 1812, Webster was serving as the town moderator of Portsmouth. He immediately began speaking openly against the war, even on occasion mentioning the possibility of disunion because of what he saw as the discrimination against New England. In the fall of 1812, the voters of his district elected Webster to Congress.

One of Webster's first actions in Congress was to call for an investigation into Pres. James Madison's response to Napoleon I's claim to have revoked the Milan and Berlin Decrees. The freshman congressman's gesture clearly called into question the president's integrity. House Republicans, apparently not feeling that the president had anything to hide, agreed to the investigation, thus robbing Webster of his chance to make the issue a public fight. Webster's spirit was undampened, and he continued to be a vocal critic of the president and his policies for the remainder of the war.

Webster voted against taxes to prosecute the war, but then he was contemptuous of the administration's efforts to defend Washington in August 1814. His attacks became quite personal when he accused the president of cowardice for accompanying the evacuation of the city before the British invasion.

In the fall of 1814, Webster's opposition to the war had become so strong that he supported the holding of a convention of New England states to discuss further action. None of his correspondence regarding this meeting, however, mentioned the possibility of secession. Yet during the same period, his resolute opposition to the institution of conscription led him to make a speech before Congress on 9 December 1814 that outlined the possibility of state nullification of obnoxious legislation. When the Hartford Convention issued its report a few weeks later, Webster supported its recommendations of constitutional amendments to protect the rights of minority sections of the country.

Following the War of 1812 until his death in 1852, Daniel Webster would evolve into one of the nation's staunchest nationalists, criticizing the growing sectionalism of the southern states. His opponents would repeatedly conjure up his own sectional past during the War of 1812 to discredit him, usually with little effect.

—*Jeanne T. Heidler and David S. Heidler*

See also: Federalist Party; Hartford Convention
Further Reading
Bartlett, Irving H. *Daniel Webster.* New York: W. W. Norton, 1978.

WELLINGTON, ARTHUR WELLESLEY, FIRST DUKE OF

1769–1852
British officer

Arthur Wellesley Wellington

Arthur Wellesley, the Duke of Wellington, was the greatest British general of his time. Born in Ireland, he entered the army in 1787 and made his reputation fighting in India from 1796 to 1805. He was first elected to Parliament as a Tory in 1806 and was appointed chief secretary for Ireland in the Duke of Portland's ministry (1807–1809). From July through August 1807, Wellington was given temporary charge of British troops in Spain and Portugal in support of the rebellion against Napoleon. He then left government office to assume permanent command there in April 1809.

Wellington reversed the British and allied armies' unrelieved record of defeat in Europe with patient generalship, wearing down the large but overextended French armies. In 1812–1813, he was preoccupied with driving Napoleon's forces out of Spain. Wellington paid little attention to the war in the United States except as a strategic nuisance making claims on the government for men and money that otherwise would have been committed to his own theater.

In February 1814, an anxious government in London asked his advice about the military situation in Canada. He replied that he knew practically nothing about the war in North America and had thought little about it. He did note, however, that Canada might be defended by controlling the Great Lakes, but to go beyond that, to attack the United States successfully, to force the Americans to peace, would be difficult. Wellington concluded that North America could not support military operations of large forces far from navigable rivers, the sea coast, or the lakes.

In April 1814, Napoleon abdicated, and in June Wellington issued the final general order of his campaign. He congratulated his army on restoring peace to Britain and the world, casually ignoring the continuing war with the United States. Wellington was named ambassador to the restored French court in July. Prime Minister Liverpool proposed in November that Wellington come home to Britain, offering him command of the U.S. war if it were not soon settled by negotiation. Liverpool hoped that when word of Wellington's possible appointment was revealed, it would be an inducement to the U.S. negotiators to make peace. Many of Wellington's battle-hardened veterans from Spain had already been sent to the United States. There was confidence that, led by their old general, they would be rewarded with military success.

Wellington did not want the U.S. command, but it would have been difficult for him to refuse it. Before he was obliged to decide, however, the Treaty of Ghent was signed in December 1814, ending the war. Wellington disapproved of the attack on New Orleans, which he thought had been done for the sake of plunder. In any event, within a few months, Napoleon was in arms again. Fortunately for Britain, its leading general was not in North America. Wellington thus had one final round in which to defeat his old enemy. From Wellington's point of view and from the perspective of the British policy makers, the war in the United States was a marginal event, an irritating and unnecessary distraction, and an unfortunate mistake.

—S. J. Stearns

Further Reading
Brett-James, Anthony. *Wellington at War, 1794–1815: A Selection of His Wartime Letters.* London and New York: Macmillan, 1961.
Gurwood, John, comp. *The Dispatches of Field Marshall the Duke of Wellington, K.G. during his Various Campaigns in India, Denmark, Portugal, Spain, the Low Countries, and*

France. From 1799 to 1818. Compiled from official and authentic documents. London: J. Murray, 1839.

Longford, Elizabeth. *Wellington: The Years of the Sword.* New York: Smithmark, 1996.

Hitsman, J. Mackay. "David Parrish and the War of 1812." *Military Affairs* 26 (winter 1962–1963): 171–177.

Landon, Harry F. "British Sympathizers in St. Lawrence County during the War of 1812." *New York History* 35 (April 1954): 131–138.

Stanley, George. *The War of 1812: Land Operations.* Ottawa: National Museums of Canada and Macmillan, 1983.

WELLINGTON, FORT

When a British military headquarters was established early in the war at Prescott, opposite Ogdensburg, New York, a stockade with gun emplacements was raised on a prominent elevation not far from the riverbank. Fort Wellington became a British strong point because its guns dominated the St. Lawrence River. On 20 February 1813, Commander in Chief Sir George Prevost visited Fort Wellington and reluctantly authorized Lt. Col. "Red George" MacDonnell's retaliatory raid on Ogdensburg as a reprisal against Maj. Benjamin Forsyth's guerrilla raids on Gananoque in the autumn of 1812 and on Morristown and Elizabethtown in February 1813. Fort Wellington was also a stopover for the British bateaux bringing military supplies and being convoyed upriver to Kingston, Lake Ontario. It became a smuggling point through which David Parrish and prominent Ogdensburg Federalists and farmers supplied the British garrisons across the river with sheep and cattle. It was garrisoned initially by the Glengarry Light Infantry Fencibles and artillery bombardiers.

Fort Wellington was not seriously threatened in November 1813 when Gen. James Wilkinson took his 8,000-strong army down the St. Lawrence toward Montreal. Wilkinson avoided the fort by ordering his army boats emptied of their troops on the U.S. shore on 6 November. As the troops marched by land, the boats passed the guns of Fort Wellington at night under a long-range bombardment that did little damage. After Wilkinson took his army into winter quarters on 11 November, Fort Wellington was not threatened again in the war.

—*Frederick C. Drake*

See also: Ogdensburg, Battle of
Further Reading
Canada, National Parks Bureau. *Guide to Fort Wellington and Vicinity, Prescott, Ontario.* Ottawa: J. O. Patenaude, 1937.

Cruikshank, Ernest A. "From Isle aux Noix to Châteauguay: A Study of Military Operations on the Frontier of Lower Canada in 1812 and 1813." *Proceedings of the Royal Society of Canada* 7 (1914): 129–173.

Curry, Frederick. "Little Gibraltar [Block Island]." *Ontario Historical Society Papers and Records* 33 (1939): 39–44.

WELLS, WILLIAM
1770–1812
U.S. Indian agent

William Wells was born in Pennsylvania and migrated to Kentucky in 1779. In 1784, he was captured by Miami Indians and taken to Indiana, where he was adopted by a Wea chief living along the Eel River. Easily adapting to Indian ways, he participated in many raids directed against white settlements throughout the Ohio Valley. Eventually, Wells made the acquaintance of the Miami chief Little Turtle, who became his lifelong friend, mentor, and father-in-law.

At the outbreak of hostilities between the Ohio tribes and the United States in 1790, Wells took an active role in the Indian resistance and participated in several engagements, including Arthur St. Clair's defeat in 1791. Shortly thereafter, Wells made contact with his white family and within a short time had reentered white society. He finished the war acting as a scout for Anthony Wayne. Appointed deputy Indian agent for the United States at Fort Wayne following the war, Wells held the post until partisan politics forced his resignation in 1809.

Reappointed in 1811, Wells was at Fort Dearborn (present-day Chicago) in August 1812. A hostile band of Potawatomis had surrounded the post after learning of the declaration of war. Although the Potawatomis gave Wells and the garrison a promise of safe passage, all fell victim to an ambush shortly after they had left the post. Killed while attempting to lead the detachment to safety, Wells died dressed in full Indian regalia and with his face painted black, a Miami custom signifying certain death.

—*Larry L. Nelson*

See also: Dearborn, Fort
Further Reading
Carter, Harvey Lewis. "A Frontier Tragedy: Little Turtle and William Wells." *The Old Northwest* 6 (1980): 3–18.

———. *The Life and Times of Little Turtle: First Sagamore of the*

Wabash. Urbana and Chicago: University of Illinois Press, 1987.

Hutton, Paul A. "William Wells: Frontier Scout and Indian Agent." *Indiana Magazine of History* 74 (1978): 183–222.

WEST INDIES

In the years leading up to the War of 1812, U.S. merchants, farmers, and lumbermen enjoyed a lucrative trade with both the British and French West Indies. As the war between the French and British grew more grave, however, both governments took steps to prevent the United States from trading with their enemy.

The British government attempted to invoke the Rule of 1756, which held that trade that was not allowed in peacetime could not be allowed in wartime. The French had opened trade between their colonies and the United States so that U.S. neutral vessels could carry products between France and its colonies. U.S. shippers tried to evade the British restriction by making a stop in the United States, in what was termed a broken voyage. In the 1800 British *Polly* Decision, a British court ruled that this practice was legitimate. In 1805, however, the court reversed itself and issued the *Essex* Decision, hence leaving open the possibility, which soon became very real, that British ships could seize U.S. ships that traded with the French West Indies.

This decision still left Americans free to trade with the British West Indies, a practice that was very popular with the British planters on the islands. Both food and lumber were in very short supply in those British colonies, and U.S. merchants made a very handsome profit from this trade. This practice was not without its critics. British merchants resented sharing the lucrative West Indies markets with Americans, and promoters of an increasing connection between Canada and the West Indies argued that the planters could obtain everything they needed from that British possession. And, of course, there was Napoleon, who in his Milan Decrees stipulated that any ship that obeyed the British restrictions was subject to seizure by France.

Many of the issues were solved temporarily, to virtually no one's satisfaction, with the U.S. embargo in 1808. President Thomas Jefferson argued that the elimination of U.S. trade in the West Indies would raise such a howl from the West Indian planters that the British government would have to relax its restrictions. The result, however, was to prove the proponents of a Canadian–West Indies connection right; the planters discovered that they could obtain almost anything they needed from Canada. As a result, the trade between the United States and the West Indies declined steadily, even after the lifting of the embargo.

During the War of 1812, the trade revived somewhat since the British needed the Canadian resources in Canada to fight the war. As a result, the British navy allowed New England to maintain its trade with the British West Indies even as it tightened a blockade on the remainder of the U.S. coastline. This policy remained in effect until the spring of 1814 and not only allowed New England merchants to make a profit from this trade but also allowed U.S. privateers to operate out of New England ports and take numerous British merchant vessels as prizes in the West Indies.

Following the war, the trade between the United States and the West Indies declined again. Not only could Canada now resume its trading relationships with its fellow British colonies, but the British demand for U.S. cotton proved far more lucrative for U.S. merchantmen.

—*Jeanne T. Heidler and David S. Heidler*

See also: Essex Decision; Milan Decree
Further Reading
Checkland, S. G. "American versus West Indian Traders in Liverpool, 1793–1815." *Journal of Economic History* 17 (1958): 141–160.
Graham, Gerald S. *Seapower and British North America, 1783–1820: A Study in British Colonial Policy*. Cambridge: Harvard University Press, 1941.

WILKINSON, JAMES
1757–1825
U.S. officer

Born on 1 January 1757 in Calvert County, Maryland, to a planter family, James Wilkinson studied medicine in Philadelphia. Ambitious, intelligent, and ingratiating, he rose quickly in the ranks of the Continental Army. Wilkinson was honored to carry the glad tidings of Saratoga to Congress, and that grateful body elevated him to brevet brigadier general at the age of 20. Wilkinson's later career in the Revolution was a checkered one, however, with his record marred by involvement in the Conway Cabal to replace George Washington and by financial irregularities that forced his resignation as clothier general of the army.

In 1784, Wilkinson moved to the Kentucky Territory, where he began a long-running secret and treasonous relationship with Spanish authorities in New Orleans. Rejoin-

James Wilkinson

ing the U.S. Army in 1791 as a lieutenant colonel, he became the senior officer of that small force in 1796, a position he held until 1798 and again from 1800 to 27 January 1812. He also served as governor of Louisiana Territory. As the ranking officer of the army, his military service was blemished by his continued flirtation with the Spanish, by his deep involvement in the Burr Conspiracy, and by his disastrous mismanagement of troops in the Terre aux Boeufs scandal of 1809. He narrowly escaped official condemnation following investigations of his conduct in 1809 and 1811.

Wilkinson bears substantial responsibility for the pathetic unreadiness of the army in 1812. At the opening of the War of 1812, Wilkinson was in command of the Seventh Military District, and his headquarters were located at New Orleans, where much of his energy was devoted to quarrels with the Louisiana militia and with Andrew Jackson, who was in charge of reinforcements from Tennessee. In March 1813, Wilkinson made his one significant contribution to the U.S. war effort, when he received authorization to take control of Spanish Florida west of the Perdido River. Moving with unusual speed, Wilkinson occupied Mobile without a fight on 15 April—the only permanent acquisition of territory made by the United States during the conflict.

Under heavy criticism from Louisiana congressmen, Wilkinson gladly accepted from Revolutionary War friend and Secretary of War John Armstrong promotion to major general and command of the Ninth Military District, encompassing Vermont and parts of New York and Pennsylvania. Despite Armstrong's injunctions to "hasten to the north... to renew the scene of Saratoga," Wilkinson's journey was slowed by numerous celebratory dinners. He arrived at Sacket's Harbor, New York, only on 20 August 1813.

There, Wilkinson announced his intention to occupy Upper Canada in a single campaign. However, the principal military authorities on the scene—Wilkinson, Secretary Armstrong, and Maj. Gen. Wade Hampton at Plattsburg—quarreled over their tangled lines of authority. Hampton and Wilkinson had long hated each other, and Wilkinson and Armstrong, initially allies, were soon feuding publicly. Additionally, Wilkinson's planning proved erratic, as he specified his military objective to be first Fort Malden near Detroit, then Montreal, and then Kingston, leading one of his subordinates to remark after almost two months of staff work that the goal of the campaign remained an "impenetrable" mystery. To make matters worse, Wilkinson's supply arrangements collapsed at his encampment, with inadequate sanitary conditions in particular felling many of the soldiers. Discouraged and physically sick himself, Wilkinson wrote Secretary Armstrong that "in case of Misfortune[,] having no retreat, the army must surrender at discretion."

In this unpromising state of mind, Wilkinson on 17 October 1813 finally left Sacket's Harbor with more than 7,000 men for the St. Lawrence River. Gales slowed the movement to a crawl, and Wilkinson's behavior became increasingly erratic as he dosed himself with laudanum and whiskey. His discouraged officers asked Armstrong for a new commander.

On 11 November at Chrysler's Farm, Wilkinson's army was repulsed by a British force of 800. The general was too sick to take the field himself, although his headquarters came under fire from British gunboats. Learning the following day that Hampton's column had abandoned its offensive in the bad weather, Wilkinson ordered his troops to winter quarters at French Mills. The fiasco of his campaign was so complete that Clintonians in New York cited it as proof of a conspiracy on the part of southern Republicans to depress the influence of the Northeast by failing to add Canada to the United States.

Wilkinson's soldiers suffered through a hard winter made worse by their commander's neglect in providing for their material needs: the men were inadequately clothed and over six months behind in their pay. In March 1814,

Wilkinson again crossed into Canada at the head of 4,000 men. Having advanced only a few miles north of the border, his force was held up by a tiny British garrison on the La Colle River. Fighting behind the thick walls of a stone mill, the 180 defenders withstood Wilkinson's artillery and inflicted 150 casualties on his infantry. Wilkinson abandoned his offensive and, with the spring thaw turning the roads to mud, retreated to Plattsburg.

He found there an order from Armstrong relieving him of his command. Wilkinson ultimately faced a court of inquiry in Troy, New York, which leveled a number of charges, including neglect of duty, conduct unbecoming an officer, drunkenness, and encouraging disobedience of orders. Surprisingly, he was acquitted on all counts. Many blamed the failure of the fall 1813 campaign on Armstrong and Hampton.

Wilkinson never again held an active command. Following the war, he oversaw his plantation south of New Orleans. He died on 28 December 1825 in Mexico City, where he had traveled in hopes of obtaining a Texas land grant.

In retrospect, it is difficult to find much of redeeming value in Wilkinson's wartime service or in his overall career. Contemporary enemies in uniform were many and vehement; Winfield Scott, for example, denounced Wilkinson as an "unprincipled imbecile." Historians have judged him harshly. Frederick Jackson Turner called him "the most consummate artist in treason that the nation ever possessed." Wilkinson offered his defense in *Memoirs of My Own Times* published in Philadelphia in 1816, a work composed of "three turgid and confused volumes of documents," according to one scholar.

—*Malcolm Muir, Jr.*

See also: Armstrong, John; Chrysler's Farm, Battle of; Hampton, Wade; Niagara Campaigns
Further Reading
Hay, Thomas Robson, and M. R. Werner. *The Admirable Trumpeter: A Biography of General James Wilkinson.* Garden City: Doubleday, Doran, 1941.

WILLIAMS, DAVID ROGERSON
1776–1830
U.S. congressman;
governor of South Carolina

Born to Anne Rogerson Williams shortly after the death of his father, David Williams spent much of his youth with his mother in Charleston, South Carolina. After coming of age and leaving college, Williams took over the management of the plantation he had inherited from his father. In addition to these activities, he dabbled briefly in newspaper publishing, and in 1805, he was elected to the U.S. House of Representatives. He served until 1809 and then returned in 1811. He considered himself a good Democratic Republican and as such supported the embargo of 1807 and the Madison administration's measures that moved the country toward war with Great Britain. He believed, however, that war would be detrimental to the nation's economy and his own financial well-being.

Still, he was associated before the war with the War Hawk faction and fought vigorously in Congress to increase the size of the military before war commenced. His rather flamboyant speaking style was often used to draw attention away from the opposition. The South Carolina delegation of John C. Calhoun, Langdon Cheves, and William Lowndes might have intimidated someone of lesser confidence than Williams.

Once war was declared, Williams urged his fellow congressmen to abandon theoretical arguments and stick to the practical side of financing and fighting a war. He had very little patience with either side when it came to their abstract arguments regarding the war's merits once the fighting began. Perhaps this practical approach to making war is what convinced the administration that Williams would be a valuable ally as one of the political generals in the field. Williams served briefly with the Army of the North in the taking of Fort George at the end of May 1813. When the army did not follow up on this victory by pursuing the British into Canada, the kind of anger Williams had displayed for desultory congressmen manifested itself for his superior officers. Williams requested a transfer to the southern theater, and when that request was denied, he resigned his commission.

Williams's various activities during the war had gained him a good reputation at home, and though not a candidate, he was selected by the South Carolina legislature as governor at the end of 1814. This would be Williams's last major foray into public life, in which he established himself as a strong proponent of states' rights. Later in life, after retiring to his plantation, he wrote extensively about the need for the southern states to become more self-sufficient to end their dependence on northern goods. He died in an accident on his plantation.

—*Jeanne T. Heidler and David S. Heidler*

See also: War Hawks
Further Reading
Cook, Harvey T. *The Life and Legacy of David Rogerson Williams.* New York: Country Life Press, 1916.

WINCHESTER, JAMES
1752–1826
U.S. officer

Born in Maryland to William Winchester and Lydia Richards Winchester, James Winchester served in the American Revolution, was captured twice, and rose to the rank of captain. Following the war, Winchester moved to Tennessee, where he became a prominent planter, political leader, and militia officer.

When war erupted between the United States and Great Britain in 1812, Winchester offered his services to the U.S. government and received a commission as a regular brigadier general in the U.S. Army. In July 1812, Secretary of War William Eustis ordered Winchester to raise 1,200 regulars and militia in Kentucky and march them to reinforce William Hull at Detroit. Before Winchester completed his task, Hull surrendered Detroit, and William Henry Harrison received a commission as the major general and commander of the Kentucky militia.

With the surrender of Hull, there arose a question as to whether Harrison or Winchester commanded U.S. forces in the Northwest. Despite his residence in Tennessee for over 25 years, Winchester was viewed by many western militiamen as too refined in his tastes, and Harrison sought to encourage this attitude by holding meetings with his officers to discuss the command situation and by writing to Secretary Eustis pointing out the attitudes of the westerners. The dispute could have turned ugly on 18 September, when Winchester arrived at Harrison's headquarters at Fort Wayne, but Harrison did not dispute the point at that time and relinquished command to Winchester. The situation changed again on 24 September with the arrival of Pres. James Madison's order of 17 September, which gave command of the Northwest to Harrison.

Harrison initially planned to attempt to retake Detroit in the fall of 1812. As part of that plan, Winchester was given command of Harrison's left flank and ordered to move forward to Fort Defiance. Winchester remained there with his army for several months under increasingly difficult circumstances. The spot proved unhealthy, and as a result Winchester moved his camp several times, trying to find a healthier location. In addition to the tremendous amount of illness in the camps, including an outbreak of typhoid fever, the supply lines to the camp were slow at first and then virtually paralyzed. Difficulties among Harrison's other commands prevented the proposed expedition against Detroit from materializing.

Then in December 1812, Harrison believed that he was finally in a position to advance and sent orders to Winchester to break camp and move to the Miami River rapids. Winchester departed on 29 December and arrived at the rendezvous point on 8 January 1813. He ordered his sick and dispirited men to begin construction of Fort Winchester but received word about 13 January from Frenchtown and area settlements on the River Raisin that the people there were about to be attacked by a combined British-Indian force.

Winchester immediately began organizing his division for the march 30 miles north to Frenchtown, sending Col. William Lewis ahead with the healthiest and best-supplied men. As the expedition got under way, Winchester received word from Harrison that he was to wait at the rapids for reinforcements, but because of the dire straits of the settlers on the Raisin and the knowledge that Harrison was not aware of all the circumstances, Winchester consulted his officers and together they decided to proceed.

When Lewis arrived in advance of the remainder of the army on 18 January 1813, he encountered a British force at Frenchtown that he easily drove off. Perhaps the ease with which this was accomplished led Winchester to neglect the security of the U.S. position after he arrived. The lack of vigilance and attention to position allowed Col. Henry Procter, commanding British regulars and Indian allies, to surprise the Americans on the morning of 22 January 1813. The Americans were caught so unawares that they were unable to combine their forces to fight off the British attack. About midmorning, Winchester was captured and convinced by Procter to order the surrender of the remaining Americans.

The surrender had occurred with the understanding that the Americans would be treated as prisoners of war and that Procter would prevent his Indian allies from harming the captives. The following day, however, this promise was broken when about 60 of the prisoners, most of them wounded, were killed by the Indians.

Winchester spent the next year as a British prisoner in Canada. Upon his exchange, he was sent to Mobile. He arrived on 21 November 1814, just before Andrew Jackson began his march to New Orleans. Jackson left Winchester in command at Mobile, where he remained until the end of the war. In January 1815, he almost had another encounter with the British when they took Fort Bowyer on the water approach to Mobile, but the war ended before they could make an attempt on the town.

Following the war, Winchester engaged in heated dispute with his detractors, including Harrison, about his role

After his capture at Frenchtown, Gen. James Winchester was turned over to British commander Col. Henry Procter, but not before he had been stripped and painted. Perhaps this embarrassment contributed to his role in convincing the U.S. troops to surrender.

in the Battle of Frenchtown. He also spent some time as an Indian commissioner before retiring to his plantation, where he died in 1826.

—*Jeanne T. Heidler and David S. Heidler*

See also: Detroit, Surrender of; Eustis, William; Frenchtown, Battles of; Harrison, William Henry; Hull, William; Jackson, Andrew; Mobile, Battles of

Further Reading

DeWitt, John H. "General James Winchester, 1752–1826." *Tennessee Magazine* 1 (1915): 79–105, 183–205.

Harrell, David E. "James Winchester, Patriot." *Tennessee Historical Quarterly* 17 (1958): 301–317.

WINDER, LEVIN
1757–1819
Governor of Maryland

Born on the Eastern Shore of Maryland to William Winder and Esther Gillis Winder, Levin Winder studied law before accepting a commission in the Maryland

Line during the American Revolution. He served throughout the conflict, rising to the rank of lieutenant colonel.

During the 1790s, Winder became increasingly active in Maryland Federalist politics and in 1806 entered the Maryland legislature. As the country moved toward war with Great Britain, Winder and his fellow Federalists spoke out against such a move. Once the war began, Winder was a vocal supporter of Alexander C. Hanson and his Baltimore newspaper the *Federal Republican*. Winder's defense of the paper and the backlash that followed the violence in Baltimore against Hanson and his supporters were responsible for Winder's election as governor in the fall of 1812.

Winder served as governor for the remainder of the war, and with the increase of British activity in Chesapeake Bay in 1813, this position would prove to be a busy one. While working to prepare the defense of the state, particularly the vulnerable sections along the bay, Winder appealed constantly to the federal government in Washington for material and financial aid. Winder believed that the Madison administration ignored Maryland's plight because of his Federalist affiliation, but unlike the Federalist governors of New England who had similar complaints, Winder aggressively managed the defense of the state and found creative ways to finance it.

As the British began their raids in Chesapeake Bay in the spring of 1813, Winder called the Maryland legislature into special session in May of that year to take measures to activate, strengthen, and pay for militia forces to protect the coastal areas. Under his prodding, the legislature appropriated money for pay and equipment for militia and authorized the government to borrow money to make up the difference.

The following year continued his active role in the state's defense, when the British returned in the summer of 1814 with a larger fleet and more landing forces. The resources that Winder now commanded probably prompted Madison to appoint the governor's nephew, William Winder, to command the new Tenth Military District, consisting of the Washington, D.C., and Baltimore areas. Nevertheless, the earlier reluctance of Madison to supply federal forces for Maryland's protection made Governor Winder hesitate to supply Maryland militia when the capital was threatened in August 1814. Not knowing if the British intended to attack Washington rather than Annapolis or Baltimore, Winder held many of his men back until the British destination was determined. Many Maryland militiamen who did report for the defense of Washington at Bladensburg ran at the approach of the British.

The response of Winder's Maryland militia to the threat to Baltimore in September 1814 was considerably different. Even before the attack on Washington, Winder had placed Sen. Samuel Smith in command of all Maryland militia forces around Baltimore. This prescient move made the city of Baltimore well prepared when the British mounted their attack there. The well-supplied militiamen in Baltimore were primarily the product of Winder's earlier preparations.

Following the war, Winder served for a few years in the Maryland Senate and died in office in 1819.

—*Jeanne T. Heidler and David S. Heidler*

See also: Baltimore, Battle of; Bladensburg, Battle of; Hanson, Alexander Contee; Maryland; Smith, Samuel; Winder, William H.

Further Reading
Johnson, Robert W. *Winders of America*. Philadelphia: Lippincott, 1902.

WINDER, WILLIAM H.
1775–1824
U.S. officer

Born in Somerset County on the Eastern Shore of Maryland to John Winder and Gertrude Polk Winder,

William Winder moved to Baltimore as a young man to establish a legal practice. By the War of 1812, Winder had acquired the reputation as one of the best attorneys in the state.

As war neared in the spring of 1812, Winder received a commission as a lieutenant colonel. Shortly after the declaration of war, he was promoted to colonel and sent to the Niagara Frontier, where he served during the first months of the war under Brig. Gen. Alexander Smyth. Following Smyth's aborted invasion of Canada, Winder was moved to the command of Brig. Gen. Morgan Lewis and was promoted to brigadier general in March 1813.

Winder participated in Maj. Gen. Henry Dearborn's invasion of Canada at Fort George in May 1813 and was sent by Lewis with 800 men in pursuit of British brigadier general John Vincent's army as it retreated to Burlington Heights, Upper Canada, in early June. On the march, Winder was joined by 500 men under Brig. Gen. John Chandler. The U.S. army approached Vincent's position at Burlington Heights on 5 June but decided to pull back to Stoney Creek to plan its offensive. Neither general had much combat experience and probably did not take the necessary precautions to protect his camp. Vincent determined not to wait for the Americans to attack him, and on the night of 5 June moved part of his army toward the U.S. encampments. Before dawn on 6 June, armed with the countersign for the U.S. sentries, Vincent entered the U.S. camps and attacked. During the chaotic battle of Stoney Creek, both Chandler and Winder stumbled into the British lines and were captured.

For the next several months, Winder was a prisoner of war in Canada before he was paroled. Until Winder was officially exchanged, he could not resume his command, so in the spring of 1814, the government chose to utilize his services in a different way. Difficulties had arisen over the issue of prisoner exchanges, so Winder was sent to negotiate an agreement with the British in Canada. He was told that while conducting his negotiations, he could unofficially broach the subject of an armistice, though this aspect of his mission never came to fruition. On 15 April, however, he did sign an agreement that smoothed the way for easier prisoner exchanges. As a result of this agreement, he too was exchanged and returned to duty as part of Maj. Gen. George Izard's command at Plattsburg, New York.

In early summer 1814, the Madison administration became increasingly concerned about the security of the capital. Rumors abounded that the British, now freed from the war against Napoleon, planned a major expedition into Chesapeake Bay. Pres. James Madison felt increasing pressure to provide a more organized defense of both Washington and Baltimore and therefore decided in late

June to create the Tenth Military District to comprise the defense of these two cities. He made this decision right before a cabinet meeting on 1 July and announced it at that meeting.

Madison had also decided that because of the importance of gaining militia support from Maryland in the defense of the capital area, he needed to appoint someone to the command of this new district who could gain the respect of the Maryland people and the support of the state's government. Probably for these reasons more than military expertise, Madison decided upon Winder, a popular Maryland native and the nephew of Maryland governor Levin Winder.

Madison made this decision without seriously consulting his Secretary of War John Armstrong. Brooding over this slight, Armstrong offered little support or assistance to Winder when he arrived in Washington. In fact, Armstrong did not even provide Winder with a staff, and for much of his short tenure in this command, Winder had to serve as his own quartermaster and adjutant as well as handle most of the paperwork for the district.

In late summer of 1814, the rumored threat materialized in the form of a large British naval squadron and army under Adm. Sir Alexander Cochrane and Maj. Gen. Robert Ross. Accompanying them was Rear Adm. Sir George Cockburn, who knew the bay intimately from his raids there the previous year. Poor William Winder, overworked and undermanned, was hardly up to the challenge.

Not only did he lack the experience of supervising the defense of a separate district, Winder was further handicapped by Armstrong's persistently sullen attitude. The secretary, even as the British threat became more immediate, refused to allow Winder to call up surrounding state militias. Winder had only about 500 regulars in his command in early July, but penny-watching Armstrong did not want to call the militia for reasons other than economy. Strangely enough, the secretary believed that militia fought better when called up at the last minute. He insisted that these men not be mustered until the British began their offensive.

As a result, when the British actually entered the Patuxent River in mid-August, Winder was in little better position to repel this invasion than he had been when he took command a month before. Winder's uncle, the governor of Maryland, was being stingy with his militia, remembering his unheeded pleas the year before for more federal protection from Cockburn's raids. And to make matters worse, not only was General Winder now short of troops, but he had wasted much of the time he did have on pointless and distracting chores.

Here Winder's inexperience in command really showed. He had spent the previous month riding around his district trying to determine the best routes to protect and to guess where the British might strike. Even as the British moved up the Patuxent to neutralize Commodore Joshua Barney's flotilla of gunboats and land at Benedict, Maryland, neither Winder nor Armstrong seemed sure about the British objective.

Knowing that the British could also move against Annapolis or Baltimore and considering both of those towns as far more strategically important than Washington, Winder finally called out additional militia. Yet, he had no idea where to place them. He continued to ride frantically around, inspecting the various approaches to the capital and supervising the preparations in the immediate vicinity of Washington.

Throughout the day on 23 August, Winder made his usual haphazard rounds, begged Armstrong in writing for advice, and sent conflicting orders to his militia commanders. All the while, the British under Ross and Cockburn marched toward Washington. Not until the morning of 24 August did Winder discern that the British were moving toward the crossing to Washington at Bladensburg.

The various militia units there, mostly under Maryland brigadier general Tobias Stansbury, were arranged in three lines to challenge the British crossing. While Winder was out riding around again, Secretary of State James Monroe appeared at Bladensburg and arranged the militia forces there in such a way that they would not be able to support one another. When Winder returned around noon, it was too late to remedy the situation because the British were approaching Bladensburg. At about 1:00 P.M., the British entered the town and prepared to cross the bridge toward Washington. Winder could only hope that his lines would hold.

They did not. As the British began the attack, the militiamen stood their ground. The firing of Congreve Rockets and a massive push of redcoats across the bridge, however, unnerved the U.S. militia. Finally, when the British troops attempted to move around the U.S. left flank, the militia began to fall back. To avoid a rout and with the hope of regrouping at another location along the Washington Road, Winder ordered a retreat. His very order, however, had the effect of throwing much of the militia into panic, beginning what became known as the "Bladensburg Races." The men scattered in so many directions that there was no hope of regrouping, even though Winder himself moved back to Capitol Hill, hoping to provide a rallying point. Within a short time, he had to abandon this hope and leave the city himself.

While Winder, then as now, receives a generous portion of the blame for the failure to defend Washington, much reproach was also directed at Secretary Armstrong. His attitude in the weeks preceding the British assault, his failure to recognize the threat to the capital, and his sulking resignation once the attack was underway resulted in his ouster.

Winder, on the other hand, was not immediately removed from his command, but he was superseded in the defense of Baltimore by Maryland militia major general Samuel Smith. Winder reluctantly placed himself under Smith's command and commanded part of the U.S. left flank in Baltimore on the morning of 13 September. Following the successful defense of Baltimore, Winder returned to the northern frontier, where he served for the remainder of the war.

Following the war, Winder left the army with the reduction of 15 June 1815 and returned to his legal practice. He continued to prosper as one of the state's most admired legal figures, but he never lived down his performance in the defense of Washington. He died in Baltimore at the age of 49.

—Jeanne T. Heidler and David S. Heidler

See also: Armstrong, John; Baltimore, Battle of; Barney, Joshua; Bladensburg, Battle of; Chandler, John; Chesapeake Bay Campaign, 1813–1814; Cochrane, Alexander; Cockburn, George; Congreve Rockets; George, Fort; Izard, George; Lewis, Morgan; Militia in the War of 1812; Monroe, James; Ross, Robert; Smith, Samuel; Smyth, Alexander; Stansbury, Tobias; Stoney Creek, Battle of; Vincent, John; Washington, British Capture of; Winder, Levin

Further Reading

Arnold, James R. "The Battle of Bladensburg." *Columbia Historical Society Proceedings* 37 (1937): 145–168.

"General William H. Winder." *Genealogical Magazine and Historical Chronicle* 21 (1919): 217–219.

Smith, Joseph H. "The Battle of Stoney Creek." *Wentworth Historical Society Papers and Records* 10 (1922): 101–124.

WIRT, WILLIAM
1772–1834
U.S. author; lawyer

Born in Bladensburg, Maryland, to Jacob and Henrietta Wirt, William Wirt was reared in modest circumstances and was orphaned at a young age. After attending local schools in Maryland, Wirt entered the study of law and eventually moved to Virginia to begin his practice. Never interested in politics as a calling, Wirt nevertheless became a supporter of Thomas Jefferson while residing in Virginia and in 1808 began a brief service in the Virginia legislature.

William Wirt

Wirt's primary interests, however, were writing and the law. In the years leading up to the War of 1812, he published a number of popular essays and gained an increasing reputation as a trial lawyer, including an impressive performance as one of the prosecutors in the trial of Aaron Burr. During the war, Wirt spent much of his time in Washington, D.C., where his insightful commentary on the operation of the government, primarily in letters to his wife and friends, has provided later generations with an inside look at the chaotic administration of the war.

During the British campaign against Washington, Wirt served briefly as a militia captain of artillery and then, after the fall of the capital, traveled to Georgetown, where he observed officials trying to restore some semblance of order. Shortly after the government's return to Washington, Wirt had the opportunity to observe the depressed and pessimistic reaction of Pres. James Madison to the destruction there.

A few months later, Wirt had an opportunity to see the president again, this time as news arrived in the capital of the impending meeting of New England Federalists at Hartford, Connecticut. Wirt noticed again the dejected attitude of the president and his obsession with the coming meeting.

Following the war, Wirt continued his literary pursuits, but because of his legal talents, he was increasingly called upon by the government. In 1816, President Madison appointed him U.S. attorney for Richmond, and a year later, Pres. James Monroe appointed him U.S. attorney general. He remained in that position until the election to the presidency of Andrew Jackson. His last foray into public life came in 1832, when he ran as the anti-Mason candidate for president. He died in Washington, D.C., in 1834.

—*Jeanne T. Heidler and David S. Heidler*

See also: Federalist Party; Hartford Convention; Madison, James; Washington, British Capture of
Further Reading
Kennedy, John P. *Memoirs of the Life of William Wirt, Attorney General of the United States.* 2 vols. Philadelphia: W. J. Neal, 1834.

WOOD, ELEAZER DERBY
1783–1814
U.S. officer

The 17th graduate of the fledgling U.S. Military Academy at West Point, New York, in 1806, Capt. Eleazer D. Wood was assigned to the staff of Maj. Gen. William Henry Harrison's Northwestern Army in 1812. Harrison placed Wood in charge of the construction of two critical forts on the Lake Erie frontier. The first, Fort Meigs, was located at the Maumee River rapids southwest of modern Toledo. The second, Fort Stephenson, located in modern Fremont, Ohio, was at the navigation head of the Sandusky River. Each fortification withstood British-Indian sieges and helped establish the reputation for excellence of West Point–trained military engineers.

For his exceptional service, General Harrison accorded Wood his first "palm of merit" and had Wood brevetted major. While simultaneously serving as Harrison's chief engineer and chief artillerist, Wood became his de facto operations officer during the invasion of Canada that followed. After the Battle of the Thames, Major Wood transferred to the Niagara Frontier, where he became the assistant engineer in Maj. Gen. Jacob Brown's army. Wood frequently participated in staff and general officer meetings, making suggestions on operational matters. He designed an expansion of Fort Erie similar to that used at Fort Meigs. At the Battles of Chippewa (5 July 1814) and Lundy's Lane (25 July), he commanded an artillery section. Following the latter engagement, General Brown paid Wood lavish compliments and had him brevetted lieutenant colonel.

After the Battle of Lundy's Lane, the Americans withdrew to Fort Erie, and Wood received command of a defensive sector. When the British assaulted the U.S. position at Fort Erie (15 August), Wood's battalion-sized command received the brunt of one British brigade's attack and brilliantly repulsed it. Lieutenant Colonel Wood was being considered for a third brevet promotion for his valor in this action when he led one of the columns attacking the British works outside Fort Erie on 17 September. This sortie was successful, but during a British counterattack, Wood was mortally wounded. Considered by many of his contemporaries as the beau ideal of professionalism and bravery, Wood was honored by General Brown with a monument placed in his honor on the parade ground at West Point. The army denominated a new fortification on Bedloe's Island in New York Harbor as "Fort Wood," which now serves as the base for the Statue of Liberty. Ohio named the county containing Fort Meigs in his honor.

—*David Curtis Skaggs*

See also: Erie, Fort
Further Reading
Cullum, George W. *Campaigns of the War of 1812–15.* New York: James Miller, 1879.
Graves, Donald E. *The Battle of Lundy's Lane.* Baltimore: Nautical and Aviation Publishing, 1993.
Nelson, Larry L. *Men of Patriotism, Courage, and Enterprise! Fort Meigs in the War of 1812.* Canton, OH: Daring Books, 1985.
Whitehorne, Joseph. *While Washington Burned: The Battle for Fort Erie, 1814.* Baltimore: Nautical and Aviation Publishing, 1992.
Wood, Eleazar [sic] D. *Journal of the Northwestern Campaign of 1812–1813 under Major-General Wm. H. Harrison.* Robert B. Boehm and Randall L. Buchman Defiance, eds. Ohio: Defiance College Press, 1975.

WOOL, JOHN ELLIS
1784–1873
U.S. officer

John Wool was commissioned captain in the 13th New York regiment soon after hostilities began. In early October 1812, Wool's company was assigned to Maj. Gen. Stephen Van Rensselaer's army along the Niagara Frontier

John Ellis Wool

to join in the offensive against the British forces holding several key posts on the Canadian side of the river.

Throughout September, Van Rensselaer concentrated his forces at Lewiston, New York, across the river from Queenston Heights. In the early morning hours of 10 October, the Americans began fording the river in an attempt to surprise the British and drive them from the Heights. Included in the first wave of 600 troops was John Wool's company, which crossed with the other U.S. forces in several small boats. The element of surprise was quickly lost, however, when British sentinels sighted the boats and sounded the alarm.

Once they detected the Americans crossing the river, the British opened fire from several directions. The Americans scrambled to coordinate their assault, but Capt. James Dennis's grenadiers scaled halfway down the steep cliff, fired with deadly accuracy, and caused the Americans to seek shelter away from the riverbank. Solomon Van Rensselaer, Stephen Van Rensselaer's nephew and commander of the first wave, took six bullets and lay unconscious. Wool was struck in the upper thigh but managed to rally his small company off the riverbank and toward the base of the Heights. One of Wool's men, Lt. John Gan-

sevoort, knew of a rarely used fisherman's trail leading up the steep and precipitous escarpment. Leaving 100 men to detain Dennis, Wool led the remainder of his company— 240 men—undetected up the 300-foot cliffs to the edge of Queenston, where the British had strategically placed an 18-pounder battery.

Meanwhile, British general Isaac Brock heard the rumbling of artillery from his headquarters at Fort George and at once struck out toward Queenston, 6 miles upriver. Arriving at daybreak, Brock went directly to the 18-pounder battery to view the U.S. assault at about the same time that Wool and his men stormed the battery. Wool's company opened fire on the British, forcing them to spike the gun and flee toward Queenston. Once Brock managed to regroup his fleeing troops, he ordered an assault on Wool's position. After two attempts to recapture the gun, Brock was mortally wounded during a third charge. Demoralized by the loss of command, the British retreated to Vrooman's Point, a short distance upriver. For the moment, it appeared that Wool's heroics would lead to a significant U.S. victory.

Weakened from a substantial loss of blood, Wool and other injured Americans were sent to the boats waiting below. Command of the Heights then passed to Lt. Col. Winfield Scott, who eagerly awaited reinforcements from the U.S. side of the river. But additional troops, primarily New York militia, were not forthcoming because most of these men refused to fight on foreign soil. Without adequate reinforcements, Scott was forced to fend off an attack by a large group of British-allied Indians at about three o'clock. One hour later, Maj. Gen. Roger Sheaffe ordered his detachment of British regulars to attack Scott's position. The Americans were driven back down the escarpment and to the river's edge, leaving Scott with no alternative but to capitulate. Thus ended the Americans' second hapless attempt to invade Canada.

Because of their heroics during the battle, both Wool and Scott received promotions. Wool, who quickly recovered from his wounds and was soon involved in further engagements, was promoted to major and assigned to the 29th Infantry in April 1813. In early September 1814, Wool distinguished himself at the Battle of Plattsburg when, with only 280 men, he successfully detained a British army of 12,000 men long enough for the main U.S. force to inflict serious damage to the British ranks. The following December, Wool was promoted to lieutenant colonel.

After the war, Wool continued in the army and in 1821 became inspector general for all U.S. forces. After a brief tour of inspection in Europe, he served as a tactician and executive officer during the Mexican-American War. With the secession crisis and bombardment of Fort Sumter in 1861, Wool was dispatched to take command of Fortress Monroe. He retired from active service in 1863.

—*Robert Saunders, Jr.*

See also: Plattsburg, Battle of; Queenston, Battle of

WOOLSEY, MELANCTHON TAYLOR
1780–1838
U.S. Navy officer

Melancthon Woolsey was born in New York on 5 June 1780, the son of Col. Melancthon Lloyd Woolsey, collector of revenue for Plattsburg, New York. He entered the navy on 9 April 1800 and served in the West Indies and during the Barbary Wars. Promoted to acting lieutenant in 1804 and lieutenant in 1807, Woolsey was ordered to Oswego, New York, in July 1808. He engaged Christian Burgh and Henry Eckford of New York to build the brig *Oneida,* carrying 18 24-pounder carronades, for $20,505.

In 1810, Woolsey selected Sacket's Harbor, New York, for a naval base on Lake Ontario, and ordered two gunboats built on Lake Champlain. In September 1812, he was superseded by Commodore Isaac Chauncey. He fought in engagements with the British at Kingston in November 1812, York and Fort George in April–May 1813, and off Niagara in August–September. Woolsey was promoted to master commandant in July 1813 and commanded the large schooner *Sylph.* On 6 May 1814, when the British captured Oswego, Woolsey retreated to safeguard the supply depot above the falls. He coordinated Chauncey's supplies between Oswego and Sacket's Harbor. After the war he purchased the *Oneida* and remained in Oswego.

Woolsey was promoted to captain on 27 April 1816 and married Susan Cornelia Tredwell at Poughkeepsie, New York, on 3 November 1817. He commanded the *Constellation* during 1825, suppressing West Indian pirates, and was given command of the Pensacola Navy Yard until 1830. He became commodore of the Brazil squadron from 1832 to 1834. He died at Utica, New York, on 19 May 1838.

—*Frederick C. Drake*

See also: Chauncey, Isaac

Further Reading
Brown, Leon N. "Commodore Melancthon Taylor Woolsey: Lake Ontario Hero of the War of 1812." *Oswego Historical Society Journal* 5 (1941): 14–21.
Cooper, James F. *Lives of Distinguished Naval Officers.* Philadelphia: Carey, Hart, 1846.
———. "Melancthon Taylor Woolsey." *Graham's Magazine* 26 (1845): 14–21.
Cruikshank, Ernest A. "The Contest for the Command of Lake Ontario in 1812 and 1813." *Transactions of the Royal Society of Canada.* sec. 2, 3rd ser., 10 (September 1916): 165–188.
———. "The Contest for the Command of Lake Ontario in 1814." *Ontario Historical Society Papers and Records* 21 (1924): 99–159.

WORTH, WILLIAM JENKINS
1774–1849
U.S. officer

William Worth was born in Hudson, Columbia County, New York, on 1 March 1774. After a common-school education in Albany, New York, Worth was employed in local businesses until the start of the War of 1812. He applied for a commission in the regular army, which he finally received on 19 March 1813. At that time, Worth was appointed as a first lieutenant in the 23rd Infantry. His first assignment was as a secretary to Gen. Morgan Lewis.

After a few months, Brig. Gen. Winfield Scott secured a transfer for Worth to become his aide-de-camp. Worth joined Scott's brigade in northwestern New York shortly before the second U.S. invasion of Upper Canada in 1814. Worth was praised in Scott's reports for his bravery and leadership in the Battles of Chippewa and Lundy's Lane. He was promoted to brevet captain after the first battle and to major after the second.

Worth was part of Scott's brigade and its supporting artillery unit that advanced northward on 14 July 1814 and took a position on the Chippewa Plain, nearly half a mile from the closest Canadian town. The combined U.S. regular army units and a militia force met the British and Canadian army in a fierce battle. The U.S. militiamen retreated, but Scott's and Worth's forces engaged the enemy and forced the British and Canadians to retire with heavy casualties. The British and Canadians had 148 dead, 321 wounded, and 46 missing. The Americans had 48 dead and 261 wounded and missing. This was one of the few major U.S. victories in Canada during the war.

William Jenkins Worth

Nearly two weeks later, a large, reinforced, British-Canadian army counterattacked the smaller U.S. forces of the ranking commander, Maj. Gen. Jacob Brown. When this happened, Brown withdrew southward back to Chippewa. Brown had earlier sent Worth, Scott, and Scott's field artillery and infantry brigade to attack Queenston, Upper Canada. While en route to their objective on the Queenston Road, which was also known as Lundy's Lane, the U.S. brigade encountered the British army about 1 mile away from Niagara Falls. Scott's forces engaged the British, who were directly across the small road. Fighting at Lundy's Lane (also known as Bridgewater) started at 5:00 P.M. and lasted until nearly midnight. Scott's forces were outnumbered 2,800 to 1,200. They fought well, but the enemy's superior forces were gaining the field when Brown's army came to assist them. In this battle, William Worth, Winfield Scott, and General Brown were all wounded. Brig. Gen. Eleazar Ripley took command of the remaining U.S. forces and retreated in an orderly manner to Fort Erie. The remaining army's presence and the arrival of the U.S. Navy's Great Lake squadron safeguarded the New York Niagara Frontier from additional attacks and occupation by the British-Canadian army.

After the end of the War of 1812, William J. Worth remained in the army until his death in 1849. He was somewhat lame from his war wounds. He was assigned as the fourth commandant of cadets at the U.S. Military Academy at West Point from 1820 to 1828, a rare honor for a non–academy man. While at the academy, Worth was promoted to lieutenant colonel. He was described by one of his colleagues as "an officer of average height but no-

ticeably strong with a trim figure and a striking military air."

After commands in infantry units, Worth again distinguished himself in the Second Seminole War, winning another battlefield promotion to colonel. His greatest fame came several years later during the Mexican-American War. Worth fought in nearly every major battle in that conflict under the command of Maj. Gens. Zachary Taylor and Winfield Scott, and in each case his conduct earned the highest honors. As a result, he was brevetted a brigadier general for "gallantry and highly distinguished services." Unfortunately for Worth, he was less talented as an administrator and a military governor of a conquered country than as a battlefield leader. He was reassigned to the command of the Texas Department in 1848, and a few months later he died from cholera in Fort Worth, Texas.

—*George E. Frakes*

See also: Lewis, Morgan; Ripley, Eleazar Wheelock
Further Reading
"William Jenkins Worth." *Dictionary of American Biography.* New York: Charles Scribner's Sons, 1936: 537.

WORTHINGTON, THOMAS
1773–1827
U.S. senator; governor of Ohio

Born on 16 July 1773 in Berkeley County, Virginia (near present-day Charles Town, Jefferson County, West Virginia), Thomas Worthington spent two years at sea, then studied surveying before marrying Eleanor Van Swearington in 1796. Moving in 1798 to Chillicothe, soon to become the capital of the Northwest Territory, he gained prominence in territorial politics as a Democratic Republican and as a member of the "Chillicothe Junto" that played a leading role in advancing Ohio's admission to the Union in 1803. Worthington was then elected one of the new state's first senators. His second term in the U.S. Senate was highlighted by a vote against the 1812 declaration of war against Great Britain. Though a devout Methodist who deplored armed conflict, Worthington's decision to side with the Federalists was based more upon his belief that the nation was militarily unprepared for such a venture. Nonetheless, Worthington actively supported the war effort once the nation became committed to the fray, serving as chairman of both the Senate's Committee on Military Affairs and its Committee on Militia. He even introduced a bill to appropriate funds to build a second military academy in Pittsburgh. Soon after the outbreak of hostilities, Pres. James Madison appointed Worthington to negotiate with Northwest Territory Indian tribes at Piqua, Ohio; the senator had successfully secured pledges of Indian neutrality at Greenville in 1807 and then entertained Tecumseh, Blue Jacket, and others at his home in Chillicothe (now maintained by the Ohio Historical Society).

Worthington's wartime stance won favor with Ohio voters, who elected him governor for two terms beginning in late 1814. In the largely ceremonial position, Worthington became an outspoken advocate of social reform, internal improvements, and a strong state militia. Higher federal office eluded Worthington, however, possibly due to his support of the Bank of the United States and its establishment of a branch at Chillicothe, and he had to settle for three terms in the state house of representatives in the early 1820s. Serving as Ohio's canal commissioner from 1818 until his death, he was instrumental in paving the way for Ohio's expansive canal network. Thomas Worthington died on 20 June 1827 while on business in New York City.

—*William E. Fischer, Jr.*

Further Reading
Barnhart, John D. "Letters of William Henry Harrison to Thomas Worthington, 1799–1813." *Indiana Magazine of History* 47 (1951): 53–84.
Knopf, Richard C. *Thomas Worthington and the War of 1812.* Columbus: Ohio State Museum, 1952.
Sears, Alfred B. *Thomas Worthington, Father of Ohio Statehood.* Columbus: Ohio State University Press, 1958.

WYANDOTS

They called themselves "Wendat," meaning "islanders" or "dwellers on a peninsula," while the French used "Huron" for the rugged, unkempt appearance of this member of the Iroquois linguistic family. They resided along the upper reaches of the St. Lawrence River and north of Lake Ontario. With an estimated population of 20,000 in 1639, the Wendats were soon forced to flee westward following their near-annihilation at the hands of neighboring Iroquois. By 1700, scattered remnants had settled in modern-day western Ontario, northern Ohio, and the Detroit area. Influential among local natives, they also claimed much of the territory between the Ohio River and Lake Erie. During the eighteenth century, they allied with those Europeans having the foremost presence in the Great Lakes region, namely the French in the French and Indian War and the British, whose term "Wyandot" became standard, during the Revolution. Later, the Wyandot chief Tarhee became the first signatory of the 1795 Treaty of Greenville with the United States.

Given that Wyandots resided in both British and U.S. territory, the War of 1812 witnessed a corollary division of allegiance. U.S.-allied Wyandot emissaries sent to an Indian council held at Brownstown in early August 1812 were rebuffed by Roundhead, whose Wyandot faction declared its loyalty to the Crown and joined British forces at Fort Malden. Yet British setbacks in the region and Tecumseh's death at the Battle of the Thames soon reduced active Wyandot participation in the war. Acceptance of a provisional armistice with the United States in October 1813 was followed by 16 Wyandot chiefs signing the July 1814 Treaty of Greenville. Refusing U.S. overtures four years later to cede their lands and move west, the Wyandots succumbed to U.S. expansionist pressures in the former Northwest Territory in 1842 and settled in Kansas.

—*William E. Fischer, Jr.*

Further Reading
Clarke, Peter D. *Origin and Traditional History of the Wyandots.* Toronto: Hunter, Rose, 1870.
Horsman, Reginald. "The Role of the Indian in the War of 1812." In Philip P. Mason, ed., *After Tippecanoe: Some Aspects of the War of 1812.* East Lansing: Michigan State University Press, 1963.
Norris, Caleb H. "Tarhee, the Crane-chief of the Wyandots." *Northwest Ohio Quarterly* 7 (1935): 1–13.
Sugden, John. *Tecumseh's Last Stand.* Norman: University of Oklahoma Press, 1985.

Y

YEO, JAMES LUCAS
1782–1818
British naval officer

Born on 7 October 1782, James Yeo was the eldest son of James Yeo, agent victualler at Minorca, and he joined the Royal Navy at the age of ten in 1793. Promoted to lieutenant on 20 February 1797, he gained a reputation for daring cutting-out expeditions at Cesanatico Harbor, Italy, in 1800; and at Muros Harbor on 4 June 1805 when, with 50 men, he stormed a fort engaging the *Loire,* and captured a French 22-gun privateer, *Confiance.* He was promoted to commander of the *Confiance* on 21 June 1805 and captain on 10 December 1807. Yeo also conquered the last French stronghold in Guiana, South America, for the prince regent of Portugal on 7 January 1809, when he led 400 British and Portuguese against a fort of 1,200 soldiers and 200 cannon. The grateful prince regent awarded him a large diamond ring, a knight's cross on 17 August 1809, and a knighthood of St. Benedict of Aviz on 20 June 1810. After the U.S. declaration of war, Yeo commanded the frigate *Southampton* (32 guns), which captured the USS *Vixen* (14 guns). Both vessels were lost off Concepcion Island, Jamaica, though Yeo was exonerated in February 1813.

On 13 March 1813, Yeo was commissioned commodore and commander in chief on the lakes of Canada. His instructions emphasized that "the first and paramount object" for which his naval force was maintained was "the defence of His Majesty's Provinces of North America." He was to cooperate with Sir George Prevost, captain general and governor in chief, and not undertake any operations without Prevost's "full concurrence and approbation." He had also to report to Adm. Sir John Borlase Warren and the Admiralty. Yeo brought with him 460 officers and men, including Commanders William Howe Mulcaster, Richard (later Sir Richard) James Lawrence O'Connor, and Frederick B. Spilsbury. Midshipman David Wingfield estimated that Yeo's arrival at Kingston on Lake Ontario "raised the drooping spirits of the inhabitants of that place... who were well aware that the fall of Kingston must necessarily involve the whole country upwards in ruin."

Yeo's squadron of six ships supported Prevost's attack on the U.S. base at Sacket's Harbor, New York, on 28–29 May 1813, which, however, failed to destroy the large ship *General Pike.* Yeo next placed O'Connor in charge of administering supplies and shipbuilding at Kingston and organized gunboat escorts for the transport bateaux operating along the St. Lawrence River. He then appeared off York and cooperated successfully with Gen. John Vincent and Col. John Harvey in the night action of 6 June 1813 at Stoney Creek, which threw back the U.S. army's invasion. Yeo's squadron of six brigs; schooners; and two ships, the *Wolfe* and *Royal George;* engaged Commodore Isaac Chauncey's larger squadron in several running actions off Niagara and York on 8–12 August, 11 September, and 29–30 September 1813, when Yeo was supplying the British army on the Niagara Peninsula.

Yeo maintained his squadron as a barrier to Chauncey, and his tactical purpose was to cooperate with the army in the upper peninsula, keep the logistical lines open, and raid his opponent's supply bases on the southern shore. His strategic goal was to preserve his squadron as a fleet-in-being for the defense of the province. None of these required him to risk all on a vainglorious search for battle. Yeo's goals obviously differed from Chauncey's, who had to support the conquest of a province.

Over the winter of 1813, in order to prevent Chauncey from dominating the lake, Yeo undertook a shipbuilding program for brigs and frigates to win control of the lake. By April 1814, the *Prince Regent* (56 guns) and *Princess Charlotte* (42 guns) had won an important lead. The shipbuilding escalated from schooners to brigs in 1813 and through corvettes, frigates, and the ship of the line *St. Lawrence,* launched in September 1814. This building contest continued until the war ended, and it worked to Yeo's advantage on Lake Ontario, though the increasing demand for seamen on that lake denied Robert Heriot Barclay on Lake Erie sufficient seamen and support in his attempt to retain control of Lake Erie in 1813.

Yeo and Chauncey raided each other's lake bases through the war: Chauncey attacked Kingston on 10 November 1812 and York on 27 April 1813, both before Yeo arrived on the lakes, and Fort George on 27 May 1813 and York in July. After the failed attack at Sacket's Harbor on 28–29 May 1813, Yeo succeeded in a raid at Sodus Bay on 18–19 June 1813 and in an attack on the supply base of Oswego, New York, on 6 May 1814, which removed large quantities of guns, ammunition, cordage, and supplies. Yeo then blockaded Sacket's Harbor, but he raised the blockade after losing some gunboats and large guns at Big Sandy in late May 1814 because his order not to pursue into small creeks was disobeyed by Capt. Stephen Popham. Yeo's logistical supply service for Gen. Gordon Drummond's army on the Niagara Peninsula in summer 1814 was crucial because he dominated Lake Ontario between May and August and was more successful than Chauncey appeared to be with Gen. Jacob Brown, though neither commander could deny the lake to the other at critical times.

Yeo's strategic initiatives helped the British army thwart Wilkinson's 1813 invasion along the St. Lawrence River and Brown's 1814 invasion of the Niagara Peninsula. His handling of Chauncey, in conjunction with Prevost's defensive war, thwarted Madison's desires for a joint navy-army sweep into Upper Canada via the Niagara Peninsula or the St. Lawrence. Ironically, in the winter of 1814, Yeo was recalled to prefer court-martial charges against Prevost for the loss of the British squadron on Lake Champlain. Prevost died before the army's court-martial was held. At war's end, Yeo was knighted by the prince regent of England and appointed to a command at Portsmouth and then, on 5 June, given the command of the African squadron, with his flag in *Inconstant*. He died of fever in 21 August 1818 en route from Jamaica to England aboard *Semiramis* and was buried with full honors at the Royal Garrison Chapel in Portsmouth.

—*Frederick C. Drake*

See also: Chauncey, Isaac; Prevost, George; Warren, John Borlase

Further Reading

Cruikshank, Ernest A. "The Contest for the Command of Lake Ontario in 1812 and 1813." *Transactions of the Royal Society of Canada*, sec. 2, 3rd ser., 10 (September 1916): 165–188.

———. "The Contest for the Command of Lake Ontario in 1814." *Ontario Historical Society Papers and Records* 21 (1924): 99–159.

Drake, Frederick C. "Commodore Sir James Lucas Yeo and Governor General Sir George Prevost: A Study in Command Relations, 1813–1814." In William B. Cogar, ed.,

New Interpretations in Naval History: Selected Papers from the Eighth Naval History Symposium. Annapolis, MD: Naval Institute Press, 1989: 156–171.

Dudley, William S., ed. *The Naval War of 1812.* Washington, DC: Naval Historical Center, vol. 1, 1985; vol. 2, 1992.

Irvine, John B. "The Role of Sir James Lucas Yeo in the War of 1812." Master's thesis, Carleton University, 1958.

Spurr, John C. "The Royal Navy's Presence in Kingston, Part I: 1813–1836." *Historic Kingston* 25 (March 1977): 63–64.

———. "Sir James Lucas Yeo: A Hero of the Lakes." *Historic Kingston* 30 (March 1981): 30–45.

Wood, William. ed. *Select British Documents of the Canadian War of 1812*, vol. 1–3. Toronto: Champlain Society Publications. 1920–1928.

YORK, BATTLE OF
27 April 1813

The raid on York grew out of confused strategic planning by U.S. leaders in the early months of 1813. Secretary of War John Armstrong, who took over from the hapless William Eustis in January, understood that the capture of Quebec or Montreal would be decisive to the U.S. war effort. Both cities were too well defended to be seriously threatened by U.S. forces then within striking distance, however. Instead, Armstrong proposed directing the next offensive at Kingston and following up with attacks upon York, Fort George, and Fort Erie. With Pres. James Madison's approval, Armstrong sent the necessary orders to Maj. Gen. Henry Dearborn, commander of the Northern Army.

Dearborn traveled to Sacket's Harbor, the jumping-off point of the invasion. There he received alarming reports that Sir George Prevost, governor in chief of British North America, was at Kingston at the head of thousands of British troops, who were preparing to attack Sacket's Harbor across the ice. When the attack failed to materialize, the cautious Dearborn nonetheless told Armstrong that Kingston was too strongly defended and therefore the plan given him by the secretary of war was not feasible. Dearborn and Commodore Isaac Chauncey, naval commander on the Great Lakes, devised instead a joint operation to raid York and to destroy the two ships being built there. This would give Chauncey the lead in the ongoing shipbuilding war on Lake Ontario. Then Chauncey would carry Dearborn's army to the western end of Lake Ontario, where it would attack and seize Fort George.

York, the capital of Upper Canada, was defended by Maj. Gen. Roger Hale Sheaffe, victor at Queenston and

Brock's successor as president-administrator of the province. Sheaffe commanded about 800 defenders, the usual mix of regulars, militia, and native warriors. Expecting a two-pronged attack that would cut off escape of his troops eastward to Kingston, Sheaffe positioned his regulars, augmented by militia and Indians, behind earthworks on both the eastern and western edges of the city. The bulk of the militia he placed in the city proper, from where it might respond to threats from either direction. At dawn on 27 April, Chauncey's fleet began landing 1,700 soldiers west of the city under the battle command of Brig. Gen. Zebulon Pike. Pike's men pushed the outnumbered defenders back toward York, assisted by heavy gunfire from Chauncey's fleet. Seeing the British regulars pulling back, many of the York militia lost heart and withdrew from the battle. Sheaffe, who had demonstrated inspirational leadership during the fighting, ordered the main magazine exploded rather than allow the gunpowder to fall into enemy hands. The resulting explosion killed or wounded over 200 Americans. Pike, who was questioning a captured sergeant, was struck on the back by a falling rock. Evacuated to a ship, Pike lived long enough to receive the British flag from his victorious troops.

Officers of the Canadian militia negotiated the surrender of their city while Sheaffe hurried his remaining regulars toward Kingston. Infuriated by the loss of so many of their comrades in the explosion, bands of U.S. soldiers destroyed public buildings and property and vandalized private homes. Dearborn, crippled by the loss of Pike, could not impose control over his ill-disciplined troops. The unrestrained soldiers were abetted in these violations of the customs of war by a sizable number of pro-U.S. citizens of York, who took the opportunity to strike back at the city's loyalists for the harassment suffered since the beginning of the war. Many tendered their parole to Dearborn's officers. By the rules of war, British authorities could not require of parolees their service in the militia nor call them up for public work connected with the war effort.

The Americans remained until 8 May. They captured one ship; the other had been destroyed by the British. Chauncey carried off naval stores intended for Capt. Robert Barclay's Lake Erie squadron, thus assisting Oliver Hazard Perry's victory later that year. Prodded on by the same militia leaders of York who could not get their men to fight, Prevost replaced Sheaffe for his unsuccessful defense of that city. Maj. Gen. Francis de Rottenburg succeeded Sheaffe as commander of British forces in Upper Canada. Dearborn and Chauncey returned to Sacket's Harbor, where the fleet was replenished and the army reinforced for the next phase of the campaign, the attack on Fort George. Long after the war, York was renamed Toronto and continued on as the capital of the province of Ontario.

—*Richard V. Barbuto*

See also: Chauncey, Isaac; de Rottenburg, Baron Francis; Dearborn, Henry; Pike, Zebulon Montgomery; Sheaffe, Roger Hale

Further Reading

Benn, Carl. *The Battle of York*. Belleville, Ont.: Mika Publishing, 1984.

Appendix 1: 12th Congress Vote on Declaration of War

Alphabetical

Name	State	Party	Vote
Alston, Willis	North Carolina	R	Y
Anderson, William	Pennsylvania	R	Y
Archer, Stevenson	Maryland	R	Y
Avery, Daniel	New York	R	Y
Bacon, Ezekiel	Massachusetts	R	
Baker, John	Virginia	F	N
Bard, David	Pennsylvania	R	Y
Bartlett, Josiah	New Hampshire	R	N
Bassett, Burwell	Virginia	R	Y
Bibb, William W.	Georgia	R	Y
Bigelow, Abijah	Massachusetts	F	
Blackledge, William	North Carolina	R	Y
Bleeker, Harmanus	New York	F	N
Blount, Thomas	North Carolina	R	
Boyd, Adam	New Jersey	R	N
Breckenridge, James	Virginia	F	N
Brigham, Brigham	Massachusetts	F	N
Brown, William	Pennsylvania	R	Y
Burwell, William A.	Virginia	R	Y
Butler, William	South Carolina	R	Y
Calhoun, John C.	South Carolina	R	Y
Carr, Francis	Massachusetts	R	Y
Champion, Epaphroditus	Connecticut	F	N
Cheves, Langdon	South Carolina	R	Y
Chittenden, Martin	Vermont	F	N
Clay, Henry	Kentucky	R	
Clay, Matthew	Virginia	R	
Clopton, John	Virginia	R	Y
Cobb, Howell	Georgia	R	
Cochran, James	North Carolina	R	Y
Condict, Lewis	New Jersey	R	Y
Cooke, Thomas B.	New York	R	N
Crawford, William	Pennsylvania	R	Y
Davenport, Jonathan, Jr.	Connecticut	F	N
Davis Roger	Pennsylvania	R	Y
Dawson, John	Virginia	R	Y
Desha, Joseph	Kentucky	R	Y
Dinsmoor, Samuel	New Hampshire	R	Y
Earle, Elias	South Carolina	R	Y
Ely, William	Massachusetts	F	
Emott, James	New York	F	N
Findlay, William	Pennsylvania	R	Y
Fisk, James	Vermont	R	Y
Fitch, Asa	New York	F	N
Franklin, Meshack	North Carolina	R	
Gholson, Thomas	Virginia	R	Y
Gold, Thomas R.	New York	F	N
Goldsborough, Charles	Maryland	F	N
Goodwyn, Peterson	Virginia	R	Y
Gray, Edwin	Virginia	R	
Green, Isaiah L.	Massachusetts	R	Y
Grundy, Felix	Tennessee	R	Y
Hall, Bolling	Georgia	R	Y
Hall, Obed	New Hampshire	R	Y
Harper, John A.	New Hampshire	R	Y
Hawes, Aylett	Virginia	R	Y
Hufty, Jacob	New Jersey	R	N
Hungerford, John P.	Virginia	R	
Hyneman, John M.	Pennsylvania	R	Y
Jackson, Richard, Jr.	Rhode Island	F	N
Jennings, Jonathan	Indiana Terr.	R	
Johnson, Richard M.	Kentucky	R	Y
Kent, Joseph	Maryland	F	Y
Key, Philip Barton	Maryland	F	N
King, William Rufus	North Carolina	R	Y
Lacock, Abner	Pennsylvania	R	Y
Law, Lyman	Connecticut	F	N
Lefever, Joseph	Pennsylvania	R	Y
Lewis, Joseph, Jr.	Virginia	F	N
Little, Peter	Maryland	R	Y
Livingston, Robert LeRoy	New York	R	
Lowndes, William	South Carolina	R	Y
Lyle, Aaron	Pennsylvania	R	Y
Macon, Nathaniel	North Carolina	R	Y
Maxwell, George C.	New Jersey	R	N
McBryde, Archibald	North Carolina	R	N
McCoy, William	Virginia	R	Y
McKee, Samuel	Kentucky	R	Y
McKim, Alexander	Maryland	R	Y
Metcalf, Arunah	New York	R	N
Milnor, James	Pennsylvania	F	N
Mitchill, Samuel L.	New York	R	N
Moore, Thomas	South Carolina	R	Y
Morgan, James	New Jersey	F	Y
Morrow, Jeremiah	Ohio	R	Y
Mosely, Jonathan N.	Connecticut	F	N
Nelson, Hugh	Virginia	R	Y
New, Anthony	Kentucky	R	Y
Newbold, Thomas	New Jersey	R	N
Newton, Thomas	Virginia	R	Y
Ormsby, Stephen	Kentucky	R	Y
Paulding, William, Jr.	New York	R	
Pearson, Joseph	North Carolina	F	N
Pickens, Israel	North Carolina	R	Y

Name	State	Party	Vote
Piper, William	Pennsylvania	R	Y
Pitkin, Timothy, Jr.	Connecticut	F	N
Pleasants, James, Jr.	Virginia	R	Y
Poindexter, George	Mississippi Terr.	R	
Pond, Benjamin	New York	R	Y
Porter, Peter B.	New York	R	
Potter, Elisha R.	Rhode Island	F	N
Quincy, Josiah	Massachusetts	F	N
Randolph, John	Virginia	R	N
Reed, William	Massachusetts	F	N
Rhea, John	Tennessee	R	Y
Richardson, William N.	Massachusetts	F	Y
Ridgely, Henry M.	Delaware	F	N
Ringgold, Samuel	Maryland	R	Y
Roane, John	Virginia	R	Y
Roberts, Jonathan	Pennsylvania	R	Y
Rodman, William	Pennsylvania	R	N
Sage, Ebenezer	New York	R	Y
Sammons, Thomas	New York	R	N
Sawyer, Lemuel	North Carolina	R	
Seaver, Ebenezer	Massachusetts	R	Y
Sevier, John	Tennessee	R	Y
Seybert, Adam	Pennsylvania	R	Y
Shaw, Samuel	Vermont	R	Y
Sheffey, Daniel	Virginia	F	
Smilie, John	Pennsylvania	R	Y
Smith, George	Pennsylvania	R	Y
Smith, John	Virginia	R	Y
Stanford, Richard	North Carolina	R	N
Stow, Silas	New York	F	N
Strong, William	Vermont	R	Y
Stuart, Philip	Maryland	F	N
Sturges, Lewis B.	Connecticut	F	N
Sullivan, George	New Hampshire	F	N
Taggart, Samuel	Massachusetts	F	N
Talliaferro, John	Virginia	R	Y
Tallmadge, Benjamin	Connecticut	F	N
Tallman, Peleg	Massachusetts	R	N
Tracy, Uri	New York	R	N
Troup, George M.	Georgia	R	Y
Turner, Charles, Jr.	Massachusetts	R	Y
Van Cortlandt, Pierre, Jr.	New York	R	N
Wheaton, Laban	Massachusetts	F	N
White, Leonard	Massachusetts	R	N
Whitehill, Robert	Pennsylvania	R	Y
Widgery, William	Massachusetts	R	Y
Williams, David R.	South Carolina	R	Y
Wilson, Thomas	Virginia	F	N
Wright, Robert	Maryland	R	Y
Winn, Richard	South Carolina	R	Y

Republicans Voting against War

Name	State
Bartlett, Josiah	New Hampshire
Boyd, Adam	New Jersey
Cooke, Thomas B.	New York
Hufty, Jacob	New Jersey
Maxwell, George C.	New Jersey
McBryde, Archibald	North Carolina
Metcalf, Arunah	New York
Mitchill, Samuel L.	New York
Newbold, Thomas	New Jersey
Randolph, John	Virginia
Rodman, William	Pennsylvania
Sammons, Thomas	New York
Stanford, Richard	North Carolina
Tallman, Peleg	Massachusetts
Tracy, Uri	New York
Van Cortlandt, Pierre, Jr.	New York
White, Leonard	Massachusetts

Republicans Abstaining

Name	State
Bacon, Ezekiel	Massachusetts
Clay, Matthew	Virginia
Cobb, Howell	Georgia
Franklin, Meshack	North Carolina
Gray, Edwin	Virginia
Jennings, Jonathan	Indiana Terr.
Paulding, William, Jr.	New York
Poindexter, George	Mississippi Terr.
Porter, Peter B.	New York
Sawyer, Lemuel	North Carolina

By State

	Party	Vote
CONNECTICUT		
Senate		
Dana, Samuel W.	F	N
Goodrich, Chauncey	F	N
House		
Champion, Epaphroditus	F	N
Davenport, Jonathan, Jr.	F	N
Law, Lyman	F	N
Mosely, Jonathan O.	F	N
Pitkin, Timothy, Jr.	F	N
Sturges, Lewis B.	F	N
Tallmadge, Benjamin	F	N
DELAWARE		
Senate		
Bayard, James A.	F	N
Horsey, Outerbridge	F	N
House		
Ridgely, Henry M.	F	N
GEORGIA		
Senate		
Crawford, William	R	Y
Tait, Charles	R	Y
House		
Bibb, William W.	R	Y
Cobb, Howell	R	
Hall, Bolling	R	Y
Troup, George M.	R	Y

KENTUCKY

Senate	Party	Vote
Bibb, George M.	R	Y
Pope, John	R	N
House		
Clay, Henry	R	
Desha, Joseph	R	Y
Johnson, Richard M.	R	Y
McKee, Samuel	R	Y
New, Anthony	R	Y
Ormsby, Stephen	R	Y

MARYLAND

Senate		
Reed, Philip	Und	N
Smith, Samuel	R	Y
House		
Archer, Stevenson	R	Y
Goldsborough, Charles	F	N
Kent, Joseph	F	Y
Key, Philip Barton	F	N
Little, Peter	R	Y
McKim, Alexander	R	Y
Ringgold, Samuel	R	Y
Stuart, Philip	F	N
Wright, Robert	R	Y

MASSACHUSETTS

Senate		
Lloyd, James	F	N
Varnum, Joseph B.	Und	Y
House		
Bacon, Ezekiel	R	
Bigelow, Abijah	F	
Brigham, Elijah	F	N
Carr, Francis	R	Y
Cutts, Richard	F	
Ely, William	F	N
Green, Isaiah L.	R	Y
Quincy, Josiah	F	N
Reed, William	F	N
Richardson, William N.	F	Y
Seaver, Ebenezer	R	Y
Taggart, Samuel	F	N
Tallman, Peleg	R	N
Turner, Charles, Jr.	R	Y
Wheaton, Laban	F	N
White, Leonard	R	N
Widgery, William	R	Y

NEW HAMPSHIRE

Senate		
Cutts, Charles	F	Y
Gilman, Nicholas	R	N
House		
Bartlett, Josiah	R	N
Dinsmoor, Samuel	R	Y
Hall, Obed	R	Y
Harper, John A.	R	Y
Sullivan, George	F	N

NEW JERSEY

Senate		
Condit, John	R	Y
	Party	Vote
Lambert, John	R	N
House		
Boyd, Adam	R	N
Condict, Lewis	R	Y
Hufty, Jacob	R	N
Maxwell, George C.	R	N
Morgan, James	F	Y
Newbold, Thomas	R	N

NEW YORK

Senate		
German, Obadiah	R	N
Smith, John	R	Y
House		
Avery, Daniel	R	Y
Bleeker, Harmanus	F	N
Cooke, Thomas B.	R	N
Emott, James	F	N
Fitch, Asa	F	N
Gold, Thomas R.	F	N
Metcalf, Arunah	R	N
Mitchill, Samuel L.	R	N
Paulding, William, Jr.	R	
Pond, Benjamin	R	Y
Porter, Peter B.	R	
Sage, Ebenezer	R	Y
Sammons, Thomas	R	N
Stow, Silas	F	N
Tracy, Uri	R	N
Van Cortlandt, Pierre, Jr.	R	N

NORTH CAROLINA

Senate		
Franklin, Jesse	R	Y
Turner, James	R	Y
House		
Alston, Willis	R	Y
Blackledge, William	R	Y
Cochran, James	R	Y
Franklin, Meshack	R	
King, William Rufus	R	Y
Macon, Nathaniel	R	Y
McBryde, Archibald	R	N
Pearson, Joseph	F	N
Pickens, Israel	R	Y
Sawyer, Lemuel	R	
Stanford, Richard	R	N

OHIO

Senate		
Campbell, Alexander	Und	
Worthington, Thomas	R	N
House		
Morrow, Jeremiah	R	Y

PENNSYLVANIA

Senate		
Gregg, Andrew	Und	Y
Leib, Michael	R	Y

House		
Anderson, William	R	Y
Bard, David	R	Y

	Party	Vote
Brown, Robert	R	Y
Crawford, William	R	Y
Davis, Roger	R	Y
Findlay, William	R	Y
Hyneman, John M.	R	Y
Lacock, Abner	R	Y
Lefever, Joseph	R	Y
Lyle, Aaron	R	Y
Milnor, James	F	N
Piper, William	R	Y
Roberts, Jonathan	R	Y
Rodman, William	R	N
Seybert, Adam	R	Y
Smilie, John	R	Y
Smith, George	R	Y
Whitehill, Robert	R	Y

RHODE ISLAND

Senate		
Howell, Jeremiah B.	F	N
Hunter, William	F	N
House		
Jackson, Richard, Jr.	F	N
Potter, Elisha R.	F	N

SOUTH CAROLINA

Senate		
Gaillard, John	R	Y
Taylor, John	R	Y
House		
Butler, William	R	Y
Calhoun, John C.	R	Y
Cheves, Langdon	R	Y
Earle, Elias	R	Y
Lowndes, William	R	Y
Moore, Thomas	R	Y
Williams, David R.	R	Y
Winn, Richard	R	Y

TENNESSEE

Senate		
Anderson, Joseph	Und.	Y
Campbell, George W.	R	Y

House	Party	Vote
Grundy, Felix	R	Y
Rhea, John	R	Y
Sevier, John	R	Y

VERMONT

Senate		
Bradley, Stephen R.	R	
Robinson, Jonathan	Und.	Y
House		
Chittenden, Martin	F	N
Fisk, James	R	Y
Shaw, Samuel	R	Y
Strong, William	R	Y

VIRGINIA

Senate		
Brent, Richard	Und.	Y
Giles, William B.	R	Y
House		
Baker, John	F	N
Bassett, Burwell	R	Y
Breckenridge, James	F	N
Burwell, William A.	R	Y
Clay, Matthew	R	
Clopton, John	R	Y
Dawson, John	R	Y
Gholson, Thomas	R	Y
Goodwyn, Peterson	R	Y
Gray, Edwin	R	
Hawes, Aylett	R	Y
Lewis, Joseph, Jr.	F	N
McCoy, William	R	Y
Nelson, Hugh	R	Y
Newton, Thomas	R	Y
Pleasants, James	R	Y
Randolph, John	R	N
Roane, John	R	Y
Sheffey, Daniel	F	
Smith, John	R	Y
Talliaferro, John	R	Y
Wilson, Thomas	F	N

Appendix 2: Executive Officers of the Federal Government during the Madison Presidency

Dates denote actual assumption of duties.

President of the United States—James Madison (Virginia), 4 March 1809–3 March 1817

Vice-President of the United States—George Clinton (New York), 4 March 1813–d. 20 April 1812; Elbridge Gerry (Massachusetts), 4 March 1813–d. 23 November 1814

Secretary of State—Robert Smith (Maryland), 6 March 1809–April 1811; James Monroe (Virginia), 6 April 1811–September 1814; acting, 1 October 1814–February 1815; 28 February 1815–1817

Secretary of the Treasury—Albert Gallatin (Pennsylvania), incumbent from Thomas Jefferson's administration until 9 February 1814; Sec. of the Navy William Jones (Pennsylvania), acting during Gallatin's absence in Europe, 21 April–9 February 1814; George W. Campbell (Tennessee), 9 February 1814–October 1814; Alexander J. Dallas (Pennsylvania), 14 October 1814–October 1816; William H. Crawford (Georgia), 22 October 1816–1817

Secretary of War—John Smith, chief clerk, acting incumbent from Thomas Jefferson's administration; William Eustis (Massachusetts), 8 April 1809–31 December 1812; Sec. of State James Monroe (Virginia), acting, 1 January 1813–February 1813; John Armstrong (New York), 5 February 1813–August 1814; Sec. of State James Monroe, acting, 30 August 1814–September 1814; James Monroe, 1 October 1814–February 1815; acting, March 1815; Sec. of the Treasury Alexander J. Dallas (Pennsylvania), acting, 14 March 1815–8 August 1815; William H. Crawford (Georgia), 8 August 1815–October 1816; George Graham, chief clerk, acting, 22 October 1816–1817

Attorney General—Caesar A. Rodney (Delaware), incumbent from Thomas Jefferson's administration, 5 December 1811; William Pinkney (Maryland), 6 January 1812–February 1814; Richard Rush (Pennsylvania), 11 February 1814–

Postmaster General—Gideon Granger (Connecticut), incumbent from Thomas Jefferson's administration until February 1814; Return J. Meigs (Ohio), 11 April 1814–1817

Secretary of the Navy—Robert Smith (Maryland), incumbent from Thomas Jefferson's administration until March 1809; Charles W. Goldsborough, chief clerk, acting, 8 March–May 1809; Paul Hamilton (South Carolina), 15 May 1809–31 December 1812; Charles Goldsborough, chief clerk, acting, January 1813; William Jones (Pennsylvania), 19 January 1813–November 1814; Benjamin Homans, chief clerk, acting, 2 December 1814–January 1815; Benjamin Crowninshield (Massachusetts), 16 January 1815–1817

Appendix 3: Documents

The Berlin Decree, 21 November 1806

ARTICLE I. The British islands are declared in a state of blockade.

ARTICLE II. All commerce and correspondence with the British islands are prohibited. In consequence, letters or packets, addressed either to England, to an Englishman, or in the English language, shall not pass through the post-office and shall be seized.

ARTICLE III. Every subject of England, of whatever rank and condition soever, who shall be found in the countries occupied by our troops, or by those of our allies, shall be made a prisoner of war.

ARTICLE IV. All magazines, merchandise, or property whatsoever, belonging to a subject of England, shall be declared lawful prize.

ARTICLE V. The trade in English merchandise is forbidden; all merchandise belonging to England, or coming from its manufactories and colonies, is declared lawful prize.

ARTICLE VI. One half of the proceeds of the confiscation of the merchandise and property, declared good prize by the preceding articles, shall be applied to indemnify the merchants for the losses which they have suffered by the capture of merchant vessels by English cruisers.

ARTICLE VII. No vessel coming directly from England, or from the English colonies, or having been there since the publication of the present decree, shall be received into any port.

ARTICLE VIII. Every vessel contravening the above clause, by means of a false declaration, shall be seized, and the vessel and cargo confiscated, as if they were English property.

ARTICLE IX. Our tribunal of prizes at Paris is charged the definitive adjudication of all the controversies, which by the French army, relative to the execution of the present decree. Our tribunal of prizes at Milan shall be charged with the definitive adjudication of the said controversies, which may arise within the extent of our kingdom of Italy.

ARTICLE X. The present decree shall be communicated by our minister of exterior relations, to the kings of Spain, of Naples, of Holland, and of Etruria, and to our allies, whose subjects, like ours, are the victims of the injustice and the barbarism of the English maritime laws. Our finances, our police, and our post masters general, are charged each, in what concerns him, with the execution of the present decree.

Source: State Papers and Publick Documents of the United States: From the Accession of George Washington to the Presidency: Exhibiting a Complete View of Our Foreign Relations since that Time. 8 vols. Boston: T.B. Wait & Sons, 1815, V:478.

British Order in Council, 7 January 1807

Whereas the French Government has issued certain orders, which, in violation of the usages of war, purport to prohibit the commerce of all neutral nations with His Majesty's dominions, and also to prevent such nations from trading with any other countries in any articles, the growth, produce, or manufacture of His Majesty's dominions; and whereas the said Government has also taken upon itself to declare all His Majesty's dominions to be in a state of blockade, at the time when the fleets or France and her allies are themselves confined within their own ports by the superior valor and discipline of the British navy; and whereas such attempts, on the part of the enemy, would give to His Majesty an unquestionable right of retaliation, and would warrant His Majesty in enforcing the same prohibition of all commerce with France, which that power vainly hopes to effect against the commerce of his Majesty's subjects, a prohibition which the superiority of His Majesty's naval forces might enable him to support by actually investing the ports and coasts of the enemy with numerous squadrons and cruisers, so as to make the entrance or approach thereto manifestly dangerous; and whereas His Majesty, though unwilling to follow the example of his enemies by proceeding to an extremity so distressing to all nations not engaged in the war, and carrying on their accustomed trade, yet feels himself bound, by due regard to the just defense of the rights and interests of his people not to suffer such measures to be taken by the enemy, without taking some steps on his part to restrain this violence, and to retort upon them the evils of their own injustice; His Majesty is thereupon pleased, by and with the advice of his privy council, to order, and it is hereby ordered, that no vessels shall be permitted to trade from one port to another, other which ports shall belong to or be in the possession of France or her allies, or shall be so far under their control as that British vessels may not trade freely threat; and the commanders of His Majesty's ships of war and privateers shall be and are hereby, instructed to warn every neutral vessel coming from any such port, and destined to another such port, to discontinue her voyage, and not to proceed to any such port, after a reasonable time shall have been afforded for receiving information of this His Majesty's order, which shall be found proceeding to another such port, shall be captured and brought in, and together with her cargo shall be condemned as lawful prize; and His Majesty's principal Secretaries of State, the Lords Commissioners of the Admiralty, and the Judges of the High Court of Admiralty, and the Courts of Vice-admiralty, are to take the necessary measures herein as to them shall respectively appertain.

Source: American State Papers: Foreign Relations. 6 vols. Washington, D.C.: Gales and Seaton, 1834, III:267.

British Order in Council, 11 November 1807

Whereas certain orders, establishing an unprecedented system of warfare against this kingdom, and aimed especially at the destruction of its commerce and resources, were, sometime since, issued by the government of France, by which "the British islands were declared to be in a state of blockade," thereby subjecting to capture and condemnation all vessels, with their cargoes, which should continue to trade with his majesty's dominions:

And whereas, by the same order, "all trading in English merchandise is prohibited, and every article of merchandise belonging to England, or coming from her colonies, or of her manufacture, is declared lawful prize:"

And whereas, the nations in alliance with France, and under her control, were required to give, and have given, and do give, effect to such orders:

And whereas, his majesty's order of the 7th of January last has not answered the desired purpose, either of compelling the enemy to recall those orders, or of inducing neutral nations to interpose, with effect, to obtain their revocation, but, on the contrary, the same have been recently enforced with increased rigor:

And whereas, his majesty, under these circumstances, finds himself compelled to take further measures for asserting and vindicating his just rights. . . .

His majesty is therefore pleased, by and with the advice of his privy council, to order, and it is hereby ordered, that all the ports and places of France and her allies, or of any country at war with his majesty, the British flag is excluded, and all ports or places in the colonies belonging to his majesty's enemies, shall, from henceforth, be subject to the same restrictions in point of trade and navigation, with the exceptions hereinafter mentioned, as if the same were actually blockaded by his majesty's naval forces, in the most strict and rigorous manner: And it is hereby further ordered and declared, that all trade in the articles which are of the produce or manufacture of the said countries or colonies, shall be deemed and considered to be unlawful; and that every vessel trading from or to the said countries or colonies, together with all goods and merchandise on board, and all articles of the produce or manufacture of the said countries or colonies, shall be captured and condemned as prize to the captors. . . .

And the commanders of his majesty's ships of war and privateers, and other vessels acting under his majesty's commission, shall be, and are hereby, instructed to warn every vessel which shall have commenced her voyage prior to any notice of this order, and shall be destined to any port of France, or of her allies, or of any other country at war with his majesty, or to any port or place from which the British flag, as aforesaid, is excluded, or to any colony belonging to his majesty's enemies, and which shall not have cleared out as is hereinbefore allowed, to discontinue her voyage, and to proceed to some port or place in this kingdom, or to Gibraltar or Malta; and any vessel which, after having been so warned, or after a reasonable time shall have been afforded for the arrival of information of this his majesty's order, at any port or place from which she has sailed, or which, after having notice of this order, shall be found in the prosecution of any voyage contrary to the restrictions contained in this order, shall be captured, and altogether with her cargo, condemned as lawful prize to the captors.

And whereas, countries not engaged in the war have acquiesced in these orders of France, prohibiting all trade in any articles the produce or manufacture of his majesty's dominions; and the merchants of those countries have given countenance and effect to those prohibitions by accepting from persons, styling themselves commercial agents of the enemy, resident at neutral ports, certain documents, termed "certificates of origin," being certificates obtained at the ports of shipment, declaring that the articles of the cargo are not of the produce or manufacture of his majesty's dominions, or to that effect:

And whereas this expedient has been directed by France, and submitted to by such merchants, as part of the new system of warfare directed against the trade of this kingdom, and as the most effectual instrument of accomplishing the same, and is therefore essentially necessary to resist it:

His majesty is therefore pleased by the advice of his privy council, to order, and it hereby ordered, that if any vessel, after reasonable time shall have been afforded for receiving notice of this his majesty's order, at the port of place from which such vessel shall have cleared out, shall be found carrying any such certificate or documents as aforesaid, or any document referring to or authenticating the same, such vessel shall be adjudged lawful prize to the captor, together with goods laden therein, belonging to the person or persons by whom or on whose behalf, any such document was put on board.

And the right honorable the lords commissioners of his majesty's treasury, his majesty's principal secretaries of state, the lords commissioners of the admiralty, and the judges of the high court of admiralty and courts of vice admiralty, are to take the necessary measures herein as to them shall respectively appertain.

Source: Commager, Henry Steele, ed. *Documents of American History.* 7th ed. New York: Appleton-Century-Crofts, 1963, pp. 200–201.

The Milan Decree, 17 December 1807

Napoleon, emperor of the French, king of Italy, and protector of the Rhenish confederation.

Observing the measures adopted by the British government, on the 11th November last, by which vessels belonging to neutral, friendly, or even powers the allies of England, are made liable, not only to be searched by English cruisers, but to be compulsorily detained in England, and to have a tax laid on them of so much per cent on the cargo, to be regulated by the British legislature.

Observing that by these acts the British government *denationalizes* ships of every nation in Europe, that is not competent for any government to detract from its own independence and rights, all the sovereigns of Europe having in trust the sovereignties and independence of the flag; that if by an unpardonable weakness, and which in the eyes of posterity would be an indelible stain, if such tyranny was allowed to be established into principles, and consecrated by usage, the English would avail themselves of it to assert it as a right, as they have availed themselves of the tolerance of government to establish the infamous principle, that the flag of a nation does not cover goods, and to have to their right of blockade an arbitrary extension, and which infringes on the sovereignty of every state; we have decreed and do decree as follows:

Art. I. Every ship, to whatever nation it may belong, that shall have submitted to be searched by an English ship, or to a voyage to England, or shall have paid any tax whatsoever to the English government, is thereby and for that alone, declared to be *denationalized*, to have forfeited the protection of its king, and to have become English property.

Art. II. Whether the ships thus *denationalized* by the arbitrary measures of the English government, enter into our ports, or those of our allies, or whether they fall into the hands of our ships of war, or of our privateers, they are declared to be good and lawful prize.

Art. III. The British islands are declared to be in a state of blockade, both by land and sea. Every ship, of whatever nation, or whatsoever the nature of its cargo may be, that sails from the ports of England, or those of the English colonies, and of the countries occupied by English troops, and proceeding to England or to the English colonies, or to countries occupied by English troops, is good and lawful prize, as contrary to the present decree, and may be captured by our ships of war, or our privateers, and adjudged to the captor.

Art. IV. These measures, which are resorted to only in just retaliation of the barbarous system adopted by England, which assimilates its legislation to that of Algiers, shall cease to have any effect with respect to all nations who shall have the firmness to compel the English government to respect their flag. They shall continue to be rigorously in force as long as that government does not return to the principles of the law of nations, which regulates the relations of civilized states in a state of war. The provisions of the present decree shall be abrogated and null, in fact, as soon as the English abide again by the principles of the law of nations, which are also the principles of justice and of honour.

All our ministers are charged with the execution of the present decree, which shall be inserted in the bulletin of the laws.
NAPOLEON

Source: State Papers and Publick Documents of the United States: From the Accession of George Washington to the Presidency: Exhibiting a Complete View of our Foreign Relations since that Time. 8 vols. Boston: T.B. Wait & Sons, 1815, VI:74.

The Embargo Act, 22 December 1807

Be it enacted, That an embargo be, and hereby is laid on all ships

and vessels in the ports and places within the limits or jurisdiction of the United States, cleared or not cleared, bound to any foreign port or place; and that no clearance be furnished to any ship or vessels bound to such foreign port or place, except vessels under the immediate direction of the President of the United States: and that the President be authorized to give such instructions to the officers of the revenue, and of the navy and revenue cutters of the United States, as shall appear best adopted for carrying the same into full effect: *Provided,* that nothing herein contained shall be construed to prevent the departure of any foreign ship or vessel, either in ballast, or with the goods, wares and merchandise on board of such foreign ship or vessel, when notified of this act.

Sec. 2. That during the continuance of this act, no registered, or sea letter vessel, having on board goods, ware and merchandise, shall be allowed to depart from one port of the United States to any other within the same, unless the master, owner, consignee or factor of such vessel shall first give bond, with one or more sureties to the collector of the district from which she is bound to depart, in sum of double the value of the vessel and cargo, that the said goods, wares, or merchandise shall be relanded in some port of the United States, dangers of the seas excepted, which bond, and also a certificate from the collector where the same may be relanded, shall by the collector respectively be transmitted to the Secretary of the Treasury. All armed vessels possessing public commissions from any foreign power, are not to be considered as liable to the embargo laid by this act.

Source: Commager, Henry Steele, ed. *Documents of American History.* 7th ed. New York: Appleton-Century-Crofts, 1963, pp. 202–203.

The Non-Intercourse Act, 1 March 1809

An Act to interdict the commercial intercourse between the United States and Great Britain and France and their dependencies; and for other purposes.

Be it enacted, That from and after the passing of this act, the entrance of the harbors and waters of the United States and of the territories thereof, be, and the same is hereby interdicted to all public ships and vessels belonging to Great Britain or France.

. . . And if any public ship or vessel as aforesaid, not being included in the exception above mentioned, shall enter any harbor or waters within the jurisdiction of the United States, or of the territories thereof, it shall be lawful for the President of the United States, or such other person as he shall have empowered for that purpose, to employ such part of the land and naval forces, or of the militia of the United States, or the territories thereof, as he shall deem necessary, to compel such ship or vessel to depart.

SEC. 2. That it shall not be lawful for any citizen or citizens of the United States or the territories thereof, nor for any person or persons residing or being in the same, to have any intercourse with, or to afford any aid or supplies to any public ship or vessel as aforesaid, which shall, contrary to the provisions of this act, have entered any harbor or waters within the jurisdiction of the United States or the territories thereof; and if any person shall, contrary to the provisions of this act, have any intercourse with such ship or vessel, or shall afford any aid to such ship or vessel, either in repairing the said vessel or in furnishing her, her officers and crew with supplies of any kind or in any manner whatever, . . . every person so offending, shall forfeit and pay a sum not less than one hundred dollars, nor exceeding ten thousand dollars; and shall also be imprisoned for a term not less than one month, nor more than one year.

SEC. 3. That from and after the twentieth day of May next the entrance of the harbors and waters of the United States and the territories thereof be, and the same is hereby interdicted to all ships or vessels sailing under the flag of Great Britain or France, or owned in whole or in part by any citizen or subject of either. . . . And if any ship or vessel sailing under the flag of Great Britain or France, . . . shall after the said twentieth day of May next, arrive either with or without a cargo, within the limits of the United States or of the territories thereof, such ship or vessel, together with the cargo, if any, which may be found on board, shall be forfeited, and may be seized and condemned in any court of the United States or the territories thereof, having competent jurisdiction, . . .

SEC. 4. That from and after the twentieth day of May next, it shall not be lawful to import into the United States or the territories thereof, any goods, wares or merchandise whatever, from any port or place situated in Great Britain or Ireland, or in any of the colonies or dependencies of Great Britain, nor from any port or place situated in France, or in any of her colonies or dependencies, nor from any port or place in the actual possession of either Great Britain or France. Nor shall it be lawful to import into the United States, or the territories thereof, from any foreign port or place whatever, any goods, wares or merchandise whatever, being of the growth, produce or manufacture of France, or of any of her colonies or dependencies, or being of the growth, produce or manufacture of Great Britain or Ireland, or of any of the colonies or dependencies of Great Britain, or being of the growth, produce or manufacture of any place or country in the actual possession of either France or Great Britain. . . .

SEC. 11. That the President of the United States be, and he hereby is authorized, in case either France or Great Britain shall so revoke or modify her edicts, as that they shall cease to violate the neutral commerce of the United States, to declare the same by proclamation: after which the trade of the United States, suspended by this act, and by the [Embargo Act] and the several acts supplementary thereto, may be renewed with the nation so doing. . . .

SEC. 12. That so much of the . . . [Embargo Act] and of the several acts supplementary thereto, as forbids the departure of vessels owned by citizens of the United States, and the exportation of domestic and foreign merchandise to any foreign port or place, be and the same is hereby repealed, after March 15, 1809, except so far as they relate to Great Britain or France, or their colonies or dependencies, or places in the actual possession of either. . . .

SEC. 19. That this act shall continue and be in force until the end of the next session of Congress. and no longer; and that the act laying an embargo on all ships and vessels in the ports and harbors of the United States, and the several acts supplementary thereto, shall be, and the same are hereby repealed from and after the end of the next session of Congress.

Source: Commager, Henry Steele, ed. *Documents of American History.* 7th ed. New York: Appleton-Century-Crofts, 1963, pp. 203–204.

Macon's Bill No. 2, 1 May 1810

An Act concerning the commercial intercourse between the United States and Great Britain and France and their dependencies, and for other purposes.

BE it enacted. That from and after the passage of this act, no British or French armed vessel shall be permitted to enter the harbor or waters under the jurisdiction of the United States. . . . except when they shall be forced in by distress . . . or when charged with despatches or business from their government, or coming as a public packet for the conveyance of letters; . . .

Sec. 2. That all pacific intercourse with any interdicted foreign armed vessels, the officers or crew thereof, is hereby forbidden, . . .

Sec. 4. That in case either Great Britain or France shall, before the third day of March next, so revoke or modify her edicts as that they shall cease to violate the neutral commerce of the United States, which fact the President of the United States shall declare by proclamation, and if the other nation shall not within three months thereafter so revoke or modify her edicts in like manner, then the third, fourth, fifth, sixth, seventh, eighth, ninth, tenth, and eighteenth sections of the act, entitled "An act to interdict the commercial intercourse between the United States and Great Britain and France . . ." shall, from and after the expiration of three months from the date of the proclamation aforesaid, be revived and have full force and effect, so far as relates to the dominions, colonies, and dependencies, and to the articles the growth, produce or manufacture of the dominions, colonies and dependencies of the nation thus refusing or neglecting to revoke or modify her edicts in the manner aforesaid. And the restrictions imposed by this act shall, from the date of such proclamation, cease and be discontinued in relation to the nation revoking or modifying her decrees in the manner aforesaid.

Source: Commager, Henry Steele, ed. *Documents of American History.* 7th ed. New York: Appleton-Century-Crofts, 1963, p. 204.

Rambouillet Decree, 23 March 1810

NAPOLEON, &c.

Considering that the government of the United States, by an act dated 1st March, 1809, which forbids the entrance of the ports, harbours, and rivers of the said States to all French vessels, orders, 1st. That after the 20th of May following, vessels under the French flag, which shall arrive in the United States, shall be seized and confiscated, as well as their cargoes; 2d. That after the same epoch, no merchandise or produce, the growth or manufacture of France or her colonies, can be imported into the said United States from any port or place whatsoever, under the penalty of seizure, confiscation, and a fine of three times the value of the merchandise; 3d. That American vessels cannot go to any port of France, of her colonies, or dependencies: We have decreed, and do decree, what follows:

ART. 1. All vessels navigating under the flag of the United States, or possessed, in whole or in part, by any citizen or subject of that power, which, counting from the 20th of May, 1809, have entered or shall enter into the ports of our empire, of our colonies, of the countries occupied by our arms, all be seized, and the product of the sales shall be deposited in the surplus fund (*caisse d'amortissement.*)

There shall be excepted from this regulation the vessels which shall be charged with despatches, or with commissions of the government of the said States, and who shall not have either cargoes or merchandise on board. . . .

NAPOLEON.

Source: Commager, Henry Steele, ed. *Documents of American History.* 7th ed. New York: Appleton-Century-Crofts, 1963, pp. 204–205.

Pres. James Madison's War Message, 1 June 1812

WASHINGTON, *June 1, 1812.*

To the Senate and House of Representatives of the United States:

I communicate to Congress certain documents, being a continuation of those heretofore laid before them on the subject of our affairs with Great Britain.

Without going back beyond the renewal in 1803 of the war in which Great Britain is engaged, and omitting unrepaired wrongs of inferior magnitude, the conduct of her Government presents a series of acts hostile to the United States as an independent and neutral nation.

British cruisers have been in the continued practice of violating the American flag on the great highway of nations, and of seizing and carrying off persons sailing under it, not in the exercise of a belligerent right founded on the law of nations against an enemy, but of a municipal prerogative over British subjects. British jurisdiction is thus extended to neutral vessels in a situation where no laws can operate but the law of nations and the laws of the country to which the vessels belong, and a self-redress is assumed which, if British subjects were wrongfully detained and alone concerned, is that substitution of force for a resort to the responsible sovereign which falls within the definition of war. Could the seizure of British subjects in such cases be regarded as within the exercise of a belligerent right, the acknowledged laws of war, which forbid an article of captured property to be adjudged without a regular investigation before a competent tribunal, would imperiously demand the fairest trial where the sacred rights of persons were at issue. In place of such a trial these rights are subjected to the will of every petty commander.

The practice, hence, is so far from affecting British subjects alone that, under the pretext of searching for these, thousands of American citizens, under the safeguard of public law and of their national flag, have been torn from their country and from everything dear to them; have been dragged on board ships of war of a foreign nation and exposed, under the severities of their disci-

pline, to be exiled to the most distant and deadly climes, to risk their lives in the battles of their oppressors, and to be the melancholy instruments of taking away those of their own brethren.

Against this crying enormity, which Great Britain would be so prompt to avenge if committed against herself, the United States have in vain exhausted remonstrances and expostulations, and that no proof might be wanting of their conciliatory dispositions, and no pretext left for a continuance of the practice, the British Government was formally assured of the readiness of the United States to enter into arrangements such as could not be rejected if the recovery of British subjects were the real and the sole object. The communication passed without effect.

British cruisers have been in the practice also of violating the rights and the peace of our coasts. They hover over and harass our entering and departing commerce. To the most insulting pretensions they have added the most lawless proceedings in our very harbors, and have wantonly spilt American blood within the sanctuary of our territorial jurisdiction. The principles and rules enforced by that nation, when a neutral nation, against armed vessels of belligerents hovering near her coasts and disturbing her commerce are well known. When called on, nevertheless, by the United States to punish the greater offenses committed by her own vessels, her Government has bestowed on their commanders additional marks of honor and confidence.

Under pretended blockades, without the presence of an adequate force and sometimes without the practicability of applying one, our commerce has been plundered in every sea, the great staples of our country have been cut off from their legitimate markets, and a destructive blow aimed at our agricultural and maritime interests. In aggravation of these predatory measures they have been considered as in force from the dates of their notification, a retrospective effect being thus added, as has been done in other important cases, to the unlawfulness of the course pursued, and to render the outrage the more signal these mock blockades have been reiterated and enforced in the face of official communications from the British Government declaring as the true definition of a legal blockade "that particular ports must be actually invested and previous warning given to vessels bound to them not to enter."

Not content with these occasional expedients for laying waste our neutral trade, the cabinet of Britain resorted at length to the sweeping system of blockades, under the name of orders in council, which has been molded and managed as might best suit its political views, its commercial jealousies, or the avidity of British cruisers.

To our remonstrances against the complicated and transcendent injustice of this innovation the first reply was that the orders were reluctantly adopted by Great Britain as a necessary retaliation on decrees of her enemy proclaiming a general blockade of the British Isles at a time when the naval force of that enemy dared not issue from his own ports. She was reminded without effect that her own prior blockades, unsupported by an adequate naval force actually applied and continued, were a bar to this plea; that executed edicts against millions of our property could not be retaliation on edicts confessedly impossible to be executed; that retaliation, to be just, should fall on the party setting the guilty example, not on an innocent party which was not even chargeable with an acquiescence in it.

When deprived of this flimsy veil for a prohibition of our trade with her enemy by the repeal of his prohibition of our trade with Great Britain, her cabinet, instead of a corresponding repeal or a practical discontinuance of its orders, formally avowed a determination to persist in them against the United States until the markets of her enemy should be laid open to British products, thus asserting an obligation on a neutral power to require one belligerent to encourage by its internal regulations the trade of another belligerent, contradicting her own practice toward all nations, in peace as well as in war, and betraying the insincerity of those professions which inculcated a belief that, having resorted to her orders with regret, she was anxious to find an occasion for putting an end to them.

Abandoning still more all respect for the neutral rights of the United States and for its own consistency, the British Government now demands as prerequisites to a repeal of its orders as they relate to the United States that a formality should be observed in the repeal of the French decrees nowise necessary to their termination nor exemplified by British usage, and that the French repeal, besides including that portion of the decrees which operates within a territorial jurisdiction, as well as that which operates on the high seas, against the commerce of the United States should not be a single and special repeal in relation to the United States, but should be extended to whatever other neutral nations unconnected with them may be affected by those decrees. And as an additional insult, they are called on for a formal disavowal of conditions and pretensions advanced by the French Government for which the United States are so far from having made themselves responsible that, in official; explanations which have been published to the world, and in a correspondence of the American minister at London with the British minister for foreign affairs such a responsibility was explicitly and emphatically disclaimed.

It has become, indeed, sufficiently certain that the commerce of the United States is to be sacrificed, not as interfering with the belligerent rights of Great Britain; not as supplying the wants of her enemies, which she herself supplies; but as interfering with the monopoly which she covets for her own commerce and navigation. She carries on a war against the lawful commerce of a friend that she may the better carry on a commerce with an enemy—a commerce polluted by the forgeries and perjuries which are for the most part the only passports by which it can succeed.

Anxious to make every experiment short of the last resort of injured nations, the United States have withheld from Great Britain, under successive modifications, the benefits of a free intercourse with their market, the loss of which could not but outweigh the profits accruing from her restrictions of our commerce with other nations. And to entitle these experiments to the more favorable consideration they were so framed as to enable her to place her adversary under the exclusive operation of them. To these appeals her Government has been equally inflexible, as if willing to make sacrifices of every sort rather than yield to the claims of justice or renounce the errors of a false pride. Nay, so far were the attempts carried to overcome the attachment of the British cabinet to its unjust edicts that it received every encouragement within the competency of the executive branch of our Government to expect that a repeat of them would be followed by a war between the United States and France, unless the French edicts should also be repealed. Even this communication, although silencing forever the plea of a disposition in the United States to acquiesce in those edicts originally the sole plea for them, received no attention.

If no other proof existed of a predetermination of the British Government against a repeal of its orders, it might be found in the correspondence of the minister plenipotentiary of the United States at London and the British secretary for foreign affairs in 1810, on the question whether the blockade of May, 1806, was considered as in force or as not in force. It had been ascertained that the French Government, which urged this blockade as the ground of its Berlin decree, was willing in the event of its removal to repeal that decree, which, being followed by alternate repeals of the other offensive edicts, might abolish the whole system on both sides. This inviting opportunity for accomplishing an object so important to the United States, and professed so often to be the desire of both the belligerents, was made known to the British Government. As that Government admits that an actual application of an adequate force is necessary to the existence of a legal blockade, and it was notorious that if such a force had ever been applied its long discontinuance had annulled the blockade in question, there could be no sufficient objection on the part of Great Britain to a formal revocation of it, and no imaginable objection to a declaration of the fact that the blockade did not exist. The declaration would have been consistent with her avowed principles of blockade, and would have enabled the United States to demand from France the pledged repeal of her decrees, either with success, in which case the way would have been opened for a general repeal of the belligerent edicts, or without success, in which case the United States would have been justified in turning their measures exclusively against France. The British Government would, however, neither rescind the blockade nor declare its nonexistence, nor permit its nonexistence to be inferred and affirmed by the American plenipotentiary. On the contrary, by representing the blockade to be comprehended in the orders in council, the United States were compelled so to regard it in their subsequent proceedings.

There was a period when a favorable change in the policy of the British cabinet was justly considered as established. The minister plenipotentiary of His Britannic Majesty here proposed an adjustment of the differences more immediately endangering the harmony of the two countries. The proposition was accepted with the promptitude and cordiality corresponding with the invariable professions of this Government. A foundation appeared to be laid for a sincere and lasting reconciliation. The prospect, however, quickly vanished. The whole proceeding was disavowed by the British Government without any explanations which could at that time repress the belief that the disavowal proceeded from a spirit of hostility to the commercial rights and prosperity of the United States; and it has since come into proof that at the very moment when the public minister was holding the language of friendship and inspiring confidence in the sincerity of the negotiation with which he was charged a secret agent of his Government was employed in intrigues having for their object a subversion of our Government and a dismemberment of our happy union.

In reviewing the conduct of Great Britain toward the United States our attention is necessarily drawn to the warfare just renewed by the savages on one of our extensive frontiers—a warfare which is known to spare neither age nor sex and to be distinguished by features peculiarly shocking to humanity. It is difficult to account for the activity and combinations which have for some time been developing themselves among tribes in constant intercourse with British traders and garrison without connecting their hostility with that influence and without recollecting the authenticated examples of such interpositions heretofore furnished by the officers and agents of that Government. Such is the spectacle of injuries and indignities which have been heaped on our country, and such the crisis which its unexampled forbearance and conciliatory efforts have not been able to avert. It might at least have been expected that an enlightened nation, if less urged by moral obligations or invited by friendly dispositions on the part of the United States, would have found in its true interest alone a sufficient motive to respect their rights and their tranquillity on the high seas; that an enlarged policy would have favored that free and general circulation of commerce in which the British nation is at all times interested, and which in times of war is the best alleviation of its calamities to herself as well as to other belligerents; and more especially that the British cabinet would not, for the sake of a precarious and surreptitious intercourse with hostile markets, have persevered in a course of measures which necessarily put at hazard the invaluable market of a great and growing country, disposed to cultivate the mutual advantages of an active commerce.

Other counsels have prevailed. Our moderation and conciliation have had no other effect than to encourage perseverance and to enlarge pretensions. We behold our seafaring citizens still the daily victims of lawless violence, committed on the great common and highway of nations, even within sight of the country which owes them protection. We behold our vessels, freighted with the products of our soil and industry, or returning with the honest proceeds of them, wrested from their lawful destinations, confiscated by prize courts no longer the organs of public law but the instruments of arbitrary edicts, and their unfortunate crews dispersed and lost, or forced or inveigled in British ports into British fleets, whilst arguments are employed in support of these aggressions which have no foundation but in a principle equally supporting a claim to regulate our external commerce in all cases whatsoever.

We behold, in fine, on the side of Great Britain a state of war against, the United States, and on the side of the United States a state of peace toward Great Britain.

Whether the United States shall continue passive under these progressive usurpations and these accumulating wrongs, or, opposing force to force in defense of their national rights, shall commit a just cause into the hands of the Almighty Disposer of Events, avoiding all connections which might entangle it in the contest or views of other powers, and preserving a constant readiness to concur in an honorable reestablishment of peace and friendship, is a solemn question which the Constitution wisely confides to the legislative department of the Government. In recommending it to their early deliberations I am happy in the assurance that the decision will be worthy the enlightened and patriotic councils of a virtuous, a free, and a powerful nation.

Having presented this view of the relations of the United States with Great Britain and of the solemn alternative growing out of them, I proceed to remark that the communications last made to Congress on the subject of our relations with France will have shewn that since the revocation of her decrees, as they violated the neutral rights of the United States, her Government has authorized illegal captures by its privateers and public ships, and that other outrages have been practiced on our vessels and our citizens. It will have been seen also that no indemnity had been provided or satisfactorily pledged for the extensive spoliations committed under the violent and retrospective orders of the French Government against the property of our citizens seized within the jurisdiction of France. I abstain at this time from recommending to the consideration of Congress definitive measures with respect to that nation, in the expectation that the result of unclosed discussions between our minister plenipotentiary at Paris and the French Government will speedily enable Congress to decide with greater advantage on the course due to the rights, the interests, and the honor of our country.
JAMES MADISON.

Source: Richardson, James D., comp. *A Compilation of the Messages and Papers of the Presidents.* 20 vols. New York: Bureau of National Literature, Inc., 1897, II:484–490.

Treaty of Ghent, 24 December 1814

Treaty of Peace and Amity between His Britannic Majesty and the United States of America

His Britannic Majesty and the United States of America desirous of terminating the war which has unhappily subsisted between the two Countries, and of restoring upon principles of perfect reciprocity, Peace, Friendship, and good Understanding between them, have for that purpose appointed their respective Plenipotentiaries, that is to say, His Britannic Majesty on His part has appointed the Right Honourable James Lord Gambier, late Admiral of the White now Admiral of the Red Squadron of His Majesty's Fleet; Henry Goulburn Esquire, a Member of the Imperial Parliament and Under Secretary of State; and William Adams Esquire, Doctor of Civil Laws: And the President of the United States, by and with the advice and consent of the Senate thereof, has appointed John Quincy Adams, James A. Bayard, Henry Clay, Jonathan Russell, and Albert Gallatin, Citizens of the United States; who, after a reciprocal communication of their respective Full Powers, have agreed upon the following Articles.

ARTICLE THE FIRST. There shall be a firm and universal Peace between His Britannic Majesty and the United States, and between their respective Countries, Territories, Cities, Towns, and People of every degree without exception of places or persons. All hostilities both by sea and land shall cease as soon as this Treaty shall have been ratified by both parties as hereinafter mentioned. All territory, places, and possessions whatsoever taken by either party from the other during the war, or which may be taken after the signing of this Treaty, excepting only the Islands hereinafter mentioned, shall be restored without delay and without causing any destruction or carrying away any of the Artillery or other public property originally captured in the said forts or places, and which shall remain therein upon the Exchange of the Ratifications of this Treaty, or any Slaves or other private property; And all Archives, Records, Deeds, and Papers, either of a public nature or belonging to private persons, which in the course of the war may have fallen into the hands of the Officers of either party, shall be, as far as may be practicable, forthwith restored and delivered to the proper authorities and persons to whom they respectively belong. Such of the Islands in the Bay of Passamaquoddy as are claimed by both parties shall remain in the possession of the party in whose occupation they may be at the time of the Exchange of the Ratifications of this Treaty until the decision respecting the title to the said Islands shall have been made in conformity with the fourth Article of this Treaty. No disposition made by this Treaty as to such possession of the Islands and territories claimed by both parties shall in any manner whatever be construed to affect the right of either.

ARTICLE THE SECOND. Immediately after the ratifications of this Treaty by both parties as hereinafter mentioned, orders shall be sent to the Armies, Squadrons, Officers, Subjects, and Citizens of the two Powers to cease from all hostilities: and to prevent all causes of complaint which might arise on account of the prizes which may be taken at sea after the said Ratifications of this Treaty, it is reciprocally agreed that all vessels and effects which may be taken after the space of twelve days from the said Ratifications upon all parts of the Coast of North America from the Latitude of twenty three degrees North to the Latitude of fifty degrees North, and as far Eastward in the Atlantic Ocean as the thirty sixth degree of West Longitude from the Meridian of Greenwich, shall be restored on each side:-that the time shall be thirty days in all other parts of the Atlantic Ocean North of the Equinoctial Line or Equator:-and the same time for the British and Irish Channels, for the Gulf of Mexico, and all parts of the West Indies:-forty days for the North Seas for the Baltic, and for all parts of the Mediterranean—sixty days for the Atlantic Ocean South of the Equator as far as the Latitude of the Cape of Good Hope—ninety days for every other part of the world South of the Equator, and one hundred and twenty days for all other parts of the world without exception.

ARTICLE THE THIRD. All Prisoners of war taken on either side as well by land as by sea shall be restored as soon as practicable after the Ratifications of this Treaty as hereinafter mentioned on their paying the debts which they may have contracted during their captivity. The two Contracting Parties respectively engage to discharge in specie the advances which may have been made by the other for the sustenance and maintenance of such prisoners.

ARTICLE THE FOURTH. Whereas it was stipulated by the second Article in the Treaty of Peace of one thousand seven hundred and eighty three between His Britannic Majesty and the United States of America that the boundary of the United States should comprehend "all Islands within twenty leagues of any part of the shores of the United States and lying between lines to be drawn due East from the points where the aforesaid boundaries between Nova Scotia on the one part and East Florida on the other shall respectively touch the Bay of Fundy and the Atlantic Ocean, excepting such Islands as now are or heretofore have been within the limits of Nova Scotia, and whereas the several Islands in the Bay of Passamaquoddy, which is part of the Bay of Fundy, and the Island of Grand Menan in the said Bay of Fundy, are claimed by the United States as being comprehended within their aforesaid boundaries, which said Islands are claimed as belonging to His Britannic Majesty as having been at the time of and previous to the aforesaid Treaty of one thousand seven hundred and eighty three within the limits of the Province of Nova Scotia: In order therefore finally to decide upon these claims it is agreed that they shall be referred to two Commissioners to be appointed in the following manner: viz: One Commissioner shall be appointed by His Britannic Majesty and one by the President of the United States, by and with the advice and consent of the Senate thereof, and the said two Commissioners so appointed shall be sworn impartially to examine and decide upon the said claims according to such evidence as shall be laid before them on the part of His Britannic Majesty and of the United States respectively. The said Commissioners shall meet at St Andrews in the Province of New Brunswick, and shall have power to adjourn to such other place or places as they shall think fit. The said Commissioners shall by a declaration or report under their hands and seals decide to which of the two Contracting parties the several Islands aforesaid do respectively belong in conformity with the true intent of the said Treaty of Peace of one thousand seven hundred and eighty three. And if the said Commissioners shall agree in their decision both parties shall consider such decision as final and conclusive. It is further agreed that in the event of the two Commissioners differing upon all or any of the matters so referred to them, or in the event of both or either of the said Commissioners refusing or declining or wilfully omitting to act as such, they shall make jointly or separately a report or reports as well to the Government of His Britannic Majesty as to that of the United States, stating in detail the points on which they differ, and the grounds upon which their respective opinions have been formed, or the grounds upon which they or either of them have so refused declined or omitted to act. And His Britannic Majesty and the Government of the United States hereby agree to refer the report or reports of the said Commissioners to some friendly Sovereign or State to be then named for that purpose, and who shall be requested to decide on the differences which may be stated in the said report or reports, or upon the report of one Commissioner together with the grounds upon which the other Commissioner shall have refused, declined or omitted to act as the case may be. And if the Commissioner so refusing, declining, or omitting to act, shall also wilfully omit to state the grounds upon which he has so done in such manner that the said statement may be referred to such friendly Sovereign or State together with the report of such other Commissioner, then such Sovereign or State shall decide ex parse upon the said report alone. And His Britannic Majesty and the Government of the United States engage to consider the decision of such friendly

Sovereign or State to be final and conclusive on all the matters so referred.

ARTICLE THE FIFTH. Whereas neither that point of the Highlands lying due North from the source of the River St Croix, and designated in the former Treaty of Peace between the two Powers as the North West Angle of Nova Scotia, nor the North Westernmost head of Connecticut River has yet been ascertained; and whereas that part of the boundary line between the Dominions of the two Powers which extends from the source of the River St Croix directly North to the above mentioned North West Angle of Nova Scotia, thence along the said Highlands which divide those Rivers that empty themselves into the River St Lawrence from those which fall into the Atlantic Ocean to the North Westernmost head of Connecticut River, thence down along the middle of that River to the forty fifth degree of North Latitude, thence by a line due West on said latitude until it strikes the River Iroquois or Cataraquy, has not yet been surveyed: it is agreed that for these several purposes two Commissioners shall be appointed, sworn, and authorized to act exactly in the manner directed with respect to those mentioned in the next preceding Article unless otherwise specified in the present Article. The said Commissioners shall meet at St Andrews in the Province of New Brunswick, and shall have power to adjourn to such other place or places as they shall think fit. The said Commissioners shall have power to ascertain and determine the points above mentioned in conformity with the provisions of the said Treaty of Peace of one thousand seven hundred and eighty three, and shall cause the boundary aforesaid from the source of the River St Croix to the River Iroquois or Cataraquy to be surveyed and marked according to the said provisions. The said Commissioners shall make a map of the said boundary, and annex to it a declaration under their hands and seals certifying it to be the true Map of the said boundary, and particularizing the latitude and longitude of the North West Angle of Nova Scotia, of the North Westernmost head of Connecticut River, and of such other points of the said boundary as they may deem proper. And both parties agree to consider such map and declaration as finally and conclusively fixing the said boundary. And in the event of the said two Commissioners differing, or both, or either of them refusing, declining, or wilfully omitting to act, such reports, declarations, or statements shall be made by them or either of them, and such reference to a friendly Sovereign or State shall be made in all respects as in the latter part of the fourth Article is contained, and in as full a manner as if the same was herein repeated.

ARTICLE THE SIXTH. Whereas by the former Treaty of Peace that portion of the boundary of the United States from the point where the fortyfifth degree of North Latitude strikes the River Iroquois or Cataraquy to the Lake Superior was declared to be "along the middle of said River into Lake Ontario, through the middle of said Lake until it strikes the communication by water between that Lake and Lake Erie, thence along the middle of said communication into Lake Erie, through the middle of said Lake until it arrives at the water communication into the Lake Huron; thence through the middle of said Lake to the water communication between that Lake and Lake Superior:" and whereas doubts have arisen what was the middle of the said River,

Lakes, and water communications, and whether certain Islands lying in the same were within the Dominions of His Britannic Majesty or of the United States: In order therefore finally to decide these doubts, they shall be referred to two Commissioners to be appointed, sworn, and authorized to act exactly in the manner directed with respect to those mentioned in the next preceding Article unless otherwise specified in this present Article. The said Commissioners shall meet in the first instance at Albany in the State of New York, and shall have power to adjourn to such other place or places as they shall think fit. The said Commissioners shall by a Report or Declaration under their hands and seals, designate the boundary through the said River, Lakes, and water communications, and decide to which of the two Contracting parties the several Islands lying within the said Rivers, Lakes, and water communications, do respectively belong in conformity with the true intent of the said Treaty of one thousand seven hundred and eighty three. And both parties agree to consider such designation and decision as final and conclusive. And in the event of the said two Commissioners differing or both or either of them refusing, declining, or wilfully omitting to act, such reports, declarations, or statements shall be made by them or either of them, and such reference to a friendly Sovereign or State shall be made in all respects as in the latter part of the fourth Article is contained, and in as full a manner as if the same was herein repeated.

ARTICLE THE SEVENTH. It is further agreed that the said two last mentioned Commissioners after they shall have executed the duties assigned to them in the preceding Article, shall be, and they are hereby, authorized upon their oaths impartially to fix and determine according to the true intent of the said Treaty of Peace of one thousand seven hundred and eighty three, that part of the boundary between the dominions of the two Powers, which extends from the water communication between Lake Huron and Lake Superior to the most North Western point of the Lake of the Woods;-to decide to which of the two Parties the several Islands lying in the Lakes, water communications, and Rivers forming the said boundary do respectively belong in conformity with the true intent of the said Treaty of Peace of one thousand seven hundred and eighty three, and to cause such parts of the said boundary as require it to be surveyed and marked. The said Commissioners shall by a Report or declaration under their hands and seals, designate the boundary aforesaid, state their decision on the points thus referred to them, and particularize the Latitude and Longitude of the most North Western point of the Lake of the Woods, and of such other parts of the said boundary as they may deem proper. And both parties agree to consider such designation and decision as final and conclusive. And in the event of the said two Commissioners differing, or both or either of them refusing, declining, or wilfully omitting to act, such reports, declarations or statements shall be made by them or either of them, and such reference to a friendly Sovereign or State shall be made in all respects as in the latter part of the fourth Article is contained, and in as full a manner as if the same was herein revealed.

ARTICLE THE EIGHTH. The several Boards of two Commissioners mentioned in the four preceding Articles shall respectively have power to appoint a Secretary, and to employ such Surveyors or other persons as they shall judge necessary. Duplicates of all their respective reports, declarations, statements, and decisions, and of their accounts, and of the Journal of their proceedings shall be delivered by them to the Agents of His Britannic Majesty and to the Agents of the United States, who may be respectively appointed and authorized to manage the business on behalf of their respective Governments. The said Commissioners shall be respectively paid in such manner as shall be agreed between the two contracting parties, such agreement being to be settled at the time of the Exchange of the Ratifications of this Treaty. And all other expenses attending the said Commissions shall be defrayed equally by the two parties. And in the case of death, sickness, resignation, or necessary absence, the place of every such Commissioner respectively shall be supplied in the same manner as such Commissioner was first appointed; and the new Commissioner shall take the same oath or affirmation and do the same duties. It is further agreed between the two contracting parties that in case any of the Islands mentioned in any of the preceding Articles, which were in the possession of one of the parties prior to the commencement of the present war between the two Countries, should by the decision of any of the Boards of Commissioners aforesaid, or of the Sovereign or State so referred to, as in the four next preceding Articles contained, fall within the dominions of the other party, all grants of land made previous to the commencement of the war by the party having had such possession, shall be as valid as if such Island or Islands had by such decision or decisions been adjudged to be within the dominions of the party having had such possession.

ARTICLE THE NINTH. The United States of America engage to put an end immediately after the Ratification of the present Treaty to hostilities with all the Tribes or Nations of Indians with whom they may be at war at the time of such Ratification, and forthwith to restore to such Tribes or Nations respectively all the possessions, rights, and privileges which they may have enjoyed or been entitled to in one thousand eight hundred and eleven previous to such hostilities. Provided always that such Tribes or Nations shall agree to desist from all hostilities against the United States of America, their Citizens, and Subjects upon

the Ratification of the present Treaty being notified to such Tribes or Nations, and shall so desist accordingly. And His Britannic Majesty engages on his part to put an end immediately after the Ratification of the present Treaty to hostilities with all the Tribes or Nations of Indians with whom He may be at war at the time of such Ratification, and forthwith to restore to such Tribes or Nations respectively all the possessions, rights, and privileges, which they may have enjoyed or been entitled to in one thousand eight hundred and eleven previous to such hostilities. Provided always that such Tribes or Nations shall agree to desist from all hostilities against His Britannic Majesty and His Subjects upon the Ratification of the present Treaty being notified to such Tribes or Nations, and shall so desist accordingly.

ARTICLE THE TENTH. Whereas the Traffic in Slaves is irreconcilable with the principles of humanity and Justice, and whereas both His Majesty and the United States are desirous of continuing their efforts to promote its entire abolition, it is hereby agreed that both the contracting parties shall use their best endeavours to accomplish so desirable an object.

ARTICLE THE ELEVENTH. This Treaty when the same shall have been ratified on both sides without alteration by either of the contracting parties, and the Ratifications mutually exchanged, shall be binding on both parties, and the Ratifications shall be exchanged at Washington in the space of four months from this day or sooner if practicable.

In faith whereof, We the respective Plenipotentiaries have signed this Treaty, and have hereunto affixed our Seals. Done in triplicate at Ghent the twenty fourth day of December one thousand eight hundred and fourteen.

GAMBIER [Seal]

HENRY GOULBURN [Seal]

WILLIAM ADAMS [Seal]

JOHN QUINCY ADAMS [Seal]

J. A. BAYARD [Seal]

H. CLAY [Seal]

JON. RUSSELL [Seal]

ALBERT GALLATIN [Seal]

Source: Miller, Hunter, ed. *Treaties and Other International Acts of the United States of America. Volume 2, Documents 1-40: 1776-1818.* Washington: Government Printing Office, 1931.

Chronology

	Political	Diplomatic	Military
1805			
May		*Essex* Decision	
1806			
21 November		Berlin Decree	
31 December		Monroe-Pinkney Treaty signed	
1807			
7 January		Order in Council	
22 June			*Chesapeake-Leopard* Affair
11 November		Order in Council	
17 December		Milan Decree	
22 December		Embargo Act	
1809			
1 March	Repeal of Embargo		
1 March	Non-Intercourse Act		
19 April		Erskine Agreement	
1810			
23 March		Rambouillet Decree	
1 May	Macon's Bill No. 2		
5 August		Cadore Letter	
5 August		Trianon Decree	
2 November		Madison invokes Macon's Bill No. 2	
1811			
16 May			USS *President* v. HMS *Little Belt*
24 July	Madison calls 12th Congress into session for 4 November		
September		Joel Barlow arrives in Paris	
4 November	Convening of first session of 12th Congress		
7 November			Battle of Tippecanoe
December		Joel Barlow dies	
1812			
8 February	President Madison purchases John Henry Letters		
9 March	John Henry Letters released		

	Political	Diplomatic	Military
1812 *continued*			
4 April	Embargo signed		
11 May		Assassination of Spencer Perceval	
22 May		*Hornet* arrives from Europe	
1 June	Madison sends war message to Congress		
4 June	House votes for war		
16 June		Withdrawal of Orders in Council	
18 June	Declaration of War		
22 June			Dearborn calls for New England militia
6 July	Adjournment of first session of 12th Congress		
12 July			Hull invades Canada
17 July			U.S. surrender of Mackinac
5 August			Battle of Brownstown
9 August			Battle of Monguagon
10 August		Dearborn-Prevost Armistice	
15 August			Fort Dearborn Massacre
22 June–August	Baltimore Riots		
16 August			Surrender of Detroit
19 August			USS *Constitution* v. HMS *Guerrière*
20 August			Harrison appointed major general Kentucky militia
17 September			Harrison given command of Northwestern army
21 September		Alexander I offers mediation	
13 October			Battle of Queenston
18 October			USS *Wasp* v. HMS *Frolic*
25 October			USS *United States* v. HMS *Macedonian*
29 December			USS *Constitution* v. HMS *Java*
1813			
18 January			First engagement at Frenchtown (Michigan Territory)
22 January			Battle of Frenchtown (Michigan Territory)
22 February			British raid on Ogdensburg, New York
23 January			Massacre of prisoners at Frenchtown (Michigan Territory)
24 February			USS *Hornet* v. HMS *Peacock*
15 April			United States takes Mobile, Mississippi Territory
27 April			Battle of York
28 April–9 May			Siege of Fort Meigs
15 May			Sack of Havre de Grace, Maryland
27 May			Battle of Fort George
29 May			Battle of Sacket's Harbor
1 June			HMS *Shannon* v. USS *Chesapeake*
6 June			Battle of Stoney Creek
22 June			Battle of Craney Island, Virginia
24 June			U.S. surrender at Beaver Dams

Political	Diplomatic	Military
1813 *continued*		
25–26 June		Battle of and Sack of Hampton, Virginia
11 July		British raid on Black Rock, New York
27 July		Battle of Burnt Corn Creek
2 August		British attack on Fort Stephenson
10 August		Battle of St. Michael's
14 August		HMS *Pelican* v. USS *Argus*
30 August		Fort Mims Massacre
5 September		USS *Enterprise* v. HMS *Boxer*
10 September		Battle of Lake Erie
5 October		Battle of the Thames
26 October		Battle of Châteauguay
1 November		Battle of French Creek
3 November		Battle of Tallushatchee
9 November		Battle of Talladega
11 November		Battle of Chrysler's Farm
18 November		Hillabee Massacre
29 November		Battle of Autossee
10 December		U.S. Burning of Newark
18 December		Fort Niagara falls to British
18 December		British destruction of Lewiston, New York
19 December		British capture of Fort Niagara
23 December		Battle of Econochaca
30 December		British burning of Black Rock and Buffalo
1814		
22 January		Battle of Emuckfau Creek
24 January		Battle of Enitochopco
27 January		Battle of Calabee Creek
27 March		Battle of Horseshoe Bend (Tohopeka)
28 March		HMS *Phoebe* and *Cherub* v. USS *Essex*
30 March		Battle of La Colle Mill
29 April		USS *Peacock* v. HMS *Epervier*
6 May		Battle of Oswego
15 May		U.S. burning of Port Dover
30 May		Battle of Sandy Creek
28 June		USS *Wasp* v. HMS *Reindeer*
July		U.S. surrender of Prairie du Chien
3 July		Battle of Fort Erie
5 July		Battle of Chippewa
25 July		Battle of Lundy's Lane
3 August		Battle of Conjocta Creek
3 August		British seizure of Hampden
8 August	Beginning of negotiations at Ghent	
9 August	Treaty of Fort Jackson	
9–11 August		Battle of Stonington
15 August		British attempt to retake Fort Erie
24 August		Battle of Bladensburg
24 August		British occupy Washington, D.C.

	Political	Diplomatic	Military
1814 *continued*			
30 August			Battle of Caulk's Field
5 September			Battle of Beakmantown
7 September			USS *Wasp* v. HMS *Avon*
11 September			Battle of Lake Champlain
11 September			Battle of Plattsburg
12–13 September			Battle of Baltimore
15 September			British attempt to take Fort Bowyer
17 September			U.S. sorties from Fort Erie
19 October			Battle of Cook's Mills
7 November			United States takes Pensacola
15 December			Battle of Lake Borgne
15 December– 5 January	Hartford Convention		
23 December			Battle at Villeré Plantation
24 December		Treaty of Ghent signed	
1815			
8 January			Battle of New Orleans
14 January			HMS *Endymion, Tenados, Pomone* v. USS *President*
11 February			British capture Fort Bowyer
16 February		U.S. Senate ratifies Treaty of Ghent	
17 February		War officially ends with U.S.-British exchange of ratifications	
20 February			USS *Constitution* v. HMS *Cyane* and *Levant*
23 March			USS *Hornet* v. HMS *Penguin*
15 April			Dartmoor Prison Massacre
30 June			USS *Peacock* v. HMS *Nautilus*

Glossary

ASTERN—(nautical usage, *adv.*) A position directly behind a vessel, or very nearly so.

BEAM—(nautical usage, *n.*) The width of a vessel, usually somewhere near its midlength; also, the direction of an object directly off the widest part of a vessel.

BOW—(nautical usage, *n.*) The forwardmost part of the vessel; also, when locating an object off the vessel, a direction somewhere between the bow and beam on either side (through an arc of 90 degrees).

BROADSIDE—(nautical usage, *n.*) The firing of all guns on one side of a vessel as nearly simultaneously as possible.

CARTEL—(diplomatic usage, *n.*) A documented compact between nations, customarily to devise a way to exchange prisoners; a CARTEL VESSEL is thus one committed to prisoner exchanges or a courier vessel protected from capture.

COMMODORE—(naval rank, *n.*) The highest rank in the U.S. Navy before 1862, it was temporarily assigned to captains in command of a squadron; abolished in 1899. As a courtesy, captains who had so served were generally referred to afterward as commodores. Similarly, a post (not rank) in the Royal Navy for captains of squadrons.

GUERRE DE COURSE—(military usage) Usually associated with privateering, the term means literally to make war on commerce; some American naval strategists, such as Stephen Decatur, urged the adoption of *guerre de course* as the best use of the small U.S. Navy.

LARBOARD—(nautical usage, *n.*) The left side of a vessel when standing aboard facing forward. In the 1840s, officially replaced in the U.S. Navy by *port* because the new word was aurally different from *starboard*.

LEE SHORE—(nautical usage, *n.*) Because *lee* means the point or place farthest from the wind, a *lee shore* is one toward which the wind is blowing (therefore a dangerous shore); likewise, *leeway* is the drift from a true course (dead reckoning) caused by wind pressure or current on a sailing vessel.

ORDINARY—(nautical usage, *n.*) Used to describe the status of a nautical vessel that is out of commission, as it would be if held in reserve; laid up; mothballed.

ORDNANCE—(military usage, *n.*) Usually gun armament (as in naval ordnance) but can mean, more broadly, any weapons and their inventories of supplies, such as ammunition.

PORT—See LARBOARD.

POST-CAPTAIN—(naval rank, *n.*) During the War of 1812, a commissioned captain of actual rank, as contrasted to the informal use of *captain* to refer to a vessel's commanding officer. In the Royal Navy a post-captain's command would normally be a *post-ship,* usually a frigate or larger vessel.

QUARTER—(nautical usage, *n.*) When locating an object off the vessel, a direction somewhere between the beam and the stern on either side.

QUARTERS (BATTLE STATIONS) (naval usage, *n.*)—When a crew was called to quarters, the men reported to their battle stations; *quartering* a crew prior to combat was essential so that each man knew his station and duties in battle.

RAKE—(nautical usage, *v.t.*) To fire down the length of an enemy vessel either from ahead or astern.

RATE—(naval usage, *n.*) An indication of the firepower of a warship; smaller numbers meant more guns, that is, first rates had 100 or more guns while sixth rates had 20 to 29.

RAZEE—(naval usage, *n.*) A ship whose upper deck(s) has been cut down to reduce her rating; (*v.*) the processing of cutting down decks; pronounced ray-*zee.*

STARBOARD—(nautical usage, *n.*) The right side of a vessel when standing aboard facing forward.

STRIKE COLORS—(naval usage) To surrender in naval combat by lowering (*striking*) the vessel's flag.

TACK—(nautical usage, *v.t.*) To change a vessel's direction by turning across, or through, the wind to make headway against the wind.

WEAR—(nautical usage, *v.t.*) To change the vessel's direction by turning across the wind when moving away from the direction of the wind.

WEATHER—(nautical usage, *adj.*) The point or place that is closest to the wind.

WEATHER GAUGE—(nautical usage) A windward (upwind) and hence desirable position in relation to an adversary, thus giving the vessel with the weather gauge the advantage of catching the wind first, dictating the speed of approach and the time of engaging.

WINDWARD—(nautical usage, *n.*) Toward the wind.

Bibliography

Adams, Donald, Jr. "The Beginning of Investment Banking in the United States." *Pennsylvania History* (1978): 99–116.

———. *Finance and Enterprise in Early America: A Study of Stephen Girard's Bank.* Philadelphia: University of Pennsylvania Press, 1978.

Adams, Henry. *History of the United States during the Administrations of Jefferson and Madison.* 9 vols. New York: Charles Scribner's Sons, 1889–1891.

———. *John Randolph.* Boston and New York: Houghton, Mifflin, 1883.

Adams, Henry, ed. *The Writings of Albert Gallatin.* 3 vols. Philadelphia: J. B. Lippincott, 1879.

Adams, John Quincy. *Memoirs of John Quincy Adams: Comprising Portions of His Diary from 1795 to 1848.* Ed. Chauncey Worthington Ford. 7 vols. Philadelphia: J. B. Lippincott, 1874–1877.

Aimone, Alan Conrad. "The Cruise of the U.S. Sloop *Hornet* in 1815." *Mariner's Mirror* 61 (November 1975): 377–384.

Ainsworth, W. L. "An Amphibious Operation That Failed: The Battle of New Orleans." *United States Naval Institute Proceedings* 71 (February 1945): 193–201.

Akers, Frank H. "The Unexpected Challenge; The Creek War of 1813–1814." Ph.D. diss., Duke University, 1975.

Akins, Thomas Beamish. *History of Halifax City.* Halifax, 1895.

Allen, Penelope, comp. *Tennessee Soldiers in the War of 1812: Regiments of Colonels Allcorn and Allison.* Chattanooga: Tennessee Society, United States Daughters of 1812, 1847.

Allen, Robert S. "Canadians on the Upper Mississippi: The Capture and Occupation of Prairie du Chien during the War of 1812." *Military Collector and Historian* 31 (1979): 118–123.

———. "Cecil Bisshopp." Vol. 5, *1801–1820,* pp. 82–83. Toronto: University of Toronto Press, 1966–1994.

———. *His Majesty's Indian Allies: British Indian Policy in the Defence of Canada, 1774–1815.* Toronto and Oxford: Dundurn Press, 1992.

———. "A History of Fort George, Upper Canada." *Canadian Historic Sites* 11 (1974): 61–93.

———. "Robert McDouall." In *Dictionary of Canadian Biography.* Vol. 7, *1836–1850.* Toronto: University of Toronto Press, 1979: 556–557.

Allen, Samuel. "Federal Ascendancy of 1812." *Narragansett Historical Register* 7 (1889): 381–384.

Allison, Joseph. *An Eulogy upon the Life, Character and Public Services of General Zachary Taylor: Delivered at the Commissioners' Hall, Spring Garden, July 29th, 1850.* Philadelphia: J. H. Jones, 1850.

Altoff, Gerard T. *Deep Water Sailors, Shallow Water Soldiers.* Put-in-Bay, OH: Perry Group, 1993.

———. "The Perry-Elliot Controversy." *Northwest Ohio Quarterly* 60 (autumn 1988): 135–152.

Ambler, Charles Henry. *Thomas Ritchie: A Study in Virginia Politics.* Richmond, VA: Bell, Book and Stationery Co., 1913.

Ambler, Charles H., ed. "Nathaniel Macon Correspondence." *John P. Branch Historical Papers* 3 (1910): 27–93.

"American Vessels Captured by the British during the War of 1812." *The Records of the Vice-Admiralty Court at Halifax.* Salem: The Essex Institute, 1911.

Ames, William E. *A History of the* National Intelligencer. Chapel Hill: University of North Carolina Press, 1972.

Ammon, Harry. *James Monroe: The Quest for National Identity.* New York: McGraw-Hill, 1971.

Anderson, Dice Robins. *William Branch Giles: A Study in the Politics of Virginia and the Nation from 1790 to 1830.* Gloucester, MA: Peter Smith, 1965.

Anderson, Thomas. "Personal Narrative of Capt. Thomas G. Anderson: Early Experiences in the Northwest Fur Trade and the British Capture of Prairie du Chien, 1814." *Wisconsin Historical Society Collections* 9 (1880–1881):136–261.

Andrews, Charles. *The Prisoners' Memoirs or Dartmoor Prison.* New York: Self-published, 1815.

Andrews, Roger. *Old Fort Mackinac on the Hill of History.* Menominee, WI: Herlad-Leander Press, 1938.

[Annals of Congress]. *Debates and Proceedings...11th Congress.* Washington, DC: Gales and Seaton, 1853.

Annals of the Twelfth Congress, 1811–1812. Washington: Gales and Seaton, 1853.

Annual Register 81 (1839): 365.

Anson, Bert. *The Miami Indians.* Norman: University of Oklahoma Press, 1970.

Anson, Walter. *The Life of Admiral Sir John Borlase Warren.* London: Wyman, 1912.

Apgar, Wilbur E. "New York's Contribution to the War Effort of 1812." *New York Historical Society Quarterly* 29 (1945): 203–212.

Arana, Luis Rafael, and George R. Fairbanks. *The History and Antiquities of the City of St. Augustine, Florida.* Gainesville: University Presses of Florida, 1958.

Armstrong, John. *Notices of the War of 1812.* 2 vols. New York: Wiley and Putnam, 1840.

Arnold, James R. "The Battle of Bladensburg." *Columbia Historical Society Proceedings* 37 (1937): 145–168.

Arthur, Stanley Clisby. *Jean Lafitte, Gentleman Rover.* New Orleans: Harmanson, 1952.

Ashe, Samuel A., ed. *Biographical History of North Carolina from Colonial Times to the Present.* 7 vols. Greensboro, NC: C. L. Van Noppen, 1906.

Aspinall, A. "The Canningite Party." *Transactions of the Royal Historical Society,* 4th ser., 17 (1934): 177–226.

Au, Dennis. *War on the Raisin.* Monroe, MI: Monroe County Historical Commission, 1981.

Averill, James P. *Fort Meigs: A Condensed History of the Most Important Military Post in the Northwest, Together with Scenes and Incidents Connected with the Sieges of 1813.* Toledo: Blade Printing Company, 1886.

Avery, Lillian Drake. *A Genealogy of the Ingersoll Family in America, 1629–1925: Comprising Descendants of Richard Ingersoll of Salem, Massachusetts, John Ingersoll of Westfield, Mass., and John Ingersoll of Huntington, Long Island.* New York: Grafton Press, 1926.

Babcock, James Locke. *Joseph Ellicott, the Founder of Buffalo.* Batavia, NY: Batavia Times, 1934.

Babcock, Louis L. *The War of 1812 on the Niagara Frontier.* Buffalo: Buffalo Historical Society, 1927.

Bailey, Thomas A. *A Diplomatic History of the American People.* 9th ed. Englewood Cliffs, NJ: Prentice-Hall, 1974.

Baldwin, Hanson W. "Fulton and Decatur." *United States Naval Institute Proceedings* 71 (1936): 231–235.

Bales, George C. "General Hugh Brady." *Michigan Pioneer* 7 (1877–1878): 573–579.

Ballard, William. "Castine, October 1, 1814." *Bangor Historical Magazine* 2 (1996): 45–51.

Banner, James M., Jr. *To the Hartford Convention: The Federalists and the Origins of Party Politics in Massachusetts, 1789–1815.* New York: Alfred Knopf, 1970.

Bannister, J. A. "The Burning of Dover." *Western Ontario Historical Notes* 21 (1965): 1–25.

Barclay, R. H. "Commander Barclay's Account of the Battle of Lake Erie." *Journal of American History* 8 (1914): 123–128.

Barker, George Fisher Russell. "Henry Goulburn." *Dictionary of National Biography.* Vol. 8. London: Oxford University Press, 1937–1938, 283–285.

Barker, Jacob. *Incidents in the Life of Jacob Barker.* Washington, DC: N.p., 1855.

Barlow, William. *The Character and Reward of a Just Man.* Albany: Packard, Van Banthusen and Co., 1839.

Barlow, William R. "Congress during the War of 1812." Ph.D. diss., Ohio State University, 1961.

———. "Ohio's Congressmen and the War of 1812." *Ohio History* 72 (1963): 175–194, 257–259.

Barlow, William, and David O. Powell. "Congressman Ezekiel Bacon of Massachusetts and the Coming of the War of 1812." *Historical Journal of Western Massachusetts* 6 (spring 1978): 28–41.

Barnard, Daniel D. *A Discourse on the Life, Services and Character of Stephen Van Rensselaer Delivered before the Albany Institute, April 15, 1839.* Albany: Hoffman and White, 1839.

Barnes, James. *Naval Actions of the War of 1812.* New York: Harper and Brothers Publishers, 1896.

Barnhart, John D. "Letters of William Henry Harrison to Thomas Worthington, 1799–1813." *Indiana Magazine of History* 47 (1951): 53–84.

———. "A New Letter about the Massacre at Fort Dearborn." *Indiana Magazine of History* 41 (1945): 187–199.

Barnhart, John D., and Dorothy L. Riker. *Indiana to 1816: The Colonial Period.* Indianapolis: Indiana Historical Bureau, 1971.

Barraud, E. M. *Barraud: The Story of a Family.* London: Research Publishing Company, 1967.

Barthorp, Michael. *Wellington's Generals.* London: Osprey, 1978.

Bartlett, C. J. *Castlereagh.* New York: Scribner, 1966.

———. *Defense and Diplomacy: Britain and the Great Powers, 1815–1914.* Manchester, England: University of Manchester Press, 1993.

Bartlett, Irving H. *Daniel Webster.* New York: W. W. Norton, 1978.

———. *John C. Calhoun: A Biography.* New York: W. W. Norton, 1993.

Basset, John S., and J. Franklin Jameson, eds. *The Correspondence of Andrew Jackson.* 7 vols. Washington, DC: Carnegie Institution of Washington, 1926–1935.

Bateman, Newton. "The Story of Fort Dearborn." In *Historical Encyclopedia of Illinois.* 2 vols. Chicago: Munsell Publishing, 1905.

Battle of Caulk's Field, 150th Anniversary Commemoration. Chestertown, MD: Kent County News, 1964.

"Battle of Sackett's Harbor, The." *Military and Naval Magazine of the United States* 1 (1833): 7–25.

Bauer, Karl Jack. *Zachary Taylor: Soldier, Planter, Statesman of the Old Southwest.* Baton Rouge: Louisiana State University Press, 1985.

Baylies, Nicholas. *Eleazar Wheelock Ripley.* Des Moines: Brewster and Company, 1890.

Bayliss, Joseph, and Estelle Bayliss. *Historic St. Joseph's Island.* Cedar Rapids, IA: Torch Press, 1938.

Beard, Charles A. *An Economic Interpretation of the Constitution of the United States.* New York and London: Free Press, Collier Macmillan, 1989.

Beasley, Paul W. "The Life and Times of Isaac Shelby, 1750–1826." Ph.D. dissertation, University of Kentucky, 1968.

Beirne, Francis F. *The War of 1812.* New York: E. P. Dutton, 1949.

Bell, Rudolph M. "Mr. Madison's War and Long Term Congressional Voting Behavior." *William and Mary Quarterly* 36 (July 1979): 373–395.

Bellico, Russell P. *Sails and Steam in the Mountains: A Maritime and Military History of Lake George and Lake Champlain.* New York: Purple Mountain Press, 1992.

Belovarac, Allan. "A Brief Overview of the Battle of Lake Erie and the Perry-Elliott Controversy." *Journal of Erie Studies* 17 (fall 1988): 3–6.

Bemis, Samuel Flagg. *A Diplomatic History of the United States.* 3d ed. New York: Henry Holt, 1950.

———. *John Quincy Adams and the Foundations of American Foreign Policy.* New York: Alfred A. Knopf, 1949.

Bender, Mark L. "The Failure of General William Hull at Detroit in 1812 and Its Immediate Effects upon the State of Ohio." Master's thesis, Kent State University, 1971.

Benn, Carl. "Iroquois Warfare, 1812–1814." In R. Arthur Bowler, ed., *War along the Niagara.* Youngstown, NY: Old Fort Niagara Association, 1991: 61–76.

Benton, Thomas Hart. *Thirty Years' View.* 2 vols. New York: D. Appleton, 1854–1856.

Berton, Pierre. *Flames across the Border: The Canadian-American Tragedy, 1813–1814.* Boston: Little, Brown, 1981.

Bethune, Alexander Neill. *Memoir of the Right Reverend John Strachan.* London: H. Rowsell, 1870.

Bickley, Francis, ed. *Report on the Manuscripts of Earl Bathurst.* London: T. B. Hart, 1923.

Bierne, Francis F. *The War of 1812.* New York: E. P. Dutton, 1949.

Billias, George Athan. *Elbridge Gerry: Founding Father and Republican Statesman.* New York: McGraw-Hill, 1976.

Biographical Directory of the United States Congress, 1774–1989. Washington, DC: Government Printing Office, 1989.

"Biographical Memoir of Sir Philip Bowes Vere Broke." *Naval Chronicle* 33 (1815): 1–22.

Birkhimer, William E. *Historical Sketch of the Organization, Administration, Materiel, and Tactics of the Artillery of the United States Army.* Washington, DC: Chapman, 1884.

Bishop, Levi. "The Battle of Monguagon." *Michigan Pioneer* 6 (1884): 466–469.

Boase, George Clement. "Sir Roger Hale Sheaffe." *Dictionary of National Biography.* Vol. 17. London: Oxford University Press, 1937–1938: 1393.

Bobbe, Dorothie. *DeWitt Clinton.* New York: Minton, Balch, 1933.

Bohner, Charles H. *John Pendleton Kennedy, Gentleman from Baltimore.* Baltimore: Johns Hopkins University Press, 1969.

Bolkhovitinov, Nikolai N. *The Beginnings of Russian-American Relations, 1775–1815.* Cambridge: Harvard University Press, 1975.

Bonner, James C. *The Georgia Story.* Oklahoma City: Harlow Publishing Corporation, 1961.

Bonney, Catharine V.R. *Legacy of Historical Gleanings.* 2 vols. Albany, NY: J. Munsell, 1875.

Boom, Aaron. "John Coffee—Citizen Soldier." *Tennessee Historical Quarterly* 22 (1963): 223–237.

Borden, Morton. *The Federalism of James A. Bayard.* New York: Columbia University Press, 1955.

———. *Parties and Politics in the Early Republic, 1789–1815.* New York: Thomas Y. Crowell, 1967.

Bourchier, Lady, ed. *Codrington's Memoirs of Admiral Sir Edward Codrington.* London: Longmans, Green, 1873.

Bowlus, Bruce. "A 'Signal Victory': The Battle for Fort Stephenson, August 1–2, 1813." *Northwest Ohio Quarterly* 63 (summer/autumn 1991): 43–57.

Boyd, John P. *Documents and Facts Relative to Military Operations during the Late War.* N.p., 1816.

Boyd, Mark F. "Events at Prospect Bluff on the Apalachicola River." *Florida Historical Quarterly* 16 (1937): 55–93.

Bradford, James C. *Command under Sail: Makers of the American Naval Tradition, 1775–1850.* Annapolis, MD: Naval Institute Press, 1985.

Bradley, Harold W. "Thomas ap Catesby Jones and the Hawaiian Islands, 1826–1827." *Hawaiian Historical Society Report* 39 (1931): 17–30.

Bradley, Udolpho Theodore. *The Contentious Commodore: Thomas ap Catesby Jones of the Old Navy, 1788–1858.* Ph.D. diss., Cornell University, 1933.

Brannon, Gary. *The Last Voyage of the* Tonquin: *An Ill-fated Expedition to the Pacific Northwest.* Waterloo, Ont.: Escart Press, 1992.

Brant, Irving. *James Madison.* Vols. 4 and 5. Indianapolis: Bobbs-Merrill, 1941, 1961.

———. "Joel Barlow, Madison's Stubborn Minister." *William and Mary Quarterly* 25 (October 1958): 438–451.

Braund, Kathryn E. Holland. *Deerskins and Duffels: The Creek Indian Trade with Anglo-America, 1685–1815.* Lincoln: University of Nebraska Press, 1993.

[Brenton, E. B.] *Some Account of the Public Life of the Late Lieutenant-General Sir George Prevost, Bart., Particularly of His Services in the Canadas; Including a Reply to the Strictures on His Military Character, Contained in an Article in the* Quarterly Review *for October, 1822.* London: T. Cadell and T. Egerton, 1823.

Brett-James, Anthony. *Wellington at War, 1794–1815: A Selection of His Wartime Letters.* London and New York: Macmillan, 1961.

Brewer, Willis. *Alabama: Her History, Resources, War Record, and Public Men.* Montgomery, AL: Barrett and Brown, 1872.

Brigham, Clarence, ed. "Letters of Abijah Bigelow, Member of Congress to His Wife, 1810–1815." *American Antiquarian Society Proceedings* 40 (1930): 305–406.

Brightfield, M. F. *John Wilson Croker.* Berkeley and Los Angeles: University of California Press, 1940.

Brighton, John G. *Admiral Sir Philip B. V Broke, bart., K. C. B.: A Memoir.* London: Low, Marston, 1866.

Brock, T. L. "Commissioner Robert Barrie and His Family in Kingston, 1819–1834." *Historic Kingston* 23 (1975): 1–18.

———. "H. M. Dock Yard, Kingston under Commissioner Robert Barrie, 1819–1834." *Historic Kingston* 16 (1968): 3–22.

———. "Sir Robert Barrie." In *Dictionary of Canadian Biography.* Vol. 7, *1836–1850.* Toronto: University of Toronto Press, 1979, 50–51.

Brooks, Charles B. *The Siege of New Orleans.* Seattle: University of Washington Press, 1961.

Broussard, James H. *The Southern Federalists, 1800–1816.* Baton Rouge: Louisiana State University Press, 1978.

Brown, Dorothy M. "Embargo Politics in Maryland." *Maryland Historical Magazine* 58 (1963): 193–210.

Brown, Jeffrey P. "The Ohio Federalist, 1803–1815." *Journal of the Early Republic* 2 (1982): 261–282.

Brown, Leon N. "Commodore Melancthon Taylor Woolsey: Lake Ontario Hero of the War of 1812." *Oswego Historical Society Journal* 5 (1941): 14–21.

Brown, Noah. "The Remarkable Statement of Noah Brown." *Journal of American History* 8 (1914): 103–108.

Brown, Roger H. *The Republic in Peril: 1812.* New York: Columbia University Press, 1964.

———. "The War Hawks of 1812: An Historical Myth." *Indiana Magazine of History* 60 (1964): 137–151.

Brown, Samuel R. *Views on Lake Erie.* Troy, NY: Francis Adancourt, 1814.

Brown, Wilburt S. *The Amphibious Campaign for West Florida and Louisiana. 1814–1815: A Critical Review of Strategy and Tactics at New Orleans.* University: University of Alabama Press, 1969.

Browne, Gary L. *Baltimore in the Nation, 1789–1861.* Chapel Hill: University of North Carolina Press, 1980.

Browne, James Alex. *England's Artillerymen.* London: Hall, Smart, and Allen, 1865.

Bruce, Henry. *Life of General Houston, 1793–1863.* New York: Dodd, Mead, 1891.

Bruce, William Cabell. *John Randolph of Roanoke, 1773–1833.* New York: G. P. Putnam's Sons, 1922; reprint, New York: Octagon Books, 1970.

Brymer, Douglas. "Capture of Fort McKay, Prairie du Chien, in 1814." *Wisconsin Historical Society Collections* 9 (1880–1881): 254–270.

Brynn, Edward. "Patterns of Dissent: Vermont's Opposition to the War of 1812." *Vermont History* 60 (1972): 10–27.

Bryon, Gilbert. *St. Michaels, the Town That Fooled the British.* Satern, MD: Eastern Publishing, 1963.

Buckie, Robert. "'His Majesty's Flag Has Not Been Tarnished': The Role of Robert Heriot Barclay." *Journal of Erie Studies* 17, no. 2 (fall 1988): 85–102.

Buckley, William E., ed. "Letters of Connecticut Federalists, 1814–1815." *New England Quarterly* 3 (1930): 316–331.

Buckner, Philip. "Sir John Harvey." In *Dictionary of Canadian Biography.* Vol. 7: *1836–1850.* Toronto: University of Toronto Press, 1979: 374–384.

Buell, Augustus C. *History of Andrew Jackson.* 2 vols. New York: Charles Scribner's Sons, 1904.

Bulger, Andrew. *An Autobiographical Sketch.* Bangalore, India: Regimental Press, 1865.

Burdick, Virginia Mason. *Captain Thomas Macdonough: Delaware Born Hero of the Battle of Lake Champlain.* Wilmington: Delaware Heritage Press, 1991.

Burnett, Kevin. "Tippecanoe and Taylor Too." *Journal of the West* 31 (1992): 44–50.

Burroughs, Peter. "Sir John Coape Sherbrooke." *Dictionary of Canadian Biography.* Vol. 6, *1821–1830.* Toronto: University of Toronto Press, 1979: 712–716.

Burt, Blanche A. "Sketch of Robert Heriot Barclay, R. N." *Ontario Historical Society Papers and Records* 14 (1916): 169–178.

Burton, Charles M. "The Fort Dearborn Massacre." *Magazine of American History* 18 (1912): 74–85.

Butler, Stuart Lee. *A Guide to Virginia Militia Units in the War of 1812.* Athens: University of Georgia Press, 1988.

Butler, William F. *Sir Charles James Napier.* London: Macmillan, 1890.

Byfield, Shadrach. "A Common Soldier's Account." In John Gellner, ed., *Recollections of the War of 1812: Three Eyewitness Accounts.* Toronto: Baxter Publishing, 1964.

Calderhead, William L. "Naval Innovation in Crisis: War in the Chesapeake 1813." *American Neptune* 36 (July 1976): 206–221.

Calloway, Colin G. *Crown and Calumet: British-Indian Relations, 1783–1815.* Norman: University of Oklahoma Press, 1987.

Campbell, Marjorie W. *The North West Company.* Vancouver: Douglas & McIntyre, 1957. Reprint, 1983.

Campbell, R. M. "The Copus Hill Tragedy." *Journal of American History* 16 (1922): 50–54.

Campbell, William W., ed. *Life and Writings of DeWitt Clinton.* New York: Baker, 1849.

Canada, National Parks Bureau. *Guide to Fort Wellington and Vicinity, Prescott, Ontario.* Ottawa: J. O. Patenaude, 1937.

Canney, Donald L. *The Old Steam Navy.* Vol. 1, *Frigates, Sloops, and Gunboats, 1815–1885.* Annapolis, MD: Naval Institute Press, 1990.

Cappon, Lesser J. "Who Is the Author of 'History of the Expedition under the Command of Captains Lewis and Clark' (1814)?" *William and Mary Quarterly* 19, no. 2 (1962): 257–268.

"Capture of Fort George." *Portfolio* 4 (1817): 3–8.

"Career of Daniel Dobbins now for the first time compiled from original documents," including "The Dobbins Papers, Early Days on the Lakes, and Episodes of the War of 1812, written by Captain William W. Dobbins from the Papers and Reminiscences of His Father," ed. Frank H. Severance. *Publications of the Buffalo Historical Society* 8 (1905): 257–379.

Carman, Francis A. "Châteauguay and De Salaberry: An Account of the Famous Campaign from De Salaberry's Own Letters." *Canadian Magazine* 42 (1913): 23–28.

Carr, Albert Z. *The Coming of War: An Account of the Remarkable Events Leading to the War of 1812.* Garden City, NY: Doubleday and Company, 1960.

Carson, Hampton L. *The Humphreys Family of Haverford and Philadelphia.* Lancaster: Wickersham Press, 1922.

Carter, Harvey Lewis. "A Frontier Tragedy: Little Turtle and William Wells." *The Old Northwest* 6 (1980): 3–18.

———. *The Life and Times of Little Turtle: First Sagamore of the Wabash.* Urbana and Chicago: University of Illinois Press, 1987.

Carter, Samuel. *Blaze of Glory: The Fight for New Orleans, 1814–1815.* London: Macmillan, 1971.

Carter-Edwards, Dennis. "The War of 1812 along the Detroit Frontier: A Canadian Perspective." *Michigan Historical Review* 13 (1987).

Cassell, Frank A. "The Great Baltimore Riot of 1812." *Maryland Historical Magazine* 70 (fall 1975): 241–259.

———. *Merchant Congressman in the Young Republic.* Madison: University of Wisconsin Press, 1971.

———. "Slaves of the Chesapeake Bay Area and the War of 1812." *Journal of Negro History* 57 (1972): 144–155.

Chambers, William Nisbet. *Old Bullion Benton: Senator from the New West. Thomas Hart Benton, 1782–1858.* Boston: Little, Brown, 1956.

Champagne, Raymond W., and Thomas J. Rueter. "Jonathan Roberts and the War Hawk Congress of 1812." *Pennsylvania Magazine of History and Biography* 115 (1980): 434–449.

Chandler, David. *The Campaigns of Napoleon.* London: Weidenfeld and Nicolson, 1967.

Chapelle, Howard I. *The History of the American Sailing Navy: The Ships and Their Development.* New York: W. W. Norton, 1949.

———. *The History of American Sailing Ships.* New York: W. W. Norton, 1935.

———. *The Search for Speed under Sail 1700–1855.* New York: W. W. Norton, 1967.

Charbonneau, Andre. *The Fortifications of Ile aux Noix: A Portrait of the Defensive Strategy on the Upper Richelieu Border in the 18th and 19th Centuries.* Canadian Heritage Parks Canada, 1994.

Chase, Philander D. "The Early Career of 'Light Horse Harry' Lee." Master's thesis, Duke University, 1968.

Chazanof, William. *Joseph Ellicott and the Holland Land Company: The Opening of Western New York.* Syracuse, NY: Syracuse University Press, 1970.

Checkland, S. G. "American versus West Indian Traders in Liverpool, 1793–1815." *Journal of Economic History* 17 (1958): 141–160.

"Chicago Massacre." In *Free Trade and Sailors' Rights: A Bibliography of the War of 1812.* Comp. John C. Fredriksen. Westport, CT: Greenwood Press, 1985.

Christie, Robert. *Memoirs of the Administration of the Colonial Government of Lower-Canada by Sir James Henry Craig, and Sir George Prevost: From the Year 1807 until the Year 1815, Comprehending the Military and Naval Operations in the Canadas during the Late War with the United States of America.* Quebec: N.p., 1818.

Claiborne, Nathaniel Herbert. *Notes on the War in the South; with Biographical Sketches of the Lives of Montgomery, Jackson, Sevier, and Late Gov. Claiborne, and Others.* Richmond, VA: William Ramsay, 1819.

Claiborne, W.C.C. *The Official Letter Books of W.C.C. Claiborne.* 6 vols. Jackson, MS: State Department of Archives and History, 1917.

Clark, George. "Military Operations at Castine, Maine." *Worcester Society of Antiquity* 18 (1899): 18–38.

Clark, James. *The British Leave Wisconsin: The War of 1812.* Madison: State Historical Society of Wisconsin, 1955.

Clark, Jennifer. "The War of 1812: American Nationalism and Rhetorical Images of Britain." *War and Society* 12 (1994).

Clark, Mary. "Willie Blount: Governor of Tennessee, 1809–1815." In *Governors of Tennessee I, 1790–1835,* ed. Charles W. Crawford. Memphis: Memphis State University Press, 1979.

Clark, Thomas D. *A History of Kentucky.* Lexington: University Press of Kentucky, 1960.

———. "Kentucky in the Northwest Campaign." In *After Tippecanoe: Some Aspects of the War of 1812,* ed. Philip P. Mason. East Lansing: Michigan State University Press, 1963.

Clark, Thomas D., and John D.W. Guice. *Frontiers in Conflict: The Old Southwest, 1795–1830.* Albuquerque: University of New Mexico Press, 1989.

Clarke, Dwight L. *Stephen Watts Kearny; Soldier of the West.* Norman: University of Oklahoma Press, 1961.

Clarke, Peter D. *Origin and Traditional History of the Wyandots.* Toronto: Hunter, Rose, 1870.

Clary, David A., and Joseph W. A. Whitehorne. *The Inspector General of the United States Army, 1777–1903.* Washington, DC: Office of the Inspector General and Center of Military History, 1987.

Cleaves, Freeman. *Old Tippecanoe: William Henry Harrison and His Time.* New York: Charles Scribner's Sons, 1939.

Clericus. "Biographical Sketch of Thomas ap Catesby Jones." *Military and Naval Magazine of the United States* 3 (1834): 27–34.

Clift, G. Glenn. *Remember the Raisin! Kentucky and Kentuckians in the Battles and Massacre at Frenchtown, Michigan Territory, in the War of 1812.* Frankfort, 1961; reprint, Baltimore: Genealogical Publishing, 1995.

———. "War of 1812 Diary of William B. Northcutt." *Register of the Kentucky Historical Society* 66 (1958): 325–344.

Cobbett, William. *Peter Porcupine in America.* Ithaca: Cornell University Press, 1994.

———. *The Autobiography of William Cobbett.* Ed. William Reitzel. London: Faber, 1933, 1967.

Cocke, John A. *A Letter to the Honorable John H. Eaton, Dec. 16, 1818.* Knoxville: Heiskell, Brown, 1819.

Coe, Charles H. *Red Patriots: The Story of the Seminoles.* 1898; reprint, Gainesville: University Presses of Florida, 1974.

Coit, Daniel. "The British Attack on Burlington." *Vermont History* 29 (1961): 82–86.

Coit, Margaret L. *John C. Calhoun: American Portrait.* New York: Houghton Mifflin, 1950.

Cogar, William B. *Dictionary of Admirals of the U.S. Navy.* Vol. 1, *1862–1900.* Annapolis, MD: Naval Institute Press, 1989.

Coker, William S. "The Last Battle of the War of 1812: New Orleans? No, Fort Bowyer!" *Alabama Historical Quarterly* 43, no. 1 (1981): 42–63.

Coker, William S., and Thomas D. Watson. *Indian Traders of the Southeastern Spanish Borderlands: Panton, Leslie and Co. and John Forbes and Co., 1783–1847.* Gainesville and Pensacola: University Presses of Florida and University of West Florida Press, 1986.

Cole, Donald B. *Martin Van Buren and the American Political System.* Princeton: Princeton University Press, 1984.

Cole, G.D.H. *The Life of William Cobbett.* London: Collins, 1924, 1947.

Coleman, Ann Mary Crittenden. *The Life of John J. Crittenden.* 2 vols. Philadelphia: J. B. Lippincott, 1871.

Coleman, Margaret. *The American Capture of Fort George, Ontario.* Ottawa: Department of Northern and Indian Affairs, 1977.

Coles, Harry L. *The War of 1812.* Chicago: University of Chicago Press, 1965.

Collins, Lewis, revised by Richard H Collins. *History of Kentucky.* 2 vols. Covington, KY: Collins and Co., 1874.

Combs, Leslie. *Col. Wm. Dudley's Defeat Opposite Fort Meigs. May 5th, 1813. Official Report from Captain Leslie Combs to General Green Clay.* Cincinnati: Spiller & Gates, 1869.

Compton, Smith C. *The Battle of Queenston Heights, U.C., October 1812: A Collection of Documents and Records Together with Factual Reports Dealing with the Events of the Day.* Toronto: McGraw-Hill, 1968.

"Conflagration of Havre de Grace." *North American Review* 5 (1817): 157–163.

Congreve, Sir William. *The Details of the Rocket System.* London: J. Whiting, 1814. Reprint, Ottawa: Ont. Museum Restoration Service, 1970.

Cook, Harvey T. *The Life and Legacy of David Rogerson Williams.* New York: Country Life Press, 1916.

Cooper, James F. *Lives of Distinguished Naval Officers.* 2 vol. Philadelphia: Carey, Hart, 1846.

———. "Melancthon Taylor Woolsey." *Graham's Magazine* 26 (1845): 14–21.

Copp, Walter Ronald. "Military Activities in Nova Scotia during the War of 1812." *Collections of the Nova Scotia Historical Society* 24 (1938): 57–58, 74.

———. "Nova Scotia Trade during the War of 1812." *Canadian Historical Review* 18 (June 1937): 141–155.

Cotterill, R. S. *The Southern Indians: The Story of the Civilized Tribes before Removal.* Norman: University of Oklahoma Press, 1954.

"Court Martial of Commander Robert Barclay, The: Important Documentary Evidence Concerning the Battle of Lake Erie Never Before Published." *Journal of American History* 8 (1914): 129–146.

Covington, James W. "The Negro Fort." *Gulf Coast Historical Review* 5 (spring 1990): 79–91.

———. *The Seminoles of Florida.* Gainesville: University Presses of Florida, 1993.

Crackel, Theodore J. *Mr. Jefferson's Army: Political and Social Reform of the Military Establishment, 1801–1809.* New York: New York University Press, 1987.

Craig, Gerald M. *Upper Canada: The Formative Years, 1784–1841.* Toronto: McClelland and Stewart, 1963.

Cramer, Clarence Henley. "The Career of Duncan McArthur." Ph.D. diss., Ohio State University, 1931.

Crane, Jay David, and Elaine Crane, eds. *The Black Soldier: From the American Revolution to Vietnam.* New York: William Morrow, 1971.

Crawford, Mary M., ed. "Journal of Mrs. Lydia Bacon." *Indiana Magazine of History* 40 (1944): 376–386.

Creason, Joe C. "The Battle of Tippecanoe." *Filson Club Quarterly* 36 (1962): 309–318.

Creighton, Don G. *The Commercial Empire of the St. Lawrence.* Toronto: Ryerson, 1937.

Crisman, Kevin James. *The Eagle, an American Brig on Lake Champlain during the War of 1812.* Shelburne, VT, and Annapolis, MD: New England Press and Naval Institute Press, 1987.

———. *The History and Construction of the United States Schooner Ticonderoga.* Alexandria, VA: Eyrie Publications, 1983.

Crockett, David. *A Narrative of the Life of David Crockett of the State of Tennessee.* Ed. James A. Shackford and Stanley J. Folmsbee. 1869; reprint, Knoxville: University of Tennessee Press, 1973.

Crouzet, François. "Bilan de l'économie britannique pendant les guerres de la Révolution et de l'empire." *Revue Historique* 234 (1965): 71–110.

———. *L'Economie Britannique et le Blocus Continental, 1806–1813.* 2 vols., 2nd ed. Paris: Economica, 1987.

———. "Groupes de pression et politique de blocus: Remarques sur les origines des Ordres en Conseil de novembre 1807." *Revue Historique* 228 (1962): 45–72.

———. "Wars, Blockade, and Economic Change in Europe, 1792–1815." *Journal of Economic History* 24, no. 4 (1964): 567–588.

Cruikshank, Ernest A. *The Battle of Fort George.* Niagara Falls, Ont.: Niagara Historical Society, 1904.

Cruikshank, Ernest A. "The Battle of Stoney Creek and the Blockade of Fort George." *Niagara Historical Society Transactions* 11 (1898): 15–31.

———. "The Capture of Mackinac, 1812," and "The Defence of Mackinac." *Canadian History Readings* 1 (1900): 158–163, 195–201.

———. "The Contest for the Command of Lake Ontario in 1812 and 1813." *Transactions of the Royal Society of Canada,* sec. 2, 3rd ser., 10 (September 1916): 165–188.

———. "The Contest for the Command of Lake Ontario in 1814." *Ontario Historical Society Papers and Records* 21 (1924): 99–159.

———. *Drummond's Winter Campaign, 1813.* Welland, Ont.: Lundy's Lane Historical Society, 1898.

———. "An Episode of the War of 1812: The Story of the Schooner *Nancy.*" *Ontario Historical Society Papers and Records* 9 (1910): 76–129.

———. "From Isle aux Noix to Châteauguay: A Study of Military Operations on the Frontier of Lower Canada in 1812 and 1813." *Proceedings of the Royal Society of Canada* 7 (1914): 129–173.

Cruikshank, Ernest A., ed. *The Documentary History of the Campaign upon the Niagara Frontier 1812–1814.* 9 vols. Welland, Ont.: Lundy's Lane Historical Society, 1896–1908.

———. *Documents Relating to the Invasion of Canada and the Surrender of Detroit 1812.* Ottawa: Government Printing Bureau, 1913.

Cullum, George W. *Campaigns of the War of 1812–15.* New York: James Miller, 1879.

Cumberland, Barlow. *The Battle of York.* Toronto: William Briggs, 1913.

Cunningham, Noble E., Jr. *In Pursuit of Reason: The Life of Thomas Jefferson.* Baton Rouge: Louisiana State University Press, 1987.

Cureton, Janet. "Catherine Lundy at the Battle of Lundy's Lane." *McLeans* (October 1960).

Curry, Frederick. "Little Gibraltar [Block Island]." *Ontario Historical Society Papers and Records* 33 (1939): 39–44.

Curti, Merle. *Peace or War: The American Struggle, 1636–1936.* New York: W. W. Norton, 1936.

Dale, Allen. "Châteauguay." *Canadian Geographic Journal* 11 (1935): 33–41.

Dallas, Alexander James. *Life and Writings of Alexander James Dallas.* Philadelphia: J. B. Lippincott, 1871.

Dameron, E.S.W. "William Rufus King." *University of North Carolina Magazine* 20 (1903): 317–322.

Darnell, Elias. *A Journal Containing an Accurate and Interesting Account of the Hardships . . . of . . . Kentucky Volunteers and Regulars Commanded by General Winchester in the Years 1812–1813. . . .* Philadelphia: Lippincott, Brambo, 1854.

Davidson, Charles Gordon. *The North West Company.* Publications in History, vol. 7. Berkeley: University of California,1918.

Davis, Dorothy. *John George Jackson.* Parsons, WV: McClain Printing Company, 1976.

Davis, Madison. "The Old Cannon Foundry above Georgetown, D.C., and Its First Owner, Henry Foxall." *Records of the Columbia Historical Society, Washington, D.C.* 2 (1908): 38–40.

Davis, Richard B., ed. *Jeffersonian America: Notes on the United States of America Collected in the Years 1805–6–7 and 11–12 by Sir Augustus Foster, Bart.* San Marino, CA: Huntington Library, 1954.

Davis, T. Frederick. "United States Troops in Spanish East Florida, 1812–1813." *Florida Historical Quarterly* 9 (1930): 3–23, 96–116, 135–155, 279–298.

Dawidoff, Robert. *The Education of John Randolph.* New York: W. W. Norton, 1979.

De Grummond, Jane Lucas. *The Baratarians and the Battle of New Orleans.* Baton Rouge, LA: Legacy Publishing, 1961.

———. *Renato Beluche: Smuggler, Privateer and Patriot, 1780–1860.* Baton Rouge: Louisiana State University Press, 1983.

Dearborn, Henry A.S. *The Life of William Bainbridge Esq., of the United States Navy.* Ed. James Barnes. Princeton: Princeton University Press, 1931.

Debates and Proceedings in the Congress of the United States...Twelfth Congress. Washington, DC: Gales and Seaton, 1853.

DeBenedetti, Charles. *The Peace Reform in American History.* Bloomington: Indiana University Press, 1980.

Debo, Angie. *The Road to Disappearance.* Norman: University of Oklahoma Press, 1941.

Derr, Emerson L. "Simon Snyder, Governor of Pennsylvania, 1800–1817." Ph.D. diss., Pennsylvania State University, 1960.

Derry, John W. *Castlereagh.* London: Lane, 1976.

DeWitt, John H. "General James Winchester, 1752–1826." *Tennessee Magazine* 1 (1915): 79–105, 183–205.

DeWitt, John H., ed. "Journal of John Sevier." *Tennessee Historical Magazine* 5 (1919): 156–194, 232–264; and 6 (1920): 18–68.

Dickinson, Henry W. *Robert Fulton—Engineer and Artist—His Life and Works.* New York: John Lane, 1913.

Dickore, Marie P., ed. *General Joseph Kerr of Chillicothe, Ohio.* Oxford, OH: Oxford Press, 1941.

Dillon, Richard. *We Have Met the Enemy: Oliver Hazard Perry, Wilderness Commodore.* New York: McGraw-Hill, 1978.

Dobbins, William W. *History of the Battle of Lake Erie and Reminiscences of the Flagships* Lawrence *and* Niagara. Erie, PA: Ashby Printing, 1913.

"Documents Relating to Colonel Edward Nicholls and Captain George Woodbine in Pensacola in 1814." *Florida Historical Quarterly* 10 (1931): 51–54.

Dodd, William E. *The Life of Nathaniel Macon.* Raleigh, NC: Edwards and Broughton, 1903.

Dolan, George R. "The Past and Present Fortification at Kingston." *Ontario Historical Society Papers and Records* 12 (1914): 72–80.

Donnan, Elizabeth, ed. *The Papers of James A. Bayard. Annual Report of the American Historical Association for the Year 1913.* Vol. 2. N.p., 1915.

Donovan, Frank. *The Odyssey of the Essex.* New York: David McKay, 1969.

Dorsheimer, William. "Buffalo during the War of 1812." *Buffalo Historical Society Publications* 1 (1879): 185–229.

Douglas, Marjory Stoneman. *Florida: The Long Frontier.* New York: Harper and Row, 1967.

Dowd, Gregory Evans. *A Spirited Resistance: The North American Indian Struggle for Unity, 1745–1815.* Baltimore: Johns Hopkins University Press, 1992.

Downey, Fairfax. *Cannonade.* New York: Doubleday, 1966.

———. *The Sound of the Guns.* New York: David McKay, 1955.

Drake, Frederick C. "Commodore Sir James Lucas Yeo and Governor General Sir George Prevost: A Study in Command Relations, 1813–1814." In William B. Cogar, ed., *New Interpretations in Naval History: Selected Papers from the Eighth Naval History Symposium.* Annapolis, MD: Naval Institute Press, 1989: 156–171.

———. "A Loss of Mastery: The British Squadron on Lake Erie, May–September, 1813." *Journal of Erie Studies* 17 (Fall 1988): 47–75.

———. "Sir John Borlase Warren." *Dictionary of Canadian Biography.* Vol. 6: *1821 to 1835.* Toronto: University of Toronto Press, 1979: 802–804.

———. *The War of 1812: Naval Operations.* Canadian Museum of Civilization, forthcoming.

Driver, Carl S. *John Sevier: Pioneer of the Old Southwest.* Chapel Hill: University of North Carolina Press, 1932.

Drugan, A. J. "Dan Dobbins—The Unsung Hero of the Battle

of Lake Erie." *Columbus Dispatch Magazine* (September 1963): 6–21.

Dudley W. Knox. "A Forgotten Fight in Florida." *United States Naval Institute Proceedings* 62 (April 1936): 507–513.

Dudley, William S. "Naval Historians and the War of 1812." *Naval History* 4 (spring 1990): 52–57.

Dudley, William S., and Michael S. Crawford, eds. *The Naval War of 1812: A Documentary History.* Washington, DC: Naval Historical Center, vol. 1, 1985; vol. 2, 1992.

Duncan, Francis. *History of the Royal Regiment of Artillery.* 2 vols. London: John Murray, 1873.

Dundonald, Thomas Cochrane. *Message from the President of the United States, Transmitting a Correspondence between Admiral Cockrane* [sic] *and the Secretary of State, in Relation to an Order of the Former to Destroy and Lay Waste the Towns on the Coasts of the United States.* Washington City: Printed by Roger C. Weightman, 1814.

Dunham, Chester G. "Christopher Hughes, Jr. at Ghent, 1814." *Maryland Historical Magazine* 66 (fall 1971): 288–299.

———. "The Diplomatic Career of Christopher Hughes." Ph. D. diss., Ohio State University, 1968.

Dunn, C. Frank. "Captain Nathaniel G.S. Hart." *Filson Club Historical Quarterly* 24 (1950): 28–33.

Dunn, Mary A. "The Career of Thomas Barclay." Ph.D. diss., Fordham University, 1974.

Dunne, W.M.P. "Pistols and Honor: The James Barron–Stephen Decatur Conflict, 1798–1807." *The American Neptune* 50, no. 4 (1990): 245–259.

Dunnell, Remark. *Barbarities of the Enemy Exposed in a Report of the Committee of the House of Representatives of the United States, Appointed to Enquire into the Spirit and Manner in Which the War Has Been Waged by the Enemy, and the Documents Accompanying Said Report.* Worcester, MA: Isaac Sturtevant, 1814.

Dunnigan, Brian. "The Battle of Mackinac Island." *Michigan History* 59 (1975): 239–254.

———. "The British Army at Mackinac, 1812–1815." *Reports in Mackinac History and Archaeology* 7 (1980).

———. "The Michigan Fencibles." *Michigan History* 57 (winter 1973): 277–295.

Dye, Ira. *The Fatal Cruise of the* Argus: *Two Captains in the War of 1812.* Annapolis, MD: United States Naval Institute, 1994.

Dyer, Brainerd. *Zachary Taylor.* Baton Rouge: Louisiana State University Press, 1946.

Eckert, Edward K. "Early Reform in the Navy Department" *American Neptune* 33 (October 1973): 231–245.

———. *The Navy Department in the War of 1812.* Gainesville: University Presses of Florida, 1973.

———. "Thomas Macdonough: Architect of a Wilderness Navy." In James C. Bradford, ed., *Command under Sail: Makers of the American Naval Tradition.* Annapolis, MD: Naval Institute Press, 1985

———. "William Jones: Mr. Madison's Secretary of the Navy." *The Pennsylvania Magazine of History and Biography* 96 (April 1972): 167–182.

Edmunds, R. David. *The Potawatomis, Keepers of the Fire.* Norman: University of Oklahoma Press, 1978.

———. *The Shawnee Prophet.* Lincoln: University of Nebraska Press, 1983.

———. *Tecumseh and the Quest for Indian Leadership.* Boston: Little, Brown, 1984.

———. "Tecumseh, the Shawnee Prophet, and American History: A Reassessment." *Western Historical Quarterly* 14 (1983): 261–276.

Edwards, Ninian Wirt. *History of Illinois from 1778 to 1833 and Life and Times of Ninian Edwards.* Springfield, IL: Illinois Journal Company, 1870.

Egan, Clifford L. *Neither Peace nor War: Franco-American Relations, 1803–1812.* Baton Rouge: Louisiana State University Press, 1983.

———. "The Path to War in 1812 through the Eyes of a New Hampshire 'War Hawk.'" *Historical New Hampshire* 30 (1975): 147–177.

Einstein, Lewis, ed. "Recollections of the War of 1812 by George Hay, Eighth Marquis of Tweedale." *American Historical Review* 32 (1926): 69–78.

Ekirch, Arthur A., Jr. *The Civilian and the Military.* New York: Oxford University Press, 1956.

Eller, E. M. *Sea Power and the Battle of New Orleans.* N.p.: 1965.

Eller, E. M., W. J. Morgan, and R. M. Basoco. *The Battle of New Orleans: Sea Power and the Battle of New Orleans.* New Orleans: Battle of New Orleans, 150th Anniversary Committee of Louisiana, 1965.

Elliot, Jesse. *A Biographical Notice of Commodore Jesse D. Elliott ... Containing a Review of the Controversy between Him and the Late Commodore Perry.* N.p., 1835.

———. *Address ... delivered, November 14, 1843, in Washington County, Maryland ... to His Early Companions, with an Appendix of Historical Facts and Documents.* N.p., 1844.

Elliot, T. C. "Sale of Astoria, 1813." *Oregon Historical Quarterly* 33 (March 1932): 43–50.

Elliott, Charles W. "The Indispensable Conquest." *Infantry Journal* 45 (July-August 1938): 334–342.

———. *Winfield Scott: The Soldier and the Man.* New York: Macmillan, 1937.

Ellison, David. "David Wingfield and Sacket's [sic] Harbor." *Dalhousie Review* 52 (1972): 407–413.

Elting, John. *Amateurs, to Arms! A Military History of the War of 1812.* Chapel Hill: Algonquin Books of Chapel Hill, 1991.

Emery, William M. *Colonel George Claghorn, Builder of the* Constitution. New Bedford, MA: Old Dartmouth Historical Society, 1931.

Emmerson, John C., Jr. *The* Chesapeake *Affair of 1807: An Objective Account of the Attack by HMS* Leopard *upon the U.S. Frigate* Chesapeake *off Cape Henry, Va., June 22, 1807, and Its Repercussions.* Portsmouth, VA: privately printed, 1954.

Emmerson, John C., Jr., comp. *War in the Lower Chesapeake & Hampton Roads Area, 1812–1815, as Reported in the* Norfolk Gazette & Publick Ledger *& the* Norfolk & Portsmouth Herald. Portsmouth, VA: N.p., 1946.

Emmons, William. *Authentic Biography of Colonel Richard M. Johnson of Kentucky.* New York: H. Mason, 1833.

Engleman, Fred L. *The Peace of Christmas Eve*. New York: Harcourt, Brace and World, 1962.

Ermatinger, C. O. "The Retreat of Procter and Tecumseh." *Ontario Historical Society Papers and Records* 17 (1919): 11–21.

Ernst, Robert. "The Aftermath: Rufus King, Violence, and the Reputation of the New Republic." *Journal of Long Island History* 10 (1973): 14–28.

———. *Rufus King, American Federalist*. Chapel Hill: University of North Carolina Press, 1968.

Errington, Jane. "British American Kingstonians and the War of 1812." *Historic Kingston* 32 (January 1984): 35–45.

———. "Friends and Foes: The Kingston Elite and the War of 1812: A Case Study in Ambivalence." *Journal of Canadian Studies* 29 (spring 1985): 58–79.

Esarey, Logan, ed. *Messages and Letters of William Henry Harrison*. Vol. 2. New York: Arno Press, 1975.

Estes, J. Worth. *Dictionary of Protopharmacology: Therapeutic Practices, 1700–1850*. Canton, MA: Science History Publications, 1990.

Evans, Sir George De Lacy. *Facts Relating to the Capture of Washington, In Reply to Some Statements Contained in the Memoirs of Admiral Sir George Cockburn, G.C.B.* London: H. Colburn, 1829.

Everest, Allan S. *British Objectives at the Battle of Plattsburg*. Champlain, NY: Moorsfield Press, 1960.

———. *The War of 1812 in the Champlain Valley*. Syracuse, NY: Syracuse University Press, 1981.

Ewing, Frank E. *America's Forgotten Statesman, Albert Gallatin*. New York: Vantage Press, 1959.

Ewing, Robert. "Portrait of General Robert Armstrong." *Tennessee Historical Magazine* 5 (July 1919): 75–80.

Fahey, Curtis. *In His Name: The Anglican Experience in Upper Canada, 1791–1854*. Ottawa: Carleton University Press, 1991.

Falconer's Marine Dictionary (1780). Newton Abbot: David Charles Reprints, 1970.

Faye, Stanley. "The Great Stroke of Pierre Lafitte." *Louisiana Historical Quarterly* 23 (1940): 733–826.

Fee, Walter. *The Transition from Aristocracy to Democracy in New Jersey, 1789–1826*. Somerville, NJ: Somerset Press, 1933.

Ferguson, Roger J. "The White River Indiana Delawares: An Ethnohistoric Synthesis, 1795–1867." Ed.D. diss., Ball State University, 1972.

Filby, P. W., and Edward G. Howard. *Star-Spangled Books*. Baltimore: Maryland Historical Society, 1972.

Fink, William Bertrand. "Stephen Van Rensselaer: The Last Patroon." Ph.D. diss., Columbia University, 1950.

Fischer, David Hackett. *The Revolution of American Conservatism: The Federalist Party in the Era of Jeffersonian Democracy*. New York: Harper & Row, 1965.

Fish, Frank L. "Jeremiah Mason." *American Law Review* 53 (1919): 269–284.

Fitzgibbon, James. *An Appeal to the People of the Late Province of Upper Canada*. Montreal: N.p., 1847.

Fitzgibbon, Mary A. *A Veteran of 1812: The Life of James Fitzgibbon*. Toronto: William Briggs, 1894. Reprint, 1972.

Flandrau, Grace. *Astor and the Oregon Country*. St. Paul, MN: Great Northern Railway, 1926.

Flournoy, H. W., ed. *Calendar of Virginia State Papers*. Vol. 10: 1 January 1808–31 December 1835. Richmond: N.p., 1892.

Foley, William E. *The Genesis of Missouri: From Wilderness Outpost to Statehood*. Columbia: University of Missouri Press, 1989.

———. *A History of Missouri*. Columbia: University of Missouri Press, 1971.

Foner, Jack D. *Blacks and the Military in American History: A New Perspective*. New York: Praeger, 1974.

Footner, Hulbert. *Sailor of Fortune: The Life and Adventures of Commodore Barney, U.S.N.* New York: Harper, 1940.

Ford, Arthur L. *Joel Barlow*. New York: Twayne, 1971.

Ford, Chauncey Worthington, ed. *The Writings of John Quincy Adams*. 7 vols. New York: Macmillan, 1913–1917.

Ford, Lacy K. *Origins of Southern Radicalism*. New York: Oxford University Press, 1988.

Forester, Cecil S. *The Age of Fighting Sail: The Story of the Naval War of 1812*. Garden City, NY: Doubleday, 1956.

Fort George. Ottawa: Parks Canada, 1979.

Fortescue, J. W. *A History of the British Army*. Vol. 10. London: Macmillan, 1920.

Foster, Vere, ed. *The Two Duchesses: Georgiana, Duchess of Devonshire, Elizabeth, Duchess of Devonshire*. New York: Charles Scribner's Sons, 1898.

Fowler, William C. "Isaac Chauncey." *Memorials of the Chauncey Family*. Vol. 1. Boston: W. H. Dutton, 1894.

Fowler, William M., Jr. *Jack Tars and Commodores: The American Navy, 1783–1815*. Boston: Houghton Mifflin, 1984.

———. *William Ellery: A Rhode Island Politico and Lord of Admiralty*. Metuchen, NJ: Scarecrow Press, 1973.

Foytik, Rodney C. "Aspects of the Military Life of Troops Stationed around the Norfolk Harbor, 1812 to 1814." *The Chesopiean* 22 (1984): 12–20.

Frame, Nat. "The Battle of Sandy Creek and Carrying the Cables for the 'Superior.'" *Jefferson County Historical Society Transactions* 3 (1895): 32–40.

Francere, Gabriel. *Adventures at Astoria, 1810–1814*. Norman: University of Oklahoma Press, 1967.

———. *Journal of a Voyage to the North West Coast of North America during the Years, 1811, 1812, 1813 and 1814*. Vol. 45. Ed. W. Kaye Lamb. Toronto: Champlain Society, 1969.

Franklin, John Hope. *From Slavery to Freedom: A History of Negro Americans*. 4th ed. New York: Alfred A. Knopf, 1974.

Fraser, Edward, and L. G. Carr-Laughton. *The Royal Marine Artillery: 1804–1923*. London: The Royal United Services Institution, 1930.

Frater, Daniel A. "Impressment in the 18th Century Anglo-American World." Master's thesis, Queens College, New York, 1995.

Frazier, Arthur H. "The Military Frontier: Fort Dearborn." *Chicago History* 9 (1980): 80–85.

Fredriksen, John C. "Niagara, 1814: The American Quest for Tactical Parity in the War of 1812 and Its Legacy." Ph.D. diss., Providence College, 1993.

———. *Officers of the War of 1812*. Lewiston, New York: Edwin Mellan Press, 1989.

Fredriksen, John C., comp. *Free Trade and Sailors' Rights: A Bibliography of the War of 1812*. Westport, CT: Greenwood Press, 1985.

Fredriksen, John C., ed. "The Memoirs of Jonathan Kearsley." *Indiana Military History Journal* 10 (1985): 4–16.

Fritz, Harry. "The War Hawks of 1812." *Capitol Studies* 5 (spring 1977): 25–42.

Frost, John. *The Pictorial Book of the Commodores: Comprising Lives of Distinguished Commanders*. New York: Nafis and Cornish, 1845.

Furlong, William R., and Byron McCandless. *So Proudly We Hail: The History of the United States Flag*. Washington, DC: Smithsonian Institution Press, 1981.

Gaines, Edward E. "George Cranfield Berkeley and the *Chesapeake-Leopard* Affair of 1807." In *America in the Middle Period: Essays in Honor of Bernard Mayo*, ed. John Bales. Charlottesville: University of Virginia Press, 1973.

Gaines, Pierce W. *William Cobbett and the U.S., 1792–1835*. Worcester: American Antiquarian, 1971.

Galbreath, Charles B. *History of Ohio*. 5 vols. Chicago: The American Historical Society, 1925.

Gallatin, Albert. *The Papers of Albert Gallatin*. Philadelphia: Historical Publications, 1969.

Galpin, W. Freeman. "The American Grain Trade to the Spanish Peninsula, 1810–1814." *American Historical Review* 28 (October 1922): 29–33.

Gapp, Frank W. "'The Kind-Eyed Chief': Forgotten Champion of Hawaii's Freedom." *Hawaiian Journal of History* 19 (1985): 101–121.

Gardiner, Robert, ed. *The Line of Battle*. Annapolis, MD: Naval Institute Press, 1992.

Gardner, Charles K. *Trial by Court-Martial*. Boston: N.p., 1816.

Garitee, Jerome R. *The Republic's Private Navy: The American Privateering Business as Practiced by Baltimore during the War of 1812*. Middletown, CT: Wesleyan University Press, 1977.

Garret, William R., ed. "Report of General Andrew Jackson to Governor Willie Blount. 'Battle of Tehopiska or the Horseshoe.'" *American History Magazine* 4 (1899): 291–296.

Gash, Norman. *Lord Liverpool: The Life and Political Career of Robert Banks Jenkinson, second Earl of Liverpool, 1770–1828*. London: Weidenfeld and Nicolson, 1984.

Gayarre, Charles. "Historical Sketch of Pierre and Jean Lafitte: The Famous Smugglers of Louisiana." *Magazine of American History* 10 (1883).

"General William H. Winder." *Genealogical Magazine and Historical Chronicle* 21 (1919): 217–219.

Gentleman's Magazine. 1839, Part ii, 650.

Gentleman's Magazine, January-June 1830, 558–559.

George, Christopher T. "Mirage of Freedom: African Americans in the War of 1812." *Maryland Historical Magazine* 91 (winter 1996).

Gilbert, Bil. *God Gave Us This Country: Tekamthi and the First American Civil War*. New York: Atheneum, 1989.

Gillett, Mary C. *The Army Medical Department 1775–1818*. Washington, DC: Center of Military History, U.S. Army, 1981.

Gillmer, Thomas C. *Pride of Baltimore: The Story of the Baltimore Clippers, 1800–1990*. Camden, ME: International Marine, 1992.

Gilmer, George R. *Sketches of Some of the First Settlers of Upper Georgia, of the Cherokees, and the Author*. New York: D. Appleton, 1855; reprint, Americus, GA: Americus Book Co., 1926.

Gilmore, J. R. *John Sevier as a Commonwealth-Builder*. New York: Appleton, 1894.

Gilmore, William E. "General Joseph Kerr." *Ohio Archaeological and Historical Society Publications* 12 (January 1903): 164–166.

Gilpin, Alec R. *General William Hull and the War on the Detroit in 1812*. Ann Arbor: University of Michigan, 1949.

———. *The Territory of Michigan, 1805–1837*. East Lansing: Michigan State University Press, 1970.

———. *The War of 1812 in the Old Northwest*. East Lansing: Michigan State University Press, 1958.

Gleaves, Albert. *James Lawrence: American Man of Energy*. New York: G. P. Putnam's Sons, 1904.

———. *James Lawrence, Captain, U.S. Navy: Commander of the Chesapeake*. New York: Putnam, 1904.

Gleig, George R. *The Campaigns of the British Army at Washington and New Orleans in the Years 1814–1815*. London: John Murray, 1836, 1847.

Goldenberg, Joseph A. "Blue Lights and Infernal Machines: The British Blockade of New London." *Mariner's Mirror* 61 (November, 1975): 385–397.

Golder, F. A. "The Russian Offer of Mediation in the War of 1812." *Political Science Quarterly* 31 (September 1916): 360–391.

Goldowsky, Seebert J. *Yankee Surgeon: The Life and Times of Usher Parsons, 1788–1868*. Boston: Francis A. Countway Library of Medicine, 1988.

Goltz, Herbert. "Tecumseh: The Man and the Myth." Ph.D. diss., University of Western Ontario, 1973.

Gomola, Christopher Ira. "Bright Victory Wasted." *Military History* 7 (1990): 30–37.

Goodwin, Daniel. *The Dearborns*. Chicago: Fergus Printing, 1884.

Gosling, D. C. "The Battle of La Colle Mill, 1814." *Journal of the Society for Army Historical Research* 47 (1969): 169–174.

Gough, Barry M. *The Royal Navy and the North West Coast of North America, A Study of British Maritime Ascendancy, 1810–1914*. Vancouver: University of British Columbia Press, 1971.

Govern, Thomas Pain. *Nicholas Biddle, Nationalist and Public Banker, 1786–1844*. Chicago: University of Chicago Press, 1959.

Graham, A. A. *History of Richland County*. N.p., 1880.

Graham, Gerald S. *Seapower and British North America, 1783–1820: A Study in British Colonial Policy*. Cambridge: Harvard University Press, 1941.

Grant, Bruce. *American Forts*. New York: E. P. Dutton, 1965.

———. *Captain of Old Ironsides*. Chicago: Pellegrini and Cudahy, 1947.

Graves, Donald E. *The Battle of Lundy's Lane: On the Niagara in*

1814. Baltimore, MD: Nautical and Aviation Publishing Company of America, 1993.

———. *Sir William Congreve and the Rocket's Red Glare.* Bloomfield, Ont.: Museum Restoration Service, 1989.

Graves, Donald E., ed. *Merry Hearts Make Light Days: The War of 1812 Journal of Lieutenant John Le Couteur, 104th Foot.* Ottawa: Carleton University Press, 1993.

Gray, Elma. *Wilderness Christians.* Toronto: Macmillan, 1956.

Gray, Marlesa A. *The Archaeological Investigations of Fort Knox II, Knox County, Indiana, 1803–1813.* Indianapolis: Indiana Historical Society, 1988.

Green, Ernest. "Some Graves on Lundy's Lane." *Publications of the Niagara Historical Society* 22 (1911): 4–6.

Green, Michael D. *The Politics of Indian Removal: Creek Government and Society in Crisis.* Lincoln: University of Nebraska Press, 1982.

Gregg, Kate. "The War of 1812 on the Missouri Frontier." *Missouri Historical Review* 33: 3–22, 184–202, 326–348.

Grenon, Hector. *Canadian Battles: De Salaberry's Victory at Châteauguay.* Ottawa: National Defence Headquarters Library, 1943

Grenville, Richard. *Memoirs of the Court and Cabinets of George the III.* 4 vols. London: Hurst and Blackett, 1853–1855.

Griffin, G. W. *Memoir of Colonel Charles S. Todd.* Philadelphia: Claxton, Remsen, Haffelfinger, 1874.

Griffith, Benjamin W., Jr. *McIntosh and Weatherford, Creek Indian Leaders.* Tuscaloosa: University of Alabama Press, 1988.

Guitard, Michelle. "Irumberry de Salaberry, Charles-Michel D'." *Dictionary of Canadian Biography.* Vol. 6, *1821–1835.* Toronto: University of Toronto Press, 1979: 341–345.

———. *The Militia of the Battle of the Châteauguay.* Ottawa: Parks Canada, 1983.

Gurwood, John, comp. *The Dispatches of Field Marshall the Duke of Wellington, K.G. during his Various Campaigns in India, Denmark, Portugal, Spain, the Low Countries, and France. From 1799 to 1818. Compiled from official and authentic documents.* London: J. Murray, 1839.

Guttridge, Leonard F., and Jay D. Smith. *The Commodores.* New York: Harper and Row, 1969.

Haeger, John D. *John Jacob Astor: Business and Finance in the Early Republic.* Detroit: Wayne State University Press, 1991.

Hagan, Horace H. "The Greatest American Lawyer." *Case and Comment* 22 (1916): 87–96.

Hagan, William T. *The Sac and Fox Indians.* Norman: University of Oklahoma Press, 1958.

Halbert, H. S., and T. H. Ball. *The Creek War of 1813 and 1814.* Chicago: Donohue and Henneberry, 1895; reprint, Tuscaloosa: University of Alabama Press, 1969.

Hall, Amos. "Militia Service of 1812–1814 as Shown by the Correspondence of Major General Amos Hall." *Buffalo Historical Society Publications* 5 (1902): 26–62.

Hall, Charles S. *Benjamin Tallmadge.* New York: Columbia University Press, 1943.

Hallahan, John M. *The Battle of Craney Island.* Portsmouth, VA: Saint Michael's Press, 1986.

Haller, Willis C., Gerard Hoard, and Robert Marshall. *The Building of Chauncey's Fleet.* N.p., 1983.

Hamer, Marguerite B. "John Rhea of Tennessee." *East Tennessee Historical Society Publications* 3 (1932): 35–44.

Hamil, Fred C. "Michigan in the War of 1812." *Michigan History* 44 (1960): 257–291.

Hamilton, Henry R. "Fort Dearborn Massacre." In *The Epic of Chicago.* Chicago: Willett, Clark, 1932.

Hamilton, Holman. *Three Kentucky Presidents—Lincoln, Taylor, and Davis.* Lexington: University Press of Kentucky, 1978.

———. *Zachary Taylor, Soldier of the Republic.* Hamden, CT: Archon Books, 1966.

Hammock, James Wallace, Jr. *Kentucky and the Second American Revolution.* Lexington: University Press of Kentucky, 1976.

Hammond, Bray. *Banks and Politics in America from the Revolution to the Civil War.* Princeton: Princeton University Press, 1957.

Hammond, Hans, ed. "Letters of John Taylor of Caroline." *Virginia Magazine of History and Biography* 52 (1944): 1–14, 121–134.

Hannay, James. *History of New Brunswick.* Saint John, N.B.: J. A. Bowes, 1909.

Hanson, George A. *Old Kent: The Eastern Shore of Maryland.* Baltimore: John P. Des Forges, 1876.

Harden, Edward J. *The Life of George M. Troup.* Savannah, GA: E. J. Durse, 1859.

Harland, John. *Seamanship in the Age of Sail.* Annapolis, MD: Naval Institute Press, 1987.

Harrell, David E. "James Winchester, Patriot." *Tennessee Historical Quarterly* 17 (1958): 301–317.

Harrington, Gordon K. "The American Naval Challenge to the English East India Company during the War of 1812." In Jack Sweetman et al., eds., *New Interpretations in Naval History,* selected papers from the Tenth Naval History Symposium, United States Naval Academy, 11–13 September 1991. Annapolis, MD: Naval Institute Press, 1993: 144–145.

Harris, Thomas. *The Life and Services of Commodore William Bainbridge, United States Navy.* Philadelphia: Carey Lea and Blanchard, 1837.

Hartmann, Gregory K., with Scott C. Truver. *Weapons That Wait: Mine Warfare in the U.S. Navy.* Annapolis, MD: Naval Institute Press, 1991.

Harvey, A. D. "European Attitudes to Britain during the French Revolutionary and Napoleonic Era." *History* 63 (1978): 356–365.

Harvey, D. C. "The Halifax-Castine Expedition." *Dalhousie Review* 18 (spring 1938–1939): 207–213.

Hassler, Warren W., Jr. *With Shield and Sword: American Military Affairs, Colonial Times to the Present.* Ames: Iowa State University Press, 1982.

Hatcher, William B. *Edward Livingston: Jeffersonian Republican and Jacksonian Democrat.* University: Louisiana State University Press, 1940.

Hatfield, Joseph T. *William Claiborne: Jeffersonian Centurion in the American Southwest.* Lafayette: University of Southwestern Louisiana, 1976.

Hatzenbuehler, Ronald L. *Congress Declares War: Rhetoric, Leadership, and Partisanship in the Early Republic.* Kent, OH: Kent State University Press, 1983.

———. "Party Unity and the Decision for War in the House of Representatives, 1812." *William and Mary Quarterly* 29 (1972): 367–392.

———. "The War Hawks and the Question of Congressional Leadership in 1812." *Pacific Historical Review* 45 (1976): 1–22.

Havinghurst, Walter. *Three Flags at the Straits: The Forts of Mackinac.* Englewood Cliffs, NJ: Prentice-Hall, 1966.

Hawk, Robert. *Florida's Army: Militia, State Troops, National Guard, 1565–1985.* Englewood, FL: Pineapple Press, 1986.

Hay, Thomas Robson, and M. R. Werner. *The Admirable Trumpeter: A Biography of General James Wilkinson.* Garden City: Doubleday, Doran, 1941.

Hayes, George H., ed. "Letters of Samuel Taggart, Representative in Congress, 1802–1814." *American Antiquarian Society Proceedings* 33 (1924): 390–440.

Heaton, Herbert. "Non-importation, 1806–1812." *Journal of Economic History* 1 (November 1941): 178–198.

Heaton, John L. *The Story of Vermont.* Boston: Lothrop, 1889.

Hecksher, Eli F. *The Continental System: An Economic Interpretation,* ed. H. Westerguard, trans. C. S. Fearenside. Oxford: Clarendon Press, 1922.

Heidler, David S., and Jeanne T. Heidler. *Old Hickory's War: Andrew Jackson and the Quest for Empire.* Mechanicsburg, PA: Stackpole Books, 1996.

Heiskel, S. G. "'Diary,' or Journal of John Sevier." In *Andrew Jackson and Early Tennessee History.* Vol. 2. Nashville: Ambrose Printing, 1920.

Heitman, F. B. *Historical Register and Dictionary of the United States Army.* Baltimore, MD: Genealogical Publishing, 1903.

———. *Historical Register of the United States Army.* Washington, DC: National Tribune, 1890.

Henderson, John H.L. *John Strachan, 1778–1867.* Quebec: Presses de l'Universite Laval, 1970.

Henderson, J.H.L., ed. *John Strachan: Documents and Opinions.* Toronto: McClelland and Stewart Limited, 1969.

Henderson, William A. *"Nolachucky Jack," Lecture of William A. Henderson to the Board of Trade of the City of Knoxville.* Knoxville: Press and Herald, 1873.

Henkels, Stanislaus V. *The Correspondence of Commodore David Conner, U.S. Navy during the War of 1812 and Mexican War.* Philadelphia: Self-published, 1914.

Henri, Florette. *The Southern Indians and Benjamin Hawkins, 1796–1816.* Norman: University of Oklahoma Press, 1986.

Hickey, Donald R. "American Trade Restrictions during the War of 1812." *Journal of American History* 68 (December 1981): 517–538.

———. "The Darker Side of Democracy: The Baltimore Riots of 1812." *Maryland Historian* 7 (1976): 1–14.

———. "New England's Defense Problem and the Genesis of the Hartford Convention." *New England Quarterly* 50 (December 1977): 587–604.

———. *The War of 1812: A Forgotten Conflict.* Urbana: University of Illinois Press, 1989.

Hill, F. Stanhope. *The "Lucky Little" Enterprise" and Her Successors in the United States Navy, 1776–1900.* Boston: F. Stanhope Hill, 1900.

Hill, Henry W. "Otter Creek in History." *Vermont Historical Society Proceedings* 8 (1913–1914): 138.

Hinde, Wendy. *George Canning.* London: Collins, 1973.

Hitsman, J. Mackay. "David Parrish and the War of 1812." *Military Affairs* 26 (winter 1962–1963): 171–177.

———. *The Incredible War of 1812: A Military History.* Toronto: University of Toronto Press, 1972.

———. "Sir George Prevost's Conduct of the Canadian War of 1812." *Canadian Historical Association Report* (1962): 34–43.

Hoard, Gerard C. *Major General Jacob Jennings Brown.* Watertown, NY: Hungerford, Holbrook, 1979.

Hoge, William A. "The British Are Coming. … Up the Potomac." *Northern Neck Historical Magazine* 14 (December 1964): 1269.

Hogg, Ian, and John Batchelor. *Naval Gun.* Poole: Blandford Press, 1978.

Hogg, O.F.G. *Artillery: Its Origin, Heyday, and Decline.* London: Hurst and Company, 1970.

Holden, Robert J. "General James Miller, Collector of the Port of Salem, Massachusetts, 1825–1849." *Essex Institute Collections* 104 (1968).

———. "Ninian Edwards and the War of 1812: The Military Role of a Territorial Governor." *Selected Papers in Illinois History, 1980.* Springfield, IL: Illinois State Historical Society, 1980.

Holland, James W. "Andrew Jackson and the Creek War: Victory at the Horseshoe." *The Alabama Review* 21 (October 1968): 243–275.

———. *Andrew Jackson and the Creek War: Victory at the Horseshoe.* Tuscaloosa: University of Alabama Press, 1969.

Hollon, W. Eugene. *The Lost Pathfinder: Zebulon Montgomery Pike.* Norman: University of Oklahoma Press, 1949.

Holt, Glen E. "After the Journey Was Over: The St. Louis Years of Lewis and Clark." *Gateway Heritage* 2 (fall 1981): 42–48.

Homfray. Irving L. *Officers of the British Forces in Canada during the War of 1812–15.* Welland, Ont.: Welland Tribune print, 1908.

"Hon. Joseph R. Underwood." *American Review* 7 (1848): 609–614.

Hopkins, Fred W. *Tom Boyle, Master Privateer.* Cambridge, MD: Tidewater Press, 1976.

Hopkins, James F., ed. *The Papers of Henry Clay.* Vol. 1, *The Rising Statesman, 1797–1814;* Vol. 2, *The Rising Statesman, 1815–1820.* Lexington: University of Kentucky Press, 1959 and 1961.

Horrid Massacre at Dartmoor Prison. Boston: Nathaniel Conerly, 1815.

Horsman, Reginald. "British Indian Policy in the Northwest, 1897–1812." *Mississippi Valley Historical Review* 45 (1958–1959): 51–66.

———. *The Causes of the War of 1812*. Philadelphia: University of Pennsylvania Press, 1962.

———. *Matthew Elliott: British Indian Agent*. Detroit: Wayne State University Press. 1964.

———. "Nantucket's Peace Treaty with England in 1814." *New England Quarterly* 54 (1981): 180–198.

———. "The Paradox of Dartmoor Prison." *American Heritage* 26, no. 2 (February 1975): 13–17

———. "The Role of the Indian in the War of 1812." In Philip P. Mason, ed., *After Tippecanoe: Some Aspects of the War of 1812*. East Lansing: Michigan State University Press, 1963.

———. *The War of 1812*. New York: Knopf, 1969.

———. "Who Were the War Hawks?" *Indiana Magazine of History* 60 (June 1964): 122–136.

Houck, Lewis. *A History of Missouri*. 3 vols. Chicago: R. R. Donnelly and Sons, 1908.

Houston, Samuel. *The Autobiography of Sam Houston*. Norman: University of Oklahoma Press, 1954.

Houtz, Harry E. "Abner Lacock." Master's thesis, University of Pittsburgh, 1937.

Howard, Frank. *Sailing Ships of War, 1400–1860*. New York: Mayflower Books, 1979.

Howard, Oliver Otis. *General Taylor*. New York: D. Appleton: 1892.

Howarth, David. *Trafalgar: The Nelson Touch*. London: World Books, 1970.

Howe, Henry. *Historical Collections of Ohio*. 2 vols. Cincinnati: C. J. Krehbiel, 1904.

Hoyt, William D. "Civilian Defense in Baltimore, 1814–1815." *Maryland Historical Magazine* 39 (1944): 7–23.

Hughes, B. P. *Honor Titles of the Royal Artillery*. Woolwich: Royal Artillery Institution, 1974.

———. *Open Fire: Artillery Tactics from Marlborough to Wellington*. Strettington, Sussex, England: Antony Bird Publications, 1983.

Hughes, J. Patrick. "The Adjutant General's Office, 1821–1861: A Study in Administrative History." Ph.D. diss., Ohio State University, 1977.

Hughes, Maj. Gen. B. P. *Honor Titles of the Royal Artillery*. Woolwich: Royal Artillery Institute, 1974.

Hull, William. *Memoirs of the Campaign of the North Western Army in the Year 1812: Addressed to the People of the United States*. Boston: Boston Statesman, 1824.

Humphries, B. "Sir Alexander Cochrane and the Conclusion of the American War, 1814–1815." Master's thesis, Liverpool University, 1960.

Humphries, Charles W. "The Capture of York." *Ontario History* 51 (winter 1959): 1–24.

Hunt, Carleton. *Life and Services of Edward Livingston: Address of Carleton Hunt, May 9, 1903*. New Orleans: J. G. Hauser, 1903.

Hunt, Charles Havens. *Life of Edward Livingston*. New York: D. Appleton, 1864.

Huntt, Henry. "An Abstract Account of the Diseases Which Prevailed among the Soldiers, Received into the General Hospital, at Burlington, Vermont, during the Summer and Autumn of 1814." *American Medical Recorder* 1 (1818): 176–179.

———. *American Medical Recorder* 1 (1818): 365–366.

Hussey, John A., ed. *The Voyage of the "Racoon": A "Secret" Journal of a Visit to Oregon, California and Hawaii, 1813–1814* [by Francis Phillips]. San Francisco: Book Club of California, 1958.

Hutcheson, Wallace S., Jr. *Robert Fulton: Pioneer of Undersea Warfare*. Annapolis, MD: Naval Institute Press, 1981.

Hutton, Paul A. "William Wells: Frontier Scout and Indian Agent." *Indiana Magazine of History* 74 (1978): 183–222.

Hyatt, A.M.J. "Henry Procter." In *Dictionary of Canadian Biography*. Vol. 6, *1821–1835*. Toronto: University of Toronto Press, 1979.

Ilisevich, Robert D. *Daniel Dobbins: Frontier Mariner*. Erie, PA: Crawford County Historical Society Publications, 1993.

Ingraham, George. "The Story of Laura Secord Revisited." *Ontario History* 57 (1965): 85–97.

Inquiry into the Present State of the British Navy Together with Reflections on the Late War with America, Its Probable Consequences, andc. andc. andc, An. London: C. Chapple, printed by W. M'Dowall, 1815.

Irvine, John B. "The Role of Sir James Lucas Yeo in the War of 1812." Master's thesis, Carleton University, 1958.

Irving, Washington. *Astoria*. Vol. 3. London: R. Bentley, 1836.

Irwin, Ray W. *Daniel D. Tompkins: Governor of New York and Vice President of the United States*. New York: New York Historical Society, 1968.

Izard, George. "The War of 1812 in Northern New York: General George Izard's Journal of the Châteauguay Campaign." *New York History* (April 1995): 173–200.

Jackson, Scott Thomas. "Impressment and Anglo-American Discord, 1787–1818." Ph. D. diss., University of Michigan, 1976.

Jacobs, James R. *The Beginnings of the U.S. Army, 1783–1812*. Princeton: Princeton University Press, 1947.

James, Marquis. *The Raven: A Biography of Sam Houston*. Indianapolis: Bobbs-Merrill, 1953.

James, William. *A Full and Correct Account of the Chief Naval Occurrences of the Late War between Great Britain and the United States of America*. London: T. Egerton, 1817.

———. *Naval History of Great Britain from 1793–1820*. Vol. 6. London: R. Bently, 1837.

Jenkins, B. Wheeler. "The Shots that Saved Baltimore." *Maryland Historical Magazine* 77 (1982): 362–364.

Jenkins, John S. *The Generals of the Last War with Great Britain*. Auburn, NY: Derby, Miller and Co., 1849.

Jenkins, William H. "Alabama Forts, 1700–1838." *The Alabama Review* 12 (July 1959): 163–180.

Jennings, Louis J., ed. *The Croker Papers: The Correspondence and Diaries of the Rt. Honorable John Wilson Croker, Secretary to the Admiralty from 1809 to 1831*. 3 vols. London: John Murray, 1884.

Jennings, Walter W. *The American Embargo, 1807–1809*. Iowa City: University of Iowa Press, 1921.

Jernegan, Marcus. *Tammany Societies of Rhode Island*. Providence: Preston and Rounds, 1897.

"John Cotton Smith Papers." *Connecticut Historical Society Collections* 5 (1948–1954).

Johnson, Allen, and Dumas Malone, eds. *Dictionary of American Biography*. 10 vols. Reprint ed. New York: Charles Scribner's Sons, 1963–1964.

Johnson, Andrew J. "The Life and Constitutional Thought of Nathan Dane." Ph.D. diss., Indiana University, 1964.

Johnson, Charles M. *The Battle for the Heartland: Stoney Creek, June 6, 1813*. Stoney Creek, Ont.: Pennell Printing, 1963.

Johnson, David R. "Fort Amanda—A Historical Redress." *Northwest Ohio Quarterly* 48 (1976): 102–106.

Johnson, J. K. "Colonel James Fitzgibbon and the Suppression of Irish Riots in Upper Canada." *Ontario History* 58 (1966): 39–55.

Johnson, Leland R. "The Suspense Was Hell: The Senate Vote for War in 1812." *Indiana Magazine of History* 65 (1969): 247–269.

Johnson, Paul A. *The Birth of the Modern: World Society, 1815–1830*. New York: HarperCollins, 1991.

Johnson, Robert W. *Winders of America*. Philadelphia: Lippincott, 1902.

Jones, F. L. "A Subaltern of 1812: Fitzgibbon." *Canadian Army Journal* 9 (1955): 59–68.

Jones, Lewis Hampton. *Captain Roger Jones of London and Virginia*. Albany, NY: J. Munsell's Sons, 1891.

Jones, Mary K., and Lily Reynolds, eds. and comps. *Coweta County Chronicles for One Hundred Years*. N.p., 1928; reprint, Easley, SC: Southern Historical Press, 1978.

Jones, Walter, Richard Coxe, and Joseph H. Bradley. *Review of the Evidence, Findings, and Sentence of the Naval Court Martial in the Case of Comm. Thomas ap Catesby Jones*. N.p., 1851.

Jones, Wilbur D. *The American Problem in British Diplomacy*. Athens: University of Georgia Press, 1974.

Jones, Wilbur Devereux, ed. "A British View of the War of 1812 and the Peace Negotiations." *Mississippi Valley Historical Review* 45 (1958–1959): 482, 485–486.

Jordon, Weymouth T. *George Washington Campbell of Tennessee; Western Statesman*. Tallahassee: Florida State University, 1955.

"Joseph Kerr." Kathryn A. Jacob and Bruce A. Ragesdale, eds. *Biographical Dictionary of the United States Congress, 1774–1989*. Washington, DC: Government Printing Office, 1989.

"Journal of the Defense of New Orleans." *Niles Weekly Register* 7 (1814–1815): 374–379.

Judd, Jacob. *Correspondence of the Van Cortlandt Family of Van Cortlandt Manor, 1800–1814*. Tarrytown, NY: Sleepy Hollow Press, 1980.

Judson, Katherine B. "The British Side to the Restoration of Fort Astoria." *Oregon Historical Society Quarterly* 20 (1919): 305–330.

Kane, John. *List of Officers of the Royal Regiment of Artillery*. 4th ed. London: Royal Artillery Institute, 1890.

Keefer, Frank H. *Beaver Dams*. Thorold, Ont.: Thorold Post Printers, 1914.

Keeling, Mildred Roberta. "John Jacob Astor and the Settlement of Astoria." Master's thesis, Southwest Texas State University, 1940.

Kellogg, Louis Phelps. "The Capture of Mackinac in 1812." *Proceedings of the State Historical Society of Wisconsin* 60 (1912): 124–145.

Kemp, Peter, ed. *The Oxford Companion to Ships and the Sea*. Oxford: Oxford University Press, 1988.

Kennedy, John P. *Memoirs of the Life of William Wirt, Attorney General of the United States*. 2 vols. Philadelphia: W. J. Neal, 1834.

Kenneth, Allen. "Broke and the *Shannon*." In *Sea Captains and Their Ships*. London: Oldham Press, 1965.

Kerber, Linda K. *Federalists in Dissent: Imagery and Ideology in Jeffersonian America*. Ithaca: Cornell University Press, 1980.

Ketcham, Ralph. *James Madison*. New York: Macmillan, 1970.

Key, Francis Scott. *Poems of the Late Francis S. Key*. New York: R. Carter, 1857.

Kieffer, Chester L. *Maligned General: The Biography of Thomas Sydney Jesup*. New York: Presidio Press, 1979.

Kilby, William. "A New England Town under Foreign Martial Law." *New England Magazine* 14 (1894): 685–695.

Kimball, Jeffrey. "The Battle of Chippawa: Infantry Tactics in the War of 1812." *Military Affairs* 31 (Winter 1967-1968): 169–186.

King, Rufus. *The Life and Correspondence of Rufus King, Comprising His Letters. …* New York: Da Capo Press, 1971.

Kinney, Joseph Lair. "The Life of Samuel Houston." Master's thesis, Lafayette College, 1934.

Kirby, William. *Annals of Niagara*. New York: Macmillan, 1927.

Kirk, Russell. *John Randolph of Roanoke: A Study in American Politics*. Indianapolis: Liberty Press, 1978.

Kirwan, Albert D. *John J. Crittenden: The Struggle for the Union*. Lexington: University of Kentucky Press, 1962.

Kline, Mary-Jo. *Gouverneur Morris and the New Nation 1775–1788*. New York: Arno Press, 1978.

Knight, Lucian Lamar. *Georgia's Landmarks, Memorials, and Legends*. 2 vols. Atlanta: Byrd Printing, 1914.

Knopf, Richard C. *Return Johnathan Meigs and the War of 1812*. Columbus, OH: Anthony Wayne Board, 1957.

———. *Thomas Worthington and the War of 1812*. Columbus: Ohio State Museum, 1952.

Knopf, Richard C., ed. *Anthony Wayne, A Name in Arms: Soldier, Diplomat, Defender of Expansion Westward of a Nation; the Wayne-Knox-Pickering-McHenry Correspondence*. Westport, CT: Greenwood Press, 1975.

———. *Document Transcriptions of the War of 1812 in the Old Northwest*. 10 vols. Columbus: Ohio Historical Society, 1956–1962.

Kolecki, John H. "Red Jacket: The Last of the Senecas." Master's thesis, Niagara University, 1950.

Kosciuszko, Tadeusz. *The Manoeuvres of Horse Artillery*. New York: U.S. Military Philosophical Society, 1808.

Kouwenhoven, John A., and Lawton M. Patten. "New Light on 'The Star-Spangled Banner'?" *Musical Quarterly* 23 (1937).

Landon, Harry F. "British Sympathizers in St. Lawrence County during the War of 1812." *New York History* 35 (April 1954): 131–138.

———. *Bugles on the Border: The Story of the War of 1812 in Northern New York*. Watertown, NY: Watertown Daily Times, 1954.

Langley, Harold D. *Medicine in the Early U.S. Navy*. Baltimore: Johns Hopkins University Press, 1995.

Langlois, Thomas Huxley, and Marina Holmes Langlois. *South Bass Island and Islanders*. Ohio State University, Franz Theodore Stone Laboratory Contribution no. 10. Columbus: Ohio State University, 1948.

Lansen, Arthur. "Scapegoat of the *Chesapeake-Shannon* Battle." *United States Naval Institute Proceedings* 79 (1953): 528–531.

Larrey, Baron D. J. *Memoires de Chirurgie Militaire*. 5 vols. Paris: J. Smith, 1812.

Latour, A. Lacarriere. *Historical Memoir of the War in West Florida and Louisiana in 1814–15*. 1816; reprint, Gainesville: University Presses of Florida, 1964.

Laughton, John Knox. "Sir Edward Codrington." *Dictionary of National Biography*. London: Oxford University Press, 1937–1938.

———. "Sir John Borlase Warren." *Dictionary of National Biography*. Vol. 20, *UB-WH*. London: Oxford University Press, 1937–1938: 869–872.

———. "Sir Philip Bowes Vere Broke." *Dictionary of National Biography*. Vol. 2. London: Oxford University Press, 1937–1938, 1294–1295.

———. "Sir Thomas Masterman Hardy." In *Dictionary of National Biography*. Vol 8. London: Oxford University Press, 1937–1938: 1243–1245.

Lauriston, Victor. "The Case for General Procter." *Kent Historical Society Papers* 7 (1951): 7–17.

Lavery, Brian. *Nelson's Navy*. Annapolis, MD: Naval Institute Press, 1989.

Lawrence, Vera Brodsky. *Music for Patriots, Politicians, and Presidents: Harmonies and Discords of the First Hundred Years*. London: Macmillan, 1975.

Laws, M.E.S. *Battery Records of the Royal Artillery: 1716–1859*. Woolwich: Royal Artillery Institution, 1952.

Lee, Francis. *New Jersey as a Colony and as a State*. 4 vols. New York: Publishing Society of New Jersey, Winthrop Press, 1902.

Lees, James. *The Masting and Rigging of English Ships of War, 1625–1860*. Annapolis, MD: Naval Institute Press, 1984.

Lefebvre, Georges. *Napoleon: From 18 Brumaire to Tilsit, 1799–1807*. Trans. Henry F. Stockhold. New York: Columbia University Press, 1969.

Leger, William. G. "The Public Life of John Adair." Ph.D. diss., University of Kentucky, 1960.

Legler, Henry E. "The Capitulation of Prairie du Chien." *Leading Events in Wisconsin History: The Story of a State*. Milwaukee: Sentinel, 1898.

Leiding, Harriet Kershaw. *Charleston: Historic and Romantic*. Philadelphia: Lippincott, 1931.

Lemmon, Sarah McCulloh. *Frustrated Patriots: North Carolina and the War of 1812*. Chapel Hill: University of North Carolina Press, 1973.

Lewis, Charles L. *David Glasgow Farragut*. 2 vols. Annapolis, MD: U. S. Naval Institute, 1941–1943.

———. *The Romantic Decatur*. Philadelphia: University of Pennsylvania Press, 1937.

Lewis, Dennis M. *British Naval Activity on Lake Champlain during the War of 1812*. Plattsburg, NY, and Elizabethtown, NY: Clinton County Historical Association and Essex County Historical Society, 1994.

Lewis, Emanuel Raymond. "The Ambiguous Columbiads." *Military Affairs* 28, no. 3 (Fall 1964): 111–122.

Lewis, Walker. *Without Fear or Favor: A Biography of Chief Justice Roger Brooke Taney*. Boston: Houghton Mifflin, 1965.

Lincoln, Abraham. *The Life and Public Service of General Zachary Taylor: An Address by Abraham Lincoln*. Boston: Houghton Mifflin, 1922

Lindley, Harlow, ed. *Fort Meigs and the War of 1812: Orderly Book of Cushing's Company, 2nd U.S. Artillery, April, 1813–February, 1814, and Personal Diary of Captain Daniel Cushing, October, 1812–July, 1813*. Columbus: Ohio Historical Society, 1975.

Little, James D., Jr. "The Navy at the Battle of New Orleans." *Louisiana Historical Quarterly* 54 (spring 1971): 18–29.

Livermore, S. T. *History of Block Island*. Block Island Committee, 1961.

Lloyd, Alan. *The Scorching of Washington: The War of 1812*. Washington, DC: Robert B. Luce, 1974.

Lloyd, Ernest Marsh. "Sir Frederick Philipse Robinson." *Dictionary of National Biography*. Vol. 17. London: Oxford University Press, 1937–1938: 11–13.

———. "Sir John Coape Sherbrooke." *Dictionary of National Biography*. Vol. 17. London: Oxford University Press, 1937–1938: 70–71.

Lodge, Henry Cabot. *Life and Letters of George Cabot*. Boston: Little, Brown, 1878.

Lohnes, Barry J. "The War of 1812: The British Navy, New England and the Maritime Provinces of Canada." Master's thesis, University of Maine at Orono, 1971.

———. "British Naval Problems at Halifax during the War of 1812." *Mariner's Mirror* 59 (August 1973): 317–333.

Lomax, D.A.N. *History of the Services of the 41st Regiment*. Davenport: Hiornes and Miller, 1899.

Long, David F. "David Porter: Pacific Ocean Gadfly." In James C. Bradford, ed. *Command under Sail: Makers of the American Naval Tradition 1775–1830*. Annapolis, MD: Naval Institute Press, 1985: 173–198.

———. *Nothing Too Daring: A Biography of Commodore David Porter, 1780–1843*. Annapolis, MD: Naval Institute Press, 1970.

———. *Ready To Hazard*. Hanover, NH: University Press of New England, 1981.

———. *Sailor-Diplomat: A Biography of Commodore James Biddle, 1783–1848*. Boston: Northeastern University Press, 1983.

Longford, Elizabeth. *Wellington: The Years of the Sword*. New York: Smithmark, 1996.

Lord, Walter. *The Dawn's Early Light*. New York, W. W. Norton, 1972.

Lowery, Charles D. *James Barbour: A Jefferson Republican*. University: University of Alabama Press, 1984.

Luxon, Norval. *"Niles' Weekly Register": News Magazine of the Nineteenth Century*. Baton Rouge: Louisiana State University Press, 1947.

MacDonell, Malcolm. "The conflict between Sir John Harvey and Chief Justice John Gervase Hutchinson Bourne." *Canadian Historical Association Report*, 1956: 45–54.

Macdonough, Rodney. *Life of Commodore Thomas Macdonough, U.S. Navy*. Boston: Fort Hill Press, 1909.

MacKenzie, Alexander Slidell. *Life of Stephen Decatur: A Commodore in the Navy of the United States*. Boston: C.C. Little and J. Brown, 1846.

MacLaren, D. H. "British Naval Officers of a Century Ago. Barrie and Its Streets—A History of Their Names." *Ontario Historical Society Papers and Records* 17 (1919): 106–112.

Maclean, D. F. "The Administration of Sir John Harvey in Nova Scotia, 1846–1852." Master's thesis, Dalhousie University, Halifax, 1947.

Macon, Nathaniel. *A Speech Delivered by Nathaniel Macon, in the House of Representatives of the United States. January 13, 1813*. N.p., n.d.

Madison, Dolley. *Memoirs and Letters of Dolley Madison, Wife of James Madison, President of the United States*. Boston and New York: Houghton, Mifflin, 1888.

Madison, James. *Letters and Other Writings*. Vol. 2: *1794–1815*. New York: R. Worthington, 1884.

Magruder, Caleb Clark, Jr. "Dr. William Beanes, The Incidental Cause of the Authorship of the Star-Spangled Banner." *Records of the Columbia Historical Society* 22 (1919): 207–225.

Mahan, Alfred T. *Seapower in Its Relation to the War of 1812*. 2 vols. Boston: Little, Brown, 1919; reprint, New York: Greenwood Press, 1968.

Mahon, John K. "British Strategy and Southern Indians: War of 1812." *The Florida Historical Quarterly* 44 (April 1966): 285–302.

———. *History of the Militia and the National Guard*. New York: Macmillan, 1982.

———. "Oliver Hazard Perry." In James C. Bradford, ed., *Command under Sail: Makers of the American Naval Tradition 1775–1830*. Annapolis, MD: Naval Institute Press, 1985.

———. *The War of 1812*. Gainesville: University Presses of Florida, 1972.

Malcomson, Robert, and Thomas Malcomson. HMS *Detroit: The Battle for Lake Erie*. Annapolis, MD: Naval Institute Press, 1990.

Mallory, Ebid L. *The Green Tiger: James Fitzgibbon, Hero of the War of 1812*. Toronto: McClelland, 1976.

Malone, Dumas. *Jefferson and His Time: The Sage of Monticello*. Boston: Little, Brown, 1981.

———. *Jefferson the President: Second Term, 1805–1809*. Boston: Little, Brown, 1974.

Maloney, Linda M. *The Captain from Connecticut: The Life and Naval Times of Isaac Hull*. Boston: Northeastern University Press, 1986.

———. "The War of 1812: What Role for Sea Power?" In Kenneth J. Hagan, ed., *In Peace and War: Interpretations of American Naval History, 1775–1978*. Westport, CT: Greenwood Press, 1978.

Manigault, George Edward. "The Military Career of General George Izard." *Magazine of American History* (June 1888): 462–478.

Mann, James. *Medical Sketches of the Campaigns of 1812, 13, 14...*. Dedham, Mass: H. Mann and Co., 1816.

Mapp, Alf J., Jr. *Thomas Jefferson: Passionate Pilgrim*. Lanham, MD: Madison Books, 1991.

"Mapping of Fort Meigs, The." *Northwest Ohio Quarterly* 58 (1986): 123–142.

Marcus, Jacob Rader. "Uriah Phillips Levy." In *Memoirs of American Jews*. Vol. 1, *1775–1865*. Philadelphia: Jewish Publication Society of America, 1955: 76–116.

Markham, Felix. *Napoleon*. London and New York: Weidenfeld and Nicolson/New American Library, 1963, 1964.

Marriott, John A.R. *George Canning and His Times: A Political Study*. London: John Murray, 1907.

Marshal, John. *Royal Naval Biography*. 12 vols. London: Longman, Hurst, Rees, Orme, 1823–1830.

Martell, James. "Halifax during and after the War of 1812," *Dalhousie Review* 23 (October 1943): 289–304.

Martin, Joel W. *Sacred Revolt: The Muskogees' Struggle for a New World*. Boston: Beacon Press, 1991.

Martin, Tyrone G. "Isaac Hull's Victory Revisited." *American Neptune* 47 (winter 1987): 14–21.

———. *A Most Fortunate Ship*. Annapolis, MD: Naval Institute Press, 1997.

Mauncy, Albert. *Artillery through the Ages*. Washington, DC: Government Printing Office, 1949.

May, George S. *War of 1812*. Mackinac State Historic Parks: Village Press, 1990.

Mayhew, Dean R. "Jeffersonian Gunboats in the War of 1812." *American Neptune* 32 (April 1982): 108–113.

Maynard, Virginia S. *The Venturers: The Hampton, Harrison, and Earle Families of Virginia, South Carolina, and Texas*. Easley, SC: Southern Historical Press, 1981.

Mayo, Bernard. *Henry Clay: Spokesman for the West*. Boston: Houghton Mifflin, 1937.

McAfee, Robert B. *History of the Late War in the Western Country: Comprising a Full Account of All the Transactions in That Quarter, from the Commencement of Hostilities at Tippecanoe, to the Termination of the Contest at New Orleans on the Return of Peace*. Lexington, KY: Worsley and Smith, 1816. Reprint, Bowie, MD: Heritage Books, 1994.

McAlister, L. N. "Pensacola during the Second Spanish Period." *The Florida Historical Quarterly* 37 (January-April 1959): 281–327.

McClellan, Edwin N. "The Navy at the Battle of New Orleans." *United States Naval Institute Proceedings* 50 (December 1924): 2041–2060.

McClure, George. *Causes of the Destruction of the American Towns on the Niagara Frontier, and Failure of the Campaign of the Fall of 1813*. Bath, NY: Printed by Benjamin Smead, 1817.

McDonald, John. *Biographical Sketches of General Nathaniel*

Massie, General Duncan McArthur, Captain William Wells, and General Simon Kenton. Cincinnati: E. Morgan, 1838.

McDougall, Robert. *Correspondence of Lt. Col. Robert McDouall and Col. McKay Relative to the Capture of Fort McKay, Prairie du Chien, 1814.* Canadian Public Archives Report, 1857.

McKee, Christopher. *A Gentlemanly and Honorable Profession: The Creation of the U.S. Naval Officer Corps, 1794–1815.* Annapolis, MD: Naval Institute Press, 1991.

McKenney, Janice. *Air Defense Artillery: Army Lineage Series.* Washington, DC: Center of Military History, 1985.

———. *Field Artillery, Regular Army and Reserve: Army Lineage Series.* Washington, DC: Center for Military History, 1985.

McLaughlin, James Fairfax. *Matthew Lyon, the Hampden of Congress: A Biography.* New York: Wynkoop Hallenbeck Crawford, 1900.

McLoughlin, William G. *Cherokee Renascence in the New Republic.* Princeton: Princeton University Press, 1986.

McMaster, G. H. *History of the Settlement of Steuben County, New York.* Bath, NY: Underhill, 1853.

McNutt, W. S. "New Brunswick's Age of Harmony: The Administration of Sir John Harvey." *Canadian Historical Review* 32 (1951): 101–125.

Meigs, William M. *The Life of Charles Jared Ingersoll.* Philadelphia: J. B. Lippincott, 1897.

Melish, John. *A Description of Dartmoor Prison, with an Account of the Massacre of the Prison.* Philadelphia: Self-published, 1815.

Melville, Herman. *Authentic Anecdotes of Old Zack.* New Brighton, MN: K. Starosciak, 1973.

Meriwether, Robert L., ed. *The Papers of John C. Calhoun, 1801–1817.* Columbia: University of South Carolina Press, 1959.

Merk, Frederick. "The Genesis of the Oregon Question." *Mississippi Valley Historical Review* 36 (1949–1950): 583–612.

Merritt, Jedediah. *Biography of the Honorable William H. Merritt, M.P., of Lincoln, District of Niagara.* St. Catherines, Ont.: E. S. Leavenworth, 1875.

Metcalf, Clarence S. "Daniel Dobbins, Sailing Master, U.S.N., Commodore Perry's Right Hand Man." *Inland Seas* 14 (1958): 88–96, 181–191.

Meyer, Leland W. *Life and Times of Colonel Richard M. Johnson of Kentucky.* New York: Columbia University Press, 1932.

Michigan Pioneer and Historical Society. *Historical Collections Volumes 15 and 16.* Detroit: Michigan Pioneer and Historical Society, 1909–1910.

Millett, Allan R., and Peter Maslowski. *For the Common Defense.* New York: The Free Press, 1984.

Mindte, R. W., U.S.N. (Retd.). "Another Navy Rodgers." *American Neptune* 19 (July 1959): 213–226.

Mintz, Max, M. *Gouverneur Morris and the American Revolution.* Norman: University of Oklahoma Press, 1970.

Mitchell, Broadus. "Hezekiah Niles." In *Dictionary of American Biography.* Vol. 7, ed. Dumas Malone. New York: Charles Scribner's Sons, 1936: 521–522.

Moir, John. "An Early Record of Laura Secord's Walk." *Ontario History* 51 (1959): 105–108.

Montross, Lynn. "An Amphibious Doubleheader." *Marine Corps Gazette* 42 (1957): 131–140.

Mooney, Chase C. *William H. Crawford, 1772–1834.* Lexington: The University Press of Kentucky, 1974.

Mooney, James L. "Isaac Chauncey." In *James Madison and the American Nation 1751–1836,* ed. Robert Rutland. New York: Simon & Schuster, 1994.

Moore, John Trotwood, and Austin P. Foster, eds. *Tennessee the Volunteer State, 1769–1923.* 4 vols. Chicago: S. J. Clarke Publishing, 1923.

Morison, Samuel Eliot. "Dissent in the War of 1812." In *Dissent in Three American Wars,* ed. Samuel Eliot Morison, Frederick Merk, and Frank Freidel. Cambridge: Harvard University Press, 1970.

———. "The Henry-Crillon Affair." In *By Land and by Sea: Essays and Addresses by Samuel Eliot Morison.* New York: Alfred A. Knopf, 1954: 265–286.

———. "The Life and Correspondence of Harrison Gray Otis." Ph.D. diss., Harvard University, 1915.

———. *The Life and Letters of Harrison Gray Otis, Federalist, 1765–1848.* 2 vols. Boston: Houghton Mifflin, 1913.

Morris, Anne Cary. *Diary and Letters of Gouverneur Morris.* 2 vols. New York and London: Charles Scribners and Kegan and Paul, 1888, 1889.

Morton, Desmond. *A Military History of Canada.* Toronto: McClelland and Stewart, 1985.

Moser, Harold, ed. *The Papers of Andrew Jackson.* Vol. 2, *1804–1813.* Knoxville: University of Tennessee Press, 1984.

Mouzon, Harold Alwyn. *Privateers of Charleston in the War of 1812.* Charleston: Historical Commission of Charleston, SC, 1954.

Muller, Charles G. *The Darkest Day: 1814, the Washington-Baltimore Campaign.* Philadelphia: Lippincott, 1963.

———. *The Proudest Day: Macdonough on Lake Champlain.* New York: John Day, 1960.

Muller, H. N. "A 'Traitorous and Diabolical Traffic': The Commerce of the Champlain-Richelieu Corridor during the War of 1812." *Vermont History* 44 (spring 1976): 78–96.

Muller, Mary H. *A Town at Presque Isle: A Short History of Erie, Pennsylvania to 1980.* Erie, PA: Erie County Historical Society, 1991.

Mutersbaugh, Bert Marsh. "Jeffersonian Journalist: Thomas Ritchie and the Richmond *Enquirer.*" Ph.D. diss., University of Missouri, 1973.

Myer, Jesse S. *Life and Letters of Dr. William Beaumont.* St. Louis: C. V. Mosby, 1912.

Nagel, Paul C. *John Quincy Adams: A Public Life, A Private Life.* New York: Alfred A. Knopf, 1997.

Napier, Elers. *The Life and Correspondence of Admiral Sir Charles Napier.* 2 vols. London: Hurst, Blackett, 1862.

Napier, William B. *The Life and Opinions of General Sir Charles James Napier.* 4 vols. London: J. Murray, 1857.

Narrative of the Life of General Leslie Combs: Embracing Incidents in the History of the War of 1812. Washington, DC: American Whig Review Office, 1852.

Nelson, Larry L. *Men of Patriotism, Courage, and Enterprise:*

Fort Meigs in the War of 1812. Canton, OH: Daring Books, 1985.

Nelson, Rodney B. *Beaumont: America's First Physiologist.* Geneva, IL: Grant House, 1990.

Nelson, William. *Some Notices of Governor Joseph Bloomfield.* Newark, NJ: Daily Advertiser Printing House, 1886.

Nevin, John. *John C. Calhoun and the Price of Union.* Baton Rouge: Louisiana State University Press, 1988.

Nicolson, G.W.L. *The Gunners of Canada.* Toronto: McClelland and Stewart, 1967.

Niles, John M. *The Life of Oliver Hazard Perry with Appendix . . . a Biography of General Pike.* Hartford: Oliver D. Cooke, 1821.

Niven, John. *Martin Van Buren: The Romantic Age of American Politics.* New York: Oxford University Press, 1983.

Norie, J. W. *The Naval Gazetteer, Biographer, and Chronologist Containing a History of the Late Wars, from their Commencement in 1793 to Their Conclusion in 1801; and From their Recommencement in 1803 to Their Final Conclusion in 1815; and Continued, as to the Biographical Part, to the Present Time.* London: J. W. Norie and Co., 1827.

Norris, Caleb H. "Tarhee, the Crane-chief of the Wyandots." *Northwest Ohio Quarterly* 7 (1935): 1–13.

Northern, William J. *Men of Mark in Georgia.* 6 vols. Atlanta: Caldwell Publishers, 1910. Reprint, Spartanburg, SC: Reprint Company, 1974.

Nova Scotia Royal Gazette (1812–15).

O'Connell, Robert L. *Sacred Vessels: The Cult of the Battleship and the Rise of the U.S. Navy.* Boulder, CO: Westview Press, 1991.

Oullet, Fernand. *Economic and Social History of Quebec, 1760–1850.* Toronto: Gage Publishing, 1980.

———. *Lower Canada, 1791–1840: Social Chance and Nationalism.* Toronto: McClelland and Stewart, 1980.

Owen, David A. *Fort Erie: An Historical Guide.* N.p.: The Niagara Parks Commission, 1986.

Owen, Thomas McAdory. *History of Alabama and Dictionary of Alabama Biography.* Vol. 1. Chicago: S. J. Clarke Company, 1921.

Owsley, Frank L., Jr. "British and Indian Activities in Spanish West Florida during the War of 1812." *The Florida Historical Quarterly* 46 (October 1967): 111–123.

———. "Jackson's Capture of Pensacola." *Alabama Review* 19 (1966): 175–185.

———. "The Role of the South in the British General Strategy in the War of 1812." *Tennessee Historical Quarterly* 31 (1972): 22–38.

———. *Struggle for the Gulf Borderlands: The Creek War and the Battle of New Orleans, 1812–1815.* Gainesville: University Presses of Florida, 1981.

———. "William Jones." In Paolo Coletta, ed., *American Secretaries of the Navy.* Vol. 1. Annapolis, MD: Naval Institute Press, 1980: 93–98.

Pack, A. James. *The Man Who Burned the White House: Admiral Sir George Cockburn, 1772–1853.* Emsworth: Mason, 1987.

Padfield, Peter. *Broke and the Shannon.* London: Hodder and Stoughton, 1968.

———. "Criticism." *Mariner's Mirror* 59 (November 1973): 453–454.

Paine, Ralph D. *Joshua Barney: A Forgotten Hero of Blue Water.* New York: Century, 1924.

Palmer, Michael A. "A Failure of Command, Control, and Communication: Oliver Hazard Perry and the Battle of Lake Erie." *Journal of Erie Studies* 17 (fall 1899): 7–26.

Pancake, John S. *Samuel Smith and the Politics of Business: 1752–1839.* University: University of Alabama Press, 1972.

"Papers Relating to the Burning of Buffalo and to the Niagara Frontier during the War of 1812." *Buffalo Historical Society Publications* 9 (1906): 311–406.

Parker, Arthur C. "The Senecas in the War of 1812." In *Proceedings of the New York State Historical Association,* vol. 15. Albany: New York State Historical Association, 1916: 78–90.

Parker, Henry S. *Henry Leavenworth, Pioneer General.* Fort Leavenworth, KS: N.p., n.d.

Parks, Joseph H. *Felix Grundy: Champion of Democracy.* Baton Rouge: Louisiana State University Press, 1940.

Parsons, Usher. *Journal of Medicine and Surgery* 7 (1818): 316.

Parsons, William B. *Robert Fulton and the Submarine.* New York: Columbia University Press, 1912.

Parton, James. *Life of Andrew Jackson.* 3 vols. New York: Mason Brothers, 1860.

———. *Life of John Jacob Astor, To Which Is Appended a Copy of His Last Will.* New York: American News, 1865.

Pasler, Margaret, and Rudolph Pasler. *The New Jersey Federalists.* Rutherford, NJ: Fairleigh Dickinson University Press, 1975.

Patrick, Rembert W. *Florida Fiasco: Rampant Rebels on the Georgia-Florida Border, 1810–1815.* Athens: University of Georgia Press, 1954.

Patrick, Rembert W., and Allan Marriss. *Florida under Five Flags.* Gainesville: University Presses of Florida, 1967.

Patterson to the Secretary of the Navy, 20 January 1815. *Niles' Weekly Register* 7 (18 February 1815): 389.

Patton, Philip. *The Observations of an Admiral on the State of the Navy, and More Particularly as it is Connected with the American War.* Fareham, Hampshire: N.p., 1813.

Paulding, James Kirke. *Letters from the South: Written during an Excursion in the Summer of 1816.* 2 vols. New York: Eastburn and Co., 1817.

Paullin, Charles Oscar. "American Naval Administration under Secretaries of the Navy Smith, Hamilton and Jones, 1801–14." *Proceedings of the U.S. Naval Institute* 32 (1906).

———. *Commodore John Rodgers, 1773–1838.* Annapolis, MD: Naval Institute Press, 1967.

———. "The Cruise of the *Peacock.*" In *American Voyages to the Orient, 1690–1865.* Annapolis, MD: Naval Institute Press, 1991: 19–23.

———. "Early Naval Administration under the Constitution." *U.S. Naval Institute Proceedings* 32 (1906).

———. "Isaac Chauncey." *Dictionary of American Biography.* Vol. 3, pp. 40–41. New York: Charles Scribner's Sons, 1936.

———. "Naval Administration under Secretaries of the Navy

Smith, Hamilton, and Jones, 1801–1814." *United States Naval Institute Proceedings* 32 (December 1906): 1289–1328.

Paulshock, Bernadine Z. "'Let Every Reader Form His Own Conclusions': Dr. James A. Tilton's Case Report of a Delaware Woman Cured of Rabies." *Delaware History* 21 (1985): 186–196.

Peabody Museum of Salem. "*Don't Give Up the Ship*": A Catalogue of the Eugene H. Pool Collection of Captain James Lawrence. Salem: Peabody Museum, 1942.

Peck, Taylor. *Roundshots to Rockets: A History of the Washington Navy Yard and U.S. Naval Gun Factory.* Annapolis, MD: Naval Institute Press, 1949.

Peckham, Howard. "Commodore Perry's Captive." *Ohio History* 72 (1963): 220–227.

Peeler, Elizabeth H. "The Policies of Willie Blount as Governor of Tennessee, 1809–15." *Tennessee Historical Quarterly* 1 (December 1942): 309–327.

Perkins, Bradford. *Castlereagh and Adams: England and the United States, 1812–1823.* Berkeley: University of California Press, 1964.

———. "George Canning, Great Britain, and the United States, 1807–1809." *American Historical Review* 63 (October 1957): 1–22.

———. *Prologue to War: England and the United States 1805–1812.* Berkeley and Los Angeles: University of California Press, 1963.

Perkins, Edwin J. *American Public Finance and Financial Services, 1700–1815.* Columbus: Ohio State University Press, 1994.

Pershing, Marvon W. *Life of General John Tipton and Early Indiana Territory.* Tipton, IN: Tipton Club, 1900.

Peterson, Harold L. *Round Shot and Rammers.* South Bend, IN: South Bend Replicas, 1969.

Peterson, Merrill D. *The Great Triumvirate: Webster, Clay and Calhoun.* New York: Oxford University Press, 1987.

———. *Thomas Jefferson and the New Nation.* London: Oxford University Press, 1970.

Petrie, Charles. *George Canning.* London: Eyre & Spottiswoode, 1930, 1946.

———. *Lord Liverpool and His Times.* London: J. Barrie, 1954.

Phalen, James M. "Surgeon James Mann's Observations on Battlefield Amputations." *Military Surgeon* 87 (1940): 463–466.

Pickett, Albert James. *History of Alabama ... Annals of Alabama, 1819–1900 by Thomas McAdory Owen.* Birmingham, AL: The Webb Book Company, Publishers, 1900.

———. *History of Alabama, and Incidentally of Georgia and Mississippi, from the Earliest Period.* N.p., 1851. Reprint, Tuscaloosa, AL: Willo Publishing, 1962.

Picking, Sherwood. *Sea Fight off Monhegan: Enterprise and Boxer.* Portland, ME: Machigonne Press, 1941.

Piers, Harry. *Evolution of the Halifax Fortress 1749–1928,* ed. G. M. Self. Halifax: Public Archives of Nova Scotia, 1947. Publication No. 7.

Pinckney, Charles C. *Life of General Thomas Pinckney.* Boston: Houghton, Mifflin, 1895.

Pitcock, Cynthia DeHaven. "The Career of William Beaumont, 1785–1853: Science and the Self-Made Man in America." Ph.D. diss., Memphis State University, 1985.

Plumer, William. "John Taylor Gilman: A Sketch." *Early State Papers of New Hampshire* 22 (1893): 830–35.

Poolman, Kenneth. *Guns off Cape Ann. The Story of the* Shannon *and the* Chesapeake. London: Evans Brothers, 1961.

Porter, David. *Journal of a Cruise Made to the Pacific Ocean . . . 1812, 1813 and 1814.* 2 vols. Philadelphia: Bradford and Inskeep, 1815.

Porter, G. W. "A Sketch of the Life and Character of the Late William Eustis." *Lexington Historical Society Proceedings* 1 (1890): 101–109.

Porter, Kenneth W. *John Jacob Astor, Businessman.* 2 vols. Cambridge: Harvard University Press, 1931.

———. *The Negro on the American Frontier.* New York: Arno Press, 1971.

Post, Waldron K. "The Case of Captain Lawrence." *United States Naval Institute Proceedings* 62 (July 1936): 969–974.

Pound, Merritt B. *Benjamin Hawkins: Indian Agent.* Athens: University of Georgia Press, 1951.

Powell, John H. *Richard Rush, Republican Diplomat.* Philadelphia: University of Pennsylvania Press, 1942.

Powell, William. *List of the Officers of the Army of the United States, 1777–1900.* New York: L. R. Hammersley, 1900.

"Prairie du Chien Documents." *Wisconsin Historical Society Collections* 9 (1880–1881): 262–281.

Pratt, Fletcher. "An Anomaly: Isaac Chauncey." In *Preble's Boys.* New York: Sloane, 1950.

Pratt, Julius. *Expansionists of 1812.* New York: Macmillan, 1925. Reprint, Gloucester, MA: Peter Smith, 1957.

———. "Fur Trade Strategy and the American Left Flank in the War of 1812." *American Historical Review* 40 (January 1935): 246–273.

Preble, George H. *History of the Flag of the United States of America.* 2d rev. ed. Boston: A. Williams and Co., 1880.

Preston, Richard A. "The First Battle of Sacket's Harbor." *Historic Kingston* 2 (1963): 3–7.

———. "The History of the Port of Kingston." *Ontario History* 56 (1954): 201–211.

———. "The Journals of General Sir F. P. Robinson, G. C. B." *Canadian Historical Review* 37 (December 1956): 352–355.

Prince, Carl. *New Jersey's Jeffersonian Republicans: The Genesis of an Early Party Machine, 1789–1817.* Chapel Hill: University of North Carolina Press, 1967.

[Procter, George]. *Lucubrations of Humphrey Ravelin.* London: G. and W. B. Whittaker, 1823.

[Procter, Henry]. "A Canadian Campaign." *London Quarterly Review* 27 (April and July 1822).

Procter, Henry. *The Defence of Major General Procter Tried at Montreal upon Charges Affecting his Character as a Soldier.* Montreal: John Lovell, 1842.

Purcell, Hugh D. "Don't Give Up the Ship," *United States Naval Institute Proceedings* 91 (May 1965): 82–94.

Quaife, Milo M. "An Artilleryman of Old Fort Mackinac." *Burton Historical Collection Leaflet* 6 (January 1928): 33–48.

———. "A Forgotten Hero [James Keating] of Rock Island." *Journal of the Illinois State Historical Society* 23 (January 1931): 652–663.

———. "The Story of Brownstown." *Burton Historical Collection Leaflet* 4 (1926): 65–80.

———. *The Yankees Capture York.* Detroit: Wayne University Press, 1955.

Quaife, Milo M., ed. "Governor Shelby's Army in the River Thames Campaign." *The Filson Club Historical Quarterly* 10 (July 1936): 135–165.

Quisenberry, Anderson. *Kentucky in the War of 1812.* Baltimore: Genealogical Publishing Company, 1969.

Raddall, Thomas. *Halifax: Warden of the North.* Rev. ed. Toronto: McClelland and Stewart, 1974.

Rauch, Steven J. "The Eyes of the Country Were upon Them: A Comparative Study of the Campaigns of the Northwestern Army Conducted by William Hull and William Henry Harrison, 1812–1813." Master's thesis, Eastern Michigan University, 1992.

Raudzens, George. "Red George MacDonnell, Military Savior of Upper Canada?" *Ontario History* 62 (1970): 199–212.

Redway, Jacques W. "General Van Rensselaer and the Niagara Frontier." *New York State Historical Association Proceedings* 8 (1909): 14–22.

Reed, John Elmer. *History of Erie County, Pennsylvania.* 2 vols. Topeka-Indianapolis: Historical Publishing Company, 1925.

Reeves, Carolyn Keller. *The Choctaw before Removal.* Jackson: University Press of Mississippi, 1985.

Reeves, James S., ed. "A Diplomat Glimpses Parnassus: Excerpts from the Correspondence of Christopher Hughes." *Michigan Alumnus* 41 (1934): 189–201.

Reid, John, and John Henry Eaton. *The Life of Andrew Jackson.* Ed. Frank Lawrence Owsley, Jr. 1817; reprint, University: University of Alabama Press, 1974.

Reid, Samuel Chester, Jr. *The Case of the Private Armed Brig of War Gen. Armstrong.* New York: Banks, Gould and Co., 1857.

———. *The New York Telegraph and Signal Book.* New York: Published by the author, 1822.

Reilly, Robin. *The British at the Gates: The New Orleans Campaign in the War of 1812.* New York: G. P. Putnam's Sons, 1974.

Remini, Robert V. *Andrew Jackson and the Course of American Empire.* New York: Harper and Row, 1981.

———. *Henry Clay: Statesman for the Union.* New York, W. W. Norton, 1992.

———. *Martin Van Buren and the Making of the Democratic Party.* New York: Columbia University Press, 1951.

"Reminiscences of the Late War." *Army and Navy Chronicle*, February 19, 1835.

Reynolds, John. *My Own Times: Embracing Also the History of My Life.* Chicago: Fergus Printing Company, 1879.

Richard, Richard C., et al. "Fort Washington Re-Discovered." *Bulletin of the Historical and Philosophical Society of Ohio* 11: 1–12.

Richards, George H., ed. *Memoir of Alexander Macomb, the Major-General Commanding the Army of the United States.* New York: McElrath, Bangs, 1833.

Richardson, John. *Richardson's War of 1812.* Ed. Alexander C. Casselman. Toronto: Historical Publishing, 1902.

Richardson, Major [John]. *The Letters of Veritas, Re-published from the* Montreal Herald *Containing a Succinct Narrative of the Military Administration of Sir George Prevost during His Command in the Canadas, Whereby It Will Appear Manifest that the Merit of Preserving Them from Conquest Belongs Not to Him.* Montreal: W. Gray, 1815.

Ringwalt, Roland. *Commodore Jacob Jones of the United States Navy.* In *Papers of the Historical Society of Delaware,* no. 44. Wilmington: Historical Society of Delaware, 1906.

Roberts, Gerald F. "William O. Butler, Kentucky Cavalier." Master's thesis, University of Kentucky, 1971.

Robinson, Ralph. "Controversy over the Command at Baltimore in the War of 1812." *Maryland Historical Magazine* 39 (1944): 117–224.

Rogers, Ann. "William Clark: A Commemoration." *Gateway Heritage* 9 (summer 1988): 12–15.

Rogers, H.C.B. *A History of Artillery.* Secaucus, NJ: The Citadel Press, 1975.

Rogers, Joseph M. *Thomas H. Benton.* Philadelphia: George W. Jacobs, 1905.

Roland, Alexander. *Underwater Warfare in the Age of Sail.* Bloomington: Indiana University Press, 1978.

Rolo, Paul Jacques Victor. *George Canning: Three Biographical Studies.* London: Macmillan, 1965.

Ronda, James. *Astoria and Empire.* Lincoln: University of Nebraska Press, 1990.

Roosevelt, Theodore. *The Naval War of 1812.* 2 vols. 3rd ed. New York: G. P. Putnam's Sons, 1900.

Rosenburg, Max. *The Building of Perry's Fleet on Lake Erie.* Harrisburg, PA: Historical and Museum Commission, 1950.

Roske, Ralph, and Richard W. Donely. "The Perry-Elliott Controversy: A Bitter Footnote to the Battle of Lake Erie." *Northwest Ohio Quarterly* 34 (1962): 111–123.

Ross, Alexander. *Adventures of the First Settlers on the Oregon or Columbia River.* Chicago: R. R. Donnelly, 1913.

Roush, J. Fred. *Chalmette.* Washington: National Park Service, 1958.

Rowland, Dunbar. *Andrew Jackson's Campaign against the British, or the Mississippi Territory in the War of 1812.* New York: Macmillan Company, 1926.

Rucker, Brian R. "In the Shadow of Jackson: Uriah Blue's Expedition into West Florida." *Florida Historical Quarterly* (January 1995).

Russell, Greg. *John Quincy Adams and the Public Virtues of Diplomacy.* Columbia: University of Missouri Press, 1995.

Rutland, Robert A. *Madison's Alternatives: The Jeffersonian Republicans and the Coming of War, 1805–1812.* Philadelphia: J. B. Lippincott, 1975.

———. *The Newsmongers: Journalism in the Life of the Nation 1690–1972.* New York: Dial Press, 1973.

———. *The Presidency of James Madison.* Lawrence: University Press of Kansas, 1990.

Ryden, George H. *Biographical Sketches of Caesar Rodney, Thomas*

Rodney, and Caesar A. Rodney. Dover: Delaware Historical Society, 1943.

Saffron, Morris H. "The Tilton Affair." *Journal of the American Medical Association* 236 (1976): 67–72.

Sands, Harold, "Canada's Conquest of Astoria: How Montrealers Peacefully Secured the American Fort on the Pacific Coast." *Canadian Magazine* 42 (1914): 464–468.

Sanford, John L. "The Battle of North Point." *Maryland Historical Magazine* 24 (1929): 356–365.

Sapio, Victor. *Pennsylvania and the War of 1812.* Lexington: University of Kentucky Press, 1970.

Schermerhorn, Hazel Fenton. "Mackinac Island under French, English and American." *Michigan History Magazine* 14 (summer 1930): 367–380.

Schroeder, John H. "Stephen Decatur: Heroic Ideal of the Young Navy." In *Command under Sail: Makers of the American Naval Tradition,* ed. James C. Bradford. Annapolis, MD: Naval Institute Press, 1985.

Schwaller, John Frederick. "Spanish Colonial Towns, from Aztec to Anglo." *Journal of Urban History* 11 (1985): 245–251.

Scott, Anne Simpson. "John Jacob Astor and the Settlement of the Northwest." Master's thesis, Arkansas State College, 1961.

Scott, Winfield. *Memoirs of Lieutenant General Scott.* 2 vols. New York: Sheldon and Company, 1864.

Sears, Alfred B. *Thomas Worthington, Father of Ohio Statehood.* Columbus: Ohio State University Press, 1958.

Sears, Louis M. *Jefferson and the Embargo.* Durham, NC: Duke University Press, 1927.

Sellar, Gordon. *The U.S. Campaign of 1813 to Capture Montreal.* Huntington, Quebec: Gleaner Office, 1914.

Severance, Frank H. "The Case of Brig. Gen. Alexander Smyth, as Shown by His Own Writings, Some of Them Now First Published." *Buffalo Historical Society Publications* 18 (1913).

———. "Documents Relating to the War of 1812: The Letter-Book of Gen. Sir Roger Hale Sheaffe." *Buffalo Historical Society Publications* 17 (1913): 271–381.

Severance, Frank H., ed. "Career of Daniel Dobbins Now for the First Time Compiled from Original Documents, Including Also 'The Dobbins Papers,' 'Early Days on the Lakes,' and 'Episodes of the War of 1812,' written by Captain William W. Dobbins from the Papers and Reminiscences of His Father." *Publications of the Buffalo Historical Society* 8 (1905): 257–379.

Sevier, Cora Bales, and Nancy S. Madden. *Sevier Family History, with the Collected Letters of General John Sevier, First Governor of Tennessee, and 28 Collateral Family Lineages.* Washington, DC: Kaufman, 1961.

Sevier, George W. "General John Sevier, a Sketch by His Son." *Tennessee Historical Magazine,* 2nd ser., 1 (1930–1931): 207–214.

Shackford, James A. *David Crockett: The Man and the Legend.* Chapel Hill: University of North Carolina Press, 1956.

Shalhope, Robert F. *John Taylor of Caroline: Pastoral Republican.* Columbia: University of South Carolina Press, 1980.

Sharp, Solomon P. *Mr. Sharp's Motion, Relating to the Conduct of Martin Chittenden, Governor of Vermont, in … Ordering the Militia of That State, Engaged in the Service of the United States, to Withdraw from Their Service.* Washington, DC: A. & G. Way, Printers, 1814.

Sheads, Scott S. *Fort McHenry.* Baltimore: Nautical and Aviation Publishing, 1995.

Shepard, Helen Louise. "The National Political Career of William H. Crawford, 1807–1825." Master's thesis, Indiana University, 1940.

Sheppard, George. *Plunder, Profit and Paroles: A Social History of the War of 1812 in Upper Canada.* Montreal: McGill-Queen's University Press, 1994.

Shomette, Donald G. *Flotilla: Battle for the Patuxent.* Solomons, MD: The Calvert Marine Museum Press, 1981.

———. "The Much Vaunted Flotilla." In *Ships on the Chesapeake: Maritime Disasters on Chesapeake Bay and Its Tributaries, 1608–1978.* Centreville, MD: Tidewater Publications, 1982.

Shomette, Donald G., and Fred W. Hopkins, Jr. "The Search for the Chesapeake Flotilla." *American Neptune* 43 (January 1983): 5–19.

Shulim, Joseph I. "The United States Views Russia in the Napoleonic Age." *Proceedings of the American Philosophical Society* 102 (30 April 1958): 148–159.

Silver, James W. *Edmund Pendleton Gaines: Frontier General.* Baton Rouge: Louisiana State University Press, 1949.

"Sir Herbert Sawyer Obituary." *Annual Register, 1834.* London: Baldwin and Cradock, 1835: Appendix to Chronicle, 245–246.

"Sir James Hillyar" (obituary). *Annual Register* 85 (1843): 279–280.

Sirey, Steven E. *DeWitt Clinton and the American Political Economy.* New York: Peter Lang, 1989.

Skaggs, David Curtis. "Joint Operations during the Detroit-Lake Erie Campaign, 1813." In William B. Cogar, ed., *New Interpretations in Naval History: Selected Papers from the Eighth Naval History Symposium.* Annapolis, MD: Naval Institute Press, 1989: 121–138.

Skeen, C. Edward. *John Armstrong, Jr., 1758–1843; A Biography.* Syracuse, NY: Syracuse University Press, 1981.

———. "Monroe and Armstrong: A Study in Political Rivalry." *New York Historical Society Quarterly* 57 (April 1973): 120–147.

Smelser, Marshall. *Congress Founds the Navy, 1787–1798.* Notre Dame, IN: University of Notre Dame Press, 1959.

Smelser, Marshal, ed. "Smuggling in 1813–1814: A Personal Reminiscence." *Vermont History* 38 (winter 1970): 22–26.

Smith, Allen W., comp. *Beginning at "The Point": A History of Northern Kentucky and Environs, the Town of Covington in Particular, 1751–1834.* Park Hills, KY: Smith, 1977.

Smith, Arthur D. Howden. *Old Fuss and Feathers: The Life and Exploits of Winfield Scott.* New York: Greystone Press, 1937.

Smith, Beatrice Merle. "Sam Houston in Tennessee." Master's thesis, University of Tennessee, 1932.

Smith, C. Charles. "Memoirs of Colonel Thomas Aspinwall." *Massachusetts Historical Society Proceedings* 3 (1891): 30–81.

Smith, Elbert B. *Magnificent Missourian: The Life of Thomas Hart Benton.* Philadelphia: J. B. Lippincott, 1958.

Smith, Francis Scott Key. *Francis Scott Key: Author of the Star Spangled Banner.* Washington, DC: Key-Smith, 1911.

Smith, Gene A. "The War That Wasn't: Thomas ap Catesby Jones' Seizure of Monterey." *California History* 66 (1987): 104–113, 155–157.

Smith, Joseph H. "The Battle of Stoney Creek." *Wentworth Historical Society Papers and Records* 10 (1922): 101–124.

Sonneck, Oscar George Theodore. *The Star Spangled Banner.* New York: De Capo, 1969.

Southall, Eugene P. "Negroes in Florida Prior to the Civil War." *Journal of Negro History* 19 (1934): 77–87.

Spaeth, Sigmund. *A History of Popular Music in America.* London: Phoenix House, 1948.

Spater, George. *William Cobbett: The Poor Man's Friend.* 2 vols. Cambridge: Cambridge University Press, 1982.

Spivak, Burton. *Jefferson's English Crisis: Commerce, Embargo, and the Republican Revolution.* Charlottesville: University of Virginia Press, 1979.

Spurr, John. "The Royal Navy's Presence in Kingston, Part I: 1813–1836." *Historic Kingston* 25 (March 1977): 63–77.

———. "The Royal Navy's Presence in Kingston, Part II:1837–1853." *Historic Kingston* 26 (March 1978): 81–96.

———. "Sir James Lucas Yeo: A Hero of the Lakes." *Historic Kingston* 30 (March 1981): 30–45.

Sridharan, Rear Admiral K. *A Maritime History of India.* New Delhi: Government of India Publication Division, 1982.

Stacey, Charles P. "The American Attack on Kingston Harbour." *Canadian Army Journal* 5 (August 1951): 2–14.

———. "Another Look at the Battle of Lake Erie." *Canadian Historical Review* 39 (1958): 41–51.

———. *The Battle of Little York.* Toronto: Historical Board, 1963.

———. "Commodore Chauncey's Attack on Kingston Harbour, November 10, 1812." *Canadian Historical Review* 32 (June 1951): 126–138.

———. "Sir Isaac Brock." *Dictionary of Canadian Biography,* F. G. Halpenny, gen. ed. Vol. 5. Toronto: University of Toronto Press, 1983: 109–115.

———. "The Ships of the British Squadron on Lake Ontario 1812–1814." *Canadian Historical Review* 34 (December 1953): 311–323.

Stagg. J.C.A. "Enlisted Men in the United States Army, 1812–1815: A Preliminary Survey." *William and Mary Quarterly* 43 (October 1986): 615–645.

———. *Mr. Madison's War: Politics, Diplomacy, and Warfare in the Early American Republic, 1783–1830.* Princeton: Princeton University Press, 1983.

Stahl, John M. *The Battle of Plattsburg: A Study in and of the War of 1812.* Argos, IN: Van Trump, 1918.

Stanley, George F. G. *Battle in the Dark: Stoney Creek, 6 June, 1813.* Toronto: Balmuir Book Publishing, 1991.

———. "British Operations on the Penobscot in 1814." *Journal of the Society for Army Historical Research* 19 (1940): 168–178.

———. "The Contribution of the Canadian Militia during the War." In Philip P. Mason, ed., *After Tippecanoe: Some Aspects of the War of 1812.* East Lansing: Michigan State University Press, 1963: 28–48.

———. "Kingston and the Defence of British North America." In Gerald Tulchinsky, ed., *To Preserve and Defend: Essays on Kingston in the Nineteenth Century.* Montreal and London: McGill-Queen's University Press, 1976: 83–101.

———. "The Significance of the Six Nations' Participation in the War of 1812." *Ontario History* 55 (1963): 215–231.

———. *The War of 1812: Land Operations.* Ottawa: National Museums of Canada and Macmillan, 1983.

Stanley, George F. G., and Richard A. Preston. *A Short History of Kingston as a Military and Naval Centre.* Kingston: Royal Military College, 1950.

Stapleton, Augustus G. *George Canning and His Times.* London, J. W. Parker, 1859.

State Archeological and Historical Society of Ohio. *93rd Anniversary of the Battle of Fort Stephenson; Reinterment of Remains of Major Geo. Croghan, Beneath the Monument Erected in His Honor on Fort Stephenson, Fremont, Ohio. Thursday August 2, 1906.* Columbus: Ohio State Archeological and Historical Society, 1907.

Steffen, Jerome O. *William Clark: Jeffersonian Man on the Frontier.* Norman: University of Oklahoma Press, 1977.

Stevens, William O. *An Affair of Honor. The Biography of Commodore James Barron, U.S.N.* Norfolk: Norfolk County Historical Society of Chesapeake, Virginia, in cooperation with the Earl Gregg Swem Library of the College of William and Mary, 1969.

Stickney, Kenneth. "Sir Gordon Drummond." *Dictionary of Canadian Biography,* F. G. Halpenny, gen. ed. Vol. 8. Toronto: University of Toronto Press, 1979: 236–239.

Stivers, Reuben Elmore. *Privateers and Volunteers: The Men and Women of Our Reserve Naval Forces, 1766 to 1866.* Annapolis, MD: Naval Institute Press, 1975.

Strange, Robert. *Eulogy on the Life and Character of William Rufus King: Delivered in Clinton on the 1st Day of June, 1853.* Raleigh: N.p., 1853.

Stricker, John. "General John Stricker." *Maryland Historical Magazine* 9 (1914): 209–218.

Strum, Harvey. "New Jersey Politics and the War of 1812." *New Jersey History* 105 (fall/winter 1987): 37–69.

———. "New York's Antiwar Campaign." *Peace and Change* (spring 1982): 7–18.

———. "The Politics of the New York Antiwar Campaign, 1812–1815." *Peace and Change* 8 (September 1982): 7–18.

Stuart, Reginald C. *The Half-way Pacifist: Thomas Jefferson's View of War.* Toronto: University of Toronto Press, 1978.

Styron, Arthur. *The Last of the Cocked Hats.* Norman: University of Oklahoma Press, 1945.

Sugden, John. *Tecumseh's Last Stand.* Norman: University of Oklahoma Press, 1985.

Sulte, Benjamin. *La Bataille de Châteauguay.* Quebec: R. Renault, 1899.

Sutcliffe, Alice C. *Robert Fulton and the* Clermont*: The Authoritative Story of Robert Fulton's Early Experiments, Persistent Efforts and Historic Achievements.* New York: Century, 1909.

Sutherland, David. "Halifax Merchants and the Pursuit of Development, 1783–1850." *Canadian Historical Review* 59 (1978): 1–17.

Suthern, Victor. "The Battle of Châteauguay." *Canadian Historic Sites* 11 (1974): 95–150.

———. *Defend and Hold: The Battle of Châteauguay.* Ottawa: Balmuir Book Publishing, n.d.

Svejda, George J. *History of the Star Spangled Banner from 1814 to the Present.* Washington, DC: U.S. Department of the Interior, National Park Service, 1969.

Swiggett, Howard. *The Extraordinary Man Mr. Morris.* Garden City, NY: Doubleday, 1952.

Symonds, Craig. *Navalists and Anti-Navalists: The Naval Debate in the United States, 1785–1827.* Newark, DE: University of Delaware Press, 1980.

Tate, Vernon D., ed. "Spanish Documents Relating to the Voyage of the *Racoon* to Astoria and San Francisco." *Hispanic American Historical Review* 18 (May 1938): 183–191.

Tebeau, Charlton W. *A History of Florida.* Coral Gables, FL: University of Miami Press, 1971.

Temperley, Harold W.V. *The Foreign Policy of Canning, 1822–1827: England, the Neo-Holy Alliance, and the New World.* London: Frank Cass, 1966.

Temple, Oliver P. *John Sevier, Citizen, Soldier, Legislator, Governor, Statesman, 1744–1815.* Knoxville: Zi-po Press, 1910.

Templin, Thomas E. "Henry 'Light Horse Harry' Lee: A Biography." Ph. D. diss., University of Kentucky, 1975.

Tennessee Historical Magazine 5 (July 1919): 75–80.

Terrell, John Upton. *Zebulon Pike: The Life and Times of an Adventurer.* New York: Weybright and Talley, 1968.

Testimony Taken before the Committee of Grievances and Courts of Justice: Relative to the Late Riots and Mobs in the City of Baltimore. Annapolis, MD: Jonas Green, 1813.

Thacher, James. *American Medical Biography.* Vol. 2. 1828; reprint, New York: Milord House, 1967: 129–141.

Thatcher, Joseph M. "A Fleet in the Wilderness: Shipbuilding at Sacket's Harbor." In R. Arthur Bowler, ed., *War Along the Niagara.* Youngstown, NY: Old Fort Niagara Association, 1991, 53–59.

Thompson, David Scott. "'This Crying Enormity': Impressment as a Factor in Anglo-American Foreign Relations." Master's thesis, Portland State University, 1993.

Thompson, J. M. *Napoleon Bonaparte: His Rise and Fall.* Oxford: Basil Blackwell, 1990.

Thomson, David W. "Robert Fulton's Torpedo System in the War of 1812." *United States Naval Institute Proceedings* 70 (1946): 1207–1217.

Thornbrough, Gayle, ed. *John Badollet and Albert Gallatin: Correspondence, 1804–1836.* Indianapolis: Indiana Historical Society, 1963.

Thornton, Anna M. "Diary of Mrs. William Thornton: Capture of Washington by the British." *Columbia Historical Society Proceedings* 19 (1916): 172–182.

Thorpe, Francis N. "The Building of the Fleet." *Pennsylvania Magazine of History and Biography* 37 (1913): 257–297.

Thwaites, Reuben Gold. "William Clark: Soldier, Statesman." *Washington Historical Quarterly* 1 (July 1907): 234–251.

Thwaites, Reuben Gold, et al., eds. *Collections of the State Historical Society of Wisconsin.* 31 vols., vol. 11, pp. 271–315; vol. 12, pp. 133–153. Madison, WI: Democratic Printing Company, State Printers, 1854–1931.

Tilton, James. *Economical Observations on Military Hospitals and the Prevention and Cure of Diseases Incident to an Army.* Wilmington, DE: J. Wilson, 1813.

Tinksom, Margaret B. "Caviar along the Potomac: Sir Augustus John Foster's Notes on the United States, 1804–1812." *William and Mary Quarterly,* 3d ser., 8 (1951): 69–107.

Tipton, John. "John Tipton's Tippecanoe Journal." *Indiana Magazine of History* 2 (1906): 170–184.

Tohill, L. A. "Robert Dickson, British Fur Trader on the Upper Mississippi." *North Dakota Historical Quarterly* 2 (1928): 5–29; 3 (1929): 83–128, 182–203.

Trofimenkoff, Susan Mann. *The Dream of Nation: A Social and Intellectual History of Quebec.* Toronto: Macmillan of Canada, 1983.

Troyat, Henri. *Alexander of Russia: Napoleon's Conqueror.* New York: E. P. Dutton, 1982.

Trumbull, James H. "The Defense of Stonington against a British Squadron, August 9th to 12th, 1814." Hartford: n.p., 1864.

Trussell, J.B.B., Jr., "Cannon Hold the Breach." *Field Artillery Journal* 39 (Nov.-Dec. 1949): 258–269.

Tucker, Glenn. *Dawn Like Thunder.* Indianapolis: Bobbs-Merrill Company, 1963.

———. *Poltroons and Patriots.* 2 vols. Indianapolis: Bobbs-Merrill, 1954.

Tucker, Lillian H. "Sir Peter Parker: Commander of the H.M.S. *Menelaus* in the Year 1814." *Bermuda Historical Quarterly* 1 (1944): 189–245.

Tucker, Spencer C. *Arming the Fleet: United States Navy Ordnance in the Muzzle-Loading Era.* Annapolis, MD: Naval Institute Press, 1989.

———. "The Carronade." *Naval Institute Proceedings* 99 (August 1973): 65–70.

———. *The Jeffersonian Gunboat Navy.* Columbia: University of South Carolina Press, 1993.

Tucker, Spencer C., and Frank T. Reuter. *Injured Honor: The Chesapeake-Leopard Affair, June 22, 1807.* Annapolis, MD: Naval Institute Press, 1996.

Tulard, Jean. *Napoleon, the Myth of the Saviour,* trans. Teresa Waugh. London: Weidenfeld and Nicolson, 1984.

Tupper, Ferdinand Brock. *The Life and Correspondence of Major-General Sir Isaac Brock, K.B.* 2d ed. London: Simpkin, Marshall, 1847.

Turner, Francis M. *Life of General John Sevier.* New York: Neale, 1910.

Tuttle, Mary M. "William Allen Trimble." *Ohio Archaeological and Historical Society Journal* 14 (1905): 225–246.

Tuttle, Mary M., and Henry B. Thompson. *Autobiography and Correspondence of Allen Trimble, Governor of Ohio, with Genealogy of the Family.* Columbus, OH: N.p., 1909.

U.S. Department of War. *A System of Exercise and Instruction of*

Field Artillery Including Manoeuvres for Light or Horse Artillery. Boston: Hilliard, Gray, 1829.

U.S. Navy Department. *The Naval War of 1812: A Documentary History.* Ed. William S. Dudley. Two vols. to date. Washington, DC: Government Printing Office, 1985–.

United Service Gazette and Naval and Military Chronicle. London, 10 April 1852.

Updyke, Frank A. *The Diplomacy of the War of 1812.* Baltimore, MD: Johns Hopkins University Press, 1915.

Utter, William T. *The Frontier State, 1803–1825.* Columbus: Ohio Historical Society, 1942.

Van Deusen, Glyndon G. *The Life of Henry Clay.* Boston: Little, Brown, 1937.

Van Fleet, J. A. *Old and New Mackinac.* Ann Arbor, MI: Courier Steam Printing, 1870.

Van Rensselaer, Solomon. *A Narrative of the Affair at Queenston in the War of 1812.* New York: Leavitt, Lord, 1836.

Vandal, Albert. *Napoleon et Alexander 1er: L'alliance russe sous le premier empire.* Vol. 2. Paris: Plon, 1891–1896: 441–445.

Vipperman, Carl J. *William Lowndes and the Transition of Southern Politics, 1782–1822.* Chapel Hill: University of North Carolina Press, 1989.

Visual Encyclopedia of Nautical Terms under Sail, The. New York: Crown Publishers, 1978.

Vogel, Robert C. "Jean Lafitte, the Baratarians, and the Historical Geography of Piracy in the Gulf of Mexico." *Gulf Coast Historical Review* 5 (1990): 63–77.

Wade, Arthur P. "The Defenses of Portsmouth Harbor, 1794–1821." *Historical New Hampshire* 33 (1978): 25–51.

Wailes, Benjamin Leonard Covington. *Memoir of Leonard Covington.* Natchez, MS: Natchez Printing and Stationery Co., 1928.

Walker Charles E. "The Other Good Guys: Army Engineers in the War of 1812." *Military Engineer* (June 1978): 178–183.

Walker, Margaret L. "The Life of William Carroll." Master's thesis, University of Tennessee, 1929.

Walker, William A., Jr. "Martial Sons: Tennessee Enthusiasm for the War of 1812." *Tennessee Historical Quarterly* 20, no. 2: 20–37.

Walters, James Raymond, Jr. *Alexander James Dallas: Lawyer, Politician, Financier, 1759–1817.* New York: Da Capo Press, 1969.

Walters, Raymond, Jr. *Albert Gallatin: Jeffersonian Financier and Diplomat.* New York: Macmillan, 1957.

Walters, Raymond, and Philip G. Walters. "The American Career of David Parish." *Journal of Economic History* (1944): 149–66.

Warner, Oliver. *A Portrait of Lord Nelson.* Harmondsworth, Middlesex: Penguin, 1958.

Washburn, H. C. "The Battle of Lake Champlain." *United States Naval Institute Proceedings* 40 (1914): 1365–1386.

Waterhouse, Benjamin. *Circular Letter from Dr. Benjamin Waterhouse to the Surgeons of the Different Posts in the Second Military Department.* Cambridge, MA: N.p., 1817.

Watson, Harry L. *Liberty and Power: The Politics of Jacksonian America.* New York: Hill and Wang, 1990.

Watts, Emma C. "New Hampshire in the War of 1812." *Granite Monthly* 30 (1901): 357–366.

Watts, Florence G. "Fort Knox: Frontier Outpost on the Wabash, 1787–1816." *Indiana Magazine of History* 62 (1966): 51–78.

Watts, Steven. *The Republic Reborn: War and the Making of a Liberal America.* Baltimore, MD: Johns Hopkins University Press, 1987.

Way, Ronald L. "The Day of Chrysler's Farm." *Canadian Geographical Journal* 62 (June 1961): 185–217.

Webster, Sir Charles. *The Foreign Policy of Castlereagh.* 2 vols. London: Barnes and Noble, 1925–1931, 1934.

Weekes, W. M. "The War of 1812: Civil Authority and Martial Law in Upper Canada." *Ontario History* 48 (1956): 147–161.

Weigley, Russell F. *History of the United States Army.* New York: Macmillan, 1967.

Wellesley, Arthur, ed. *Supplementary Dispatches, Correspondence and Memoranda of Field Marshal Arthur Duke of Wellington K.G.* 15 vols. London: N.p., 1858–1872.

Welsh, William J., and David C. Skaggs, eds. *War on the Great Lakes: Essays Commemorating the 175th Anniversary of the Battle of Lake Erie.* Kent, OH: Kent State University Press, 1991.

Wertenbaker, Thomas J. *Norfolk: Historic Southern Port.* 2nd ed. Marvin W. Schlegel, ed. Durham, NC: Duke University Press, 1962.

Weslager, C. A. *The Delaware Indians: A History.* New Brunswick, NJ: Rutgers University Press, 1972.

Westcott, Allen. "Commodore Jesse Duncan Elliott: The Stormy Petrel of the Navy." *United States Naval Institute Proceedings* 54 (1928): 773–778.

Wheeler, George A. "British Occupation in 1815." In *Castine Past and Present.* Boston: Rockwell, Churchill Press, 1896.

———. *History of Castine, Penobscot and Brooksville.* Bangor, ME: Burt, Robinson, 1875.

White, George. *Historic Collection of Georgia.* New York: Pudney and Russell, 1855.

White, Patrick C.T. *A Nation on Trial: The War of 1812.* New York: John Wiley & Sons, 1965.

White, Robert H., ed. *Messages of the Governors of Tennessee.* Vol. 1, *1796–1821.* Nashville: Tennessee Historical Commission, 1952.

Whitehorne, A. C. *A History of the Welsh Regiment.* Cardiff, Wales: Western Mail and Echo, 1932.

Whitehorne, Joseph. *While Washington Burned: The Battle for Fort Erie, 1814.* Baltimore: Nautical and Aviation Publishing, 1992.

Whitely, Emily S. "Between the Acts at Ghent." *Virginia Quarterly Review* 5 (1929): 18–30.

Whitfield, Carol. "The Battle of Queenston Heights." *Canadian Historic Sites* 11 (1974): 9–59.

Whitfield, Carol M., and Wesley B. Turner. "Sir Roger Hale Sheaffe." *Dictionary of Canadian Biography.* Vol. 8, *1851–1860.* Toronto: University of Toronto Press, 1979: 793–796.

Wilcox, Orlando B. "Sacket's Harbor and the War of 1812" and "The War of 1812." *Jefferson County Historical Society Transactions* 1 (1886–1887): 23–31, 97–100.

Wilder, Patrick. *The Battle of Sacket's Harbor*. Baltimore: Nautical and Aviation Book Company, 1994.

Wilkie, Katherine E. *John Sevier, Son of Tennessee*. New York: Messner, 1958.

"William Jenkins Worth." *Dictionary of American Biography*. New York: Charles Scribner's Sons, 1936: 537.

Williams, Eugene Ellis. "The Copus Battle Centennial." *Ohio Archaeological and Historical Publications* 21(1912): 379–395.

Willson, Beckles. "Foster Fails to Avert War." In *Friendly Relations: A Narrative of Britain's Ministers and Ambassadors to America, 1791–1930*. Boston: Little, Brown, 1934.

Willwerth, Mary Elizabeth. "John Quincy Adams as Minister to Russia, 1809–1814: The Ideals and Realities Confronting His Mission." Master's thesis, Eastern Illinois University, 1992.

Wilson, Clyde. "Nathaniel Macon." *Dictionary of North Carolina Biography*. Vol. 4. Chapel Hill: University of North Carolina Press, 1991: 185–187.

Wilson, Edwin M. "The Congressional Career of Nathaniel Macon." *James Sprunt Historical Monographs*. Chapel Hill: University of North Carolina Press, 1900.

Wilson, John P. *Fort George on the Niagara: An Archaeological Perspective*. Ottawa: National Historic Parks,1976.

Wilson, Joseph T. *The Black Phalanx: A History of the Negro Soldiers of the United States in the Wars of 1775–1812, 1861–1865*. Hartford, CT: American, 1888.

Wilson, Samuel, Jr. *Plantation Houses on the Battlefield of New Orleans*. New Orleans: Battle of New Orleans, 150th Anniversary Committee of Louisiana, 1965.

Wiltse, Charles M. *John C. Calhoun: Nationalist, 1782–1828*. Indianapolis: Bobbs-Merrill, 1944.

Winslow, Richard Elliott. *Wealth and Honour: Portsmouth during the Golden Age of Privateering, 1775–1815*. Portsmouth, NH: P. E. Randall, 1988.

Winton-Claire, C. "A Shipbuilder's War." In Morris Zaslow, ed., *The Defended Border*. Toronto: Macmillan of Canada, 1964: 165–173.

Woehrman, Paul W. *At the Headwaters of the Maumee: A History of the Forts at Fort Wayne*. Indianapolis: Indiana Historical Society, 1971.

Wolfe, James Harold. *Jeffersonian Democracy in South Carolina*. Chapel Hill: University of North Carolina Press, 1940.

Wood, Eleazar D. *Journal of the Northwestern Campaign of 1812–1813 under Major-General Wm. H. Harrison*. Robert B. Boehm and Randall L. Buchman Defiance, eds. Ohio: Defiance College Press, 1975.

Wood, H. F. "The Many Battles of Stoney Creek." In Morris Zazlow, ed. *The Defended Border: Upper Canada in the War of 1812*. Toronto: Macmillan of Canada, 1964: 56–60.

Wood, William H., ed. *Select British Documents of the Canadian War of 1812*. 3 vols. Toronto: Champlain Society, 1920–1928.

Wooden, Allen C. "James Tilton, Outstanding Military Medical Administrator." *Delaware Medical Journal* 47 (1975): 429–441.

Woodress, James. *A Yankee's Odyssey: The Life of Joel Barlow*. Philadelphia: Lippincott, 1958.

Woodward, Frank B. *Lewis Cass: The Last Jeffersonian*. New Brunswick, NJ: Rutgers University Press, 1950.

Woodward, Thomas S. *Woodward's Reminiscences of the Creek, or Muscogee Indians*. N.p., 1859. Reprint, Mobile, AL: Southern University Press for Graphics, 1965.

Wright, Frances Fitzpatrick. *Sam Houston, Fighter and Leader*. Nashville: Abingdon Press, 1953.

Wright, J. Leitch, Jr. *Creeks and Seminoles: The Destruction and Regeneration of the Muscogulge People*. Lincoln: University of Nebraska Press, 1986.

———. "A Note on the First Seminole War as Seen by the Indians, Negroes, and their British Advisors." *Journal of Southern History* 34 (1968): 565–575.

Wrobel, Sylvia, and George Grider. *Isaac Shelby: Kentucky's First Governor and Hero of Three Wars*. Danville, KY: Cumberland Press, 1974.

Wyckoff, William. "Joseph Ellicott and the Western New York Frontier: Environmental Assessment, Geographical Strategies, and Authored Landscapes, 1797–1811." Ph. D. diss., Syracuse University, 1982.

Wyllie, John C. "Uriah Phillips Levy." In *Dictionary of American Biography*. Vol. 6. New York: Charles Scribner's Sons, 1936: 203–204.

Young, Bennett H. *The Battle of the Thames*. Louisville, KY: John P. Morton, 1903.

Young, Mary E. "The Creek Frauds: A Study in Conscience and Corruption." *Mississippi Valley Historical Review* 47 (1955): 411–437.

Zaszlow, Morris, ed. *The Defended Border. Upper Canada and the War of 1812*. Toronto: Macmillan, 1964.

Zimmerman, James F. *Impressment of American Seaman*. New York: Columbia University Press, 1966.

List of Contributors

Capt. John Abbatiello
U.S. Air Force Academy

Dr. Thom Armstrong
Mt. Hood Community College

Mr. Sandor Antal

Dr. S. K. Bane
Arkansas Tech University

Mr. Richard V. Barbuto

Mr. John Barron

Dr. James Biedzynski
Ocean County College

Charles H. Bogart

Dr. Charles H. Bowman

Prof. Blaine T. Browne
Broward Community College

Dr. Robert J. Bunker

Dr. Michèle Butts
Austin Peay University

Mr. Stanley D. M. Carpenter
Florida State University

Dr. Jennifer Clark
The University of New England,
   Australia

Mr. David Coffey
Texas Christian University

Dr. David Coles
Florida State Archives

Dr. Rory Cornish
Northeast Louisiana University

Mr. James Tertius de Kay

Dr. Frederick C. Drake
Brock University, Ontario, Canada

Mr. R. Blake Dunnavent

Mr. Richard Eddy

Dr. J. Worth Estes
Boston University School of Medicine

Lt. Col. Peter R. Faber
U.S. Air Force

Capt. William E. Fischer, Jr.
U.S. Air Force

Prof. Michael Fitzgerald
Pikeville College

Dr. George E. Frakes
Santa Barbara City College

Prof. Donald S. Frazier
McMurry University

Dr. John C. Fredriksen

Mr. Tim A. Garrison
University of Kentucky

Capt. John Grenier
U.S. Air Force

Dr. Mark Granstaff
Brigham Young University

Dr. Lowell H. Harrison, Emeritus
Western Kentucky University

Dr. Donald R. Hickey
Wayne State College

Elizabeth Lutes Hillman
Yale University

Mr. Robert J. Holden
George Rogers Clark National
   Historic Park

Dr. Reginald Horsman
University of Wisconsin–Milwaukee

Dr. Charles Howlett

Prof. Eric Jarvis
King's College, London, Ontario,
   Canada

John M. Keefe

Prof. Phillip E. Koerper
Jacksonville State University

Dr. Harold D. Langley
National Museum of American
   History

Dr. Kurt E. Leichtle
University of Wisconsin, River Falls

Dr. John K. Mahon
University of Florida

Prof. Henry S. Marks
Alabama A&M University

Dr. Thomas S. Martin
Sinclair Community College

Comdr. Tyrone G. Martin (Ret.)
U.S. Navy

Prof. Joseph M. McCarthy
Suffolk University

Mr. Chuck McArver

Michael McCulloch
Brock University, St. Catherines,
   Ontario, Canada

Mr. Gary L. Morrison

Prof. Malcolm Muir, Jr.
Austin Peay University

Dr. Larry L. Nelson
Fort Meigs State Memorial, Ohio
   Historical Society

Lt. John Newbill
U.S. Air Force

LIST OF CONTRIBUTORS

Mr. Ricky Earl Newport
Indiana University

Dr. William A. Paquette
Tidewater Community College

Dr. Edwin J. Perkins
University of Southern California

Mr. Stephen Piscitelli
Jacksonville Community College

Mr. Mark Pitcavage
The Ohio State University

Prof. Eugene L. Rasor
Emory and Henry College

Dr. Miles S. Richards

Dr. Junius Rodriguez
Eureka College

Dr. Robert Saunders
Troy State University

Prof. James E. Scanlon
Randolph-Macon College

Mr. Jeffrey J. Seiken
The Ohio State University

Prof. Kyle S. Sinisi
The Citadel

Prof. David Curtis Skaggs
Bowling Green State University

Prof. Gene A. Smith
Texas Christian University

Prof. S. J. Stearns
The College of Staten Island

Prof. Harvey J. Strum
Sage Junior College of Albany

Prof. Reginald C. Stuart
Mt. St. Vincent University, Halifax,
   Nova Scotia, Canada

Dr. George D. Torok
El Paso Community College

Dr. Frank Towers
Clarion University of Pennsylvania

Dr. Spencer C. Tucker
John Biggs '30 Cincinnati Chair in
   Military History
Virginia Military Institute

Dr. Wesley Turner
Brock University, St. Catherines,
   Ontario, Canada

Dr. Harry Ward
University of Richmond

Dr. William Weisberger

Dr. Leigh Whaley
Acadia University, Nova Scotia,
   Canada

Dr. T. Howard Winn
Austin Peay University

David T. Zabecki
American Military University

620

Index